AMERICAN ODYSSEY

By Robert Conot

American Odyssey

Rivers of Blood, Years of Darkness

"Riot Profile: The Police Reaction" in Law Enforcement
    Science & Technology II (IIT Research Institute)

"Profiles of Disorder" in Report of the National Advisory
    Commission on Civil Disorders

Ministers of Vengeance

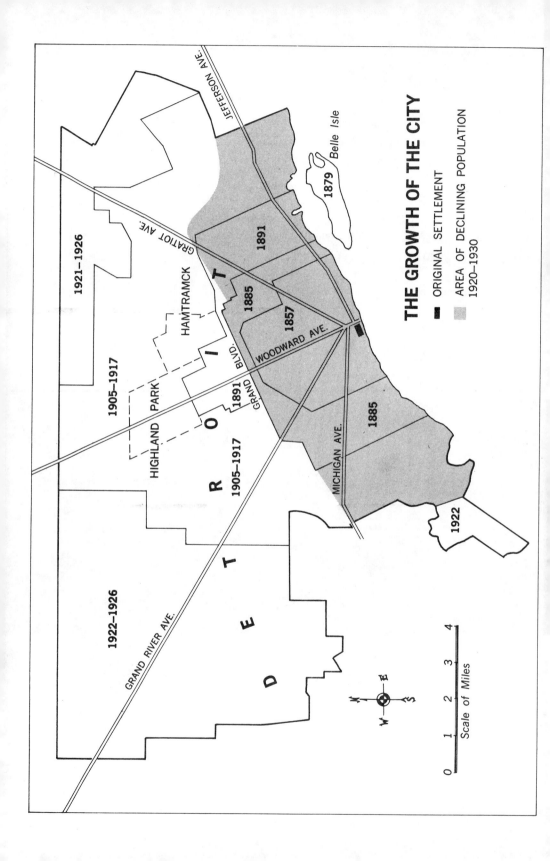

THE GROWTH OF THE CITY

■ ORIGINAL SETTLEMENT

▨ AREA OF DECLINING POPULATION
1920–1930

Scale of Miles
0   1   2   3   4

JEFFERSON AVE.

Belle Isle

1879

1891

GRATIOT AVE.

HAMTRAMCK

1885

1857

1921–1926

1905–1917

D E T R O I T

WOODWARD AVE.

1891
GRAND BLVD.

HIGHLAND PARK

1905–1917

MICHIGAN AVE.

1885

1922

1922–1926

GRAND RIVER AVE.

D E T

by ROBERT CONOT

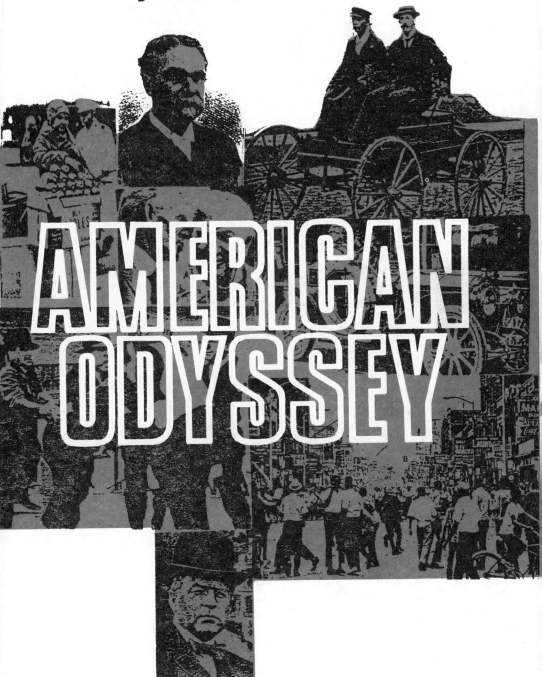

AMERICAN ODYSSEY

WAYNE STATE UNIVERSITY PRESS   DETROIT   1986

PHOTO CREDITS

Burton Historical Collection, Detroit Public Library—# 13.
City of Detroit—# 1.
Detroit Free Press—# 47, 48, 55, 61-64.
Ford Archives: Henry Ford Museum; Dearborn, Michigan—# 8-10, 12,
    14-18, 20, 23, 28, 42, 46, 52, 54.
Ford Motor Company—# 43.
Library of Congress, Washington, D.C.—# 2-7, 19, 21, 22, 26, 29, 32, 34, 35,
    37, 49, 53, 60.
Motor Vehicle Manufacturers Association—# 24, 25, 27, 30, 31, 33, 36, 38-41,
    44, 45, 50, 51. 56.
Author's Photos—# 57-59.

MAPS BY DYNO LOWENSTEIN

PRINTED IN THE UNITED STATES OF AMERICA.

Library of Congress Cataloging in Publication Data
Conot, Robert E.
    American odyssey.
    Reprint. Originally published: New York : Morrow, 1974.
    Bibliography: p.
    Includes index.
    1. Detroit (Mich.)—History. 2. Cities and towns—United States—History—Case
studies. I. Title.
F574.D457C66   1985   977.4'34   85-26393
ISBN 0-8143-1806-1 (pbk.)

for Flick
who endured

and Eric and Gigi
that theirs may be a brighter future

Acknowledgment and Methodology

RESEARCH FOR THE BOOK WAS UNDERTAKEN IN DETROIT AT VARIOUS PERIODS between April of 1968 and June of 1973, and in Washington, D.C., primarily during 1968 and 1969.* No person played a greater role in making the book's writing possible than Mayor Jerome P. Cavanagh, who for a number of months made an office available to me in the mayor's suite and permitted me to observe the operations of the city from their most critical point.

Many of the mayor's associates, former associates, and staff members provided valuable information and insights. Foremost among them are Richard Strichartz and Conrad Mallett. Strichartz's association with the mayor goes back to the time of Cavanagh's decision to run for office. Mallett was executive secretary and director of the Housing Commission.

Joe B. Sullivan, commissioner of the Purchasing Department, and Robert Toohey, general manager of the Detroit Street Railways and former commissioner of Public Works, contributed not only their expertise in municipal government but much information stemming from their long-time personal relationships with the mayor. Mrs. Rose Cavanagh, the mayor's mother, related to me much of the family history.

I am no less indebted to the following: Harold Black, former community development coordinator and director of the Community Renewal Program, and a twenty-five-year employee of the city; David Nelson, assistant to the mayor; James D. Wiley, director of the Community Renewal Program; Dr. Bernard W. Klein, controller; Robert Roselle, executive secretary; James T. Trainor, press secretary; James L. Trainor, community development coordinator; Anthony Ripley, *New York Times* correspondent and former member of the mayor's staff; Maurice Kellman, special counsel; Sandy McClure, of the mayor's staff; Jack Casey and Paul Borman, formerly of the mayor's staff; Frank Beckman, assessor; Walter I. Stecher, budget director; Dr. Robert Kearns, commissioner of Building

* For the purpose of simplification, the positions and titles of persons are given, in general, as they were at the time of the author's interviews. Titles may reoccur when the position was held at different times by different persons.

and Safety Engineering; Robert Banyai, of the Operations Analysis Division; Charles Blessing, director of city planning; Robert G. Hoffman, principal city planner; Juliet Sabit, principal social economist; Charles A. Mayer, secretary-chief examiner of the Civil Service Commission; Richard V. Marks, secretary-director of the Commission on Community Relations; Robert Reese, corporation counsel; John Smith, director of elections; Morton Sterling, air pollution control director; Dr. George Pickett, health commissioner; Edward P. Henry, administrator, Detroit General Hospital; Dr. Margaret Zolliker, Detroit Department of Health Maternal and Infant Care project; Robert Knox, director of the Housing Commission; Al Legatt, director of labor relations; Thomas F. Ashcraft, co-ordinator of the Mayor's Committee for Industrial and Commercial Development; William H. Bannon, superintendent of the Detroit House of Correction; Delbert R. Jay, supervisor of community services of the Mayor's Rehabilitation Committee on Skid Row Problems; David Cason, director of the Model City Program; Richard Fanning, assistant general superintendent of the Department of Parks and Recreation; Gerald Remus, general manager, Water Commission; Councilman Ernest C. Browne, formerly of the city's Budget Analysis Division; and Councilman Mel Ravitz.

The following persons assisted me in examining the operations of the anti-poverty program: Richard Simmons, Jr., director; Georgia Brown, assistant director; Carl Westman, deputy director; Myron Liner, director of program planning, research, and development; Ralph Rosenfeld, director of community-development center operations; Leon Shearer, director of manpower development; Herman Snead, director of Target Area I; Brad Nichols, director of Target Area IV.

For an understanding of the police department I am indebted to four former police commissioners of the city, George Edwards, Jr. (1962–1963); Ray Girardin (1964–1968); Johannes Spreen (1968–1969); Patrick Murphy (1970); and to the many men of the department whom I accompanied as they performed their duties.

Judge James H. Lincoln of the Juvenile Court, by permitting me to observe the operations of the court, by making available to me records spanning a period of forty years, and by giving generously of his time, played a key role in the researching of the book.

Paul Conlan, director of the Wayne County Department of Social Services, and Robert Shelton, his administrative assistant, aided me immeasurably by making departmental records available and by discussing with me the history and problems of welfare services in Detroit.

Dr. Norman Drachler, superintendent of the Detroit School System, met with me on several occasions over a period of years and provided his assistance in my investigation of the school system. Valuable information was also provided by the following persons:

Dr. Carl Marburger, commissioner of education for the state of New Jersey, who played an important role in setting up the Great Cities Program in Detroit; Dr. William Simmons, deputy superintendent, Division of Governmental Relations and Fiscal Planning; Julia McCarthy, deputy superintendent for administration; Arthur L. Johnson, deputy superintendent for school-community relations; Dr. Louis D. Monacel, associate superintendent, Office of Federal, State, and Special programs; Dr. William Wattenberg, associate superintendent for child accounting and adjustment; Dr. James Neubacher, director of the Great Cities

Program; Dr. Robert S. Lankton, divisional director of the Department of Research and Development; Mrs. Elsie M. Jinks, divisional director of evaluative services, child accounting and adjustment; Mrs. Dorothy Ware, director of the psychological clinic; Miss Ann McCarthy, director of field services; Dr. Theodore Mandell, director of special education-speech correction; Mel Chapman, principal of Northwestern High School; Lewis B. Schulman, principal of Cooley High School; Arthur W. Rosenau, principal of Redford High School; Mrs. Martha R. Sanders, acting principal at Butzel Junior High School; Mrs. Mary Ellen Riordan, president of the Detroit American Federation of Teachers local; Maurice Silver, of the psychoeducational project; Louis Starks, Joseph McGlynn, Charles Reich, and Nettye Buchalter of the psychological clinic staff; Stan Webb, of the Division of Intergroup Relations.

Prosecutor William Cahalan and Judge Henry L. Heading (formerly chief of the criminal division on the prosecutor's staff) provided many insights into the administration of justice in the city.

William Patrick, president of the New Detroit Committee, enabled me to attend meetings of the committee and observe its deliberations.

Mrs. Josephine Gomon, grande dame of the Democratic party in Detroit, spent several hours with me discussing her contributions to the history of the city.

For an understanding of the operations of the county government, I am indebted to Richard Austin, Wayne County auditor.

Other persons who provided me with information and assistance are: the late Walter Reuther, president of the United Auto Workers; Irving J. Rubin, director of the Detroit Regional Transportation and Land Use study; Edward Robinson, director of the Metropolitan Detroit Citizens Development Authority; Bob Turner, director, and Robert Farley, deputy director of the Southeast Michigan Councils of Government; Paul Silver, chairman of a special Board of Supervisors committee on OEO; Chuck Allegrino, supervisor of the General Accounting Office audit in Detroit; Alan Canty, executive director of the Detroit Recorders Court psychological clinic; Chris Alston and Roy J. Robinson of Forest Park; and Dr. Elliot Luby, associate director of the Lafayette Clinic.

The histories of the Jansen, Norveth, Lentick, Mirow, and Stallings families were compiled through records made available by the Juvenile Court, the Wayne County Department of Social Services, and the Detroit public school system, and by interviews conducted by the author with various members of the families. In the instance of some of the early history prior to World War I, the author has added details regarding general events and conditions.

The lives of a number of multigenerational, multiproblem families were examined; five of these histories were ultimately chosen for inclusion in the book. In order to conform to public law, and to protect the privacy of the persons involved, *all names of families and persons have been changed, and many additional details, relationships, occurrences, places and dates have been altered in order to preclude identification.*

In Washington, D.C., I received much information and assistance in examining the operations of the departments and their relationships to the cities, in tracing the history of the antipoverty program, and in analyzing the impact of Federal operations on the urban economy. The following persons were interviewed, some of them a number of times:

Department of Housing and Urban Development—Undersecretary (and later

Secretary) Robert Wood; Dwight Ink, assistant secretary for Administration; H. Ralph Taylor, assistant secretary for Model Cities and Governmental Relations; Philip N. Brownstein, assistant secretary for Mortgage Credit and Federal Housing commissioner; Robert E. McCabe, deputy assistant secretary for Renewal Assistance; Thomas F. Rogers, director, Office of Urban Technology and Research; James Banks, director, Office of Community Development; Arnold Diamond, economist, special assistant to the Joint Economic Committee of Congress.

Department of Health, Education, and Welfare—Harold Howe, commissioner of Education; James F. Kelly, assistant secretary and comptroller; Jule Sugarman, chief, Children's Bureau; Samuel Halperin, deputy assistant secretary for legislation; Alice M. Rivlin, deputy assistant secretary for program analysis; Richard Warden, deputy director, Civil Rights Division; James Alexander, director of the Center for Community Planning (CCP); Natalie Spingarn, CCP assistant director for communications and training; Lee Lendt, CCP assistant director for technical assistance; Francis Hennigan, CCP assistant director for Program Development and Evaluation; and David Seidman, expert in population and family planning.

Department of Labor—Jack Howard, executive assistant to Secretary Willard Wirtz; Stanley Ruttenberg, assistant secretary for Manpower; Mark Battle, administrator, Bureau of Work-Training Programs; Philip Rutledge, acting deputy director of Manpower Development (and former director of MCHRD in Detroit); and Arthur Chapin, special assistant for equal opportunity in Manpower Programs.

Office of Economic Opportunity—Robert Perrin, acting deputy director; Robert A. Levine, assistant director for research, plans, programs, and evaluation; William Bozman, deputy director for Community Action Programs; Don Hess, associate director for Program Planning; Paul Cain, chief, Office of Evaluation, Community Action Programs.

Bureau of the Budget—William D. Carey, assistant director in charge of the Human Resources Division; William B. Cannon, chief, Education, Manpower, and Science Division; Alexander J. Green, associate division director, Human Resources Division; Ken Kugel and Al Patterson of executive office management; Mark Alger, Detroit liaison on the staff; and Dr. Michael S. March.

Department of Justice—Warren Christopher, deputy Attorney-General; Thomas Finley, associate deputy Attorney-General; Wesley Pomeroy, assistant director, Office of Law Enforcement Assistance Administration; Dante R. Andreotti, chief, Municipal Services Division, Community Relations Service.

Department of Transportation—Langhorne Bond, special assistant to the Secretary; and E. H. Holmes, director of policy planning.

General Accounting Office—Henry Eschwege, associate director.

Bureau of the Census—Dr. Herman Miller, chief, Population Division; and Meyer Zitter, assistant chief, Population Division.

Congress—John Stark, executive director, Joint Economic Committee; and Richard Kaufman, of the Urban Areas Subcommittee; Charles Ferris, general counsel, Senate Committee on Democratic Policy; Stewart McClure, chief clerk, Senate Committee on Labor and Public Welfare; and Roy Millenson, minority clerk; Carl A. S. Coan, staff director, Housing Subcommittee of the Senate Committee on Banking and Currency; Casey Ireland, minority clerk of the House of Representatives Subcommittee on Housing; Wyn Turner, of the Senate

Government Operations Committee; Dr. Steve Ebbin, of the Senate Subcommittee on Governmental Research.

Advisory Commission on Intergovernmental Relations—John Shannon and David Walker, assistant directors.

The Brookings Institution—Kermit Gordon, president, and former director of the Bureau of the Budget; James Sundquist, former Undersecretary of Agriculture; William Capron, former staff member on the Council of Economic Advisers; and Richard Nathan (assistant director in charge of the Human Resources Division of the Office of Management and Budget in the Nixon Administration.)

The Urban Coalition—John Gardner, president, and former secretary of Health, Education, and Welfare; Lowell Beck, executive director, Urban Coalition Action Council; Brian Duff, director of communications; Ron Linton, co-coordinator, and former director of the Environmental Task Force at HEW.

National Planning Association—Dr. Leonard Lecht and Philip Golden, of the Institute for Priority Analysis; Dr. Sidney Sonnenblum, of the Center of Economic Projections; and the late Dr. Gerhald Colm.

United States Conference of Mayors—John Gunther, executive director; John Feild, former executive director, President's Committee on Equal Employment Opportunity; Bob Walter; and Gene Murphy.

Persons who provided me with information on the inception of the War on Poverty, as well as on other matters, are: Jack Conway, former administrative assistant to the late Walter Reuther; Richard Boone, director, Citizens Crusade Against Poverty; Paul Ylvisaker, commissioner for community affairs of the state of New Jersey; David Hackett, special assistant to the late Attorney-General (and Senator) Robert Kennedy; and Sy Rotter, former deputy director of the United Planning Organization, District of Columbia.

Other persons to whom I am indebted are: Jim Martin, executive secretary, National Governors Conference; Alan Pritchard, assistant executive director, National League of Cities; Mark Keane, director, International City Managers Association; David Selden, president of the American Federation of Teachers; Nat Goldfinger, director of research, AFL-CIO; Ken Young, AFL-CIO legislative specialist; George Jones and Father John Devlin of the National Education Association; and Dr. Earle Shaefer, director of an early-childhood study at the National Institute of Mental Health.

The following persons assisted me in understanding the operations of the Federal government's regional offices in Chicago: Frank Fisher, regional administrator, Department of Housing and Urban Development; Don Morrow, deputy regional director, HUD; Ed Levin, Detroit liaison man and expediter, HUD; Alan Goldfarb, Model Cities regional director; Lewis F. Nicolini, regional director of the Manpower Administration, Department of Labor; James G. Brawley, regional director of the Department of Health, Education, and Welfare; Frank Olivierre and Bob Ford, community development, HEW.

Research was conducted at the Library of Congress in Washington, D.C.; the Burton Historical Collection of the Detroit Public Library; the Detroit Municipal Reference Library; the Wayne State University Library; the archives of the Henry Ford Museum; and the Library of the University of California at Los Angeles.

Contents

II. THE PERNICIOUS PROSPERITY

Illustrations appear between pages 306 and 307

List of Maps

Reference Guide

THE FOLLOWING REFERENCE GUIDE IS INTENDED TO AID THE READER IN IDEN-
tifying persons who appear in the book at different points. Some important
persons whose appearance is limited to primarily one section are not included.

Oliver Barthel—auto pioneer who worked with Henry Ford and designed more
than eighty different engines.

Harry Bennett—Henry Ford's "man Friday" who attained immense power in
the Ford Motor Company between 1920 and 1945.

Harold Black—the son of Polish immigrant Abraham Schwartz, he was one of
the first members of the Detroit Planning Department, and became a leading
executive in the Cavanagh Administration.

Charles Blessing—director of the Detroit City Planning Department and nationally known authority on planning.

Dr. Samuel Brownell—commissioner of education in the Eisenhower Administration and Detroit superintendent of education from 1956 to 1966.

William J. Cameron—unstable and eccentric writer for Henry Ford's newspaper, the Dearborn *Independent*.

Lewis Cass—governor of the Michigan Territory, Secretary of War in President
Jackson's administration, and Democratic candidate for President.

Jerome P. Cavanagh—son of Sylvester J. Cavanagh, a Canadian immigrant
who went to work in the Ford plant in 1919. Jerry Cavanagh was elected
mayor of Detroit in 1961 and became a leading spokesman for American
cities.

Zachariah Chandler—nineteenth-century merchant who became mayor of Detroit, played a key role in the founding of the Republican party, and was
elected the first Republican senator from Michigan.

Roy Chapin—sales manager for the Olds Motor Company in the early 1900's,
he was the principal organizer of the Hudson Motor Company and was appointed Secretary of Commerce in the Hoover Administration.

Walter Chrysler—son of a Kansas locomotive engineer, he became a railroad mechanic and manager of railroad shops before being appointed general manager of Buick. In the early 1920's, he founded the Chrysler Motor Company.

Albert Cobo—Detroit city treasurer from the mid-1930's until 1949, when he was elected mayor.

Father Charles Coughlin—pastor of the Shrine of the Little Flower in Royal Oak, a suburb of Detroit. A dynamic figure, he attained political influence and national power through the medium of radio.

James Couzens—a brilliant administrator who came to Detroit from Canada as a youth. Next to Henry Ford himself, he played the most important role in the formation and success of the Ford Motor Company. He was appointed police commissioner of Detroit in 1916 and elected mayor in 1918. From 1922 to 1936 he served in the U.S. Senate.

John and Horace Dodge—Detroit machine shop operators who began manufacturing engines for automobiles, became partners in the Ford Motor Company, and then quarreled with Henry Ford and built an auto plant of their own.

Dr. Norman Drachler—son of Ukrainian Jewish immigrants, he was named Detroit superintendent of education in 1967.

William C. Durant—grandson of a Michigan governor and lumber tycoon, he made his first million dollars by paying fifty dollars for the patent of a road cart. He took over the nearly bankrupt Buick Motor Company, and through financial manipulation and acquisition of other companies built it into General Motors.

Thomas Edison—a hawker and paper boy on the train from Port Huron to Detroit before and during the Civil War. Learning telegraphy, he patented numerous telegraphic inventions and founded the first electrical engineering firm in the United States. He devised a new system of electrical transmission to complement his perfection of the incandescent bulb. With the backing of a Wall Street syndicate he founded General Electric. His later inventions included the gramophone and the kinetoscope, which laid the basis for the motion picture industry.

George Edwards, Jr.—Brilliant UAW organizer during the late 1930's, he was appointed Detroit housing commissioner, and elected to the city council. Later he was named judge of the Wayne County Juvenile Court. He was elevated to the Michigan Supreme Court, but resigned to accept the Detroit police commissionership in the Cavanagh Administration.

John M. Forbes—Boston shipper who made a fortune in the China trade while still in his twenties. He became the key backer of the Michigan Central and other railroads, and a member of the Republican coalition.

John, Samuel, and George Ford—the sons of William Ford, an English leaseholder and middle-class farmer in County Cork, Ireland. They emigrated to America between 1832 and 1847, and became prosperous farmers in Dearborn, Michigan.

William Ford—the son of John Ford. A well-to-do farmer and participant in civic affairs.

Henry Ford—the son of William Ford, he showed an early mechanical bent. As a sixteen-year-old he went to Detroit to learn steam and internal combustion engine mechanics. In the 1890's he became chief engineer for the Detroit

Edison Illuminating Company. He built one of the first autos in Detroit, and was noted for his racing cars. After several false starts, he became one of the founders and the president of what today is the Ford Motor Company.

Edsel Ford—the only child of Henry Ford, he was overshadowed by and often at odds with his father.

Henry Ford II—the eldest son of Edsel, he was the architect of the modernization of the Ford Motor Company after World War II, and has played an active role in civic affairs and the operations of the Ford Foundation.

John Gillespie—Detroit water commissioner and police commissioner, he was later hired by the Ford Motor Company and played a significant role in company intrigues during the 1930's.

Ray Girardin—noted crime reporter for the Detroit *Times,* he was appointed executive secretary and then police commissioner by Mayor Cavanagh.

Josephine Gomon—grande dame of the Detroit Democratic party, she entered politics as executive secretary to Mayor Frank Murphy in 1930 and later was named first director of the Detroit Housing Commission.

James F. Joy—Detroit attorney who promoted private acquisition of the Michigan Central Railroad, and became one of the foremost American railroad builders and a power in the Republican party.

Henry B. Joy—the son of James F. Joy, he organized a group that purchased the Packard Motor Company and transferred it to Detroit.

Albert Kahn—the son of a German Jewish rabbi and peddler, he became the foremost industrial architect of his time and built most of the auto plants in the Detroit area.

Ernest Kanzler—Edsel Ford's brother-in-law, he became a Ford executive and Detroit banker.

Charles B. King—Detroit engineer, inventor, and auto pioneer whose construction of a car stimulated Henry Ford to build his first vehicle.

Robert Knox—director of the Detroit Housing Commission in the Cavanagh Administration.

William Knudsen—Danish immigrant who became an executive at the Ford Motor Company before heading the Chevrolet operations and attaining the presidency of General Motors.

Henry Leland—mechanic and engineer who established a machine shop in Detroit, was the first head of the Cadillac Motor Company, and founded the Lincoln Motor Company. He was instrumental in the formation of the Employers Association of Detroit and the Good Citizens League.

Ernest G. Liebold—A bank clerk who became Henry Ford's personal secretary and contended against Harry Bennett for power in the Ford organization.

Alexander Y. Malcomson—a coal dealer who was Henry Ford's principal backer in the formation of the Ford Motor Company.

Conrad Mallett—the son of a poor Texas farmer, he worked his way through college as a postman and police officer. He became an official in the Detroit antipoverty program, executive secretary to Mayor Cavanagh, and the first Negro director of the Detroit Housing Commission.

Thomas, William, and Henry Maybury—acquaintances of the Fords in Ireland, they migrated to America in the 1830's and prospered in Detroit. William Ford was married to Mary Litogot in the parlor of Thomas Maybury's house.

William Maybury—the son of Thomas Maybury, he was a lawyer, politician, and friend of Henry Ford. As mayor of Detroit he gave Henry Ford a permit to operate his first car on the streets, and later backed Ford in the formation of an auto company.

James McMillan—Detroit railroad and industrial tycoon, he took over as boss of the Michigan Republican party after the death of Zachariah Chandler.

Frank Murphy—Democratic judge who was elected mayor of Detroit in 1930 and went on to become governor of Michigan, United States Attorney-General, and justice of the U.S. Supreme Court.

William Murphy—son of well-to-do lumberman Simon Murphy, he was a Detroit builder and backed Henry Ford in the formation of an auto company that ultimately produced the Cadillac.

John Newberry—member of a prominent Detroit and Chicago merchant and shipping family, he was one of the founders of the Republican party and a builder of railroad rolling stock.

Truman Newberry—the son of John Newberry, he was a conservative Republican who defeated Henry Ford in a bitter race for the U.S. Senate in 1918.

Ransom E. Olds—founder of the Oldsmobile and R.E.O. Motor Companies.

Robert Pelham—Negro freedman and artisan who fled from the South in 1859 and became a well-to-do Detroit contractor.

Benjamin Pelham—the son of Robert Pelham, he published the Detroit *Plaindealer*. During the late 1890's he obtained two key positions in the county government and entrenched himself so strongly that for forty years he was known as "the czar of Wayne County."

Alfred Pelham—the son of Benjamin Pelham, he was appointed controller by Mayor Cavanagh, the first time a Negro was placed in a key position in the Detroit municipal government.

Hazen Pingree—shoe manufacturer and one of the "Big Four" of the Michigan Republican Club. He became a maverick after being elected mayor of Detroit, and pioneered Progressive Republicanism and urban reform.

Walter Reuther—young tool-and-die maker hired by the Ford Motor Company. A Socialist, he was one of the founders of the UAW and later attained the presidency of the union.

Father Gabriel Richard—leader of the French community in Michigan during the early nineteenth century.

George Romney—general manager of the Automobile Manufacturers Association and president of American Motors. He came to prominence as head of the Detroit Citizens Advisory Committee on School Needs during the late 1950's and subsequently was elected governor of Michigan.

Robert Roselle—Detroit municipal official and executive secretary to Mayor Cavanagh.

Alfred J. Sloan—president of General Motors in the 1920's and 1930's.

Charles Sorensen—production boss at Ford's River Rouge plant.

Richard Strichartz—a key executive and the "Federal man" in the first Cavanagh Administration.

Eber Brock Ward—a shipping, lumber, and steel magnate, he built the first Bessemer converter in America at Wyandotte.

David Ward—nephew of Eber Brock Ward, his survey of the Michigan pine lands earned him a fortune from lumber.

G. Mennen Williams—scion of a prominent Republican family, he became a

Democrat and a protégé of Frank Murphy. After World War II he revitalized the state Democratic party and was elected governor six times.

Childe Harold Wills—brilliant designer and engineer who played a prominent role in the development of Ford's Model T.

Judge Augustus Woodward—a friend of President Thomas Jefferson, he was appointed judge of the Michigan Territory in 1805. For twenty years he was the most powerful figure in Detroit.

The following names used are fictitious in order to protect the privacy of the actual persons:

Adam Jansen—a Swedish immigrant to the Michigan lumber country.

Peter Jansen—the son of Adam Jansen, he went to work for Ford in 1914 and later became a truck driver. He married Marie Norveth and developed into an alcoholic. He earned too little money to support his numerous children, and the family had a host of problems.

Rita Jansen—eldest child of Peter and Marie Jansen, she was born with congenital cataracts. She married an auto worker from Alabama named George Devers, and their life moved from one crisis to another.

Jim Jansen—eldest son of Peter and Marie. He was a juvenile delinquent and spent much of his adult life in jail.

Joella Jansen—feebleminded daughter of Peter and Marie. She married Ned Black Bear, an auto worker of Indian descent, and gave birth to ten children.

Katherine Jansen—sensitive and intelligent daughter of Peter and Marie, she tried desperately to escape from the environment of poverty.

Alfred Lentick—Cornish copper miner who immigrated to the northern Michigan peninsula during the 1860's.

Ralph Lentick—grandson of Alfred Lentick, he migrated to Detroit and went to work for Ford.

Harold Lentick—son of Ralph Lentick, he married Elmira Norveth. After experiencing difficult times during the Depression, he obtained steady work in the auto industry and achieved middle-class status.

William Norveth—immigrant from Hungary who went to work on the American railroads in the 1890's. During the early 1900's he was drawn to Detroit by the nascent auto industry, and sent for his wife Theresa and their children.

Wallace Mirow—a middle-class Negro who abandoned his farm in Kansas during the Depression and moved with his wife Antoinette and daughter Irma to Detroit, where he became a coal and ice dealer and assembly-line worker. Antoinette and Irma were unable to cope with the urban environment. Antoinette was afflicted by schizophrenia. Irma began to drink.

Odie Stallings—an illiterate Virginia Negro who came to Detroit and went to work for Ford after World War I. He and his wife Freda had three children, and had a difficult time surviving the Depression.

Donald Stallings—eldest child of Odie and Freda Stallings, he became a garbage collector for the city of Detroit and married Irma Mirow. Donald was a compulsive gambler and Irma an alcoholic. Their six children grew up amidst turmoil and poverty.

Mirabel Stallings—eldest daughter of Donald and Irma Stallings. She married a poorly educated Georgia migrant, Tom Winesberry, who deserted her. She went on welfare and became an alcoholic and prostitute. Her daughter Dinah became pregnant at thirteen and was prostituting at fourteen.

Natalie Stallings—daughter of Donald and Irma Stallings, she graduated from high school and obtained a job in the antipoverty program. Her husband Nick Palmerill was jailed, but on release obtained a job with Ford's inner city program.

Brett Stallings—youngest son of Donald and Irma Stallings, he did poorly in school and was a "typical" juvenile delinquent, getting into more and more serious trouble as he grew older.

Introduction

IN THE SUMMER OF 1967, RIOTS ERUPTED IN CITIES THROUGHOUT THE NATION. Following the outbreak of the Detroit riot during the last week of July, President Lyndon Johnson announced the formation of a National Advisory Commission on Civil Disorders. He asked the commission to determine "What happened, why did it happen, and what can be done to keep it from happening again and again?" I joined the commission as a special consultant, and directed the work of the staff in preparing the *Profiles of Disorder,* the historical section of the report.

The President had said, "You will have all the support and cooperation you need from the Federal government." Funds were obtained from four agencies concerned with urban affairs: the Office of Economic Opportunity, and the Departments of Labor, Housing and Urban Development, and Health, Education, and Welfare. In the fall of 1967, however, the President was preoccupied with the Vietnam War. Congress demanded reduction of the budgetary deficit, and all departments found themselves short of money. The President had believed the riots to be organized, and when the commission—working in conjunction with the FBI—discovered they had been unorganized and spontaneous, he lost interest in the work of the commission. Funds dried up. The commission had intended to issue two reports: a preliminary report in early 1968, and a final report six months later. Instead, a single, *final* report was issued on March 1, 1968.

The report served a critical need. It raised, however, almost as many questions as it answered. It never came to grips with the long-range history of the American city and its polyethnic population. It did not attempt to deal with all of the city's varied institutions. Except for an examination of black-white relations, it did not examine the social pathology. The staff of the commission found considerable material on urban history, but it was fragmented and compartmentalized. There was no lack of record of *what* had happened. But there had been little exploration of the interrelationships of these happenings: *how* things had happened, and *why* they had happened.

To fill the gaps, to tell *how* and *why,* as well as what, is the purpose of this book.

No probing of our institutions and our problems is practicable without uncovering their roots. No understanding of the American city is possible without a comprehension of the national political, social, and economic forces with which it interacts, for we have become a nation of cities. No analysis of those forces can be meaningful without an examination of how they affect the everyday lives of the people. I attempt to show not only how institutions develop and how decisions are made, but what their effect is upon ordinary men, their families, and their children. I believe that history is not merely a record of the past; but that like all experience it provides a vital guide to actions in the future.

To provide a sharper picture, I have focused on one city, Detroit, within the larger American context.

Why Detroit?

"You can see here," Edmund Wilson wrote during the Great Depression, "as it is impossible to do in a more varied and complex city, the whole structure of an industrial society." [1]

Wilson's declaration was an oversimplification, for Detroit is not only the principal but the most diversified manufacturing city in the United States. It is a financial center. Unlike New York, Chicago, or Los Angeles, however, Detroit has retained a sense of oneness and a sense of order. Its lines of development are clear, and its complexities are comprehensible. Over the course of a century it was involved in many major historical developments. As the world center of the automobile industry, it has exerted tremendous social and economic influence. It has been the headquarters of two of the world's three largest corporations, and it is America's most unionized city. Detroit is the heart of American industry, and by the beat of that heart much of America's economic health is measured.

I

THE WELDING
OF THE LINKS

1

The Shantyman

AT NOON THE MILL'S GREAT HORN TREMBLED THE BRANCHES OF THE TREES. The saw's rasp and the cannon shots of axes biting into tree trunks ceased.

The boots of Peter Jansen crunched deep into the snow, punching down the shallow tracks of squirrels, deer, snowshoe rabbits, and occasionally a mink. But mink and bear and wolf, driven ever farther north by the destruction of their environment, were rare. Dogs and cats, abandoned by their owners whenever logging camps broke up, were replacing them as predators.

It took Jansen only a few minutes to reach the clearing where the chore boy had the fires hugging the fifty-pound cans of "bull meat," beans, potatoes, and tea. From all directions the notchers, sawyers, swampers, and teamsters tramped in. Rising at 4 A.M., they had long since expended the energy generated by their huge breakfasts. During the winter months the sun's rays, chipped and broken by the trees, often failed to bring the temperature up to zero. Since food not eaten hurriedly soon froze to the tin plates, Jansen wolfed down the meal. The unchewed chunks of meat he flushed down with drafts of hot tea. Sitting down on a stump, he took out a small bag of Myrtle Navy tobacco, and, shaking it into the square of thin paper, rolled a cigarette.

The men were not talkers. In a few of the larger, well-established mill towns there were men who had families with them. But the camps were populated by single men—single, even if they were married. Usually all one knew was a man's name, and names were shed as easily as jackets. At night in the bunk-house, stories would be recounted, but they were tall tales told competitively. Whatever they revealed of a man's background was tangential.

Many of the men, like Jansen, seemed almost to have no past. His parents had been Swedish. His father, Adam, had emigrated in the 1880's. A fisherman in summer and a logger in winter when the Baltic froze, Adam Jansen had come to Michigan to be a fisherman in summer and a logger in winter when the Great Lakes froze.

Adam Jansen had been drowned on the Lakes in 1900, when Peter was four years old. Peter's mother had died five years later. Since the age of nine,

Peter Jansen had been earning his keep in the camps and the small towns of the Michigan Peninsula.

Of average height, he was stocky and thick-muscled. His face was plain but not displeasing. Below the light brown hair, the weather-tanned forehead seemed never to have been perplexed by a frown.

In a half hour the men were back at work. Jansen's crew was loading the fourteen-foot logs onto the heavy sleds for transport to the narrow-gauge railway that would take them to Lake Huron. At the beginning of winter, teams had tramped down the snow and mixed it with water to form a surface of ice for the runners. In the early afternoon the forest was already settling into twilight as the huge horses, steaming from the exertion, pulled the sled. At each downgrade a "road monkey" tended a fire to thaw sand—sand that he threw into the path of the runners to brake the sled.

As the logs were being loaded onto the flatcars by the jamming crews, the torn page of a newspaper, blown from the wood tender, landed at Jansen's feet. Reading matter was in no great demand at the camp. Peter would have paid no attention to the paper except for the extraordinary size of the headline and its reference to "FIVE DOLLAR DAY." Folding the sheet, he tucked it inside his jacket.

Not until he returned to the bunkhouse after dinner and settled himself upon the deacon seat, the bench running along the line of bunks from one end of the building to the other, did he have an opportunity to look at the paper again.

Long and narrow, the bunkhouse was lined with twin rows of double-decker bunks. The air was pungent with sweat, tobacco, and the steaming odors of wet clothes. In one corner a group of men had broken out a deck of cards for a game of smear. Across the way from Jansen a notcher struck sparks as he sharpened his ax. At the wash trough a jack, stropping his razor, peered at his murky reflection in the metal mirror.

Jansen shifted his position to better catch the light from the kerosene lantern. Reading for him was torturous; almost like breaking a code. He had obtained his schooling in a one-room schoolhouse from a husky female teacher who had been hired as much for her ability to cope with unruly boys as for her eighth-grade education. Jansen had attended school for most of two years, and for portions of two others. Depending on the difficulty of the reading matter, of every four words he could usually make out two; one he might be able to guess; and one would be beyond his grasp.

Once he realized that the headline heralded the paying of five dollars a day in *wages,* he concentrated until the blood vessels at the sides of his head bulged. Dated January 6, 1914, the article stated that Henry Ford was hiring five thousand more men to work in his automobile company, and was raising wages to five dollars a day.

As a lumberjack, Jansen was being paid twenty-six dollars a month—a dollar a day. The five-dollar figure was almost beyond his comprehension, for he could not multiply five by six. But by laboriously adding six fives together, he came to the realization he could make more in one week in Detroit than in a month in the lumber camp.

When he looked up, he felt dizzy from his concentration and the smell of kerosene. The kerosene was being used by one jack to kill the lice in his red-flannel underwear, while another picked the cooties out of his hair and bisected them with his thumbnail. As Jansen wove out of the door, the night air hit him like a sheet of ice. Clasping the newspaper page to him, he made his way to the pitch-black privy and collapsed onto the log that served as a seat.

In warm weather the open trench was a pesthole that had the reputation of transmitting "swamp fever." But in winter the feces and the urine froze in less time than it took a man to pull up his pants. Compared to the bunkhouse, teeming with *crawlers* that came up through the floorboards, and with *creepers* and bedbugs from the straw-ticked mattresses, the privy was antiseptic. Detroit was two hundred miles away, and Jansen had made up his mind to go there. If he were to arrive by Monday morning, he had little more than three days in which to make the trip. He must leave at daybreak, and without alerting the rest of the jacks—or there would be a stampede for the city.

Before dawn he had slung his "turkey," containing his belongings, over his shoulder, and, wearing his stags—boots with the tops cut off—was firing up the wood-burning locomotive of the logging train. In the darkness, the locomotive spewed smoke speckled with sparks as it began to move over the frosted terrain.

For Jansen it was the happiest day of his life—he was on his way to make his fortune. As he hurled the logs into the flames he sang lustily:

> *"When our youthful days are ended,*
> *We will cease from winter toils,*
> *And each one through the summer warm*
> *Will till the virgin soil;*
> *We've enough to eat, to drink, to wear,*
> *Content through life to go,*
> *Then we'll tell our wild adventures o'er*
> *And no more a-lumbering go;*
> *And no more a-lumbering go,*
> *So no more a-lumbering go,*
> *O we'll tell our wild adventures o'er*
> *And no more a-lumbering go."* [1]

Daylight framed the puffing, swaying engine against the ermine cover of the denuded land. Fifty years before, primeval forests of pine had ranged the breadth of the state. All that remained were isolated stands too mean for the logger's ax, stumps blackened by fire, and some struggling saplings of new growth. Much of the territory had been surveyed by David Ward between 1847 and 1857, when the "pine land craze" had been set off by Congress. By taking one fourth of the land surveyed in return for his services, Ward had become one of Detroit's wealthiest citizens.

Behind him, he and others like him had left a land ravaged by a rapine seldom equaled. Forests were mowed like wheat. The prime lumber was selected; the remainder burned or left to rot. Fires started as the result of carelessness turned tens of thousands of acres into furnaces. In 1871, on the heels of the great Chicago fire, flames had swept two hundred miles across the Michigan Peninsula from Benton Harbor to Port Huron. Entire towns had been wiped out. Ten years later, another fire had killed 125 persons.

At the turn of the century, thirty acres of hard woods daily were being fed into the kilns of iron smelters. In 1890 nearly two thousand mills were producing 4.5 billion board feet of lumber annually. By 1900 the prized white pine was all but extinct. By 1910 the Norway pine and other original growth was disappearing. Mills shut down. Lumber towns were abandoned to fire and to snow and to wind—the wind that now swept unopposed from Great Lake to Great Lake. In 1912 even the giant saws of the mill at Deward, named after David Ward, ceased to turn. The buildings of Deward bleached and rotted in the desert they had helped to create. Onto the land that Peter Jansen's train crossed like a tiny caterpillar, a long winter of penance was settling.

Thousands of men pressed against the walls of the Ford plant to gain shelter from the gusts of wind. Snow swirled along the streets. Here and there a fire lit in a can or drum was overwhelmed by the nine-degree temperature. From all over Michigan, from the Midwest, from the East, from the South, workers earning no more than thirty cents an hour even when highly skilled were heeding the clarion call of the $5 day. By the time the gates opened there would be more than ten thousand. They were a portion of the seventy-five thousand men in Detroit and millions throughout the nation who in the economic downturn of 1913–1914 were again walking the streets and standing in bread lines.

Thirty-nine-year-old William Norveth had lined up in front of the plant every day since Tuesday, January 6. Born in Hungary, he had come to America shortly before the turn of the century. A ten-year resident of Detroit, he had worked at a different job almost every year. With a large family to support, he had not had steady employment since the fall.

Neither Ford, who went off to the auto show in New York, nor any other company executive had anticipated such an outpouring of men, roughly equal to the entire work force of General Motors. It was an indication of management's lack of understanding of economic conditions and the lives led by the men. Having no machinery to process such numbers, the company hung out "No Hiring" signs in several different languages.

The signs had no effect. By Thursday, the packed crowd before the gates contained men from as far away as Chicago, Indianapolis, Dayton, and Cleveland. Trying to head off a job rush that rivaled the Oklahoma land rush, the company announced it would hire no one who had not been a resident of Detroit for at least six months. But that was like trying to halt a tidal wave by announcement.

Beneath their frayed pants and coats the men who gathered in the darkness of Monday, January 12, wore pieces of blankets, flannel nightshirts, and newspapers wrapped around their chests with twine. Their heads were protected with caps and old rags wound like bandannas. Their feet protruded through cracked footwear. Some, coming from as far south as Missouri and Tennessee, were dressed in clothing that failed to break the wind at all.

A month before, Ralph Lentick had been living in Calumet on the Keweenaw Peninsula of Upper Michigan, five hundred miles away, and had never been to Detroit. For fifty years his Cornish family had worked in the copper and iron mines. Then, in the summer of 1913, the great strike had broken out. Of fiercely independent spirit, Lentick had little use for either the company or the union. The day after Christmas, in the aftermath of a tragedy that had brought death to seventy-four people, he had packed up his family and headed for the farm of his wife's sister near Lansing in central Michigan. It was there that the news of the $5 day had reached him. Traveling on the interurban electric system, he reached Detroit two days later and was melded into the legions in front of the plant.

Many of the men had arrived on the interurban electrics. From Detroit the system radiated for more than nine hundred miles across Michigan to Toledo, Lansing, Kalamazoo, and Bay City. At Bay City, Peter Jansen had boarded one of the cars. Now, stepping down the street, he was slightly drunk. Glowing in the warmth of his boots, heavy trousers, and heavy jacket, he bellowed out the words:

> *"Once I was a shantyman and was a lively lad,*
> *I flung away my money till no more was to be had.*
> *And now I'm old and feeble, boys, and left out in the cold,*
> *So save your money when you're young*
> *You'll need it when you're old."* [2]

Turning in half circles this way and that, he looked up at the block letters that, suspended from the tall smokestacks, spelled F O R D. On what a half dozen years before had been sixty-two acres of racetrack and farmland, Albert Kahn, the son of a Jewish peddler, had constructed for Henry Ford the world's largest automobile factory.

2

The Paris of the West

THE LAND ON WHICH FORD HAD CONSTRUCTED HIS PLANT HAD BEEN PLATTED*
during the first part of the nineteenth century by Judge Augustus Woodward.
Tall and angular with piercing eyes, the judge was a friend of Thomas Jefferson;
and a member of the first city council of the new United States capital. In June,
1805, the President had appointed him as one of five officials to administer the
newly organized Michigan Territory.

The Detroit in which Judge Woodward arrived on the last day of June was
a demoralized town of a few hundred persons. Only a solitary building remained
standing amidst the charcoal and ashes and skeleton chimneys.

Between eight and nine o'clock on the morning of June 11, baker John
Harvey had set out to replenish his supply of flour. Climbing into his cart, he
had rapped his clay pipe against his boot. The coals, caught by a gust of the
constant and vigorous breeze that blew off the Lakes, had been swirled into the
barn. Within seconds the pile of hay in which they landed was ablaze.

The citizens carried buckets of water from the river and tried to damp the
flaming thatched-moss roofs with swabs at the end of long poles. They were
overwhelmed by the flames. Loading their belongings onto canoes and bateaux,
they watched the town burn. When another baker, Jacques Girardin, returned
to the batch of fresh dough he had left in his unlighted oven, he found it
baked to perfection. Since most of the food supply was destroyed, Father
Gabriel Richard, the unofficial but acknowledged leader of the community,
organized an expedition to call on the farms up and down the river.

It was Father Richard who greeted Judge Woodward. An aristocratic
Sulpician priest, he had barely escaped the Paris militia after refusing to take
the oath of loyalty to the French Republic. Vaulting out of a rear window, he
had made his way to a seaport and boarded ship for America. Soon he had
been in the wilds of Illinois and working among the Indians. In 1798 he had
arrived in Detroit.

* A term denoting the drawing up of a plan, map, or chart, usually of a town site.

8

Left to themselves, Detroit's people would have rebuilt the frontier town with its narrow streets and small, clustered lots in the form in which it had existed since its founding in 1701 by Antoine de la Mothe Cadillac, the younger son of a Gascon nobleman. But as they chafed to get started so that they could have shelter before winter, the judge refused to permit them to proceed. While they muttered, *"Mon Dieu,"* and stared at this strange American, he sat on a chair amidst the rubble. Meditating, he paid no heed to sun, lightning, or pouring rain, but waited until he could obtain a copy of L'Enfant's plans for the city of Washington. Once he had the plans in his hand, the judge announced that work could now commence on laying the foundations for the Paris of the West.

From Canada, the judge imported a surveyor. "For the space of thirty days and thirty nights," wrote John Gentle, the community's self-appointed cynic and social commentator, "he viewed the diurnal evolution of the planets, visible and invisible, and calculated the course and rapidity of the blazing meteors. To his profound observings of the heavenly regions the world is indebted for the discovery of the streets, alleys, circles, angles, and squares of this magnificent city." [1]

In place of the Old World village, there was laid out a city of interlocking hexagons, bisected by broad avenues and studded with plazas. Each hexagon was composed of twelve triangular units of eight blocks. In the center of each, one block—or one ninth of the land—was reserved for public purposes. Each triangle was to be a small community, in which citizens would be able to find all conveniences needed for everyday living. At the hub of each hexagon was a large, open, circular area from which the avenues radiated. The first of these, designated the Grand Circus, was located eight tenths of a mile from the river front in an area that had been part of the commons.

The townspeople, contemplating the devastation of the fire, wondered at the judge's sanity. In its hundred-year history the community had never had a population of more than twenty-two hundred, including soldiers and Indians. One upheaval after another had retarded its prosperity. A majority of the French settlers had departed for St. Louis after the British conquest of Canada during the French and Indian Wars. The town was just recovering from that conflict when the American Revolution had broken out. For more than a decade after the end of the war, its status had remained unclear, and it had continued to be occupied by the British. Not until July, 1796, had the American flag been raised over Detroit.

During this entire period the community had existed primarily as a trading post. As a trading post it had maintained—except for some brief intervals—cordial relations with the Indians. The Indians had found the manufactured goods imported from Europe useful additions to their way of life. Most of the French settlers, intent on trading not farming, had been dependent on the Indians not only for furs but for many of their provisions.

Cadillac had encouraged the Indians to raise their huts and establish their villages along *de trois*—the straits—where they long had had meeting grounds and a village. (He had been opposed by Jesuit missionaries, already alarmed at the corrupting effect of European influence on the Indians' civilization.) While the Wyandot and Ottawa warriors hunted and engaged in sports, the women tended the fields. Beneath their skilled and diligent hands, beans, peas, squash, and melons grew to gigantic proportions. As the Europeans looked on in astonishment, the corn reached ten to twelve feet high.

The whites seldom bothered to lock the doors of their homes and storehouses. They watched the Indians play lacrosse, and at night attended their dances. Romantic attachments developed between the largely womenless pioneers and the Indian maidens. Since the future of the settlement depended upon an expanding population, and the French monarchy discouraged emigration, Cadillac encouraged the settlers to marry Indian girls.

When the British ousted the French in 1763, Dutch, New England, Scotch, and Jewish merchants made their way up the Hudson and Mohawk Rivers to Lake Erie. Replacing the French in the fur trade, they established themselves in Detroit. They stocked their stores with snowshoes, large brass locks, pewter plates, ink powder, scalping knives, nightcaps, mounds of blankets, hair powder, burning glasses, candles, animal traps, Dutch ovens, tea, silver buckles, ear bobs, breast plates, rolls of tobacco, barrels of rum, and mococks of maple sugar.* In 1781 a single fur shipment consisted of the skins of 12,132 deer, 9,482 raccoons, 682 wildcats and foxes, 413 bears, and countless mink. "Hard money"—mostly in the form of the Austrian silver *Thaler* (dollar)—was scarce. In its place, the settlers used furs, slaves (usually Indians, but occasionally Negroes and whites), tobacco, and clam and oyster shells manufactured by the New York Dutch and carried by the Indians as wampum.†

A thoroughly cosmopolitan population developed. Scotsman John Askin, the town's leading merchant, raised in succession two families—one by a French, and a second by an Indian wife.

This tolerant and mutually productive relationship between the whites and the Indians was changed to a fierce struggle for land and survival by the expansion of the English settlers from the Atlantic seaboard. Reproducing prolifically, they were more than doubling themselves each generation, and relentlessly pushing westward. The mixed nomadic-agricultural culture of the Indians needed vast tracts of land to sustain it. (Indian agent Henry Schoolcraft estimated that one hunter required fifty thousand acres to support his family.) Wherever the whites went, they cleared the forests. With their guns, they destroyed the ecological balance. The Indians were driven into each other's hunting grounds, and forced to fight each other.

In the West, the Revolutionary War became a savage conflict between the frontiersmen and the British-led Indians. From British-held Detroit, party after party, some outfitted with artillery, descended on Kentucky and the Ohio River Valley. With the British paying five dollars per scalp, they returned laden with hundreds of scalps and prisoners.

The Treaty of Paris, which ended the war in the East, had no effect upon that in the West. Repeatedly, American expeditions sent out from Kentucky and Pennsylvania were defeated, and their commanders burned at the stake. Throughout the 1780's an average of four hundred settlers—as prisoners or in the form of scalps—were represented annually in the Indian parades around Detroit.

* The only sweetening agent of the settlers, maple sugar was tapped from the trees and the syrup boiled down by the Indians. Since the Indians used the boiling liquid to cook their fish, a tea drinker occasionally found himself coming eye to eye with the skeletal remains of a fish head.
† Paying for furs with shells, the Dutch obviously reaped fortunes. However, so long as the shell money could be used to purchase other goods, and had not been "counterfeited" or "debased," it served its purpose as well as silver money or paper money.

Many of the first Negroes in the community were slaves captured by Indians in their raids on the border states.

One of the whites taken prisoner along the Ohio River and brought to Detroit in 1782 was John Fitch. A clockmaker, brass worker, gunsmith, and surveyor, he recognized that the vast distances of the West were an insuperable barrier to development until an efficient means of transportation could be devised.* Following his release, he devoted the rest of his life to the invention of a steamboat. But the period was one in which the United States was in economic depression, and the Indians and the British still made the Northwest unsafe. Although he constructed four steam-powered boats, Fitch was unable to find the backers to carry his experiments to a successful conclusion.

The experiments, however, induced Robert R. Livingston, a patrician New Yorker, to finance Robert Fulton's construction of a steamboat. (Fulton had achieved a worldwide reputation as a canal builder, and developer of a submarine.) On August 17, 1807, Fulton's sidewheeler, the *Clermont,* paddled at a speed of five miles per hour from Manhattan to Albany. Four years later a steamboat was able to make its way upriver from New Orleans to Pittsburgh.

The effect on Detroit was electrifying. When the British had departed, the community had been left dangling like a broken blossom at the end of a limb —the natural and traditional flow of trade was from the Straits of Mackinac along the Great Lakes to Montreal, a territory and route that remained largely in control of the Hudson's Bay Company and the British. There had seemed little future to an outpost separated by 250 miles of hostile Indians and some two to three weeks of travel from the nearest American settlement. The population had plummeted to five hundred.

The steamboat promised to bridge the wilderness and end the isolation of Detroit. Settlers streamed up the Mississippi—which had become an all-American river when President Jefferson in 1803 acquired the Louisiana Territory— and along the Ohio River. The Indians, abandoned by their former British and French allies, and already outnumbered ten to one by the whites, were left to contend alone against the flood. Foreseeing the advent of an Armageddon for his people, the "Shawnee Prophet," the most prestigious of the Indian leaders, preached a "holy war" against the whites. In Detroit the townspeople locked their doors and at dusk ejected the Indians from within the town's walls—even though the Indians might be visiting their "white" cousins. The town was rife with rumors and anxiety. Fearful of the ragged, worm-ridden, ever more impoverished Indians, the people repeatedly appealed to Washington for protection.

By 1811 when the Indians rose under Tecumseh, the Prophet's brother, the whites had the advantage of numbers, and of transportation. Most of all, they had the advantage of weapons.

Until the late 1790's gunsmithing had been an art. The United States Arsenal at Springfield was producing 245 handmade muskets a year. Then Eli Whitney, the inventor of the cotton gin, had reacted to the nation's need for arms in the threatened war with France and turned his ingenuity to the production of muskets. To replace the workmen departing in droves to settle upon the Western lands, Whitney invented machines. For the machines he made patterns and

* Detroit was so isolated that when Fitch arrived the news of Cornwallis's surrender, which had taken place more than six months earlier, had not yet reached the community.

guides to perform the tasks previously carried out by hand. Since the machines did not have the eccentricities of the individual workmen, each part turned out to be like every other part.

In 1798 Whitney had obtained an audience with the Secretary of the Treasury and President Adams. As the President, other members of the government, and various arms experts reacted with astonishment, he invited them to pick parts at random for the assembly of ten guns. Successfully completing the demonstration, Whitney proposed that he be given a contract for the manufacture of ten thousand weapons, a number breathtaking to men used to seeing guns turned out by the dozens. It was the world's introduction to the mass production of hardware.

Whitney obtained the contract. Employing water power, and machines for forging, rolling, boring, and grinding, he ultimately completed the weapons. (It took him eight years instead of the two projected.) New England was established as the center of the world's light-arms industry.

The weapons Whitney produced, far less expensive than any ever made before, went to arm the swarms of settlers that Generals William Hull and William Henry Harrison pressed into their militias. Down the muzzles of the muskets was poured one of the world's finest powders, developed by Eleuthère Irénée du Pont—like Father Richard a refugee from the French Revolution and like Judge Woodward a friend of President Jefferson. Du Pont, appalled by the coarseness and inaccuracy of the powder he found in America, had induced the United States Government to support him in the construction of a powder works.

Tecumseh, and the poorly armed, ammunition-short Indians had no chance. On November 7, 1811, General Harrison, sweeping across the Northwest Territory, won a decisive battle at Tippecanoe. From west of the Wabash to Lake Michigan, the Midwest was turned into white man's country.

The war hawks of the West were jubilant. Allied with John Jacob Astor's New York-based American Fur Company, they would now be satisfied with nothing less than the annihilation of the Hudson's Bay Company, and the annexation of Canada.

On the outbreak of the War of 1812, however, Detroit was ignominiously surrendered to the British. Although retaken the next year, and made safe from the Indians by the defeat and death of Tecumseh in Canada, the town had been ravaged by the war. Indians, Americans, and British troops had vied with each other in destroying fields and tearing down fences and barns for firewood. Food, never abundant, had disappeared. People were reduced to eating boiled hay. Cholera killed seven hundred soldiers, more than died in all the Western battles. The peaceful Indians (and all but a handful now were peaceful) were more and more dependent on subsidies and handouts from the white man. Scavenging amidst the garbage, they lived on entrails and putrefying offal. When, starving, they threatened in 1813 to overrun the town, barrels of whiskey and rum were broken open for them. Within a few hours dead-drunk Indians littered the streets. No brigade of riflemen could have dispatched the *menace* more efficiently.

Judge Woodward wrote: "The desolation of this territory is beyond all conception [with] more than half of the population destitute. . . ." [2]

The war did not bring the conquest of Canada, but it did serve to turn the eyes of the nation westward. Congress appropriated six million acres—one third in Michigan—for veterans of the war. The Detroit *Gazette* published pie-in-the-sky stories encouraging settlers to come to the territory. The vast majority of the migrants, however, continued to settle in the Ohio Valley, which the steamboat provided with a dependable means of transportation.

Not until Michigan could be tied to the East via water transportation would it prosper. Scarcely had Fulton's steamer arrived in Albany in the summer of 1807 than New Yorkers began urging the construction of a canal along the Mohawk Valley to connect the Hudson to Lake Erie. In 1808, a resolution was introduced into the New York Legislature. A canal committee, to which Fulton and Livingston were added in 1811, was formed. Fulton bombarded Congress with canal-building schemes.

With the end of the war, the canal promoters, buttressed by land speculators, succeeded in convincing the New York Legislature to pass an act authorizing $5 million for the building of the Erie Canal.

Preceding the canal, a host of *Bostonians,* as New Englanders came to be generically named, made their way through the Mohawk Valley to Lake Erie and Detroit. Their influx generated not only a clash of languages and of nationalities, but of cultures.

Even as Father Richard had continued to gain in stature as the leader of the French community, Judge Woodward had ruled as the challenged but unbowed dictator of American government and policy in Detroit. Pale and cadaverous, he wore as his customary court dress a swallow-tailed coat with brass buttons, a buff vest, and a red cravat. Ruffles, seldom laundered, bloomed from beneath his coat and sleeves. The single room in which he lived and worked was a labyrinth of books and papers. Men gaped openmouthed and uncomprehending as he delivered himself in Latinized English. Never intoxicated, yet never appearing entirely sober, he sat every night smoking a pipe and consuming a half pint of whiskey in Mack and Conant's store. On the bench he kept a brandy snifter within reach. Unquestionably erudite, evidently fair, the law was as he made it. In one action he was both complainant and judge. In another he was the accuser, the prosecutor, and a witness, as well as the judge. His arm reached into every important activity. He acquired extensive holdings of land. When the first bank was incorporated in 1806, he was its president.

The life of the community, however, continued to be dominated by the Romance culture of the French. Except in Judge Woodward's cluttered room, books were scarce. Church was attended faithfully, if only because, in the medieval European tradition, Sunday was also market day and racing day, cockfighting day and courting day. Along the narrow streets the men, despite an official ban, raced their horses in breakneck fashion. Teen-age marriages were the custom. It was not unusual for the ages of the bride and groom to total less than thirty. (The bride of Dr. G. C. Anton walked to the altar with a doll in her arms.) Households drew their water from piers projecting into the river. Maidens "walking the plank" with their buckets had a fine view up and down the banks, and in turn presented a fine appearance as the wind entwined itself in their skirts.

French continued to be the principal language of the town, Catholicism its dominant religion, and the atmosphere of a French provincial town its pervading aura. It was a paternalistic and easygoing society, which did not enshrine hard work and competitiveness as virtues. Since there were few books and few complicated business transactions, and the priest was the acknowledged interpreter of the Bible, literacy was limited largely to the upper class.

The *Bostonians,* in contrast, brought with them diametrically opposed traditions. They were literate, they strove to get ahead, they applied themselves diligently to their work and their businesses, and they believed every child was to be taught to read. In 1816 the Reverend John Monteith arrived from Princeton to become the first permanently established Protestant minister in the territory. He immediately founded a common school.* It came, however, to an untimely end when the teacher, a Mr. Danforth, hurled a knife at one of his obstreperous scholars, and was thereupon chased across the river by the vexed parents.

Father Richard had even less luck in trying to bring education to the community. In 1804 he had started a church school, and five years later he had imported the first printing press into the territory. The French population, however, had provided little demand for either. He had worked diligently to promote an Indian school to prepare Indian children for life in the rapidly changing culture. President Jefferson had backed him wholeheartedly. President Madison, however, had decided that the United States Government could not constitutionally support the school. Father Richard had been dispossessed of the farm on which he had set up the school and sued for the debts he had contracted.

In 1817, Judge Woodward, who hardly would allow such an opportunity for abstruse semantics to slip by, organized the *Catholepistemiad,* or University of Michigania. Thirteen *didaxiim* † were established. The Reverend John Monteith was appointed to seven of these; Father Richard to six. Their combined annual salary was set at $181.25.

Simultaneously, the demand for reading material stimulated by the *Bostonians* led to the establishment of the territory's first newspaper, the Detroit *Gazette.* Written four fifths in English and one fifth in French, it reflected the literacy and comparative demand for reading material of the two populations. Father Richard in an "anonymous" editorial admonished the French Catholic population, "There are many young people, of from eighteen to twenty years, who have not yet learned to read." Frenchmen were exhorted to have their children educated, because otherwise the *Bostonians* soon would hold all of the important positions. Judge Woodward aptly but impolitically commented that the French were spending too much time in church, and not enough time attending to business.

The French might be spending too much time in church, but they were not observing the Sabbath in the manner to which the Reverend John Monteith and the *Bostonians* were accustomed. Although it was natural for farmers coming to church to bring their produce and make Sunday the market day, it outraged the Reverend John Monteith's sense of propriety. He succeeded in having the Sunday market abolished. He did not, however, succeed in eliminating the horse racing, card playing, and general revelry that were also a part of the day.

As men migrated to Michigan to seek their fortunes, the town soon had a licensed saloon on every corner, and as many more unlicensed saloons between. Although the announcement of the construction of the Erie Canal had been

---

* Since paper was far too expensive to be used by children, a sandbox was employed to teach writing and arithmetic.
† Professorships. The subjects included *catholepistemia, anthropoglossica, physiognostica, iatuca, diegetica,* and *ennoeica.* Or, respectively: universal science; literature; natural history; medical science; historical science; intellectual science.

greeted with derision by skeptics, within a year a host of men were successfully digging westward. In the summer of 1818 a Hudson River steamboat builder transferred his skills to Lake Erie. Late in August the *Walk-in-the-Water* puffed from Buffalo to Detroit in less than forty-eight hours—a distance it had taken sailing vessels as long as a month to negotiate. Sitting like a nix astraddle the bowsprit, grinning, waving, and spitting tobacco juice, was Judge Woodward.

As the gateway to the Northwest, Detroit was booming. In five years the population nearly doubled, reaching fourteen hundred by the end of the decade. Mushrooming as a center of commerce, the town contained 232 businesses.*

The expanding economy created a shortage of money. There was one small bank, but its capital of $10,000 disappeared with the cashier. Of the nineteen Ohio banks whose money circulated, that of seven was classified as "good," and that of about an equal number as "good-for-nothing." Merchants issued their own due bills, which were accepted or not according to individual reputations. Father Richard, embarking on the erection of a new church, printed his own money to pay the workmen (and was embarrassed when the type was stolen and used in the printing of a *counterfeit* issue). The construction of the capital and the courthouse was financed by $22,500 worth of scrip issued by the governor and Judge Woodward.

The question of the manner in which the territory was to be developed had been settled by Judge Woodward in 1807. Five years earlier, when its entire white population had been little more than four thousand, the shortage of labor had led territorial delegates to petition Congress to suspend the Northwest Ordinance's Article VI, which banned slavery in the territory between the Ohio and Mississippi Rivers. In response, Virginian John Randolph, chairman of the committee to which the petition was referred, had stated: "The committee deem it highly dangerous and inexpedient to impair a provision wisely calculated to promote the happiness and prosperity of the northwestern country." [3] The Virginians, in general, had been dubious about the economic efficiency of slavery and increasingly concerned about its destructive moral effect.

Judge Woodward had interpreted Article VI as making slavery illegal except for those persons held in bondage on the date the American flag had replaced the British. By 1815 there were not more than two dozen slaves in the territory. The encouragement of the migration of free labor was a necessity. In order for free labor to respond to that encouragement, land, plentiful and cheap, had to be available.

There was scarcely a man in the territory, including its governor, Lewis Cass, and its judge, Augustus Woodward, who was not involved in land promotion and speculation. They were, however, hampered by the fact that the Indians had been induced to give up only the southeastern part of the territory around Detroit. If the promoters were to prosper, it would be necessary to dispossess the Indians of Michigan as, within the span of less than two decades, the Indians of Ohio, Indiana, and Illinois already had been dispossessed.

In the fall of 1819 Governor Cass invited the Indian chiefs to a council meeting. Only thirty-seven years old, Cass, a schoolmate of Daniel Webster, had

---

* Including five bakers, twelve blacksmiths, sixty carpenters and joiners, three cabinetmakers, six coopers, one coach and chaisemaker, ten gunsmiths, twenty-four grocery and dry-goods merchants, sixteen grocery and provision stores and alehouses, six hatters, five harness makers, eight innkeepers, twenty-three masons, three painters, three printers, twelve shoemakers, seven watchmakers and five wheelwrights.

been an Ohio legislator and a colonel in the militia that retook Detroit. Dynamic and strong-willed, he was skilled in the art of applying pressure.

Placing three thousand dollars in silver on the table, he remarked pointedly that those Indians who had opposed the white settlement had been ousted anyway, and had nothing to show for it. Why should not the forty thousand Indians of Michigan be wiser, accept three thousand dollars, cede all of their lands, and move across the Missisippi (where, of course, they would have to go to war against the existing tribes to establish hunting rights).

Indignant, the Indians rejected the offer. Plied with whiskey, they quarreled among themselves. Betrayed by the French-Indian traders on whom they depended, but who now recognized far greater profits could be gained by participating in the land grab, the Indians wilted beneath the governor's pressure. General Cass, making pikers out of the Dutch who had bought Manhattan for twenty-four dollars, forced the Indians to relinquish the eastern half of Michigan for three thousand dollars and the promise of a one-thousand-dollar annuity.

As the Indians were pushed westward, their numerous French-Indian cousins in Detroit, many of whom were shortly to grow rich, were ever more separated from them, not only in distance but in manner. Soon many a delicate young lady, picking up her skirts at the sight of a ragged Indian, would have no inkling that the Indian's great-grandmother might have been the sister of her own.

In 1823 the French community, profiting from a split among the Yankees, managed to carry the day for their candidate, Father Richard, in the territory's third election for delegate to Congress. The only priest ever to serve (until 1970) in Congress, Father Richard appeared at the Capitol in knee breeches and an ankle-length coat like an apparition from the court of Louis XVI. His thick-accented English was still sometimes more comprehensible in French. He was, nevertheless, a successful lobbyist. In 1825 he was influential in the passage of a bill to build the first road through the wilderness. Named Michigan Avenue in Detroit, the road was to end as Michigan Avenue in Fort Dearborn (or Chicago, as Fort Dearborn subsequently came to be known).

By 1823, 220 miles of the Erie Canal were open. In October, 1825, the canal was completed along its entire 263-mile length. The next spring there were seven steamboats on Lake Erie. *Bostonians* and upstate New Yorkers—many of whom, in fact, had also been born in New England—poured into Detroit.

Father Richard was defeated for reelection. Judge Woodward, his eccentricities increasingly out of place as the community was transformed from a frontier post to the replica of a New England township, was toppled from his position.

Turning to land promotion, and choosing his sites shrewdly, the judge laid out along the Pontiac Road the village of Woodwardville, a village that was to stand empty for more than three quarters of a century until occupied by Henry Ford. Another township that he platted on the Michigan Road he named, with Byronesque flourish, Ypsilanti, in honor of a Greek prince engaged in the war of independence against the Turks. Both townships were planned far better than the cities that ultimately were to rise on the sites.

In the days when the journey from Detroit to New York had taken two months, there had been no way any of the Northwest's products, except furs, could profitably be shipped to the East. The canal cut both the travel time and the shipping expense from Detroit to New York to one tenth of what they had been previously. Even as the canal was being opened, the "singular fact" was recorded of the arrival in Detroit of a wagon load of flour from the mill in

Pontiac. It was the first ever from the interior. Two years later the first bag of flour was loaded onto a boat for export. The next year it was followed by the initial shipment of tobacco, the first of many that were to make Detroit a leading cigar-manufacturing center.

The vast fishing grounds of the Great Lakes could now be commercially exploited. Sturgeon, pickerel, pike, perch, bass, and bullheads ranged up to 125 pounds. In a single day in 1824, thirty thousand whitefish were caught almost within sight of Detroit. By 1830, seven vessels were engaged in shipping salted fish to the East. Others carried products like ice and cider, and returned with oysters and manufactured goods from the Atlantic. In 1833, with the completion of the Welland Canal—the Canadians' response to the Erie—Niagara Falls was bypassed. The Great Lakes were connected to the St. Lawrence.

Suddenly, the orientation of the entire American nation was shifted, as if a giant hand had superimposed itself upon the continent and rearranged its geography. The route of trade had been from the East Coast to Pittsburgh, and then along the Ohio and Mississippi Rivers to New Orleans. Philadelphia and Baltimore were both located closer to the West than New York, and they, together with Boston and New Orleans, had laid claim to being the leading American cities.

But with the completion of the Erie Canal, the route of trade and the growth of population shifted to New York and the Great Lakes. Philadelphia, Baltimore, and Boston watched astonished as New York pulled away in population and prosperity. Everywhere there was agitation for canal building.

Within a quarter of a century the inventions of Whitney and Fulton had had as much effect upon the course not only of American, but of world history, as the Revolutionary War. In Europe they were a major force in the economic revolutions that were being wrought. The application of steam power to transportation ended the historic isolation of communities and linked town to town, country to country, nation to nation, and continent to continent. By the middle of the century Detroit was closer, in time, to Liverpool than it had been in 1800 to Cincinnati. People whose world had been limited to within a few miles of their birthplace had a vast new universe opened. As the cotton gin and the steamboat bound England and Ireland to America much more closely than political connections ever had, they pushed the Western world into an era of upheaval.

3

The Irish Aphrodisiac

FOR THE FORD FAMILY, WHICH HAD SETTLED IN THE FERTILE BANDON VALLEY north of Clonakilty in County Cork, it was Whitney's cotton gin that was bringing hard times.

The Fords were English, members of the Anglican Church. Educated, skilled as carpenters, the family had come to Ireland from Essex.* They were part of the movement of people that had begun in the latter part of the sixteenth century when, with a rapidly multiplying population of about five million, England had found itself in the initial stage of a land shortage.

Ireland, more than half the size of England and Wales but with a population of less than one million, had seemed a convenient area in which to settle the overflow from England and Scotland. Repeated uprisings against British rule, and invasions by the Spanish and the French, had led the British government to declare forfeit the lands of the Irish nobles in Ulster in the north and in Munster—Cork, Kerry, Limerick, Waterford, and Tipperary—in the south. The lands were assigned to English "undertakers" (nobles) on the proviso that they be settled with English emigrants and men of arms. The Fords and their middle-class compatriots, coming as leaseholders onto the large estates, had founded Bandon as a fortified town for protection against the hostile countryside.

By 1690, when the Irish were crushed at the Battle of the Boyne, the enmity between the two nationalities had been etched beyond redemption onto the characters of men. The English, viewing the Irish as barbarians whose will and capacity to resist was to be stamped out forever, imposed a rule designed to create and reinforce the inferiority that they ascribed to their subjects.

To eliminate popish influence, the English expelled the Jesuits, and made the education of children by Catholic schoolmasters a penal offense. For Protestants, on the other hand, charter schools were established to educate children at public expense. In practice, this meant the end of what little education had existed for Catholics. Illiteracy became synonymous with the native Irish.

* One of the most heavily wooded regions of England, Essex long had been known for the skills of its "mechanics" and woodworkers. The ancestors of John Fitch had also taken ship from Essex.

Catholics were barred from holding civil and political offices. They could not be freemen of corporate towns, and were banned entirely from the limits of Bandon, Galway, and Limerick. Above the gates of Bandon was inscribed the legend:

> *A Turk, a Jew, or an Atheist,*
> *May live in this town, but no Papist.*[1]

Catholics could not purchase land from Protestants. They could lease land from Protestants for no more than thirty-one years, and only if the rent represented two thirds of the profits. Since Catholics were forbidden to own horses worth more than £5, any Protestant could claim a Catholic's horse for £5 and 1 pence. Unable to enforce the laws without the cooperation of at least part of the populace, the government built into the system large rewards for informers.

Made by the English for Englishmen, and by Protestants for Protestants, the laws forfeited all moral force in the Irish-Catholic community. Regarding the law and its enforcers as the enemy, the Irish abided by their own codes, and turned into a nation of *law breakers.*

What made the situation worse and exacerbated the conflict was that the Irish, while losing their liberty, had acquired the potato. A hardy root that would grow anywhere and with practically no care, the potato had been transplanted by the Spanish from its native America to Europe. In the latter part of the sixteenth century it had been introduced into Ireland.

Throughout Europe the middle class harbored a strong prejudice against the potato—as late as 1795 a French waiter was arrested on a charge of sedition for exclaiming that the French people were "reduced to . . . eating potatoes . . . only good for swine." [2] But for poor people everywhere it was a godsend that saved many from starvation.

Providing the most abundant source of food in the history of Europe, the potato affected the Irish like an aphrodisiac. The population *exploded.* The production of manpower became the leading industry of the Catholic population. Since there was no longer warfare, and little else (besides sex) to employ Irishmen at home, they were exported in the form of mercenaries for European armies.

Poland enlisted them for the war against the Turks. The Spanish army sometimes seemed more Irish than Spanish. Between 1691 and 1745 at least a half million served in France's Irish Brigade. During the eighteenth century the French fleet was commanded by Admiral *Macnamara.* The "French" governor of the occupied city of Dresden was *Maguire.* An Austrian army was commanded by General *Lacy.* The British army often was as Irish as it was English.

Despite the continuing drain of young men, the Irish population quadrupled from less than one million to nearly four million in the century after 1660. In a land that had seemed underpopulated a fierce struggle for survival developed. The poverty was so appalling that Dean Swift, in a savage satire, suggested as a solution that Europeans cultivate a taste for one hundred thousand roast Irish babies annually.

Vermin-ridden families lived in earthen-floored, sod-covered, daub-and-wattle huts, damp and without heat. With the Irish family lived its pig, virtually the only product that it could raise for cash.

The degradation, backwardness, and retention of barbaric customs—such as the attachment of the plow to the horse's tail—were the concomitants of poverty.

The English, however, ascribed the poverty to the degradation. Abject poverty was looked upon as a national characteristic of the native Irish.

The invention, in the second half of the eighteenth century, of the spinning jenny, followed by the establishment in Lancashire of the world's first "factory," brought prosperity to the English of Bandon, but further misery to the Irish. The jenny multiplied the production of yarn eight times at first, and more later. In the factory, water power and, beginning in 1785, steam power were substituted for human power in the running of the machinery. As the capacity to manufacture cloth multiplied, a huge demand for wool was created. In Cork, as throughout England and Ireland, land was withdrawn from tenant farming and devoted to sheep raising, which required little manpower.

Generating a demand for Irish foodstuffs, the Napoleonic Wars brought a temporary halt to the eviction of tenants, and a general prosperity to Irish agriculture. Ireland was brought under the protection of the Corn Laws—designed to protect English agriculture through restriction of imports of grain, and to make the British Isles self-sufficient in food production. More Irishmen succeeded in maintaining themselves by renting small plots of land. While they themselves continued to subsist on potatoes, they raised corn and pigs, which they could sell for cash.

As the price of agricultural products had increased, so had the demand for land. Rents rose. Among the Catholics, outlaw organizations like the Defenders and the Whiteboys sprang up to discourage the practice of open bidding for land. By beatings, burnings, floggings, and, if necessary, killings, they intimidated anyone who attempted to outbid and drive another man off the land. In Northern Ireland, the Presbyterians formed the Peep O' Day Boys to deal with the Catholics who, willing to accept a lower standard of living, were driving the Scotch-Irish from their holdings.

With the end of the Napoleonic Wars, however, agricultural prices collapsed. The inflated rents, which no tenant could any longer afford, brought tens of thousands of evictions, and a return of land to pasturage. Even the potato crop was insufficient to feed a population whose number was approaching seven million. In the early 1820's there was famine.

Concurrently, the demand for wool declined. Since it was all but impossible to work cotton fibers in hand looms, throughout history weavers had relied mostly on wool and flax. The new power machinery, however, was ideally suited for cotton. Traveling to Georgia in 1792, Eli Whitney had heard planters lament that they could not meet the surging British demand for cotton. Though "green seed" or short-staple cotton would grow almost like a weed, the separation of the seed from the boll required so much labor as to make its production economically impractical. Whitney, setting to work, within ten days devised a working *gin,* or mechanical separator that removed the seed from the boll. Thanks to Whitney's ingenuity, cotton, now infinitely cheaper than wool, became the staple raw material for the textile industry, the first in the world to be converted to mechanized production. British imports of cotton increased from 31 million pounds in 1790 to 273 million pounds in 1831.

The 157,000 Irish artisans were unable to compete with mechanized British industry. Nearly all of Protestant English or Scotch descent, they streamed out of the towns to the factory gates of England and New England.* Although all

---

* Although skilled workers were forbidden to emigrate, Samuel Slater, carrying the "secret" of the factory in his head, smuggled himself out of England in 1789. He supervised the establishment of the first factory in America.

of Ireland was hurtled into depression, the most poverty-stricken areas were the south and the west. There a man could not hope to earn more than sixpence or eightpence a day, little more than a third of what even the most menial agricultural laborer in England was paid. By 1830 the Fords, together with the other English landlords and middlemen, were islands in a bog of despair and hatred. Everywhere the roads were lined with begging families. Hundreds of thousands of people were starving, diseased, and deformed. Everywhere the attempts of the landlords to collect rents and tithes were met by obstruction, defiance, and resistance. Economically hard-pressed themselves, they were forced continually to be ready to defend themselves. Crime and guerrilla warfare covered the countryside. In one day in December, 1831, eleven police officers died in an encounter at Carrickshock.

If it was Whitney's cotton gin that was bringing despair to Ireland, it was Fulton's steamboat that was beginning to offer an escape from that despair. Steamboats, small in size but heavy consumers of fuel, had not yet been developed to the stage in which they could be used as carriers across the Atlantic. They were well suited, however, for the short, relatively calm run across the Irish Channel. The first steamboats appeared in the harbor of Cork in 1825 within a few months of the completion of the Erie Canal and of George Stephenson's demonstration of the first commercial railroad. Offering cheap passage to deck passengers, the boats carried Irish laborers back to England.

To transport the bulky raw materials required by their rapidly developing industry, the British were building the largest sailing vessels in history. With the opening of the Erie Canal, the ships carried wheat from western New York's vast grain-growing belt, in addition to cotton from the South. Needing *bulk* cargo to carry back to America along with manufactured goods, the shippers found it in people. The price of passage was reduced to between twenty and thirty dollars.

In the latter 1820's the Michigan Fever, which was causing thousands of Americans to trek westward, crossed the Atlantic to Ireland. Only 125,000 Europeans had emigrated to the United States during the first quarter century of its nationhood. Between 1820 and 1825, 39,000 took ship. In the five years following the completion of the Erie Canal, more than 90,000, nearly half of them Irish, embarked.

Among them were three young Bandon townsmen, Thomas, William, and Henry Maybury. The Mayburys were friends and neighbors of the Fords—even to the extent of sharing an affinity for the same Christian names.* Arriving in Detroit in 1830, the Maybury brothers purchased land in the Springwells area to the west of the town. Sending back glowing reports of Michigan, they urged the younger sons of William Ford to follow them.

Early in 1832, Samuel, George, and Henry Ford took ship for America.

---

* They may also have been distantly related by marriage. Thomasina Smith, who married John, the oldest of the five Ford brothers, is said to have been a cousin of the Mayburys. There is a discrepancy among sources as to whether Thomas Maybury came to Detroit at the time his two brothers did, or not until 1834.

4

The Warm Wave of the White Man

WITH THE FORDS TRAVELED AN EPIDEMIC OF CHOLERA THAT HAD BROKEN OUT in the congested and sanitationless cities of Europe. Flourishing on the fetid ships, with their slop buckets and barrels of stale water, the disease rooted itself in the immigrants, and was spread by them over America. Henry Ford made it up the Hudson, but was taken sick in Pennsylvania. While Samuel and George continued along Lake Erie to Detroit, he was left behind and never heard from again.

Since pioneering required a sizable stake, many of the immigrants interrupted their journeys at the small manufacturing and agricultural centers that were forming along the length of the Erie Canal. Hiring themselves out as laborers, they established the nuclei of population that were to grow into such cities as Schenectady, Syracuse, Rochester, and Buffalo.

Those slightly more solvent or adventurous were making Detroit the prototype of the Western boomtown. In 1830 a total of fifteen thousand disembarked, increasing the population of the territory by 50 percent. In 1832 as many as two thousand crowded into the town each week. Townsmen who had been speculating on a boom were unprepared for its reality. Along Jefferson Street, paralleling the river, every house was outfitted as a store. Householders sold out at profits of 100 percent, only to see the buyer himself sell at a profit of 100 percent the next year. Thomas Maybury, who had been trained as a carpenter in Bandon, abandoned farming and set to work building houses and speculating in real estate.

Such was the shortage of buildings, and so great the demand of the new arrivals, that men with a few dollars bought what goods they could and set themselves up as auctioneers in open fields. (Angry at being undersold, the regular merchants exercised their political strength for passage of an ordinance banning the auctioneers.)

A block from the water's edge Samuel and George Ford found a thriving seed farm that stood ready to sell them the seeds they would need to pioneer in the wilderness. It was the beginning of a business that was to make Michigan the world's leading seed producer.

The Ford brothers set out on Michigan Avenue, the road that Father Richard had convinced the Federal government to blaze to Ypsilanti and Chicago. Soon they were amidst one of the world's finest primeval forests. Ash, birch, butternut, cedar, cottonwood, elm, hickory, maple, red oak, white oak, pine, and walnut rose above the tangled undergrowth of the swampy land. The road, whether of corduroy construction or dirt, was uniformly bad. Only horsemen could make their way with some degree of speed. Families of settlers, trudging on foot, pushed handcarts loaded with their belongings. Periodically they were forced to wade through mud and water. Those driving wagons discovered that their affluence did not necessarily give them an advantage. Not only did the wagons sink into the mud, but the road's rough transverse logs, settling here and rising there, broke axles and wheels with maddening regularity. Everywhere the travelers faced the danger, not of wolves, which were being systematically exterminated, or of Indians, but of legions of gnats and mosquitoes. "Swamp fever," consisting of chills, fever, and the ague, struck almost everyone in his first years in the forest.

Samuel Ford bought eighty acres for a hundred dollars. (George, after helping his brother, was later to acquire eighty acres at the same price.) Months of hard labor followed. With little more than an ax, the men had to establish themselves in a forest so thick the sun appeared above it only like a dancing bauble. Once enough trees had been felled to make a clearing of a half acre or acre, other trees had their bark circled, and were left to die of their own accord. Without heavy draft animals, the men could not pull the stumps, with their massive root systems, out of the ground. While corn and melon and vegetable seeds were planted in the open spaces between, the stumps often were allowed to remain in the fields for twenty or thirty years.

The forest was full of strawberries, whortleberries, cranberries, and raspberries. The fields were shaded by maple, walnut, plum, and apple trees. Turkeys, quail, pheasants, partridges, woodcocks, doves, swans, geese, ducks, pigeons, and bustards filled the sky. Passenger pigeons, abundant and unafraid, could be killed with sticks.* Fish darkened the lakes and the streams.

Buffalo, elk, moose, bears, rabbits, and bisons had existed in an ecological balance with the bow-and-arrow culture of the Indians. But they fell easy prey to the New England muskets. Sometimes the settlers set fire to the woods, and potted the bears and the deer as they fled.

Under the assault of the large number of newcomers, the forest quickly became unequal to the task of supporting the population. The settlers, especially in winter, suffered from "Michigan appetite," a condition of arising from the table hungry.

The Indians, horrified by the destruction of their environment, were desperate. From their villages they watched as the white men felled the trees and settled in the forest around them. A generous people, they made white visitors welcome and shared with them the corn they raised and the fish they caught in the lakes. When the whites were at a loss as to how to prepare the corn, the Indians taught them. When the whites came into the forest without shelter, the Indians showed them how to build their twenty-by-thirty-foot cabins, sloping the roofs to fifteen feet and shingling them with bark. At many logging or raising bees the majority of the workers were Indians, and the whites found them "a happy

---

* So within a few decades they were exterminated.

set of fellows to work with." [1] As late as 1846, Albertus Van Raalte, leading the first contingent of Dutch immigrants to Michigan, paid twenty-six dollars to the chief of an Indian village for a building to use as a church.

Supplying each Indian family with eight dollars' worth of pork, flour, and tobacco annually, the Federal government attempted to get them to take up a permanent agricultural existence. The Indians, however, could not understand why they must abandon the life of hunting, trapping, and fishing in which they were happy. They "objected to settling on farms, claiming that by doing so they would become slaves of their cattle and hogs. They would rather obtain their living with rifles and when they returned to their wigwams lie down and rest instead of waiting upon and feeding dumb brutes." [2]

Such an attitude was unsustainable in a territory which, by 1835, contained over one hundred thousand whites, more than twice the number of Indians it had supported. The settlers acted like lords of the land. They placed fences across old Indian trails, appropriated fruit trees the Indians had planted, horse-whipped a chief who tried to collect tolls from the whites who crossed Indian land, and could not understand why the Indians should then enter their homes to demand food from them.

By 1835 the rapid increase of population qualified Michigan for statehood.* (Only some three thousand persons, less than 3 percent of the population, voted in the statehood election.) In the frenetic boom, men who arrived with modest stakes were growing wealthy. Laborers had no difficulty hiring themselves out at a dollar to a dollar and a half a day to the builders of houses, mills, ships, roads, wagons, and wharfs. If they were diligent, in a season or two they could save enough to purchase their own plots of land. Settlers could more than recoup their investment from the sale of the timber alone. If, somehow, they were able to wrestle the produce of the cleared land over the rough roads to Detroit, they were assured of a good price.

The boom was due, in large part, to the policies of Andrew Jackson. Taking office in 1829 as the first "Western" President, Jackson was committed to the expansionist policy that the Westerners had been demanding since before the War of 1812. Blaming the Eastern establishment of banking and commercial interests and their self-serving monopolistic and "tight money" policies for the recession of 1828–1829, Jackson refused to renew the charter of the United States Bank. Instead, the U.S. Treasury deposited its funds in "pet banks," picked for the political inclinations of their directors. Money poured into the Treasury from the burgeoning cotton and wheat exports, and from land sales. For the first and only time in American history, the national debt was reduced to zero. In 1836 President Jackson ordered the surplus distributed to the states. Between 1830 and 1837, as the amount of money in circulation nearly doubled, the number of banks jumped from 329 to 788. The total of their loans increased from $137 million to $525 million. [3]

A large proportion of these loans were going for land speculation. Michigan's spectacular population growth and application for statehood focused attention on the Northwest. Tales were broadcast of men who bought land for $1.25 an

---

* Michigan was engaged in a border war with Ohio over Toledo and a thin strip of land. Congress delayed Michigan's admission to statehood until settlement of the dispute in 1837. In return for relinquishing claim to the Toledo strip, Michigan received the Upper Peninsula across the straits of Mackinac—a territory that proved to have rich resources of minerals and timber.

acre and resold it for as much as $500 an acre. Even staid Baltimore and Philadelphia bankers joined the stampede for Western lands.

In 1830, sales at the government land office in Detroit had been 147,000 acres. In 1834, they were 498,000 acres. In 1835, they rose to 1,817,000 acres. In 1836, as long lines formed in front of the office, they jumped to 4,190,000 acres—a quantity that had never before been equaled in world history.[4]

One of the principal beneficiaries of this phenomenon was General Cass, who had been appointed Secretary of War by President Jackson. Cass's extensive landholdings in Michigan—five hundred acres along the Detroit riverfront alone—were making him one of the richer men in America. Fifteen years before, when Cass had obtained the eastern half of the state from the Indians, the prospects of its ever being completely settled by whites had been remote. Suddenly, however, in the surge of speculation, it seemed as if the Federal government might run out of land to sell.

The administration already had established its policy of forcibly removing Indians from the Southern and Eastern states to an area west of Arkansas.* General Cass was posing as the best friend the Indians had ever had. Claiming he wanted only to separate them from the deleterious influence of the white man, he was determined to complete the removal of Indians from Michigan.

Three times, the Indians of Michigan had been called to the council table. Three times, they had been coerced into parting with huge portions of their land and been given to understand that those were the last demands the government would make upon them. In 1819, Chief Ogemaw-ke, present with 113 other Indian chiefs, had told Cass, then Michigan's governor:

"Your people trespass on our hunting grounds. You flock to our shores. Our waters grow warm. Our lands melt away like a cake of ice. Our possessions grow smaller and smaller. The warm wave of the white man rolls in upon us and melts us away. Our women reproach us. Our children want homes. Shall we sell from under them the spot where they spread their blankets?"[5]

Nevertheless, the chief recognized that there was nothing for the Indians to do but "smoke with you the pipe of peace." Governor Cass, in turn, assured the Indians that the government was reserving for them one hundred thousand acres in choice locations.

Only two years later, at the 1821 Treaty of Chicago, Governor Cass had expropriated the southwestern corner of Michigan from the Indians. Then in 1836, the promises of 1819 were repudiated. In a land grab that roughly equaled the total of all previous ones, the Indians were dispossessed of the western half of Michigan, as well as the eastern half of the Upper Peninsula.

Once again they were assured they were receiving a good deal: 142,000 acres were reserved for the Ottawas and Chippewas. And once again expediency soon dictated the making of a new "treaty." When explorations indicated the location of rich copper deposits in the western portion of the Upper Peninsula, those lands were taken from the Indians in 1842.

Many of the Indians were bewildered. As white men whom they had believed to be their friends aided the troops of General Cass in rounding them up, they scurried into the wilderness in an effort to escape. Mothers searched

---

* The Cherokees of Georgia, the Creeks of Florida, the Chickasaws of Alabama, the Choctaws of Mississippi, the Seneca of New York, the Delaware of Delaware, and the Osage of Missouri were all jammed into Oklahoma, where they had to contend for the hunting grounds of the infuriated Comanches.

frantically for their children who disappeared into the woods to hide from the soldiers. Old men led villagers in attempts at passive resistance. Lying face down, they refused to move from the ground on which they had dwelled for generations.

It was of no use. The old, the sick, the infants, the pregnant—all were rounded up to begin the march to the North.

The whites had the land. But, without transportation, the land could not be exploited. Over the Indian trails and the one or two execrable roads that meandered through the wilderness, it was all but impossible to ship produce to market. The cost of transporting a barrel of flour eighty miles was five dollars. Farmers burned a large part of their crops in the fields and converted their grain to whiskey for easier shipment. Detroit, with a population of less than ten thousand, had ten distilleries. Even as the cost of food in the mushrooming cities skyrocketed—the price of flour increased 140 percent in little more than two years—barrels and barrels of hard liquor were rolled off the wagons. If workingmen lacked the price of bread, let them drink booze!

The need for transportation led to agitation throughout the West for canal construction; and, after the completion of the first successful public railroad in England in 1825, for railroad building.* In 1830 Detroiters received a charter for a railroad to Pontiac. Slightly more than twenty miles from Detroit, Pontiac consisted of no more than two dozen shacks set in a clearing in the woods. It had, however, an abundance of wheat and a flour mill. Within the next half dozen years more than a score of railroads were chartered in the state.

The railroad promoters soon discovered that their plans were as grossly overoptimistic as the difficulties of their implementation had been underestimated. They appealed to the state government for help. After Michigan was admitted to statehood in 1837 one of the first acts of the legislature was to authorize a five-million-dollar bond issue for railroad construction.

Scarcely a city and no state in the West was without its railroad or canal project. From less than $13 million in 1820 the debt of the states burgeoned to $172 million by 1837, of which $60 million went for construction of canals, $42 million for railroads, and $54 million for the financing of banks.[6]

By 1836 the boom was out of hand. As money was siphoned off for speculation in the West, inflation pushed up the cost of living in the cities of the East. Workingmen's wages lagged. Disorders, erupting first in Philadelphia in 1835, spread to other urban centers. In an effort to halt the rampant speculation, President Jackson issued in July of 1836 the Specie Circular, ordering that henceforward all payment for United States land was to be made in *hard* money; gold or silver.

The effect of the President's action was to take out of circulation the specie that was the backing for the paper on which the boom was based. The deflation that resulted was devastating. The five-million-dollar bond issue Michigan had floated had been sold to a New Jersey banking and canal company, which in

---

* A steam-powered wagon had been built by Nicolas Joseph Cugnot, a Frenchman, as early as 1769, the same year Watt patented his steam engine. In 1803 Richard Trevithick, an Englishman, had built a steam road carriage that looked like a giant watch movement. Its weight, however, mired it in the road. The same factor of weight had doomed experiments to use steam engines on rails laid in coal mines—the rails had broken and fragmented under the heavy load. It had taken two decades for iron technology to improve enough to make rails practical.

turn had marketed it at a discount to a London banking firm. Michigan had received only two million dollars of the notes when the New Jersey company went down in the nationwide crash. Having been *taken,* the state repudiated the bonds. As other states also defaulted, their actions aggravated the financial crisis. The American credit rating in Europe plummeted. The flow of funds into the United States was constricted. A desperate shortage of money developed.

As in the past, the citizens resorted to issuing their own. Detroit was flooded with paper notes or "shin plaster," of 6¼, 12½, 18¾ cents and up. Wages dropped 30 to 50 percent.

Throughout the West the depression generated a groundswell against Eastern bankers and proponents of hard money. Based on grass-roots economics, a forerunner of the Greenback, Populist, and Free Silver movements emerged.

What was the sense of marketing in the East and in Europe bond issues whose security was the land and resources of the West? Why not free the Western economy from the capricious supply of specie?

The logic was so compelling that the Western states moved in unison to set up their own banking systems. The Michigan Legislature made the land expropriated from the Indians legal tender. In December, 1837, it passed a law granting any twelve persons the right to organize a bank. Only 10 percent of the minimum fifty thousand dollars capitalization was required to be subscribed in specie. The remainder of the backing for the bank's notes could be supplied by a first mortgage on land.

Within months, forty-nine banks were organized in the state. Since the value of the land was a matter of judgment, appraisers were bribed and cajoled to outdo each other. The land boom of the early 1830's paled before the land boom of 1838. While lots in what was to be downtown Chicago were selling for one hundred dollars, lots platted in mythical towns in the Michigan wilderness were going for as much as five thousand dollars. Men, who the year before had been in despair as deflation faced them with ruin, paid off their debts, and still had left fistfuls of "wildcat" and "redhorse" money (so called because of the symbols used on the bank notes). The banks they represented were almost as wild as the beasts. The Bank of Shiawassee was a shack in a forest clearing. The Bank of Sandstone sat at the bottom of a quarry.

Since there was not nearly enough specie to provide the backing for such an expansion, the bank owners ignored the requirements. The single examiner provided by law was incapable of supervising forty-nine banks, many of which conspired to deceive him. Kegs of specie were in reality kegs of nails with a thin covering of silver. After the examiner had counted them at one bank, they would be rushed out of the back door to await his arrival and be counted again at the next. Before long, the directors of some banks did not know themselves how much paper money they had issued.

Stories of chicanery spread. A crash became inevitable. Before it arrived, however, the combination of worthless money and the land boom served to bring into operation the initial stretches of three railroads in Michigan. The first built west of the Appalachians, they gave Detroit a leadership in railroad construction that was to prove of importance for decades to come.

On the morning of February 3, 1838, a train huffed its way into Dearbornville on the Detroit and St. Joseph Railroad—the first in the West to have a locomotive in operation. As most of the community's sixty families turned out for the occasion, Samuel and George Ford must have speculated on how much the railroad would mean to them, and how much it would increase the value of their land. Yet even in their most optimistic mood they would have had difficulty envisioning the impact it would come to have on the history of their family. The mechanical skills that had been nurtured in Essex and passed on from generation to generation in Ireland would blossom to their full potential in the industrial culture that the railroad was about to establish in Detroit.

Nevertheless, as the train, its passengers coated with soot, stopped at Dearbornville on the return journey from Ypsilanti, the future of the railroad seemed in doubt. With a hiss and a sigh, the locomotive expired. Nothing could coax it back to life. The train that had departed with a glorious display of black smoke, white steam, and crimson sparks, returned to Detroit ignominiously, towed by a team of horses.

There were those in the crowd who would have agreed with the city fathers of an Ohio town who declared: "There is nothing in the Word of God about them. If God had designed that His intelligent creatures should travel at the frightful speed of fifteen miles an hour by steam, He would have certainly foretold it through His holy prophets. It is a device of Satan to lead immortal souls down to Hell."

In fact, spearing through the wilderness, the railroad was shortly to *raise* hell. But it would also make farmers ten miles from the city competitive with those two miles from the city. Within a dozen years it would make farmers one hundred miles from the city competitive with those ten miles from the city. As it opened the vast hinterlands, it removed the limitations on urban populations. No longer was a city dependent on the food it could grow in its immediate environs or import via water. No more need great cities be restricted to waterfront locations. Within a decade the economies of European nations would be reverberating from the strokes of the sledgehammers driving the spikes on American railroads.

5

The Epidemic Tax

IN ANOTHER DECADE, THE RAILROADS WERE TO ABSORB THOUSANDS OF THE Irish laborers. But in the 1830's, after a voyage that left them weak and debilitated, the Irish took work in the nearest city that offered it. The vessels furnished only water, the passengers had to provide all of their own food. One authority advised each person to carry 160 pounds of provisions, including 10 pounds each of pork, ham, and beef; 20 pounds each of rice, flour, blue peas, and gray peas; 15 pounds of potatoes; 30 pounds of the best bread; plus butter, cheese, sugar, prunes, sweet cake, wine, brandy, gin, vinegar, salt, mustard, pepper, coffee, tea, and medicines. In contrast, most of the Irish poor took with them little more than a few potatoes.

The American cities, which lacked all but the most rudimentary municipal services, were ill prepared for the arrival of a swarm of immigrants. In 1830 only 8 percent of Americans lived in places with a population of over 2,500, and there were only eight sizable cities: New York (213,000), Philadelphia (161,000), Baltimore (80,000), Boston (61,000), New Orleans (46,000), Charleston (30,000), Cincinnati (25,000), and Washington (19,000).[1] During the decade the urban population increased 64 percent, proportionately twice as fast as the rural. As in the English industrial cities, the influx of people produced a building boom with no other plan or purpose than the greatest private profit. Stables were converted to rooming houses, rear gardens were turned into tenements, mansions were divided and subdivided into warrens. The tendency to build higher and higher, which had originated in the overcrowded European Jewish ghettos, now encompassed entire cities. Streets and alleys took on the appearance of tunnels burrowed by moles.

In towns without sanitation, or water, or street cleaning, children waded and played amidst excrement. Courtyards were filled with huge piles of manure. Dogs trotted in and out of houses with pieces of dead animals left to decay in the alleys. The stink of offal was blotted out by the stench of factory smokestacks. Belching sulphurically, the ducts of slime that had once been rivers received the acids, offal, sewage, gases, animal dead, and human dead.

Cholera thrived. It spread from sailing ship to seaboard city, from seaboard city to steamer, and from steamer to inland city. On July 4, 1832, the *Henry Clay* docked in Detroit with a contingent of 370 soldiers for the Black Hawk War.* Several were already ill. The next day, the first died. The vessel was ordered to cast off. But as men were felled by the score, it made land near Port Huron, fifty miles above Detroit. About one hundred fifty of the troops deserted, and made their way back toward Detroit.

The disease had no difficulty taking root among the pioneers who, camping near the waterfront, drew their water and passed their water indiscriminately along the riverbank. On July 6, Detroit recorded its first death.

Cows, pigs, goats, and other domestic animals which were allowed freely to wander and root about the garbage-littered streets spread the epidemic. A mass exodus of the population began. Heading for Dearbornville, Pontiac, and Ypsilanti, the refugees were met by barriers, burned bridges, and posses who threatened death to anyone who tried to proceed.

With autumn and colder weather the epidemic subsided. The summer of 1834, however, brought its recurrence. As the governor himself died, those people who could afford to leave dashed helter-skelter out of the city.

The custom of ringing the church bells to announce a death was abandoned, for the ceaseless tolling only added to the panic of the residents. With bells, horses' hooves, and hawkers' cries stilled, the city was eerily peaceful. The streets were choked from the smoke of pitch, which people burned in the belief it warded off the disease. The sick, pallid and desiccated, were carried to the impromptu hospital that Father Martin Kundig, a German priest, established in his church. Their beds were composed of pews and wooden planks. Their best chance of recovery was to escape the eyes of the doctors. Those patients who, already dehydrated, were bled, at least had their suffering shortened. Those plied with liquor expired in an alcoholic stupor. Those dosed with opium died in hallucinatory delirium. Those unfortunate enough to have calomel, rhubarb, or cayenne pepper administered to them went off in screaming agony. The only effective prescription was a dose of arsenic. Its recipient shortly arose and departed under his own power.

During the month of August death claimed 7 percent of the city's population. As with all epidemics, it was concentrated most heavily among the poor, and the poor were mostly Irish and German Catholics. About half of those who died were *strangers,* that is, people who had only recently arrived.

Crammed together, sometimes two families to a shanty, the Irish congealed into a ghetto that was quickly nicknamed Cork Town (after County Cork). It was typical of the "Irish Towns" that were forming huge slums in the industrial cities of England and along the East Coast of America. The age-old, clannish feuds that had subverted attempts to form a united front against the British continued to flourish. Immigrants from Cork would not live in the same neighborhood with immigrants from Kerry. The men fought over jobs, and settled their quarrels with their fists. Having been encouraged by the British— even as the Indians were encouraged by the American whites—to consume quantities of alcohol to forget their misery, they drank themselves into stupe-

---

* The Black Hawk War was, in reality, a series of skirmishes. A segment of the Sacs and the Foxes, having been driven from Michigan to Wisconsin, became strangely resentful at being forced from Wisconsin to Minnesota and Iowa by a new wave of settlers. Led by Chief Black Hawk, they rebelled.

faction in a land where whiskey was cheaper than beer, and often more easily obtainable than good drinking water. For seven months of the year the men labored for a dollar and a dollar fifty per day. Then, as the leaves turned yellow and red, families gathered huge piles of cordwood, sacks of potatoes, and other provisions to carry them through the five months of winter; months during which the lakes froze and the snows fell, and Detroit went into a state of virtual hibernation.

Corktown had no resources to fall back on in times of disaster. Traditionally on the frontier relatives would come to the assistance of a family struck by death or misfortune. If the family had no relatives, then the congregation of the church would assume the responsibility. Thus it had always been among the closely knit French Catholics of Detroit.

The appearance of the poor Irish and Germans, at the same time that the French were growing wealthy from the appreciation of their lands, brought an end to the Catholic homogeneity. Father Richard managed for a brief time to bridge the gap between the ethnic groups. But in September, 1832, after exhausting himself ministering to the sick, he died. The Irish and Germans, moving out of the French church, formed a congregation of their own. They lacked, however, the means to support the fifty children who had been orphaned. The immigrants, who were procreating prolifically in their crowded quarters, had neither the room nor the resources to assume the burden of more children.

It was a pattern familiar to emerging cities throughout the world. An impersonal society was developing in which the unfortunate, the crippled, the women, the children, and the elderly were thrown upon the mercy and the charity of the community. It was a development for which Detroit was unprepared. Falling back upon English precedent, the county at a cost of $950 constructed a poorhouse, and contracted its operations out to the Sisters of Charity.

The question arose of how to support the poorhouse. In 1830 municipal expenses had totaled but $2,889, of which $1,600 had gone for the maintenance of streets, and $31 for poor relief. Rather than levy taxes, the city had been paying its expenses through the sale of lands—the ten-thousand-acre tract to the north of the city, and the military preserve in its heart—which Judge Woodward in 1805 had induced the Federal government to reserve as a municipal resource. By the early 1830's Detroit had frittered away a potential source of revenue that could have relieved it of taxation for decades. Thus faced with the necessity of finding other funds for maintenance of the orphans, the state legislature imposed a tax of ¼ of 1 percent on real and personal property. Even as in England two hundred fifty years earlier, the modern property tax was introduced into Michigan to raise funds for the support of the poor.

The revenues, however, were inadequate to cope with the new outbreak of cholera in 1834. Since most of the approximately three hundred unfortunate were already in Father Kundig's charge, the government acknowledged the fact by appointing him to the position of Director of the Poor. The sixteen cents per capita it allowed him for their daily care was but half the actual cost.

With the depression of 1837-1838, Father Kundig's situation became desperate. One third to one half of the work force was idled. Hungry men, roaming the streets, abandoned their families to charity. Beseeching the city for more money, the priest mortgaged himself, the poorhouse, and the church. When it became evident that the city neither had the money, nor would raise it through taxation, his creditors descended upon him. Beds, clothing, and eating utensils were carried off. Left with nothing but the clothes they were wearing, the poor were abandoned.

In despair, some turned to thievery and robbery to support themselves. Following the epidemic of 1834, so many children resorted to pilferage to keep from starving that Detroiters formed the Society for the Suppression of Felony. In January of 1835 a night watch was established.

The next month it was disbanded. The captains, as well as most of the twelve men, were seldom sober enough to catch a thief.

Whether in Detroit or New York, London or Liverpool, citizens associated their multiplying problems of sanitation, epidemics, poor relief, and crime with the influx of the Irish Catholics. With their "high-water" trousers (to keep out of the mud), distinctive dress, brawling ways, and "peculiar habits" the Irish were highly visible. Willing to work for "Irish wages," they took jobs away from unskilled native Americans and undermined the efforts of inchoate labor organizers to form unions and improve working conditions.* Mobs of Protestants, sometimes led by Scotch-Irish Presbyterians, rioted through the Irish-Catholic sections of Philadelphia, Boston, and other cities. Composed mainly of young toughs, they sacked and burned convents, churches, and homes. Here and there Irishmen were lynched.

In New York the reaction was political. In 1835 the Native American party ran its first candidate for office. The next year it chose Samuel F. B. Morse as its candidate for mayor.† Although Morse was badly beaten, a fusion with the Whigs brought the party its first victory. Before the end of the decade the Native American movement spread to Louisiana and to the nation's capital. There it influenced the Senate to direct the Secretary of State to collect information on the supposed relationship between immigration, pauperism, and crime.

* The workday of half the labor force was eleven hours and more. In New England, women and children as young as seven years of age were working fourteen- to sixteen-hour days in damp, freezing, earthen-floored factories for $1.56 a week.
† Morse was a talented painter who had turned to investigation of electrical phenomena, and was on the verge of patenting the telegraph.

6

Liberty and Learning

RESIDENTS IN CITIES THROUGHOUT THE NATION WERE COMPLAINING THAT THEY were unable to "leave their homes at dark without some fear." The *Bostonians* believed that the answer was to implement the principal of universal free education, since "fearful experience" showed that "liberty and learning, domestic quietude, and the pursuit of happiness lean on each other for support." [1]

It was a belief that had been handed down to the *Bostonians* from their Puritan ancestors, who regarded the Bible as the bulwark against both popism and the Established English Church. Massachusetts nourished a tradition of literacy and a determination to teach every child to read that the world never before had seen.* In 1642 the colony enacted a statute making the failure of parents to ensure the education of their children an actionable offense. Five years later another law required every township of more than fifty households to hire a teacher and to build a schoolhouse.

Every New England colony except Rhode Island followed the leadership of Massachusetts. The Michigan territorial legislature passed an education bill in 1827. Two years later it established the post of superintendent of public instruction, and so set an American precedent.† Since, however, the well-to-do had their children tutored or sent them to private schools, the public schools law remained a dead letter. By 1832 there was so much alarm at the spread of idleness and ignorance among children that female volunteers formed a Free School Society.

When the Michigan Constitution was enacted, two *Bostonians,* lawyer Isaac Crary and the Reverend John Pierce, succeeded in including an article for the

---

* During the 1630's some eight thousand well-educated town-dwelling Dissenters, mostly of the merchant and artisan classes, emigrated to Massachusetts to escape the erratic persecution of Charles I. They thereby formed the nucleus of the colony. Since Dissenters and Non-Conformists were barred from preaching in England, they had kept and propagated the faith by turning out vast numbers of tracts and pamphlets. In order for these to have an effect, the faithful had to be able to read them. Universal literacy became a central tenet of the Puritans.
† New York had established the position earlier, but then abolished it.

establishment of the first centralized educational system in the United States. While other Western states conveyed the lands set aside for public education by the Northwest Ordinance to the townships, the Michigan Legislature retained control over the lands, and prevented them from being siphoned off by speculators. Judge Woodward's *Catholepistemiad*, which had expired in 1827, was revived as the University of Michigan, the first state university in the country. Eight branches—actually the equivalents of high schools—were established in the more populous communities.

Detroit opened its first public school above a grocery store on the riverbank in 1836. Although during the Panic of 1837 the school funds vanished along with the speculative ventures in which they had been invested, only a temporary setback resulted.

Michigan and Massachusetts were moving in tandem to pioneer the modern American educational system. Horace Mann, the strong and dedicated head of the Massachusetts system, battled the well-to-do as he sought to have education supported by a property tax. Declaring that he could think of no more heinous an act than "embezzlement and pillage from children," he asserted that property was not a private right, but a common trust. "The property of this commonwealth is pledged for the education of all its young," he said, "up to such a point as will save them from poverty and vice, and prepare them for the adequate performance of their social and civil duties." [2]

Detroit's mayor, Dr. Zina Pitcher, echoed his words. Since the 1841 school tax was only a dollar per child, schools were closing down. No more than a fourth of the school population of 2,100 was actually enrolled. The children, said Dr. Pitcher, "are coming up in ignorance, the offspring of which are vice and wretchedness." If the children of the Irish and the German poor were in school, he argued, they would not be running about the streets committing pilferage and vandalism. If they were not illiterate, they would not later become a burden on the community. A property tax of ¼ of 1 percent for support of the schools, Dr. Pitcher and a coalition of progressive Detroiters suggested, "was the cheapest insurance that could be put upon property. . . . If the school tax were omitted, then the jail tax and the criminal court costs must take its place." [3]

The tax became the issue of a bitter mayoralty campaign in the spring of 1842. Ranged against the tax were large property owners who insisted that pauper schools were good enough for the poor; proprietors of twenty-seven private academies who were educating seven hundred children at eighteen dollars apiece annually; and some churchmen, who contended that education was the function of the Church. What ultimately carried the day for the free-education slate and Dr. Douglas Houghton,* its candidate for mayor, was the argument that an educated populace was necessary not only for the safeguarding of property, but for the conduct of commerce and industry. With Dr. Houghton's election, the city established the principle of free schools for all between the ages of five and seventeen.

---

* Only thirty-three years old, Houghton had graduated from college at the age of twenty with a degree in botany, chemistry, and geology. The next year he accompanied a doctor on his rounds, and soon absorbed enough medical knowledge to be certified as a physician. Subsequently, he added dentistry to his professions. No more successful during his four-year practice of medicine in Detroit than his colleagues, he was appointed the first state geologist in 1837. Between 1837 and 1842 his surveys and explorations laid the groundwork for what was to become history's greatest mineral and timber exploitation (and for the final removal of the Indians from the state).

(Opposition to free public schools, however, remained strong, especially in rural areas, where farmers did not see the connection between the ability to read and the skill to milk a cow. Free public schools were not extended throughout Michigan until 1869, and most states lagged even further behind.)

While in America the *Bostonians* advocated education as the solution to the Irish "problem," in Ireland the people remained mired in destitution. The letters which John Ford received in Bandon from his brother George in America (Samuel died in 1842) must have contained astonishing news of the rapid progress in the wilderness. Not only did the railroad enable George Ford and his neighbors to ship their crops to market, but it ended the isolation of Dearbornville. Coffee, tea, sugar, salt, candles—all of them high-priced *luxuries* seldom seen before the arrival of the railroad—were becoming staples. In Detroit Thomas Maybury, building houses and dealing in real estate, was accumulating wealth so rapidly that he could have purchased one of the largest estates in County Cork.

John Ford gave serious thought to following his brothers. Fifty thousand Irishmen were yearly emigrating to England to work on the construction of railroads, which were spiderwebbing the island. When they couldn't get work on the railroads, they took jobs digging, hauling, and carrying. They became part of a ragged army that swept horse dung off the streets, and peddled it for fuel. Sometimes they returned to Cork, their teeth crumbling like chalk, their lungs and stomachs seared from the bases in the alkali industry where they worked in the jobs that no one else would take.

Thousands of others were going to America. Yet despite the emigration, the Irish population continued to grow. In the early 1840's, as the number of the Irish neared 8.5 million, between 2.25 and 2.5 million were on the edge of starvation. Studying the problem, the British Devon Commission concluded in 1843 that to provide relief at least 200,000 families would have to be encouraged to emigrate.

Disaster was restrained by nothing more than a tenuous dike of potatoes. In 1845 blight crept through the fields. Half of the crop was destroyed. The British government's endeavors to import food were bedeviled by the nation's restrictive trade laws. The Navigation Acts required that the corn that was being contracted for in Russia be carried in British bottoms. But British shipowners were unwilling to divert ships from their regular runs. The corn rotted on the docks of Odessa.

While the Irish starved, carts and wagons loaded with meat and dairy products rolled down Irish roads toward Irish seaports for export. Beseeching and begging families, watching them pass, hobbled after them all the way to the sea. There was no shortage of cash crops. But the Irish peasants had no cash with which to buy them.

A situation so dramatically intolerable was grist for the arguments of the Free Traders. Repealing the Corn Laws, Great Britain in 1846 switched to a policy of free trade. Since the new policy removed protection from agriculture, it imposed new hardships on Irish farmers.

The blight that had devastated half the potato crop in 1845 destroyed all of it in 1846. Already heavily in debt, many English landlords and leaseholders were faced with the devil's choice of marketing their cash crops and paying the installments, so dooming their tenants, or of diverting the cash crops in an effort to save the tenants. Those who chose the latter course saw the income from both rents and crops vanish. Thousands went into bankruptcy.

Famine and depression were the consequences of Ireland's past. The repeal of the Corn Laws was a portent of the future. Twenty years after the first barrel of flour had been carted out of the wilderness from Pontiac, 2,175 barrels of Michigan flour arrived in Ireland for famine relief. John Ford decided to delay no longer. Gathering his family and his belongings, he set out on the road for the port city of Queenstown (Cóbh).*

As the Fords traveled in their wagon, they passed scores of families trudging in the same direction. Never before had there been such a rush to empty an overflowing land. A hundred thousand left in 1846. Double that number in each of the next four years. Roughly half went to England; the other half to the United States and Canada.† For every three or four who managed to board ship, one fell by the wayside. Only a few thousand died of actual starvation. The others succumbed to whatever viral, bacterial, or bronchial infection first happened to lodge in their emaciated bodies. Carried to burial grounds in coffins with sliding sides, they were dumped into mass graves. The coffins were returned to the carts to pick up new loads—scarce and expensive wood could not be consigned to the earth with abundant and cheap people. Many died forlorn and abandoned. Their skeletons were to be discovered for years to come in ditches, fields, and bogs.

By 1851 the population was reduced to 6.5 million. By the end of the century it was half of what it had been in 1845.

Thousands of the Irish who left Europe never arrived in America. The vessels carried a razor-thin margin of provisions. If they were delayed in leaving port or were forced to fight headwinds, the last days of the journeys became agonies of forced rations. In the damp and fetid holds, men, women, and children lay in their own excrement and puke, and feverishly begged for water. Typhoid and scurvy, typhus and dysentery, smallpox and cholera carried them off. Thousands of others survived only long enough to reach shore. Thomasina, the wife of John Ford, was one of the seven thousand who, in 1847, died at the quarantine hospital on Grosse Isle, just outside Quebec.

The surviving twelve to sixteen members of the party traveled down the St. Lawrence to Lake Erie. Fifteen years earlier, when John's brothers had traversed the lake, it had been a lonely expanse on which an Indian sailing canoe might be seen darting from some inlet, the shoreline of solid forest broken only occasionally by a church steeple. Now the villages were emerging as respectable towns, and the wilderness between was spotted with dozens of new communities. The traveler was rarely out of sight of the masts of a sailing ship or the smoking funnel of a steamer.‡ By the 1850's the tonnage of Great Lakes shipping exceeded that of the Western rivers. The steam tonnage of the Western rivers exceeded that of the British Empire.

As the Fords traveled west, the first shipments of Michigan pine—destined to bring a shift of the lumber industry from east to west of the Appalachians—passed them on the way to Buffalo. Fellow travelers heading west were participants in the first great mining rush in American history; a rush set off by the transportation

* The precise makeup of the party is in some doubt. It included, besides John Ford's wife and his children, his mother and other members of the family.
† Irish immigration to the United States increased from 33,000 in 1844 to 106,000 in 1847 and 221,000 in 1851—the latter year marking an all time high. Between 1847 and 1854, 1,188,000 Irish, one of every seven persons in the population, came to the United States.
‡ The slower sailing ships were holding their own against the steamers, which were handicapped by the necessity of carrying large stocks of wood for fuel.

of the Ontonagon Boulder, three tons of copper and rock, from the northern Michigan wilderness to Washington, D.C., in 1843. As soon as news of the discovery spread, men streamed toward the Upper Peninsula. Lacking know-how, and money to invest in equipment, most of them straggled back to Detroit, Chicago, and other Midwestern towns. It would take Eastern and British capital, and the importation of skilled Cornish miners, to turn the copper rush into a copper boom.

From Henry Maybury, John Ford bought eighty acres near Dearborn. It was a prospering community with several flour mills and stores, a sawmill, and an iron foundry. Since land was appreciating rapidly, the $350 he paid was probably a cut-rate price.*

Dearborn was a strategic way station on the carriage road to Chicago and on the Michigan Central Railroad. Both the road and the railway, however, were in an execrable state. The two stages a week that made the trip to Chicago regularly suffered broken axles and overturned in the swampy ground. The railroad was the possessor of but a single locomotive, and had bogged down in Kalamazoo, halfway across the state.

---

* Some years earlier the municipality of Detroit, deciding to establish a new "poor farm," had paid eight hundred dollars for one hundred twenty acres twice as far from the city.

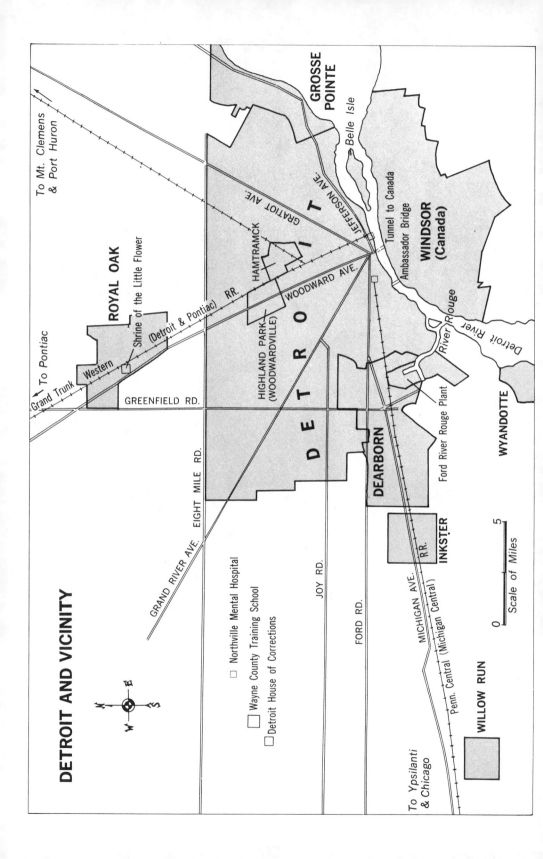

DETROIT AND VICINITY

□ Northville Mental Hospital

□ Wayne County Training School

□ Detroit House of Corrections

0   5
Scale of Miles

7

The Heathen Altar of the
Michigan Central

THE STATE OF THE DETROIT AND ST. JOSEPH RAILROAD HAD BEEN OF CONCERN to Detroit businessmen ever since recovery from the Panic of 1837 had begun injecting new vigor into the city's boom.

By the mid-1840's, the city population was nearing fifteen thousand. Two canals, the Portsmouth to Cleveland, and the Toledo to Cincinnati, linked Detroit to the Ohio River and Pittsburgh, Memphis, St. Louis, and New Orleans. The city was now connected by water to New York, the Gulf of St. Lawrence, the Southern border states, and Chicago and the West; and its strategic location was about to be further enhanced.

Following his term as mayor, Dr. Houghton in 1844 had returned to surveying the lands from which the Indians had been evicted in the Upper Peninsula. The Indians long had been aware of the area's deposits of copper and iron. But having no way to market the ore, they had mined it in sporadic fashion. Crossing the peninsula together with William A. Burt,* the Deputy Surveyor of the United States, Houghton was amazed to see his compass spinning, and indicating the north magnetic pole to be first east, then north, then south, then west. The men soon realized that they were in the midst of one of the world's great deposits of iron.

The Jackson Mining Company was organized to exploit the discovery. In 1846 it initiated operations near Marquette. Other mining companies were being organized to dig down into the earth for copper. One of these was in the process of bringing out of the Minesota Mine the largest single mass of copper ever discovered. From that day in 1847 until late in the 1880's Michigan led the world in copper production.

Even more important than copper and iron to Detroit's development as a

---

* William Burt was a descendant of Richard Burt, who arrived in Massachusetts in 1634 and became surveyor of highways for the state. William Burt was not only a restless explorer, but an inventor. In 1829 he received U.S. Patent Number 259 for a "typographer," the precursor of the typewriter. Without the solar compass he invented in 1836, the surveying party would not have been able to establish the location (Marquette) of the iron deposit.

manufacturing center was lumber. Michigan's vast stands of timber, some of the most extensive and finest in the world, had made the town a shipbuilding center ever since its days under the British flag. As commerce on the Great Lakes flourished, Detroit was well on the way to becoming the leading shipbuilder in the United States.

Lumber was being used to build not only ships, but furniture, carriages, and wooden articles of all kinds. Carpenter shops sprang up to supply the immigrants who, fanning out from the city, were transforming the incredibly fertile soil of southern Michigan into one of the nation's great agricultural areas. It was a process that was being accelerated and mechanized by John Deere's development of the steel plow, which was able to turn over the deep, rich soil as it never had been before, and by Cyrus McCormick's invention of the reaper.* So efficient was the reaper, and so greatly did it enable farmers to expand the amount of land that they cultivated, that McCormick instituted a policy of allowing purchasers to pay the stiff price of $115 over the span of three harvests. The risk of nonpayment was negligible, since in those three years the reaper would more than pay for itself.

It was the world's introduction to installment selling.

In this climate of exponential expansion, discovery, and inventiveness, Detroit's men of commerce and industry prospered. They continued, nevertheless, to be frustrated by the bottlenecks that existed in transportation. Though the city was linked by water to every point of the American compass, in its hinterlands transportation was as difficult and uneconomic as it had been a hundred years before. The three partially completed railroads had been acquired by the state during the Panic of 1837. The legislature, however, refused to appropriate further funds for capital development. Trains operated at tortoiselike speeds over strap-iron rails that bent and broke. Running more on whimsy than on schedule, they halted for anyone who flagged them down. In large part the railroads were failing to make the connection between the ever larger harvests garnered by farmers and the goods being manufactured and sold in Detroit. Both farmers and merchants were dissatisfied and restless.

The railroad in which the city was particularly interested was the Detroit and St. Joseph. Though its tracks were supposed to traverse the peninsula to Lake Michigan, the railroad was stuck at Kalamazoo. One of its first directors had been Oliver Newberry. A *Bostonian* who had arrived in Detroit in 1826 as an agent of the American Fur Company, he had become the city's leading shipbuilder and financier. Known as the Admiral of the Lakes, he had committed himself at the time of statehood to the purchase of $100,000 in Detroit bonds. It was a staggering sum considering that the city's annual expenditures were still less than $25,000. Together with other civil leaders, Newberry was outspoken on the issue of the railroad, and its retarding effect on the city's development. Something had to be done.

---

* Deere was a Vermont blacksmith descended from a British officer in the Revolutionary War. Migrating to Illinois in 1837 and perceiving the difficulties farmers were experiencing with their old-fashioned plows, he developed and year by year improved a new plow. By 1846 he was making, out of steel imported from England, 1,000 plows a year.

McCormick was the grandson of a Scotch-Irish weaver who had emigrated from Ulster in 1734. His father, a comfortably situated western Virginia farmer, was an inveterate inventor who lacked the persistence to perfect his inventions. In 1831 Cyrus, then twenty-two, had taken up work on a reaping machine where his father had left off. It was not until the family was bankrupted by the Panic of 1837, however, that Cyrus had decided to take the reaper west. After some years of indifferent success, sales picked up. In 1847 he erected a factory in the frontier town of Chicago.

What could be done, suggested James F. Joy, was to buy the railroad from the state.

Descended from Puritans,* Joy, with visionary eyes and the chiseled profile of a patriarch, had graduated from Dartmouth at the head of the class of 1833. Subsequently he had attended Harvard Law School. Arriving in Detroit in 1836, he joined George F. Porter in a law partnership that established itself as the most prestigious in the city. They were the counselors for the city's leading merchants. They were the attorneys for the Bank of Michigan, the only bank in the state recognized in the East after the fiasco of 1837–1838. They had continuing contacts with financiers in Boston and New York. As a participant in municipal politics, Joy was allied with the free-school forces. In 1838 he had become one of the first three "inspectors" of the school system.

In 1845 Joy commenced a campaign to get the state to sell the railroad. From New York came John Brooks, the twenty-seven-year-old superintendent of the Auburn and Rochester Railroad. After appraising the property, Brooks prepared a favorable *Report Upon the Merits of the Michigan Central Rail-Road As an Investment for Eastern Capitalists.* It was read in Boston by John Murray Forbes,† a thirty-two-year-old millionaire shipper who had been speculating in Western lands since the 1830's. He grasped the implications of the Irish and the European famines, and of the British repeal of the Corn Laws. If means could be found to transport Western agricultural products to the East Coast and to Europe, the potential of the Western trade exceeded that of the China trade. So Forbes set to work purchasing the Detroit and St. Joseph Railroad.

Part of the financing Forbes obtained from the British Baring Brothers, a banking firm with which he had established his reputation and credit while a trader in Canton. A syndicate of Bostonians and New Yorkers provided the rest.‡

In Michigan, Joy was having the devil's own time persuading the legislature to get the state out of the railroad business. Legislators were reluctant to let the state's lifeline fall into the hands of "Easterners." Nevertheless, the measure authorizing the sale squeaked through. The price was $2 million—$500,000 down, and $1.5 million to be paid in twelve months. The railroad was not to violate the injunction of the Lord by running trains on the Sabbath, and all of the directors were to be true believers who attended church every Sunday—twice.

Under the direction of Brooks and Joy, a frenetic attempt was launched to repair the railroad and drive it the remaining length across the peninsula to St.

---

* The first American Joy, Thomas, had been an architect and builder. In 1657 he had received the contract for the erection of the largest building in the colonies, a structure for the housing of the Boston council, courts, and market.
† Although orphaned at an early age, Forbes was descended from several patrician Boston families. At the age of eleven he entered the counting house of his uncles, James and Thomas Perkins, who pioneered in the China trade. Forbes's older brother Bennett had, at the age of twenty, captained one of the first ships in the trade. In 1830, seventeen-year-old John Murray Forbes had been shipped out to Canton to take charge of the firm's trading post. Becoming a confidante of the mandarin, Houqua, who controlled foreign trade, he dealt in tea and opium, and became a millionaire by the age of twenty-four.
‡ The syndicate consisted of John Forbes's brother Robert, sole or part owner of sixty-eight ships; his uncle, Thomas Perkins, whose Granite Railway Company, the first in America, had hauled the stones for the Bunker Hill Monument; John E. Thayer, a banker; David Neal, president of an Eastern railroad; Josiah Quincy, Jr., son of the Harvard president; and Erastus Corning, former mayor of Albany, president of the Utica and Schenectady Railroad, founder of Corning, New York, and owner of an iron works that was being kept in white heat supplying rails, tools, and rolling stock for the railroads.

Joseph on Lake Michigan. All along the one-hundred-fifty-mile route from Detroit to Kalamazoo the rails were rusted and broken. Ties had rotted. In places the tracks sank into the swamp under the weight of the locomotive. As in England. the Irish Catholics provided cheap and abundant labor. Twenty-five hundred of them were put to work as section hands, "swampers," and track layers.

Also going to work for the railroad was William Ford. The twenty-one-year-old son of John, he was literate and skilled, and probably employed in a supervisory capacity. Brooks, thinking of the $1.5 million payment that would have to be made in a year, drove the men relentlessly. Battling outbreaks of cholera, the swampers and sawyers set the virgin forest to ringing with the sounds of their axes. Saws rasped as they cut the ties. Iron clanged against iron. Sweating, cursing, brawling, and swilling beer, the men laid the new English rails that Forbes was buying with Baring Brothers money. The construction of the Michigan Central Railroad—the Detroit and St. Joseph's new name—created the prototype of the "hell-on-wheels" camp that was to give the laying of the Western railroads their own special aura.

In 1848 the Michigan Central reached New Buffalo on Lake Michigan, cutting the travel time between Detroit and Chicago to one third of what it had been previously. The next year the company's own steamers, the largest and fastest on the Lakes, initiated the first water-rail through service between Buffalo and Chicago.

Throughout the United States, railroads resembled bits of broken string scattered about on the map. Crossing and recrossing each other, they were the enterprises of local promoters. They formed no coherent pattern.

The Michigan Central was the first railroad to be built with an eye on the long haul as well as the short. For Forbes and the Boston group, it presented the opportunity to counter the challenge of the Hudson-Erie Canal traffic, and to place Boston once more in competition with New York. Two major obstacles, however, remained. One was the fragmentation of the lines between Buffalo and Albany. The other was winter—when the Great Lakes froze, traffic halted, and Michigan and Chicago were again isolated from the East.

In New York, Erastus Corning set to work merging the lines between Buffalo and Albany into the New York Central Railroad. To bridge the gap between Buffalo and Detroit, the men of the Michigan Central and would-be New York Central proposed to build the Great Western Railroad across Canada. (Not only was this the most direct route, but, in the parochial and state-oriented society of the day, Pennsylvania was blocking railroad construction across its territory by out-of-state groups.) Although the Canadian government viewed any American enterprise with the suspicion of a householder who recognizes this month's door-to-door salesman as last month's housebreaker, the negotiations were concluded successfully.*

In the West, Indiana and Illinois were as adamant against allowing "foreigners" to cross their territory as Pennsylvania was in the East. Once more Joy applied himself to working his magic on legislators. To lobby the Illinois Legislature, he retained a gaunt Springfield attorney: Abraham Lincoln.

Senator Stephen A. Douglas of Illinois had been trying since 1846 to get Congress to authorize a land grant for the building of the Illinois Central Railroad.

---

* However, just to make certain no American jingoists could chug right across the border into Canada, the Great Western was laid with a different gauge than the New York Central and Michigan Central.

He was still trying in 1850. Then, in a complicated series of trade-offs involving Michigan's Senator Lewis Cass and Kentucky's Henry Clay, Douglas got his grant of 2,595,133 acres. Precedent setting, it was the first for any railroad, and represented one tenth of the land area of the state.

Forbes marketed the land bonds in Europe. Baring Brothers loaned the Illinois Central $5 million. The Michigan Central chipped in with $800,000, its stockholders thereby acquiring a major interest in the Illinois Central. The Michigan Central was granted access rights to Chicago. Its first train pulled into Chicago in May, 1852, beating the Michigan Southern Railroad by one day. (The Michigan Southern, with its eastern terminus at Toledo, had been acquired by a group of New York investors as a counter to the Forbes group.)

The coming of the railroads was greeted with far from universal approval. Collisions became frequent as the growing population vied with the locomotives for use of roads and streets. Horses bolted at the sight of the high-stacked ambulatory boilers. Woods, barns, haystacks, and houses were set afire by sparks sprayed from the locomotives.

As long as the railroads had been operated at slow speeds in their ramshackle fashion by the state, which paid off damage claims promptly and generously, they had been tolerated. Private operators, however, faced with the necessity of making a profit, were less responsive to the public's convenience and the public's interest. Friction increased. Farmers who allowed their cattle to forage freely around the unfenced countryside were irate when the locomotives, not yet equipped with "cow catchers" but now traveling at the eye-popping speed of thirty miles per hour, took the animals for a last ride. Instead of paying damages generously, Joy contended that the railroad was not responsible when cows trespassed on its property. Inhabitants of communities through which the Michigan Central passed were upset by its imperious, noisome, countryside-destroying operation. Stage operators and innkeepers were dismayed as their clientele disappeared.

The core of opposition was at Jackson and Marshall in the center of the state. The railroad was setting whatever rates the traffic would bear, and the rates from the center of the state to Detroit were higher than from New Buffalo to Detroit. From New Buffalo on Lake Michigan, the railroad had competition from steamships.

Leaders of the opposition to that "damned monopoly" were Abel Fitch and the Reverend John Pierce. Pierce, who had become the state's first superintendent of public instruction, thundered:

"No heathen altar ever smoked more continuously with the blood of its victims." [1]

Fitch, a tavern operator, had grown rich by speculating in real estate. He had been a captain in the state militia, had helped organize the state's Democratic party, and was a supervisor of Leoni Township. Under his exhortations the tracks became a gauntlet of stones, bricks, bottles, and musket shots aimed at the exposed locomotive engineers. Tracks were greased, switches jammed, woodpiles set on fire, and trees felled across the rails. There was wild talk of blowing up the railroad and being rid of it once and for all. Joy attempted to bring action against some of the suspected perpetrators in Jackson County, but it was impossible to obtain a conviction. The county was united in its hatred of the railroad.

On November 19, 1850, the Michigan Central freight depot in Detroit burned to the ground. At first no one questioned that the fire in the huge $140,000 structure, topped by a five-story dome, was accidental. Then Henry Phelps, a horse stealer, forger, and ex-convict was retained by the railroad as a $1.25-a-day spy. He soon asserted that George Washington Gay, a gimpy-legged character with an advanced case of syphilis, had admitted setting the fire, and that Fitch had put him up to it. Sheriff Lyman Baldwin announced that the fire had resulted from an "infernal machine" placed at the top of the dome.

On April 19, 1851, a special train, carrying the sheriff and one hundred deputized railroad hands, headed for Jackson County. More than thirty of the antirailroad citizens were hustled aboard and brought back to Detroit to face charges of a conspiracy to burn down the depot.

While the Detroit press viciously attacked the "organized band of desperadoes," the outstate papers just as stoutly defended them. To middle-class Detroiters the railroad meant business and prosperity. They regarded the attacks upon it as sabotage of their interests. To the outstaters the railroad had become precisely what many legislators had feared it would in private hands—a dragon-like, monopolistic monster. In pursuit of profit, the railroad operators set whatever rates they wished, fleeced the farmers, and rode roughshod over anyone who dared oppose them.

Whipping up the citizens of Detroit, Mayor Zachariah Chandler warned of a "crime wave," and organized a night watch to purportedly keep the city from being burned to the ground. The city's leading merchant and a close associate of Joy, the mayor set off an hysteria that spread all the way to New York.

To put some spine into the prosecution, the city marshaled six of its top lawyers, including Joy, to assist the county prosecutor. The defense retained New York's most prominent Whig, Senator William H. Seward.

The purported perpetrator, Gay, died in jail before the start of the trial. But that did not prevent it from becoming the most sensational railroad trial in American history. More than five hundred witnesses were presented between June and September. One hundred and twenty witnesses testified that Phelps was a liar and scoundrel. In the fetid jail one after another of the prisoners took sick. Two died in early August. On August 12, Fitch himself came down with dysentery.

"If this railroad company must rule this State why the sooner we know it the better," he wrote, "and perhaps I may as well be the first victim as the last." [2]

On August 24 he died. As the foul nature of the prosecution's case became evident, public sentiment shifted in favor of the prisoners. People began to ask why the railroad should be capable of burning down everything except its own buildings. Joy attempted to influence public opinion through largesses, railroad passes, and dire threats of "crime waves" if the accused were not convicted. The jury did, in fact, find twelve of the defendants guilty, and they received sentences of up to ten years.

The prosecuting attorney received five hundred dollars from Joy for services rendered.

Joy's intent had been to cow the antagonists of the railroad. He had failed, and instead generated more ill feeling. Yet so rapid was the flow of events in Europe and America that the trial already had lost much of the importance it had had for the railroad six months earlier.

8

The Republican Genesis

NOT ONLY DID THE POTATO BLIGHT SET OFF A MASS EXODUS FROM IRELAND, IT was a principal factor in the revolutions that swept over the entire European continent in 1848. In France, Germany, and all of central Europe the rapidly increasing population had been flooding into the cities since the end of the Napoleonic Wars. Although the French had not yet descended to eating potatoes, potatoes were a principal animal fodder. As the blight destroyed the crop, food prices in the cities rose daily. People were spread-eagled between the accelerating prices and the twenty-five cents a day wages that the archaic and inefficient manufacturers were paying in order to attempt to compete with more efficient British and American industry. Workers set up barricades and rioted in the cities.

As much as 40 percent of the urban population was unemployed. When the French government set up a public works program, 120,000 Parisians applied for the 6,000 jobs offered. Demanding reform, the Protestant and Jewish industrialists, progressives, and "liberals" of the cities were pitted against the Catholic agrarians who controlled the governments and the military. When, after a bitter struggle, the revolutions were crushed, the Protestant refugees from northern Europe, added to the Irish, created the most massive human movement since the time of the Mongols. The number of immigrants arriving in America increased from 599,000 in the decade of the 1830's to 1,713,000 in the 1840's and 2,598,000 in the 1850's.

Nearly all of these immigrants were from seafaring lands with long ties to America.* The Napoleonic Wars had interrupted trade with America, but in the 1820's and the 1830's European interest in the United States gradually re-

---

* Holland and Sweden had established two of the earliest colonies: New York and Delaware. Germany was linked to America by the fact that the German-descended British royal house had continued to hold the principality of Hanover as a personal possession. Hesse, which was part of Hanover, suffered from the same problem of overpopulation as Ireland, and like Ireland was a producer of manpower for various armies. An estimated one third of the Hessians in the British army deserted during the Revolutionary War and settled in America.

vived. The opening of the West through the building of the Erie Canal not only quickened that interest, but had a major economic impact on the northern European nations whose ships carried on trade with the United States. The 1840's saw the publication of a number of German, Dutch, and Swedish books that described the United States in glowing, almost Utopian terms.

Limitations of communications and transportation largely restricted the "American fever" to communities near the seaboard. Language barriers prevented news of America from penetrating deeply into central and, especially, rural Europe. The lack of land transportation and railroads made travel on much of the continent almost as difficult as in the United States, and precluded any mass migration from the interior. The religious chasm between Protestant America and Catholic southern and eastern Europe further inhibited immigration from those lands.

Much of the Protestant migration of the 1840's from England, the Netherlands, Germany, and Scandinavia was, like the Irish immigration, economic in origin. The forty thousand Dutch of the Reformed Church that Albertus C. Van Raalte led to Michigan had just had "for the time being at least, freedom of worship granted. . . . Famine and poverty, however, were more insistent." [1]

The drama, nevertheless, was provided by the revolutions and the persecutions. It was these that gripped the imaginations and the hearts of Americans. In the United States, Van Raalte emphasized his pleas for assistance with stories of the religious persecution his followers had undergone. Fueled by tales of Catholic and monarchial repression, American public opinion again flared up in violent anti-Catholicism.

(Repeated popular uprisings in the Papal States were put down as ruthlessly as rebellions elsewhere. The encyclical *Mirari vos* not only condemned revolt against any established government for any reason, but took a dim view of the practices of liberty of conscience and liberty of the press. In 1849 the skies of Rome were lighted by an orgy of Protestant Bible burning. It was, therefore, natural for Americans, whose nation had sprung from revolution, whose Constitution guaranteed those liberties that the Vatican denounced, to consider the papacy "un-American.")

At the same time that Protestant refugees were welcomed as champions of freedom, the Irish were damned as pestilential. Tens of thousands were stampeding into Detroit, Boston, New York, Philadelphia, Cincinnati, and the other Northern cities. They squatted on every vacant lot, invaded gardens, and dug into cellars. The wealthy fled their "downtown" mansions and turned them over to managers, who cut them up into airless and lightless cubicles. Since these were nothing more than dormitories, the streets during the daytime were transformed into swarms of humanity. While men, women, and *older* children (nine and ten years of age) went off to work from dawn to dusk for a few pennies a day, infants and five-year-olds were left in the care of seven- and eight-year-olds. Swarming, filthy and half naked, they formed gauntlets of begging gamins, petty thieves, and pickpockets.

Used to relieving themselves in the bogs and the fields and provided with almost no sanitary facilities in the cities, the Irish dug holes in the floors in the middle of their rooms, and otherwise relieved themselves wherever their bowels and their bladders moved them. Without furniture and without washing facilities, they slept on beds of straw and feathers, not infrequently laid on the bare earth.

Emerging caked with dirt and feathers, they were objects of contempt and derision.

Into cities whose water supply consisted of "slaughter wells" and inadequate penstocks—where water might be obtainable only at certain hours and on certain days—both the immigrants and the returnees from the Mexican War again introduced cholera.

In Detroit, schools were closed on June 22, 1849, which was made a day of "prayer, fasting, and thanksgiving" because the epidemic seemed to have spared the city. Residents turned out en masse to clean up the rotting piles of debris and refuse and the festering mudholes. The streets were corrugated with open private sewers which, steaming and stinking, not infrequently ran backward to deposit their effluence in the cellars of outraged householders.

Although a "toilet saloon" featuring hot and cold showers and salt baths was set up in downtown Detroit in 1846, most Detroiters, like people the world over, continued to have a fearful aversion to bathing. Citizens listened intently as men of medicine and men of God warned that the practice would wash away a man's virility and a woman's virginity.

(The first bath tub in the United States, installed in Cincinnati in 1842, had been met by newspaper editorials calling it undemocratic and a plaything of the rich. As the dangerous device spread eastward, Philadelphia restricted its use to between March 1 and October 31, and Boston, not surprisingly, banned it entirely except when prescribed by a physician.)

Given these conditions, it was soon evident that Detroit's day of thanksgiving had been premature. As the epidemic spread across the nation, the city in July, 1849, recorded 360 deaths from cholera, plus 421 from a variety of other diseases. Imploring divine intercession, President Zachary Taylor decreed the first Friday in August a day of fasting and prayer. But Washington, apparently, was no more influential than Detroit.

So it was that the unwashed, slum-dwelling Irish Catholics were charged with responsibility for the epidemic. Their concentration in the urban centers was viewed with the greatest alarm. Was this not a popish plot? The sight of a Catholic with a shotgun or a musket generated rumors of weapons' caches and plans to overthrow the government. The democratization of the American Revolution * and the abolition in the 1820's of property requirements for the franchise provided the Irish and the urban poor with the kind of political clout that was unknown in Europe. Since most cities did not impose citizenship requirements for voting in local elections, the Irish were able to step off the ships and market their votes for jobs, beer, or whatever else they could obtain. Political bosses, riding upward on the tide of humanity, organized the newcomers and voted them in blocs.

No other challenge could have caused such alarm among the urban-oriented Protestants. The Supreme Order of the Star Spangled Banner was organized to contest for control of the cities. Originating in New York, it spread with prairie-fire rapidity across the nation. Requiring members to swear that they had been free from the taint of Catholicism for two generations, the order became known as the Know-Nothings—those who belonged to it gave a standard "I don't know" response to all questions asked. Protestant ministers urged vigilance and the

---

* Of the white population of approximately 3,000,000, only 160,000 had voted on the ratification of the Constitution: 100,000 in favor.

strengthening of the public schools as the surest defense against a Catholic take-over. They warned that the future of America as a Protestant nation with a Protestant ethic was at stake.

The clannish and separatist tendencies of the Irish Catholics provided fuel to the opposition. In the opinion of Detroit's bishop, to let Catholic children attend public schools was to risk having them weaned away from their religion. Acting to set up a system of church schools, he objected to the taxation of the Catholics for the support of the public school system and demanded a pro rata distribution of public funds for the maintenance of separate Catholic schools.

The bishop's demands split the city asunder. They showed a remarkable lack of the political sensitivity that had led Horace Mann to conclude that in a multi-religious society the survival of the public schools system depends on the separa-tion of religion from education. Mann had had to overcome the opposition of Protestant ministers who denounced him and preached that juvenile delinquency, crime, and "children of wrath" were the consequence of his ban on (Protestant) Bible instruction. No sooner had Detroit's bishop spoken, than the smoldering issue burst into flame. If the Catholic demands were to be granted, other denomi-nations demanded equal treatment in setting up their own church schools. The city's school system was threatened with death in its infancy.

Although they were hardly models of efficiency, the Detroit schools were offering all the children of the city the opportunity to acquire the rudiments of education. The nineteen small schools scattered around the city were almost all one-teacher schools. The 1850 census showed 6,306 children of school age in a population of 21,000. Luckily, since the city engaged only 21 teachers, the average attendance was but 1,743. Throughout these years the pupil-teacher ratio was near 100 to 1. Textbooks and paper were scarce and expensive. Each child obtained whatever book he could. Often one book was shared by two, three, or four children. Since each teacher taught according to his own inclinations, the transfer of a child from one school to another was all but impossible. Edu-cation-conscious Negroes who demanded equal opportunity for their children were furnished with one teacher, who conducted class in a church for approxi-mately a hundred pupils.

The decision of the Democrats to support the Catholic bishop split the party. In the mayoralty election of 1853, the future of the school system was the critical issue. Amid verbal and physical violence, the Independent Democrats united with Whigs, Know-Nothings, and Free-Soilers to carry the election by a convincing two thousand votes.

Yet the victors were uneasy. They had beaten back the challenge, but only through the fusion of several diverse groups who, in the past, had seemed to have little in common. Unless the fusion could attain a measure of permanence, the danger was likely to remain. The fusion, furthermore, was one that Joy and his railroad associates could regard with interest.

Forbes was no longer thinking in terms of a railroad stretching merely from the East to Chicago. Scarcely had the news of the discovery of gold in California reached Boston in 1849 than Forbes, whose clippers often made stops on the West Coast, envisioned a railroad spanning the continent. The land grant for the building of the Illinois Central established a generous precedent, and Forbes found the bonds readily marketable in Europe. The agricultural reforms and removal of trade barriers instituted by European governments following the Revolutions of 1848 offered the promise of a vast European market for American wheat, corn, and meat—a potential market no one could appreciate better than a shipper like Forbes.

By 1853, within a year after the Michigan Central reached Chicago, the Forbes group was pushing its railroads toward Iowa and Missouri.* In the meantime, to the east, the tracks were being rapidly completed across Canada. In the late afternoon of January 17, 1854, a crowd of thousands in Windsor, Canada, burst into cheers as a plume of black smoke appeared on the horizon. It was the first train on the newly completed Great Western Railroad. Except for a short ferry ride across the Detroit River, Boston, Albany, Detroit, and Chicago were connected by rail. By the end of the year the tracks reached Davenport on the Mississippi River.

No longer was the West isolated from the East in winter. Travel time from the East Coast to Detroit was reduced to twenty-seven hours. Chicago could be reached from Detroit in nine hours. In one day in 1854, fourteen thousand passengers arrived in and departed from Chicago on the Michigan Southern—equal to the city's entire population in 1846!

The American axis which, with the building of the Erie Canal, had begun to shift away from its North-South orientation, completed its movement and locked into place: East-West.

Pushing their railroads westward, Forbes and Joy were brought into direct confrontation with the ambitions and interests of the South.

Like locusts, cotton bolls raped the land. In a few years they exhausted the most fertile soil. In little more than a generation the cotton armies, marching out of South Carolina and Georgia, swept through Alabama and Mississippi. Gorging themselves on the loam of the Mississippi Delta, they crossed the river and invaded Louisiana, Texas, and Arkansas. No one knew how long such a process could continue. But as planters abandoned their old plantations to establish new ones farther and farther west, they perceived the horizon stretching all the way to the Pacific Coast.

The prospect of a land planted with cotton from the Mississippi to the Pacific was anathema to the Railroaders. Railroads required an economic base of small farmers and consumers, not an economic base of large plantations composed of slaves without purchasing power. They needed land to provide the backing for the bonds which, marketed in Europe, were the means by which they could obtain British and German steel rails and rolling stock.

Conversely, Southerners were alarmed by the fingers the railroads were extending southward. Canals were already redirecting the economic orientation of the border states away from the South and toward the North. As the railroads connected Kentucky and Missouri with Chicago, Cleveland, Indianapolis, and Detroit, they promised to multiply the effect of the canals many times over. If Kentucky and Missouri should waver—and if they wavered, Maryland and Delaware would scarcely be far behind—the balance between the sixteen free and the fifteen slave states would be upset.

Such a development seemed ever more likely as the railroads encouraged immi-

---

* Joy was counsel not only for the Michigan Central, but for the Illinois Central. He was president of the Chicago and Aurora. He was piecing together the lines between Chicago, Burlington and Quincy. He was participating in negotiations for acquisition of the Hannibal and St. Joseph, whose large land grant, coupled with the promise of control of northern Missouri, made it an enticing investment.

gration. Northern Missouri and the Ohio River Valley were becoming second *Heimatlanden* for the Germans fleeing from the repressions of the revolution. Spilling over into Iowa, Kansas, and Nebraska, they threatened to destroy once and for all the political equality of the South in the national government. Without immigration, the South would have gained five seats in the House of Representatives during the 1840's.* With immigration, the North gained twelve.

A plentiful supply of cheap, immigrant labor threatened to depreciate one of the South's two principal assets: slaves. Even more, the canals and the railroads were aiding the escape of a significant number of the most valuable of those slaves.

The constitutional ban on the overseas slave trade, coming just at the time (1808) when the demand for slaves skyrocketed, had created a domestic industry in the breeding and trading of slaves. In the forty-five years since John Randolph had admonished the Northwest on the evils of slavery, Virginia, with no need for a large labor supply, had made a business of the breeding and exporting of slaves. The nation's capital, Washington, D.C., was the largest slave market in the world, one so vile that Randolph declared:

". . . Every day that passes things are done in it at which the despotisms of Europe would be horror-struck and disgusted. . . . In no part of the earth—not even excepting the rivers on the Coast of Africa, was there so great, so infamous a slave market, as in the metropolis, in the seat of government of this nation which prides itself on freedom." [2]

Slaves, together with raw land, were the sine qua non of cotton growing. A rough rule of thumb held the value of a field hand at $100 for every cent in the market price of a pound of cotton. With the coming of the 1840's and 1850's, the demand for and production of cotton hit new peaks. The price of a field hand jumped to between $1,200 and $1,800.[3]

Yet slaves were not restricted to employment as field hands. They were used in industries, on the docks, and in construction. Trained on plantations, they made up a major portion of the artisans: carpenters, bricklayers, barbers, blacksmiths, tanners, and tailors.† If a blacksmith became noted for his skills, a planter would hire him out to other plantations, or even set him up in a shop in town.

For educated slaves, the increasing railroad and canal connections to the north offered avenues of escape—the underground railroad was an adjunct of the steam railroad, and many of its "stations" were along the tracks. Both skilled artisans and agricultural laborers were welcomed in the North, and easily absorbed into the economy. Observing their wealth seep northward, the Southerners gained passage of the stringent Fugitive Slave Law of 1850, and in state after Southern state passed laws making the teaching of a slave to read and write a capital offense.

(Nevertheless, the punitive laws had little effect. Adopting the guise of washing machine salesmen, a group of thirteen Southerners, driven to desperation, traveled north in covered wagons, and began a roundup of fugitives. Discovered

---

* The slave population had grown from 500,000 to 3,500,000 in seventy-five years. For purposes of representation, each slave was counted as three fifths of a person.
† In testimony before the National Advisory Commission on Civil Disorders, Dr. Benjamin Quarles, a historian, estimated that 100,000 of the 120,000 Southern artisans prior to the Civil War were Negro.

with their black cargo, they were arrested and charged with assault and kidnaping.)

In one more attempt to reconcile sectional differences, Senator Douglas of Illinois proposed a deal. Douglas wanted the eastern terminus of the proposed Pacific railroad in the North, so as to channel the traffic through Illinois. Secretary of War Jefferson Davis was determined to direct the railroad through the South. Since no organization except the army had the resources to run the survey for the railroad, Davis held the upper hand.

In return for the railroad, Douglas proposed that the Northern wing of the Democratic party would agree to the nullification of the Missouri Compromise—which barred the extension of slavery beyond 36° 30′ latitude, roughly the northern boundary of Arkansas. Each territory could choose whether it wanted to be slave or free at the time of admission to statehood. That portion of the Louisiana Territory west of Missouri and Iowa would be divided into the territories of Kansas and Nebraska. Implicitly, Kansas, if its settlers so willed, would be admitted as a slave state.

Undoubtedly, each side thought it was outwitting the other. Douglas could contend that he was giving away nothing; the destiny of Kansas would be decided by its people, and, with the railroad linking the territory to the North, the settlers would opt for a free state. (Further, to anyone familiar with soil and climate, it was obvious that Kansas was unsuitable for the raising of any of the slave crops: cotton, rice, sugar cane, or indigo.) The Southerners, conversely, were confident that they had the inside track. Kansas was unapproachable except through Missouri. And Missouri (though wavering) was a slave state.

There was no question that Douglas had the votes in the Senate to pass the Kansas-Nebraska Act. But what the preponderance of public sentiment was, no one knew. Condemning the bill as morally untenable, a petition signed by 3,050 Northeastern clergymen warned that it would be "exposing us to the righteous judgment of the Almighty." When, on March 3, 1854, the bill easily passed the Senate, opponents marshaled their forces to block its passage in the House of Representatives. In Detroit an anti-Kansas-Nebraska Act group was already organized, and other "anti" groups were meeting in Jackson, Michigan, in Ripon, Wisconsin, and elsewhere. On April 3, an "anti" ticket carried the municipal election in Grand Rapids, Michigan. Nevertheless, on May 22 the bill squeaked through the House by a vote of 113-100. It was a foregone conclusion that President Pierce, a Vermont Democrat with Southern predilections, would sign it.

Hardly had the clerk announced the tally, than Democratic Congressman Kinsley Bingham jumped aboard a train for New York, Albany, Buffalo, and Detroit. Within three days he was in consultation with Joy, former Mayor Chandler, and the *Bostonian* coalition that continued to dominate the city.

Developments in the nation had outstripped the debates in Congress. The proposal to let slavery spread—no matter how unlikely that it would—goaded the passions of the Abolitionists to a new fury, and aroused widespread opposition among Northern intellectuals who were otherwise indifferent to Southern practices. Most of all, it sent chills of apprehension through manufacturers and merchants.

Detroit was just beginning to receive shipments of iron ore and copper from the North; it had vast forests to be converted to lumber and consumer goods;

its seed industry was thriving; it was manufacturing cigars for sale to prospering Midwesterners *; and it was acquiring its first heavy industry. Prominent Detroiters were envisioning their city as a giant alembic into which humanity would be funneled from the East, agricultural products from the West, and iron, copper, and lumber from the North. They were adamantly opposed to any action that might inhibit the rapid growth of population and of industry. The Forbes-Joy Hannibal and St. Joseph Railroad was directed like an arrow at Kansas, and needed for its success not only Kansas but northern Missouri as *free* territory. The prospect of the railroad having to pass through a thousand miles of slave territory between the Midwest and the Pacific Coast was intolerable. In mid-June the *Bostonians* issued a call for a mass meeting in Jackson on July 6, 1854.

It was without doubt the most amazing political gathering in all American history. Men who shortly before had been at each other's throats found a cause to unite them. Chandler declared:

"Misfortunes make strange bedfellows. I see before me Whigs, Democrats, and Free-Soilers, all mingling together to rebuke a great national wrong. I was born a Whig [but] I have laid aside party to rebuke treachery." [4]

In fact, there were far more than Whigs, Democrats, and Free-Soilers. Gathering on "Morgan's Forty Acres" were up to five thousand pro-Railroad men, anti-Railroad men, public education advocates, Know-Nothings, Homesteaders, European Revolutionaries, Prohibitionists, Abolitionists, and picnickers. What brought them together was their hatred of the Southern way of life, their boiling anger at Southern domination of the national government, and the realization that unless they merged their interests they would never be able to contend successfully against the North-South coalition in the Democratic party. (Joy's Free-Soilers had demonstrated their impuissance by gathering only 156,000 votes in the 1852 presidential election.)

The Homesteaders in the coalition dated their origins to 1844, when George Evans, editor of the New York *Working Man's Advocate,* had proposed that the immigrants in the slums of Eastern cities be encouraged to settle in the West. To help them, Congress should enact a law to dispose of the public domain through free grants of 160 acres to any person settling upon and farming them. Horace Greeley of the New York *Tribune* had eagerly adopted the idea. The Southern opposition, however, killed every congressional attempt at enactment of the law. Complementing each other, the Homesteaders and the Railroaders were driven together.

The European Revolutionaries not only were in contention with the Southerners for the lands of the West, but discerned in the South the same kind of agrarian oligarchy against which they had battled in Europe. The North was developing an egalitarian school system, supported by property taxes and guaranteeing every child a basic educaton. The South retained the English system of pauper schools for the common people. Since few parents would send their children to such schools, education was a privilege of the children of the well-to-do. The North had opened politics to mass participation. The South retained a system of patrician political control. The North promoted one-family farming and widespread ownership of land. The South was wedded to the plantation—and the

---

* Starting out with homegrown tobacco, Detroit became a cigar-manufacturing center as a result of its canal and railroad connections with Kentucky. The power for the cutting machinery of the first tobacco factory was provided by a blind horse. Lowered into the basement, it spent the rest of its life going in circles around a capstan.

plantation was merely another form of the large European estate with its serfs and dirt-poor peasants. To keep from breaking up their plantations, Southern gentlemen directed their excess sons into the United States Army, whose officer corps was made up largely of Southerners, just as the European aristocrats relied on the armies to absorb their second sons. In the South as in Europe the result was a culture of conservatism, exaggerated concept of honor, and militarism.*

The Prohibition movement was a product of bad water, plentiful beer, and cheap whiskey. Irish laborers arriving from Europe were accustomed to drinking beer, sterilized in the process of brewing, rather than urban water, which frequently was equivalent to death. Discovering in America the "hard stuff" could be bought just as cheaply, the Irish on the weekends turned the streets of their quarters into streams of drunkards, seined by hordes of prostitutes. The Washington Movement, a Baltimore organization of reformed drunkards advocating temperance, was gaining strength. The scandalized *Bostonians* supported it. In 1851 Maine passed the first prohibition law.

The Abolitionists, a suffering, derided, lonely minority of Quakers, Moravians, and moralists, provided the drama. The Southerners' determination to keep their slaves in ignorance was as "un-American" to the *Bostonians* as the papacy's authoritarianism. Ministers were outraged by the planters' indifference to the religious instruction of the slaves, by their violation of marriage mores, and by their destruction of the family. Since a field hand's value depended on his physical attributes, planters encouraged their most powerful males to impregnate as many females as possible. Families were ripped apart, and the offspring sold to provide revenues for the plantations.

(Since males were the primary commodity of the slave trade, the trade brought about a shortage of males in the slave-raising state of Virginia—which between 1830 and 1860 shipped 220,000 human beings South—and an excess of males in the slave-importing and cotton-exporting states of the Black Belt. The imbalance between the sexes thus created naturally led to promiscuity.)

Detroit's location across the river from Canada, and its accessibility from the border states made it the focal point for the underground railroad. A sizable and energetic Negro community was developing in Windsor, and from there Henry Bibb's *Voice of the Fugitive* eloquently furthered the antislavery cause. Ever since 1833, when Detroit's black community had resorted to arms to rescue Thornton Blackburn and his wife from a sheriff preparing to return them to Kentucky, there had been periodic confrontations between the people of Michigan and of the South.†

"Slavery," thundered the orators at the Jackson gathering, "is a violation of the rights of man . . . a relic of barbarism . . . weakness in the midst of the state . . . greatly injurious to the free states, and to the territories themselves,

---

* The military school, to which boys were shipped at an early age, became a fixture in the South.
† In 1847 the Adam Crosswhite case almost led to a declaration of war between Michigan and Kentucky. The offspring of a white father, Crosswhite had been given as a servant to his white half-sister, the wife of a slave dealer, who sold him for two hundred dollars. Crosswhite was forty-four and had four children when he learned that his owner was planning to separate and sell part of the family. He escaped and settled in Marshall, Michigan. When Kentucky slave hunters attempted to spirit him back to the South, a riot broke out. The Kentuckians were arrested and fined one hundred dollars. Although the Southerners brought suit in the U.S. Circuit Court, they failed to regain Crosswhite, who was ably defended by a number of lawyers, including Joy. The case played a leading role in the Compromise of 1850 and the passage of the new Fugitive Slave Law.

tending to retard the settlement and to prevent the improvement of the country by means of free labor [and to] reduce the North, with all her industry, wealth, and enterprise, to be the mere province of a few slave-holding oligarchs of the South—a condition too shameful to be contemplated."

To the public education forces, the platform promised "a careful preservation of the primary school and university funds, and their diligent application to the great objectives for which they were created."

The anti-railroad forces managed to push through a plank calling for a "general railroad law" opening Michigan to competitive railroad construction—a small pill for Joy to swallow considering the gains that were promised.

"Be of good cheer," the orators exhorted the free settlers in the territories, "persevere in the right, remember the Republican motto, *The North Will Defend You!*"

Leaving no doubt about where they stood, the gatherers announced "the necessity of battling for the first principles of republican government, and against the schemes of an aristocracy, the most revolting and oppressive with which the earth was ever cursed, or man debased."

And so, they declared, "We will cooperate and be known as Republicans." [5]

9

The Predictable War

ELSEWHERE IN AMERICA, 1854 SAW THE CRESTING OF THE KNOW-NOTHING TIDE. In Michigan, however, the slate headed by Representative Bingham smashed Democratic control of the state, and won the governorship and the legislature by a margin of more than ten thousand votes. From the men in attendance at Jackson were to come six governors, six senators, and nineteen representatives. Governor Bingham pardoned the last two of the railroad "conspirators" still in jail, and Joy even paid indemnities to some of the defendants. William Howard, one of the defense attorneys, ran on the Republican ticket and defeated the prosecutor, Democrat David Stuart, for Congress. A general railroad law and Prohibition were enacted.

(On May 15, 1855, all of the bars in Detroit were shut down. By the end of June they were wide open again. Recognizing that the law was impossible to enforce in the city, the state practiced de jure Prohibition, but left Detroiters to enjoy their pleasures.)

Michigan's natural ties to New England carried the Republican genesis to Massachusetts. At Worcester, in September, a gathering of the same diverse elements that had met at Jackson greeted with tumultuous applause Amasa Walker's speech defining the struggle as "between Slavery, Romanism, and Rum, on the one side, and Freedom, Protestantism, and Temperance, on the other." [1]

Never before had the nation been in such turmoil. Politically, it was fragmenting. In 1854 the Know-Nothings gained control of both the governorship and the legislature of Massachusetts, elected forty members to the New York Legislature, and won nearly fifty congressional seats. Not until the sixtieth ballot was the House of Representatives in 1855 able to elect a speaker: a Know-Nothing. The fall elections, possible the most confusing in American history—in Connecticut twenty-three different parties entered candidates—sparked untrammeled violence and riots between Irish and Know-Nothings. In Louisville an Election Day fight brought a mob surging through the Irish "Quinn's Row." Looting, burning, and murdering, the rioters threw some of the injured into burning buildings, and killed anywhere between twenty and one hundred persons.

After the votes had been tallied, the governors of Connecticut, Massachusetts, Rhode Island, New Hampshire, New York, Maryland, Kentucky, Texas, and California were Know-Nothings. Eight legislatures were controlled by Know-Nothings, or Know-Nothing and Whig coalitions. In four others the Know-Nothings had significant minorities.[2]

But, even if the lack of a constructive program did not doom the Know-Nothings, they resembled the disintegrating Whigs and the sorely tried Democrats in their orientation along the decaying North-South political axis. It was the East-West Republicans who were attuned to the new political forces.

With "Pathfinder" John Frémont * as their presidential candidate, the Republicans in 1856 won 1.3 million popular votes, only 500,000 fewer than the Democrats.† It was an amazing showing for a party that had not been in existence three years before, and whose candidate was damaged by charges of being a secret Catholic.

When Congress convened, the House was unable to agree on a speaker until the one hundred and thirty-third ballot. When it did, he turned out to be an ex-Democrat turned Know-Nothing who had jumped to the Republicans.

In the West, the Republicans were engaged in a little-disguised war against the South. In Michigan they passed a "personal liberty law" that prohibited the detention of fugitive slaves in county jails, directed prosecuting attorneys to defend them, and in effect nullified the national Fugitive Slave Law. Perfervid orators whipped up adventurers to go to Kansas and battle for the Lord. Chandler, who replaced Lewis Cass in the Senate in 1857, proposed that Detroit send one hundred men to Kansas. Together with the other *Bostonians,* he launched a campaign to collect ten thousand dollars for Kansas aid. When three Michigan men were killed in "bleeding Kansas," the orators had their martyrs.

The principal beneficiary of the tens of thousands of dollars that the "emigrant aid societies" poured into Kansas to battle against the proslavery Missouri "border ruffians" was a hypnotic religious zealot, John Brown. As adept at wielding the sword as waving the Bible, Brown had no compunctions about massacring innocent Southerners in the cause of "righteousness." Periodically he appeared in Detroit with his "trains" of fugitive slaves, and replenished his war chest. Financing the war, the Railroaders were delighted to use him to make it appear that they were engaged in a noble cause against slavery, instead of an economic conflict for control of the West.

When Brown ventured east to Boston, Forbes entertained him in his house, but scarcely revealed his dispassionate viewpoint to him. "I am essentially a conservative," Forbes wrote, "and have been anti-slavery more because anti-slavery is anti-republican, anti-peace, anti-material progress, anti-civilization than upon the higher and purer ground that it is wicked and unjust to the slave! I have no special love for the African, any more than for the low-class Irish, but don't want to see either imposed upon." [3]

Neither had Forbes any special love for John Brown. The night after secretly entertaining Brown, he hosted the proslavery governor of Missouri, who had placed a three-thousand-dollar price on Brown's head. The interest of Forbes

* Frémont was the somewhat unstable army officer who had surveyed the route for the Pacific railroad.
† The crushing rejection of the Know-Nothings, whose candidate, former President and Democratic-reject Millard Fillmore garnered only 874,538 votes, brought about the death of the party.

and Joy was the security and profitability of the Hannibal and St. Joseph Railroad.

In February, 1859, the railroad reached the Missouri River across from Kansas. The conflict was coming to a head. There was little prospect of its being settled peacefully. From 1856 onward, the fratricidal Congress conducted no business. Any debate was likely to erupt into a fist fight. Members challenged each other to duels with weapons ranging from bowie knives to rifles. On February 5, 1858, the floor of the House of Representatives was the scene of a full-blown gang fight.

On March 12, 1859, John Brown arrived in Detroit with a "train" of fourteen liberated slaves. The Railroaders expected him to continue in the forefront of the battle for Kansas. But Brown was growing restive. Why should he content himself with fighting against slavery on the periphery? Armageddon would never come in Missouri or Kansas—it would have to come in the South.

Brown was at the zenith of his influence. The more he was vilified by the Southerners, the more his stock rose with the *Bostonians*. While Southerners demanded the implementation of the "law and order" that would return fugitive slaves to their owners, abolitionist Wendell Phillips told a Boston Music Hall audience:

"Law and order are only means for the halting ignorance of the last generation." [4]

Frederick Douglass * was in Detroit to present a lecture on the evening of Brown's arrival. After the lecture, Douglass met with Brown and a number of other men in a quiet, two-story frame house on Congress Street. By candlelight Brown outlined his plan for the organization of simultaneous slave uprisings all across the South. George de Baptiste suggested that the rebellion be punctuated by the wholesale elimination of planters. All the churches should be blown up one Sunday.

Douglass was far too perspicacious to commit himself to such a course. The slaves lacked education and leadership. They had no knowledge of the affairs of the world beyond the horizon of their own plantations. They were among the world's least likely candidates for successful revolutionaries. The history of the rebellions of Denmark Vesey, Gabriel, and Nat Turner was one of failure, followed by greater repression.

Nevertheless, Brown, communing with the Lord, was not to be dissuaded by temporal considerations. To obtain the weapons with which to arm the slaves, he attacked the United States Arsenal at Harpers Ferry on the evening of October 16, 1859. Harpers Ferry was close enough to Washington for the raid to have the maximum impact on the nation's capital.

As the blood spilled over the arsenal, the nation's festering sores burst open. In the six weeks between Brown's capture and his execution, an infuriated South read about the plot for its destruction. Captured with Brown was correspondence linking him to prominent Northerners. Abstruse documents, although undecipherable, seemed to indicate the locations for slave revolts and massacres of whites. If Brown had hoped to unify the North, the effect of his action was to unify the South.

Three fourths of Southern whites did not own slaves. There was no love

---

* Douglass was a former slave who, escaping in his youth, had educated himself. A brilliant writer and lecturer, he was used by Abolitionists as the example of what Negroes could make of themselves if given the opportunity.

between the small white farmers (who might keep a slave or two) and the owners of the large plantations, 10,600 of whom possessed one fourth of all the slaves. But the specter of hordes of unleashed slaves put the lower-class whites—as well as many of the half million American free blacks, who disdained the rude field hands—in the same camp with J. H. Hammond, the patrician governor of South Carolina, who intoned:

"In all social systems there must be a class to do the menial duties, to perform the drudgery of life . . . a class requiring but a low order of intellect and but little skill . . . or you would not have that other class which leads progress, civilization and refinement. . . . Fortunately for the South, she found a race adapted to the purpose of her hand . . . slaves." [5]

A hysteria of rumors swept across the South in a "Great Fear." New England missionaries, German peddlers, New York salesmen—anyone who did not speak with a Southern accent—was suspected of being an agent of the Abolitionist conspiracy. A boycott of Northern businesses was organized. People were ridden out of town on rails, and lynched on the slightest suspicion. A loyal Southerner, Hinton R. Helper was forced to flee for warning in his book, *The Impending Crisis of the South,* that slavery was retarding industrialization and destroying the economy. His books, along with those of other authors, were seized and burned. Months before the Southern states seceded, they were recoiling from the North.

If they were not as outraged as the Southerners, the Republicans were scarcely less shocked. Neither the Railroaders nor the Homesteaders had intended, or foreseen, that their mercurial protégé would turn his brimstone and fire directly against the South. The Railroaders denounced him. Abraham Lincoln deplored him.

When the Republican convention of 1860 assembled in Chicago, New York Senator William H. Seward was the leading candidate. The public education forces, however, opposed him because he advocated aid to Catholic schools. The railroad men remembered his defense of the "conspirators" against the Michigan Central and packed the galleries with Lincoln supporters. Lincoln had shown well in his debates against Stephen Douglas in 1858. As a former railroad lobbyist, he seemed reliable. His views on slavery paralleled those of the conservative Forbes.

When the North-South Democratic party split three ways, Lincoln was elected President with less than 40 percent of the popular vote. It was the smallest winning percentage in American history. The agrarian Southerners were convinced that their own party had broken apart beyond redemption, that the Republicans would push their railroads and their settlers westward at Southern expense, and that they would encourage more John Browns to carry off their slaves. They decided upon divorce from the industrializing North.

Southerners were certain, although purblindly so, that in any confrontation with the North they held the advantage. In 1858, a Southern senator declaimed: "Without firing a gun, without drawing a sword, should they make war upon us we could bring the whole world to our feet. . . . If no cotton was furnished . . . England would topple headlong and carry the whole civilized world with her. No. You dare not make war upon cotton . . . cotton is king." [6]

Responsible for two thirds of the dollar value of American exports, cotton was the principal earner of revenue for the Federal government. Four fifths of the cotton used in England and three fifths used in France came from the

South. It was the propellant for the triangular trade from the South to England, from England to the North, and from the North to the South. Whitney's cotton gin had transformed the South into the most affluent region of the nation. The per capita wealth of the South's free population was twice that of the North's. Without Southern officers, the Northern army was likely to disintegrate into a rabble.

Following Lincoln's election, the three Southern members of President Buchanan's six-man Cabinet directed a steady flow of supplies southward. Under the guidance of the Secretary of War, a Virginian, and his Southern generals and colonels, scores of thousands of muskets and cannons were cached in the Southern states. The Southerners not only prided themselves on their military prowess, but believed that England and France would have to assume the role of their protectors. They were confident that the North would have to *cotton* to the South.

To the *Bostonians,* the Southern posturing resembled that of a blowfish. The Northern and border states had four times the free population of the South, and ten times the industrial capacity. The annual value of manufactured products, reaching $1.8 billion in 1860, had doubled since 1850. The North had *networks* of railways and canals; the South had only chopped-up segments. Nearly 40 percent of the Southern wealth—$2 billion out of $5.5 billion— was tied up in slaves. Much of the remainder was in land. Neither would be negotiable in a conflict. The navy had as great a New England orientation as the army had a Southern, and could sever the link between the South and Europe. Western agriculture and Eastern and Midwestern factories, whose mechanization outstripped the world's comprehension, were producing at a rate that threatened to swamp the markets.

If strong, and perhaps prevailing, sentiment in the North was to let the South go in peace, amicable divorce was a practical impossibility. It would leave unsettled the question of the Western lands and of the war in Kansas. It would leave the New England textile industry dependent upon cotton imports from a "foreign" country. It would deprive the Federal government of its principal revenue from foreign exchange through the sale of cotton. It threatened the reestablishment of a strong British influence along the Atlantic seaboard. It would give the South control of the mouth of the Mississippi, and place the burgeoning Ohio, Mississippi, and Missouri River Valleys at its mercy. Such a development would be intolerable to the Westerners, who were counting not only on the river but on the new Illinois Central–Mobile and Ohio Railroad link for lucrative commerce through the Gulf Coast outlets.

"We own that river," Detroit's Senator Chandler said of the Mississippi. "It was a desert when we bought it, and we will make it a desert again before we will let you steal it from us." [7]

In Detroit, the *Bostonians* and the Republicans greeted the outbreak of war with patriotic huzzahs. In response to President Lincoln's request for seventy-five thousand volunteers for ninety days, the 1st Michigan Infantry—the initial troops from the West to arrive on the Eastern front—left in May of 1861 with banners flying and bands playing. From the German Revolutionaries, the immigrants, and the Homesteaders there was an extraordinary response.*

* For example, the 150 Jewish families in Michigan, most of whom had settled in the state since the latter 1840's, furnished 181 men, of whom 38, or 21 percent, were killed—a death rate 40 percent above that for the Michigan contingent as a whole.[8]

Seldom has there been a war that followed a more predictable course. In July the badly trained, badly led Union forces were routed and slaughtered at the Battle of Bull Run. In the East, the South managed to convert the war into a campaign of attrition that it could not afford. On the seas, the New England navy established its dominance and blockaded the Southern ports.

The dissaffection of the border states that Southern politicians had feared was, in fact, far advanced. Though the states might be slave, the people and economies of Delaware, Maryland, and Kentucky were linked to the North, not to the South; so were the people and economies of western Virginia and eastern Tennessee. In Missouri, a decade of German settlement had turned the politics of the state upside down. There were numerous communities whose language and culture were not English but German, and identification with the South had steadily decreased. Carl Schurz, the leader of the German community, became a Union general, and a power in the Republican party and American politics for a generation.

In Washington, the members of the Republican coalition took control of the government and enacted one after the other of their programs over the nominal and demoralized Democratic opposition. Under the prodding of Senator Chandler, who was chairman of the Committee on Commerce and a member of the Joint Committee on Conduct of the War, the building of the Pacific railroad was authorized. Jacob Howard, Joy's old associate and now the junior senator from Michigan, was named Chairman of the Committee on the Pacific Railroad.

Slavery was forever banned from all territories.

The Homestead Act, granting 160 acres to anyone who would settle upon and improve the land, was passed.

The Morrill (college land grant) Act established the principle of Federal aid to higher education, and extended nationally the Michigan concept of public education on the university level. This was followed by the establishment (in 1867) of a Federal Department of Education, which was mandated to report on the state of education in the United States.

Influenced by Michigan's establishment of the nation's first agricultural college in 1857, Congress voted in 1862 to create a United States Department of Agriculture.

To deal with the growing labor shortage as the Northern armies removed more than a million men from the labor force, the Contract Labor Law was passed. It permitted manufacturers to recruit and import laborers from Europe.

While the war was stalemated in the East, the Western-oriented Republican war hawks pushed it with vigor along the Mississippi. Samuel Colt, who had taken over and improved Whitney's machinery, had turned New England into the world center of small-arms manufacturing. (In contrast to Colt's mass production of weapons, European gunsmiths were still wrestling muskets into shape in the same fashion as their forebears in the sixteenth century. At the 1851 World Fair in London, Colt exhibited his revolver. The British military mission sent to the United States to study his methods was amazed. As a result, New England became the arms supplier for England, Denmark, Egypt, Sweden, Spain, Turkey, Prussia, and Russia.) Tens of thousands of the eighty-five thousand small arms that were being manufactured monthly were shipped to the West. By the late spring of 1862 the Union forces were in command of New Orleans and Memphis, and of all of the Mississippi except the portion between Baton Rouge and Vicksburg. A year later, with the victory at Vicksburg, Ulysses S. Grant completed the sundering of the Confederacy.

But as the victories in the West were offset by the disasters of the Peninsula Campaign in the East, each train filled with volunteers scarcely had departed from Detroit before it was returned from Washington with the plea that it be filled again. The Republicans staged rally after rally to exhort the men of Michigan to demonstrate their patriotism. On July 15, 1862, at a gathering on the Campus Martius in front of the city hall, Joy, the mayor, the sheriff, and even old and feeble General Cass pleaded with the throng to provide the recruits to fill the ranks of the 24th Michigan Infantry.

The crowd, however, was in an ugly mood. Rumors of an impending draft incensed the men. Speakers were shouted down. Calls to come to the defense of Old Glory were drowned in hoots of "Rich man's war! Rich man's war!" Men in the crowd taunted the speakers. Why were they not putting their words into action on the Mississippi and the James? The exchanges grew more acerbic. There was a rush on the grandstand. The rally disintegrated into a riot. Protected by the sheriff and his deputies, who flailed at the charging mob, the recruiters fled to the sanctum of the city's leading hotel.

When August brought the draft, there was an enthusiastic rush for the Canadian side of the river. So massive was the exodus that the government closed the border.* Not until the end of the month was it possible to form the 24th Infantry and dispatch it to the East. Two brothers, Barney and John Litogot, were among its privates. John was being paid one thousand dollars by a wealthy draftee to take his place.

The sister of the Litogot brothers was twenty-two-year-old Mary Ford. Not quite a year and a half earlier, on April 25, 1861, she had married William Ford in the parlor of Thomas Maybury's home. In the thirty years since his arrival, Maybury had become the leading real estate operator in Detroit. He was the builder of the first Woodward Avenue sewer, and was the largest taxpayer in the city.

William Ford had paid his father $600 for forty acres of land in 1858. He stopped working on the railroad, spent less time carpentering, and concentrated on farming. The war was a boon to agriculture. Like thousands of other farmers, William invested in a McCormick reaper, a mower, and other machinery. (In 1864, seventy thousand reapers were manufactured in America, seventeen times the number McCormick had made in 1858.) The reaper increased productivity ten times, and made possible the reaping of fourteen acres and the threshing of three hundred bushels a day. Together with the price of wheat, the price of land shot up. Forty acres that cost John Ford $175 in 1848, William sold for $2,500 in 1865.

But if the war brought prosperity, it also brought heartache. Shortly before Christmas, 1862, Mary Ford received word that her brother John had been killed at the battle of Fredericksburg. She was, then, not quite two months pregnant. When her and William's first son was born at the end of July, 1863, he was baptized Henry, one of the traditional family names.†

---

* The difficulty of obtaining recruits led Forbes to propose the establishment of a "German Legion," to be brought over from Europe.
† In addition to William's Uncle Henry, who had died in Pennsylvania in 1832, there was William's younger brother Henry, who had caught the California gold fever in 1849, and was now prospecting in Idaho.

10

The Education of
Thomas Edison

FIFTEEN YEARS BEFORE, DURING THE MEXICAN WAR, THE NEWS OF BATTLES
and casualties had taken weeks to reach American communities. In the Civil
War newspapers were carrying reports of conflicts while they were in progress.

What brought the war closer to the people than any before in history was a
revolution in communications equaling that in transportation.

In 1844, after several years of frustration, Samuel Morse had convinced
Congress to finance the construction of an experimental telegraph line from
Baltimore to Washington. On May 24 the first message was transmitted. By
1848 Detroit was linked to Chicago, Buffalo, and New York. Nevertheless,
practical application of the telegraph languished.

In the meantime, on the Michigan Central's high-speed, long-distance line
from Detroit to Chicago trains were running hell-for-leather without any control.
Daredevil locomotive engineers, seldom knowing what was ahead of or behind
them, raced each other at thirty miles per hour for the crossings of rival tracks.
Crashes and wrecks were spectacular. They added spice and excitement to
railroading, but they were not conducive to public confidence or to profits.

Then, in 1855, as traffic continued to increase, the Michigan Central became
the first railroad to use the telegraph to control the movement of trains. With
that innovation, the future of Morse's invention was assured.

Concurrently, thanks in large part to the efforts of the *Bostonians,* the schooling received by Americans was increasing from an average total of 80 days in
1800 to 434 by the time of the Civil War. America was by far the world's most
literate nation, a literacy that astonished Europeans.* Hoe's invention of the
rotary press introduced an economy to printing that brought the monthly magazine and the daily newspaper within everyone's reach. In an age when it was
possible to know the name of every newspaper printed in one of the European

* Per Adam Siljestrom in *A Trip in the United States,* published in Sweden in 1852, wrote:
"The Americans are the most practical people in the world; they are also its most inveterate
readers." When Sweden began establishing its school and library systems, they were based
partly on the American model.

countries, the United States had 400 dailies and 2,800 or more weeklies and monthlies. Stimulated by the instantaneous reporting from the war fronts made possible by the telegraph, their combined circulation topped 10 million.

Obtaining advance news of every major battle from the telegraph, a teen-aged newsboy on the daily train from Port Huron to Detroit increased his stock of papers on "big news" days. Thomas Alva Edison was the great-grandson of a well-to-do New Jersey landowner who had fought on the British side in the Revolutionary War and narrowly escaped being hanged as a spy. Migrating to Canada, the family had grown progressively poorer. Tom's father, Samuel Edison, Jr., had fled back to the United States after participating in Mackenzie's Rebellion, an uprising of small farmers. Passing through Detroit, which was in the doldrums of the Panic of 1837, he settled in Milan, Ohio, a town that withered when the city fathers refused to grant a right-of-way to the Cleveland-Toledo railroad. In 1854, Edison moved his family to Port Huron, fifty-five miles northeast of Detroit. As the location of the first railroad crossing from Canada to Michigan, the town was expected to grow rapidly.

The railroad, however, had taken its time in coming. Following the Panic of 1857, the educated, middle-class family was on the edge of poverty, and even hunger. In 1859, when the railroad from Detroit reached Port Huron, Tom obtained a job as a vendor of newspapers, apples, sandwiches, berries, and anything else that might appeal to the passengers on the journey. Departing Port Huron at 7 A.M., the train arrived, if on time, in Detroit at 10 A.M. It did not leave on its return journey until 6:30 P.M.

Tom, therefore, had all day to explore the city. Rebelling at the dry chaff dispensed by the Reverend G. B. Engle, he had spent only three months of his life in school. Despite the fact that the Reverend Engle reported that he was "addled" and incapable of learning, his mother had taught him to read and instilled in him a liking for books. Paying two dollars for a library card—for the first public library was not to be opened until 1865—he spent hours in the reading room of the Young Men's Association in Detroit. (Nevertheless, he was throughout his life to be confounded by grammar and spelling.)

When Tom first started making his run, the city was still in the initial stages of recovery from the Panic of 1857—a part of the industrial-railroad boom-and-bust cycles that were to plague the world's economies until the Great Depression. For months hungry bands, made up mostly of adolescents and young men, roamed the streets and looted stores. "No Irish Need Apply" signs proliferated, and hundreds of ragged children daily begged from door to door.*

By the latter part of 1859, however, Eastern and European capital was once more pouring into the railroad industry, and Detroit recovered. Along the railway tracks that spidered out in every direction—to Port Huron, Pontiac, Chicago, Toledo—locomotives chugged all day long. In the railroad yards Edison watched George Pullman building experimental sleeping and "hotel cars" for the Michigan Central and Great Western—which, boasting some of the best and fastest trains in the world, were the first railroads to add sleepers and diners. Along the docks he picked up a full vocabulary of Anglo-Saxon four-letter

---

* In the western part of the state, new settlers who had not had time to bring in their first crop had been unable to obtain loans. While the land basked in plenty—wheat production increased 75 percent during the decade, and in some counties farmers were reaping a million bushels a year—they had been reduced to setting traps, hunting for roots and berries, and beseeching handouts from their neighbors.

words. The river was alive with stately single and twin-stacked sidewheelers, with ferryboats, and with sailing barques and schooners—which often were hitched to each other like camels to be towed through the straits by furiously clanking tugboats. Occasionally a ship might be bound directly for Europe— the first vessel to make the voyage had left Chicago in 1856.

From scores of smokestacks and chimneys, black smoke and white steam was brushed across the sky. In the evenings, the downtown area glowed with gaslights. Since most of the buildings continued to be built of wood, a repetition of the fire of 1805 was a constant threat.

There was no greater spectacle than the volunteer fire companies. Splendiferously outfitted, they whipped their horses and each other as they raced to the scene of the frequent fires. Since it was the custom for citizens to fete the company that saved their property, firemen went all out to keep their rivals from the scene. In the shadows of the dancing flames they brawled with fists and axes. Although more than one structure burned to the ground while the melee went on, the battles were crowd pleasers. The company that acquired the reputation of a winner could take its pick of new recruits. Its political and social powers were enhanced. These powers were frequently of more importance than the company's firefighting abilities.

From docks to railroad depots, from warehouses to the ironworks in Wyandotte and Hamtramck, the streets were raucous with the curses of draymen and teamsters urging their horses through the rich mixture of mud and manure. After a rain a dozen wagons might be bogged down in a single block. The drabness of the unpainted clapboard buildings was shaded by the magnificent trees which, paralleling the thoroughfares, interlaced their leaves overhead. Many of the houses still had gardens planted with pear, apple, and cherry trees introduced by Cadillac.

The expansion of communications and of the railroads, and the application of the telegraph to the movement of trains, brought about a great demand for telegraphers. One day in 1863 Thomas Edison dropped off the train at Mt. Clemens, halfway between Port Huron and Detroit, and apprenticed himself to the telegrapher. Numerous other youths drawn by the good pay, one hundred dollars a month and more, were finding telegraphy the stepping-stone to success. But none would come close to making an impact upon the world comparable to Edison's.

11

The Great Boom

As the war progressed, the Republican businessmen of the city were able to rejoice that the great boom they had been seeking for two decades had at last arrived. The Southern congressmen who had been intent on keeping the cost of manufactured goods low were gone. No longer could they block the increases in the tariff that Northern industry sought. The Republicans raised tariffs 47 percent.

The effect was to make much of America's heavy industry competitive with England's. The demand for iron to manufacture guns, plows, railroads, and sewing machines not only brought Pennsylvania's coke ovens to red heat and set Pittsburgh off on its great expansion,* but raised the prices of the raw materials of which Michigan was one of the world's great storehouses. The price of lumber doubled. That of copper nearly tripled—from seventeen cents to forty-six cents a pound.

Through their acumen, shrewdness, and rapacity, the *Bostonians* were reaping the lion's share of that boom. When the copper mines in the Upper Peninsula had begun operation, the twenty-dollars-per-ton cost of shipping the metal to the East Coast had priced it too high for competition with Cornish and Chilean copper. The principal bottleneck was St. Mary's Falls, blocking the passage between Lake Superior and Lake Huron. In 1852 Detroit's men of commerce, spearheaded by the Railroaders, had prevailed upon Congress to provide a land grant of 750,000 acres for the construction of the "Soo" Canal, bypassing the falls. Assigned the task of building the canal, Brooks, the Michigan Central's general manager, pushed his men relentlessly. Ten percent of the Irish and German laborers died of cholera, but he never allowed a day of work to be interrupted. The canal cut in half the shipping cost of copper and assured the success of the mines.

To pick the choicest of the pine lands from the 750,000-acre grant, the Rail-

---

* The key to Pittsburgh's economy was its strategic river location and the unlimited reserves of coal in its vicinity. By the laws of economics, it was cheaper to bring iron and other raw materials to coal than to carry coal to other raw materials.

roaders sent out a surveying party. Challenging them was another of the canal's promoters and investors, Eber Brock Ward. A *Bostonian,* he and his uncle, Samuel Ward, were the principal competitors of both "Admiral of the Lakes" Oliver Newberry and the Railroad men. (Since the day when Samuel Ward's schooner had been one of the first through the Erie Canal, the Wards' fleet had grown to more than forty vessels.) David Ward, Eber's nephew, was dispatched to race the Railroad surveyors. With a one-hundred-pound pack, an ax. and a rifle, Ward set up his instruments in thirty-degrees-below-zero weather, killed bear to supplement his diet of salt pork, and on his dash back to Detroit appropriated the canoe of the Railroad surveyors—an act equivalent to stealing a man's horse. He arrived at the United States land office in Ionia a few hours ahead of his rivals, and was on the way to ownership of lands containing a billion board feet of timber.

Detroit and Chicago were the points at which the raw materials—the copper, the iron, and the timber—came together and were linked to the railroads. For half the year the ice that closed the Lakes still presented a transportation bottleneck. Copper and iron were mined and timber was cut during the winter, but they had to be stockpiled until spring. Transported to Detroit, they were converted into manufactured goods; goods that, from Detroit, could be distributed via the railroad all year long. On 2,200 acres at Wyandotte, Eber Brock Ward built a huge blast furnace and rolling mills, Detroit's first heavy industry.* In 1864 he installed the first Bessemer converter in America.

Railroad cars had been manufactured in Detroit since the late 1830's. But as the consequence of higher wages and a dearth of craftsmen in America, railroads had continued to order most of their equipment from British, and, to a lesser extent, from German manufacturers. The tariff brought about a drastic change in comparative costs. The Republican administration, in which Michigan's influence was challenged only by that of Massachusetts and Illinois, directed toward Detroit a huge order for railroad cars to be used on the new lines of the West, and in captured territory in the South.

As it happened, there was no firm in Detroit to build the cars. But there were several alert and enterprising young men.

One was John S. Newberry. The nephew of "Admiral" Oliver Newberry, he had graduated from the University of Michigan in 1847. For two years he had worked as a civil engineer on the Michigan Central. He had been admitted to the bar, and had become a specialist in railroad and maritime law. He had come into the Republican coalition as a Prohibitionist. (In 1852 he was nominated for governor on the Temperance ticket.) In 1862, President Lincoln named him provost marshal of the state.

The other was James McMillan. Twenty-five years old, he was the grandson of a Scottish sea captain, and the son of William McMillan, who had settled in Ontario, Canada. William had been associated with Joy and Forbes in the building of the Great Western Railroad across Canada, and subsequently had become one of its officers. In 1858 the twenty-year-old James had been hired as purchasing agent for the Detroit and Milwaukee Railroad.

Rushing to the aid of the government in its time of great need, Newberry and McMillan, together with two other men, founded the Michigan Car Company to commence construction of rolling stock.

---

* He constructed other steel mills in Chicago and Milwaukee, and lumber mills in Ludington, Michigan, and Toledo, Ohio.

The interaction of railroads, the tariff, and the availability of raw materials led to the conversion of other metal manufacturing enterprises from local to mass production. The Fulton Iron and Engine Works, falling into the McMillan domain, was soon turning out one hundred fifty steam engines a year. The Detroit Bridge and Iron Works, established in 1863, became the builder of the Mississippi and Missouri River bridges for Joy's railroads. The Detroit Stove Company, organized in 1864, led the way in making the city the world's stove manufacturing capital.

The mines and mills of Michigan had difficulty keeping up with the demand. In the Upper Peninsula new copper mines competed for miners with old copper mines, and iron mines competed with copper mines. So great was the economic effect that it crossed the Atlantic to the Cornish Peninsula of England, and drew a new set of immigrants to the United States.

12

The Coming of the
Cousin Jacks

ALFRED LENTICK HAD BEEN WORKING WITH HIS FATHER IN THE COPPER MINES of Cornwall since the age of seven. The family, like most Cornish families, was large. Alfred had six brothers and sisters, and several others had died—nearly half the children never reached the age of five. He himself had been married at the age of sixteen, and already had two children. Since 1700 the population of Cornwall had multiplied from 100,000 to nearly 350,000. Thousands of people made their living in the tin and copper mines. Except for the mines, the Methodist Cornish would have been in as dire economic straits as the Catholic Irish.

Copper mining had been given a new lease in the second decade of the eighteenth century by Thomas Newcomen, a Dartmouth ironmonger. Watching horses being used to pump out the water that regularly flooded the mines at a shallow level, he had been inspired to construct an atmospheric steam engine. By the 1770's, these engines, inefficient and heavy consumers of fuel, could no longer operate economically at the new depths reached by the miners. James Watt, a Glasgow instrument maker, came to the rescue with the invention of the modern steam engine.* By the middle of the nineteenth century the Cornish mines reached depths beyond fifteen hundred feet. Sometimes extending underneath the ocean floor, the shafts were the deepest in the world.

The machinery necessary for the operation of the mines led increasingly to their control by "foreign adventurers" (London capitalists). But the system of working the mines remained essentially the same as in the days when a landowner, discovering a vein of copper on his property, would hold an auction among local miners for developing it. Alfred Lentick's father was a "tributer." At two- to three-month intervals the "captains," or agents of the mine owners, would hold auctions for the working of the "pitches" into which a lode was divided. The better the bargain a tributer could strike—that is, the less tribute, or royalty, he could obtain a pitch for—the greater would be his remuneration.

---

* Since steam engines replaced horses in the pumping out of the water, their efficiency was measured in terms of the number of horses they replaced, or *horse power*.

If he were experienced, shrewd, and lucky, and able to obtain a pitch in a "brave keenly lode" for a reasonable tribute, he might make as much as twenty to twenty-five dollars a month. Usually, as he was forced to bargain against both the captains and his fellow tributers, his remuneration was closer to twelve or fifteen dollars a month. If he tried for a pitch in a nearly worked-out "hungry mine" and guessed wrong, he and his family faced ruination and starvation.

At first Alfred worked "on the grass" (the surface) separating the "deads" (rubbish) from the ore. As he grew older he became part of the "pair" (a group of anywhere from two to twelve men who together bid for a pitch and worked it in twelve-hour shifts), and went down into the mine to trundle a wheelbarrow filled with ore. The only light came from the candles carried by the miners, so that in the underground passages the men appeared like rodent fireflies. The walls were wet with saline water. It accumulated into pools, and soaked the flannel clothing of the miners. There was no danger of gas explosions as in coal mines. But the air was sickly hot and damp, oxygen starved, full of dust, and reeking with the odor of black powder used for blasting.

Scarcely a miner who had worked twelve to fifteen years was not suffering from silicosis or salivation, rheumatism or tuberculosis. By the time that the fifteen-year-old Alfred took his place beside his father as a tributer, his father, still in his midthirties, already was broken-winded. Every year he had more difficulty climbing the hundreds of feet up the ladder to the "grass." (In some of the deeper mines the climb took as long as an hour.) Most of the miners, if they were not dead, were "tuckered out" by their early forties. Any man who reached fifty was looked upon as a patriarch.

When Alfred married, his relatives and friends pitched in to build him a two-room thatch cottage with walls of clay and wattle. The barren Cornish moors and hills had neither wood nor coal, so fires were made out of peat and turf cut from the fields. The people ate barley bread and turnips fried in grease purloined from mining machinery, kiddley broth and stanning pie, pig's fry and figgy hobbin. They ate pasties, in which everything that could be thrown together was baked into a kind of pie. But mostly they existed on taaties (potatoes) and pilchards.

The potato had become a staple of the Cornish diet during the last half of the eighteenth century when "short commons" were becoming all too common, and it had saved much of the population during the "starving times" of the Napoleonic Wars. The pilchards' ability to keep pace with the Cornish reproduction rate made the catching of the silvery little fish an industry second only to mining.* A single village might net up to one and a half million of the fish during one season.

Isolation made the Cornish fiercely independent—the first railroad link to London was not completed until 1859—but it also left them vulnerable if anything happened to their mines, their pilchards, or their potatoes. The potato blight of the 1840's hit them as hard as the Irish, and if the effect upon them was less it was only because riots brought relief from the government: public works, subsidization of wages, soup kitchens, blankets, and price controls on corn. Nevertheless, many men emigrated and sought work where they could find it—in Australia, Canada, and Michigan, whose mines were just being opened. Radiating to the gold fields of California and the silver mines of Nevada,

* Pilchards are better known today by the name of their young: *sardines*.

they brought with them skills and experience where none had existed before. American mining took on a distinctly Cornish aura.*

Already, during the early 1850's, one Cornish mining company had purchased 1,240 acres on the Upper Peninsula, and found the ore there ten times richer than that of the mines in Cornwall. As the Cornish mines went deeper and deeper, the struggle against water became so difficult that more energy was being expended in pumping out the water than in getting out the ore.

Uneducated and illiterate, Alfred Lentick and his compatriots remained unaware of the new economic forces rapidly closing in: the Republican tariff favoring Michigan copper and American copper products; the continuing and rapid improvements in the American transportation network that reduced the price of Michigan copper in Eastern United States markets; the technological breakthrough in steel production that came with the development of the Bessemer process (1857) and resulted in the conversion of the manufacture of many articles from copper to steel; and the revolution that was occurring in the shipbuilding industry, which was changing rapidly from the construction of wooden to steel vessels. (Wooden ships used copper for sheathing.)

The impact upon Cornwall came with dramatic suddenness at the end of the Civil War, and the return to "normalcy" in international commerce. One by one the Cornish mines were "knocked" (shut down). In 1866 a single parish lost four mines. As wages in the remaining mines dropped by a third, strikes and riots broke out, and blacklegs (strikebreakers) and troops were brought in. By the spring of 1867, the families of half the miners were near starvation, and some were going without food for days at a time.

In the meantime, the mines of Michigan were so desperate for experienced men that by 1865 wages had risen to sixty-five dollars a month—five or six times what a miner in Cornwall earned. American recruiters were sent to Cornwall. In some Cornish grocery stores it was possible to book passage straight through to Houghton on the Upper Peninsula. The fare was often advanced under the Contract Labor Law. Miners who had emigrated earlier urged their "Cousin Jacks" to follow them. (The Cornish tended to have so many cousins that Cousin Jack became a generic nickname.) If that were not enough to bring on a mass migration, one prominent mine-owning family all but crated up its mine and moved it to America—the machinery was sent to the Upper Peninsula and the engineering works were relocated in Pittsburgh.

One day Alfred Lentick kissed his wife good-bye and joined the stream of fellow miners who were boarding ships. They were the vanguard of an emigration that by 1900 reduced the Cornish population from 341,000 to 230,000. Most of the men left their families behind and anticipated returning to Cornwall after making their fortunes in America. Some of them did return. The vast majority, however, never made it back. With illiteracy prevalent, communication was haphazard. Although many of the wives and children—including the family of Lentick—ultimately joined the men in America, in countless other cases miners disappeared into the wilderness of Michigan, Montana, Nevada, or Australia, and abandoned their families in Cornwall to charity.

To the Upper Peninsula, the Cornish brought their way of life, their way of work, and their clannishness. The miners' occupation continued to make them sallow, lung-wracked, stoop-backed men with broad shoulders and thick-

* The white frontiersmen who first tried to exploit the deposits of lead, copper, and iron in the Midwest frequently were clumsier and had made less headway than the Indians.

muscled arms. They engaged in Sunday wrestling matches. They continued, despite their Methodism, to be "whiskey-soaked beerbellies" who roiled in the streets and frequently beat their women [1]—Michigan's Prohibition laws had even less effect in the "North country" than in Detroit, and mining towns were among the few places where saloons remained open on Sundays. They despised the "popish" Irish who were unskilled laborers, and brawls between the nationalities were common.* The women continued to be engaged as *bal* (mine) maidens, who crushed and separated the ore. The men transferred intact the system of bidding for pitches and their status as semi-independent contractors. They continued to light their way by candles, and to heat their pasties by means of "Cornish stoves" (two candles placed beneath a shovel). There continued to be grisly accidents—in one cave-in seven men were buried and devoured by rats before their bodies could be recovered from the earth.†

But there were also important changes. Few men could have survived a Michigan winter in a Cornish cottage, so the companies built housing for the workers. In the middle of the forest, the houses were cheaper to build and infinitely better than the hovels left behind in England. Since fuel was no problem, the men ate better-cooked meals and were able to keep warm. Except when late winters kept the lakes frozen longer than normal, and a food shortage resulted, there were few periods of short commons.

In accordance with Michigan law, the companies established schools for the children, and so presaged the end of the culture of illiteracy. In contrast to the surfeit of manpower in Cornwall—a surfeit that not only held down wages but retarded the introduction of labor-saving machinery—the manpower shortage in the Upper Peninsula acted as a stimulant to mechanization. Ladders were replaced by "man-engines" that took the workers into and lifted them from the mines. Before long the ancient rock-drilling wedges, pounded with sledgehammers, were replaced by pneumatic drills fed with air from the surface. Deep in the galleries and adits, wheelbarrows were replaced by tramways. The cars that traveled the rails ultimately were hooked to miniature electric locomotives, creating a *literal* underground railroad.

---

* In one memorable encounter in 1857 the Cornish drove the Irish out of Rockland in Ontonagon County. The battered survivors fled to Portage Lake. There, four hundred Irishmen, vowing vengeance, set out for Rockland. Before they had traveled more than three miles, however, the expeditionary force was felled by a common malady—drunkenness —and the only split heads were the consequence of hangovers.
† A classic description of a mining accident in England was given in the Liverpool *Mercury* of February 7, 1845: "A fellow-workman . . . hearing a noise of something coming down, hastily stepped out of the way, when two legs and a thigh and arm fell where he had been standing; also a hat and lamp, and immediately after the head, body and remaining arm and thigh, all of which he gathered up, put in a sheet and conveyed to the top."

13

The Irish Riots

EVERYWHERE IN AMERICA THE CIVIL WAR WAS PLACING A PREMIUM ON SKILLS —both old and new. Everywhere it brought a surge of mechanization. The conversion from hand to machine labor that had occurred in gunsmithing two thirds of a century before was repeated in other fields. Crafts were turned into industries.

German Jews who grasped the revolutionary character of the sewing machines invented by Elias Howe and Isaac Singer turned Detroit, New York, Boston, Philadelphia, and Cincinnati into centers for the production of uniforms. A ready-made clothing industry sprang up. The sewing machines, which like reapers could be purchased "on time," multiplied productivity tenfold! They reduced the cost of clothing as dramatically as had Arkwright's transfer of weaving from the home to the power looms of the factory. When New England shoe makers enlisted, sewing machines adapted to work with leather replaced them. (Howe, who a few years before had had to pawn the model of his machine and work his way back from England to the United States as a cook in steerage, was receiving royalties of four thousand dollars a week.)

Guns, clothing, shoes, sewing machines, stoves, railroad rolling stock, farm implements—mechanization enabled industry to turn out goods in numbers unprecedented in world history. By 1864, in the midst of a full-scale war effort, the American market was so glutted with sewing machines that fifty thousand were exported to Europe. The demand for skilled workers, and the growth of factories, generated a drive, paced by frequently successful strikes, toward the organization of craftsmen. In Detroit, the iron molders organized in 1860; the machinists, blacksmiths, cigar makers, carpenters, and plasterers followed in 1864. Combining into the Detroit Trades Assembly, the unions by war's end had a total membership of about five thousand.

By organizing, skilled workers were able to obtain wage increases and protect themselves against inflation. The unskilled and the unorganized, however, had no such leverage. To finance the war, the Federal government sold bonds to Dutch and German investors, and placed in circulation $450 million worth of "greenbacks" not covered by gold. Consequently, by 1864 prices were 80 percent higher than they had been in 1860. Detroit schoolteachers, who at the beginning of the war were being paid two hundred to three hundred dollars a year, saw the buying power of their wages decrease by a third. The purchasing power of unskilled laborers was even more severely affected.

Inflation, high casualties, lack of success in the field, and Lincoln's own vacillations created waves of revulsion against the war. Detroit's draft riot in the summer of 1862 was followed by disastrous Republican losses in the fall congressional elections. While Michigan's Senators Chandler and Howard and many New England Republicans who had connections with the Western railroads attacked the President for not prosecuting the war more vigorously, the Northern Democrats denigrated him for prosecuting the war at all. Unenamored of Negroes, he said that "wrong as we think slavery is, we can yet afford to let it alone where it is." [1] When, in May, 1862, General David Hunter issued a proclamation freeing the slaves in the occupied territory of the South under his control, Lincoln repudiated him. A month earlier, Congress had abolished slavery in the District of Columbia and provided a maximum of three hundred dollars per slave compensation for the owners. But Lincoln's suggestion that the same principle be applied to the border states was greeted by their politicians with a lack of enthusiasm that would have done justice to Jefferson Davis.

It was as an economic threat and as a retort to his critics that the President, on September 22, 1862, issued an ultimatum: if, within one hundred days— that is, by January 1, 1863—the South did not lay down its arms, he would issue a proclamation freeing the slaves in those states which remained in rebellion. What was to be done with the slaves after they were freed he did not know but he thought they might be resettled in Liberia or Haiti.

The threat of economic destruction failed to sway the planters, who were more impressed by the ineptness of the Northern armies. Though emancipation opened the way for the enlistment of Negroes, it also generated further division and bitterness in the North. The Detroit *Free Press,* with its Negro-hating editor Wilbur Storey, was a leader in the trumpeting of Democratic charges that the war was no longer being fought to save the Union, but to promote "nigger domination." The Ohio Legislature moved to amend the constitution to bar Negroes from the state. After Michigan's Senator Howard introduced the Thirteenth Amendment to abolish slavery in the United States, he needed two years to rally the votes for its passage. In 1863 and 1864 Negroes were walking about as free men in occupied areas of the Confederacy while they continued to be enslaved in the loyal border states. Not until 1865 was the amendment adopted.

Playing on the fears of the lower-class workers and the Irish, the Democrats warned them that their days were numbered. Emancipation was a plot by anti-Catholic Republicans to replace the Irish with Negroes; by industrialist Republicans to use the freed Negroes to depress wages and reduce working men to European-type peonage; by "nigger-loving Republicans" to work and tax the poor whites for the benefit of the blacks. Negroes would be supported by the Poor Commissions and dwell in indolence, Democrats predicted.

Spearheaded by a new crop of publications specializing in racist literature, the Democratic press worked itself in a lather over the baby-roasting and virgin-raping that previously had been attributed to Indians. Nothing stirred up lower-class whites more than the vision of black-white sexual contact. Lurid posters and pamphlets poured off the presses. Words such as *miscegenation* and *melamigleukation* were coined to describe race mixing.

Affected by the climate of hysteria that the Detroit *Free Press* was generating by its frequent report of Negro "outrages," two adolescent girls, one white and one Negro, early in 1863 accused one William Faulkner of having attacked them. In a state in which more than 40 percent of the Negroes were reported to be of mixed ancestry, and Indian blood flowed in the veins of countless prominent families, it was often difficult to tell just who a man's progenitors had been. In the Negro community it was said of Faulkner, who was of Spanish-Indian extraction, that "if he thought he had one drop of colored blood in his veins, if he could, he would let it out." [2] Nevertheless, he was tried, convicted, and sentenced to life imprisonment * on the testimony of the two young girls who, in fact, were prostitutes. Incendiary tales of sexual outrages committed by a Negro sped around the city.[†]

Throughout the Northern cities many of the unskilled immigrant workers were economically inferior to the Negroes, and strove to move into the jobs and businesses held by them. Agitators whipped them up by shouting that the savage and ignorant blacks were able to retain their position only because of a Republican conspiracy. (In fact, for twenty-five years immigrants had been moving into trades blacks previously had dominated. In 1853 Frederick Douglass complained that "a few years ago a white barber would have been a curiosity." [3])

Detroit's unskilled Irish and German immigrants were incensed over the passage a few days earlier of a national conscription law. Since the affluent could escape the draft by paying a three-hundred-dollar fee, the immigrants associated it with the kind of discrimination that had caused them to flee their homelands. The impressment of the Catholic poor for cannon fodder was an old story. The families of the soldiers would be thrust upon the untender mercies of the Poor Commissions. Teen-aged girls would resort to prostitution to support themselves.

Shouting, therefore, that white men were being sent off to die so that black men could take their jobs and rape their daughters, a mob carrying guns, clubs, axes, and a rope gathered on Friday, March 6, 1863. Attacking the military guard that was conveying Faulkner to prison, they attempted to lynch him. Driven off by gunfire, they turned their attention to the Negro district along Croghan and Beaubien Streets. Rumors of treasures hidden in the shops and houses of the Negro shopkeepers and artisans swept the throng.

"Kill all the damned niggers!" the men shouted as they surged down the street. "Come out, you sons of bitches," they yelled at three black men who were working in their cooper's shop. Throwing bricks and stones, they charged the building and were met by a shotgun blast. Throughout the area they attacked anyone they found on the streets. Battering down doors, they ransacked stores and homes. An expert mechanic who had escaped from slavery in West Virginia was stamped and beaten to death. An eighty-year-old former Kentucky slave who had been freed after his master was killed at the Battle of Tippecanoe was beaten and kicked into unconsciousness as he defended the African Methodist Episcopal Church.

As evening settled, flames lighted the sky and smoke drifted through the

---

* In 1830 the public hanging of a white man had generated such revulsion among Detroiters that Michigan had taken the lead in America in abolishing capital punishment. Numerous Indians previously had been hanged without occasioning outrage.
† Six years later, the girls confessed their stories had been fabrications, and Faulkner was released.

streets of the city. In the Negro quarter building after building was put to the torch. When firemen arrived, their hoses were slashed and they were attacked by the mob. The city as yet had no police department. The provost marshal feared that, if he put troops into the area, the mob would use the opportunity to free the recalcitrant draftees he had under guard. Not until troops were dispatched from Fort Wayne and Ypsilanti was the rampage brought under control.*

The riot, plus the fear of Rebel raids from Canada, catalyzed the Detroit city council into thinking about organizing a police department.† Its formation took on a new urgency when the worst riot in American history broke out in New York City in early July following the Battle of Gettysburg.‡ Immediately cries of outrage arose from Detroit's marshals, deputy sheriffs, ward constables, and property owners. Politicians feared the loss of patronage. Property owners objected to any increase in taxation. The legislature, nevertheless, passed the enabling act in 1865. Not trusting Detroit's Democrats, it provided for control of the department by four commissioners appointed by the governor.

* Among the Negroes who escaped into the woods or across the river to Canada were Robert and Frances Pelham. The Pelhams had been farmers in the Petersburg, Virginia, area, and were members of the class of educated "free" Negroes in the South, most of whom *were* free because they had a liberal admixture of white male blood. Pelham, a good mathematician, bricklayer, mason, and contractor, had left the South during the hysteria that followed John Brown's raid on Harpers Ferry. For three years the family wandered about the North. In 1862 they arrived in Detroit and rented a house on Congress Street, only a few blocks from where Brown had presented his scheme for the slave rebellion. During the next hundred years the Pelhams were to become one of the leading families in the city.

† Police were a byproduct of the Industrial Revolution and the development of the over-populated, undercapitalized cities and their wildly oscillating economies. As the number of England's poor had increased in concert with new wealth, and more property had been available for theft and robbery by more desperate people, crime had shot up exponentially and in direct proportion to an area's industrialization. In England, the number of crimes quadrupled between 1805 and 1830. The Metropolitan Police Act of 1829 had created in London the world's first municipal police force. During the next decade, police departments spread to major cities in the American Northeast. Neither in England nor in America, however, did they prove a deterrent to crime.

‡ On Saturday, July 11, 1863, the first drawings were held for New York City's quota of thirty-three thousand men, established under the National Conscription Act. When the draft resumed Monday morning, a paving block shattered the window of the district office at Forty-sixth Street and Third Avenue. A wave of seven hundred men, predominantly Irish, poured into the office. Scattering the records, they set the building ablaze. Firemen responding to the alarm were attacked and beaten. By noon, as flames sprouted from building after building, the heart of Manhattan was in control of the mob.

Not only were the police actions hesitant and confused, but many of the Irish police were in sympathy with the mobs. Smashing store windows and invading the homes of the well-to-do, looters roamed the city. The police arsenal was attacked, captured, and set on fire. Night after day, day after night, rioters attacked draft offices, Republican newspapers, and public buildings. Negroes were set upon, beaten, lynched, and burned. Late Tuesday, as the stench of death rode everywhere on clouds of smoke, the governor declared the city to be in a state of insurrection. Five regiments of troops were dispatched. Before they were able to restore order, between seventy-four and fifteen hundred persons lay dead. In an age when people arrived in and disappeared from the teeming districts without anyone's knowing or caring, there was no possibility of accurate assessment.

14

Republican: Spelled
RAILROAD

THROUGHOUT THE WAR, FORBES WAS ABLE TO NEUTRALIZE SOUTHERN INFLU-
ence in England through his connections with the Baring Bros. and other
bankers, whose heavy investments in the Western railroads placed them in the
Republican camp. By 1864 the prospects of a Northern victory appeared certain enough for the flow of European capital into American railroads to be
resumed.

Joy drove his railroads westward at full speed. In July of 1864 the com-
plaisant Congress granted the Burlington and Missouri Railroad more than two
million acres of land in order to enable it to connect with the Union Pacific at
Pacific Junction, near Council Bluffs, Iowa. Between 1865 and 1867 Joy was
elected president of the Chicago, Burlington and Quincy, the Burlington and
Missouri, and the Michigan Central. Thus controlling the lines from Council
Bluffs to Chicago, Detroit, and the East, he planned to make the Hannibal and
St. Joseph, lying to the south, a link in a system that stretched all the way to
California as a competitor to the Union Pacific. In 1867 the Hannibal and St.
Joseph reached Kansas City. Once more Joy prevailed upon Congress, and
Congress enacted a "treaty" separating the Cherokees from 800,000 acres of
land, which were passed on to the railroad. Ejecting Indians and squatters from
their holdings, the United States cavalry cleared the way for the railroad across
Kansas.

The frenetic railroad construction that followed the war ensured a continuation of the boom for Detroit and Michigan. As the Pennsylvania, Ohio, and
Illinois coal mines were developed, and the railroad reached the treeless plains
of the Midwest, locomotives were converted from wood- to coal-burning. The
conversion necessitated the replacement of iron flutes with copper, and played
a part in the expansion of copper production. In 1867, the Burlington and
Missouri laid the first rolled steel rails, which were purchased from Eber Brock
Ward. The huge demand for rolling stock brought hundreds of thousands of
dollars into the coffers of Newberry and McMillan. The Detroit Bridge and
Iron Works manufactured the first iron bridge to span the Mississippi River.

The first bridge across the Missouri River was built in 1867 by the Hannibal and St. Joseph at Kansas City.

To provide the population for the lands that the railroads were receiving as subsidy, Joy and other railroad magnates dispatched hundreds of agents to recruit immigrants. The agents fanned out across Germany, England, France, Scandinavia, and Bohemia with tales of opportunity in the golden lands of the West. Immigration was placed on a business footing. It was a big, profitable business.

What made it so was mechanization. Mechanization of agriculture; mechanization of shipping; mechanization of land transportation in the form of the railroads.

The McCormick reapers and the other mechanical devices were revolutionizing agricultural production, but they also made the lives of Europe's small farmers miserable. American wheat sold for less in London, Berlin, Paris, and Vienna than wheat grown but fifty miles away. Peasants abandoned the land. In the three decades following the 1850's, American wheat exports increased from an annual average of 5.5 million bushels to 150 million bushels. Millions of people displaced by this American tide swarmed into the industrial areas of England, Germany, and Austria-Hungary. There they discovered that American industry was not far behind American agriculture in underselling European industry in its own markets.*

Driven off the land, unable to find work in the cities, the surplus European population became the commodity exchanged for the surplus American wheat. The 700,000 immigrants who came between 1860 and 1865 were followed by 1.6 million during the next five years. The decade of the 1870's brought 2.8 million more.

They traveled on the steamers that the British shipping industry year by year turned out in greater quantities. With many times the annual capacity of sailing vessels, steamers carried 33 percent of the immigrants in 1862; 58 percent in 1865; and 91 percent in 1870.

The effect upon New England's shipbuilding and lumber industries, geared to building wooden sailing vessels, was devastating. Lumbermen and shipbuilders migrated to Michigan and to Detroit, where ships were still being built out of wood, and where the production of lumber was having difficulty keeping up with the demand. Wood was used in railroad cars, in carriages, in packing crates, and in furniture. Entire houses were being prefabricated in Chicago and shipped by railroad to the plains of Iowa, Kansas, and Nebraska.

Detroit's population jumped from fifty-four thousand in 1864 to nearly eighty thousand in 1870. By 1873, four fifths of the children in the schools were of foreign parentage. Each nationality tended to segregate itself in its own districts. There was little mingling between the children of Germans (36 percent), Irish (20 percent), Americans (20 percent), English and Scotch (11 percent), French (2 percent), and Scandinavians, Bohemians, and a smattering of other foreign-born (11 percent).[1]

Between genteel Jefferson Avenue and the riverfront, the railroad created a reeking slum the likes of which were plaguing every industrial city. Enwreathed in the smoke belching from steamships, locomotives, and factories,

---

* The Lancashire watch industry, which twenty years before had dominated world production, was dying. In 1872 America was turning out three times as many watches as England.

it was a district of unpainted and blackened wooden buildings. Cheap lodging-houses, whorehouses, and tenements proliferated. Since lack of public transportation inhibited the expansion of the city, warehouses, stables, and even churches were converted into tenements. As the district spread outward, the wealthy abandoned their mansions and placed them in the hands of managers. Left to do with them as they pleased so long as they channeled a fixed income to the owners, the managers discovered they were in possession of property more valuable than the mines of Michigan. The more intensively they mined the property, the greater their personal profit. Windowless cubicles as small as fifty square feet were occupied by as many as two families each. Twenty persons sometimes slept in two beds. Thousands of others camped in cellars. Water dripped on them from the walls. Their dreams were swathed in the stench from piles of stored manure.

Pushcart peddlers sold vegetables, fish, needles, horse dung, and opium. Itinerant artisans, purchasable females, cripples and blind men, children, chickens, and pigs choked the narrow streets and alleys. (The pig was the Irishman's neurosis. America was so glutted with hogs that all but the choicest parts were discarded. At Cincinnati, a slaughtering center, the Ohio River stank with the pigs' feet, entrails, heads, tails, and skins dumped into it. The Irish, however, continued to cling to their pigs long after they ceased to serve as an economic resource.) The death rate rose more than 50 percent in a half century, and children died in fearful numbers. But, in a land with an abundant supply of food, men and women had the energy to breed two to replace each that was lost.

It was a district where no respectable citizen would venture, into which the neonate police rarely went, and in which violence and death were so common that it was derisively named The Potomac, a name derived from a caustic Civil War song:

> "All quiet along the Potomac," they say,
> Except now and then a stray picket
> Is shot, as he walks on his beat, to and fro,
> By a rifleman hid in the thicket.[2]

The knots of humanity forming along the waterways and the railroads and, especially, at intersections of the two, reflected the fact that only land within twenty miles of either was economically viable. Because of the lack of roads, no farmer more than twenty miles from a railroad could profitably ship his produce to market. Those at a greater distance were as isolated as ever.

With the population at his mercy, Joy pursued the same policies that he had with the Michigan Central twenty years earlier. Wherever the railroad had a monopoly, rates were set at whatever the traffic would bear. It was a policy adhered to by railroads throughout the country.

In 1867 the farmers revolted. Squeezed between exorbitant railroad rates, declining income, and large debts, they organized the Patrons of Husbandry, or Grangers. To reduce the price-fixing power of the railroads, the Grangers encouraged farmers to form cooperatives, and to construct their own elevators for storing grain. In Chicago, the movement stimulated the birth of Montgomery Ward and the mail-order business. In several states—Iowa, Illinois, Minnesota, Wisconsin—the Grangers succeeded in enacting legislation setting up public bodies to regulate the rates of railroads and grain elevators.

Antipathy to the South had acted as a catalyst to bring about the fusion of the Republican party. With the South defeated, the diverse elements that had formed the party once more began to go their separate ways. In Michigan, Senator Chandler, the party boss, and Joy remained so firmly in control that throughout the latter part of the century Republican could be spelled two ways: R E P U B L I C A N or R A I L R O A D. But elsewhere, the former Whigs resumed their pursuit of business profits, and the Abolitionists set out on a crusade to reform the South. The Homesteaders, Western agrarians, and former European Revolutionaries became the bitter enemies of the Whigs and the Railroaders. In 1872 they adopted the label of Liberal Republicans. With the support of the disorganized Democrats, they nominated Horace Greeley to oppose President Grant.

(It was the only time in American history one major party endorsed the nominee of another.)

Once the Granger revolt spread across the Midwest, it was evident to the Railroad Republicans that they would need a new base of power in order to retain control. The Abolitionist interest in the welfare of the Negro offered an opportunity to develop and exploit Negro voting strength—if the South could be swung into the camp of the *regular* Republicans, it would more than make up for the Midwestern defections. The Railroad-Abolitionist alliance was personified by Detroit's senators—from 1861 to 1875 Chandler, as the chairman of the Committee on Commerce, was the most powerful man in the Senate in economic affairs, and Howard, as a member of the Joint Committee on the Reconstructed States, was a leading advocate of Negro rights.*

By trying to return to Congress the men who had precipitated the war and then led the Confederacy, and by the enactment of the Black Codes,† the Southern politicians played into the hands of the Republicans, and brought on Reconstruction.

While Northern educators and New England spinsters poured South to organize an educational system,‡ the Railroaders and their allies set about restructuring Southern politics. The means used—graft, bribery, jobs—were the same used to control legislatures in Northern states, and were, in fact, employed by all parties on all levels of American government.

Hand in hand with political exploitation came economic exploitation. With many of its facilities destroyed, with the capital that had been invested in slaves wiped out, and with cotton exhausting the soil, the South was not only a devastated but an impoverished land. Much as the South might object to the infusion of Northern capital and carpetbaggers, without them economic revival would have been even slower.

In agriculture, the shortage of money brought about the adoption of a European invention tailored to the problems of a semibarter economy—the sharecropper system. Without public schools and without an appreciable middle class, economically the South was now America's Ireland. It was not surprising, therefore, that a half dozen Tennessee Protestants of Scotch-Irish descent should

---

* He was of course also, as indicated by his chairmanship of the Committee on the Pacific Railroad, a *Railroader.*
† The Black Codes provided for compulsory apprenticeship of Negro children, and the restriction, essentially, of Negroes to farming. They thus would have converted the status of the Negro from slavery to peonage.
‡ By and large they were successful. Ironically, their efforts were to benefit lower-class whites far more than Negroes.

revive the Peep O' Day Boys and call it: the Ku Klux Klan. Like the Peep O' Day Boys, the Klan rode at night. Like the Peep O' Day Boys, the Klan tried to intimidate a former underclass so as to keep it from thrusting itself into economic and social competition with the Protestant whites.

But while the Republicans worked to enfranchise Negroes in the South, they were indifferent, and not infrequently hostile to the establishment of Negro rights in the North. At the end of the war, Negroes were able to vote in only seven of the twenty-five Union states. In the years immediately following, voters refused to grant the ballot to blacks in Republican states like Connecticut, New Jersey, Minnesota, Wisconsin, Ohio, and Michigan. The schizoid Republican platform of 1868 demanded the suffrage for Negroes in the South, while insisting upon "states' rights" in the North. Gideon Welles, Secretary of the Navy in Lincoln's Cabinet, objected to the enfranchising of "negroes and fools." * Before the Fifteenth Amendment was ratified, largely as the result of control of Southern legislatures by Radical Republicans, Negroes were voting in the former Confederate states, but were still excluded from the polls in half of the Union states, including Michigan. Robert Pelham and the other Detroit Negroes had fewer rights than the former slaves. Their children could not obtain the kind of public education that was being made available to Negroes in the South. In 1869 the city's Negroes sued, successfully, to integrate the school system. As it turned out, it was an important victory not only for Negroes, but for women. Since there was only one high school, segregation had prevented Negroes from obtaining a high school education.† But the University of Michigan, like virtually every institution of higher learning, had barred not only blacks but females. In 1870, unwilling to argue that Negroes were superior to women, the university decided that women, too, should be admitted.

The regular Republicans were able to win the national election in 1872, but Joy saw dark clouds gathering. Together with Forbes, he deplored the "overbuilding" of railroads—much of the "overbuilding" taking the form of competition—and the internecine wars in which the top railroad magnates engaged against each other.

Shortly after the election, the Crédit Mobilier scandal broke. Involving Vice-President Schuyler Colfax, it brought the revelation that $23 million of the Union Pacific's $93 million construction cost had been siphoned off into private pockets. The consequent public revulsion led to the end of land grants to railroads. In September, 1873, Junius S. Morgan bested Jay Cooke in the scramble for the administration's favors; and Cooke's banking house, which had been backing the building of the Northern Pacific, collapsed. The Northern Pacific went into bankruptcy. Investor uneasiness spread to other railroad stocks. Unable to cope with the huge selloffs, the stock market closed for ten days. The Panic of 1873 was on.

To help him weather the panic, Joy, without the knowledge of Forbes and

---

* In California, where in 1860 the superintendent of schools had demanded the exclusion of "Africans, Chinese, and niggers," and where in 1871 fifteen Chinese were lynched in a Los Angeles riot, there was as great alarm at the thought of giving the ballot to the Orientals as to Negroes. Ignorant of the fact that they were using a Chinese invention, paper, and a Korean invention, printing, with which to issue their report, a study commission appointed by the California Legislature declared: "The Chinese are inferior to any race God ever made. These people have got the perfection of crimes of 4,000 years." [3]
† In fact, only the exceptional student reached high school. In 1861, out of 7,437 students, only 112 were in high school. [4]

the Boston directors, diverted money from the construction funds of the Chicago, Burlington and Quincy, which was thrusting northwestward. Forbes's discovery of the action resulted in a showdown with Joy. In 1875 Joy was ousted from the presidency of the C.B. and Q. Two years later he resigned, also, from the presidency of the Michigan Central, control of which was in the process of passing to the New York Central.

An era was coming to an end. The men who had made the Republican party were splitting apart. The Democrats, benefiting from voter reaction to the depression, gained eighty seats in the House of Representatives and dominated it for the next twenty years. In Michigan, which had become known as "the most Republican state," a coalition of Democrats and Liberal Republicans in the legislature succeeded in ousting Chandler from his seat in the U.S. Senate.

Appointed Secretary of the Interior by President Grant, Chandler in 1876 employed Federal troops in Louisiana, South Carolina, and Florida to "steal" the election from the Democratic nominee, Samuel J. Tilden. It was, however, a Pyrrhic victory. The new President, Rutherford B. Hayes, replaced Chandler with Liberal Republican Carl Schurz, the German revolutionary who had helped keep Missouri in the Union. The Hayes-Tilden Compromise brought about the withdrawal of Federal troops from the South, and ended the plans of the Railroad Republicans for control of national politics.

15

A Ford Comes to the City

THROUGHOUT THE NATION, THE DEPRESSION FORCED FARMERS TO TIGHTEN their belts. The Ford family of Dearborn was no exception.

In his middle forties, William Ford had prospered as Detroit had grown. He had bought considerably more acreage, and the farm, with its orchards, fences, cattle, and machinery was well ordered. In the substantial, two-story house children were being born at regular two-year intervals, until there were a half dozen in all. (Two others died in infancy.) No longer was cooking done in an open fireplace, and baking in a brick oven set to the side of the chimney or in a tin reflector placed before the flames—the cast-iron stoves manufactured in Detroit were lightening the chores of the farmwife. No longer was salt, which the pioneers sometimes did not see for six months at a time, a luxury. In 1859 the legislature authorized a subsidy for salt production, and the salt wells drilled at Saginaw were the beginning of a burgeoning industry. No longer did farmers set fire to a pine cone or use pork fat with a twisted rag to provide a flickering, uncertain light; the drilling of the world's first producing oil well (also in 1859) by a sometime Michigan hotel clerk and steamship conductor named Edwin Drake had led to the invention of the kerosene lantern.

The railroad had made Dearborn virtually a suburb of Detroit—it took no more than an hour to reach the city from the farm. The rapidly growing city absorbed all the dairy products, meat, fruit, and vegetables the farmers could ship, and in turn provided them with mass-produced manufactured goods at the cheapest prices in history.

Many of William's neighbors were related to him—everywhere in Dearborn and its vicinity the Fords had established their farms. William's father, John, and John's brother George who had preceded him to America, had survived until the early 1860's, and the Fords were of hardy and prolific stock. (William was one of six children, and his uncles, brothers, sisters, and cousins were producing children no less rapidly than he.) Within a generation of their coming to the United States, the Fords were spreading over Michigan and establishing themselves as far away as Idaho and California.

On January 11, 1871, Henry Ford started for the neat, red-brick school building constructed by the literate, middle-class Protestant community. He was seven and a half, the usual age at which children entered school. His teacher in the glass-windowed schoolhouse with its glowing stove, blackboard, piano, and two-pupil desks was seventeen-year-old Emily Nardin, not more than a year older than some of her pupils. More often than not the principal criterion for the employment of a teacher was how cheap he or she came. The average salary for men was thirty-seven dollars and for women twenty-six dollars a month. They were "boarded round," staying with a different family every month. Girls as young as fourteen were hired. Teaching was considered an interim period between adolescence and marriage, and a good preparation for motherhood. Many people believed too much education spoiled children, encouraged indolence, and resulted in snobbery. The Michigan superintendent of schools lamented that education was "scarcely worth the time and money," and that "save the ability to read and write a little, and to make some simple computations with figures, naught remains." [1] Even so, in the small, homogenous community where fathers enforced the discipline that the young teacher herself might not be able to, the atmosphere was more conducive to learning than in the confused polyethnic classrooms of the city.

In Detroit, district inspectors were used to discipline the fourteen-, fifteen-, and sixteen-year-old grammar-school boys who cursed and spit tobacco juice onto the floors. Birch rods, leather thongs, shillelaghs—all served as instruments to keep youths in line. The pupil-teacher ratio had been halved—from over 100 to 1 to slightly more than 50 to 1 (about the same as Chicago's). But there were only 5,896 places available for 20,353 children. (That was not a particularly bad showing. Cincinnati had less than one place for every five children.) Half-day schools were held in shacks and barns not fit for cowsheds or pigsties—in fact, hogs, dogs, geese, pigeons, and a variety of other animals wandered in and out. The new compulsory attendance law of 1871 required the schooling of all children between eight and fourteen for a minimum of twelve weeks a year. It was, however, never enforced. Children ran about in the streets. In 1873 Detroit Superintendent J. M. B. Sill warned that "reckless and vicious boys [were] forming, in effect, an organization for the training of future criminals." [2]

William Ford placed an emphasis on education far above average. He was an avid reader of newspapers, and became a member of the school board. In the Protestant, middle-class community, Henry must have heard many conversations about the issues of the day: the damnable "tight money" policies of Eastern bankers, and the antidemocratic actions of the pope. The dogma of papal infallibility, promulgated in 1870 by Pope Pius IX in reaction to a new surge of liberalism and nationalism, was resulting in a wave of anti-Catholicism all over the world. Rumors of papal conspiracies and plots were widespread. As the Catholics expanded the system of parochial schools, the controversy over public school funds flared anew. The 1876 Republican platform included a proposal for a constitutional amendment "forbidding the application of any public funds or property for the benefit of any schools or institutions under sectarian control." [3]

Listening to such discussions, the teen-aged Henry was having implanted in his mind ideas that four decades later were to have a major impact not only upon his own life but upon history. Never much taken with books, he was fascinated by machinery. He had a knack for taking things apart and putting them back together. He never missed an opportunity to examine mills and steam engines, whose number grew as agriculture mechanized. (In California and the Dakotas there were farms thousand of acres in size where steam power was replacing manpower.)

In the summer of 1876, while driving to Detroit with his father, he came upon a steam engine propelling itself along the road by means of a chain drive. It was as if he had fallen through the looking glass. Fascinated, he explored it minutely.*

By the fall of 1879, the sixteen-year-old Henry was out of school and working on the farm. He was, however, no lover of mud and manure, and was aching to work with machinery. His father, conditioned to the Irish respect for landownership, was shocked to discover that his son saw no great status or satisfaction in being a farmer.

In December, after the harvest was in, Henry quietly took leave, and trudged along the rotting planks of the Michigan Road toward Detroit. On the western edge of the city, five miles from the farm, he came upon the huge plant of the Michigan Car Company.

The largest manufacturing enterprise in the state, it was the hub of the Newberry-McMillan industrial empire. Although the company's growth had been slowed by the disasters that had overtaken the railroads in 1873,† business was now reviving briskly. The company that had come into existence thanks to Detroit's influence in Washington had turned out nearly forty-nine thousand railroad cars. Railroad car production accounted for $1.5 million of the $27 million value of goods annually manufactured in the city.

Needing men, the plant foreman hired Henry Ford at $1.10 a day, the prevailing wage for laborers. In the plant's setting-up shop a primitive assembly line was in operation. The trucks with the wheels were first set on parallel rails. Upon them carpenters mounted the sills, or frames. As the cars gradually were moved down the tracks, the roofs and siding were added. At the end of the line the cars were painted.

Henry, however, was with the company only a few days. The following week found him at the Flowers Brothers Machine Shop. The three Flowers brothers had arrived from England in 1852 and gone to work as mechanics for the Michigan Central. They were acquaintances of William Ford, and knew Henry. Their shop at Woodbridge and Brush Streets occupied the first brick building to be erected after the 1805 fire. Henry was working within earshot of the railroad depot at which Edison had arrived daily twenty years before.

---

* Although for Henry Ford the machine was a novelty, nonrail steam propulsion had developed in parallel with rail. Cornish mining engineer Richard Trevithick not only had built a steam-powered road carriage in 1803, but had constructed engines for threshing and for use on West Indian sugar plantations. In the 1820's and 1830's, Sir Goldsworthy Gurney, Colonel Macaroni, and Walter Hancock had built steam carriages that operated on various stage runs in England. Sometimes they achieved speeds as high as twenty miles per hour. The lack of all-weather roads and the greater efficiency of steam propulsion on rails ended their development.

† Between 1874 and 1877, one fourth of American railroad mileage had gone into receivership. In 1875, only two thousand miles of rails were laid compared to seventy-five hundred in 1871.

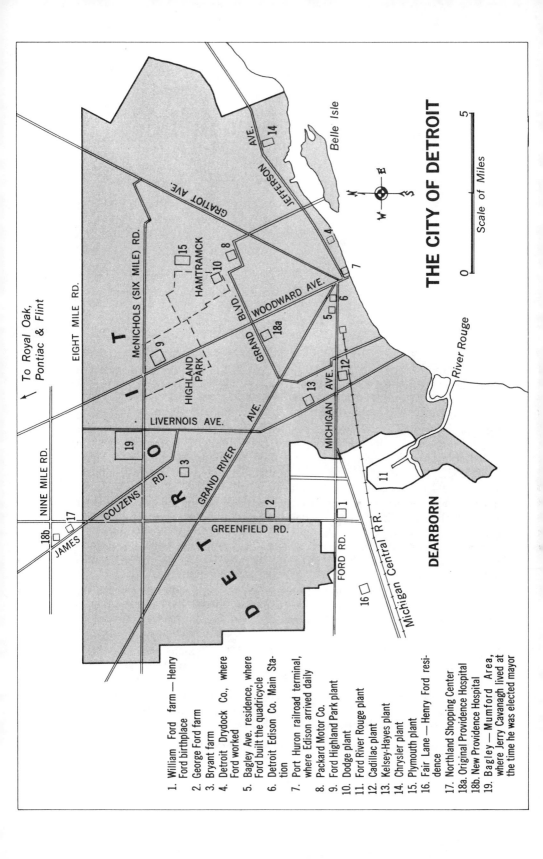

THE CITY OF DETROIT

Scale of Miles

0   5

1. William Ford farm — Henry
   Ford birthplace
2. George Ford farm
3. Bryant farm
4. Detroit Drydock Co., where
   Ford worked
5. Bagley Ave. residence, where
   Ford built the quadricycle
6. Detroit Edison Co. Main Station
7. Port Huron railroad terminal,
   where Edison arrived daily
8. Packard Motor Co.
9. Ford Highland Park plant
10. Dodge plant
11. Ford River Rouge plant
12. Cadillac plant
13. Kelsey-Hayes plant
14. Chrysler plant
15. Plymouth plant
16. Fair Lane — Henry Ford resi-
    dence
17. Northland Shopping Center
18a. Original Providence Hospital
18b. New Providence Hospital
19. Bagley — Mumford Area,
    where Jerry Cavanagh lived at
    the time he was elected mayor

16

The Subdivision of Light

A<small>N OCCASIONAL VISITOR TO DETROIT, EDISON WAS ESPECIALLY INTERESTED IN</small> what was happening in Charles Van Depoele's shop, set up in what had once been the First Methodist Church.

The son of a Flanders railroad mechanic, Van Depoele had emigrated to America in 1869, and established himself in Detroit as a manufacturer of church furniture. In 1870, nine years before anyone else in Detroit, he demonstrated an electric arc light. Three years later he discovered that since electrical power could be produced from the mechanical power of steam engines, the process could be reversed, and machines could be run by electric power.* The next year he applied the principle to running machines in his shop. Laying rails in a long shed on Pine Street, he demonstrated the first electric-powered railroad.

In addition to Van Depoele, a number of Americans and Europeans had been working for years on the problem of utilizing electricity for lighting.† In 1878 Broadway in New York and the streets of Paris were illuminated by high-powered, intense arc lights. In Philadelphia, John Wanamaker installed the lights in his store. But the most prominent inventor in the field of electricity had not evinced interest in applying electricity to lighting.

Edison, only thirty-one years old, was the leading developer of telegraphic equipment. Following his apprenticeship in Mt. Clemens, he had bounced around the country as a telegrapher until he had arrived in New York in September, 1869. When the stock ticker had broken down amidst Jay Gould's attempt to corner the gold market, Edison had fixed it. Catapulted into instant prominence, he had formed with Franklin Pope the first electrical engineering firm in the United States. Backed by both Western Union and Gould's com-

---

* The same discovery was being made almost simultaneously at an electric exhibit in Vienna.
† Two Frenchmen, De La Rive in 1820 and De Moleyns in 1841, a Briton, Sir William Grove in 1840, and an American, J. W. Starr in 1845, attempted to develop an incandescent light by heating various substances in a vacuum. Moses Farmer, William Sawyer, Hiram S. Maxim, St. George Lane-Fox and Joseph Swan had been experimenting off and on with incandescent lighting.

peting Atlantic and Pacific Telegraph Company, Edison had taken out numerous patents, and had close ties to Wall Street.

More a perfecter than a pioneer, Edison made a habit of visiting other inventors like Van Depoele and exchanging ideas with them. His brilliant insights and painstaking experiments often were stimulated by the inventions of others.* In 1878, after it was suggested to him that he ought to take an interest in electric lighting, Edison went to inspect the Connecticut laboratory of William Wallace, the partner of Moses Farmer. Farmer had lighted the parlor of his home with an incandescent bulb as early as 1859, and in 1868 had wired and lighted an entire house.

Excited by what he saw at the laboratory, Edison decided to turn his attention to the development of electric lighting. Two factors distinguished him from other inventors. He recognized the necessity of developing an electric light that would have practical application. And he could turn to Wall Street for the large amounts of money required to take the experiments out of woodshops and sheds.

Edison concluded that it would be necessary to apply to electricity the principles of the $150-million-a-year American gaslight industry, which directed small amounts of gas into individual homes and establishments. The huge amount of electricity fueling the arc lights would have to be broken into small units. There would have to be a "subdivision of light." To realize this concept, it would be necessary to develop not only a long-lasting bulb, but an entire *system* of electrical transmission.

Financed by a Morgan-Vanderbilt syndicate, the Edison Electric Light Company was capitalized at $300,000. It was the first time a syndicate was formed to underwrite not the practical development of a proven invention, but the experiments to develop an idea.

With ample funds to draw on, Edison set about expanding his already extensive work force. Although he derided theoretical scientists, he hired them to work out the formulas that converted his intuitions into realities. Ignoring a multitude of scoffers, he constructed a revolutionary new constant-pressure dynamo. Producing 110 volts, it was but one ingredient in a system of supply, conductors, and circuits. From Princeton, Edison borrowed a high-efficiency vacuum pump. Just developed in England by Sir William Crookes, it was the only one of its kind in America. Week after week, laboratory workers pumped, pumped, pumped to achieve the near-perfect vacuum that had always eluded other inventors. From Germany, Edison imported an expert glassblower, Ludwig Boehm, to blow bulbs in a variety of shapes and sizes.

Often frustrated, Edison expressed his frustrations in the explicit language he had learned on the railroad and along the docks of Detroit.

"Shit! Glass busted by Boehm!" he wrote in his notebook.[1]

Hundreds of materials were tested for use as filaments in the bulbs. Unwilling to reject out of hand any substance, Edison received his first glow from a piece of carbonized limburger cheese. On October 21-22, 1879, a piece of carbonized

---

* After Alexander Graham Bell in 1876 patented the electric speaking telegraph, Edison developed a telephone receiver working on a different principle. While applying himself to the development of a telegraph repeater, he hit upon the principle of the diaphragm. From this came the primitive phonograph, which he patented in 1877. Capable of only a squeaky reproduction of the human voice, it placed Edison in the forefront of the world's inventors. Nevertheless, the phonograph was considered a scientific curiosity that lacked practical application. Putting it aside, Edison was not to return to it for ten years.

Number Twenty-four thread lasted, possibly, as long as forty hours. (The records are contradictory.)

Rapid improvement in the longevity of filaments followed. A piece of Bristol cardboard glowed for one hundred seventy hours. Plucking a strip from a bamboo fan, Edison carbonized it. It remained incandescent for twelve hundred hours!

For Christmas, Edison wired the trees around his laboratory. As they glowed in the night, people thronged from far and wide to gasp at the world's newest wonder.

17

The View from the Tower

QUITE NATURALLY, IT WAS THE LIGHT BULB THAT CAPTURED THE IMAGINATION of the world. But without a system for distributing electricity, the bulb could not have revolutionized living habits. It was the system, in combination with Van Depoele's discovery that electric power could be used to run machinery, that transformed the factory. Thirty-five years later another Detroiter would seize upon it to initiate a new era of technology.

But as Henry Ford trudged through the city's wintry streets, windows cast only a pale glow from gaslights, kerosene lamps, and occasional candles upon the snow. In the central area some 1,760 gas lamps were an aid in picking one's way over the muddy streets and plank sidewalks with their projecting nails and splintered boards. To conserve the public funds the gas lamps were lighted only three weeks out of every month—on the fourth, the full moon was depended upon to take their place.

Since public transportation was all but nonexistent, the central part of the city was packed with public and commercial buildings, factories and machine shops, and the residences of the wealthy. Those who could afford to, built as close as possible to downtown and the waterfront. During the boom of the 1860's, George Hendrie, the operator of a trucking business hauling goods from one railroad depot to another, had obtained through James McMillan the franchise for the horse-powered Detroit City Railway. The cars, however, traveled at no more than six miles per hour, and often halted as long as ten minutes at the switches. The five-cent fare was a stiff price for dollar-a-day workers.

To supplement his fifty-cents-a-day wages, which were not enough for him to live on, Henry took a night job repairing watches. Since the movements being mass produced in New England were rough and simple, the job was not difficult. It was, however, complicated by the fact that he had only the light from a kerosene lantern to work by. Gas lighting had been introduced in the city thirty years before, but it was expensive, dirty, and evil-smelling. Since it required the laying of pipes, it was used mostly in the central part of the city.

The average Detroit home was illuminated by less than one tenth of the twenty-five candlepower considered necessary for reading.

In the fall of 1880, Henry Ford switched jobs once more and went to work for the Detroit Drydock Company, the largest of the city's shipbuilding firms. There he came into contact with a development stemming from Drake's oil well drilling that was of incalculably more importance to the future of Detroit and the world than the kerosene lamp: the internal combustion engine.*

The first patent for an internal combustion engine had been taken out by Englishman Robert Street in 1794, but not until Étienne Lenoir displayed his engine in Paris in 1860 had development reached the point of commercial applicability. In oil-short Europe the engines were designed to run on gas or naphtha. But the availability of oil from Drake's wells in Western Pennsylvania led a British-born American, George Brayton, to develop in 1872 an internal combustion engine fueled with petroleum. Since the supply of wood on the periphery of Lake Erie was being exhausted, steamships were increasingly fueled with coal; on smaller boats internal combustion engines were installed. Although oil-burning engines could not develop the high power of steam, they had the advantage of being light, and could be manufactured in units of less than one horsepower.

As the leading shipbuilding center, Detroit developed experience in internal combustion technology. Since Michigan lacked commercial-grade coal, emphasis on perfecting the engines was greater in Detroit than elsewhere in America.† Henry Ford, therefore, was introduced to the mechanics of both steam and internal combustion engines.

From daybreak to dusk the clangorous sounds of shipbuilding penetrated into the city. From the mansions along nearby Jefferson Avenue nurses brought their charges to look at the hulls taking shape or being repaired in the drydocks. Masts and smokestacks towered into the air. Propeller-driven vessels lay next to sidewheelers. Seven to eight ships a year were launched, and numerous others refitted by the company.

Within less than three years Henry gained enough experience to be hired by Westinghouse to set up and service steam engines for farmers in southeastern Michigan. Traveling the countryside, he displayed a competence that earned him a high reputation. On occasion he was called upon to fix engines in Detroit. Undoubtedly he was familiar with the heavy, steam-propelled vehicle that John and Thomas Clegg of St. Clair constructed in 1884, and with the problems it encountered in attempting to traverse the muddy tracks known as roads. Although his specialty was steam, he was familiar enough with internal combustion engines to be able to repair a "Silent Otto" for the Eagle Iron Works.

At a ball on January 1, 1885, he was introduced to Clara Bryant, a friend of his sister Margaret. Smitten, he bought a cutter to take her sleigh riding. Handsome, of average height, he had a leanness that made him appear taller.

---

* Drake was a tragic figure. Unschooled in the ways of law and business and lacking money, he failed to patent his inventions. Coming out of the venture with but sixteen thousand dollars, he lost all of it speculating in oil stocks. For the last fifteen years of his life he was sick, and very nearly starving.
† Michigan does have large deposits of coal, but it is of low-grade, poor quality. As a consequence of the lack of coal, Detroit was losing ground to Pittsburgh, Chicago, and the Ohio lake shore in iron manufacturing. The Wyandotte ironworks established by Eber Brock Ward were shut down in the mid-1880's.

Frequently called away on trips, he wrote her letters laced with sloshy Victorian verses:

". . . It don't seem mutch like cutter rideing to night does it but i guess we will have some more sleighing. there is a great many Sick in this neighborhood i have called on five sick persons this afternoon three in one house. it seems to bad colds our folks are about over it John is going back to school tomorrow i hope you and your folk are all well . . .

> "May Floweretts of love around you bee twined
> And the Sunshine
> of peace Shed its joy's o'er your Minde . . ." [1]

Such composition would not earn him a passing grade in a twentieth-century junior high school, but it was representative of the literacy of the 1880's.

On April 11, 1888, he and Clara were married. Like many other honeymooning couples, they climbed the 180-foot-high tower of the city hall. Since the land was flat as far as the eye could range, they were able to see to the edge of the city, and to the farms and scattered tracts of forest beyond.

The heart of the city was contained within a half dozen square blocks. Most of its business—government, commerce, education—was conducted there. Across from the city hall, where the Soldiers and Sailors Monument stood as a centerpiece, the three-story Central Market Building raised its three towers. On the first floor were the meat stalls; on the second and third the Board of Health, the Superior Court, and other government agencies.

Fueled by the railroad boom of the 1880's, the city was sprouting wildly without plan or control. The population increased from 116,000 in 1879 to 206,000 in 1889. The city's area nearly doubled, from 12.75 square miles in 1870 to 22.19 square miles in 1885. Farmlands and wasteland were annexed as far out as the Grand Boulevard, conceived as a parkway for riding and biking.

At the river the boulevard connected with Belle Isle, a marshy seven-hundred-acre island full of hogs and snakes. During French rule the island had been part of the commons, but after the arrival of the British, a Lt. McDougall had managed to have title conveyed to him. In 1879, when it became evident that there was need for a new commons, or park, the city had paid $200,000 to reacquire the island. Wealthy property owners, who considered such frills as parks and parkways unnecessary, looked for crooked real estate promoters behind the bushes and trees, and howled "Graft!" It was too bad, they mused, that Joy's plans for using the island as a freight yard and stepping-stone for a railroad bridge to Canada had fallen through.*

Launches and ferries, steamships and tall-masted sailing vessels swarmed upon the river. The world's first railroad ferry, transported in sections from England and assembled at Windsor in 1867, had multiplied into a fleet carrying an average of fifteen hundred cars daily. Numerous fishing vessels and iceboats attested to the fact that the Great Lakes provided the world's greatest ice harvest and catch of freshwater fish.

Looking down from the tower, Henry Ford saw a city that since his first

---

* Blocked by shippers' objections from constructing a bridge across the river, Joy had attempted to bore a tunnel underneath it. But, as the tunnel progressed, the workmen had been enveloped by hydrogen sulfide gas. Two had been killed. When the others rebelled, drilling had been abandoned.

arrival had been spiderwebbed by telegraph, telephone, and electric lines. The arc lights illuminating the streets were so intense that they were placed in clusters of four to six on skeletal towers up to one hundred sixty feet high. Painted a garish red, the towers looked like the three-pronged tuning forks of a giant mad musician. On some nights the lights were enveloped by the smoke and haze of the city until they seemed like moons in the sky.

A mile west of the city hall, the Union Station created its own acrid atmosphere. Constructed by a group headed by Joy, McMillan, and Newberry, it was transmuting the substantial homes in its neighborhood into celluled roominghouses and railroad hostelries. Killing the century-old fruit trees, the station was converting gardens into junk piles, and cultivating the land for a crop of factories.

At troughs spotted on squares and intersections, drivers jockeyed for position to water their horses. Such was the multiplication of horses, carriages, and wagons, that on the side streets traffic not infrequently came to a standstill behind double- and triple-parked vehicles. Horses became entangled, and the wheels of wagons locked against each other. Draymen and coachmen cursed and threatened to whip each other.

Before Henry Ford spread a panorama of the machine age. It was a panorama of which he considered himself a part. Yet, his days as a traveling mechanic at an end, he was leaving it behind. Clara shared the feeling prevalent among well-to-do farm families that the city was a nice place to visit, but that it was corrupt and full of vice, and that only the very rich and the very poor lived there. The newlyweds were returning to Dearborn, and the forty acres of farmland offered to Henry by his father.

18

The Industrial Aristocrats

THE DIVISION BETWEEN THE RICH AND THE POOR WAS, IN FACT, BECOMING more pronounced. Since the Civil War, a city of modest homes had been planted lushly with mansions. Broad and tree-lined Woodward and Jefferson Avenues were as stately as New York's Park Avenue. Of the various aristocracies of wealth, the oldest one was that of the French settlers. Their original land grants had made a number of families millionaires. The fur traders, the shippers, and the *Bostonian* merchants had grown rich on commerce. The mineral and timber kings had acquired the land that Congress had so generously dispensed. The wealthiest and most powerful of all were the Railroad men. And they, in turn, were giving rise to the industrialists.

Almost every month witnessed the organization of a major new concern. In the eight years since its establishment, the Peninsula Car Company had built thirty-five thousand freight cars and was pressing the Michigan Car Company for leadership. Founded only in 1881, the Detroit Copper and Brass Rolling Works were the largest in the world. Deposits of lead made the area a center for paint manufacturing. Mass production dramatically lowered the cost of paint. The nation's weathered and unadorned appearance was rapidly becoming more pleasing and colorful.

From the modest beginning of salt-well drilling had come the discovery that southeastern Michigan contained vast deposits of chemicals and salt. These were transforming Detroit and nearby cities into one of the world's centers for the manufacture of pharmaceuticals and chemical products. Frederick Stearns, who had started bottling drugs in one room in 1855, now had a work force of four hundred. Among his competitors were Parke, Davis and Company, and Upjohn. A hundred miles to the north at Midland, the Dow Chemical Company was soon to establish itself. Along Detroit's western riverfront Belgium's Solvay Company would erect the plant for producing soda ash and alkali that was to make the city the principal soap manufacturing center in the Western hemisphere.

With the advent of the chemical industry, the rivers turned corrosive. The sulphurous smoke killed trees and bushes and was powerful enough to scour the paint off anything in its path. Near the plants, residents were so enveloped by the rotten-egglike stench that eventually many had their sense of smell destroyed.

Beyond the limits of the smoke, the rich Michigan soil continued to supply one of the most abundant agricultural harvests in the world, a harvest for which Detroit was the funnel. The enterprise of raising seeds for pioneers had grown into the D. M. Ferry Company, the largest in the world.

In central Michigan, Kellogg and Post had brought into being the world's dry cereal industry. In Detroit, Pingree and Smith, the largest shoe factory west of the Alleghenies, manufactured 490,000 shoes yearly. Despite the depredation of the forests, the state annually shipped a half million dollars' worth of furs to Europe.

Refrigerated railroad cars were the invention of fish merchant William Davis. In May of 1869, thirty-year-old George Hammond * had agreed to risk a shipload of beef in a refrigerator car built by Davis. When the shipment arrived unspoiled in Boston, another industry was born. Branching out, Hammond established slaughterhouses and packing plants in Omaha, Nebraska, and on the rail lines directly south of Chicago. There the town of Hammond grew into Indiana's sixth largest. By the mid-1880's the firm was utilizing eight hundred refrigerator cars.

For spectacular expansion, however, it was difficult to surpass the stove industry. Jeremiah Dwyer's father had bought a farm at Springwells at about the same time the first Fords had settled in Dearborn, three or four miles away. During one of its early runs the fire-spewing locomotive of the Detroit and St. Joseph had panicked a team of horses. The elder Dwyer had been killed. Forced to make his own way, Jeremiah had gone to work in a foundry. In the late 1850's he had set up a business for the manufacture of reapers and stoves. Like dozens of other entrepreneurs who had crowded into the field after the expiration of McCormick's patent, he had discovered that manufacturing reapers produced a poor harvest.

Everywhere, however, people were anxious to abandon their open hearths and improve their cooking and heating devices. The market for stoves was vast. The Upper Peninsula iron mines were spewing out the ore needed in their manufacture. The organization of the Detroit Stove Company in 1864 marked the beginning of large-scale production.

Such were the economics of mass production and of steam transportation that Detroit manufacturers, yearly making 150,000 stoves in 700 models, could undersell European manufacturers in their own markets. Agencies were established in Stockholm, Frankfurt, London, and Australia.

To provide space for the burgeoning plants, James McMillan organized the Rouge Improvement Company. Located along the River Rouge, which was dredged for three miles inland to admit oceangoing vessels, the Improvement Company was a forerunner of the industrial park. Eight million dollars was invested in the project. That was more than half as much as the total capital investment in plant and equipment in Detroit in 1880. During the decade of

---

* Descended from William Penn's sister, Hammond had arrived from New England in 1854. In 1857 he opened a neighborhood meat shop. The prosperity the Civil War brought to Detroit enabled him to expand, and he became head of the largest meat packing firm in the state.

the 1880's investment in, employment by, and output of industry nearly tripled. (Investment rose from between $13 and $15 million to $39 million; employment from less than 18,000 to 38,000; and output from $27 million to $77 million.)

The industrial boom of the 1880's and the concomitant expansion of the American railroad network all but buried Joy, McMillan, Newberry and their associates beneath mounds of gold. Joy and the other investors in the Soo Canal were reaping a dual harvest—one from the seven hundred and fifty thousand acres of timber and mineral lands that the government had donated to them, the other from the canal itself. Even though the canal was closed during the winter months, the ore carriers made it by far the busiest in the world, with many times over the traffic of Suez.

Detroit, whose egalitarian character had struck Alexis de Tocqueville in 1830, now contained a significant number of the nation's four thousand millionaires.*

Not only were they the leaders of the city's "society," but, through intermarriage, they were forming what was, in effect, an interlocking financial directorate. Seeking an outlet for their money, the Detroit wealthy bought real estate near and far,† and plunged heavily into the inchoate field of public utilities, where large outlays were required, but huge dividends promised.

In 1877 James McMillan was among the group that obtained the telephone franchise. (The next year the first directory of the *Speaking Telephone,* containing 125 names, was published.) In 1881 McMillan, his brother Hugh, James Joy, and Russell Alger were the leaders of the group that formed the Edison Electric Light Company.‡

The Detroiters actually obtained the electric lighting franchise before New York, but like investors in ten other cities they were left to chafe while Edison devoted his energy to setting up the system in Manhattan. Since "electrical engineers" were all but nonexistent, he was attending to everything—from the most complex theoretical problems to laying wires. It took him two years to establish factories to manufacture the dynamos and the bulbs. (The bulbs cost $1.21 apiece.) The wires, which were laid underground with rudimentary insulation, not infrequently electrified the people walking over them in the streets.

(Edison had chosen a system operating on a direct current—which shocked, but was less likely to kill—over the alternating-current system adopted by his competitor, Westinghouse. The Westinghouse system, Edison pointedly indicated, was doing an excellent job of killing people at Sing Sing.)

Not until November 8, 1886, was the switch thrown on Detroit's system.§ Within two months demand exceeded the four-thousand-lamp capacity of the six-hundred-horsepower plant. Three more engines and six more dynamos were ordered from the Edison Machine Shops.

---

* At the end of the Revolutionary War, there was not a single millionaire in the colonies. When New York Central Railroad magnate Cornelius Vanderbilt died in 1887, he left a fortune of $100 million.

† Traveling on land-promotion trains arranged by the railroads, they founded the city of Riverside, California.

‡ Joy, though in his seventies, continued to be an alert, vigorous man. From 1884 to 1887 he served as president of the Wabash, St. Louis and Pacific Railroad. Alger, related by marriage to the Joy family, was the world's largest dealer in pine lumber, the president of the Detroit, Bay City and Alpena Railroad, and the principal stockholder in the Peninsula Car Company. In 1884 he was elected governor of Michigan.

§ The company in the meantime had been reorganized as the Edison Illuminating Company. Among the additional investors were Simon J. Murphy, a lumberman who had moved from Maine to Michigan, and James E. Scripps, the founder of the Detroit *News.*

19

The Reformation of the City

THE ELECTRIC INDUSTRY WOULD SET OFF A NEW BOOM IN THE COPPER MINES, and make Michigan's Calumet and Hecla the most lucrative mine in the world. But it was lumbermen who were coming almost to rival the wealth of their railroad acquaintances. It was, in fact, the unparalleled expansion of the railroads that created the demand for lumber. Lumber for railroad cars and ties. Lumber for every kind of article needed on the treeless Western plains that the railroads were opening to cultivation.

When the railroads were expanding, their appetite for manpower was voracious; and during the 1880's the United States constructed railroads at a world-record pace that would never be surpassed.* People were needed to settle the lands that the railroads opened. Men were required to grade the roadbeds and lay the rails, to build the locomotives and the rolling stock, to labor in the ironworks and the sawmills, to mine the ore and cut the timber. Thus the peak years of railroad expansion—1882 and 1887-88 corresponded with the peak years of immigration.

Thousands of immigration agents—from American railroad and steamship companies, from various state governments, from mining and industrial concerns—combed Europe for workers and settlers. They had little difficulty in inducing young men like Adam Jansen (who was to become the father of Peter Jansen) to leave homelands whose economies could no longer support their populations.

The Jansen family were "torpare," who rented their torp (cottage) from a landlord in return for their labor a certain number of days each month. The people of rural Sweden, where money was almost nonexistent, operated essentially in a barter economy. They slept, without taking off their clothes, huddled together against the cold on a straw mattress in one room. They sharecropped a patch of land, but it was not nearly large enough to support them. Living in

---

* In 1878 there were eighty-two thousand miles of track in operation. During the next fourteen years another eighty thousand miles were built, twice the mileage that existed in any other country in the world as late as the 1920's.

a country blessed with extensive forests and a long coastline, the boys grew up learning to be fishermen and woodsmen. They were Lutherans, but a few hundred years of Christianity had not succeeded in eradicating the ancient Nordic mythology. Prey to a hundred and one superstitions, they conducted much of their lives according to folklore. A toothache was cured by rubbing a horse-shoe nail over the gum until it bled, then imbedding the nail in a tree; smallpox could be caught by coming into contact with a blighted potato; the call of the first cuckoo in spring could bewitch a person; a child must not be loused on Sunday; the "evil eye" roamed about the countryside. They drank great quantities of "finkel" (potato brandy), swore vigorously, and were not particularly chaste. They suffered from no shortage of fuel, and they tended to be more substantially housed and better clothed than their Irish and Cornish counterparts. But their fare was much the same. They ate potatoes, porridge, and vegetables, and seldom came into contact with fresh meat.

They suffered from the same problem of increasing population as almost every European nationality. A population of 1,780,000 in 1750 had multiplied itself to 4.7 million by 1880. In a land that continued to be 90 percent rural—there were but twelve cities with a population of more than 10,000—they were immensely affected by the industrial and transportation revolutions in the United States, Great Britain, and Germany.

The first significant wave of Swedish immigrants had come to the United States as a consequence of the potato blight of the 1840's. They had been followed by small farmers and agricultural laborers who, at the close of the Civil War, were bankrupted by the flood of American wheat and corn that cascaded into Europe. The American depression of the 1870's put a brake on the immigration. But at the close of the decade the Swedish economy went into such a steep decline that one fourth of the population expressed itself ready to cross the seas.

Paid five cents an hour, and sometimes sleeping in the snow, Adam Jansen had supported himself by cutting timber in the winter and working as a fisherman and field hand in summer. But the end of wooden shipbuilding had the same effect upon the Swedish lumber industry as upon the Maine lumber industry and the Cornish copper industry. Having overharvested the most accessible timber, lumber companies saw their costs rise at the same time that their sales slumped. Men were laid off. Wages, already at a bare subsistence level, were reduced further. The men struck. But they might as well have been striking against a storm on the ocean. A number of publications, led by the newspaper of Isidor Kjellberg, who had traveled extensively in the United States, urged them to emigrate.

Adam Jansen went. If he were surplus at home, he would be welcomed in the lumber country of Michigan. The number of Swedes in the state rose from 2,400 in 1880 to 27,000 in 1890. He traveled on a ship whose decks were so low that he could not walk upright, and which provided slop buckets for toilets.* He was one of 5,237,000 immigrants to America during the 1880's. They represented 41 percent of the increase in the nation's population, and 62 percent of the increase in the urban population.

On the one hand, industrialists saturated Europe with agents, and fostered immigration to keep American wages down and workers in line. On the other,

---

* Although an act of Congress in 1882 was designed to end the abuses of ship packing, it contained no provisions for enforcement, and so was ignored.

they viewed every new worker as a potential recruit for the city's political bosses, and a threat to the delicate balance between the Democratic and Republican parties.

A major portion of the Republican party's constituency came from the artisans of New England. But as the moving force behind industrialization, the Republicans were cast in the role of the antagonists of labor. By the end of the Civil War union members numbered about 200,000, roughly one out of seven men employed in manufacturing. Eight years later the number was 300,000. By 1873, mechanics and laborers in Federal employment had achieved an eight-hour day, which, it appeared, might soon be accepted as the national norm.

The Panic of 1873 and subsequent depression eroded all of labor's gains. Union members, laid off by the tens of thousands, were blacklisted when the time came for rehiring. When the unemployed picketed and attempted to keep workers from entering the plants, police and militia were marshaled against them.

After the 1875 Irish "Molly Maguire" riots in the anthracite coal fields, ten workers were executed. In 1877, when one fifth of the New York work force was unemployed and another two fifths underemployed, a massive protest parade was assaulted and dispersed by the New York police. A strike against the Baltimore and Ohio Railroad united tens of thousands of workers and farmers. When the Allegheny County militia was mobilized, it mutinied and joined the strikers. As the Eastern United States was plunged into a condition bordering on anarchy, President Hayes ordered Federal troops into action. Before The Great Strike was broken, scores were killed—twelve in Baltimore, twenty or more in Chicago, sixty-six in Pittsburgh—and $10 million worth of property was destroyed.

The railroad strike brought the Knights of Labor, which had originated in the Philadelphia garment district in 1869, to national prominence. The Knights broke with the tradition of a union movement that had followed in the footsteps of the guilds, and tried to protect skilled workers against the inroads of the unskilled, and of machines. The first unions had continued to operate on the guild theory that wages depended on supply and demand. They had attempted to establish an artificial shortage of workers by restricting apprenticeships and by establishing stiff entrance requirements. Since every worker excluded from a union became a potential strikebreaker, such a theory was self-defeating. The Knights of Labor initiated a policy of "industrial unionism." Membership was opened to all workers, both skilled and unskilled.

With the prosperity of the 1880's, unions flourished. Despite management's employment of Pinkerton detectives, and use of foreign workers and Negroes as strikebreakers, numerous strikes succeeded. Union membership reached 700,000. On May Day, 1886, a general strike broke out in Chicago. The actions of the police, as usual, were directed against the strikers. Several men were shot. The violence culminated in the Haymarket Riot. When a bomb was set off, the police reacted by shooting point-blank into the crowd, killing ten persons and wounding more than fifty. Seven labor leaders were sentenced to death.

Chicago, a city of fewer than a million people, had 450,000 foreign-born. It had the third largest German and the third largest Scandinavian populations of any city in the world. The situation in other Eastern and Midwestern cities was comparable. New York and Brooklyn had twice as many Irish as Dublin and two and a half times as many Jews as Warsaw. In Detroit a third of the 216,000 people were foreign-born. A majority of the foreign-born were industrial workers and their families. Almost to a man the agitators who tried to organize them spoke with foreign accents.

Native Americans, propagandized by industrialists that a wave of anarchists was engulfing the country, reacted by reviving the patriotic Know-Nothing fervor of the 1850's. States vied with each other in passing antilabor legislation.

But the widespread unrest among workers and the decline of farm prices brought on by a glut of agricultural products was too much for the Republican party to overcome. Rebelling against the banker-railroad domination of the party, the Western Republicans in 1884 deserted the Republican nominee, James G. Blaine, and backed the Democratic nominee, Grover Cleveland, the reform mayor of Buffalo. Emerging from a Fifth Avenue meeting with Blaine, Presbyterian clergyman Samuel Burchard paraphrased Amos Walker's wildly received declaration of thirty years earlier:

"We are Republicans, and don't propose to leave our party and identify ourselves with the party whose antecedents have been rum, Romanism, and rebellion." [1]

The upshot was that New Yorkers, voting against the Reverend Burchard's abstinence, Puritanism, and concept of loyalty, gave the election to Cleveland, the first Democrat to attain the White House since 1856. It was the clearest manifestation yet of the growth of political power of the Irish.

To revitalize the party and heal the wounds of its various factions, McMillan, Joy, Alger, and other leading businessmen in January of 1885 founded the Michigan Republican Club. Among its twelve hundred members were latter-day Know-Nothings, temperance advocates, antilaborites, and would-be reformers of both the city's morals and its politics. It was in the reformation of the city that many could find a common cause similar to that of the anti-South crusade a generation before.

Despite the prosperity of the 1880's, thousands of men and boys worked only on and off and seldom slept in the same bed more than a few nights at a time. To make ends meet it was usually necessary for both parents to work. Children continued to be left largely to their own devices in the streets. One fifth of the criminals were juveniles. Although jails were described as "the public schools of crime," it required less soul searching to attribute problems of delinquency to the "laxity of the courts" and the new immorality in literature. [2] Lewd material—especially contraceptive information—was banned from the mails. Crime rose and fell inversely with the condition of the economy—following the Panic of 1873 a group of Detroit citizens had been so aroused by the increase of drunkenness and crime that they formed the Law and Order party.

Saloons, brothels, and gaming dens flourished twenty-four hours a day. In an era when men had little home life save between the sheets, the saloons served as neighborhood clubs. The saloon keeper acted as father confessor, banker, referee, and adviser. It was only natural that he should become, if not himself a political boss, one of the lieutenants of the ward boss.

Where roominghouses were operated in conjunction with the saloons, their operators often offered free bed and board on election eve. Came the dawn, the lodgers were marched to the polls before being returned to the bar. Jobs were always scarce before an election and plentiful afterward—for those who had demonstrated their loyalty. No laws governed the printing of ballots, which were supplied by the party committees. Fraudulent ballots, carrying phony names, were circulated in districts controlled by the rival party. Many ballots were deliberately confusing, so that only the most sophisticated voters could decipher them. Illiterate and half literate voters relied on their friend the boss to make the choice for them. To frustrate poll watchers, the first man in the booth, instead of casting his ballot, brought it out and turned it over to the boss. Marking it, the boss handed it to the second man, who, taking it into the booth and casting it, brought out his own unmarked ballot. So, as the procession continued, the boss cast every vote.

Police officers, knowing their jobs depended on the victory of the incumbent party, harassed opposition voters. As a last resort, word would be passed to "let the bluebirds fly." Concealing stubs of blue pencils in their palms, bribed election officials would re-mark, and so void, unfavorable ballots at the same time that they were counting them.

To ensure that no reformer or antimachine candidate could win, and that the "regulars" of both parties could retain power in the city, Democrats and Republicans commonly practiced "vote swapping."

The Michigan Clubbers' interest in "reform" was stimulated by the fact that aldermen repeatedly threatened the owners of public franchises with restrictive legislation and "strike bills" unless they contributed to the aldermen's favorite cause—themselves. And while the Republicans were no less experienced in bribery than the Democrats, they disliked extortion.

Following the death of Senator Chandler in 1879, the leadership of the state party fell to James McMillan. (McMillan had gained stature by successfully managing the congressional campaign of his close friend and partner, Newberry, in 1878.) By 1885 McMillan was state chairman, and but a step removed from being elected to the U.S. Senate by the state legislature. Pondering who could head the reform ticket for mayor, McMillan decided upon Hazen Pingree.

Forty-nine years old, a charter member and one of the "Big Four" of The Club, Pingree had all the proper Republican credentials. One of eight children, he had left his home in Maine at the age of fourteen because the area, like rural Europe, was producing too many children and too little else. Migrating to Massachusetts, he had become a leather cutter and shoe maker. During the Civil War he had enlisted in the artillery and participated in numerous battles before being captured by Mosby's guerrillas.

Surviving several months in Andersonville Prison, and hearing much of Michigan from fellow prisoners, he had come to Detroit. In 1866, together with Charles H. Smith, he had formed the firm of Pingree and Smith. In twenty years their investment of $1,360 grew into a plant with a payroll of seven hundred and an annual gross of more than $1 million. As the proprietor of the largest shoe factory west of New York, Pingree earned a reputation for liberality and for good relations with his employees.

Although he had never been one of the Joy-McMillan railroad "crowd," there was every indication that Pingree would complaisantly respond to their desires. Bald-headed and squeaky-voiced, he seemed undynamic. Protesting that he knew nothing about running the city government—an asset, since the old pols would have been horrified had he expected to run it—he was ushered forth as the candidate of public virtue.

Within a short time of taking office, however, he was startling the city with the kind of independence that led him at a later date to roar: "This town needs somebody to tell the public utilities crowd to kiss something else besides babies!" [3]

Had President Richard Nixon removed his cloak to reveal John Lindsay beneath, the Republicans could not have been more shaken.

20

The Strong Mayor

CONTRARY TO PRECEDENT, PINGREE DID EXPECT TO RUN THE CITY. DEDICATED and efficient, he was dismayed by the rotten condition of the municipality and his lack of power. Most major decisions, notably those on taxation and finance, needed the approval of the state legislature. Anything the legislature did needed the approval of Senator McMillan, ensconced in Washington. Locally, the thirty-two members of the city council met but one evening a week. The sessions, which were full of invective, resulted in little action. Sometimes the Democrats and Republicans refused to meet together, and held separate sessions. Most business actually was conducted by committees in executive session. Accountable to no one, their chairmen were the principal wielders of power in city hall. Commonly failing to notify opposition members where and when the meetings would be held, the committees gathered in lofts over saloons, and similar out-of-the-way places.

It was a city in which the old and the new, the obsolete and the modern, clashing, repelling, and merging, were forming a society full of turmoil and vitality. Directly across Cadillac Square from the city hall the Hammond Building was rising. Financed by a small portion of the returns from George Hammond's meat packing business, it was Detroit's first skyscraper.*

Upon the 10-story building's completion in 1889, a state holiday was declared. People came hundreds of miles to gawk. Bands played. Orators praised the marvel. A tightrope walker, wearing baskets on his feet and pushing a wheelbarrow, negotiated a cable strung from the city hall tower to the top of the new building. Fireworks rocketed into the sky.

From the tenth story of the Hammond Building, office workers descended in

---

* Chicago's 10-story Home Insurance Company Building, constructed in 1885, was the world's first skyscraper. The new heights were made feasible by the development of the electric elevator and structural steel. The elevator was dependent upon the work of Edison, and Edison's German counterpart, Werner von Siemens. Architect W. L. B. Jenny used iron and steel to create a structural framework that took the load off the walls, whose thickness previously had had to be increased with every foot of height. Foundations, however, still presented something of a mystery. It was not unusual to find two-hundred-foot-high buildings settling like the Tower of Pisa.

electric elevators. Once they reached the street, however, they were enveloped in an urban technology that had changed little since the Civil War. The horse-cars they boarded, their floors insulated with layers of foul-smelling straw, were heated by small, pungent gas stoves that threatened to asphyxiate and incinerate the passengers. The homes at which they arrived continued to be supplied with water from penstocks—only one fifth of the houses had running water. The sanitary facilities they utilized were still back-alley privies—although the water trap had greatly improved indoor plumbing since the 1870's, when toilets had belched such noxious fumes that it was like living with a dyspeptic whale, indoor plumbing continued to be a luxury.

Until the latter 1870's, as ever greater amounts of garbage, raw sewage, and industrial wastes had been dumped into the river, the city's water had tasted like the brew concocted by *Macbeth*'s witches. Then a tunnel had been dug beneath the riverbed, and the intake had been relocated at the head of Belle Isle, three miles above the city's northeastern limits. The largely open sewage system competed with the systems of cities like Baltimore and New Orleans in the breeding of disease. Overflowing with every heavy rain, it turned the streets themselves into sewers.

Hospitals staffed with doctors who needed only to attend lectures for a couple of semesters to obtain their M.D.'s and commence on-the-patient training retained their Civil War reputations as *pesthouses* serving as way stations to the mortuary. Conditions at the "crazyhouse" had improved only in degree since the 1860's, when inmates, housed in the same building with hogs, had been chained to the walls, fed through iron grates, and bedded down on straw.

Fire hazards continued to increase. In the city hall tower the bell, connected to a system of alarm boxes, pealed night and day. The development of water mains and firefighting equipment continued to lag behind the expansion of incendiary materials, fuel, and machinery. A decade earlier the city had experimented with a "self-propeller" steam engine that was an impressive five tons of spit and polish. But, bogging down in the muddy streets, it had been abandoned as impractical.

The condition of the streets was a scandal that stood out among scandals. Before the 1870's the city had had reasonably good cobblestone pavement. But as the lumber industry developed, lumbermen convinced the citizens that cedar blocks would provide a smoother pavement. Absorbing the clop of the horses' hooves, they would generate less noise. Throughout cities of the Midwest the cobblestones were torn up and replaced. The cedar blocks were all that the lumbermen claimed; and more. Tamped down with gravel and asphalt, they soon worked loose. During heavy rains they rose and floated on the streets; small boys discovered that they made great rafts. In summertime they caught fire. It was not unusual to see literally an entire street burning.

Portions of four principal streets had been paved with asphalt. Although $550,000 was spent on the paving, widespread graft combined with lack of know-how produced a material more akin to molasses. The asphalt clung to shoes, skirts, and the wheels of vehicles, and was eaten by children.

Objecting to pavement that burned, floated, and glued, the nation's one million bicyclists * formed a strong lobby for better streets. Together with other citizens

---

* The safety, or modern bicycle evolved between 1876 and 1885. With its seat placed low between the wheels and a chain connecting the pedals to the rear wheel, the machine was transformed from an acrobat's pedestal to a practical mode of transportation. In Europe,

they stormed at the railroads, which caused massive traffic jams and frequent accidents as they shunted long strings of cars back and forth across the thoroughfares.

Catering to the rising number of middle-class independents, Pingree made street improvement his first priority. He initiated a program of repaving the entire city, and directed himself to the removal of traffic bottlenecks. He ended the practice of charging the cost of paving to the residents of each block, a policy that was unfair to people living on the main thoroughfares, and generated great resistance to any paving at all. Henceforward, through the issuance of bonds, the burden was to be spread equally over the community. In a half dozen years Detroit was turned into one of the best-paved cities in the nation.

Recognizing that most of his program depended on the reform of municipal finances, Pingree retained Robert W. Oakman as his tax expert. The former editor of a labor newspaper, Oakman was a disciple of Henry George, Jr. George, born in 1839, was a San Francisco printer who, during the economic tailspin of the 1870's, had pondered over the "vague but general feeling of disappointment; an inward bitterness among the working classes; a widespread feeling of unrest and brooding revolution. . . . Everywhere [there was] the increasing intensity of the struggle to live, the increasing necessity for straining every nerve to prevent being thrown down and trodden under foot in the scramble for wealth. . . . In every civilized country pauperism, crime, insanity, and suicides are increasing. In every civilized country the diseases are increasing, which come from overstrained nerves, from insufficient nourishment, from squalid lodgings, from unwholesome and monotonous occupations, from premature labor of children." [1]

In his book *Progress and Poverty,* published in 1879, George put forward the theory that the economic malaise was due to the private ownership of land. Land, he asserted, was the common property of all the people. No monarch or government had the right to dispose of it in huge grants. Growing rich, land speculators and railroad men were soaking up the capital that should, instead, be applied to the expansion of productive facilities. It was this misdirection of capital that brought on depressions. It was the control of an inelastic commodity, land, whose rent spiraled upward with increasing population, that was responsible for the miseries of the urban population. As an increasing portion of the cost of production was devoted to rent, wages fell. Material gains from the use of labor-saving devices were going to the landowners, not to the workers.

In contrast to Karl Marx, George advocated not confiscation of the land, but taxation to take the profits out of rent. As the profits were taxed away, speculation would cease. Since the conflict was not between labor and capital, but between labor and capital on the one hand and property on the other, only the raw land, not improvements on it, would be taxed. The tax on land would replace all other taxes.

Both in America and in Europe, George's "single tax" theory was received with enthusiasm. It became one of the principal bases for Populism. Employment of the property tax was vastly expanded.

---

costing twenty pounds apiece, bikes were the latest novelty to come into fashion among the elite. In America, the Pope Company of Connecticut applied the mass production techniques developed in the light-arms and sewing machine industries to the manufacture of bicycles. Costs were lowered to the point that the popularity of the bicycle outstripped even that of the six-shooter.

In Detroit, Oakman found that tax assessments were so inequitable that real estate speculators and businessmen were assessed at a rate 50 percent less than homeowners. The street railroad which, in lieu of property taxes, was supposed to pay 1 percent of its gross revenue to the city, refused to let the city inspect its books. So it paid anything it wished. Companies that were headquartered and doing business in Detroit escaped municipal taxation by establishing *official* addresses in shacks or taverns beyond the city limits.

Pingree could initiate the equalization of assessments. But while the regular Republicans controlled the state legislature and the governorship, there was little hope of obtaining the enabling legislation to institute meaningful reforms. Then, in 1890, the Democrats, in part of a national sweep, captured control of the state for the first time in nearly forty years.

At once Pingree began planning a reordering of municipal affairs. At the time of his entry into office, the lighting franchise of the Brush Company was expiring. By underbidding (or overbribing), a new group, the Detroit Electric Light and Power Company, succeeded in having the franchise transferred to it. The Brush Company proclaimed that their rivals might have the franchise, but that they did not have the 142 light towers and the wires. Unable to buy or lease the installations, the Detroit Electric Light and Power Company constructed its own towers. Although these sometimes mysteriously toppled, within a few months the city could boast of a dual set of towers and a further tangle of wires. Proleptically, the town appeared like a vast radar installation.

Pingree was convinced that the unseemly performances of the two electric companies had prepared citizens for getting rid of both. He proposed that the municipality build its own power plant.

While the wealthy lived within a horse trot of the center of the city, workers commuted from outlying districts. In the 1870's, New York, attempting to relieve its brutalizing congestion, built an elevated railway. In 1879, von Siemens produced the first commercial electric streetcar, and its use spread quickly. "Detroit's Edison" as the *Free Press* referred to Van Depoele (even though in 1881 he had moved to Chicago), was receiving contracts to electrify the street railways of city after city. In 1885 he put his system into operation in South Bend, which vied with Baltimore for the distinction of being the first American city to replace its horsecars with electric streetcars. By the end of the following year he had electrified the systems of eight cities. In Detroit, however, the citizens were left to stew behind the bell-jangling collars and swishing tails of the horses, which, proceeding leisurely, fertilized the streets.

Appearing in Detroit in 1889 to recruit workers in a tobacco industry that was paying women and children four cents an hour, organizers for the American Federation of Labor were attracted by the plight of the streetcar employees.* Theoretically working twelve hours a day, they were required to work one shift in the morning and one in the evening to coincide with the periods of peak loads, and so spent up to eighteen hours on the job.

In April, 1891, a Democratic legislator introduced a bill to reduce the work-

---

* Organized in 1886, the AFL was primarily the handiwork of Samuel Gompers, a Dutch-English Jewish cigar maker who had emigrated to the United States in 1863. Becoming president of the New York cigar makers local, he rejected the industrial unionism and complex theorizing of the Knights of Labor, which seemed to invite disaster during depressions. He eliminated competitive locals, and linked the locals in each trade into federated national unions. He emphasized the improvement of working conditions within the system, rather than a change of systems.

ing hours on the cars from 12 to 10. Immediately, the company circulated handbills warning that, if the hours were cut, wages would have to be reduced accordingly. A dozen or more men were discharged for labor agitation. Were it not for "outside professionals assisted by a few agitators," the company asserted, there would be no problem with its cheerful, well-satisfied employees.

At a meeting that lasted until four o'clock in the morning, the well-satisfied employees voted cheerfully to strike. When the company attempted to continue operations, workers blocked the tracks with lamp posts, trees, and overturned cars. Battles between employees, and company police and strikebreakers raged on car platforms.

When the company issued revolvers to strikebreakers, an incensed mob of five thousand men, women, and children gathered on the third day of the strike. At 4 P.M. they began attacking streetcars along Woodward Avenue with clubs and rocks. Mayor Pingree arrived. The officers of the company implored him "to save the city," and the captain in charge of the police pleaded for him to urge the people to return to their homes. But Pingree, the memory of his own days as a worker not forgotten, indicated he might not be averse to throwing a few rocks himself. He refused to interfere. Led by Don M. Dickinson, President Cleveland's Postmaster-General, the mob rolled a streetcar to the foot of Woodward Avenue and, cheering wildly, dumped it into the river.

21

A School of Philosophy

In washington, senator mcmillan instinctively must have ducked away from the splash.

Not only had the Michigan Republican Club failed to reunite the various factions, it had enabled a covert adherent of Liberal Republicanism to attain the mayoralty of Detroit. The 1890 elections were a disaster for the Republicans, both in Michigan and nationally. The westward push of the population was portending a shift of power that endangered the economic and political control of the railroad, industrial, and banking Republicans.

The astonishing expansion of the railroads and the competition between lines had driven down rates. Between the early 1870's and the 1880's the charge for carrying wheat from Chicago to New York fell from thirty-three cents to thirteen cents a bushel. Unable to compete with railroads, canals lowered their tolls or, like the Erie Canal, removed them altogether.

On the high seas, competition was even fiercer. Ships were constructed of a size and tonnage impossible before the development of controlled-quality and low-cost steel. The cost of transporting wheat from New York to Europe declined from twenty cents to two cents a bushel.

Breakthroughs in industrial technology halved the price of steel between the 1850's and the 1870's and reduced the price of some industrial chemicals by three quarters. The reductions were quickly reflected in the prices of consumer products, such as stoves, pots, flatware, clothing, soap, and glass. The 45 percent decline in the price of glass between 1876 and 1888 resulted in an architectural revolution that threw buildings open to the sun.

In 1870, Great Britain had manufactured more than five times as much steel and three times as much iron as the United States (the second largest producer). By 1890, although British steel production had increased 1,800 percent, the United States was producing 500,000 more long tons of steel, and 1.3 million more long tons of pig iron. In 1870 Britain had produced 31.8 percent of the world's manufactured goods; America 23.3 percent. By 1885, the United States led the world with 28.9 percent, Britain was second with 26.6 percent, and Germany third with 13.9 percent.

While population, industry, and agriculture were growing at a record rate, the world's monetary supply, hinged to the amount of gold in existence, expanded slowly. The consequent deflation * brought on savage labor struggles and agricultural upheavals. In fact, since prices were dropping faster than wages, the last four decades of the nineteenth century were producing an unparalleled *increase* in *real wages* (income evaluated according to purchasing power). Between 1860 and 1900 real wages appreciated more than 80 percent. But this was too complex for the comprehension of American farmers and workers, who were seeing less money come their way. (Income in *current wages* declined by a third between 1873 and 1896.) Farmers wanted agricultural prices to *increase,* and workers wanted more *cash* in their pockets. Damning gold and bankers, they demanded the remonetization of silver.

In 1889–1890 six new Western states, all of them intent on promoting their mining industries, were admitted to the Union. Suddenly, the thirty senators from west of the Mississippi † held the balance of power. The promotion of silver linked miners' interests with those of Homesteaders and Liberal Republicans. Followers of Henry George, Free-Silverites, small farmers, antibankers, and antimonopolists were coming together in a new coalition. Demanding a graduated income tax and the nationalization of the telephone, telegraph, and railroad industries, the People's party, or Populists, burst upon the consciousness of the nation.

To McMillan and his associates, events could not have been more disheartening had the plagues of Egypt befallen the regular Republicans. Reacting to the increasing competition and declining profits, railroads were establishing "pools" to divide business and raise rates. Industrialists were forming "trusts." (The most notable was the Standard Oil Company trust organized between 1879 and 1882. It controlled 90 percent of the oil business.) But, as the American public became fed up with the high-handed operations of railroads and industry, Congress in 1887 outlawed pools and established the Interstate Commerce Commission. In 1890 the Sherman Anti-Trust Act was passed. In Washington's School of Philosophy Club, founded by McMillan and other conservative Republican senators, discussions swirled long into the night about what could be done to counter the antibusiness sentiment, and the growing voting strength of farmers and laborers.

Support grew for a major increase in the tariff to make European industrial goods less competitive in the American market. British and German railroad-equipment manufacturers presented a greater threat to McMillan's Michigan Car Company than the Peninsula Car Company in Detroit. But the tariff bill introduced by Representative William McKinley stood little chance of passage unless it could attract Western and Southern support—and as exporters of agricultural products and purchasers of manufactured goods the West and the South traditionally were opposed to high tariffs.

In the South, however, there were signs of change. Textile mills were being

---

* In simplified terms, what happened was that where previously one pair of shoes had been manufactured per dollar of money, now two pairs of shoes were manufactured for each dollar of money. So that for both pairs to be sold (disregarding the further complicating factor of the *velocity* of money) the price had to drop to fifty cents a pair.

† Not including the senators from the *Southern* states of Louisiana, Texas, and Arkansas.

erected. Discoveries of coal and iron deposits in Tennessee and Alabama were creating a steel industry centered on the new city of Birmingham. In 1889, Andrew Carnegie led a party of businessmen and bankers south to investigate opportunities for large-scale Northern investment in Southern industry.

Ever since the Hayes-Tilden Compromise of 1876 and the withdrawal of Federal troops, Southerners had been chipping away at Negro rights. As Negroes were disenfranchised, Republican alarm had grown. In 1890, Representative Henry Cabot Lodge of Massachusetts authored a Force Bill, authorizing the introduction of Federal registrars into districts where there was a concerted attempt to deprive citizens of the ballot. On June 19 the bill was passed by the House of Representatives.

To the planter oligarchy, the Force Bill was as great a threat as the Federal troops of Reconstruction. Small farmers, both white and black, were flocking to the Populist movement. If they were to vote according to their pocketbooks instead of their skin colors, they might overthrow the Bourbon hegemony.

But might the Force Bill facilitate the registration not only of Negroes in the South, but of workers and foreign-born in the cities of the North? That question animated discussions in the School of Philosophy Club, which frequently met at Senator McMillan's Washington residence. For a quarter century virtually every one of the club's members had been a supporter of Negro voting rights in the South. But the support had not achieved the ends toward which it had been intended, the establishment of a strong Republican presence in the South. There was, therefore, little politically to be gained by the support of the Force Bill. There was, on the other hand, a danger of considerable loss. McMillan was well aware Pingree's power was growing and his own being undercut by the expansion of the electorate. Pennsylvania's two senators were sensitive to the problems Andrew Carnegie and Henry Frick were having with labor in their coal mines and steelworks.* Other members of the School of Philosophy Club had comparable considerations.

The Western senators needed Northern and Southern support for the remonetization of silver. The Railroad-industrial Republicans needed Western and Southern support for the passage of the McKinley tariff. The Southerners needed Northern support to kill the Force Bill.

On July 14, 1890, the Sherman Silver Purchase Act was passed.

On October 1, the tariff was enacted.

The Force Bill was not heard of again.

While the passage of the first two measures had the more immediate impact on American history, it was the death of the Force Bill that had the greatest long-range effect—an effect that McMillan and his fellow School of Philosophy Clubbers never considered or bargained for.

The demise of the bill signaled to the South that the way was clear for the disenfranchisement of the Negro. Beginning with the Mississippi constitutional convention of 1890, one Southern state after another all but deprived Negroes of the vote. Negroes had no way to inhibit the enactment of the Jim Crow laws—laws that were at first ridiculed by many Southerners themselves, but were to reach full flower during the Wilson Administration, when Washington and the Federal government became as segregated as the South. In the segre-

---

* Especially at Homestead, where a labor-management confrontation was soon to erupt into a bloody war.

gated school system, the bulk of the inadequate appropriations was pumped into the white schools. Negro schools were left to atrophy.

(Not surprisingly, the movement to deprive the poor, the minorities, and the "radicals" of the vote spread from the South to the North. After Louisiana enacted the "grandfather clause"—exempting anyone whose ancestors had voted before 1867 from the literacy tests designed to disenfranchise Negroes —a number of prominent Republicans suggested that Northern states adopt the clause to disenfranchise immigrants.)

Despite the fact that he was abandoning the masses of Negroes in the South, McMillan retained the support of Detroit's 3,500 blacks. Generally prospering, they regarded the immigrants with disdain and certainly would never have aligned themselves with the Democrats. Robert Pelham, putting to use the skills he had learned as a free Negro in the South, had become one of Detroit's better known contractors and builders. One of the first families in the city to have a telephone—a clear sign of status—the Pelhams were members of Detroit's Black Society, which included seven attorneys, six physicians, three contractors, two bank managers, and numerous college graduates. Participating in politics, they elected their first city councilman in 1882.

Of Robert Pelham's seven children, one became a teacher, one a high school principal, one a seamstress, one the wife of a law school graduate who was elected to the legislature, one an editor, one a civil engineer, and one, Benjamin, the founder and publisher of *The Plaindealer,* the city's first Negro newspaper. "Webster's unabridged dictionary does not contain words strong enough to express the hatred we bear against the southern democracy," Benjamin Pelham wrote. An advocate of *black power,* he lamented: "We are strong in numbers, but the trouble is, the majority of our people are too weak in spirit." [1]

After a decade of publication, *The Plaindealer* became one of the many casualties of the Panic of 1893. The next year McMillan asked Pelham to campaign for Alex McLeod, his candidate for Wayne County treasurer. When McLeod won, the thirty-two-year-old Pelham was appointed a junior clerk in the treasurer's office. It was the beginning of one of the more remarkable political careers in Detroit's history.

22

An Electric Beginning

LIKE THE CAREER OF PELHAM, THAT OF ANOTHER DETROITER IN HIS EARLY thirties was just beginning to take shape.

For three years after 1888 Henry Ford worked on the forty acres at Dearborn. Cutting down the trees that still covered most of the acreage, he built a nine-hundred-square-foot house for his bride. With his steam engine he sawed both his own and his neighbors' timber. He seemed, however, little interested in farming. As the city spread outward, the distance between it and the farms of the Ford family was shrinking. (Two of Henry's brothers, John and Will, had a milk route in the city.) In September, 1891, Henry Ford learned that the Edison Company was looking for an engineer. To Clara's dismay, he applied for the job.

The forty-five dollars a month that was offered him was considerably more than he had been earning in Dearborn. Moving his family into the city, he went to work as night engineer at the new "substation." Since the service area of the Edison direct-current system was limited to within less than two miles of the power source, the substation was actually an independent unit erected in response to the demand of the affluent Woodward Aveune residential district.

Within two years Ford was raised to the station's chief engineer. Teaching a class at the YMCA machine shop, he had as a pupil a brilliant seventeen-year-old, Oliver Barthel. Barthel was employed by a young engineer, Charles B. King, whose workshop was located above the Lauer machine shop on St. Antoine Street. Five years younger than Ford, King was a developer of railroad equipment. Through Barthel, or while having parts for Edison machined at the Lauer shop, Ford met King.

When King attended the Chicago World's Fair in 1893, he was struck by the lack of automobile exhibits. It was twenty-five years since Siegfried Marcus, a German Jew, had begun experimenting in Vienna with carriages propelled by

110

gas-combustion engines.* It was eight years since a German engineer, Gottlieb Daimler, had mounted a one-cylinder internal combustion engine on a bicycle, and another German, Karl Benz, had mated an engine to a tricycle. By the early 1890's, two Frenchmen, Armand Peugeot and Emile Levassor, were the leading automobile developers in the world. (Levassor, who placed a vertical engine in the front of the vehicle so as to counterbalance the weight of the passengers, evolved the basic design of the modern automobile.) France's excellent system of roads, constructed under the two Napoleons, provided a stimulant for experimentation.

In the United States, on the other hand, where the emphasis was still on railroad construction, there was little public interest. (Similarly, the British, with their long experience in building steam engines and their land reticulated by rails, lagged in internal combustion and automobile technology). Obtaining the American rights to Daimler, William Steinway was unable to strike a responsive chord with any of the financiers he approached for support, and went back to making pianos.

It was left to a number of the readers of *The Scientific American,* which carried extensive articles on the European development of motor carriages, to become excited about building automobiles. On September 21, 1893, two young bicycle mechanics, Charles and Frank Duryea, took to the streets of Springfield, Massachusetts, in a vehicle modeled on Benz's.

Returning from the fair, King was stimulated by the feat of the Duryeas. Assisted by Oliver Barthel, he set to work building an automobile.†

Ford, who previously had given no indication of an inventive mind, caught the fever. In December, 1893, he was promoted to chief engineer—at a salary of one hundred dollars a month—at the main Edison plant on Washington Street. On the fifteenth of the month he moved his wife and his newborn son, Edsel, into one half of a small two-story brownstone duplex three blocks from the plant. It was an important move. For the house was one of fewer than four thousand in the city wired for electricity.

Late in the evening of the ninth day in his new home, Ford brought a primitive, toylike engine into the kitchen. Its cylinder consisted of a one-inch diameter gas pipe fitted with a piston and connected to a flywheel made from an old lathe. It was Christmas Eve, and as Clara bustled about preparing dinner for a host of relatives expected the next day, Henry clamped the engine to the sink. Since the house was on direct current, he was able to split the electric wire and use it to provide a spark. Beckoning to Clara, he had her drip gasoline into the cylinder from a can. As he spun the flywheel, the engine exploded into life. Spurting flame, popping wildly, filling the house with smoke and fumes, it shook the sink and brought coughing protestations from Clara.

Henry was elated. It was a beginning.

---

* Marcus had exhibited a vehicle at the Exposition of 1873, and road-tested an improved version in 1875. But he lacked capital to develop the machine. The authorities opposed its operation on the roads. Discouraged, he consigned it to a museum.
† Barthel had been born in Detroit, but was educated in Germany, where his father was an agent for the Michigan Stove Company. Fluent in German, Barthel was able to keep abreast of developments in German automobile technology.

23

Pingree's Progress

As a member of the middle class and a technician in an expanding industry, Ford was insulated from the economic crisis that was clamping an icy grip on the city. Ragged men and women huddled in doorways, and hungry, hollow-eyed children begged from door to door. Once more, the villain was gold. In 1889, reaction had set in to the wild and uncontrolled expansion of the railroads and other capital projects throughout the world. Money became scarcer. The French Panama Canal Company had folded. Amidst sordid scandals, that staunch backer of American railroads, Baring Bros., had gone under. The rise of the Populist party shook the confidence of investors in the future of American capitalism.

The wealthy hoarded their gold. The Treasury's stock of gold fell below the legal minimum. Six hundred banks closed their doors. In July, 1893, the Erie Railroad went into bankruptcy, to be followed by 155 other railroads, including the Northern Pacific and the Union Pacific. One fifth of the total American railroad mileage went into receivership.

The effect on Detroit was catastrophic. One after another, the railroad-equipment manufacturers, the stove works, the shipbuilders—all the heavy industries—either shut down or continued operations with only skeleton crews. By winter more than twenty-five thousand men, one third of the work force, were unemployed. Most affected were the unskilled foreign-born, the last to be hired and the first to be fired. Foreigners, half of them recently arrived Poles and Germans, made up 85 percent of the relief rolls. Of the city's ninety thousand foreign-born, twenty-four thousand were thrust upon the Poor Commission, which was totally unprepared to cope with an emergency of such magnitude. Private charitable organizations were geared to aid a small number of families for a few days, not an entire population for weeks and months. Yet beyond those receiving aid there were many, speaking little or no English, who had no knowledge of what help was available or where to go to apply for it. Outcasts in the city, five thousand families starved and froze in unheated rooms, in cellars, in back-alley sheds, and on the streets themselves.

Anathematizing the McMillans and their associates as "bloodsuckers," Mayor

Pingree pointed his finger at the Michigan Car Company for paying wages "barely enough to keep body and soul together," and then jettisoning five thousand men onto the charity of the community. Every year, he complained, the railroad-equipment manufacturers and machine shops were cheating the city of some $5 to $6 million in taxes. The railroads owned property valued at $35 million, yet were paying nothing for municipal services.

Like private businesses, the city was hard pressed for cash. Unable to sell its bonds, its tax revenues dropping, the municipal government discharged nearly half its workers and reduced the pay of the remainder.

While Detroit's millionaires warmed themselves by their fires and contributed parsimoniously to charity, the mayor dispatched teams of house-to-house surveyors to search out the needy. For the unemployed, he initiated a large-scale program of public works. Gangs of men were put to work on the streets. Others were assigned to improvement projects that, ultimately, turned Belle Isle into one of America's most beautiful parks.

Without money, the people of the cities were unable to buy the produce of the farms. As prices plummeted, farmers lost money on every ear of corn or kernel of wheat they shipped. While children were crying with hunger in the cities, farmers burned their crops in the fields.

The failure of the economy to improve in the spring of 1894 caused Pingree's thoughts to turn to the winter ahead. If people had no money with which to buy food, they would have to grow their own. The mayor appealed to landowners to make available plots of land on which the unemployed could raise vegetables. In response, fewer than 500 acres were donated. Only 945 of the more than 3,000 families who applied for the half-acre plots could be accommodated.

For money to buy tools and seed, Pingree appealed to the churches. The total collected came to $13.80. "Pingree's potato patches" were the laughingstock of the well fed, well clothed, and well housed. The mayor responded by auctioning off his prize horse to obtain the seed money, a dramatic gesture that reduced the ridicule. In the autumn the truck gardens produce a harvest of beans, corn, squash, cabbages, carrots, and potatoes.

But, so far as the needs of the unemployed and, more generally, the American people were concerned, the measures were as effective as blowing the nose of a man whose lungs are full of water. As Pingree tried to spread the inadequate resources over the immense needs, the drowning fought each other and the city. A mob nearly lynched an inspector for the Poor Commission in front of the city hall.

The Poles were constant troublemakers. They rioted and repeatedly threatened the Italians who, they charged, were unfairly taking work from Polish family men who had up to a dozen children to feed.

The Italians were bearing the brunt of a wave of anti-immigrant feeling. Every increase in the size and density of the cities brought an increase in crime. Between 1880 and 1898 the number of homicides recorded annually more than sextupled: from 1,266 to 7,840.[1] And with every increase in homicides, the murders committed by the southern Italians stood out. Like Chinese and Mexicans, whose tendency toward violence was even more pronounced, the Italians came from a rural land where the police were few and not to be trusted.* The settling of their own quarrels was not only a matter of custom but a question of honor. The Irish-

* The Italian homicide rate was nearly ten times the English. Murders and robberies were five times as frequent in agricultural southern Italy as in the industrializing north.[2]

American police, whose grandfathers had lain in the brambles to cut the throats of the hated constables, and whose fathers had rioted through the streets of American cities, looked upon them as bloody barbarians.*

The importation of ethnic antagonism from Europe enabled employers not only to play off the Negro against the foreign-born, and the foreign-born against the white native American, but the French against the German, the German against the Irish, the Irish against the Pole, and the Pole against the Italian. There was little intermingling among the first generation of ethnic groups. Detroit had Corktown (Irish) on the west, Dutchtown (Dutch and German) along Gratiot Avenue on the east, Sauerkraut Row (German) along Grand Boulevard, and Kentucky (Negro) and Polacktown adjacent to each other on the east. Even as the French Catholics had looked down upon the Irish, so now to the Irish bishop the fourteen thousand Poles represented a "church commenced in rebellion and continued in rebellion." The *Michigan Catholic* chided the "howling Poles." [3] Throughout the country native Americans, children of immigrants, and even the immigrants themselves were demanding an end to immigration and the influx of new workers. The people of Michigan voted four to one to end the practice of allowing aliens to vote in state and local elections. In 1892 the platforms of both parties contained anti-immigrant planks.†

With the depression, the anti-Catholic American Protective Association, a reincarnation of the Supreme Order of the Star Spangled Banner, blossomed into an organization of a million members. Antibanker as well as anti-immigrant, its power was centered in a Midwestern band running from the industrial districts of northern Ohio and eastern Michigan to the plains of Kansas and Nebraska. Purchasing arms, electing candidates, forging inflammatory documents, it published magazines like *The Menace* and *The Rail Splitter* to expose purported Catholic plots to take over the United States and burn "heretics." In 1894 the organization helped stimulate the march on Washington by "General of the Commonwealth of Christ" Jacob Coxey and his "army" of a few hundred farmers, unemployed, and mentally unbalanced.

Malnutrition weakened the poor's resistance to disease, and so brought epidemics. In Detroit diphtheria was followed by smallpox. In the charnelhouses that went by the name of "hospitals," the sick were bundled into beds with the dying, and the dying were left to lie next to the dead. Wielding shotguns behind barred doors, people refused to allow sick family members to be removed by the quarantine teams. Gravediggers with gauze wrapped mummylike around their faces wore ankle-length rubber coats and fishermen's helmets as they knocked on marked doors and carted off the dead.

Without the potato patches, the toll would have been higher. Throughout the United States, Pingree was the hero of the reformers and of the new crop of social workers who were establishing settlement houses in the slums. For all the agonizing that had been done over corruption, slums, and boss control of the cities, Pingree was the first to "put the cusses on record." Everywhere his potato patches were imitated. Innumerable stories were written about his new, *Progressive* Republicanism. From Boston to Seattle citizens called out for "Pingrees" of their own.

---

* When, in 1891, the police chief of New Orleans was murdered, a mob reacted by lynching eleven Sicilians and Italians. A protest by the Italian government brought the haughty rejoinder from Secretary of State Blaine: "It is a matter of indifference what persons in Italy think of our institutions. I cannot change them, still less violate them." [4] It was a rejoinder that led Italy to break off diplomatic relations with the United States.
† The Chinese had been excluded by law from the United States in 1882.

In the jungle of urban politics, the mayor had become a wily hunter. If alder-men could be bribed, he was not averse to bribing them himself. Outraged to discover once that he had been outbribed, he stormed into the council chamber and yelled:

"Al Diemel, you are so damn crooked you don't even stay bought!"

Nowhere was corruption more prevalent than on the school board. Elected by the same system and through the same organization as the aldermen, the in-spectors like the aldermen were commonly half literate. Bribed by book agents, school-furniture salesmen, and contractors, they frittered away the inadequate school funds. Handpicking teachers and obtaining kickbacks, they demoralized the system.

Under attack from several directions, the schools were severely affected by the drop in revenue resulting from the depression. Salaries were reduced. Al-though the pupil-teacher ratio was still approximately fifty to one, twenty-five teachers were dismissed. Conservatives demanded an end to *modern* methods which, corrupting youth, were responsible for juvenile crime, and called for a return to the four "r's": reading, 'riting, 'rithmetic, and the rod.

When the old Capitol High School burned in 1893, and plans were drawn to replace it with the most modern school building in America, a surge of resistance swelled up from workers and immigrants. Since the school was populated almost exclusively by the children of the well-to-do, the suggestion was made that the city of more than a quarter million population could do without a high school. Lower-class parents charged that their children were being sacrificed to academic education and not being properly prepared for "the world of work."

With his New England respect for the public schools, Pingree tackled the task of throwing out the "cusses." Bursting into a meeting of the Board of Education, he announced: "You are a bunch of thieves, grafters, and rascals! As your names are called, the police will take you into custody!" [5]

Pingree's proposal for a municipal lighting plant was fought by all of the competing companies, including Detroit Edison. Both sides employed well-known tactics. Appearing in the council chamber, Pingree waved two hundred dollars in bills with which, he charged, the manager of the Detroit Electric Light and Power Company had bribed one of the aldermen. That bit of drama, as much as a study showing municipal lighting would reduce charges in half, ultimately carried the day. In 1893 voters approved the municipal power plant by a ratio of fourteen to one.*

Shortly afterward, William Maybury walked into the mayor's office. In his middle forties, heavy-set, thick-moustached, he was the son of Thomas Maybury, in whose parlor Henry Ford's parents had been married. A member of a firm of prominent attorneys, he was a popular, baby-kissing Democratic politician who had been city attorney in 1876 and had served in Congress from 1883 to 1888. To Mayor Pingree, Maybury suggested that he had just the right man for the superintendency of the new city power plant: Henry Ford.

Pingree, however, was not taken with Ford's managerial capability. He was more impressed by a thirty-one-year-old Scotsman, Alex Dow, who had received his education in the British electrical industry, and seemed better able to protect the city's interests than the apolitical, slow-speaking, self-conscious Ford.

---

* Although he fought a nation-focusing battle for lower fares, the mayor had less success in obtaining municipal control of the streetcar system. A "thirty years' war" for public ownership was only beginning.

24

The Olds-Powered Ford Cadillac

HAD FORD OBTAINED THE POSITION, IT IS DOUBTFUL HE WOULD HAVE HAD TIME to continue working on his car. In later days, as writers wondered when a man working a twelve-hour shift had opportunity to construct an automobile, the myth arose that Ford, abjuring sleep, displayed heroic endurance in his single-minded dedication. In fact, the demand for electric power was such as to require attention to the machinery only between 6 P.M. and 8 P.M. The rest of the time the company was trying to bring about an increase in consumption. While the machinery idled, there was little for the engineer to do. He could putter about to his heart's content in a basement room next to the station, or even return to the workshed in the back of his house from which he could be recalled in two minutes. If he had happened to work late the previous night, there was opportunity for him to nap during the day. Making his way to St. Antoine Street, he could compare notes and progress with Charles King.

King, a brilliant inventor and the son of a Union general, had entree to Detroit's Jefferson and Woodward Avenue society. Henry B. Joy and Truman Newberry, the sons of James Joy and John Newberry, were business associates of King and liked to drop by his shop.* Ford probably met both of them there. Although neither King nor Ford suffered personally during the anxious days of depression and epidemic, the uncertainty of the times and the lack of capital slowed their work. (In 1893 King had been asked by James W. Packard, an Ohio electrical manufacturer, to build an internal combustion engine with which to power a vehicle. But the depression had killed the project.) King, better prepared than Ford to plunge ahead, was pulled into the orbit of his friends and, with them, spent time and money making the nineties gay. (As so many times before and since, the perspective of an era depended upon who wrote its history.) For both King and Ford, the building of the cars was an avocation, not an occupation.

Not until March 6, 1896, did King, with Ford following behind on his bicycle, take to the streets at eight miles per hour in his motorized carriage. That

---

* Joy and Newberry were brothers-in-law. James Joy, his life spanning most of the nineteenth century, had died in 1896.

116

was nearly two years after Elwood Haynes, the superintendent of the Indiana Natural Gas and Oil Company, had completed a workable car. It was one year after Hiram P. Maxim, a graduate of MIT, had duplicated Benz's feat of motorizing a tricycle.

Close on the heels of King came Ford. His $1,900-a-year salary gave him a comfortable surplus over his living expenses. (His rent was $16 a month.) He drew freely on the expertise of King, Barthel, and a number of others. Between 2 A.M. and 4 A.M. on June 4 he tightened the last nut on the *quadricycle,* with its two-cylinder engine. As he looked about, ready to wheel the vehicle from the shed, he was struck by a minor problem.

The shed's single door was too narrow for the vehicle.

So Ford broke out one side of the shed. In the predawn drizzle, he was soon pop-popping down the street. In front of the Cadillac Hotel a group of night owls gaped as his explosive apparition loomed out of the mist.

Technically, Ford's vehicle was inferior to those of the French automobile pioneers and of the Duryea brothers. But, capable of attaining a speed of twenty miles per hour, it was an improvement over King's.

Proudly Ford, with King accompanying him, drove the quadricycle the nine miles to Dearborn. As he brought it to a halt in front of the open kitchen door, neighbors came running across the fields. William Ford, tall, dignified, justice of the peace and church warden, stepped out to look at the pony-sized, five-hundred-pound machine. He shook his head. How could a grown man waste his time building toys? Laughing and ridiculing the quadricycle, the neighbors sympathized with him.

Crushed, Henry turned to King. "Come on, Charley," he said. "Let's get out of here." [1]

That was not his only disappointment of the summer.

Affected by the depression, the Edison Company was not doing well. A rate war during 1894–1895 had resulted in the defaulting of the competing Peninsular Company. But, with electricity costing 50 percent more than gas, there were still nearly four times as many families lighting with gas as with electricity. Two thirds of the homes in the city had neither.

The directors cast about for a new manager. Ford applied. But when the new manager was installed on July 1, who should it be be but Dow! In the final reckoning what counted was not his association with Pingree, but the fact that he had gotten the municipal power plant off to a resounding start.

Once more Ford was saved from attaining a position that would have absorbed all of his time.

The next month he and Dow went east for the annual convention of the Association of Edison Illuminating Companies.* Pointing out Ford at the ban-

---

* Edison, not inclined toward business management, interested himself less and less in the operation of the Edison General Electric Company. Returning to work on the gramophone, he patented an entirely new invention, the kinetoscope, in 1891. At Menlo Park he built the world's first motion picture studio, and began filming ninety-second shorts starring celebrities like Buffalo Bill and Gentleman Jim Corbett. Beginning April 14, 1894, crowds were strung along New York City's Broadway night and day in front of the "kinetoscope parlor."

General Electric was the brainchild of Henry Villard, a German-American railroad capitalist, who envisioned it as the first step toward a worldwide electrical monopoly. Backed by the Deutsche Bank of Berlin and J. P. Morgan, he merged G. E. with Thomson-Houston (which had acquired, among others, the 249 patents issued to Van Depoele), leaving only Westinghouse as a major competitor in the United States.

quet, Dow jokingly asked Edison what he thought of a man in the electrical field who wasted his time building a gasoline-powered buggy. Somewhat to Dow's surprise, Edison displayed an intense interest. In the East, except for the Duryeas, automobile experimentation was centered on steam- and electric-powered vehicles. His experience with storage batteries had convinced Edison that electric vehicles were impractical. He questioned Ford closely.

"That's the thing!" he exclaimed. "Keep at it!"

Privately he noted: "Damn fool." [2] Given Ford's nature, and his record of building an automobile in a shed without egress, the comments were not mutually exclusive.

Detroit's other automobile pioneer, Charles King, was trying to convince his friends Joy and Newberry that they should back him in an enterprise to manufacture automobiles. They, however, looked upon his vehicle as an amusing but commercially impractical gadget. Since the country had not yet fully recovered from the Panic of 1893, and the wealthy were casting fearful glances at the rising Populist tide, it was not a good time to be seeking venture capital.

As huge yields depressed prices, small farmers were losing their struggle to keep pace with the gains in productivity of Big Agriculture and Big Industry. Nine out of ten of the late-arriving homesteaders on the marginal lands of western Kansas and Nebraska were abandoning their farms. In four years banks foreclosed on eleven thousand Kansas farms. Under pressure to open up the better of the remaining Indian lands, the Federal government set off the 1889 Oklahoma stampede.

Throughout the West, breaking treaty after solemn treaty, the government confiscated 50 million acres on reservations, and left the Indians with 2 million acres, mostly of parchland and desert. But the despoliation of the Indian brought little relief from the inexorable laws of economics.

In the South, where there had been 700,000 farmers in 1860, there were 1,800,000 in 1890. Whether in the South or in the West, whether sharecroppers or owners of their land, they were in a running battle to escape debt and poverty. Flocking to the banner of the Populist party, they enabled it to capture control of the Democratic convention and nominate William Jennings Bryan. A Fundamentalist spellbinder, he denounced the "conspiracy of international bankers," and orated that "you shall not crucify mankind upon a cross of gold."

Not since the 1870's had the image of the Republican party been more tarnished. The shooting of workers during the 1892 Homestead strike in Pennsylvania and the 1894 Pullman strike in Chicago had alienated labor. Quiet and colorless, William McKinley, who won the Republican nomination on his third try, paled even more before the flamboyant Bryan. With every indication of a Bryan victory in Michigan as well as nationally, Senator McMillan directed his attention to salvaging the state's Republican party from the debacle.

In 1892 McMillan had blocked Pingree's nomination for governor. Since then he had directed the legislature in decreasing Detroit's powers of "home rule" further. With his friends he had used every device at his command to bring the mayor to heel. They had requested him to resign his bank directorship. They had attempted to restrict his credit. They had initiated whispering campaigns against him. They had advised businessmen it would be imprudent either to sell to or to buy from Pingree and Smith.

Finally, in desperation, they had taken away his pew in the Woodward Avenue Baptist Church.

Pingree espoused all of the *progressive* causes—the state regulation of public utilities and transportation, the graduated income tax, the abolition of child labor, the direct and open primary, and the direct election of senators. He was scarcely less abhorrent to the regular Republicans than Bryan.

However, elected four times to the office of mayor and immensely popular, he could undoubtedly carry Detroit and Michigan. He was a politician of national stature, and his presence on the ticket would enhance the image of the party everywhere. So the Republicans nominated Pingree for governor.

The 1896 campaign proved to be a harbinger of twentieth-century politics. Bryan whistle-stopped across the country. Traveling eighteen thousand miles and making more than six hundred speeches, he was the first nominee to take the campaign directly to the people. McKinley, meanwhile, sat at home, and let his multimillionaire manager, Marc Hanna, levy an assessment of ¼ of 1 percent on the assets of frightened big businessmen and bankers. Spending between $7 million and $16 million—probably more than the Republicans had expended in all previous campaigns combined—Hanna exploited the national literacy and the improvement in lighting that was responsible for the world's greatest publication boom. For the first time working people could go home at night, and *read!* Magazines and dime novels were created for the new public. More than half the world's newspapers were being published in America!* Hanna ordered the printing of one hundred twenty million pamphlets in every immigrant language. Eight thousand speakers were sent out with the message that to elect Bryan would be to turn the country over to wild-eyed radicals and Socialists. Workers were warned to support McKinley. At Steinway they were told:

"Men, vote as you please, but if Bryan is elected tomorrow the whistle will not blow Wednesday morning." [3]

Even so, it was barely enough. The Democrats took four hundred more counties than the Republicans. A shift of 50,000 votes in key states would have swung the election to Bryan.

Pingree was swept into the governorship by more than 84,000 votes. He announced that, since he had been elected both governor and mayor, he intended to serve as both governor and mayor. When his consternated opponent challenged him, and the state's supreme court ruled that he would have to give up one office or the other, he had a salty Great Lakes ship captain run for mayor as a stand-in. Campaigning on the platform, "If I'm elected, I will do just what the governor tells me to do," he was defeated by his Democratic opponent by 248 votes.[4]

Into Pingree's former office in the city hall moved William Maybury.

Twenty-five years earlier Siegfried Marcus had had his car banned from the streets of Vienna. Mayor Maybury not only gave Henry Ford a special permit

* James E. Scripps, the scion of a British newspaper family, had initiated a new newspaper era when he had founded the Detroit *News* in 1873. In contrast to other papers, it was not controlled by either the Democrats or Republicans, and directed itself at a mass audience. Selling for two cents, it thrived on exposés and scandals. Within a year it had twice the circulation of any of its competitors. Out of it grew the world's first newspaper chain.

to drive on the streets of Detroit, but talked him up at every opportunity. Ford, who had sold his first car for two hundred dollars, was working on a new machine. Maybury and three other prominent Detroiters agreed to put up five hundred dollars each to back him. While King, with his friends Joy and Newberry,* joined the navy and went adventuring in Cuba upon the outbreak of the Spanish-American War, Ford at a critical time was left as the leading automobile developer in Detroit.

William Murphy, son of the former Maine lumberman who was one of the principal investors in the Edison Illuminating Company, naturally was acquainted with the company's chief engineer. An automobile buff, he told Ford that when he had a vehicle that could travel to Farmington, Pontiac, and back —a triangular course of some sixty miles—he would be interested in forming a company.

One Saturday afternoon in July of 1899 the two men set out, and completed the journey in Ford's new car.

In the meantime, the Edison Illuminating Company was following the grand strategy plotted by General Electric and engaging in a policy of driving its competitors into bankruptcy.† Thus paving the way for expansion, Dow took Ford aside and offered him the general superintendency, the second-ranking position in the company. That would mean, however, in view of the demands on his time, that he would have to give up his automobile building.

Having twice before been saved from an executive career in the electrical industry, Ford was now boosted out of it by the revitalized economy. A score of the city's investing fraternity, including Murphy, Mayor Maybury, and William C. McMillan (the son of James), put up fifteen thousand dollars to incorporate the Detroit Automobile Company. In August, 1899, Ford went to work full time constructing a car. Throughout the United States the financial euphoria was resulting in similar backing for other pioneers.‡

Leadership in building internal-combustion-powered automobiles meanwhile passed from the Duryea brothers to Alexander Winton. A Scotsman trained as a marine engineer, Winton was the proprietor of a bicycle business in Cleveland, Ohio. In 1895 he mounted an engine on a bike. During the next year he constructed a *dos-a-dos,* which had one seat facing to the front and the other to the rear. The next summer he drove from Cleveland to New York in ten days: the first long-distance automobile trip on record. Soon he held the speed record as well. Getting into production in 1898, he sold the cars for one thousand dollars, realizing a profit of four hundred dollars on each.

* The Secretary of War was Russell Alger, Railroad Republican, former governor of Michigan, and intimate of the Joy, Newberry, and McMillan families. Although he bungled the conduct of the war—the troops were fed "embalmed beef" and outfitted in woolen winter uniforms for the campaign in the tropics—he saw to it that the three young men received appointments on the cruiser *Yosemite.*
† The Peninsular Company was acquired at auction in 1898. The next year the Detroit Electric Light and Power Company went into receivership. The only "competitor" remaining was the small East Side Electric Company. Operating from a shed in back of clothing merchant Abraham Jacobs's store, it supplied the Jewish business district along Gratiot Avenue.
‡ In Lansing, Ransom E. Olds had taken over his father's machine and motor shop in 1890. He built a steam-powered vehicle that he sold to a maharaja, and then, in 1895, constructed his first gasoline-motored buggy. He now found a backer in Samuel L. Smith. Smith was a lumberman and stockholder in the Calumet and Hecla copper mine, the richest in the world. As the mining company's stock appreciated from $1 to $1,000, Smith became a multimillionaire. He agreed to back Olds with $200,000. Moving to Detroit, Olds—continuing for the time being to build engines for a variety of purposes—was starting to make cars even as Ford's company was being organized.

Ford was devoting most of his time to fashioning a racer. Playing a leading role in designing the engine was young Oliver Barthel. (During his lifetime, Barthel designed eighty-five different internal combustion engines.) It took more than a year to prepare a machine for the "big car" event that was to crown a day of racing at the Grosse Pointe track on October 1, 1901. When the other contestants dropped out, Ford was matched head-to-head against Winton. Averaging forty miles per hour, he passed Winton, the holder of the record for the mile, at the eight-mile mark of the ten-mile course. Emerging from the car as if he had been dipped in oil, Ford was the city's hero of the moment.

Since there was division among his backers between those who were encouraged by the victory and those who were discouraged by its messiness, the Detroit Automobile Company was reorganized as the Henry Ford Motor Company. It was the impression of Murphy and the remaining backers that Ford would now produce a commercial auto. Cars were open, fair-weather conveyances whose engines froze in cold weather and whose wheels lacked the traction to negotiate mud and snow. The selling season began in spring. Ford, therefore, had all winter to put together a salable machine.

But nothing in Ford's background had prepared him for this role. An excellent and often ingenious mechanic, he floundered when it came to organizing his thoughts. Faced with a deadline, he puttered about devising means of improving the racer. Incubating innovations for a commercial car, he had difficulty translating his ideas into reality. Lacking technical training, he was dependent on time-consuming "cut and try" methods. Both Mayor Pingree and the Edison Company had rejected him as an administrator.

Aware of these judgments, Murphy, seeing no motor carriage being spruced up as spring approached, was increasingly disturbed. As he talked about the problems, he found an apt listener in Henry M. Leland, a Woodward Avenue neighbor and fellow member of the Presbyterian Church.

In his late fifties, Leland had been born in the rugged hills of Vermont. Able to sustain only small families and a limited number of people, this beautiful country had been cast by industrialization and Western large-scale farming into the same kind of depression as Cornwall and other rural, isolated parts of Europe. The trapped inhabitants turned the valleys into chasms of illegitimacy, incest, idiocy, and drunkenness. Ministers lamented that "people are degenerates." [5] Leland's father, like countless of his neighbors, abandoned the farm and moved his wife and children to Massachusetts. Since the unskilled job he found in a gristmill did not pay nearly enough for him to support his family, everyone was forced to go to work.

What distinguished Henry Leland from Alfred Lentick and Adam Jansen was that, by the time he went to work at the age of eleven, he had had the benefit of New England's educational system. In some of the world's most advanced industrial plants he came under the tutorship of foremen, many of them British, who were the direct first- or second-generation descendants of the master mechanics developed by the Industrial Revolution.

Eventually becoming a foreman himself, Leland was schooled in a system that had its roots in the guild culture. The "putting-out" system that was the precursor of the capitalistic era had changed the guild master from an independent workman to a contractor who produced goods with the raw materials furnished by the merchant. With the advent of industrialization, he had moved to a central location, where the "factor" provided machinery as well as raw materials. Yet, as the master had become the foreman, he had remained an independent contractor. He hired and fired his workmen. He bid against other foremen for contracts. Since the job normally went to the lowest bidder, the system was a test not only of the foreman's efficiency, but of his adeptness in holding down wages. While the foreman might sympathize with the plight of an individual laborer, he was usually a bitter foe of unions, which he looked upon as trespassing on his prerogatives and restricting his freedom to operate competitively.

During twenty-five years in the New England arms industry, Leland became an expert in precision technology. As a journeyman and foreman at the Springfield Armory, at Colt, and at Brown and Sharpe, he gained an incomparable knowledge of machine tools, and of the methodology of quantity production. Intensely religious, he had an abhorrence of the drunkenness and immorality he had witnessed as a boy. He read much. In 1890 he was drawn to Detroit. The rapid expansion of manufacturing enterprises had brought about a shortage of machine shops, and of men with the expertise to operate them. Backed by forty thousand dollars of Robert Faulconer's lumber fortune, he established the enterprise of Leland and Faulconer.

A perfectionist, Leland soon built an international reputation. In 1899 he began manufacturing transmissions for Oldsmobile.

In 1901, fire destroyed the Olds factory. The only car to be saved was a small model with a curved dash, a long steering tiller, and racy lines. Necessity forced Olds to concentrate production on it. Roy D. Chapin, a test driver for Olds, maneuvered one of the cars over execrable cow paths and the towpath of the Erie Canal to the second annual New York auto show. The feat created a sensation. The little three-horsepower runabout, priced at an unprecedentedly low $650, suddenly was the best known car in America. Orders rose from 425 in 1901 to 3,300 in 1902. The Oldsmobile became the world's best-selling car, and the first to go into mass production.

Following the fire, the engines for the car were turned out by Leland and Faulconer, and by the Dodge brothers.

The next year Leland developed an improved ten-horsepower engine. However, a rift was developing in the Olds firm between the inventor-engineer and his financial backers. Samuel Smith and his son Fred, who was taking an increasingly active part in the management of the company, thought the runabout undignified. Millionaires, they wanted to produce a luxury model. As Olds argued with the Smiths, Leland was unable to obtain a commitment. Olds soon sold his interest for one million dollars, and turned to the production of a new car, the R.E.O.

Leland, therefore, had what Murphy needed: an engine. If Leland were to manufacture the engine, transmission, and steering mechanism, it would still be possible to get a "Fordmobile" on the market by summer. Since nearly every car being built consisted of an assembly of parts from various manufacturers, the plan was scarcely novel. But when Murphy broached it to Ford, he rejected it. Any car he made would be *his* car. On March 10, 1902, taking the plans for the new racer and a payment of nine hundred dollars with him, Ford departed.

Left with a plant and the skeleton of a car, Murphy appealed to Leland to assume control of production. Leland equipped the car that had been envisioned as the Fordmobile with the howling *one-lung* engine intended for the Oldsmobile, and rolled it out of the plant as the Cadillac.

25

The Mile-A-Minute Company

WATCHING THE WINTON-FORD RACE AT THE GROSSE POINTE TRACK HAD BEEN two of the world's foremost bicycle racers. Tom Cooper and Barney Oldfield had participated in a race against each other earlier in the day. The popularity of bike racing, however, was waning. When Ford some months later showed Cooper, who was moderately wealthy, the plans for two new racing cars, The Arrow and The 999, Cooper agreed to become the backer.

The 999 was a fearsome machine, larger than any previous American car, and a prototype of the racers to come. Ford and Cooper were so shaken by the experience of driving it that they approached Oldfield. Totally miscast as the manager of a boardinghouse, Oldfield had never driven a car. Joking that "I might as well be dead as dead broke," he jumped into the driver's seat of the vibrating machine.[1] A career was born! A year after the Ford-Winton race, Oldfield, averaging almost sixty miles per hour, choked Winton and two other competitors in The 999's exhaust.

In the meantime, just as Murphy had found a more congenial plant superintendent in *his* church, Ford was fashioning a new partnership through the Episcopal Church he attended. Scotch-born and thirty-six years old, Alexander Malcomson had bought a distressed coal yard on credit during the Panic of 1893, and ridden the wave of prosperity of the late 1890's to success. Although heavily in debt, he owned by 1902 ten coal yards, a West Virginia mine, one hundred ten wagons, and one hundred twenty horses. The possessor of a Winton, he listened interestedly as Ford described his plans for a car mounting a vertical engine instead of the standard horizontal engine. It was a design intended to reduce noise, vibration, and wear.

Once more, the triumph of a Ford racer led to the formation of a company. In November, 1902, the two men agreed to organize the Ford and Malcomson Company.

Malcomson and his limited resources were a far cry from the millionaires who had backed Ford in his previous ventures. Word had spread around the city's investing fraternity that Ford was impractical, stubborn, and a tinkerer.

In turning out cars that went faster than anybody else's, he had burned up the money of his backers, and given no indication of a business mind. Even Mayor Maybury had lost some of his enthusiasm for his protégé.* To raise money for the company that as yet existed only on paper, Malcomson directed his office manager and general factotum to start knocking on the doors of potential investors.

The office manager was thirty-year-old Jim Couzens. His English parents had migrated to Chatham, Ontario, fifty miles from Detroit, in 1870. Like many English "Independents," the elder James Couzens, a Presbyterian, was educated but poor. Foreseeing little future clerking in England, he had gone to work in a soap factory in Chatham.†

Taking soap ash in trade, the elder Couzens peddled hard soap from a wagon. During the depression of the 1870's, the family was so poor that every member worked and scrounged for money to buy a kerosene lantern. But, gradually, the family's economic position improved. In 1881, when his wife inherited fifteen hundred dollars from her father, Couzens opened the Chatham Steam Soap Works. Becoming an entrepreneur, he dealt in ice, coal, and cement blocks, as well as in soap.

Young Jim resented what he considered his father's menial occupation, and hated the stench of soap that enveloped the household. Stubborn, self-confident, and contemptuous of authority, he was also intelligent. At a time when only three of every one hundred youths was finishing high school, he graduated near the top of his class.

When a friend wrote of the money to be made working for the railroad, he came to Detroit. His superior education enabled him to obtain a job as a car checker in the Michigan Central Railroad yards. Working twelve hours a day, seven days a week, he made forty dollars a month. The fact that he had to walk six miles a day did not dispose him favorably toward the horsecar lines—he was a member of the mob that attacked the streetcars and dumped one of them into the river. But though he might, philosophically, be a "radical," he was the most efficient checker in the yards. At the age of twenty-one, he was promoted to boss of the freight office. Malcomson was so impressed by Couzens's handling of his coal shipments that he hired him.

Confident, his jaws set like John Bull, Couzens was not prepared for the rejection he encountered in offering the stock certificates handed him by Malcomson. Not only had Ford acquired a bad reputation, but November, 1902, saw the onset of the Rich Man's Panic. The stock market was inundated with new, speculative issues arising out of the boom and the formation of giant syndicates and trusts, and there was not enough money to go around.

Malcomson, Ford, and Couzens were thus forced to proceed with the organization of the Ford Motor Company in a patchwork fashion that would have seemed to doom it. In December, Malcomson leased a coal yard and wagon shop owned by Albert Strelow, one of the larger carpentering and painting contractors in the city. In return for fifty shares of stock, Strelow agreed to remodel his shop as an assembly plant.

* But Maybury and his law firm were, nevertheless, to be richly rewarded. They became the attorneys for Ford.
† Commercial *hard* soap was still fighting an uphill battle agisnt homemade *soft* soap, concocted out of waste fats and lye obtained by leaching hardwood ashes with water. Boiled together, the fat and lye made a nauseous jelly. Such soap could take off the top layer of skin along with the dirt, and made bathing an excruciating experience.

Two months later, in February, 1903, Ford ordered 650 chassis at $250 each from the Dodge Brothers machine shop. The Dodges had a reputation as roughhousers and brawlers harking back to frontier days.* They would pick the worst dive in town, get roaring drunk, challenge everyone to a fight, and occasionally pull revolvers and shoot up the joint. Nevertheless, they operated one of the best machine shops in the Midwest. (Horace had received part of his training at Leland and Faulconer.) After an abortive fling at manufacturing bicycles, the brothers had switched to producing engines and parts for launches and cars. According to the contract, Ford was to pay five thousand dollars on March 15, and ten thousand dollars later.

By mid-March there was no money to meet either the first or second payments. Malcomson, therefore, went to his uncle, John Gray, the president of the German-American bank. Gray, who had obtained control of the small, shirt-sleeve bank during the difficult times following the Panic of 1893, was not pleased with his nephew's operations.† But rather than let the Ford venture collapse— a failure that would have reflected on Malcomson's coal business—Gray agreed to advance ten thousand dollars in return for 105 shares of stock. Since Ford was notoriously careless about money, Couzens was installed as business manager. Over the course of the two or three months in which the car was taking shape in the plant, a variety of Malcomson's relatives and associates borrowed and scraped money together to keep the enterprise going. Malcomson's two attorneys contributed five thousand dollars each, most of it borrowed. (While making the loan, one of the bankers protested that he had never seen a worse investment.) The only "outsider" to buy stock was Charles H. Bennett, originator of the Daisy Air Rifle, who, looking for a car, had been steered to Ford.

When the company was incorporated in June, 1903, there were thirteen stockholders.‡ Gray was named president. In the meantime, Ford had been joined by a brilliant toolmaker and self-educated engineer, Childe Harold Wills. As Ford talked out his ideas, Wills translated them into designs. Thus filling the gap between concept and concretion, he reduced the time required by Ford's trial-and-error methods.

Desperate for money, Malcomson began in the spring to advertise for orders. By July 4, however, when a seemingly endless line of Oldsmobiles paraded in Lansing, not a single car had been sold. Then, on July 15, Dr. E. Pfennig of Chicago paid $850, and became the first purchaser of a Fordmobile.

Ten days later Oldfield, driving The 999, sped over a measured mile in 55⅘ seconds. Breaking the mile-a-minute mark created a sensation. Orders poured in.

As long as Ford had been left to his own devices and had had the security of millions of dollars in backing, he had resisted pressure to direct his work toward financial remuneration. Couzens, however, kept after him like a demon. While Ford seemed intent on transforming each vehicle into another 999, Couzens

* The first John Dodge of record in Michigan was an eighteenth-century Indian agent. By the time John and Horace Dodge arrived in Detroit from Niles in the 1880's, there were fewer than seven thousand Indians left in the state.
† Born in Edinburgh, Scotland, in 1841, Gray was the son of a crockery merchant who had come to America in 1849 and settled on a Wisconsin farm. Discovering that he was not cut out to be a farmer, the older Gray had moved to Detroit and opened a toy store. John Gray had gone into the candy business and ultimately become the largest candy manufacturer in the state.
‡ Ford and Malcomson each held 255 shares; Gray 105; the two Dodges, Bennett, Horace Rackham and John Anderson (Malcomson's attorneys), Strelow, and Vernon Fry (Malcomson's cousin) 50 each; Couzens 25 (one of which was for his sister); and Charles Woodall 10.

literally snatched them from beneath his hands and directed them onto the freight cars.

Compared to the noisy, vibrating, one-cylinder Oldsmobile and Cadillac, the Fordmobile was a joy. Generating eight horsepower, its two-cylinder engine was twice as powerful as that of the Olds. With a top speed of thirty miles per hour, it outperformed models costing twice as much. By October 1, sales totaled $142,481, and profits were $36,957. By the end of June, 1904, when production was more than 350 cars monthly, gross sales topped $1 million, and dividends equaled a 98 percent return on investment. The next year they increased to 200 percent.

26

The Joy of Packard

UNLIKE FORD, KING FAILED TO FIND HIS COUZENS. AN IMMENSELY TALENTED man, he tended to be disorganized, and was pulled thither and yon by his many interests. In 1900 he went to work for Olds. Later he developed the Silent Northern, one of the better engineered cars of its time and the first to introduce left-hand drive. He went to Paris to study art and design, and he invented a seventy-five-millimeter airplane gun. When, finally, his Detroit society friends decided to invest in an automobile, they turned to the man who had first contacted King in 1893.

Following the Panic of 1893, James W. Packard of Warren, Ohio, had been too occupied pulling his electrical company through the depression to concern himself further with the development of an automobile. In 1898, however, he had bought the twelfth car manufactured by Winton. When he complained about the car's many defects, Winton had suggested that if he thought he could do better, he should build an automobile himself.

A mechanical-engineering graduate of Lehigh University, Packard accepted Winton's challenge. On November 6, 1899, the first Packard was road-tested. Early the next year the car went into production.

Attending the 1901 New York automobile show, Henry Joy was standing outside the exhibition building when a fire engine raced by. A man dashed to his car, spun the crank once, jumped in, and was off to chase the engine. Greatly impressed, Joy discovered that the vehicle was a Packard, and bought the only other one available in New York.

Shortly thereafter, Joy visited the plant at Warren, and realized that Packard lacked the capital and facilities to produce more than a few dozen cars a year. Returning to Detroit, he convinced the second generation of the Railroad Republicans that Packard was the car of the future. Together with Philip H. McMillan, John and Truman Newberry, Frederick M. and Russell Alger, Jr., D. M. Ferry, Jr., and one or two others, Joy acquired 62.5 percent of the stock of the company. He was named president. Since all the new investors lived in Detroit, and the city was much superior to Warren as a production center, the company was transferred to Michigan.

Joy thereupon turned his attention to building a plant. Throughout the 1890's, Detroit, along with the rest of the United States, had been plagued by fires. The combination of wooden buildings and incendiary materials created holocausts. The loss of life among workers on upper floors was enormous. In 1895 the explosion of a steam boiler in downtown Detroit set fire to two adjacent buildings, and trapped fifty persons. In a factory explosion in November, 1901, thirty workers lost their lives. Some burned to death; others were drowned in the basement during the firemen's all-night battle against the flames. The Oldsmobile plant was destroyed only two years after being constructed. Insurance companies, loath to issue policies at all, were charging higher and higher rates.

Industrial architects searched desperately for a fire-resistant material. In Detroit, the newest landmark was the Palms Apartment Building, constructed of concrete. Concrete, obviously, would not catch fire, but because of its tendency to crumble, it was considered a poor building material. It appeared that the architect responsible for the solidly built Palms Apartments had a special knack, or had discovered something new.

The architect was Albert Kahn. Born in 1869 in the Rhineland, he was the eldest of six children. His father, a rabbi who made his living as a peddler,* had decided to emigrate to the United States. Albert had received a sound basic education in the demanding Prussian educational system, but after coming to America at the age of eleven he had never returned to school.

In Detroit, Albert's father became a peddler of fruits and vegetables. Albert's mother, Rosalie, cooked in a small restaurant near the Michigan Central Railroad station. Albert worked nights as a busboy in the restaurant, then helped his father groom and stable the horse. During the day he was an office boy for an architect. In a city in which only one fifth of the houses were connected to the water supply, Saturday night baths were still the norm. Inevitably, toward the end of the week, Albert smelled of both the horse and the kitchen. One day in 1883 the odor became too much for the other people in the office. He was fired.

As he stood, crying, in the hallway, he was discovered by Julius Melchers. An architect and sculptor, Melchers had been commissioned to sculpt the four huge statues that an affluent citizen was donating for the top of the city hall. Sympathizing with the boy, Melchers took him under his wing. In 1890 Kahn won *The American Architect*'s traveling scholarship to Europe. (There his companion became Henry Bacon, Jr., who was later to design the Lincoln Memorial.)

Returning to Detroit, Kahn in 1895 set up his own office. Like Malcomson, he was carried upward by the industrial boom. In 1903, he won the commission to design the University of Michigan's new $150,000 engineering building.

His younger brother Julius, who was studying engineering at the university, asked him how he calculated the strength of concrete. He didn't, Albert replied. It was a matter of knack and intuition. Startled, Julius devised a means to calculate the strengths and stresses. That accomplished, Julius decided that concrete could be improved by reinforcing it. Developing the Kahn Bar—for the manufacture of which he founded the Truscon Steel Company—he laid the basis for modern concrete construction.

To Joy, concrete construction seemed the answer to the fire problem. He commissioned Albert Kahn to build the Packard factory. On forty acres on Grand Boulevard, Kahn erected a large-windowed, airy, sunlighted, reinforced-concrete factory that became the prototype for twentieth-century industry.

---

* It was not an unusual combination in the Jewish culture. Learning was highly esteemed, but the scholar was expected to earn his living like anyone else.

27

The Making of Detroit

THERE WERE ELEVEN THOUSAND CARS, MORE THAN ONE MILLION BICYCLES, and seventeen million horses in the United States. But 1903 doomed the horse and the bicycle.

Everywhere, manufacturers of bicycles and a variety of other goods were turning to the assembling of automobiles. Peerless, which had started out in 1869 as a producer of clothes wringers and switched in 1891 to bicycles, switched again to automobiles. In Buffalo, an erstwhile bird-cage manufacturer who had added a line of bicycle spokes, then bicycles themselves, produced the first Pierce. In Kenosha, Wisconsin, Thomas B. Jeffery converted from bikes to autos, but called them by the same name: Rambler. Another bike manufacturer put together the Thomas Flyer that was to win (disputedly) the 1908 New York to Paris race. The White Sewing Machine Company commenced manufacturing steamers. In Detroit, David Buick, a plumbing manufacturer, added wheels and valve-in-head engines to his bath tubs. So it went with company after company. In 1900, there were seventy-two American firms producing cars. In 1901, thirty-eight more were organized; in 1902, forty-seven; and in 1903, fifty-three.*

In the early years it appeared that the center of the automobile industry would be in the Northeast. New England had a century of experience in mass production technology and the making of machine tools. The Pope Company was the largest bicycle-manufacturing concern in the country. Colonel Albert Pope was one of the leading advocates of better roads in the United States.† In 1895, he had invited Hiram P. Maxim, who had like Benz and Winton powered a bicycle with an engine, to become head of a new motor carriage department.

---

* In 1903, also, two bicycle mechanics named Wright added wings to wheels and an internal combustion engine, and initiated the history of powered flight. The importance of the improvement of internal combustion engines in the development of flight has generally been overlooked. In 1894, Hiram S. Maxim, the inventor of the mechanical machine gun, had succeeded in getting a flying carriage a few feet off the ground, but the steam engine that powered it had been too heavy to sustain the flight. His son, Hiram P., became an inventor in the automotive and electrical fields.

† He was influential in the establishment of the Bureau of Roads in the Department of Agriculture, and in setting up the first course in road engineering at MIT.

To Maxim's chagrin, however, what Pope had in mind were not internal combustion engines but electric motors. No one, Pope insisted, could be induced to sit on top of an explosion.

During its first two years of production, the Pope Company turned out 500 electric but only 40 gas-engined vehicles. By 1899 New England was producing 734 of the American total of 1,575 electrics, and 1,191 of the 1,661 steamers; but only 171 of the 1,207 gassers.

Electrics and steamers, however, were showing themselves incapable of competing with gasoline-powered vehicles. In New York City, Isaac L. Rice, a brilliant attorney of Bavarian Jewish antecedence and a strong believer in electric transport, organized a company to operate a fleet of electric hansom cabs. The storage batteries, however, weighed a ton and had to be recharged after every trip. Even in a city of short-distance hauls the cabs proved themselves impractical.

The handicaps of steamers became obvious after the first coast-to-coast trip in a gasoline-powered auto was made by Dr. H. M. Jackson of Vermont and his chauffeur in 1903. (Equipped with rifles, camping gear, and all the paraphernalia of the forty-niners, they astonished the families in covered wagons whom they passed on the Overland Trail.) In wide swathes of the West there simply was not enough water to sustain the steamers.

Pope, despite his earlier opinion about the American public's intolerance for explosions beneath their rumps, changed his mind and began manufacturing gasoline-powered cars. But by then the center of the industry had shifted to the environs of Detroit.

Why Detroit?

It was a question that, in later years, intrigued many writers and economists, who looked back no further than Henry Ford, and failed to comprehend what had been an orderly evolutionary development.

For better than a half century the city had been a major production center. Joy, McMillan, Newberry, Alger, and their associates had turned it into one of the world's great producers of railroad rolling stock. The technology for manufacturing frames, bodies, wheels, axles, and bearings was developed. From the vast deposits of chemicals and salt came the ingredients that were turned into paint and glass. The cheapness and availability of lumber had made southeastern Michigan the hub of the American carriage-building industry; and in the first two decades of automobile construction wood was used for bodies and wheels. The carriage industry had developed a skilled force of leather workers, upholsterers, and carpenters, all of whom were able to transfer their skills to the making of automobiles. The importance of the concentration of so many elements became evident as soon as the industry passed beyond the bicycle and quadricycle stage.

But the key factor in New England's failure to obtain the automobile industry was the internal combustion engine. The concentration of the petroleum industry in Pennsylvania, Ohio, and Indiana gave the Erie lake shore and Detroit the leadership in internal combustion technology. Due to its shipbuilding experience, Detroit was the center of that technology. In no other place in the United States were there so many men—Olds, King, Barthel, Ford, Leland, Buick, the Dodge brothers, and a host of others—with experience in the building of internal combustion engines.

The men were the sparks that ignited the fire. What fueled it and concentrated it further in Detroit was the capital that had been accumulated through the exploitation of Michigan's natural resources and the development of the railroad industry. Olds was financed by lumber and copper. Leland had established himself in Detroit as the consequence of Faulconer's lumber fortune. The Ford-Cadillac money came from lumber, and to a lesser extent iron, copper, and the railroads. Packard was transferred from Warren, Ohio, to Detroit with the fortunes of the Railroad Republicans.

While auto makers in other sections of the country faced the danger that a downturn in the economy or a single mistake would end in bankruptcy, in Michigan there was frequently someone to pick up the company. Even Pope, as well financed as any of the early manufacturers, went under in the Panic of 1907. But when Olds after quarreling with his backers sold the company to them for $1 million in 1904, a group of Lansing businessmen quickly subscribed $300,000 to finance the building of a new car, the R.E.O. (Ransom E. Olds).

When Buick floundered, selling only sixteen cars in 1903 and thirty-seven in 1904, William Crapo Durant appeared on the scene to take over.

Durant was the grandson of Henry Crapo, who had come to Michigan in the migration of New England lumbermen, built the largest lumber mill in Flint, and become a Republican governor of the state. In his youth Durant had paid fifty dollars for the rights to an improved road cart. The cart proved so successful that by the turn of the century Durant was a millionaire. A student of the stock market, he was as at home in New York and in Boston as in Michigan.

Capitalizing Buick at $1.5 million, Durant himself went out to sell the stock. At the time, Oldsmobile had by far the largest sales in the world (6,500 in 1904). By 1908, however, Buick, with sales of 8,487 cars and a profit of $1.7 million, was the leader.

In the same decade that the era of railroad expansion was coming to an end, the automobile industry was developing in Detroit. Although ten years earlier there had been twenty-five thousand unemployed in the city, by 1906 as many as fifteen thousand jobs were going begging. Tailors, painters, carpenters, machinists, furniture makers, bicycle mechanics, metalworkers, glaziers—skilled workers of every kind were needed by the seventy auto manufacturers. Recruiting widely, they sucked men to the city from America, from Canada, and from Europe.

One of those who arrived in Detroit during the early years of the new century was William Norveth.

28

The Wretched Refuse

THE VILLAGE IN WESTERN HUNGARY IN WHICH NORVETH HAD BEEN BORN WAS essentially unchanged from the eighteenth century. There was little differentiation between town and country. Some villagers owned small plots of their own. But, in a land where more than half of the holdings consisted of less than seven acres, everyone walked to and worked in the fields of the aristocratic landowners, as their ancestors had for centuries. (The feudal system had not come to an end until the Revolution of 1848.) The three-field system was still in use. Each year one field was allowed to lie fallow. No one had heard of the rotation of crops, or of artificial fertilizers. Horse and wagon were the only transportation. In inclement weather, when the dusty road turned into a quagmire, the town was isolated. Possession of a kerosene lantern was a sign of affluence. So was ownership of a well—most families carried their water from the village pump. Only a handful of men, and even fewer women, could read. Social life centered on the church. For an interpretation of the world, people relied on the priest and the few men who had spent some time, however briefly, in one of the big cities like Buda or Pressburg.

It was a static society, and it was unable to cope with the growth of population. In 1715 the population of Hungary and Transylvania had totaled 2.5 million. In 1850 the population of Greater Hungary was 13 million. By 1900 it reached 19 million. Since no new jobs were created, there was an increasing division of the old. More than two thirds of the population was dependent on the land, but there was not nearly enough land to support them. Hungarian wheat could not compete with Russian and American wheat even in Budapest and Vienna. Wages, with board, for workers in the fields were twenty-two cents a day for men, fourteen cents for women, and ten cents for children. Pushed out of their villages, young men streamed into the industrial cities of Austria, Moravia, and Bohemia.

At the age of eighteen, Norveth had been married to Theresa, at the time not quite sixteen. Since she came from a family who owned a lantern and a small orchard, he was much congratulated on the match. They lived in her father's house. Four years later, despite having lost one infant, they were the parents of two children. Since both Theresa's mother and older sister were bearing children, scarcely a season went by without a blessed event. William's father-in-law began musing whether it would not be better for a young man to seek his fortune elsewhere.

Early in 1897, a youth who had moved to the city returned to the district and spread the news that an agent would soon arrive to invite men to become rich in America. The youth was a "runner," whose job it was to prepare the way for the coming of the great man himself.

Excitement spread through the village. Norveth pored over the guide book the runner left. It declared that now was the time to emigrate, because there was a great shortage of labor. On the one hand the booklet painted a roseate picture of life in America; on the other it warned of the traps for the inexperienced. The newcomer would need someone to look out for him. The agent would provide such a person to "afford protection against extortion of vicious beguilers," and to prevent the unwary from falling into the hands of "swindlers, cheaters, and thieves who will rob him of everything." [1]

One day, the great man himself arrived, and established himself in the coffee-house. Norveth learned that the fare was $95. He would have to take with him about $20 as "show money" to indicate that he was not a pauper. He would need another $20 to obtain documents circumventing Hungary's anti-emigration law and postponing his obligation to serve in the army. The total of $135 was completely beyond the means of many. However, it was not necessary to have cash, the agent explained. In America a man could earn $2 a day. Therefore, if he or one of his relatives had property, it could be mortgaged to obtain the passage money.

There was long and earnest conversation between Norveth and his father-in-law. If in America one could make so much money, it must be a magic land. In Hungary even carpenters, blacksmiths, and masons made no more than $2.50 a week. William returned to the agent with his father-in-law. It was agreed he would mortgage the house and the orchard to pay for the passage.

Carrying his belongings in a cardboard box and wearing the distinctive button that would identify him to the agent's man in Hamburg and New York, William Norveth boarded a train for the first time in his life. After a journey of two days, the train discharged the emigrants at the gates of the *Auswanderhallen,* the camp constructed by the steamship line in Hamburg.

There, Norveth was given a medical examination. His eyes received the most rigid attention; for in many sections of Europe trachoma was almost pandemic. The decision as to who would be turned back because of some defect was made by the American vice-consul. Looking over the nervous, docile ranks, he indicated those to be rejected. No appeal, no tears could move him. When he had to pass judgment on tens of thousands of persons yearly, there was no room for emotion.

A self-contained community, the *Auswanderhallen* had dormitories, mess halls, chapels, hospitals, and laundries. Its scenes were duplicated at the other principal ports of embarkation: Liverpool, Bremen, Naples, and Trieste. In Hungary, Italy, the Balkans, and Poland, young men were deserting villages where conditions were similar to those in Ireland fifty years before. Peasants continued to live in mud huts without windows and with earthen floors. They cooked on earthen stoves. They slept with their animals, because fuel was limited and costly, and the animals provided warmth.

Communities, however, no longer were isolated. Railroads were penetrating into previously remote areas and enabling people to emigrate from the deepest parts of central and eastern Europe. Some villages lost a fourth of their population in twenty years. Unable to find work in Italy—Fall River, Massachusetts, had 50 percent more cotton spindles than all of Italy—half as many men were leaving the country every year as were employed in all its industry.

The average annual wage of farm laborers in southern Italy was $80, and in northern Italy $103. Miners were paid from 42 to 58 cents per day. American industrial wages were double those in Britain and three times those in Germany—a reflection of the greater and more efficient use of machinery. Yet the cost of food in European cities equaled and sometimes exceeded the cost in American cities.

After three days in the *Auswanderhallen,* Norveth was taken aboard ship. One section of the steerage was set aside for men, another for women, and the third for families. Berths were mounted on an iron framework that allowed each person two feet six inches of vertical space. Mattresses were filled with straw and kelp. The life preserver served as pillow. Since there were no lockers or shelves, everyone slept with his belongings, and sometimes carried them around with him during the day.

When they put to sea, the compartment turned into a chamber of horrors. Sick bags or receptacles were lacking. At first people tried to make it to the toilets—an open trough with iron steps that only a contortionist could use. But the toilets, which were never cleaned, soon sloshed a soup of icy saltwater, puke, and excrement over the floor. Women and children slipped, and were carried back and forth with the pitch of the ship as if trapped in a crazyhouse slide. By the second day out, the children were screaming, the women crying, and the men groaning. All were sure that they would die.

Once the weather and their stomachs calmed, the task of cleaning up began. Women used chamber pots to wash their clothes, their hair, and their children. The floor was swabbed with disinfectant, whose stench was as nauseous as the weather had been.

Many of the ship's personnel regarded the immigrants as cattle. The Irish and German stewards, whose fathers and grandfathers had looked more ragged and traveled in worse conditions, missed little opportunity to make loud remarks about the filthy habits of the wops and the yids. Any unattached woman was fair game. A moment's inattention, and a girl would find a steward's hand sliding under her dress or down into her bosom. Women defended themselves with their teeth and their hatpins. Every day the screams of girls and the oaths of men were heard on the deck.

Stewards, in fact, sometimes served as agents for the procurers who gathered at Ellis Island to watch the passengers debark. Tipped off by the stewards, the procurers attempted to "cut out" the single, attractive girls. The approach was, seemingly, innocent. Work was waiting for them, the girls were told, in a candy shop or laundry. The wages quoted exceeded their highest expectations. Free rooms were available in the "boardinghouse."

When the immigrants arrived in America, labor agents for the railroads, steel mills, and other industries circulated among them and looked for the distinctive buttons identifying men as theirs. Could they have seen the inscription on the statue they had passed in the harbor, the immigrants would have been uncomprehending. *"Give me your tired, your poor . . . The wretched refuse of* *your teeming shore . . ."* Poor they were; but if they had been *tired* and *refuse* they would have been floated right back out to sea.*

What America was looking for was hard workers; cheap labor—cheap, at any rate, in comparison with the going wages for American workmen—for sweatshops and railroads, for mines and quarries, for steel mills and road building; for the innumerable unskilled jobs created by capital projects.

Groups of immigrants were herded this way and that in preparation for dispersal across the United States. Norveth was placed aboard a boxcar with bunks arranged in tiers. After a slow one-and-a-half-day journey southward, the car was detached at a siding. The railroad was ready to have Norveth go to work for it.

Shoveling, digging ditches, sloping the sides of cuts, carrying crossties and rails, Norveth worked harder than ever before in his life. Paid a dollar and a half a day, he continued to live in the boxcar, for which he was charged a dollar a month "rent." Separated according to nationality, the workers were nearly all Hungarians, Italians, Slavs, and Negroes. Each group had its own "walking boss," an earlier arrival who interpreted the orders. Negroes were paid the same as immigrants. They were used as teamsters, woodsmen, and carpenters —in general, for the more skilled jobs.

Food, tobacco, and other necessities were sold at the commissary car, run on a concession basis by an Austrian, who had arrived ten years earlier. Norveth spent about forty cents a day for food, and ate better than ever before in his life. Each group cooked its own meals on iron grills propped on stones. Men unaccustomed to being able to pick up wood wherever and in any amount they wanted delighted in building huge fires.

The men seldom left the self-contained community that traveled along the tracks, and so were able to bank twenty to twenty-five dollars a month. Only the Negroes, laughing and shouting, went off to nearby towns. The Europeans, warned of what might happen to them in the South, stayed close to the camps.

The abominable conditions on plantations and turpentine farms made it almost impossible for Southerners to obtain workers. Negroes could not be rounded up unless coerced. For a few years southern Italians and Sicilians had been tricked into signing up. But the rural and small-town South attained such notoriety that the Italian Commissioner of Emigration was moved to "pray . . . that no passports for the southern region of the United States, and especially Mississippi, be given to compatriots." [3]

Convict labor, therefore, was widely employed. Since there were never enough convicts, there was a widespread and organized practice of creating more. Immigrants were rounded up and charged with vagrancy. Fined ten dollars and "costs"—which were usually greater than the fine—they were consigned to peonage at seventy-five cents a day. Incarcerated in barns, fed like pigs, worked from daybreak to darkness, they had additional "costs" charged to them until, inevitably, both their sentences and the harvest expired concurrently. For the Southern plutocracy, it was a system that had some decided advantages over slavery. There were no families to be supported, and the men did not have to be fed after the season was over.

* The circulars distributed in Europe were more realistic: "The healthy, industrious and temperant can attain economic prosperity in America, but the lazy and intemperant will fall into greater poverty there than here." [2]

By the time work concluded in late autumn, Norveth had earned enough to pay off his father-in-law's mortgage. With a group of his countrymen, he scattered to one of the various "Hungary Hollows" in the big cities—New York, Cincinnati, Chicago, Detroit. Paying twenty-five cents a night at a men's roominghouse, he slept in a bed consisting of canvas stretched between parallel frameworks.

Jobs were hard to come by during the winter, and there was little to do. He never ventured from the neighborhood. Spending his time in the ethnic saloons and coffeehouses, he played backgammon and began to pick up some elementary knowledge about the operations of American society. Here and there an English word crept into his conversation. The saloon keeper was his man of the world. He relied on and trusted him. The saloon keeper put him on jobs. It was with him that Norveth "banked" the fifty dollars he had saved.

There were thousands of immigrant bankers in the country. They were operators of saloons, grocers, butchers, barbers, notary publics, steamship agents, book dealers, and labor agents. They were earlier immigrants who spoke English and had learned the system. They transmitted money to the old country, wrote letters for illiterates, and, through their political connections, helped extricate men who got into jams. In contrast to the American banks, with their imposing and awesome façades, their tellers who spoke only English, and their inconvenient hours, the immigrant banks were neighborhood places, open nights and Sundays. Individual bankers had as little as a few hundred dollars and as much as $600,000 on deposit. Some of the money they placed in interest-drawing accounts in regular banks. Some they invested in their own businesses. Some they loaned to their countrymen to start small businesses and to buy real estate. In each ethnic district there was a growing number of immigrant slumlords.

On occasion, especially during an economic downturn, the immigrant bankers failed. One, owing his depositors $75,000, fled back to Hungary when he was unable to keep up the payments on the $90,000 worth of property he had bought.

Norveth learned that this was a different kind of world from the static society in which he had been raised. In America everyone expected to "get ahead." There were Hungarians who were making fortunes out of restaurants patronized by Americans, and Hungarians who had worked their way up in the political world until they were big shots in city hall.

The Bohemians dominated the cigar industry. Paid $4.50 per thousand cigars, a man and wife working fifteen hours a day in their tenement room could make $13.50 a week. Spending $12.50 a month for rent and $15 for food, they could save $20 to $25 a month. Eventually they might open a small tobacco store. If that prospered, they might become jobbers themselves.

In the Polish-Jewish district, windows were filled with the figures of men and women hunched over their sewing machines. Turning out pants at 42 cents a dozen, a pants maker earned between $7.50 and $8 a week. Working long into the night by the light of kerosene lamps, stripped to the minimum clothing demanded by decency, the tenement dwellers *sweated* alongside the red-hot stoves that, winter and summer, heated the irons used to press the garments. Families strove to save money to rent extra machines at $2 per month. Employing as many as a dozen persons at $1.50 to $3 a week each, they became operators of "sweatshops." After a man learned English, he could advance into the ranks of the "sweaters": the middlemen who let out the contracts. Eventually he might become a small manufacturer, or open a direct-sales outlet. In an economy turning out goods in historic quantities at unprecedently low prices, a new suit could be bought at retail for less than $2.

A Jewish pants maker made more in New York than a Jewish lawyer in Poland; an unskilled Hungarian laborer three times as much as a skilled worker in Budapest; and an illiterate Italian girl as much as a miner in Sicily. Millions of Europeans were aching to escape the charnelhouses of their dead societies to plunge into the cauldrons of the American cities.

For five years Norveth wintered in one or another American city. From spring to fall he worked on the railroads. The second year he went west, where the pay was better and he could make up to $2.50 a day. As his English improved, he learned of other jobs that were available. In 1902 or 1903 he came to Detroit. Soon he was working for 22 cents an hour at a plant making wheels for automobiles. By 1905 he had saved enough money to send for his family.

29

The Posthumous Revolution

BETWEEN 1880 AND 1890, DETROIT'S POPULATION INCREASED FROM 116,000 TO 286,000. During the first decade of the new century it rose to 466,000. In 1895, the city expanded beyond what had once been thought of as its "ultimate limits" of Grand Boulevard. In 1905, following industry westward along the Detroit River, it pushed to the River Rouge, within a mile and a half of the school Henry Ford had attended. Although the city nearly doubled its area between 1895 and 1910, population density continued to increase. From 3,500 persons per square mile in 1860, it rose to 11,400 in 1910. All over the United States reformers were proclaiming that public transportation would reduce density, break up slums, and halt the upward spiral of crimes. But New York's newly completed subway proved no more effective than Detroit's rickety street-railway system.*

Landlords were collecting premiums on the rent of every dilapidated building. Norveth and his family lived in two rooms in a complex of clapboard shacks that had been thrown together behind the stables of a mansion. There was a central kitchen with a gas stove. But in the apartments themselves there was neither gas nor electricity.

Water came from a penstock in the courtyard. Next to the penstock were two privies, which froze in winter and overflowed in summer. Excrement was piled a foot deep on their floors. Oozing out of the doors, it mingled with the manure of horses, and the droppings of pigs and sheep that the residents allowed to wander in and out of their rooms. Children made mud pies out of the ordure, wrestled in it, and sometimes ate it. The bakery man came, tramped it into his wagon, then piled the uncovered loaves of bread where he had stood.

There was nearly always someone sick, and often someone dying. Most often the cause was pneumonia, or one of the other lung diseases. Next door to the

---

* In 1906 Detroit obtained a tentative commitment for the building of a subway from a group of New York financiers, but the project expired in the Panic of 1907 and in the factory of the Ford Motor Company.

Norveths, however, an old man had a more exotic illness—a "live" leg out of whose ulcers the children watched the maggots crawl.

Only one out of seven immigrants had an annual income of $900, considered the minimum necessary for a family of five to maintain an adequate standard of living. Since the average wage of immigrants in industry was but $455 a year, in nearly every family the wife and older children worked.[1]

Despite the hardships, they were living and, especially, eating better than they ever had in Europe. So, even with the lack of sanitation, fewer were dying. Children were so numerous that they traveled in swarms. The Poles, with an average of 6.2 children per family, were the most prolific. The Catholic French-Canadians, who were migrating largely from rural areas, had an average of 5.6 children. The Protestant and rural Finns had 5.3. The Protestant but urban English only 3.4. With each generation of urban living the number of children declined. The offspring of the immigrants had an average of 4.7 children, and they, in turn, an average of 3.9. Negroes living in the cities had but 3.1. Native urban whites 2.7.[2]

With a new baby to mind, Theresa Norveth learned from her neighbors that in America it was easier to care for infants than in the villages of Europe. It was easier because there were magic potions that soothed them and would keep them quiet. Thesesa gave the baby patent medicines like Dr. Fowler's Strawberry and Peppermint Mixture and Dr. Moffett's Teething Powders. The active ingredient of the first was morphine; of the second, opium. There were dozens of such mixtures on sale. Dr. Fahrney's Teething Syrup contained morphine and chloroform; Dr. James' Soothing Syrup heroin; Dr. Miller's Anodyne for Babies morphine sulphate and chloral hydrate (knockout drops).[3] Since the harried mothers often worked as domestics or did piecework for twelve hours a day, docile children were a necessity.

Once the children could no longer be doped, they were left to shift for themselves. Lacking playgrounds or supervision, they congealed into neighborhood gangs, in which the older boys served as fathers to the younger. Many of the gangs practiced organized thievery.

Girls fourteen and fifteen years old continued to marry as they had on the farms. Others were seduced by procurers who then sold them to whorehouses for twenty-five dollars apiece. No one, least of all the mother herself, knew what to do with all of the babies. Scarcely a night went by without an abandoned infant being discovered on the streets. In New York City there were twelve hundred to thirteen hundred foundlings yearly. In Detroit, the problem had been recognized as early as the Civil War. In 1869, the Catholic Sisters of Charity had founded the House of Providence to care for foundlings, and for pregnant women who were begging, sleeping, and giving birth on the streets.

In 1869, most of the foundlings had been Irish. But by 1900 the Irish constituted a large proportion of the American population,* and people stopped speaking of Irishmen and pigs in the same breath. The Irish had gained respectability through their votes. Their votes brought them thousands of municipal jobs. In their brass-buttoned uniforms and Keystone Cops helmets, the Irish

---

* America continued to act as an overflow receptacle for the Irish population. Irish immigration to America between 1900 and 1910 still averaged 35,000 a year, topped only by Italian immigration of 187,000 annually, by Jewish—88,000, Polish—79,000, German—61,000, and English and Scottish—38,000. Between 1820 and 1910, 4,212,000 Irish came to the United States, a number approximately equal to the population remaining in Ireland.

police often looked like gingerbread men all stamped out by the same cookie cutter. But they were not comic figures in the Polish, the Italian, and the Greek slums.

If there was enmity between the Irish cop and the "new wave" adults, there was warfare between him and the juveniles. Walking his beat in the tenement district, the cop learned to duck the nightly barrage of rocks.

Despite Michigan's compulsory education law, thousands of children were employed in sweatshops. Two million children, one out of every five between the ages of ten and fifteen in America, held jobs. Where children were barred from working, they often were left with nothing to do but roam the streets. Police used truancy laws to round up juveniles suspected of delinquency. Ten-year-old truants were thrown into cells with adult criminals.

Commenting on the unsatisfactory conditions, the Detroit Board of Education in its 1910 report declared that children often "come from neglected homes, have cruel stepparents, are feeble minded, suffer from malnutrition, nervous diseases, vicious habits, or physical conditions, many of which can be cured and the child saved from a criminal life. The policeman and the delinquent are not friends, the psychic effect of the policeman is association with crime, hence branding the child as a criminal." [4]

To cope with the ever-growing problem, a juvenile division of the Wayne County Probate Court was established in 1908. A little over three years later, in January, 1912, its judge, Henry S. Hulbert, told an audience of business executives:

"With them [the immigrants] it is largely a matter of economics. They rear large families, and they begin . . . in poverty, and rise through a gradually increasing line of prosperity to a point where the maximum number of their children are of the work age and at home in the family, and then as the children marry or go out the parents . . . go down the poverty side again. The children are kept in the school only so long as the law compels them to be there. They then force them into work, and confiscate their entire wages. . . . The child is going to become rapidly sick of the employment because he gets no benefit from it. . . . He gets his money in some other way, and then I get him as a delinquent child." [5]

Along with other native whites, the judge believed that immigrants were begetting so many children deliberately, and for the purpose of exploiting them. What schools these children were supposed to attend, and who was supposed to teach them when businessmen and property owners resisted every measure to increase taxes was, of course, irrelevant. When Professor Franklin H. Giddings of Columbia University investigated the charge that immigrants exploited their children by putting them to work instead of sending them to school, he found that where classroom space was available 88 percent of the children of Italian immigrants and 93 percent of the children of Bohemian and of Russian-Jewish immigrants were in school. Immigrants had, in fact, an overwhelming desire to have their children learn. But since every major city had a shortage of school facilities, there was an "army of enforced truants." [6]

When the poorly dressed, bathless, often pungent, barely English-speaking immigrant child arrived in school, he was likely to be met by teacher indifference, if not hostility. Frequently he was consigned to the rear of the room. Teachers who did take an interest thought nothing of lecturing immigrant children on the need for cleanliness in front of the class, or of taking them to the wash-room to be scrubbed.

In 1895, a teacher-retirement law had been passed for the specific purpose of ridding the Detroit school system of its numerous incompetents. But the standard of education for a teacher was still no more than eight years of grammar school followed by one year of "normal school." Teachers continued to be gauged not by their efficiency, but by the economy of their employment. Since women came cheaper than men—the average annual salary was but slightly over seven hundred dollars—there was only 1 man among the 1,436 teachers in regular classes in the elementary schools in 1908.

It was a system that facilitated failure. By the time children reached the fifth grade, 47.6 percent of them were "retarded"—two years or more behind in grade. By then nearly one of every three who had entered the first grade had already dropped out. By the eighth grade only 2,143 out of 6,765 were left, and of these a third were hopelessly behind. Of every thirteen who entered grammar school, only one reached the fourth year of high school.

How well the children did in school seemed unrelated to the educational system, but was directly dependent upon the degree of a family's urbanization and the emphasis the parents placed on education.

The children of German Jews had the best record. Only 27.6 percent of them were behind in grade. After them came children of native white parentage, 31.3 percent of whom were behind, then those of Scotch, Irish, English, and English-Canadian parentage: between 36 and 37 percent behind. Doing the poorest were children of Negro and Indian parentage, 53.6 percent of whom were "retarded." They were followed by southern Italian children, 51.7 percent "retarded," Polish, 49.7 percent, and French-Canadian, 46.4 percent.* [7]

Not until the turn of the century did Detroit have more than one high school. Then the proposal to build Eastern and Western High Schools to supplement the Central High School was denounced as but another extravagant scheme. But since 56 percent of high school students (compared to 45 percent of elementary school pupils) had native white and voting parents, the schools were built.

Consistent with their elementary school records, German-Jewish children had the best record of advancing to high school. They were followed by English, English-Canadian, native white, Irish, Russian-Jewish, Scotch, and German children. There were only two Negro, two Polish, and no Italian children in high school. [8] There was no inducement to retain the children in school. There was, however, good reason to get those who were lagging behind out of school.

For decades the building of new schools had been neglected. Classes were being held in shacks, lofts, and basements. As mayor, Pingree had tried to clean up the waste and graft in education. Now, posthumously—for he had died in 1901 after a trip to Africa—he was to bring about a revolution in the Michigan schools.

Within two years of attaining the governor's office, Pingree had succeeded in

---

* The more than thirteen thousand students in parochial schools had even worse records. With an enrollment 40 percent Polish and 13 percent German—compared to 29 percent native white and 4 percent Irish—the schools conducted some classes in the native languages. Nevertheless, by the fourth grade 70 percent of the pupils were "retarded." Only one of every seven who entered the first grade reached the eighth. One out of every one hundred graduated from high school.

outmaneuvering Senator McMillan and the Railroad Republicans. He captured control of the state central committee, and purged many of the Old Guard from the legislature. For nearly a half century the railroad, public utility, and mining interests had manipulated the electoral process to control the state government. The lightly populated rural areas of the Lower and Upper Peninsula were dominated by them. As a consequence of the continuing misapportionment of the legislature, these areas had a larger representation than the cities.

Pingree's coup created a Progressive Republican-Democratic majority in the lower house. McMillan was forced to fall back upon the senate's "Immortal 19," each of whose hands he could raise, and mouths open and close, at will. They were a bloc capable of barring the passage of any legislation.

Pingree was able to demonstrate that the railroads owned 38 percent of the property in the state but paid only 3.5 percent of the taxes. He proposed the repeal of the law requiring railroads to pay 1.5 percent of their gross earnings in lieu of property taxes. The railroads never paid close to that much of their earnings, but nearly $200 million of railroad property was escaping taxation. Pingree urged the enactment of a constitutional amendment establishing an *ad valorem* tax on railroad property. To assure equalization, all property was to be taxed at "true cash value."

The electorate approved the amendment by a margin of five hundred thousand votes. The lower house overwhelmingly passed the bill for its implementation. But by means of the Immortal 19, McMillan was able to block passage in the senate for five years. Not until Pingree mousetrapped his opponents into a *deal* during the election of 1900 was he able to overcome the opposition. Retaining a University of Michigan professor to appraise the railroad property —the first such appraisal in America—he succeeded in adding $350 million to the tax rolls.

Through appeals in the courts, the railroads were able to delay implementation of the new law until 1905. When, thereupon, they succeeded in pressuring the state board of assessors into reducing their assessment by $82 million, the Detroit Board of Education sued.

The court's decision in favor of the Board of Education brought the tax on railroad property to $3.3 million. Since the entire state budget was less than $5 million, the additional revenue provided a windfall for education. Teachers organized themselves to get their share of the money, and in one year, from 1905 to 1906, membership in the Michigan Teachers Association jumped from nine hundred to forty-five hundred. More school districts began planning to build high schools, and enrollment in secondary schools was to increase dramatically.

As far back as 1873, the Kalamazoo school board had won a court test against three citizens who challenged its right to levy taxes for the support of a high school. The decision was the first of its kind in the nation. But until 1903, families living in districts without a high school were forced to pay tuition if their children attended high school in another district. In 1908, there were still only 169 accredited high schools in the state.*

* Rural education had all but remained at a standstill since Henry Ford's boyhood. Schools commonly did not open until after Thanksgiving, and then ran only for twelve to sixteen weeks. There continued to be a strong emphasis on moral instruction, and boys and girls had separate recesses. Pay for teachers was but $36 to $40 a month. The typical superintendent of a rural school district, paid $1,350 a year, made his rounds on horseback or in a buggy.

By bringing the railroads to account, Pingree set a national precedent and facilitated the establishment of a school system capable of accepting all children for education *if their families were motivated, and financially able to send them.* However, since most families expected boys to be working by the age of sixteen, there was a growing disparity between the number of boys and girls who graduated from high school. Nationally, of the 156,000 graduates in 1910—seven times the number a generation earlier—three out of five were girls. The three to two ratio continued during the next decade as the number of graduates doubled to 311,000.

30

A Car for All People

PINGREE'S FORMER FINANCIAL ADVISER, ROBERT OAKMAN, WAS LUNCHING IN A Woodward Avenue restaurant in the summer of 1906. At a nearby table was Henry Ford. Oakman overheard Ford discussing the company's need for a site at which to construct a new plant. It happened that Oakman, despite his philosophical adherence to Henry George, was making a lucrative living as a real estate agent. Oakman suggested to Ford that he take a look at a piece of land some five and a half miles from downtown Detroit that was being used for farming and horse racing. It was the land platted by Judge Woodward on the road to Pontiac.

The Ford Motor Company had experienced the same division of opinion between the *producers* of cars and the financial backers that had caused the split at the Olds Motor Company. Although at Olds the dispute had caused the decline of the company, at Ford it was leading to greater prosperity and plans for expansion.

From the beginning, relations between Ford and Malcomson had been tenuous, and sometimes tempestuous. Introverted, stubborn, Ford would agree to anything to avoid an argument, and then do as he pleased. Reared in an atmosphere in which bankers were looked upon as manipulators, he disliked owing money to anyone, and could develop a liberal distaste for someone who used money to try to control him.

Three years younger than Ford, Malcomson thought of himself as the leading executive in the company. He did not trust Ford as a manager. It was a mistrust more than a little justified. When F. L. Klingensmith was hired as a bookkeeper in 1905, he discovered three wastebaskets stuffed with mail, bills, checks, and orders, some of them two years old.

Malcomson was not only irritated by Ford; he was angry at Couzens. Couzens had been introduced into the company to monitor the accounts. But, given free reign, he was demonstrating himself to be an immensely strong and confident man, whose primary allegiance had shifted from Malcomson to the motor company. Adept at handling men, unafraid of a verbal slugfest, he became Ford's breakwater against Malcomson. Malcomson was infuriated when the salary of his former bookkeeper, whom he had paid $1,500 a year, was raised to $8,000 at Ford. He demanded that Couzens return to his old job with the coal company. This capricious demand was voted down by the board of directors.

Between Malcomson and Ford there was basic disagreement about whether to concentrate on a cheap or an expensive car. As was to happen during every period of prosperity, from 1903 to 1906 sales of the more expensive models increased. Except for Brush, and one or two little known companies, all of the auto manufacturers, including Olds, were building larger and more luxurious cars. The more expensive the car, the greater the profit per unit.

Ford, to the contrary, was talking about bringing out a five-hundred-dollar Model N. The upshot was a sharp break between the company's affluent investors, who regarded the market for cars as limited to the wealthy, and the men of middle-class background, who, having scraped and borrowed to invest, believed that Ford was right: that there was a mass, middle-class market for automobiles. In the social composition of its investors, and their perspectives, the Ford Motor Company was unique.

When Malcomson brought matters to a head he was chagrined to discover that his friends and relatives voted according to their economic outlook, not their blood lines. Unalterably opposed to the Model N, Malcomson demanded concentration on the more expensive models.

Ford and Couzens, backed by a majority of the other stockholders, thereupon conceived the idea of forming a separate company to manufacture the Model N. It was not unusual for a company to act as the sales agent for cars manufactured by another concern. If Malcomson was not interested in the Model N—well and good. They would show him just what kind of success could be made of it. As a stockholder in the Ford Motor Company, he would share in the profits from the car's sales, but not its manufacture. The Ford Manufacturing Company was incorporated to make the Model N.

Malcomson, in turn, formed the Aerocar Company to produce a luxury car with an air-cooled engine. The Ford Motor Company divided like an amoeba. Its business suffered. Sales dropped from 1,745 in 1904–1905 to 1,599 in 1905–1906. Profits declined to a third of what they had been.

Both sides agreed the time had come to part. Ford, as usual, wanted nothing to do with money and haggling; he allowed Couzens to handle negotiations for his purchase of Malcomson's 255 shares of stock. A price of $175,000 was agreed on.

The automobile men, the investors who had borrowed money, and John Gray, who had considerable experience in dealing with the middle class, cast their lot with the company. Woodall, Fry, Bennett, and Strelow decided to go with Malcomson. Couzens bought 35 of Bennett's 50 shares, and all of Strelow's 50.*

Following the shakeout, Ford owned 585 shares; Couzens, the treasurer and general manager, 110 (of which 1 belonged to his sister, who was soon to be the richest schoolteacher in the city's history); Gray, 105; the Dodge brothers 100; and Anderson and Rackham, 50 each.

Since Ford's lack of production experience had been one of the reasons for the company's poor showing, Walter E. Flanders was hired as production man-

---

* Strelow invested the $25,000 he received in a gold mining venture, and lost all of it. In later years he was once seen in a line of men applying for work at Ford's gates.

ager at a salary of $7,500 a year. Trained at the Singer Sewing Machine Company, he had, like Leland, emerged from the New England industrial establishment to become an engineer.

What Flanders perceived was chaos. There was little order and no rhythm to the production. Since cars were individually ordered, and finished to the specifications of each buyer, the plant might be so busy one week that the streets had to be scoured for workers, and so idle the next that half the force would have to be let go. Because there were few buyers for cars in the winter, plant and machinery were all but unemployed for several months of the year. Flanders drafted a plan to pace production over fifty weeks. The result was that while gross sales in 1906–1907 quadrupled over the previous year, the work force shrank from 700 to 575.

So great was the public's response to the Model N that, raising the price to six hundred dollars, Couzens stopped taking orders. There were six thousand orders for which the company had no cars.

Meanwhile, in May of 1907, New York fell under the spell of a Wall Street and banking panic stemming largely from overcapitalization and grandiose schemes for monopolies. Two thousand wealthy New Yorkers sold their cars, and thousands of others canceled their orders. In Detroit five auto companies went bankrupt. Four of them were the Detroit Auto Vehicle Company, the Huber, the Marvel, and the St. Clair.

The fifth was the Aerocar.

On sales of 8,403 cars, more than five times the number sold the previous year, Ford netted $1,163,000.

During the thirteen-month recession, Couzens continued to ship cars out on sight drafts on the presumption that dealers would be able to sell them. April and May of 1908 were the best months in the company's history. Together with Buick, R.E.O., and Maxwell-Briscoe—all located in or about Detroit—Ford became one of the industry's Big Four. The devastating effect of the panic on automobile manufacturers catering to an elite clientele and the correctness of the judgments of Ford's "middle-class" managers were demonstrated graphically.

The tremendous success of the Model N and of the cost-cutting production techniques installed by Flanders indicated the direction for the future. Sewing machines were not turned out according to the specifications of each sewer. Why should cars be tailored to the eccentricities of each driver? If the company were to have a smooth-functioning and economic production operation, such customizing was impossible.

During the latter part of 1907 Ford closeted himself in a specially fitted twelve-foot-by-fifteen-foot room with C. H. Wills and Joseph Galamb, two of the extraordinarily talented engineers whom he and Couzens had attracted to the company.

Ford knew what he wanted. A car simple enough for anyone—not just a chauffeur or a mechanic—to drive; rugged enough to reduce maintenance to a minimum; responsive enough so that one did not need to be a wrestler to control it; and cheap enough to appeal to the middle class.

As Ford talked out his ideas, the men took turns sketching them on a blackboard so that he could *see* them. The new car assumed form. It was impossible to divide Ford's imagination and intuition from Wills's engineering expertise, or Wills's engineering expertise from Galamb's patternmaking.

In keeping with simplicity, the car had no gas gauge, no shock absorbers, no fuel pump (gas was fed to the engine by gravity), and no water pump. (If the engine overheated, one lifted the sides of the hood.) Since the shifting of the rough, soft-metaled gears of the times was one of the mysteries baffling drivers, Ford substituted a planetary transmission for the gear shift. Operated by means of two foot pedals, it enabled drivers to go directly from forward into reverse, and so rock the car out of any mudhole.

By building a magneto into the flywheel, thus making the electrical ignition system an integral part of the engine, Ford eliminated the need for costly, often malfunctioning storage batteries. By making the cylinder head detachable, he simplified repairs to the point that any reasonably competent fourteen-year-old could take the engine apart and put it back together.

The car also had its perversities. To save a dollar or two on tires, Ford designed the front wheels a fraction of an inch smaller than the rear. A driver seldom had peace of mind unless he carried two spares for the front, and two for the rear wheels. Setting the spark and cranking the engine was an art that caused mechanics to write page after page of lyrical instructions. Despite their efforts, numerous drivers were knocked senseless and kicked in sensitive parts by ornery crank handles.

So, uniformly painted Brewster green (later black) with red striping, the Model T rolled out of the plant late in the fall of 1908. Priced at $850, it cost as much as the Cadillac. The public received it as if it had sprung from Aladdin's lamp. The twenty-horsepower engine mounted on the light, 1,200-pound chassis, gave the car enough pep to climb mountains, to nose into the Grand Canyon, and to set a transcontinental speed record, New York to Seattle, in twenty-two days.

But, most of all, the Model T conquered the rural areas and the farmers. In a day when roads ended at fences and crossed cultivated fields, farmers had come to hate the "flying red devils" whose drivers cut through wire, routed chickens and pigs, and even shot in and out of barns. The Model T dawned on them as the first car that could replace the horse. It could negotiate the same abominable roads. It could be hitched to a plow. (Various devices to increase the effectiveness of converting it into a team of mules were patented.) It could have its rear wheels jacked up, and be used to saw wood or pump water. It was taken out on the range to herd cattle.

As Ford's destiny would have it, the period from 1897 to 1920 was the longest era of agricultural prosperity in American history. Beginning in 1901, vast new oil fields were discovered in Texas, Louisiana, and California, so that—in contrast to Europe—the price of gasoline kept dropping, and automobiles became more and more economical to operate.

It was an era marked by an unprecedented expansion of the monetary supply, and by the rapid spread of new industries. By demanding greater technical skills and more education, these industries were creating a middle class of managers and "professionals." Engineers, doctors, lawyers, accountants, and teachers could not in a day of modest salaries and cash sales afford the $2,000 to $3,000 price tags of a Pierce or a Packard. But they were often able to save up for a low-priced car. (The price of a Ford was roughly equivalent to a year's salary for a teacher.)

In 1909 Ford sold 10,600 cars, one fourth of all those produced in Detroit, and 10 percent of the American total. Two years later company sales reached nearly 35,000. The United States, which, in 1906, had passed France to become the world's leading automobile producer, in 1910 was turning out as many cars as the rest of the world combined.

For production of the Model T, Albert Kahn was building the world's most advanced factory on the sixty-two-acre tract Ford had purchased for $55,800 through Oakman. When construction started, Woodward Avenue, on which the property fronted, was a poorly surfaced muddy track. Between 1908 and 1910, however, Woodward Avenue was transformed into a concrete highway from the Ford plant to the city of Pontiac. Twenty-four miles long, it was the first in America.

By coincidence, Ford was a charter member of the Wayne County Roads Commission, established in 1906.

The construction of the plant, as well as of the road, owed a good deal to Ford's friend and idol, Thomas Edison. For an iron mining venture, Edison had devised giant rock crushers and other machinery. The venture had been a disaster, but the machinery proved perfectly adaptable to the manufacture of cement. After Kahn demonstrated the workability of concrete, Edison, unable any longer to obtain fire insurance for wooden buildings, switched to reinforced concrete construction.* In 1907 he incorporated the Edison Portland Cement Company. Highly mechanized, it greatly reduced costs.

Adopting Edison's machinery, Kahn and the road builders began exploiting Michigan's vast deposits of marl, gypsum, and lime. At a time when the state's iron, lumber, and copper resources were showing signs of the hard wear to which they had been subjected, a new industry was born.

Not only did Ford get the county to pave Woodward Avenue, he also persuaded Detroit Water Commissioner John Gillespie to run a pipeline several miles to the new factory. The plant, however, was far beyond the reaches of the Detroit Edison Company. So Ford, using his electrical engineering experience, erected a massive power plant. Capable of supplying a city of a quarter million people, it rivaled Detroit Edison as the largest producer of electricity in the state.

* The housing shortage, he asserted, was solved. With cement he would mass produce modular houses of six rooms for three hundred dollars.

31

The Birth of Empire

IN THE WAKE OF THE PANIC OF 1893, INDUSTRIALISTS AND FINANCIERS DIS-
illusioned with the intense competition of the laissez-faire system had commenced forming giant combinations to control output and prices. While the
Justice Department let the Sherman Anti-Trust Act lie dormant, the holding
company, first legalized in New Jersey, was devised to serve the same purposes
as a trust. Local and family firms which, however avaricious, had had an interest
in the areas in which they were located, were swallowed up by national and
international enterprises that were faceless and operated by remote control.*
Detroit's Michigan and Peninsula Car Companies, like railroad-equipment manufacturers elsewhere, were merged into the American Car and Foundry Company.
The copper works were absorbed by Anaconda. Local paint manufacturers were
mixed into national concerns like Sherman Williams. The tobacco industry was
organized into a giant trust. In the late 1880's, Eber Brock Ward's Illinois
Steel Company had still been the largest of numerous competing firms. During
the first decade of the new century, however, J. P. Morgan's United States
Steel Corporation became the first company to be capitalized at over $1 billion.
In addition to dominating the steel industry, the House of Morgan controlled
scores of railways, streetcar systems, the International Mercantile Marine, International Harvester, American Telephone and Telegraph, and General Electric.
A little competition he did not mind, Morgan said, but "ruinous" competition
he believed, in concord with his fellow industrialists, ought to be ended.

To reduce global competition, industrialists erased national borders and established international trusts and cartels. An international syndicate set prices in
the glass industry. Royal Dutch Petroleum was to the world what Standard Oil
had been to the United States. The Lever Brothers trust sought control over the
European soap and allied chemical industry. Britain's Nobel Dynamite Trust,
Germany's Vereinigte Köln-Rottweiler Pulverfabriken, and America's Du Pont
divided up the world's munitions markets between them.

* Pope even tried to organize the forty-five competing American bicycle manufacturers into
a trust.

149

In Detroit, William Durant, who had made a spectacular success of Buick, had ambitions to organize a similar combine in the auto field. In the Lafayette Street bars where the hard-drinking auto pioneers gathered, rumors bubbled that the charter members of "The International" were to be the Big Four—Buick, Maxwell-Briscoe, Ransom Olds's R.E.O., and Ford.

When approached by Durant, Ford, like Ransom Olds, demanded $3 million —in *cash*. With one out of every five automobile companies being taken to the junkyard each year, stock like that offered by Durant had a history of plunging in value until a whole issue was worth less than one automobile.

Stymied, Durant turned his attention to the Olds Motor Company. In October, 1908, he bought Olds for $3 million in stock, and incorporated Olds and Buick into the General Motors Corporation. In January of 1909 he added the Oakland Motor Company (which, in 1932, was to become Pontiac). Acquiring companies right and left, he brought into his domain the Cartercar, which had its genesis in King's first vehicle.*

Durant's greatest coup was the acquisition in July of 1909 of the Cadillac Motor Company for $4.5 million in cash. (The company's earnings the year before had been $2 million.) Under the direction of Leland, Cadillac had the finest workmanship and quality control in the industry. Leland amazed the British automobile industry by having his mechanics disassemble three stock Cadillacs, scramble the parts, then reassemble the cars from parts picked at random. To Europeans, who were customizing their cars as they had their muskets, it was a demonstration as revealing as Colt's. Who would have thought it possible to standardize the production of large, complex pieces of machinery like automobiles!

At the end of its first year of operations, General Motors reported a net of $9.1 million on sales of $29 million.

Flushed with success, Durant once more tried to induce Ford to sell. The Model T having proved itself in the meantime, Ford upped his sales price to $8 million. Durant scurried from banker to banker in the East to raise the sum, but was rebuffed. The men of New York's financial district were horrified that the American public was spending $300 million a year on automobiles instead of investing the money in bonds. They refused to market the bonds of Midwestern and Western cities which, in their opinion, had too high a ratio of automobiles to population. They scoffed at the suggestion that any automobile company could be worth $8 million.

Once, in spite of himself, Ford had been saved from a career in the electric power industry. Now, destiny in the form of the bankers denied him the comfortable life of a millionaire in order to make him the world's richest man.

Durant, to the contrary, had so overextended himself that less than a year after his offer to Ford he was unable to meet the Buick and Cadillac payrolls. In two years he had bought twenty companies, several of which were little more than corroding relics.

(He paid $7 million for the Heany Lamp Company, whose principal asset was the patent for a tungsten lamp that could produce three times as much light

---

* Supervisor of the machine shop at the Michigan State Prison, Byron D. Carter had purchased the chassis of King's car. Commissioning Barthel to design an engine for it, he had it made in the prison machine shop. In commercial production by 1905, the vehicle was unique in its use of friction drive in place of a clutch.

per electrical unit as the lamps then in use. Shortly thereafter the United States Patent Office declared the patent invalid.)

Desperate, Durant was forced to accept the terms of a syndicate, headed by James J. Storrow of the Eastern banking firm of Lee, Higginson, and Company. For a loan that, actually, amounted to $12.5 million, they charged a commission of $2.5 million, plus 6 percent interest, plus $6 million in General Motors stock as security. Durant was forced to relinquish the presidency. Only Leland's reputation and the fact that Cadillac was a money maker saved General Motors from dissolution. Charles Nash, the works manager at Buick, was picked to run the corporation.*

To replace Nash as works manager of Buick, Storrow turned to the American Locomotive Works, a firm of which he was a director. The works manager of the shops in Pittsburgh was thirty-five-year-old Walter Chrysler.

Born in Ellis, Kansas, Chrysler was the son of a Union Pacific locomotive engineer, and a descendant of the Dutch and German Republicans who had fought the slave owners for possession of the state. The Chrysler home was one of the more substantial in the town. When Walter's father had bought a windmill to provide the house with running water, it had been an event noted throughout the community.

In 1892, Walter Chrysler had been one of only twenty thousand boys in the country to graduate from high school. His parents wanted him to go to college, but he was determined to be a railroad mechanic. He regularly read *The Scientific American*. Before he was twenty he knew more about locomotives than master mechanics who had been on the job for decades. By the age of thirty he was a general foreman.

Bluff and competent, he had one passion—automobiles. At the 1908 Chicago Automobile Show he fell in love with and bought a $5,000 Locomobile. Since he was an expert mechanic but had no idea of how to drive, the first thing he did was take the car apart and put it together again several times. Gaining confidence, he drove it out into the country, gave an exhibition of the kind that sent farmers running for their shotguns, and wound up in a ditch.

Although the job at Buick paid only half the $12,000 he had been earning, Chrysler accepted Storrow's offer to manage the automobile company. After twenty years of experience in heavy production and cost accounting, he was startled by the slapdash horse-and-buggy methods that prevailed at the plant. Organizing production along the lines of Leland at Cadillac and Flanders at Ford, Chrysler in a short time tripled production. In a little more than five years he would be president of Buick, with a salary of $500,000 a year.

---

* Orphaned at an early age, Nash had been a migrant farm laborer until he had found a job as a trimmer at the Durant-Dort carriage works.

32

The Union Wreckers Association

DURANT'S ATTEMPT TO MONOPOLIZE THE AUTOMOBILE INDUSTRY FAILED. SO DID the attempt of William C. Whitney (descended from the same John Whitney as Eli), to obtain control of the industry through a monopoly on patents.* The legions of auto companies were left to form, merge, and dissolve in bewildering designs of their own making. As scores of cars were marketed, some for not more than a year or two, men flitted from firm to firm, so that it was difficult to know who was working where on any particular day.

Departing from Ford, Flanders in 1908 formed EMF with B. F. Everitt, general manager of the Wayne Automobile Company, and William Metzger. Metzger, the first automobile dealer in Detroit, had been one of Ford's original backers, and thus had become the first sales manager for the Olds-powered Cadillac. With King as chief engineer, he had organized the Northern Motor Car Company.

Wayne and Northern were merged into EMF. Two years later EMF was acquired by Studebaker, a South Bend, Indiana, carriage-making concern that had entered the automobile field in 1904. In another two years Flanders rejoined Metzger and Everitt to form the Flanders Motor Company. Scarcely had it been organized than it was bought by Benjamin Briscoe, whose United States Motor Company was intended to emulate General Motors. In 1912, United States Motors went into receivership and was renamed the Maxwell Motor Company.

If an automobile purchaser had difficulty knowing whether today's Silent

---

* Intending to form a taxicab monopoly in the United States, Whitney in the late 1890's bought Pope's electric vehicle manufacturing operation, and obtained rights to George B. Selden's patent for an internal combustion powered carriage. (Although Selden never built a car, he was one of the first promoters of the automobile in America.) Auto pioneers were almost unanimous in their ridicule of Selden's obsolete patent, but Whitney set up the Association of Licensed Automobile Manufacturers. Through suits and threats of suits, he attempted to collect a royalty on every car made. Although the first suit was filed against Winton, Ford ultimately became the principal defendant. The case dragged through the courts for a decade before the United States Court of Appeals ruled against Whitney in 1911.

Northern was tomorrow's EMF, how was he to choose between a Hackett, a Hollier, a Handley, and a Harroun? Some of the manufacturers tried catchy advertising: Maxwell was "Perfectly Simple—Simply Perfect"; the Cartercar had "No Clutch To Slip—No Gears To Strip"; for Jackson there was "No Hill Too Steep—No Sand Too Deep."

But it was far more reassuring to buy a Ford, one of the few cars that had established an identity. The New England production controls and techniques instituted by Flanders made Ford, along with Cadillac, the only car whose parts were machined finely enough to be interchangeable. While the owner of another make might have to wait weeks to have a part repaired or replaced by the factory, the owner of a Ford could drive into a garage, wait for a part to be changed, and drive out again. With every car serviced Ford's reputation grew, the number of cars sold increased, and the number of agencies to service the cars expanded.

In 1909, when sales in each of the various regions of the country reached thousands of cars annually, Sales Manager Norval Hawkins pointed out the tremendous savings in transportation costs that could be achieved by shipping components instead of cars, and assembling them at their destination.* The first branch assembly plant was built in Kansas City. By 1911, one out of every five cars sold was a Ford; two years later, two out of every five—a total of 168,000.

To expand his production facilities, Ford purchased the John R. Keim Steel Mill of Buffalo in 1912. The general manager of the mill was John R. Lee. The superintendent was a young Dane, William Knudsen.

Knudsen's father had lost his cooperage business in 1873 when Danish farmers, buried beneath mounds of American wheat and corn, had been all but swept off their land. Earning $350 a year as a customs inspector, the elder Knudsen had spent a good part of his life paying off the debts of the business whose downfall had been wrought on the American prairies.

William had come to the United States in 1900. Two years later he had taken a job with the Keim firm, at the time a maker of bicycles. When bike sales slumped, Keim turned to making brake drums, washing machines, telephone housings, and anything else that would keep the company going. In 1905, Knudsen accompanied the plant's superintendent to see "a man named Ford, who is in the automobile business." The result was a contract for seventy-five thousand dollars, largest in the history of the firm, to supply rear axle housings. The continuing relationship ultimately led to Ford's acquisition of the company.

Scarcely had Ford acquired the plant than the workmen struck for higher wages. Taking a cue from Edison,† with whom he shared a vehement hatred of unions, Ford moved stealthily to solve the strike. One day the fifteen hundred workers arrived at the plant to discover that it was a shell. All of the machinery had been crated and shipped to Detroit.

Knudsen was ordered to convert the empty factory into an assembly plant.

---

* Californians, affluent and with year-round motoring weather, bought far more automobiles than residents of any other state: 1 for every 29 persons. Mississippians were last, buying 1 for every 580.
† When workers had struck at the Edison Machine Works in New York City, Edison had packed up the machinery and moved the whole plant to Schenectady. On another occasion, when eighty men, trained to insert and seal filaments in bulbs, had formed a union, Edison had devised a machine that would seal the filaments mechanically. After completing thirty of the machines, he had fired all eighty workmen.

Such was his efficiency that, when he completed the task, Couzens called him to Detroit, presented him with a five-thousand-dollar bonus, and assigned him to set up branch assemblies in fourteen other cities.

In Detroit, Ford had no great need to worry about unions and strikers.

Organized labor had had its ranks decimated by the depression of the 1890's and had been handed a further setback by the Supreme Court in 1895. The judges ruled that the Sherman Anti-Trust Act, all but unapplied for its intended purpose of breaking up trusts, could be used to prosecute "monopolistic" labor unions. Industrialists, thereupon, broke strike after strike with injunctions, police, and Negro and foreign laborers employed as strikebreakers.

In such a climate the AFL was unable to maintain even a semblance of the industrial unionism that had been promoted by the Knights of Labor. In 1901, the Federation adopted a policy of "craft autonomy." Emphasizing the unionization of skilled labor—which could, presumably, not be replaced in the event of a strike—it excluded unskilled labor. In 1903, membership passed the 1.5 million mark. In 1898, there had been 1,098 work stoppages involving 263,000 workers. Five years later there were 3,648 strikes, involving 788,000 workers, the largest number in American history up to that time.[1]

To combat the threat of the AFL in a labor-short market, Leland and a number of his friends in 1902 organized the Employers Association of Detroit (E.A.D.). Declaring that he was not an enemy of the worker and that he believed in unions as protection against *unscrupulous* employers, Leland insisted that he was interested only in protecting employers against the *abuses* of labor. But what was unscrupulous and what were abuses was left to anyone's definition.*

By 1904, the E.A.D., which earned for itself the name of the Union Wreckers Association, had attained such a measure of control that Leland could recommend to a labor-troubled friend, Joseph Boyer, that he transfer the Burroughs Adding Machine Company from St. Louis to Detroit. (Boyer was associated with William Burroughs in construction of the first successful adding machine.) Employing spies, the E.A.D. kept a master list of forty thousand workers, half the labor force in the city. Through lockouts, the restriction of credit, threats of mortgage foreclosures, and the importation of labor from other areas it broke one strike after another. Not only did it seek to control labor, but it forced employers who treated workers too liberally to conform to the wage and hour standards that it established (a sixty-hour week with pay averaging about fifteen dollars a week for skilled workers and ten dollars for unskilled). It set up a labor bureau that in effect made it the employment agency for the entire city.

Before 1907, union men had still been able to find employment. But after the "panic" of that year, the craft unions were reduced to impotence. When employees in the metal trades struck, the E.A.D. replaced them with nonunion workers. The expansion of industry resulted in hundreds of skilled workers becoming foremen and voluntarily leaving the union.

A powerful political force in the city, the E.A.D. maintained a lobby in the state capitol. It killed bills prohibiting child labor, setting safety standards,

---

* For President Baer of the Reading Railroad, abuse was anything that discomfited "the Christian men to whom God in His infinite wisdom has given the control of the property interests of the country." [2]

and requiring factory inspections. Through its influence on the courts it obtained omnibus injunctions against picketing. Through its control of the police department it routed strikers at one plant after another. The police forbade the workers to meet in public places. On May Day, 1909, the police waded with swinging truncheons into a peaceful parade. The Progressive Republican Detroit *News* commented:

"The assault on these few score men was as unwise as it was unprovoked. . . . It is a strange thing that this FREE COUNTRY does not allow half the liberty in this respect that is enjoyed under the monarchical governments of Europe."

Tens of thousands of new workers streaming into the city were screened by the E.A.D. By 1911, the association could pride itself that, of a labor force of 175,000, 160,000 were free from union taint.

33

The Strike Against the
Widow Maker

THE FAILURE OF THE AFL'S CRAFT UNION POLICY TO INHIBIT UNION BUSTING RE-
sulted in rebellion within the Federation. In 1904, the Western Federation of
Miners and a number of other groups denounced the AFL for attempting to build
an "aristocracy" of workers, while simultaneously failing to deal with the problems of mechanization. The next year a number of unions, including the Western
Federation of Miners, pulled out of the AFL to form the International Workers
of the World. The militant and socialist IWW countered the repression and
force employed by management with a policy of violence. Both sides resorted
to murder and kidnaping. Obeying only such laws as were convenient, they
denounced each other for breaking the laws.

From West Virginia to Idaho, the conflict was especially bitter in the
mines. At the Calumet and Hecla copper mine in upper Michigan, fifteen
thousand miners struck on July 22, 1913. One of the men involved was twenty-
nine-year-old Ralph Lentick, the grandson of Alfred Lentick, who had arrived
from Cornwall not quite fifty years before.

Unlike his illiterate grandfather, Ralph had completed grammar school in
the solid, steam-heated building seating twelve hundred children that the Calumet and Hecla mining company had constructed. But like his father, his grandfather, and his forebears for generations, he was a miner.

Much had changed in the depths of the earth in those fifty years. In 1880,
three-hundred-pound, two-man pneumatic drills had replaced the three-man
teams of miners relying on muscle power. At about the same time dynamite
had taken the place of black powder for blasting, thus enabling the company
to increase productivity 50 percent. A forest of huge timbers had grown underground to shore up the galleries and adits. Telephone lines were strung along
the passages. Miners' lamps replaced candles. Huge steam engines hoisted
eight-ton skips at speeds of forty miles per hour. The Red Jacket shaft, sunk
in the 1890's, had not bottomed out until it reached forty-nine hundred feet.
Never before had men dug to such a depth.

Above ground, Calumet was transformed from a wilderness into a city of twenty thousand people. The world's biggest copper-smelting plant, employing forty-five hundred men, was constructed. Electric streetcars ran beneath electric lights. Electric interurban cars connected Calumet with other Upper Peninsula communities. Electricity lighted the homes of the miners.

In some ways Calumet was a more modern city than Detroit. The pollution it generated was even worse. Rivers of waste were channeled into Lake Superior. Mountains of "deads"—the material that remained after the ore was extracted —challenged in height the smokestacks wreathed in their own black effluence.

Financed by Boston money, Calumet had its culture (a sixteen-thousand-volume public library) and its elegant *society,* consisting of transplanted *Bostonian* managers and executives, who patronized the Red Jacket Opera House to see Maude Adams, Lillian Russell, and Sarah Bernhardt.

In its relations with the men, the company exercised an enlightened, nineteenth-century paternalism. For the nominal rent of about a dollar per room per month, the men were provided with well-built, two-story frame cottages. There was a prepaid medical plan to which married men contributed a dollar and single men fifty cents a month. An Employees Aid Society financed by equal contributions from the miners and management paid sick benefits of twenty-five dollars a month, and disability and death benefits of three hundred to five hundred dollars.

In return, management expected the workers to acknowledge that the company knew best, and to accept decisions without questions. The company owned everything: the mines, the school, the library, the stores, the hospital, the coal supply, the water pumps, the garbage wagons, the church, and the hymnbooks in the church. It owned the houses. It owned the red paint that added the identical finishing touch to every identical house. It even owned the toilets.

It was a paternalism that had worked reasonably well in a community that was fairly tightly knit, but which was breaking down in a polyglot city. The Cornish and the Irish had arrived first. Then had come Swedes and Finns, to be followed by French-Canadians, Germans, Hungarians, Italians, Norwegians, Lithuanians, Poles, Slovenes, and Croatians. Rippling outward from the mines like the rings of a tree, the groups formed distinct and separate districts, whose social standing could be determined by the distance from the center. Farthest away, in the outer circle, lived the *Bostonians.* Next to them were the Cornish and the English-Canadians, many of whom now occupied supervisory positions and earned $85 to $125 a month. The most recent immigrants settled in the Red Jacket district, containing the oldest and poorest housing, next to the mines and the mills.

Nationality differences and old European animosities were exploited by the company to channel grievances against itself into ethnic antagonisms. Paternalism was expanded. Social workers knocked on the doors if there were family problems, or if the children got into trouble.

For decades the Calumet and Hecla mine was the world's most profitable, and it made the fortunes of Bostonians and Detroiters. The investment in Calumet, below and above ground, was the largest for any copper mine. But with the beginning of the new century there were indications that many of the "eyes of the mine" (the richest veins) had been taken out. It was costing 50 percent more to remove the ore from under the ground in Michigan than to strip-mine it in Arizona and Montana. If profits were to be maintained, the company would have to increase efficiency and reduce costs. Less than a half century after going into production, Calumet was reaching the stage of Cornwall in the 1840's.

In 1911, the company introduced thirty-nine-pound one-man drills to replace the three-hundred-pound two-man drills. Productivity increased up to 91 percent. But opposition of the miners to the one-man drills was intense.

A generation before, mining had been a group enterprise, in which the loneliness and fear of the underground was ameliorated by the camaraderie. Mechanized tramways and pneumatic drills had reduced the "group" to two men. Now it was proposed that one man should work in an isolated stope (excavation) at the end of a gallery where during a ten-hour shift he would have no one to talk to, and no one to help him in case of an accident. Yet he was being paid only $2.36 a day compared to the $3.87 received by a Montana miner.

The men rebelled.

Denouncing the one-man drills as "widow-makers," they flocked to the ranks of the Western Federation of Miners. They demanded union recognition, an eight-hour day, a graduated scale of wages (based on the price of copper) rising to $4 a day, and, most of all, two-man drills. Although union organizers urged restraint and caution, the men walked out. So tense was the atmosphere that by July 27, five days after the beginning of the strike, Governor Woodbridge Ferris dispatched the entire 2,600-man Michigan National Guard to Calumet.

The company was determined to break the strike and the union. It influenced the sheriff to deputize 1,700 men and bring in 52 strikebreaking experts. It hired 120 detectives from the Waddell-Mahon agency, a strikebreaking firm whose men had gained such a notorious reputation that even the manager of the mine compared them to gangsters.

(The agency publicized its employment with an advertisement: "We ask you to watch the progress of the present strike, because we know it will be a triumph for law and order, a triumph for the mine owners, and will furnish still another evidence of the success we have always met with in breaking strikes.") [1]

At the same time, in keeping with its record of paternalism, the company adopted the position that everything could be settled peacefully within the family. If the men would return to work, all the issues could be negotiated. All, except union recognition. There could be no question of dealing further with the "Red Socialists" and "outside agitators" who were responsible for the disruption of a tranquil and contented community.

But as the weeks passed and the men remained determined, the attitude of management hardened. A half dozen Waddell-Mahon men shot and killed two miners, and when they were indicted for murder, it was the sheriff who sent them into hiding and refused to surrender them for trial. Eviction notices appeared on the doors of the cottages. (The evictions were enjoined by court order.) Credit was cut off. Clamping the men in an economic vise, the company demonstrated the stanglehold it held on the community.

In answer to complaints, Major Roy Vandercook of the National Guard wrote Governor Ferris:

"I am aware that every mine locality is a little kingdom of itself with the mine manager practically king of that domain; I know this is not American, but they are not dealing with American citizens." [2]

The strike attracted the attention of the nation. Charles Moyer, the union's president, established himself in Calumet. Clarence Darrow, its attorney, and John L. Lewis, a rising power in the labor movement, came to bolster the morale of the strikers. But month by month additional strikebreakers were imported, until there were nearly three thousand in all. Month by month miners watched their jobs being taken away. Men began drifting back to work. Bitterly the holdouts watched them go. Fights flared between strikers and workers; between friends and between neighbors. On December 7, 1913, three strikebreakers were murdered, and four days later a pitched battle erupted at a union headquarters.

Ralph Lentick's education would have qualified him for a job as a shift boss, and many of the Cornish were working in managerial capacities. But he had no stomach for bossing men. He wanted the restoration of the two-man drills. Otherwise, he wanted to be left alone, both by the company and the union. He would not participate in the strike, but neither would he cross the picket lines. He had a wife and two children, and, as the strike continued, his savings vanished. He had listened to his father coughing his life away, and had watched him sleep sitting up at the kitchen table because he could no longer breathe lying down. And already, as he spit up the dust and smoke that he sucked into his lungs in the mine, Ralph knew that the miner's inexorable fate was catching up with him.

To provide some cheer, the Women's Auxiliary of the Western Federation of Miners scheduled a Christmas Eve party for the children. Ralph's wife Rebecca had a cold, so she remained home with four-year-old Harold while eight-year-old Cissy went to the party with a friend.

Some seven hundred persons, mostly children and women, crowded into the hall of the Societa Mutua Beneficenza Italiana, located on the second floor above an A and P store. On the stage was a Christmas tree bright with electric lights. The children fidgeted as they were made to sit through a program of recitations and carol singing before the glorious moment when Santa Claus would hand each a present. At last the time came, and they crowded into the aisles to make their way to the stage.

Through the single door at the top of the staircase the head of a man appeared.

"Fire!" he cried.

There was no fire. But the cry was echoed around the hall. *"Fuoco!" "Feuer!"* "Fire!" It was sounded and resounded in several languages.

There was a stampede for the door. The children who were the first to reach the landing were shoved and tumbled down the stairs. Others were pushed on top of them. A human avalanche poured down the stairwell, an avalanche that was transformed into a pillar of bodies reaching all the way to the ceiling, a pillar compacted as if by the force of a giant press.

Within it, thirty-seven girls, nineteen boys, thirteen women, and five men were asphyxiated and crushed to death.

Before an hour passed the news spread over the town. Ralph and his wife rushed toward the hall. Thousands of people congregated in the damp, freezing darkness. The process of untangling the dead was slow and excruciating.

Pressing against the cordon set up by the police, men cursed and women wailed. Hysterically they called out the names of their children. Rumors spread that the tragedy was the result of a company plot. There was little disagreement that the man who had precipitated the stampede should be hanged as soon as he was identified and caught. (He never was.)

While the parents waited at the hall, children who had survived went home and, finding no one there, ran through the streets searching for their mothers. Frantic parents were going down one block, their frantic children down the next. As mangled bodies were brought out from the stairwell, men and women identified children as their own and carried them home, only to discover that their own child, unhurt, was in fact waiting for them there.

Three hours of waiting, searching, and chaos passed before the Lenticks discovered Cissy had survived unscathed. Ralph decided he had had enough of Calumet. On the day after Christmas he took his family, boarded the train, and headed for the farm of Rebecca's sister and her husband near Maple Rapids in the central part of Michigan.*

The long hours of the search had aggravated Rebecca's cold. A train ride of more than a day made her feel even worse. By the time the family reached the farm, her temperature was over 105. Before the week was out she was dead from pneumonia. It was a few days after the funeral that Ralph, grieving and wondering what he would do, heard that Henry Ford was going to pay workers five dollars for an eight-hour day. It seemed as if all, and more, that the men were striking for in Calumet was being offered to them by an auto manufacturer in Detroit.

---

* On the same day the union's president, Moyer, was shot in the back. Seriously injured, he was hustled onto a train for Chicago by company detectives.

34

The Dawn of the Assembly Line

CONSTRUCTED OF STEEL, CONCRETE, AND GLASS, THE "CRYSTAL PALACE" IN Highland Park was occupied by Ford on New Year's Day, 1910. The main building contained 260,000 square feet of floor space spread over four stories. A sixth of a mile long, it was paralleled by the sawtooth-roofed machine shop. A 57-foot-wide covered craneway occupied the space between the buildings. Facing the craneway were galleries where the huge, traveling cranes picked up and delivered goods and materials. The vast, uncluttered expanse of the interiors emphasized mobility and flexibility, and facilitated experimentation in the arranging and rearranging of production. Openings in the floors permitted vertical movement. The five-stacked power plant (to which Ford's office was connected by an overhead walkway), the 40,000-square-foot foundry, the metallurgical laboratory—all emphasized self-sufficiency and the smooth flow of production.

Initially, the move to the new plant proved a mixed blessing. Under the management of Flanders, productivity at the Piquette plant had increased 150 percent; from 5.8 cars per worker per year in 1905, to 14.6 in 1907.*

At the new plant, however, production executives were forced to cope with vastly increased quantities of everything. The number of cars made multiplied from 6,400 in 1908 to 78,000 in 1912. Simultaneously, efficiency plunged. The number of cars per worker per year dropped to 6.7 in 1910, then rose slowly to 11.7 in 1913.† [1]

Grappling with a continuing shortage of skilled workers, and an off-and-on shortage of unskilled workers, executives gave increasing attention to "Taylorizing" the plant. Frederick Winslow Taylor, the prototype of the efficiency expert, was urging industrialists to adopt his measures of "scientific management."

* The company had constructed the Piquette plant in late 1904 after it outgrew its original Mack Ave. facilities.
† At Highland Park, Ford had his own power plant, and he produced a great many more of his own components in the new factory. The figures, therefore, are not entirely comparable. Nevertheless, they do indicate that there were major production problems.

To increase productivity, Taylor planned every task for every workman, the manner in which he was to do it, and the time it was to take him. The old-style foremen, with their close and personal relationship to the men, were replaced by eight *efficiency experts*—an inspector, a gang boss, a speed boss, a repair boss, a time clerk, a route clerk, and a disciplinarian. Since an unskilled worker was "too stupid to properly train himself," Taylor declared, he must be given an overseer who, like a drill sergeant, would control his every motion from dawn to dusk, and curse him at every misstep. "With a man of the mentally sluggish type of Schmidt it is appropriate." * [2]

In 1909, Taylor spoke to a group of Packard executives. His theories rapidly gained credence in Detroit. At Ford the thinking went a step further. If efficiency depended upon transforming men into robots, even greater efficiency should be achieved by then mating the robots to machines.

The turn-of-the-century development of high-speed tool steel made possible a whole new generation of machine tools. By 1914, the company had fifteen thousand machines, more than one for every worker. The machines' sophistication increased as rapidly as their numbers. One automatic multidirectional steel drill was able to bore forty-five holes simultaneously in four different directions in a cylinder block.

But the machining of parts did not cut through the swamp of confusion that existed in the main assembly plant. Gangs of workers moved from chassis to stationary chassis. Runners taking parts to and from the depots on the floor dodged and twisted through the maze. Foreign workmen unable to follow instructions or read labels lost their way and did not return for hours. Parts were directed to the wrong stations. Tools vanished. Despite Taylorization, lack of coordination resulted in periods of frenzied activity followed by periods in which workers sat on their machines.

If the solution to the shortage of skilled workers was to transfer the skills to the machines, then evidently the solution to the problem of the delivery of parts was also mechanization. Overhead delivery belts had been used in the Cincinnati meat packing industry since shortly after the Civil War. If a moving hook could be used to carry a carcass, there was no reason why it could not be rigged to deliver an engine block.

In fact, there was little novel about the individual components going into the new mode of production at the Ford plant. Johann Bodmer had invented the traveling crane for a Manchester factory in 1853. Ford during his boyhood had watched railroad cars rolled from point to point in the production shed of the Michigan Car Company. What was unprecedented was the application of such principles and devices to heavy industry and a product as complex as an automobile. What was unique was the coordination between scores of diverse productions, operations, and feeder and assembly lines.

What made the new mode of production possible, first, was the standardization that Ford had built into the Model T. If each part were not like every other equivalent part, and each assembly not like every other equivalent as-

---

* Taylor was able to triple and quadruple production in many plants that adopted his system. Costs were often reduced to less than half of what they had been previously. Only the young, the strong, the healthy—the most productive third of the work force—needed to be retained. About what was to happen to the two thirds of the workers who were dismissed, Taylor was cavalier. They would find work elsewhere—sooner or later.

sembly, the dehumanization and coordination of production could never have been achieved.

What made it possible, second, was the layout of the factory. Technological developments in steel and reinforced concrete had brought into being a plant offering unprecedented mobility and flexibility. Never before had there been a production line a sixth of a mile long.

What made it possible, third, was electricity, and the concept, originating with Van Depoele, of applying electric power to the driving of machinery. At the Piquette plant, Ford had benefited from the low-rate "energy contract" Dow had devised to induce manufacturers to switch from steam to electric power, and thus increase the usage of electricity during daylight hours.* By 1909, the seventy automotive manufacturers were using 10 percent of the system's capacity, a capacity that had increased some tenfold in five years. But the Highland Park complex was unique in having an in-plant system capable of generating enough electricity to light most of the cities of the world. It was a system that made feasible the operation of a virtually unlimited number of machines, and their arranging and rearranging to the best advantage.

The devising of feeder lines to carry parts for the assembly of components like magnetos and axles was relatively simple. But to have dozens of feeder lines converging on numerous stationary assembly points was a practical impossibility. The assembly itself would have to be placed in motion. There would have to be parallel feeder lines reticulating the assembly line.

The first assembly line to go into operation was the one for the magnetos. By December, 1913, after months of experimentation, the final assembly line—on which the engine, wheels, and body were to be mounted on the chassis—was being readied for production.

As the company's executives met for a year-end assessment, they could congratulate themselves on the great strides—strides that would show up in 1914 when the company sold an almost unbelievable 19.2 cars for each worker it employed. But the problem of the labor supply, and its quality, remained unsolved.

The result of a production study was astonishing. For every 100 jobs, 963 men had to be hired annually. Two decades earlier a worker had remained with the same company an average of thirteen and a half years; the average now was little more than a month. Floating from job to job, workers showed up one day and disappeared the next. Sometimes they were half drunk when they did appear, and at other times they were so ill that they passed out. Foremen who continued to be semi-independent masters of their own departments hired and fired whomever they pleased whenever it pleased them. Within the limits established by the company they set their own pay scales. An investigation by John R. Lee, the former Keim executive who was concerned principally with personnel at Ford, discovered sixty-five different scales. Men performing the same jobs were being paid different wages in different departments. Foremen often confined their hiring as much as practicable to their own neighborhoods and their own ethnic groups. Kickbacks were common. Favoritism and division along ethnic lines created bad blood. Fist fights were frequent. Men had no incentive to remain on the job.

* In 1908, Detroit Edison installed thirty-one motors to drive sewing machines, a little-noted development that would bring about the shift of clothing manufacturing from tenement to factory, just as mechanization had moved textile production from cottage to factory.

Ever since the inception of industrialization, factories had plucked unskilled men, women, and children off the streets, given them a few hours of training, then ushered them back onto the streets when orders slackened. But in the complex organization of production at Ford there were fewer and fewer jobs for which men needed no skills. For many positions the training required was no longer to be measured in hours but in weeks. Literacy and the ability to speak English were becoming essential. The company was unable to produce cars as fast as they were being sold, and had a backlog of one hundred thousand orders.

In order to increase production, Couzens, Wills, and the other executives who were gathered with Ford in his office decided to scrap the schedule of two nine-hour shifts and operate around the clock. For over half a century workers had struck and fought unsuccessfully for an eight-hour day. Now Ford, faced with the arithmetic necessity of dividing a day into equal periods, came to the only practical decision: three eight-hour shifts.

At the same time, it was imperative to upgrade the work force and reduce turnover. Since 1909, Ford had had "profit sharing" in the form of Christmas bonuses for steady employees. At the end of 1913, the company distributed $60,000 in bonuses to 640 employees, an average of less than $100 each. Yet profits for 1913 were $27 million. Dividends, of which more than half went to Ford, were $11.2 million. Evidently the company could afford to be more generous.

Someone, possibly Lee, asked why the "profit sharing" could not be extended into a year-round plan. Since the company had to make a considerable investment in many of its employees, such a plan would encourage them to improve themselves, and to remain both on their good behavior and with the company. In accordance with Taylorization, hiring would be taken out of the hands of the foremen and lodged in a separate department.

In October, Lee had revised the company's pay scale and fixed wages at a minimum of 26 cents an hour for the unskilled and 54 cents for the skilled. During further discussion, the company's pay scale and the concept of "profit sharing" blended into each other, and were thereafter never to be separated.

At 54 cents an hour, skilled workers were earning $4.86 a day. But in a factory that had more machines than it had workers, the difference between skilled and unskilled was being blurred. By learning to operate a machine, a man could move from an unskilled to a skilled position in a matter of weeks. It appeared that unskilled labor would be less and less of a factor in the company's operations. Why not, then, pay everyone a wage on which he could live and support his family decently? A wage that would enable the company, which needed to add five thousand men for its new, three-shift operation, to attract and choose from the most desirable of the labor force? Why not pay everyone $4.86, or, in effect, $5 a day?

When economic practicality dovetails so perfectly with altruism, it is only human to emphasize the altruism. To the reporters who gathered at the plant late in the afternoon of January 5, 1914, Ford and Couzens announced "the greatest revolution in the matter of rewards for its workers ever known to the industrial world"—the eight-hour, $5, *profit-sharing* day.

It was, in fact, the advent of a revolution; but a revolution that had nothing to do with "social justice" or workers' rewards. It was a revolution as epochal as that generated by Watts's improvement of the steam engine, by Arkwright's devising of the factory, and by Whitney's development of standardized production. These had brought about the end of the guild and of the independent workman. They had led the excess rural population, unlettered and unskilled, to flock toward great factory cities in which they could earn a living.

The Five-Dollar Day was the announcement that this epoch was coming to an end. It drew men from the mines, the forests, and the railroads. But it wanted only the best of those men. It did not want, it could not use, it would not keep the sluggards, the illiterates, the unintelligent. It was a warning of new standards. A warning that the new, ultramechanized industrial society would have decreasing use for the large number of people who continued to be procreated on the farms.

II

THE PERNICIOUS
PROSPERITY

35

The $5 Day

PETER JANSEN'S EXUBERANCE WAS COWED BY THE SULLEN STARES OF THE other men. They all could see the "No Hiring" signs in English, German, and Polish that hung on the factory gate. Some of them had been standing there for six days. Shivering in the nine-degree temperature, they were buffeted by a wind that blew swirls of snow along the street. Many of them were desperate. The city's Poor Commission was doling out pittances to more than nineteen thousand persons—a greater number than at any time since 1896–1897.

As other men arrived, forming row upon row, Jansen was knitted into the mass. "Workers! Comrades!" an IWW agitator appealed to them. Nearby two or three thin, pallid girls were passing out copies of the union's publications, *Solidarity* and *The Emancipator*.

Every day the soapboxes were set up near the gate. Every day the police, swinging their truncheons, hauled the orators away. With no more than a few hundred adherents, the Communist-leaning "Wobblies" were no great threat to anyone. But the Employers Association of Detroit had been made uneasy even by the AFL's International Union of Carriage and Wagon Workers, a convivial guild of less than four thousand members that had not added the word *automobile* to its name until 1913.

Coughs, like the barks of dogs, swept fitfully through the thousands. Legs locked against legs, bodies pressed against bodies, men rubbed their hands together and tried to warm their frozen cheeks with their own breath.

A stocky man, about five foot six in height, was pushed against Jansen. His red nose sniffled into a full moustache. Jansen reached into his "turkey" and brought out a heel of bread. As he bit into it, he noticed that the man stared hungrily. Ripping the heel in two, he offered him half. The man pretended not to see it. Again Jansen thrust it forward. The man accepted it. From the difficulty he had chewing, it was apparent that he had bad teeth.

Bringing forth a jug of whiskey, Jansen took a swallow and offered it. William Norveth declined. Speaking with an accent, he warned Jansen that a young man, fresh from the country, was sure to be taken advantage of by the

sharpers in the city. He should not trust anyone. He should not give anything
to anyone.

As the day shift arrived, they found the gates of the plant plugged solidly.
Workers wearing small Ford badges tried to force their way through the job
seekers. They were beaten back with blows and curses. No one was going to
work until there was work for all.

The guards were unable to open a passage through to the gates. Hurling
expletives in a half dozen languages, the men shouted for "Jobs!"

"No jobs," the guards shouted back. There would be no jobs until the regular
workers had been allowed to enter. The men swore and jeered. Mr. Ford had
promised jobs. They had been waiting hours and days for those jobs. No one
was going to take those jobs away.

"No jobs," the guards kept repeating. "No jobs." The declaration infuriated
the men. The plant was immobilized. Inside the plant a crew appeared with a
water hose. The men were warned if they did not make way before the gates,
the hose would be turned against them. Jeers and curses were the response.

A jet of water hissed from the hose. The men were knifed back. Cries of
anguish, dismay, anger, and pain blended into a guttural roar. Stumbling, shoving, knocked to the ground, the men fought to escape. Frozen by the water, the
job seekers dispersed into a mob. Rocks were hurled against the guards, and
then through the windows of the plant.

Jansen, roaring, wielded the stick on which he had carried his turkey against
a row of windows. Spreading this way and that, the men vented their anger at
anything in their path. They flailed at policemen and ripped off their uniforms.
They overturned and plundered the lunch and cigar stands of the vendors who
catered to the factory workers.

Shots of whiskey were two for a quarter in the bar; and Jansen had spent
almost two dollars. That was more than he could afford. But he did not know
what to do. Not knowing what to do, he was getting drunk. For the first time
in his life he had to *find* a place to sleep; *find* a job; *find* a way to stay alive.
In the lumber towns and logging camps, on the farms of the Peninsula, if a
boy were willing to work for whatever might be offered, a farmer would put
a plate in front of him, a bed of straw beneath him, and a blanket over him.

Like thousands of other men arriving in Detroit, Jansen was lost. Coming
into the bar, he had stamped his boots against the sawdust floor, and stood in
front of the hot stove to thaw and dry his frozen clothes. Pausing only to eat
the free sandwich provided for lunch, he drank his way through the daylight
into dusk.

Gradually, Jansen acquired a drinking companion. He was taller than Jansen,
and had the same broad shoulders, muscular arms, and calloused hands. He did
not talk much. When he did, he spoke in disconnected expletives. "The day
will come . . . Goddam capitalist adventurers . . . We'll get 'em, you bet
. . . Bastards . . ." Periodically he was shaken by cavernous coughing. Occasionally a sob issued from him. Over the course of the hours Jansen learned
that Ralph Lentick had heard about the $5 day in Maple Rapids. On Thursday,
three days after the original announcement of the $5 day, the Ford manage-
ment, appalled at the rush to the factory gates, had announced that only men
who had lived in Detroit for at least six months would be hired. Lentick said
he did not believe that. It was just another way to "trick the workers."

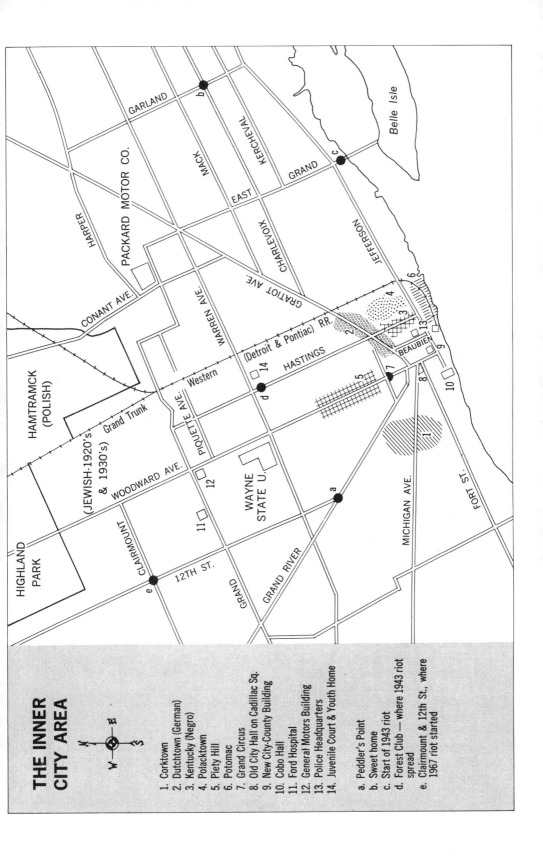

THE INNER CITY AREA

1. Corktown
2. Dutchtown (German)
3. Kentucky (Negro)
4. Polacktown
5. Piety Hill
6. Potomac
7. Grand Circus
8. Old City Hall on Cadillac Sq.
9. New City-County Building
10. Cobo Hall
11. Ford Hospital
12. General Motors Building
13. Police Headquarters
14. Juvenile Court & Youth Home

a. Peddler's Point
b. Sweet home
c. Start of 1943 riot
d. Forest Club — where 1943 riot spread
e. Clairmount & 12th St., where 1967 riot started

HIGHLAND PARK

HAMTRAMCK (POLISH)

(JEWISH-1920's & 1930's)

Belle Isle

PACKARD MOTOR CO.

WAYNE STATE U.

GARLAND

HARPER

CONANT AVE.

MACK

EAST

KERCHEVAL

GRAND

CHARLEVOIX

JEFFERSON

WARREN AVE.

GRATIOT AVE.

Western

HASTINGS

(Detroit & Pontiac) RR.

Grand Trunk

PIQUETTE AVE.

WOODWARD AVE.

CLAIRMOUNT

12TH ST.

GRAND

GRAND RIVER

MICHIGAN AVE.

FORT ST.

BEAUBIEN

It was dark when Jansen heard the voice with the accent addressing him. Turning, he saw the man with the moustache with whom he had shared the bread in front of the plant. Norveth suggested that the bar was no place for a boy. He said that he had room in his house for a lodger. Jansen asked if he had room for *two* lodgers. Norveth shrugged. Together the three men boarded the Woodward Avenue streetcar.

Not even knowing each other's names, they traveled in silence. The glow projected from the windows of the mansions painted the street a soft yellow. Occasionally the streetcar passed an automobile struggling by the side of the tracks. As the car neared the Grand Circus, the street took on a commercial appearance. Shop windows were alight. The headlamps of a truck flickered across a horsedrawn cart. Since Henry Ford's appearance in the city on a winter evening thirty-five years before, electricity had transformed it. No longer was there a sharp division between the activities of daylight and darkness. No longer was the height of buildings limited by the number of flights of stairs one had to climb.

Jansen stared at the skyscrapers that had risen to dwarf the ten-story Hammond Building: the Pontchartrain Hotel, the Union Guardian Building, the Penobscot Building, and others. The electric signs fascinated him. The most astonishing of all hovered over Cadillac Square. High in the sky, a woman, her scarf blowing in the wind, was riding a motor car and advising all of Detroit to "Watch the Fords go by."

As the men changed streetcars to a crosstown line, their path took them by a small restaurant. The odor of food caused Jansen to turn his head. He had eaten nothing but a sandwich and a few pieces of bread during the day. He was accustomed to huge meals. His stomach growled angrily. As his eyes focused on the vapor escaping from the kitchen's ventilator into the alley, they were alerted by a movement in the shadows. He halted. Beneath the vapor, seemingly stretching toward its warmth, was a skeletal, rag-clad woman. Trembling violently, she appeared very old. Yet her skin was unwrinkled, almost diaphanous. Clinging to her was a small child. Wedged between a garbage can and the shallow indentation of a doorway, the two were almost invisible.

Rooted to the spot, Jansen felt a tug on his arm.

"What is she doing?" he asked Norveth.

"Waiting. When they bring the garbage out, they eat."

"Where do they go?"

"They don't go anywhere. They stay."

"She's sick!"

"She dies. This morning. The next morning. Soon."

"The child?"

"She belongs to church, they take her if they find her. I don't think they find her. I think they both die."

"But you can't let them die like that!"

"God lets them. He lets them be born. So he lets them die. There are many children."

There were many children in the two-story frame house to which Norveth took Jansen and Lentick. Of the nine born to William and Theresa, eight were still living at home.

In the confusion in front of the plant, Norveth had picked up a badge, walked in with the regular shift, and been taken on when one of the crews showed short. In the city, survival as one grew older depended on one's wits. It depended on slipping past guards and bribing foremen; on lying about experience and age—at thirty-nine Norveth cut his hair short so that it stood straight up, and smudged his moustache black so that the gray could not be seen. It depended on keeping up with the younger men in the shop—if the foreman suspected that a man was faltering because of his age, out he would go.

The house had five rooms and a kitchen. In back, by the alley, was the privy. Downstairs the house had electricity. In each room a low-wattage bulb hung from a cord in the ceiling. Electricity had only recently become competitive with gas, and the capped pipes of the gas lights still protruded from the walls.

To reach the kitchen table, Jansen and Lentick had to run a gauntlet of wet shirts, long johns, nightgowns, and drawers that hung drying in parallel lines. Norveth was already sitting down. Facing toward the crucifix suspended from the wall, he said grace. He told Jansen and Lentick that he would help them get work in the Ford plant. Once employed, they could board with the family for four dollars a week. They could share an upstairs bedroom with two of the boys.

The double bunk with its mattress and sheets was fancier than any Jansen had ever slept in. But the thin blanket was hardly suitable for the unheated room. When Jansen saw that the two boys in the other bed were embracing each other for warmth, he threw his own blanket over them. The bunk-shaking coughing of Lentick, above him, made him twist and turn. Finally, still dressed in his heavy pants and jacket, he drew the last ounce from his jug of whiskey and slept soundly through the night.

Two weeks later both Jansen and Lentick were working at Ford. Assigned to the final assembly line, Jansen was one of a dozen men who helped guide the body onto the chassis. As the chassis was moved through at ground level, the body, suspended from scaffolding at second-story level, was slid down on top of it. Thus the two were mated together.

Through the new production techniques, the time required for assembling an engine was being cut from 9 hours and 54 minutes in October, 1913, to 3 hours and 46 minutes in April, 1914. The time required for assembling the chassis was reduced from an average of 12½ hours to 93 minutes!

With the addition of Jansen and Lentick, the number of persons in the Norveth household reached sixteen. (The oldest daughter, with her husband and three children, was still living at home. Her mother took care of the children so that she could supplement her husband's meager income by working in a cigar factory.)

Humorless, Norveth dominated the family. Raised in the culture of the Austro-Hungarian Empire, in which the Hungarians were simultaneously servants and masters, he was a petty tyrant. Although he would drink beer and wine, he disliked hard liquor. Peter learned to skirt him in order to avoid his fatherly admonitions.

After dinner, Norveth always settled down with a large, curved pipe. Occasionally he would read, or try to read, the *Detroiti Ujsag,* the local Hungarian-language weekly. The family's prize possession was a hand-cranked phonograph. The collection of seven records, three of which were cracked, consisted solely of martial band music. On Sundays, his family trailing like a school of fish, Norveth led the way to mass. In the afternoon, if the weather were nice and a band concert scheduled, they headed for Belle Isle.

Like other families, the Norveths for nine years had skirted the edge of economic disaster while dollar by dollar struggling to improve their standard of living. The $5 day produced a different crisis: how much of the additional money to spend on necessities, such as clothing and food—on which the family had always skimped—and how much to save for major purchases and for the future. Although Ford reasoned that the $5 day should enable the women and children of employees to stop working, many families were concerned not with reducing the number of working members, but with raising their standard of living.

The neighborhood in which the Norveths lived would not have been considered a slum, but like blue-collar districts throughout the city—and throughout the world—it was lacking in amenities and all but bereft of city services. Pigs, geese, and goats no longer roamed the streets, but it might have been better if they had. The dogs and cats that had replaced them were not as useful and not as good at scavenging. In the mounds of garbage that piled up in the alleys, rats, flies, and vermin bred prolifically. Since the area had no playground, children poured out of the overcrowded homes and occupied the streets and the empty lots. Enviously they clustered around the ubiquitous neighborhood bars and poolrooms. In boardinghouses, men slept four to a bed, four beds to the cramped, dank, airless and foul-smelling rooms. Such was the shortage of housing that every room, from parlor to kitchen, was likely to be a "bedroom." Indoor toilets were a rarity. Since they were placed wherever there was plumbing—even in the kitchen—they were often more a curse than a blessing. Many houses had no indoor water supply, but only a backyard pipe that froze in winter.

"There are thousands of men out there in the shop who are not living as they should," Ford declared. "Their homes are crowded and insanitary. Wives are going out to work because their husbands are unable to support the family. They fill up their homes with roomers and boarders in order to help swell their income. It's all wrong—all wrong. It's especially bad for the children." [1]

So Ford, faced with ranks upon ranks of men with inflamed gums, swollen jaws, and toothless mouths, with skin lesions and abscesses, with watery and infected eyes, initiated a program of hygiene counseling and urged workers to "avoid the congested and slum parts of the city." He advised them that trunks should not be used as savings banks, and counseled them to be thrifty and save toward buying their own homes. The company's legal department would assist workers in purchasing houses. By 1916 it was estimated that one out of every eight or nine Ford workers was buying his own home: a home that had running water, electricity, and a bathroom; a small, narrow, wood-frame home without foundation or insulation that would become the slum of the next generation.

"By underpaying men we are bringing on a generation of children undernourished and underdeveloped morally as well as physically; we are breeding a generation of workers weak in body and in mind. . . . Industry will, therefore, pay the bill in the end," Ford prophesied.[2]

But Ford's fellow industrialists could see only their own labor demanding parity with that at Ford, their factories wracked by strikes and denuded of workers. Unable to comprehend what was occurring, they excoriated the "mad socialist" of Highland Park. Ford was denounced as a "traitor to his class" and attacked viciously in the *Wall Street Journal,* and other financial papers. The Employers Association of Detroit was aghast. By "sharing profits" with the workers instead of the stockholders, he was undermining the structure of the capitalistic system. By increasing wages, he was creating millions of dissatisfied workers and so breeding revolution. By establishing the eight-hour day he was violating the dictum of business that the only good worker was an occupied worker. What use would the workers make of all their excess cash and time? They would, according to the theory of Frederick Winslow Taylor, drown themselves in dissolution. They would fall prey to agitators. They would lose respect for work. Pay a worker twice what he needed for a minimum existence, and he would show up for work only every other day!

While businessmen exaggeratedly denounced Ford, social workers went to the other extreme and hailed him as a paragon, the new industrialist with a social conscience. No one understood what Ford meant when he called the $5 day a "piece of efficiency engineering, too." No one paid notice to the firing of nine hundred Orthodox Greeks and Russians who had thrown the plant into an uproar by celebrating Christmas in January.* No one grasped the implication of Ford's statement that his workers "must observe American customs and holidays." No one looked beyond Ford's altruistic proclamation of "social justice," or examined how the rules laid down to make men eligible for that social justice would benefit the company.

It was right that a man be paid enough so that he could raise his family decently, organize his life, and get to work on time. It was not right to pay a man five dollars to conduct himself improperly, or to get drunk, so that he was hung over on the job. To teach workers the proper way of life and to ensure that they follow the company's rules, the Sociology Department was organized. Headed by Lee, it consisted of thirty social workers and investigators, each furnished with a car, an interpreter, and a driver.

Only family men deemed worthy would be admitted to the "profit sharing" of the $5 day. Women, who had been averaging $2.07 a day, were not included in the $5 day. When Ford was asked why, he replied that he thought they would get married. In fact, women did not work on the assembly line, and were not likely to drink and fail to show up for work. They did not jump from job to job. So there was no reason to include them.

Similarly, anyone who had not yet proven that he fit into the great machine assembled under the roof in Highland Park was not admitted to the $5 day, but languished on "probation" at $2.72 a day. Probationers were workers who had been with the company less than six months, unmarried men under twenty-two years of age, men separated or involved in divorce—anyone not hewing to the "code of conduct." The code was all-embracing. Employees were admonished not to "spit on the floor at home," and to "use plenty of soap and

---

* To fix dates for holidays, the Russian and Greek Orthodox Churches continue to follow the old, uncorrected Julian calendar, in which dates are thirteen days behind the Gregorian calendar.

water." They were to "avoid . . . making purchases on the installment plan." The smoking of cigarettes engendered suspicion. Marital discord, gambling, and the excessive consumption of alcohol were social felonies. The "evil custom" of taking in male boarders demanded explanation.

No one discerned anything improper in investigators knocking on the doors of workers' homes to check that the beds were made up, in demanding to see savings account passbooks, or in requiring an itemization of household debts. Fellow workers, neighbors, wives, children, and even the doctors of workers were interviewed. Each scrap of information, each piece of gossip was entered on a card in the man's name, and filed. The Sociology Department bred suspicion, mistrust, and silence. Through the department, men could exploit their grudges; wives could coerce their husbands; neighbors, landlords, and creditors could threaten.

If a man were found unworthy, his pay was reduced to that of a probationer. He could regain his full wages only by satisfying the investigator that he had recovered his "strength of purpose." Each month that he was derelict he lost money from his "bonus." If he had not reformed at the end of six months, he was discharged. Because Ford employment was the most sought after in Detroit and perhaps the world, workers submitted to the regimen. Like other companies, Ford had been wont to hire anyone who appeared at the gates. Now the company delved into every cranny of a worker's life.

It was midsummer when an investigator called at the Norveth house. It seemed she was really interested in Lentick. The man was reported to be drinking, and not to be living with his family. Nevertheless, her investigation soon included Jansen and Norveth. She asked Theresa if her husband mistreated her; if he brought home all of his money; if he had any vices. She looked at the bedroom in which Lentick and Jansen slept. She wanted to know why two of the children were not in school. She talked to the neighbors. She noted everything.

Norveth was called to the Sociology Department and questioned. He was keeping male boarders. Was he not concerned about their influence on his daughters? What kind of example was the dissolute Lentick? Did not the company pay a fair wage so that he could avoid this evil custom?

Norveth was adept at manipulating bureaucrats. He convinced the investigator that his motive in boarding Jansen was to provide guidance to a fatherless youth, and that he was being victimized by Lentick.

The investigator warned Norveth that he would be watched. Lentick was fired. The Sociology Department was the medium through which Ford was transforming his employees into the most disciplined work force since the beginning of the Industrial Revolution.

36

The Americanization of Detroit

THE $5 DAY WAS THE BEST COST-CUTTING MEASURE EVER UNDERTAKEN, FORD
exulted. The 10 percent per week turnover was reduced to .3 percent. In 1913,
between 55,000 and 60,000 men had filled 12,000 jobs during the course of the
year. In 1914, 85 percent of the men who were employed by Ford stayed with
Ford. In 1915, only 6,508 new men were hired.

(At the old rate of turnover, 200,000 would have had to be hired, a number
that, according to Ford, would have been "an impossible proposition.") [1]

Among those new men were the Schwartz brothers from Bialystok in Russian
Poland. Coming from a family of tailors, they were part of the exodus of more
than a million Jews who left Russia in the twenty years before the World War.
Forty-five thousand of them settled in Detroit.

Ever since the Jews had been invited into Poland by Boleslav the Pious and
Casimir the Great in the thirteenth and fourteenth centuries to practice their
skills and trades in an agricultural and backward land, they had made up the
greater part of the middle class. (The same was true in most other eastern
European lands, such as Romania, the Ukraine, and White Russia.) It was a
middle class of capitalists, of managers and professionals, and of workers; of
the wealthy, but mostly—an estimated nine out of ten—of the poor and near-
poor.

In a Russia that was 88 percent rural, the 2.4 million Jews made up 37.7
percent of the urban population. They owned 38 percent of the factories. They
controlled from one half to four fifths of the textile, soap, tobacco, lumber,
leather, and dairy industries, and major portions of the iron and steel, brewing,
glass, paper, and chemical industries. As both industrialists and workers they
fought bitter battles against each other—the Jewish *khevras* were one of the
principal antecedents of the industrial union movement in the Western world.
In a nation that was two centuries behind the West in industrialization and in
which money was chronically short, everyone worked long hours, and even the
professionals and "capitalists" commonly were poorer than an American farmer.
Artisans worked thirteen to eighteen hours daily. Doctors received fifteen to
twenty cents a visit, and lawyers earned from five dollars to six dollars a week. [2]

In a land that had no public schools and whose education policy had not

177

changed since Catherine the Great had told the governor of Moscow, "The day when our peasants shall wish to become enlightened, both you and I will lose our places," the Jews were the only group who supported their own system of universal male education.[3] Composing less than 2 percent of the population, they accounted for more than half of the applicants to the universities.

During the worldwide depression of the 1890's, the czarist government once again sought to channel the grievances of the peasants away from itself and the nobility, and toward the Jews. A special double tax was placed on Jewish artisans, thirty thousand of whom were expelled from Moscow. When uprisings followed the Russo-Japanese War, several hundred Jews were among the eighteen hundred revolutionaries hanged. The secret police established a special section for the incitement of pogroms, and encouraged mobs to storm Jewish homes. Jewish areas of cities were put to the torch, the men were killed, the women raped, the children carried off to be baptized into Christianity.

Jewish boys as young as twelve were impressed into the army and coerced into accepting baptism. Frequently they would not be released for twenty or thirty years. Army service was looked upon as the equivalent of a sentence of life imprisonment, if not death.

Faced with entering the army, Hymie Schwartz and his brothers had fled, and made their way to England and America. With their coreligionists they carried the center of the world's clothing industry from Lodz to New York.

In America, however, they found that they could earn a better living making screws and bolts for the Ford Motor Company. In contrast to the western European Jews, the Polish and Russian Jews tended to be highly visible. Bearded and dressed in black, stooped and shriveled from sedentary labor and an inadequate diet, they were segregated and regarded as inferior—not only by the Christians, but by their western coreligionists. (In the same fashion, rural Negroes were looked down upon by their skilled, urbanized, and bourgeois cousins.) In Detroit they congregated in the area that had been the old Negro district, and pushed northward along Hastings Street.

Yet if their speech and habit were strange, they were scarcely more so than those of the fifty-two other nationalities working at the Ford plant. As wars ravaged the Balkans, and Christians were persecuted in the Turkish Empire, Greeks, Armenians, Syrians, and Lebanese streamed to America. Detroit developed the most numerous Bulgarian and Macedonian communities in the United States. There were immigrants from the largest nations in the world and from some of the smallest, but Malta had more representatives than China.

To bridge the Babel of tongues and enable workers to comprehend the operation of their machines, Ford instituted Americanization and English classes. For foreign workers who expected to share in the five-dollar day they were mandatory. Workers were pressured to take out citizenship papers. Between 1914 and 1916 the number of aliens at Ford dropped from two thirds to one half of the work force. On July 5, 1915, six thousand Ford workers marched several miles from the Campus Martius to Belle Isle in celebration of "Americanization Day."

With the start of the World War, Ford's program was adopted as the pilot model for Detroit, and Detroit became the pilot model for the nation. The city was plastered with five hundred posters urging foreigners to enroll in evening English classes. Schoolchildren were told to bring in their mothers if they could not speak English.

37

The American War

INITIALLY, THE WAR REDUCED AMERICAN EXPORTS TO EUROPE TO A TRICKLE. The unemployment problem in Detroit was aggravated. One could scarcely go a block in the downtown section of the city without meeting a sight such as that which had greeted Peter Jansen. Between seventy-five thousand and eighty thousand people—three fourths of whom did not speak English, and the great majority of whom had come from the rural Catholic areas of southern and eastern Europe—were out of work. Deserted wives, many with a half dozen children, made up at least a fifth of the applicants for relief. Ninety percent of people in their middle sixties and older did not have enough money to live on. Old couples begged arm in arm on the streets. Children cadged pennies and had to be driven away from the doors of restaurants. The sick and the dying huddled in doorways, in woodsheds, beneath tarpaulins, and in cellars.

Despite the establishment of a new Poor Commission in 1880, the city was no more prepared to deal with the problem than it had been in the days of Father Kundig. The Poor Commission's funds were soon exhausted. Separated by sex, old couples and children were placed in poorhouses that were not too different from the Industrial Revolution horrors of England a century before. Since no hospital would accept the mentally ill, they were thrown into the tank at police headquarters or caged in the basement of the Red Cross Hospital.

Little treatment of any kind was available to the poor. Eighty percent of those receiving care were at St. Mary's Hospital. But when the Poor Commission proposed the allocation of funds for an addition to the hospital, Protestant ministers were outraged. A drive was initiated to have the city build its own hospital. Opened in October, 1915, the hospital admitted nearly eleven thousand patients during its first nine months of operation.

To alleviate the plight of the aged, an Old Couples Support Fund of five thousand dollars was established, and forty-nine couples were selected as the beneficiaries. The fund ultimately grew into an Old Age Pension plan, the first in America.

To bring some coordination to the halfhearted and penny-ante charities, the

179

Bureau of Public Welfare was established in 1914. Supplementing the Poor Commission, it was intended as a clearinghouse for the needy.

But all this was patchwork and provided minimum relief. Only an upturn in the economy could help most of the needy. That upturn, beginning in 1915, was provided by the war. It was a war that came to be known as the World War.

It would better have been named the American War.

For it was American technology that dominated it, and American industry that largely came to support it.

It was the technology for mass producing weapons perfected by Whitney and by Colt, and exported to Europe by Colt, that enabled the warring nations to arm millions of men. It was the barbed wire devised to contain cattle on the Western plains that immobilized the men. And it was the machine gun developed by three Americans—first Richard Gatling, then Hiram S. Maxim, and finally John Browning—that slaughtered them by the hundreds of thousands.

It was the Wright brothers' airplanes that added a new dimension to war. It was an American Holt caterpillar tractor that Winston Churchill converted into the first tank, and it was the tank that ultimately played a major role in breaking the stalemate. It was the submarine that carried warfare beneath the sea. And it was Isaac L. Rice who in 1899 had incorporated the Electric Boat Company of Groton, Connecticut, after he had failed to develop an electric cab. The Electric Boat Company became the world's principal manufacturer and licenser of submarines—two thirds of which were built for foreign powers, and used by both sides in the conflict. (As the war progressed, the company's stock shot up from $10 to $125 a share.)

America had become the world's leading industrial nation in the 1880's, and by 1913 its dominance was complete. It produced more iron and steel than Germany, Great Britain, and France combined.* From its factories came 36 percent of the world's manufactured goods. To cope with the German industrial establishment which had supplanted Britain's as the second largest, the Allies turned to the United States. To raise money with which to buy armaments, they floated a $500 million loan through J. P. Morgan, shipped gold to America, and liquidated their foreign investments. The balance of trade, which had been in favor of the United States since 1896, reached proportions unprecedented in world history. The world's financial center shifted from London to New York.

The blood of the Western Front was grist to the mills of American arms manufacturers. Colt, Remington, and Winchester could not expand fast enough to meet the orders. Ninety percent of the small arms of the Allied armies were manufactured under the Colt patent. Between 1915 and 1916 the company's sales doubled. Du Pont almost overnight became the world's greatest manufacturer of gunpowder.

Harking back to the Civil War, the industrial Republicans perceived the war as the best thing that could have happened. Many were Anglophiles through ancestry; others through their financial connections with London banking houses; others because before the war Germany had dominated world markets in electrical and chemical products, and with the war these markets were falling to American manufacturers by default. A German victory would endanger re-

---

* The United States had 48 percent of the world's steel production compared to 25 percent for Germany, 12 percent for Great Britain, and 7 percent for France. Russia, Austria-Hungary, and Italy, the other three major powers involved in the war, had much smaller industrial establishments.

payment of the loans by the Allies, and would place Germany in an even stronger position in world markets than before. With every battle the Germans won, the industrialists and bankers became more insistent on American "preparedness," a preparedness that would, of course, increase the orders of materiel from heavy industry.

The industrialists, however, were bedeviled by the maverick in their midst, Henry Ford. Violating the most sacred theories and dogma of economists, Ford and Couzens were turning the Ford Motor Company into the most successful business in the world's history. With mechanical regularity, Model T sales multiplied from year to year. They were 6,398 in 1908, 78,000 in 1912, and 472,000 in 1916. With such skyrocketing sales, any other manufacturer would have raised prices in order to maximize profits. Ford, to the contrary, passed on to the consumer the cost reductions achieved through greater efficiency, and kept cutting prices. (In July of 1915 he even rebated 10 percent to every purchaser of a Model T during the previous twelve months; a total of $15.5 million.) Instead of the company's falling to ruin through such practices, as had been freely predicted, its profits rose. They were $30 million in 1914, $24 million in 1915, and $60 million in 1916.

Having discovered a mass market not only for a "luxury" product, but for a product of heavy industry—a feat that a half dozen years before would have been considered impossible—Ford did not understand the necessity of production for destruction. "New York wants war, but not the United States," he declared. The Navy League was a "tool of war profiteers." On August 22, 1915, the Detroit *Free Press* headlined:

HENRY FORD TO PUSH WORLD-WIDE CAMPAIGN FOR UNIVERSAL PEACE

"I hate war," said Ford, "because war is murder, desolation and destruction.

"If one-tenth of what has been spent on preparedness for war had been spent on the prevention of war the world would always have been at peace."

Such assertions could not go unanswered by Detroit's industrialists and Navy Leaguers.

On September 1, Henry Joy, crying "Remember the Maine!" warned that Germany would "lay heavy tribute" on the United States if the Allies were defeated.

Four days later Ford established a $1 million education fund against "war." He praised President Wilson for his firm stand against the "militarist clique." In an unveiled reference to Joy he denounced the "local apostle of murder," who was "known to be interested in manufacturing munitions of war."

"Loud-mouthed bleaters for peace at any price . . . ought to be shot," Joy derided Ford.[1]

The feud split Detroit.

In 1913 Ford had not even been listed in *Who's Who,* but in 1915 he was one of the half dozen best known men in the United States, and a hero to the opponents of the war. In the second week of October, an International Peace Conference in San Francisco proposed that a Neutral Conference for Continuing Mediation to end the war be established by President Wilson.

The formation of such a conference had been advocated by Mme. Rosika Schwimmer since the beginning of the war. Jewish and Hungarian by birth, she was the London correspondent for several European newspapers and the press secretary of the International Women's Suffrage Alliance. She was one of the world's most militant advocates of women's rights and a leader of the International Committee of Women for Peace. Through Edwin Pipp, the editor of the Detroit *News,* she obtained an interview with Ford for herself and Louis P. Lochner, secretary of the International Peace Conference.

Ford believed that one "international banker" by himself was responsible for keeping the war going. After meeting with the financially hard-pressed peace advocates on November 19, he was convinced that the world was waiting for him to take over leadership of the peace movement. Two days later Ford and his entourage were in New York. Spontaneously during lunch an idea emerged that Ford should charter a ship and lead a peace delegation to Europe. Shortly thereafter Ford was on his way to the White House to obtain a presidential blessing.*

Invitations to join the peace delegation were sent to the governors of all the states, former President Taft, William Jennings Bryan (who had just resigned as Secretary of State in protest against Wilson's pro-Allies policy), and other notable Americans. Almost unanimously they declined. Even old friend Thomas Edison, with whom Ford had Thanksgiving dinner, exclaimed, "Oh, hell, I beg to be excused!" [2]

Ford was called upon to address a peace rally at the Belasco Theater. Since confrontations with an audience were terrifying to him, he had to be pushed out onto the stage to acknowledge the wild chants of "We want Ford." Blushing, he managed to stammer one sentence:

"Out of the trenches by Christmas, never to return again!" [3]

"Out of the trenches by Christmas" became the motto for Ford's "Peace Ship," and was promptly ridiculed by the cynical realists of the newspapers. On December 4, 1915, eleven days after the idea had first been broached, the *Oscar II,* a Danish ship chartered by Ford, weighed anchor. Aboard were eighty-three "peace delegates," fifty members of the "technical staff," fifty-four reporters, eighteen students, a couple who had decided that a European honeymoon could be combined with peace promotion, and a Jewish telegraph boy who stowed away and became Ford's messenger boy.

In the short time since Ford had sprung upon the consciousness of America, a legend of genius had been spun about him. In fact, brilliantly intuitive in areas in which he had experience, he was hopelessly adrift in those in which he did not. In his early fifties, he represented a generation whose education, except for that of the elite, had been rudimentary. Many of his ideas had been shaped by the prejudices and folklore of rural, nineteenth-century America. Unable to express himself or to spell out what he had in mind, he uttered pronouncements as equivocal as those of Greek oracles. His close associates had learned that it was necessary to "interpret" what he said, analyze it, come to a conclusion, and then go back and discuss with him if that was what he had meant. Meetings with the press had to be "well guided." An "interpreter" intimately familiar with his thoughts had to stand by and state: "What Mr. Ford means is . . ."

Aboard the ship Ford had no such protection, and rubbed ideas with fifty-four newsmen. The war had broken out, he suggested, because "liquor had made Germans and Frenchmen suspicious of each other." The history of crime was the history of the "inveterate cigarette smoker." Granulated sugar cut the walls of blood vessels. Asked how he intended to end the war, he indicated it would

---

* Ford, who remained a "country boy," sat swinging his leg back and forth over the arm of the chair while telling jokes to the President.

be sufficient to demonstrate to the belligerents that they could derive greater profits from making tractors than from making war.

As Ford's reputation of genius crumbled, the newsmen, at first incredulous, then delighted, magnified his follies. The expedition came to seem like a sally by the Don Quixote of Highland Park against the mills of war. Michigan newspaper editor Arthur Vandenberg * renamed the Peace Ship the "loon ship."

It was the cosmopolitan Madame Schwimmer who emerged as the leader of the expedition. It was she to whom reporters paid homage and to whom they gave most of the publicity. Autocratic, heavy-set, with the face and steely determination of a Russian commissar, she had fully as much sense of the dramatic as Ford, and she loved being on stage. Day and night she surrounded herself with secretaries pouring out statements and press releases. She always carried with her a large black bag that quickly attained an aura of mystery and was rumored to contain top secret documents—a rumor she did nothing to dispel.

(In actuality the bag held such exotic items as perfume vials, family photographs, a diary, a miniature deck of cards, a package of Sen-Sen, and some baby powder.)

Ford, who was unable to compete with her and uncomfortable with the reporters, disappeared into the ship's engine room, where he was in his element. Halfway across the ocean a wave nearly washed him overboard. Catching cold, he closeted himself in his cabin. There he was kept company by Dr. Samuel S. Marquis, dean of the Episcopal Cathedral in Detroit, whom Clara Ford had sent along as a monitor. Dr. Marquis was Clara's bridge to Detroit's Anglophile "society," and he set about convincing Ford that he should separate, if not disassociate himself from the venture.

By the time the ship arrived in Norway, Ford had lost his euphoria, and his conviction that he could end the war in one stroke. He had scarcely been lodged in his hotel before he murmured, "Guess I had better go home to Mother." [4] Unable to face the delegation to tell them that, he slipped out of the hotel at four o'clock in the morning and caught a ship back to the United States.†

Ford's belief that he had been "used," and that there were mysterious persons in the world who carried international secrets in black bags, was soon to be skillfully exploited by one of his executives. His resentment at having been exposed to ridicule opened his mind to a virus which, as it developed into a disease, was to have a significant effect on the Ford Motor Company, on the city of Detroit, and on the world.

---

* Vandenberg subsequently became a power in the Republican party and the U. S. Senate.
† Ford continued to support the committee until the United States entry into the war in 1917. Mme. Schwimmer was appointed minister to Switzerland by the first democratic Hungarian government after the war. When she refused to swear allegiance to the Communists who overthrew the government, she was dismissed. Nevertheless, she was denounced as a "Bolshevik agent" and a "German spy" when she returned to the United States in 1921.

38

"No Stockholders . . . No Parasites"

For some time relations between Ford and Couzens had been strained. Ford's peace campaign carried them to the breaking point.

Following completion of the Highland Park plant, management of the company devolved upon Couzens. In less than five years he built a network of seven thousand dealers, almost as many as the rest of the industry combined. Initiating a policy of depositing company funds in communities where Ford had assembly plants or important dealerships, he established for Ford a financial influence in every region of the country.

Ford possessed neither patience nor talent for the details of day-to-day operations. He hated paper work. Once, when asked to sign a requisition, he had all the carefully contrived forms and reports of Sales Manager Norval Hawkins gathered up and dispatched in a bonfire. With an absent-mindedness that came to be legendary, he would stick important papers into nooks and crannies and then forget that he had ever seen them.

Abhorring disputes and seemingly incapable of meeting any issue head on, Ford was neurotic about avoiding arguments. He tiptoed past the office of "Old Bear" Couzens, and even took to climbing in and out of the windows of his own office in order to evade disagreeable visitors or topics. He countermanded the directives of other executives behind their backs, and left a trail of confusion.

With an ego as sensitive as a barometer and as easily bruised as a flower, he was determined that the success of the company should be publicized as due to one genius: Henry Ford.

When Ford had returned from his first trip to Europe in 1912, Wills had presented him with a surprise—a new Model T. It was a car for which Wills, who headed the engineering staff, had designed numerous improvements. Ford had circled it like a panther. Then he had pounced. A door had flown off. Snarling, he had ripped and kicked loose part after vulnerable part. Calling for a sledgehammer, he had smashed the vehicle to pieces.

He was not going to allow Wills to intimate a Model T could be designed without the inspiration of Henry Ford.

Couzens thought that Ford was making a fool of himself and hurting sales by expounding his views on the war in company publications. Ford avoided a confrontation, but undercut Couzens's authority, and finally made his position untenable. Exclaiming, "I've had enough of his goddam persecution," Couzens stalked out.[1]

Ford was left to run the company as he pleased. He made decisions without consulting the board of directors. He was at odds with the Dodge brothers, who were dissatisfied with their role as parts suppliers for Ford, and in 1915 put their own car on the market. As owners of 10 percent of the Ford stock, they were applying the huge dividends from the Model T to the construction of their own plant. In the summer of 1916 Ford announced that since minority stockholders had collected $28 million in dividends in thirteen years, future profits over $1.2 million a year would be reinvested in the company. Although unable to keep up with orders, he dropped the price of the Model T another $75, until the cheapest runabout cost only $345.

For several months the Dodges waited for Ford to alter his stand. On Boston Avenue in the exclusive upper Woodward Avenue area, the Fords, the Dodges, and department store magnate Joseph L. Hudson * were neighbors. On November 2, 1916, Edsel Ford married Eleanor Clay, Hudson's niece and ward. (Her parents had died some time previously.) Attending the wedding, the Dodge brothers talked to Ford, but became convinced they would be unable to sway him.

On November 3, they filed suit, seeking a court order that Ford declare "reasonable dividends."

Ford's reaction was to announce the formation of the Henry Ford and Son Tractor Company, with "no stockholders, no directors, no absentee owners, no parasites."

It was the beginning of Ford's isolation not only from the associates of his meteoric rise to power, but from the city of Detroit.

---

* Hudson, descended from an English merchant family, had built Detroit's largest department store. In 1909 he backed Roy Chapin, who had risen to sales manager at Olds, in the production of a new motor car. It was duly named the Hudson.

39

The Three T's

WHEN THE DETROIT UNITED RAILWAYS (D.U.R.) HAD THREATENED IN 1910 TO discontinue service because of a dispute over fares, Ford and Couzens had offered one thousand Model T's to replace the streetcars. Three years later Mayor Marx had appointed Couzens commissioner of the street railways. It was the beginning of a distinguished political career.

In three annexations the city had increased its area to nearly eighty square miles. The D.U.R., however, embroiled in its "thirty years' war" with the city, let its cars and its tracks deteriorate and failed to provide service to many of the outlying districts. Couzens spearheaded another attempt to have the city take over the system. But it was the company, warning that municipal acquisition would bring higher taxes and more corruption, which won a narrow victory at the polls.

The city, in fact, was being shaken by another of its periodic scandals. In order to obtain a street closing, the Wabash Railroad paid off virtually every one of the forty-two aldermen. "Honest Tom" Glinnan, the council leader, received one thousand dollars. Most citizens had no doubt that such bribery was routine.

To put an end to the corruption, Cadillac's Henry Leland and thirty-six other members of the Westminster Presbyterian Church in 1912 had founded the Good Citizens League. The league drew its support not only from the traditional anti-Catholic, anti-immigrant wing of the Republican party, but from the party's Temperance faction, frustrated for more than a half century, and from a powerful and rising political force: women. Women were breaking out of their Victorian subservience as a result of the mass employment opportunities offered by the three T's: typing, the telephone industry, and teaching.

The typewriter was an outgrowth of American literacy and the mushrooming newspaper industry.* Its development had stemmed from the need to mechanize

* Christopher Sholes, a Wisconsin newspaper editor, enlisted a machinist, Samuel W. Soulé, in the development of the prototype machine. A typewriter operating on a different principle was patented by John Pratt, a South Carolina newsman.

the writing of reporters, even as printing was being mechanized by the linotype. The Remington Arms Company, applying the mass production techniques of weaponry, had initiated the commercial manufacture of the typewriter in the 1870's. The prosperity of the 1880's had brought about its rapid application to the paper work of business; and the male amanuensis was supplanted by the female secretary.

The telephone industry had started its spectacular expansion after the expiration of Bell's patent. (Prior to 1893, the American Bell Telephone Company had held a monopoly, and like most monopolies had attempted to earn the highest profit through the highest rates, rather than through the expansion of service.) During the economic revival of the latter 1890's, thousands of local telephone companies were incorporated. Needing tens of thousands of English-speaking operators, the companies turned to the cheapest domestic source of labor—young native white women.

In the rapid expansion of American education between 1900 and 1910, 119,000 additional women found jobs as teachers. As educated men were drawn off by the higher pay and greater opportunities in industry, four out of every five of America's 523,000 teachers by the end of the decade were women.

Since it was the American industrial and educational boom that was creating the positions, the emancipated woman became another of the American phenomena. Her emancipation gave her both economic independence and economic power. As taxpayers, women had had the right to vote in Detroit school tax elections since 1865. Remaining longer in school, women tended to be better educated than men. Their numbers in white-collar jobs gave their spokesmen a new authority. (Militant feminist Laura F. Osborn denounced the Detroit superintendent of schools because, although four fifths of the teachers were women, all the department heads and assistant department heads were men.)

Essentially native American, antisaloon, and reform-minded, the women's suffrage movement was kicking its heels as never before. It presented a vast reservoir of votes for virtue to combat and more than offset the votes that the city bosses were drawing from the immigrants. So reformers embraced women's suffrage.

In 1912 a proposed Michigan constitutional amendment to enfranchise women lost by only 760 votes out of a half million cast. It left little doubt as to what was in store, despite Cardinal Gibbons's dark warning that female suffrage would "increase the searing social evil, divorce," and bring about "moral looseness, discord, and dishonor in the sacred family circle."* [1]

But in Detroit, as in other major cities, the "sacred family circle" was more often than not absent. The massive migration of young workingmen from Europe to America, and from the farms to the cities had created a serious imbalance between the sexes.

In 1870 there had been only 430,000 more men than women in America. By 1900 the disparity was 1.6 million. In 1910 it reached 2.7 million.† (Actu-

---

* Gibbons was the second American cardinal. His parents were immigrants from County Mayo, Ireland. He was the archetype of the turn-of-the-century Christian Socialist. Considered a "liberal" who was vitally interested in improving the lot of the workers, he nevertheless did not believe workers mature enough to have control over their own destinies.
† Seventy percent of the immigrants between 1900 and 1910 were men. The Irish immigration during this period was unique in that 52 percent of the immigrants were women—a reflection of the earlier drain of men from Ireland, the demand for Irish maidservants in America, and the need of Irish-American men for girls to marry. Jews had the second high-

ally, since the census tends to *lose* unattached males, the differential may be assumed to have been considerably greater.)

There were at least 3,643,000 more men than women of marriageable age. In the major cities there were tens of thousands of men without women. Having not even a bed they could call their own—in roominghouses they slept in shifts synchronized with the shifts of the factories—the workers congregated in pool halls and saloons. Detroit had sixteen hundred licensed bars, and at least one thousand unlicensed ones known as "blind pigs." No records were kept of how many men whiled away their hours in the opium dens that flourished in the Chinatowns of many cities.

To compensate for the imbalance between the sexes, prostitution was a major and organized business, catering to every taste and pocketbook. In a day of haphazard statistics, no one could tell just how big a business it was. (Estimates of the number of whores in New York City varied from nineteen thousand to forty thousand.) In Detroit, where the heart of the city alone contained more than five hundred whorehouses, there were more brothels than churches, and far more prostitutes than deacons. Even as each nationality frequented its own saloons, so each nationality had its ethnic whorehouses. Some of the places, like Hattie Miller's elegant brick fortress or the House of All Nations or the Bucket o' Blood Saloon, were notorious. Whenever a street became too disreputable, its name was changed. So Croghan Street disappeared in favor of Monroe; and if one asked for Champlain Street, he was directed to Lafayette East.

Girls as young as twelve worked up to sixteen hours a day as laundresses and shop girls. If a shirt were burned or an article stolen from a counter, they were held responsible, and the loss was deducted from their two-dollar-a-week wages. Half starved, they were easy prey for anyone with a kind word or an offer that seemed to promise a better life. Youths roamed in organized bands, seducing the girls, then selling them to houses of prostitution.

Like the railroads and factories, the sex industry recruited the European and Asiatic poor. Depending on the quality of the "goods," an "importer" received from five hundred to fifteen hundred dollars. (Up to three thousand dollars for Chinese girls, who were in short supply because of the Chinese Exclusion Act.) Talent scouts ranged over Europe to report that "her beautiful teeth alone are worth a million" and to message in code that "the cigars . . . are fine, young, and good-looking." [2]

Troupes were taken to wherever the action was: the Chicago World's Fair, the Klondike, the Seattle Exposition. The auto boom generated a migration of prostitutes to Flint and Detroit.

In a check of twenty-two licensed employment agencies, investigators found that seventeen agencies readily agreed to supply girls for sportinghouses. Some of the immigrant homes and mission houses, purportedly established to shelter single girls who had no place to go, channeled them into prostitution. Commonly the police demanded payment into the police fund of a fee for each prostitute. (The annual take from the owner of one chain of brothels in New York was thirty thousand dollars.) Throughout America there were organizations that

---

est proportion of women, 43 percent, among immigrant groups. Like other immigrants from eastern and southern Europe, Jews were drawn to America by the economic opportunities; but unlike the others they had no intention of returning to Europe, so most men brought their families along.

functioned as guilds for procurers and operators of whorehouses and handled their members' business with the police, the magistrates, and the politicians.[3]

Such flourishing of vice, and the participation of the police in its profits, was intolerable to the Good Citizens League and its supporters. Under the police commissionership of former Water Commissioner John Gillespie, money flowed into the police department; and suspects who had been arrested flowed out. With money, a miscreant could buy virtual immunity from arrest. If he were arrested, he could buy dismissal of the charges. If he were brought to trial, he could buy acquittal. And if he were convicted, he could buy quick release.

Police officers were badly paid, worked twelve-hour shifts, and often owed their appointments to politicians. They had no esprit de corps, and tended to bounce back and forth between factory and police work depending on the economic situation. Paid $2 to $2.50 a day—only in Boston and New York were they paid over $3.50 a day—and needing to supplement their income, officers could not help it if nimble fingers filled their pockets while they walked their beats.

Poorly educated, they were frequently illiterate or semiliterate. As late as 1921, lieutenants on the Detroit force averaged 57.80 on the U.S. Army's "Alpha" test (roughly equivalent to an IQ test), and sergeants 54.71, compared to 77.3 for apprentices in industry.* [4] Mostly born in the United States, with a large percentage of second- and third-generation Irish and farmboys among them, they were subservient in dealing with the middle class, and rough and authoritarian in handling immigrants and the poor.

Not until 1911 had Detroit—together with New York City, Philadelphia, and Berkeley—pioneered in the establishment of a training school for police. Before then, men had been given a revolver, a club, a pair of handcuffs and a badge, and instructed to go out and enforce the law. What the law was, normally was left to the discretion of the sergeant or lieutenant, who usually was beholden to the ward boss. "Crime investigation" consisted of beating confessions out of suspects. The "curbstone court" was an accepted custom.

In 1901, the four-member Detroit Police Commission had been replaced by a single commissioner. Mayor Maybury had filled the post with Frank C. Andrews, thirty-one years old, self-made "boy millionaire," and vice-president of the City Savings Bank. The reputation of the department was not enhanced when, as the bank failed and it was revealed that Andrews had milked it for his million dollars, the commissioner was sentenced to the penitentiary for fifteen years. (Within a year the governor pardoned him.)

When Frank Croul, one of the city's Brahmins, had been appointed to the post in 1909, he had taken over a ramshackle department that had just adopted fingerprinting, but still kept no file of criminal records. To deal with the expanding area of the city and the new mobility afforded by the automobile, Croul replaced the bicycle squad with a "minute motorcycle squadron," and formed a motorized "flying squadron" capable of responding to calls from any part of the city. To cope with the increasing congestion of streets on which pedestrians, horsedrawn vehicles, streetcars, and automobiles vied for the right of way, he organized the first traffic squad.

Mayor Oscar Marx replaced Croul with former Water Commissioner John Gillespie, a politician tutored in the spoils system. The mayor was severely criti-

* A score of 100 is considered average on an IQ test.

cized, and when he ran for reelection in 1916 he fired Gillespie and appointed James Couzens in his place.

Couzens discovered fourteen hundred saloons operating twenty-four hours a day, seven days a week, in violation of the Sunday and 2 A.M. closing laws. Bookies, numbers runners, and agents for bordellos hustled in the streets. Announcing the findings of his survey, Couzens called for a "disciplined city." He ordered the department to enforce all laws. His declaration brought a reaction of astonishment—everyone knew laws were passed to satisfy the mores of one section of society, but then ignored so as not to disturb the habits of another. When it became evident that Couzens meant what he had said, the astonishment turned to horror. A delegation of businessmen, pretending not to hear his offer to join them in lobbying for legalized prostitution, trooped to his office to implore him to save the red-light district for the "public welfare."

In fact, as the United States drifted into war, the rapidly expanding and disorganized city became so potentially explosive that Couzens found his attention demanded by more important problems than the red-light district.

40

The City at War

WITHIN SIX MONTHS OF SQUEAKING THROUGH TO REELECTION ON A PLATFORM of peace, President Wilson allowed himself to be pushed into war. The collapse of Russia exacerbated the threat of a German triumph. The bellicose and impolitic German diplomatic and naval policies gave credence to the warnings of the interventionists that a German victory would bring about German domination of the world. A German victory would probably make uncollectible American loans for munitions purchased by the Allies—loans which after two and one half years had reached $2.4 billion.

America's entry into the war set the Federal government off on a $34 billion spending spree. Detroit, repeating its Civil War experience, was propelled into a boom dwarfing all previous booms. Once again the principal beneficiaries were the men of industry.

Before the war the American aircraft industry was minuscule. The need for airplane engines brought representatives from Cadillac, Packard, and the Hall-Scott Motor Company together. They designed the Liberty airplane engine, contracts for which went to several manufacturers. One of them was the Lincoln Motor Company, a new concern formed in June of 1917 by Henry Leland and his son. Resigning as managers of Cadillac, they used Federal funds to construct a huge new factory with 616,000 square feet of floor space.

During his peace campaign, Ford had announced he would burn down his plant before manufacturing one item of war material. But no one turned the war to greater advantage than he. One by one he had been adding to his own inheritance the farms of uncles, nephews, cousins, in-laws, and neighbors, until he owned virtually all the land adjacent to the Rouge River in Dearborn. On part of that land he had been planning to construct the plant for the Henry Ford and Son Tractor Company. But he scarcely envisioned what was about to happen to those plans.

Not only did Ford receive an order for 20,000 tractors and 16,000 tanks, but, drawing up plans for a new type of antisubmarine ship, he got an order for 112 Eagle submarine chasers. To complete such a large number of ships for service in the current war, he proposed to fabricate them, like automobiles, on an assembly line.

Ford had no factory to build his subchasers. The Federal government, however, was willing to underwrite any project that had the label "war" attached to it. The government assumed the $10 million cost of dredging and widening the Rouge River, of cutting a canal to the Detroit River, and of constructing a turning basin in which ships that went up the river could be swung around to go down. A huge industrial complex that came to be known as the River Rouge plant was laid out. Designed by Albert Kahn, it dwarfed not only Highland Park, but any other in the world in both its size and the degree of its mechanization.

Just as the Civil War had been a watershed in the development of the railroad industry, the World War was a turning point in the development of motorized transport.

In 1910 the "truck" was still a local delivery wagon on which an engine had been mounted—and only six thousand of these vehicles were sold in the United States yearly. By 1916, however, trucks were proving their value on the battle fronts—a caravan of trucks supplied Pershing's cavalry hunting Pancho Villa in Mexico, and six thousand trucks were used to carry materiel to Verdun after the rail lines were cut. When the United States entered the war, the government ordered hundreds of thousands of trucks from the auto industry.

Initially the trucks were transported to Atlantic Coast ports on boxcars. Hudson's Roy Chapin regarded the shipping of trucks by rail as a misuse of both the trucks and the hard-pressed and overworked railroads. (Chapin was head of the Highway Transport Committee of the Council for National Defense.) Plotting a course over the best of the execrable roads, he had the trucks loaded with supplies and driven to the ports. Their service in supplementing the railroads was an eye-opener. Once more attention was focused on the nation's roads—or lack of them.

During the first decade of the twentieth century, responsibility for building and maintaining roads still lay with the counties—a system of administration that dated back to the Roman Empire. Roads tended to be centered on the county seat, and there was little or no coordination between one county and the next. A good road in one county might end at a fence on the county line. In much of the West the only roads were wagon trails. Fewer than 10 percent of the nation's roads had any kind of improvement, even gravel.

In July, 1913, Chapin, Leland, Henry Joy, and a number of other auto pioneers had incorporated the Lincoln Highway Association to promote the building of a coast-to-coast highway. Dedicating themselves to collecting $10 million from the auto industry, they proposed that the association furnish the plans and materials for the road, and that the localities contribute the machinery and labor.

The next month the Governors' Conference endorsed the project. By 1915, with 2.5 million vehicles in use, the automobile industry was developing into one of the stronger lobbies in America. The demand for a national road, as well as road improvement in general, was carried to the floor of Congress.

In 1916 Congress passed a five-year highway act authorizing $75 million to aid states in road construction. The "matching" formula conceived by the Lincoln Highway Association was adopted.

The act set a precedent in Federal-state relations. It established the concept of matching grants that was to come to play a major role in American government. By requiring that as a condition of eligibility each state set up a highway department, it injected the Federal government into the affairs of state governments. It acknowledged for the Federal government an interest and a role in public transportation that had been rejected in the eras of canal and railroad construction.

The measure set off highway construction in every state. Following the example of Oregon, states enacted gasoline taxes to raise funds for construction. Michigan passed a $50 million bond issue that by 1924 brought three thousand miles of hard-surface and gravel roads into existence.

More vehicles stimulated better roads. Better roads stimulated more vehicles. More vehicles choked cities that had been having difficulty coping even with the proliferation of horses and wagons.

During Couzens's tenure as police commissioner, the number of motor vehicles in Detroit approached one hundred thousand. Along the city's principal arteries, the streetcar lines had concentrated population. These concentrations, plus the availability of transportation, led to the buildup of commercial strips. The commercial strips attracted more traffic. Automobiles competed with streetcars for the right of way. Parked and double-parked, the cars often brought traffic to a halt altogether.

To accommodate the multiplication of private transportation, principal thoroughfares were widened. To widen them, century-old trees were extirpated. The gracious avenues that were the spokes in Judge Woodward's elegant radial plan became lined with cheap buildings. They were transformed into scars across the surface of the city.

Judge Woodward had envisioned a city of multiple, self-contained hexagons; but after his departure, planning had been jettisoned, and the spokes created only a single downtown hub. Increasing the flow of traffic by widening the spokes served only to exacerbate congestion in the hub. At a dozen or more principle intersections, where up to twenty-one thousand cars were counted in a ten-hour period in 1916, traffic congestion "reached a point which during the busiest hours made it quite impracticable to traverse these streets at all." [1]

Despite the tangle of streetcars, pushcart peddlers, trucks, dirt wagons, manure wagons, bicyclists, junk peddlers, and pedestrians, this hub continued to attract the business and commerce of the city. Land that a hundred years earlier had sold for ten dollars an acre was commanding one thousand dollars and more per foot of street frontage.

Steam transportation, by facilitating the conveying of large amounts of provisions over great distances, had removed the limitations on urban population. Edison's system of electrical distribution, by making practical the high-speed elevator and the layering of people to greater and greater heights, had all but removed the limitations on population density.

The cost of horizontal space was prohibitive. Vertical space, however, was free. Construction expanded upward. Buildings went higher and higher. Hardly had five stories been added to the ten-story Pontchartrain Hotel than the entire structure was torn down to make way for a skyscraping bank and office building. William Murphy erected a twenty-two-story tower on his Penobscot Building in 1914, and then kept adding to the structure until in 1928 it topped out at forty-seven stories, the tallest ever raised in the city.

The architects of the vertical city, however, failed to take into account that

Ford's popularization of the automobile was vastly expanding the metropolitan boundaries, thus setting in motion a giant pumping action. Every morning the automobile pumped people from a ten-mile radius to the tenth stories of downtown office buildings, and every evening it pumped them back. Meanwhile, the conveyances were left to sit in the streets—one large office building, populated by the owners of five hundred cars, had parking spaces for ten. The city tore down the Central Market Building, and converted the plaza between the city hall and the county building into a huge parking lot. Detroit, however, needed scores of such lots. Automobile owners continued to park their cars in alleys, on sidewalks, and on green strips. The parking problem was critical in the downtown area and little better in the industrial districts.* It soon became serious even in residential areas, since houses built before the age of the automobile lacked garages.

Before 1909 there had been no control of street traffic,† and under the commissionership of Gillespie the laws had been honored mostly in the breach. When traffic fatalities tripled in two years—from 50 in 1915 to 148 in 1917— Couzens ordered the police to enforce all traffic laws. Leading citizens and automobile owners thought the order tyrannical, and spoke of "rebellion." Nevertheless, officers wrote 30,000 tickets in 1917 compared to 6,800 in 1915.

The traffic problems reflected not only the multiplication of automobiles, but the explosive increase in the city's population that came as war industry was superimposed upon the automobile industry. In the summer of 1918 Lincoln was employing 5,600 men and women in a factory that had been farmland a year before. General Motors employment, which had been little more than 10,000 in the early years of the decade, approached 50,000. The Ford work force rose from 32,000 in 1916 to 48,000 in 1919.

Since immigration from Europe had been interrupted by the war, industry sought new sources of labor. One hundred thousand workers were recruited from Puerto Rico and the Virgin Islands. As American farm workers were enticed into the cities, Mexican nationals were imported to take their place. For unskilled laborers, manufacturers turned to the American Black Belt. While plantation owners howled in protest, trainloads of Negroes were collected and sent north. The number of Negroes in steel plants nearly quintupled. Similar, if less dramatic expansion of the number of black workers occurred in coal mining, meat packing, and other industries. From 5,741 old and well-established residents in 1910, the number of Negroes in Detroit multiplied to 40,838 by 1919. They were part of the explosion that saw the city's population more than double during the decade, from 466,000 to 994,000. A nation that entered the decade with 8 million more people in rural areas than in the cities ended it with 2½ million more in the cities than on the farms.

---

* When Ford and Couzens had built the Highland Park plant, they had not anticipated the advent of the $5 day, the repeated lowering of the price of the Model T, and the effect upon the workers' mode of transportation. The plant had every convenience except a parking lot for the employees. By the time of the war, the streets around the factory were nearly impassable.
† The initial attempt to control traffic at intersections involved stationing police officers in the middle of them. Motorists, however, failing to understand their signals, plowed right through both officers and pedestrians. To protect the officers, kiosks were erected on pedestals in the center of the intersections. To make the signals more comprehensible, railroad-type semaphores, with which most of the public was familiar, were set up on the corners. The semaphores were equipped with ancillary lamps, which ultimately developed into traffic signals.

The crowding into the cities, the demand for farm produce by the multi-million-man armies, the diversion of production from consumer goods to war materiel, and the unprecedented infusion of money into the American economy fueled a wildfire inflation. As the monetary stock grew by $6.4 billion between 1915 and 1920, the cost of living doubled. Rents skyrocketed. In Detroit and other cities mansions were once again divided and subdivided into warrens. Jerry-built dwellings went up on every vacant lot. Houses were crammed together, window looking into window, as many as twenty to an acre. The inflation benefited industrialists and property owners, but eroded the gains workers had made. The $5 day was replaced by the $6 day, and then the $7 day—but wages failed to keep up with the rise in prices. Among the hardest hit were the families of soldiers—when the Michigan National Guard was called up, the wives and children became dependent upon charity.

The schools were in bad shape. The number of pupils grew from 54,500 in 1913 to 91,000 in 1918. Some 60 percent were in ramshackle and makeshift classrooms, in basements and in old firetraps. Teachers' salaries—$70 a month for women, and $122 a month for men—increased only half as much as the cost of living, and were $200 a year less than the wages of janitors. Veteran teachers departed for industry. Thousands of pupils were on double session, and 29,000 were in classes of more than 45. More than half the children were not in school at all. Hanging out in poolrooms and saloons, they ran errands, cadged tips, were given an occasional beer, and became wise in the petty larceny of the streets.

The number of juvenile offenders increased 57 percent in three years. The youths overflowed the second floor of the county building, which had been used as a detention area since 1907. (Before then, children were held in the county jail.) A juvenile detention hall was built. "It is manifest," said Couzens, echoing the words of Horace Mann and Mayor Pitcher three quarters of a century before, "that the first great effort must be made in schools, and that is where the earliest effect will be felt."

The social dislocation, the crowding, the poverty on the one hand and the spread of affluence on the other, generated a crescendo of crime. Between 1915 and 1917 murders in Detroit multiplied from 25 to 89, robberies from 308 to 843, and auto thefts from 1,097 to 4,405.* Police made 31,000 arrests in 1915, and 53,000 in 1917.

Nevertheless, Couzens believed that "bending all energies to catching and punishing crooks has never had an effect on decreasing crimes," and "to encourage officers to make large numbers of arrests . . . would be . . . to make crime-increasing agencies out of the police departments." Depreciating officers who had the largest number of "scalps at their belts," he instituted a "merit system" for officers and precinct commanders who had the best record for maintaining order and reducing the number of crimes and arrests.[2]

Couzens's philosophy of police work resulted in precinct commanders reporting as few crimes as possible, and was to affect the department's statistics-keeping operation for the next half century.

Not the least of the police commissioner's tasks was keeping the peace among the city's 289,000 foreign-born. Most of the immigrants had sympathies for one side or the other in the war, and read one of the numerous foreign-language

* One of the Detroiters who had his car stolen was none other than Police Commissioner Couzens. It was a Packard, not a Ford.

newspapers that fanned support for the Allies or the Central Powers. The Irish bombed "preparedness" parades and staged rallies to denounce the English. The Jews, the Finns, and the Swedes hated the Russians. The Italians were at war with the Austrians. The Dutch, like the Irish, were anti-English. The Germans despised the French and the Italians. The French and Belgians thought the Germans barbarians. The Romanians and the Bulgarians spat in each other's faces. The Syrians and the Greeks, living next door to the Turks, cast murderous glances upon them. The Serbs and the Croats were ready to slit the throat of any Austrian or Hungarian they encountered. The Poles were against everybody —Russians, Germans, Austrians, and Jews.

When the United States declared war, a wave of anti-German hysteria swept the city. The police were run ragged checking on spies and saboteurs who were reported to be popping out of sewers, descending from zeppelins, grinding glass into sugar, and poisoning the water supply.

For two and three generations the Germans had clung to their ethnic identity. In the Lutheran parochial schools the children were taught half in German and half in English. At the beginning of the war, the president of the German-American Alliance, three million strong, declared:

"We have long suffered the preachment that 'you Germans must allow yourselves to be assimilated, you must merge in the American people,' but no one will ever find us prepared to descend to an inferior culture. No! We have made it our aim to elevate the others to our level. . . . We must not allow our two-thousand-year-old culture to be trodden down in this land." [3]

Taking stock, the *native* Americans were agitated by the fact that a quarter of the population was composed of "foreigners." Foreigners who might or might not be trustworthy.

From the Ford plant, the emphasis on Americanization swept over the nation like a tidal wave. German was eliminated in the schools. Sauerkraut was replaced by cole slaw. Hamburger became Salisbury steak. Frankfurters turned into hot dogs. The Norveth children came home and told their mother it was a disgrace she spoke only Hungarian, and that she should go to school to learn English.

41

The Progressive Tide

IN THE SUMMER OF 1918 COUZENS ANNOUNCED HIS CANDIDACY FOR MAYOR. AS a youth throwing rocks he had received Mayor Pingree's support. As a politician he was a believer in Progressive Republicanism.

Since the day Pingree had split the Republican party, there had been not two parties in the state, but three: the Democrats, the Old Guard Republicans, and the Progressive Republicans. In 1912 the state had sent two delegations to a Republican convention that resulted in a memorable brawl. The Progressives, charging the "assassination" of the convention, had stalked out. When Theodore Roosevelt ran as a third-party candidate on the Bull Moose ticket, Michigan had supported him wholeheartedly.

Throughout the nation there was a Progressive tide. In the drive to transfer American politics from back rooms to the people, constitutional amendments for women's suffrage and the popular election of senators were enacted. State legislatures passed bills authorizing the initiative and referendum, the direct primary, and cross-filing. The Sixteenth Amendment, reversing a reactionary Supreme Court's decision, provided for the institution of a graduated income tax—the most equitable means of taxation. Four decades of frustration came to an end in 1908 when Congress, its conscience roused by one and a half million industrial and railroad injuries and deaths yearly, passed the first meaningful labor legislation. Four years later the Children's Bureau and the Department of Labor were established. Pressing on, the Progressives demanded nationalization of communications, railroads, and industries based on natural resources such as minerals, oil, and water power. They wanted the Federal government to commit itself to a program of full employment, a minimum wage for workers, old age pensions, and, if necessary, price controls.

Disillusioned with Big Business, the Progressives urged the substitution of Big Government in its stead.

In Michigan they succeeded in enacting a new state constitution that laid the bases for the regulation of public utilities and for the granting of home rule to Detroit. The citizens of Detroit followed by passing a new city charter. Abolishing the ward system and the forty-two-man city council, the charter provided for citywide election of a new nine-member council. The Board of Education was reduced to seven members elected at large, and the school system was made independent of the municipal government. Throughout the United States municipal leagues hailed the Detroit charter as a model for ending graft and corruption, for ending the power of the bosses, and for providing for "majority" rule: the majority of white Protestants represented by the Good Citizens League.

Running in the first election under the new charter, Couzens split the Good Citizens' vote. He represented "clean" government. But he also represented the kind of "radicalism" the Citizens League abhorred. Bluff and forthright—on occasion he called his best friends "sons of bitches"—he had told a Board of Commerce meeting during the depression of 1914–1915:

"You can't give these men work during the summer and then discharge them in the winter while you take your golf sticks and go to California. . . . You don't give a damn what becomes of your workmen." [1]

He repeated Pingree's campaign stunt of boarding a streetcar and refusing to pay the fare, which over public objection had been raised from five cents to six cents. Hundreds of citizens followed his example. The company ordered all cars to halt until nonpaying passengers had been put off. Couzens countered by decreeing that all operators who stopped their cars were to be arrested for blocking traffic. Rioting broke out. John Dodge, who had replaced Couzens as commissioner of the street railways, accused him of inciting Communists and anarchists.

During the campaign, Couzens received a suggestion to call John Dancy, Detroit director of the Urban League. Couzens was surprised. The political leader of the Negro community was considered to be Benjamin Pelham. Since being appointed a junior clerk at the behest of Senator McMillan, Pelham had risen to be Wayne County accountant and clerk to the Board of Auditors. So diligently had he applied himself and so encyclopedic had his knowledge become that he was credited with being the man who actually ran the county government. He was referred to as the "czar of Wayne County." The growth of the city, however, had diminished the importance of the limited number of Negro votes. And Negro support had traditionally gone to Old Guard Republicans.

Dancy, in fact, was representative of a new current in black-white relations. Like Pelham, he was descended from a family of Southern Negro artisans. His father, a typesetter for the Tarboro, North Carolina, *Southerner,* had been appointed customs collector for Wilmington, North Carolina, by President Harrison, and Recorder of the Deeds for the District of Columbia by President Theodore Roosevelt. By the turn of the century, however, Negroes in the South had been abandoned by the Republican party. Conditions of servitude almost as onerous as those existing during slavery were imposed upon them.* The white society attempted to justify these conditions by making Negroes the victims of a campaign of denigration that attributed a hopeless racial inferiority to them.

To counter this campaign, the Liberal Republicans—who were the lineal descendants of the Abolitionists and the European Revolutionaries—organized the National Association for the Advancement of Colored People in the wake

* On January 6, 1914, the Reverend I. N. Ross, charging the complete violation of Civil Service rules, urged an enthusiastic black audience in Washington, D.C., to stop buying toys and to start buying guns to fight against a "new era of slavery." [2]

of the Springfield, Illinois, riot of 1908. In 1910 three other small organizations merged into The National League on Urban Conditions Among Negroes.

The Urban League had hardly anticipated the northward flood of Negroes that was soon to follow. It was this migration that brought the league to prominence and gave it much of its importance.

Meeting with Couzens, Dancy and other leaders of the black community pointed out that the number of Negroes in the city had grown from six thousand to nearly forty thousand. Since numerous companies, including Ford, were discriminating against them, they were having a difficult time. Why didn't Ford hire more Negroes, Dancy asked Couzens, who was still a Ford director.

Couzens was taken aback. Ford did not discriminate, he insisted.

Ford did not have a policy of discrimination. But the foremen, who had been doing the hiring, favored workers from their own ethnic groups. Since there were no Negro foremen, the company had not hired its first Negro until 1914; and he was an acquaintance of Ford's from the days on the farm. In 1917 Ford still had only two hundred black employees, nearly all in low-paid positions. Every other company in the automobile industry except Packard, which employed eleven hundred Negroes, had fewer.*

Couzens was elected in a landslide. Setting a precedent, he made the first Negro appointment to a municipal commission.

---

* During the last six months of 1917 the Detroit Urban League reecived 5,542 requests for Negro workers, of which at least 95 percent were for unskilled jobs. Wages averaged between seventy dollars and ninety dollars a month. Packard, due to its Railroad Republican heritage, was the largest employer of Negroes in the city.

42

"A Great Business Is Really Too Big To Be Human"

WHILE COUZENS WAS RUNNING FOR MAYOR OF DETROIT, THE SENATORIAL CAM-paign turned into a bitter battle between two old acquaintances.

To bolster congressional support for his forthcoming peace proposals, President Wilson encouraged Ford to run for the Senate. To vindicate the honor of the Old Guard of industrialists, the Republicans picked Henry Joy's brother-in-law, "Commodore" Truman Newberry.

Pitting the peace advocate against the war hawks, and the maverick upstart against the city's established "society," the campaign was a continuation of the feud Ford had initiated three years earlier. The Newberry forces hired hundreds of workers. Every county, and every ethnic and special-interest group had its own organization. The Republicans even assumed the expenses of Ford's Democratic primary opponent. Newberry spent $176,000 in the primary. Before the campaign was over, his expenditures topped $500,000.

Ford, a man who confessed "I have been a voter for thirty-one years and I never voted more than six times—I voted then only because my wife made me," was too shy and too unreliable in his utterances to make speeches.[1] He depended on Ford-for-senator committees to carry his campaign. Nevertheless, the spectacular success of the Model T gave Ford a political base in every community.* Despite Newberry's efforts, Ford, cross-filing, showed well in the Republican primary, and won the Democratic nomination handily. When, therefore, Newberry defeated him in the general election by 7,500 out of the 433,000 votes cast, there was chagrin in Washington. Ford's election would have given the Democrats a 48-48 standoff in the Senate, and, with the Vice-President casting the tie-breaking vote, enabled them to organize the Senate and control the committees.

Ford had been unwilling to spend anything to win the election. Now, how-

* By 1918 the Model T accounted for more than half the car sales in America. Land rushes and copper rushes paled in comparison to the rush for Ford franchises. From small-town mayors to senators and governors, men were casting themselves at Ford's feet and hailing him as a demigod in the hope of being granted a share in the pot of gold.

ever, goaded by his claque into believing that he could have been defeated only through fraud, he established a forty-thousand-dollar fund to attempt to prove that he had not lost it. Dozens of detectives were hired. Herded together for pep talks, they were organized like auto salesmen into competing teams.

U.S. Attorney-General Mitchell Palmer, still hopeful of swinging control of the Senate to the Democrats, took his cue from Ford and launched an investigation of his own. The result was the indictment of Newberry and 133 other members of the G.O.P. on a charge of violating a Federal law limiting campaign expenditures in a primary to ten thousand dollars. When the defendants were assembled in Federal Court in Grand Rapids, one wag remarked: "This is just like an old-time Republican convention." [2]

Senator Newberry was convicted and sentenced to two years' imprisonment. He appealed to the United States Supreme Court. The Court, by a vote of five to four, reversed the conviction on the tenuous grounds that the Federal government lacked jurisdiction to regulate primaries.

In the Senate, with Old Guard Republicans in control, a resolution to oust Newberry failed. In Detroit's Republican society, Ford was mentionable only as a four-letter word.

Ford suffered a further blow when the Michigan Supreme Court ruled in February, 1919, that the Dodges and the other minority stockholders were entitled to a special dividend of $19¼ million, and that Ford must not withhold dividends in the future.

In response, Ford decided to buy out the "parasites." Except for Couzens, the minority stockholders agreed to sell for $12,500 a share, or a total of $76¼ million. Couzens held out for, and received, an extra $500 a share. The payment came to $30 million—$29,308,857.90 for Couzens and $691,142.10 for his sister Rosetta who had invested $100 sixteen years earlier.

No longer did Ford need to justify his actions. No longer was there anyone within the company who could dispute with him as an equal. No company of a comparable size in the history of the world was ever so completely under the domination of one man.

He was determined to be master not only in his own house, but over the materials that went into production. He purchased four hundred thousand acres of timber (automobile bodies were still made of wood), lumber mills, coal mines, and iron mines. He launched a rubber plantation in Brazil. He acquired a fleet of ships. When the ramshackle but strategic Detroit, Toledo and Ironton Railroad lacked the money to build a new bridge over the widened Rouge River, he purchased the railroad for $5 million, and by drastic cost-cutting measures turned it into an asset.

Knudsen—one of a number of executives without portfolio since Ford hated "titles"—attempted to point out to him that in many cases he was increasing his costs by centralizing processing and manufacturing operations at the Rouge. But Ford neither knew anything nor cared about accounting. He followed his intuition and his hunches. It was up to others to implement them profitably. More often than not—as with the railroad, which he sold for $36 million in 1928—he came out ahead.

In May of 1920 the first blast furnace of the world's largest industrial complex went into operation. The foundry and the 500,000 horsepower electric plant were the largest in existence. The concrete bins into which ships could directly discharge their cargoes of ore and fuel had a capacity of 2 million tons. On 24 miles of railroad tracks freight cars were operated by remote control. By 1923, the plant was turning out 102,000 tractors annually. The next year, the time from the moment raw materials were delivered at one end and a finished tractor was rolled out at the other was reduced to 28 hours and 20 minutes.

In the postwar boom, the automobile industry was selling every car it could produce. Manufacturers engaged in helter-skelter expansion. In 1920, however, the Federal budget was reduced to $6.4 billion. The Federal government curtailed its purchases of goods and ended its financing of capital expansion. Industrialists started borrowing money to supplant the funds they were no longer receiving from Washington. By March of 1920 they reduced the *free* reserves in the Federal Reserve System to $131 million. That was barely above the limit of 40 percent required by law. To brake the inflation, the Federal Reserve Board raised the discount rate from 4¾ to 6 percent—the most drastic increase during the first fifty years of the System. By late summer the constriction of the monetary supply was affecting everyone.

The auto makers reacted to the pressure of increasing costs of labor and materials by raising prices even as money and credit became tighter. During the latter part of the summer a steep decline in sales set in.

Ford was endeavoring to pay back as quickly as possible the money he had borrowed to acquire the $106 million of minority stock. He had to disburse, by court order, $21 million in back profits and interest. He was in the midst of an expansion that in three years had seen the company expend $80 million. He was thus trapped in an acute cash squeeze.

F. L. Klingensmith, the treasurer, and other executives urged that the emergency be met through borrowing. But Ford, terrified at the thought of falling under the control of bankers just at the time he had freed himself from the *parasites,* decided on another of his unorthodox actions. Overriding the almost unanimous opposition of his executives, on September 21, 1920, he reduced prices on the Model T by 25 to 30 percent.

Since he would lose money on every car already produced, the action seemed to make little sense. However, because of his dominant position, he was able to force his suppliers to roll back their prices. They, in turn, during a year of violent labor strife, forced a rollback in wages. Not only did Ford's action collapse the price structure of the automobile market, but it helped thrust a drastic deflation down the gullet of the economy. By June, 1921, wholesale prices dropped to 56 percent of their May, 1920, level.

At the plant, Ernest Kanzler, Edsel's brother-in-law,* discovered tens of millions of dollars that Ford didn't know he had. A graduate of the University of Michigan and Harvard Law School, Kanzler was struck by the lack of inventory control, and found $88 million tied up in parts and supplies. Some $28 million of this inventory was worked off and shipped to dealers in the form of cars and parts. The spare parts that automatically went out with each car turned a theoretical loss into an actual profit. Ford's financial position improved rapidly.

Dealers were inundated with stock that they could not refuse if they wanted to keep their franchises. Since the cars and the stock had to be paid for when received, the dealers went heavily into debt and held cut-rate sales. By such force feeding, Ford used his dealers to borrow for him the money that he himself would not.

---

* Kanzler was married to Josephine Clay, the sister of Edsel's wife.

Concurrently, Ford conducted major surgery on the administrative departments. Desks, chairs, and office equipment were collected and sold. Sixty percent of the telephones were removed. Every pencil sharpener was taken out, and employees were told to bring knives in their stead. Without *firing* anyone, the company made massive cutbacks in personnel. Eighty people came to work one morning to discover their desks removed or smashed and their offices stripped—their jobs no longer existed.

Dr. Marquis, appointed head of the Sociology Department after the Peace Ship journey, complained to Ford that the department could not function if people were to be treated in this fashion. Ford promised to look into the matter. As usual, he was willing to agree to anything in order to avoid a dispute. In fact, Charles Sorensen, the production boss, had his instructions on reducing costs. How he did it was not Ford's concern. Dr. Marquis could fight with Sorensen over the details.

(The Ford way of showing disapproval was inimitable. Ford disliked a set of coke ovens that Edsel had ordered constructed. Rather than argue with his son, Ford let the ovens be completed. Then he had them demolished.)

The Sociology Department, of course, had lost the purpose management had foreseen for it. Ford's pay scale no longer was superior to the rest of the industry's. He could no longer pick and choose his workers. To threaten men with dismissal was meaningless when they could find work elsewhere at the same pay.

On the other hand, the war years' Americanization of the work force had wrought its concomitant industrialization. With fewer foreign-born and single men in the labor force, more workers were capable of following instructions. They understood that if they wanted to be able to buy their share of the increasing quantity of material goods, they had better show up daily and on time. Youngsters remained longer in school, and emerged better educated and readier to assume their places on the assembly lines.

The staff of the Sociology Department could not, in any case, keep tabs on 70,000 workers. When each investigator was assigned 727 workers, meaningful sociology was impossible. Social workers who intervened in behalf of men drew the ire of the production bosses.

Over Christmas and New Year 1920–1921, the entire plant was shut down for six weeks. When it reopened, 20,000 of the 70,000 workers were not rehired. Among the missing were Dr. Marquis and the Sociology Department.

"A great business is really too big to be human," Ford explained.[3]

43

The "American Plan"

AT THE END OF THE LAYOFF, WORKERS WERE REHIRED AT BEGINNERS' WAGES, no matter what their experience or seniority. It was a cost-cutting measure employed not only at Ford but throughout industry. Savage labor struggles were the consequence of it and similar pernicious practices.

The labor shortage created by the war had served to strengthen unions. In the rampant inflation, wages of unskilled workers had increased only half as much as those of skilled workers. Hundreds of thousands of dissatisfied workers joined the ranks of the industrial unions. By the end of the war there were 5.1 million union members. A general strike that closed down the city of Seattle in February, 1919, signaled the beginning of the greatest year of labor strife in American history.

In September, 375,000 steelworkers struck. The Boston police force walked off the beat. Detroit teachers, fed up with making $200 a year less than janitors, threatened to boycott classes. The 3,630 strikes during the year involved 4,160,000 men, 20.8 percent of the labor force.

Notwithstanding the ancestry of Samuel Gompers, there was a native American hue to the craft union AFL. In contrast—and despite the IWW's "Big Bill" Haywood and the United Mine Workers' John L. Lewis—the leaders of the industrial unions seemed mostly to speak with German-Jewish and Russian-Jewish accents.

Jews had, in fact, fathered both the German and the Russian labor movements.* In Russia the repressions of the czarist government had radicalized the labor movement. Many of its leaders were Communists. When the Communists

---

* The origin of the Russian labor movement lay in the *khevra*. The Jewish equivalent of the guild, the *khevra* had split into organizations of masters and journeymen as the interests of the two groups had diverged. Strong enough in many cases to establish the principle of the "closed shop," the journeymen *khevras* had followed the workers into the factories, most of which were owned by the former Jewish masters. In the great migration from the Russian Pale, the *khevras* had been transferred to America in the form of unions like the International Ladies Garment Workers and the Amalgamated Clothing Workers.

Similarly, the German labor movement had been nurtured by well-educated but poor Jews and by Jewish intellectuals who split away from their well-to-do families. Ferdinand Lassalle, the son of a wealthy Breslau merchant, had founded the Social Democratic party, the progenitor of all the European labor parties.

in March, 1919, founded the Third International to foment world revolution, many Americans began to associate the Russian-accented labor leaders in the United States with the Jewish revolutionaries in Russia.

The effect was to set off an hysterical Red Scare. If Trotsky had sailed from New York to help launch the Bolshevik Revolution in Russia, whom had he left behind? Wasn't the answer self-evident in the host of foreign-accented agitators fomenting strikes? Calling upon the patriotism of Americans, management resorted to proven tactics of strikebreaking. Thirty thousand Negroes were imported as scabs by the steel industry. Thousands more were used to undermine strikes in coal, meat packing, and other industries. The "open shop" was promoted as the "American Plan."

Inevitably, violence spread. In the spring of 1919 a revolutionary blew himself to pieces as he tried to plant a bomb in front of the house of Attorney-General Mitchell Palmer. The act proved a godsend for those who contended that revolutionaries were tumbling off every ship. Badly shaken, Palmer was convinced that it was part of a Red plot. Suspecting a revolutionary hiding behind every door, he ordered the compilation of a list of every possible suspect organization, including the NAACP. On January 1, 1920, a nationwide raid was staged. Six thousand persons, including most of the radical labor leaders, were arrested. But the total of three revolvers that were found would hardly have sustained Tom Mix through one movie.

Nevertheless, eight hundred aliens were deported. Newspapers and magazines ran sensational stories. Progressive Republicans were equated with Communists. Couzens, Governor Hiram Johnson of California, and Senators Burton K. Wheeler of Montana and Robert La Follette of Wisconsin were denounced as Bolsheviks.

Millions perceived the red blotting out the white and the blue. The strikes, businessmen said, were part of the plot. The Negroes and the Catholics, the Ku Klux Klan asserted, were part of the plot. College professors, the anti-intellectual descendants of the Populists alleged, were part of the plot. Wall Street and international Jewry, Henry Ford said, were part of the plot. That old Bolshevik Henry Ford, oilman Edward L. Doheny declared, was part of the plot.

In Detroit, Mayor Couzens labored to maintain a rational atmosphere. He forbade the police to interfere with a speech by the IWW's Haywood, despite the American Legion's threat to break up the gathering if the police would not. He prohibited municipal cooperation in Palmer's raids and called them disguised efforts to halt social progress. Nevertheless, scores of labor leaders were rounded up, incarcerated by the army at Fort Wayne, and held indefinitely, while their families were reduced to beggary.

The depression, in fact, like every depression before, was more effective than the Attorney-General in combating the unions. Over four fifths of the 175,000 auto workers, and tens of thousands in other industries were thrown out of work. Wages were rolled back 20 percent. The Detroit teachers were cowed by the school superintendent, who warned that anyone joining the newly formed American Federation of Teachers would not have his contract renewed. The prosecution of labor leaders for "criminal syndicalism" destroyed the IWW and much of industrial unionism—a fact that did not particularly perturb Gompers and the AFL. Union membership declined by a third. For a decade after 1922 the principal characteristic of labor was its docility.

44

The "International Jewish Conspiracy"

LELAND COULD TAKE SATISFACTION THAT ONCE AGAIN DETROIT HAD BEEN DE-livered from unionism and made safe for industry, but the cost to him was high. For as auto maker after auto maker failed under the double onslaught of the depression and Ford's tactics, Leland's Lincoln Motor Company became one of the more celebrated victims.

At the end of the war, Leland had decided to switch from making Lincoln aircraft engines to manufacturing Lincoln motorcars. His reputation as a craftsman was unequaled. For the 1912 Cadillac he had designed the prototype of the modern ignition and electrical system, a development as revolutionary in the history of the automobile as the appearance of the Model T.*

Backed once more by William Murphy, Leland shipped the first Lincoln the week before Ford announced his September, 1920, price cuts. In the pattern of every recession, cars priced the highest suffered the most in sales. Limping along on sales averaging seventy cars a month, Lincoln lost $100,000 and more monthly. In September, 1921, the company went into receivership.

Ford presented himself as the good Samaritan. Doubtlessly deriving satisfaction in thinking of the time twenty years earlier when the inefficient Ford had been replaced by the efficient Leland, he acquired Lincoln for $8 million. He promised Leland and his son that they would be left in full control.

As usual, Ford's promises remained good only so long as one had hold of the sleeve of their author. Soon Sorensen appeared on the scene to enforce the same kind of efficiency in the Lincoln plant as he had at River Rouge.

---

* In 1910, Byron Carter, who had come to be Leland's close friend, was driving on Belle Isle when he encountered a woman motorist whose car had stalled. Carter offered to crank the engine, but unwittingly failed to retard the spark. Kicking back, the crank broke his arm and smashed his jaw. Gangrene set in, and he died within a few days.

Leland vowed that he would develop a self-starter. A short-action but powerful electric motor for opening cash registers had been devised by Charles Kettering, a former employee of the National Cash Register Company, who had become a partner in the Dayton Engineering Laboratory Company (DELCO). Combined with a notched flywheel and a more powerful storage battery, the motor proved to be the solution to the self-starter problem.

While the Lelands appealed to the ever more inaccessible Ford, Sorensen broke open drawers, removed desks, and swept tools onto the floor. The Lincoln plant was in turmoil.

On June 10, 1922, Ford dispatched his secretary, Ernest G. Liebold, to inform the Lelands that they were through, and had to be out of the factory by the end of the day.

It was Liebold who had emerged as the man second in power only to Ford in the upheavals that followed the buyout of the minority stockholders.

Born in 1884, Liebold was descended from middle-class German-Lutheran farmers who had settled in the vicinity of Detroit. After graduating from business college in 1904, he had gone to work for twenty-five dollars a month at the Peninsula Savings Bank. A hard worker who thought nothing of staying at the office until midnight even on New Year's Eve, he caught the eye of J. H. Johnson, the president of the bank. When Johnson and Couzens together founded a new bank in Highland Park, Liebold came to the attention of Couzens.

Couzens, who was bedeviled by Ford's absent-mindedness and disorganization,* assigned Liebold to look after Ford's business affairs. Soon Clara Ford was letting Liebold take care of the household bills, too. As he brought order to what had been disorder, he made himself indispensable. It was he who catalogued Ford's holdings in Dearborn—Ford himself had been hazy about what he owned. After Couzens separated himself from active participation in company affairs, Ford relied more and more on Liebold.

A squat, heavy-set, bull-necked man with short-cropped hair, Liebold could be depended upon to do the "dirty work" from which Ford himself shrank. When reproached for his roughshod tactics, Liebold responded: "We don't care whose careers we wreck." [1] When things went wrong, he accepted without a murmur the scapegoat role that Ford assigned to him. Whatever feelings and emotions he had, he suppressed. His overriding sense was one of *pflicht:* duty. Liebold was not just a cold fish. He was frozen stiff.

Ford was determined to be rid of all those who might consider themselves to have been his equals in the rise of the Ford Motor Company. Undercutting one executive with another and murmuring, "well, well," if cornered and reproached, he used Liebold as his hatchet man.

Out, with a check for $1.6 million, went Wills, whom Ford never had trusted after the episode of the "new" Model T. Out went Norval Hawkins, who had developed by far the most efficient sales organization in the automotive field, but whom Ford derided for his emphasis on reports and paper work. Out went Lee, who had provided a humanizing influence on the production lines. Out, together with the advertising department which Ford now perceived as being a waste of money, went the advertising manager, Charles A. Brownell. Out went Hubert E. Hartman, the general attorney. Out went Knudsen, who had supervised the construction of the branch assembly plants and the assembly line at River Rouge, but who, in 1918, had repeated Wills's error of suggesting that the Model T needed improvement.

Explaining the dismissal of Knudsen, Ford said:

"This is my business. I built it, and as long as I live, I propose to run it the

---

* Matters had come to a head when Ford forgot that he had placed a $70,000 check in a coat pocket, and sent the suit to the cleaners.

way I want it run. . . . I let him go, not because he wasn't good, but because he was too good—for me." [2]

Not only did Ford intend to be the autocrat of Highland Park and River Rouge. He thought that what was good for the Ford Motor Company might also be good for America:

"I have definite ideas and ideals that I believe are practical for the good of all, and intend giving them to the public without having them garbled, distorted, or misquoted." [3]

For an organ, he purchased the rundown, weekly Dearborn *Independent,* and converted it to the "Ford International Weekly," dedicated to "social justice." To manage the paper, he hired Edwin Pipp, the editor of the Detroit *News.* Pipp brought with him William J. Cameron, an occasionally scintillating, but erratic and alcoholic columnist who resembled W. C. Fields.

Urging his reporters to be "good mechanics," Ford proposed that stories be written according to assembly-line techniques; one writer would deal with the facts, another would insert the humor, a third the editorial comment, and so on. Espousing the Progressive line, the paper backed striking workers in the steel and coal industries and urged the nationalization of transportation and communications.

In the eyes of Ford, who continued to see himself as the rugged individualist struggling against Wall Street, Big Business was the enemy of Free Enterprise. The paper, however, failed to attract much notice. During the first year of its publication, it lost $284,000.

During the summer of 1919 the staff was given the task of reporting from Ford's perspective the trial of his $1 million defamation suit against the Chicago *Tribune.** In 1916 the *Tribune* had responded to Ford's protest against the American intervention in Mexico by calling him an "anarchist" and an "ignorant idealist." The suit went to trial in Mt. Clemens, a town in which people prided themselves on having known Edison when he studied telegraphy there.

For fourteen weeks in the humid, midsummer heat, the largest legal batteries in Michigan history addressed themselves to a jury of eleven farmers and one public-roads inspector. Each day as they entered the small, red-brick courthouse a sign admonished them: "If you spit on the floor in your own house, do it here. We want you to feel at home." [4]

As the witnesses lounged about the courthouse, the town looked as if it had been transplanted from the Southwest. The *Tribune*'s defense was supported by cowboys in wide-brimmed hats who recounted horror stories of Mexican rape and pillage. One hundred Mexicans in their sombreros countered in behalf of Ford with tales of depredations committed by American troops. The star witness, however, was Ford. As he took the stand, it became apparent that two trials were in progress: one was Ford's before the jury; the other Ford's before the nation.

Daily the *Tribune* attorneys hammered at his intellectual capacity, knowledge of history, and comprehension of world events. On the stand Ford described a "large mobile army" as "a large army mobilized." In response to the question:

---

* The *Tribune* was owned by a branch of the McCormick family that had descended from William, the brother of Cyrus. Joseph Medill McCormick was an ardent supporter of Theodore Roosevelt, and, like him, a Progressive and Imperialist. He was elected to the Senate in 1918.

"What was the United States originally?" he replied: "Land, I guess." Asked to identify Benedict Arnold, he said that he was a writer. The American Revolution, he thought, had taken place in 1812.[5]

Predictably, the different trials produced different verdicts. The city slickers' attack on Ford's IQ misfired, for the upbringing, education, and values of the jurors were much like those of Ford. Ruling for Ford, they awarded him six cents and court costs (which totaled more than the one million dollars sued for). Rural and small-town Americans, who bought two thirds of the Model T's, acclaimed the verdict. In the cities, Ford was laughed at.

Like the Scopes "monkey trial" soon to follow, the trial was a microcosm of the conflict between small-town and urban America, between Fundamentalism and cosmopolitanism, between a return to insularity and internationalism, between nineteenth-century and twentieth-century education. For the moment, the tide seemed to be running backward to the nineteenth century.

"The real United States lies outside the cities," Ford concluded.[6] Alienated from most of the other auto men, ostracized by Detroit's "society," afflicted with a keen sense of his intellectual inferiority, he withdrew to his new two-million-dollar mansion, "Fairlane." There he resided in magnificent isolation among the hundreds of acres he owned in Dearborn.

Brooding upon the source of his troubles, he was encouraged by Liebold in the belief that certain people were out to "get him." Who had suggested taking out a loan with the bankers, a loan that would have placed the company in their power? Klingensmith, the treasurer. And was not Klingensmith half Jewish? Who had upstaged him, and, according to Liebold, was making critical and derogatory remarks about him? That "Hungarian Jewess," Madame Schwimmer, whom Liebold despised. Who was the publisher of *The New York Times,* which had editorialized that Ford's election to the Senate "would create a vacancy both in the Senate and in the automobile business?" A Jew. Who held 1 percent of the stock in the Detroit, Toledo and Ironton Railroad and refused to sell it so as to give Ford 100 percent control? Two Jews. Who was the chief justice of the Michigan Supreme Court that had ruled against Ford in the Dodge suit? Henry Butzel—a Jew. Who were the fomenters of revolution, and the leaders of the IWW? Jews. Who could be found prominently among the "monopolists" and the "international bankers?" Jews. Who were among the supporters of Senator Newberry? An "influential gang of Jews."[7]

What was going on?

Liebold assumed the task of finding out. The detectives who had been on Newberry's trail were put to work ferreting out the Jewish "secrets." Designated by numbers like 202X and communicating in code, the detectives infiltrated Jewish organizations, slunk around temples, and looked for arcane handshakes. From all over the world Liebold collected anti-Jewish tracts and books.

He considered his prize acquisition to be the *Protocols of the Wise Men of Zion.* Purportedly this was a document issuing from a secret conclave of world Jewish leaders. It described in exhaustive detail plans for the establishing of a universal Jewish supergovernment through the medium of revolution. In fact, it had been forged by the czarist secret police in their efforts to discredit the Jewish revolutionaries, and was a plagiarism from a satire on Napoleon III.

In the spring of 1920, Liebold advised Ford that he had uncovered "those wonderful documents known as the 'Protocols,'" and that Ford's troubles could be explained by the fact that Jews, whether capitalists or Socialists, whether judges or pimps, whether rich or poor, were all under the control of a secret supergovernment directing them toward a takeover of the world.

Ford was enlightened. Conditioned by the prejudices and culture of the rural Midwest, he had harbored a lifelong anti-Catholicism. It was a prejudice that—as he came to believe Catholics were "tools of the Jews"—he projected upon the Jews. He could observe, Ford declared through his ghost writer, "certain streams of influence which were causing a marked deterioration in our literature, amusements, and social conduct; business was departing from its old-time substantial soundness; a general letting down of standards was felt everywhere. It was not the robust coarseness of the white man, the rude indelicacy, say, of Shakespeare's characters, but a nasty Orientalism which has insidiously affected every channel of expression. . . . all traceable to one racial source. . . ." [8]

Ford told Liebold to expose the "international Jewish conspiracy" in the Dearborn *Independent*. "Of course," Liebold complained, "Mr. Ford's ideas and theories were sometimes very difficult to carry out, and he didn't seem to have the faculty of being able to go into very much detail to explain them." [9] So Liebold was left to conduct the campaign according to his own design.

As the direction in which the *Independent* was heading became manifest, most of the original staff, including Pipp, left the paper. Cameron, however, remained. A Presbyterian preacher born in Canada, he considered himself a "British Israelite," descended from one of the "lost tribes" of Israel. He was assigned the task of ghost writing for Ford.

On May 22, 1920, the first article in a ninety-one-part series on "The International Jew: the World's Problem," appeared on "Mr. Ford's Own Page."

Five days earlier the first furnace had been fired up at River Rouge, a complex designed by Albert Kahn, the son of a German rabbi.

"If you read the Protocols it is all very clear," declared the Ford-Liebold-Cameron ghost, "Jewish idealism is the destruction of Gentile society and the erection of Jewish society. . . . All powerfully contributed to by murder, rapine, theft, and starvation."

To further that goal, it was Jews who had "provoked the war," and who aimed at "the destruction of order by revolution. . . . The Jewish revolution in Russia was manned from New York. The present Jewish government of Russia was transported almost as a unit from the lower East Side of New York. . . . Bolshevism is Jewish. . . . The conclusion, when all the facts are considered, is irresistible, that the Bolshevik revolution was a carefully groomed investment on the part of international Jewish Finance."

Why would the "international Jewish financier" support communism? Because "The Red Revolution is the greatest speculative event of human history," and "speculation and gambling are known historically as special propensities of the Jewish race." Because Jews have "taken a whole rich country, without the cost of war."

With the end of the war and the consummation of the Russian Revolution, the supersecret Jewish high command was devoting itself to "moving an army, which having done duty in Europe for the subjugation of that continent, is now being transferred to America . . . to bring the Bolshevik revolution to the United States."

The Jews were the bane of the farmer by burdening him with "mortgage indebtedness." They were the bane of the worker, because they helped him to force up wages, but then secretly eroded the gains through inflation. They were the bane of all Gentiles because they made them lust for "all-enticing luxuries."

Stupefying workers by encouraging them to drink, they were converting them to anarchy by inciting them to strike for better working conditions. In accordance with Liebold's "wonderful Protocols," they were "turning the witless heads of the Gentiles by the word 'progress'." They were demoralizing Gentiles through the spread of the doctrines of "Darwinism, Marxism, and Nietzscheism" —a curious combination, unless one keeps in mind the rural, Populist audience at which the propaganda was directed. They were responsible for introducing "the poison of liberalism." They were encouraging the breakdown of the family, and of morality and order. They were leading youth astray. Through their control of the textile industry they were shortening skirts, and through their control of the schools they were introducing sex education for the purpose of softening up Gentile girls for their "downright, dirty immorality." [10]

Ford himself was affected by the propaganda. He began to regard the "international Jew" as ubiquitous. Undoubtedly, Ford thought, Lincoln had fallen victim to a Jewish conspiracy, and he spent thousands of dollars trying to find John Wilkes Booth's body in order to prove his theory.

Jewish drugs, Jewish liquor, Jewish sex, Jewish jazz, the Jewish press, and the Jewish fur trade—all were linked in the great plot. But, "speaking of furs," as Cameron wrote with unintentional irony, "it is very funny to see how some affairs turn out." [11]

Jewish fur traders had made their appearance in the Northwest territory in the 1760's. They had played a prominent part in the territory's development. Jacob Franks and his nephew John Lawe had been among the founders of Green Bay, Wisconsin, and Lawe had been appointed associate justice on the first Michigan territorial court. (He founded a thoroughly "American" family by marrying the daughter of a British officer and a Chippewa Indian girl.)

In 1844, twenty-year-old Edward Kanter had arrived from Breslau via Paris, New Orleans, St. Louis, and Chicago. The son of a prosperous linen merchant, he had received an excellent education and spoke six languages. He had gone to work for the American Fur Company and three years later opened a store on the Apostle Islands in Lake Superior. Learning Chippewa, Huron, and Pottawatomi, he established himself as a favorite of the Indians, who nicknamed him "Bosh-Bish 'gay-bish-gon-sen," meaning "firecracker." He had prospered and become a shipper and trader on the Lakes. Marrying the daughter of State Senator Lyman Granger, he had engaged in Democratic party affairs and been elected to the legislature. In 1871, with a capital of $100,000, he had incorporated the German-American Bank.[12]

When the German-American Bank, like most other financial institutions, found itself in difficulty during the Panic of 1893, Kanter had retired, and John S. Gray had taken over as president. Nevertheless, Kanter's son remained as vice-president, and the board of directors continued to have predominantly German and Jewish backgrounds. The money that had saved the Ford Motor Company from bankruptcy in 1903 had come from a bank founded by an "international Jew."

While "Mr. Ford's Own Page" vilified Jews and painted the horns of Satan upon them, Henry Ford could not understand why his Jewish friends should be shocked and upset. Wasn't it clear that the calumny was intended only for the evil "international Jews"—like Rosika Schwimmer? (Nevertheless, when referring to a Jew or a Catholic whom he liked, he would say: "He's mixed," or, "He's not a good Catholic.")[3] He was chagrined that Rabbi Leo Franklin, titular head of Detroit's Jewish community and a man even Liebold liked, should send back the new Model T that Ford had been giving him every year. He was pleased that Albert Kahn pretended never to have heard of "The International Jew." While 121 prominent non-Jewish Americans, including William Jennings Bryan, and ex-Presidents Taft and Wilson, wrote a letter of protest to Ford, he kept running the articles—which were then compiled into book form—and insisted nothing that was being printed was hurting anyone.

It was, in truth, not a question of whether it was hurting, but how much. Two hundred thousand copies of the *Independent* were distributed weekly. No Ford dealer could hold a franchise without circulating the paper. In cities it brought protest marches and riots in front of Ford showrooms. In Detroit, where before the war there had been no discrimination against Jews, the *Independent* nourished the roots of a virulent anti-Semitism.

"The International Jew" made its appearance during the depression of 1920–1921, and when prosperity returned to the United States people lost interest in the alleged economic and political machinations of the Jews. In a Germany wracked by turmoil, the publication of the articles in book form had a more significant and long-lasting impact.*

---

* No American was better known or a greater hero in Germany than Ford. Industry was rushing to "rationalize" and "Taylorize" production on the Ford model. Ford's *My Life and Work,* which vigorously defended *The International Jew,* was a best seller in Germany. Hitler wrote in *Mein Kampf* that "a single man, Ford, to their [the Jews'] fury, still maintains full independence."[14] Baldur von Schirach, one of the top twenty Nazi leaders, testified at the Nuremberg Trial that his first knowledge about anti-Semitism had come through reading *The International Jew.* The Nazis translated the book into twelve languages and distributed it all over the world.[15]

One morning when Ford was in Munich a "shabbily dressed fellow" knocked on his hotel door at 7 A.M. and asked for a contribution. When Ford, with Liebold acting as interpreter, turned him down, "the fellow felt very much put out about it and was rather mad when he left."

Four hours later Liebold received a telephone call from Louis Lochner of the Peace Ship, who had become Associated Press correspondent in Berlin. Lochner asked if it were true that Ford had just turned down Hitler's request for a contribution.[16]

45

The Scab Millionaire

WHILE FORD PURSUED HIS INDEPENDENT COURSE, MAYOR COUZENS WAS WRES-
tling with the problems of the city.

The population had more than doubled in a decade. Tens of thousands of
people were packed into leaky and unheated barns and shacks without plumbing.
Thousands of others were camping out in tent communities. Badly housed,
badly nourished, and badly clothed, they were the principal victims of the
1919 influenza epidemic that, sweeping the world, replaced cholera as the
concomitant of wars and "urban rushes." Conditions for these wartime migrants
to the city grew even more serious when the depression of 1920–1921 followed
the epidemic. One hundred thousand persons were unemployed in Detroit.
Mayor Couzens established a public works program. But like Pingree before
him, Couzens found that the resources were entirely inadequate for the needs.

Although Detroit was synonymous with the automobile industry, the city
really served as a huge bedroom community. The auto plants located within
its boundaries were primarily those of the smaller "independents" like Packard,
Hudson, and Maxwell. The major manufacturers had placed most of their
facilities beyond the city's taxing power. Ford was in Highland Park and Dearborn. Dodge was in Hamtramck, settled mostly by Poles. General Motors produced only the Cadillac and some components for other makes in Detroit.

When the city in 1922 expanded its limits, Ford and Dodge influenced the
people of Highland Park and Hamtramck to incorporate as separate munici-
palities. Detroit completely surrounded the new communities, but the revenues
from the auto plants lay just beyond the city's reach.

Nevertheless, the city's assessed valuation quadrupled from $350 million to
nearly $1.4 billion between 1910 and 1920. Couzens used the additional
revenues from the property tax to implement the Progressive philosophy that
government exists to serve the needs of the people. Since the city had suffered
neglect from the day it was incorporated, and its facilities had never caught
up with its growth, these needs were enormous. Couzens spent $243 million
during his three years in office. Since the city's tax budget ten years before had

213

been only $6.3 million, it was an astonishing figure. Yet the sum was still insufficient.

(Most of the other major cities in the world were in comparable states of neglect.)

The capacity of the sewer and water systems had been surpassed when the population had topped 500,000. The water department began building a filtration plant that, capable of handling 320 to 360 million gallons daily, was the largest in the world. Nevertheless, like the industrial plants, the city continued to dump its effluences raw into the river. Detroiters occasionally might be chagrined at the pollution enveloping their city, but they could always rationalize it in the context of Edison's "beautiful" evidence of the progress of industrialization.*

Since 1904, the Detroit Edison Company had increased its output of electricity from 16 million kilowatts to 1 billion kilowatts. The Book Building alone used as much power as the entire system had generated in 1894, and it was but one of a host of high-rise buildings—Detroit was third in the world (behind New York and Chicago) in skyscraper construction. The city that four decades earlier had depended upon the moon to light its streets now presented a brilliant spectacle at night.

It was a different picture in the daytime. From the top floors of the Book Tower, office workers amused themselves trying to pitch pennies down the fuming stacks of the original Detroit Edison plant in the heart of the business district. From Edison's huge new "Seven Sisters" plant along the river, from the chemical complex at Wyandotte, from Ford's furnaces on the Rouge River, from auto factories, rubber factories, and railroad yards, and from ships steaming by on the river, a noxious mix of smoke and fumes enveloped the city. Only the wind saved the population from asphyxiating on the wastes of its own prodigious production.

To clean up the streets, Mayor Couzens acquired some of the 146,000 surplus trucks that were part of the huge and unnecessary stock of war materiel acquired by the Federal government during its spending spree. (Others were going to the Post Office Department, the Public Health Service, the Bureau of Public Roads, the inchoate state highway departments, and private contractors.) Put to work hauling earth, garbage, and building materials, the trucks presaged the end not only of the common workhorse, but of many of the jobs filled by the common laborer.

To improve the operations of the police department, Couzens initiated the building of a new, eight-story police headquarters. Increasing the motorization of the force, he had some of the cars linked to headquarters through the new medium of radio. Strung with innumerable parallel antenna wires, they looked like ambulatory harps, and received their instructions from station KOP.

The measures to increase efficiency nevertheless failed to be reflected in a reduction of vice, crime, and corruption. These were being nurtured by a phenomenal new illicit activity: bootlegging.

There was no doubt that corrupt politics and corrupt police had been an adjunct of the saloons. Alcoholism went hand in hand with illness, crime, and broken families. The thesis of the Temperance advocates was that the pro-

---

* EDISON: "Do you see that valley?"
PRIVATE SECRETARY: "Yes, it's a beautiful valley."
EDISON: "Well, I'm going to make it more beautiful. I'm going to dot it with factories." [1]

hibition of alcohol would lead to solution of all the other problems. For two generations the Prohibitionists had been the only group within the original Republican fusion to have their aims frustrated. Then, through the enfranchisement of women and the drive for urban government reform, they gathered new support. With the aid of a propaganda campaign against German-American brewers who purportedly were undermining the war effort by converting grain and barley into alcohol, they pushed the Eighteenth Amendment over the top.

The Eighteenth Amendment, however, was an anachronism. Supported mainly by rural, Protestant Fundamentalist America, its passage came at a time when the cities, which overwhelmingly voted "wet," for the first time contained a majority of the American population. It was an anomaly generated by the disproportionate power that rural areas exercised in Congress and in state legislatures as the result of the misapportionment of electoral districts.*

Anticipating passage of the Volstead Act, Michigan went dry in May, 1918, a year before the rest of the nation. Detroit, which had exempted itself once before from Prohibition through the expedient of nonenforcement, now became the prototype for the roaring twenties.

Boatload after boatload of liquor was ferried across the river from Canada. Other loads were trucked in via the Dixie Highway leading south to Ohio (which was still wet). Because of its proximity to Canada, Detroit established itself as the country's principal port of entry for bootleg liquor, a position it would hold throughout the Prohibition era. Saloons went underground and became "blind pigs." Speakeasies blossomed in the back rooms of restaurants, in the basements of apartment houses, in the lofts of commercial buildings, and in shacks along back alleys. People who had never taken a drink in their lives took to drink because it was chic. Girls who would have been ushered from any respectable saloon became the adornments of blind pigs. Drugstores sold both the ingredients and the instructions for making gin.

Over the highways radiating out from the city the liquor was trucked to other locations in the Midwest. The proliferation of highways and motor vehicles made it all but impossible to control the traffic.

The proliferation of highways also took people ever farther beyond the radius of service provided by the Detroit United Railways, and brought more and more of them downtown in their cars. Couzens, therefore, under enabling provisions of the revised state constitution, spearheaded a renewed drive for acquisition of the D.U.R. In April, 1922, the electorate voted five to one for acquisition of the system. A price of $33,659,913 was agreed on. With 1,457 cars and 373 miles of track, the Detroit Street Railways became the largest public-operated municipal transportation system in the United States. But the rundown tracks, poor trolley lines, and dilapidated cars made it anything but a bargain. The peculiarities of a manufacturing city with three shifts creating three peak traffic periods—from 6 A.M. to 9 A.M., 3 P.M. to 6 P.M., and 11 P.M. to 1 A.M.—resulted in high operating expenses. The new Rapid Transit Commission produced a plan for a combination of superhighways and subways. The cost of such a network was prohibitive, however.

The new city charter enabled Couzens to acquire the streetcar system and do things that mayors before him had been unable to do. He controlled the

* With a third of Michigan's population, Wayne County (Detroit) had 14 out of 100 seats in the state assembly and 4 out of 32 in the senate.

preparation of the budget. He could appoint commissioners and some department heads. In theory, the government had become a "strong mayor" type. In actuality, the mayor was only as strong as he was determined to be, and had only as much power as he chose to exercise.

Couzens quickly discovered that the government would function as he wanted it to only if he were continuously alert and prepared to whip it into line. Unless he stormed at department heads to perform the services they were supposed to, the clerks worked their way through the day in routine slow motion. Unless the mayor were willing to battle for his prerogatives, the council would usurp them. His relations with the council became tempestuous. He said he would seek the impeachment of its president, and was thenceforward banished from the council chamber. Councilman John Lodge called him a "scab millionaire."

In the 1922 election, voters reacted to the previous year's depression by replacing enough Old Guard Republicans with Progressives to give a Progressive-Democratic coalition control of the U.S. Senate. Newberry, who had escaped ouster from the Senate only because of the Old Guard's control, decided to resign.

Michigan's Progressive Republican governor, Alexander J. Groesbeck, thereupon appointed Couzens to serve out Newberry's term.

46

The Government of Business

THAT WAS NOT EXACTLY THE DENOUEMENT FORD HAD FORESEEN WHEN HE had set his detectives on the trail of Newberry.

If Couzens could be senator, Ford would be President.

Couzens called his candidacy "ridiculous," but in July of 1923 a poll showed Americans favored Ford two to one over President Harding. The August 8 issue of *Collier's* carried a ghost-written article, "If I Were President," under Ford's by-line.

As an alternative to President Harding, whose own assessment of his presidency, "I am not fit for this office and should never have been here," [1] was now shared by a majority of Americans, Ford seemed an attractive choice. Only the "Jewish propaganda societies" could keep Ford out of the White House, Liebold and Cameron stridently asserted.

Three years earlier the selection of Harding as a compromise candidate had appeared like an accidental stroke of genius. President Wilson's romantic illusions of the "war to make the world safe for democracy" and the "peace without victory" had ended in the greedy nationalistic shambles of Versailles. The American public had been repelled by the decadence it perceived in Europe. For much of the foreign-born population, the war had been the scalpel that severed the umbilical links to their former homelands. The patriotism of the war followed by the patriotism generated by the Red Scare had made everyone conscious of proving his "Americanism."

"Americanism," Republican leader Boies Penrose said in 1920, should be the Republican theme in the election.

Asked what Americanism was, he replied:

"Damned if I know, but you will find it a damn good issue." [2]

Silver-haired and handsome, Harding seemed the epitome of the Norman Rockwell America. Many women found him irresistible. Those who registered to vote in the first presidential election since being granted the ballot were mostly Anglo-Saxon, Protestant, and Republican. The vote for Harding was 16,143,000, nearly double the total for Hughes (8,534,000) four years earlier.

By the greatest landslide of any contested presidential election up to that time —60.4 percent of the popular vote—the electorate made clear that it was not interested in making the world safe for democracy; but in making America safe for Main Street.

By 1923, however, farmers were restive because twenty-five years of agricultural prosperity were showing signs of coming to an end. The Puritans were in a huff because the President, shutting himself up with his cigars, his whiskey, his poker-playing cronies, and his women, was turning the White House into a bawdyhouse. Setting an example for his fellow Americans, he flouted Prohibition, and speculated heavily in the stock market. He let each Cabinet member run his own department and peculate to his heart's content. If the government is best that governs least, Harding could lay claim to being one of the best Presidents of all time.

When he died in the summer of 1923, he left a legacy of scandal, graft, and corruption.

Sober, rural Calvin Coolidge, who took the oath of the presidency by the light of a kerosene lantern in a Vermont farmhouse, was more in keeping with the electorate's image of the President. In resources and reputation, however, the taciturn New Englander was scarcely a match for the Dearborn industrialist who, day by day, was coming closer to becoming the world's first billionaire. As a Ford presidential boomlet was launched in Nebraska, the new President cast anxious glances over his shoulder toward Detroit.

A deal was arranged. As part of its war program, the Federal government had begun construction of a huge project to dam the Tennessee River at Muscle Shoals, Alabama. The electricity generated was to have been employed in the production of nitrate for explosives and fertilizer. With the end of the war, the project had been abandoned. Several industrialists coveted the facility. The principal one was Ford.

In December, 1923, the President invited Ford to the White House. Ford came away from the meeting convinced that Coolidge was one of the great Presidents of all time.

"I would never for a moment think of running against Calvin Coolidge for President," he declared.* [3]

A few days later the President announced his wholehearted support of Ford's plans for Muscle Shoals.

The Federation of Farm Bureaus, the AFL, the Senate Committee on Military Affairs, the House of Representatives—all backed the plan. A speculative land boom was set off. A mythical city was platted. Only Nebraska's Senator George Norris, chairman of the Senate Agriculture Committee, Couzens, and a few other Progressive Republicans opposed what they considered to be another subordination of the public interest to private greed. Muscle Shoals was saved for the future. In the 1930's it was to become the keystone of America's first great power project—the Tennessee Valley Authority.

Throughout the 1920's the Progressives were carrying on a lonely vigil as the conscience of the nation. For if the replacement of Harding by Coolidge changed the dress of the presidency from smoking jacket to Sunday suit, the attitudes and

* Clara Ford had already told Liebold: "You got him into it so you can get him out of it. . . . If Mr. Ford wants to go to Washington, he can go, but I'll go to England!" [4]

perspectives changed hardly at all. Coolidge conducted a five-year sit-in in the White House. "Don't you know that four fifths of all our troubles in this life would disappear if we would only sit still?" he asked a senator.[5]

To make sure he would do little to disturb the troubles as they disappeared, he slept twelve hours a day. His theory of government was that it should be self-liquidating. Business, on the other hand, was holy. He compared a factory to a temple, and suggested that a worker should feel privileged to be allowed to worship in it.

The business of government had become a government of business.

Business was playing a major role in the withdrawal to isolationism. Only one nation had profited from the war: the United States. Between 1915 and 1921 the country had a favorable balance of trade of $20 billion, a sum unprecedented in world history. The cost of the war had been greater than the cost of all previous wars combined. The Central Powers had spent $63 billion. The European Allies had spent $123 billion, and wound up owing the United States $10 billion in war debts. Following the war, American factories produced two fifths of the world's manufactured goods, 25 percent more than Germany, England, France, and Italy combined. America's factories were the most modern and her production techniques the most efficient. America had become the very heart of the world, and as such it should have been evident that she was the crux of the peace.

England's rise to industrial greatness had been predicated upon exporting and she was dependent upon the rest of the world for a significant proportion of her raw materials. Germany's prosperity hinged almost as much as England's upon her ability to market her goods in foreign lands. America's principal rivals in industrialization had been committed to keeping the arteries of trade open.

In contrast, the end of the war found America in a unique position. She was the world's financial center. She was the world's industrial powerhouse. She was the world's breadbasket. She was essentially self-sufficient in raw materials—her discovered reserves of coal, iron, and oil were the greatest on earth. With the world's largest middle-class population, America possessed the largest market for industrial goods—it was, as the Ford Motor Company had shown, the world's first mass market.

America was self-contained. The concern of her industrialists was to protect their backyard against the intrusion of foreign competition.

Nowhere was this truer than in the chemical and electrical fields, dominated by Germany before the war. Not only had American manufacturers been able to move into the previously German markets, but after the American declaration of war they had been able to seize all the German patents. They were now desperate to obtain protection against the expected German resurgence.

"We want more than the ordinary tariff for the reason that this is an intricate industry and cannot be developed except under unusual conditions," C. K. Weston, a Du Pont executive declared. "It really requires an absolute embargo of competitive products so that we can secure an income over the sale of these which will be sufficient to pay for the development of the products which we have not yet learned to make." [6]

In the Fordney-McCumber Tariff of 1922, by far the highest in American history, the protection-demanding industries achieved their aims. Europe, and especially Germany, was in dire straits. Couzens, returning from a trip to Germany after his appointment as senator, reported that the people were "in great distress. . . . The extreme isolationists have forbidden or intimidated the United States from having a voice in world affairs. We cannot go on that way." [7]

But it was precisely the way the United States was intent on going. For two centuries America's vast expanses of land had been able to absorb people. For two centuries the white inhabitants had imported additional labor—first indentured servants, then slaves, then immigrants. Beginning with the Civil War, industry had made a practice of importing labor from Europe in order to depress wages. Immigration had become a regular part of trade.

But the greater and greater mechanization of industry reduced the need for unskilled labor. The mechanization of agriculture, given a special impetus by the development of the tractor, was reducing the need for farm laborers. It was a reduction that farmers, continuing to harvest bumper crops of children as well as wheat and corn, were slow to recognize. The labor that previously had been imported from the rural areas of Europe was now coming from the rural areas of America—at an opportune time, too, considering the extent to which business had been shaken by IWW agitation among foreign workers and by the Red Scare. Among those rural migrants were hundreds of thousands of blacks— blacks who were welcomed in many industries. Ostracized by the unions and lacking leadership, they presented less of a threat than the foreign workers. Unlike the foreign workers, they did not have to be "Americanized."

So even as the government of business acted to constrict the flow of trade, it moved also to shut off the flow of immigrants to the United States.

47

The Source of All Evils

THE BELIEF WAS WIDESPREAD THAT IT WAS THE IMMIGRANTS WHO WERE RE-
sponsible for the multiplication of crime, alcoholism, vice, and the general ills
of the cities. In 1907 Congress had authorized the formation of a nine-member
commission to investigate the problems of immigration. Under the chairmanship
of Senator William P. Dillingham, a Vermont Republican, the commission had
engaged in a four-year investigation, the most exhaustive sociological survey in
American history. The results of that survey were far different than the commissioners had expected; and the report of the commissioners was far different
than the results of the survey.

The immigrants were, the commission's staff discovered, held responsible for
"poisoning the pure air of our otherwise well-regulated cities; and if it were
not for them there would be no congestion, no filth, and no poverty in the great
industrial and commercial centers of America." [1] Because of the "aversion of
the native American . . . there is a sharp line of division in the occupations
or the departments in which recent immigrants and persons of native birth are
engaged." [2] Even in the parochial schools, "a considerable proportion of the
children of foreign-born parents are also segregated." [3]

The "most significant feature," a staff member decided, "is the almost complete ignorance and indifference of the native American population to the recent
immigrant colonies and their condition . . . but even when acquainted with
them, natives are usually indifferent so long as they do not become too pronounced a menace to the public health and welfare." [4] Another of the commission's experts wrote that "in spite of the social and race prejudice and other
almost unavoidable conditions which practically compel the herding of immigrants in little communities of their own . . . the showing of the immigrants
is on the whole a decidedly good one." [5]

Since most of the immigrants settled in the cities, where the schools were
better than in rural areas, and in the North and West where they were better
than in the South, the children of immigrants actually were attaining a higher
degree of literacy than native-born children.

Income was correlated with literacy and the ability to speak English. The southern Italians and the Poles had the lowest income. Russian Jews and northern Italians about the same as urban Negroes. The Irish were in the middle. The Germans and Swedes on top. Second-generation Jews, whose centuries-old skills enabled them to break out of the ghetto as soon as they learned English, made the most dramatic gains, increasing their average income 14 percent. They thus overtook the Irish, who remained largely in the same jobs as their fathers.

Since people do not change their habits and characters merely because they move from one country to another, and since children tend to imitate their parents, northern and western Europeans, with their heritage of drinking "hard liquor," produced a far greater proportion of alcoholics than southern and eastern Europeans. Native Americans, living in the only land where an excess and not a shortage of grain was a chronic problem, were the biggest drunkards of all.

That, certainly, was an unexpected finding. Almost as startling was the commission's discovery that the Irish were the most susceptible to insanity—a large proportion caused by alcoholism and venereal disease. Since the Germans were not far behind the Irish, the commission was compelled to declare that "insanity is apparently most prevalent in the nationalities who were among the earliest immigrants to this country and contributed the sturdiest of their people. . . . It may therefore be that an explanation of these discrepancies is that conditions of American life are conducive to an increase in insanity." [6]

The foreign-born committed not only proportionately fewer crimes than native whites, but the offenses were less likely to be serious. Crimes of personal violence were characteristic of those nationalities—Chinese, Mexican-Americans, Italians, Negroes—who came mostly from rural areas. The sexual mores of the southern Italians produced a plethora of rape and abduction charges. The French and Jews led in the commission of gainful offenses and of violation of laws against prostitution. Robbery was an almost purely American crime.

Juvenile delinquency was a product of the cities. The heavily urbanized North Atlantic states contained slightly over one fourth of the population of the country, but had half of all the juvenile delinquents.*

Dominated by rural, Protestant, New England and Southern members, the commission in 1911 issued a report that reflected little of the forty volumes of data, but many of the prejudices of the members.

"The old and the new immigration differ in many essentials," the commissioners asserted. "The former was . . . a movement of settlers . . . from the most progressive sections of Europe [who] mingled freely with the native Americans and were quickly assimilated. On the other hand, the new immigration has been largely a movement of unskilled laboring men . . . from the less progressive countries of Europe [who] congregated together in sections apart from native Americans and the older immigrants to such an extent that assimilation has been slow." [8] In this respect, the commission's *Dictionary of Races*—the most egregious of its pseudoscientific compilations—indicated that the *Norse* "Americanize more rapidly than do the other people who have a new language to learn," and "the place of the German race . . . is too well known in America to necessitate further discussion." [9]

* The Irish produced 20.5 percent of second-generation juvenile delinquents. The Germans were next with 19.4 percent; followed by the Italians, with 16.4 percent; the Russians, with 11.1 percent (much of this Jewish); the Canadians, with 6.9 percent; and the English and Welsh, with 5.7 percent. In the South Atlantic states, children of foreign-born parents, mostly Mexicans, were nearly three and a half times as likely to be jailed as children of native whites. [7]

In fact, the Germans had resisted assimilation with greater vigor than any other ethnic group, and there were second- and third-generation German communities in Wisconsin and Missouri where people would have been hard put to hold a conversation in English. In backwoods Louisiana, the Cajuns, after more than a century under the American flag, still conversed in their own bastardized French, and many did not understand English. Contrary to the commission's assertions, it was in the polyethnic cities where assimilation occurred—assimilation in which ethnic origin was not a factor.

What troubled the commissioners was that the immigrants were contributing to the growth of the cities; for the commissioners believed, like Henry Ford, that the cities were the source of all evils. "In European countries, as in the United States, the poorest and least desirable element in the population, from an economic as well as a social standpoint, is found in the larger cities. . . ." [10]

That statement was patently false. The report itself pointed out that there was a consistently higher illiteracy rate in the rural than in the urban population, and that illiteracy and poverty were correlated.* Nowhere in the world did the rural population have a higher income or standard of living than the urban population.

The commission's assertion that the *old* immigration had been as "skilled" as the new was "unskilled" was erroneous. The correlation was between skill and the degree of industrialization of the region of origin. Jews, Armenians, and Czechs joined English, Scotch, and Welsh as the most skilled of the immigrants. The Irish were grouped with Poles and Greeks and Slovaks among the lesser skilled.

Since the results of the research failed to substantiate the conclusions that they wanted to propound, the commissioners ignored much of the forty volumes of data. The consequence was a report notable for its casuistry and obtuseness. In order to "redress the apparent lack of balance now threatening to exist between the cities and country districts, due to the apparent disproportionate growth of city populations," one of the commission's experts suggested that the immigrants be redirected to the country districts. There they would be able to duplicate "the remarkable success of the early German and Scandinavian immigrants." [12]

That America twenty-five years before had run out of "country districts" able to sustain an increase in population was beyond their comprehension. Even while they were praising the Norse for supposedly not settling in the cities, the Norse were doing precisely that. Swedish Professor Helge Nelson, without the bias of the commission, later wrote:

"The three prairie states, Iowa, Nebraska, and Kansas, all of them typical agricultural areas [had] received most of their Swedish immigrants before 1890, and the number of Swedish-born thereafter greatly decreases, since no industry exists which affords the possibility of making a living." [13]

By 1930 only 16.6 percent of Swedish-Americans would remain on farms. Like Peter Jansen, and like rural Americans no matter of what ethnic origin, they were migrating to the cities, especially to Chicago and Detroit.

There was no way the commissioners could get around the facts that the new immigrants were not criminally inclined, that they were not asking for handouts,

---

* In Italy, the illiteracy rate in rural Calabria was 78.7 percent, and in urban Piedmont 17.7 percent. In Austria-Hungary there was a close correlation between urbanization and literacy: Dalmatia was 73 percent illiterate, Galicia 56 percent, Styria 14.3 percent, and Bohemia 4.1 percent. [11]

that they did not fill up the insane asylums, that they kept their homes in remarkably good condition, and that they were anxious to have their children go to school.

So the commission recommended restricting the immigration of the unskilled and the illiterate, and suggested a quota based on the country of origin.

The Dillingham Commission's report lay dormant during World War I, but was revived at its conclusion. The House of Representative's Immigration Committee in 1921 framed a bill that, by taking the 1910 rather than the 1920 census as a quota base, allocated 198,000 of the 357,000 slots annually to "old immigration" lands.

That, however, left the door open for the "international Jewish revolutionaries." Consequently, the Immigration Act was revised in 1924. Reducing the quota to 165,000, the revision rolled the base back to 1890. Since most eastern and southern Europeans had immigrated after that date, the "old immigration" lands were allocated 141,000 of the slots; the rest of the world 24,000.

The Dillingham Commission's report was, like Ford's *International Jew,* a twisted and tortured attempt by men to find explanations for dynamic forces that they did not understand. It reflected not only a xenophobia but an urban phobia that was sweeping rural and small-town America. It reflected fear of the economic power of the big cities and hatred of the potential political power of the latecomers—"potential," not actual, because in most states unequal apportionment enabled small-town America to fight a delaying action for decades. Most inimically, it appeared to give the endorsement of the American government to the theorists dividing the world into superior and inferior races and people— the *masters* on the one extreme and the *slaves* on the other.*

---

* In *Mein Kampf,* Hitler was moved to admire "the American Union, in which . . . by simply excluding certain races from naturalization, it professes in slow beginning a view which is peculiar to the folkish state concept." [14]

48

The Age of Intolerance

ORGANIZATIONS AND LODGES OF THE FOREIGN-BORN MIGHT PROTEST THE BIAS contained in the new Immigration Act. Individual immigrants, however, concentrated on blending into the American culture and on improving their standard of living. There were twenty-seven thousand people enrolled in Americanization classes in Detroit. But what was Americanizing the Norveths and the other families even more effectively than these programs were the products of the factories in which they worked, and the schools to which they sent their children.

For forty-five years Norveth had been blowing his nose with his thumb and wiping it on his sleeve. When his children came home from "handkerchief drills" and reported that the school demanded that they all have their own handkerchiefs, he was astonished. For forty-five years Norveth had not brushed his teeth. When his children came home from "toothbrush drills" and insisted that they all must have toothbrushes and toothpaste, he was unbelieving. One toothbrush, maybe. But each to have his own toothbrush? That was too much! Next they would be demanding that each have his own glass, instead of drinking out of the long-handled pan that hung by the faucet. Sure enough, they returned to say that the teacher had told them that "hygiene" required that each should drink out of his own glass.

The Norveth children accepted the American way of life as a matter of course. For Norveth and Theresa, who had grown up hauling water from the village well and considering a kerosene lantern a luxury, the American standard of living was a wonder. On an eleven-year "land contract" requiring a down payment of 1 percent, they were buying the house that they had been renting. It was a house that had electricity, a gas stove, and a hot-water heater. Back home they would have ben considered rich beyond measure.

In Detroit, however, it was hard to keep up with the "all-enticing luxuries" that were being pressed upon them. In 1905 Dow, in his drive to increase the consumption of electricity, had begun sending salesgirls door to door to publicize electric appliances, which Detroit Edison sold at cost. The first device was a six-dollar iron. Next, in the summer of 1906, came the fan. Then the washing machine. By the end of 1906 there were 3,500 electric irons and 350 electric washing machines in use in the city.

That was only a beginning. Following the war, the system devised to supply power to the incandescent bulb was directed toward electrifying the home, thus changing forever the concept of housework. Norveth bought Theresa an electric toaster. He bought her an electric iron. The entire family contributed twenty-five dollars for an electric vacuum cleaner.*

The most amazing device of all was the radio. On August 31, 1920, the Detroit *News* broadcast election results over a "wireless telegraph" apparatus to which amateur enthusiasts tuned their crystal sets. It was the first news broadcast. On September 4, Charles F. Hammond, Jr., of the meat packing family, and his young friends danced in the basement of his home to music from the same station, WWJ. On November 2, the Westinghouse Electric Company in Pittsburgh broadcast the results of the general election. At the end of the month, its station, KDKA, scheduled the first regular evening program.†

In the summer of 1924, Norveth, taking advantage of the spreading practice of installment purchases, bought a radio. Hooked to the same cord in the ceiling as the light bulb, the three-foot-high set became the centerpiece of the living room. Theresa, who had accepted the other modern marvels with scarcely a thought, couldn't understand people talking out of a wooden box. She was afraid of the "black magic." But she was also fascinated. As the family gathered around the set every evening, she kept asking what the people were saying. Since she had been restricted in her associations to her Hungarian neighbors, her English continued to be limited to the rudimentary phrases of a tourist in a foreign land.

To the surprise of her family, the radio began to Americanize her. Asking what this meant, what that meant, she was picking up an understanding of English. American slang phrases popped up in the Hungarian she continued to speak.

Throughout the nation radio had a similar effect. More so than newspapers, magazines, and movies (still silent), it was creating an American culture. Even as the proliferation of highways was tying America together physically, the radio was bridging sectional differences and beginning to tie the land together psychologically.

Historically, workers had had difficulty buying the goods produced in the factories in which they labored. Now, even though wages still averaged less than twenty-five dollars a week, the cost-cutting achieved through mass production was turning them into consumers. The standard of living was rising dramatically. Nevertheless, the means through which that mass production was achieved made the lives of Norveth and the other workers a continuing purgatory.

On the assembly lines, speed took precedence over everything else. As machine tools became the specialists, men were, literally, degraded. Although within the work force, classes still existed—sweepers and cleanup men at the bottom, tool-and-die men at the top—the assembly line itself was a classless society.

---

* The war years had brought a conversion of the vacuum *system* to the portable vacuum machine. Vacuum systems operated by means of a basement suction pump connected, like central heating, to a series of ducts had been limited to the homes of the wealthy.
† KDKA lays claim to being the first commercial station on the air, since it received its Federal license before WWJ.

Machines had become the master mechanics. Machines were the aristocrats. Efficiency experts stood with stopwatches to clock how long it took to fasten each bolt or to cover a seat with fabric. If one worker took thirty seconds for a job completed by another in twenty-nine, the reason had to be found. Second by second the time for each operation was reduced.

Production was a race between the inexorable belts on which parts and cars moved forward, and the men. The human goal was to "work up the line" so as to exceed the speed of the belts, and thus be able to take a five-minute breather every hour. The job of the efficiency expert was to convert that five minutes into increased production. The workers hated the men with the stopwatches and clipboards.

Conditions were back to what they had been in 1913. But the psychology of the workmen had changed. They ached for the better life that industry was advertising they should have. So they submitted to the tongue-lashings, the taunts, and the provocations of the line bosses. In what was a new form of the old system of group piecework, foremen used every trick and prejudice to turn worker against worker. "If you can't cut it, you lazy dago, go back to spaghetti stringing!" Micks were stupid. Krauts were born losers.

Nobody could stop the lines. If a worker, faltering, threatened to upset the delicately coordinated mechanism, a relief man would be rushed to help him. Then would come the study: why had the quota not been met?

Men were discharged because they would not, or could not, keep up with the line; because they returned insult for insult; because they broke under the pressure. Hour after hour the din of metal on metal reverberated across the acres of space.

Norveth had increasing difficulty maintaining the pace of production. His hearing was damaged by the ceaseless screech of metal being pounded, ground, and sawed. Like hundreds of other workers he developed an ulcerous "Ford stomach." Chronic tension raised his blood pressure. Yet he saw no alternative to working until he dropped.

A steady worker, Peter Jansen did not have the family responsibilities of Norveth. He took "vacations" whenever there was a slowdown in the industry. He bought a Model T. With a Model T, he could look upon himself as a success. Cramming eight members of the Norveth family into the car, he whirled them around the neighborhood.

During the 1923 recession, Jansen began using the car as a jitney. He charged five cents to carry people on short trips. The occupation of chauffeur was more to his liking than the confinement and discipline of a factory job. He did not return to Ford.

In the blue-collar speakeasies he frequented, Jansen heard much talk about a true-blue American organization that was going to run the niggers, yids, and bead counters out of the country. The renascent Ku Klux Klan found a favorable climate at Ford, and established itself strongly in Detroit. It was the demotic wave whose crest was manifesting itself in Congress in the immigration acts.

As people flocked from rural areas into the cities, native whites were thrust into competition with Catholic immigrants and Negroes for blue-collar jobs. (In the South, the number of agricultural workers increased from approximately 1.1 million in 1860 to 2.1 million in 1930, even though the amount of land under cultivation remained constant, and the ravages of the boll weevil reduced the harvest in some counties to half what it had been twenty years before.)

Willing to work longer hours for less pay, Negroes were undercutting the whites. The auto industry was using between 23,000 and 26,000, almost all in the back-breaking and lung-searing foundry, which came to be known as the "black department." Laboring for eighty-nine cents a day (seventy cents in the South), there were 58,000 Negroes in the coal mines. By the end of the 1920's there were 177,000 working twelve-hour days in the iron and steel industry.

During the 1920's, Pennsylvania gained 265,000 Negroes, Illinois 214,000, New York 200,000, Ohio 190,000, New Jersey 122,000, and Michigan 117,000. Michigan, having had only a little over 17,000 Negroes in 1910 (but uncounted others who had disappeared into the white population), was the state with the greatest percentage gain. Of the seven U.S. cities with more than 100,000 Negroes, six were in the North.* [1]

Once more, as in eighteenth-century Ireland and the South after the Civil War, an underclass was threatening the economic position of the lower stratum of its "superiors." Drafted into the army during World War I, Negroes had appeared as "equals" in the form of soldiers. During the labor troubles that followed the war they were widely used as strikebreakers. Once again, as in the Civil War, riots spread through the cities: Houston, East St. Louis, Chicago, Tulsa, Omaha, and Washington, D.C. The onset of the 1920–1921 depression knocked white migrants a rung or two down the ladder and generated a fierce scramble for jobs. Publication of a Communist plan for creation of a separate Negro republic in the Black Belt provided grist for racial propaganda.

From Atlanta, the KKK seeped northward into the Midwest, and established itself in the same territory that had been the stronghold of the American Pro-tective Association. Like the Nazis in Europe, the KKK directed itself at two segments of the population: the people who presented an economic threat from below, and the minority within the middle class who could safely be attacked for the purported "exploitation" of the masses—the Jews.

The Klan cast itself as the purifier of corruption, upholder of American values, and maintainer of law and order. A 1921 exposé in the New York *World,* followed by a misdirected and cursory investigation by the Rules Committee of the House of Representatives, gave it national publicity. In keeping with the xenophobic spirit of the times, Americans rushed to join. In less than five years Klan membership rose to somewhere between 4 and 8 million. Michigan's estimated 875,000 members were the largest number in any single state. The huge sums of money that flowed into the coffers of the Klan made it a political power. Many politicians became secret members. Their campaign funds were swelled by Klan contributions.

In at least two states, Georgia and Indiana, the Klan controlled the state governments. In others, politicians prudently stayed in the good graces of the Klan. Opposition to the Klan forced Senator Oscar Underwood of Alabama from office. The Populist liberal, Hugo Black, who replaced him, like so many other ambitious men of the time was a KKK fellow traveler.

At the Democratic convention of 1924, an estimated three hundred delegates were controlled by the Klan. Once again, the Democrats were in reality two parties: a Northern urban and a Southern agrarian. A proposed plank in the platform opposed intolerance and denounced the KKK. But William Jennings

---

* They were Washington, Baltimore, New York, Philadelphia, Chicago, and Detroit. The only Southern city with more than 100,000 Negroes was New Orleans.

Bryan, the ghost of Populism, arose for the last time and exhorted: "It requires more courage to fight the Republican party than it does to fight the Ku Klux Klan." [2]

For the first time radio carried a blow-by-blow account of the proceedings. People listened with fascination as delegates tore down and smashed each other's standards, and wrestled each other to the cement floor of Madison Square Garden. During the roll-call vote on the plank, spectators and delegates turned the garden into an arena of flying fists, chairs, and bottles. The anti-Klan plank was defeated by a vote of 542 3/20 to 541 3/20. It was an indication of just how matters stood.

The delegates deadlocked between the Catholic candidate of the urban wing, Governor Alfred E. Smith of New York, and the candidate of the agrarians, William G. McAdoo, Wilson's son-in-law. When on the one hundred and third ballot they picked a corporation lawyer, John W. Davis, it scarcely mattered. The party was in even greater disarray than it had been in 1920.

49

Sweet Justice

AMONG THOSE NEGROES WHOSE MIGRATION CATALYZED THE KU KLUX KLAN was Odie Stallings.

Born in the middle 1890's in the James River country of Virginia, Stallings was a member of the first generation of blacks abandoned by the Republican party. He had never seen the inside of a school. As a boy he had lived in a three-room cabin with thirty-seven other persons, twenty-one of them his brothers and sisters.

His mother had lost count of the number of children to whom she had given birth. She was, in truth, unable to count that high. She used to say that as many as were living "had done died." That was probably an exaggeration. But, married at the age of thirteen, she could well have had more than thirty children.

The Stallings family lived with two score other families in a compound of huts that had once been slave quarters. With the end of slave breeding for export, the Virginia economy was incapable of sustaining a static population, much less a multiplying one. It was a barter economy that resembled Ireland's fifty years before. Odie's father chopped wood, helped harvest tobacco, picked fruit, and worked a few days at pig-killing time. But a generation after emancipation he was as shackled by poverty and the lack of education as his father had been by law.

Since he no longer had economic value to anyone his diet was worse than that of the slaves. No one cared about his health. Four of the people in the cabin were blind, three had "the shakes," and none over twenty-five had more than a half dozen teeth. Intestinal parasites were chronic. There were no privies. Water was drawn from a small stream. Doctors and nurses and medicine were unknown. Sickness and injury were treated with herbs, mud, and poultices. Flies and worms and mosquitoes fought over the well and devoured the sick.

When Odie's sister fell out of a tree and broke her arm, it was set in a poultice. Ten days later Odie watched the maggots pouring out of the wound like meat from a grinder. The smell was terrible, but there were so many bad smells it blended into the general putrefaction. Because she was sick she was allowed to sleep on the only mattress. Five people slept with her, even though she was thrashing and screaming in delirium.

Most of the time while she was sick, rain fell. The water rose through the loose boards that had been placed on the dirt floor. The mud that had been used to chink the holes in the walls melted. The roof leaked like a tattered umbrella. While Odie's sister lay dying on the dripping mattress, thirty-six people, wet and shivering, stood around the room, and tried to find a place where the water did not come through the roof or the walls, or the floor.

Beneath the weight of the people, the floor boards sank into the mud. Water rolled ankle-deep over Odie's bare feet. For three days and nights they stood like that, with nothing to eat, no place to lie down, and nowhere to go. The children cried. The babies wailed themselves into exhaustion. The adults called unto the Lord. And still it rained. It rained and rained until it had seemed they would all be driven mad.

That was the worst death. But death from typhoid, pneumonia, and general debilitation resulting from malnutrition and intestinal parasites was present all the time.

During World War I the army drafted Odie and took him out of the back country. Among the soldiers of 1918 as among the soldiers of 1865, Detroit attained a reputation as a city of promise. After he was discharged in 1919, Stallings joined the throng of Negroes crowding into Hastings Street and "Paradise Valley."

Like the immigration from Europe, the black migration consisted largely of young men. (There were still 125 foreign-born men for every 100 foreign-born females in Detroit.) Southern cities were deserted by Negro men. In some there were only 75 males for every 100 females. Conversely, steel cities like Homestead and Aliquippa in Pennsylvania had 120 or more Negro men for every 100 Negro women, and Saginaw, Michigan, had 136 to 100, the highest proportion in the country.[1] (Since it is now known that in urban areas the census has been undercounting Negro men by about 10 percent, the ratio probably went as high as 150 to 100.)

The disparity produced the expected sexual stresses. Like the foreign-born girls who had responded to the law of supply and demand, Negro women were drawn into prostitution. Black men transferred their sexual drives to drinking, gambling, and fighting. Sweaty and dirty from their jobs in the foundries, they boarded streetcars and so inadvertently reinforced the negative image of Negroes held by whites. For Dancy and the Urban League it was an exhausting struggle to open up opportunities and find housing for the new arrivals. All Dancy could do was appeal to the consciences of the Progressive Republicans. He startled upper-class whites by introducing them to a Negro who was an expert on Greek art—and then revealing that the Phi Beta Kappa graduate from Amherst was earning his living as a railroad porter in the Michigan Central depot.

Through J. L. Hudson's niece, Margaret Jackson (whose husband was Chapin's associate in the Hudson Motor Car Company), Dancy persuaded the management of the city's largest department store to accept light-skinned, pretty Negro girls—several of them college graduates—as elevator operators. It was the first time any major store had hired Negroes for jobs where they were visible to the public.

In a city that had miserable housing for whites, the housing for blacks was atrocious. In the blighted area between St. Antoine and Hastings Streets, where

Civil War Negroes had been replaced by German Jews, and German Jews by Russian Jews, the Russian Jews were being displaced by Southern Negroes. One out of every six or seven families was living in a single room, and "doubling up" was common. In some tiny rooms occupied by two people, the most practical way to dress was to stand in the middle of the bed. Each block was studded with saloons, gambling parlors and brothels. Poolrooms and dance halls were everywhere. One motion picture house confounded the Negroes who entered it by staging, between the films, vaudeville acts—in Yiddish.

Stallings drifted around the city for several months before he found work in the "black department" at River Rouge. Since Ford had its own steel- and glassmaking operations, it had more hot and "dirty" jobs than any other auto company and had replaced Packard as the largest employer of blacks in the industry.

All of the communities bordering the plant, however, were lily white and determined to remain so. Dearborn, where most of the white Ford workers lived, had a strong chapter of the Klan (and even in 1970 had only thirteen Negro residents). When the Melville Brass Company in Wyandotte hired some Negroes and tried to build housing for them, whites formed a vigilante committee and drove every black out of the town. Stallings and his black co-workers at Ford were forced to commute ten miles from downtown Detroit.

To alleviate the situation, Dancy, with a real estate developer from Florida, mapped a subdivision west of Dearborn. Stallings, marrying a woman two years older than himself, settled into a small, neat house with a good coal stove in the new community of Inkster. His wife Freda had a daughter, Janice, by a prior marriage; and Freda and Odie quickly produced two boys.

For Negroes able to pay the price, housing had always been available in Detroit. Although blacks had to pay 50 percent more for one side of a duplex than whites for the other, they were not segregated. More than half were living in predominantly white areas and fewer than one sixth in all-black areas. In 1925 Dr. Ossian Sweet, a gynecologist who had graduated from Howard University and later studied under Madame Curie in France, purchased an eighteen-thousand-dollar, two-story brick house in a comfortable middle-class neighborhood on the far East Side.

Polish and other "new wave" immigrants were buying heavily into the neighborhood. They were being hard pressed by the competition of the Southern Negroes, and in many ways were not as acculturated as the urban blacks.* While the KKK burned crosses around the city in demonstrations against Negroes and Catholics, the immigrants developed their own virulently anti-Negro bias.

Between the time the Sweets bought the house and the time they moved in, mobs attacked the homes of other Negroes in the area. (Such attacks had become common in Northern cities.) A newly formed "improvement association" held meetings at the neighborhood school and called for action against the Sweets. Under police protection, Dr. Sweet, his wife, and young child occupied the house.

Dr. Sweet enlisted the aid of his two brothers—one a dentist, and the other

---

* The illiteracy rate of Detroit Negroes in 1920 was 3.9 percent, that of the foreign-born 9.7 percent. Black children were staying in school longer than foreign-born children.[2]

a student at Wilberforce University—and six other men to defend the house. On the second night of their stay, scores of people gathered from all over Detroit. At about eleven o'clock, when the number on the street had grown to four or five hundred, people started hurling rocks through the windows of the darkened house. From the interior came the flash of a shotgun. Leon Breiner, sitting on the porch of a house across the street, fell dead. Another man was wounded.

The eight to ten police officers stationed in the neighborhood had failed to take any action against the crowd. Now, in Inspector Norton Schuknect's words: "I goes over into the house, comes up on the steps there, rings the bell. . . . I seen Dr. Sweet, the first man I seen." All eleven persons in the house were arrested and charged with murder.

The case united the middle-class Negroes. The NAACP undertook the defense of the Sweets. Clarence Darrow,* sixty-nine years old, was persuaded to become the counsel for the defense.

The judge to whom the case was assigned was Frank Murphy. One of the four children of an Irish Democratic lawyer and politician in rural Huron County, and the grandnephew of a man hung by the British in Ireland, Murphy had barely squeaked through the University of Michigan Law School. A liberal, he had been elected to a Detroit Recorders Court controlled by a reactionary bloc of four judges. His assignment to the controversial Sweet case was widely regarded as a device to put an end to his career. Detroiters predicted that, whatever the outcome of the case, Judge Murphy would be convicted and not heard of again.

In an age when there was an average of one lynching a week, many Americans approved of summary justice, and most of the rest were apathetic. Except for Mayor John Smith, scarcely a single leading citizen could be found in Detroit to speak up for the rights of Negroes.

The trial was the most notable in the city since the "railroad conspiracy" case seventy-five years before. People began lining up in the courthouse at five o'clock in the morning. Newspaper correspondents came from all over the nation. In the jam-packed courtroom Negroes sat in one section, whites in another. Darrow had difficulty finding any white person willing to testify for the defense. More than fifty whites, however, swore that there had been no shouted threats, no throwing of rocks—the street had been practically empty of people when the Sweets, without provocation, had fired.

Darrow, in turn, attempted to pin the firing of the fatal shot on a policeman with a reputation as a "nigger hater." He took seven hours for his closing argument. In the sweaty, packed courtroom people were fainting without falling down. For days the jury remained deadlocked. They screamed "nigger lover" at each other, and threw chairs across the room. In the end, Murphy had to declare a hung jury.

The retrial was attended by judges from other cities where the racial issue

* The careers of few men reflected the urbanization of America more accurately than Darrow's career. Born in Kinsman, Ohio, a farming community near the Pennsylvania border, he had been attending Allegheny College when the Panic of 1873 had forced him to interrupt his education. For the next three years he had been paid thirty dollars a month to teach school. Then, after attending the University of Michigan for one year, he had passed the law exam. A disciple of Henry George, he had been the defense lawyer in numerous cases involving union officials. Only a few months before he had represented evolution against Fundamentalist reaction at the Scopes "monkey trial."

was coming ever more to public attention. Darrow changed his tactics. For one of the first times in a twentieth-century trial, he turned the focus onto civil rights. He assured himself of a jury of native whites. Henry Sweet, Dr. Sweet's younger brother, admitted firing the fatal shot in defense of the home and the family. Darrow emphasized the sociology of the Negro, and the injustices he had suffered. He played up the contrast between the cultured, educated Sweets and the inarticulate, foreign-accented members of the mob.

"This great state and this great city . . . must face this problem and face it squarely," he said.

"If eleven white men had shot and killed a black while protecting their home and their lives against a mob of blacks . . . they would have been given medals instead.

"I haven't any doubt but that every one of you is prejudiced against colored people [but] I want you to do all you can to be fair in this case, and I believe you will." [3]

The jury deliberated only briefly before bringing in a verdict of acquittal.

The trial led Mayor Smith to appoint an interracial committee, the first in the city's history, to find jobs and housing for Negroes. Headed by Reinhold Niebuhr, pastor of the Bethel Evangelical Church, the committee suggested that the city follow a policy "not imperiling Negro rights [but] not ignoring the cultivated race prejudices of large sections of the community." [4]

50

One Family—Like Cain and Abel

SINCE DETROIT WAS UNDER THE INFLUENCE OF SOME OF HIS MOST DISILLU-sioned and bitter acquaintances, Ford separated himself from the city more and more. Detroit was the city of Mayor John Smith, and Smith, a protégé of Truman Newberry, was an old antagonist.* Detroit was the city of Edwin Pipp and his Detroit *Saturday Night*—supported by Newberry—which missed no opportunity to expose Ford's foibles and follies. Detroit was the city of the Good Citizens League and its "grand old man," Henry Leland, to whom Ford was Judas Iscariot. Detroit was the city of the Butzels and the other patrician German-Jewish families, who were outraged by Ford's anti-Semitic diatribes. Detroit was the city of the Packard Motor Company controlled by the Joys and the McMillans, the Algers and the Newberrys.

To America and the world, Detroit was Ford, and Ford was Detroit. They were, in fact, one family—like Cain and Abel.

Surrounded by people who dared not dispute a word he spoke, Ford tried to create a world of his own in the splendid insularity of Dearborn. He had few people who could associate with him as equals. His friendship with Thomas Edison was increasingly restricted by Edison's age and his failing health. Ford meddled in relatives' affairs and tried to patch up broken marriages—a trait that was not welcomed by members of the family. He wanted Edsel to build a house near him on the "Fairlane" estate. But Edsel bought an estate in the eastern suburb of Grosse Pointe. The distance-spanning automobile had con-verted Grosse Pointe from the summering place of the wealthy into the all-year residential district of Detroit's most fashionable society. In Grosse Pointe, Edsel not only was geographically far removed—thirteen miles—from River Rouge; he was separated even further from his father by the friends he made. They

---

* Smith had been circulation manager of the Dearborn *Independent* at the time Ford pur-chased it, but had left almost immediately. Notwithstanding his name, he was of Polish ancestry and had organized the Polish wards for Newberry in the 1918 Senate race against Ford. As a senator, Newberry had promoted Smith's appointment to the Detroit postmaster-ship, thus starting him on a long and prominent career in city politics.

were friends who brought him within the orbit of that same Detroit "society" with which his father was at odds.

At "Fairlane," Henry Ford would gather his claque and discourse with the air of an oracle upon Wall Street, the Jews, international bankers plotting wars in secret conclaves, and synthetic cows. He suggested that "reading can become a dope habit, I don't like to read books; they mess up my mind." He attempted to convince Ford workers to drink soybean milk and soybean coffee. Believing in "harmonious foods" and in the avoidance of coffee, tea, and meat, he urged that eating be made "a part of religion." [1]

He flitted from project to project, many of them bordering on the eccentric. Since everyone knew that he did not want to hear that an idea of his could not be carried out, everyone plugged on and on at such projects as the X-engine, whose cylinders pointed in four different directions.

He initiated the Greenfield Village project to recreate the romantic, kerosene-lamp America of his boyhood and record the evolution of mechanization. Dozens of steam engines, farm implements, primitive horseless carriages, and artisans' workshops were brought to Dearborn. Edison's laboratory was transplanted intact. So was Luther Burbank's workshop (except for the remains of Burbank's dog, which, like John Wilkes Booth's body, Ford wanted to have exhumed).

But if Ford was looking back, he also continued to move forward.

The end of World War I left Detroit as dominant in the aircraft industry as in the automobile business. Following enactment by Congress of an airmail subsidy in February, 1925, Ford organized a Detroit-Chicago airline. Since all airplanes in service were obsolescent, he had the company develop a new craft. In June of 1926 Ford began testing the Trimotor, an eight-passenger plane that was the largest built in America up to the time, and the first specifically designed for commercial service.

(Later, by producing a "flivver plane" that set a small aircraft endurance record, Ford stimulated rumors that he was developing the Model T of the air. Actually, although he was employing sixteen hundred men in aircraft production in 1929, the Depression crushed the nascent flying boom.)

Financing all of these endeavors was the most successful car in the history of the world—the Model T. Any proposal for replacement of the Model T continued to be received by Ford like a suggestion for progenycide. And why not? Farmers, whose income rose steadily if unspectacularly during the early 1920's, bought hundreds of thousands of the cars. One million were sold in 1921; nearly 1.4 million in 1922; and more than 2 million—some 55 percent of all American automobiles—during each of the next three years. (Not till 1955 would the company surpass its 1923 sales of 2,120,000.)

Yet even while sales were peaking, the age of rural America symbolized by Ford and the Model T was coming to an end. In 1921 Congress, under pressure from the suddenly powerful highway lobby, passed legislation to create a national network of primary roads—a network that within a decade would be without parallel in the world. In 1921, of 203,000 miles of state highways, 84,000 had been surfaced. In 1925, of 275,000 miles, 145,000 were surfaced. About 15,000 miles of roads continued to be improved every year.

The nature and uses of the automobile were undergoing rapid change. Until 1920 most trips were limited to a few miles—only the most rugged adventurer would think of driving cross-country. Only the most intrepid would venture out in rain or snow or dark of night in an open car even in the city, where side streets were likely to be as muddy as any country lane.

But paving changed all that. Chapin, with his experience in pioneering highways, was the first to recognize the new demand. In 1921 he introduced the closed body on Hudson's Essex coach. The closed body converted the automobile into not only an all-weather but a long-distance conveyance. By 1925, 56 percent of all cars sold had closed bodies, and the next year the proportion climbed to 72 percent. Only Ford continued to manufacture a large number of "open" cars, for the Model T's high clearance and light chassis made the car top-heavy and unstable when a closed body was added. In 1927, when 85 percent of all cars manufactured were "closed," 42 percent of Model T's sold were still "open."

From 2,332,426 cars registered in the United States in 1915, the number multiplied to 17,439,701 by 1925. In the cities, droves of people abandoned the inadequate public transportation systems.

Naturally, the trend was most pronounced in Detroit. As the area's car registrations multiplied from 100,000 in 1920 to 500,000 in 1930, streetcar rides per capita declined more than 50 percent, from 335 in 1920 to 160 in 1930.* There was a direct correlation between the economics and efficiency of public transportation and population density. Five-Mile Road became a dividing line. Between the road and the river, people were public-transportation oriented. Beyond the road in the newer, middle-class districts, they were auto oriented.

For intercity travel, the automobile mated to the paved road was the most convenient means of transport ever devised. Much of the fuss and labor that previously had attended trips was eliminated. From door to door, four could travel for the price of one. Between 1920 and 1933 the number of passengers carried annually by railroads plummeted from 1.3 billion to 435 million. By the mid-1920's the commuter service of Michigan's once great system of inter-urban electric lines was in disarray. Ten of the seventeen lines were in receivership, and the last was to be abandoned in 1934. In the shipping of freight, trucks, especially on shorter hauls, were beginning to provide serious competition for railroads.

When Henry Joy had taken a prominent role in the promotion of the Lincoln Highway, he scarcely had anticipated that he would undermine the railroad system that his father had worked so diligently to build.

In nearly twenty years the Model T had remained essentially unchanged. Its drivers were still required to be rugged. Its nondemountable wheel rims were an intolerable nuisance. Its spark plugs had to be cleaned every two hundred miles. Its planetary transmission, once a wonder, was now an oddity. Its "muffler" was a series of tin cans with asbestos that, when the engine backfired, popped off as if fired from a shotgun. Its magneto-linked headlights, which died entirely when the car came to a standstill, were a menace on the highways.

* Year	Auto Registration	Streetcar Rides per Capita	Revenue
1920	100,000	335	$365 million
1926	300,000	235	382 million
1930	500,000	160	320 million

The lawyer on his way to court or the teacher on her way to school did not have the patience to stand in the rain and crank a recalcitrant engine. Yet it was the middle class of the cities who were taking to the road en masse: and the cities, gaining 1.5 million people every year, were growing nearly seven times as fast as rural areas.

But who was intrepid enough to tell that to Henry Ford?

In January, 1926, Ernest Kanzler tried. In an obsequious memorandum he pointed out to Ford that "most people when with you hesitate to say what they think," and suggested changes in the Model T.[2]

The consequence was predictable. Ford was infuriated.

Kanzler was already in Ford's bad graces because Ford resented the close relationship between the sisters, Josephine Kanzler and Eleanor Ford, and believed Edsel was being corrupted and turned against him by it. Ford resorted to his usual devices to make Kanzler's position untenable. Less than six months after Kanzler wrote the memorandum, he resigned.

The Model T, Ford insisted, was successful precisely because it was "old-fashioned," and Americans yearned for the days gone by. Once more a reduction in price would correct matters.

But the magic was gone. Farmers were used to running their Model T's until they died in a furrow. But as urbanites traded in their old cars for newer models, a *used*-car market developed. Able to buy a more advanced *used* car of another make for the same price or less than a new Ford, an increasing number of people turned away from the Model T. In 1926, while Chevrolet sales gained 43 percent, Ford's slipped 20 percent.

Once more as things went awry Ford turned against the Jews. The Dearborn *Independent* reported that farm prices were falling because Jews were trying to corner the wheat market. The paper singled out a renowned and respected Chicago attorney and leader of the farm-cooperative movement, Aaron Sapiro, and accused him of cheating his clients.

Sapiro filed a $1 million libel suit.

When the case came to trial in Detroit in March, 1927, Ford sent a substitute. The man pushed into the spotlight was Harry Bennett.*

Bennett was the kind of "tough guy" that Ford would have liked the sensitive Edsel to be. Lonely, Ford needed a man Friday who would cater to his whims, talk with him on his own intellectual level, provide entertainment, and obey the injunction: "never try to understand me." Amid lurid newspaper stories of gangsters and kidnapings, Ford was receiving some 250 threatening letters a year. The pistol-packing Bennett gave Ford, who himself carried a brace of Magnums in his car, a sense of security.

Through his personal relationship with Ford, Bennett was usurping some of the power of the model bureaucrat, Ernest Liebold. Liebold had responsibility for Ford's personal finances, his correspondence, public relations, political activities, the *Independent,* Ford Hospital, the railroad, and the Dearborn State Bank. Even more importantly, he held the power of attorney for both Henry

---

* Bennett was the stepson of an engineering professor at the University of Michigan. At the age of seventeen he had joined the navy. Seven years later he had just been discharged when he became involved in a brawl in New York. New York columnist Arthur Brisbane had bailed him out and taken him to meet Ford. The first question Ford asked Bennett was:
"Can you shoot?"
Bennett was hired as a guard for the new River Rouge plant. He moved up quickly as the plant expanded, and soon was in charge of the Ford "service men," or security guards.

and Clara Ford. Viewing Kanzler as a threat to himself, Liebold had worked to undermine Kanzler as he had once undercut Klingensmith.

Kanzler's downfall, however, produced bitter recriminations within the family, and caused Ford and Edsel to drift further apart. Ford relied on Bennett all the more. He called upon him day and night, and virtually adopted him as a surrogate son.

At the trial, Sapiro's lawyers were determined to bring Ford to the stand. Bennett was just as determined to preserve Ford from a repetition of his experience during the Chicago *Tribune* trial. Ford, who kept dodging subpoenas, was involved in a strange and suspicious automobile accident that was said to preclude his appearance. Bennett accused Sapiro of bribery and jury tampering, and did his best to abort the trial. When Bennett impugned the competence of a woman juror, she declared publicly that Ford seemed anxious to keep the case from going to the jury. Her statement caused the judge to declare a mistrial.

For the moment Bennett had accomplished his aim. But Ford still faced the likelihood of having to make an appearance at a retrial. Edsel and the family were chagrined at the regeneration of Ford's anti-Semitism, and urged a settlement.

Ford, who was agonizing over the fate of the Model T, gave in. Bennett negotiated an apology and disclaimer with Brisbane, Samuel Untermeyer, and Louis Marshall of the American Jewish Committee.

"I have been greatly shocked as a result of my study and examination of the files of the Dearborn *Independent* and of the pamphlets entitled *The International Jew,*" the statement declared.

"I am deeply mortified that this journal . . . has been made the medium for resurrecting exploited fictions. . . .

"Had I appreciated even the general nature, to say nothing of the details, of these utterances, I would have forbidden their circulation. . . .

"I deem it to be my duty as an honorable man to make amends for the wrong done to the Jews as fellow men and brothers . . . by giving them the unqualified assurance that henceforth they may look to me for fellowship and good will."

The signature read "Henry Ford"; but the signer was Bennett.[3]

The settlement was supposed to include the firing of Liebold and Cameron. But Ford had learned that the departed tell tales. He was not about to dismiss Liebold, who knew more about Ford's affairs than Ford himself.* Liebold was humiliated; but his position was not affected. Cameron became the spokesman for Ford's "Sunday Evening Hour" on radio.

The publicity of the trial further damaged the Model T's faltering sales. People continued to stream into the cities from the "real America." The KKK, racked by scandals and subverted by prosperity, was disintegrating. The constituency for the Model T shrank. Chevrolet, which had been outsold fifteen to one in 1921, was selling more than half as many cars as Ford in early 1927.

Ford's fear of the Catholic Du Ponts, who controlled G.M., was as great as his animosity toward the "international Jews." Like an automotive Jonah he

---

* Liebold wrote in his memoirs: "Mr. Ford knew everything that was going on. Of course, it put Cameron and I in a rather embarrassing position to be blamed for what went on. . . . Nobody was ever doing anything around Dearborn or anywhere else that Mr. Ford didn't agree with 100 per cent."[4]

kept looking over his shoulder for the General Motors whale. With the whale approaching closer, Ford did an abrupt about-face.

On May 25, 1927, he told a nation that had come to regard the Model T as a national monument similar to the Capitol or the Statue of Liberty that he was discontinuing production of the car. Five days later the number 15,007,003 was stamped on the last chassis. The assembly lines, some of which had been in continuous operation for fourteen years, were shut down.

51

The Model of the
Modern Corporation

SIX YEARS BEFORE, FORD HAD FIRED THE EXECUTIVES WHO WERE "TOO GOOD" for him. Now the same men were making Chevrolet the industry's best seller.

In 1911, the year after Durant had been forced to relinquish the presidency of General Motors, he began production of a new, light car designed by French immigrant, Louis Chevrolet. Its success was extraordinary.

General Motors, in the meantime, doubled its profits year after year. As its stock gyrated,* Durant used the profits from Chevrolet to play the market and to add to his holdings of G.M. stock. At the November, 1915, meeting of the General Motors board of directors, Durant revealed to the shocked bankers that they no longer had control of the company. Since neither side commanded a majority, an agreement was reached that Pierre S. Du Pont, who had acquired two thousand shares, should name the three swing directors.

In June, 1916, Durant succeeded Nash as president.† Three months later he astonished the financial world by declaring for General Motors, which had earned $58 million between 1913 and 1916, a dividend of $50 a share, the largest in the history of Wall Street.

By 1917 the Chevrolet Motor Company held 450,000 of the outstanding 825,589 shares of General Motors stock. Merging the two companies a year later, Durant retained General Motors as the parent corporation.

An empire builder, Durant was bored by the routine of administration. As soon as he regained control of G.M., he renewed the pell-mell acquisition of other companies. The Remy Electric Company and DELCO, together with Charles Kettering, were brought into the fold. Sixty percent of the stock of the Fisher Body Company, a family firm of carriage makers that had become the auto industry's most prestigious maker of bodies, was acquired. With a personal check for $53,366.50, Durant purchased the Guardian Refrigerator Company of Detroit, the maker of a primitive mechanical refrigerator. (It became the

* Between 25 and 40 in 1913; 35 and 99 in 1914; 82 and 558 in 1915.
† Nash bought out Jeffery. So the Rambler, which had been one of the more popular bicycles before growing into an automobile, became the Nash.

Frigidaire Division of G.M.). He induced Alfred P. Sloan, Jr., to merge the Hyatt Roller Bearing Company of Newark, New Jersey, into General Motors.* Airplane manufacturers, steel mills, a tractor company—all became part of the expanding corporation.

While Ford was turning his company into the world's first vertically integrated, Durant was organizing General Motors into the prototype of the conglomerate. The postwar economic euphoria rocketed G.M. sales from $270 million in 1918 to $510 million in 1919. On Grand Boulevard the foundations were poured for the General Motors Building. Designed by Albert Kahn, it was to be the world's largest office building.

Division managers, anxious to outperform each other, committed tens of millions of dollars to capital expansion. The collection of economic data, however, was still in a primitive stage. Decisions involving huge sums of money were made on the spur of the moment.

In the suddenly "tight money" market of 1920 the company was unable to raise the cash it needed; and, when Ford made his cut in the price of the Model T, sales of G.M. cars plummeted. By November all divisions except Buick and Cadillac were shut down.

Using his G.M. stock as collateral, Durant had speculated heavily in the market. As the G.M. stock was caught in a long slide—it was to hit bottom at $9.50 per share in early 1922—his creditors called in their loans. In his wild wheeling and dealing Durant had lost track of how much he owed. In November, 1920, he told Sloan and Du Pont that he believed he had contracted an indebtedness of $20 million for the company; and that he had a personal indebtedness of $14 million that he could not cover. If even a hint of Durant's financial situation were to leak out, a general Wall Street panic might be precipitated.

Since Durant's 1915 coup, control of the company had shifted to Du Pont. Of all the American beneficiaries of the war, none was more blessed than Du Pont. The company had manufactured 40 percent of all the propellant powder used by the Allies. Between 1914 and 1918 it had profits of $238 million on gross sales of $1,157 billion. In pursuit of "reasonable profits," Pierre Du Pont said, "we cannot assent to allowing our own patriotism to interfere with our duties as trustees." [1] He refused to accept a cost-plus contract from the Federal government. For three months after American entry into the war he held up construction of a badly needed powder plant until he obtained his terms, which the War Industries Board considered exorbitant.

As the war progressed, the "reasonable profits" filled the company's treasury. In 1917, Treasurer John J. Raskob informed the finance committee that, although the company already had invested $40 million in new industries, a $50 million surplus remained for which it was imperative to find an investment outlet. For $43 million, Du Pont acquired 26.4 percent of outstanding General Motors stock.

To extricate Durant from his financial dilemma, Du Pont arranged a new stock issue of 3.2 million shares, priced at $20 per share. Britain's Explosives Trades, Limited, bought 1.8 million shares, and J. P. Morgan the remainder. Ousting Durant, Du Pont took over the presidency of General Motors.

* An 1895 electrical-engineering graduate of MIT, Sloan had borrowed $5,000 from his father, another one of those prosperous New England merchants, to buy control of Hyatt, a manufacturer of antifriction roller bearings. Sloan received $13.5 million, including a large block of stock, from Durant.

Responsibility for actual operations was lodged with Sloan. Ford's purge enabled Sloan to acquire two of the ablest executives in the business. Knudsen took over the stewardship of Chevrolet. The decision was made not to attempt to compete with the Model T, but to make Chevrolet a "quality" low-priced car. Hawkins, Ford's former sales manager, set to work unraveling the tangled price structure and ending the internecine competition among G.M.'s seven automotive divisions.

Sheridan and Scripps-Booth were dropped. The remaining divisions—Chevrolet, Oakland (subsequently Pontiac), Oldsmobile, Buick, and Cadillac—were assigned individual brackets in a price structure ranging from $450 to $3,500 and up.

Under Durant, General Motors had been, essentially, a holding company, in which each division operated independently. The corporation was now transformed into an organization delicately balanced between overall policy control by top management and internal autonomy for divisions. The Du Pont practice of decision making by committee was adopted and expanded. There were separate committees to oversee finance, operations, production, sales, and policy (the executive committee). There were interdivisional committees to provide coordination. In 1922 G.M. became the first large corporation to set up a system for consolidated cash control.

Despite these measures, the corporation failed to anticipate the recession of 1924. To provide an economic barometer, a sales forecasting system reaching all the way down to the dealer level was installed. Even as at Ford—albeit in a different manner—the retailer lost much of his independence and was forced into the mold of the giant corporation. Decisions were made by committee. Faceless bureaucracy was carried to the ultimate, and humanity was submerged within *the system*.

In 1925, General Motors created the concept of "standard volume." Cars were priced so as to bring a 15 percent return on capital investment or a 20 percent return on net worth when facilities were operating at 80 percent of capacity—the "standard volume." In determining standard volume, the period during model changes, holidays, etc., was discounted, so that the number of production days was reduced to approximately 180. In reality, standard volume represented nearer 50 percent than 80 percent of capacity.

General Motors was separating itself from the competitive operations of the marketplace, and from the variable pricing of the "law" of supply and demand. The concept of "administered prices" was being substituted for laissez-faire. Administered prices, with the large margin of profit built into them, insured that the corporation would have impressive profits during good times, and would not have to operate at a loss even in the worst. By 1927 G.M. was one of ten American firms valued at over $1 billion.

Most of the other auto manufacturers were whipsawed between the giganticism of Ford and General Motors. Durant, who departed with $3 million in stock from G.M., organized a new company, Durant Motors.* Despite the "prosperity" of the 1920's, he had nearly as much difficulty staying in the black as the small, independent auto makers. One by one they were shutting down. Haynes went

* Durant marketed four models. The luxury Locomobile was the lone survivor of New England's automobile industry. The Star was one of the dozen most popular cars of the 1920's.

bankrupt in 1924. Apperson and Rickenbacker * in 1926–1927. Franklin, Peerless, Pierce–Arrow, Stutz, and Willys were all in trouble. From 113 exhibitors at the New York automobile show in 1923, the number was down to 44 in 1927.

The one man who was moving successfully against the trend was Chrysler. Quarreling with Durant over his diverting of Buick profits to undisciplined expansion, Chrysler in 1919 had chucked his $500,000-a-year presidency of Buick. Slamming his office door on the way out, he had sworn he was through with the auto business.

Within a few months, however, he was retained as a million-dollar-a-year consultant to reorganize Willys. From Willys, he went to Maxwell, which was loaded down with a huge inventory and $26 million in debts. Reorganizing the company as the Chrysler Motor Corporation, he employed three brilliant young engineers to design a new car. The first automobile powered by a high-compression engine, it was unveiled at the January, 1924, New York auto show. Costing $1,500, it was superior to most of the $5,000 cars on the market. Chrysler was able to obtain his own terms on a $50 million loan from New York bankers. Thus, after two reorganizations, the company that had started out as U.S. Motors became a major competitor in the automobile industry as Chrysler.

With C. H. Wills † soon joining the team, Chrysler had the best engineering talent in the industry. Within three years the company skyrocketed to third place among auto makers. It expanded by acquiring Dodge.‡ When Ford discontinued the Model T in 1927, Chrysler jumped at the opportunity to begin marketing a new low-priced car: the Plymouth.

To Detroit, the advent of Chrysler was of inestimable importance. The Chrysler facilities—designed, of course, by Albert Kahn—were located within the city limits. For the first time since the early 1900's the city could claim one of the top four auto makers for its own.

* The principal contribution of Eddie Rickenbacker to the company was his name. Actually, it had been organized by Flanders following his departure from Maxwell.
† Following his departure from Ford, Wills had combined with Lee to build a model industrial community near Port Huron. There they produced the Wills St. Claire, a car so advanced and so complex no auto mechanic could fix it. Only five hundred were sold in 1921, and early the next year the company went into receivership.
‡ The Dodge brothers had died in 1920. General Motors offered $125 million for the company in 1925, but was outbid by the banking firm of Dillon, Read and Company, which discovered it lacked the talent to market a car, and sold out to Chrysler.

52

An Aristocracy of Wealth

MANY OF THE SMALLER AUTO MANUFACTURERS SUFFERED BECAUSE THEY lacked the capital to finance credit purchases of cars. Installment selling of automobiles had originated with Willys in 1915. The practice received its biggest boost when Durant, following the war, incorporated the General Motors Acceptance Corporation. By the mid-1920's G.M. was selling nearly two thirds of its cars on credit.

Ford, to the contrary, had continued to sell only on a cash-and-drive basis. The fact that the American public did not have enough cash to buy all the goods being turned out by the factories had helped Chevrolet draw closer to Ford. The architect of the policy that was causing Americans to resort increasingly to credit was Treasury Secretary Andrew Mellon.

The son of a Pittsburgh judge and banker, Mellon was one of the principal organizers of the Aluminum Company of America, a founder of Gulf Oil, and president of the Mellon National Bank. He had been a banker for forty-six years and was a behind-the-scenes power in Pennsylvania Republican politics when Harding had appointed him Secretary of the Treasury.

True to his background, Mellon set out to maximize business profits while minimizing the effect of the hated income tax upon the wealthy. In office during the entire decade of the 1920's, he authorized $3.5 billion in tax refunds and abatements to Republican stalwarts and favored corporations, including his own. His rulings helped millionaires avoid taxes altogether, and his obvious propensities made the Bureau of Internal Revenue adopt the role of a benign granduncle to the wealthy.

While he acted as Santa Claus to the privileged few, he played Silas Marner to the public at large. He was obsessed with reducing the national debt—a debt that the government was collecting disproportionately from low- and middle-income taxpayers, although it had been incurred by the generous payments to the Fords, the Lelands, and the Du Ponts. Between 1920 and 1930 he reduced the debt from $24.3 billion to $16.2 billion. Three times—in 1924, 1926, and 1928—he was responsible for killing farm-relief measures. In a representative year, 1925, when the Federal budget totaled $2.88 billion, $882 million went for interest on the national debt, and only $652 million for all domestic programs combined.

In a decade when the population was increasing by 17 million, more than in any like period before, the Federal government was ignoring the enormous needs of both the people and the land. It was up to local governments to try to meet the needs; or to ignore them. By 1927 local governments were spending twice as much as the Federal government, and state and local governments combined were accounting for three quarters of the total—$63.05 of $86.10 per capita. Since state and local governments obtained their revenues from regressive taxes on sales, gasoline, and property—preponderantly the latter—the burden of taxation fell heavily on low- and middle-income groups. In Detroit, the per capita tax doubled, from $26.84 to $53.44 between 1920 and 1930, and the per capita debt multiplied sixfold from $26.85 to $162.83.[1]

To Senator Couzens, the "scab millionaire" who was experienced in local government, the policies of Mellon were inimical to the welfare of the nation. On February 21, 1924, he charged that thirty-eight corporations with which Mellon was affiliated were receiving huge tax rebates, and introduced a resolution in the Senate calling for investigation of the Bureau of Internal Revenue.

A coalition of Progressive Republicans and Democrats passed the resolution. Mellon wrote Coolidge that the investigation would "threaten the institution of government itself." The President, in turn, asserted that it would violate the Constitution and turn the country over to a "government of lawlessness." Attempting to intimidate Couzens, Mellon filed suit charging that he was $10 million in arrears on the payment of taxes on the sale of his Ford stock, even though the Bureau of Internal Revenue itself had computed the tax. The upshot was a determination by the court that Couzens had overpaid his tax by $900,000. Couzens thereupon took $10 million from his fortune and established the Children's Fund of Michigan.[2]

Couzens could win the personal battle. But in the prevailing political climate he and the Progressives were reduced to the role of Cassandras. They could warn of the dire consequences, but lacked the power to bring about a more equitable distribution of income.

The labor unions were impuissant. "That faction," said Chief Justice Taft, "we have to hit every little while."[3] Workers were forced to sign "yellow dog" contracts which specified they were subject to dismissal if they joined a union. Strikes were broken by court injunctions and by the use of police. The steel industry, still sticking to the twelve-hour day, in 1929 achieved an output fifty times that of 1869 with but ten times the number of employees. In many industries the work week was fifty hours or more. In a labor force of 49 million, only 3.6 million were union members. AFL President William Green was derisively referred to as "Sitting Bill."

Productivity was increasing so rapidly that between 1923 and 1929 industry hired only 91 new workers for every 100 displaced. The total number of production workers was 700,000 less in 1928 than in 1919. Weekly wages of production workers rose only about one fifth as much as productivity. In 1929 the average worker still earned less than twenty-five dollars a week.

The share of total national income being received by the lower 50 percent of the population was dropping steadily—in ten years it declined 18 percent.

The total income of 60 million persons at the bottom was less than one third of the income of the 13 million at the top.

Sixteen million families, 74 percent of the non-farm population, could not afford to spend the eight hundred dollars a year on food that the Agriculture Department considered as providing an adequate diet at moderate cost.

A society whose outstanding characteristic a century earlier—so far as its "free" population was concerned—had been its egalitarianism, was becoming the greatest aristocracy of wealth in the history of the world. America's 125,000 wealthiest persons had a greater total income than the 49 million citizens at the lower end of the economic order. It would take a worker twenty years to match Henry Ford's daily personal income.

53

The Curse of Progress

FORD'S SHUTDOWN CREATED A CRISIS FOR THE MANY AMERICANS PARTICIPATING only marginally in the "prosperity." Automobile production in 1927 fell by 750,000, about 25 percent, from its 1926 high. Sixty thousand men were laid off by Ford in Detroit, and 40,000 in the rest of the country. As many ancillary and satellite industries were affected, industrial failures were near their all-time high of 1922. Hundreds of Ford dealerships went out of business. There were 400,000 fewer workers employed in manufacturing than four years earlier. Unemployment increased by 1.2 million.

In Detroit the shutdown was responsible for 45 percent of the relief cases. The relief load went up by $1 million.

One of the unemployed walking the streets was William Norveth. He was fifty-two years old. No longer was he able to disguise his age by dyeing his hair and his moustache. His elbow was stiff from arthritis, and his rotting teeth made it difficult for him to chew. When Ford in 1926 had reduced the work week from six days to five, but had speeded up the lines so as to turn out as many cars in five days as in six previously, Norveth had been brought to the verge of collapse. Instead of an average of three machines, each worker at Ford was running from five to six. The only break during the shift was fifteen minutes for lunch. If a man took so much as a deep breath at his machine, he faced dismissal. Humming, whistling, any communication with a fellow worker was forbidden. Bennett's "service men" were everywhere. Norveth's "Ford stomach" had given him no rest. He was aching and exhausted.

He had no illusion that he would be rehired by Ford. Long lines of men gathered at plant gates throughout the city. Disheartened, Norveth no longer had the persistence and the aggressiveness that had obtained jobs for him in the past. Theresa, working twelve hours a day in a small bakery, became the family breadwinner. To supplement her income, Norveth withdrew five dollars each week from the three hundred dollars in their savings account.

All his life Norveth had emphasized to his children the importance of work. Work was the most important education for a boy. He couldn't understand why the authorities, for the first time, were making a real effort to see that parents kept their children in school until the age of sixteen.* Now he was out of work, and his children, more knowledgeable on many subjects and infinitely wiser than he had been at their age, were barely suppressing their rebellion. *Work,* they were saying, was not nearly as important as who you knew.

Throughout the neighborhood, parents with old-country backgrounds were complaining that they were having difficulty controlling their children. The city offered innumerable distractions. The movies were full of sex. The streets were full of speakeasies. The dance halls were full of girls. It seemed impossible to keep the boys from smoking cigarettes, and the girls from putting on lipstick. They wanted cars, radios, electric appliances—all the good things that the modern world not only was offering to them, but through advertising insisting they should have. When Norveth had told his children that the family could not afford a car, they had pointed out that Jansen could afford a car. Anyone could afford a car on credit.

In 1926 the city had banned jitneys in an attempt to reverse the decline in the patronage of streetcars and reduce the traffic congestion that was congealing the downtown business district. Peter Jansen had gone to work as a truck driver for the Kroger grocery chain.

Now, in the late summer of 1927, he was on his way to Maple Rapids to attend the funeral of Ralph Lentick. For twelve years Lentick had shuttled between Lansing and the farm of his sister-in-law Jenny and her husband, Arthur Yarman. For a time he had worked in the Oldsmobile factory. But his hatred of regimentation and "the bosses" had always gotten him into trouble. He would hold a job for a few weeks, then walk off or be fired. When he tired of Lansing, he would return to the farm. When he tired of the farm, he would go back to the city. His two children, Harold and Cissy, were cared for by his sister-in-law.

Never an easy man to get along with, Ralph acted stranger and stranger as he grew older. Standing in the fields he bayed at the moon. He dug holes into the ground and said he could "feel copper in his bones." Had he lived in the city he would, undoubtedly, have been committed to an asylum. (He had, in fact, once been remanded for observation when he took a pickax down into a manhole and started chopping at the sewer.) But the countryside, with its open spaces, was more tolerant of aberrations.

As it had for Lentick, the city sometimes became too much for Jansen. Then he would drive out to the farm. The family was always glad to see him, for the Model T provided them with transportation.

Jansen and Lentick had not really been friends; yet for each the other had been the only friend he had. When Jansen drove along the dirt road to the farm with its kerosene lamps and the well with the hand pump, he felt as if he were returning home. He helped milk the cow, he fed swill to the pigs, and he churned butter. He couldn't understand why they kept talking about maybe having to make the move to the city.

A Hollander, Yarman's grandfather had been the kind of immigrant of which the Dillingham Commission approved, and with which it wanted to populate American farms. But the increase in agricultural population and the wartime

---

* In 1920, out of every one hundred sixth graders, only twenty-three had gone through the tenth grade, and sixteen had graduated from high school; in 1930, fifty-two went through the tenth grade, and thirty graduated, nearly five times the number in 1900.

expansion of acreage cultivated were now principal factors in depressing farm prices.* Gross farm income dropped from $17.9 billion in 1919 to an average of $12.3 billion between 1921 and 1927. While the top 10 percent of farms were producing more than 40 percent of the value of all crops, the bottom 40 percent were producing only 10 percent. The per capita income of farmers in Michigan was less than one third that of the people in the cities.†

It was impossible for a small farmer like Yarman to buy a tractor, and without a tractor he couldn't compete. Most farmers, instead of churning their own butter, were buying it at the red-fronted A and P store. The A and P chain was driving the Gleaner and Grange stores out of business.

In 1910 there had been no more than 1,000 tractors in the whole country. By 1927 there were nearly 700,000. In 1918 fewer than 100,000 farms, about 1.5 percent of the total, had had electricity. By 1927, as rural cooperatives filled the gap left by public utilities unwilling to serve low-density areas, nearly 400,000 farms had electricity. The minority of farmers beginning to use the power tools of mass production only aggravated the problems of the majority.

Progress seemed more and more like a curse. With cars and the new roads, people were going to the county seat to do their shopping. Communities at a distance from improved roads were withering, as communities without railroad service had withered three quarters of a century earlier. The blacksmiths and the cracker-barrel stores were disappearing. With them went the market for the small farmers.

Without electricity, indoor plumbing, a gas stove, or running water, the farm was unchanged from a half century before. The Lentick and Yarman children were itching to get to the city. They wanted to listen to the radio, to go to the movies, to make big money in the factories so they could buy clothes and cars. The world had become a cornucopia from which manufactured goods tumbled. It did no good for Jansen to try to disillusion them. He himself, with his car and packaged cigarettes, was an example of success. The stories he told to discourage them only made their eyes open wider.

After Ralph Lentick's funeral, Jansen took Harold, now almost eighteen, back to Detroit. They left the farm before daybreak, so that Harold would have a full day to look for a job. They arrived in the city at eight thirty. Dropping him off, Peter Jansen headed for the Norveth house. He was surprised to find Marie Rose puttering around the kitchen. Sixteen years old, she was still attending school, but working part-time at the Kresge five-and-dime store. Peter asked her if she would not be late for school. She replied that she already was. He offered to drive her. Without enthusiasm, she said okay.

Thin, five feet three inches in height, Marie was cute without being pretty. She thought she could be prettier, but her father would not let her use cosmetics. When she suggested that a boy might ask her for a date, he ridiculed the notion, declaring that she was nothing but a baby.

Marie was in love with the movies. She could have spent twenty-four hours a day in the theaters. But her father let her go only twice a month, and only if another member of the family went with her.

---

* The war increased the number of farms to 6,448,000, more than ever before or since. They occupied 50 percent of the land area of the nation, compared to 33 percent thirty years earlier.
† In 1929, $295 annually compared to $984.

"I don't want to go to school," she said after she had started off with Peter. "I want to go see *A Kiss for Cinderella.*"

Peter protested. But strength of will was not one of his characteristics. When they emerged from the theater in the early afternoon, rain was falling. In the open car Peter and Marie soon were chilled and wet.

When they reached home, the house was empty, its interior gray and lonely. Marie Rose said she would change clothes and then fix something for them to eat. From beneath the seat of the car Peter was trying to sneak a bottle of liquor into the house.

"What's that?" Marie asked. Grinning sheepishly, he told her. She said she wanted to try some. He said it was not for girls. "Do you think I'm just a baby, too?" she asked, and reached for the bottle. A moment later, choking and laughing, she went up the stairs.

After taking a swallow from the bottle, Peter started for his own room. As he passed Marie's room, he saw that the door was open. Her back was to him. She had stripped to her panties. Stopping, he stared. Suddenly, she turned. After the initial moment of shock, she started laughing. He did not know what to do. Outside of a house of prostitution it was the first time he had ever seen a girl exposed like that. So he started laughing, too.

The second month Marie wasn't sure. The third month she acted as if, by ignoring it, she could make it go away. The fourth month she began to bulge.

When Theresa told William, it was as if William had never before been angry. He threatened to have Marie Rose declared mentally incompetent and placed in an institution. Taking off his suspenders, he vowed to give her a thrashing that would teach her not to repeat her error. Theresa replied tearfully that it could not have been Marie Rose's fault. Jansen must have forced his will upon her.

Norveth dashed up the stairs in search of Jansen, but discovered he was not at home. Opening the window, Norveth threw Jansen's belongings into the street.

When Jansen returned, the police were waiting for him. Norveth had filed a complaint of rape. Jansen was taken to the station. After he had been held three days, the charge was reduced to statutory rape. One of the assistant prosecuting attorneys appeared and asked if he would be willing to marry the girl. Although Peter had never thought of getting married, he was not opposed to marriage.

The priest who came to visit the thirty-one-year-old degenerate who had violated a sixteen-year-old girl soon was convinced that Peter was not such a bad fellow. At the age of six Peter had learned from his mother that he was a Lutheran. Since then his religion had not been a matter of major concern to him. He said it would be quite all right if his children were brought up as Catholics. An investigator from the League of Catholic Women reported that he seemed to be a steady worker, and, except for some minor scrapes on account of his drinking, had stayed out of trouble.

The wedding was so quiet it was almost secret. Theresa was the only member of the family who attended. The others were ashamed even to talk about what had happened. Peter and Marie set up housekeeping in one room. They shared the kitchen with other boarders. They went to the movies often. Peter always had a bottle. When Marie became depressed or frightened, she would have a drink with him. Then they could laugh. Theresa had given birth to all her children at home, and so Marie's older sisters had absorbed at first hand some knowledge of childbearing. But Marie had never had the benefit of that experience. (When Stephen and Elmira, fifteen and fourteen, had been born, she had been too young to understand what was happening.) She wanted desperately to know how children were born. But she had no one whom she could ask.

Norveth was overcome by his sense of defeat, and humiliated by a world with which he had more and more difficulty coping. On some days after being turned away from a plant gate he would sit down in the park, or go to the riverfront to look at the boats. Although he had forbidden her to talk about the *shame,* Theresa had said that Marie Rose would be going to the hospital to have her baby. To the hospital! Theresa had never gone to the hospital.

"It serves her right to be sick," he had said, thinking there must be something wrong.

The benches were full of old men, men who were old because they had no jobs, and could perceive no future. They sat, their eyes staring blankly, waiting to die.

One blustery day at the end of October, Norveth was in the vicinity of the County Building. Downhearted and cold, he went into the mildew-green and gold building. The "crime wave" battering the nation was keeping the courts busy. In a corridor he caught sight of a notice announcing an opening for court interpreter. Since he spoke Hungarian and German, he applied, and was hired on a part-time basis.

54

American Roulette

In the midst of a city of unemployed men, one type of worker was in demand as never before: the tool-and-die man. To produce the 5,500 new parts required for the Model A, Ford had to replace 15,000 machines and rebuild another 25,000. Tool-and-die men, who made the machines that made the cars, were the elite of the workers. Tool-and-die leaders, who supervised a half dozen other workers, invariably were men of long experience in their forties or late thirties.

At the Ford factory gate, the guards laughed at the stocky twenty-year-old who insisted that he was a die leader. Yet, having walked through a glass factory on stilts in his home town of Wheeling, West Virginia, as a boy, he lacked neither courage nor daring to go with his persistence. From the age of eleven he had watched the die makers cutting patterns at the glass factory. At the age of sixteen he had started his apprenticeship in a machine shop. He was convinced he could handle the job. His conviction was reinforced by the thirteen hours a day he was working at the Briggs plant, which had the reputation of being the worst sweatshop in the auto industry. To the guards he insisted that Ford could not afford to lose him. That he must be taken to the foreman. To the foreman he insisted that he must be given a tryout.

For $1.05 an hour Ford hired Walter Reuther.

In addition to designing a new car, Ford was phasing out production at the Highland Park plant. The new automobile would be made at River Rouge. The executives at Highland Park who had played a leading role in the introduction of the assembly line, who were in rapport with Edsel, and who, ironically, had fought for modernization of the Model T were fired. One of the chief production men, Frank Kulick, was literally taken for a ride. Bennett ordered him to lie on the running board of a car and listen for an engine noise. He then drove him outside the gate. Sharply swerving the car, he threw Kulick off. After Kulick picked himself up, he found the gates of the plant barred against him.

Not until December 1, 1927, was Ford ready to advertise the Model A. Although at the January auto show it created a sensation, it had so many bugs—including a faulty brake system—that only one hundred thousand cars were produced in the first six months of the new model run.

Then, in the spring of 1928, Edsel broached the question of how the company would be able to sell all the cars it was capable of producing. What made the question a demanding one were the policies of Treasury Secretary Mellon, the movement of the population from the farms to the cities, and the ever greater concentration of economic power in the hands of the wealthy.

Between 1916 and 1929 the United States had an aggregate favorable balance of trade of nearly $23 billion. Between 1914 and 1927 the American stock of gold—which determined the amount of money in circulation—increased by 140 percent. Not since the early days of the Industrial Revolution had a nation so dominated world trade and finances,* and never had a nation been so indifferent to the effect of such dominance on others.

While one European nation after another hovered on the brink of financial crises, and the majority of Americans borrowed money to participate in the "prosperity," Mellon pursued his scheme to enrich the wealthy and make multimillionaires out of millionaires. The well-to-do† made up 2.4 percent of the population, but accounted for 67 percent of all savings. Bank deposits rose from $17.4 billion in 1914 to $52.7 billion in 1928.

The first outlet for this accumulation of capital was a traditional one: real estate. As the urban population increased by 14.8 million during the decade, housing grew by 5.5 million units, the greatest for any ten-year period until after World War II. In 1926 the outlay for private construction was nearly double what it had been in 1920.

By 1927, however, the segment of the population financially capable of improving its housing standards was exhausted. The pace of construction sagged. Between 1926 and 1927 building expenditures in Detroit dropped nearly in half.

American savings were redirected to money-short Europe, where interest rates were 8 percent and higher. Money flowed from low- and middle-income American taxpayers to the bank accounts of the wealthy; from the bank accounts of the wealthy to investments in foreign countries, especially Germany; ‡ from Germany to France and Great Britain in the form of reparations; and from France and Great Britain to the United States Treasury in payment of war debts. Between 1924 and 1931 the Treasury received more than $2.7 billion, which Mellon squirreled away to reduce the national debt or directed toward tax rebates for the favored few.

As the money was withdrawn from circulation, it contributed in 1928 to the unique manifestation of a contracting monetary supply in the midst of an expanding economy.

America's rural population was the first to feel the squeeze of Mellon's policies. The restrictive trade policy of the administration resulted in a 20

---

* Lacking a mass market, Morris Motors, the largest of the British automotive manufacturers, did not install a moving assembly line until the middle 1930's.
† Individuals with incomes over $5,000 a year, and families with incomes over $10,000.
‡ Germany's capacity to earn money had been sharply curtailed by Du Pont's attack upon the chemical industry and the American tariff of 1922 at the same time that the Versailles Treaty was forcing the nation to pay billions of dollars in reparations. Both General Motors and Ford made major investments in Germany. For $33 million, G.M. bought Opel, the largest of the German car manufacturers. Between them, G.M. and Ford manufactured nearly half the cars made in Germany.

percent decline of farm exports from the previous decade. Per capita income of farmers dropped to one fourth that of nonagricultural wage earners. People used up their savings. Forty-three hundred banks, most of them in rural communities, failed between 1923 and 1929.

In contrast, big-city banks were experiencing a boom. As dollars flowed into the accounts of the wealthy, new banks were opened. In June, 1927, Edsel, Kanzler, Kahn, Roy Chapin, and Frank Couzens, the son of the senator, organized the Guardian Detroit Bank.

In the two decades since Ford had demonstrated that there was a mass market for the automobile, Detroit had turned into one of the world's great financial centers. Since workers were outproducing their earnings, it was necessary to find some means by which they could continue to buy the goods they were producing. Experience with the "good risk" salaried class—professionals, teachers, civil servants—indicated that the vast majority of people who were loaned money would repay it. Soon even blue-collar workers, whose jobs were far less secure, were being encouraged to mortgage their future earnings, even though their future earnings might not be enough to pay the installments.

A new phenomenon was born in America: the credit economy.

Edsel convinced his father that Ford would have to join the credit economy if the Model A were to compete successfully against Chevrolet and the other makes being sold on the installment plan. The Universal Credit Corporation was organized. Of the 15,000 shares, the Ford Motor Company held 7,501, the Guardian Detroit Bank 5,000, and Kanzler 2,499.

During 1928 Ford manufactured only 758,000 of the industry's all-time high of 3.8 million cars. Finally, in December, the company was ready to resume full production and issued a call for workers. In the snowy, fourteen-degrees-below-zero darkness of January 2, 1929, thirty-two thousand men lined up before the gates. Many dropped from the effects of frostbite and exposure. Eight thousand were hired during the week. No one questioned why or from where an army of men had materialized at a time of such great prosperity.

The Model T had occupied a niche of its own. The Model A was pitted head to head against Chevrolet. Knudsen, president of the G.M. division, reacted by outfitting Chevrolet with a six-cylinder engine, the first in the low-price field. In July, 1928, Chrysler, taking advantage of the Ford hiatus, introduced the Plymouth. Competition took on a fierce new cutthroat character.

Dealers of all makes were soon overstocked. If a dealer did not sell his "quota," the manufacturer could revoke his franchise within ninety days. Dealers, dependent on sales of accessories for most of their profits, resorted to the marginal practices that were to cloud the reputation of the industry for decades.

The customer was stuck with a largely fake transportation charge. His car was overloaded with *extras* which, in reality, were often standard equipment. Insurance charges were computed at a much higher than actual rate as one means of providing a "pack" for the dealer. Finance charges were double and quadruple what they were represented to be. Huge "balloon payments" were tacked on, so that not until the last installment came due would the purchaser discover that he still owed several hundred dollars.

Despite the efforts of dealers to milk the business, many salesmen were earning as little as twenty dollars a week and hundreds of dealers were failing monthly. In the period of "greatest prosperity" between 1927 and 1929, there were seventy thousand industrial and commercial failures, a larger number than ever before.

Squeezing their dealers and the American public at one end, the corporations were able to squeeze their unorganized workers on the other. As productivity in the auto industry more than doubled during the decade, a surplus of manpower developed. Manufacturers were able to turn worker against worker to knock down wages. Wages in the auto industry were $500 less per employee in 1928 than they had been in 1923. With every layoff, men lost their seniority and were rehired at the minimum wage. Trimmers making 90 cents an hour in 1927 earned only 60 cents an hour in 1929. Thirty-five-cents-an-hour women replaced $1.25-an-hour men as stripers.

In 1929 the American automobile industry produced 4.6 million cars and 771,000 trucks, 85 percent of the total manufactured in the world. For corporations, times were plush as never before. Between 1922 and 1929 corporate profits after taxes rose 76 percent, and dividends 108 percent. The Ford surplus blossomed from $592 million in 1928 to $717 million in 1930; the General Motors surplus from $139 million in 1927 to $333 million in 1929. The G.M. return on investment was not the generous 15 percent projected on "standard volume." It was 36 percent! The corporation created some eighty millionaires. In 1929 it disbursed to the average stockholder almost half as much as it paid a full-time worker: $780 to the stockholder; $1670 to the worker.

Little wonder that bankers, contemplating their swollen funds, were attracted to the stock market. Not only did stocks offer a 10 to 15 percent return, but they were far more easily convertible to cash than real estate or foreign bonds. Stocks were considered such secure investments that in 1927 the interest rate for stock purchases on credit was lower than the prime commercial rate. Since stocks, like everything else, could be purchased on credit—one fourth down— the market gyrated upward along with the industrial output. Between 1926 and 1929 the averages doubled. At their high point they were more than three times what they had been in 1922.

In an age when "conflict of interest" was interpreted by the White House as the difference between 4 percent and 5 percent, President Coolidge, Secretary Mellon, and other members of the government speculated heavily in the stock market. J. P. Morgan and Company established a "preferred list" of customers to whom stock was sold as much as 40 percent below market value. The list, beginning with Coolidge, included Democratic presidential candidates and aspirants like John W. Davis and William G. McAdoo, former Secretary of War Newton D. Baker, national heroes like General Pershing and Lindbergh, *éminences grises* like Bernard Baruch, and industrialists like Raskob.

Americans outside of the charmed circle were propagandized with tales of the effortless profits made by these men through their "financial wizardry," and fell into the trap of believing they too would find Wall Street paved with gold. Instead they became the victims of a shell game of phony financial statistics, stock-pool manipulations, and pyramidal holding companies through which financiers milked companies while inflating the value of their stocks. For the corner shoeshine boy the stock market replaced the numbers game as the way to strike it rich. The stock market had been turned into American Roulette.

A contracting money supply, greater and greater concentration of wealth in the hands of the few, the need for more and more credit to enable people to keep buying, an increasing amount of money siphoned off from banks and consumer credit into the stock market—it was not a question of whether the financial merry-go-round would break down, but when.

By February, 1929, the Federal Reserve Board was so concerned that it issued a statement deploring security speculation. But it refused to raise interest
rates because the board's governor, Charles Hamlin, believed it would result in
a deflation greater than that in 1920, a deflation that in turn would bring on a
congressional investigation in which Democrats and Progressives would unite
to deal President Hoover a decisive defeat at the outset of his administration.

Toward the end of the summer, the American public, supersaturated with
cars, was running out of both cash and credit.* People began to curtail their
purchases. At G.M., statisticians received a continuous flow of reports. Within
two weeks they were charting the decline. On Wall Street, a few perspicacious
insiders like Joseph Kennedy, the father of the future President, quietly sold
their stock and took their profits.

But for the overwhelming majority of Americans, including those who
gathered at Greenfield Village on Monday, October 21, 1929, the illusion of
ever upward was just as persistent as it had been. Great men from all over the
world gathered to pay tribute to the eighty-two-year-old Edison as Ford staged
the fiftieth anniversary jubilee of the development of the incandescent bulb.
President and Mrs. Hoover, J. P. Morgan, Albert Einstein, Madame Curie, Will
Rogers, and Orville Wright—they were a cross-section of the men and women
who had created the twentieth century. It was a century of pulsating industry,
undreamed-of masses of material goods, the automobile, the airplane, and, most
of all, electric power.†

Everywhere people were turning on. As never before they turned on their
radios to listen to the broadcast of the festivities from Greenfield Village. Since
the first commercal broadcast in 1920, 606 stations, linked by networks, had
gone on the air. Ten million families had purchased sets.

"And Edison said: 'Let there be light!' " the announcer intoned.

And there had been light. Just like that!

It was a reflection of the slickness, the oversimplification, the buddy-buddy
familiarity, the have-it-good-today-and-it'll-be-better-tomorrow hucksterism that
Hollywood and Madison Avenue were employing to reshape the American
psyche. As Greenfield Village blazed into light, the gathering clouds were lost
in the glare. Yet many of those present who had played such prominent roles
in the raising of the boom were about to have equal importance in the lowering
of the boom.

---

* In August, as outstanding brokers' loans reached $6 billion, the Federal Reserve Board
felt forced to act. Lacking means of selective credit restriction, it authorized the New York
Federal Reserve Bank to raise the discount rate.
† From 6 billion kilowatt hours in 1902, American power production soared to 117 billion
by 1929.

55

The Lowering of the Boom

TWO DAYS AFTER THE GREENFIELD JUBILEE, ON WEDNESDAY, OCTOBER 23, THE sell-off on the stock market began. The next day it reached avalanche proportions. Speculators were unable to find anyone to cash in their paper profits. On October 10, the Standard and Poor stock index registered 245. By October 29 it was down to 162.

Once more the "financial wizards" attempted to restore confidence through manipulation of the market, buying with a flourish, then selling in secret to protect themselves. During the week following the crash, New York banks extended $1 billion in loans to stockbrokers and dealers. But once the great golden beacon began flickering, the magic was gone. As brokers called in or attempted to call in their loans in order to cover their losses, Black Monday followed Black Thursday and was in turn followed by Doomsday Tuesday. A week after the panic began, *Variety* chided: "Wall Street Lays an Egg."

Wall Street, however, was not a cause, but a symptom. Had the economy been built on a sound base, money would have been available to come into the market. But to cover the $26 billion paper losses—a 40 percent decline in value of stocks listed on the New York Exchange—would have taken almost the entire total of time deposits (savings) in the country. An economy that had become used to conducting its business on credit was not accustomed to extending credit to an establishment that was on fire.

The fissure created in society by the upheavals of the technological age was now rending that society asunder. On one side were some twelve million people, highly educated, skilled, and shrewd. Straddling the fissure, tumbling this way and that, were fifty million who had been making their way upward in the economy. On the other side, sinking and abandoned, was half a nation.

Cars were the leading durable product bought on credit. Car sales were the weather vane of the economy. During the 1920's automobile production had become the leading American industry. It was responsible for one out of every six or seven jobs.* Detroit had 2,700 industrial establishments employing 311,000 workers, and more than 75 percent of the city's economy was linked to auto manufacturing. Since its organization, General Motors had had the largest earnings of any corporation in the world.

As auto sales went into their skid, manufacturers' gross dropped from $3.4 billion in 1929 to $2 billion in 1930. Unemployment rose exponentially. In May, 1929, 15,400 people were out of work in Michigan; in September, 56,800; in November, 212,500.†

The collapse of the stock market did not surprise President Hoover, who had deplored the speculation of the 1920's. Peering through the wrong end of the telescope, he came to the conclusion that, despite the crash, the economy was sound.

Since the economy was sound, what was necessary was to stimulate it. Taxes must be cut. The Federal Reserve Board must expand the money supply. Construction outlays must be continued. Tariffs must be increased in order to protect domestic industry. Employment and purchasing power must not be reduced. The public must be encouraged to keep buying. On November 22, Hoover called a conference of business leaders, and asked them to maintain wages at the current level.

Ford, with his flair for the dramatic, said he would not maintain wages. He would *raise* them to seven dollars a day.

Many business and financial leaders concurred in Treasury Secretary Mellon's belief that laissez-faire was experiencing one of its normal, cyclical shakeouts. A little depression always served a salutary purpose in bringing labor to heel. The unemployment rate of 8 percent was not as bad as the rate of 11 percent at the height of the 1921 depression. (However, because of the addition of 8 million persons to the labor force, the *number* of the unemployed was nearly as large.)

The *Literary Digest* called it a "prosperity panic." Mellon asserted that after a period of *liquidation* the system would correct itself. "Liquidate labor, liquidate stocks, liquidate the farmers, liquidate real estate," he suggested. He could see nothing to "warrant pessimism." [1]

The assessment was a quarter century out of date. It failed to take into account the effect of concentration, credit, and the secretary's own policies on the economy. The greater the industrialization and complexity of an economy, the less capable was it of self-correction.

The very factors that had accentuated the boom portended to accelerate and aggravate the bust. Classically, the drop in demand should have stimulated a decline in prices, until price and demand were again brought into equilibrium. But with the concentration of economic power, the large corporations had taken pains to separate themselves from the vicissitudes of the marketplace. Their price structure was such that they could suffer a 50 percent loss in sales, yet still operate profitably. They were not about to tear down the carefully erected

* Automobile manufacturers consumed 28 percent of American aluminum production, 14 percent of copper, 19 percent of hardwoods, 28 percent of nickel, 74 percent of plate glass, 85 percent of rubber, 18 percent of steel, and 24 percent of tin. The fortunes of the petroleum industry were interwoven with those of Detroit. In 1859, 2,000 barrels of oil had been produced in the United States. In 1929 the number topped 1 billion. There were 350,-000 service stations and 40,000 car dealers.
† According to official figures. There was, however, no adequate means of determining the number of men who were looking for work. Evidently, many of the unemployed were not being counted.

walls and return to "ruinous competition" just because there seemed to be a temporary and normal economic downturn.

On the other hand, smaller businesses and individuals who had not accumulated vast reserves continued to be subject to classic economic forces. As demand declined, they attempted to stimulate sales by reducing prices. In reality, then, two economies were in operation. One administered by Big Business, in which prices were fixed. And one that was free, in which prices fluctuated. General Motors and Ford had no problem continuing to ship cars to dealers at the same prices. Dealers, however, were forced to hold cut-rate sales, to employ gimmickry, to sell cars at a loss in an effort to ride out the *temporary* downturn—to "liquidate."

In the four years following 1929, the income of farmers declined 65 percent; that of proprietors of unincorporated businesses in wholesale and retail trade 79 percent; that of persons engaged in contract construction 80 percent.

The price of consumer durable goods, however, decreased a mere 8 percent.

Obviously, persons operating in the free economy were more and more incapable of buying the goods produced by the enterprises of the administered economy. Yet even while the two economies were separating and growing further apart, people were still paying off at the old prices and high interest charges goods they had "bought ahead."

The result was a catastrophic drop in demand.

At first, the narcotic of optimism served to dull the pain of the economic injury. In every pinpoint of light, businessmen were persuaded to see the breaking of the dawn. In Detroit, banks funneled funds to their executives and employees so that they could continue speculating in stocks—in the inevitable recovery they would recoup their losses. Having been on the winning side in the game, people refused to face the fact that it was now cleaning them out.

In the spring of 1930 unemployment did, in fact, recede from its high point in January. In April, in Michigan, it fell to 190,000. On May 1, the President was encouraged to declare that "we have now passed the worst and . . . shall rapidly recover." [2]

In fact, the full impact of what was happening to demand was just manifesting itself. The sine qua non of the credit economy is anticipation and confidence. If things are good today, they will be better tomorrow. Encourage borrowing, expand credit, and the anticipation will be fulfilled. But credit will not be extended to men who have no jobs, or whose prospect of retaining their jobs is doubtful. Like a snail, the credit economy is a fair-weather animal that contracts into its carapace of cash when danger threatens. It has an exponential effect not only on expansion, but also on contraction. Some of the President's measures, like the tax cut, simply put more money into the pockets of the upper-income group, and catered to the economic distortions.

Thus in May unemployment commenced to increase rapidly again. At General Motors, Sloan scanned the discouraging reports from around the country even as inventories remained at record levels. He decided that the time had come to trim sales to weather the storm. Consolidations were effected between the Chevrolet and Pontiac sales forces and divisions, and between Buick, Oldsmobile, and Pontiac. Expenditures were slashed.

The corporation would survive by living off the fat it had accumulated. The corporation's obligation was to its stockholders. Its workers would have to shift for themselves. Between 1929 and 1930 employment in the auto industry dropped 28 percent: from 471,000 to 341,000.

56

The $150 Marriage

AMONG THE TENS OF THOUSANDS OF MEN WANDERING ABOUT THE CITY SEEK-ing work was Harold Lentick. The foundry at which he had been employed had shut down in January. He had saved only a few dollars. He seldom slept two nights in the same place. Twenty-five cents bought a bed in a flophouse or men's dormitory, but twenty-five cents could be put to better use. It was cheaper to sleep in an all-night movie. The streets were lined with cars that could be curled up in. Each day empty garages and abandoned buildings became more plentiful.

The battle to find a job was a struggle against cold and sickness—he conserved what money he had for food. He was on the verge of going back to the farm when he heard that the Yarmans were in such desperate straits they wanted to know if he could put them up in the city.

Like many of the other four million unemployed, Lentick was attracted to the International Unemployment Day that the Communists staged on March 6, 1930, in industrial cities throughout the nation. He could not have told a Communist from a Christian Socialist. He went because he had nowhere else to go, because it was a means of demonstrating that he was a person, someone looking for help. If the Communists were offering to bring that fact to the attention of the government, what did he care whether they were red, green, or yellow?

Throughout America, there was growing irritation with a government that seemed obsessed with sticking a thermometer in the mouth of business, while oblivious to suffering and hunger. When thousands congregated in Cadillac Square and Grand Circus Park, Detroit's most prominent gathering places, the police reacted as if they were faced with full-scale revolution. Flailing away with nightsticks, they chased and slashed indiscriminately at demonstrators and spectators.

Harold was knocked flat by a boy fleeing from a police officer. Scrambling out of the way, he found himself at the edge of the melee. He was at a loss to understand why the police were so angry and why they attacked the crowd. He was hungry. He began walking to the Jansens' lodginghouse.

Marie was happy to see him, as she was always happy to see anyone. She said she had nothing to eat in the house. But she gave him a candy bar.

The children were asleep. Marie's cheeks were sunken, but her stomach was distended. Harold would have preferred to stay in the house and go to sleep. But she tugged him down the stairs. She wanted to see a movie. He told her he had no money. She said she would take him.

Not more than a few months past her eighteenth birthday, Marie was pregnant for the third time. Rita, her first child, had been born in the spring of 1928. Even though Marie had not seen a doctor until the day she gave birth, the baby had appeared quite healthy. When she began crawling, and banging into things, Peter and Marie had thought it was funny that she was so clumsy.

At the age of thirteen months, Rita's clumsiness had increased. When she tried to walk, she constantly knocked things over and bloodied her nose. In the late summer of 1929 Marie had taken her to a doctor. He had examined her eyes. She had congenital cataracts.

Two months earlier, Rita's brother Jim had been born. The family continued living in the one housekeeping room. The bathroom had to be shared with two other families. The kitchen was on the floor below. Trying to care for two babies, one of them nearly blind, had Marie in tears more days than not.

William Norveth had never allowed Marie to do anything on her own. Literally, she did not know how to arrive at a decision. The responsibility of a family had fallen upon her like a boulder, pinning her beneath its weight. She wanted only to go back to being a little girl.

Her parents and her older brothers and sisters continued to ostracize her. After the discovery of Rita's blindness, Marie went to them for help. But her father replied that it was the judgment of God against her. She should pray.

Since no one in the Norveth family had cataracts, Marie blamed Rita's affliction on Peter. They drank no longer for laughs, but to break the tension between them. Neither was prepared for the responsibilities of parenthood. Since Marie did not know how to take care of children, the babies were continually squalling. There was scarcely a day when one or the other did not have a rash, a cold, or some minor ailment. Marie had only a few diapers and seldom washed them more than once a week. She penned the children in one corner of the room, and let them go bare-bottomed.

The room smelled like a privy. After two or three weeks she became so conditioned to the odor she hardly noticed it. Peter, explaining that he was ordered on overnight trips out of the city, started staying away one night a week; then two; then three.

Marie messed the bathroom, and left it in a mess. She broke things in the kitchen. Going into the boarding house's communal parlor to sit before the radio, she would leave the children crying and screaming alone upstairs. Fed up, the other lodgers indulged her only because of her youth. The landlady kept threatening to evict the family. Instead, she raised the rent until they were paying eight dollars a week.

Whenever Marie thought of the movies, she was caught by a self-stimulated excitement. The excitement would grow until she would be unable to resist the temptation. Explaining that she had had an urgent call, she would abandon her children to one of the other women. The moment she dashed out of the house and was on the streetcar her mood changed from depression to elation. When she entered the theater she felt as if she were immersing herself in a luxurious bath.

Marie paid for Harold's ticket. They did not emerge from the movie until late afternoon. Marie told Harold she wanted to stop by the Kresge store on Woodward Avenue. Her younger sister Elmira, now seventeen, was working at the store.

Elmira was pleasant and had a good figure. Her face was scarred by acne, but she let her hair fall over her cheeks so as to hide some of the blemishes. Harold's clothes were shabby. Every day, however, Elmira was serving customers whose dresses and shirts were frayed and mended. She was anxious to escape from the dictatorial household of her father. Harold was reasonably good-looking. He was polite, and he seemed attracted to her.

During the two years she had worked at the store, Elmira had saved $150. Four days after meeting Harold, she told her father that she was going to get married. William Norveth objected. Harold was unemployed, he was Protestant, and he was the son of Ralph Lentick, whom Norveth did not recall favorably.

These arguments made no impression on Elmira. She wanted to be independent. Harold managed to start earning a dollar or two a day by working at odd jobs. On March 24, eighteen days after they had met, Elmira and Harold were married.

57

Blood and Gin

WILLIAM NORVETH LAMENTED THAT HE NO LONGER HAD INFLUENCE OVER HIS children. His words were echoed by parents in every American city. On May 31, 1930, eleven hundred Chicago youths were arrested at a "wild rum party." The National Commission on Law Enforcement and Observance * reported that "because of automobiles and movies, family life as it was known a few years ago has almost entirely disappeared." There were more separations and divorces of young married couples, more unmarried mothers, more children abused and neglected, more children exposed to "vicious and degenerative practices in the home," more broken homes than ever before. Furthermore, the commission observed a "close relationship between divorce and crime." [1]

Evidently, Cardinal Gibbons had been right. Women's suffrage had brought on divorce; and divorce had brought on juvenile delinquency and crime.

Many youths of foreign-born parents gained "upward mobility" through bootlegging. They started as "runners" delivering bottles of liquor and worked their way up. The overwhelming sentiment of the urban population placed bootleggers in a category similar to traffic violators; arrest involved no stigma. Prohibition was as unenforceable in American cities in the 1920's as it had been in the 1850's. (Chicago had voted 406,000 to 147,000 to remain wet. The Detroit vote was 62,500 to 54,000.)

The bootlegging industry offered employment during a decade when jobs were being preempted by machines or eliminated entirely by new techniques and products. In economically depressed areas, people who would otherwise have had to go on relief set up stills in their cellars. Stills became family enterprises in which everyone from old granddad to toddlers was involved. When one woman's husband died, neighbors took up a collection to put her in business. In some communities, the liquor business contributed to the urban infrastructure. Tunnels were dug and pipelines laid. Any kind of establishment

---

* Often referred to as the Wickersham Commission. The commission was formed to investigate the widespread lawbreaking associated with Prohibition and the great increase in crimes of all kind.

was likely to be used as a front: a hospital, delicatessen, florist, or nursery.

Young men of Sicilian, southern Italian, and Polish-Jewish descent often continued illegally in a business in which their parents had engaged legally.* Profits were high. Competition was fierce. Individual entrepreneurs fell by the way as syndicates were formed in emulation of trusts in legitimate industry. Tables of organization were set up that would have done justice to General Motors. Gangs diversified and became "conglomerates" that tried to establish control over other growing businesses—both legitimate and illegitimate—like cleaning and dyeing establishments, taxicabs, bookmaking, and the numbers racket. Detroit's Jewish mobsters—the Oakland Sugar House Gang, the Little Jewish Navy Gang, and the Purple Gang—battled each other and the Sicilian and Italian racketeers. City streets resounded with gunfire and bomb explosions.† But so long as the gangsters stuck to killing each other, they did not need to worry about facing intensive prosecution or receiving extended jail sentences.

When a bootlegger did get arrested, people generally believed that he was an "outlaw" who had not paid off the police. Sometimes, police used an arrest as a shakedown for more money. "Successful violation is rather a matter of boasting. . . . Fines are often regarded as license fees," the Wickersham Commission reported.[2]

Detroit had been a brewing and distilling center since the days when farmers had been unable to market their grain except in the form of alcohol. Its location across the river from Canada made the city the principal port of entry for liquor in the United States. Canadian officials refused to cooperate with the United States Government in halting the traffic. Instead, Canada collected an export tax. The number of gallons shipped from Windsor to Detroit rose from 666,000 in 1925 to 1,169,000 in 1928. The river patrol had been so corrupted that liquor could be ferried across the river in the daytime as well as at night. The Wickersham Commission called the situation among American customs officials "bad beyond expression." Bootlegging was one of the half dozen largest industries in Michigan and had an estimated gross of $215 million a year.

The Detroit police department, like hundreds of other departments around the country, made only perfunctory efforts to crack down on the gangs. In a state like Illinois half of the sheriffs failed to enforce the law, and refused to cooperate with Federal authorities. In Hamtramck, the enclave city within Detroit, in Rockford, Illinois, and in other places, the bootleggers were the police and deputy sheriffs themselves. Although the Detroit police force increased from 1,770 officers in 1920 to 3,769 in 1930, its quality was as questionable as ever. Twenty-four of the 73 men in the class of 1926 had resigned under charges or been dismissed by 1932. They frequented blind pigs, they slept on their beats, they were involved in burglary rings, and they committed armed robberies. The class of 1928 averaged 83 on mental testing equivalent to IQ. While the fire department required a minimum score of 100 for accep-

---

* Sicily and Italy were wine-producing areas. In Poland the Jews had dominated the grain and sugar trade. When it was difficult or unprofitable to ship cargoes in bulk, the merchants had converted them into alcohol. In this fashion they had become distillers and liquor dealers. Polish Jews in Detroit, furthermore, monopolized the junk business. With the onset of Prohibition, the boilers, pipes, and plumbing fixtures sometimes were diverted to the construction of stills.

† In one year, 1929, the Detroit police force's "Black Hand" squad, organized before the World War to deal with the Italian Black Hand, the forerunner of the Mafia, made 1,378 arrests.

tance, the police department was satisfied with 65. The older the officers, the dumber they were. Sergeants and lieutenants scored in the 50's.* Naturally they were sensitive about smart-alecky kids coming in and telling them how to run the department. As in military and paramilitary organizations everywhere, the good soldier was the soldier who did as he was told and didn't ask questions. The best ways were the old ways, even though the old days in which they had been the "best" were long gone.

To protect their status and promotional opportunities against the better-educated younger men, the old-timers made certain that longevity was the principal criterion for moving up. Any officer who refused to conform to departmental mores could be controlled by being down-rated on the regular reports. Since these were subjective evaluations, it did a man no good how well he might, in actuality, be performing his job. If he appeared too smart for his police breeches, he was encouraged to don another pair of working pants. For decades, departmental operations had been geared to lackadaisical performances by officers, and there had been little improvement of efficiency. Constituting a monopoly, protected by civil service, the police could afford to be inefficient.

Riven by feuds and by factions, the police all but turned the city into a shooting gallery. During 1927–1928 the police killed 70 persons and wounded 134, while suffering 8 dead and 25 wounded of their own.

Disillusionment with "reform" was widespread. People talked about the "good old" ward system. In a city whose population grew from 994,000 to 1,569,000 between 1920 and 1930, nine tenths of the electorate no longer knew the candidates for whom they were voting. Primary ballots contained as many as 500 names. Candidates encouraged people with the same name as prominent opponents to enter the primary simply to create confusion. Frequently a half dozen persons with the same name were listed.

In election after election the challengers campaigned on the promise to end the high crime rate and the high taxes promoted by the incumbents. The belief was widespread that city hall was being run by an "invisible government" controlled by the Good Citizens League.

In 1927 the league had run its elder statesman, courteous, patrician John Lodge for mayor.† When Lodge won he told Joe Garvin, a cop renowned for his toughness, to halt the shooting on the streets. Garvin did. He organized the city into one huge syndicate.

Two years later, Charles Bowles campaigned against Lodge on an anti-Citizens League, reform-the-police-department platform—a combination that would have been unbelievable twenty years before. Suddenly, all deals were off.

The streets were alive with gang warfare. Inevitably, as the Depression became more serious, crimes against property increased dramatically. The total number of robberies, burglaries, and larcenies rose from fewer than 15,000 in

---

* Test scores, of course, are determined not only by intelligence, but by verbal skill, and by experience in taking tests. Yet even if one grants the officers the benefit of every doubt, the department was staffed with men of no better than low-average intelligence.
† Born in 1862, Lodge at the age of forty had asked his mother's permission to run for alderman. Well, all right, she had assented; but no speeches! Without once violating her injunction in a political career spanning four decades, he was elected again and again to the council. A good friend of Benjamin Pelham, his knowledge of the city government was equivalent to Pelham's grasp of county affairs.

1929 to more than 31,000 in 1933.* The Citizens League blamed Mayor Bowles. Six months after the mayor took office, the league launched a recall campaign.

Ford, still battling the Citizens League and convinced that another "Jewish plot" must be afoot, came to the support of Bowles. While the recall campaign became more vitriolic, the city was introduced to a "Bloody July." On July 4 two Chicago dope peddlers were killed in front of the La Salle Hotel, and scarcely a day went by thereafter without a murder in Detroit.

On the eve of the recall election, one of Ford's former employees, Jerry Buckley, bitterly attacked Bowles and the inept police. Buckley had been an investigator for Ford on the Newberry case. With the advent of radio, he had risen to fame as an exposé reporter and became a powerful influencer of public opinion. Each of his broadcasts was a social event for which friends gathered and sipped bootleg liquor. Hundreds of Buckley fan clubs were formed throughout the city.

The election was held on July 22. Late that night Buckley went on the air to announce Bowles's recall. At one o'clock in the morning Buckley was waiting for a tipster in the lobby of the La Salle Hotel. On brightly lit and busy Woodward Avenue the movie theaters were still open. Prostitutes sauntered by. Three men walked into the lobby and approached the chair in which Buckley was sitting. A moment later, as shots splintered the furniture, Buckley was dead.

The police did not exert themselves to find his killers. No broadcast went out over the police radio. Two patrolmen following a promising lead were transferred to less arduous duty. The commissioner went on vacation.

In the mayoralty campaign that followed, Bowles attempted a comeback against six other candidates. The victory, however, went to Judge Frank Murphy.

---

* No national tabulation of crime statistics yet existed. In compiling records from forty-six cities, the Wickersham Commission discovered that the 1920's had produced an unprecedented "crime wave." The total number of offenses rose from 739,000 in 1920 to 1,842,000 in 1929. Even excluding the "statistical lie" of traffic offenses, the number increased from 539,000 to 973,000. Robberies, burglaries, and thefts, which the Dillingham Commission had regarded as "American" offenses, jumped from 17,000 to 53,000.

58

The Flapping of the Hoover Flags

ON SEPTEMBER 23, 1930, MURPHY WAS INAUGURATED AS THE NEW MAYOR. He had run on a platform of fiscal responsibility, public works, unemployment insurance, and old-age pensions. But like most Americans in leadership positions, he had no idea of the degree of the economy's distress. Employment was down only 6.5 percent from 1929. Wages and salaries had been maintained remarkably well.

Only by probing the vitals of the economy could one gauge the extent of the danger—and in 1930 that was too sophisticated for all but a few professional economists. The more one narrowed the probe, the greater the alarm. Employee income in manufacturing was down 13.9 percent; in durable goods 18.7 percent; in the automobile industry, the bellwether of the entire system, a catastrophic 35.2 percent!

Two decades of chaotic expansion, in which the city had nearly quadrupled its area, had strained its finances to the limit. Between 1915 and 1930, 3,200 miles of new water mains had been laid. During the 1920's a total of $260 million in bonds had been issued for capital improvements. The tax budget had leaped from $6.3 million in 1910 to $76 million in 1930. The net debt had multiplied from $7.2 million to $255 million.

The municipal government's personnel were woefully unprepared to run the enlarged establishment. Most city departments were hardly more efficient than the police. For the insecurity of the spoils system, civil service had substituted another evil: total security. Seniority and the policy of "automatic promotions" created an upward osmosis of incompetence. Departments were overweighted with colonels and generals who feasted on the budgets. Management was a mysterious science beyond their capabilities. Departments routinely ran out of money well before the end of the fiscal year, and had to request supplemental appropriations. Planning was all but unknown. Coordination between different departments was unheard of.

The expansion had been sustained by the boom. As the boom lowered and money became increasingly difficult to obtain, the city in July, 1929, three months before the crash, had discovered itself unable to market its bonds. At the end of 1929 the city council invited Ralph Stone, chairman of the board of the Detroit and Security Trust Company, to organize a special Committee on City Finances.

The committee applied Mellon's remedies of economy and "liquidation" to the city government. But as the traditional autumn upturn in the automobile industry failed to materialize, Mayor Murphy realized that he faced a gigantic task if he were to implement his social welfare program on even a minimal level. Since the Stone committee was unsympathetic to the Irish Catholic Democrat who had broken more than a decade of Republican rule, the mayor cast about for another means of mobilizing the wealth of the city.

From the Democratic debacle of 1928, only one man in the party had emerged with increased stature. Still crippled from infantile paralysis, Franklin D. Roosevelt, Democratic nominee for Vice-President in 1920, had been elected governor of New York. By heritage a Progressive, he formed in 1930 a Commission for the Stabilization of Employment and suggested plans for old-age pensions and unemployment insurance. More and more he loomed as a contender for the 1932 presidential nomination.

In Detroit, Mrs. Eleanor Roosevelt's only brother, Hall Roosevelt, was vice-president of the American Bank. Mayor Murphy, a shrewd calculator and politician, sent Josephine Gomon,* his executive secretary, to contact Hall Roosevelt.

Roosevelt agreed to become chairman of an Unemployment Committee established by the mayor. A municipal employment bureau was set up. To find work for the 112,000 men that registered in the first seven months, Roosevelt enlisted a corps of Grosse Pointe millionaires. But work could be found for no more than 24,000—work that invariably did not last more than a few days. As sales slumped and businesses closed, a survival psychology set in. Everyone cut corners. Slashing pay and increasing hours, employers squeezed labor in an effort to maximize unit profits and compensate for declining sales—perversely they thus cut consumption further. At the factory gates men waited for a week to obtain one day's work, for which they might be paid two or three dollars. By January, 1931, 125,000 families, approximately one out of every three in the city, had no money and no means of support.

Murphy diverted millions of dollars from other city funds toward their relief. He thereby, of course, reduced municipal employment, placing more people on relief. He instituted a wage-work plan through which the men purportedly worked off the forty cents a day they were receiving. By December the mayor had all but exhausted the city's treasury. The mechanization of city services initiated by Couzens ten years earlier was steadily reducing the work to which laborers could be assigned.

Through the summer of 1930 Harold Lentick looked for a job. Between March and October he worked fewer than ten days. Everyone was hanging

---

* Mrs. Gomon had met Murphy when both were students at the University of Michigan. She was the only child of a rocky marriage between an Irish-Catholic waitress and a Scotch-English Protestant professor. She worked her way through college by grace of the second of the three T's—for twelve hours a night she manned the telephone switchboard, then attended classes during the day. After becoming a physics teacher at the City College of Detroit, she married Louis Gomon, an electrical engineer. Brilliant and dynamic, Mrs. Gomon had just had the youngest of her five children enter school, and took the city hall job because she thought she needed something to keep her busy.

on grimly to his job, no matter how menial. Men not only stopped seeking advancement, but "bumped downward," displacing men in lower-paying positions. "Overqualification" for jobs was pandemic. With his rural tenth-grade education and brief work experience, Lentick was better qualified than Henry Ford when he had first come to the city. But he was near the bottom of the job pool. For a few months Elmira's employment at Kresge supported them both. But by the end of August she was so rotundly pregnant that the store manager told her she would have to quit.

Lentick stood in the long lines of men in front of the factory gates and the municipal employment bureau. Their clothing disintegrating, their shoes splitting, the men sometimes remained all night so as to get first crack at the handful of jobs. Their eyes vacuous, they had become conditioned to expect nothing. They talked of "the good old days" that had passed only the year before. The twenties took on a glamour and gaiety that had not been, somehow, fully perceived during their presence.

When in November the wind drove the temperature below freezing, the likelihood of catching pneumonia became considerably greater than that of finding a job. Fewer and fewer men stood in the lines. Like animals digging into the ground, they huddled in cellars and shacks.

By November Harold and Elmira had only $22 left from her savings of $150. They lived in a partitioned loft with eight other families. The loft was without heat, or water, or toilet facilities. Since the roof was peaked, the partitions did not reach to the ceiling. Babies' screams, children's cries, family quarrels, living habits—all were communal. The only way to cook food was on Sterno cans. The odor of petroleum and boiled cabbage mingled with the smell of dirty diapers, and never left the air.

Children sickened. The loft was racked with coughs and fevers. Occasionally the city physician came and ordered someone to the hospital. Men no longer made the pretense of looking for work. Families spent days huddled together in bed. They seldom took off their clothes and never bathed. In December, Harold and Elmira spent twelve of their last fifty cents to ride the streetcar to the welfare office. All day long they waited in the overheated room. There were three persons for every seat. Most, like the Lenticks, had had nothing to eat. Despair spread from person to person like a virulent infection. On and off women broke into uncontrollable sobs. At closing time, Elmira and Harold still had not been interviewed. They were told to come back the next day. Since the city was all but out of money, the implicit policy of the department was to be as discouraging as possible.

One man refused the guard's order to clear the room. Within moments others joined the rebellion. The interviewers agreed to see everyone who was an emergency case. Everyone was. The Lenticks were given an order for $1.25.

Before Christmas a basket of food was delivered to each family in the loft. Each basket contained a chicken. But there was no way to cook it. The people who had jammed together in the loft to minimize their rents looked at the house next door. It was vacant. Its owner had moved beyond the Boulevard years before, and the tenants had been evicted for nonpayment of rent.

One man suggested that the house could be stripped for firewood. Three dozen men, women, and children tore at the building with their hands. The wood was collected into a huge pile. As it blazed upward, the chickens were thrust over the flames. In the bitter cold, the people warmed themselves by the huge fire, and feasted. Sparks drifted through the broken windows of the house. Soon it, too, was afire. In the glorious heat of the flames the children danced. When the firemen came to extinguish the flames, the darkness returned not only to the night, but to their spirits.

Buildings were being burned not only accidentally but deliberately—some so that owners could collect the insurance, others so that they would not have to pay the property taxes. The inflation of property values had resulted in an increase in assessed valuation from $1.37 billion in 1920 to $3.68 billion in the latter 1920's. During this period the revenue derived from many of the deteriorating buildings had far outstripped their intrinsic value. Some had been insured for up to five times their actual worth. The inner city became littered with destroyed and abandoned buildings.

As an $11 million tax delinquency compounded an unbudgeted, $14 million expenditure for welfare, Mayor Murphy in January of 1931 was forced to acknowledge the insolvency of the city. The committee of bankers was convoked. Despite the mayor's objections, they insisted, as financiers around the country were insisting, that only thrift and bone-scraping financial surgery could be employed as therapy. Expenditures would have to be reduced by $24 million. Murphy and Stone accused each other of irresponsibility. Angrily they fought over the future of the city.

To relieve the city of the burden of as many of its unemployed and non-productive citizens as possible, Hall Roosevelt concocted a plan to subsidize their transportation back to the rural areas from which they had come. It was as if the industrial era itself were going under in the cataclysm.

In emulation of Pingree's potato patches, Murphy had the welfare department search out empty lots and encourage recipients to plant "thrift gardens." Harold Lentick decided there was a lot more ground on which to plant a thrift garden in Maple Rapids. With Elmira and the recently born baby he started for the Yarman farm. More than one hundred thousand other Detroiters were making similar journeys back to small towns and farms. All over America, people were on the move; urban dwellers to the farms, farmers to the city, Southerners north, and Northerners west. Two million boys and girls went "on the road." Highways were lined with hitchhikers. Railroads sometimes carried more hobos than goods. Everyone believed that the money must be greener, or at least more plentiful, someplace else. After all, James A. Farrell of United States Steel had stated that the Depression had peaked in December, and that economic conditions were improving.

The journey Harold had made in less than four hours when he came to Detroit took ten days. The Lenticks slept in abandoned barns, woodsheds, and the hulks of cars. They were given a few short rides; but most of the time they walked. One night they spent in a hobo camp. From there they were guided to another "Hooverville." There they ate horse-meat "Hooverburgers," and watched men turn their empty pockets inside out to fly "Hoover flags."

Hoovervilles were going up all over the country as the new nomads of America moved from hunting ground to hunting ground. Living off the land, asking no questions, harassed by the law, hating the sheriff and the police, they existed outside of the economic system and were alienated from the government. Mostly they were the underskilled and undereducated: people who had never made it even to the lower rungs of the middle class. But hidden within their ranks were men of talent: someone who could coax an old motor to life, or knew how to treat a child that had fallen ill.

Elmira objected to leaving the city. But once they were on their way, the simple fact of moving seemed to give their life direction. When they reached the farm, Harold found his sister and the Yarmans living in the barn. The farm had been repossessed by the bank. The house had been padlocked. But the bank had been unable to auction off the farm. The sheriff had indicated he would overlook the Yarmans' presence in the barn.

Except for a few chickens running around half wild, all the animals were gone. The Yarmans had no money with which to farm; no mules; no implements. Grass and weeds were growing over the fields. There were rumors that the government might provide seeds with which to plant vegetable gardens. In one of the largest seed-growing areas in the nation, farmers lacked money to buy seeds.

It was Yarman's shotgun which played a large role in keeping the family alive. He killed rabbits, squirrels, birds, chickens, anything that ran outside the bounds of anyone's backyard. It was the way the pioneers had lived a hundred years before when the land had been unspoiled, and they had not yet had time to bring it under cultivation. The new economics appeared to dictate that men, camping on the land, should starve while the land returned to the wilderness.

The Yarmans were not overjoyed by the arrival of the Lenticks. No matter how Harold tried to explain how bad things were in the city, the Yarmans did not believe him. It was clear to them that no one could be worse off than they. The Yarmans told Harold that they had heard the President had said things were picking up for people; obviously, the *other* people. They all but accused him of malingering. Why should they have the burden of three more persons to feed, when they couldn't feed themselves?

Elmira complained day and night. To get milk for the baby, Harold had to walk two miles to a farm that was still operating. In less than two months they started back for the city.

59

The Ford Circus

IN MARCH, 1931, THE PROGRESSIVES MET IN WASHINGTON. THEY ALWAYS HAD represented more of an ideology than a party; and there was little to differentiate Progressive Republicans from Progressive Democrats, or Farmer-Laborites. The economic slide was the most severe since 1893, and it was that depression which had given the Progressives, as well as the Populists, their first great impetus. Swamped in the business-oriented politics of the 1920's, the Progressives could claim that the past eighteen months had vindicated their philosophy of governmental activitism; that government did not exist merely to preside over its own dissolution. Many of the men at the conference believed that the Progressives should run their own candidates in the 1932 presidential election. Mayor Murphy suggested Senator George W. Norris of Nebraska as the logical man. But Norris responded that the best hope of the Progressives was "another Roosevelt."

Of all the people at the conference, no one was faced with more pressing problems than the mayor of Detroit. In April the city was forced to borrow five million dollars to meet its payroll. In May all public improvement projects were suspended.

Galled that the Ford Motor Company contributed nothing to the Detroit welfare fund, Mayor Murphy charged that one third of the men on relief were former Ford workers. Harry Bennett retorted that in seven years Ford had employed 300,000 men, and that the dispensation of relief was ridden with scandal and chiselers. A clerk had, in fact, made off with more than $200,000. In the chaos resulting from tens of thousands of applications, little track was being kept of the payments.

At the beginning of June, 1931, the news leaked out that the city had run out of money; the June 15 payroll was the last it would be able to meet. Day after day from dawn to dusk hundreds of people milled about the corridors of the city hall. Jo Gomon's office was a maelstrom of people. Early one morning she received a visit from former court clerk Frank Nolan. Nolan had been hired by Ford after Murphy had dismissed him because of his drinking and unreliability.

Nolan told Mrs. Gomon that Harry Bennett would like to have the pleasure of her company for lunch and would send a car to pick her up.

Without informing the mayor, Jo Gomon decided to accept. Toward the close of a luncheon of partridge in Ford's damask-appointed private dining room, Bennett asked:

"What do you think of Hall Roosevelt as a banker?"

"He knows more than all the rest put together."

"Tell him to call me. Mr. Ford wants to lend the city five million dollars. There will be no interest."

For Ford, who believed one should "never give anything without strings attached," it was a way of showing up the bankers and answering his critics. For Bennett, who had become the behind-the-scenes power in the state's politics, it was a typical operation.

Between Ford, Liebold, and Bennett, the Ford Motor Company had turned into a cross between a medieval Borgian principality and a three-ring circus. Whenever someone who could be useful to the Ford Motor Company was in financial difficulties, Bennett offered money. Whenever a person with some special knowledge or contacts fell on hard times, Bennett hired him. The company was studded with cashiered Detroit police officers, faded athletes, and political hacks. The state's prisons paroled thousands of convicts to Bennett —they were men whom he could control with the threat of sending them back to the penitentiary. To allay Ford's fears of the underworld, Bennett put many of its key members on the Ford payroll. Chester LaMare of the Black Hand received the fruit concession at River Rouge and was given a Ford agency, which he promptly turned into a gang headquarters.

More and more, Ford leaned upon his "Harry." Unlike Edsel, Bennett readily agreed to build an estate, replete with tunnels and secret exists, near "Fairlane." There, Ford, after seeing him every day, called him every night.

Ford wanted "tough guys," and Bennett played the role of tough guy like Humphrey Bogart. Raising lions and tigers, he trotted them about on leashes, drove them about in his car, and played practical jokes by slipping them into the back seats of visitors' cars. One lion, undiscovered, awakened in the middle of the ride back to the city, and fondly draped his paw over the driver's shoulder. After the driver fled, the lion roamed about town. Finally he wound up at the Dearborn police station, where the officers, not knowing what to do with him, reported he "hanged himself," the world's only known leonine suicide.

Bennett and Ford regularly held target practice by shooting at rows of pencils and the crystals of chandeliers. When the state boxing commissioner appeared smoking an evil-smelling cigar, Bennett shot it out of his mouth.

In a safe shared by Ford and Bennett was a four-million-dollar "kitty," which Bennett could use for whatever purpose suited him. Although Bennett's official "salary" was never more than sixteen thousand dollars a year, he owned speedboats, fast cars, and three princely residences.

Obsessively superstitious, compulsively suspicious, Ford continued to find security in turning one man against another. The struggle for power was never-ending. Sorensen controlled production. Edsel held 40 percent of the stock. Liebold's mind was like a computer in which the secrets of the company were stored. Bennett, using his service men as goons, spies, and private detectives, had his finger on the pulse of everything. He planted microphones, kept an eye on everyone's movements, and accompanied Ford on "raids" of Edsel's home. He was Ford's eyes and ears.

But Ford was uneasy even about his surrogate son. So he used John Gillespie to spy on him. Gillespie was the former water commissioner who had run a line to the Highland Park plant, and subsequently been police commissioner of Detroit. A neighbor of Liebold's, he lived in John Dodge's former home on Boston Avenue. Gillespie had helped elect Mayor Bowles, and then had started fitting out his home as an elegant gambling casino. The recall of the mayor had reduced Gillespie's plans to nothing but an accumulation of bills.

Naturally Bennett hired him. As unprincipled and dishonest as he was shrewd and clever, Gillespie seized the opportunity to become Ford's monitor of Bennett. Ford set up an elaborate system of "secret" meetings to receive his reports; meetings which, given Liebold's and Bennett's spy networks, were seldom secret very long. Another contender for power had been added to the company.

Such was the management of one of the world's two leading auto manufacturers in the midst of the nation's greatest economic crisis. Throughout 1930, Ford tried to duplicate his feat of the 1921 depression by force-feeding dealers with cars. This time he only succeeded in bankrupting them. A third of the Ford dealerships in America folded.

In 1931, total car sales in America dropped below two million for the first time since 1921. Model A purchases plummeted from 1.4 million in 1930 to 620,000. The company lost $37 million. Once more Ford came to a heroic decision. In August, 1931, he repeated his action of May, 1927, and closed down the production lines. Not until December would he decide what the new car should be.

If the 1927 shutdown had resulted in a crisis in Detroit, the 1931 shutdown produced a catastrophe. In the state the number of unemployed and their families reached nearly 2.5 million, 40 percent of the population. Those who were thrown out of work *knew* no other jobs were available. Ford, who opposed unemployment insurance as leading to "permanent unemployment," expressed the opinion that it was only lazy workers who could not find jobs.

The month before, Detroit's conservative city council had ordered the $14 million welfare expenditure for 1930–1931 cut in half for 1931–1932. A family of two received $3.50 per week; a family of five $37.50 per month. The lodges for homeless men were closed. Whites, "bumping down," demanded that Negro garbage collectors be fired so that they could take their jobs. Mayor Murphy refused the demand. In much of the remainder of America, however, whites were ousting Negroes from even the lowest-paying positions.

The council reduced the public works budget from $17 million to $6 million. It ordered the cessation of all improvement work in districts with substantial tax delinquencies. These, of course, were the blue-collar districts. The poverty-stricken were to be punished for having been thrown out of work. The inner city areas were abandoned to weather and decay. The men that were pulled off the jobs were added to the welfare rolls.

With the Ford shutdown, the mayor said that the city would need at least $10 million to carry its citizens through the winter. Couzens, who in 1930 had been overwhelmingly reelected to the Senate, asked the President to call a special session of Congress to act on the emergency. When Hoover continued to insist "we cannot legislate ourselves out of this depression," Couzens offered to contribute $1 million to a Detroit relief fund if the remainder of the city's wealthy would furnish the other $9 million. The city's Brahmins, ensconced in their elegant mansions, refused.

The mayor, attempting to juggle a deficit of $32 million, appealed once more to Stone and the committee of bankers. A syndicate of Detroit and New York bankers reluctantly agreed to provide $40 million in short-term financing, but only with the proviso that the city cut another $6 million from its budget. The city council ordered $500 million worth of tax-delinquent property sold at auction. But the speculators who had responded in swarms to such auctions during the 1920's had disappeared. Only 15 percent of the property was sold. Homeowners were saved by default.

60

The Patriarch of Inkster

IF THE PLIGHT OF THE WHITES WAS DESPERATE, THAT OF THE BLACKS WAS very nearly mortal. Few executives emulated Mayor Murphy's refusal to fire Negroes. Since machines could not be fired, managers hung on to those workers whose skills could be employed ever more intensively to reduce costs. The most expendable jobs were those of the unskilled laborers. Even when a job was not eliminated, the Negro holding it often was. Not more than one out of three blacks held a steady job.

In his darkened house in Inkster, Odie Stallings despaired of the future. Even before the Ford shutdown, the community had been in critical straits. When the shutdown came, the town's meager resources were already exhausted. Like a bankrupt business, it ceased to operate. The people slid back toward the standard of living of the Dark Ages from which most had emerged.

Not a police officer remained on duty. The power company disconnected the electricity. Children were not going to school. The doors of the bank were locked. Storekeepers who during the winter of 1929–1930 had extended credit were bankrupt or on the verge of bankruptcy.

People who had subsisted for two years on starches and water were dying of malnutrition. Odie's weight had dropped from 160 to 125 pounds. With an old army bag slung over his shoulder, he crisscrossed Wayne County on foot. Working for anything he could get, he would swap or try to swap it for food. After a few days he would return home with a few cans of beans, a piece of rancid bacon, and an egg or two. But by the autumn of 1931 his last pair of shoes was in tatters, and he could no longer make the excursions.

Odie's and Freda's baby, a boy, was born with the aid of a midwife in September. For two months Freda tried to nurse him from her dried breasts. Crying continually, he clung to life.

To supplement her own milk and the occasional bottle of milk she was able to buy, she fed the baby a mix of flour and water. To retain heat in the house, Odie lined the walls with newspapers. But the wind sliced through the paper. The children coughed and sneezed and shivered. Freda and Odie cradled the baby between them in the bed to keep him warm. But one morning he woke up coughing. The next morning he was dead.

Toward the close of 1931 Ford prepared to bring out the first automobile with a V-8 engine as replacement for the Model A. As he began rehiring, he discovered the agonies of Inkster. Wages had been reduced to four dollars a day, and were not enough for the men to live on and simultaneously make payments on the debts they had accumulated with Inkster's mostly Jewish merchants. Ford, who believed that "the Negro had not yet developed a sufficient intellect to be able to be on his own [and] had to be guided and supervised," thereupon decided to save the community from the Jewish "exploiters." [1]

To keep the Jews from getting the Negroes' money, he paid only one dollar of the black workers' daily wages in cash. In lieu of the other three dollars, he adopted Inkster, and turned it into a communal enterprise. A public commissary was set up to provide food and clothing. Ford reopened the school. He furnished seeds and had the men cultivate the fields. He bought sewing machines for the women and taught them how to sew. To his great satisfaction, Ford became the patriarch of Inkster.

Litle by little, the community returned to life. The lights went on. In Odie's house, the stove glowed. For the first time in eighteen months the family ate a meal that did not leave them hungry.

A few days later Odie was notified by the police that Donald had been found. At ten the oldest of Odie's and Freda's three boys, he had run away after Odie had carried the baby in a cardboard box and buried it next to the small church. The burial had frightened Donald. He had lapsed into total silence. Two days later he had disappeared.

He was picked up in the freight yard, where he had joined a gang that rifled boxcars for food. He was suffering from frostbite. At the hospital, doctors amputed three toes.

Ford's offbeat beliefs had never made much of an impression upon the white population. But as his stature among Negroes grew, so did a cult whose "prophet" surfaced in Detroit's black community in the summer of 1930.

W. D. Fard—also known as Wali Farrad, Farrad Mohammad, and Professor *Ford*—appeared as a house-to-house peddler of coats and materials. No one knew his true origins. Since the Mideastern migration to Detroit had established in the city the second largest Moslem population in America, he could have walked across the street from the Moslem to the black enclave. Perhaps he had worked at Ford. Certainly he was familiar with Ford's writings and faddisms, and attempted to capitalize on his name. Ford felt that eating should be made "a part of religion." Fard made it a part of his religion. Ford warned against alcohol and smoking. Fard banned both. Ford was anti-Semitic. Fard preached against the Jews.

But more was needed to rally the Negroes of the ghetto than Henry Ford. With the concentration of Negroes in the Northern urban areas, the first mass black social and political movement had come into being in the early 1920's. Generated by the same economic forces as the Ku Klux Klan, the Universal Negro Improvement Association had emerged as the brainchild of Marcus Garvey, one of the thousands of West Indians drawn to the United States after 1900. Garvey had taught a "black is beautiful" racial consciousness, and preached separatism and racial purity. In 1921 he had proclaimed the "Empire of Africa" and turned the movement into a back-to-Africa crusade. Attracting perhaps a million adherents, he had staged demonstrations in New York, Chicago, Detroit, and other Northern cities. The middle-class, Republican Negroes had viewed the movement as subversive. The Coolidge Administration had indicted Garvey on a charge of mail fraud, and deported him. With Garvey's departure, the movement had collapsed.

Emulating Garvey, Fard taught black pride. To kindle that pride in a people whose sense of inferiority continued to be reinforced by the white culture, Fard developed the theory that the white man was the incarnation of Satan. Whites had imposed Christianity on Africans in order to enslave them. To regain their liberty, black men must free themselves from the white man's religion and rediscover the true religion of the Koran.

Fard's customers became listeners. The listeners became adherents. Fard's message that the whites were devils and the blacks were children of God excited and uplifted his followers. It gave them a weapon with which to counter the white racial propaganda.

The Detroit police, discovering a new militancy among the black youths whom they routinely stopped and frisked, suspected Communist subversion. Tracing the militancy to its source, they were relieved to discover only the "Supreme Ruler of the Universe."

As the movement gained believers, home economics classes were set up for girls, literacy classes for men and women, and the "University of Islam"— actually an elementary and secondary school—was established for black youth. In a community in which vice and gin making were the most profitable and frequently the only possible occupations, Fard preached chastity, abstinence, respect for women, and cleanliness.

But, as time passed, Fard appeared to become disenchanted with the progress of his movement. His apathy, and the growing hostility of influential Negro Christian ministers handicapped the organization. One day, four years after his appearance, his followers discovered he was gone.

After his disappearance, his disciples quarreled among themselves. The more viable faction, led by Elija Poole, a Georgia migrant, went to Chicago. Except for the hard core, the followers drifted away. A generation would pass before the Black Muslims, as they later were to be known, became a significant force in American society.

61

A First-Class Promoter

THROUGHOUT THE ECONOMIC ROLLER COASTER OF THE 1920'S, SYLVESTER J. Cavanagh had never been laid off for more than two or three weeks in succession from the Ford assembly line. The end of Model A production left him out of work. Returning home in the middle of the day, he engaged his wife Rose in anxious conversation in the kitchen—the scene became engraved in the memory of his three-year-old son Jerry.

The Cavanaghs had left Ireland in the great migration, and settled on farms a few miles from Toronto, Canada. By the time Sylvester grew to manhood, the continuing fecundity of the rural Catholic population was beginning to re-create some of the Irish problems. Only one or two of the numerous Cavanagh children could remain on the family's 150-acre farm. Sylvester went to work in a lumber camp. In 1919 he was drawn to Detroit by the production boom at the Ford Motor Company.

When Cavanagh was laid off during the economic shakeout of 1920–1921, he returned to Canada and married Rose Timmins. The Timmins family owned a 500-acre farm, and was a notch above the Cavanaghs in wealth and social standing. Both families were pious and conservative Catholics. Sylvester had only a grade-school education, but Rose had graduated from the public high school and then had attended teacher's college for two years.

After their marriage, the Cavanaghs settled in a house within the Boulevard area of Detroit. From a culture of kerosene lantern and wood stove, they moved into the age of gas and electricity. In 1925 they bought their first car. Five children were born during the first eight years of their marriage. All were enrolled in parochial school. From Canada, brothers and sisters of Rose and Sylvester followed to find jobs as assembly workers or schoolteachers.

To survive jobless 1932, Rose's sister moved her family into the Cavanagh home. One brother returned to the farm. The Cavanaghs' savings went nickel by nickel and dime by dime for essentials. Like the people who thronged Jo Gomon's office, they hoped for some sign that the economic plague was nearing its end. Like millions of other Americans, the entire family gathered around the radio every Sunday to listen to the inspiring and hypnotic voice of Father Charles Coughlin.

Father Coughlin was the son of a dominating Irish mother who had ardently desired to see him achieve priesthood. He had a natural theatrical flair and liked to stage Shakespearean readings in which he took a half dozen roles. To raise funds in his rural parish near Flint, he had organized a fair that netted more money than the county fair. His parishioners admiringly described him as "a first-class promoter."

In 1926, at the age of thirty-five, he had moved to the small parish of Royal Oak, nine miles from Ford's Highland Park plant. A Protestant farming community, Royal Oak was in the path of the urban auto expansion. The simple, wood-frame Catholic church was hardly completed before the Ku Klux Klan burned a cross in front of it.

Father Coughlin was struck by the widespread ignorance of Catholic history and dogma. He was amazed, simultaneously, by the multiplication of radio sets. The priest approached Leo J. Fitzpatrick, the manager of Detroit station WJR, and asked to be granted air time on Sundays. In response to the inquiry as to what he could do, Father Coughlin said he could play the organ and sing a little.

Father Coughlin's initial broadcast was on October 17, 1926. Royal Oak's "Shrine of the Little Flower" became the first Catholic church on the air. Contributions were solicited to pay for the broadcasts.

Within six months, mile-long traffic jams developed around the church on Sundays. Mailbags full of money were delivered weekly. As the number of radios multiplied, the audience grew.

Father Coughlin was congenial, commanding, and worldly. He recognized the power of attraction of girls with "lithe and sinuous figures." For the penetrating and intimate medium of radio he devised a formula of religion spiced with sex. A mild report by the Federal Council of Churches that "abstinence" might be used to limit the size of families generated his thunder against this "most heinous and vicious of sins." He called birth control an unfit subject of conversation for decent people and a "surrender to the ideals of paganism." The council was spreading Communist propaganda to undermine the virility of free nations. Every week listeners could expect a new issue, a fresh approach, a dash of sensationalism, with usually an element of sex or rapine—properly denounced—to add prurience. In 1929 the rolling phraseology of his mellifluous voice spread to Chicago and Cincinnati.

He espoused the philosophy of paternalistic Christian Socialism, and he had the ardent support of Detroit's archbishop, *Commonweal,* and the "liberal" wing of the Church. With the onset of the Depression, his message gained more and more relevancy and immediacy. On the one hand, he gave America a choice between "Christ or the Red Fog of Communism." On the other he denounced Wall Street and the "international bankers." In 1930 the Columbia Broadcasting System began carrying him. When a congressional committee held hearings on subversion in Detroit, he testified and threw a thunderbolt at Henry Ford by lumping him with the "bankers" and the "capitalists." By their treatment of workers, Ford and his fellow industrialists were the principal instigators of the Communist threat to America, Father Coughlin charged.

Father Coughlin was receiving an average of fifteen thousand letters a week and spending $300,000 a year on his radio broadcasts. To handle his correspondence, he employed 4 secretaries and 106 clerks. Millions of dollars poured into the "Shrine." Much of the money he invested in stocks and commodities. The rest he devoted to the construction of a $500,000 Charity Crucifixion Tower. One hundred and eleven feet high, it was topped by a thirty-five-foot floodlighted statue of Christ. Joining Christ were representations of the Blessed Mother, St. John, Mary Magdalene, Longinus, four evangelists, and the archangels.

He was at odds with the Catholic Establishment and much of the American hierarchy, who regarded his attacks upon capitalism with horror. By April, 1931, his broadcasts were so controversial that CBS refused to renew air time for the program. Unable to purchase time on any of the established networks, he formed one of his own. Ten million persons—one out of every three or four with a radio—listened to him weekly. He had become a figure of national renown, and Hall Roosevelt urged his brother-in-law Franklin to seek his support for the 1932 presidential campaign.

Roosevelt clearly was emerging as the front runner for the Democratic nomination. For the past half dozen years the party apparatus had been under the control of the Du Ponts. John J. Raskob, a registered Republican until Pierre S. Du Pont had succeeded in capturing the 1928 nomination for Al Smith, was the party's national chairman. Except for the fact that Hoover was the candidate of Republican Protestant "prosperity" and Smith of Democratic Catholic "prosperity," the campaign had seemed like a contest between Tweedledum and Tweedledee. Smith's hopes had expired in the ashes of the Klan's crosses. Yet there was every indication that much of the party's leadership intended to wage the same kind of campaign that had taken it to three straight national election disasters. Since 1860, the Democrats had been able to elect only two Presidents, Grover Cleveland and Woodrow Wilson. And Wilson had attained the presidency primarily as the result of Republican disarray.

Franklin D. Roosevelt set out to woo liberal Catholics in the hope that their support would counterbalance the influence of the conservative Catholic businessmen at the nominating convention. In the spring of 1932 he invited Father Coughlin and Mayor Murphy to Hyde Park.

62

The Hunger March

IN NEW YORK'S GOVERNOR ROOSEVELT, MAYOR MURPHY FOUND A SYMPATHETIC listener. Both were Progressives who believed in governmental activism, and it was evident that government action was desperately needed. Unemployment would recede slightly, then, like the waves of a still-gathering storm, crest toward new heights. The unemployment rate of 16 percent was grossly understated. Many persons *working* were doing so only one or two days a week. Millions of others had dropped out of the labor force, and were in a statistical limbo.

In the fall of 1931, the Detroit Unemployment Committee had put Harold Lentick on the street with a basket of apples. They might just as well have given him and hundreds of others pencils or shoelaces to sell. The businessmen of the city were setting up panhandlers. It was the last refuge of free enterprise.

Local governments, many of them insolvent, were incapable of feeding and housing the destitute, whose numbers kept increasing. In most Northern cities those families able to obtain relief were existing on an average of less than fifteen dollars a month. In Detroit nearly one out of every seven persons was on relief. Children scavenged through the streets like animals for scraps of food, and stayed away from school. The attendance department made little pretense of tracking them down. Among high school students in the inner city the incidence of tuberculosis tripled. Each day four thousand children stood in bread lines. With their sunken, lifeless eyes, sallow cheeks, and distended bellies, some resembled the starving children in Europe during the war.

By the end of 1931, the city was attempting the impossible in paying back the short-term loans while its revenues declined and the needs of its citizens increased. Tax delinquencies in some of the poorer wards topped 50 percent. Of the $57 million collected, $27 million was allocated to debt service. Revenues fell $19 million short of the budget. Mayor Murphy appealed to public utilities to reduce their rates. But, like other businesses operating in the administered economy, they refused. In January, 1932, Murphy went to Washington and told a Senate committee that urban society was on the point of disintegrating unless Federal help were forthcoming.

Under pressure from the committee of bankers, the Detroit welfare department chopped the case load to 21,500 families. Only bread and flour were distributed for food. As welfare ceased paying rents, approximately 4,500 families with no money and no place to go were evicted every month. While hundreds of buildings stood empty, thousands of persons had no shelter. Families carrying their belongings trudged through the streets. Tent cities reappeared. People squatted in abandoned houses, shacks, garages, and warehouses.

By paying no rent, by pursuing what welfare and charity was available, by stealing, by virtually dropping out of the money economy, the Lenticks dragged themselves through the winter. Twice the baby, critically ill, went to the hospital. Once Elmira was admitted. The social system, which no longer seemed to have the capacity to enable them to conduct useful lives, still felt obligated not to let them die.

Even AFL President "Sitting Bill" Green, who often had seemed as business-oriented as the most conservative businessman, questioned the continuing existence of the capitalistic system, and warned that the nation's leaders were "taking no account of the history of nations in which governments have been overturned. Revolutions grow out of the depths of hunger." [1]

The president of the National Association of Manufacturers, however, contended that workers who were contributing to the rising "Communistic chorus" were men who had "either struck on the jobs they had or don't want to work at all." [2] For the first time in American history, the Communists—appealing to the outrage of intellectuals, and the growling stomachs of the unemployed— were gaining a major foothold. In December, 1931, they rallied the hungry for a March on Washington. Shivering in the wind and cold, the ragged men contrasted startlingly with the glowing façades of the Capitol and the Library of Congress. At the central portico of the Capitol they were turned back by a line of policemen backed by machine guns.

Slightly over two months later, the Communists directed their attention toward Ford. Consistently, Mayor Murphy had refused to give them the pretext for the violence they sought. In October, 1930, he had debated several Communists before a crowd of three thousand at Grand Circus Park. In July, 1931, he had faced down six hundred protestors who blocked the entrance to city hall. When the Communists announced that they intended to stage a Hunger March to River Rouge, he granted them a parade permit and provided them with a police escort.

Ford was the target because he was the largest employer in Detroit and had shut down in the middle of the Depression. The symbol of the $5 day, he had reduced wages to two thirds of what he had been paying in 1914. (Five $4 days in 1932 compared to six $5 days in 1914.) He was employing Negroes at $1 a day plus subsistence—the whites looked upon them as scabs who were undercutting wages even further. He was pressuring his workers to tend *"thrift plots"* in their backyards and on his Dearborn acreage. In effect, while cutting their wages he increased their hours. Not only did they have less money to spend; they had less need to spend it at the corner grocery store.

On March 7, 1932, three thousand men marched under the red banner toward the Ford plant. Their "radical" demands were the elimination of kickbacks in hiring, a six-hour day without reduction in pay, free medical care for

Ford workers, a fifty-dollar unemployment "bonus," and the right to organize. Considering that the participants in the march were not likely to see the inside of a Ford plant again, their demands were scarcely a threat.

But Bennett was determined not to risk contamination of the workers by allowing the marchers near the gates. At the Dearborn city line the marchers were met by forty Dearborn police under the command of Carl Brooks. Brooks, a former Ford service man, had been head of the Highland Park plant police before being appointed chief in Dearborn. The Ford and Dearborn police were, in actuality, interchangeable, and men moved back and forth freely.

Chief Brooks ordered the marchers to turn back. When they refused, the police fired tear gas canisters into their midst. The gas scattered the marchers, and the breeze scattered the gas. Breaking into small groups, the people continued to make their way over open fields and along side streets toward the Ford plant. As the police chased them, hand-to-hand fighting broke out. The officers wielded truncheons; the marchers used fence posts, rocks, pieces of rusted metal—whatever objects fell to hand.

Appearing on Miller Road adjacent to the plant, the marchers overran the two fire engines whose high-pressure hoses were intended to turn them back. As the battle continued along the road, two of the plant's hoses were unrolled onto the pedestrian bridge spanning the roadway at Gate Three. Freezing water was sprayed onto the crowd below.

Bennett, ever ready to prove himself afraid of no man, dashed out of the plant to personally confront the marchers. As he argued with Joe York, a nineteen-year-old organizer for the Young Communist League, the crowd turned toward him. A piece of slag hit him on the side of the head. Blood poured down his face. Bennett grabbed York, and both fell to the pavement. A moment later, York, disentangling himself, got up.

Police and service men at the gate opened fire. Shots slammed into York, marchers, and spectators along Miller Road. Workers, responding to the echo of the shots, arrived to look at a score of dead and injured, screaming and twisting on the cold, wet pavement.

Among the observers was a delegation of Russian technicians, who were at River Rouge as the result of a thirty-million-dollar contract negotiated between Ford and the Soviet government.

Perceiving no contradiction, Ford blamed a Communist conspiracy for the incident. Cameron characterized the marchers as Red hoodlums, intending to precipitate revolution.

County Prosecutor Harry Toy was virulently antilabor and an ally of Bennett and Gillespie. Placing sixty of the marchers under arrest, he ordered two of the seriously wounded men shackled to their hospital beds. At the request of Chief Brooks and Prosecutor Toy, and without the authorization of Mayor Murphy, Detroit police rounded up Communist suspects all over the city. Three women who had picked up two wounded men and taken them to Detroit Receiving Hospital were arrested and turned over to the Dearborn police. Toy announced wholesale prosecutions for "criminal syndicalism."

The unemployed of the city responded by gathering nearly fifteen thousand strong to march in the four-mile funeral procession for York and the three others who had been killed. They formed a sea of red—red banners, red armbands, red berets, red-draped caskets—bobbing slowly up and down to the muffled beat of drums. At the graveside, thirty thousand gathered to hear the band play "The International" and the funeral march of the 1905 Russian Revolutionaries.

Ford, frightened and alarmed, fortified the plant and his Dearborn residence. Searching for allies, he began mending his fences. He came to an agreement with the American Legion to give preference in hiring to five thousand war veterans. With Police Chief Brooks one of its charter members, the Knights of Dearborn, a paramilitary group, was organized. Ford promised to take over the Dearborn welfare load if officials would remove from the ballot a proposition calling for a special welfare tax. (Ford property accounted for 62 percent of the city's assessed valuation.) Relief recipients were given a daily food order of sixty cents at the Ford commissary. If they were reemployed at Ford, fifteen dollars a month was checked off until their accounts were settled.

63

The Verge of Destruction

EMPLOYMENT IN THE AUTO INDUSTRY WAS ONLY SLIGHTLY MORE THAN HALF what it had been three years before. As wages were cut, the payroll fell to a third of what it had been in 1929. There was an abysmal decline in purchasing power.* At first people had reduced principally their purchases of durable goods: automobiles, radios, furniture, electric appliances. But, as the Depression knifed into the marrow, they also cut back on their food purchases. Expenditures for food dropped 9 percent between 1929 and 1930; 15 percent between 1930 and 1931; and 17 percent between 1930 and 1932.

In Detroit, tax delinquencies for 1932 jumped to $25.1 million—one third of the assessment—bringing the three-year total to $48.2 million. In three years taxes collected by the school district dropped in half. Continually teetering on the edge of bankruptcy, the city in April was unable to scrape together enough money to make the payments on the special assessment bonds. Mayor Murphy and Stone, the head of the banker's committee, again assailed each other—the banker charging excessive welfare expenditures, the mayor retorting that the bankers had laid the groundwork for the city's insolvency by encouraging the wild speculation and extravagances of the 1920's that had loaded the city with debt.

The city was out of money. The bankers were not about to lend more. This time Henry Ford was not riding to the rescue. To make it through April and May, Murphy cut all municipal salaries in half. The welfare budget for the fiscal year beginning July 1, 1932, was cut to three million dollars, a totally unrealistic figure. Yet it was evident that, because of the continuing outlays, all but a pittance of the money would be spent before the first of July arrived.

Convinced that the city could not survive without state and Federal aid, Mayor Murphy called for a meeting of Michigan cities.

While eighty thousand Detroiters gathered at a rally in Cadillac Square to

---

* Per capita purchases which had declined 35 percent between 1929 and 1930, and 28.8 percent between 1930 and 1931, nosedived 42.7 percent between 1931 and 1932.

berate President Hoover for failing to act, eighteen mayors assembled in Detroit in the third week of May. Denouncing the Michigan Legislature for appropriating $20 million for highways but not a cent for the cities, they called for enactment of newspaper magnate William Randolph Hearst's proposed $5 billion "prosperity loan" for public works. A resolution was passed to expand the gathering to a national conference of mayors.

Jo Gomon got busy on the telephone. The mayors of all cities over one hundred thousand population were invited to meet in Detroit on June 1. From New York, Boston, Cleveland, Minneapolis, New Orleans, Milwaukee, Denver, Indianapolis, Richmond, and other cities the mayors came to Detroit.

New York's Mayor Jimmy Walker declared: "This country is on the verge of destruction." Having accomplished the impossible and resurrected American Populism in the cloak of a cassock, Father Coughlin damned "the modern Pagans who have crucified us upon a cross of gold," and demanded the expansion of the money supply through the monetization of silver.[1] Mayor Murphy was appointed to head a committee to call upon the President and request the initiation of a massive program of public works and the refinancing of municipal debt through loans from the Reconstruction Finance Corporation.

President Hoover, eleven years younger than Henry Ford, had grown to manhood at a time when the period of expansionist free enterprise was entering its final stage. It was a period of Victorian romanticism and Horatio Alger; and Hoover, whose origins were middle class and Middle Western, had lived a Horatio Alger story. Orphaned early in life, he displayed little academic excellence, but flunked the admission examination to newly founded and tuition-free Stanford University. After a summer of tutoring, he was permitted to enter the university conditionally in the fall of 1891. Four years later he graduated as a mining engineer. It was an era when mining engineers were few and industry was scouring the world for mineral deposits. By his middle thirties he was a millionaire.

President Hoover conceived it to be his mission to preserve the system that had made his success possible: a system in which the "rugged individualist" (a Hooverian coinage) free of governmental interference and restraints could make his way upward to success; a system in which the Federal government stayed out of local affairs, and did not impinge upon the right of the people to govern themselves as they saw fit; the system of "free enterprise" established by the American middle-class revolutionaries in reaction to the repeated British fetterings of the economy.

He was trapped in an illusion. The Herbert Hoover of the 1920's probably would not have gained admission to Stanford University. If he had, he would not have been able to pay its tuition. "Rugged individualism" was being submerged in corporate enterprise. Durant had been replaced by the General Motors policy committee. The Edison of the twentieth century was one of scores of researchers at the General Electric laboratory. The Ford Motor Company had been started on capital of less than fifty thousand dollars. A quarter century later it would have taken many millions of dollars to organize a new automobile company with any chance of success.

Faced with the alternatives of abandoning his dogma or the American people, the President took refuge in rationalization.

Since 1893 the nation had been exporting far more than it was importing.

Its industry and agriculture were the most efficient in the world. Yet in 1930 the President backed the Smoot-Hawley Tariff to *protect* American industry and agriculture against European competition.* Despite the warning of a thousand economists of the catastrophic consequences, he viewed the tariff as an anti-Depression measure. Twenty-five of the world's principal nations retaliated. Between 1929 and 1932 United States trade declined 70 percent. Automobile exports fell from 11.6 percent of production in 1928 to 4.8 percent in 1932.

For a decade, American loans had propped up European economies. But as Secretary Mellon had reacted to the onset of the Depression with a program of governmental economy and "liquidation," the amount of money in circulation steadily decreased.† American loans to Europe dried up. European exports to the United States, still the world's only mass market, withered. In the summer of 1931 the European financial structure collapsed. In Germany, blue-collar unemployment soared toward 50 percent, and the nation headed into the night of Naziism.

Perceiving effect as cause, and cause as effect, the President from 1931 on placed the blame of the American Depression on the European collapse. Waving fistfuls of billion- and trillion-mark notes printed in Germany during the runaway inflation of the early 1920's, he insisted that, if the experience were not to be repeated in the United States, the budget would have to be balanced. (The $2.1 billion Federal deficit in 1931 was the largest in peacetime history.) For the budget to be balanced, government spending would have to be slashed, and taxes would have to be raised. It was an opinion reflecting a lack of economic know-how not only within the administration, but within the business community in general.‡ Having prescribed applications of ice for frostbite, yet being unable to comprehend why the gangrene kept spreading, American leaders were now proposing to shrink the nation to the size of its financial blood supply.

The President worked at his desk until midnight and was up again before dawn. His face turned ashen. He haunted the corridors of the White House like a living ghost. Repeatedly, month after month, year after year, he emphasized that he was protecting the integrity of the individual against government encroachment, and that if business were only given the chance to recover the economy would right itself. But it was the administration of business, not of government, that was imperiling the individual, both as an entrepreneur and as a person. The President sought to be the defender of laissez-faire. But laissez-faire, both domestically and internationally, had been killed off by the very men who kept citing it as the reason for government to stay aloof from the debacle. The President placed his faith in the resiliency of a system of commerce that no longer had faith in itself. The patient that the President diagnosed as ready to leap out of bed calling for a doctor and a priest.§

* One of the companies crying the loudest for "protection" was Mellon's Aluminum Company of America, which had no domestic competition at all.
† It declined from the inadequate total of $26.5 billion in 1929 to $20.6 billion in 1932. Between August 1931 and January 1932, 1,860 banks with deposits of almost $1.5 billion closed their doors, and the money supply contracted another 12 percent.
‡ The German *inflation* had been generated by the government's printing of money far beyond the capacity of the industrial establishment to produce goods. The American *deflation* was the result of the maldistribution of income and the people's lack of money to buy the huge volume of goods industry was capable of turning out.
§ In September of 1931 Gerard Swope, president of General Electric, suggested the interment of the free enterprise system. Competition would be replaced by industry-wide planning. Every industry would organize self-regulatory trade associations in which all firms of

In a series of clandestine meetings with the President at the end of 1931, the nation's leading bankers told him they were not prepared to lend money, and not willing to place a moratorium on the collection of debts and mortgages. They were prepared only to liquidate. They would liquidate farmers. They would liquidate homeowners. If necessary, they would liquidate themselves.

So the Reconstruction Finance Corporation was established with a capital of $2 billion to make loans to businesses.* Mayor Murphy asked the RFC for a $10 million loan to finance welfare expenditures during the coming year. (The $10 million figure was as unrealistic as the $14 million figure had been the year before.) There was, literally, no other institution left from which to borrow the money. The mayor told the President that what government could do for business, it could do for the people. At the instruction of the conference of mayors, Murphy urged him to initiate a large-scale program of public works.

In the past the President had been inclined favorably toward public works to decrease unemployment. However, his obsession with the need to balance the budget now led him to state that attempting to cure poverty by law was futile. As administrator of American relief in Europe during and immediately following the war, he had been all but apotheosized as a humanitarian. Unable to reconcile his lifelong beliefs with the truth, he convinced himself that "our people have been protected from hunger and cold." The hoboes, he said, were "better fed than they have ever been. One hobo in New York got ten meals in one day." [2]

When the Southwest had been struck by drought, he had moved promptly and decisively to bring Federal aid to the cattle. People, however, were not to be treated like cattle. Cattle were not rugged individualists whose self-reliance could be subverted. Provide Texans and Californians and Michiganders with aid, and their self-reliance would be sapped, their self-determination undermined. When Congress passed the public works bill in July, he vetoed it.

---

more than fifty employees engaged in interstate commerce would participate. The associations would regulate production, set prices, and establish systems of unemployment insurance and old-age pensions to which both workers and management would contribute. Some segments of Big Business, which had opposed and broken unions on the argument that they were intolerable interference in management's prerogative to run industry as it pleased, now appeared ready to submit to a controlled economy.

* That was enough to convince former Democratic presidential nominee John W. Davis and a good many other conservatives of both parties that Hoover was moving the country toward socialism.

64

"In No Year Did the Corporation Fail To Earn a Profit"

IN DETROIT, GENERAL MOTORS PRESIDENT SLOAN WAS CONVINCED THE ECONomy had passed beyond the point of righting itself, and organized a committee of industrialists to deal with the Depression. The committee, however, proved as unproductive as other committees, and accomplished little.

General Motors, in fact, was reinforcing the Depression by continuing to act as a redistributor of income from the public at large to the upper 5 percent of the population. Between 1929 and 1932, while its payroll declined by nearly two thirds, it paid out $343 million in dividends to its stockholders. "Standard volume" provided such a large cushion that during the first three years of the Depression the corporation had profits of $248 million. In 1932, while auto manufacturers were losing an aggregate of $191 million, G.M. earned a 1.1 percent return on investment after taxes. Sloan was able to boast that "in no year did the corporation fail to earn a profit." [1] Despite the largesse to its stockholders, its surplus was still $105 million greater than it had been in 1927. While the economy was desiccated, General Motors floated in liquidity.

Until 1932, professionals and white-collar workers who formed the savings and capital class had been relatively insulated from the Depression. The average income of individuals in the legal profession had decreased only 16 percent; in banking and in the Federal government, 13 percent; in public education, 12 percent; in utilities, 8 percent. In certain occupations—the Federal government, the legal profession, broadcasting—employment actually was *increasing*.

In the third year of the Depression, however, even the people in the topmost layer of the economy were beginning to shiver in its icy blasts. President Hoover cut Federal salaries 25 percent. Personal savings, which had fallen $1.5 billion between 1929 and 1931, plunged $3.3 billion between 1931 and 1932. Harvard graduates haunted bread lines in increasing numbers. Churches closed because their parishioners no longer could support them. Ministers took to tending garden plots. The wholesale value of auto production, $2.8 billion in 1929, dropped to $617 million.

Few independent automobile manufacturers survived. Stearns Knight and Peerless folded in 1929.* Durant Motors and the Moon Motor Company went under in 1930. They were followed by Gardner, Elcar, Jordan, Franklin, and Kissel in 1931–1932, by Nordyke-Marmon in 1933, and by R.E.O. and Auburn in 1935. (R.E.O. continued as a manufacturer of trucks.) In the "class" market, Packard was the only independent to survive, and it lost $14 million between 1931 and 1934 despite the fact that it accounted for 43 percent of the sales of all high-priced cars.

Like suns attracting to themselves the fragments of economic debris, the giant corporations amassed greater and greater power. While the share of the auto market held by independents declined from 25 percent in 1929 to 10 percent in 1932, General Motors increased its share from 32 percent to 42 percent. (Ford and Chrysler divided the other 48 percent.) As company after company struggled in the financial quicksand, General Motors pulled them out and gathered them in.

The Packard Electric Company, from whose womb the Packard motorcar had sprung, was brought into the G.M. fold. The Electro Motive Corporation and the Winton Engine Company of Cleveland, both of which had done extensive research on Diesel engines but lacked the money to convert the research to commercial application, were purchased by G.M. in 1930.†

The result of bringing all the research together was dramatic. In 1932, two years after the acquisition of Winton, General Motors demonstrated a new, lightweight Diesel engine capable of being used in locomotives.

The railroads considered it little more than an oddity. Forming one of the most introverted and conservative of American industries, they spent insignificant amounts on research and discouraged "outsiders" from concerning themselves with their problems. Locomotives continued to be handcrafted to the specifications of the buyers. Diesels were looked upon as unfit for railroad use.

However, Ralph Budd, president of the Burlington Railroad built by James F. Joy, was interested in introducing a lightweight passenger train. From the E. G. Budd Company, a manufacturer of automobile bodies, he ordered three lightweight passenger cars. From G.M. came the locomotive. Cheaper than coal, oil could produce three times as much power per weight. The Diesel was far cleaner and did not require the many service and refueling stops of the steam locomotive. In November, 1934, the Burlington inaugurated Diesel service between Chicago and Denver. Running time was reduced to one half, and operating cost to one sixth of the conventional train that had been on the route.

Already as dominant in the aircraft industry as in the automotive,‡ General

---

* Peerless moved with the times. The company had started out making clothes wringers. It then turned to bicycles, and from them to cars. With the end of Prohibition, it began brewing Carling's Ale.
† With his marine background, Alexander Winton had always had a passion for Diesel engines. (Rudolph Diesel had received his patent in 1892, but the engine's weight restricted its use.) Away from the Detroit mainstream, Winton had never capitalized on his early lead in auto production, and the Winton Motor Carriage Company had been liquidated in 1924. But, working on Diesel power plants for industry, ships, and railroads since 1912, he had advanced Diesels further than anyone else.
‡ As holder of 48.6 percent of the stock of the General Aviation Company, General Motors had working control of Dayton-Wright, Allison, Bendix, Fokker, and North American Aviation. Through North American Aviation it controlled Douglas Aircraft Company and

Motors proceeded to establish a monopoly in the manufacture of railroad locomotives. When, after the success of the initial trial, General Motors decided to
mass produce Diesel engines, railroad men scoffed. Who would purchase a
mass produced locomotive?

By 1940, one hundred thirty Diesel engines would be operating passenger
trains. By the mid-1950's, as G.M. broadened production to include freight
engines, the manufacture of steam locomotives for American railroads would
come to an end. In another ten years the steam locomotive would disappear
from the American scene. With the exception of switch engines, General Motors
would be making 100 percent of all American locomotives.* Piece by piece
the railroad industry, which had been one of the parents of the automotive
industry, was being chewed and swallowed by its offspring.

Insofar as railroad operating costs and efficiency were concerned, G.M.'s
development of the Diesel locomotive unquestionably was progress. But it was
progress at a price. With a monopoly, G.M. could apply the concept of
"standard volume" to the pricing of Diesel engines. Tens of thousands of craftsmen who had been engaged in the making of steam locomotives would find
their profession eliminated.

In virtually every field in which General Motors and the other giant corporations applied their research and ingenuity, the result was the same: gains in
efficiency and convenience; losses in the labor needed, and, therefore, in jobs.
As early as 1914, Kelvinator had marketed a mechanical refrigerator. For more
than a decade, however, refrigerators continued to be wooden monsters of
up to 1,000 pounds that sold for $700 and $800. In 1926, G.M.'s Frigidaire
division had introduced a steel-cabineted refrigerator weighing 362 pounds
and selling for $468. Other manufacturers entered the field. Within a genera-
tion the refrigerator would retire the breadman and the milkman, and play a
significant role in boarding up the corner grocery store.

Operating not only as a state within a state, but as a state crossing international boundaries, General Motors pursued policies affecting tens of millions of
persons. Yet the formulators and directors of those policies did not think—and
could not be expected to think—in terms of the welfare of the general public.
It would have been phenomenal had they not conceived their responsibility to
be the corporation's prosperity and the maximization of its profits.

As great a power as could be wielded by one corporate giant, not infrequently
more than one combined to dictate new economic directions. When in the
early 1920's Charles Kettering developed a lead additive for gasoline, three
corporations—General Motors, Du Pont, and the Standard Oil Company of
New Jersey—joined to form the Ethyl Corporation to market the additive.
Leaded gasoline soon acquired the reputation of "looney gas." Numerous
communities attempted to ban its sale. But individual communities could not

---

Northrop in the production fields; and Eastern, Transcontinental Air Transport (subsequently TWA), and Western Air Express (later Western Air Lines) in the transportation
field. Receiving Federal subsidies through the Air Mail Act, three giant holding companies
—Aviation Corporation, United Aircraft, and North American General Motors—had been
awarded twenty-four out of twenty-seven airmail contracts by the Hoover Administration
despite the fact that smaller lines had on occasion submitted lower bids. After the collusion
between the administration and the air giants was revealed and remedial legislation was
passed in 1934, General Motors withdrew from the air transport field and retained control
only of the aircraft production concerns.
* As well as 85 percent of American Diesel buses, and a large percentage of trucks.

prevail against the propaganda of three of the world's most powerful corporations, who together now had a mutual interest in the production of larger cars with more powerful engines requiring greater quantities of "Ethyl." For nearly half a century lead would be spewed into the air before the harmful effects of "Ethyl" would again be brought to the public's attention.

Thus, immense power wielded within the limited perspective of self-interest had far-ranging effects on the economy and the environment. The Depression gnawed at the vitals of the world's social body. But for General Motors and other large corporations it served as a temperer of the corporate structure and a consolidater of power.

65

The Coming of Christ's Deal

WHILE GENERAL MOTORS TURNED THE DEPRESSION TO ITS ADVANTAGE, FARMERS and workers strove to survive. In the cities people went hungry at the same time that farmers had crops pile up in their fields and barns. Iowa farmers, fed up with the inability even to recoup their cost of production, organized the Farmers Holiday Association. In Detroit and other cities, pasteurization plants controlled by the large milk-distributing companies formed "bottlenecks." Paying farmers a low price for milk in the "free" economy, the distributors jacked up the price in the "shared monopoly" they administered in the cities. Bedeviled by the dual economy, in which farm income had dropped 50 percent while the *administered* prices of farm implements had declined but 14 percent, farmers decided to starve the cities. Picket lines were set up to prevent farm goods from traveling the highways between rural and urban areas. Milk trucks were halted, and their contents dumped on the side of the roads.

The attempted embargo, leapfrogging across the Midwest, set city against farm. Although it proved ineffective, its ineffectiveness resulted more from lack of organization than from lack of will.

It was the smaller farmers who were hurt the most. Heavily in debt, they were being squeezed off the land. (Eleven percent of farm income was going to pay off interest.) At homestead after homestead, farmers banded together and brandished shotguns to prevent foreclosure sales. Thousands of farmers joined the "Bonus Expeditionary Force" of war veterans who journeyed to Washington in May and June, 1932, to demand prepayment of the "bonus" due in 1945. Twenty-five thousand strong, they set up camps on the greens, in abandoned government buildings, in parks, and on the mosquito-ridden Anacostia Flats. Parading nostalgically, comically, pathetically on Pennsylvania Avenue like the spectral army of a bygone age, they intruded upon the image of American life the administration had painted on its mirrors. Marching like zombies around and around the White House and standing like accusing pickets in front of public buildings, they all but immobilized the President. Hoover believed the B.E.F. to be a bunch of criminals and ne'er-do-wells controlled by

Communists. The U.S. Army's deputy chief of staff suggested that the entire group of veterans be shipped to detention camps in the Hawaiian Islands.

At the end of July the President, increasingly jittery about having the Bonus Expeditionary Force encamped in Washington during the election campaign, ordered General Douglas MacArthur to clear the veterans out of Washington. Astride his horse, weaving in and out of the traffic on Pennsylvania Avenue, General MacArthur led his force of cavalry, infantry, and tanks against the veterans. Routing them with tear gas and bayonets, he razed the camp on Anacostia Flats.

"I have released in my day more than one country which had been held in the grip of a foreign enemy," he declared.[1]

In a climate in which the American people and the army veterans could be referred to as the "enemy," the feeling was spreading across the land that the people no longer had a government. Walter Waters, a former Oregon cannery superintendent who was the leader of the B.E.F., suggested that in a nation in which "there were billions for the bankers, [but] nothing for the poor," the time had come to organize the poverty-stricken. Such an organization might be called the "Khaki Shirts." [2]

Among veterans, farmers, workers, and the owners of small businesses operating in the "free" economy, there was a mood of rebellion against the government of Big Business.

Others, unable to see their way out of the morass, were willing to accept dictatorship, if dictatorship were the sole means of salvaging the economy. As early as the fall of 1931, Columbia University President Nicholas Murray Butler praised totalitarian systems as superior to democracies in enabling men of great intelligence and character to attain power. In 1932 Bernarr MacFadden suggested that "the President should have dictatorial powers." Senator David Reed of Pennsylvania, an Old Guard Republican, declared: "I do not often envy other countries their governments, but I say that if this country ever needed a Mussolini, it needs one now." [3]

Since President Hoover and the conservatives were firmly in control of the Republican party and were able to squash every uprising of Couzens and the Progressives, the people who hoped to achieve change through the electoral process could only look to the Democrats. But with Raskob of Du Pont and General Motors as the chairman of the Democratic National Committee, the Democratic party seemed as firmly in the control of big business as the Republican. Despite President Hoover's record, Raskob looked on the Republican party as the party of big government, aiming to concentrate power in Washington. The Democratic destiny, he believed, was to win the coming election and reverse this trend; to give business, despite its abysmal record, carte blanche to run the economy as it saw fit. He recognized no inconsistency between the absolute control General Motors exercised over its dealers and the absolute freedom from governmental control that he wanted for General Motors.

Continuing to favor Smith for the 1932 presidential nomination, Raskob received the backing of the party's 1920 and 1924 nominees, Cox and Davis, for his choice. Opposing him was the Populist-rural wing, whose strength lay in Congress and whose candidate was John Nance Garner, Speaker of the House of Representatives.

The leading candidate, nevertheless, was Franklin Roosevelt, who had gained the support of the urban and liberal votes. Although the liberals and the proponents of governmental activism had doubts about him—they thought he was too complaisant, too closely associated with business, and not enough of a "fighter" *—he had espoused the Progressive philosophy during most of his twenty-year politcal career. He was a proponent of public power and of conservation. As governor he had pushed social welfare legislation. New York, in 1931, was the first state to establish an Emergency Relief Administration. Roosevelt was not afraid to say that if the advocacy of programs for the welfare of people was socialistic, then he was a Socialist. It was time, he said, for the government to stop worrying so much about the welfare of business, and to start concerning itself with the welfare of the little man, the "forgotten American."

When it appeared that Roosevelt might lose the nomination because of the two thirds majority rule that had brought on the deadlock in 1920, Garner acquiesced to William Randolph Hearst's request and threw his delegates to Roosevelt. Smith, in high dudgeon, refused to make the nomination unanimous. Raskob, questioned as to whether he would support Roosevelt, turned and asked for the stock market quotations.

Roosevelt was attuned to the modern era as no presidential candidate before him and had made up his mind well before the convention to make use of technology to hold an unprecedented dialogue with the American people. After sitting beside the radio all night to listen to the balloting from Chicago, he decided to break tradition by accepting the nomination in person. It was a decision made possible by Ford's Trimotor. Stopping in Buffalo and Cleveland for the refueling of the plane, he flew from Albany to Chicago.

In 1924 radio had broadcast the doom of the Democrats from the shambles of the convention floor in Madison Square Garden. Taking the rostrum in Chicago, Roosevelt was determined to turn radio to the Democrats' advantage. Addressing himself more to the American people than to the delegates, he declared:

"I pledge you, I pledge myself, to a new deal for the American people."

Within a short time, Father Coughlin was to apotheosize his declaration:

"The New Deal is Christ's Deal," he said.[5]

* Walter Lippman wrote that he "simply does not measure up to the tremendous demands of the office of President." [4]

66

The End of Illusion

ROOSEVELT MIGHT OFFER HOPE. IN THE MEANTIME, HOWEVER, THE PLIGHT of Detroit and other cities grew more desperate. Although financial institutions were receiving hundreds of millions of dollars from the RFC, banker Stone and his finance committee opposed Detroit's making application for a $10 million loan. Instead they proposed a $7 million reduction in the budget, a permanent 13 percent cut in municipal salaries, an emergency bond issue of $20 million, and prepayment of taxes by wealthy property owners.

The committee prevailed. But in the face of a massive tax revolt, the measures weren't enough. Tax delinquencies in Detroit reached $26 million. After the allocation of funds for debt service, the city had only $16 million on which to operate for the year.

Raging at "welfare chiselers," real estate operators formed the Association for Tax Reductions and demanded a statutory limit of $57 million on the city budget. Amendments to the state constitution were passed. The vote on property taxes was restricted to property owners, and the state property tax was limited to 1½ percent of assessed valuation. The fiscal crisis that ensued resulted in enactment of a 3 percent state sales tax, the burden of which fell heavily on lower-income families.

Unemployment continued to rise, seemingly without surcease. In October, 1932, 725,000 Michigan citizens, 43 percent of the work force, were jobless. Including the families of the unemployed, more than half the population of the state was affected. Nationally, unemployment was somewhere between 13 million and 17 million—no more accurate assessment was possible.

Hundreds of thousands of people lined up at soup kitchens for week-old bread and a watery mix containing a few vegetables. To get even half enough to eat, it was necessary to stand in as many lines as possible—the President's assertion that hoboes sometimes were getting ten meals a day was quite true.

Unshaven and unkempt, men wandered directionless on the streets of the cities. The immigrants disembarking from the boats and the workers in the sweatshops of New York had presented a better appearance.

Finally venturing out of the White House to commence his campaign for reelection, President Hoover had little concept of true conditions in the cities. Arriving in Detroit, he was still confident. Never had he expected to be greeted at the railroad station by an army of tatterdemalions whose rotting teeth were crumbling on the iron-hard doughnuts handed out by the welfare department. Never would he have dreamed that many of these men came from families that for generations had been staunch Republicans. Ejected from the middle class into the streets, believing themselves betrayed by their own party, they were in some ways the most bitter of all.

The cutting jokes and outright threats against Hoover reached such a crescendo that Mayor Murphy feared for his safety. As the President's train pulled into the station, a line of police officers beat back the mob that, flying "Hoover flags," booed, hurled epithets, and sang, "Hang Hoover from a sour apple tree!" Driven to the auditorium in a limousine provided by Henry Ford, the President stumbled through his speech like a malprogrammed robot. The Republican illusion that the big cities would produce their usual large turnout for the party was shattered. The image of the land and the people with which Hoover had emerged from the White House was splintered into a thousand pieces in Detroit.

In the Ford plant, signs warned the workers that their jobs depended upon their voting for Hoover. In one form or another Steinway's message of 1896— "Men, vote as you please, but if Bryan is elected tomorrow the whistle will not blow Wednesday morning"—was repeated throughout industry. Bennett's service men cracked down hard on any show of independence—when the proud tool-and-die makers indicated signs of rebellion, they returned to their benches one morning to find their tools smashed and scattered.

On Walter Reuther, however, Ford's warning failed to make an impact. Thoroughly imbued with the socialism his grandfather had brought with him from Germany, he was campaigning for Norman Thomas.

At a time when auto workers were making as little as 12½ cents an hour, Reuther earned $1.45 an hour at Ford. (That was within a few cents of the pay his father had received for a day's labor.) At the age of twenty-five, in the middle of the Depression, he was prospering modestly. He owned a Model A, he had made a down payment on a lot in Dearborn, and he had nearly $1,000 in the bank. He represented the elite group of professionals and highly skilled workers who, if they had not lost their savings in the stock market crash, were better off than they had been before the Depression.

Yet even if the elite did not suffer the physical deprivation of their fellow Americans, huge numbers were in psychological turmoil. As the election approached, Reuther fitted a platform over the rumble seat of his Model A, drove onto his lot in Dearborn, and exhorted passersby to vote for Thomas. The police appeared to warn him he could not hold a political rally on public property without a permit. Reuther retorted that he was not on public property, but on his own.

That was a victory for Reuther, the speaker. But before the end of the year Reuther, the worker, was dismissed by Ford.

As the election campaign drew closer to the day of decision and Hoover's realization of the extent of the country's rejection of his presidency grew, he warned stridently that Roosevelt would destroy "the very foundations of our American system." Yet it was the people's continuing faith in the ability of the electoral system to bring about the drastic changes Hoover abhorred which kept the despair from being transformed into violence and revolution.

Roosevelt captured 57.4 percent of the popular vote and 91 of 106 cities with a population of over 100,000. It was the first clear-cut Democratic victory in forty years. The Socialists received nearly a million votes. The Communists, for the first and only time in American history, topped 100,000.

In fact, tens of thousands of Americans were speaking of Soviet Russia as a model. Hundreds of thousands of others were willing to investigate its merits. And millions would have accepted communism to solve America's economic problems. Authors, businessmen, and national folk heroes jumped on the Soviet bandwagon. Will Rogers declared that the Russians "have got some mighty good ideas. . . . Just think of everybody in a country going to work." On Broadway, plays with social content were larded with allusions to the superiority of the Communist system. John Strachey wrote that "to travel from the capitalist world into Soviet territory is to pass from death to birth." Lincoln Steffens asserted: "All roads in our day lead to Moscow." [1] Every year, more than 100,000 Americans, taking him literally, made inquiries about obtaining jobs in Russia.

Walter Reuther decided to see what life in the Soviet Union was like. In the first week of February he withdrew his savings of eight hundred dollars and started on a journey to Gorki, where hundreds of Americans were working in the factories.

67

The Collapse of the Pyramids

WITH A NEW GOVERNMENT ELECTED, BUT THE OLD ONE REMAINING IN POWER for four more months, the machinery of government was frozen. The people who had elected Roosevelt were deriving no benefit from his victory. The people who had voted for Hoover were jittery and confused.

In Detroit, auto employment dropped to less than 40 percent of the 1923–1925 average. Harold Lentick was working at the Briggs Manufacturing plant, which turned out automobile bodies for Ford. He was paid twelve and a half cents an hour. Along with the other men, he went to the factory early in the morning and stayed until late at night. The production line no longer was a smooth, continuous operation. It moved in stops and starts, two to three hours at a time. The men were paid only for the time the line was in operation. On a good day, after spending ten to fourteen hours at the plant, Lentick would get one dollar.

In January, 1933, Briggs reduced wages again. Together with nine thousand other men, Lentick walked out. The immobilization of the plant put sixty thousand additional men out of work. Walter Briggs refused to negotiate with "Communists," and Ford was unable to understand why the men should be striking. When the workers milled around the plant and attempted to set up picket lines, the police arrested them or chased them away. Briggs hired strikebreakers, and by mid-February was back in full production. The minimum wage was raised to twenty-five cents an hour, but half the men who had walked out lost their jobs. Lentick reapplied for relief.

By February, Detroit had received $13 million in loans from the RFC. But with the continuing economic deterioration, the city was on the verge of defaulting on $56 million in loans. Once more Mayor Murphy was forced to go to Stone's committee of bankers.

During the first few weeks of 1933, however, the Senate Banking and Currency Committee launched an investigation into banking practices. As the "savings class" began hoarding money and gold, banks in the United States lost almost $2 billion in deposits. It became apparent that many of the Detroit banks were in little better shape than the municipal government. A tale of financial manipulation and cynical self-interest commenced to unfold.

The 1920's had brought a tremendous drive toward concentration of power and giganticism in the banking world. Because many states prohibited the establishment of branch banks, banks were often combined into groups and chains in order to achieve greater flexibility and interchange of funds. By 1928, fourteen hundred banks had been united into various groupings. The smaller and weaker banks, afraid of being unable to meet the competition of the larger, sought to gain strength through consolidation. The concept of the holding company spread rapidly. One large, prestigious bank would become the mother organization beneath whose umbrella the smaller could nestle. Banks, like companies, were layered into pyramids as intricately structured and as laced with hidden passages and secret chambers as the pyramids of Egypt.

In 1928 the Guardian Detroit Bank, a year after it had been organized by Edsel Ford and Ernest Kanzler, became the nucleus of the Guardian Detroit Union Group, a holding company encompassing twenty-five Michigan banks. (One of the group's members was the Guardian National Bank of Commerce, which had once been the German-American Bank.) Kanzler was chairman of the board of the holding company. Edsel Ford, with fifty thousand shares, was the largest stockholder.

To counterbalance the tremendous power of the Guardian Detroit Union Group, forty other banks backed largely by General Motors and Chrysler money merged into the Detroit Bankers Company in January, 1930. The two groups controlled 87 percent of the banking in Detroit, and held 57.5 percent of all loans and investments in the state.

If the advantage of a holding company was that the weaker members could gain strength from the stronger, the disadvantage was that the process worked also in reverse. The poison from one bank could spread through the system. If the holding company itself were to be debilitated, even the strongest of the members would be endangered. The holding company enabled a group of banks to exercise greater power and flexibility through a combining of assets. But through its internal channels, the holding company also provided opportunity for limitless abuses.

The Guardian Group invested heavily in real estate, especially office buildings. It bought a securities firm that gave it entry to Wall Street, and it acquired a large portfolio of stocks. By October, 1929, it had stretched its resources to the limit. In the "Depression-was-over-yesterday" atmosphere of 1930 and 1931, the group's directors engaged in financial manipulations to maintain the price of the shares of the holding company, so that they would not have to liquidate investments at depressed prices. By October, 1930, the group's stock had dropped to $75 a share from its high of $350 in August, 1929. A stock pool was formed by 110 directors who agreed to purchase at least 60,000 shares and hold them for one year in an effort to keep the stock from slipping further. A trustee committee of five, including Kanzler, Hudson's Roy Chapin, and Charles Warren, former ambassador to Japan, was formed.

Once started, the members of the pool borrowed more and more money to support the price of the stock. The Guardian holding company borrowed $14 million with heavy interest charges to enable member banks to put up a good front. While the mortgage and consumer markets were starved for funds, and the bankers' committee damned "welfare chiselers" and insisted on further reductions in the municipal budget, the banks cannibalized the money of savers and investors. In 1930, the Guardian Group held 48,431 of its own shares as security for loans; in 1931, 57,531; in 1932, 149,574. This was a clear violation of both state and national banking laws.

By 1932, the Guardian National Bank of Detroit had loaned officers and directors of the bank $3,481,000, equivalent to 34 percent of its capital. Another bank had loaned 122 junior officers and employees approximately $1 million on collateral of $15,000. The First National Bank of Detroit had loaned directors, officers, and employees $33,296,000, more than the total capital of the bank. In order to bolster the price of its stock, the Detroit Bankers Company continued to pay the 17 percent dividend it had promised when it was organized.

To maintain public confidence, the Guardian Group issued false reports as to its strength. Whenever it became time for a member bank to issue its statement, money was shifted into it. The device was essentially the same as that employed a century earlier, when kegs of nails and silver had been transported from bank to bank ahead of the examiner. Even though unit banks had small earnings or were running in the red, they continued to declare substantial dividends on their stocks so that the group could pay dividends on its stock, held for collateral on loans to officers and employees.

The stock held for collateral, however, was all but nonnegotiable. If a bank attempted to sell the stock, its price would be driven down, and in 1932 the group had already disposed of $1.7 million in securities for a pittance. The moment public confidence was the least shaken, the structure would collapse. Three years after the Wall Street crash, officers in the Detroit banks were still engaging in the same practices that had brought it on.

At a meeting in June, 1931, the public relations committee of the Guardian Detroit Union Group discussed means of continuing to pull the banks' statements over the public's eyes. "It was finally decided that this consolidated statement would be printed in the same standard form rather than the understandable form [because] the understandable form was devised at a time when conditions warranted such a statement whereas the situation is now entirely different." [1]

Since not even incomprehensible financial statements would suffice, huge sums were juggled in the credit and debit columns. The 1930 report of the Guardian Group declared earnings "more than sufficient to pay during 1930 regular dividends at the rate of $2 per annum and an extra dividend at the rate of $1.20 per annum," when, in truth, the group had lost $39,387. In 1931, net earnings before charge-offs were publicly reported as $3,887,052, but the official report to the Michigan Securities Commission listed a loss of $288,930.

In the meantime, as banking irregularities and favoritism in the granting of RFC loans became public through congressional investigations, public confidence in the banking system sank. During the first few months of the RFC's existence in early 1932, the President had insisted that its grants be kept secret so as not to start runs on banks to which it loaned money. He had asserted RFC loans would not be made to help *big* banking and *big* business. Now it was revealed that more than half of the $126 million in loans had gone to three large banks. Charles Dawes—the Vice-President of the United States under Coolidge, and the president of the RFC—abruptly resigned in order to try to save the Central Republic Bank of Chicago, of which he was one of the founders. Behind him, although the RFC's total deposits at the time were but $95 million, trailed a $90 million loan. Detroit's Union Guardian Trust Company, with which Secretary of Commerce Roy Chapin was associated, received $14 million.

In January, 1933, under the grilling of the Senate Banking and Currency Committee, witness after witness began to unveil the sordid story.* The men of finance were revealed to be fools, mountebanks, tax dodgers, manipulators of stocks, and speculators rivaling Mississippi riverboat gamblers. Endorsing and floating stock and bond issues that their own experts knew to be dangerous, the banks had taken their profits and foisted the securities upon the public. The integrity of the judicial system was brought into question as the investigation disclosed that more than forty judges had $600,000 in loans outstanding at one Detroit bank. A loan of $100,000 had been made to the state treasurer. While banks were auctioning homes and farms, they failed to press for collection of large overdue loans made to friends of bank officers.

For months Alfred P. Leyburn, the chief national bank examiner for the Fourth Federal Reserve District, had been sending reports to Washington about the irregularities occurring in Detroit banks. He was given to understand that "the Comptroller of the Currency was instructed by the higher command not to do anything to rock the boat, and not to have any more bank failures." [2]

On January 24, 1933, the Guardian Group issued its report to stockholders, noting that "1932 was a year of notable improvement [in] the safety of funds which our depositors have entrusted to us." The statement declared a net income of $1,316,952. In actuality, in Kanzler's words, there had been a "profit for the year 1932 in the red" of $1,789,069. Asked if this were not a prevarication, he replied, "It really was not a figure that the stockholders should have been or would have been interested in." [3]

At the same time that the 1932 statement indicating a profit was issued, the Union Guardian Trust Company was applying to the RFC for another loan of $20.5 million. As collateral it could offer securities worth only $6 million at face (not market) value. Kanzler told the RFC that if the Union Guardian Trust Company were forced to close, the entire Guardian Group—which had banks in sixteen communities with deposits of $900 million—would be brought down. If that happened, the Michigan banking structure would collapse.

By the first week in February, Detroit was rife with rumors. The assets of the Union Guardian Trust Company lacked some $14 million of the amount depositors had banked. The Guardian National Bank of Commerce was able to meet routine withdrawals only because it had the city's welfare funds on deposit.

It soon developed that what the Group actually needed was an emergency loan of $51 million. The loan was to be secured by $90 million in mortgages, which were valued at only $35 million in the depressed market. Since the law required that every RFC loan be insured by full collateral, the $51 million obviously could not be lent without violating the law.

President Hoover, nevertheless, appeared willing to violate the law if the alternative was the suspension of business of the Group's banks and the widespread panic that would almost certainly follow. On February 9, 1933, he invited the state's two senators, Couzens and Arthur Vandenberg, to the White House.

Couzens was outraged by the President's proposal. Day after day in the

---

* Couzens, the committee's leading Republican member, enthusiastically supported the investigation.

committee hearings he was listening to a litany of bankers' follies. He had been rebuffed by the White House in his efforts to have little-used army camps opened to the tens of thousands of homeless youths who were roaming the country. The RFC had done next to nothing to aid the populaton at large, and only $60 million of the $300 million authorized by Congress for loans to localities had been disbursed. The record of the RFC already was soiled by the conflict of interest of the Central Republic Bank loan. Now the President was proposing to rescue the bankers of Michigan and an institution with which his Secretary of Commerce was intimately connected even though the action would circumvent the law. Couzens rejected the President's suggestion that he, Sloan, and Chrysler each contribute $2 million to the rescue, while Ford would subordinate (i.e., give preference to other depositors) $7.5 million in deposits. If the President persisted, Couzens said, he would denounce the loan on the floor of the Senate.

The only remaining hope was to convince Henry Ford to shore up the banks. The Fords had loaned the Union Guardian Trust Company some $12 million in three years. Edsel had permitted the institution to use $5 million of the Ford Motor Company's municipal bonds as collateral. On December 29, 1932, he had committed the company to another loan of $3.5 million. In return the bank had all but placed itself under a Ford trusteeship.

On February 10, a Friday, President Hoover dispatched Chapin and Undersecretary of the Treasury Arthur Ballantine to Detroit. If anyone could prevail upon Ford, it was Chapin, who through the Hudsons had a long personal relationship with the Ford family. He and Henry Ford had made their entry into banking together in 1910, when they had been elected directors of the Detroit National Bank. He and the Fords were among the principal organizers of the Guardian Detroit Union Group. Lincoln's birthday, which fell on Sunday, was to be celebrated on Monday. Chapin and Ballantine thus had three days in which to attempt to work out a solution.

Proposals and counterproposals were shuttled back and forth between Ford's officers in Dearborn and the banking offices in the ornate, gilded tower of the Guardian Trust Company, where bankers from Michigan and elsewhere gathered with Chapin and Ballantine. The bankers asserted they would not be able to raise the $6 million needed to keep the banks operating even temporarily. In truth, no one wanted to risk more of his own money to rescue what looked like a hopelessly insolvent enterprise. Henry Ford offered to purchase two of the banks for $8.5 million. But since the offer did not include an agreement to assume the outstanding liabilities, it was rejected.

On Monday, Chapin and Ballantine went to Dearborn in a final effort to obtain Ford's commitment. Ford's impression that he was an object of persecution was growing. He was shocked, he said, that the United States Government should ask him, its largest taxpayer, to take on an obligation that was clearly its own. If the RFC would not make a loan to the Guardian Group, then he refused to prop it up with any more of his money. He was not about to risk $50 million, he said, "to keep Jim Couzens from making a speech." He retracted Edsel's commitment to subordinate $7.5 million in deposits. He spoke of an international plot of bankers against him. If the Union Guardian Trust Company did not open on the next day, he said, he could see no reason why the Butzels' First National Bank of Detroit should, either. He would withdraw not only his $32.5 million in deposits from the Guardian Group, but $25 million from the First National. Although it was pointed out that if he did, he would bring down every bank in the state, he was immovable. If the crash had to come, he quoted Couzens, then "let the crash come." [4]

That evening, Michigan's Democratic governor, William Comstock, joined the marathon session in the Union Guardian Building. Ford's threats made it clear that only closing the banks could prevent a statewide panic the next day. The bankers demanded he declare a bank holiday. Already reports were spreading through the city that the RFC, the Treasury, Senator Couzens, and "Wall Street" were responsible for the crisis. Comstock, well aware that as soon as the emergency was over the bankers might deny it had even existed and blame the closing on him, refused to declare the holiday unless the bankers submitted a signed request. One by one they affixed their signatures.

It was midnight when the governor went out to take a walk in the cold, misty, and smoke-shrouded night to make his decision. Stopping at a hot dog stand, surrounded by the skyscrapers of the industrial era that was now in disrepair and disrepute, he munched on a hot dog and came to his decision.

At 1:32 A.M. on Tuesday, February 14, 1933, he signed the proclamation declaring the bank holiday.*

The Michigan bank holiday froze deposits of more than $1.5 billion in the state. A total of 436 banks and trust companies closed. To meet payrolls, industrialists like Chrysler went out of state and returned carrying sacks of money. But even that tactic was a temporary expedient. The automobile and Detroit had come to symbolize America. If Detroit had gone into receivership, could the rest of America, where more than 5,000 banks had closed in three years, be far behind?

Panic spread across the nation. On February 23 the banks in Indiana closed; on February 25, those in Maryland; on February 27, Arkansas; February 28, Ohio; March 1, Alabama, Kentucky, Nevada, and Tennessee; March 2, Arizona, California, Louisiana, Mississippi, Oregon. By March 4, banks in only a handful of states remained open.

The economic system of the country had broken down. Laissez-faire had expired.

---

* The next day an immigrant Italian bricklayer, unemployed and ill, fired at the President-elect's car in Miami. Roosevelt was not hurt. But Mayor Anton Cermak of Chicago, who was riding with him, was fatally wounded.

1. The view of Detroit from the Canadian shore shows the L-shaped City-County Building on the right and the Ford Auditorium directly in front on the river. Across Woodward Avenue from the City-County Building is the new Michigan Consolidated Gas Company skyscraper. Behind it and to the left, the forty-seven-story Penobscot Building completed in the 1920's continues to tower over the downtown area. Along the riverfront on the left is Cobo Hall, the largest convention facility in the world at the time of its construction.

2. One hundred and fifty years earlier, in 1820, the same perspective from the Canadian shore showed the *Walk-in-the-Water*. The first steamer on Lake Erie, the ship had been built two years earlier. The advent of steam transportation transformed Detroit from an isolated outpost to the gateway to the Northwest. **3-4.** Within a decade Irish peasants (left and above) whose abysmal poverty resulted partly from their fecund multiplication were streaming to labor-short Detroit and other American cities.

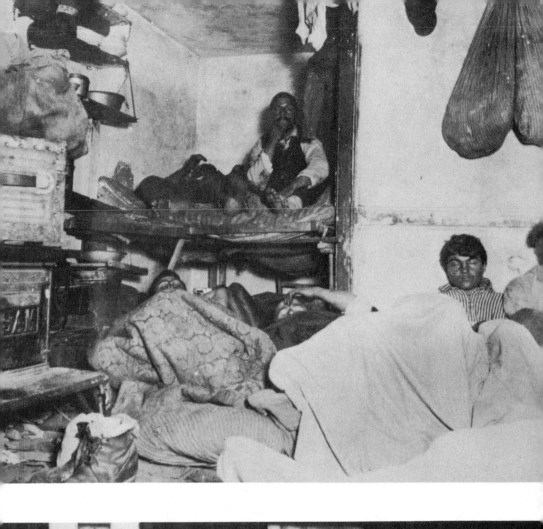

5. In America the immigrants were crammed into airless and lightless tenements. Six or more men bedded down on two or three mattresses in tiny cubicles (left above). **6.** Families lived and worked in sweatshops (left). **7.** Streets like those in New York's Jewish district (pictured above about 1890) were turned into market and meeting places.

8. One of the few middle-class immigrants from Ireland was William Ford (above left) who arrived in America in 1847 when he was twenty-one years old. William prospered as a farmer, but his son Henry was more interested in machinery than farming and came to Detroit at the age of sixteen. 9-10. Henry Ford went to work for the Detroit Drydock Company (below), where his picture was taken (center of photo above) about 1880 when he was seventeen years old.

11. William Ford had worked for the Michigan Central Railroad promoted by James F. Joy (above left), one of the great railroad developers and a founder of the Republican party. 12. Joy prepared the way for railroad industrialist James McMillan (above right) who became the boss of the Michigan Republican party. 13. McMillan was challenged by Mayor Hazen Pingree, pictured as he broke ground for the paving of Grand Boulevard in 1891 (below). Pingree was the spear carrier for the new, Progressive Republicanism.

14. Pingree's view from the city hall was of the Campus Martius with its sky-scraping arclight towers, horsecars, and Soldiers and Sailors Monument (top). Behind the monument is the Central Market Building and to the right the famed Russell House Hotel. 15. Pingree turned down Henry Ford for manager of the municipal power plant, and the moustachioed Ford (below, far right of picture) continued working as chief engineer for the Edison Illuminating Company.

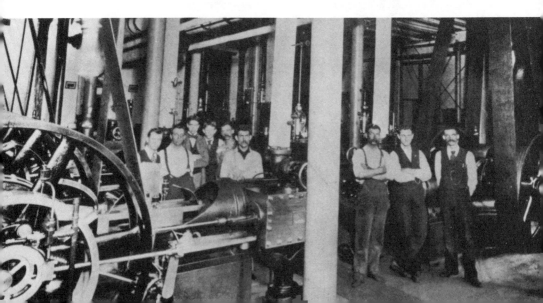

16. Pingree's drive for street improvement was enthusiastically supported by the Detroit Rambler Bicycle Club, whose photo (above) was taken in 1896. **17.** In March of the same year Charles B. King (below, seated right) with the help of Oliver Barthel (left) completed the first motor carriage built in Detroit. (The manufacturer of Rambler bikes began making automobiles, and the company survives today as part of American Motors.)

18. Ford apparently caught the automobile fever from King and Barthel. He concentrated on building racers. In the big race at the Grosse Pointe track in October, 1901 (above), Ford is shown taking the lead against Winton. Afterward a group of Detroiters put up money for him to produce a commercial car. 19. In January, 1902, however, Ford wrote his brother-in-law on company stationery (below) that he was determined to continue racing. "My company will kick about me following racing but they will get the advertising and I expect to make $ when I cant make ¢s at manufacturing." 20. Ford's obsession with racing resulted in his backers withdrawing and turning to Henry Leland (above right) to manufacture the car.

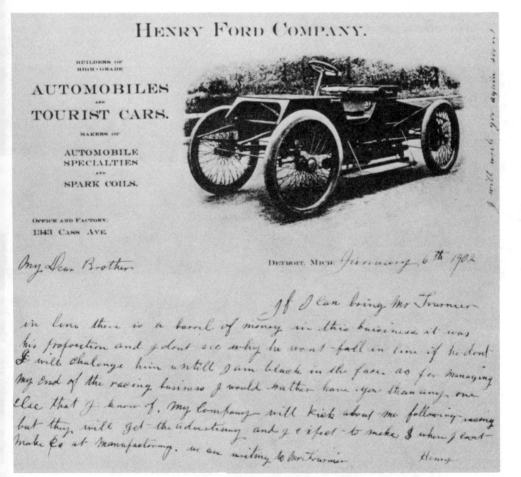

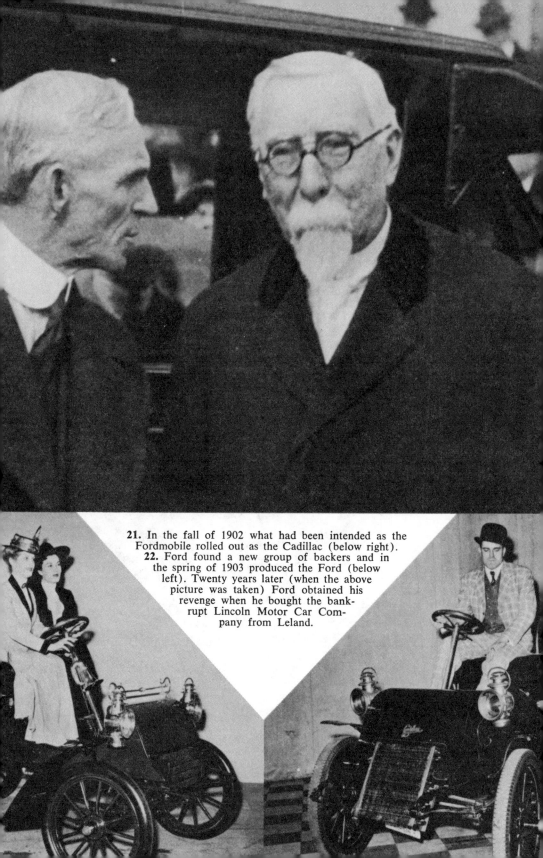

21. In the fall of 1902 what had been intended as the Fordmobile rolled out as the Cadillac (below right).
22. Ford found a new group of backers and in the spring of 1903 produced the Ford (below left). Twenty years later (when the above picture was taken) Ford obtained his revenge when he bought the bankrupt Lincoln Motor Car Company from Leland.

23. The spreading employment of steam engines, gas, and electricity resulted in devastating fires. Thirty-seven persons lost their lives in the fire that followed the explosion of a boiler adjacent to Detroit's Journal Building on November 6, 1895.

24. Shortly after the picture (above) was taken, the Olds Motor Works was destroyed by fire in the spring of 1901. The only model saved from the first auto factory established in Detroit was a small, curved-dash runabout. 25. The Olds runabout was demonstrated in 1902 with a stunt that seems out of a 1970 television commercial (below), and became the first car to be sold in large numbers.

26. When Henry B. Joy formed a syndicate that moved the Packard Company to Detroit in 1903, he wanted a fire-resistant factory constructed. The reinforced-concrete building (above) that Albert Kahn designed heralded a new era in industrial architecture. 27. The 1906 Packard being driven by Joy (below) was one of the first models produced at the plant.

28. At the Ford Motor Company, James Couzens (left) combined his managerial ability with Ford's engineering expertise and proved how wrong Ford had been when he said he couldn't make money at manufacturing. **29.** The Model T, whose engines were started for the first time by rollers at the factory (below), became the most successful car in American history.

30. General Motors had its beginnings when David Buick, a manufacturer of plumbing fixtures, started buildings cars in this shop in 1903 (left above). 31. Because Buick lacked the capital to market the cars, William C. Durant, who had become a millionaire by building road carts at a factory in Flint (above), acquired the business. 32. The success of the 1907 Buick (below left) enabled Durant to expand. He bought Oldsmobile and Cadillac, and incorporated General Motors. 33. After Durant lost control of the corporation in 1910, he formed a new association with French auto designer Louis Chevrolet (shown below driving a Fiat in the 1905 Vanderbilt Cup race).

The industrial boom drew men to the cities from the forests and the mines.
34. In the Michigan lumber country (above) the timber was being exhausted.
35. At the Calumet and Hecla copper mine (below) a 1913–1914 strike against
the one-man drills called "widow makers" failed disastrously.

36. In cities throughout the United States the vehicles of the mushrooming population generated huge traffic jams (above), as horsedrawn wagons, automobiles, streetcars, and electric cabs (first vehicle foreground) competed for the streets.
37. On Sunday, Detroiters went to Belle Isle (below) where they gathered along the banks and in canoes to listen to the concert coming from the bandstand arcing the Grand Canal.

38. In the countryside, dirt roads that became impassable when it rained continued to give the horse an advantage over the automobile (above left). 39. In the summer of 1912 a Philadelphia firm sponsored the first transcontinental delivery of goods by truck, shown (above) at the theoretical midway point across the United States. The next year the Lincoln Highway Association was formed to promote a coast-to-coast highway. 40. As building of the highway began in 1916, a road grader worked in Iowa (below left). 41. The success of American trucks during the war (shown below supplying Verdun in 1917) led to the development of the trucking industry.

42. As the Federal government poured billions of dollars into American industry, Henry Ford developed the River Rouge plant, and helped his grandson Henry Ford II light the fire in the first blast furnace in May, 1920. **43.** The largest industrial complex in the world, the River Rouge plant rivaled the Detroit chemical industry (seen in the distance along the river) in pouring huge billows of smoke and pollutants into the air.

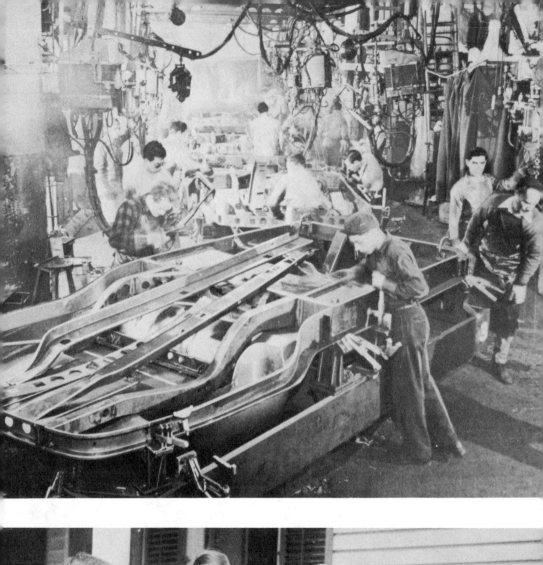

44. The frantic pace of the assembly line (above left) and the leisurely operations of the government of business symbolized the roaring twenties. **45.** Calvin Coolidge holds a maple sap bucket (left) as he talks (left to right) with Harvey Firestone, Henry Ford, and Thomas Edison, at the President's Vermont home. **46.** On October 21, 1929, Ford shouted into Edison's ear (above) at the Greenfield Village celebration of the fiftieth anniversary of Edison's development of an incandescent light. Two days later the stock market crashed, and the end of the pernicious prosperity was at hand.

47-48. When the United States sank into its Great Depression, formerly affluent Americans sold apples on the streets (above) and the Communists led protesters at the nation's Capitol (below).

49. In 1931, the skyscrapers erected during Detroit's boom of the 1920's towered over the soot-blackened buildings of the nineteenth century. Directly to the left of the city hall is the ten-story Hammond Building, completed in 1889. The skyscrapers (left to right) are the Guardian Building, the Buhl Building, the Ford Building, the Penobscot Building, and the Dime Building. (The Ford Building was constructed by John Ford, who made his fortune in the chemical industry and as far as is known was not related to Henry Ford.)

When legislation was passed giving workers the right to organize, strikes broke out all across the United States in the mid-1930's. **50.** In January, 1937, workers and police battled amid tear gas bombs in front of the General Motors plant in Flint (above). **51.** The United Auto Workers staged a giant rally attended by tens of thousands of workers in Detroit's Cadillac Square (below). **52.** But when Walter Reuther led a delegation to talk to workers at Ford's River Rouge plant, they were met by Harry Bennett's service men (right). Richard Frankensteen was one of several labor leaders attacked and beaten in the Battle of the Overpass.

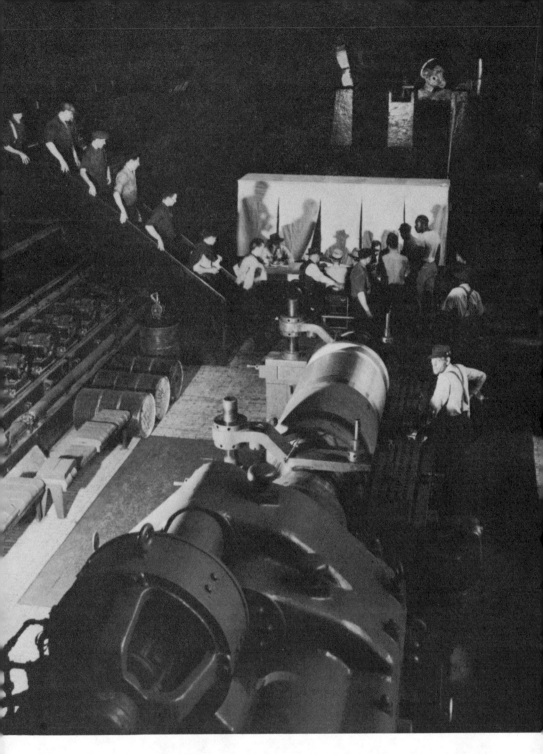

53. Four years later when the National Labor Relations Board forced Ford to allow workers to hold an election on union representation, the men cast their ballots amid the giant, brooding machinery and voted overwhelmingly to have the United Auto Workers bargain for them.

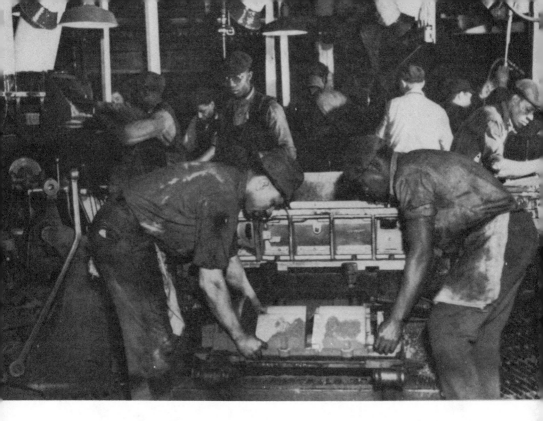

54. Negroes continued to be restricted largely to the "black department"—the foundry—at River Rouge (above) and other auto plants. 55. When the Detroit Housing Commission built the Sojourner Truth project for Negroes adjacent to a Polish residential district, whites picketed the city hall (below) and attacked black tenants trying to move into the apartments.

56. After World War II, whites began a mass exodus for new residential districts on the urban fringe. Six lanes of cars are outward bound on Second Avenue during the evening rush hour (above). 57. The city's older housing was abandoned like this home in the Forest Park area (below). Although the area is now occupied almost totally by blacks, the Catholic church testifies to its Polish antecedence.

58. Negroes and poor whites were left to contend against the decay. They lacked the resources for renovation and upkeep. Junked cars and blighted buildings with boarded and broken windows came to cover the inner city (above). 59. The population could no longer support local businesses, and proprietors moved away and boarded up their stores (below).

HIGHWAYMAN AT 17

BURGLAR AT 17

MURDERER AT 19

PICKPOCKET AT 15

BURGLAR AT 18

HANGED AT THE TOMBS

60. Throughout history, as in the New York of the 1880's (above), the slums have produced juvenile delinquents. **61.** During periods of national stress, delinquency is likely to be channeled into rioting, as exemplified by the youthful faces of the arrestees in the 1943 Detroit riot (below).

62. Economic riots erupt when normal restraints break down. Police formed a picket line across Twelfth Street on the morning of July 23, 1967, but did not interfere with the crowds milling about and already breaking store windows (above). **63.** When fires were set, residents of the area were among the principal victims (below), and piled their belonging on the sidewalks as wind-fanned flames swept through the buildings.

64. Trying to govern a city in economic crisis, Mayor Jerry Cavanagh was confronted by a black youth in the ashes of Twelfth Street.

III

THE NEW POLITICS

68

The Faded Mask

With the closing of the banks, Detroit defaulted on its bonds. A food panic swept the city. People with money cleaned out the grocery stores, and prices skyrocketed. Both the city and the Board of Education resorted to the nineteenth-century substitute for money, scrip, to pay their employees. Over a period of several months, $42 million was placed in circulation. (Nationally, the figure was approximately $1 billion.) Accepted as "legal tender," the scrip helped to start commerce flowing again.

Mayor Murphy was convinced that the cities must obtain, and keep, the ear of the new Democratic administration and Congress. The United States Conference of Mayors was transformed into a permanent organization, headquartered in Washington.

On March 4, Roosevelt was inaugurated as President. Two days later, he declared a national bank holiday. Exhibiting the pragmatic mixture of conservatism and radicalism that was to mark his administration, he resisted the urging of the Progressives that he nationalize the banking system. Instead, the administration prepared a bill to prohibit the hoarding of gold, and thus return the money in private hands to circulation. Closed banks were to be reorganized and reopened under Federal supervision.

On Sunday, March 12, Roosevelt gave the first of his "fireside chats" over the radio. In his inaugural address he had said: "The only thing we have to fear is fear itself." Now, seemingly addressing each listener individually, he added: "Let us unite in banishing fear."

The next day the banks reopened. General Motors purchased all the stock of the new National Bank of Detroit, which was chartered to take over the remaining assets of the First National Bank and the Guardian National Bank of Commerce. From the shambles of the Ford-backed banks emerged the Manufacturers National Bank. The Guardian Bank of Dearborn and the Dearborn State Bank, which Liebold had been running—and mismanaging—for Henry Ford, crashed along with the rest and were taken over by the Manufacturers Bank. Liebold, who had cracked under the strain and fled to northern

309

Michigan, was tracked down by Bennett's spies and returned in humiliation to Detroit. Stripped of much of his power, he was nevertheless retained by Ford, who was afraid of what he knew and might disclose.

As the country began to believe that the new President would *act,* the psychological depression lifted. Although nothing, in fact, had changed, a mood of euphoria swept the land. A "God-sent man," said Cardinal O'Connell. New York Congressman Hamilton Fish hailed the administration as "an American dictatorship based on the consent of the governed without any violation of individual liberty or human rights." [1] Yet the number of Americans calling for a Mussolini was growing larger, not smaller. Had the President been so inclined, he could have obtained congressional enactment of bills that would have given him almost dictatorial powers.*

In contrast to the immobilizing dogmatism of Hoover, Roosevelt adopted a pragmatic activism that astonished both his friends and his critics. During the first three months of the new administration, the famous "One Hundred Days," the relationship between the Federal and state and local governments, and between the Federal government and the people themselves underwent the most fundamental change since the adoption of the Constitution.

The concept that the Federal government could deal directly with the American people without using the states as intermediaries—a concept articulated before only in wartime—was accepted in fact, without being spelled out, by both the executive and the Congress.

On the heels of legislation placing the banking system back in operation, a bill to establish a Civilian Conservation Corps was passed. The Labor Department recruited the eligible—unmarried and unemployed men, ages eighteen to twenty-five—from families on relief. The army operated the camps. And the Forestry and National Park Services set up and supervised the projects of conservation, reforestation, camp building, and trailblazing.

By midsummer, three hundred thousand men were scattered in thirteen hundred camps over America. By the direction of its recruiting effort, the operation made an impact on the economy. Removing three hundred thousand hard-core *surplus* workers from the population centers, it employed them constructively. The pay of thirty dollars a month, however minimal, not only transformed the youths from potential delinquents into consumers, but helped alleviate the economic plight of their families. The number enrolled in the CCC made up approximately 10 percent of the decline in unemployment between the spring and the fall. The economy showed signs of stirring from its deathbed.

In April, the President appointed Mayor Murphy governor-general of the Philippines. That elevated Frank Couzens, the president of the city council, to the mayoralty. At thirty-one he was the youngest mayor in Detroit's history.

To extricate the city from its fiscal morass, the new mayor installed Albert Cobo, a financial expert from the Burroughs Corporation, in the city treasurer's office. Cobo worked out a plan to enable homeowners in arrears to pay their taxes over a period of seven years. In conjunction with the Home Owners Loan Act (the eleventh bill of the Hundred Days), the tax plan altered the climate of hopelessness in which small property owners had been living.

The Home Loan Act provided for long-term Federal refinancing of small

---

* In the world's second leading industrial nation, Germany, the population had abandoned hope that the economy could be righted by normal means. On March 23, 1933, Hitler, a minority chancellor, was granted dictatorial powers for *four years!*

homeowners' mortgages, and reversed the upward trend in nonfarm fore-closures; during the winter and spring of 1933, one thousand families a day had lost their homes. Ultimately, the Home Owners Loan Corporation was to be responsible for financing one out of every ten urban home loans.

In the southwest neighborhood, where the Norveths lived, as in every low-income neighborhood, four years of neglect had taken their toll. It was seven years since the Norveth house had had a coat of paint. In the damp, board-warping winters, the smoke, salt, and chemicals in the air had gnawed at the wood. Throughout the older portions of the city there was a shabbiness that had not been present in 1929. Short of money and uncertain whether they would be able to keep their property, both homeowners and owners of rental property had failed to make needed repairs.

Since the onset of the Depression, nearly 10 percent of the city's population had left. Hundreds of businesses and industries had gone bankrupt or moved out of obsolete structures. Stores, warehouses, and factories were abandoned to decay. Though the city had never had many amenities, the pace of activity had created a tawdry mask. But now the ball was over, and the mask was faded and torn. The city, quite literally, was rotting.

There was little the municipal government could do to halt the deterioration. The city's credit rating was so poor that bankers charged $125 million in additional interest to refinance Detroit's $278 million debt. Revenues were not enough for allocations to capital projects. Not until 1938 were appropriations again made for the sinking fund.

When Congress, therefore, in June, 1933, established the National Industrial Recovery Administration and the Public Works Administration, Detroit seized the opportunity to obtain Federal funds for construction. In the fall, Acting Mayor John Smith journeyed to Washington to see Secretary of the Interior Harold Ickes (who also ran PWA). On November 23, the Federal Emergency Housing Corporation granted the city $3.2 million for slum clearance and the construction of low-cost housing. The next day Smith appointed a five-member Housing Commission to administer the program. For secretary-director he chose Josephine Gomon, who thereby became the first director of the first housing program in the United States.*

Hiring two thousand people, many of them college graduates, Josephine Gomon set about making a survey of housing in the city. She found that it was not unusual for two or three families to be sharing one room. The full picture of the inflated real estate values, the deterioration that had taken place, and the dreadful physical condition of the city became apparent. Construction in the city had all but ceased—$183 million in 1926, it was down to $4 million in 1933.

The Public Works Administration proceeded slowly in Detroit, as every-where. Not until a sweltering day in midsummer of 1934 did the project direc-tor, Ray Carman, a Southerner, appear from Washington. When Carman saw that one of Jo Gomon's two secretaries was black, he halted and stared at her:

"I'm not used to niggers sitting in my presence," he declared.

"*She* belongs here," Mrs. Gomon retorted. "Where you belong, I don't know." She suggested he find an office someplace else.[2]

* The legislation ultimately was responsible for the building of public housing projects in thirty-seven cities.

That was only the beginning of the conflict. When Mrs. Gomon set up a consortium of architects to design the housing, she was unable to discover any Negro architects in the city. She therefore included two black draftsmen. Carman returned the list to her with the names of the two blacks scratched out. An impasse developed. Jo Gomon carried her case directly to Washington. Colonel Horatio Hackett, head of the housing division, arrived from Washington. Handing Carman a contract, he said:

"This is it."

"Not as long as those niggers are on there," retorted Carman, who was unaware that Ickes had been president of the Chicago chapter of the NAACP.[3]

The Negroes stayed. On September 9, 1934, Eleanor Roosevelt officiated at ceremonies marking the start of the razing of slums on the east side of Woodward Avenue. Nevertheless, like many other Federal housing developments, the project was to go through numerous twists and turns before a single new unit was erected. Jo Gomon's victory over Ray Carman was more the exception than the rule. In most Federal programs, especially in the South, Negroes continued to be discriminated against. Nowhere was this truer than in agriculture.

69

The Bubbling Earth,
the Drifting Land

PRICES OF SOME AGRICULTURAL PRODUCTS WERE THE LOWEST IN THREE HUN-
dred years. Huge surpluses of cotton, wheat, hogs, and tobacco bubbled like
lava out of the earth. In a renewal of the movement launched a year earlier
by the Farmers Holiday Association, farmers blocked roads, halted trucks,
and scattered and burned their contents. Throughout the Midwest sheriffs were
challenged by groups of shotgun-toting farmers protecting their homes from
foreclosure.*

Since increasing the demand for crops seemed impossible, the only alternative
was to reduce the supply. To bring about the reduction, farmers would have to
be paid to produce less and to destroy their crops.

On May 12, 1933, Congress passed the Agricultural Adjustment Act. Insti-
tuting a planned system of agriculture, it caused Republican conservatives to
agonize that it was "Bolshevistic."

The agricultural extension service and its network of county agents were
pressed into service to administer the AAA. Before fall, enough farmers had
signed up to plow under one fourth of the cotton crop; in return they received
more than one million dollars. Six million piglets were slaughtered in an heroic
measure of porcine population control.

The Commodity Credit Corporation was established as a mechanism to
stabilize prices. In the fall of 1933, with cotton selling for eight to nine cents
a pound, the CCC offered to lend ten cents a pound to farmers who would
participate in the acreage reduction program for 1934. In security for the
interest-free loan, the government would take the cotton. If the price rose above
ten cents a pound, the farmer could redeem the cotton and sell it on the open
market at a profit. Soon the concept was extended to wheat, corn, tobacco, and,
ultimately and inevitably, to dairy products and other commodities.

* In late April, 1933, when a county judge in northwest Iowa refused to halt foreclosure
proceedings, five hundred infuriated farmers kidnaped him, drove him out of town, twisted
a rope around his neck, looped it over a telephone pole, and only at the last moment desisted
from lynching him. As the threat to authority continued to grow, the governor mobilized the
national guard. A large portion of the state took on the appearance of occupied territory.

The AAA appeared a rational prescription for the ills of agricultural prices.*
It represented, however, a fragmentary approach. No cognizance was taken of
the impact upon small farmers, or upon the economy as a whole. No attempt
was made to study or to project the long-range effects.

The depression in agriculture had been brought about by overproduction,
which pushed down prices. The depression in industry was generated by the
attempt to meet the problem of overproduction through the curtailment of
production and the concurrent maintenance of prices; the result was a self-
reinforcing cycle of unemployment and reduced purchasing power. The AAA
was now applying, inadvertently, the industrial solution to the agricultural
problem.

The price-support payments aided larger farms to electrify and mechanize.†
Since one tractor could do the work of three men with mules, either: 1) three
men would have to share one tractor, each working four hours a day instead
of twelve; or 2) the acreage under cultivation and the yield would triple; or
3) if the number of hours worked and the yield were to remain the same, the
number of workers would have to be reduced by two thirds.

In practice, farmers worked shorter hours. The surpluses, following a temporary reduction in the mid-1930's, grew larger than ever. (The 1937 cotton
crop was the biggest in history.) The farms supported fewer people. Smaller
farmers, for whom support payments were not enough to aid in mechanization
—and for whom large capital investments would, in any case, be inefficient—
saw their competitive position eroded further. In North Carolina, a petition by
318 white farmers complained that "Two years of the AAA . . . had the
effect of making the powerful farmer more powerful and the weaker farmer
weaker. . . . He had no opportunity to expand unless he could get a pull
somewhere further up in the endless chain of governmental machinery so designed as to make all little farmers completely helpless." [1]

The smaller farmers were pushed off the land. With them, as production was
cut back, went hired hands and sharecroppers, the agricultural equivalent of
the unskilled workers.‡ Starting in 1935, even as the rural birth rate continued
to outpace the urban, there was an uninterrupted ten-year decline in farm
employment. In 1938, 1,111,000 fewer persons were working on farms than
three years earlier. In the next three years, nearly another million left. In six
years, one out of every six farm workers abandoned the land.

Especially hard hit were the Negroes. Both the Agriculture Department and
the congressional committees dealing with agriculture were dominated by
Southerners, many of them unabashedly bigoted. ("Cotton Ed" Smith, chairman of the Senate Agriculture Committee, filled his committee's hearing records

---

* Between 1932 and 1937 cash farm income rose from $4.7 to $9.2 billion. The index of
farm prices rose from 68 to 122 of the 1909–1914 average, and the price of some commodities as much as septupled. While the prices farmers paid for manufactured goods increased
7 percent, the prices received by farmers went up 79 percent.
† Between 1935 and 1938 the number of tractors on farms went up by 332,000, an increase
of nearly a third. Between 1935, when the Rural Electrification Administration was established, and 1940, the number of farms with electricity increased from 744,000 to 1,853,000,
30 percent of the total.
‡ By 1939 the top 10 percent of farms accounted for 48.1 percent of production, 4.5 percent more than a decade earlier. The bottom 50 percent, on the other hand, accounted for
less than 12 percent of production. As the number of farms decreased from 6,812,000 in
1934 to 6,097,000 in 1940, *per capita* farm income rose 50 percent more than total cash
income.

with jokes about "great big buck niggers.") [2] The conservatives easily squashed a challenge by the Agriculture Department's left-wingers—notably the Communist cell led by Alger Hiss and Lee Pressman—and left control over disbursements to local committees. The committees, which were dominated by the Bourbon landowners, channeled the Federal payments into their own pockets, not to the needy tenants and sharecroppers. When, in the middle 1930's, the system was changed and checks were sent directly to the persons farming the land, the landowners either increased the rents as a form of kickback, or forced the tenants off the land and substituted hired workers with tractors in their stead.

During the decade the number of Negro tenants and sharecroppers in the South dropped by two hundred thousand, 30 percent of the total. Including the families of the dispossessed, well over a million blacks were trudging the dusty roads toward the cities. Illiterate, ignorant of modern society, they were in the true sense *plantation* Negroes, for whom time had stopped in 1865. Thrust into urban areas, they could perform only the most rudimentary manual labor in a market in which such labor was not merely superabundant, but irrelevant. Three fourths of the Negro families in the South had an income below that considered adequate only for an emergency budget, and many were spending no more than four cents per person per meal. Between 1933 and 1935, even as the economy was gaining strength, the number of Negroes on relief increased from 18 to 30 percent.

On the Oklahoma-Kansas border a brown-skinned Negro named Wallace Mirow was desperately trying to hold on to his land, and every day finding it more impossible to do so.

Wallace Mirow's father, David, had been the offspring of a white Southern physician and his mulatto mistress. David Mirow had been sent North to obtain an education. After attending Oberlin, in Ohio, he had become a pharmacist in Cleveland. Wally's older brother had inherited the business. His younger sister had become a schoolteacher.

Wally had been one of the hundreds of thousands of boys and young men who had responded to the plea for help during the agricultural boom years of the war. In the summer of 1918 he had gone to work on the farm of an uncle in southwestern Kansas. There he had fallen in love with a handsome, high-cheeked girl of part-Negro and part-Cherokee extraction, whose ancestors had been marched from Georgia to Oklahoma by General Cass. Much to his surprise, Wally found himself a farmer. Although he was a poor farmer, he was a good manager. For the first few years the farm did well.

Then had come the steady decline in farm prices. The first reaction to the bad times of the 1920's had been to borrow money to keep planting in anticipation of the recovery. But prices had continued to fall. The burden of the accumulated debts had become heavier. Farmer after farmer had been bankrupted. Much of the land west of a line running roughly from Corpus Christi, Texas, up through the Oklahoma Panhandle and North Platte, Nebraska, to the Missouri River was semiarid and should never have been cultivated. The railroads had received large sections of it as part of their land grants. During a period of unusually heavy rainfall in the nineteenth century, the railroads had sold the land to settlers.

From then on, the land was alternately farmed and abandoned according to rainfall and agricultural prices. Denuded and depredated, it was defenseless against the new and greater drought that appeared almost simultaneously with the onset of the Depression.

By 1932 the area had hardly a farmer who was not on the brink of bankruptcy. In the small towns grass was growing in the unpaved streets and between the boards of the wooden sidewalks.

In 1934 the winds came to gather the harvest sown by man. Hundreds of thousands of acres of topsoil, carrying fields of wheat and corn with them, blew across the sky. The sun was turned into a red moon, and the moon swayed like a faded Chinese lantern. The wind powdered the leaves and stalks of crops with earth, silted the wells, and piled chest-high drifts of dirt against the doors and windows of the Mirow house. Wally and Antoinette Mirow slept in dirt, ate dirt, and drank dirt. Day by day their resistance was worn away. Ultimately, like tens of thousands of others, they gave in.

Neither Mirow's wife, Antoinette, nor his twelve-year-old daughter, Irma, had ever been more than forty miles from home. Mirow loaded them into the family's truck, and headed for Cleveland. Myriads of other people were streaming off the land into the cities of the East, the North, and the West.

Wally's brother was not overjoyed to see him. Business was bad. The colored coming up from the South, he complained, were ruining the neighborhood. White families, one after another, were moving out. An acquaintance visiting from Michigan suggested that since auto production was on the upswing, Wally might find opportunities better in Detroit. Wally decided to drive back with him.

In Detroit, Mirow was able to hire out his truck for short hauls. In a few months he set himself up as a coal and ice dealer. Clearing more than $150 a month in the winter and averaging about $135 a month the year round, he was able to establish his family in moderate comfort.

Nevertheless, Antoinette, lonely, unable to adjust to the city, was unhappy. She communicated her unhappiness to her daughter Irma, whose country schooling, informal and personal, had failed to prepare her for the demanding, organized, formalized, and inflexible city schools. She did poorly. The other children made fun of her. Together with her mother she took refuge in frequent illnesses. These allowed her to stay home, and reduced the demands made on her by the urban environment.

70

The Destroyer of the Spirit

HARD HIT BY TAX DELINQUENCIES, A 40 PERCENT DECLINE IN ASSESSED VALUA-tion, and the measure limiting state property taxes to 1.5 percent of assessed valuation, the schools were unable to cope with the new influx of migrants. Of the 1.5 percent tax, only .4 percent went to the schools. Since the median assessed valuation of homes in the city was but $3,000, state support for the schools was an average of $12 a year per family. Although in 1935 there were 260,000 pupils in the schools, more than twice the number there had been in 1920, the budget was reduced to $23 million, $8 million less than in 1920. There was talk of keeping the schools open only six months of the year.

Amidst the crisis, Congress in May, 1933, established the Federal Emergency Relief Administration. For the first time in American history, there was acknowl-edgment that people besides drunks, bums, and ne'er-do-wells were unable to find jobs. Schoolteachers and other professional and white-collar workers joined the lines. Relief became "respectable."

Michigan's Governor Comstock, in conformance with the Federal law, estab-lished the state Emergency Welfare Relief Commission, which was empowered to appoint county commissions to administer relief locally. Some 624,000 persons began drawing checks. To provide work for unemployed teachers, the Federal Emergency Relief Administration (FERA) set up adult education classes. By the end of the year, 3,000 teachers in the state were back in the classrooms.

FERA ended the chaos of locally administered relief. The practice of detailed case investigations to separate "moochers" from those who were worthy of relief was instituted. Since FERA was aiding some four million families in the nation, and funds were never adequate, supervisors emphasized to their growing number of caseworkers that marginal applicants were to be rejected. Politically it was advantageous to be able to show to the critics of relief a high percentage of applicant rejections. A caseworker was expected to turn down between 25 and 30 percent of applicants. If he averaged fewer rejections, he was subject to suspicions of leniency; if more, he was likely to be praised for his diligence.

His lifelong experience as a social worker led Harry Hopkins,* the director of FERA, to believe that relief degraded and demoralized people. He was determined, therefore, to channel relief funds into a program of reemployment.

In November of 1933 his determination became a reality in the form of the Civil Works Administration (CWA). Joining the Public Works Administration and the CCC in putting the unemployed to work, the CWA created more than four million jobs. Engineers, teachers, writers, clerks, mechanics—all were placed in positions utilizing their skills. During its brief existence—the program was terminated in May, 1934—the Civil Works Administration built roads, schools, airports, parks, sewers, and recreation areas.

In Michigan, 170,000 workers were enrolled in CWA. Half were drawn from relief cases, and half from the unemployed not on relief. As all of the various Federal programs—the CCC, PWA, FERA, CWA—put people to work, or at least took them off the streets, unemployment in Michigan dropped dramatically. By May, 1934, it was down to 242,000, one third of what it had been a year earlier. As unemployment dropped, so did the incidence of crime—in Detroit the number of economic crimes was down 15 percent from the previous year.

But as soon as CWA was terminated, unemployment shot up again. The Michigan Relief Administration set up its own projects. People were put to work cannning surplus food. In a little more than a year, they packed 1.7 million cans. Hundreds of thousands of household articles and items of clothing were manufactured. The program of public works was continued. Similar projects were under way in Ohio and other states.

Although no one spoke of it in such terms, the division of America into two populations was receiving official recognition. The productivity of one population was competitive. That of the other was not. Common sense dictated that the people in the subeconomy should be restored to useful work. Nevertheless, as government subsidies helped the economic dropouts resume functional lives, the effort was resented and opposed by farmers, shopkeepers, food processors, manufacturers of furniture, clothing, and the like, who regarded the self-help enterprises as being in competition. In truth, the people who were employed and to whom the finished goods were distributed had ceased to be consumers in the regular economy years before.

Roosevelt, by this time, was as opposed as Hopkins to the dole. The average monthly grant of twenty-five dollars per family served little purpose other than to prevent starvation (but not malnutrition). The Keynesian concept that government itself was the heart of the economy and could, therefore, control its tempo through increasing or decreasing the flow of money, was having a hard time bursting through the covers of the books in which it was contained. But if Roosevelt were still committed, in theory, to governmental economy and a balanced budget, he was a pragmatist who knew that America could not much longer exist as a democracy if millions of its people were not able to participate in its economy.

The administration's public works program, PWA, had been intended to get people off relief. But much had happened since the days when Pingree had used public works to provide jobs for the unemployed. More than a dozen years before, Couzens had found it impractical to take work from efficient machinery

* The son of an Iowa farmer, Hopkins had been born the year before Hoover entered Stanford University. After graduating from Grinnell College, he had by chance been directed into social work in the slums of New York. Roosevelt, as governor, had named him director of the New York state relief agency, and he became the "social worker" in the President's administration.

and give it to far less efficient men. As overseer of PWA, Secretary of the Interior Ickes, a Progressive who had broken with the Republicans, insisted on efficiency and a maximum return to the government for its money. Seldom was a government department run in such shipshape fashion. During the 1930's PWA was the principal construction organization in America. It built airports, cruisers, and the Hoover, Bonneville, and Grand Coulee Dams, the largest in American history. In the Tennessee Valley—saved by Senator George Norris and the Progressives from falling into the domain of Henry Ford—it transformed a backwater into a pulsating industrial-agricultural area that was the prototype of regional development. In Detroit and other tax-starved cities PWA provided the principal financing for school construction and for the renovation and building of physical facilities. It emphasized the reduction of pollution—in 1936, Detroit, like most other cities and nearly all industry, was still dumping its sewage raw into the river. (The Ford plant had polluted the Rouge River so badly that the plant itself was unable to use the water any longer.) With PWA funds the city began construction of a sewage treatment plant, and, to go with it, the Conners Creek sewer, the largest in the world.

The PWA emphasis on projects that required heavy capital investments and employment of a large percentage of skilled labor did wonders for business. But it made only peripheral inroads into the masses of the unemployed. By the end of the summer of 1934 it was evident to the President and to Hopkins that a new, permanent agency would be needed to get the unemployed off the relief rolls and back to work.

During the fall of 1934, the concept of a massive government employment program took shape. Since its primary aim was to put men to work, it was intended to complement the Public Works Administration, which expended only 30 percent of its funds for labor. In contrast, the program proposed by Hopkins aimed at allocating 75 percent of expenditures for labor.

In the January, 1935, budget message to Congress, the President proposed putting 3.5 million men to work. The "security wage" would be more than relief, but less than prevailing wages in private enterprise, so that men would return to private employment as soon as the economy revived. Roosevelt was emphatic that "the Federal government must and shall quit the business of relief. . . . Continued dependence upon relief induces a spiritual and moral disintegration fundamentally destructive to the national fiber. To dole out relief in this way is to administer a narcotic, a subtle destroyer of the human spirit." [1]

After lengthy debate, Congress passed the bill. To the chagrin of Ickes, the efficiency expert, the President placed Hopkins, the social welfare man, in charge of the new agency. Hopkins named it the Works Progress Administration (WPA). Not only the nation but the District of Columbia post office had difficulty distinguishing between the PWA and the WPA.*

Considering a Federal deficit of nearly $3 billion in 1934, and a total four-year deficit of $7.77 billion, Hoover Republicans viewed WPA and its projected $5 billion yearly expenditure as outrageous. Small businessmen and shopkeepers, affected only indirectly by the outpouring of social and economic legislation from Washington, thought of it as a vast boondoggle. Businessmen had nearly given up on the free enterprise system when it appeared on its deathbed in 1933. Now, as the economy regained vigor, they complained of the bitter taste of the medicine. The President was accused of trying to "sovietize America."

---

* There were already two CCC's; the Commodity Credit Corporation, and the Civilian Conservation Corps.

71

The National Runaround

IN FACT, IT WAS THE EARLY MEASURES OF THE NEW DEAL, ENTHUSIASTICALLY
supported by businessmen, which threatened far more to impose an authoritarian
state-planned system on American life.

Throughout the latter years of the Hoover Administration, business had
clamored for a system of controls that would curtail competition, fix prices,
and allocate production. Organized labor and most members of Congress, conversely, demanded an end to sweatshops and the exploitation of labor. Only by
reducing hours and raising wages could the available work be spread and the
purchasing power of workers be increased.

In the late spring of 1933, the demands of labor and of business were melded
together into the National Industrial Recovery Act. When Roosevelt signed the
bill in June, he called it "the most important and far-reaching legislation ever
enacted by the American Congress." [1]

On one hand it granted the right of collective bargaining to labor, protected
union members from intimidation by employers, and established a maximum
work week (forty hours) and a minimum wage (thirty cents an hour) in the
production of goods shipped in interstate commerce. On the other hand, exempting industries from antitrust laws, it promised to promote trade associations to
establish codes of fair competition within industries.

The proponents of statewide economic planning, who established a strong
foothold in the Federal government with the advent of the Roosevelt Administration, regarded the National Industrial Recovery Act as a means to create
order out of chaos. Each industry was to be governed by a council that would
establish standards and regulations. The councils were to promote fair labor
standards, eliminate overproduction, and end cutthroat competition. The end
effect, through exemption from the antitrust laws, was to be price fixing.

By December, 1933, approximately two million employers were signed up,
and seven hundred codes were agreed to by industries. But, as small businessmen had feared, the trade councils, with their enormous powers, were dominated
by the larger companies, who established industry codes favoring themselves.

Within each industry the administrators of the codes and the officers of the trade associations commonly were one and the same person. The price fixing and restraint of trade that would have been cause for antitrust prosecutions before the advent of the National Recovery Administration (NRA) became part of government policy within it. But the Federal machinery that was supposed to supervise operations and manage the economy remained skeletal.

Thousands of establishments displayed the Blue Eagle emblem of compliance while violating the codes. Controls and penalties were nonexistent. The national economic council that was supposed to oversee the entire operation and maintain the balance between different industries was never organized. In an experience that was later to be repeated with the Office of Price Administration, it became evident that it was nearly impossible to institute national economic controls without establishing a large bureaucratic apparatus, the existence of which would be as great a threat to the economy as the malpractices it was intended to curb.

The handful of survivors of the once diversified and individualistic automobile industry adopted the code—and adhered to or ignored it as suited their purpose. After attempting and failing to write an open-shop clause into the code, management succeeded in substituting a "merit clause" that worked just as effectively. Although NRA guaranteed workers' rights to organize, it was soon apparent that any worker who joined a union lacked "merit." The companies had no more intention of permitting unionization in 1933 than in 1929, when they had unanimously ignored a feeler from AFL President Green.

Throughout the United States, businessmen viewed the provisions of the act conducive to unionism as communistic. It was only after the most bitter wrangle that the textile industry agreed to outlaw child labor.

Ford, at first, indicated that he would participate in drawing up the auto industry code and become a member of the association. But after the AFL sent its first full-time organizer to Detroit in May, 1933, and Ford was given to understand that he was expected to negotiate with the union, he abruptly changed his mind. Still considering himself the best friend the worker had ever had, he believed that it was *he* himself who represented and bargained for the workers at the Ford Motor Company.

In September, 1933, when twenty-five hundred Ford workers formed an AFL local at the Chester, Pennsylvania, assembly plant, Ford closed down the plant, and a short time later reopened it with nonunion labor. The secretary of the local, it turned out, was one of Bennett's spies. The AFL failed to support the workers. NRA officials were indignant, but inactive.

During the winter, the Mechanics Education Society formed a chapter among the tool-and-die workers at River Rouge. As the aristocrats of labor, the tool-and-die men felt secure, and some even began wearing union buttons around the plant.

Bennett soon knew every man that belonged to the union. One by one, he transferred all two hundred fifty into the same department. He then abolished the department. No one had been "fired," but they all were out of work. The lesson was not lost on other workers.

Referring to the NRA as the "national run around," union leaders threatened a nationwide strike in March, 1934. President Roosevelt, in his inimitable fashion, proposed a compromise: the manufacturers would not obstruct organization, but the locals that were formed could be "company unions." Fewer than half of the auto workers joined unions. Nine tenths of the locals were weak and company-controlled. Bennett organized the Ford Brotherhood of America, and shortly had the signatures of 80,698 out of 82,064 employees on a "loyalty pledge." When workers at the General Motors and Hudson plants struck, they were provided with no more protection against company retaliation by the NRA and AFL than the workers at the Ford assembly plant. G.M. President Sloan expressed the opinion:

"All's well that ends well." [2]

After three years of inventory liquidation, industrial production had bottomed out in 1932. Federal expenditures increased $2.4 billion, or 60 percent, between 1933 and 1934. Of this sum, approximately $1.5 billion went into the hands of consumers through outright relief, or through projects such as the CCC and CWA. On the local level these expenditures had an enormous effect. Between 1933 and 1937 Federal aid in Detroit and Wayne County totaled $102 million. Since much of this was, in essence, "new money," created by deficit spending, it acted as a stimulant to purchasing power and production.

By 1935, the index of industrial production was 50 percent above its 1932 low. The durable goods index had increased 100 percent. Annual expenditures by consumers were up $7.1 billion. Production of passenger cars more than tripled, from 1.1 million in 1932 to 3.7 million in 1936.

By 1934 the General Motors share of the resurgent auto market was inching toward 50 percent. In 1934, the Chevrolet division was unable to meet demand. In 1935, the company took the first steps toward a new program of expansion.

Yet if business indicated every sign of recovery, the effect of this recovery on the depressed population was negligible. Hard times had exacerbated the trend toward replacing less productive human workers with more productive machines and more efficient assembly lines. The establishment of minimum wage rates under the NRA served, actually, to precipitate additional marginal workers out of the economy. An estimated half million Negroes lost their jobs. Development of new chemicals and metal alloys created spectacular breakthroughs. Technical journals were filled with articles describing new methods to reduce costs and increase productivity.

Thus, while politicians and economists in the early New Deal years continued to place emphasis on a business revival in the belief that there was an inflexible link between an increase in production and a reduction in unemployment, in truth the link was rubbery; as production increased, the link stretched, so that employment increased at a slower rate than production. Inevitably, the result would again be overproduction.

The economic cycles themselves were a factor pushing industry toward more intensive use of machinery. During a downturn the oldest, most inefficient plants, employing the largest amount of labor, are the ones closed first. Any long-term drop in production, therefore, tends to have a multiplier effect on unemployment. As the depression continues, the remaining plants are operated further and further below capacity. Productivity drops. More workers are employed than warranted by the output.

During the initial stages of the recovery, therefore, an enormous amount of slack can be taken up. Output increases more rapidly than the number of workers on the assembly lines. The old, obsolete plants which had the highest employment of labor will never be put back into operation. In their stead—if the recovery lasts long enough—new plants will be built; more mechanized plants using even less manpower. Not until there is a major upsurge in capital investment and plant construction will the recovery bite deeply into unemployment. And then, because of the tendency for production to outpace consumption, the surge in employment will be difficult to sustain.

Between 1932 and 1935, as the production index increased 50 percent, employment in manufacturing rose by only 2.1 million, approximately 30 percent. Payrolls increased only 20 percent. In the auto industry fewer men, working shorter hours, were turning out more vehicles in 1936 than in 1928. Corporations, which had lost $2.3 billion before taxes in 1932, showed profits of $3.6 billion in 1935. In Detroit, 17 percent of the labor force—compared to 13 percent in 1930—remained out of work. Nationally, nearly eleven million Americans—two of every seven outside of agriculture—were still unemployed.

It was difficult to comprehend—and scarcely anyone did. If business was once again prospering, why wasn't there more work for people? Since the reasons were obscure, anyone could create his own interpretation. It was a culture conducive to demagoguery and violence.

72

"Roosevelt or Ruin"

To FATHER COUGHLIN, THE SOLUTION SEEMED SIMPLE. SMITE THE BANKERS, abandon gold as a basis of the monetary system; use silver to inflate the money supply.

On November 27, 1933, fifteen thousand persons crowded into the New York Hippodrome to hear Coughlin and Senator Elmer Thomas of Oklahoma denounce the bankers, who continued to contend that the future of the country lay with "gold dollars as against baloney dollars." The future of the country, Father Coughlin predicted, would be "a revolution that will make the French Revolution look silly" if the President were not given the power to revalue the dollar. "It is either Roosevelt or ruin." [1]

In January, 1934, Congress passed the Gold Reserve Act. Roosevelt, raising the price of gold to thirty-five dollars an ounce, thereby devalued the dollar slightly more than 40 percent. Overnight the value of the Treasury's stock of gold increased by three billion dollars, enabling the government, if it wished, to print that much more money without affecting the gold reserve ratio. Bankers and financiers, who had regarded gold as the constant sun around which the financial world revolved, were shattered by the thought that henceforward the United States Government might manipulate the value of gold. Budget Director Lewis Douglas believed it meant "the end of Western civilization." [2]

It marked, in fact, the initiation by the Federal government of "managed" monetary and fiscal policies; policies designed to make more money available and stimulate the economy when it showed signs of slowing down, and to contract the money supply during periods of inflation.

Father Coughlin, however, continued to press the administration to engage in a policy of silver purchases that would bring about an increase in the price of silver. Confident of his influence, he was speculating heavily in the silver market. From his retreat atop the 150-foot tower in Royal Oak he unleashed thunderbolts at the financiers who "without either the blood of patriotism or of Christianity flowing in their veins have shackled the lives of men and of nations with the ponderous links of their golden chains."

Father Coughlin's influence on the American public continued to be immense. Roosevelt's attempt to save capitalism, he believed, was hopeless and misguided. Legislation like the Banking Act, which appeared to cater to the interests of business, incensed him. "Democracy is doomed," he intoned. "It is [either] fascism or Communism." [3] Only a benevolent dictatorship could save America.

To counter the priest's relentless pressure for the expansion of silver purchases, the Roosevelt Administration revealed his speculations. That revelation, naturally, sent Father Coughlin into paroxysms of fury. Roosevelt, nevertheless, was not prepared to write Father Coughlin off as an adversary. The President used two prominent Catholics, former Mayor Murphy and Joseph P. Kennedy, as emissaries to cajole him and to bargain with him, and invited him to Hyde Park and the White House.

Yet wooing Father Coughlin was one thing. Toning him down was quite another. So long as the American population continued to be divided into two parts, one economically viable and the other not, and so long as unemployment persisted, Father Coughlin was a rallying point for the downtrodden and the poor, and for the politicians who demanded not only a New Deal, but, in Father Coughlin's words, a "new deck."

Author Upton Sinclair, who was running for governor of California on a semi-Socialist platform, made a pilgrimage to the tower and received the priest's blessing. Sinclair was well on his way to victory when the motion picture industry, under the leadership of the Republican state chairman, Louis B. Mayer, launched the most vicious smear campaign in the history of American politics against him. (Producing fake newsreels, the studios used actors to impersonate cranks, Communists, and anarchists who loudly voiced their support for Sinclair, while other actors in the guise of "Mom" and "Pop" declared forthrightly for his opponent.) To Father Coughlin, the campaign seemed a declaration of war. A week after Sinclair's defeat in November, 1934, the priest announced the formation of the National Union for Social Justice.

The next month he proposed a ten-billion-dollar public works program of road building, agricultural reclamation, and slum clearance, coupled with nationalization of natural resources, and a guaranteed annual wage. In April, 1935, he drew fifteen thousand to a rally in Detroit. The next month he had twenty-three thousand at Madison Square Garden in New York. To President Roosevelt's alarm, the National Union for Social Justice was one of a trio of political movements beginning to congeal into a "third party."

The second was a movement launched in the fall of 1933 by a retired California physician, Dr. Francis Townsend. Appalled by the callous disregard for the poverty-stricken aged, whom he watched scavenging through garbage cans, Dr. Townsend suggested that everyone over the age of sixty should be retired on a pension of $150 a month (soon raised to $200 a month). The pension would enable the aged to live decently, reduce the supply of labor (and hence raise wages), and stimulate the economy, since the aged would be required by law to spend, not to bank, their pensions.

The idea spread across the country with the rapidity of the telegraph and radio. By the fall of 1934 hundreds of thousands of the aged, singing "Onward Townsend Soldiers," were organized into clubs in every city of the nation.

The organization was strong enough to play a significant role in the election of a number of congressmen. In January, 1935, one of them introduced a bill that incorporated the essentials of the Townsend plan and provided financing through a transaction tax. The only hitch was that at a time when the Gross National Product was $65 billion, and the total of all taxes collected $12 billion, the estimated cost of the pension was $24 billion.

The third movement was the "Share Our Wealth Society" of Senator Huey P. Long, Jr. Emerging from the Fundamentalist and Populist-oriented hill country of northern Louisiana, Long rallied the hill folk and the swamp people, the slum dwellers and the unschooled, the men with blue collars and dirty fingernails. Casting himself as the Robin Hood of the bayous who would tax the rich and better the lot of the poor, he made the state his personal fiefdom, and pronounced: "I'm the constitution around here now." He became estranged from Roosevelt—whom he had supported in 1932—when the President refused to give him control over Louisiana patronage but reinstituted an Internal Revenue Bureau investigation initiated by the Hoover Administration. On the floor of the Senate, Long announced:

"It will not be long until there will be a mob assembling here to hang Senators from the rafters of the Senate. I have to decide whether I will stay and be hung with you, or go out and lead the mob." [4]

Long proposed to confiscate all personal income over $1 million and all inheritances over $5 million, and to grant everyone a homestead allowance of $5,000 and a minimum annual income of $2,000. In January, 1934, he incorporated his "Society." Its direction was assigned to the Reverend Gerald L. K. Smith, an eloquent, Fundamentalist, fire-breathing, anti-Semitic preacher. By 1935 the society had established 27,000 clubs with 7 million adherents. Its weekly publication, *American Progress,* had a paid circulation of over 300,000.

These movements were the "respectable" reactions to the continuing trauma of the Depression and its aftermath. But as in major economic crises of the past, there was also a violent undercurrent. Following in the footsteps of the Supreme Order of the Star Spangled Banner, the American Protective Association, and the Ku Klux Klan, came the Black Legion.

The father of the Black Legion was Isaac "Peg Leg" White, a former Detroit police officer. After a violent internal dispute in the KKK, White in 1931 organized two hundred former members into the Black Legion. Mortal enemies of the KKK, the Legion adopted black robes with a skull-and-crossbones insignia.

"The native-born white people of America are menaced on every hand from above and below," the Legion oath declared. "Our ancestors won this land from the savages and paid for it with their blood. . . . The Republicans stand for the rich, while the Democrats seem to be in the grasp of the Pope of Rome."

Recruits were taken to cellars or remote spots in the woods. With spotlights and guns trained on them, they were made to swear "in the name of the God and the devil [to] consecrate my heart, my brains, my body and limbs," and to pray that if they violated the pledge an "avenging God [will] tear my heart out and roast it over the flames of sulphur." [5]

At the same time that the Legion spread through the Midwestern "native American belt," bloody confrontations between labor and management were taking place. In Minneapolis, a middle-class Citizens Alliance confronted the Trotskyite-led teamsters. In May, 1934, two Alliance members were killed in a battle, and the National Guard occupied the city. In a second confrontation in July, the police, shooting into a crowd of pickets, killed two and wounded more than sixty. In San Francisco a two-month-long strike exploded into bloodshed when the Industrial Association attempted to force open the docks. When two strikers were killed and dozens injured by police, enraged workers paralyzed the city by a general strike. So it went from Rhode Island to Oregon, and from Wisconsin to Georgia.

Right-wingers seized upon the opportunity to appeal to the "Americanism" of the mainly Protestant, church-going, blue-collar workers and family men in their twenties and thirties who composed the Black Legion. They gave secret financial support to the Legionnaires and urged action against Commies, Catholics, niggers, foreigners, radicals, and Jews. Front organizations, like the Michigan Relief Association, recruited members by offering welfare benefits.

Like a parasitic disease, the Legion infested the entire social body of Detroit and southeastern Michigan. In Detroit, some sixty to seventy police officers were members. In Father Coughlin's Royal Oak, the chief of police and virtually the entire department were Legionnaires. The Legion's chief recruiter was an employee of the Detroit Board of Health. Wayne County Prosecutor Duncan McCrea signed up—though he later claimed he had joined so many organizations that one more membership meant nothing.

Into the aimless lives of its members, the Legion injected "thrills," excitement, and the opportunity to release their frustrations through violence coated with a patina of approval. Though whippings, bombings, and burnings multiplied, the police failed to make a single arrest. The attraction of the Black Legion increased. Organized into a "guerrilla army" with ranks up to "general," it grew to some two hundred thousand members in Michigan alone. WPA workers, trade unionists, and the treasurer of the Auto Workers Union were among the growing number of murder victims. The statewide coordinator of the Legion suggested to a Department of Health bacteriologist the mass elimination of "class enemies" through the contamination of their milk.

Only when the Black Legionnaires' apparent immunity led to flagrant "mistake" and "thrill" killings were the citizens aroused enough to demand action. Once the crackdown got under way in 1936, scores of Black Legionnaires were rounded up and brought to trial. Thirteen received life sentences, and thirty-seven others were sentenced to prison terms of up to twenty years. But when it became evident that further investigations would snare increasingly prominent persons, the Black Legion was allowed quietly to fade from the public eye.

While the Black Legion was thoroughly in the American tradition, other organizations aimed at producing a Hitlerian solution were springing up. The Khaki Shirts proposed the elimination of the Jews and a policy of American imperialism. A former California real estate promoter and motion picture writer, William D. Pelley, organized an American S.S.—the Silver Shirts. Inevitably, the would-be Nazis of America linked up with the Nazis of Germany. In the anti-Semitic, antiunion climate of the Ford plant at River Rouge, where KKK and Black Legion cells were flourishing, a chemical engineer named Fritz Kuhn joined the Friends of New Germany, and in 1936 founded the German-American Bund.*

---

* Kuhn, who had spent four years in the German infantry during World War I, lost his job in 1923 when the new American tariff further disrupted the German chemical industry. Unable to come to America because of the new quota restricting immigration, he emigrated to Mexico, and finally arrived in the United States about 1928. He went immediately to Detroit, and worked for Ford for eight years until he was fired for trying to seduce a nurse in an elevator at Ford Hospital. Kuhn's brother was appointed to the German Supreme Court by Hitler.

Ford's refusal to have anything to do with the NRA had degenerated into a bitter feud between Ford and the administration. Boycotting Ford products, the Federal government caused the company to lose millions of dollars in orders. At Ford, the Blue Eagle was referred to as the "Roosevelt buzzard," and the New Deal became the "Raw Deal."

All this, however, was but prologue. Determined to bring back into circulation the billions of dollars salted away in corporate treasuries and in a few private hands, the administration prepared two measures. One was a 60 percent tax on undistributed corporate profits. The other was an inheritance tax that in the upper brackets went as high as 70 percent. "The transmission from generation to generation of vast fortunes . . . is not consistent with the ideals and sentiments of the American people," President Roosevelt told Congress in 1935.[6]

The second of the two measures was immediately recognized as being directed at Ford. Furious and consumed by anxiety, Ford called it a "soak-the-rich" scheme and a "Ford-wrecking" plan that would drive the company into the hands of Wall Street and the "money changers."

Although Ford once referred to endowment as "the opiate of the imagination," he had as early as 1923 considered establishing a Ford Foundation whose purpose would be "a chance not a charity." To avoid payment by the family of over three hundred million dollars in taxes when Ford died, company attorneys devised a scheme to split the company stock into voting and nonvoting shares. The voting stock would remain entirely in family hands. The nonvoting stock would be assigned to a Ford Foundation.

In January, 1936, without any public announcement, the foundation was incorporated. Edsel made out a check for twenty-five thousand dollars as an initial contribution. "It will be on a small scale and I have no intention of making it larger," he declared.[7] *

---

* Horace Rackham, one of the two attorneys who had drawn up the incorporation papers for the Ford Motor Company in 1903 and borrowed money to buy stock, had left fourteen million dollars with which to establish a foundation when he died in 1933. Couzens had set up the Children's Fund of Michigan. Several other auto pioneers, especially those participating in G.M.'s success, established foundations.

73

The Middle of the Road

AS OLD-LINE DEMOCRATS WERE ALIENATED FROM THE NEW DEAL AND LONG drained off the Populists, Roosevelt's problem was to shape a winning coalition for the 1936 election. Still hoping to mollify Father Coughlin, the President was having lunch with him at Hyde Park when word was relayed that Long had been assassinated in Louisiana.

That removed the expected third-party presidential nominee from the scene. Father Coughlin, however, viewing himself as a kingmaker, had come to the realization that Roosevelt was not a king he could manipulate. In 1936, Father Coughlin, Dr. Townsend, and Long's heir-apparent, the Reverend Gerald L. K. Smith, drew together into one of the more unlikely fusions in American political history. In July, 1936, they met in Cleveland under the banner of the Union party to nominate Congressman William Lemke of North Dakota for President. Lemke was a Populist Republican whose district literally was shriveling up and blowing away under the combined influences of foreclosures, drought, and wind. With his glass eye and haggard features, he looked like a fifth Horseman of the Apocalypse emerging from the red dust of the windstorms.

The Republican nominee, Governor Alfred Landon of Kansas, a political moderate, was occasionally referred to as the "Kansas Coolidge." It was a description hardly tailored to excite anyone except diehard Main Street Republicans.

Roosevelt, in contrast, was a master at occupying the middle ground and preempting the programs of others for his own designs. He lured away the Townsend supporters by introducing his own, milder version of the Townsend Plan, the Social Security Act of 1935, which provided assistance to categories of the "worthy needy": the aged, the blind, and children in families where the father was absent. He kept farmers from flocking to Lemke by pacifying them with price support payments. He employed potential supporters of Father Coughlin on WPA projects, and kept potential recruits for the Silver Shirts working in CCC camps. He was doing more to implement the program of the Republican Progressives than any President since Theodore Roosevelt. By adopting a neutral stance and refusing to identify his administration with big-otry, he conveyed the impression of being in sympathy with the demands of minorities for better treatment.

By not interfering in the administration of Federal departments, he en-couraged the process of liberalization in those departments that were not Southern-controlled.*

In the Agriculture, State, Army and Navy Departments discrimination con-tinued as part of an unwritten code. But in the Interior, Labor, Commerce, and Post Office Departments opportunities began opening up for Negroes for the first time in a quarter century. In seven years 103 Negroes were appointed to posts in the administration.†

The Depression had precipitated hundreds of thousands of Negroes out of the economy. When the Republican party continued to present itself as the advocate of the affluent, Negroes began to shift their allegiance to the party catering to the interests of their stomachs. In the mad scramble for work, Ne-groes had been bumped downward from one position to another, until they lost even the most menial jobs. By the early 1930's, unemployment among Negro males was as high as 80 percent in some Southern cities. Ten percent of the nation's population was subsisting on 3 percent of its income.

After Hoover's sanctimonious declarations about the destruction of the American system if the Federal government were to undertake relief, Negroes viewed the programs of the New Deal as a deliverance. If they still were pushed to the back of the line and got the worst jobs, the worst were better than what they had had before. Although the Federal "security wage" of $12 a week was supposed to be less than that in private employment, in depressed areas and especially the South it invariably was higher. (The annual income of *unbroken* black families in 1935–1936 averaged $726 in Chicago, $632 in Atlanta, and $481 in Mobile.) Southerners complained of Roosevelt's "spoiling the niggers," who would no longer work for fifty cents a day. They were echoed by patrician Northerners who were seeing their faithful, "happy-go-lucky" servants running off into Federal programs.

In truth, as whites discovered they could make more money working on WPA projects than on the porter and bootblack jobs from which they had forced Negroes during the most desperate days, these jobs began opening up again to blacks. The complaint, really, was that blacks wouldn't work for $5 a week when they could get $12.

Approximately 200,000 black youths were enrolled in the CCC, and their $30-a-month pay helped their families take a step upward from the level of starvation to that of bare subsistence.‡

* Nevertheless, Washington remained a *Southern* town in which even facilities in Federal buildings were segregated.
† With Ickes as Secretary, the Interior Department led the way. Mary McLeod Bethune, president of the National Council of Negro Women and a noted educator, was appointed to the newly created post of Director of Minority Affairs in the National Youth Administra-tion. Dr. Clark Foreman of the Julius Rosenwald Fund was named to a free-wheeling position that amounted to looking after Negro interests. Dr. Foreman opened the door for Dr. Robert Weaver, a Harvard economist, and other Negro professionals followed through.
‡ The latest in the series of vitamins, D, was discovered in 1932. With it came the revelation of widespread malnutrition in the United States. Throughout the 1930's, educators, phy-sicians, and pharmaceutical firms campaigned to get the American people to take their vitamins and improve their diets. For half the population, however, the campaign was mean-ingless, since it did not suggest how a family of a half dozen members should go about ingesting vitamins on an income of a dollar a day.

The public works program helped Negro schools, as well as white, to improve their facilities. Under the emergency education program, several hundred thousand illiterate Negroes learned the rudiments of reading and writing.

Roosevelt and the Democrats, with their silent acquiescence to discrimination and segregation, scarcely warmed the hearts of the Negroes. But the Republicans, taking a reactionary stand on issue after issue, did everything to alienate them.* In Detroit, Benjamin Pelham, more than ever the "czar of Wayne County," continued to think of Hoover as one of the great men of American history—and his sentiments were those of a good many of the old, patrician Negro families. But they had as little identification with Stallings and the poverty-stricken blacks as Sloan and Ford had with the Norveths and the Lenticks. Pelham occupied simultaneously the three key positions in the Wayne County government—clerk to the Board of Supervisors, clerk to the Board of Auditors, and county accountant. He established the tax rate, prepared all departmental budgets, controlled all purchases, prepared the agenda, and dominated the county government like no man before or since. Through his control of patronage he had built up a legion of "Ben's Boys."

But most of Ben's Boys, like most of the men to whom he loaned money during the Depression, were white. Politically he was more and more alienated from John Dancy, the Urban Leaguers, and the NAACP.

Similarly, more and more Jews were finding affinity with the Democratic rather than the Republican party. Like the patrician Negroes, many of the patrician Jewish descendants of the German revolutionaries who were one of the elements of the early Republican coalition stuck with the party. But for the later arrivals—especially the eastern Europeans, who were as hard hit by the Depression as anyone—it was Roosevelt who was saving them from ruin.

When the four Schwartz brothers had immigrated to Detroit from Bialystok, Poland, before the war, Abraham, the youngest, had been left behind. The war had made it impossible for him to follow, and, immediately thereafter, Poland had been torn by the dual Polish-versus-Russian, Reds-versus-Whites conflict. The Jews were suspected of being Communists by the Poles, bourgeois by the Russians, and German sympathizers by the nationalists. Thousands had been slaughtered. After serving his apprenticeship in the family tailoring business, Abraham had been impressed into the Polish army that was fighting the Russians. In 1921, leaving his wife Leah and his year-old son Harold behind, he had made his way to the port of Danzig. There he had discovered that because of the new American immigration law, the Polish quota was filled.

Unable to enter the United States, he wound up in Mexico City. He established a tailoring shop that flourished, and sent for his family. In 1923 he received his visa for the United States. But then the even more restrictive act of 1924 closed the quota against his family. Making a difficult decision, Abraham Schwartz moved to the United States. His wife and their Mexican-born daughter—for whom there was no quota—were soon able to follow. But the "Polish" Harold had to be left behind. Harold spent five years in Juarez, across the border from El Paso, and did not arrive in Detroit until 1930. The Schwartzes

* The overriding issue for the Negro leadership was antilynching legislation. Between 1890 and 1920 the United States had averaged more than one hundred lynchings a year. Despite a decline in the number of lynchings during the 1920's, mobs still killed twenty-eight people in 1933. When two Democratic senators, Wagner of New York and Costigan of Colorado, introduced an antilynching bill in 1934, a coalition of Southern Democrats and conservative Republicans staged a successful filibuster against it.

were, in fact, an "international Jewish" family—one child born in Poland, one in Mexico, and a third in the United States.

Like their neighbors, they were thrust into poverty by the Depression. Living in a rodent-infested house, Leah once accidentally baked a rat along with her cake. Sometimes there was not enough money to buy milk. Harold was sent to an Americanization class. Attuned to the Mexican culture, he mistook a handwriting test in which the teacher filled the blackboard with numbers for a lottery, and was ready to risk all on the number 130.

The Schwartz family lived north of Grand Avenue in the corner of Detroit formed by Hamtramck and Highland Park. From downtown Hastings Street and Polacktown, the Polish Jews and Polish Catholics who could afford better housing had pushed northward. The Catholics had occupied Hamtramck. The Jews, stopped from continuing northward by Highland Park and the Ford plant, moved west of Woodward Avenue. There, in the geographic heart of Detroit, they established Twelfth Street as the new Jewish district.

The area was ethnically homogeneous but economically diverse. Twelfth Street was densely packed with shops, laundries, restaurants, and gas stations. Adjacent to the commercial strip were apartment houses interspersed with modest single-family residences. Beyond them, a block or two to either side of Twelfth Street, were large, fashionable houses.

The economic hetereogeneity generated ferment. The Jewish youths growing up in the postwar era were *American,* and many of them were alienated from their *foreign* parents. They formed neighborhood gangs which, during the 1920's, developed into bootlegging mobs that fought bloody battles for control of the rackets.

By 1935, with the improvement in the economy, the Schwartzes were able to cross Woodward Avenue to Twelfth Street. They bought a four-thousand-dollar duplex from a real estate salesman who had survived the Depression by being the neighborhood numbers runner. As they moved into the house, a refugee from the Depression who had been squatting in the dirt-floored garage emerged, and, smelling like ancient cheese, trundled off with his handful of belongings. The parents of one Purple Gang member were neighbors of the Schwartzes. But the glory of the gangsterism of Prohibition was vanishing, and the younger children were growing up in a different environment. The brother of one gangster convicted of murder became an assistant district attorney, and then a judge.

In the tightly knit neighborhood the daily trip to the butcher shop, the bakery, the creamery, and the grocery was a social event. One could not walk a block without being caught up in a discussion. On any street corner where there were three Jews, there were likely to be a dozen political opinions. They ranged from support for the Spanish Communists, who were recruiting for the civil war that had just broken out, to sympathies for Father Coughlin, who had a not-insignificant audience in the Jewish community. Few people, however, expressed confidence in Landon, or willingness to risk a return to the Republican policies that had brought on the gloomy days from which they were just emerging.

So it was throughout the lower- and middle-income neighborhoods of the city.

After stoutly resisting advancing age, William Norveth had capitulated suddenly. His abscessed teeth, which he lacked money to have fixed, had helped bring on arthritis. By 1936 his joints were so swollen that he had to give up his part-time job at the court. Since he could not chew solid food, he lived on liquids. Together with the huge number of aspirins he took, his diet soured his stomach.

His pride was broken. All day long he sat by the radio. Heartily he joined Father Coughlin in denouncing the Republicans and the international bankers. "They kill me. They murder me!" he muttered with his gummy intonation. The *they* were Coolidge and Hoover. For once his views were those of the entire household.

By fall the Federal programs of categorical assistance were having a major impact not only on people directly affected, but also on relatives who were relieved of much of the burden of supporting the needy. In the Norveth household the terrible tension of the past few years was dissolving. Marriage had mixed the Hungarian Norveths with Germans, with Swedes, with Swiss, and with Slovaks. But not with a single Republican.

In September, however, polls indicated Lemke receiving 8.6 percent of the vote, most of which in a two-party race would have gone to Roosevelt. The election appeared to be in doubt.* To neutralize Father Coughlin and improve his chances of carrying Michigan, the President had brought Frank Murphy back from the Philippines to run for governor. Nevertheless, in the Democratic senatorial primary, a Coughlin supporter came within seventy-five hundred votes of upsetting the regular party candidate.

On October 15, flanked by Murphy, Mayor Frank Couzens, and Senator Jim Couzens, Roosevelt was accorded an ovation at a mass rally in Detroit. Senator Couzens, who was seriously ill, rose from a hospital bed to stand with Roosevelt. Although he refused to change his registration from Republican to Democrat, he supported the President strongly, and his support represented that of the Progressives.

If the support for Roosevelt was widespread, the opposition to him among the industrial-financial Republicans and among those whom the government programs had not reached was deep. The economic recovery was making 1936 the second most profitable year in the history of American business. General Motors paid dividends of $202 million, the highest in its history. Yet industrialists and bankers were frustrated because the Roosevelt Administration was not cracking down on labor in the fashion of the Wilson and Harding Administrations, but instead was sponsoring legislation to assure workers, farmers, and the "forgotten Americans" a share in the prosperity. The nation's Brahmins and business leaders seemed prepared to roll the economy back to the Depression, if only the New Deal could be rolled up with it.

Henry Joy had retired from the presidency of Packard. But he was a member of the American Protective Tariff Association and the American Fair Trade League, and an ardent advocate of those policies that had contributed much to bringing on the Depression. He raged at the Department of Justice's "stupid prejudice" for attempting to curb price fixing in the automobile industry. During the latter 1920's, the Packard Motor Company, while making some of the highest profits in its history, had reduced wages and kept "obedience charts" on its workers. Repeatedly criticizing newspapers, Joy called for a "responsible" press—responsible to business—and advocated advertising boycotts to bring

---

* Relying on a telephone poll, the *Literary Digest* showed Landon winning convincingly. But only one out of four blue-collar households had a telephone.

liberal papers into line. He was a prominent member of the American Liberty League, organized in 1934 to provide a conservative bulwark against the Roosevelt Administration's social legislation, and a supporter of extreme right-wing organizations like the American Vigilance Intelligence Federation.

It was the American Liberty League—backed by Sloan, Knudsen, Raskob, the Du Ponts, and former Democratic presidential nominees Al Smith and John W. Davis—which spearheaded the right-wing attack on the administration. In 1935 the Liberty League spent twice as much money as the Republican party. In lavishly printed literature it depicted the administration as bringing on fascism, communism, and "the end of democracy." In their frenzy to defeat the President, some of its members like Sloan and Lammot du Pont were ready to supply funds to any man that was anti-Roosevelt, be it Gerald L. K. Smith or Georgia Governor Eugene Talmadge. (Talmadge warned it was dangerous to encourage niggers who were only a few short years removed from cannibalism.) At a climactic League banquet in the Mayflower Hotel in Washington, Al Smith arose to "give this solemn warning: There can be only one capital, Washington or Moscow. There can be only one atmosphere of government, the clean, pure, fresh air of free America, or the foul breath of communistic Russia." [1] The League's attacks grew so vitriolic that even the Republican party asked it to disassociate itself from the Landon campaign.

As the campaign moved toward a decision, both the Right and the Left lost their composure. The Red Scare of the 1920's was revived. The Republican National Committee charged that administration policies were leading "to the destruction of the capitalistic system. . . . Stalin over in Russia knows it and has ordered his following in the United States to back Roosevelt." Congressman Lemke declared: "I do not charge that the President of this nation is a Communist but I do charge that Browder, Dubinsky, and other Communist leaders have laid their cuckoo eggs in his Democratic nest and that he is hatching them." Father Coughlin denounced Jews, Republicans, and the administration with equal fervor. He likened the choice between Roosevelt and Landon to picking between "carbolic acid and rat poison." The "road of fascism" was to be preferred. In mid-October the Reverend Gerald L. K. Smith announced that his purpose was the formation of a movement to "seize the government of the United States." [2]

Not surprisingly, Roosevelt's moderate, middle-of-the-road position attracted a growing number of Americans. When Detroit Republicans launched a national campaign against Social Security as a confiscation of wages and infringement on personal liberty, they merely reinforced the impression that Republicans were opposed to all social and welfare legislation. When the Townsendites, in turn, attacked Social Security and Old Age Assistance as inadequate, they reminded middle-class Americans of the reasonableness of the programs. Thus the Republicans pushed the Townsendites toward Roosevelt, even as Townsend pushed more-conservative Americans toward the President. So it went, on issue after issue. The more the two sides attacked, the more they canceled each other out.

The economy, meanwhile, was booming. Unemployment was moving toward its lowest point in seven years—although nine million were still unemployed, five and a half million more were employed than three years earlier. The auto industry was making more cars than in any previous year except 1929. Since 1933 wages had risen 13 percent. In manufacturing they were up 18 percent.

Between the upper and lower extremes, the middle half of the American population was better off than it had ever been before.

In River Rouge, Henry Ford avowed that, although he had not voted in twenty years, he would most surely vote for Landon, and his employees were exhorted to follow his example. In his pay envelope Sylvester J. Cavanagh, who had returned to Ford after a layoff of more than a year, found a slip warning him to vote for Landon lest he suffer the terrible fate of having ½ percent of his pay deducted for Social Security. The warning served, instead, as a potent reminder of the insecurity of assembly-line jobs, and the auto industry's callous policy of casting aging workers into the streets. Emotionally the Cavanagh family was drawn to Father Coughlin, and on weekends eight-year-old Jerry peddled Coughlin's *Social Justice* publication. But it was Roosevelt who challenged that "business and financial monopoly, speculation, reckless banking, class antagonism . . . are unanimous in their hate for me—and I welcome their hatred." [3] And it was he who stood between Sylvester Cavanagh and a return to the conditions before 1933.

So the Coughlin supporters silently slipped away. Lemke received fewer than 900,000 votes. Nearly 28 million voters, 60.8 percent of the total, cast their ballots for Roosevelt. Topping even Harding's percentage, he carried with him the largest congressional majority since Reconstruction. Murphy won the governorship by 40,000 votes. The President, whom he was supposed to help pull through, carried the state by 300,000. Only 2 of 116 cities with a population of over 100,000 went to the Republicans.

74

The Labor of Union

THE SHOCK WAS TOO MUCH FOR HENRY JOY. THREE DAYS AFTER THE ELECTION he collapsed, and died of a heart attack.

Two weeks earlier, seven days after standing on the platform with Roosevelt, Senator Couzens had died. His funeral procession, two miles long, was the largest and most spectacular in the history of the city.

The deaths of Joy and Couzens marked, in truth, far more than the end of two men who had played leading roles in shaping the automobile industry. They represented the death of a coalition, and the funeral of an era.

When James F. Joy had found himself politically isolated, he had pursued the interests of the Michigan Central Railroad by participating in the formation of a new coalition. It was a coalition that his Railroad Republicans soon dominated. Although segments of that fusion started splintering off within two decades, for eighty years the Republicans showed a capacity for renewing themselves by attracting fresh elements. Henry Joy and the leadership of the party that steered the economy into the disaster of 1929, however, had by their political egocentricity isolated themselves not only from the body of the nation, but from the grass roots of the party. By their rigid insistence that they must do nothing to disturb the American structure, while that structure was cascading down about their heads, they ended up standing in the rubble of the Republican party. The coalition was shattered beyond redemption. The years from 1930 to 1936 produced as great a metamorphosis in the American political and social structure as the years from 1854 to 1860.

The Progressives, who had been wandering in the political wilderness since 1912 and repeatedly had been rejected by the Republicans, settled en masse in the Democratic party. Any Republican of liberal inclinations, including many of the offspring of Detroit's Woodward Avenue society, deserted the party. When Couzens ran in the Republican senatorial primary in 1936, he found his constituency had disappeared. The party remained only a citadel of conservatism, and Couzens was swamped by Wilbur Brucker. But three fourths of the 200,000 voters for Couzens in the primary shifted allegiance, and provided the Democrats with their 150,000 vote margin in the general election. While the Progressive infusion revitalized the Democratic party and significantly affected the balance of power between its Southern (conservative) and Northern (generally liberal) wing, the reciprocal migration of conservative and business Democrats established the Republicans as a party of the affluent who yearned for a return to the 1920's.

The shift of the Negro vote, just at the time when it was beginning to become a factor in the Northern cities, was dramatic. In 1932 blacks had given Roosevelt 36.7 percent of the vote in Detroit. In 1936 it was 63.5 percent. With the black vote went that of Jewish liberals and civil righters—the latter-day descendants of the Abolitionists.

With Americanization and the continuing gains in education, participation in the electoral process was growing. (High school enrollment in Michigan was up 29 percent since the onset of the Depression and the number of high school graduates in the nation nearly doubled during the 1930's.) When women had been granted the vote, the Republican party had been the beneficiary. The new voters, however, were affiliating themselves with the Democratic party. Between 1928 and 1936 the number of voters increased from 1 out of every 3.3, to 1 out of every 2.8 persons in the population; and the Democrats gained nearly 13 million votes.

Roosevelt's overwhelming victory was widely interpreted as a mandate for the continued transformation of the Federal government from an aloof arbiter and overseer of the national structure to a body intimately concerned with the lives and welfare of the American people.

The "rugged individualism" President Hoover had espoused was looked upon by the majority of Americans as an anachronism. The Depression had made it clear that the individual, rugged or otherwise, was at the mercy of economic forces manipulated by large organizations; that the only way he could protect himself was by combining with other individuals to form an influential economic unit of his own.

Security was collective. It must be achieved through a community of interest; and, even as the large corporations had done, by ending "ruinous competition."

A new element was injected into American life. In field after field, both unions and professional organizations moved to protect their members against competition by making the entry of newcomers more difficult and, in some cases, almost impossible. In reaction to young "normal school" graduates "bidding" for jobs against veteran teachers, the Michigan Education Association in 1936 prevailed upon the state to raise certification requirements for new teachers to four years of college training. Since tens of millions of people lacked the money to pay doctors' fees, a strong belief developed in the medical profession that there were far too many doctors, and that "unethical practices" (i.e., fee cutting) would result. Seeking cartel powers, the American Medical Association kept raising the standards for licensing, and was unenthusiastic about expanding the facilities for medical training. Medical schools initiated an unwritten "quota system." In some of the motion picture guilds, it became necessary to have a job in order to obtain guild membership, but one could not obtain a job unless one were a member of the guild. Trade unions not only initiated examinations for which an applicant had to have a knowledge of higher mathematics and Shakespeare in order to be accepted for apprenticeship training as a plumber or a carpenter; they also required the applicant to show before he was accepted for training that a position was waiting for him upon his completion of the course. "The Lawyers' union," Clarence Darrow said, was "about as anxious to encourage competition as the Plumbers' union, or the United States Steel Company, or the American Medical Association." [1] Qualification after qualification was added for passage of the bar examination.

Whereas at the turn of the century a person could become a teacher with less than a high school education, a plumber with the ability to fit two pipes together, and a lawyer with a year or two of college study or experience clerking in a legal office, the requirements for one occupation after another were placed so high as to put them beyond reach of an increasing proportion of the population.

That, of course, was the intent. The open competition of laissez-faire and "free enterprise" having proved too great a strain on the system, the United States was moving toward the kind of closed, stratified society that had existed in Europe before the Industrial Revolution. It was a mercantile society in which each guild regulated its own craft, and in which membership in that guild was the most valuable inheritance a father passed on to his son.

In this climate, the Democratic-controlled Congress reversed the tradition of its predecessors, and, beginning in 1932, passed one piece of legislation after another strengthening the rights of labor. The Norris-LaGuardia Act outlawed the "yellow dog" contract (which prevented workers from joining unions), and the use of court injunctions to prohibit men from organizing and striking. The National Industrial Recovery Act granted workers the right to organize and to bargain collectively. Industrial-relations boards that acted as informal, industrywide collective bargaining agents were set up. To supervise the codes and to act as an investigative and mediating agency, the President established a National Labor Relations Board, headed by Senator Robert Wagner.

In May, 1935, the Supreme Court declared sections of the NIRA unconstitutional. The effect, as Congress and the administration speedily reacted, was to strengthen the hand of labor. Concerned about the chaos of attempting to regulate labor relations through separate mechanisms in each industry and about the inability of unions to generate bargaining strength, Senator Wagner earlier in the year had introduced the National Labor Relations Act. Containing elements of both the NIRA and the National Labor Relations Board, the act placed the force of law behind its provisions. (Under the NIRA, labor had had to depend on the government's persuasive powers.)

The Wagner Act guaranteed the rights of employees to organize and to bargain collectively. It prohibited employers from interfering with that right, from threatening to close a plant if it were unionized, from organizing company unions in order to thwart independent organization, from spying on union meetings, from threatening and discriminating against union members, and from refusing to bargain in good faith with elected worker representatives. To enforce and adjudicate the act, a National Labor Relations Board was created.

No sooner had the Supreme Court invalidated the NIRA than Congress passed the Wagner Act.

The prolabor mood of Congress and the nation was so strong that 1935–1936 produced the greatest outpouring of labor legislation in American history. An antistrikebreaker law made it a felony to transport across state lines any person hired to interfere with peaceful organization of and picketing by employees—it was a law directed at the long-time practice of engaging Pinkerton detectives to break up strikes. Minimum wage and maximum hours legislation was enacted for workers in the coal and textile industries, in Federal highway, housing, and public works programs, and on projects under government contract. A new workmen's compensation act was passed.

The effect of Roosevelt's victory was to confirm the permanence of this legislation. There was no possibility of congressional repeal in the foreseeable future. Some companies rushed to increase wages in the hope of damping the growing militancy of labor.

In 1935, Walter Reuther returned from Russia to Detroit. Disillusioned with communism but still a Socialist, he was blacklisted by the major auto companies, and became a recreation director for the WPA. The auto workers were restless, dissatisfied, and beset by anxiety. Amidst the economic upsurge they kept looking for a trapdoor to be sprung beneath their feet. Without security in their jobs, unhappy with their wages and working conditions, they had been granted the right to organize by the NIRA, but had no one to organize them. The Auto Labor Board, appointed in March, 1934, was weak, convoluted in its own bureaucracy, and haunted by the image of Henry Ford. Sitting on the sidelines, refusing to subscribe to the code, he set the example for the other auto makers, whose subscription was pro forma. When the board held an industry election in the spring of 1935, nearly 90 percent of the workers voted "no union."

Nevertheless, the industry was streaked with wildcat strikes. In April, 1935, when workers at the Toledo Chevrolet plant walked out, they were soon joined by workers at the Fisher Body Plant in Cleveland and the Chevrolet plant in Norwood, Ohio. That brought the total number of General Motors workers on strike to thirty thousand.

As early as June, 1934, 157 delegates from 77 auto locals meeting in Detroit had sent feelers to United Mine Workers President John L. Lewis. The son of a Welsh coal miner, Lewis had been president of the miners since 1920, and was a vice-president of the American Federation of Labor. As leader of a union which was one of the Federation's strongest and which cut across the lines between craft and industrial unionism, he was a natural focal point for progressives like David Dubinsky of the International Ladies Garment Workers and Sidney Hillman of the Amalgamated Clothing Workers.*

The enactment of the National Industrial Recovery Act expanded UMW membership from 60,000 to 360,000, and brought 350,000 new members into the textile unions. The passage of the Wagner Act, which provided unprecedented opportunity for organizing, brought the matter of industrial unionism to a head.

At the Federation's October, 1935, convention in Atlantic City, the majority report of the resolution committee upheld the AFL's traditional opposition to industrial unionism. The AFL's primary concern continued to be the protection of the craftsman's job from liquidation resulting from the mating of machines with unskilled workers. Even during the construction boom of the 1920's, skilled workers, because of the seasonal and on-and-off nature of the work, had never averaged more than $1,200 to $1,500 a year. By 1933, construction activity had been one third of the 1925–1929 average, and total wages had fallen to

---

* Both born in Russia, they were steeped in the tradition of eastern European Jewish unionism. Nondoctrinaire Socialists, they were dedicated anti-Communists.

one fourth of their 1929 level. At times 90 percent of the union members had been out of work. Throughout the trades, unemployment had been averaging more than 60 percent. In 1935, 1.7 million building-trade workers were still unemployed.

With his mane of hair, shaggily burgeoning eyebrows, full jowls, and huge bulk, Lewis had the steely presence of an English bulldog. He pleaded for the Federation to adopt industrial unionism. Since, however, the admission of hundreds of thousands of new workers would menace the power of the conservatives and traditionalists, the AFL hierarchy had additional reason to reply that "the American Federation is going to carry on just as it has in the past." [2]

When the delegates from the rubber workers and the newly organized Consolidated Auto Union were denied the chance to speak, Lewis engaged Bill Hutcheson of the Carpenters in a vitriolic argument. Hutcheson muttered, "Bastard." Lewis swung. Hutcheson, a towering figure, fell against a table. His face bloody, he leaped back to his feet. As the antagonists clinched, the convention disintegrated into pandemonium.

The next day Lewis called a meeting of the progressive and militant leaders. They decided to bypass the Federation leadership by forming a committee to organize industrial unions within the Federation. Early the next month a Committee for Industrial Organization was established. Two weeks later Lewis resigned his vice-presidency in the Federation. When members of the Committee refused to appear before the executive council to answer charges of fomenting insurrection, they were expelled from the Federation in September, 1936.

These were heady developments for the young and aggressive unionists in the auto industry. They had had their fill of AFL equivocations and vacillations. But they had little except determination with which to organize the industry. On April 27, 1935, when Reuther's local met in Detroit to pick its delegate to the UAW organizing convention in South Bend, Indiana, only seven workers showed up. Selected as the delegate, Reuther was presented with the five dollars in the union treasury for expenses.

Hitchhiking the 175 miles to South Bend, he ate hamburgers and on arrival shared a room with five other men. The convention was split three ways between conservatives, Communists, and non-Communist radicals like Reuther. The conservatives succeeded in placing the Reverend Homer Martin, by far the best known and most popular of the candidates, in the presidency.* The Communist-supported candidate, Wyndham Mortimer, was elected to the vice-presidency. Reuther was named to the executive board.

Back in Detroit, Reuther, borrowing three hundred dollars, rented a sound truck, a mimeograph machine, a typewriter, and a dingy West Side office across from the Cadillac plant. He placed his bride, a Jewish schoolteacher from the Twelfth Street area, behind the keyboard of a typewriter, and commenced organizing. As a first step, he succeeded in merging the disputatious, minuscule West Side locals.

Half the membership worked at the Kelsey-Hayes plant. Reuther planned to halt operations at the plant by means of a sit-down strike. Sit-downs had been

---

* The Reverend Homer Martin was a Fundamentalist Baptist preacher from Kansas City. He had been kicked from his pulpit when he supported members of his congregation on strike at the local auto plant. His commanding voice and ringing biblical phrases launched him on a career as a union organizer.

staged throughout Europe, and had been employed in the 1935 strike in the Akron rubber industry. They required only a small body of disciplined men to shut down an assembly line, and avoided bloody clashes with police on picket lines.

Reuther had one tactical problem. He was unable to get into any plant in the Detroit area.

His brother Victor was enlisted as a surrogate. Obtaining a job at the Kelsey-Hayes plant as a punch-press operator at thirty-six cents an hour, he became the "inside" man. In November, in the midst of the workers' euphoria following the national election, sentiment for a strike grew strong. When a Polish girl "fainted" on the assembly line and confusion momentarily ensued, union men pulled key switches. As five thousand workers milled about and unionists barred foremen from the switches, Victor mounted a box and harangued the workers.

For Harold Lentick, listening to Victor Reuther was a puzzling experience. Federal programs had helped him through the Depression. He had canned food for the Civil Works Administration, and been paid twenty dollars a month by the Federal Emergency Relief Administration to take a mechanics course. The course had aided him in getting the sixteen-dollar-a-week job at Kelsey-Hayes, the first steady employment he had held in six years. The sixteen dollars was half again his weekly earnings of a year earlier. Victor Reuther's promises that unionization would bring better wages and job security were fine. But, like other workers, Lentick was not inclined to jeopardize his job for promises. He had heard vivid stories from his father and sister about what had happened when the men had struck at the Calumet and Hecla copper mine. The auto unions were noted for their lack of success. Workers who joined unions had succeeded only in winding up on the blacklist.

But if modern technology had given a comparatively small number of workers the capability to produce masses of goods, it had also enabled a small number of men—as management discovered to its consternation—to paralyze production by capturing control of the nerve centers. Most of the workers were not ready to defy management. But neither were they prepared actively to defy the union. Continuing their passive roles, they waited to see who would gain the upper hand.

The worker who took charge in the building that housed the brake assembly line was George Edwards, Jr. Twenty-one years old, he had been born in Dallas, the grandson of the first judge of Dallas County, and the son of a classics scholar and a lawyer. Edwards's father was that rarity, a Texas liberal. (In the 1920's he had taken on the KKK, represented union leaders when no other lawyer would even allow himself to be seen talking to them, and served as the Texas manager for the 1924 presidential campaign of Progressive Robert LaFollette.) Brilliant and precocious, George Edwards, Jr., had graduated from Southern Methodist University at the age of eighteen and received his master's degree from Harvard in 1934. Becoming a researcher and lecturer for Socialist Norman Thomas's League for Industrial Democracy, he had come to Detroit with less than fifty dollars and the intent to write a novel. Together with ten thousand other men, he had stood all night in five-degree-below-zero weather in a snakeline that wound through the parking lot outside Gate Four at River Rouge. Not hired at Ford, the master in sociology had taken a dirty, lung-wracking, 37½-cents-an-hour job in the paint department at Kelsey-Hayes. He played a prominent role in organizing the strike, and was named chairman of the workers' bargaining committee.

Company executives frantically tried to get the assembly lines moving again, but were unable to break the stalemate. The strike's leaders asserted that only Walter Reuther could get the men back to work. A car was dispatched for Reuther. As a unionist, he was chauffeured into a plant from which he had been barred as a worker.

Instead of urging the men to return to work, however, Walter took Victor's place on the soapbox and exhorted them to join the union. To the horror-stricken plaints of management, "You were supposed to get them back to work," he replied, "How can I get them back to work if they're not organized?" [3]

If this argument did not impress management, they lacked the strength to counter it by recapturing control of the assembly lines. The morale of the strikers went up. More of the workers threw in their lot with the union. Walter Reuther, climbing out of a window, organized a feeder line of sandwiches and coffee into the plant. Day after day the impasse continued. On the fifth day management caved in. The minimum wage was raised to seventy-five cents an hour. Agreement was reached on other union demands pertaining to working conditions and the right to organize.

It was an amazing victory for men who had been dehumanized to the point that they were identified and called, prisoner-like, not by name but by number. Wildcat sitdowns flashed around the area. There were strikes at Midland Steel in Detroit and the Bendix Corporation in South Bend in December; at Chrysler, Briggs, and Fisher the next month. As Edwards became an organizer and, subsequently, national welfare director for the United Auto Workers, applications for membership poured in. Union headquarters had difficulty keeping up with the chapters that sprang up spontaneously at plant after plant. In less than six months membership in the West Side local grew to twenty-four hundred.

75

The Sparks of Flint

IMPORTANT AS WAS THE UNION VICTORY AT KELSEY-HAYES, IT HAD NOT DEM-
onstrated that the auto workers could successfully take on one of the major
manufacturers. The principal General Motors facilities continued to be in
Flint, where Durant had had his carriage factory.* With 50,000 of its 165,000
people working in the General Motors plants, Flint came as close to being
dominated by one company as any major modern city was likely to be.

In 1934, in the first surge of enthusiasm, auto union membership in the
area had reached 26,000. But by 1936, the combination of AFL ineptitude, a
$1 million G.M. espionage campaign, and worker apathy had reduced it to 120.

General Motors executives, who continued to think of their workers in terms
of Frederick Taylor's oxen, oxen who now were being led astray by Communists, had no intention of negotiating over what they considered the in-
alienable rights of property and of management to run operations as they saw
fit.

Their greatest scorn was reserved for the Wagner Act. "Industry," said
G.M. President Sloan, "will fight this proposal to the very last." Earl F. Reed,
counsel for the Weirton Steel Company, said he would "advise a client not to
be bound by a law that I consider unconstitutional." [1] Since the Supreme Court
had struck down the much less stringent provisions of the NIRA, a host of
businessmen proposed to stage delaying actions until the Wagner Act could
meet a similar fate at the hands of the "nine old men."

General Motors, said Executive Vice-President William Knudsen, had no
objection to negotiating with the union so long as it was done on a "gentle-
manly" basis and without strikes. However, since each plant within the corporation was operated semiautonomously, the management of G.M. could not
presume to speak for the manager of each plant, and so could not negotiate as
a corporation. The union would have to negotiate on a plant-by-plant basis.

* Durant, listing $250 worth of clothing as his assets and debts of $914,000, filed for bankruptcy in 1936. David Buick, his money squandered in oil speculation, had died penniless
and forgotten in 1929.

Casuistic as this was, it was an ingenious ploy. If company unions were out-lawed by the Wagner Act, the solution was to fragment and emasculate the union by splitting up the process of negotiation.

The General Motors organization was so intricate that the corporation could plead decentralization when it suited its purpose, yet implement a decision by the board of directors at all of its plants within hours. Beyond a point, nevertheless, its size militated against efficiency. Sloan himself lamented:

"In practically all our activities we seem to suffer from the inertia resulting from our great size. It seems to be hard for us to get action when it comes to a matter of putting our ideas across. There are so many people involved and it requires such a tremendous effort to put something new into effect that a new idea is likely to be considered insignificant in comparison with the effort that it takes to put it across.

"I can't help but feel that General Motors has missed a lot by reason of this inertia. You have no idea how . . . frequently we fail to put the idea into effect until competition forces us to do so." [2]

That was in 1925, when the corporation was hardly out of its adolescence, yet already suffering from bureaucratization. But if size added nothing to efficiency, it contributed wondrously to the capability of administering prices. The divisions of G.M. were run like units in a planned economy.

The Supreme Court had brought down the governmental structure of the National Recovery Administration. But, in 600 out of 850 code associations, the code secretary and the secretary of the trade association had been one and the same person. Thus, many industries continued to control prices and compe-tition as they had before, but without even nominal government supervision. They established powerful lobbying organizations to assure the passage of favorable legislation. The drug industry originated the concept of the "Fair Trade" law, under which the moment a manufacturer and one retailer signed a resale price agreement all other retailers were forced to market the manu-facturer's wares at the same price. In a deliberate campaign to administer the medicine to the American people without their knowledge, the "Fair Trade" laws—an egregious misnomer—were *hushed* through the legislatures of forty-three states. Of the first thirty-two legislatures that enacted "Fair Trade," only three held public hearings.

In one fashion or another, industry after industry controlled or attempted to control the market and competition. In the construction industry, suppliers of materials, contractors, and the craft unions combined to lobby for the passage of building codes that had the same effect as the establishment of monopolies. Codes became so restrictive that in some communities it was a violation of law for an electrical engineer to splice a wire in his own house without obtain-ing a license, or for a person to hammer a nail without becoming a member of the carpenters' union.

In the oil industry, the interstate oil compact served to limit production and fix prices through the proration of production. The "integrated" companies, which controlled the pipelines, charged themselves high rates (which, of course, made no difference to themselves, since the money was simply shifted from one balance sheet to another) so that they could charge the same high rates to independents.

In its 1934 *Report to the President,* the Federal Trade Commission de-clared: "There is growing doubt whether the capitalistic system, whose basic assumption is free markets and a free price system, can continue to work with an ever widening range of prices fixed and manipulated by monopolies." ³

Administering consumer prices, and failing to pass on to workers an adequate share of the profits, American industry was working itself right back to 1929. The plants were operating at capacity. Men were drawing overtime pay. But all the old grievances remained: the speedup, which increasingly became an issue as management tried to get more units off the assembly lines; the status of the foremen, who continued to practice favoritism, bribery, and forms of extortion; the lack of security and seniority—a man never knew what day on the job would be his last, or, if he were laid off, whether he would be rehired. In a climate of worker dissatisfaction, slowdowns were frequent. There were "quickies," in which a few men downed their tools; and "skippies," in which every fourth or fifth task on the assembly line was skipped, so as to create total confusion.

On December 28, 1936, the workers at the Fisher Body Plant in Cleveland sat down. The next day, five union leaders in the Flint Body Plant Number Two were fired by General Motors. As the word spread rapidly through the plant, the chant began:

> *"When they tie the can to a union man,*
> *Sit down, Sit down.*
> *When they give him the sack they'll take him back,*
> *Sit down, Sit down.*
> *When the speedup comes, just twiddle your thumbs,*
> *Sit down, Sit down.*
> *When the boss won't talk, don't take a walk,*
> *Sit down, Sit down."*

Suddenly the assembly lines were moving, but the men were sitting. The next day, the men in Body Plant Number One, noting that a number of dies were being removed from the plant and crated for shipment, began to suspect that the transfer was a precautionary measure against a sitdown. They, too, promptly sat down. Shortly, the strike spread to the Cadillac and the Fleetwood plants in Detroit.

The men were forcing the decision on their own leaders, and, simultaneously, frustrating the machinations of the company. Through the frosty New Year's Eve the workers boiled cups of coffee on Sterno cans, sang the union hymn, "Solidarity Forever"—which had been taken over from the IWW—played cards, and slept fitfully on benches, on automobile upholstery, and on the floor. Their wives and children, bringing food, cigarettes, and coffee, appeared outside the plants. Ladders were set up against the windows to establish pipelines. UAW President Martin, wiring Knudsen, requested a conference on collective bargaining. Knudsen replied that the strikers were trespassers and that there could be no talks until the plants were vacated.

The battle lines hardened. Walter and Victor Reuther, driving their sound truck, headed a reinforcement of union organizers. George Boysen, former Buick paymaster and the owner of a small spark plug factory, formed the "Flint Alliance," purportedly representing a cross-section of the community, including local labor leaders opting for a company union. Prompted by General Motors public relations men, the Alliance, which later changed its name to the Flint Law and Order League, promoted a back-to-work movement.

From County Judge Edward Black the corporation obtained an injunction ordering the strikers to vacate the plants.

The UAW attorney, Lee Pressman, then revealed that the judge owned 3,365 shares of General Motors stock worth $219,000. Since Michigan law forbids a judge to preside over a case in which he has an interest, the injunction was invalid.

As the strike drew into the longest sitdown in American history, management decided to attempt to starve and freeze the workers out of the plants. On January 11, General Motors shut off the heat. In late afternoon, 150 guards blocked all access to the plants. When the culinary auxiliary made its usual evening appearance with the strikers' supper, they were barred. A contingent, evading the police, managed to secure a ladder to a window.

As soon as the police saw the ladder, they rushed toward it. Strikers fought them for possession. The battle spread to the gate. Bill Carney, a rubberworkers organizer, and Victor Reuther took turns on the sound truck. Directing the men, they urged them not to let themselves be intimidated. News of the ruckus spread, and additional workers arrived. In the bitter cold they stamped their feet, slapped their arms, and chafed for action. To the tune of "The Battle Hymn of the Republic," the verses of "Solidarity Forever" rang out.

> "They have taken untold millions that
>   they never toiled to earn,
> But without our brawn and muscle
>   not a single wheel could turn;
> We can break their haughty power,
>   gain our freedom when we learn
> That the union makes us strong.
>   Solidarity Forever,
>   Solidarity Forever,
>   Solidarity Forever,
> For the union makes us strong." [4]

It was approximately seven o'clock when the workers, charging the plant from two directions, overwhelmed the police and opened an alley through which the food could be carried to the men inside. Two hours later, the police, reinforced by fifty additional men, counterattacked. By this time the workers had armed themselves with lengths of iron pipe, maces fashioned from jagged pieces of metal, and a variety of clubs and implements. At the plant's windows, the strikers waited with brickbats, bolts, car hinges—an endless supply of metal missiles. In the chiaroscuro of light and darkness along the walls, knots of men battled fiercely, their breaths freezing, their faces caked with blood.

Through a broken window, police fired tear gas into the plant. Soon the tear gas canisters began exploding amidst the men milling about the walls. The gray-greenish gas swirled like a veil about the combatants. Shotguns loaded with buckshot came into play—here and there a man crumpled to the ground. When the sheriff drove onto the scene, his car was surrounded and overturned. Three police cars met the same fate.

While police prepared for another charge on the gate, workers seized a fire hose. Reaching the gate, the police were caught in the rapierlike jet of freezing water. Knocked off their feet, gasping for breath, they scrambled out of the way, then broke and ran. "The Battle of the Running Bulls!" the workers yelled triumphantly.

Murphy, who had been inaugurated as governor only ten days earlier, drove to Flint, and then ordered twelve hundred National Guardsmen into the city. Executives of General Motors and members of the Flint Alliance expected the governor to direct the guardsmen to clear the plants. When, instead, he ordered them to keep the peace, he was assailed for capitulating to lawlessness and communism. Around Body Plant Number Two, the union threw up a massive picket line composed of workers and their families. Schoolchildren and even toddlers carried the signs: "We're behind our dads 100%"; "My daddy strikes for us little tikes: On to Victory!"

Murphy now took a personal hand in mediating between the corporation and the union. Knudsen was an old friend. On January 15 Murphy brought him and Homer Martin together in the governor's office. After fifteen hours of negotiations, they reached an agreement: the men would vacate the plant; for the following fifteen days, while negotiations took place, G.M. would not operate.

The evacuation was ready to begin when, at the twelfth hour, a United Press reporter discovered a telegram from G.M. to the Flint Alliance. It seemed to indicate that the corporation would recognize the Alliance, as well as the UAW, as a bargaining agent. Although Knudsen repudiated the telegram, the union leaders refused to believe him. The men stayed.

Secretary of Labor Frances Perkins invited Sloan to meet with Lewis under her auspices. Lewis did not trust women generally and Madame Perkins specifically. Referring to the half million dollars labor had contributed to Roosevelt's reelection campaign, the union leader rumbled: "The workers of this country expect the administration to help the workers in every legal way and to support the workers in the General Motors plant." [5]

Sloan, who had gone to Washington with the greatest reluctance, interpreted Lewis's statement as confirmation that the administration was biased. He boarded a train back to Detroit.

The impasse continued.

The Flint Alliance tightened the vise, legally and economically, on the workers' families. Its more extreme elements were preparing for vigilante action to clear the plants.

The leadership of the UAW decided pressure would have to be increased. If strikers could seize Plant Number Four, the engine assembly plant for Chevrolet, they would be able to halt operations at all Chevrolet assembly plants around the nation. Well aware of the crucial nature of the plant, management was fully prepared to prevent a sitdown. The union had few adherents among the workers in the plant.

Calling a meeting at Fisher Body Plant Number One, Roy Reuther, another of Walter's brothers, told the twenty-five men assembled that the union had decided to seize Plant Number Nine, which manufactured ball bearings. Company spies present at the meeting informed management. Shortly after 3 P.M. on February 1, one hundred fifty union supporters inside Plant Number Nine commenced the now-familiar chant: "Sit down! Sit down!"

The two hundred guards who had been assembled were ready. Tear gas was shot into the building. As the men, gasping and coughing, rushed to open doors and windows, the guards engaged them. Fighting broke out. From the street outside the plant the UAW sound truck spurred the men on. A women's auxiliary used long poles to smash the plant's windows so the tear gas could escape.

Now Reuther sprang the trap. A handful of union men from the day shift had hidden in the toilets on the balcony of Plant Number Four. However, when they went onto the floor to urge the workers to sit down, they were too few to be effective. In Plant Number Six, to the contrary, the union was strong. At 3:30 P.M., Ed Conk, the UAW committeeman in Plant Number Six, unfurled a miniature American flag from his pocket. Waving the flag over his head, he shouted to the workers: "Follow me!" and stormed across the open ground toward Plant Number Four.

"Sit down! Sit down!" the UAW men already inside Number Four were yelling as they ran up and down the lines. But they received little support. Then Conk, hairy-chested, stripped to the waist, followed by a score of grease-smeared men wielding large hammers and lead pipes, burst in.

Although Reuther's ruse had worked to perfection, and the plant was only lightly guarded, it contained three thousand workers and almost as many machines. Men who had watched the month-long deadlock between the company and the union were without enthusiasm for a strike. Many were from the middle South, especially Kentucky and Tennessee. Migrating back and forth as work became available or slackened, they were not interested in organizing. Like the men at Kelsey-Hayes, they were determined to remain neutral until there was an indication as to which side would prevail.

When the men refused to turn off their machines, Conk sent back to Plant Number Six for reinforcements. Dozens of additional UAW men poured into Plant Number Four. Running down the lines they turned off the machines, chanting: "Sit down! Sit down! When they tie the can to a union man, sit down! Sit down! When they give him the sack they'll take him back, sit down! Sit down!"

Desperately the foremen tried to control the situation, threatening to fire the men if they did not remain at their machines. But the workers were no more inclined to take positive action in favor of the company than they had been to take positive action in favor of the union. As dusk fell and not a machine was running, the silence of the normally clangorous building was eerie. The strikers climbed to the rooftops of the captured plants and shouted "Solidarity Forever!" to each other.

For Sloan and Knudsen, the coup represented bolshevism unbridled. The UAW had taken over by force the property of General Motors. If this were not revolution, then it was the prelude to revolution. Most liberals, while backing the workers, were almost as horrified as management by the sitdowns and, especially, by the seizure of the plant. AFL President Green thought it outrageous. President Roosevelt was shocked. Governor Murphy regarded it as a betrayal of his own studied impartiality. Furious, he told union leaders that if they did not order their men out, he would order the National Guard in.

The UAW leadership placed an emergency call to Lewis in Washington. Grumbling about being awakened at three o'clock in the morning, he agreed to come to Michigan. Before leaving the capital, he paid a visit to the White House.

Get the men out of the plant, the President told him.

In Flint, General Motors obtained a new court order. On pain of imprisonment and a fifteen-million-dollar fine, the men were to vacate the plants within twenty-four hours. Picketing was enjoined.

The sheriff issued an ultimatum: the men were to be out by 3 P.M. the next day, or he would use all the forces at his command to evict them.

The workers at Fisher Plant Number One sent a telegram to Governor Murphy:

"The introduction of the militia, sheriffs or police with murderous weapons will mean a bloodbath of unarmed workers. . . . We freely expect that if a violent effort is made to oust us many of us will be killed, and we take this means of making it known . . . that if this result follows from the attempt to eject us, you are the one who must be held responsible for our deaths." [6]

When Lewis arrived in Detroit, Knudsen refused to meet with him. To do so, Knudsen contended, would be to give de facto recognition to the seizure. There could be no negotiations until the men were out of the plants.

Detroit seethed with rumors. Remembering that the Reuther brothers had returned from Russia less than two years before, business leaders interpreted the sitdowns as a Communist-led attempt to seize American industry. The Roosevelt Administration's coddling of the Reds was about to bear fruit. The police were placed on alert. Men stocked their houses with food and barricaded their doors. There was widespread conviction that America's 1917 was at hand.

The National Guard had isolated Fisher Body Plant Number Two. But as the three o'clock deadline approached on February 3, five thousand workers marched two abreast behind an American flag toward Fisher Body Plant Number One. Circling the plant, they sang:

> *"In our hands is placed a power*
> *greater than their hoarded gold,*
> *Greater than the might of atoms,*
> *and magnified a thousand-fold;*
> *We can bring to birth a new world*
> *from the ashes of the old*
> *For the union makes us strong!"* [7]

In Detroit, bowing to Governor Murphy's exhortations, Knudsen finally agreed to meet with Lewis. But he only reiterated his declaration that there could be no negotiation without evacuation. Reminding Lewis of the court order, Murphy warned him that the hour was late.

Drawing himself up with all the histrionic majesty of which he was capable, Lewis replied:

"I do not doubt your ability to call out your soldiers and shoot the members of our union out of these plants, but let me say that when you issue that order I shall leave this conference and I shall enter one of those plants with my people." [8]

To Knudsen the issue was a strike against General Motors. President Roosevelt, however, knew it was far more than that. The strike had already idled 125,000 workers in 117 plants. These were men who had passed through the most bitter years of their lives. Through the 1920's they had worked for the prosperity to which they had been spectators, but in which they had participated little. Now they perceived the pattern repeating itself. Business and industry profits were soaring, while they lived from day to day and wondered when they would again be thrown out of work.

Throughout the 1920's the government had acted to suppress labor and to accord special privileges to industry, until the entire economic system had been thrown out of kilter. Now the electorate had installed in Washington a man professedly a friend of labor. The Wagner Act accorded labor the right to organize. But if industry could circumvent the act, if the power of government was to be used once again to favor one segment of society at the expense of another, the credibility of the American system of government itself would be placed in jeopardy. The workers marching in Flint were determined they would not be pushed back into the ranks of the economic dropouts. To fire on them, and on a man of Lewis's stature, would be to push America to the brink of revolution—a revolution not of scattered bands of farmers, but of tens of thousands of workers under organized leadership in key industrial centers. As in Spain, or Italy, or Germany, the consequence might well be the division of the country between the extreme right and the far left.

Placing his prestige at stake, the President asked General Motors to bargain. Governor Murphy wired the sheriff of Genesee County to take no action against the strikers.

As the deadline passed and neither the sheriff nor the National Guard appeared, rumors of victory swept the ranks of the workers circling the plant. An impromptu celebration began. Hillbilly songs mingled with "Solidarity Forever." Men and women danced in the street. Wives passed children through the windows of the plants so that they could become reacquainted with their fathers. Although there was no indication that the deadlock had ended, the breaking of the tension gave the workers a sense of triumph.

On February 4, negotiations commenced in the Detroit court of Judge George Murphy, the governor's brother. Since the two sides refused to meet face to face, the governor, himself acting as the go-between, shuttled proposals between them from the courtroom to the jury room. At 2:35 A.M. on February 11, after a week of continual maneuvering and bargaining, an agreement was signed. General Motors would recognize the union as the bargaining agent for all workers designating it as such. The plants would be evacuated. Negotiations would follow.

Carrying American flags, the bedraggled men marched jubilantly out of the plants amidst the cacophony of impromptu bands featuring rattles, harmonicas, whistles, guitars, accordions, cymbals fashioned from pieces of steel—any implement that could be used to make noise. With them, wearing red and green berets, marched the women's emergency brigade. Union membership in Flint soared to forty thousand. Overall, auto union membership climbed to two hundred thousand.

The settlement that followed brought a wage increase averaging only five cents an hour. Nevertheless, the starting hourly wage reached its highest point in history: 20 percent over 1936 and 28 percent above 1929. Most importantly, the union would never again have to fight for recognition.

76

The Battle of the Overpass

AN EPIDEMIC OF SITDOWNS SPREAD AROUND DETROIT. ALUMINUM WORKERS, ironworkers, drug workers, grocery workers, shoe makers, cigar makers—all emulated the Flint sitdowners. Thirty members of the National Guard who had been in Flint sat down because they had not been paid.

In mid-March the UAW sat down in the Chrysler plant. Outside the plants, police clashed with workers. Protesting the "police brutality," the union called a mass rally in Cadillac Square. Tens of thousands of people poured into the square and jammed every street leading to it. The gathering was by far the largest in the city's history.

Fearful that the workers' continued violations of the law would bring on counteraction by vigilantes, Governor Murphy sponsored a Law and Order Committee to mobilize public support for peaceful settlement of labor disputes. Despite his dim view of the sitdown, he took the lead in negotiating the Chrysler strike. When a court ordered an injunction, the Wayne County sheriff tucked it into his pocket and did not serve it. On April 6, 1937, Lewis and Walter Chrysler signed an agreement. Other independent auto companies fell into line.

Ford was a different matter. General Motors might dominate Flint. But Ford totally controlled Dearborn. In April the Supreme Court declared the Wagner Act constitutional, removing the legal straw to which the auto magnates had been clinging. Edsel, nominally the president of the company, was in favor of negotiating with the UAW. But Henry Ford was convinced that the union was but the latest device of the Wall Street-Communist conspiracy against him, and that Lewis, Reuther, and the rest of the union leaders must all be Jewish.

Seventy-four years old, he was descending into senility, and was soon to suffer a stroke. Yet the grip he and Bennett held on the company was as iron as ever. In the plant nothing the men did escaped the eyes of the ubiquitous service men, who made up one fifth of the work force. Outside the plant, Bennett, liberally sprinkling money about, extended his tentacles into every facet of the area's life. Many of the Negro ministers were beholden to him. The mayor of Dearborn was a Ford concessionaire. The Wayne County Republican organization was under his influence. So thoroughly had he infiltrated the UAW that service men were spending much of their time reporting on each other. The Knights of Dearborn were injected with new life, and assigned the task of fighting labor organizers and Communists.

With the sitdown at General Motors, Bennett increased the size of his force even further. No pirate ship ever had a more motley crew. They consisted of gangsters, discharged police officers, and athletes who had gone astray. There was Eddie Cicotte, banned from baseball in the Black Sox scandal; Norman Selby, alias Kid McCoy, a battered ex-fighter who would have married eleven times but reduced his total by one when he murdered one of his sweethearts (a mishap for which he served eight years in San Quentin); Angelo Caruso, the former head of the Downriver Gang; Sam Cuva, who had shot his mother-in-law; "Legs" Laman, a kidnaper and rumrunner.

For union activists to shut down an assembly line as at Kelsey-Hayes was impossible. To assault and capture an entire plant like Chevrolet Number Four was unthinkable. The events of Flint had served to reinforce the beliefs of Ford and Bennett that the law would bend to accommodate whoever showed himself the stronger. Despite the criticism heaped upon the company for the killing and wounding of the 1932 hunger marchers, the event quickly had been forgotten, but the status quo had been preserved.

Flushed with their victories over General Motors and Chrysler, the UAW obtained permission from the Dearborn city council to pass out handbills. It was a brisk spring day as a quartet of UAW leaders, Walter Reuther, Richard Frankensteen, Richard Merriweather, and Ralph Dunham climbed the flights of stairs leading to the overpass across Miller Road to the plant. Behind them, mostly on streetcars, came other proselyters, many of them women. The overpass offered a panoramic view of the surroundings: the Rouge River, dirty and polluted, leading vaginally into the interior of the huge Ford complex; the ore freighters being unloaded by the massive cranes; the smokestacks exhaling into the wind; the railroad yards with row upon row of boxcars; the famed "rotunda"; the acres and acres of parking giving proof that the American worker was the world's most affluent.

Reuther, natty, a gold chain across the front of his vest, a fountain-pen-and-pencil set sticking out of his pocket, was in the lead. Frankensteen, a former Dayton University football player who now looked paunchy, was slightly out of breath as he followed. Trailing were the other two men, both wearing glasses.

From the direction of the plant came a group of men, their hats pulled low over their eyes. Among them were a professional wrestler, a boxer, an ex-convict with twenty-one arrests, Caruso, and Sam Taylor, a Ford foreman and the president of the Knights of Dearborn. One had a cigarette dangling from the corner of his mouth. Another, coatless, exhibited a colorful vest. In the lead was a sparrow of a man, not more than five feet four inches tall. As Reuther, expecting a verbal barrage, watched their approach, they so resembled the stereotype of the hoods in gangster movies that he smiled.

In the next instant, he was cracked across the back of the head, and went down. Picked up, he was pummeled, then thrown to the concrete again and again. Frankensteen's coat was whipped over his head so that it formed a straitjacket. As he stood, helpless, he was slugged repeatedly. Dunham and

Merriweather were beaten and kicked. All four were pushed, rolled, and knocked down the several flights of stairs of the overpass.

When other UAW members tried to get off the streetcars, the leaflets were ripped from their hands. The men were beaten. The women were manhandled back onto the cars.

Dunham's injuries required ten days of hospitalization. Merriweather's back was broken. If, as in 1932, there were cries of outrage, among other people there was a sense of satisfaction that, at last, a company had shown it had the courage to stand up to the union. In Dallas, Kansas City, and at Ford facilities around the country, the service men beat union organizers with as much savagery.

After extensive hearings, the National Labor Relations Board accused the company of violating the Wagner Act. Ford retorted: "The things the board charged never happened and could not happen here." Asked if he knew the facts, he snapped: "I don't want to know the facts." [1]

77

The Permanent Depression

FOR HAROLD AND ELMIRA LENTICK, THEIR THIRTY-DOLLAR-A-WEEK INCOME WAS a windfall they could hardly believe. They acquired a 1932 Hudson. In one of the subdivisions that had sprung up during the 1920's near River Rouge Park in northwest Detroit, they purchased a two-bedroom frame house. Like all the other houses in the neighborhood it was set on a small lot and had a matchbox appearance. It had neither a basement nor central heating. Although the subdivision had been as jerry-built and planless as those in the older sections of the city, the fact that it was newer and that the residents had higher incomes gave it a better appearance. Most of the houses were neatly kept. Nevertheless, the streets and the empty lots, inadequately patrolled and cleaned by the city, were littered with paper, refuse, and old cars in various stages of decay.

While a telephone continued to be a luxury, and about a fourth of the houses had no indoor toilet, most of the people in the area were working and living more comfortably than they had in years. Making thirty to forty dollars a week, they saved a little toward the inevitable layoffs, but spent most. They spent money on cars and on furniture, on movies and on radios. Scarcely a family was without a radio—to be without a radio was to be really poor. Knowing that if they were laid off they could always go back on a job with WPA gave them a new sense of security and confidence. Talking with his neighbors, Lentick was amazed by how many of them suddenly had become outspoken union supporters—a year before you could have talked "union" only with your most trusted friends.

Elmira rejoiced over the improvement in her life and kept thinking she would have to visit Marie Rose. The Norveth children were all going their own ways, and although there were close ties between certain of the sisters and brothers, family feeling was not strong. No one was more isolated than Marie. It was only occasionally that Elmira would hear a secondhand story about what a difficult time the Jansens were having.

Eight-year-old Rita Jansen dug her fingernails into the windowsill. The man, speaking to her kindly, kept saying: "Little girl, now little girl," trying to persuade her to let go. But the silent screams within her drowned out his pleas. The man, who had told her when he came to the door that he was a constable, said that they had to move because the building was being torn down.

Rita felt as if she could not move. As far back as she could remember, she had moved every few months of her life. If it was difficult for others, it was torture for her. Her perception of the world was through frosted glass. She could discern movement, and light and shadow, but little else. Each time the family moved she had to become familiar with an entirely new world: new rooms, new neighborhood, new dangers. Now she was determined to hold on to her world. As the constable pulled, her fingers, scraped and bloody, brought a small piece of the sill with them.

The constable carried Rita out to the sidewalk and placed her on top of the couch. The remainder of the family's belongings were grouped around the couch. Immediately thereafter the wrecking crew moved into the building. A few minutes later, with creaking and crashing sounds, the structure came apart. Its demolition had been ordered by the city housing authority, which was engaged in Detroit's first slum-clearing project.

Rita was terrified. Dust drifted down on her. Marie and Peter had left at seven o'clock to look for a new place to live, and told Rita to look after the four younger children. But Rita could barely see them, much less keep track of them all. Seven-year-old Jim had disappeared. For nearly two years he had been roaming the city on his own. Becoming wise to the ways of the adult world, he had developed an instinct for discriminating between people who were likely to buy him a hamburger at the White Tower Restaurant, and those who would try to turn him over to the police. His favorite place was the entrance to the Windsor Tunnel. Not only was it exciting to watch the cars, but every so often a motorist would not bother to get out of his car after dropping a coin. Then Jim would scramble across the road to pick it up.

Other days he went to watch the trains in the railroad yards—the same yards in which Thomas Edison had arrived daily seventy-five years before. Near the warehouses he could sometimes find a banana or a carton of cookies. Once he had rifled a sandwich from a workman's lunch box. The second time he had tried it, he had been caught. The whipping he received left him bruised for a week.

It was less dangerous to scour the cars that were parked on the side streets. Most were unlocked. In them he was able to find an amazing number of articles, as well as loose change. The articles were always negotiable—people never questioned his declaration that his mother had sent him to sell them or to exchange them for food.

The marriage of Peter Jansen and Marie Norveth, brought about by an accident of pregnancy, had grown less sustainable with the birth of each child. Marie did not know how to manage money, keep house, or care for children. When Peter gave her money, she spent it within a few days. Sometimes Peter's next pay day was still three or four days off when the family's food supply ran out. Then, as the children cried with hunger, Marie would rush out and buy candy bars for them with forty of her last fifty cents. With her remaining dime she would escape to the movies, and forget the world in which she lived.

Peter's resentment increased with every manifestation of Marie's failure as a mother. His accusations became more frequent and bitter. Since, however, he lacked the ability to articulate, she was usually able to gain the advantage.

She would yell that he was a drunkard and not a proper father and provider, and that he could not expect her to remain home all day seven days a week and have no fun. She would taunt him until he hit her. Then he would storm out of the house to get something to drink.

The larger the family grew, the more difficulty they had renting a place to live. The roach and rat and vermin populations were drawn from the walls of the decrepit roominghouses by Marie's slipshod housekeeping, the stale food scattered about, and the urine-soaked beds. The children continually had bites and sores, upset stomachs and diarrhea. In the bathroom-short dwellings, they often relieved themselves in the hallways. In the last three years the Jansens had never stayed more than six months in one place without being asked to move.

All the children, in accordance with the marriage agreement, were baptized in the Catholic faith. The Society of St. Vincent de Paul and the League of Catholic Women took occasional interest in the family. But at a time when resources were lacking to take care of all the families who were destitute through no fault of their own, there was little sympathy for people whose misery stemmed from their own inadequacies and inability to manage their income.

Until a few months before, Peter had continued working as a truck driver for Kroger's. Although he was forty years old, he looked ten years younger. His muscles, developed in his youth, were awesome; he could lift more than two hundred pounds. He was a simple man, well liked. He even laughed when the other drivers made him the butt of their practical jokes. His likableness had led the company's manager to put up with him far longer than his work record warranted. He repeatedly was involved in minor accidents. Although he was able to follow simple instructions, if anything out of the ordinary occurred he did not know what to do. He had difficulty reading maps, and sometimes he became lost. Often he could not decipher a bill of lading. He tried to be diligent; but when he was frustrated by a problem, he took refuge in drinking. After three or four drinks, a solution seemed easier—though it was seldom the right one. Peter Jansen was being overwhelmed by complexities for which his rudimentary education and boyhood in the woods had not prepared him. Several times he received suspensions and warnings. Finally, in the summer of 1936 he had been discharged. When he was unable to find a job, he was put to work on a WPA project. His reduced income resulted in a further deterioration of the family's situation.

Marie seldom had a "baby-sitter" for the children. She would merely tell a neighbor that she was leaving. If a neighbor were not handy, she would indicate to Rita that she expected her to take charge. From the time she was six years old, Rita was left alone. Shivering with loneliness and anxiety, she huddled and cried. Sometimes her crying would rouse another tenant, who might call the police. The Jansen file at the women's division of the police department grew steadily.

The wreckers left. Behind Rita the house, which four hours before had represented home, was a heap of rubble. Rain began falling. Although she threw a blanket over herself and the baby, she was soon soaked through, and shivered in the forty-degree temperature. Jim had not come back, but his two younger brothers begged pennies from passersby, and splashed them with mud when they did not respond.

It was nearly five o'clock when Marie and Peter returned. The couch, the two ragged mattresses, and the few clothes the family possessed were sodden. When she saw them, Marie began crying. Then she realized that Jim was missing. Since he did not know the family's new address, the police would have to be notified. She sobbed that she did not know what to do. She could not take care of so many children, and wished someone would take them off her hands.

The Jansens' new quarters consisted of an upstairs flat that was reached by an outside stairway. The fifty-year-old wooden building was damp and mildewed. There was no bathroom, only a sink in an alcove, and a privy in the backyard. A wood-burning stove served for both cooking and heating.

Under the hard wear to which the children subjected the stairs, several of the slats soon gave way. One of the boys plummeted ten feet to the frozen ground and broke a rib. Instead of repairing the staircase, the landlord nailed a ladder to the landing. Although he said the ladder was temporary, he did nothing to repair the broken steps.

At the end of November, 1936, the WPA project on which Peter was working was terminated. Its director suggested to Peter that the economy had improved sufficiently for him to find private employment. When Peter was still jobless ten days later, however, he had no recourse but to seek help from welfare. Public assistance provided the Jansens with money for rent, groceries, and fuel, but it was seldom enough, and there was no provision for paying other bills. The family had few clothes, little bedding, and no furniture except the beat-up couch. For three months, from January through March, there were only two bushels of coal to heat the rooms. The freezing wind was a constant visitor in the uninsulated, crack-streaked house.

Odoriferous, sneezing, feverish, their eyes red, their throats sore, their bodies aching, the children breakfasted on dry cereal, crackers, bread; perhaps bananas. There was never enough to eat. Whenever Jim went to school, he smelled so badly and was dressed so poorly that the other children mocked and avoided him, and, as a last resort to drive him away, gang-beat him. Roaming the city, stealing, cadging food, he did not often go to school. Rita had only one dress and no underwear, and did not attend the "sightsaving classes" in which she was enrolled. The smaller children wandered half naked through the streets, and begged food and pennies.

Marie smoked to drive away her hunger. She bought the cheapest cigarettes. But two or three days before the next welfare payment was due she would be out of both money and cigarettes. Desperately she would sift through the meager stock of food for items she could swap for cigarettes. In the hope of making the big hit she played policy with the Yellow Dog Company; so another dollar disappeared weekly.

Rita, sleeping on the mattress with her parents, was an intimate witness to their copulations. Although she did not fully understand what was going on, at the age of nine she was more *experienced* than most middle-class college girls.

In April of 1937, Peter was hired by a trucking company. His pay was fifteen dollars a week, and sometimes he was able to work overtime to make more. Conditions in the household improved. Occasionally he drank while driving to bolster his confidence. But for nearly a year he stayed out of trouble.

Early in 1938, he was ordered on a trip to the north of Michigan. It was his first return to the lumbering country he had left more than twenty-three years before. Roads cut through what had been a wilderness. But the land was as sparsely populated and far less prosperous than it had been in the early years of the century. Lumbering operations were a third of what they had been when Peter had left. Lumber production in Michigan was one twelfth of what it had been in 1890. Here and there smoke rose from a farmhouse. But the skeletal remains of other farmhouses and barns evidenced the difficulties of cultivation in the harsh climate. The rust-encrusted rails of one of the abandoned narrow-gauge railways briefly skirted the highway.

At the roadside cafés at which Peter stopped there was lament at economic conditions. People talked of "stranded" families who were unable to make a living off the land, yet had nowhere else to go. The small towns were laced with boarded-up buildings. Before the Depression, small farmers had been able to make ends meet by tilling the soil in the summer and working part-time in the mills or the mines in winter. But employment in the iron mines was a third of what it had been. As more machinery was introduced, productivity increased: one man was mining twice as much ore as he had twenty years earlier. There was less need for casual labor. Employment in the copper mines had all but disappeared. Michigan copper cost over eleven cents a pound to mine. Yet, as a result of competition from African and other foreign mines, the price of the metal hovered at about five cents a pound.* With the encouragement of the United States Government a land of vast riches had been ruthlessly despoiled. Scores of men had made their fortunes from it. Now, having lost its allure, it was withering in a state of permanent depression.

In the rest of the United States the economic euphoria of 1936 and early 1937 was ending in an economic slide whose swiftness exceeded that of 1929. In the three years after 1933 the Roosevelt Administration pumped up the economy with record peace-time expenditures. The Federal government spent $9 billion more than it received. In 1936 the World War I veterans were paid their bonus, which acted as a one-time, $1.4 billion infusion into the economy. Most of the Federal money went to people who had been able to buy only essentials for four or five years, and they went on a spending spree. Business prospered. Corporate dividend payments for 1936 and 1937 totaled $9.2 billion, only 18 percent below 1929–1930.

The dividends, of course, siphoned money from the pockets of the general population into those of the upper tenth. In 1937 Americans in the upper half of the economy were receiving 79 percent of all income, the highest proportion ever. The bottom third of the population was subsisting on less than 10 percent of the total American income. The end of the Depression had generated a new upsurge in productivity. Fewer unskilled workers were needed than ever before. (The proportion of unskilled workers in auto factories dropped from 20 percent of the labor force in 1930 to 11 percent in 1940.) During the peak of production in 1937, six million persons remained unemployed, and millions of others, not actively looking for work, were "nonstatistics." The Michigan Emergency Welfare Relief Commission reported that it continued to be "necessary to support as many as a half million Michigan men, women, and children through some form of public assistance. This represents about

---

* The "cut-over" counties from which the timber had been removed were averaging between 24 and 37 percent of their populations on relief, and during a period of three years one out of every two persons had been assisted. During the peak months of each year, between 43 and 63 percent of the people in the four mining counties were on relief.

one out of every ten persons in the state who, given conditions as they have been during the past ten years, will be permanent public charges." The "contradiction between relative prosperity and public dependence has become . . . pronounced." [1] President Roosevelt himself was unable to understand the "paradox."

Evidently the lower third of the population was now dependent upon at least partial support from the government. But, greatly pleased by the economic resurgence, the administration cut WPA and CCC expenditures by more than a fourth, and in other Federal work programs reduced the number assisted by more than half. The Federal deficit, which was acting as an agent to redistribute income from the upper to the lower portion of the population, fell from $3.6 billion in 1936 to $358 million in 1937.

The economic repercussions were immediate. Like the production of 1929, the auto production of 1937 swamped the new-car market, still essentially limited to the upper fifth of the population. Between 1937 and 1938 vehicle production fell 48 percent, and the many industries dependent upon auto manufacturing went into comparable declines.

Of the men laid off from WPA in 1937, two out of five were unable to find jobs at all. Two fifths were forced to take jobs at a lower wage than the unskilled security wage—the amount essential for a minimum standard of living —they had been receiving at WPA. More than half the men separated from WPA between April and July of 1937 made application for relief by August. By March, 1938, 310,000 of Detroit's 760,000 workers were unemployed. Unemployment nationally was near 11 million. The Michigan Emergency Welfare Relief Commission could see no solution except a *"continued outlay of Federal funds for a permanent public works program."* * [2]

On his return trip from the north Peter made good time. It was the early afternoon of a bright spring day when he reached the outskirts of the city. Ahead he saw a beer garden. He decided to stop there for lunch.

An hour and a half, five beers, and two shots of whiskey later, he started for the trucking terminal. He was swinging the truck around a corner when, suddenly, he noticed a bus turning the same corner. The two vehicles jammed together side by side. The accident was not serious; but of course it brought the police.

In November, 1936, the Recorder's Court had established the office of Traffic Psychotechnologist to examine chronic traffic offenders. The office was headed by a psychologist, Alan Canty, who had developed the then-novel theory that certain drivers are responsible for an unusually high number of accidents, and should be weeded out as poor risks. After testing Peter Jansen, Canty wrote:

"He is classified as feeble-minded on the basis of his test performance, a rating which is in keeping with the fact that after five years of schooling he was able only to complete the second grade. His work record has been erratic, and his industrial activities have been of a consistently inferior level. More important, perhaps, is the matter of alcoholism. And in this respect, his appetite has already become chronic. In view of the patient's alcoholic interests, coupled with his feeble-mindedness and unsocial attitudes, we may reasonably suspect

* Original italics.

that future traffic depredations will be committed. In view of the patient's de-
viations we might say that the permanent revocation of his driver's license
should be seriously considered."

Peter's driver's license was suspended. In the midst of a new depression, he
was deprived of the only occupation he had practiced in fifteen years. The family
went back on relief.

Two months later Marie was admitted to Providence Hospital to have her
sixth child. From a charity establishment for foundlings and for women who
had gone astray, the hospital had grown into a huge, solid-stone structure
occupying an entire square block. More Catholic children were born there
than in any other hospital in the city. Three days after Marie gave birth, she
followed a sister's suggestion and went to the chapel. The chapel was a high-
ceilinged structure of stained-glass windows and statuary. As patients had contributed to it in gratitude for their recovery, it had taken on the magnificence
of a cathedral. Marie, who had not been to church in years, cried as she sat
in its peaceful splendor.

The obstetrician, shaking his head, said she should have something done
about her teeth. Bit by bit they were breaking off and crumbling. The dentist
who probed her sore and receding gums told her he suspected she had abscesses.
At the age of twenty-five, she looked at least ten years older, and felt exhausted.
Joella was her sixth child. She did not want her. She told the sister that she
could not cope with five children, and that a sixth child was entirely beyond
her. The sister, expressing a mixture of shock and understanding, replied that
postparturient depression was common. Marie should pray and she would feel
better. But the more Marie compared the surroundings of the chapel with
those to which she would return, the more she cried.

On the fifth day of her hospital stay, a police patrol car discovered Jim and
the other two boys scavenging through garbage cans for food. Only Jim had
shoes. The officers did not believe the boys when they said they lived in a
house with a ladder. But when the police arrived at the flat, they found it
necessary to climb the ladder. Rita was alone. The boys' mattress was soaked
with urine, covered with flies, and infested with bedbugs, which had left bloody
marks on the children.

When the landlord was cited for not repairing the staircase, he responded
by evicting the Jansens. They were lodged in the city's emergency shelter.
Caseworkers from the Department of Public Welfare, the women's division of
the police department, the St. Vincent de Paul Society, and the Juvenile Court
met to decide what to do about the family. They concluded that Marie was
right, and that she could not care for six children. The Juvenile Court assumed
supervision over the family. Two-year-old Alice was placed with foster parents
in the city, and Jim and his two brothers were boarded with farm families.
The court would pay the cost of $5.25 per child per week—more than Marie
had been able to spend on all three together. All had innumerable cavities in
their teeth. Jim had abscesses between his toes, skin lesions, and a chronic infection of the genitalia that contributed to his enuresis. The other two boys
needed orthopedic and neurological care. The court assumed responsibility for
the medical treatment—treatment the children would probably not have received had Peter and Marie been more capable, if equally poor, parents.

Rita underwent the first of a series of operations to remove her cataracts.
Frightened, she developed psychosomatic symptoms: asthma and chronic sinus-

itis. An additional operation was scheduled to remove her tonsils and adenoids. After the operations she would be so tense and in so much pain she was given barbiturates.

The caseworker even arranged for Marie to begin treatment on her own teeth, a half dozen of which would have to be extracted. With only Rita and the baby, Joella, remaining at home, Marie's housekeeping improved. Peter was assigned by the WPA to a surveying team and paid sixty-six dollars a month. Since the tensions were fewer, he drank less.

78

Monuments to Genius

Demolishing the ancient, rat-infested buildings inhabited by the Jansens and other unfortunate families had not been difficult for Josephine Gomon and the Detroit Housing Commission. Getting new housing built was far harder. In 1937 the program Eleanor Roosevelt had inaugurated with such fanfare nearly three years earlier had yet to produce a single new housing unit.

Since 1929, private construction of homes for low- and middle-income families had all but ceased.* Even though 14 million new housing units would be needed by 1945, in 1935 more housing was being demolished than was being built.† Yet Detroit's realtors, like real estate interests throughout the nation, fought bitterly against the erection of public housing by the city. It "would destroy all incentive for home ownership and break down that great barrier against the spread of communism." A spokesman for the New York Real Estate Associations predicted it would bring about "the end of our country." [1]

The opposition of the Wider Woodward Association was vehement. Since almost all the slum housing demolished had been occupied by Negroes, there had been an assumption that the new housing project would be built for blacks. In 1930 there had been scarcely a single Negro beyond Beaubien Avenue, three blocks east of Woodward. The growth of the black population, however, combined with the destruction of housing in the ghetto and the movement of the white population from within the Grand Boulevard area, was bringing on an outward rippling of the black population. By 1937 Negroes were to be found as far east as Mt. Elliott Avenue, as far north as the edges of Highland Park and Hamtramck, and as far west as Woodward Avenue.

It was the westward expansion which generated shivers of apprehension in the merchants, businessmen, and real estate owners who composed the Wider Woodward Association. Seeking to reverse the steady decline of business in the

---

* During the second half of the 1920's, an average of 447,000 houses had been built yearly in cities of more than 25,000; in the first half of the 1930's, the number was 74,000.
† In three years New York City had torn down 36,000 housing units without replacing them. Yet more than 60 percent of Manhattan continued to be a slum in which 66,000 "old law" rookeries, occupied by "people living . . . under conditions repulsive to every human instinct," remained standing. [2]

downtown area, the association lobbied for a program of renovation and slum clearance. To brake the Negro expansion, the association wished to use the housing project to implant a white colony in the midst of the black ghetto.

Complicating the issue, Negroes and liberal whites of the Urban League and the NAACP wanted to employ public housing to break down racial segregation, and were opposed either to an all-white or an all-black project. In the atmosphere of the Detroit of the 1930's such a stand promised to kill the project altogether. Even as congressional committees launched investigations to prepare legislation to deal with the abysmal housing situation in the United States, Detroit's project still had not progressed beyond the architect's plans.

Calling John Dancy and two dozen of the city's Negro leaders together, Jo Gomon told them bluntly: "Either we have a segregated project, or we won't have any. So make up your minds." After a day-long debate, the participants voted for an all-black project.

To counter the opposition of the Wider Woodward Association, Mrs. Gomon devised the policy that "no housing project shall change the racial characteristics of a neighborhood." The policy was designed to cater to the fears of whites, but also to undermine the position of the association. Her language accurately reflected the mood of the nation and was incorporated into the Wagner-Steagall Act creating a United States Housing Authority.

The hearings on that act were moving toward a denouement. Surveys showed the desperate straits of the lower-income population of the cities. Sixty percent of American families had incomes under one thousand dollars a year, and were unable to afford decent housing. A major portion of Schenectady's General Electric work force, earning sixteen to twenty dollars a week, was paying twenty-five to thirty dollars a month rent for accommodations in the slums. In Pontiac, north of Detroit, people working in the auto plants were again living in tents.

There were three hundred square miles of slums in American cities of over one hundred thousand population, of which nine square miles were in Detroit. (New York City alone had seventeen square miles.) And the slums were economic millstones. The cost of providing services in Detroit's slum area was fifteen times the city average. Chicago's cost for services in the slums was six times the amount returned in taxes. In Cleveland the ratio of services to taxes collected was ten to one.

The residential construction program initiated as an adjunct to the Public Works Administration was proceeding slowly, and only whetting the appetite for more. Only nine projects had been completed. Many cities were so near their debt limits that they were unable to participate fifty-fifty even in slum clearance.* Yet there were up to twenty-five applicants for each finished unit of public housing.

Following the pattern established by the proponents of public education and Prohibition, the proponents of public housing grasped at the chance to demonstrate the association between the slums and crime, poverty, and disease. Detroit's East Side ghetto had seven and a half times the crime rate of the rest of the city, six and a half times the tuberculosis rate, and ten and a half times the juvenile delinquency rate.† Half of Birmingham's 105,000 blacks—living in a

---

* In New York state, eight of the nineteen large cities were in default on their bonds.
† The Cleveland ghetto, representing 2.5 percent of the population of the city, had 21 percent of its murders, 26 percent of its prostitutes, and 10 percent of its illegitimate births. Manhattan's West Side, with 1.7 percent of the Jewish population, had 12 percent of Jewish juvenile delinquency.

cloaca in which 50 percent of the houses had no electricity, 85 percent no toilets, and 95 percent no bathing facilities—had three times the juvenile delinquency and illegitimacy rates of the rest of the city, and were responsible for half of all major crimes. The chairman of the Birmingham Housing Authority warned that "the children will spread to other sections of the country." Secretary Ickes was indignant that "some people are more interested in highways than they are in children. . . . You are breeding children in surroundings that are conducive to degeneration and crime and vice. . . . We have been going along in housing from bad to worse ever since the Republic was founded." [3]

Once more, as with alcoholism, a symptom was inverted into a cause. Since wretched housing and wretched people went together, a rising school of environmentalists proclaimed that if the wretched housing were corrected the wretchedness of the people would disappear.

A New York slum-clearance project was cited as proof of the marvelous effect of public housing upon an area's sociology. To be accepted in the housing project that replaced the slum, tenants had to have been employed for at least one year. They needed a savings account of $100 to $1,000, and insurance of $1,000 to $3,000. The family had to be unbroken. Except under extraordinary circumstances, there could not be more than one child.

With that, crime, disease, and immorality had disappeared.

Why?

What other reason than that the moldering buildings had been replaced with neat new brick tenements?

So the Wagner-Steagall Act was passed. The Federal government would finance construction of housing projects. After they were erected, the cities would operate them. The deadlock in Detroit came to an end, and work on the Brewster project commenced.

Jo Gomon's survey had shown large families had the greatest need for housing. The project, however, was designed for families with no more than two children. After all, replacing large families with small had been shown as the proper way to bring about the reformation of a slum. Furthermore, smaller units meant *more* units could be built for the same number of dollars—an important factor in congressional justification. Although it had been demonstrated that "low-cost housing" was a myth, and Secretary of the Interior Ickes warned that "we get nowhere if we replace a slum with a building that would be a slum in five or ten years," [4] Congress aimed for a construction cost of $4,000 per unit—half of what prototype projects in New York had cost. The financial restrictions meant that the units would have to be small and the projects would have to be barren and devoid of amenities. Since the projects were intended to be self-supporting, they could not accept people who were on relief, who were sporadically unemployed, or who had incomes of less than $750 a year—two thirds of the families who were living in the slums. What would happen to the slum dwellers as their housing was torn down, or what would happen to the new areas they moved into, no one was prepared to delve into. Certainly no one was going to suggest that sweeping people from one area to another would simply spread the blight—such a suggestion would not only be heresy to the environmentalists, but provide a devastating argument against the legislation. Since the estimated cost of providing decent housing merely for working-class Americans was $60 to $64 billion, the time was not right to worry about the plight of the economic dropouts.

Directing himself toward the housing projects in Williamsburg and Harlem, New York's Mayor La Guardia lauded the legislation:

"One hundred years from now people will be looking at those houses . . . as monuments to the genius and the vision of American statesmen." [5]

79

"The End of the
Ford Motor Company"

THE CONTROVERSY OVER HOUSING WAS ONE OF THE ISSUES THAT HELPED Richard W. Reading win Detroit's mayoralty election in November, 1937. Fifty-five years old, a roly-poly five foot three inches tall, he had built a political following during his twelve-year tenure as city clerk, and was the champion of all that was traditional in the city. His opponent was a New Deal Democrat backed by the CIO and the auto workers.* Charges that the Communists were attempting to take control of the city government drew twice as many voters to the polls as in 1935, when Frank Couzens had been victorious. Reading's triumph by better than one hundred thousand votes was cause for jubilation among the Republicans and businessmen—a year after the liberal tide had crested in 1936, it seemed to be rapidly ebbing.

No sooner had Reading taken office than he complained that his fifteen-thousand-dollar salary was not enough to support him in the style to which he had become accustomed as city clerk. Appointing his son as his executive secretary, he proceeded to utilize his powers as a "strong mayor" to establish himself as the vice-czar of the city—a development the members of the Good Citizens League had not foreseen when they had succeeded in eliminating the corruption of the ward bosses. Nicknamed "Double Dip" Dick because he demanded a rake-off not only for himself but also for his son, Reading had a take as high as $55,000 a month. Top jobs in the police department were so lucrative that there was open bidding, and promotions went to the highest bidder.

Affable and punning, Reading might well have presided for years over his citywide gaming establishment had it not been for the fatal despondency of a jilted lover. In August, 1939, a bookkeeper in a policy joint murdered her child and committed suicide after being spurned by her boyfriend. On her body she left letters addressed to the FBI, the governor, and the newspapers, charging that her boyfriend was a "bag man" for the police department. Payoffs to top officials were detailed.

* The CIO also ran a slate that included Walter Reuther for the city council. Reuther, however, finished last in the fifteen-man field.

366

Never had a greater sensation burst upon the city. Circuit Judge Homer Ferguson was appointed as a one-man grand jury (and later capitalized on the publicity to win a United States Senate seat). Among the 135 persons indicted were the mayor and his son, the county prosecutor, the sheriff, the superintendent of police, Joe Louis's manager, and 80 police officers.

The situation was ideally suited for the operations of the Ford Motor Company's Harry Bennett. Spending money liberally, Bennett knew more of what was going on in the police department than the commissioner himself. When two of his service men were identified as the attackers who attempted to kidnap Walter Reuther in August, 1938, the police proved as incompetent in gathering evidence as they had in the Buckley murder, and the men were acquitted.*

In more than a dozen cities where Ford had plants Bennett employed thugs and gangsters to intimidate, beat, and sometimes cripple and blind suspected union members, as well as citizens who gave assistance to them. Not only in Detroit, but in Dallas and Kansas City he worked hand in hand with the police. In the latter community he threatened to move the plant to Omaha if the city itself did not crack down on and bust the union. Gillespie, who had assembled an arsenal of tear gas and other noxious gas bombs in the Ford film vault, took to disrupting union meetings with stink bombs.†

These activities led the UAW to file charge after charge with the National Labor Relations Board. Edsel, frustrated and humiliated, urged his father to negotiate with the union. Henry, increasingly affected by cerebral arteriosclerosis, would hear none of it. Instead Bennett initiated a campaign to destroy the menace of the UAW through a Ford coup.

Turmoil within the union offered him the opportunity. Split between the Populist Fundamentalism of its president, the Reverend Homer Martin, the socialism of the Reuthers, and the communism of Secretary-treasurer George Addes and Vice-president Wyndham Mortimer (with a small Trotskyite splinter group thrown in for good measure), the UAW had mushroomed from 35,000 to 350,000 members in two years. Even the best of administrators would have had difficulty putting order into such an organization, and Martin had no administrative talent at all. By far the best organized, the Communists dominated the union, and gained even more power when Martin turned against the Socialists, and fired Roy and Victor Reuther. For a few months John L. Lewis managed to patch up an accommodation between Martin and the Communists. But in June of 1938 Martin suspended Addes and Mortimer, as well as Frankensteen, who was suspected of being allied to them.

In June of 1938, Father Charles Coughlin organized the Workers Council for Social Justice at Ford. P. E. "Pete" Martin, a French-Canadian who was one of the few surviving executives from the early days at Ford, was a member of Father Coughlin's parish. Martin was trying to bridge the gap between the one-time antagonists, Henry Ford and Father Coughlin. Anti-communism and anti-

* The assault came to be known as the "Chop Suey" incident, because a delivery of Chinese food was expected when the gunmen barged in on a birthday celebration being held in Reuther's apartment. When the pair ordered Reuther to come with them, he grabbed a floor lamp and swung it at them. One of the women threw a pickle jar, and in the ensuing bedlam one guest jumped out of a second-story window and ran for the police.
† Constantly watched by Bennett, whom he was watching for Ford, Gillespie became convinced that people were after him, and that he was destined for elimination. In the midst of the union battle in 1938 he blew his mind and turned his arsenal against Michigan Republican boss Frank D. McKay and Governor Fitzgerald, stink-bombing their homes.

Semitism were the bonds that drew them together. As usual, Ford blamed his troubles on the Jews; and Father Coughlin had become increasingly strident in his denunciations ever since the debacle that had befallen his political coalition in 1936.

Designed to marshal the latent anti-Semitism of the blue-collar workers against the "Jewish" UAW and CIO, the Workers Council for Social Justice excluded all non-Christians. Pronouncing anathema on any Catholic who joined the UAW, Father Coughlin in July, 1938, announced the organization of a Christian Front. He proposed the formation of a fascist corporate state as the only means to provide full employment, and hailed Mussolini as "Man of the Week" in his *Social Justice* publication.

From Ford, Coughlin obtained the *Protocols of the Elders of Zion.* A decade after Ford had renounced the material published by the *Independent,* Coughlin commenced its republication in *Social Justice.* When it was emphasized to him that the material had been proven false, Coughlin retorted that whether it was true or not did not matter, because "some unseen force has taken Christianity out of government, business, and industry, and, to a large degree, education." [1]

Ford worked desperately to bring down the Democratic administration in Washington before the courts could catch up with his flagrant violations of the National Labor Relations Act. He gathered the Roosevelt haters under his wing and set them to work denouncing Communists, the CIO, and Jews. He provided financial assistance to Gerald L. K. Smith. Smith became a radio preacher in Detroit, and began to influence Protestants as Coughlin was influencing Catholics. Ford supported Charles Lindbergh's Germanophilic "America First" committee. Cameron founded the Anglo-Saxon Federation and established a "speakers' bureau" to send people across the nation to warn against Communist, CIO, and Jewish subversion. Through Cameron, even William Dudley Pelley and his Silver Shirts were linked to the company. The Nazi-fronting National Workers League, fulminating against Jews and Negroes, established one of its strongest cells at River Rouge.

On July 30, 1938, Ford was awarded the second highest German decoration, the Grand Cross of the German Eagle, at a public ceremony in Dearborn.* A lesser decoration, the Order of Merit of the German Eagle, went to Liebold. Passing out a hundred swastikas in the Ford offices, Liebold urged everyone to put them on. Ida Steinberg, a secretary whom Liebold described as a "very efficient girl . . . it took three to take her place when she went on vacation," was told to pin on one of the swastikas. She burst into tears.

Liebold tut-tutted: "You are just one of a lot of other Jews who have to go through the same thing. Don't pay any attention. Let it roll like water off a duck's back." [2]

Criticized for accepting the decoration in light of Nazi persecution of the Jews, Ford said he thought the reports of persecution were greatly exaggerated but he would be glad to give refugees jobs on the Ford assembly lines. Coughlin explained the Nazi persecutions as a "self-defense mechanism against Communists and Jews." Stories of atrocities were merely "Communist propaganda." It was only the "international Jews" who were being punished. "Good Jews" had nothing to fear. [3]

---

* Hitler had offered Ford a partnership in development of the Volkswagen, but Ford rejected the offer. Both Ford and General Motors had a low opinion of the VW, which G.M. President Knudsen decided had no future in the American market.

Even as the Ford-Coughlin anti-Semitic, antiunion drive was rising to a crescendo, Homer Martin was locked in a desperate struggle to retain control of the UAW. In the late summer-early fall of 1938, Bennett discerned his chance. At his behest, Father Coughlin invited the Reverend Homer Martin to dinner in Royal Oak.

At the conclusion of dinner, Coughlin went into a tirade against John L. Lewis as a stooge of the Communists. Then suddenly he asked:

"Homer, how would you like to have the auto workers organize the Ford Motor Company?" [4]

Martin, Coughlin suggested, should meet with "kindly, old Henry Ford." Ford had no idea of the things that were being perpetrated in his name, and he would not object to a union if it were not a Communist, subversive union controlled by the "international Jews." It was impossible to negotiate with Walter Reuther, who undoubtedly was controlled by the Jews. But if Martin would rid himself of the UAW and these people, who knew what might happen?

Martin took the bait. In October he entered into secret negotiations with Ford. Inevitably, before long the secret was out.

The union split asunder. In January, 1939, Martin called one convention and the Communists, now the major and controlling force, called another. Discredited by his behind-the-back dealings, Martin was able to command the loyalty of only one out of every seven union members. Taking his splinter group into the AFL, he was financed by Ford and offered a union building by Coughlin. In plant after plant the workers voted for the UAW, despite its Communist leadership. In fact, only the opposition of Reuther and the pressure applied by Lewis and the CIO prevented Mortimer and the Communists from gaining control of the UAW.

During 1939 and 1940, the NLRB served one "cease and desist" order after another on Ford. Ford, however, delayed compliance by appealing to the courts. One of his hopes was destroyed in the fall of 1940 when Roosevelt was reelected to a third term. On February 10, 1941, the United States Supreme Court turned down his appeal. All avenues of delay were exhausted.

Eight days later compliance notices, granting workers the right to organize, went up in the plants. Decades of pent-up frustrations and resentment exploded in a massive flowering of union buttons. Prounion signs were tacked on walls and machines. In the radio department a worker clandestinely set a selector button onto the frequency of the small union station, which was broadcasting to Ford workers in several languages. In some departments, workers elected shop stewards.

Bennett, nevertheless, continued his harassing tactics, transferring some union men and firing others. Don Marshall, the Negro "boss," passed the word to blacks that Ford wanted them to support Martin and the AFL union. If an election were held and the workers voted for UAW representation, Ford warned that he would refuse to bargain. With the company and the union on a collision course, Edsel on one side and Reuther on the other worked behind the scenes to avoid a potentially bloody confrontation.

Throughout March there were sporadic sitdowns. On the afternoon of April 1, when 8 union stewards in the rolling mill were fired, 1,500 men sat down and immobilized the mill. Bennett summoned the Dearborn police. As 110 officers moved in and tempers flared, a pitched battle threatened to erupt. Since the Supreme Court had declared sit-ins illegal, Reuther did not want a sit-in.

Promising that the workers would not try to occupy the plant, he averted a show-down, and the police withdrew.

At 12.30 A.M on April 2, fifty thousand workers at River Rouge walked off their jobs and into the night. In an impromptu parade, singing "We don't give a damn for the A. F. of L.," "Solidarity Forever," and "Old Hank Ford, he ain't what he used to be," they marched four abreast to union headquarters a mile away. The strike was on.

The UAW's strategy was to seal off the plant. Barricades of cars, junk, rail-road ties, and telephone poles were erected on every road. Along the railroad tracks and on the drawbridge across the river, union men took control of the switches, so that neither trains nor ships could travel in or out of the plant.

Ford was furious. He proposed to arm the nonstrikers so that, if necessary, they could fight their way into the plant. On the morning of April 2, squads of Negroes armed with iron bars and other implements charged out of Gate Number Four to try to break through the union lines. Wielding clubs, pipes, and baseball bats, the union men repulsed the charge. Thirty-six were injured.

Bennett asserted the strike was a Communist conspiracy to take over the plant and that sitdowners, rampaging on drunken sprees, were sabotaging machinery. He asked President Roosevelt and Governor Murray Van Wagoner to send the National Guard and Federal troops to Dearborn. If the National Guard intervened, the CIO retorted, Detroit would be shut down by a general strike.

The men who remained in the plant—some four or five thousand in all—were not, in fact, sitdowners but Ford supporters. Most were service men. A few hundred whites were Martin adherents or members of the Workers Council for Social Justice. A thousand, including Odie Stallings, were Negroes.

The blacks hated the service men—who were even more ready to beat up a "nigger" than a white worker—and there were brawls between the two groups amidst the brooding machinery, storage bins, and giant furnaces of the eerily quiescent plant. Negroes had little more liking for Ford than white workers had for him—since 1937, Ford's wages had been below average for the industry, and the wages of blacks were below those of whites. In the foundry where the fierce red heat turned the sweating bodies of the men to glistening black marble, and the pounding, screeching din of metal was a cacophony dredged up from Dante's *Inferno,* speedup had followed speedup. Stallings was participating in the dismantling of two hundred old cars daily.

But for Negroes things were better at Ford than elsewhere. Since 1930, Negro employment in the automobile industry had dropped from 30,000 to 21,000—less than 4 percent of the total—and 10,000 of the 21,000 were at Ford. While Ford had upgraded Negroes, and had virtually the only black tool-and-die work-ers and foremen in the industry, the advent of unionization had made things even more difficult for Negroes at the other plants.

The leadership of the UAW was committed to nondiscrimination, and there were nondiscriminatory clauses in the contracts. But at the plant level the white union leaders—dependent upon the votes of the many Southern and Polish workers for reelection—ignored the clauses. Blacks were not upgraded and placed in charge of whites, nor admitted to all-white departments.

For years many of the Negro ministers in the ghetto had been in Bennett's pay. On the second night of the strike Martin organized a meeting in "Paradise Valley," and urged three thousands blacks to march in a body back into the plant. Such a course would have set off a racial holocaust. John Dancy of the Urban League, Walter White, executive secretary of the NAACP, and other "liberal" Negro leaders firmly backed the UAW and thwarted Martin.

But when White went out to River Rouge and, using a megaphone, called to the blacks to leave the plant and join the strike, only a few responded. To Stallings and the blue-collar workers, the NAACP was an organization of the upper class that meant nothing to them (many of them had never heard of it), and they saw little advantage but much danger in casting their lot with the UAW.

If the Ford strike resulted in as much sensation as the General Motors sit-in four years earlier, it caused far less alarm. Curiosity was the general reaction among the public; sightseers crowding the roads to River Rouge added to the effectiveness of the UAW blockade.

At Wayne University, which had grown into the second largest municipal university in the country,* the left-wing American Student Union mobilized students to aid in the picketing of the plant.

One of those who responded was a sociology major named Harold Black, the twenty-one-year-old son of Abraham Schwartz. To finance his education, Black was working a fifty-six-hour week as a barker at a busy amusement park in East Detroit. He did most of his studying on the ninety-minute streetcar rides each way.

His ambition had been to teach English in college. But a counselor had told him he was foolish. No college would hire a Jew by the name of Schwartz to teach English. Americanization and the necessity for assimilation continued to be shibboleths. So he had Anglicized his name and changed his major to sociology.

At River Rouge, Black passed leaflets through the fence—a chancy business since service men were grabbing arms, pulling them through, and breaking them. Sporadic fights between pickets and service men, between whites and blacks, and between Martin and UAW adherents were erupting all around the perimeter. So effective was the blockade that a youth who wanted to collect his pay check in order to buy an engagement ring attempted to swim the River Rouge to get into the plant. But the river was so badly polluted that it was like trying to stroke through molasses. Coated with oil, grease, and chemicals, he was pulled out half drowned.

In the Cavanagh household, feelings about the strike were mixed. From the assembly line, Sylvester J. had worked himself up to the position of boiler-maker, a skilled job with a good deal of security. In 1939 his eldest son, Paul, had joined him at the plant. Both carried home the tensions created by Bennett's spies, the speedups, and the dehumanization. Sylvester knew that on a service man's whim he might be dropped back to the assembly line or fired; that if he fell ill, he would be discharged without a second thought. A union was needed. Yet as a staunch Catholic, an admirer of Father Coughlin, and a believer in "social justice," he was affected by the charges that the UAW was controlled by Communists. He therefore tended to lean toward Martin and the AFL.

Both the Federal government and Edsel applied pressure on Henry Ford. The administration warned that Ford would not receive a single government contract. On April 11, 1941, ten days after the onset of the strike, Ford agreed to let the National Labor Relations Board hold an election.

---

* The City College of New York was by far the largest.

In 1937, after the Battle of the Overpass, Bennett had sent his service men around the plant to collect the signatures of workers on a loyalty pledge to Ford; and 98.3 percent had signed. Ford felt confident that the new election would produce a vote of vindication. At most, he predicted, a fourth of the workers had been deluded to the point that they would vote for a union.

In the secret election held on May 21, 58,000 Ford workers voted to join the UAW, 23,000 voted for Martin and the AFL, and fewer than 2,500 voted "no union."

Having suffered a stroke in 1938, Ford believed more and more that he had "divine guidance." Suddenly he felt himself, Job-like, to have been struck down. His grandson and heir, Henry II, a sociology student at Yale, had in 1940 married Mary Anne McDonnell and been converted to Catholicism. It was a conversion Ford regarded as little less than a catastrophe—if only young Henry could have heard William Ford's tales of the wretchedness and depravity of the Catholics in Ireland! On June 19, when Henry Ford saw the contract prepared by Edsel and Bennett and the UAW leadership, he went into a tantrum. He refused to sign. Rather than hand over River Rouge to a Communist-Jewish conspiracy, he would close down the plant. It was the end of the Ford Motor Company!

Throughout the day and evening, Edsel, Clara, and Bennett worked to convince him that John L. Lewis, Walter Reuther, and R. J. Thomas, who had succeeded Martin as president of the UAW, were neither Communists nor Jews. Bennett pointed out that he had always been able to infiltrate every organization, and that he had a multitude of spies within the UAW.

The next day Ford signed the contract. Not only did Ford agree to match the highest wages paid anywhere in the industry, he consented to pay back wages to four thousand workers discharged for union activity. Bennett, confident of his ability to work from within, volunteered to have the company check off union dues from the workers' pay, and to make Ford a closed shop—agreements the union had been unable to obtain from any other manufacturer. It was a victory as great as that at General Motors in 1937.

80

Sojourner Truth

FOR THREE YEARS AFTER HE HELPED DIRECT THE KELSEY-HAYES STRIKE IN November, 1936, George Edwards was an active unionist. He was one of the first members of the Ford Organizing Committee. In 1938 he organized the sitdown at the Yale and Towne Company. When a judge ordered the plant vacated, Edwards refused to obey the order. Showering nuts, bolts, and locks down on officers from the roof of the building, he led the defense against the police assault. One hundred and twenty workers were arrested. Edwards was sentenced to thirty days in jail.

Shortly thereafter he was appointed national director of the UAW's welfare department. A friend from his days at Harvard heard he was in Detroit and suggested:

"Why not look up Peg McConnell?"

Peg McConnell was the daughter of an arch-Republican who had been one of the city's leading brokers and investment bankers before the Depression. When Edwards rang the doorbell, he was greeted with all the enthusiasm of a Robespierre calling on the daughter of Louis XVI.

Nevertheless, like many of the other offspring of Detroit's society, Peg McConnell had reacted against the pre-Depression conservatism of her parents by swinging into liberalism. There was an immediate attraction between her and Edwards. In April, 1939, they were married.

The marriage precipitated a crisis in the boardrooms of General Motors second only to the one occasioned by the sitdown. Just ten months before, Peg's sister had married Semon E. "Bunkie" Knudsen, the son of G.M. President William Knudsen and himself a rising young executive in the corporation. Suddenly the president of General Motors was linked through two marriages to the welfare director of the UAW—and God only knew what intimate corporation secrets might find their way into union hands through that route!

It was an intolerable situation, one that seemed to G.M. executives as improbable and unreal as the plot from one of Horatio Alger's books. In real life, assembly-line workers simply did not marry the genteel daughters of the upper class.

That was essentially true in the age of Horatio Alger. But at the same time that education was raising the intellectual level of the American population, the Depression had pushed millions of the educated down to assembly-line jobs. Edwards was a match in brilliance and background for any General Motors executive. When workers had erupted in 1936 they had been able to draw upon an educated leadership from their own ranks. It was this leadership that brought unprecedented success to the organizing efforts. College-educated men like Reuther, Edwards, and Frankensteen had consistently outorganized and out-maneuvered business executives, who were thinking in outdated terms.

G.M.'s dilemma was solved when Detroit's new mayor, Edward Jeffries, Jr., appointed Edwards director of the Housing Commission. (Jo Gomon had been dismissed from the post two years earlier when Reading had come into office.)

Between 1930 and 1935 fewer than 7,400 residential structures had been erected in the city, and the number for the decade was less than one third that built during the 1920's. Since 1937 a combined total of 1,500 public housing units had been completed at Brewster, the downtown Negro project, and at Parkside, a white project near the city airport. But as the outbreak of a new war in Europe stimulated Detroit's industry, there was a growing shortage of housing. Edwards was faced with the necessity of quickly expanding the housing supply.

New units were added to Brewster and Parkside, and ground was broken for three additional "white" projects.* A mile north of Hamtramck work started on the Sojourner Truth Homes, a new project for Negroes. Construction had barely commenced before the Polish neighborhood on which the project intruded rose up in arms. Edwards held steadfast against the pressure. In November, 1941, however, he was elected to the city council—at twenty-five the youngest man ever to take his seat in that body. On January 4, 1942, three weeks after the completion of the project, the Federal Housing Director sent a telegram stating that Negroes must be admitted to Sojourner Truth. On January 5 he sent another, advising city authorities to "disregard the previous wire." On January 20 under pressure from Representative Rudolph G. Tenerowicz, whose mostly Polish district consisted of Hamtramck and six adjacent Detroit wards, the Federal government redesignated Sojourner Truth Homes as a "white" project.†

Detroit's Negro leaders were incensed. In January of 1941, the most prestigious black union leader, A. Philip Randolph, of the Brotherhood of Sleeping Car Porters, had threatened a March on Washington if the Federal government would not act against the rampant discrimination in industry and government. Assuming the role of mediator, Eleanor Roosevelt had persuaded her husband to establish a Fair Employment Practices Committee in return for cancellation

---

* Herman Gardens and the John W. Smith Homes in the northwest, and Charles Terrace on the east side.
† A former mayor of Hamtramck, Tenerowicz had been involved in the scandals of the 1920's and 1930's, but, after his release from prison, had been elected to Congress in a landslide in 1938. Called the "Wild West of the Middle West," Hamtramck was an inimitable example of Polish society transplanted to the United States. Most of the residents were blue-collar workers at Dodge, Briggs, and Ford. Strongly Catholic, they preferred a wide-open town whose vice dens put even Detroit's to shame. (One gambling parlor flourished in the building housing the director of public safety.) Economic control was shared, as in Poland, between Jews and a few well-to-do Poles. Anti-Semitism was widespread, deep-rooted, reinforced by Father Coughlin and often supported by the parish priests. Candidates commonly ran on such platforms as "throw the Jews out of Hamtramck."

of the march. On pain of termination of government contracts, Roosevelt's order banned "discrimination because of race, creed, color or of national origin." But in the face of political and industrial antipathy and resistance, the FEPC sat like a stuffed owl, peering down but incapable of action. Unemployment among Negro men in Detroit was still 16 percent. The razing of slums near the downtown area had only aggravated the problem of housing for blacks.

Under pressure from Negroes and white liberals, Mayor Jeffries sent a telegram to Washington protesting that converting Sojourner Truth into a project for whites "would be tantamount to saying to the Negroes that there is no place within the city of Detroit where they can have new housing." [1] As Detroit Negroes threatened to revive the March on Washington, the administration reversed itself again, and on February 2 reconstituted Sojourner Truth as a "Negro" project.

Rioting would be the result, Representative Tenerowicz predicted on the floor of Congress. Pickets marched day and night in front of the Detroit city hall. On the night of February 27, 1942, one hundred fifty pickets patrolled the project to prevent Negroes from moving in, and a cross was burned in a nearby field.

Father Coughlin had first taken to radio when the Ku Klux Klan burned a cross in front of his church. A decade and a half later, amid the continuing hate propaganda spewed out by Coughlin and Gerald L. K. Smith, the Catholics and the Klanners—whose Michigan organization had revived following the demise of the Black Legion—marched side by side around Sojourner Truth. Real estate dealers and parish priests joined in exhorting them on.

Early in the morning of February 28 the crowd grew to twelve hundred. When the first Negro tenants arrived and saw the gathering spread out along the roads and across the fields, they turned around and left. Shortly after ten o'clock fighting started between whites and a few score Negroes. Sixteen mounted police officers moved into the middle of the road to keep the two sides apart. But when a truckload of Negroes armed with pipes appeared, fighting broke out anew. A hundred police officers were rushed into the area and stationed there for the next several days to keep the mobs separated.

In fact, the police acted principally in support of the whites. Whenever fighting broke out, the police arrested the blacks, not the whites. (Of seventy-eight persons arrested, seventy-six were Negro.) Investigating the riot, the Federal Office of Facts and Figures reported that "in order to keep the peace . . . police seem bent on suppressing the Negroes," a policy that "seems to point straight to civil warfare." A police lieutenant expressed the opinion that "if you locked them up, they just ate free," and "if you shot them, they didn't have to worry any more." [2]

For two months the impasse continued. Mayor Jeffries demanded that the Federal government take responsibility for moving in the tenants, and the Federal government responded that it was a local problem. When the first tenants took up residence in the project on April 30, they had to be protected by 1,750 police officers and army troops.

81

"Detroit Is Dynamite"

IN THE EIGHTEEN MONTHS AFTER PEARL HARBOR AND AMERICA'S ENTRY INTO
World War II, 350,000 people converged on Detroit. The city's effort to increase
the housing supply was overwhelmed. Houses that had been abandoned a half
dozen years before were commanding rents of one hundred dollars a month and
more. Real estate operators paid off the delinquent taxes on ramshackle structures and reaped fortunes.

Once again war brought a spectacular surge of industrial construction, and
once again Ford erected the most innovative and gigantic complex. In 1917 he
had built a factory at River Rouge to mass produce ships. In 1941 he decided
he would show the world how to mass produce airplanes. For the assembly of
the B-24 bomber, Albert Kahn designed a factory building a mile long and a
quarter mile wide that could accommodate one hundred thousand workers under
its roof.*

The factory was located twenty-seven miles from downtown Detroit in the
farming community of Willow Run, near Ypsilanti. But when the U.S. Housing
Authority began to survey land for the construction of housing for workers,
both Ford and the people of rural, Republican Washtenaw County objected.
They did not want hordes of blue-collar Democrats coming to live in the community, nor thousands of children for which schools would have to be built.

* Kahn immediately surpassed himself by designing an even larger factory on the outskirts
of Chicago for aircraft engine production by Chrysler. When he died in 1942, he was the
world's foremost industrial architect. The factories designed by him in the United States and
in Russia played a major role in the outcome of the war. In 1928, upon Ford's recommendation, Kahn had agreed to design a twenty-million-dollar tractor plant for the Soviet Union.
It turned out to be only the first of 521 Russian factories for which he drew the plans.
When the Germans reached Stalingrad in the winter of 1942–1943, the Russians converted
Kahn's massive steel and concrete factories into fortresses. It was among these that the
German attack bogged down, in what is generally considered the turning point of the war.
    In America, no architect of his time dominated a city more. He was the designer of the
Ford, General Motors, Chrysler and Packard plants; of all three of the city's newspaper
buildings; of the General Motors and Fisher Buildings; and of scores of others.
    Upon his death, his home on Mack Ave. was sold to the Detroit Urban League for the
knockdown price of $20,000. It continues to be the League's headquarters.

Ford and Bennett themselves plodded over the squishy ground and pulled out the surveyor's stakes. When the regional director of the housing administration protested, Ford drew a revolver and threatened to shoot him.

By the fall of 1942, twenty thousand people were employed at the plant. Most were commuting from Detroit.* To reduce the commuting time and the number of accidents, the city began construction of its first expressway. (It was America's second urban expressway. The Arroyo Seco Parkway in Los Angeles was built in 1940.)

The expansion of production and the siphoning of men into the armed forces provided job opportunities for Negroes for the first time since 1929. Few were "desirable" jobs. Nevertheless, the pay was far more than the blacks were used to. Between 1941 and 1943 the number of Negroes in Detroit jumped from 150,000 to 200,000.

Donald, the son of Freda and Odie Stallings, had come to the city in 1936. Sixteen years old at the time, he had finished the eighth grade. He had a permanent limp—the result of having lost three toes from frostbite when he had run away from home in 1931. Working on and off at dishwashing and other menial jobs, he would go home to Inkster when he ran out of money. In early 1939 he was hired by WPA. Soon thereafter, in a bar, he met Irma, the daughter of Wallace and Antoinette Mirow.

In the booming city, Wallace Mirow was doing well with his coal and ice business. After expenses, he netted between three hundred and four hundred dollars a month. He had bought a neat, comfortable house near Mack Avenue and St. Aubin Street, a Polish neighborhood that was being infiltrated by blacks. Having grown up in a middle-class environment in Cleveland, he had successfully made the transition to farmer, and then back to small urban entrepreneur.

Antoinette and Irma had been far less successful. Lonely, unable to make friends, Antoinette acquired a reputation for being "strange," and this increased her isolation. Irma, awkward, shy, indrawn, dropped further and further behind in her schoolwork. She was teased without respite by the neighborhood children. Like her mother she had no friends, and dreaded meeting anyone on the street. Her father was a good provider, but he worked long hours and offered little companionship. Only when she discovered the darkness and anonymity of bars, where a glass of cheap wine acted as a bridge between one human being and another, did the loneliness leave her. When she came across Donald Stallings, and he made no demands on her and did not make fun of her but accepted her as she was, she fell into his arms.

They were married in 1939. A year later, their first child was born. They tried living with her parents, but Donald could not get along with Antoinette. Their quarrels upset not only Antoinette, but Wallace. In the summer of 1942, Irma and Donald moved out.

Donald was hired by the city sanitation department as a garbage collector at 50 percent more than his WPA wage. Yet the cost of the family's food and lodging was three times as much as at the home of Irma's parents. They paid twenty-two dollars a month for a single room. They used a communal water tap and had no bathing facilities. The backyard privy consisted of a hole dug down

---

* The lack of living accommodations for workers helped produce chaos at Willow Run. Labor turnover was 50 percent a month. The goal of the plant was "a bomber an hour," but during all of 1942 it produced only fifty-six planes. Derisively it was referred to as "Willit Run?"

into a city sewer line—there were thirty-five hundred of these outdoor accommodations almost within smelling distance of the downtown business district.

Living in a hovel, more isolated and lonely than she had ever been, Irma
made the neighborhood bar her recreation center. Since few people in Paradise
Valley and Black Bottom had decent living accommodations, the bars, streets,
ten-cent movie houses, and poolrooms were jammed with people. Except that
the faces were black, the atmosphere was that of the immigrant districts at the
turn of the century. All but a handful of the Jews who had lived on Hastings
Street twenty-five years earlier had moved on to Twelfth Street, but they still
owned the groceries and pawnshops, the tailor shops and second-hand stores—
all the cheap-goods places designed to cater to a low-income population. After
more than a decade of hard times, they were reaping bonanzas.

Hemmed in geographically, repressed occupationally, restricted to the *leavings*
of the wartime economic feast, the Negroes were restive and deeply unhappy.
(A poll indicated 83 percent of the city's black population was dissatisfied, the
highest such percentage in the nation.) President Roosevelt's "equal opportunity"
order was not being enforced. Of the 185 war plants in the Detroit area, producing 35 percent of all American ordnance, 55 hired virtually no blacks. Like
the Irish a hundred years before, the rural, mostly Southern whites who flooded
into Detroit expected the Negroes to take the back seats; they could not understand how their "inferiors" might have better jobs and a higher economic standing than they. Conversely, the urbanized Negroes, often better educated than
the newcomers, were incensed at being passed over for upgrading and training
in favor of the neophytes. Both management and shop stewards ignored governmental directives and union policy.

At one factory after another there were bitter disputes, sitdowns, and walkouts. Repeatedly Negroes struck over the lack of enforcement of regulations,
and their failure to receive promotions at Packard, Chrysler, Hudson, and the
Timken Detroit Axle Company. When two Negro metal polishers were transferred to war work at Packard, white workers struck, and management rescinded
the transfer.

The city was a cauldron of hate propaganda. Following the Sojourner Truth
riot, the archdiocese ordered Father Coughlin to say no more; but the KKK,
the Nazi-fronting National Workers League, and Gerald L. K. Smith more
than made up for his silence. The Negroes were said to be universally syphilitic
—their contaminated blood purportedly oozed from their fingers onto the
machines at which they worked; if a white man were forced to use the same
machines, he too would become diseased. As thousands of white men contracted venereal disease from the whores they patronized on Hastings Street,
the propaganda mills attributed the epidemic to integrated working conditions.
Running against Judge Homer Ferguson in the 1942 Republican senatorial
primary, Gerald L. K. Smith polled an astonishing 109,000 out of 308,000
votes.

Conversely, from the large number of educated Negroes, from the liberal
Jewish element, and from the descendants of the Progressive Republicans, the
NAACP had built its largest and most powerful chapter in the country. In
Walter Reuther's West Side local, the strongest in the UAW, Negroes working
at Ford held important posts.

The leadership of the NAACP, the Urban League, and the UAW were proclaiming that the battle against fascism and intolerance abroad was meaningless

unless there was a simultaneous destruction of bigotry in America. How could freedom and self-determination be right for Europeans and Asians, but not for American blacks?

On April 11, 1943, ten thousand persons attended an "equal opportunity" rally sponsored by the NAACP and UAW in Cadillac Square. In the first week in June, delegates from thirty-nine states met at an "Emergency War Conference" in Detroit. Denouncing discriminatory practices by the U.S. Employment Service, Civil Service, industry, and the armed forces, the conference declared, "American Negroes and colored peoples all over the world will justly regard the Four Freedoms as hypocrisy unless the President acts to end discrimination." [1]

But when three blacks in the Packard foundry exercised the greater militancy that they were being urged to, and forced the company to agree to upgrade them according to seniority, twenty-five thousand white workers walked out. Over a loudspeaker a voice shouted that it was better to let Hitler and Hirohito win than to work "next to a nigger!" [2]

The city was a beaker of nitroglycerin with the ever-present potential for explosion. A series of secret reports by the Federal Office of Facts and Figures warned that "hell is going to be let loose in every Northern city where large numbers of immigrants and Negroes are in competition," and that the situation was most critical in Detroit. In August, 1942, *Life* magazine found that "Detroit Is Dynamite," and that it "can either blow up Hitler or it can blow up the U.S." On June 3, 1943, Walter White declared, "A race riot may break out here at any time." [3]

The competition for overcrowded public facilities caused repeated flareups. Hundreds of thousands of whites were outraged that blacks did not have to stand in separate queues at movie theaters, that they could sit on streetcars while whites stood, and that first-come, first-served rules prevailed. Black and white students rioted at Northwestern High School. Repeatedly incidents occurred on the rickety transportation system that was carrying two million riders a day. On the Sunday after the Packard walkout a fight broke out in a park in Inkster, and battling spread over nearby Romulus Township. Two days later, on June 15, a small riot erupted in the East Detroit Amusement Park at which Harold Black had worked.

But no one in Detroit, including Mayor Jeffries, recognized a pattern in the disturbances or anticipated that they might explode into something bigger. The city's leaders had grown so accustomed to the staccato of small explosions that they were deaf to the thunder on the horizon.

Belle Isle was a persistent trouble spot. Every weekend, as soon as the weather turned warm, tens of thousands of Detroiters swarmed to the island. A near-equal mixture of whites and blacks competed for the boats, horses, bicycles, rides, picnic spots, tables, hot dog stands, and pavilion. All of the facilities were overtaxed. Even without the racial antagonisms there would have been bumping, shoving, and short tempers. Feeling was especially bitter between Poles and Negroes—the two major ethnic groups in the lower economic stratum —who everywhere in the city rubbed against each other.

June 20, 1943, was like any other Sunday, except that with the temperature near ninety degrees the park was even more jammed than usual. An estimated one hundred thousand persons were bumping about in less than two square miles. Footloose youths of both races roamed about making a nuisance of themselves, insulting people, and acting like small gangs. In an atmosphere in which people were tired of being pushed around, everyone was being pushed around.

Still, there was no ominous portent, nothing more than a rash of the normal cursing, purse snatching, and minor incidents of assault and battery. In the warm evening the crowd stayed late, and many people did not start leaving until twilight settled about nine o'clock. On the island, lines of people waited to get on the buses, of which there were far too few. Tens of thousands set off on the three-quarter-mile hike across the bridge to the mainland.

Even under normal circumstances, the intersection of Grand Boulevard and Jefferson Avenue at the end of the bridge was a bottleneck. Streetcar and bus lines crossed each other, Jefferson Avenue was lined with large industrial plants, and on the southeast corner stood the U.S. Naval Armory. By ten o'clock traffic was not only backed up along the bridge toward Belle Isle, but was strung out for blocks along Jefferson Avenue. Amid the streams of pedestrians on the bridge, there was inevitable jostling between whites and whites, between blacks and blacks, and between whites and blacks.

Following an altercation, a group of Negro teen-agers chased a white man along the bridge. Two sailors came to his rescue. Within the hour, two hundred sailors were roaming up and down the bridge from the intersection. Fighting was not generalized. Whites and blacks formed small, battling knots that would quickly break up and swirl someplace else. The intersection was like an arena, in which first one match, then another took place. Several thousand people coming from the island and from industrial plants, which were changing shifts, milled about in an area of three or four blocks. All but a handful were spectators. Police rushed 166 men to the intersection. By two o'clock they had dispersed the crowd. A few people had suffered injuries, none serious.

At midnight, Hastings Street in Paradise Valley was still carpeted with people. Jazz and boogie-woogie intermingled with the aroma of frying food and drifted like mist over the small neon signs. Darkness veiled the shabby, tawdry street with a patina of mystery. Doors stood open, revealing nothing of the black caves of the buildings into which they led. Occasionally a prostitute, leading a customer—more often white than black—disappeared into one. In the pleasant evening, people lingered in the street.

Donald Stallings was sitting in a bar just south of Forest Avenue. Irma had been with him until a little after ten o'clock. But, pregnant with their third child, she had grown tired, and he had told her to go on home. After she had left, he had gone into the back room, where a crap game was always in progress. Loaded dice continually floated in and out of the game, and hustlers feasted off ducks like Stallings. He seldom came out ahead, and frequently lost heavily. But when he watched a game, looked at the bills and coins forming a hypnotic pile, and listened to the exhortations of the shooters, the compulsion to join overwhelmed him. He stayed in the game for not much more than a half hour, and then went back to the bar to brood about the five dollars he had lost.

Around midnight a man came in and excitedly started talking about a "war" on the Belle Isle Bridge. The white people had called in the navy, and the black folk were getting their heads knocked in. At first nobody paid much attention to him. But then suddenly everyone was gathering around and voicing indignation. Every day Negroes heard on the radio that the war was being fought for democracy and to free people from Nazi oppression. At the same time, however, Negroes, who were fighting in that war, continued to be oppressed at home.* Blacks deeply resented the biased and segregationist policies of the armed services. Riots broke out at several army posts and "service towns." †

At the corner of Forest Avenue and Hastings Street, a young Negro jumped to the stage of the Forest Club, the largest establishment in the Negro ghetto.‡ Impersonating a police officer, the youth shouted that white people were attacking Negroes on Belle Isle and that a black woman and her baby had been thrown off the bridge and killed.

Stallings had emerged from the bar and was standing in the street when seven hundred people exploded out of the Forest Club as if a family of skunks had been let loose inside. Most of them were young, like Stallings, and many were eager for action. Someone heaved a rock at a white motorcyclist going by. Struck cleanly, he toppled off the bike, which skidded and burst into flames.

Down the street Stallings heard a crash of glass. One after another, the windows of the liquor stores, the groceries, the clothing stores, the cleaners, and the *Hock with Yock* pawnshops crashed down. With their Jewish proprietors sleeping on Twelfth Street, there was no one to protect them. In the rooms and apartments above the stores, Negroes had replaced the Jews. Awakened by the noise, many drifted down into the street.

The police headquarters on Beaubien Street was on the edge of the ghetto, and scarcely five minutes removed from the heart of Hastings Street. Police arrived within a half hour of the first trouble. But they received no orders and had no training in how to cope with such an outburst. Taking isolated actions, shouting, "Move, nigger!", "Get the hell out of there, niggers!", "Where you going, nigger!" they were not numerous enough to restrain the looting. Staying on the edge of the area, some of them grabbed and beat Negroes who were uninvolved, and by their abrasiveness merely inflamed the situation.

While most of the crowd turned to looting stores, some black men were bent on "revenge" for the rumored beatings and killings of Negroes on the Belle Isle Bridge. Several major east-west arteries crossed the ghetto. In the early morning hours there was a continuous traffic of workers changing shifts at industrial plants. Sporadically, cars driven by whites were stoned as they crossed Hastings Street. A score of Negroes attacked a streetcar and beat the motorman, conductor, and a half dozen pasengers. Harold Black's uncle, Hymie Schwartz, the first of the brothers to have arrived in Detroit, was driving to Eastern Market to pick up produce for the grocery store he now operated; as he crossed Hastings Street, a rock hurtled through his car window and struck him on the head, injuring him painfully but not seriously.

It was after three o'clock in the morning when fourteen-year-old Jim Jansen

---

* Negroes who entered a *white* U.S.O. or a *white* latrine were courtmartialed. In Indiana, one hundred Negro officers had been locked in the stockade for attempting to integrate a *white* officer's club. Black military personnel—both men and women—were frequently beaten and occasionally lynched. Isaac Woodward returned from overseas to have his eyes gouged out by a South Carolina sheriff. In a riot in Alexandria, Louisiana, twenty-eight black soldiers were shot down by civilian and military personnel. German prisoners of war guarded by Negro soldiers ate on the diners of Southern trains. If one of the black American soldiers had sat down, he would have been arrested.
† In a navy that was almost pure white—only a few thousand Negroes were admitted as mess boys and in other menial positions—sailors were quick to erupt in racial attacks. During a few weeks in the summer of 1943, ship workers and sailors rioted in three port cities: Mobile, Alabama, Beaumont, Texas, and Los Angeles.
‡ Nearby was the mansion belonging to the family of Charles Lindbergh's mother, as well as the first Edison Co. substation at which Henry Ford had worked.

emerged from the all-night movie theater on Woodward Avenue. Five years before, he and his two younger brothers had been separated from Peter and Marie and placed in farm boarding homes. When Jim was expected to conform to a discipline he had never known, he became morose and anxious. He did not rebel against doing chores like carrying wood, gathering eggs, and feeding the chickens. But he did them without enthusiasm. So long as the weather was good he roamed for hours by himself across the fields and woods. But when winter confined him indoors, he quarreled and fought with the other boys. He responded alike to reward and punishment with a shrug of the shoulders. Never having owned anything himself, he considered property impersonal. He took anything that was left unguarded. Admonitions that taking other people's belongings was "stealing" did not impress him, for the *concept* of stealing was alien to him.

Theoretically, the boarding homes to which children were sent were carefully checked. But there was conflict between theory and the practical consideration that the demand for homes was greater than the supply. The homes *were* decent. The obvious boarding-parent misfits *were* usually eliminated. But most farmers kept the children for the supplemental income they brought and the extra hands they provided. Few, if any, were qualified to deal with the variety of psychological and behavioral problems the children brought with them from the city. The children were simply being removed from the deleterious urban environment and placed in rural isolation until they were sixteen.

Jim failed to adjust. The Juvenile Court moved him from one boarding home to another. In December, 1942, he ran away after a violent quarrel with his boarding parents. Caught shoplifting, he wound up in the jail at Mt. Clemens.

A caseworker thought Jim might do better with a member of the family. His grandmother, Theresa Norveth, offered to take him. William Norveth had died in 1939 at the age of sixty-four. More than thirty years of industrial labor followed by the spirit-destroying Depression had worn him out. Between the early 1890's and 1915 William and Theresa had had ten children who survived. The youngest boy had been ensnared in the juvenile delinquency of the Depression, and was in prison. Several of the children had had difficulty in school. The boys had become blue-collar workers, and the girls had married men employed in the automobile plants or one of the ancillary industries. Some like Elmira and Harold Lentick were doing reasonably well. Others like Marie and Peter Jansen were in continual difficulty economically and were failing in the care of their children.

As soon as he was back in the city, Jim's spirits picked up. He resumed his old habits and returned to his old haunts as if he had never left them. The disorganized wartime town with its well-paid workers, frenetic bars, and crowded stores offered far more opportunities than the city of the 1930's. As the days turned warm in the spring of 1943, Jim roamed around downtown Detroit. He stole, ran errands, loitered about pimps, peddled pornographic postcards in the railroad and bus stations, and made himself useful in the underground of the flourishing black market. Theresa Norveth could control him no better than Marie Jansen and the boarding mothers had been able to control him. He returned to her house only when he needed "rest."

The city was full of youths in their teens and twenties with backgrounds similar to his. In the early morning darkness of June 21 a group of them sauntered in front of the Woodward Avenue theater. Someone came up and said that "the niggers in Paradise Valley have gone wild." The youths began talking about "getting us a nigger." Soon someone yelled, "There goes one now!" and they chased helter-skelter down the sidewalk.

They cornered him in an alley, and beat and kicked him to the ground. They ripped open his pockets, snatched off his watch, and fought over the money and ration stamps that tumbled from his wallet.

Not only was nigger hunting exciting, it could be profitable. Small gangs of white youths congealed along Woodward Avenue. The police ignored them. When a Negro complained, an officer told him: "You don't belong here. Get the hell back to Paradise Valley!" Other officers laughed as they watched the Negroes being chased down the street. Seeing what was happening, some of the Negro patrons about to emerge from the theaters scurried back inside.

For a couple of hours, Jim roamed along the avenue. Then, tired out, he searched for a car parked along a side street, jimmied open the door, crawled inside, and fell asleep.

At 4 A.M., a conference got under way in the police commissioner's office between Commissioner John Witherspoon and Mayor Jeffries. Shortly after the outbreak of the disturbance on the Belle Isle Bridge, the 3,400-man force had been placed on twelve-hour shifts, enabling the city to put more than 2,000 officers on the streets. Almost all of the persons arrested were Negro. Watching them being brought into the building, the police commissioner and the mayor could not decide whether to ask for Federal assistance—several hundred military police were stationed in the Detroit area, and could be on duty within the hour. Arrests, however, steadily declined in number and at dawn ceased almost entirely. Commissioner Witherspoon decided that the "serious rioting" was over. He advised the mayor that the police should be able to handle the situation. He was mistaking momentary exhaustion for surcease—an error that has been repeated in every American riot to the present day.

On Hastings Street people emerged into the morning, saw windows shattered, goods strewn about the pavement, and no police to protect the stores. Looting resumed. Making sorties into the area, the police used their guns on anyone who attacked them, offered resistance, or tried to make a run for it. Negro casualties mounted.

The police sealed off Hastings Street, and warned whites to stay out of the area. Some, nevertheless, ventured in. Most were not molested. A few were attacked by small gangs or individuals with rocks and knives. A handful lost their lives. One was saved only because he was stabbed in front of the hospital toward which he was heading to pick up his wife and newborn child—several of the city's "white" hospitals, which continued to refuse to add Negroes to their staffs, were in the ghetto area. A light-skinned "Negro" woman had her skull crushed on Hastings Street by a black who thought she was white.

The shots echoing from Hastings Street inflamed the imaginations of the whites gathering a half dozen blocks away on Woodward Avenue. Rumor after rumor swirled through the crowd. Niggers were raping white women. Niggers had killed a twelve-year-old girl. Niggers had murdered a police sergeant. Niggers had killed fifteen people on Hastings Street.

"There's one of them rich, fat niggers!" someone shouted as a car driven by a Negro slowly made its way down the avenue. A brick arced out of the crowd and smashed into the windshield. The car skidded to a halt. The mob surged forward, pulled the driver out, and struck and kicked him as he staggered off. The car was tipped over. A match was lighted. From the middle of the avenue. a column of smoke rose into the sky.

The smoke acted as a beacon that attracted more people, most of them merely curious, but many soon caught up in the excitement. By nine or ten o'clock Jim Jansen was in the midst of a mob of approximately a thousand persons that surged up, down, and across Woodward Avenue. Traffic stalled in the tangle of cars and people. Car after car was overturned and set afire. Yet the police, directing all traffic away from Hastings Street, continued to wave Negroes down Woodward Avenue.

But black motorists did not arrive with enough frequency to keep the mob occupied. "Let's get 'em on the trolleys!" someone shouted. Jumping aboard streetcars, white youths attempted to drag off any black man aboard. Some Negroes who saw them coming tried to get away through the second door and even dived out of windows, but few escaped without being battered and beaten.

The mood of the crowd was more frenzied than murderous. They spit and hated, but did not kill. Everywhere white men who attempted to help Negroes were denounced as "nigger lovers." But routinely the mob backed off. There was none of the fury of a lynching.

The actions of the police were confused, and due more to individual inclination than departmental directive. With most of the force concentrated on Hastings Street, they made no attempt to break up the mob on Woodward Avenue. They did little about Negroes being beaten—in the normal course of events a white man was seldom arrested for battery on a black. But they did pull Negroes out of the grasp of the mob and protect them when it appeared that they would be subjected to serious injury.

From the high-rise buildings occupied by executives and office personnel the street scenes had an air of unreality about them—it was as if Woodward Avenue and Hastings Street were two separate stages upon which one play was being performed simultaneously. At 8:30 A.M. a Negro delegation called on the mayor and urged him to ask for Federal troops. But he put them off. Shortly before ten o'clock, however, he telephoned Governor Harry Kelly to report that the situation was rapidly getting out of control. In the city hall, the councilmen stood around lamenting, speculating whether the riot had been organized by the Axis Powers, and commenting that Detroit had always had excellent race relations. None of them had had any expectation of an eruption. Councilman George Edwards asked Mayor Jeffries what he could do to help, and Jeffries replied that there was nothing any of them could do. So, since the council sessions were limited to mornings, at noon Edwards went off to the Timken Detroit Axle Company, where he worked the afternoon shift from 2 to 10 P.M.

Negro and white leaders meeting with the mayor suggested that "martial law" be declared. None, however, realized that martial law entailed the suspension of all civil government and liberties, and the assumpton of control by the military. The confusion over martial law continued during a meeting between the mayor, the governor, and military leaders later in the afternoon. When the governor left the meeting at 4:30 P.M., he had the erroneous impression that he would have to ask for a declaration of martial law before Federal troops could be committed to the city—actually all that was necessary was a presidential proclamation. Reluctant to ask for martial law, the governor decided to mobilize the State Troops. The Troops were a ragtag outfit of one thousand volunteers that had been organized after the National Guard had been sent off to war. At 6:30 P.M. the governor went on the radio, declared a state of emergency, and ordered the State Troops to duty.

Hours later, when stragglers were still shuffling in, it appeared that the total complement of the State Troops was thirty-two men.

All afternoon the mayor's office was deluged with calls along the line that "those Jews up along Joy Road are ruining the niggers and the town with them." On Cadillac Square, in front of the city hall, and at various downtown intersections, hate literature was passed out. As the sun fell behind the tall buildings and the long twilight settled, a number of cars belonging to Negroes were burning in the downtown area. Workers leaving their jobs drifted to Woodward Avenue to see what was going on. The crowd grew to more than ten thousand. Its mood turned uglier. Suddenly, along two or three different streets, hundreds of people surged eastward toward the ghetto.

Hurling rocks, bricks, and pieces of iron through the windows of the houses, they flowed down the streets. Negroes trying to protect themselves and their homes responded in kind. Numerous persons were struck—and one subsequently died—in the primitive, stone age battle. Flames leaped from one house as whites set it afire. Some Negroes fled toward Hastings Street. A few with rifles and shotguns fired at the mob.

At barricades along John R. and Brush Streets, the police were caught in the midst of the turmoil and crossfire. Many Negroes identified the police not as a neutral force but as an adjunct of the mob. In a parking lot next to the six-story Frazer Hotel, a Negro fired and hit a police officer with the charge from a shotgun. The Negro was killed instantly by the return fire. Some fifty police officers rushed up, and upon a report of "sniper fire" from the hotel, turned their weapons against it. Revolvers, shotguns, high-powered rifles, machine guns sent up a deafening staccato, their bullets shattering the windows, ricocheting, and sending pieces of brick flying through the air. Round after round of tear gas was shot into the building. By the time the terrified residents were brought out of the hotel and lined up against its wall to be searched, a thousand rounds had been fired. Seeking weapons and snipers, the police ripped the interior of the hotel apart, but found nothing.

The mob was rampaging within sound and almost sight of city hall. A few minutes after nine o'clock Governor Kelly told military authorities that the situation was out of control, and that only the troops could restore order. By ten o'clock, 350 military police were clearing Woodward Avenue—an action that the mayor and the police had not lacked the manpower, but the will to order earlier in the day. Two hours later when President Roosevelt signed the proclamation authorizing the use of Federal forces, the troops had cleared the rioters from the cross streets, and had the city under control. Another day would be needed to mop up. But, with nine whites and twenty-five blacks dead, the Detroit riot was over.

A sociologist who did a study of the arrestees was surprised by their youth. Approximately half of the whites and a fourth of the blacks were under the age of twenty-one,* and nearly two thirds of both races were under thirty-one. A fourth were illiterate.

---

* If police had arrested only the more active participants in the riot among blacks as they did among whites, the ages would probably have matched more closely. Negro arrestees were *older* because many were picked up for curfew violations and other peripheral activities, while whites were not. The fact that twice as many blacks as whites, proportionately, were in their twenties, also reflected the much greater unemployment among blacks than whites.

An officer on the arson squad commented, "I recognized a lot of those fellows. We've had lots of trouble with them before. The whites that did most of the car burning were from gangs of Italians, Syrians, and others who hang around bars and poolrooms, and in 'peace time' pull false alarms and that sort of thing." [4]

In the aftermath, Negroes were more bitter than ever about the police. NAACP Executive Director Walter White charged the police with having been "in sympathy with the mobs." The leadership of the National Urban League, the Federal Council of Churches of Christ, the YMCA, and the YWCA asserted that "Negroes have been victimized by police in the name of law and order as well as by lawless mobs." They were supported by Brigadier General William Guthner, the army commander on the scene, who wrote:

"They've been very handy with their guns and clubs and have been very harsh and brutal. . . . They have treated the Negroes terribly up here, and I think they have gone altogether too far, as that kind of treatment of course will keep this thing going longer than if they get back to normal."

Mayor Jeffries retorted that the police "role in the riot needs no defense . . . it was splendid and at times magnificent. . . . I am rapidly losing my patience with those Negro leaders who insist that their people do not and will not trust policemen." [5]

Councilman Edwards suggested that 43 Negro policemen on a force of 3,400 were not enough, and that the number should be expanded to 200. A grand jury should be empaneled, he declared, to determine the truth of the charges and investigate the causes of the riot.

He was voted down. After all, said councilman and former governor William Comstock, "The racial conflict has been going on . . . since our ancestors made the first mistake of bringing the Negroes to this country." [6]

A fact-finding committee of city, county, and state law-enforcement officials charged that it was the "exhortation by many Negro leaders to be 'militant' in the struggle for racial equality [which] played an important part in exciting the Negro people to violence." The Wayne County prosecutor went further and said that the leaders of the NAACP "were the biggest instigators of the race riot. If a grand jury were called, they would be the first indicted." [7]

On July 15, after concluding an investigation, U.S. Attorney-General Francis Biddle submitted a confidential report to the President:

"I believe that the riots in Detroit do not represent an isolated case but are typical of what may occur in other cities throughout the country. The situation in Los Angeles is extremely tense."

Biddle suggested that "careful consideration be given to limiting, and in some instances putting an end to, Negro migrations into communities which cannot absorb them, either on account of their physical limitations or cultural background. This needs immediate and careful consideration. When postwar readjustments begin, and jobs are scarcer, the situation will become far more acute. . . . It would seem pretty clear that no more Negroes should move to Detroit." [8]

IV

THE BLIGHT OF POVERTY

82

The Chameleons

ONE NEGRO WHO ARRIVED IN THE CITY A FEW MONTHS LATER WAS SIXTEEN-year-old Conrad Mallett:

Conrad's mother, Mary Lonnie, had been raised in Alton, Louisiana, a dusty crossroads in the pine and bayou country across Lake Pontchartrain from New Orleans. Her father looked white. Her father's mother was an Indian. On her mother's side, her grandmother was a blonde, and her grandfather had the appearance of a Mexican. Nevertheless, in the small rural community they were a *colored* family. As such, the white-skinned, fair-haired Mary Lonnie and her brothers and sisters, together with the other *colored,* could only "look at white children going to school and wish I could go." When the parish "built a large school for Catholic children, the priest didn't care. He thought it okay we didn't learn to read and write. Lord, if I'd had a third-grade education, that would have been wonderful!"

Instead, at the age of eight, Mary Lonnie started baby-sitting for white children in order to supplement the family's meager earnings. Her father worked in the rice fields, but sometimes, on Saturday night, he gambled away what little he earned, and at other times "there was no work. We was hungry. We cried in the morning and we cried at night."

When her father died, she went to live with an aunt in Raywood, Texas, halfway between Beaumont and Houston, where "the whole town was kin to me." There she married; and there Conrad and his sister were born.

In the farming country of eastern Texas in the late 1920's "all they ever knew was a depression," and when the great Depression itself came, the Malletts' farm was borne down with it. The family was unable to make ends meet, and the quarrels became more frequent. In 1932 Mary Lonnie Mallett took her two children and followed her sister to Houston. A few months later, her husband walked all the way to join her.

In Houston, her husband was seldom able to keep a job for more than a few months. But he made twelve dollars a week on WPA, and Mary Lonnie worked as a domestic. "He didn't care about nothing and never hardly talked."

Nevertheless, "they was happy times for us. People was working. They didn't get much. But they could work."

When Mary Lonnie Mallett lived among fair-skinned relatives in Alton and Raywood, she had no difficulties over her white appearance. But in the colored community of the city, her and her husband's light skins engendered resentment, taunts, and fights. In 1938, her husband was killed in a brawl in a bar. For Mary Lonnie Mallett the trauma went beyond the normal shock. "It was a black man that killed my husband, and I already had this black on my mind. One side's just as prejudiced as the other. I wanted to get away from blacks because they give you hell!"

Without revealing her background, she obtained a job as a live-in domestic with a wealthy white family. In order to have her children with her, she smuggled them into her room during the summer of 1939.

For twelve-year-old Conrad and his ten-year-old sister, it was a silent, soul-trying summer. There was a great deal of rivalry between them, and they had often bickered and fought. But confined in their mother's room they could make no noise—they could flush the toilet only between two and three o'clock in the afternoon when their mother had an hour off. So they quarreled in sign language; and then burst into noiseless laughter. Trapped in the sweltering heat, they turned the mirror on the dresser so that through the window they could watch the family's children romping in the swimming pool. In the garage were stacks of old *Redbook, Cosmopolitan,* and *Liberty* magazines, as well as seventeen volumes of Zane Grey. On the way back from the 6 A.M. visit to the kitchen with their mother—long before anyone in the family was stirring—Conrad and his sister would pick up reading material to last through the day. It was during those ten weeks of enforced isolation that Conrad, bright and quick, learned to read well.

The next year he was accepted by St. Augustine in Bay St. Louis, Mississippi, the only seminary in the country for Negroes. There he was introduced to a classical education that bore no resemblance to the schooling he had been receiving in Houston. During summer vacations he worked as a houseboy. He discovered he was more than a match intellectually for white youth, and lost his awe of the social system and gained confidence. But when he returned to the seminary in the fall of 1943, he was troubled. He told his adviser that he couldn't keep his eyes off girls, and that a life of celibacy seemed impossible for him.

A few months earlier, Mary Lonnie Mallett, drawn by the frenetic war boom, had followed her sister to Detroit. When she arrived, she "wanted to do what a white woman does. I didn't want this housework. I had done it so much." The employment agency she went to assumed she was white. "Lord, if I'd had told them this is a nigger woman, I wouldn't have had a job. It's tough, passing all the time. You have it on your mind all the time. But I've been white most of all my days 'cause I've had to make a living."

As a white, she became a meat cutter in a cafeteria in Grosse Pointe, Detroit's most fashionable community, from which Negroes were for all practical purposes excluded. In a society of strange classifications and segregation, in which she looked white but was black, she was one of the thousands who moved back and forth between the two worlds.

As other members of her family scattered north and west, a cousin told her: "Two of my boys went for white, and two for colored." Another cousin married a Greek, and no one in her husband's family suspected that she was "colored." Mary Lonnie Mallett's aunt had passed over into the white society and married a white man without enlightening him, and when the aunt's son came to visit Mary Lonnie all he knew was that the family had come from the South. Unsuspecting, he ranted about the "damn niggers." Mary Lonnie did not tell him that back in Louisiana or Texas he would have been talking about himself.

In November, Conrad arrived in the city. His mother, believing he had lost the chance for a good education, was furious. He found a room downtown, and went to work four hours a day as a busboy in a cafeteria. Earning twenty dollars a week and meals, he enrolled in Miller High School, and graduated in 1945.

83

A Master Plan

WHEN HAROLD BLACK HAD GRADUATED FROM WAYNE UNIVERSITY IN JANUARY of 1942, he had attempted to enlist in the armed forces, but had been rejected because of his poor eyesight. The demand for liberal arts graduates had not yet caught up with the supply, and when the city advertised competitive examinations for the position of technical aide, four hundred men took the test. In the twelve years since his arrival from Mexico via Poland, Black had improved his English to the point that he spoke the language better than many Americans; and he was one of the six men hired.

Various WPA projects were still active in the city, and Black's job was to make the rounds of foremen's shanties, pick up the work slips and total the costs. When examinations were held for junior appraiser in the assessor's office —a step up—Black, who could not have distinguished an appraisal from an assessment, picked up a dictionary of appraisal terms, studied it for one night, and, while real estate people were flunking, successfully bluffed his way through. Discovering that he hated the job, he tried to get work in a war plant, but was too clumsy even to solder two wires together. One day he and a friend, Bill Goodman, were discussing their dislikes for their work. Goodman said a great many jobs were opening up at city planning. Black, who didn't know the department existed, asked: "What is it?"

"I don't know," Goodman replied, "but it can't be any worse." *

Zoning regulations to control development had been authorized by the city's new charter at the time of World War I. Not until 1940 was the first zoning ordinance passed by the city council, however. Mayor Jeffries directed the planning commission to draw up a master plan. But for three fourths of the city, a master plan came ex post facto. Even for land still vacant, zoning had little meaning, because a property owner with political pull could usually obtain a variance. On arguments that a project was to the economic benefit of the city or essential to the war effort, the Board of Zoning Appeals was granting nearly 85 percent of requests for variances.

Nevertheless, it was an enthusiastic group that came together in the planning

* Goodman is today professor of planning at the University of Illinois.

department to work on the master plan for a "new Detroit" in the postwar era. Although the concept of city planning was now more than a quarter century old, it had been frustrated by the laissez-faire boom of the 1920's followed by the financial constrictions of the 1930's. As a science it was scarcely out of the womb. Like Black, many of those in the planning department were receiving their training on the job. There was great élan. They believed they were charting the city's future, that their research and ideas would turn it into a thing of beauty. As the assessed valuation rose from the Depression low point of $2.25 billion to $2.9 billion in 1945 (in 1930 it had been $3.8 billion), and property owners paid off their tax delinquencies, the city found revenues exceeding expenditures for the first time in fifteen years. Physical deterioration was present everywhere, and the needs were enormous, but wartime restrictions made it impossible to conduct any but housekeeping projects. In conjunction with the drawing up of the master plan, Mayor Jeffries put together a postwar package of capital improvement projects totaling $730 million. Councilman Edwards complained that it was inadequate. But in a city that had spent a total of only $46 million for capital improvements between 1932 and 1944, the sum seemed enormous.

The end of the war, however, brought new turmoil. By the spring of 1945, as Germany crumbled, the overproduction of war materiel began to plague the government, and major cutbacks were ordered. Returning veterans got their jobs back. Tens of thousands of war migrants were laid off. Some of the rural whites went back to the Blue Ridge Mountains and the Ozarks to wait for better times, but the Negroes had no such retreats to which they could return. Though unemployment among them rose rapidly, they stayed in the city.

While wages had increased 15 percent during the war, the cost of living had risen 30 percent. (UAW statisticians claimed the rise was 45 percent.) Workers had harbored their frustrations through the war. But they were now itching for a showdown with management.

Detroit was the most unionized city in the nation. Of 15 million American union members, nearly a half million were in the city—350,000 in the CIO and 100,000 in the AFL. In the coming negotiations, labor would benefit if a unionist were in control of the city hall. Richard Frankensteen, UAW vice-president and director of the CIO's Political Action Committee, declared his candidacy for mayor.

A sludge-slinging campaign that was to prove the harbinger of the McCarthy era resulted. The Communists had entrenched themselves firmly in the CIO, were in control of some unions, and were threatening to capture the UAW. Although not a Communist, Frankensteen had cooperated with them and was considered a fellow traveler. In the UAW itself, the supporters of Reuther, who had fallen out with Frankensteen in 1943, were singing:

> *Who are the boys who take their orders*
> *Straight from the office of Joe Staleen?*
> *No one else but the gruesome twosome*
> *George F. Addes and Frankensteen.*[1]

In a city of rundown services and facilities, dissatisfaction with the Jeffries Administration was widespread. Rats, cats, and dogs fought over the garbage— which might be picked up once every two weeks, or once a month. Streetcars and buses creaked and literally cracked. The schools, most of which within the

Boulevard area had been erected in the previous century, were facing the same kind of population expansion that the First World War had brought. Municipal employees demanded the right to organize. The need for greatly increased revenues to renovate the city portended an increase in taxation. Amidst the continuing housing shortage, real estate interests clawed and fought against the demands made by unions and liberals for more public housing. To avoid further violence, Jeffries in 1943 had taken a stand against "race mixing," and had forbidden the Housing Commission to introduce Negroes into white neighborhoods. The result of what the Negroes considered a "damnable and inequitable housing policy" was that blacks occupied only 2,000 of the 45,000 permanent and temporary housing units that had been erected.

In the primary held on August 7, exactly one week before the Japanese surrender, Frankensteen won 90 percent of the Negro vote, 61 percent of the Polish blue-collar vote, and 59 percent of the Jewish vote. The turnout was small. Frankensteen led the field with only 83,000 votes, followed by Jeffries with 69,000, and former Wayne County auditor James D. Friel, representing the "regular" Democrats, with 36,000.

Frankensteen's success in the primary generated an all-out campaign to defeat him in the November general election. Both the KKK and Gerald L. K. Smith's forces intensified their campaigns. In the Polish neighborhoods Frankensteen was called a Jew and a nigger lover. When Frankensteen, a lifelong Episcopalian, took out ads in the Polish press announcing that he stood for the "Christian ideals of democracy," a whispering campaign was started in the Twelfth Street area that Frankensteen was anti-Semitic and associated with Father Coughlin. (They had been allies in 1935, when both had been fighting Ford.)

When a returning Negro war veteran, Charles Johnson, demanded accommodations on a first-come first-served basis in a "white" housing project,* and the Housing Commission refused him, the Jeffries camp charged that Frankensteen (who would no more commit himself to integration than Jeffries) would back a Negro "invasion."

Linking Communists and the CIO Political Action Committee, Jeffries charged that they were "out to use Detroit as a springboard, as a jumping-off place for their revolutionary crusade [to] knit together a political empire that will rule the United States." The Detroit *News* editorialized, "A vote for Jeffries is a vote against communism." [2]

Unlike the primary, the general election produced a massive turnout. Frankensteen retained most of his supporters from the primary, but the Friel vote went to Jeffries. Jeffries won reelection by 275,000 to 217,000. George Edwards, Jr., who was running in the city council race while serving with the army in the Philippines, topped octogenarian John Lodge for the largest number of votes. At the age of twenty-nine, Edwards became the youngest president in the council's history.

The election demonstrated that although Detroit now had a solid Democratic majority, the Democrats were split between the "left-wingers" of the UAW and CIO, and the more conservative traditionalists and former Republican Progressives. Labor could play a significant role in helping a candidate to victory; but it could not by itself win an election.

---

* In the limited Negro projects the waiting time was measured in years.

84

Metamorphosis and Death

ON NOVEMBER 21, 1945, TWO WEEKS AFTER THE ELECTION, THE UAW, WRACKED by internal dissension, struck General Motors. The 200,000 workers who closed down ninety-six plants set the pattern for 1946—the year saw 4.6 million men involved in strikes, nearly a half million more than in 1919. It was the greatest number in American history. Reuther based his demands on the findings of union economists that profits and the cost of living had risen three times as fast as wages. He wanted a wage increase of 30 percent, coupled with a company agreement not to increase the prices of its cars. It was pointless, he said, for workers to attempt to improve their standard of living by bargaining for higher pay if industry promptly erased the wage gains by upping prices.

General Motors executives, led by Chairman of the Board Sloan and President Charles Wilson (who had replaced Knudsen) were adamant against any such deal. The corporation had resigned itself to living with a union. But the specter of that union having an influence over company policy through a voice in production schedules, worker standards, discipline—and especially pricing—generated as much management opposition as ever. Sloan asked: "Is American business to be based on free competition or is it to become socialized, with all activities controlled and regimented?" [1]

When a fact-finding board appointed by President Truman sided with the UAW and declared that wages should be raised according to the "ability to pay"—in effect making company profits a criterion in the negotiations—General Motors negotiators walked out. Board Chairman Sloan believed that "increased efficiency flows not so much from the increased effectiveness of the workers, but primarily from more efficient management and from the investment of additional capital in labor-saving devices." [2] The old argument over whether workers and consumers should share equally with management and investors in the benefits from increased productivity was as critical as ever.

As the strike dragged on, and entered its fourth month, Reuther came under increasing pressure from all sides to abandon his anti-inflation formula. For ninety-nine out of one hundred workers on the assembly lines what was important was the cash they received, not an abstruse issue over economics that they could not understand. Within the union, Reuther was campaigning against President R. J. Thomas and the Communists, a campaign he would almost certainly lose if the strike were not settled before the election. When steel and electrical workers obtained an 18½-cent-an-hour increase, the price of steel was promptly raised $5 per ton. But even CIO President Philip Murray advised Reuther to accept price increases as a fact of life, and not to try to fight a one-man battle against inflation. Harry Coen, G.M.'s assistant director of personnel, snapped at Reuther:

"Why don't you . . . talk about money . . . and let the labor statesmanship go to hell for a while?" [3]

Reuther's theoretical reach always exceeded his practical grasp, and under the combination of pressures he buckled. After 113 days, the longest strike in the automobile industry's history, a settlement was reached without an anti-inflation clause. Two years later G.M. President Wilson outmaneuvered Reuther by presenting his "broken-hip" formula (he had worked out the basic concept while recuperating in the hospital from a fracture) which would enable workers to share the benefits of increasing productivity through the principle of an "annual improvement factor."

The settlement aided Reuther in squeaking through to the presidency of the United Auto Workers by a vote of 4,444 to 4,320, and so established him as one of the prominent labor leaders in the country.

More importantly, the agreement kept the automobile industry firmly on the road of *administered enterprise* on which it had started in the 1930's. Clearly, for the management of General Motors, which was the industry's price-setter, any formula tying wages to prices and profits would have undermined the concept of "standard volume," and the corporation's freedom and capacity to exact the maximum prices from the marketplace.

In administered enterprise, however, the union presented no great hazard. As a purveyor of manpower, it could be treated like any other supplier. The price of its product could be negotiated. Increases could not only be passed on to the consumer, but be rationalized to the public as the cause for even greater hikes in prices.*

The "free competition" that G.M.'s Sloan apotheosized was in a shambles. The situation at Ford was chaotic. Walter Chrysler was dead, and the status of the Chrysler Corporation as one of the Big Three was shaky. The remainder of the auto workers, from graybeard Packard to infant Kaiser-Frazer, had been reduced to scavengers, cleaning up what was left after the behemoths had munched their way through the market.

Few other American industries were dominated so thoroughly by a "Big One." Since money in the bank and the demand for cars had built up in concert during the war, G.M. had no difficulty in imposing upon the public a massive increase in prices. Between 1941 and 1949, while auto workers obtained wage increases averaging 61 percent, the average factory prices of cars rose 91 percent (from $679 to $1,299). Industry profits after taxes tripled: from $398 million in 1941 to $1,205 million in 1949. In the decade following the war, General Motors *averaged* 37.5 percent of return on investment after taxes—somewhat

---

* Walter Reuther testified before the U. S. Senate Subcommittee on Antitrust and Monopoly in 1958 that a $30 increase in wages brought $85 to $135 increases in the prices of cars.

better than the 15 percent projected through "standard volume," and topping the two previous individual golden years of 1929 and 1936, when the returns had been 36.2 and 29.5 percent.

A quarter century before, following World War I, the management of General Motors had been in disarray and had benefited immensely through the absorption of Ford executives. During World War II, a group of air force officers in the Pentagon had observed the production agonies and management chaos at Ford. In November, 1945, ten of them, under the leadership of thirty-two-year-old Colonel Charles B. "Tex" Thornton, sent Ford's grandson Henry Ford II a telegram:

"We have a matter of management importance to discuss with you."

Not until 1943 had Sorensen, the Ford production boss, injected enough organization into Willow Run to begin turning out combat planes in large numbers. Ultimately, the plant assembled 8,685 B-24 bombers. Throughout the company, however, the intrigues and power battles Ford had set in motion were playing toward a denouement. Confusion was everywhere.

Ford had made a remarkable physical recovery from his stroke in 1938. But his mind, more jumbled than ever, deteriorated steadily. His paranoia became worse, and he saw Jews and President Roosevelt emerging from fire and brimstone with horns and tails. He had hallucinations in which he held conversations with people who had been dead for years. Edsel contracted undulant fever from the milk that his father insisted on serving unpasteurized from his cows. Though Edsel recovered from the fever, his health rapidly worsened. His ulcers turned cancerous and on May 26, 1943, he died.

When Edsel died, Henry Ford went on a hunger strike, and would eat nothing but cracked wheat. Blaming the doctors at Ford Hospital for Edsel's death, he wanted to replace them with chiropractors. He insisted on resuming the presidency of the company himself. The surrogate son, Bennett, was now the only son, and Ford depended upon him totally. When Ford suffered another stroke and was unable to go to his office, Bennett in effect took over the presidency of the company. No one knew whether orders came from Ford or Bennett. In fact, since Bennett was the only executive who saw Ford regularly and was able to influence him in any manner he wished, it did not matter. Bennett even prevailed upon Ford to draw up a secret codicil to his will; a codicil that nullified the foundation plan and gave Bennett power to appoint a board of trustees to run the company.

One of the nation's principal defense manufacturers was overrun by crackpots, ex-convicts, and suspected subversives. The administration in Washington was intensely concerned. Edsel had been the steadying influence, and had worked closely with the Pentagon. John Bugas, the FBI director in Detroit, who had established his own information network in the plant to counter that of Bennett's, had been in continuous touch with Edsel. To inject someone whom the administration could trust into the upper echelons at the plant, the Federal government discharged twenty-six-year-old Henry II from the navy. Henry brought in Bugas to watch Bennett. Bennett, in his inimitable fashion, made Bugas his assistant so that he could watch the former FBI man.

An epic struggle was developing between Bennett and Henry II. The other contenders for power, who had been dependent upon the protection of Ford himself, were purged. In March of 1944, Bennett telegraphed Sorensen, who was on vacation, and informed him he need not bother to return. He pressured Liebold into turning over the power of attorney he held for Henry and Clara Ford. Thereupon both the pro-British Cameron, and the German-loving, British-hating Liebold were booted out.*

In the tense atmosphere, Bennett, Bugas, and Henry II were all packing guns—no one would have guaranteed that the struggle would not explode into a shoot-out at River Rouge. Ford, who was still upset over his grandson's marriage and conversion to Catholicism, supported Bennett. But Henry II had the backing of the family's two strong-willed women, his grandmother Clara and his mother Eleanor, and they threatened to sell their stock unless he was installed in the presidency.

On September 21, 1945, Ford, helped to his chair, listened as his letter of resignation was read to the board of directors and his grandson was elected president of the company. When, a short time thereafter, Bennett revealed that he had the codicil to Ford's will delegating power to himself, Henry II said he would resign. Evidently, however, Ford had so encumbered the "codicil" with scribblings, biblical verses, and other evidence of a disintegrating mind that it never would have stood up in court. In a dramatic gesture, Bennett touched a match to the codicil. With its burning, his own power crumbled to ashes, and he resigned. Henry II assigned the task of a management study of the company to the contingent of air force officers from the Pentagon—a contingent that included future Secretary of Defense Robert S. McNamara and future Ford president Arjay Miller. For four months they probed into every aspect of operations, and were nicknamed the "Quiz Kids"—later changed to "Whiz Kids." Conditions were more chaotic than even they had expected. (One manager when asked the cost of a project under his direction replied he did not know, because "we don't talk about costs around here.") The result was that Tex Thornton was installed as director of planning,† and Ernest Breech, president of the General Motors subsidiary, North American Aviation, was hired to make Ford over in the General Motors image.

In the twilight of his life, Henry Ford knew little of these activities, and repeatedly called for and wondered where Harry was. In the first week of April, 1947, the Rouge River, flooded by spring rains, overflowed its banks. As the water poured into the powerhouse on the "Fairlane" estate—which still relied solely on its own electric-generating facilities—the lights and furnaces in the mansion flickered out. On April 7, twenty minutes before midnight, in a house heated by wood fires and lighted by candles and oil lamps, eighty-three-year-old Henry Ford suffered a massive cerebral hemorrhage and died. Almost exactly one hundred years had passed since his father had left Ireland in the spring of 1847.

* Liebold's tunnel vision and Anglophobia is summed up by one of his observations. The best thing he had to say about the English was that "they built a car like the Rolls-Royce, but anybody who knew that car would know that it didn't compare with our automobiles." 4
† Thornton stayed with the company only briefly. He moved on to Hughes, and then founded Litton Industries.

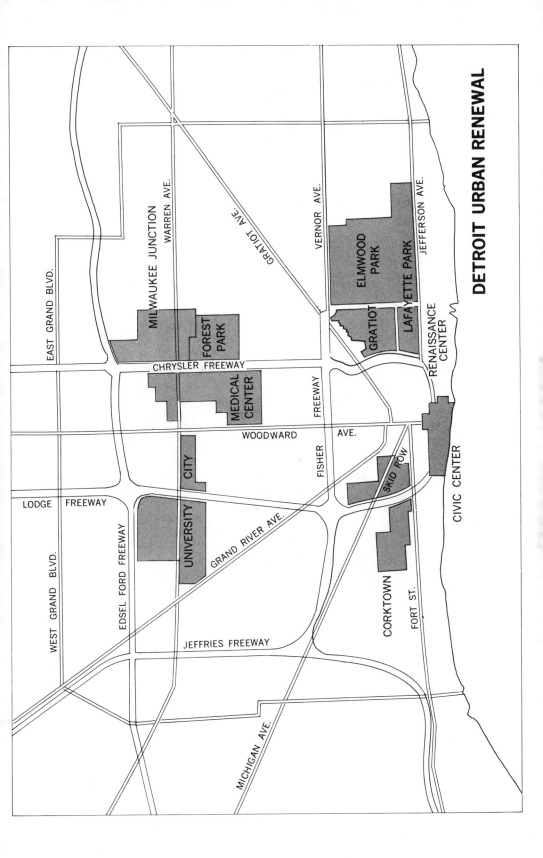

DETROIT URBAN RENEWAL

85

The "Detroit Plan"

WITH THE COMPANY REORGANIZED, FORD IN 1950 HAD ITS FIRST TWO-MILLION-vehicle year since 1925. In a world much of whose heavy industry had been destroyed* or else was obsolete, the United States and Detroit occupied a position of unprecedented dominance. The personal savings of Americans during the four war years totaled $128 billion, and the income of both farmers and workers continued to increase.† The result was an automotive explosion that surpassed even that of the 1920's—1949 topped 1929 by nearly a million vehicles as the best production year in the industry's history, and between 1945 and 1950 the number of automobiles registered in the United States jumped from 25 million to 40 million.

Detroit reaped immediate economic benefits from this production. But in the long run, the more automobiles existed the less the city was able to cope with them. The master plan, completed in 1946—but not approved by the city council until 1948 and published in final form until 1951—made no provision for any improvement in the public transportation system. Twice Detroit had attempted to obtain a subway system—the second time, during New Deal days, Secretary Ickes had allocated the money to Chicago instead—and twice the attempt had proven futile. The city, therefore, pegged its future on a system of freeways patterned after the Willow Run Expressway, which had gone into operation in 1943. The planners convinced the citizenry that since freeways would be "landscaped strips approximately 300 feet wide [they would] be an asset to the sections which [they] pass through." [1]

* Planes manufactured in Willow Run bombed Ford plants in Germany and France, and many other American corporations found themselves engaged in self-destructive missions. Conversely, these European plants of American concerns, staffed with Nazi production men, furnished a considerable portion of Germany's war materiel. Hitler diverted at least two billion dollars in American investments made in the 1920's toward his war machine.
† The United States had 60 percent of the world's stock of gold and one third of the world's exports. Between 1946 and 1948 it had a favorable balance of trade of nineteen billion dollars. With much of the world in need not only of industrial goods but also of food, American farm income was three times what it had been in 1940.

In the central city, however, motorists were as much at a loss where to park their automobiles as they had been in the 1920's. Two acres of parking space were needed for each acre of commercial construction—an impossibility in the built-up core of the city where land values were exorbitant. Concurrently, as land was used up voraciously in the construction of single family homes, builders pushed beyond the city limits at Eight-Mile Road. The population center of the city continued to move steadily northwestward.

The downtown business district had prospered because of its central location, and the high population density in the area encompassed by Grand Boulevard. Volume sales had enabled the merchants to reduce their prices, to expand, and to increase their sales even further. But as the population moved outward, "downtown" had less and less meaning as a focal point, and travel to it became more and more inconvenient. New business districts were building up beyond Six-Mile Road. Though their stores were smaller and their merchants charged more, they were more convenient to people living in the better residential areas.

The management of the J. L. Hudson Company, whose downtown skyscraper was one of the largest department stores in the world, decided to follow the people. Just beyond the city limits at Eight-Mile Road and Couzens Drive, at the point where the migrations—northwest from Detroit, south from Pontiac, and north from Dearborn—were intersecting, the Hudson Company began construction of Northland, the first suburban regional shopping center in America. The center's success was immediate and beyond expectation. Oriented horizontally rather than vertically, with unlimited parking, it became the new shopping center for northern and western Detroit.

Industry, also, lacked land for expansion. Although some plants had been built between 1942 and 1945, most of the city's factories had been erected before 1929. They were jammed into industrial corridors along railroad tracks and on the riverfront. Typically three to five stories high, and predating the age of truck transportation, they had been built for compactness. When the time came for expansion, there was no room to expand them. New industrial plants, freed from the limitations of locale by the grids of highways and electric power lines constructed in the 1930's, were being located in suburban areas, where raw land was cheap. Like residential and commercial construction, they were oriented horizontally, spreading one-story high over scores of acres, and accommodating their workers with as many acres of parking. (Frequently a manufacturer recouped the entire cost of a new plant by buying more land than he needed, holding the excess acreage for a few years, then selling it at a large profit.) Far more efficient than the older factories, the new, one-story plants generated pressure on industries to abandon their obsolescent facilities.

The master plan revealed that more than one third of the central business district and the industrial areas in the city were blighted.

To counter the trend toward abandonment and blight, Mayor Jeffries in 1946 unveiled the "Detroit Plan." Since it was uneconomic for private enterprise to acquire and build on high-priced slum land, the city would take on the role of broker. Declaring a district a redevelopment area, the city would condemn the land, acquire the individual parcels from the many owners involved, demolish the slums, and then offer the cleared land for sale to developers. To make the price of the land competitive with that of the suburbs, the city would resell the land at between a fourth and a fifth of the acquisition cost. The city planned to recoup this loss over a span of fifteen years through the greater tax revenues derived from the increased assessment of the redeveloped area. To finance the slum clearance, Mayor Jeffries proposed that $2 million of the city's annual $100 million tax budget be placed in a revolving fund. The sum would enable about 100 acres to be cleared annually—a pace at which it would take one hundred years to rid the city of the nearly 10,000 acres of existing slums.

The first site chosen was 129 acres of the Hastings Street area south of Gratiot Avenue. The second site, consisting of 77 acres between Michigan Avenue and Fort Street, encompassed most of Corktown. Balancing each other out, one on each side of the central business district, the two roughly triangular sites were composed largely of structures erected before or around the turn of the century. Both were occupied by families of the poor. The Hastings Street Negroes had median incomes of $1,800 a year, the Corktown whites of $2,700 a year. (Citywide, median family income was $3,600.)

Throughout the United States, fifteen years of almost continuous depressions and war had brought about deterioration and shortage of housing. The U.S. Senate Committee on Postwar Economic Policy and Planning recommended an expansion of the Housing Act of 1937 to provide Federal aid for slum clearance and the construction of public housing. A bipartisan-sponsored bill was passed by the Senate. But in the House of Representatives, the Republicans, winning control of Congress in 1946 for the first time since 1930, bottled it up. When the Democrats regained control, the measure was passed and signed into law by President Truman in 1949. It incorporated the central feature of the Detroit Plan for "urban renewal": condemnation and acquisition of slum areas by municipal governments, with resale—if local authorities desired—to private developers at knockdown prices. Before the development of the Detroit Plan, most urban planners had looked upon slum-cleared land primarily as sites for public housing. But the continuing bitter opposition of realtors and conservatives to housing projects resulted in Congress separating slum clearance from public housing within the Housing Act of 1949.

Testifying in favor of the act, Detroit Council President George Edwards told congressmen that 70,000 families in the city were doubled up and that 37,000 married veterans lacked decent living accommodations. Prewar restrictions on cost had made it impossible to build any more public housing at postwar construction prices. Between 1946 and 1948 only 8,000 houses were built in the city yearly, fewer than in the last three prewar years, and less than one fourth of the total in the metropolitan area. The decay of the inner city, where neither construction nor renovation were taking place, was accelerating. Negroes, it was clear, were the principal sufferers. So rapidly were whites moving to the suburbs that 150,000 of the 225,000 people the city gained during the 1940's were black. In Paradise Valley, the worst slum section, the number of Negroes increased from 87,000 in 1940 to 140,000 in 1950. Edwards was unequivocal in his declaration that one of the city's principal priorities must be the construction of housing for Negroes.

The city had so many needs, and much of its population was so frustrated that an air of discontent billowed about it along with the rotten smells of garbage, and the smoke and foul odors exuded from myriad smokestacks. The tensions of the assembly lines and the repeated battles over speedups spilled from the factories into the life of the city—a life of overflowing bars, "blind pigs," wide-open gambling, and vice. Anxious fathers did not want their sons to follow them onto the assembly lines—by 1948, with the seniority protection gained through unionization, more than half the workers in the auto factories were over forty. Many parents were unhappy with the education provided by the schools. The general discontent manifested itself in the 1947 defeat of the incumbent, Jeffries, by Eugene Van Antwerp, and the failure of Van Antwerp even to make the runoff in 1949. Pitted against each other in the general election were Council President George Edwards and Albert Cobo, the "financial wizard" from the Burroughs Corporation who had been brought into the city government during the Depression and had devised the "seven-year plan" for payment of delinquent taxes. Elected city treasurer in 1935, he had been reelected to seven consecutive two-year terms since.

The liberal Democrat, Edwards, should have been an overwhelming favorite to defeat the conservative Republican, Cobo, who had had many bitter disputes with Jeffries and the liberals of his own party. In state and national elections Detroit consistently voted nearly two to one—and sometimes better than two to one—Democratic. In 1948 Edwards had been part of the liberal-labor coalition, led by Gerhard Mennen "Soapy" Williams,* which revitalized and captured control of the state Democratic party from the Catholic-conservative wing. Although the Democrats had been so disorganized that the Republicans had won 123 of the 132 seats in the legislature and 14 out of 17 in Congress in 1946, Williams led the party to victory in the 1948 election.† Edwards had the hearty endorsement of the leadership of both the CIO and the UAW—and he would be able to win the mayoralty handily if no one but the union members in the city voted for him.

But the contest was not so much between "liberal" and "conservative," as between private homeownership and public housing, between "fiscal responsibility" and the threat of increased taxation, and, most of all, between black and white.

The racial issue clearly delineated the division within the UAW between the rank and file and the bureaucratic leadership. The Depression had provided workers with leaders by forcing college-trained liberals and intellectuals down onto the assembly lines. But unionization and prosperity separated the blue-collar from the educated once again.‡ Assembly-line workers derided the educated, white-collar men who had stepped up into the union bureaucracy as "pork choppers." While the union leadership promoted racial amity and equality, the whites on the line, competing with Negroes, harbored their old prejudices. When the interests of whites and blacks coincided, as in a strike,

* Descended from settlers who had arrived in Detroit before the Civil War, Williams had had a Woodward Avenue Republican upbringing, but had been part of the 1930's migration to the Democratic party. In 1937 he had received an appointment in the Murphy Administration in Lansing, and when President Roosevelt named Murphy Attorney-General of the United States, Williams went to Washington with him as his adminstrative assistant.

† Williams benefited from public reaction to continuing revelations of graft, scandals, and vice. Organized crime, having entrenched itself in Detroit during Prohibition, continued to make the city one of its headquarters in the nation. In 1945, after Republican State Senator Warren G. Hooper testified on payoffs and was responsible for sending several legislators to the penitentiary, he was rubbed out in a gangland killing. In 1946 Republican State Chairman Frank D. McKay had been charged with corrupting the Liquor Control Commission (which purchased all alcoholic beverages sold throughout the state) in return for a 25 percent kickback from the distilleries. Although it was shown that he had exerted influence in favor of certain distilleries and had been involved in setting up dummy companies and splitting commissions, he was acquitted on the judge's instructions that "salesmanship isn't criminal."

‡ For example, after his political defeat by Jeffries and his union defeat by Reuther, Frankensteen established a labor relations firm and later became a businessman himself.

they walked the picket lines together. But when four Negroes were upgraded at Chrysler's Kercheval plant, four months of turmoil resulted. At the nearby Hudson plant a "racial" strike broke out in the fall of 1948. Similar disturbances took place at other plants. When union leaders suggested that white workers should help Negroes gain admission to eating places around the Chrysler plant, the whites reacted with hostility. When the Hudson local held a Halloween dance, tickets were sold to everyone regardless of race; but when three Negro couples appeared at the door they were turned back by the white police, who had been told "to keep the niggers out."

"Keeping the niggers out" was a continuous theme in every lower-class white neighborhood. Seemingly, it was dealt a blow when the U.S. Supreme Court in May of 1948 ruled "restrictive covenants" * unenforceable. But even if Negroes could no longer be kept out of a neighborhood legally, the determination to keep them out in fact was as strong as ever. Pickets were likely to appear whenever a Negro moved into a previously "white" block.

A plan by the Detroit Housing Commission to relieve the housing shortage by building twelve public housing projects at sites scattered throughout the city generated apprehension. Most neighborhoods were opposed to any kind of housing project. And while the Housing Commission adhered to Josephine Gomon's formula that a project should not affect the racial composition of a neighborhood, realtors and other opponents kept reminding the public that Sojourner Truth, constructed while Edwards had been director of the commission, had violated the pattern.

Repeatedly, as juvenile crime increased in the high-density slums and adjacent downtown areas, Edwards had taken the side of Negroes who were critical of the police. Negroes complained that the police were as prejudiced as ever, that they continued to shoot black youths with little provocation, and that they enforced laws selectively. (A juvenile curfew law passed in 1948 was employed almost solely against blacks.) Edwards's clashes with reactionary and antilabor Harry Toy, the former prosecutor who had been appointed police commissioner by Van Antwerp, were notably bitter.

The steadfast, unspectacular Cobo, on the other hand, was the choice of business interests and substantial property owners. He disliked public housing or any other governmental activity that competed with private enterprise and smacked of socialism. He supported the Detroit Plan, but objected to the use of the cleared land for public housing, and wanted redevelopment to be left entirely to private enterprise. His reputation was enhanced in the summer of 1948 when he was chosen chairman of the Detroit-Wayne County Joint Building Authority —a body that was to supervise construction of a new City-County Building.† The $26 million skyscraper was to be part of a new civic center complex rising on what once had been the slums of the Potomac. Adding to his reputation as a sound financial administrator, Cobo was gaining prominence as a builder and a planner of the city's future.

It was a year of cold-war conflict, in which attacks on Communists and fellow-

---

* In a neighborhood governed by a "restrictive covenant," no one could purchase a home without signing a document agreeing not to sell to an "undesirable"—a classification that always embraced Negroes, usually Orientals, frequently Jews, and sometimes members of the Mediterranean "unwashed," like Syrians, Greeks, and Sicilians.
† Both the existing city hall and the county building were nineteenth-century edifices, which had ceased to be adequate for governmental needs decades before. Agencies were housed in thirty-one separate buildings, rental charges for which totaled nearly $375,000 a year.

traveling "pinkos" were becoming steadily more strident. The leveling-off in the postwar auto boom gave indications of layoffs and belt tightenings for auto workers. The anti-Communist and anti-Reuther Cobo, descended from one of the city's long-established French families, represented the old virtues and promised homeowners that he would look after their interests in the future as he had looked after them in the past. The thirty-three-year-old liberal and dynamic Edwards, heartily disliked by the police, unacceptable to old-line Democrats because of his association with the left-wingers, was suspected of wanting to impose on the city a Reuther-like program of race mixing and socialism. He represented change and uncertainty; even danger.

In the heaviest turnout for a mayoralty election in the city's history, Detroiters registered their preference for Cobo by 313,000 to 206,000 votes. For Edwards, who had seldom tasted anything but success, it was a stunning and a bitter defeat.

In 1951, however, Governor Williams appointed Edwards judge of the Wayne County Juvenile Court, the largest such jurisdiction in the nation.* In this capacity Edwards came closer to the human misery and learned more about the malaise of the city than he ever would have as mayor.

---

* In the 1950 biennial gubernatorial election, Edwards had played the key role in pulling victory out of what appeared certain defeat for Williams. (Peg Edwards and Nancy Williams both came from families that were part of the state's Republican "society," and had been girlhood friends.) After the final tally of the nearly 1.9 million votes, Williams trailed former Republican Governor Kelly by approximately 1,000. Edwards, however, discovered discrepancies in suburban Macomb County, which usually voted Democratic.

On demand of the Democrats, a statewide recount began. Day by day Edwards directed the workers and pored over the returns. After ten days, 2,000 votes were moved from the Republican to the Democratic column—Williams was the victor by 1,154 votes.

86

The Jurisdiction of the Juvenile Court

Among the children who had come under the jurisdiction of the Juvenile Court were those of Irma and Donald Stallings.

Irma had been twelve years old when she had come to Detroit with her parents, Wallace and Antoinette Mirow, in 1934. But she had never adjusted to the city. Before she was eighteen she was escaping from her loneliness and fright into the darkness of bars. Alcohol, then, had been a comfort. In her marriage to Donald it became a refuge.

Donald Stallings had grown up in his parents' house in Inkster during the Depression, and those years had left both physical and mental scars on him. He limped, and he had only an eighth-grade education—which was more like a sixth-grade education. He wanted to do right. He was concerned about his children. But, lacking the ability to help himself, he lacked the ability to help them. He was a man betrayed by the false hope that someday he would be a winner.

From Monday to Friday of every week he worked hard as a garbage collector. On Friday afternoon, like some of his coworkers, he felt he deserved a reward. He never intended to have more than a drink or two before going home to Irma. He never intended to become a participant in the crap game that followed. But a crap game was the one event in his life that raised him from his drab existence and set his blood bubbling. Unable to quit either as a loser or a winner—when he lost, he kept playing to win back his losses, when he won, he kept playing because he would tell himself it was no time to quit—he was destined forever to be a loser. Commonly, having lost anywhere from $20 to $75 of his biweekly $96 pay in the game, he would not return home until sometime Saturday. Conscience-stricken, he would placate Irma by bringing her a bottle. No matter how she might upbraid him for the money lost, they could find comfort and escape in drink and fornication.

Almost every year after their first child, Mirabel, was born in early 1940, they had another. When Mirabel was two years old, a doctor discovered that she had advanced tuberculosis of the hip. From 1942 to 1947 she was in Children's

Hospital. By the time she returned home she had three brothers and sisters, and another child had died in infancy. Natalie, the fifth surviving child, was born in 1948.

Irma could not bear to stay alone in the miserable flats and furnished rooms they rented. At every opportunity she slipped out to the neighborhood bar. Friday nights, when Donald did not return home, were the worst. Her anxiety and tension would rise until she had to scream to let them out. As soon as the children were asleep, she left. After four or five drinks she could no longer distinguish between one face and another, between one man and another. If he spoke to her quietly, held her hand and stroked her hair, she fell into his arms. In June of 1948, she took a man back to her room. She had left the two older girls sleeping in her bed, and when eight-year-old Mirabel awoke it was to the vision of a strange man pressing down repeatedly and violently upon her mother. Terrified, Mirabel fled from the room and at three o'clock in the morning ran shrieking down the street. Not until dawn was she found, shaking and incoherent, hiding in a coal bin. When police tried to question Irma, she was still too drunk to speak intelligibly.

When Donald returned home and pieced the story together, he was enraged. He slapped Irma, beat her, shook her, and flung her against the walls. Again the neighbors called the police. Donald was jailed, Irma was taken to the hospital, and the children went to the juvenile detention home. The Donald Stallings family was enrolled in the records of the Juvenile Court.

Donald spent five days in jail, and Irma was placed on probation. The caseworker learned that Donald's pay seldom lasted through the two weeks, and that he frequently pawned possessions or borrowed money at 50 percent a month interest. The caseworker thought that Donald's "income would seem sufficient to care for the family properly," and tried to teach him "budgeting." But addictions are not restrained by budgets. A condition of Irma's parole was that she stay away from alcohol. In February of 1949, however, the police picked her up as she was staggering down the street. Having violated her probation, she was ordered to spend sixty days in the Detroit House of Correction.*

After Irma was released, she and Donald rented a basement apartment in the Gratiot Redevelopment Area. The "apartment" consisted of little more than a partitioned basement utility room. One "wall" of the combination kitchen-bathroom was made up of the building's furnace. Every morning when the stoker poured on the coal, the furnace protested long and hackingly like the lungs of an old smoker at an early morning cigarette. For hours it filled the basement with smoke. Soot lay on the walls, the table, the dishes, and the bed. Every item of clothing and bedding turned black. Donald bought a washing

---

* The women's section of the Detroit House of Correction—known popularly as DeHoCo— is unique among American municipal prisons. In 1861, when Detroit was still the only sizable city in Michigan and produced most of the female offenders, the state had decided to use the city's facilities to house all female convicts. Since the state never did get around to building a separate prison, DeHoCo has continued to be the state penitentiary for women. In the heterogeneous population, life-termers are mixed with thirty-day drunks, habitual criminals with first offenders, and prostitutes with homosexuals. (Homosexuality runs rampant—even more so than in the men's facility.) Psychotics and psychopaths sometimes go for months without being identified—in the entire Michigan prison system there is no appropriation for a staff psychiatrist. For short-term prisoners like drunks and alcoholics there is almost no remedial treatment. Some of the short-term recidivists spend almost as much time in DeHoCo as the lifers. There are drunks, petty thieves, and misdemeanor violators who have been back as many as two hundred times—some of them deliberately commit an offense in front of a policeman in November so that they can serve a sentence till April.

machine, but within the month it broke down. During the winter a pipe began to leak. Seeping across the concrete floor, the water froze during the night when the furnace was damped down. Every morning when the family awakened the floor was slippery with ice.

Once again pregnant, Irma, twenty-eight years old, felt worse than she ever had in her life. She froze, she suffocated, her eyes smarted and watered, and she drank. The apartment was littered with piles of soiled clothing and with empty bottles. She had neither the energy nor the will to care for the children. Since "soothing syrups" concocted of opium and morphine no longer were available to discourage activity and keep the children quiet, she laced the baby's bottle with wine, and encouraged ten-year-old Mirabel to drink with her. In December of 1949 she began bleeding from her vagina. She had terrible cramps and could not stomach food, so she drank more wine. When the Juvenile Court worker was unable to contact the family, she went to the apartment. She found Irma lying in a bed putrescent with blood and the baby's urine. Irma was so weak from loss of blood she was semidelirious. When she arrived at the hospital, the doctor discovered she was hemorrhaging because she was suffering a miscarriage. An operation had to be performed to remove stillborn twins.

After Irma's release from the hospital, she and Donald moved from furnished room to furnished room. Of Donald's $96 biweekly check, $18 was being garnisheed for the junked washing machine, so they had less money than ever. By March of 1950 Irma was pregnant again. Malnourished, anemic, and unsteady on her feet, she spent most of the time in bed with her bottle. Sometimes in her alcoholic stupors she picked up a man, and the children became spectators to her sex acts. From ten-year-old Mirabel to two-year-old Natalie they received only the most rudimentary care. They wandered the streets. Their clothes were ragged, patched, and held together with pins. At times they had only one pair of pants, one dress, one set of underwear, one pair of socks. Mirabel had large sores on her body from dirt and infected bedbug bites. Although Irma had given birth to eight children (three of whom had died), she was incapable of motherhood.

In the autumn of 1950, Irma and Donald received a letter from the Detroit Housing Commission. The letter informed them that the commission was embarking on the eradication of the slums and their problems, and that as a consequence of clearance and renewal, the people in the area could look toward a better future. The commission suggested that the Stallings family would "undoubtedly move back into the area when redevelopment is completed."

There was no mention of public housing. One of Cobo's first acts as mayor had been to scrap the plans for all the housing projects, except for two already well advanced—Douglass, adjacent to Brewster in the Negro area, and Jeffries, on the other side of Woodward Avenue, in a poor-white area. Implicitly, he was establishing a "containment" policy, the purpose of which was to keep not only Negroes but the poorest whites clustered in the districts they already occupied, and to prevent the blight of poverty from spreading.

The city had received a $4.3 million Federal grant, one of the first allocated under the new Housing Act. At a time when the outbreak of the Korean War was bringing a new expansion of industry and population, the Cobo Administration moved steadfastly ahead to demolish nearly three thousand dwelling units in the largely black Gratiot area. The intent of the proponents of redevelopment and of Congress was to get people out of execrable housing and into better accommodations. The goal of the Cobo Administration, despite casuistic declarations to the contrary, was to raze what was the city's highest crime area and part of its worst slum—become what might of its residents.

The population of the Gratiot area was 98 percent black, but during the clearance between mid-1950 and the end of the 1951, the Housing Commission leased six out of seven of the limited public housing units to white families. The upshot was that in these eighteen months the "white" waiting list shrank from 2,247 to 574, but the "Negro" waiting list increased from 5,226 to 7,571. Many of the families were not eligible for public housing because their incomes were too low to make the rent payments or because their families were too large for the small apartments. Frequently, as the consequence of war inflation and housing destruction, they ended up paying higher rents for no better accommodations.

Theoretically, the commission was responsible for finding new housing for the families. But by the end of 1952 nearly two hundred families, approximately 10 percent of those in the area, still had not been relocated. One third of the people were going into public housing and one sixth were finding permanent rentals or buying homes. The remaining half were simply disappearing—a great relief to the commission!

Among the people who faded from the purview of the commission was the Stallings family. In December of 1950 Irma gave birth to her sixth surviving child, Brett. Six weeks later she was discovered writhing, screaming, and hallucinating in the street. At the receiving hospital, her condition was diagnosed as delirium tremens. She was kept in the psychopathic ward for a few days, then released. Two weeks later she was again drunk. Carrying the baby in her arms, she tried to leave the rooming house, and staggered from wall to door, and door to street. When other roomers refused to let her go, she became hysterical and fought them. Again the police were called. Again she was taken to the hospital. Donald wanted to leave the baby at the hospital, too, because "he belongs with his mother." Informed that was out of the question, Donald said that as a workingman he did not know what he could do with him.

At a court hearing, Irma was adjudged a chronic alcoholic and committed to the state hospital at Northville.

Donald went to live with his mother, Freda Stallings. He took Mirabel and the baby Brett with him. Donald's father Odie had died in 1947. He had been only about fifty years old, but his childhood in rural Virginia and a lifetime of hard labor in the Ford foundry had taken their toll—throughout the United States life expectancy for Negroes continued to be several years less than for whites. In the upsurge of the real estate market that came with the Korean War, Freda had sold the little house in Inkster and moved into Detroit. She leased a venerable, ten-room house in the old Jewish section west of Hamtramck where Harold Black had lived when he had first come to Detroit, and planned to support herself by subletting to boarders.

Irma's father, Wallace Mirow, agreed to care temporarily for the other four children. Not until the summer of 1951 was a hearing held in the Juvenile Court to determine the permanent disposition of the children, and then it only confirmed the existing arrangement. Donald was ordered to contribute approximately two thirds of his weekly pay for support of the children—twenty-two dollars to Wallace Mirow and fifteen dollars to Freda. Most weeks, however, he gave ten dollars to each, and in addition might buy some groceries. But when he had a "bad week," he would empty his pockets of two or three one-dollar bills and some loose change, and say that's all there was left.

At Northville, Irma was diagnosed as an "ambulatory schizophrenic" who "probably would not be able to live successfully in the community." Nevertheless, after a few months she was released to Wallace Mirow. She was to attend meetings of Alcoholics Anonymous and receive treatment as an outpatient at the psychiatric clinic at Kiefer Hospital in the city.

In the economy of the Korean War, Wallace not only was operating his coal and ice truck, but also working at the Dodge Main Plant in Hamtramck. Since it was he who cooked breakfast, he made the children get up with him at five o'clock every morning. Not until he returned from his truck route at seven or eight o'clock in the evening would there be dinner.

In addition to working at two jobs, Wallace was the housekeeper because his wife Antoinette was less and less able to perform even simple tasks. Her eyes would focus on something, and if anyone touched or attempted to move into the spot at which she was staring, she would scream. Her sense of taste went through periods of distortion in which she would dump an entire container of pepper into a pot of stew before it "tasted right," cook oatmeal with vinegar, and scramble eggs with their shells. The children refused to eat the food she cooked. Regarding her as "queer," they would pay no attention to her even when she was lucid. She regarded them as an intrusion, and kept begging Wallace to "do something with them."

Wallace took the oldest boy, Windsor, on the truck with him, but he had no time to see that Irma attended Alcoholics Anonymous. Only if someone were with her and watching over her constantly could Irma be prevented from drinking; and Irma was quite on her own. Within three months of her release she was back in the hospital. From Northville she went to the state asylum at Kalamazoo, from Kalamazoo back to Detroit, and from Detroit back to one or another of the institutions. In an institutional setting she could function. But an institution could not "cure" her. Short of money, space, and personnel, the institutions had to give priority to cases more acute than hers. So, since she was not dangerous, they kept bouncing her back into the community. When she was again drinking heavily enough to lose control of herself, and stole the money that no one would give her to buy wine, the community would return her to an institution. In twentieth-century American society she had, quite literally, no place.

A considerable portion of Wallace's coal and ice business had been in the Gratiot Redevelopment Area. As people were moved out and the buildings were torn down, his business suffered. Only the slums continued to support the ice trade; elsewhere it was being replaced by mechanical refrigeration. Coal sales, too, were declining as people moved out of buildings heated by potbellied stoves and old coal furnaces. For some of Wallace's customers, urban redevelopment was an even harder blow—the small corner grocer and the operator of the neighborhood hand laundry found it impossible to relocate their obsolescent businesses elsewhere. Some had no choice but to go on relief.

When the Korean War ended and the economy of the city went into a recession in early 1954, Wallace lost his job at the Dodge plant. With his business also declining, his income dropped to the lowest level since 1938. Friction increased. Antoinette complained that Wallace was spending all his money on the grandchildren and none on her. Her antagonism toward Windsor, who did not hide his belief that she was crazy, grew stronger. Windsor was the only one of the children doing well in school. The others attended irregularly, and frequently traveled back and forth by themselves between Freda's and Wallace's houses, a distance of two and a half miles. Their attendance dropped off even further when Wallace said he could no longer give them money for clothes. In school, clothes were a status symbol, and all the girls knew whose parents were "making it." Mirabel complained that she was being made fun of because "all I've got to wear is Goodwill dresses."

The household in which Mirabel lived resembled a disorganized commune. Freda Stallings had Donald, Mirabel, and Brett living in a room in the attic. Three other families were scattered over the main two stories and the basement. A woman on welfare and her four children rented the second floor. Freda's only daughter, Janice, and Janice's eldest daughter and her children were on the first floor and in the basement. Altogether nineteen persons spanning four generations occupied the house. Janice had been married four times and divorced four times. She helped support herself by making whiskey in the basement. Since taxes had all but priced legitimate alcohol out of the reach of the poor, home brew continued to be in demand in the blind pigs (illegal bars) and underground of the ghetto. The liquor was used mostly at gambling and rent parties. Janice and her boyfriend sold it for a set price, or took a percentage of each pot.

People were constantly going in and out of Freda's house. The children lived in turmoil. Mirabel stayed awake late at night, and did not go to school more than one day in three. Donald, who was seldom home, expected her to take care of Brett. Mirabel fed him, she washed his diapers, she cleaned the room, and she cooked. Although she had just reached the age of puberty, she was already an adult. She seldom played with other children. The games the children did play were based on the adult world around them. They were imitations of adult sex, gambling, and violence.

The police raided the house, and Mirabel once more came to the attention of the Juvenile Court. She was small but tough, self-conscious about her lack of clothing, her physical appearance, and the slight limp that was the heritage of her tuberculosis. She was four grades behind in school. The court decided that Donald was not providing a proper home for her and that she should be placed with boarding parents.

There were, however, no Negro farm families to which black children could be sent for isolation from the city. Since boarding parents were of the same socio-economic background as the masses of the blacks and lived within or on the fringes of the ghetto, the children could not even be sent to a different environment within the city. Mirabel resented being separated from the rest of her family. She craved affection, and made advances to her boarding fathers. Although she was moved from one boarding home to another and one school to another, she kept making trouble and running away.

Mirabel and children like her faced Judge Edwards and the Juvenile Court with an insoluble dilemma. They were being processed through the court by the thousands, yet for most the state had no facilities. For the hard-core cases there was the Boys Vocational School at Lansing, a dirty, overcrowded, unkempt firetrap that served principally as a prep school for a life of crime. The Wayne County Training School was intended only for the mentally deficient. For children with emotional problems, for the children whose parents were unfit to care for them, for children who were being corrupted by their environment, there were no facilities.

The psychotic, the promiscuous, the delinquent, the maladjusted, the homo-sexual, and the homeless—all were crowded together into the juvenile deten-tion home. Intended to serve as a processing center, it frequently held children for months at a time. Children with severe problems were mixed with children with few problems. Since security had to be tailored toward the dangerous and violent, the detention home was run more like a jail than the Wayne County Jail itself.

Mirabel spent three weeks in the juvenile home. Then the court, not knowing what else to do with her, returned her to Freda's home. To save face, the court placed her in Freda's care instead of Donald's.

In the spring of 1954, when she was fourteen years old, Mirabel attended a dance at a neighborhood school. It was eleven o'clock when she and a girlfriend left the dance. They were followed by three boys. The boys cornered the girls at an alley and demanded that they all go "someplace where we can have some fun." When the girls refused, one of the boys pulled a knife, put it to Mirabel's throat, and warned that "you're gonna get stuck! One way or the other, you're gonna get stuck!" Mirabel's girlfriend, with two of the boys in pursuit, ran. Pressing the knife against Mirabel, the third boy forced her into the alley and against the side of a garage. Reaching under her dress, he attempted to pull down her panties. She bit into his arm, pushed him away, and tried to run. With a yell of pain, he caught her, tripped her, and slammed her to the ground. As she lay there stunned, he ripped off her panties and raped her. She was still on the ground when one of the other boys returned and, brandishing a bottle, told her she would "get her head bashed in" if she did not stop crying. But the headlights of a car turned down the alley, and he fled.

87

A Black Man on a White Force

THE DRIVER OF THE CAR TOOK MIRABEL TO THE POLICE STATION. A MEMBER of the women's division interviewed her. She was given a physical examination. The case was then assigned to the youth bureau.

The case load of the youth bureau was increasing more rapidly than that of any other division in the police department. The slump following the end of the Korean War brought a sharp rise in major economic crimes—from fourteen thousand in 1952 to nearly eighteen thousand in 1954. Even more than usual the perpetrators of these crimes were youth, and an increasing number of these youth were black. Experience had shown that because of the antagonism between black youth and white police officers, Negro officers often dealt more effectively with Negro juveniles. But of the eighty officers in the bureau, only two were black. When in 1955 the bureau's black complement was expanded to five, Conrad Mallett was one of those chosen.

After graduating from high school in 1945, Mallett had gone to work in the post office. A year later he had been drafted. Routinely he was asked to state his "race." In that moment, Mallett, who looked Spanish or Sicilian, had his choice between "white" and "colored."

"Colored," he said.

After his release from the air force in 1948, he returned to a job at the post office, and simultaneously enrolled at the University of Detroit. Lack of a background in science and mathematics hindered him, and he pursued his studies in a desultory fashion. For a Negro, the police department offered a better salary than most other employment—during the decade after World War II the pay scale was raised 60 percent—and in 1952 Mallett took the examination.

Although between a fourth and a fifth of those who took the test were black, the department operated with an implicit "quota" system under which the number of Negroes did not rise above approximately 3 percent—140 of the 4,200-man force. The department enforced the quota by downgrading Negroes on the oral examination, which was largely subjective, and by developing unfavorable material on their past lives, associates, and families in the background checks—in the ghetto, few blacks had had the prophylactic, middle-class up-bringing that the police set as the standard for recruits. The decade-long de-pression of the 1930's had enabled the department to pick and choose among applicants—both black and white. By 1940 a four-year high school education was the norm, and the intelligence test scores of new patrolmen were double the scores of those who had joined the force twenty years earlier. Since only the very best black applicants were selected, most, like Mallett, had had some college education, and quite a few had received their diplomas.

Once on the force, the black officer found himself, for all practical purposes, segregated from the white. Many white recruits were unprejudiced, but they quickly learned that any white officer who indicated signs of friendliness toward a black would be labeled a "nigger lover," given all the dirty assignments, and blackballed so far as promotion was concerned. A white officer who might, covertly, go fishing with a black would refuse to speak to him in the station-house. At one time white and black officers had been assigned to walk beats together, but that practice had ended with the 1943 riot. No black officer had ridden in a squad car until after World War II. Then one special car was set aside for blacks, allowing six Negroes (three shifts) to ride instead of having to walk beats.

Following the revelation of police department scandals under the administra-tion of Double Dip Dick Reading, Detroit voters in 1940 had adopted a charter amendment establishing a "merit system" for promotions. The system could be circumvented, however, since the written examination was weighted as only 40 percent of the total. Both the "service rating," which was weighted at 30 percent, and the "promotional evaluation," 20 percent,* were manipulated to work against Negroes and those whites who did not hew to departmental mores. Since it was inconceivable that Negroes would be placed in command over white personnel, promotional opportunities were severely limited. Only five blacks held the rank of sergeant, and none that of lieutenant. (There had been one detective lieutenant, but he had retired.)

After a brief stint on the vice squad, where he was instrumental in breaking a conspiracy case against a numbers operator, Mallett was assigned to walk a beat in the Third Precinct. He learned quickly that "reform" had been pri-marily a matter of degree, and that some practices had changed little since Mayor Pingree's day.

Frequently police officers knew the location of the blind pigs and numbers houses on their beats. If the officers were not in on the take, they nevertheless could participate in the fringe benefits—free plays on the numbers, free drinks, free girls, and free apartments for assignations. Some officers rolled drunks and shook down prostitutes. On occasion when a burglary was reported, a procession of squad cars would appear to "investigate." The policemen would load up with goods overlooked by the burglars and drive off. Sometimes the police took more than the burglars, and the store owner reported to his in-surance company a loss beyond what had been taken by both.

Since the war years, the department had increased its strength from 3,500 to 4,200, and its budget had doubled, but the additional money and manpower added little to efficiency. At four o'clock on winter mornings Mallett and seven or eight other officers would drink coffee and warm themselves for an hour in

---

* Seniority made up the other 10 percent.

the kitchen of a restaurant whose manager was making preparations for the day's opening at six o'clock. In such informal, *unseen* situations there were no blacks and no whites, only "cops." In public, a white officer who dared to sit down to drink coffee with a black would have been identified as a rebel. Negro officers were even discouraged from frequenting the same restaurants as white officers.

Although Michigan had had a nondiscrimination statute since 1885, Detroit continued to be essentially segregated. If a Negro objected to not being served in a public place, the police not only would refuse to take a complaint, but sometimes would warn him that he was subject to arrest for disturbing the peace. A Negro officer was charged fifty cents for a cup of coffee in a café where the price for whites was ten cents, and where white policemen drank their coffee free. When the officer protested, his superiors advised him that it would be better for his career if he did not pursue the matter of the operator's violation of the civil rights statute.

Transferred to the youth bureau, Mallett and his fellow black officers were assigned to infiltrate and break up Negro gangs. This proved a difficult assignment. The city had hordes of black juvenile delinquents but, except in the minds of the police hierarchy, no Negro gangs. When Mallett reported to the lieutenant he could find no gangs, the lieutenant retorted, "Just do as you're told." So the gang detail spent its time in parks, moviehouses, and pool halls ferreting out the nonexistent gangs. Since they were expected to report on the imaginary gangs, they made up their own, and titillated their superiors with the activities of such fictitious groups as the "Stilettos."

When repeated requests for a more useful assignment were met with the response: "Do you want to go back to walking a beat?" Mallett and one other officer jeopardized their careers by going out of channels to see the police commissioner.

That brought the breakup of the gang detail. Reassigned to the Third Precinct, Mallett was given the task of visiting schools and talking to youth about delinquency and police work. He discovered he had a knack for communicating with kids, and began to think about returning to school and obtaining his degree.

Once before, during his first year on the force, Mallett had attempted to continue his education. Derided as a "schoolboy" for enrolling in the University of Detroit Law School, he had discovered the anti-intellectual tradition of the department. He had been harassed, and his shift had been changed every month, so that it had been impossible for him to continue. He volunteered for the afternoon shift—usually considered an undesirable assignment—so that he could go to classes at Wayne State University. Keeping his school attendance secret, he explained that he had a "sick wife" whom he had to take care of.

The Third Precinct encompassed a major portion of the black Paradise Valley area. When Mallett had first started walking his beat on Gratiot Avenue, the last of the structures was being torn down in the Gratiot Redevelopment Area to presumably herald a new era in the city. Nearly five years later, when his stay on the police force was nearing its end, the leveled acres were still flat and empty, and the wind blew unobstructed from the river. In the area, crime, disease, and all the other problems associated with people had been wiped out. In the areas adjacent, crime, disease, and all the other problems associated with people were multiplying.

88

The Master Mistake

THE CITY PLANNING DEPARTMENT WAS NEVERTHELESS DETERMINED TO DO FOR the poor, white population of Corktown what it had accomplished for the poor, black population of Gratiot.

For the planning commission staff it seemed a matter of elementary statistics. According to the scale of "blight ratings" devised for each of the city's thirteen thousand blocks, Corktown presented a compelling case for elimination from Detroit. Industrial development along the railroad tracks had made the area a hodgepodge of factories and houses. It was an unattractive district in which to live or to build. Four fifths of the structures, most of which had been put up before the turn of the century, were substandard. The median income was only three fourths that in the city as a whole. Most of the thirty-three hundred people living there were unassimilated Catholics who had supplanted the Irish in the lower economic reaches. Two thirds were Maltese and Mexicans, many of whom spoke English poorly or not at all. About half the remainder were remnants of the southern European immigration. With the minority status, the language barrier, and the lower income came overcrowding, and the higher disease and crime rates that the planning staff converted into "blight." Only 7 percent of the people living in the area were homeowners. Most of the property was owned by families who had long since moved away. Unable to sell their property for what they considered an equitable price, they had rented the houses and become "absentee landlords." Even as the English and French once had become the landlords of the Irish, German, and Jewish slums, the Irish, Germans, and Jews had become the landlords of the Maltese, Mexican, and Negro slums.

But while the Negroes of the Gratiot area, unorganized and lacking ethnic cohesiveness, had moved out with scarcely a whisper of protest, the residents of Corktown, dismayed by the example of Gratiot, organized to prevent the razing of their area. One rallying point was the Most Holy Trinity Roman Catholic Church. Another was the much smaller St. Peter's Episcopal Church, whose pastor, the Reverend John F. Mangrum, became the most articulate leader of the opposition to redevelopment. Such organizations as the Maltese Benevolent Society and the Corktown Home Owners Association were the spearhead of the attack on the planning commission.

Harold Black and others of the planning commission staff at first thought of the opposition as the offspring of ignorance nurtured by the well of reaction. The planners had a diversity of educational backgrounds, they had come into the department from routine and boring jobs in other agencies, and they had developed a sense of mission. Believing they were engaged in eliminating slums and in building the city of tomorrow, they were shocked to discover people who wanted to continue living in their slums. It was as if they had found pigs who wanted to go on living in their pigsties. Evidently more intelligent people, people with any sense of the future, would not dispute the prescription of the "professionals." The disdain with which the planners regarded the residents and talked down to them generated bitter personal animosities.

Asserting that "the city's master plan was a master mistake," and that "we are not slummy people," residents laid the responsibility for what blight there was at the door of city hall. The area had, in fact, suffered from Detroit's "no taxes-no services" policy during the Depression, and since then had had low priority with department heads.

The atmosphere was scarcely improved when a planner retorted: "It's the people's obligation to improve the area. They have had all these years to improve. But they didn't. It's not our problem. We merely study problems." [1]

Appealing to their congressman, residents became the ball in a Ping-Pong game between the city and the Federal bureaucracy. When the homeowners prepared their own study to refute the data of the planning commission, they were advised that it would have to be submitted to the regional office of the Urban Renewal Administration. The regional office of the Urban Renewal Administration returned it with the notation that it should be brought to the attention of city officials.

As the battle continued, the residents became more sophisticated. They charged that the proposed renewal was nothing but a land grab to provide industry with subsidized property on which to build. That, in fact, since Mayor Cobo was desperately trying to stem the flow of industry from the city, was what it was. The planning commission staff, continually being prodded by the mayor, objected to what they considered political interference by Representative Charles Diggs, the black congressman who represented the area, and by members of the city council in a nonpolitical project. They made every effort to circumvent the public hearings and the polemics of the Reverend John Mangrum, who declared:

"Destroy families, tear up homes and supplant them with questionable business development and the wrath of God will fall on our city." [2]

Although as many as four or five hundred residents—nearly 15 percent of the total number—attended some of the hearings, the planning staff contended that Mangrum and the president of the homeowners association were "troublemakers" who were not representative of the people in the area.

The charge that they were "unrepresentative" contained a good deal of truth. They were the small percentage of homeowners still living in the area, the people who had a personal stake in it, who were activitists and participants in community affairs, who created neighborhoods and a sense of community within the faceless heterogeneity of the city.

For five years after June, 1952, when the planning commission first announced its approval of the project, the residents sustained a delaying action. Through their fight they were able to obtain far more official interest and better terms than the people of the Gratiot area. But because the leaders of the opposition *were* a small minority and *unrepresentative,* the planning bureaucracy prevailed. The planners were able to refute the data of the homeowners association and reinforce their own. The people who *were* representative of those living in the area were Marie and Peter Jansen.

89

The Inner City Syndrome

KATHERINE, THE JANSENS' SEVENTH AND LAST CHILD, HAD BEEN BORN IN 1942. Peter was working in a war plant. Depending on the amount of over-time he put in, he made from forty to sixty dollars a week. Marie had enough money to buy cigarettes, to go to five or six movies a week, and yet feed the children adequately. With Katherine, there were now three children living in the two rooms Marie and Peter rented. Marie relied on Rita to help care for the two younger girls. Rita's eyesight had been improved by the operations on the cataracts, and in her teens she could cope better with children than she had been able to as a small, blind girl. The Juvenile Court had established some stability in the home by removing Jim and three other children, and placing them in boarding homes. The arrival of Katherine, however, threatened the family's tenuous stability; and one more child to feed and care for would bring a renewal of chaos. Neither the Juvenile Court, nor the Catholic Church, nor any of the numerous social agencies that had impinged upon the Jansens' life would encourage Marie to employ contraception. So Peter subconsciously di-rected himself toward preventing another conception. He drank more. The more he drank, the less he copulated with Marie.

During the layoffs that came in the summer and fall of 1945, Peter lost his job. A semiskilled laborer, he was about to turn fifty. He discovered, as William Norveth had twenty years earlier, that the men who did the hiring looked right past him. By November, 1945, he had used up his unemployment insurance. As the family's money ran out, the animosity between Peter and Marie flared anew. Since Peter had no money, he stopped going home, but loitered on the Michigan Avenue skid row. He was actually drinking less than when he had been working. The craving, however, gnawed at him continuously, so that when-ever he was hired for an odd job and received a dollar or two he immediately spent it on a bottle. Marie had no alterative but to go on welfare.

When Marie applied for relief, a nonsupport warrant was issued for Peter. On an occasion when he was picked up for being drunk, the police discovered the warrant outstanding against him. The judge lectured him on supporting his family, and sentenced him to thirty days in the Detroit House of Correction.

In the summer of 1946 the automobile industry was reaching its postwar production stride, and Peter found work again. He moved back in with Marie and the two younger girls.

Rita was no longer living with the family. Two years earlier, in the winter of 1944, she had been taken ill with rheumatic fever. Her heart valves were scarred. By the next fall, she was past the age of sixteen. Despite her continual absences and failures, the school system had pushed her up to the seventh grade. The system, however, was not geared to provide meaningful education for a child such as she. Technically, she could read, but because of her poor eyesight she had difficulty deciphering lower-case print. She could write block letters, but not script. Since the school system was not anxious to have her return, its employment office helped her find a job as an occasional baby-sitter and light houseworker.

Rita's physical ailments, insecurity, and rootlessness caused her to respond exaggeratedly to any display of affection. By early 1945 she was pregnant. The baby, born prematurely, was deformed, and died within twenty-four hours. Rita went to work in a convalescent home. After a few months she became involved with the husband of one of her patients. Rita's second child, Betty, arrived in the fall of 1947. A social worker suggested that Betty be placed in a boarding home. Rita screamed, "I'm never going to let that happen to *my* baby!" Claiming she could not work and look after the baby at the same time, she filed an application for welfare. The application was approved.

For the next few months she moved from one rundown boardinghouse to another, and repeated the pattern of disorganized misery to which she had been subjected as a child. Since the Aid for Dependent Children grant was not enough to buy necessities for herself and the baby, she chose boyfriends who agreed to contribute to her support. When a doctor warned that unless she took better care of her eyes she might lose her sight entirely, she reacted by increasing the pace of her activities. Soon she was little more than a prostitute. Men flowed in and out of her room.

In the fall of 1948, her swelling abdomen indicated another pregnancy. To the welfare worker, however, Rita, now twenty, claimed that the doctor had told her she had complications and a tumor from her previous pregnancy. Even after she gave birth, she insisted that she was in the hospital to have the tumor removed. When the baby was brought to her, she refused to recognize it as hers. One of her boyfriends, believing the child to be his, took it to his mother's house, and paid for Rita's confinement.

After her release from the hospital, Rita accepted a job caring for the three children of a family. She said it was hard to care for other people's children when she could not care for her own. In the summer of 1949 she met George Devers.

Seven years older than Rita, Devers worked at the Dodge Main Plant. He had grown up in the vicinity of the northern Alabama town of Decatur and could remember when, in his teens, the modern world had burst in on him as the TVA earth-moving equipment gouged through the hills, and the towers of the electric power lines were raised. Daryl, George's father, quit sharecropping and went to work on the project. In 1942 he left Alabama and went to work for the Veterans Administration in Chattanooga. Eighteen months later he was transferred to the VA hospital in Detroit. George, who was 4-F, came to visit him in 1944. He had no difficulty finding a job in a defense plant, and remained.

As George kept talking about getting married, Rita agreed in November, 1949, to let the Society of St. Vincent de Paul place Betty in a boarding home. At a cost of ten dollars a week Betty was placed, "the people of Wayne County to be reimbursed for the cost of maintenance, care and education of the said ward by the parents or the person standing in *loco parentis,* when able, or from any estate which may come to the said ward." Officers of the court had difficulty recalling a case in which the people of Wayne County *had* been reimbursed. But the stipulation was necessary to satisfy the law.

In January, 1950, Rita and George were married. Trilby was born in the fall. At the Dodge plant the Korean War brought activity to a high pitch. George worked overtime and made good money. Rita had never known such good times. She bought furniture, a refrigerator, and a television set. The struggles of her childhood seemed past. She wanted to bring Betty to live with them, but George refused to accept another man's child in his home. Reluctantly, Rita agreed to have Betty placed for adoption.

Between 1946 and 1949 Peter Jansen worked eight or nine months out of each year. But in the recession of 1949 he was laid off again, and went back onto skid row so Marie could draw welfare. The roominghouse in which the family lived was nearby, on the edge of Corktown. The owner was an Irish-German auto worker who had migrated along with the automobile assembly plants and was spending much of his time in California. He had been notified that his house was in an urban renewal district, and so was making no effort to arrest the termites and rot. Throughout the area, the unpainted and bleak buildings sagged and sighed, and were boarded up. (Skid row itself, however, was not eligible for urban renewal because more than half the people living along it were unrelated individuals, and the law was intended to improve the living accommodations of families.)

A one-eyed Maltese named Madriga managed the property for the owner.* Marie became Madriga's housekeeper. Since Peter was absent most of the time and seldom interested in sexual intercourse even when he was home, a liaison developed between Marie and Madriga.

Marie's youngest two children lived with her and Madriga. Thirteen-year-old Joella was of low intelligence. She was a chronic pilferer of cigarettes, for which she had developed a craving. Occasionally she was caught. In the fall of 1951, a drugstore clerk would not release her despite her pleas and tears, but turned her over to the women's division of the police department. The officer asked her what she did with the cigarettes. She replied that she smoked them. When the officer chided her, she replied: "I ain't little like you think." To indicate her maturity she recounted her knowledge of sex, which was considerable.

Katherine, four years younger than Joella, was the brightest and most verbal of the children. She was Peter's favorite, and she responded to his affection.

* Malta, a small-scale Ireland, had been exporting its surplus population for hundreds of years. Immediately after World War I hundreds of Maltese streamed to Detroit. When the immigration acts reduced the annual Maltese quota to fourteen, wives and girlfriends were prevented from following. The men were left largely without women until they became Americanized enough to look beyond their own ethnic group for female companionship.

She cried over his absences, and she deeply resented Madriga. She was far more articulate than Madriga, whose conversation consisted mostly of grunts. She would taunt him until he reacted violently, and then dodge around him and escape into the street. A week after Joella was taken to the juvenile home, Katherine for once was not nimble enough to elude Madriga. He caught her and whipped her with his belt. When Katherine finally wrenched away from him, she ran to the police station, exhibited the welts, and reported that they had been inflicted by "a man who's fucking my mother!"

That brought the entire Jansen family to the Juvenile Court again. Four children had been removed from the home in 1938, and Peter and Marie could hardly recall what they looked like. Alice, the two-year-old girl who had been placed in boarding care, was an attractive, blonde child, and after some time she had been adopted by a middle-class family in Dearborn. The two younger boys had been kept on farms until they were seventeen. Neither of them had done well in school, but they had not gotten into major difficulties. After they were dismissed from the jurisdiction of the Juvenile Court, they faded into the adult world. Jim, the oldest boy, was drawn to trouble wherever it existed. A few weeks after he had participated in the 1943 riot, he was picked up again. He was placed in one boarding home after another without success. In 1947 he enlisted in the army. Unable to adjust to discipline, he stole a .45 automatic, went on a binge of armed robberies, and was sentenced to the penitentiary.

To Peter and Marie these children were like strangers who had come and spent a while with them, then disappeared into another existence. Peter had a greater sense of failure than Marie. When Judge George Edwards asked him if he was not ashamed, he shook his head: "I like to do right by my children, but I don't get jobs."

So Katherine was boarded in a home, and Joella, whose IQ was in the mid-70's, was committed to the Wayne County Training School.

"That's all right," Joella told Judge Edwards, "I ain't gonna be there long." When he asked her what she meant, she continued: "I'll just get myself a baby."

The brighter children, those who presumably should have benefited the most from the training at the school, were the ones who disliked the school most. Wayne County had begun operation of the school in 1926 when, following World War I, the number of retarded children in the public schools had risen astronomically. A generation earlier, when the compulsory attendance law was not enforced, they would have dropped out and been used to fill menial jobs, and no one would have noticed. But with the changed attitude toward the use of eleven-year-olds as child labor, and with the migration of the population from rural to urban areas, an "epidemic" of mental deficiency had suddenly been noted in Detroit, in Michigan, and in America. The public schools had not known what to do with the children who did not respond to the traditional methods of teaching. The children that the Wayne County Probate Court had been trying to commit to the Lapeer State Training School, the only school for feeble-minded operated by the state, had been placed on a five-year waiting list. Most never had been admitted to the school, but were abandoned to the hazards of the city's streets.

That was when the county had decided to erect its own training school at Northville, twenty-three miles from downtown Detroit. Across the road was the Detroit House of Correction and nearby was the Maybury TB Sanitorium—

all conveniently lumped together on the borders of the county and far removed from the city's consciousness.

By the late 1950's and early 1960's, children were being sent to the Wayne County Training School not so much because of their mental deficiencies—two thirds of them tested high enough to qualify for service in the army—but because of a whole host of mental, emotional, and social disturbances that combined into what could be called the Inner City Syndrome.

Although the training school served the entire 2.6 million population of Wayne County, six out of ten of the children came from the half million people living within or adjacent to the inner Boulevard area of Detroit. (As the population of the Boulevard area turned predominantly black, so did the population of the training school.) Increasingly it was a dumping ground for children with difficult problems for which no solution could be found. The Detroit school system kept referring children to the training school in the hope that a more structured and disciplined setting would make them better learners, and the Juvenile Court committed them in order to remove them from the inimical environment of their families and the slums. It was like hoping for improvement by a transfer from hell to Siberia. In the training school the children were immersed in a dehumanized culture that treated them as "a biological machine, so to speak, which must eat, sleep, and work."[1]

Nearly nine out of ten of the children were in the school because of psychological problems associated with their families, their upbringing, and their environment.* At least one third of those admitted were suffering from "cultural deprivation"—malnutrition, physical neglect, and child abuse. The problems, and the causes of the problems of many children were so complex and so well hidden in the labyrinths of their pasts that they were all but undiagnosable, and classified as "unknown."

Yet the school was still operated as if it were dealing with mentally retarded and epileptic cases. Only nineteen thousand dollars a year was budgeted for psychiatric services. Although the table of organization provided for seven psychologists, three were actually employed, and none of these had a Ph.D. The teaching staff was 25 percent under strength. The psychologists and the social workers felt as if they were operating in a vacuum. Counselors, who were assigned more than a hundred cases each, worked in essentially the same manner as the Juvenile Court's probation officers—they concentrated on alleviating crises.

In theory, since its population was supposed to consist of the mentally handicapped, the school had an "open" setting, with no physical restraints placed on the children. In actuality, two thirds of the children presented behavior problems. There was an explosive mixture of the mentally retarded, the physically handicapped (whose "mental retardation" might be due to a lack of hearing and whose lack of hearing might be rooted in psychological trauma),

---

* Nearly half the children exhibited severe behavior disorders that formed a delinquent or predelinquent pattern. More than a fourth of the remainder were there because they had been unable to withstand the tremendous stresses imposed upon them by unstable, chaotic, or violent family situations. One out of seven had severe, chronic personality disorders that might be characterized by hysteria, aggressiveness, antisocial activity, or explosive outbursts. Many exhibited overt sexual aberrations—promiscuity, homosexuality, exhibitionism, and sexual assaultiveness.

and the emotionally disturbed. The administration of the school, therefore, directed its principal efforts to maintaining peace and order.

At the time of its construction, the school had been isolated and difficult to reach. It was conceived as a self-contained community—a village of subintelligent children. It had its own electric power plant, medical clinic, fire department, and employee housing. It raised its own food on its own farm, it baked its own bread in its own bakery, it sewed its own clothes, and then washed them in its own laundry. Since the children had been placed there because they were thought incapable of intellectual achievement, the emphasis of the "training" was on manual labor. They were set to hoeing and planting and picking in the fields; to hauling coal and firing the furnaces in the powerhouse; to sewing and washing, mending and ironing clothes; to endless sweeping and scrubbing of floors, polishing furniture, and washing windows. They were serfs, paying their own way, satisfying the requirement that they be in "school," but learning little or nothing, and being "trained" for jobs that in the real economic world were being transferred to machines.

Joella hated the ritual, the endless routine, the reform school sense of confinement and repression. It heightened the tensions, anxieties, and frustrations of the children. Screaming tantrums and fights were common, and almost necessary to clear an atmosphere that would grow taut beyond endurance. The malefactors were penned in barren isolation rooms, and sometimes kept there for weeks. They were assigned the hardest and dirtiest work details, so that in the minds of the children work was equated with punishment. Since recreation and exercise were inadequate, and, like the work, mind dulling, the one escape and entertainment offered to the adolescents was sex. Girls and boys were separated and watched—though that did not prevent an occasional tryst—so most of the sex was onanistic and experimentally homosexual. Since the children came from lower-class backgrounds they had an abundance of raw sexual experience, but, conversely, almost total physiological ignorance. Superstitions were rampant—one could get a baby from a snake or from being kissed during a full moon. Most of the girls looked upon sex as a kind of magic potion.

"There isn't nothing sex can't get you," Joella said.

One third of the children ran away every year. Nearly 90 percent of them had had contacts with the police and the courts, either through their own actions or those of their parents, before they entered the school. Like the Boys Vocational School (reformatory), the Wayne County Training School was a means of removing the most troublesome juveniles from the society of the city. Yet almost without exception the school failed to help them in any but the most marginal way; and they returned to that society with the same problems that had caused them to be removed from it. Like carriers of a disease that temporarily has been arrested, but not cured, they would not only themselves suffer recurrences, but infect others with it.

When Joella was allowed to go home for the Christmas holidays in 1953, she made up her mind she was not going back to the school. Lying about her age—she was fifteen and a half—she obtained a job as a waitress at a hamburger stand. Before the end of January she met twenty-six-year-old Ned Black Bear—who was married but was separated from his wife—and went to live with him.

Black Bear was of Indian descent. He knew little of his heritage, but in the

1850's the name still had been prominent enough among Michigan Indians for Joy and Brooks to name one of the Michigan Central locomotives the *Black Bear*. During the latter part of the nineteenth century, while Joy and Alger, Newberry and McMillan, Ward and Murphy, and all the other economic buccaneers had basked in the glow of the gold they were reaping from the Michigan lands, the Black Bear family had experienced a bitter harvest. Black Bear's grandfather had been able to make a tenuous living as a woodsman and guide for hunting parties, but by the second half of his lifetime the ruthless rapine of the lumbering industry had destroyed that livelihood, too. Black Bear's parents had eked out a miserable and degrading existence as itinerant farm workers in the Michigan fields. They had no home. After the harvest was in, they wandered from place to place. They scavenged in the cities, and slept in shacks and lean-tos. In the bitterness of the Depression their lot was the most bitter, for they were not only poor but outcasts. Even in the most miserable of Hoovervilles someone would raise the cry, "Get those goddam dirty Indians outa here!" Black Bear's early memories were of constant cold and hunger; of his mother giving him sips of corn liquor to warm him and make him drowsy so as to still his crying. Not until his father had gotten a WPA job had Black Bear attended his first class. By then he was nearly ten years old.

When Joella met him, he was earning $1.90 an hour as a sweeper and cleanup man at Packard. They moved into a "single" apartment with kitchen and private bath in the Twelfth Street area—the most luxurious accommodations either one of them had ever had. Black Bear owned a 1947 Plymouth—so they could go places. With Joella continuing to work, their combined income after deductions came to $85 or $90 a week, a sum that Joella thought fabulous. Although occasionally she worried about being sent back to the training school, for the first time she was enjoying life.

In fact, economic circumstances over which she had no control, plus her ignorance of contraception, made this a brief interlude. It was a year before she became pregnant. By then, Packard, still in middle age, was tottering like a senile old man. Control had passed out of the hands of Detroit's Railroad Republican families—who were multiplying and scattering—and become diversified. Ever since 1940 the company had been depending on war contracts to ward off insolvency. With the end of the Korean War these contracts were phased out, and a terminal illness set in. The first of the "Eisenhower recessions" in 1954—a recession that like all economic downturns affected the sale of high-priced cars the most—was like a paralytic stroke. In a heroic, desperation maneuver, management abandoned the large, Kahn-built plant on East Grand Boulevard, and moved production to a smaller factory. In many ways the move reduced overhead at the cost of efficiency. Assembly-line workers grumbled that it made no sense. An anxiety, endemic to dying enterprises, pervaded the plant. Every time a machine stopped running a score of men would swivel about, as if expecting the shutdown of all the assembly lines.

The end came early in 1956. When the company announced it was merging with Studebaker and closing its Detroit facilities, the reaction of the men was almost one of relief. The dreaded sentence had been passed; but would there not be a reprieve? The four thousand workers engaged in an explosive verbal purging. Rumor was piled upon rumor. There was widespread belief that the company was the victim of a "plot." Some men thought that the officers of the company had conspired against it. Others that the Big Three had ganged up to drive it to the wall. Others that Secretary of Defense Charles Wilson had shifted defense contracts away from Packard to General Motors, so as to eliminate a competitor of Cadillac.

Until the layoffs actually began, there was a new and unusual sense of community among the workers—a sense of oneness in the same sinking company. Men who had been used to greeting Black Bear with the condescending and snide, "Lo, the vanishing Indian!"—a reference to his habit of occasionally disappearing—put their arms around him, offered to buy him a beer, and told him, "You goddam Indians have had it pretty rough!" Two thirds of the workers believed that the Federal government had an obligation to save the company, be it through the allocation of defense contracts or outright subsidy, or to find new jobs for the workers who were laid off.

But then the disintegration began, and it was every man for himself. Unskilled and with no seniority, Black Bear was one of the first to be let go. Although the economy was purportedly expanding, he discovered that jobs were scarce for men who had no special skills. At first he looked for work enthusiastically; then more and more sporadically. Week by week his unemployment benefits ticked away. One Monday in spring they were gone. He was part of a statistic. Only one out of four Packard workers, nearly all of them skilled, were reemployed in other auto plants.*

When Black Bear had been working, he and Joella had gotten high on weekends and had a good time. Out of work, he lay on the studio bed and sipped whiskey straight from the bottle. Two months after Black Bear was laid off, Joella lost her job because of her advanced state of pregnancy. By the time the baby was born in May, the money was gone, and so were the good times. Joella could not understand why Black Bear could not find another job. Her irritation, heightened by her fear of sliding back into the circumstances she had known all her childhood, led to frequent quarrels. Three weeks after the birth of Eliza, Joella and Black Bear were evicted for not paying their rent. Dropping the infant off with her mother, Joella said that she was going with Black Bear to look for work in other cities.

---

* Only 43 percent of the unskilled workers were unemployed for less than seven months; 28 percent were unemployed for more than a year. Although 42 percent of the whites—in general, better educated and more skilled—found work after going to no more than five places, a third of the Negroes had to apply at more than thirty.

90

"What's Good for General Motors..."

PACKARD HAD FALLEN VICTIM NOT TO AN EGALITARIAN TREND IN AMERICAN society—the segment of the American population that had bought Packards in the 1920's was more affluent than ever in the 1950's—but to the Hollywoodization of the automobile industry that had begun with the Depression; to rising costs; to automation; and, most of all, to the continuing centripetal forces that were concentrating vast economic power in ever fewer and more gigantic financial and manufacturing enterprises.

On a trip to Hollywood in 1926, Cadillac President Lawrence P. Fisher had discovered Harley J. Earl, a young Stanford graduate whose father had developed one of Southern California's largest carriage making businesses. Earl was custom-designing automobiles for movie stars. Detroit, with its nuts-and-bolts orientation, had no experience in building cars with emphasis on styling. Fisher invited Earl to come to Detroit and design a General Motors car. The result was the 1927 La Salle. The first mass produced car to be "styled," it marked a watershed in the automobile industry almost equal to the introduction of the Model T.

With the Model T, Ford had put an end to what the auto pioneers had come to consider a "curse": the annual model change. For more than twenty-five years thereafter manufacturers had stuck to producing the same model year after year, until such time as they came out with a completely reengineered automobile. During the Depression, however, executives at General Motors became convinced that, since the corporation had the capacity to manufacture far more cars than people needed, the public would have to be stimulated into purchasing *more* cars than they needed. Talking to Earl, G.M. President Sloan mused:

"What can we do to create an obsolescence? Every other year, a new model with slight changes—advertise to the public that G.M. is improving each year?" [1]

What General Motors could do was resurrect the "curse": each year come out with a new model. For that purpose, G.M. in 1937 dedicated a styling center to rival its research facilities.

The corporation thereupon set out to convince Americans that it did not matter if their housing were inadequate, or if their marriage were on the rocks, or if their medical treatment were often too little and too late, they were a success as long as they were "in style" with their automobiles. To be in style they had to buy a new car every other year.

Radio proved a highly effective medium for that kind of indoctrination. Following the war, television far surpassed it. Television also far surpassed radio in cost. Between 1952 and 1956 advertising outlay per car increased 190 percent for Chevrolet, 126 percent for Ford, and 235 percent for Plymouth. The Big Three combined were spending over $1 billion a year to create "obsolescence." At Ford, styling costs alone ranged from $150 to $270 per vehicle annually, depending on the extent of change. At General Motors, overhead costs—sales, administration, advertising, amortization of special tools, depreciation, and obsolescence—multiplied over seven times between 1937 and 1957. They accounted for approximately 60 percent more of the price of the car than labor, and a fourth of the total wholesale price of the average General Motors car ($550 per vehicle). As the result of its giganticism, General Motors could absorb these costs.* Its design teams were restyling not one line, but six lines simultaneously—Chevrolet, Pontiac, Oldsmobile, Buick, La Salle, and Cadillac; and all these cars were in most part variations of only three basic designs. (In 1959 the company standardized further and began using only one basic body shell for *all* its cars.) The corporation's break-even point was at 40 to 45 percent of capacity—above that, it earned $31.60 for each $100 in sales.

In contrast, the independent manufacturers, whose *combined* share of the market was one tenth that of General Motors, were being forced to restyle and retool continuously for *one* line of cars. Unable to break even at anywhere near their 1956 volume, they lacked the huge amounts of capital the Big Three were investing in research, in automated equipment, and in advertising. While General Motors had so much surplus capital it could make multimillion-dollar loans to enterprises like Jones and Laughlin, Republic Steel, and Pittsburgh Coke and Chemical Company, the independents became less and less competitive. When Packard needed fifty million dollars to carry it through 1956, "the roof fell in. The banks refused to refinance our loans and we had insufficient money to tool, build, and market our new 1957 line." [2] The bankers could see no way for Packard to compete with General Motors and Ford.

In 1953, G.M. President Charles E. Wilson, nominated for Secretary of Defense by President Eisenhower, told a Senate committee: "What's good for the country is good for General Motors, and what's good for General Motors is good for the country." His statement had been considered not only gospel, but a truism, at the corporation for decades. As early as 1927, Sloan had declared:

"There are several cities of importance in the United States whose prosperity is absolutely linked up with the prosperity of General Motors.

"I have estimated that a very appreciable percent of the total population of the United States is directly affected by the prosperity of General Motors." [3]

Emerging from the General Motors executive offices, Wilson had had no

---

* The corporation not only had 50 percent of the American automobile market but was one of the top four companies in twenty-two other product classifications, and had a monopoly on the manufacture of some products.

inkling what a furor his statement would create, a furor reflective of the naiveté of the American public about the American economy and the role played in it by far the largest and most powerful corporation in the world.

What was good for General Motors certainly was not proving good for Detroit. In the "new America" of the late 1940's and the 1950's, as the Federal government financed no-down and low-down housing construction on the urban fringes, Americans purchased automobiles as never before. The auto industry's sales were twice what they had been in the 1920's. To transport the larger families that were a concomitant of prosperity, Americans demanded larger cars. Since the suburban scattering of the population made public transportation economically unfeasible in the outlying areas, the suburban family was as dependent upon its automobile as the farm family had once been upon its horse. When the man drove off in one car, the woman needed another to do her shopping in the regional shopping center or to drive the kids to the doctor. In the "new America" tailored to the automobile, everything was neatly separated and packaged into residential, commercial, and industrial areas. Shopping centers provided acres of parking, but neighborhoods did not provide a single store. Without a car, a woman was stranded in a forest of houses.

So the two-car family, once an indication of the utmost affluence, turned into the suburban norm. With the advent of the two-car family, the demand for new automobiles went up. Each year after 1948 the industry sold more vehicles than it had in 1929. In 1955 the number sold topped nine million.

But while the family car might be a basic commodity, suburbanites soon realized that two *family cars,* with their high initial and repair costs, as well as gas-gobbling tendencies, were a little too much. As the family's second, or used car wore out, they searched for something smaller to replace it.

They had difficulty finding it in Detroit. So did singles and young couples, who were coming to play an increasingly important role in the market. On the evidence that the public apparently bought more cars the bigger they were made, Detroit had set out to blur the boundary between a large car and a small truck. Since American automobile manufacturers had had a virtual monopoly on the American automobile market for fifty years, the industry did not emphasize "consumer research." Executives worried more about what General Motors would do, what prices it would set, and what new styles it would introduce, than what the public wanted. The public, presumably, would want what the industry through the mouth-watering gimmickry of television was promoting—an automated, air-conditioned, overpowered, oversized, orchestrated ambulatory bordello.

The automobile industry accommodated itself to the enormous power the UAW had gained by wielding even greater power over the American economy, and by passing every wage increase on to the consumer.* While American manufacturers steadily priced themselves out of the low-priced market that Henry Ford had tapped with the Model T, the consumer sought a means to escape their steely domination. He found it in the reborn European auto industry, and most notably in the Volkswagen.

Without a gas gauge or other "frills," and with a top speed of seventy miles per hour, the Volkswagen was rugged, economical to operate, and simple to

---

* Between 1949 and 1961, while the consumer price index rose 25 percent, average annual earnings in the automobile industry increased 84 percent, and the average factory price of a car went up 43 percent.

fix. Essentially, it was a reincarnation of the Model T. Like the Model T it lacked "style," and remained unchanged year after year.

In the late 1930's G.M.'s President Knudsen had voiced the opinion that a Volkswagen could never sell in the American market. Twenty years later, however, American cars cost three times as much as they had in those days. The Volkswagen price, on the other hand, was not loaded down with the 25 percent overhead resulting from continual model changes and the effort to convince the public that a car with 1956 grille and chrome was better than a car with 1955 grille and chrome. The VW filled the second-car, basic-transportation gap that Detroit was ignoring. In the mid-1920's the better values offered by used Chevrolets and Hudsons had led Americans to shift away from buying new Model T's; in the mid-1950's Americans shifted from used Chevrolets to the better value offered by new Volkswagens.

Between 1955 and 1960 imports of foreign cars increased from 57,000 to 445,000, even while exports of American cars were dropping by more than 100,000. This difference of a half million cars translated itself into the loss of 50,000 jobs in the automobile industry, and multiplied as it spread over ancillary industries. The effect on the independent auto manufacturers and on the city of Detroit was devastating. In addition to Packard, Hudson closed down, and with Hudson went 35,000 jobs.* As suppliers went out of business or moved from the city, the East Side alone lost 71,000 jobs in the 1950's and early 1960's. With the plants went the taxes and the revenues they had produced—the Packard plant was sold for 10 percent of its assessed valuation. Chrysler, the city's bread-and-butter manufacturer, was one of the Big Three but lacked the resources of Ford or General Motors. In the latter 1950's, Chrysler attempted to emulate General Motors styling, but instead produced finned aberrations that caused company sales to nosedive. For a time Chrysler's existence was threatened, too. In its four Detroit plants employment skidded from 46,000 in the mid-1950's to 22,700 in 1958.

* Hudson merged with Nash to become American Motors, and all production was moved to Nash's Kenosha, Wisconsin, plant. Packard merged with Studebaker and moved to the Studebaker plant in South Bend, where production of the car was continued only briefly. Studebaker itself lingered on only until the early 1960's.

Another manufacturer, Kaiser-Frazer, led a tenuous existence for a decade after its formation in 1945. Organized by Henry J. Kaiser, a steel and shipping magnate, and Joseph W. Frazer, president of Graham-Paige, the company bought Ford's Willow Run plant and other surplus war property to begin production. Subsequently, it acquired Willys-Overland, one of the pioneering auto firms. By 1955, however, Kaiser-Frazer's heavy losses and inability to make headway against the giants forced the company's dissolution. (Willys was continued as a jeep and commercial-vehicle manufacturing enterprise.) General Motors bought Willow Run for an automatic-transmission manufacturing plant.

91

The Bad Seed

THE FORTUNES OF GEORGE AND RITA DEVERS WERE LINKED CLOSELY TO THE prosperity of Chrysler and Dodge. The ups and downs in the life of the family directly reflected the ups and downs in Chrysler stock. Since the family income was mortgaged for years in advance to buy the car, the furniture, and the television set, any layoff of more than two or three weeks presaged disaster. During the "Eisenhower recessions" in 1954 and 1958 the family came close to disintegrating.

The interaction between the genes of George Devers and the former Rita Jansen was not favorable. Rita herself had been born with congenital cataracts, and her first child had been deformed. George's and Rita's firstborn, Trilby, was healthy, and so was their fourth child, Ryan. They, however, proved to be the exception. The second child was stillborn. The third, Georgia, had club feet.

Rita had difficulty caring for three children. Remembering the chaos of her own upbringing, she was determined not to have any more. She was, however, indecisive and lackadaisical about obtaining information on how to prevent conception. She did not know where to go. Governmental agencies were not permitted to dispense information. The Catholic Church, to which she still belonged, continued to express its disapproval of birth control. Sporadically she used contraceptive jelly, which she could buy in a drugstore, and which she regarded as a compromise between "being unnatural and pregnant." Mostly, however, she hoped "I'd be lucky!"

When it became evident in the fall of 1954 that she was with child again, Rita broke down. She blamed George for forcing himself upon her and giving her inadequate time to prepare for the sex act. The birth of the baby nearly wrecked the marriage. Hilda had congenital cataracts and was blind.

When George's father, Daryl, came to visit, he and George would sit at the kitchen table and during the course of the evening gradually get drunk. The drunker Daryl became the more he questioned his son's judgment, and the more he taunted him about marrying a girl who had had affairs with all kinds

431

of men. He made lewd remarks to Rita about her "experience." It was no wonder, Daryl said, that the children were afflicted by the "bad seed" in Rita and her family. Rita was terrified of the drunken men. She did not want her children subjected to the sufferings she had experienced as a child. Tears streaming down her face, she would take the children and flee.

So long as George was a good provider, Rita stifled her resentment against his father. In 1954, however, he was laid off for several months. When the family was unable to make the payments on the furniture, it was repossessed. Rita was reduced to living in a barren room again. Her children slept rolled up in blankets on the floor, as she and her brothers and sisters had slept. Rita began to see similarities between George and her father. She called George a "lousy father and a drunken bum." Occasionally her quarrels with him erupted into violence. Once, when he hit her, she slapped him back. Immediately she was terror-struck. "Hit me! Hit me!" she pleaded with him. "I deserve it."

George had superficial insight, and would "talk things out" more than Rita. Sporadically he appealed to a social agency for help. In seeking help, however, he was mostly trying to justify himself and shift the burden of problems he could not handle onto someone else. Insecure and dependent, he was disturbed that Rita needed him for a father as well as for a husband.

When their fourth child, Hilda, was born, George was working again. But the debts had not been paid off, and the apartment continued to lack furniture. Two months after the birth, George and Rita slid into another quarrel—he accused her of failing to bear healthy children, she screamed that the kind of children she gave birth to made no difference, because he could not provide for them. Taking the children, she stormed out of the house. Following her, he called the police when he found the children alone at a neighbor's home. He was so intoxicated and incoherent that the police took him to the station to sober up.

Like Rita, George was deeply attached to his children. When she refused to return to him, he appealed to the caseworkers at the Juvenile Court for help. He wore his work clothes, whose splotched and unkempt appearance matched that of his hair and face. His breath smelled of the sour odor of yesterday's alcohol and tobacco, but he was sincere in wanting a reconciliation.

As soon as Rita returned to him, however, and life settled back into its routine, he was satisfied. Not only was it too much trouble to go for continued counseling, but since he thought the counselor abrupt and unsympathetic, he did not think it would do any good.

Norman was born in December, 1957, and Laura, their sixth child, followed in September, 1959. Norman had congenital cataracts and was blind. Laura had cerebral palsy and was totally disabled.

Having experienced blindness, Rita had great sympathy and affection for Hilda and Norman, and watched over them diligently to see that they did not hurt themselves. But forgetfulness, chaos, disputes, and lack of time caused many things to be neglected. Hilda was supposed to be returned to the hospital for an operation on her cataracts when she was a year old. But perhaps because Norman was being born then, perhaps because of Rita's fears of eye operations, Rita never took Hilda back.

Laura required even more time than the two blind children. As she grew older, doctors discovered that, in addition to the cerebral palsy, she had a septal defect. Twice she had mild heart attacks. She was in and out of the hospital two or three times a year. Whenever these periods coincided with troubles in the home, Rita would leave her at the hospital and ignore the exhortations of the staff that "the hospital is not a foster care agency and the child *must* be taken home." Once, when the family visited Laura, the nurses were so upset by the ragged appearance of the children that they took up a collection for them.

Although Rita agreed to an operation to have her Fallopian tubes tied, it came too late to save the family. On George's income Rita was unable to cope with six children, three of whom were invalids. When George was laid off, unemployment insurance and a $125 monthly aid-to-the-blind grant cushioned the shock. But as soon as George was rehired as a $105-a-week hi-lo driver at Dodge, the aid-to-the-blind check was discontinued. After dues and tax checkoffs the family's income was only about $15 a week more when he was working than when he was not. His job seemed unimportant.

Overwhelmed by problems with which they could not deal, George and Rita gave in to them. George found refuge in drinking. Rita was obsessed by guilt feelings.

Her energy was sapped by the complications and heavy menstrual bleeding that were the aftermath of the operation. Her eyesight was almost imperceptibly yet steadily deteriorating. Half the time she verged on hysteria, and the rest of the time she was exhausted. Ever since as a girl she had been in the hospital for her eye operations, Rita had liked cough syrup. As her troubles increased, this liking grew into a craving. She would drink anything that contained codeine or other narcotics such as paragoric or terpinhydrate. Forced to spend what time and energy she had on the three younger children, she left the three older to their own devices.

While the Juvenile Court was thus already engaged in trying to salvage the grandchildren of Peter and Marie, it was still struggling to bring order into the life of the youngest Jansen child, Katherine.

Katherine had an IQ of 114, but her intelligence only added to her loneliness and isolation. The court placed her in one foster home after another, but the placements never worked out. Since she had experienced only disappointment, she continually created difficulties to guard herself against the expected buffeting. She had become wise in the way of social agencies, and would brook no slight from a boarding mother. When a boarding mother told her she was eating hot dogs while the family ate steak because "they don't pay us enough to feed you steak," Katherine ran for the telephone to call the caseworker.

One caseworker wrote that Katherine had "been greatly aggravated by social workers and psychiatrists." She had learned to disbelieve and distrust them and would not allow them to put her off. Boarding mothers did not know how to handle her and kept asking that she be removed from their homes. Her intelligence and susceptibility to bronchial illness made her one of the court workers' more difficult cases. In January, 1957, fourteen-year-old Katherine wound up in the juvenile home again. Since the court did not know what to do with her, she was kept in the home "temporarily" for half a year. She enjoyed school and liked her job as an assistant nurse. She was probed and tested, reprobed and retested. Finally, a Catholic girls' academy in Ohio agreed to accept her.

For the next three years, Katherine attended the academy and maintained a C-plus average. The $100 a month that was directed toward supporting her there was ten times the amount Marie had spent on her at home. Nevertheless, there were repeated and unseemly disputes between the academy, the Juvenile Court, and Catholic Social Services about who was to pay for incidental expenses. (One semester they amounted to $23.74.) When the caseworker wrote that the court had no funds for such expenses and suggested that Katherine was being extravagant, her counselor at the school wrote back:

"Katherine did not incur unnecessary debts, and is as frugal as it is possible. Because of her desperate need, we have even provided clothes for her; but it is our policy that the academy guild fund should be used only for diocesan girls. Since your agency is unable to assume the debt, will you please make arrangements with Mrs. Jansen to make regular weekly payments until the debt is paid."

The middle-class academician had no idea of how humorous she was being, and no concept of the environment from which Katherine had been propelled into the academy. Katherine's "vacations" were trips to another world. Had she taken back to the academy only a small sampling of the everyday language and behavior of her family, she would have been expelled. Her mother and her sisters, both spiteful and envious, ridiculed her "ladylike airs." As her June, 1960, graduation neared, she was beset with anxiety as to what would become of her. If she returned home, Katherine told her probation officer, she was afraid she would fall back into the pattern of life that existed there.

Katherine's ambition was to be a nurse, and she asked her probation officer to help her. She needed, first, the ten-dollar fee for the entrance examination—ten dollars that no one seemed to have—and then two hundred dollars for tuition. After many telephone calls, the probation officer found that the Rotary Club would lend her the money.

On the entrance examination Katherine scored three points over the passing grade. The clinical psychologist who interviewed her, however, decided that she was too nervous and excitable, especially in view of the fact her records showed that, as a child, she had been hospitalized for St. Vitus dance. (That was an erroneous diagnosis that had been made when, hysterical, she had been brought to the hospital by the police during one of the family conflicts. Nevertheless, the records had not been corrected, and the psychologist accepted them at face value.) He recommended against her acceptance for training. The director of training of the hospital at Northville followed the recommendation. In view of her marginal score on the examination and the negative psychological evaluation, he believed that she would not be able to withstand the pressures.

The probation officer indicated she was sorry, and tried to console Katherine by saying it was better not to start something than to find out that she would not be able to finish it. But Katherine was crushed. She did not know what else she could do, or even where she could live.

In July, 1960, Katherine found a job paying ninety cents an hour as a salesgirl at Kresge's. She was removed from the court records. Her sister Joella had married Black Bear. Joella now had four children, and was living in an apartment on Twelfth Street. Since Black Bear was driving a truck and was out of town much of the time, Katherine moved in with Joella.

92

The Crossroads of the City

A SOCIOLOGIST STUDYING THE TWELFTH STREET AREA IN THE LATTER 1950's when it was a mixture of old Jewish families, Negroes, and both lower-class and middle-class whites might have come to the conclusion that here was integration at work. In fact, just as middle age is not "integration" between youth and old age, Twelfth Street was not integrated, but in a stage of transition. Both geographically and demographically it was the crossroads of the city. Here the social and economic forces buffeting the city were at their strongest and creating the most violent conflict.

With the closure of Packard, Hudson, and scores of other marginally efficient plants, the retreat from the city turned into a rout. The construction of the Edsel Ford Freeway, crossing the city from east to west, and the John C. Lodge Freeway, bisecting it from north to south, enabled motorists to travel four miles in the same time required to travel one mile on surface streets. Simultaneously, the city administration was pushing ahead to raze additional sections of the inner city.

Both Albert Cobo, and Louis Miriani, who succeeded him as mayor in 1957, were concerned about the "image" presented by the Michigan Avenue skid row section, sitting astraddle the old route to Chicago that was considered the "gateway to the city." As soon as the change in Federal guidelines enabled the city to designate skid row as an urban renewal district, Mayor Miriani ordered the planning commission to initiate its redevelopment.

In the Corktown, Gratiot, and Lafayette Park (an extension of Gratiot) Redevelopment Areas, the problem was how to relocate the residents in upgraded housing. In Central Business District Number One—the euphemistic designation of skid row—the problem was simply what to *do* with its mostly alcoholic habitués. As far as Mayor Cobo had been concerned, "Under my program there wouldn't be much room in Detroit for a complete alcoholic." Harold Black and another member of the planning staff suggested that the solution might be to build a skid row somewhere else. The reaction to this suggestion was hilarity—but Black, who had majored in sociology, was quite serious.

No one, however, was willing to face up to the sociological problem of the skid row denizens. Like the poverty-stricken Negroes, like the whores and the hustlers of Paradise Valley, like the lower-class whites plowed aside by urban renewal and freeway construction, the alcoholics were left to their own devices.

Freeways and renewal, therefore, had no therapeutic effect on the economic and social cancer, but merely pushed it out of the way and let it spread where it might. As the freeways channeled through the city, they tapped the pool of middle-class whites, long chafing at their urban entrapment. Like water they poured into the channels and out of the city.

The transformation was most pronounced in the Twelfth Street area, where block after block of high-rise apartment buildings had been erected. As Jews and other middle-class whites emptied out of the apartments, the housing shortage was suddenly transformed into a housing surplus. For the first time in a quarter century, rents dropped and tenants were in demand. The city's poor could rent apartments on Twelfth Street for less money than they had been paying for slum accommodations within the Boulevard area. Since two or three families often combined to rent a single six-room or eight-room flat, the density of the area was further increased.

The shift of the lower-class white population was directly northward along the west side of Woodward Avenue. The Negroes, who had been moving northward in parallel along the east side of Woodward, crossed over and shifted west. By the end of the 1950's, one fourth of all the housing within the Boulevard area stood vacant.

Twelfth Street, with its bustling commercial district, still had a residue of vice and rackets from the roaring twenties and Depressed thirties. The area had always been a scene of action, but the participants in the action had been ethnically homogeneous. "Integration" mixed Paradise Valley vice with Twelfth Street vice. The action was transformed into conflict, and the conflict commonly was expressed in terms of crime. More and more of the substantial number of old-time residents who had remained were frightened out of the area, or pressured out of it by the deteriorating conditions in the schools.

(Harold Black's parents moved after an old lady on the street was attacked by Negro youths one Friday night and had her skull cracked open with her own candlestick.)

It was in the schools that the reaction to the infusion of Negroes and lower-class whites was most volatile, and it was there that the transformation was the most accelerated. The children of George and Rita Devers and the children of Donald and Irma Stallings attended school erratically. Ofter they stayed awake late at night. In school, they fell asleep at their desks. Poorly fed, inadequately clothed, seldom if ever treated by a doctor or a dentist, they had frequent illnesses. If they did not have physical handicaps such as deafness, they were likely to have been subjected to psychological trauma. Raised in nonverbal environments, they lacked the ability to express themselves. In the schools within the Boulevard area, they had made up a homogeneous, largely segregated population—blacks on the east side of Woodward Avenue, whites on the west—and these schools had, in effect, been written off and quarantined by the administration. (Since remedial reading courses were expensive to conduct, only children with a C average were eligible for remedial reading. The others, a great many of whom were doing below-average work because they could not read, were dismissed as educationally terminal cases.)

Money was being spent for new schools in the city's outer ring, where subdivisions had risen on the last of the city's vacant land and existing facilities were overloaded, not for renovation of the nineteenth-century and turn-of-the-century schools in the inner city. For teachers the Boulevard area was Siberia. It was where new teachers, substitute teachers, and misfits were assigned. As soon as a teacher had acquired seniority he usually requested a transfer to a more desirable area—a policy that did not include Negro teachers, who were all but barred from white schools.

The conditions in the Boulevard area were abominable. But the administration expected nothing more from the children and the teachers. The parents lacked the drive and ability to organize and demand something better. So apathy prevailed.

When, however, the children from these schools erupted into the middle-class schools beyond the Boulevard, they created havoc. Between 1955 and 1960 one Twelfth Street elementary school, MacCullough, was transformed from an essentially Jewish to a largely Negro school. During that period the number of A students plummeted from 45 to 12 percent. In 1955, 80 percent of the parents were businessmen, professionals, white-collar workers, and skilled tradesmen; and none were on public assistance. In 1960, 45 percent were unskilled laborers, and 18 percent were supported by welfare. In 1955, 90 percent of the children had both parents in the home, and illegitimacy was virtually unheard of. In 1960, 40 percent of the children had only one parent in the home, and 9 percent were illegitimate.

The effect of this transformation was multiplied by the fact that families with a great many more children were crowding into the same accommodations. Between 1955 and 1960, the Center District (Twelfth Street) gained 6,826 elementary pupils— *two thirds of the citywide total!* As the Center schools were inundated, class sizes shot up—nearly 15 percent of the classes had more than forty children.

As long as children from problem homes had constituted no more than about 20 percent of enrollment, they had benefited from the improved facilities, the better teaching, and the atmosphere provided by the middle-class emphasis on education and achievement. But by the time the proportion of problem students reached one in three, a teacher, no matter how well motivated, was overwhelmed. His class lost its homogeneity. He was simultaneously attempting to teach children who belonged in his grade and those who were two, three, or four grades behind and had been "promoted" simply because it was incongruous to continue to retain a ten-year-old in the first grade or a thirteen-year-old in the third grade. His basic ability to teach suffered, and the quality of education for all went down. Much of the energy of the staff was taken up in merely keeping order.

The newcomers could not read the textbooks, and could not even understand much of the language that was being used. Feeling ill at ease among their middle-class classmates, they were envious of their "riches"—their clothes, their possessions (watches, knives, purses), and pocket money. Anxious, bored, and frustrated, they channeled their energy into aggressive behavior, aimless destruction, attacks on teachers and students, and *crimes:* crimes aimed at obtaining a share of the wealth of their more privileged classmates.

Well before conditions in the neighborhood became intolerable for residents, parents felt that their children were endangered in the schools. Their first reaction was to transfer their children to schools that continued to be middle class in character; their second was to transfer their homes as far as practicable away from the tide of poverty sweeping out of the inner city—in effect, as far as the freeway would carry them back and forth to their work in reasonable time.

In 1956, the school district obtained one of the more prestigious educators in the nation as its new superintendent. A Nebraskan by birth, fifty-six-year-old Dr. Samuel Brownell, the brother of Attorney-General Herbert Brownell, had been professor of education administration at Yale. In 1953 he had become the first commissioner following the reorganization of the United States Department of Education. An expert in management, Dr. Brownell was apprehensive about the conditions and trends in the school system he was taking over. The Detroit Board of Commerce and much of the business community were opposed to any further increase in taxes. Since the end of World War II, the school district's budget had nearly tripled, from $39.5 million to $118.6 million a year, and school taxes had risen 72 percent. Yet, more money would be required if inner city schools were to be improved. (Half of the 52,500 high school students in Detroit, mostly in economically disadvantaged areas, were on half day sessions.) Dr. Brownell therefore decided to let the citizens themselves determine what the schools' needs were. In 1957 the Board of Education established a Citizens Advisory Committee on School Needs to set goals for the next decade. George Romney, president of American Motors and former general manager of the Automobile Manufacturers Association, was recruited to head the committee.* Russian-born Dr. Norman Drachler, who had graduated from Twelfth Street's Central High School, was appointed director of research for the committee and charged with the responsibility of finding out what was going on. For both men the committee positions were platforms from which they were to rise to public prominence.

The committee report, issued eighteen months later, placed the focus on the inner city as never before. In some schools the pupil turnover was 100 percent every year. The attendance department was making eighty thousand home calls a year, and of these 40 percent were related to poverty. The deleterious economic environment and the family disorganization were having a strong negative impact upon the children's performance in the schools. Parents did not involve themselves in their children's education, and the schools did not communicate with the parents. Coming from different cultures, the children often did not understand the teachers, and the teachers lacked understanding of the children with whom they were dealing. Eighteen thousand children with physical and psychological handicaps were in special education classes.

Before World War I, a child who stayed in school until the age of sixteen was considered well educated. Until the early 1950's a youth who left school at sixteen or eighteen was able to obtain a job. But as industry moved out of the city and automation replaced even more manpower than mechanization had, the

---

* The Mexican-born son of American Mormons, Romney had left college in 1929 to go to work as a stenographer for Massachusetts Democratic Senator David I. Walsh, a member of the Senate Finance Committee. The committee was soon embroiled in thrashing out the Smoot-Hawley Tariff of 1930. As a result of that experience, Romney was hired by Alcoa as lobbyist, then in 1939 joined the Automobile Manufacturers Association. In 1948 he became an executive of Nash, and after Nash merged with Hudson he assumed the presidency of American Motors. In 1958, going counter to the trend of all other American automobile manufacturers, Romney brought out a compact car: the Rambler. American Motors had its headquarters, but no plant, in Detroit.

sixteen-year-old who stopped going to school became a "dropout." In the nation's inner cities up to three fourths of the high schoolers were dropping out, and the dropout could seldom obtain a job. Susceptible to delinquency and crime, the dropout raised the concern of the police, the courts, and the Citizens Advisory Committee.

The committee recommended the increase in school funding Dr. Brownell wanted. At the millage election that followed, Detroiters voted to raise their school taxes another 32 percent. Dr. Brownell was in agreement with the committee on the need to concentrate spending on inner city schools, so as to improve the educational atmosphere in them. He concurred on the need to strengthen the central administration and reduce the power of the special-interest bureaucratic organizations that had sprung up within the system.

Educationally, Dr. Brownell was a progressive. Sociologically, he was anything but a revolutionary. From 1927 to 1938 he had been superintendent of schools in Grosse Pointe, Detroit's most fashionable suburb, and one of the most lily-white, Anglo-Saxon, Protestant communities in the United States. Dr. Brownell was eager to improve education, but he was unwilling to do much to disturb the long-established practices and mores that had brought about de facto segregation. Transfer regulations permitted white parents to shift their children out of schools that were being overrun by the inner city population. Catholic parents took their children out of the schools in the Mumford High School area to which the Jews from Twelfth Street were flocking. Teachers continued to be assigned according to race, whites to white schools and blacks to black schools, as well as on occasion according to their religion, Jews to "Jewish" schools.

The redrawn boundaries that followed the advisory committee study placed all schools that had turned or were turning Negro in the Center District, but took those schools that were still predominantly white out of it. When students were bused out of the overcrowded schools in the Center District, the Negro children were taken back to schools in the inner city, sometimes passing uncrowded white schools on the way.

Dr. Brownell had been United States Commissioner of Education at the time (1954) that the U.S. Supreme Court in *Brown v. (Topeka) Board of Education* had held segregated schools unconstitutional.* But when civil rights leaders assailed the continuing segregation of the Detroit schools, the administration replied that the segregation was due to housing patterns and racially differentiated neighborhoods and was beyond the power of the school system to correct.

Dr. Brownell nevertheless became a leader in directing the attention of the nation's educators toward the urban areas' problem schools. Following a meeting between Dr. Brownell and Dr. Benjamin C. Willis, superintendent of the Chicago school system, superintendents of fourteen of the nation's largest school systems were invited to meet in Chicago. There they established the Great Cities Research Council. Working with a grant from the Sears, Roebuck Foundation, they first turned their attention to vocational education, with the goal of providing dropouts with skills they could use to obtain jobs. They soon realized that, in order

---

* The legacy of Andrew Carnegie, who had played a significant role in the 1890 accommodation between Republicans and Southern Democrats, helped to chronicle the abandonment of the Negro and bring his plight to the attention of the Supreme Court. In the late 1930's the Carnegie Foundation commissioned a Swedish sociologist, Gunnar Myrdal, to study the condition of the American Negro. Myrdal's exhaustive study, *An American Dilemma,* was published in 1944 and became a source book for the court in its ruling that separate was inherently unequal.

to provide those skills, schools would have to reach outward into the social and economic pathology that was producing dropouts, and would have to involve themselves with the families and the community.

In September, 1959, Dr. Brownell initiated a pilot project in three inner city schools close to the Jeffries Housing Project: Couzens Elementary, populated by Negroes; Burton Elementary, serving the poor-white area west of Woodward Avenue; and Jefferson Junior High School, to which children from both of the elementary schools advanced.

Each school received three additional staff members: a coaching teacher, whose job it was to work with individuals and small groups on remedial reading and arithmetic; a visiting teacher or social worker, whose job it was to work with emotionally disturbed children and their families, and to improve the conditions under which the children came to school; and a school-community agent, whose assignment was to bridge the cultural gap between the school and the community, to involve the parents in the school, and to make the school more relevant to the neighborhood. To widen the horizons of the children, most of whom never went more than a few blocks from their homes, extra bus service was provided to take them on field trips. To involve the schools in the community, they were kept open at night and on weekends for a variety of activities. New materials and teaching methods were tried, and some ungraded classes were established.

Evidently, the assignment of 9 more persons to three schools with a total staff of 130 and an enrollment of 3,500 could have only a limited effect. But, after six months, Dr. Brownell felt there were enough encouraging signs to warrant the continuation and expansion of the project. In February, 1960, in conjunction with other cities that were taking part in the Great Cities School Improvement Project, he applied for a Ford Foundation grant.

93

The Ford Foundation

As long as Henry Ford had remained alive, the "small-scale" Ford Foundation had been little more than an in-house charity. It supported the Ford Hospital, the Ford Museum, and the Detroit Symphony Orchestra. In 1948, however, 90 percent of the stock of the Ford Motor Company came into the possession of the foundation.*

Henry Ford II thereupon commissioned H. Rowan Gaither, chairman of the board of the Rand Corporation, to conduct a study on the role of the foundation. In November, 1949, Gaither's study committee submitted its report.

"The aim of the Ford Foundation," the report declared, "is to advance human welfare." Special attention was given to education and minority rights. There is, the committee said, "an unusual degree of dissatisfaction with educational institutions and influences which now operate in our society. . . .

"Without equal educational opportunity, equality of economic opportunity cannot exist. The effects of unequal opportunity in education are aggravated as industry, business, and the professions become more and more complex . . .

"Prejudice and discrimination abridge the educational opportunities of the members of our minority groups. Persons of all races and colors do not have equal access to education. The advantages of education are also walled off behind economic barriers. . . . [Because of] the decreasing proportion of the national income going into higher education . . . higher education threatens to become increasingly the prerogative of the well-to-do." [1]

By the standards of the 1940's, the tone of the report was ultraliberal. While the board of trustees, chaired by Henry Ford II, was digesting its contents, dividends poured into the foundation's account from the revitalized company's sales of 5.5 million cars between 1947 and 1950—by far the best showing since the early 1920's. In 1948 and 1949 the foundation's share of dividends

---

* The foundation stock was nonvoting. All voting stock, the remaining 10 percent, passed into the hands of Henry Ford's widow and Edsel's family. Had it not been for the foundation, inheritance taxes would have taken 77 percent of the estate. As it was, the taxes came to only $42 million, all of which was paid out of the foundation stock.

was $50 million; its 1950 share was $87 million. But, during the first fourteen years of its existence, the foundation had disbursed only $19 million.

The Internal Revenue Service grew restive. Pressure increased for the implementation of the study group's report in the form of grants. Following publication of the report, twenty-five thousand grant applications were received.

The annual total of disbursements grew from $24 million in 1950, to $68 million in 1954. (The latter figure was equal to the total annual value of all foundation grants only six years before.) As the foundation's impact and influence increased, so did the reaction of those infuriated by its liberal stance. Its opposition to McCarthyism drew the ire of the Communist-hunters—even though in its "foreign policy" the foundation was a firm supporter of anti-Communist activities. Its anticipation of the 1954 Supreme Court school desegregation decision and support of Negro rights caused apoplexy among Southern segregationists and brought threats of boycotts of Ford products. During congressional investigations in 1952 and 1954 the foundation was accused of being a Communist front and a Communist plot against America. The investigations reinforced the study committee's observations that American freedoms were being threatened "as a result of the emotions aroused by current international tensions."

Not until the mid-1950's, however, did the foundation initiate the massive disbursement of funds that had an immense impact on American education and medicine, and turned the spotlight on the human problems in the cities. In 1956 the foundation obtained the Ford family's approval to place a large block of Ford stock on the market. The single biggest issue in the history of Wall Street, it netted $643 million.

With assets exceeding $2.5 billion, the foundation was one of the world's largest financial or industrial enterprises, and capable of wielding massive power. During the next eighteen months, using the money acquired from the sale of the Ford stock, it made grants of $500 million.*

Some members of the study committee regarded "emotional maladjustment as the most characteristic and widespread ill of our civilization." So the fifth of the foundation's five program areas, "individual behavior and human welfare," was concerned with "the scientific study of the causes of personal maladjustment, neurosis, delinquency, and crime, and the improvement of methods for prevention and cure." [2] The issuance, in 1955, of a $600,000 grant to the National Probation and Parole Association for a five-year study of juvenile delinquency became a precipitant for the foundation's involvement in the problems of the cities.

The comprehension of the difficulties facing the nation's cities was still limited to a handful of people. In 1957, when Senator Joseph Clark, the former mayor of Philadelphia, warned on the floor of the Senate that the cities were broke and in danger of collapse, he was greeted with laughter—in the minds of the senators, the cities were equated with wealth and privilege. Clark's former administrative assistant in Philadelphia, Paul Ylvisaker, in the meantime

* Of this, $290 million was directed toward nonprofit private hospitals and medical institutions, and $210 million, on a matching basis, went to liberal arts colleges to raise faculty salaries, which were at such a low level that universities were having great difficulty in retaining professors. Concurrently, scholarship programs were initiated to attract more people into the teaching profession. Henry Ford, with his jaundiced view of higher education, would have been horrified.

had joined the public affairs division of the Ford Foundation. The foundation was making a number of grants for metropolitan studies. Urbanologists, however, were emphasizing the physical rejuvenation of cities—there was little awareness of the far greater importance of economics and of population. Ylvisaker began to nudge the foundation's personnel toward dealing with the human problems in the cities—especially those arising out of the large influx of Negroes.*

In Oakland, California, the foundation prepared to launch its first "Gray Areas" program, focusing on the needs of inner city residents. Dr. James B. Conant's book, *Slums and Suburbs,* was soon to dramatize the inability of urban schools to cope with the complex problems of "deprived" pupils—as they had been unable to cope with the problems of immigrant children fifty years earlier.

The officers of the foundation, therefore, were more than receptive to such experimental approaches as those offered by the Great Cities project. In June of 1960, the foundation made grants totaling $3.2 million to the school systems of Detroit and nine other cities.† In the fall, Dr. Brownell expanded the Detroit program from three to seven schools.

---

* Ylvisaker hired Robert Weaver as a consultant. Weaver had gained entry into government when Harold Ickes had opened the doors of the Interior Department to Negroes. He had been New York housing administrator in the administration of Governor Averill Harriman.
† Chicago, Philadelphia, Cleveland, Pittsburgh, Buffalo, Milwaukee, St. Louis, San Francisco, and Washington, D.C. New York City had previously launched its own, similar Higher Horizons program.

94

The Big Builder

NOT UNTIL 1959, THIRTEEN YEARS AFTER THE INITIATION OF THE PROJECT, WAS the first new building—the twenty-two-story Pavilion Apartments—completed in the Gratiot Redevelopment Area. One snag after another had snarled the project. At the first auction of the land, in July, 1952, not a single bid had been submitted to the city. A year later the Housing Corporation of America purchased a fifty-acre site. But in another year the contract was canceled. The Federal Housing Administration demanded that the new housing be available at a price that the former residents of the area could afford. The builder insisted such low pricing could be obtained only by cutting corners and by *economical* construction. The city planning commission objected that this kind of construction would simply recreate the pre-existing slum. In June, 1954, Walter Reuther stepped in and, offering the financial backing of the UAW, suggested formation of a citizens committee to deal with the problem.

Throughout his political career Mayor Cobo had fought the "Communists" of the UAW. In the cold war-McCarthy era he considered himself one of the front-line warriors, and established the Mayor's Loyalty Investigating Commission to check on Communists and subversives in the municipal government and in the city. At his behest, the commission had collected a file on Walter Reuther that, the mayor said, was nearly a foot thick. It was a reflection of the mayor's desperation—the Gratiot area was now referred to as "Ragweed Acres"—that he responded by naming Reuther one of twelve members of a Citizens Redevelopment Committee.

The following year the Redevelopment Committee evolved into a private, nonprofit corporation. It drew up new plans for an extended Gratiot area (renamed Lafayette Park) and took over marketing of the property. To operate the corporation, some $450,000 was raised. Henry Ford II, who was involving himself in civic affairs as much as his grandfather had divorced himself from them, was the leading contributor.*

* The Ford Motor Company gave $80,000; Chrysler, General Motors, the J. L. Hudson Company, the Kresge Foundation, and the UAW $50,000 each. In 1948, Henry II, continually beleaguered by requests from charitable agencies, had originated the concept of the Detroit United Fund. One collective drive for funds was substituted in place of a multitude of individual appeals. The Detroit organization set a national pattern.

First construction on the site began in January of 1957. Initially some housing was to be reserved for low-income families, but gradually the reservation disappeared. When the corporation finally purchased the St. James Baptist Church, which had been left standing so that the old Negro congregation eventually could return to it, the permanent removal of the old population became a fait accompli. A few Negroes moved into the shiny glass-and-steel skyscrapers that rose on the site, but they were middle-class Negroes who blended almost invisibly with the other tenants, most of whom were liberal, small-family whites.

The basic difficulty with the Gratiot project was that, despite the subsidy provided by urban renewal, developers continued to feel the inner city did not offer a good climate for investment.

Nevertheless, since the municipal administration had no other means to raze slums and provide land for new development, the Boulevard area became checkerboarded with one project here and another there. University City was planned to enable Wayne State University to expand. The new Medical Center was intended to renovate the area in which many of the city's hospitals were located, and to stem the flight of the hospitals and their patients to the suburbs. But the time lag between the announcement of a project and its implementation was great. Whenever it became known that an area was designated for urban renewal, all rehabilitation work by property owners ceased. The effect was to create deterioration by announcement and further aggravate the formation of slums.

Mayor Cobo brought to Detroit the new City-County Building (which, nevertheless, was inadequate and obsolescent on the day it was completed). Construction started along the riverfront on the modernistic Ford Auditorium and on Cobo Hall, the largest convention facility in the world. Cobo Hall led to the erection of the new Pontchartrain Hotel, a major landmark. Sitting in his new eleventh-floor office with its panoramic view of the river and the $112 million civic center, Cobo predicted that he had launched the revitalization of the downtown area. He prophesied that the freeways—known as Cobo's Canyons—would provide express transportation, and bring people back into the city. He called the police department "one of the best in the country" and the health department "second to none." He took pride that the city was building a huge new water plant that would relieve what had become a chronic water shortage.*

By bonding the city to the limits of its capacity, Cobo was able to avoid raising taxes. He was eulogized as a financial "magician," as "the mayor who started Detroit on its comeback," and as "Little Al—the big builder." On September 13, 1957, in the nick of time to keep his reputation unsullied, he died.

---

* The Water Board, operating out of its own revenues, was a semi-independent agency. It supplied water not only to Detroit but to many of the burgeoning communities. A five-year controversy over who should supply water to the new areas ended in 1959 with the Water Board's purchase of the Wayne County water system. In effect, the purchase made the Detroit water department the supplier for the entire metropolitan area.

95

Jerry the Giant Killer

FROM HIM THE NEW MAYOR, LOUIS C. MIRIANI, INHERITED A BUDGET DEFICIT and the necessity for a whopping tax increase.* Property taxes for running the municipal government were raised to $24.53 per $1,000 of assessed valuation, the highest in the city's history.† Between 1950 and 1957 the assessed valuation in Detroit had risen from $4 billion to $5 billion, thereby providing an "automatic" 25 percent increase in tax revenues. By 1958, however, industries moving out of the city were vacating entire blocks. The freeway builders were in the process of removing 1,500 acres with an assessed valuation of $43 million from the rolls.

The "automatic" revenue increases stemming from increases in assessed valuation càme to an end.

Two months after Cobo's death, Miriani was elected to a four-year term as mayor. (The city charter had been changed in 1953 to extend the mayor's term from two to four years.)

Fifty-one years old, owlish and dumpy, Miriani was the son of Italian farmers and a graduate of the University of Detroit Law School. He had spent his career in the Legal Aid Bureau, the welfare system, and labor relations. Between 1931 and 1934 he had been legal advisor to Mayor Murphy's Unemployment Committee. He had served ten years on the city council.

Mayor Miriani reacted to the financial crisis—a crisis that encompassed not only the city but the state government ‡—by announcing a "shotgun savings"

---

* As president of the city council, Miriani automatically assumed the position of mayor on Cobo's death.
† County and school taxes were, of course, separate.
‡ Michigan's population growth during the 1950's trailed only California's and Florida's. But the state was forty-seventh in the amount of increase in its government expenditures, ahead only of Delaware. With the end of the Korean War, Michigan lost at least 125,000 jobs in defense industries and more than 100,000 through the decentralization of automobile manufacturing and assembly. Although the state's voters reelected G. Mennen Williams to the governorship every two years between 1948 and 1960—an affirmation of confidence unprecedented in the state's gubernatorial history—the archaic apportionment of the state enabled the Republicans to dominate the legislature through their control of the rural

plan reminiscent of the Depression. He placed a freeze on the hiring of new municipal employees, reduced the work force, withheld the city's contribution to the fire and police pension funds, and cut back on services. Although he "saved" over $20 million in three years, he was still unable to balance the budget. Nevertheless, when the city council in May, 1960, passed a 1 percent income tax in order to eliminate the revenue gap, he vetoed it.

By nodding liberally but acting conservatively he managed to please both the labor movement and the business community. The mayor cared less about the politics of his supporters than their number—twenty years after Double Dip Dick, Detroit had another occupant of city hall determined to leave office far richer than he had entered it. As a boy, Miriani had wrestled produce crates at Eastern Market for twelve cents an hour; as a lawyer and city councilman he had never been able to achieve financial security. For the first time money slid into his reach, and he could not resist it. Much of it came in the form of "political contributions" about which the donors asked no questions. During the last three years of his administration, he had an "outside income" of at least $259,495.*

Frequently popping off, feuding with the city council and with department heads, Miriani had little charm and no charisma. At political functions he made peremptory appearances. Watching him perform at a banquet one night in 1960, thirty-two-year-old Jerome P. Cavanagh decided he could defeat the mayor.

Jerry Cavanagh had been involved in Wayne County Democratic politics since he was a political science major at the University of Detroit in the late 1940's. He was, in the tradition of the family, a supporter of the party's moderate, Irish Catholic wing. As a Young Democrat he had opposed G. Mennen Williams and the CIO Political Action Committee when they had captured control of the party in 1948.

Encouraged and pushed by his mother, Cavanagh had helped pay his way through the University of Detroit by working as a mailboy at Ford, an IBM salesman, and a deputy sheriff. His father, Sylvester, employed at Ford continuously for nearly half a century, had attained the "skilled" position of boilermaker. Thanks to the 1941 strike, he was earning enough and had sufficient job security for his wife, Rose, to maintain a firm discipline over the children. In 1952, Jerry married beautiful, vivacious Mary Martin, the university's "carnival queen." In 1954 he received his law degree. Handsome, slightly over average height, he had charm enough to reduce a cobra to a lap pet and a wit sharp enough to hone a rusty blade for a television commercial. He was living

---

counties even when the Democrats outdrew them at the polls. (In the 1958 election, with a minority of the popular vote, the Republicans captured twenty-two of thirty-four senate seats.) The Republicans blocked every attempt to raise new revenues through a corporation profit or other "progressive" tax. In 1958, when the second of the "Eisenhower recessions" sent unemployment in Michigan to more than 400,000 and increased welfare rolls 50 percent, the state government ended the year with a budget deficit of $110 million. The continuing deadlock between the governor and the senate over the type of revenue measure to enact (one Republican senator proposed collecting tuition from the first grade up) left the state hopping from one fiscal crisis to another. Local school districts were forced to borrow $80 million in place of funds they had not received from the state. The culmination was the "Payless Pay Day" of May 7, 1959, when the state treasury had no money to pay its employees.

* In 1966 he was charged with, and later convicted of, failing to report that sum on his income tax returns.

the American success story: overalls to pinstriped suit in one generation.

Jim Friel, the former county auditor and old pol who had run third in the 1949 mayoralty race behind Cobo and Edwards, adopted Cavanagh as his protégé. He took him to party functions, introduced him to people, and helped him build experience and confidence. After sizing up Miriani, Cavanagh asked Joe B. Sullivan, a friend from law school days and fellow Democratic party activist:

"What do you think of my running for mayor?"

Sullivan didn't think too much of it. Neither did Cavanagh's family, who believed at first that he was joking. When it became evident that he was serious, his father suggested that a city council race might be more realistic.

But Jerry Cavanagh had made up his mind. And there were few minds that could be made up with greater conviction. On July 29, 1961, Cavanagh, a television repairman, and an unemployed cook filed for mayor. Most people considered Cavanagh's chances no worse than those of the other two.

Jerry Cavanagh had no public record and was all but unknown outside the Democratic party circle, where he was not universally admired. But in a nondescript field his vigor, charm, and famous Irish name were enough to make him the runner-up to Miriani, and so put him into the runoff against the mayor.

Miriani was hardly worried. Cavanagh had won 35,897 votes to Miriani's 80,645, and had carried only 35 out of 1,154 precincts. The mayor had the financial and political backing of almost every leading organization in the city —both business and labor—and was confident enough to pocket more of the money than he spent. The UAW-CIO had seventy to one hundred people out working for him in each congressional district. He had the endorsement of all the daily newspapers and most of the politicians.

But the support for Miriani was the cream at the top of the political order, and it was deceptive. Just as Detroit's business, political, and social leaders had greatly underestimated the decline in the city's fortunes that had set in during the middle 1950's, so they also failed to realize the discontent generated by the backwater of the urban economy.

That discontent was greatest among Negroes. Thirty-four percent of black families (compared to 10 percent of white families) had incomes of less than $3,000 a year and were officially poverty-stricken. Eighty-three percent of black families had incomes lower than the *median* family income of whites, $7,219 a year. (The Negro median income was $4,385.) Of Negro men, two thirds in their late teens, nearly half in their early twenties, and four out of ten of all ages were not working.

Their unemployment was a major factor in the rapidly rising urban delinquency and crime rate. In a "crime wave" second only to that which had occurred with the onset of the Depression, the number of crimes reported in the city jumped from 54,700 in 1957 to 68,500 in 1960, and major economic crimes * increased 40 percent—from 18,000 to over 25,000. During the latter 1950's black suspects began to outnumber white suspects (in 1960 there were 18,936 blacks and 13,603 whites arrested), and as a result the spotlight was turned upon "Negro" crime. The newspapers sensationalized incidents of attacks on white women by black youths in the inner city.

When Mayor Miriani ordered a "crackdown," relations between the police

---

* Robbery, burglary, and grand larceny.

and Negroes became more abrasive than at any time since the 1943 riot. White officers were still seething from a limited attempt to integrate scout cars in 1959, an attempt they had defeated by going on a ticket-writing strike. They welcomed the crackdown order and opportunity it offered to show their independence from civil rights pressure. Negro youths were manhandled in full view of newspaper reporters. Although most victims of crimes by Negroes were Negroes, police were likely to regard any Negro as a "suspicious character." Officers frisked middle-class Negroes on the street. Despite the incensed reaction of blacks, Police Commissioner Herbert W. Hart, who planned to "go back to being an orange peddler when I resign from police commissioner," was insensitive to the complaints:

"I do not understand why a good law-abiding citizen would object to being patted down and questioned," he proclaimed.[1]

Exploiting the black disenchantment with the mayor, Cavanagh took a firm stand in favor of equal rights for Negroes, and won the support of most of Detroit's liberals. The Trade Union Leadership Council, formed three years before by a group of Negro unionists fed up with the lack of black representation among union executives, broke with the UAW to back Cavanagh. The prestigious Negro Cotillion Club endorsed him. "Phooie on Louie" buttons appeared everywhere in the black community.

Miriani struck back by picturing Cavanagh as the candidate of the Negroes, planning to install a Negro as police commissioner. Ignoring the Negro vote, he drummed on the fear of the whites. Such a campaign might have been successful in 1953, or even 1957. But during the 1950's nearly one out of every four whites who had lived in the city had moved to the suburbs, and the white population had plummeted from 1,545,847 to 1,182,970. At the same time the black population had increased more than 50 percent: from 300,506 to 482,229. In antagonizing 29 percent of the population Miriani placed a heavy handicap on himself.

Cavanagh, to the contrary, built a coalition of minorities. Sullivan plotted the strategy for the general election. Wayne State University Law Professor Dick Strichartz, Cavanagh's neighbor, wrote position papers and brought the economic issues into focus.*

Cavanagh was cast as "Jerry the Giant Killer" whose destiny and interests were the destiny and interests of the working people of Detroit. By the beginning of November, 1961, the momentum was clearly with the challenger. Winning by 200,413 votes to 158,778—including 85 percent of the Negro vote —Cavanagh was the second youngest man elected to the office of mayor.

Animated, chain smoking, ordering coffee and beer, Cavanagh gathered his close supporters for a midnight strategy session. The members of the group knew little about running the municipal government and less about managing an enterprise with a budget of nearly $400 million a year.

For a financial analysis of the city, Cavanagh called on Alfred Pelham. One of Detroit's most distinguished citizens, he was descended from Robert Pelham, who had fled from the South during the agitation that followed John Brown's

---

* Strichartz's grandfather had owned one of the factories that had made Lodz the textile center of the world. Strichartz's father, a Jewish intellectual, had fled Russia to escape the hangman after the 1905 Revolution, and had made his living repairing shirts in a New York cold-water flat. Dick Strichartz had obtained his college education in the United States Navy during World War II. After the war he had used the G.I. Bill to acquire a law degree.

raid on Harpers Ferry and had prospered as a contractor. Alfred's father, Benjamin, had become the "czar of Wayne County." Alfred Pelham had graduated from Harvard Business School, and had been appointed county budget director in 1939. He was now associate professor of political science at Wayne State University. No one had a better grasp of the intricacies of the urban government and its finances than he. Pelham estimated that unless a new source of revenue were established the deficit in the city's budget the following year would be between $34 milion and $43 million—nearly equal to the annual *total* of taxes collected during the Depression.

Familiarizing himself with the municipal government, Cavanagh became aware of the weaknesses in the "strong mayor" structure. Offsetting the 69 positions * to which he could appoint people to establish his policies were 21,000 Civil Service "untouchables," who knew that mayors come and go, but that their jobs continue. In the normal course of events, department heads, many of them Civil Service appointees, conducted their operations with a minimum of interference from the boards and commissions. Among the Civil Service department heads were the director of the planning commission, the general manager of the water department, the general superintendent of parks and recreation, and the secretary of the Civil Service Commission—all positions of pivotal influence. Since the health department was now a combined city-county operation, with each arm of government holding the right to appoint its own department head, the commissioner had to be someone acceptable to both the mayor and the Wayne County Board of Supervisors. The city and the county still had their own separate, overlapping welfare departments. The city treasurer and the city clerk were elective positions.

Some members of the nine-member city council served term after term, and formed unofficial but powerful alliances with key departmental officials. Reflecting a general suspicion of corruption in government, the city council required that every departmental expenditure of more than one thousand dollars be submitted to it for approval. The requirement gave the council impressive influence over departmental operations. The council had been a major source of frustrations for almost every mayor. (The council, of course, considered every mayor a source of their frustrations.) In the entire history of the city probably only Pingree and Jim Couzens could be considered to have been "strong" mayors—mayors who really had come to grips with the problems.

Cavanagh appointed Pelham controller, the most important position next to that of mayor. It marked the first time a Negro was installed in a major post in the city government. Joe B. Sullivan was appointed executive secretary—the mayor's alter ego. Strichartz was named assistant controller. (The title did not reflect the importance of Strichartz's role. Since the table of organizations provided only two staff positions for the mayor—executive secretary and press secretary—it was necessary to slide Strichartz into a slot from which he would be able to act as a free-wheeling member of the mayor's staff.)

But Cavanagh's major coup was in his appointment of police commissioner. Although he did not name a Negro, he would not have startled the city or the police force more if he had.

The man who agreed to take the post was George Edwards. With that stroke Cavanagh confirmed his overnight reputation as a political Svengali. From a

* An additional 181 appointive positions were nonpaying and largely honorary.

union organizer who had been sent to jail in 1938, Edwards had advanced to Juvenile Court judge, and in 1954 had been appointed to the Michigan circuit court. Two years later Governor Williams had elevated him to the state supreme court. That a supreme court justice would resign to accept the thankless job of Detroit police commissioner would have been thought incredible. Edwards, however, had recently suffered a setback in his quest for the chief justiceship, a position that was not likely to open up again for many years. Cavanagh convinced Edwards that a man of his caliber was needed to defuse a situation that made "Detroit the most likely candidate for a major race riot of any big city in the country." [2]

Police officers were incredulous. Some of the older men remembered when Edwards had hurled nuts and bolts at them from the factory roof during the Yale and Towne Company strike. Officers went around popping off that the new commissioner would have to "wise up" and "forget some of his constitutional law enforcement ideas" if he expected to run the department.

Suddenly Cavanagh, who had fought the left wing of the Democratic party, was the hero of the liberals. The appointments of Edwards and Pelham won him the approbation of the UAW, of Negroes, and of liberals in general. The appointment as housing commissioner of Bob Knox, a realtor who was active in Democratic politics, offered a rapprochement to the regular party organization. Strichartz was Jewish. Sullivan and Jim Trainor, Cavanagh's press secretary, were Irish. In fact, Cavanagh's appointments—45 percent white Protestant, 34 percent Catholic, 14 percent Jewish, and 7 percent Negro—accurately reflected the ethnic mix and educational levels in the city. The Negroes, lagging behind in education, were greatly underrepresented. The Jews, with proportionately almost twice the number of college graduates as the population as a whole, were considerably overrepresented.

The immediate task was to prepare the new budget; a budget of $351 million that could be balanced only, Mayor Cavanagh told the state legislature, with enactment of a 1 percent city income tax. The legislators applauded him—until he said he also wanted to tax suburbantites working in the city. Then the battle lines were drawn, suburban and rural versus city legislators. Instead of an income tax, the legislature passed a bill prohibiting the city from taxing nonresidents. Democratic Governor John B. Swainson vetoed the bill, a courageous act that was to contribute to his narrow defeat by George Romney in the fall gubernatorial race.*

(Nevertheless, it was to be the last hurrah for the rural legislators. The next year the United States Supreme Court, in *Baker v. Carr,* established the one man-one vote rule. Ironically, since the decision came at a time when population was moving out of the cities, its principal beneficiaries were the suburbs.)

Cavanagh succeeded in having a municipal income tax enacted—1 percent on residents and ½ percent on nonresidents working in the city. For the first time since the Depression Detroit was on such sound financial footing that its bonds were accorded a prime rating. He threatened a municipal takeover of

---

* The state's Payless Pay Day crisis, and his experience on the school committee had led Romney to the forefront of the movement to rewrite the state's constitution. When the constitutional convention met in 1961, he was elected chairman. As a liberal Republican, he engineered a compromise that apportioned the legislature partly on the basis of population and partly on area. Rejecting the compromise, the Democrats filed briefs in support of the Tennessee suit that led to the *Baker v. Carr* decision.

Cobo Hall if the unions, which had usurped power at the convention center, did not curb their excesses and reform themselves. He cracked down on the Department of Public Works, which had an annual budget of $38 million and was the largest single city department. Employees were shaking down trash contractors, they were "overweighing" garbage trucks in order to justify increased departmental appropriations, they held card parties on the job, they took hour-long coffee breaks—all while picking up the garbage every other week.

Cavanagh's sound business practices earned him the approbation of the financial and industrial communities. The liberals were pleased by his first executive order: an edict prohibiting discrimination in municipal employment.

Reporters and journalists found him the most open and delightful politician they had encountered in years. They never tired of writing about him, and nearly everything they said was complimentary. He was full of enthusiasm, full of zest for his job, confident that it was his destiny to turn the city around.

"Only under Cavanagh does a city hall take on the appearance of a launching pad," the Detroit *Free Press* said.

Nevertheless, the inherent conflicts between the council and the mayor were not long in reappearing, especially when it became evident that the mayor intended to take a firm grip on the government. The council soon was eyeing the mayor's projects with suspicion—what was his purpose in asking for a $50,000 annual appropriation for the establishment of a municipal office in Washington? The business of the city's government was in Detroit, not in the District of Columbia! But Cavanagh was convinced that the destiny of Detroit lay ever more in the hands of the Federal government—the city's most important business acquisition in years was the Internal Revenue Service's new $30 million computer center.

96

The Embattled City

IN FACT, OVER DETROIT'S MOST CRITICAL PROBLEM, ITS DETERIORATING economy, the mayor had little control. For years Detroit had been a leader in the Midwestern agitation for construction of the St. Lawrence Seaway—a canal to enable modern oceangoing vessels to enter the Great Lakes. Railroads and Eastern shippers had opposed the seaway because of the commerce it would divert from the Atlantic Coast. Not until Canada had threatened to build the canal alone had the United States Congress appropriated the money.

Completed in 1959, the canal was hailed as a breakthrough in making Midwestern products more competitive in foreign markets. But, quite unexpectedly, the seaway was having the converse effect of aiding foreign manufacturers to undersell domestic goods in the American heartland.

For a half century United States industry had exercised unprecedented dominance in the world. In 1945 America was the only major nation whose industrial establishment had not been shattered by war. With one third of the world's exports, it annually exported from $5 billion to $8.5 billion more than it imported. Sixty percent of the world's gold supply was already lodged in this country, and more was being siphoned off daily into Fort Knox. Not since Roman times had one nation been in such a position of power.

The preeminence was too great. It threatened the stability and viability of every other industrial nation in the Western world. If there still had been unrestricted immigration, half the population of the world would have flocked to America's shores. Living in misery, much of that population was turning toward what appeared the only alternative: communism.

To reduce the inclination toward communism, the American government had to find a means to alleviate the impact of the unfavorable balance of trade on Europe. Beginning in 1947, the Truman Administration devised the Marshall Plan, Point Four, and other foreign-aid programs. These, in effect, returned to foreign nations the dollars they were spending for American goods in excess of their exports to America, so that they could buy more American goods. It was a unique subsidy by the American government to both foreign nations and its own industry. It worked to keep plants operating at high capacity, and it kept unemployment at a relatively low level until 1958.*

Inevitably, the foreign industries that American aid helped to rebuild began to compete with American industry. In Europe the Common Market was organized. As the middle-class and workingmen's share of national incomes increased, a mass market comparable to that in America emerged. Manufacturers had incentive to "Taylorize" and "Fordize" along American lines.

The accommodation between American labor and industry had driven up United States wages and prices far beyond those in other parts of the world. In industries that were labor-intensive,† foreign goods began to drive domestic products out of the American market. Since American manufacturers were unable to respond by reducing wages, they reacted by attempting to increase productivity. Manpower could be reduced through greater mechanization and automation, and costs could be reduced through modernization of plants and transfer of operations from high-outlay to low-outlay locations. An industry that might not be profitable in a high-rent, high-tax Northern urban area might be economically viable in a low-rent, low-tax Southern semirural setting.‡

In the clothing and textile industries, shoe making, metal manufacturing, and automobile production, the United States had had a favorable balance of trade ever since electricity had been mated to "American ingenuity" in the nineteenth century. Suddenly, the balance of trade was reversed. The United States began to import more of these goods than it was exporting. Employment in Northern cities declined. Jobs disappeared because of declining sales and because plants moved away. The jobs that were lost were largely the unskilled and low skilled, in which it would have been impossible for a worker to maintain an "American" standard of living at anywhere near the wages paid workers in foreign countries. These were the jobs traditionally held by the more recent migrants to the cities—Negroes, Puerto Ricans, Mexican-Americans, and Appalachian whites.

For Detroit, whose fortunes more than those of any other city in the nation were linked to manufacturing, the implications were as serious as those of the Depression.

In the automobile industry, automation was enabling 641,000 workers to produce almost a half million more cars and trucks in 1961 than 735,000 had produced in 1949. Employment for unskilled and lower-skilled workers in the Detroit metropolitan area dropped more than 13 percent between 1950 and 1960. The city had 78,000 unemployed, and an equal number were out of work in surrounding communities. There were over 12,000 persons on public welfare, and the city and the county were spending more than $26 million annually for relief—although thousands of others, theoretically eligible for welfare, were not on the rolls.

The industrial upheavals were bringing about cataclysmic changes in the entire commercial structure of the city. As factory after factory disappeared, and the population exited for the suburbs, enterprises that had been dependent

* The unemployment rate was under 5 percent except in 1949, 1950, and 1954.
† Industries in which a relatively large part of the final product's cost is due to the labor involved. In 1960 average hourly wages were $2.26 in the United States, 90 cents in England, 62 cents in Germany, 53 cents in France, 34 cents in Italy, and 30 cents in Japan.
‡ One of the firms that moved from the Detroit area to a Southern location (Arkansas) was the Daisy Air Rifle Company, whose founder, Charles Bennett, had been one of the original investors in the Ford Motor Company.

on the patronage of blue-collar workers went under. In 1959, Kern's, the city's second-largest department store, had closed its doors, removing from the tax rolls most of an entire downtown block. Kern's had been followed by the Detroit *Times,* one of the city's three major newspapers.*

At three o'clock in the morning of November 7, 1960, Western Union messengers knocked on the doors of *Times* employees with telegrams informing them that their jobs had been terminated. The *Times* had been sold to the Detroit *News.*

Trained and educated during an era that was rapidly ending, the employees— like the employees of Packard, Hudson, and scores of other former enterprises—were thrust into a chronically depressed labor market. Thirty-five percent were grammar school dropouts; 42 percent had gone only through the eighth grade; 5 percent had graduated from high school; and 2 percent had had some college education. Most of them were second-generation urbanites, but there had been little upward mobility among them.†

Even *Times* professionals had a hard time finding new jobs—28 percent were still looking for work after six months. For others the situation was catastrophic: of the technical editorial employees 41 percent were unemployed longer than six months; of the skilled workers in the commercial department, 49 percent; of the unskilled, 64 percent. The two most critical factors were age and education. Two thirds of men over forty-five and three fourths who had not graduated from high school became part of the long-term unemployed.

The state employment service, created as part of the Roosevelt Administration's anti-Depression effort to couple people to jobs, proved almost useless. Only one out of every one hundred workers was able to find employment through it.

A photoengraver lamented:

"I wasn't worried with twenty-five years' experience and a good work record. What a shock to find out that I wasn't needed! . . . Those new machines let one man do the work of five." [1]

Mayor Cavanagh personally hired two of the paper's former employees. One was James Trainor, the city editor, who became the mayor's press secretary. The other was Ray Girardin.

For thirty years Girardin had been one of the top crime and police reporters in America. He had aged along with the police force and the mobsters—the informers and tipsters he could call on among both were legion. He knew the city well, and had first met the mayor when the young Cavanagh had been working his way through college as a sheriff's deputy. When Joe B. Sullivan resigned to run for Wayne County Prosecutor, Cavanagh asked Girardin (who

---

* Feasting on crimes and scandals, the *Times'*s yellow journalism and wild red headlines had boosted its circulation from 26,000 in 1921—when Hearst had bought it—to 434,000 in 1951. But the violence and "entertainment" featured in the paper were portrayed more graphically on television. The *Times* depended heavily on central city, newsstand sales, and the population was disappearing from downtown. By 1960 *Times* circulation had dropped to 380,000—compared to 500,000 for the *Free Press* and 480,000 for the *News.*
† There was a close correlation between their father's status and the education they had received. In the circulation department, 24 percent of the workers' fathers had held white collar or skilled jobs, and 24 percent of the workers had gone to or graduated from high school. In the editorial department, 52 percent of the fathers had held white collar or skilled jobs, and 68 percent of the employees had gone to high school or beyond.

meanwhile had become chief probation officer for the Recorder's Court) to take his place as executive secretary.*

That was twenty months after the end of the *Times,* yet any number of its employees were still seeking jobs. Tens of thousands of Detroit's citizens were struggling in that kind of economic quagmire. The state legislature was unsympathetic and almost oblivious to the urban problems. Only 56 percent of the money paid in taxes by Detroit residents and businesses to the state was allocated back to the city. In August, 1962, Cavanagh went to the convention of the American Municipal Association (now the National League of Cities) in Philadelphia, and made an historic speech.

Political and economic circumstances, he declared, were forcing the nation's cities into a partnership with the Federal government. It "will be impossible for cities to retreat from involvement with and dependence on the Federal government. . . . In a whole host of new programs, the Federal government, either directly or by grant . . . is coming to the aid of the embattled cities." [2]

The speech focused national attention on the festering condition of the cities. It made Cavanagh the man on the white charger to the urbanologists.

"An unknown Republican," said *Look,* had made himself the celebrity of the convention. The administration in Washington took note. A few weeks later, President Kennedy made it a point to get together with Cavanagh. Both were young, both were handsome, both were Irish Catholics, both were middle-of-the-roaders who were gaining an awareness of economic problems, and becoming more liberal. The President felt more comfortable with Cavanagh than with the Williams-UAW wing of the Michigan Democratic party.† Cavanagh became one of the White House's two or three favorite mayors. A continuous interchange of information and ideas began between members of the mayor's and the President's staffs.

---

* Girardins have played a prominent role in the history of the city. Charles Girardin was an associate justice on the first regular court established in Detroit in 1788. Baker Jacques Girardin was the first overseer of the poor in the late eighteenth century. P. N. Girardin was one of the first captains on the Detroit police force, serving from 1865 to 1882.
† The organized-labor vote had become so important, and Detroit was so generally recognized as the most unionized city in the United States, that between 1948 and 1968 every Democratic presidential nominee inaugurated his campaign with a Labor Day speech in the city's Cadillac Square.

V

A NATION OF CITIES

97

"What About the Poverty Problem?"

PRESIDENT KENNEDY HAD CAMPAIGNED ON THE ECONOMIC ISSUE AND PLEDGED to "get this country moving again." He was, therefore, increasingly perturbed by the economic inertia.

The economy had never fully recovered from the recession of 1958, and it had suffered a relapse in 1960. Pockets of chronic unemployment existed throughout the nation. In the hills of Appalachia, the coal miners were undergoing slow starvation as a consequence of the mechanization of mining, the replacement of steam locomotives by the Diesels of General Motors, and the widespread substitution of oil for coal as a fuel. (Between 1950 and 1961 coal mining employment decreased from 470,000 to 159,000, and railroad employment from 1,373,000 to 813,000.) In New England and Southern textile towns workers lost jobs as Du Pont developed one synthetic fiber after another, and the disparity between domestic and foreign wages increased. (Textile employment dropped from 1,256,000 to 897,000.) In the shoe industry production was diverted to Italy, Japan, and Brazil, where manufacturers switched to American machine technology but workers were decades behind in translating increases in productivity to gains in wages. (Leather work employment decreased from 396,000 to 356,000.) In Michigan's Upper Peninsula, miners and lumbermen fought an unequal battle against diminishing resources and suffered the consequences of the depredations of the past. (Lumber industry employment decreased from 800,000 to 580,000, and metal mining employment from 97,000 to 89,000.)

Twice Congress had passed an Area Redevelopment Act, and twice President Eisenhower, who showed little interest in domestic affairs and regarded the act as but another pork barrel, had vetoed it.

Within five months of taking office President Kennedy signed a new Area Redevelopment Act. But with more than half the nation's industrial areas suffering from severe unemployment, awareness grew that the problems were of national rather than local character. In the decade between 1950 and 1960, farm employment had dropped from 6.5 million to 4.7 million. Construction employment remained at a level of about 3.5 million, while the industry's annual income rose from $12 billion to $21 billion. Manufacturing employment was

lower in 1961 than in 1951, even though manufacturing income increased from
$76 billion in 1950 to $126 billion in 1960.

In 1962 Congress passed two more administration measures: the Public Works
Acceleration Act, designed to pump additional Federal funds into construction,
and the Manpower Development and Training Act, aimed at retraining workers
displaced by technological and economic changes.

The effect of these measures on the economy was marginal. A majority of
the administration's economic advisers believed Federal taxes were acting as a
"brake" on industrial expansion. In late 1962 a Cabinet committee on economic
growth headed by Walter Heller, chairman of the Council of Economic Advisers,
recommended a tax cut of $12 billion as a remedy both for the lagging economy
and the chronic deficits in the Federal budget. The committee in effect was applying to the business of government the classic solution for declining sales—a
reduction in the price per unit aimed at stimulating greater revenues through a
greater volume of sales, even though the profit per unit would be less.

It was a philosophy that major American industries, operating in an economy
increasingly administered by themselves, had abandoned. It was a philosophy
whose efficacy was open to question in a nation with a tax structure favoring the
well-to-do. It left out of account the fact that American industries were directing
a large part of their investments into overseas plants—plants whose products
would compete not only in the burgeoning foreign markets but would come back
to the United States to compete against domestically manufactured goods. Since
capital investments could often be made more profitably in foreign than in
domestic industries, American investment abroad mushroomed from $29.1 bil-
lion in 1955 to $50.4 billion in 1960. Continuing to accelerate, these investments
contributed to the development of an unfavorable American balance of payments * which first reached alarming proportions in 1958. It raised the question
whether the drain of money from the average American consumer to the savings
elite and then to foreign investment that had proven so devastating in the 1920's
was beginning to repeat itself.

Nevertheless, President Kennedy, who had known little about economics when
he took office and was by instinct a fiscal conservative, agreed to propose the
tax reduction to Congress.

The tax reduction, however, could be expected to help the poor only marginally, if at all. Michael Harrington's book, *The Other America,* shocked
the President and many members of the administration with its depiction of the
plight of the poor. Mayors of big cities were restive, and dissatisfied with the
scope of the measures so far enacted. Mayor Cavanagh, who had asked for
$118.7 million under the Public Works Acceleration Act, had received only $5.5
million and was wondering aloud if what was needed was "a domestic peace
corps."†

At the year-end review in December, 1962, the President turned to Heller
and said:

"Give me facts and figures on the things we still have to do. For example,
what about the poverty problem in the United States?" [1]

---

* *Balance of payments* includes all financial transactions. *Balance of trade* is the difference
between exports and imports. The balance of trade, after being in America's favor since
1893, finally tipped against the nation in 1971.
† The Peace Corps was the display piece of the Kennedy Administration. The agency sent
volunteers with technical skills to underdeveloped countries to provide people-to-people
assistance.

98

"Twelfth Street Is Not the Milky Way"

THE PRESIDENT NEED HAVE LOOKED NO FARTHER THAN MAYOR CAVANAGH'S sanitation division. There, Donald Stallings, nearing the end of his second decade of picking up garbage cans, was trying to support himself, six children, his drinking, and his gambling on wages less than half those considered adequate for a moderate standard of living by the Department of Labor.* Even had the sanitation division not had a reputation of frustrating advancement for its Negro employees, Stallings would have had difficulty making ends meet.

Donald's six children continued to be divided between the households of Donald's mother, Freda Stallings, and Irma's parents, Wallace and Antoinette Mirow. The oldest child, Mirabel, and the youngest, Brett, were at Freda's, the other four children were in the Mirow home. It was a division that had occurred more or less by chance when Irma had been adjudged an alcoholic in 1950.

Wallace continued to work at two jobs. He was employed at Chrysler, and he operated his coal truck. When he could afford to, he hired a neighborhood woman to cook and do the housekeeping. But when in 1958 and again in 1960 the auto industry went into a recession and he was laid off, conditions in the house were chaotic.

Antoinette had been diagnosed as a paranoid schizophrenic, and Wallace had "put her away" for one extended stay of several months in a sanitarium. But since she, like her daughter Irma, was of no danger to anyone, the state preferred to have her live at home, and to administer only "crisis" treatment. Antoinette was incapable of doing housework. Seldom a day went by when she did not disorganize the house. She broke the dishes, hid things in nooks and crannies, and buried articles. She took the clothes out of all the drawers and closets, mixed them in huge piles, then cut them and sewed them together in random fashion— socks to shirts, shirts to dresses, dresses to pants. One day the children returned home to discover every item of clothing in the house sewn together and winding from room to room like a monstruous python.

The Juvenile Court probation officer on her way to visit the home encoun-

---

* Stallings's pay was $3,350 a year. The Bureau of Labor Statistics estimated annual expenditures in Detroit for a family of *five* at approximately $7,500.

tered Antoinette rambling down the street. Antoinette was filthy. Wearing bobby sox, her hair streaming in long strands, her clothing in tatters, her sunken breasts swaying pendulously, she was naked to the waist. Finding the house in a condition not unsimilar to Antoinette's, the probation officer told Wallace that this was no environment in which to raise children, and that the court might have to place them in foster homes.

Wallace reacted belligerently. He said the state doctors thought Antoinette could live at home, and the court had placed the children in his home. He could "not understand why there should be a complaint now, when Antoinette has been going around naked for years."

Wallace often did the cooking and housekeeping himself, and tried to create a livable environment for the children. How well they functioned was conditioned largely by their relationships to Antoinette. The oldest boy, Windsor, terrified Antoinette. He extended his protection to Natalie, the youngest of the girls. (Natalie also benefited from the summers she spent in Cleveland with Wallace's college-educated sister and brother.) Both Windsor and Natalie were progressing in high school—Windsor graduated and joined the army in 1960. The other two girls, however, were cowed and frightened by their grandmother. Both exhibited emotional aberrations stemming from their association with Antoinette. They frequently fell asleep in class. One of them rocked back and forth at her desk for hours and picked compulsively at her arms with a tweezer or needle until she began to bleed.

Occasionally when Irma was released from the hospital she moved in with her parents. But within a few months she was always recommitted. Donald continued to rent the attic of his mother's house in the old Jewish section west of Hamtramck. In 1960 Freda Stallings was sixty-five years old. She had arthritis and no longer could perform the domestic work that had paid her twenty to twenty-five dollars a week. She made application for Old Age Assistance. The application was denied on the basis that her son Donald could support her on his $110 weekly salary from the sanitation division.

(Donald, of course, was making only $64.44 weekly before deductions. Since he was paid biweekly, the investigator had mistaken his income as double what it actually was.)

Freda's only income was the money she obtained from roomers. In addition to her son Donald, Freda had her daughter Janice and Janice's daughter Ruth and their families living with her. A woman on welfare with three children rented a room. There were six adults and ten children in the house.

Janice continued to make her living by brewing liquor and hosting parties. Mirabel, Donald's oldest child, began helping her. For the first time in her life Mirabel had "fun." The parties often led to lovemaking. In the fall of 1954, a few months after she had been raped, Mirabel met Tom Winesberry. Six months later she was pregnant. At the age of fifteen she was married to Tom.

Winesberry was twenty-four years old. One of twelve children of a Georgia sharecropper, he had grown up in a frame shanty without foundation and flooring, without gas, electricity, or plumbing. With the equivalent of about a fourth-grade education, he had been drawn to Atlanta, where he had worked as a bootblack. During the latter part of the Korean War he had come to Detroit. He worked in a small foundry that had difficulty operating profitably. He performed the same kind of back-breaking labor as Mirabel's grandfather, Odie Stallings, when he had arrived from Virginia nearly forty year before.

Tom was an easier mark for the city slickers than Donald Stallings had ever been. When he received his pay, he drank, he gambled, he got rolled. Mirabel discovered to her horror that she had married the image of her father. In a desperate attempt to keep some kind of control over Tom, she drank with him. Hating what was happening to her, she wished that she had never gotten pregnant, that she had never gotten married, and that she had never met her husband. She railed at him that he was a bum like her father. He beat her and blackened her eyes.

By 1961 Mirabel had three children. Despite the quarrels, Mirabel had stayed with Winesberry because he worked steadily. The recession of 1960–1961, however, combined with the ever greater competition from imports of foreign steel resulted in the shutting down of the foundry. Throughout Detroit and the Midwest marginal business after marginal business closed its doors during the 1960's, and with the businesses went the jobs of the marginal workers.

Tom's unemployment benefits were soon exhausted. The fights between Tom and Mirabel grew more violent. One Friday night when she tried to wrench away from him, a switchblade knife fell from his pocket. Grabbing the knife, Mirabel plunged it into his chest. She nearly killed him; but after a two-week stay in the hospital, he recovered. Mirabel was jailed for three days and then allowed to return home to care for the children.

Tom disappeared. Mirabel made application to the county welfare department for Aid for Dependent Children (ADC) and rejoined her Aunt Janice in party giving. Within a month she met a man who paid her $7 a week to sleep with her. The additional money supplemented her $125-a-month ADC check just enough to allow her to get by.

The caseworker, who had commented on Mirabel's lack of bedding, was suspicious when Mirabel purchased a bed and a mattress. "Are any men frequenting the house? For what purpose?" the worker asked.

Mirabel replied that no man was frequenting the house, but the caseworker called in the Special Investigation section. Three times, on November 22, 1961, at 3 A.M., on December 22 at 1:30 A.M., and on January 22, 1962, at 3:30 A.M., an investigator knocked on Mirabel's door and insisted on searching her rooms.

He did not discover Mirabel's paramour. Mirabel, however, became pregnant. She contacted a Twelfth Street abortionist and paid him fifty dollars. But he bungled the operation, and Mirabel was rushed to Detroit General Hospital with an "incomplete abortion."

That brought her to the attention of the caseworker again, who chided that she had violated the law. "You should have a legal marriage before having sexual relations."

"I have a legal marriage, but I don't know where my husband is."

"Your ADC grant will be discontinued because you are not setting a proper example for your children to follow."

That, of course, was punishing the children. Mirabel had only one means of supporting herself—she became a prostitute. Mirabel's mother, Irma, had been released from the state hospital in 1960. A sixty-year-old man took her in, and for three years she lived with him. She drank as much as always. But she no longer had the responsibility of children; in the Twelfth Street area people were used to bizarre behavior; and police did not pick up drunks as quickly as they once had. So Irma was not returned to the hospital. In 1963, when she was in her early forties, she looked twenty years older. The man kicked her out.

Irma moved in with Mirabel, and lived on the money her father and occasionally Donald gave her. Once more Mirabel tried to obtain welfare assistance. The social worker came to the apartment and told her she should obtain a job. Mirabel responded that she had three children to take care of.

"Your mother can take care of them," the social worker said. Looking at Irma, she saw a woman who resembled a Raggedy Ann doll; a woman with a silly smile and missing teeth. For the moment, Irma was sober, and the social worker, who knew nothing of her history, considered her perfectly capable of baby-sitting.

"No, she *can't!*" said Mirabel.

"Yes she *can!*" the social worker insisted and refused to be swayed.

Repeatedly Mirabel's application for ADC was denied with such comments as: "The application needs further study. It seems very improbable that Mrs. Winesberry and her children could live for three years on the amount of money her mother and her father give her. An investigation is needed to determine her source of income."

In the summer of 1964 Mirabel was arrested by the vice squad, and charged with accosting and soliciting. She did not have the fifty dollars she needed for bail. When she did not return home, Irma, drunk and confused, staggered off into the street to look for her. The children were left alone. The next afternoon a grocer called the women's division of the police department and reported three hungry children were begging in his store. The police picked them up and took them to the juvenile home. When Mirabel was released from jail and called to find out what had happened to them, she was rearrested for abandonment and neglect.

In September, 1964, Mirabel sat in the Juvenile Court where her mother had sat before her. It was not, she explained plaintively, a life of luxury. She lived in a dark, converted attic, whose walls were black with dirt and age. She had almost no furniture, and the only heat came from an electric heater. "The rats are bad and they won't do nothing about it. I am afraid one of the kids nearly got bit. I could get a place if I could get some furniture. But they cut off my welfare, so what can I do? Believe me, judge, Twelfth Street is not the Milky Way."

A generation before, the children would probably have been placed in foster homes. But with few foster homes and no institutional care available, there was nothing to be done but to leave the children with Mirabel under the custody of the court. To make that possible, the court prevailed upon the Department of Social Services to ignore thé Federal regulations it was supposed to enforce and reclassify Mirabel as a *worthy* mother. The court thus assumed responsibility for a new generation even while it was still struggling with Mirabel's youngest brother, Brett.

Until she had married Tom Winesberry in 1955, the teen-aged Mirabel had been Brett's "mother." At the age of five Brett was left in his grandmother Freda's communal household with no adult to whom he could relate. His father, Donald, seldom was home, and Brett had no sense of kinship to him. As Freda aged, she was less able to care for Brett. The young boy was buffeted about among four women who squabbled, pulled each other's hair, and threw things at each other. He had nothing of his own except the clothes he wore, and even clothes lost their identity as they were interchanged among the ten children. He had to fight for food and battle for a toy to play with. He grew up combative. When he was small, he was victimized by the older children, and as he grew bigger he in turn became a bully. When he entered the first grade he was a C student. But his performance steadily deteriorated. He was a troublemaker and he could not concentrate on anything for very long. He was classified as "hyperactive."

His only friend was Garry Gatling, a year younger than he.* Brett was considerably bigger than Garry and watched over him. The boys had no concept of *private* property, and they transferred their battle for material things from the household to the streets. Before they were ten they would rob smaller children of licorice sticks, beat them up, and extort money from them. By the time Brett was eleven, he and Garry were slipping through open doors of houses and climbing through windows.

At three o'clock one morning in May, 1962, police officers noticed two boys coming out of the door of a candy store on Woodward Avenue. The officers chased the boys and cornered them in an alley. Brett was carrying a coffee can with $7.40.

Brett and Garry were held six weeks in the juvenile detention home. A hearing was held, but almost inevitably it was pro forma. Since there were no facilities available in which they could be placed, they were returned to Freda's house.

---

* Garry was Brett's stepcousin, once removed. He was the grandson of Janice, who was the stepsister of Donald Stallings, Brett's father. Janice was Freda's only child by her first marriage.

99

The River of Hate

IN DETROIT AND THROUGHOUT THE UNITED STATES, JUVENILE DELINQUENCY and crimes committed by Negroes were increasing.

The number of juvenile boys arrested for major offenses jumped from 4,000, the majority of them white, in 1940 to 6,600, most of them black, in 1963. There had been 9,500 Negroes among the 35,000 persons arrested in Detroit in 1940. There were 23,000 among the 36,000 arrested in 1963. Since the economy and crime acted like the opposite balances of a scale, the more that Negroes were victimized by economic conditions, the more crimes they committed. In 1963 the number of major economic crimes was nearly double what it had been in 1952, and almost four times what it had been in 1939. Most of the victims of crimes committed by Negroes were Negroes.* Negroes were one of the most vocal segments of Detroit's population demanding better police protection.

In his capacity as police commissioner, George Edwards was trying to reorient the performance of his officers toward equal treatment of Negroes. Shortly after taking office, he had come face to face with the practices of the entrenched bureaucracy and learned the truth of "police brutality." When a Negro prisoner complained that he had been beaten in the stomach, attacked with a baseball bat, and threatened with a saw, the officers involved reported that the prisoner had accomplished the remarkable feat of assaulting six policemen while his arms were handcuffed behind his back, and that they had used only the "necessary force" to subdue him. When a trial board composed of Edwards, the chief of detectives, and the superintendent of police was convened, the two career officials outvoted Edwards and acquitted the men.

Edwards launched an investigation of his own. The precinct inspector told him that the officers had admitted the beating and that he had reported their admission to the deputy superintendent of police. Edwards concluded that there

---

* In one typical Detroit inner city precinct, 78 percent of identified assault offenders were Negroes, and 76 percent of the people upon whom assaults were committed were Negroes.

had been a conspiracy to find the officers innocent, and confronted his fellow trial-board members.

"Of course, they're guilty," the chief of detectives agreed, "but I couldn't go back and run the department if I found them guilty."

It was obvious to Edwards that this had been trial-board policy for years except when officers violated the department's own code of standards. Furious, he warned the department's top officials that the continuation of this policy would see their removal—the commissioner and the mayor controlled promotions and demotions to the rank of captain and above. Subsequently, in thirty out of thirty-two trial boards held in 1962 the officers were adjudged guilty.

To bridge the "river of hate" between the police and the black community, Edwards set up precinct-level meetings between officers and residents. He warned officers that he would not tolerate "alley courts" and tried to impress upon them that by viewing every Negro as a probable criminal they were making their own task more difficult. Yet many patrolmen believed only that Mayor Cavanagh, Commissioner Edwards, and all those associated with the administration were a bunch of "nigger lovers." *

When a Negro purchased a house in northwest Detroit near "Copper Valley"—so named because of the multitude of police officers living there—two attempts were made to burn down the dwelling. Edwards assigned police to watch the house around the clock.

The harassment and vandalism continued.

To Edwards it was evident that the police themselves were involved. He removed the precinct commander and replaced him with a lieutenant who lived in the neighborhood. "I want you to take off every officer," Edwards told the lieutenant, "and you, personally, will be held responsible that there is no more trouble at that house."

There was no more trouble.

Edwards could deal with issues that could be met head-on. Yet like the mayor in his confrontations with the Civil Service bureaucracy, he was unable to penetrate deeply into the labyrinths of the police bureaucracy. It remained a mystery why so many Negroes who wanted to be police officers were rejected— of 455 who applied in 1962, only 2 were finally appointed. The KKK continued to operate within the department—when a Detroit civil rights activist, Viola Liuzzo, was murdered during the 1965 demonstrations in Selma, Alabama, the Klan was able within a few days to publicize her Detroit police record. Edwards was convinced that the tentacles that organized crime had extended into the department in the days of Prohibition had never been eliminated and that a good deal of police brutality stemmed from Negro infringement of Mafia territory. But he had little hope that he could ever crack the department's tight, clannish atmosphere to prove it.

For the city's Negroes there was a new kind of frustration—they had helped elect an administration dedicated to equal rights, yet in most ways those rights seemed as far beyond reach as ever. The most blatant forms of discrimination—

---

* When Cavanagh's executive secretary, Joe B. Sullivan, was running for county prosecutor in 1962, a police officer questioned him:
"What would you do if someone filed a complaint against a police officer?"
"First thing, I'd investigate it."
"That's what a bastard would do. No one should investigate a police officer. We have enough problems without being investigated."

including the barring of Negroes from Detroit's fashionable hotels and restaurants—had ceased in the latter 1950's with the establishment of a Michigan Fair Employment Practices Commission. Negroes were able to receive a fair hearing at city hall. The police had curbed their more roughshod ways. But in the slums the blacks were still isolated. In the schools they were confronted with the ironic fact that, nine years after the United States Supreme Court had declared "separate and equal" unconstitutional, Superintendent of Schools Brownell was working diligently to make them more equal in their ever greater separateness—72 percent of Negro children were going to schools that were 90 to 100 percent black, and only 8 percent were going to what could be termed "integrated" schools.

Dr. Brownell said the school system could do nothing about housing segregation. But whereas thirty years before more than half the Negro population had lived in predominantly white neighborhoods, now 85 percent were living in totally or predominantly black neighborhoods. Until 1948 the underwriting manual of the Federal Housing and Home Finance Agency had adhered to the code of ethics of the National Real Estate Board. In 1948 President Truman, following the Supreme Court decision outlawing restrictive covenants, had ordered the agency to revise its segregationist policies. But both the FHA and the VA practiced "red-lining," prohibiting loans on houses in deteriorating areas. Since red-lining affected the older housing, and older housing was all Negroes could afford, the practice was an oblique continuation of discriminatory policies. Only about 1 percent of FHA loans were being made to Negroes.

Buttressed by the policies of the Federal agency, Detroit's board of realtors and most of its financial institutions continued their biased operations. Fearing adverse reaction from white depositors, banks and lending institutions refused to finance mortgages for Negroes moving into white neighborhoods. "Gentlemen's agreements" between brokers and white property owners not to show houses to "undesirables" prevailed.* Any broker who violated the implicit rules of the Real Estate Board risked losing his membership and his access to multiple listings. In one case, a broker unable to turn away a buyer with the usual stratagems deliberately clouded title to the house. Missing the irony of his statement, William R. Luedders, the president of the Detroit Real Estate Board, defended the realtors' position, because "it is by the chipping away at such basic rights as that of private property that countries eventually lose their democratic forms of government."[1]

Since employment followed the pattern of housing segregation, up to 60 percent of the work force in the old factories in the city was black. As white workers ceased applying at plants once they "tipped"—just as white parents ceased enrolling their children in schools more than one third black—the percentage

* Suburban Grosse Pointe had developed the most elaborate system in the United States to exclude "undesirables." The property owners association, in conjunction with the brokers association, devised a point system to determine the "eligibility" of prospective buyers. Buyers were rated according to such criteria as swarthiness in appearance, religious affiliation, club membership, accent, neatness, education, conservatism, and whether their "way of living [is] typically American." Negroes, Mexicans, and Orientals were excluded automatically. A "passing grade," in general, was 50 out of a possible 100 points. Southern Europeans, however, had to score 65 points. For Jews, who almost invariably were able to "pass," the acceptance grade was raised to 85 points—a level that excluded a half-Jewish doctor who was a descendant of one of the signers of the Declaration of Independence. Jews had difficulty purchasing homes from more than half the brokers in the Detroit metropolitan area.

of Negroes in industry within the city continued to rise. But since it was the older, marginally efficient plants that were bearing the brunt of economic downturns and foreign competition, the black workers were the most severely affected by the recessions.

Conversely in the new suburban plants, Negroes could be counted on one's fingers. There were 20 Negroes out of a work force of 2,384 at the General Motors Fisher Body Plant in Livonia, and 6 out of 4,153 at the General Motors Technical Center.

For decades the downriver chemical industry, bowing to the prejudices of its white employees, had excluded Negroes. By the 1960's, when pressure was placed upon the industry to open jobs to Negroes, employment was declining. Hundreds of whites, who had seniority and had to be rehired before any new workers could be taken on, were idle because jobs had been eliminated by automation and repeated recessions.

In the third generation of the automobile industry, Negroes continued to be stuck in the lowest-grade jobs and excluded from professional, supervisory, white-collar, and skilled positions. Twenty-three percent of General Motors employees in the Detroit area were Negro, but of 11,125 skilled workers, only 67 were black; of 775 workers in a preparatory program for skilled jobs, 10 were black. Twenty-six percent of Chrysler employees were Negro. But of 7,425 in skilled jobs, 24 were black; of 3,000 in clerical positions, 10 were black; and of 1,890 engineers, none was black. Forty percent of Ford employees at River Rouge were Negro. But of 7,000 in skilled categories, fewer than 250 were black. Altogether, Negroes made up ½ of 1 percent of skilled craftsmen.

Every year, 2,000 unskilled and semiskilled jobs were disappearing in Detroit, while 20,000 more eighteen- to twenty-one-year-olds entered the labor market. Mayor Cavanagh pleaded with the unions to open up jobs to Negroes. But Walter Reuther himself was unable to pry open the doors of the skilled unions within the United Auto Workers.* Continuing to suffer from the trauma of the Depression, unions attempted to wall themselves off from competition by restricting membership. To be accepted in the city's apprenticeship training school, a youth had to go to the joint apprenticeship board of the trade in which he was interested and obtain a declaration that there would be a job for him after he finished school. To exclude "outsiders" all the board had to do was say no jobs were open—no jobs, no training; no training, no jobs. In 1960, out of 2,626 apprentices in the Detroit metropolitan area, 68 were black—8 fewer than in 1950. General Motors and Chrysler each had a single Negro apprentice. The vice-president for industrial relations of the Burroughs Corporation could not recall his company having had any.

Only slightly more than a fourth of black job seekers had graduated from high school. Yet there was an intimate correlation between employment and education. Ford required at least a tenth-grade education and a C average for its apprenticeship training program, and General Motors demanded a high school diploma—Henry Ford or Thomas Edison would not have been eligible for either.

Two thirds of the unemployed were dropouts. But in the inner city high

---

* Only 1.5 percent of tool-and-die workers were black; .5 percent of structural steel workers; .9 percent of printing craftsmen; .2 percent of carpenters; 2.1 percent of electricians; and 5.2 percent of machinists and job setters.

schools between 55 and 60 percent of the students were dropping out. Many of those who did receive their diplomas were graduated mostly for "good behavior." (Nevertheless, the record of the children of Negro migrants was better than the record of the children of foreign immigrants—a fact that reflected English-speaking ability and the improvements that had taken place in teachers and schools.)

The average sixteen-year-old in the Wayne County Youth Home was over four years behind in reading ability. It was not uncommon for a high school graduate to be reading at the sixth-grade level. Yet even a job as a service-station attendant required seventh-grade reading ability.

"The majority of these children," said Judge James Lincoln of the Juvenile Court, "face almost certain failure. If I could tell these kids you have to stay on the job if you're on probation, we might make a dent. But I can't tell a boy he's got to have a job when there aren't any jobs. The child labor laws that were passed to protect children are now cruel. A seventeen-year-old can work on moving equipment in training school, he can join the army and become a truck driver, but the law says he can't do it in industry. So he's out on the streets. I had a boy out of training school. He was on a crappy thirty-five-dollar-a-week job. For eight months he stayed out of trouble. The job was eliminated. Three weeks later he was in a holdup." [2]

The economy was the ship on which the people traveled. And with the economy full of holes, it was the inner city's blacks, traveling in steerage, who were drowning. There was a direct relationship between employment and family breakup—half the husbands in young black families were unemployed, and between one third and one fourth of the fathers were missing from the home. There was a direct relationship between the economy and the percentage of Negroes on welfare—even in better times three fourths of welfare rolls were made up of Negroes; in recession the proportion went over 80 percent. The city's whites thought of Detroit as "the best town for Negroes in the United States," but in fact it was almost exactly average. It did have one negative distinction. Of sixty-eight cities surveyed by the Urban League, it had the highest black unemployment rate.*

While the "white" economy was giving every indication of an upswing, the number of jobs provided by the recovery for the people at the bottom lagged as usual, and the gap between white and black was widening. During the 1950's income in the inner city failed even to keep pace with the rise in the cost of living.†

Out of the turmoil of dissatisfaction in the Negro, community a new grass-roots leadership was emerging. For a half century the Negro intelligentsia had chipped away at discrimination through an alliance with liberal whites. The new militants, however, regarded the Urban League and the NAACP as having "gone white" in their pursuit of middle-class aims and lost touch with the poverty-crusted black masses.

Ever since a Negro minister named Dr. Martin Luther King had promoted a successful boycott of the Montgomery, Alabama, bus system in 1955, the

---

* The city was thirty-third in median family income, thirty-third in infant mortality, thirtieth in the number of dropouts, and twenty-seventh in employment commensurate with training (an index of discrimination).
† Nationally, the median family income of whites increased by $3,400 between 1947 and 1963, while that of blacks rose but $1,850.

focus of the black struggle for equal rights had been on the South. In early May, 1963, Negroes were demonstrating in Birmingham, Alabama, against continuing economic discrimination. When the police chief, Bull Connor, sicked his dogs on the marchers, television carried the picture all over the United States.

The Birmingham events catalyzed the Detroit Council for Human Rights, the new grass-roots Negro organization, into planning a march of its own. Asserting that "the same basic, underlying causes for the disturbance are still present," the council's chairman, the Reverend Clarence Franklin, scheduled a "Walk to Freedom" for Sunday, June 23, 1963, to commemorate the twentieth anniversary of the Detroit riot. It was "a warning to the city that what has transpired in the past is no longer acceptable to the Negro community. We want complete amelioration of all injustices." [3]

The old-line civil rights leadership was aghast. They viewed the council as upstarts and took the position that the riot was not an event to commemorate. At first most of them indicated that they would not participate. In light of what was happening in the South, many people believed such a march could get out of hand and provoke another riot.

Mayor Cavanagh, discussing with his advisers how to respond to the Reverend Clarence Franklin, saw the march as no threat to himself. If it was no threat, then why not preempt it? Redirect it from a march of protest into one of affirmation for the rights of Negroes. Calling upon all citizens and organizations of good will to participate, he declared that he himself would serve as one of the leaders of the march. Dr. King also agreed to participate.

In the heat of midafternoon the marchers gathered on Woodward Avenue, a mile from the civic center. With banners and signs they surged, 125,000 strong, down the broad avenue toward the riverfront. Not since the days of the Depression had the city seen a demonstration like it. Fifteen thousand crowded into Cobo Hall, and there, in his resonant, theatrical voice, the Reverend Dr. King revealed "a dream." In that dream white men and Negroes had been "walking together, hand in hand, free at last, free at last." [4]

100

An Unconditional War on Poverty

CONDITIONS IN OTHER NORTHERN AND WESTERN CITIES, TO WHICH NEGROES were migrating at a rate of 150,000 a year, were no better. The *eminence grise* among Negro leaders, A. Philip Randolph, whose threat of a March on Washington in 1941 had led to President Roosevelt's antidiscrimination order, was calling for the organization of a new march.

President Kennedy was apprehensive, and at first opposed the march. But after observing events in Detroit and talking with Mayor Cavanagh, administration officials decided to follow Cavanagh's example and identify themselves with the march. On the steps of the Lincoln Memorial in August, Dr. King once more recounted the "dream" that had been accorded a rousing reception in Detroit.

The march added a note of urgency to the deliberations of the "Saturday Club," * an informal group of Kennedy Administration officials who were attempting simultaneously to educate themselves and to answer President Kennedy's question: "What about the poverty problem in the United States?" By May a number of Walter Heller's staff on the Council of Economic Advisers had prepared an analysis that showed that "upward mobility" in the economy had slowed to a crawl. Between 1956 and 1961 the number of families with incomes under three thousand dollars—the accepted poverty line —had increased.† In the Northeastern-Midwestern industrial belt, the number of people earning less than three thousand dollars was rising. Professional and skilled workers, clerical and sales personnel, and strongly unionized workers were increasing their incomes at a much faster pace than laborers, service workers, and farm workers. The top 40 percent of the population, the affluent Americans, continued to receive two thirds of all income; the bottom 40 percent one seventh of total income.

Analyzing statistics was one matter. Applying statistics to the individual and devising programs to aid him was quite another.

* So named because they met on Saturdays.
† The *proportion* of families in poverty had declined slightly, however, from 23 to 21 percent.

The administration's primary effort to penetrate directly into the poverty jungle was through its juvenile delinquency program. Various versions of a measure to deal with juvenile delinquency had been introduced in Congress during the latter 1950's, but President Eisenhower had not regarded them as priority legislation. In contrast, President Kennedy's Attorney-General, Robert Kennedy, was determined to come to grips with the problem of delinquency. In September, 1961, Congress passed the Juvenile Delinquency and Youth Offenses Control Act, designed to focus the efforts of a spectrum of government and community agencies on youth.

In Detroit, which was one of sixteen cities funded, the juvenile delinquency program came under the purview of Richard Strichartz, who had taken on the role of the "Federal man" in the Cavanagh Administration. Since the city had been turned down by the Ford Foundation for a "gray areas" grant, Strichartz was hoping to supplement the city's resources through the yet largely nebulous Federal-city partnership.

Strichartz found that there was no coordination among agencies and no unified approach. Facilities were lacking. "The vast majority of troubled youth [were] currently receiving only token, or makeshift assistance." [1] The juvenile was handled, mishandled, and buffeted between the *city* police department, the *county* Juvenile Court, the school system's psychological clinic, three—city, county, and state—welfare departments, thirty-three children's agencies, and between seventy and one hundred social service agencies. The Community Action for Detroit Youth (CADY) program pieced together by the city proposed to establish "community intervention teams" to bring about a measure of coordination. These teams would be brought into contact with a youth when he was picked up by the police and assume supervision over him on his return to the community.

Inevitably, some of the agencies felt that their jurisdictions were being infringed upon and reacted with a passive campaign of noncooperation. Not only was the proposal for the program written with rose-colored ink, but its authors were as ignorant of the facts of social and family disorganization among the poverty population as the devisers of the Great Cities program. There was no realistic assessment about the effort and costs that would be involved in dealing with the poor. Though CADY was to be limited to the Tenth Police Precinct, which had the highest crime rate and included the Twelfth Street area, the proposed funding of $190,000 was so inadequate as to presage the program's failure. Washington was dismayed by a presentation that included such social science gobbledygook as "educational expediters," and proposed to create paralegal "neighborhood lawyers"—which smacked of "jailhouse lawyers." Yet Detroit's proposal was in many ways typical of those being received from other cities.

It was in this atmosphere of disappointing returns from the juvenile delinquency program that the Saturday Club labored. In addition to the regular participants, people from a variety of government departments and agencies drifted in and out. The project still had not progressed beyond its weekend status on October 20, 1963, when an article by *New York Times* writer Homer Bigart graphically depicted the poverty and blight in eastern Kentucky. President Kennedy was so upset that he ordered emergency Federal aid for the region.

William Capron, a staff member of the Council of Economic Advisers, sent memoranda asking for ideas and suggestions to all relevant government agencies and departments. He got back, in his words, "a file drawer full of crap. Warmed-over proposals, dying ducks shot down over and over, a mess of bureaucratic hash." [2]

Locking themselves in a conference room, members of the Saturday Club sifted through the material. By the first week in November they developed a memorandum, euphemistically titled "Widening Participation in Prosperity," for the signatures of Walter Heller and Budget Director Kermit Gordon. A meeting was arranged with Theodore Sorensen, President Kennedy's aide, in his White House office.* It became evident that no one had any idea of what should be done or how. Even agreement on principles was lacking. The problem of organizing programs cutting across the tangle of Federal agencies made it impossible to talk about proposals. Sorensen was disgusted.

In view of the confusion and the fact that an attack on poverty was not likely to win many votes, Heller asked President Kennedy on November 19 whether he wanted the project pursued. The President replied that he did: that he intended to make remedial action against poverty part of his 1964 legislative program.

Friday, November 22, was set aside for a total review by the combined Council of Economic Advisers-Budget Bureau group working on the problem. Several members were returning from lunch when they encountered a messenger, rushing down the gloomy corridors of the Executive Office Building.

"The President has been shot!" he exclaimed.

The next day Heller mentioned to the new President, Lyndon B. Johnson, that preparations were under way for a campaign against poverty. Johnson, who had not previously been informed, declared: "That's my kind of program . . . full speed ahead." [3]

Instead of "full speed ahead," however, the participants tacked this way, then that, as they continued to grope for a course of action. It was nearly mid-December before the Budget Bureau's William Cannon, once more sifting through the stacks of papers, was struck by the idea of an "umbrella agency" to coordinate programs. The umbrella agency had been devised by the Ford Foundation in its "gray areas" program to tie together the multitude of competing and often conflicting programs in each community.† Cannon suggested that "development corporations" be established in ten "pockets of poverty" to initiate demonstration projects.

Since Budget Director Gordon and Council of Economic Advisers Chairman Heller were skeptical, Paul Ylvisaker, the Ford Foundation's director of public affairs programs, was asked to give a presentation on his experiences. Ylvisaker convinced Gordon and Heller. They in turn took the concept of a program of "community action" to President Johnson. Localities were to organize nonprofit corporations through which the Federal government could channel assistance to deal with the problems of poverty.

---

* Included in the meeting were the Secretaries of Labor, and of Health, Education, and Welfare (Willard Wirtz and Anthony Celebrezze), and Housing and Home Finance Agency Director Robert Weaver.
† David Hackett, Attorney-General Robert Kennedy's delegate to the Saturday Club, had written three memoranda suggesting the adoption of the umbrella agency concept by the Federal government.

President Johnson accepted the concept. In his January, 1964, State of the Union message, he announced that he was "declaring an unconditional war on poverty in America."

It was one thing to declare unconditional war. It was another to fight it. The President had established Poverty as the enemy. But what resources were to be mobilized to attack it and who was to lead the effort were undetermined. The Department of Health, Education, and Welfare was momentarily considered as the coordinating agency, but then eliminated. For HEW was not so much a department as a department store. Each bureau went its own way, and each Secretary of HEW was forced to struggle to establish even a semblance of control. On one point there was near unanimity among the men working to develop an antipoverty program: the existing Federal agencies and departments were failing and in many ways irrelevant to the problems, just as the private social agencies were failing. During his years in the Senate President Johnson had come to distrust the competency of other people and to believe that only those projects over which he kept personal control were likely to be carried out well. He decided to establish the Office of Economic Opportunity as part of the Executive Office of the President. On February 1, 1964, he announced that the late President's brother-in-law, Sargent Shriver, would head the new office. As director of the Peace Corps, Shriver had established a reputation as a "doer."

On Tuesday, February 4, the organizers of the antipoverty program gathered in the Peace Corps conference room. Once again all the government participants, plus selected outsiders like Ylvisaker and author Michael Harrington, came together. Several of the men who were veterans of the juvenile delinquency program advocated a year of careful planning prior to the inception of operating programs. They, together with Gordon and most of the Budget Bureau people, thought of the Office of Economic Opportunity (OEO) as a coordinating, not an operating agency. As a direct arm of the President its function would be to pull the programs together, monitor them, and end the chaos, inefficiency, and bureaucratic drag within the Federal government.

The expectations of the planners, however, were in conflict with the intentions of the politicians. The 1964 election was not far off. The President wanted to see the program in action as speedily as possible, and he wanted direct control. Neither a long planning period nor a limited number of demonstration areas could produce political capital. Instead, the War Against Poverty, with a projected annual budget of $500 million, was to get under way as soon as possible in as many places as feasible—once again the government was setting out on a confused path of dribbling money here and dribbling it there instead of concentrating it where it was most needed. And Shriver, who declared, "I don't intend to spend my time in Washington jabbing my elbow into other people's ribs," was not a man willing merely to monitor and coordinate the actions of other officials.[4]

The conflict between the existing departments and the neonate OEO manifested itself immediately. Budget Director Gordon considered the Department of Labor to be "in a state of semiparalysis." The Employment Security Service was controlled by the states, and all but inactive in the poverty areas of the inner city. The Bureau of Apprenticeship Training had become a sinecure for old union war-horses who could be depended upon to protect the restrictive apprenticeship policies of the unions. Few of the hard-core unemployed were being retrained under the Manpower Development and Training Act. More than half the trainees were high school graduates, nearly one in ten had had some college, and only one in seven had had merely a grade school education. No more than one in five was black. In many cases the jobs they were being retrained for were obsolescent, and in some areas they did not exist.

In the Department of Health, Education, and Welfare, the Children's Bureau was afflicted with hardening of the bureaucratic arteries, and had little relevance to the society of the 1960's. The Office of Education was a captive of the National Education Association, which opposed anything that threatened the status quo. (A proposal to establish a system to rate the effectiveness of different schools, teachers, and education methods was killed forthwith.) The Public Health Service was so closely connected to the American Medical Association that it was sometimes difficult to tell whether it was subordinate to the President of the United States or to the president of the A.M.A.*

Even as in Detroit city council members had established long-standing liaisons with bureaucrats in the various departments, so in the Federal government the chairmen of congressional committees wielded immense influence over the diverse departments and agencies. While Presidents came and went, the congressmen and the bureaucrats remained. Every civil servant knew that cooperation with the members of the committee upon which his agency depended for funds could be of signal importance to his career. And every secretary who took over a department was soon aware that the committee chairman knew more about the department—its operations, its personnel, its skeletons, and not infrequently its current goings-on—than he did.

Shriver, therefore, made up his mind to establish an entirely new structure. He would bypass not only the old-line Federal agencies but also the existing *state* agencies, who were even less highly regarded. Federal aid would be channeled directly to the cities and to the people. At the local level it would be disbursed through the independent community action agencies. The maternalism of social welfare agencies had fallen into as much disrepute as the paternalism of industrial concerns a half century earlier, and much discussion revolved about what could be done to give the people themselves greater voice in and control over the programs. As the experiences of the Peace Corps, the Appalachian volunteers, and the Ford Foundation's Mobilization for Youth program were blended together, Richard Boone came up with the phrase "maximum feasible participation" of the poor.† No one was quite certain what this meant or entailed, or to what degree it was practical; but for the moment that was unimportant. It seemed a step in the right direction.

The participants in the organization of OEO were thus working to bring to an end the Federal system that President Hoover had insisted must be protected at all cost—destitution, hunger, even the risk of revolution. The

---

* After President Kennedy announced the program of crash aid for the people of Appalachia, Sorensen called the Public Health bureaucrats to a meeting in the White House Cabinet Room to tell them that the President wanted them to provide direct services to the children in Appalachia. The Public Health people replied that they couldn't do that, because it would be a violation of the separation between private and public medicine. The more Sorensen insisted, the more they resisted. He finally delivered a stinging lecture that the PHS was not some independent barony within the Federal establishment, but was subject to the direction of the President. Whether the lecture had more than a momentary shock effect, however, is doubtful.[5]
† Boone was a former Cook County, Illinois, police captain who had joined the Ford Foundation's juvenile delinquency program.

Civil War and the evolution from a rural to an industrial society had brought about the first shift of power toward Washington. The telegraph and telephone, the railroad and the highway had woven together the myriad communities set amid a vast expanse of land. A system of government designed to serve the needs of a geographically isolated and parochial people was archaic, and often cumbersome and inefficient. Recognizing the new reality, President Franklin D. Roosevelt had steered the Federal government on a pragmatic course that had broken down the old separations between national and local government while largely preserving the old forms. The effect of the Depression and of World War II had been to expand the Federal government to an elephantine size and establish its controlling influence over the economy. But nothing since the Constitutional Convention quite matched the revolution that was progressing in the conference room of the Peace Corps.

By shaping OEO as both an operating agency and a coordinating agency, Shriver intended to inject vitality and élan into the "war" against poverty. Nevertheless, by bringing OEO into competition and conflict with the old-line agencies, he also diluted its potential influence and control, and risked making it but one more segment of the Federal establishment's "overlapping, duplication, backbiting, competition, conceit, and bureaucratic rigidity." [6]

Secretary of Labor Willard Wirtz was disturbed by the undermining of his department's control over manpower programs. He contended that the key to the problem of poverty was jobs, and he was unable to see how the antipoverty program was going to generate those jobs. The massive employment program he advocated was, however, impractical from a budgetary standpoint —in exchange for the passage of the tax cut, the administration had had to promise Harry Byrd, chairman of the Senate Finance Committee, to keep the budget below one hundred billion dollars. HEW Secretary Celebrezze disrupted one meeting, at which the suggestion was made to include a modest family planning component, with a forty-five-minute lecture on the evils of birth control.

The programs that finally were brought together under the OEO umbrella were a mixture of old and new, rejuvenations and innovations. The idea for a "domestic peace corps" was implemented in VISTA (Volunteers in Service to America). The proposal for a Youth Conservation Corps, patterned on the New Deal CCC, was translated into the Job Corps.* The aim of the Job Corps was to take the sixteen- to twenty-one-year-old dropouts and hard-core unemployed and channel them into conservation work while simultaneously training them for skilled jobs or a return to school. (Both Shriver and the President believed that the Job Corps would lead to a dramatic and highly "visible" reduction of unemployment and juvenile delinquency in the cities.) "Community action" was intended to stimulate local effort, local organization, local innovation, and to permit individual communities to tailor Federal assistance to their own needs. But even its most ardent advocates had only a foggy notion of how community action was to work.

Shriver was thus shaping OEO to bypass the states, which had always been the intermediaries between the Federal government and the citizens. The relationship between the states and the central government was the backbone of

* The establishment of a Youth Conservation Corps had first been proposed by Senator Hubert Humphrey and Representative John Blatnik of Minnesota during the Eisenhower Administration.

the Federal system. But the people involved in the organization of OEO—all of them civil libertarians—feared that if the system did not provide direct delivery of funds to the needy, the experience of the agricultural subsidies would be repeated. Negroes would not receive a fair share of the money. The establishment of Community Action Agencies fashioned a detour around not only state but local governments. It laid the basis for the creation of a new "power structure" of the poor. Jump-wiring the Federal system, OEO was constructing a direct connection between the central government and the people; a connection that threatened to make all the intermediate governmental bodies irrelevant.

101

A Social Portrait

IN FORMULATING THE PROGRAM, SHRIVER DREW ON ALL THE URBAN EXPERTISE available. Within a month he assembled officials from ten major cities. Strichartz came from Detroit. Asked how much he thought Detroit could use the first year, Strichartz said $15 million, perhaps even $20 million, tripling the figure Mayor Cavanagh had pulled out of his hat.

Even the maximum amount would be only a small addition to a city budget of $350 million, but the fact that it would be "free money," not committed to any specific department or to routine operations, multiplied its importance. Since funds from several other Federal sources were drying up, Cavanagh and Strichartz were even more anxious to plunge the city into the antipoverty program. The juvenile delinquency program was dead. So was Area Redevelopment, which had helped construct badly needed new hotel and motel facilities downtown, and additions to the library and museum. It had proven to be, Cavanagh said, "a bonanza to the private contractors and the urban construction industry and building trades people." But, like the PWA of Harold Ickes, "it did very little to reduce hard-core unemployment." [1] New York City Republican Congressman John Lindsay charged that the "program has utterly failed . . . leaving in its wake a shameful record of mismanagement, stodginess, and waste," and helped fellow Republicans and conservative Democrats to kill it. [2]

To prepare the ground for Detroit's participation in the antipoverty program and to write the application, Strichartz chose Robert Roselle and Harold Black of the Community Renewal Program.

Community Renewal had had its genesis in Detroit in 1953, immediately after Charles Blessing had become director of the planning commission. Detroit, like cities throughout the country, had no system for collecting data, and the government was in ignorance of what was occurring in the city. Blessing initiated a series of neighborhood studies to determine blight, property values, and land use. Three years later, when the study was completed, he was asked by U. S.

Urban Renewal Commissioner Dick Steiner, a former schoolmate at MIT, to bring the results to Washington. By then, the chaotic, hit-and-miss implementation of urban renewal throughout the nation was apparent. The cities needed to be given the capability to conduct research and analyses, a capability which, hopefully, would lead to comprehensive planning. In the Housing Act of 1959, Congress authorized funds for Community Renewal on a matching basis of two dollars in Federal contribution to each dollar of local money. Detroit's program, funded in June of 1962 with a grant of $900,000, was the largest in the nation.

Before coming to Detroit, Blessing had been regional planning engineer for the Greater Boston Development Committee and director of Chicago's master plan commission. He had served two terms as chairman of the urban design committee of the American Institute of Architects, one term as chairman of the city planning division of the American Society of Civil Engineers, and two terms as president of the American Institute of Planning. He had a reputation unmatched in the planning field. But planning departments, as conceived by urban planners, were all but obsolete by the time they were established. To make possible the implementation of Detroit's master plan would have required another 1805 fire, so that the city could be rebuilt from the ground up. Gathering dust, the master plan became more outdated with each passing day. In his frustration, Blessing set his staff to work drawing up a new master plan —a never-ending labor that was looked upon by some as an exercise in urban science-fiction.

A visionary and a perfectionist, Blessing like most urban planners did not concern himself with social aspects, but looked upon the city as a physical framework in which people were to fit. (Later his perspective was to undergo considerable change.) He disliked politicians. But within a short time of Cavanagh's accession to the mayoralty, Richard Strichartz was coming into Blessing's office and demanding that the planning department concern itself with the immediate needs of the city. The whipcracker in the administration, Strichartz was gaining a reputation as "the son of a bitch on the eleventh floor."

To implement its policies, the Cavanagh Administration needed to find sympathetic bureaucrats in the old-line departments. In the planning department Harold Black came to Strichartz's attention. With his sociological orientation, Black, who headed the department's research division, had come to be more and more at odds with Blessing.

Having initiated the Community Renewal Program, Blessing expected it to be made part of the planning department. Cavanagh, however, intended to use it to come to grips with the social problems. He saw it—as President Johnson regarded OEO—as an opportunity for the executive to establish a new agency over which he would have direct control. In the city's efforts to obtain Federal funds, the Community Renewal Program could be a vital element.

Blessing already was engaged with Housing Commissioner Bob Knox in one of the more celebrated feuds in the city's history. (With his antipathy for politicians, Blessing could get up a real hatred for Knox, who always had an eye on the political capital to be gained from a decision.) Since the Federal Housing and Home Finance Agency was supplying the funds for the Community Renewal Program (CRP), Knox contended that the CRP should be under the control of the housing department. Blessing vigorously opposed him. Cavanagh used the dispute to yank the CRP away from both men and place it under the jurisdiction of a committee headed by the controller, Al Pelham.

In November, 1962, Pelham called in Robert Roselle, the head governmental analyst in the budget bureau, and asked him if he would like to become head of the Community Renewal Program. Roselle said he wasn't sure. In fact, he didn't know what CRP stood for, or what it was supposed to do.

During the next few days he talked to the planning staff, found out, and was appointed director. Thirty-five years old, of German Lutheran descent, Roselle was the son of an auto worker, and the family had experienced all the trauma of the Depression. While attending Wayne State University in 1947, Roselle had applied for a job as payroll clerk with the Street Railway system. The clerk who was handing out the examination papers had told him that, since he had no experience, there was no point in his taking the test. Only when Roselle insisted did the clerk grudgingly thrust the papers at him—with Civil Service it was almost standard procedure to send people away unless they put up some kind of argument. Like hundreds of other city workers, Roselle was disenchanted with Civil Service—even while Civil Service projected itself as the champion of the interest of municipal employees.*

With Harold Black joining him as assistant director of the Community Renewal Program, Roselle undertook a street-by-street research of the city's thirteen thousand blocks. When Cavanagh returned from one of his trips to Washington, the mayor called the heads of various departments together and told them: "There's a new term they're using. Social Renewal. And no one knows what it is. I'd like to have each of you do a paper on what it means." [3]

So *social renewal,* in effect the rehabilitation of the city's "poor and huddled masses," was added to the urban lexicon, and became part of the CRP study. In February, 1964, the CRP applied for and received a further grant of $175,000 from the Federal government. A consulting firm, Greenleigh Associates, was retained to conduct a survey of inner city families.

During the spring and summer of 1964, while the antipoverty bill was being debated in Congress, Strichartz, Roselle, and Black made trip after trip to Washington. Roselle and Black worked hand in hand with the OEO staff in Washington to draw up the proposal for the city's program, and were even given an office in the Urban Renewal Agency. In the meantime, interviewers from Greenleigh were going from door to door. From a total of 2,081 families, the first such intensive survey of a poverty area ever undertaken, they drew a social portrait of the "old city" within Grand Boulevard and along the riverfront.

Although the combination of the Kennedy Administration's economic meaures and the introduction of compact cars by the Big Three had brought about a dramatic upsurge in automobile production, the effect on families living in the poverty area was negligible. While Detroit's official unemployment rate fell from 10.9 to 4.3 per cent between 1961 and 1964, in the poverty area

---

* Later Roselle was informed that he had failed an examination for junior accountant. When he challenged the result, he found out that he had been failed *automatically* because he lacked a degree. Since the city in fact did not require a degree if the applicant were already in municipal employ, Roselle interviewed for a job in the Budget Bureau and was hired.

Negroes, less articulate and less skilled in handling such rejections, were especially affected by these Civil Service practices. They naturally viewed the rejections as due to racial bias.

2 persons remained unemployed for every 5 who were employed—an effective unemployment rate of 30 percent. In many cases the businesses they had worked for had moved out of the city or no longer existed. Forty percent of families had an income of less than $3,000 annually, and only 17 percent received more than $6,000—considered by the Labor Department the minimum adequate budget for a family of four in Detroit.*

Almost one out of four families was receiving public assistance. But it was clear that many more, entitled to welfare aid, were not receiving it, either because they did not know their rights or did not want to subject themselves to the humiliation the system imposed. Most of the recipients were long-time residents in the city—better than 99 percent had lived in Detroit more than five years, and 93 percent had lived there more than ten years.†

Almost without exception, the houses in which they lived were blighted. Seventy percent required major repairs to the basic structure or were beyond repair. Because of deteriorated wiring and heating devices, crumbling floors and stairs, and infestations by rats and vermin, two of every five houses were health and safety hazards. The economics of the inner city were such, however, that it was unfeasible to make repairs. Since plumbers, carpenters, and electricians earned five dollars an hour and more, repair costs were more than the value of the houses warranted. For owners of rental property, repairs would produce no economic gain—in a poverty area property in mint condition did not command much more rent than property in a state of advanced dilapidation. (A new house built in the area would, on the date of its completion, have been worth several thousand dollars less than it had cost to build.)

Therefore, those people whose economic condition improved did not fix up; they moved out. Like tens of thousands of automobiles that were yearly towed to the city's junkyards, thousands of houses were long past the day when they should have been treated as "junkers."

Inadequate housing contributed to the health problems of the people. But the Wayne County Medical Society opposed privately financed general-care medical programs, the expansion of government health programs, and even free medical treatment for schoolchildren. (Many individual physicians disagreed with the society's position.) In nearly three out of five households adults had chronic illnesses—tuberculosis and respiratory diseases, arteriosclerosis and heart conditions, arthritis, diabetes, and cancer. Yet a fourth of the ill were receiving no treatment—either because it was too expensive or too difficult to obtain. A muscular distrophy victim was supposed to be receiving regular checkups at General Hospital, but since he had to be there by seven thirty in the morning and usually was not seen until late in the afternoon —a delay that left him exhausted—he did not go. A seventy-five-year-old

* Most of those employed had marginal incomes—17.4 percent earned less than $3,000, and only 26 percent earned more than $6,000. In comparison to an annual per capita income of $2,416 in the state, whites in the inner city had a per capita income of $1,056, and Negroes a per capita income of $816. Among larger families—and Negro families were, in general, larger—the per capita income dropped as low at $444.

† Although 93 percent of the blacks and 75 percent of the whites had been born elsewhere, over 90 percent of both had lived in Detroit more than ten years. Most blacks had been born in the South. Among whites, migrants from the South and from foreign countries were almost equally divided, 28 percent from the South and 20 percent from overseas. Many of the foreign-born were long-time residents who had bought homes and settled in the inner city, and lacked the income to move out.

widow with a heart condition and rotting teeth was living on a sixty-dollar-a-month Social Security check. Treatment by a private physician, at eight dollars a visit, had exhausted the twenty-one hundred dollars she had had in savings. He had told her not to come back until she had more money, and she did not know where else she could turn.

The poorer people, if they were willing to put up with the insults, day-long waits, and cattlelike treatment, could obtain care at General Hospital. But those whose incomes were marginally higher were not eligible for treatment at a public clinic, and private medical care was a luxury they commonly could not afford. Thus, while chronic health conditions were going untreated in 28 percent of families with incomes under $3,000, they were also going untreated in 21 percent of families with incomes over $6,000.

As the problems reacted upon and reinforced each other, they created an area not only of economic depression, but mental depression. In more than one fifth of the households there were adults with mental problems, problems for which little medical help was available. Over 72 percent were not receiving treatment.

The lower the income, the more severe were the problems. The people on public assistance had the most aggravated problems. And the people with the most aggravated problems tended to have the most troubled children.

Two parents, legally married, were present in but one third of households on public assistance. One fourth of households with incomes under $3,000 had illegitimate children, twice as many as households with incomes over $6,000. Thirty-six percent of households on welfare had illegitimate children, three times as many as those not on welfare. Contrary to the common conception that welfare mothers wanted more children, they desperately wanted to have fewer. While HEW Secretary Celebrezze filibustered against providing birth control information and Superintendent Daniel J. Ryan of the welfare department enforced a see-no-squalor, hear-no-squalling "policy of silence" on his caseworkers, women were in despair because they did not know how to stop having unwanted babies.

The stereotype of the welfare mother having more children to increase her income was a myth—welfare payments never adequately supported either an adult or a child. Welfare payments, however, did take into account the number of persons in the family. So the economic effect of too many children in a family on welfare was less critical than in a family of working parents whose budget was already strained. The effect of one more child on working families was to push them over the brink, sometimes disintegrate them, and not infrequently drive them onto welfare.

The consequence of the lack of birth control information, therefore, was to add an increasing number of families to the welfare rolls.

The consequence of the lack of birth control information, the lack of medical care, the lack of employment, and the lack of income was to impose a life sentence of deprivation upon the children before they were born. *In nearly one out of every eleven families there was a child afflicted with mental retardation—* and some families had more than one. Seven thousand mentally retarded children were in special classes conducted by the Detroit school system—and this number included only those who could derive some benefit from education. Children presented serious behavior problems in 22 percent of the households. In over a third of the families children were having problems in school. Among welfare families, the figure was one in two. One out of every six families had at least one school dropout. An uncounted number of children suffered from malnutrition.

Obviously the antipoverty program would have to concentrate heavily on the young. The school district would have to participate. But when Cavanagh approached Dr. Brownell, the superintendent reacted as if the mayor, with his free-wheeling disdain for precedents and regulations, was carrying a cattle prod in one hand and a lasso in the other. He suspected that the antipoverty program would become a device for the mayor to subvert the independence of the school system. Referring to the Great Cities Program, Dr. Brownell said the schools "have been fighting delinquency all along." If the schools were to be included in the antipoverty program, he wanted the money to come directly from Washington, not through the city.

Yet in some ways the schools were in worse shape than the city. Between 1961 and 1963 the racial composition of the students shifted from 153,000 whites and 131,000 blacks to 151,000 blacks and 141,000 whites. As a consequence, according to Roselle, Dr. Brownell was "finally dragged in kicking and screaming." [4]

102

The Bridging of the Moat

IN FACT, ALTHOUGH IT HAD ITS INDIVIDUAL "SUCCESSES," THE GREAT CITIES Program overall was having a minimum effect. Limited to seven schools, its per pupil expenditure was only forty dollars a year. Realistically, it could not expect to alter the massive community pathology. Within the education system it had to overcome bureaucratic drag, resistance to change, and resentment at innovation. In one school the program was breaking down because the principal, while praising it with pedantic clichés, did not attempt to break down the old barriers and move his teachers in new directions. In another, the principal reported that "many of our teachers are relatively inexperienced and too large a proportion of them have average or below-average abilities. These will very likely never be able to perceive or become interested in the complex problems of a school such as ours." [1]

In all the schools the lack of male teachers was a serious handicap—the boys, coming from female-dominated homes, resented the female domination of classrooms and reacted by developing a precocious, hyperactive, independence-asserting sexuality. Twelve-year-old boys sometimes fought over who could claim a girl in the class for his "old lady." A young and pretty teacher who attempted to develop a rapport with the boys risked having her gesture misinterpreted as a sexual advance.

The school administration, in the natural desire to demonstrate that things were "happening" and that the program merited continuing support, highlighted the successes and glossed over the weaknesses. Expectations were raised unreasonably, so that on the "morning after" what was mild progress was likely to be looked upon as a major failure.

No one knew the limitations of the program better than Dr. Carl Marburger. Young and dynamic, he had been a principal in the school system before assuming charge of Great Cities. Reporting directly to Dr. Brownell, Dr. Marburger was able to operate outside the well-worn channels of the system. He acquired a national reputation and was asked to chair the Disadvantaged Youth Program for all of the Great Cities. In the spring of 1964 Dr. Marburger was invited by Dr. Francis Keppel, U.S. Commissioner of Education, to take a leading role on the departmental task force that was seeking means to maneuver around the traps that for decades had been the downfall of most of the programs for Federal aid to education.

Although President Jefferson had suggested using Federal funds for support of education as early as 1806, not until the Smith-Hughes Vocational Education Act of 1917 had the Federal government begun channeling money to the states. During the 1930's it had slipped aid through the back door; the Federal Emergency Relief Administration had given employment to teachers, and the Public Works Administration had built schools. Commencing in 1950 the government provided assistance to "impacted areas" (school districts in which Federal activities, such as defense bases, generated a large student population but reduced the amount of taxable property). But efforts to use Federal resources to alleviate the lack of school buildings and correct the general shortcomings of American education became snagged on one of the new three r's: race, religion, and Reds.

The racial issue became critical after the Supreme Court's school desegregation decision in 1954. The chairman of the Senate Committee on Labor and Public Welfare was Alabama's Lister Hill, a liberal who no matter what his personal views had to reflect Southern racial mores if he wanted to be reelected. In the committee's hearings on education in 1955, Clarence Mitchell of the NAACP was asked:

"Do you believe the Federal government should provide funds for education to districts refusing to abide by the Brown [desegregation] decision?"

"No," Mitchell replied.[2]

That was that. No Southerner, no matter how strongly he backed education, would vote for a bill that would withhold funds from segregated districts. And few Northern liberals would vote for a bill that did not.

The religious issue, of course, was whether Catholic parochial schools should be allowed to participate in the aid. The issue of "Reds" was raised by states' righters who warned that Federal money would become the means for Federal control of education.

Nevertheless, it was the "Reds" who were responsible for the initial breach of the barricades. When the Russians orbited the first Sputnik in the fall of 1957, Americans were alarmed. President Eisenhower blamed the lag in the nation's space program on the fact that Russian schools were turning out more scientists and engineers than American schools. The result was passage of the National Defense Education Act of 1958, offering financial assistance to schools and students in order to reverse this human "missile gap."

But the act had been precedent breaking rather than precedent setting, and after its passage the impasse reestablished itself. It still existed in February, 1964, when Democratic Senator Wayne Morse of Oregon, chairman of the subcommittee on education, proposed a bill aiding children residing in areas of poverty and substantial unemployment. If assistance could be provided to Federally *impacted* areas, could it not be provided to *poverty impacted* areas as well?

That was the question the Department of Education sought to answer. At first the task force concentrated on the role the schools would play in the antipoverty program, but by summer it was focusing on means to overcome the state-Church impasse on the Morse bill. Dr. Marburger, who came from one of the half dozen cities of greatest Catholic power in the United States, sat in on the "cabinet meetings" of both Keppel and Shriver. Out of these meetings and the deliberations of a group headed by Assistant HEW Secretary Wilbur Cohen, a former University of Michigan professor, a new concept evolved. The aid would not be provided to the schools per se, but to the *children*. If Catholic schools could not be assisted by public funds, Catholic children could.

In the fall of 1964 a "kiddy corps" of experts, focusing on the critical nature of early childhood education, suggested that a summer preschool program for children entering kindergarten be transformed into a national "Project Head Start." In his original memo on Head Start, Jack Conway suggested that what had been a Detroit program for 30 kids be expanded to 50,000.* But the reaction to the Head Start program was so favorable during its first summer of operation in 1965 that Shriver enlarged the enrollment to 356,000, and Head Start became the jewel of OEO.

Marburger's constant companions on his travels back and forth between Detroit and Washington were Strichartz and Roselle. Despite Superintendent Brownell's reluctance, a close liaison developed between the Detroit schools and the city administration. With a grant from the Ford Foundation, Mayor Cavanagh put his energy into organizing the antipoverty program. In April, 1964, he convened a meeting of leaders from the public schools, the Catholic archdiocese, the UAW, the Greater Detroit Employers Association, the Board of Commerce, the three welfare departments, various state departments, and private social agencies. With Strichartz and Roselle supervising the staff work, Cavanagh brought all the diverse elements together for the first time in the city's history. By June they were organized into the Policy Advisory Committee, the city's community action agency for the antipoverty program, which was named TAP (later TAAP)—Total Action Against Poverty. The Policy Advisory Committee (PAC) was established as a forty-one-member body, of which the mayor was chairman. Private and public service agencies were represented by ten members; labor, business, religious, and minority groups by fourteen—all appointed by the mayor. Sixteen members were to be elected by residents of the poverty "target areas." The mayor thus could appoint a comfortable majority of the Policy Advisory Committee—and, if necessary, could exercise a veto power. There was never any question in Detroit, as there was to be in other cities, of the poor taking control of the community action agencies and obtaining power over the disbursement of Federal funds.

The inner city was divided into six target areas—only four of which ultimately became operational. Roselle and Marburger went into the areas, ferreted out community leadership, and urged the residents to organize themselves. By the time the Economic Opportunity Act was passed by Congress in August, 1964, Detroit was the best organized city in the nation. While Congress dragged its heels on appropriating the funds until after President Johnson's defeat of Barry Goldwater, Roselle was all but perched on Shriver's desk.

On November 23 the city received its first grant. At $2.8 million, it was the largest per capita grant and the second largest total grant in the nation. By December 15 the first of the target area centers was in operation. Roselle was appointed director of the Total Action Against Poverty Program and Black moved up to director of the Community Renewal Program.

With the antipoverty program launched, President Johnson in January, 1965,

* Conway was Walter Reuther's administrative assistant, and one of the men involved in the development of the antipoverty program.

sent to Congress his program for "full educational opportunity." Developed by the education task force, the program quintupled the size of that conceived by Senator Morse. It was a program close to the heart of the President, a former schoolteacher who had started his political career in the anti-Depression National Youth Administration, which provided part-time employment for college students. It followed closely the lines of proposals made in 1938 by the U.S. Advisory Committee on Education, appointed by President Roosevelt. In any ordinary year it would probably have stood little chance of passage. But in 1964 the electorate gave the Democrats their most overwhelming victory in history— President Johnson received 61.1 percent of the popular vote compared to 60.8 percent for President Roosevelt in 1936. The landslide produced a 155-vote Democratic majority in the House of Representatives and a 36-vote majority in the Senate. Nearly all the new congressmen were liberals. Voting en bloc, they passed not only the Elementary and Secondary Education Act, providing aid to school districts on the basis of the number of children from families earning less than $2,000,* but the Higher Education Act of 1965. In 1965–1966 they enacted 42 percent of all Federal education programs, and, according to President Johnson, "did more for the wonderful cause of education in America than all the previous one hundred seventy-six regular sessions of Congress did, put together." [3] Ninety-eight years before, the Republicans had succeeded in establishing a United States Department of Education after the conservative, Southern Democrats had seceded and ceased to be a factor in national politics. In 1965, after the conservative Republicans had committed political hara-kiri by making Barry Goldwater the 1964 Republican presidential nominee, the liberal Democrats bridged the moat separating the Federal government from public education.

In the Detroit school system, Dr. Marburger was named Deputy Superintendent for Special Projects—a new position that made him coordinator and overseer of Federally funded projects. Federal educational expenditures, which had been $29 million in 1947 and $273 million in 1957, burgeoned to $4.2 billion by 1968.

---

* There were five "titles" to the act in all. They included support for research, for innovative teaching methods and programs, for books and instructional material, and for measures to strengthen state departments of education. School districts had to coordinate requests for grants with the local Community Action Agencies set up through the antipoverty program.

103

The City of Promise

SUDDENLY, LEGISLATION IN THE FIELDS OF EDUCATION, LABOR, HEALTH (MEDI-care and Medicaid), housing, and pollution control poured out of Congress. The "Great Society" and the "Creative Federalism" partnership between Federal, state and local governments that President Johnson had proclaimed during his delivery of the 1964 commencement address at the University of Michigan was at hand.

The site of the speech had been appropriate, for the mayor who typefied the promise of that Great Society was Detroit's Jerry Cavanagh. President Johnson was pleased by the thirty thousand people the mayor helped turn out at the airport to give him a cheering reception, and asked Cavanagh to fly back to Washington with him. Cavanagh became the only elected official chosen by the President for his Task Force on Urban and Metropolitan Development. (There were fourteen such presidential task forces, designed to suggest programs and legislation for the Great Society. Informal groups that operated under the aegis of the President and reported directly to him, the task forces were an innovation in national politics.) From the Metropolitan Development task force came the recommendation and organizational plan for the new Department of Housing and Urban Development—the agency that was to deal with the affairs of the cities—and many of the concepts that President Johnson presented in his message to Congress on the cities in January, 1965.

The message marked the first time a President directed himself unequivocally and exclusively to the problems of the cities. Mayor Cavanagh interpreted it as the announcement that the Federal-city partnership he had proposed was coming to fruition. Cavanagh's reputation as the spokesman for the cities and as the harbinger of a new era increased. He had been elected when Detroit's and the nation's economies were seemingly suffering from chronic dysfunction, and every day that he occupied the mayor's office Detroit's latest cyclical boom ac-celerated. The Kennedy-Johnson tax reductions, the billion of dollars that the Federal government was pouring into the economy for the Vietnam War, and the compact cars with which the American automobile makers were attempting to counter the imports all played their part. Automotive employment was the highest it had been in a decade. Chrysler, said Cavanagh, had made a "miraculous comeback." * The population flight had been arrested and, Cavanagh believed, even reversed. Although a 1963 study by Thomas F. Hoult and Albert J. Mayer of Wayne State University predicted that by 1970 more than 40 percent of the city's population would be in the economically nonproductive category (under fifteen and over sixty-four years of age), the prediction was regarded by civic leaders as an exaggeration.

As a consequence of the income tax, the economic upsurge boosted the financial health of the municipal government. The mayor announced that the property tax rate was being reduced 5 percent at the same time municipal salaries were being increased 3 percent. Two hundred men were added to the police department, and additional funds were allocated to social programs. The urban renewal programs initiated more than fifteen years before were finally bringing returns—the West Side Industrial Project was filling up, and more high-rise buildings and townhouses were going up in Gratiot-Lafayette Park. The assessed valuation of real estate, after decreasing since 1960, was up for the first time in five years. A period of twenty-five years during which there had been no major private construction downtown was brought to an end by the erection of three spectacularly designed thirty-story skyscrapers—the Pontchartrain Hotel, the Michigan Consolidated Gas Company headquarters, and the National Bank of Detroit Building. Other structures, such as the First Federal Savings Building, were rising to join them. Planning Director Blessing unveiled the $250,000 model he had built of the "dream city"—including a "Versailles-like" cultural center—that was to replace the entire 10,000-acre inner Boulevard area. The Detroit *Free Press* ran a fourteen-by-fourteen-inch full-color overhead view of the model under the headline: "Our New Detroit—An Aerial Spectacular." Suddenly Detroit was the "city on the go" and the "city of tomorrow." Presiding over it all was Jerry the Giant Killer.

During the last week of July, 1965, the National League of Cities gathered in Detroit for its annual convention. Cavanagh had already been chosen vice-president of the U. S. Conference of Mayors—the big-city organization whose founding had been engendered by Mayor Frank Murphy—and would become its president in 1966. Now, amidst a "coronation air" of lighted fountains, spectacular floral displays, and red carpets, Cavanagh was elected president of the National League of Cities—he would be the only man ever to hold the top offices of both organizations simultaneously. Detroit was establishing a computerized "social data bank," he told the mayors, into which statistics would be fed continuously from every block in the city. When a neighborhood began to change, danger signals would "flash" and the city would move in to arrest the blight. The mayor created a vision of the blinking lights and whirring reels of the electronics age applied to the management of the city.

Imaginative, a magnetic conversationalist, Cavanagh held the attention of the mayors and enraptured the press. His wife, Mary, was dazzling even after having given birth to eight children. Master of Ceremonies Bop Hope sat at the mayor's side. Vice-President Hubert Humphrey, the featured speaker and himself a former mayor, praised Cavanagh highly.

---

* In 1965 the factory value of cars and trucks was $22.1 billion, $9.7 billion more than in 1961. The unemployment rate in the Detroit area was down to 3.5 percent, a third of what it had been.

Two weeks after the National League of Cities meeting, the Los Angeles riot erupted. It was the nation's most serious internal upheaval since the Detroit riot of 1943. The summer before had seen a major riot in Harlem. Much of the nation suddenly was aware of an "urban crisis." To the news media that had covered the League of Cities meeting, New York, Los Angeles (and Chicago, Philadelphia, Baltimore, Washington, D.C., and a host of additional cities) seemed to be on one side of the crisis, and Detroit on the other. Detroit had a mayor who had met the crisis and mastered it. While other cities were decaying, Detroit—from the impression the reporters and editors absorbed—was building. While in other cities there was animosity between blacks and whites, in Detroit the white mayor had the approbation of an overwhelming number of the blacks.

In the genial and dynamic Cavanagh the news media had found a hero. Stories spread his fame across the United States. He was cited as "the mayor who knows how." *Time* Magazine said he was "restoring the heart." *Life* picked him as one of the one hundred young men of the "take-over generation." *Look* Magazine featured him as "The mayor who woke up a city." The Washington *Post* editorialized that "Cavanagh has succeeded where other big city mayors have failed." The aura being built around him passed almost beyond the boundaries of mystique into those of magic. One magazine photographer taking pictures of him in the evening atop the roof of the Veterans Memorial Building, with the city in the background, lamented that there were not more lights on in the buildings. Thereupon, it was reported, the mayor whispered to an aide—and the darkness was parted by crystals of light.

"On a clear day," said Fred Romanoff, a long-time associate, "Cavanagh can see the White House." But as he ran for reelection in the fall of 1965, he insisted he had no ambition other than to be mayor for four more years. Walter Shamie, the conservative businessman who ran against him (and only briefly before had acknowledged his inability to package an "international village" of shops and restaurants in the skid row urban renewal area), was little more than a straw opponent. Cavanagh defeated him by a margin of two to one.

At his inauguration in January, Cavanagh proclaimed, "Today we enjoy the greatest prosperity in Detroit's history." In his second term, he said, he would seek to build new dimensions in urban living, he would bring suburban amenities into the city, he would create a network of neighborhood centers—each center having its own special aura to reflect the needs and desires of the people it served. He no longer spoke of the "embattled city," but of "The City of Promise."

How was this City of Promise to be brought into being?

The Greenleigh study spotlighted the confusion in social services. The experiences with public housing and urban renewal were demonstrating the futility of dealing with the physical aspects of the city without a concurrent program for the rehabilitation of people. Federal programs were coming into the city in an uncoordinated jumble. Above all, there was the fact of "not enough"—of a sprinkle here and a sprinkle there of funds that disappeared like raindrops in the sand. Cavanagh had suggested during his participation in the Urban Development task force the selection of one demonstration city. Into this city Federal funds would be poured in massive amounts. The disparate programs would be coordinated. For the first time a city would have the wherewithal to counter the forces of decay. If not *one* city—of course, Detroit—then three: Minneapolis (for Vice-President Humphrey), and Houston (for President Johnson).

That Congress, with its interest blocs and home-district sensitivities, would agree to spend hundreds of millions of dollars of Federal revenues for the special benefit of three American cities was a Candide-like view of the political process. After the President's message on the cities in January, 1965, Cavanagh had declared, "We stand on the threshhold of being Demonstration City, U.S.A." But then, while Detroit was standing on the threshhold, the door seemed to slam, and for months nothing more was heard.

In fact, although the Urban Development task force had been dissolved, a new, "secret" task force had been formed under the direction of Robert Wood, the youthful chairman of the Department of Political Science at MIT. Cavanagh was not on the task force, but Walter Reuther was. While the bill creating the Department of Housing and Urban Development was wending its way through Congress, the task force met on weekends in a small, cramped upstairs room in the West Wing of the White House. Reuther, backed by some of the other members of the task force, kept alive the idea of the "demonstration city." According to Wood, "The President's legislative staff almost died when the issue kept being brought up." Reuther, however, told President Johnson: "We've got to do something on a greater scale." [1] After considerable thought he sent the President a memo suggesting that he pick *ten* cities. Already the concept of concentration was being diluted.

Budget Director Charles L. Schultze was in favor of the demonstration city concept. He had continually urged putting Federal money where it was needed most rather than scattering it about, and was concerned about the lack of coordination of Great Society programs. After the passage of nearly nine months, Mayor Cavanagh was invited to meet with the task force in the White House. Pledged to secrecy—for the President would still not concede that the task force even existed—he was asked to have Detroit's proposal for a "demonstration city" in Washington by the first of December.

The job of readying the proposal in three weeks was given to Strichartz, Black, and Anthony Ripley. (Ripley, a 1950 Harvard graduate, had been hired away from the Detroit *News* a few months before. He was such an excellent writer that one Cavanagh aide thought he "could turn out five Gettysburg addresses in a week.") What they threw together was a grab-bag of generally unrelated requests that chilled many of the city's well-wishers in Washington. The cost added up to $982 million over a 10-year period, most of it for a vastly expanded program of physical construction and reconstruction—$550 million for water and sewer facilities, $204 million for freeways, and $50 million for slum clearance. Included—in a city that had arisen out of a forest—was $4.8 million for the planting of 120,000 shade trees. There were several innovative proposals—the realization of the "computerized city," the joining together of the municipal government and Wayne State University to form an "urban observatory" to study urban problems,* and the establishment of sixteen $7-million "family centers," each to serve a "neighborhood" of 100,000 people.

On January 26, 1966, President Johnson unveiled the idea of the "demonstration city" in a special message to Congress. But instead of $982 million for one city, the President proposed $2.4 billion for sixty or seventy over a six-year period. Cavanagh was disappointed. More and more he was recognizing the realities of the Federal-city partnership, a partnership in which the Federal gov-

* The concept of the "urban observatory" is generally credited to Mayor Henry Maier of Milwaukee.

ernment teased the urban appetite, but never came close to satisfying the hunger.

Cavanagh had reached a climax of power and popularity. But much of the image of a revitalized city was based on illusions. The downtown "building boom" was like the false fronts on a movie set. More office space—55 percent of the total—was being erected in the suburbs than in the city. The city was unable to dispose of additional land it had cleared under urban renewal in the central business district. Except in urban renewal areas, industrial, commercial, and residential construction had all but ceased—70 percent of industrial and 80 percent of commercial construction was outside the city. The mayor was engaged in never-ending efforts to keep the industrial base from eroding further. He convinced General Motors not to remove one of its plants from the city but, instead, to remodel it. By political logrolling he got Chrysler to shoehorn a $15 million foundry into twenty-three acres within the city rather than build in the suburbs.* But there was a limit to how often the mayor could successfully employ his political capital when economic and social factors indicated it was far more profitable to build outside the city than within it.

That was the illusion of the building boom. Then there was the illusion that the mayor somehow was connected with the economic resurgence—the city's economy was utterly dependent upon decisions made in Washington, and in the boardrooms of Ford and Chrysler, General Motors and Fruehauf, Uniroyal and Parke-Davis. There was the illusion that in tapping the Federal well Cavanagh had brought in a gusher that would oil the city with money. There was the illusion that Jerry and Mary were a replica of John and Jackie.

Cavanagh could marvel at how far he had come. From his eleventh floor office he looked at the sparkling lights of the riverfront and Canada. He was driven in one of the limousines supplied to the mayor's office by Chrysler and Ford. He was regularly met in Washington by Henry Ford II's personal car. He attended meetings in the White House and hobnobbed with the "beautiful people." He became a gourmet and a wine connoisseur. To dress appropriately for the new circles in which he moved he wore two-hundred-dollar suits and Italian ties. Mary, similarly, acquired the expensive tastes that befitted her emulation of Jackie.

It was quite a strain on a salary of thirty-five thousand dollars a year. Thirty-five thousand dollars was infinitely more than he had ever earned as a young lawyer, but as a young lawyer he had not yet had eight children, he had not moved in such expensive circles, he had not been expected to send flowers to funerals and presents to weddings.

In 1965 a Lebanese by the name of Manogian donated his $300,000 riverfront mansion to the city for use as the official mayor's residence. But, in January of 1966, Mary publicly balked at making the move to the mansion. She did not want to move away from the vicinity of the Gesu Church, where the children went to parochial school and where she had her friends. She was worried that the mansion was an "impractical home to raise children in" since it had only four bedrooms, in contrast to the eight in their present house. She

---

* Industrialists had been trying for fifteen years to obtain repeal of a state tax on locally assessed personal property such as tools, dies, fixtures, etc. Opposition by the cities, especially Detroit, had killed all attempts at repeal. Cavanagh told Lynn Townsend, president of Chrysler, he would switch his stand and support repeal if the plant were built in the city. The tax was repealed, and the plant was built, but the mayors of other Michigan cities regarded Cavanagh's reversal as little short of heresy.

thought the mansion would be a nice place in which to entertain, but not in which to live. She complained:

"I'm the one who would have to move in with the children. I'm the one who would have to do the work.

"They call my husband—what is it now—yes, a strong mayor. Well, I'm kind of a strong mother."

The glamorous beauty queen and the brilliant and handsome politician who formed the ideal couple—was that an illusion, too?

It was. Mary Cavanagh thought that Jerry spent far too little time with her and the children, and that when he had gained the mayoralty she might have lost a husband. While Jerry was the toast of the city, her life revolved about "Kirche, küche, and kinder." For a year, since shortly after the birth of their eighth child, Mary and Jerry Cavanagh had merely been keeping up appearances. But it was increasingly difficult to continue the pretense. Throughout the adulation and the rocketing to fame, throughout the romanticizing and the stories that failed to probe beyond the outer layer of the city's skin, Cavanagh had not allowed himself to be swept away by the glorification. He retained a remarkable self-deprecatory humor and sense of reality. With reason he had the feeling that "it was too good to last."

If he remained mayor of Detroit for another four years, some and perhaps all of the illusions would most surely vanish. As mayor he had nowhere to go but down. If he were to have a long and rewarding political career, he would do well to move on from Detroit before his domestic troubles became public knowledge. One possibility of moving to Washington had seemed to offer itself in September, 1965, after Congress had passed the bill establishing the Department of Housing and Urban Development (HUD). President Johnson had traced him to a Grand Rapids steak house. Cavanagh took the phone next to the bar. While the mayor shielded his ears against the laughter, music, and clinking of ice, the President asked him to come to dinner at the White House the next evening. But although President Johnson elicited his ideas on HUD and talked around the possibility of appointing a mayor as secretary of the new department, the post ultimately went to Housing and Home Finance Agency Director Robert Weaver, as it generally had been assumed that it would.

That left one other road to Washington open—the 1966 Senate race. G. Mennen Williams had already resigned his State Department post and filed in the Democratic primary. Williams was the most successful Democratic politician in the history of the state. In February, 1966, however, Cavanagh indicated he too might enter the primary.

The Michigan Democratic party leadership was appalled. A primary contest between Williams and Cavanagh would be divisive. It might lead to the Republicans' winning the general election. If Cavanagh had ambitions to move to a higher office—that was fine. Let him run for the governorship against Romney. Williams and Cavanagh together would give the Democrats the strongest state ticket they had ever had.

But a move to Lansing would not give Cavanagh the graceful, long-distance separation from Mary that Washington would. Lansing was not where the action was—the national action affecting the urban scene in which he was knowledgeable. If Williams won the Senate race, liberal Democrats would occupy both Michigan seats in the U. S. Senate, and Cavanagh was afraid that "it might be twenty years before another opportunity came along." [2]

In March he gathered his aides and advisers together. The majority were strongly against his running. Many of the top Democrats—such as George Edwards and Walter Reuther—who had come to be his supporters would back Williams. They would resent being forced into making personal choices. But Cavanagh believed in his instinct. No one had given him a chance in 1961 when he had decided to run for mayor—and he had won. "Look," Strichartz finally said. "We're wasting time: If you want to run—you're going to run." [3]

Williams was a protégé of Frank Murphy. But it was Cavanagh, the Catholic middle-of-the-road liberal, who was cast in the Murphy image. Murphy's long-time friend and executive secretary, Josephine Gomon, was the grande dame of the Michigan Democratic party. Calling Cavanagh on the telephone, she asked: "What about the Vietnam War?"

Cavanagh's impulse was to say, "What about it?" He had never given it much thought. Like nineteen out of twenty Americans, he had gone along with President Johnson's policies. During the President's first nine months in office, Johnson had been praised for his domestic accomplishments, but criticized for not paying more attention to foreign policy, and for allowing the war to drag on toward what seemed an inevitable Communist victory. Johnson did not want to go down in history as "the President who had lost Vietnam," and when the Gulf of Tonkin Incident offered the opportunity for a firm, strong response, he took it. In that response he had received the overwhelming support of both the American people and the American Congress. So long as the war had retained a semilimited character and the casualties had consisted primarily of professional soldiers and lower-class draftees unable to obtain exemptions, the cycle of escalations had done little to arouse opposition. (It was not by accident that the communities hardest hit by the war were an Ohio farming village and a small Southwestern Mexican-American mining town, or that over 20 percent of the casualties were Negroes, double the number of blacks in the American population.) Only when regulations granting exemptions to college students were tightened and the war began to affect the articulate campus population and the politically powerful white middle class did opposition to it increase.

"You must have a position on the war," Jo Gomon told Cavanagh. She suggested that he meet with a number of people interested in Southeast Asia.

"All right. You arrange it," Cavanagh responded.

All along Cavanagh had been confronted with the problem of how to counter Williams's appeal to the Negro and liberal vote, and how to find an "issue" in the campaign. Williams supported President Johnson and the Vietnam War. If Cavanagh came out against the war, he would cast himself in the role of leader of the opposition.

On April 20, he issued a position paper. It proposed an immediate cease-fire, free elections, massive social reforms, the "neutralization" of the country, and the recognition of Communist China. Cavanagh thus became one of the first prominent politicians to break with the President on Vietnam.

It was a hazardous course. President Johnson regarded it as little short of betrayal. If Cavanagh should lose the Senate race, Detroit's White House status as a "favored city" would be at an end. It was an all-or-nothing gamble, just as the 1961 mayoralty race had been. In 1961, however, Cavanagh had had everything to gain and nothing to lose. In 1966 he had much to lose.

Cavanagh's race turned out to be a textbook example of how not to run a campaign. Trying to appease both blue-collar whites and Negroes on the "law-

and-order" issue, he flip-flopped on the hated "stop-and-frisk" ordinance that had helped bring down Miriani. On Vietnam, he was making the fatal mistake for a politician of being ahead of the times. Opposition to the war had not yet matured, and his stand probably lost him far more votes than it gained him— as a middle-of-the-road anti-Communist he might have pulled away some of the Catholic, blue-collar labor vote, but suddenly Williams appeared more anti-Communist than Cavanagh. Cavanagh had the endorsement of Henry Ford II (who had switched his registration from Republican to Democrat during the Kennedy Administration, in which Ford's Robert McNamara had become Secretary of Defense) and of Detroit Edison Company Board Chairman Walker Cisler, who became his financial director. But the business community did not have many Democratic voters.

To woo the Negro labor vote, Cavanagh elevated TAAP's deputy director, Phil Rutledge,* to the directorship in place of Bob Roselle. (Roselle was made the city's budget director.) But Williams went after the Negro vote on a personal basis. He attended Negro churches and sang hymns with the congregations. As governor of Michigan, he had established a Fair Employment Practices Commission and ended legal segregation.

While the CIO's Political Action Committee organized every urban precinct for Williams, Mayor Cavanagh wasted time making whistle-stop railroad tours of the state and recurrent trips out of the state. Detroit *Free Press* columnist Judd Arnett said Cavanagh was campaigning as if he had "forty pounds of dead weight in each hip pocket."

The result was foreordained. In the August 4 primary, Williams—taking Negro districts by margins of six to one and ten to one, and swamping Cavanagh in Wayne County two to one—won by 426,000 to 290,000 votes.

---

* Raised in Chicago, the forty-one-year-old Rutledge was the son of a Georgia sharecropper. After returning from service in World War II he had been unable to obtain a job. Finally he went to the ward boss, who sent him to Chicago's Public Health Department, where, two weeks previously, he had failed to get past the doorman. He was put to work as an interviewer on VD cases. Going back to school, he obtained an M.A. in public health from the University of Michigan. Before joining TAAP, he had been supervisor of public health education for the city.

104

The Changing of the Guard

THE LOSS WAS NOT ONLY THE LOSS OF A CAMPAIGN, BUT OF PRESTIGE AND mystique. Bitterness had been generated, and friends had been turned into enemies. Cavanagh once more was branded as a maverick. Some Democrats blamed Williams's loss in the general election on Cavanagh. Most important was the damage to the morale of both the mayor and his staff—Cavanagh would have to find another solution to the problems that had led him to enter the race.

In the autumn the last of the men who had moved into office with Cavanagh began to leave the administration. Strichartz joined General Motors as a general counsel. (He did not thrive in the atmosphere, and seven months later returned to Wayne University.) Fred Romanoff, the executive secretary, also wanted to leave.* This departure of the "first team" would have consequences far beyond the loss of the individual talents of the men.

One of the men who moved into the mayor's office was Harold Black. In the summer of 1966 the Community Renewal Program completed its initial four-year study, begun under Robert Roselle and completed under Black. In his 133-page report entitled, *Detroit: the new city,* Black pointed out that "in many cases where interdepartmental programs are being carried out, the existing administrative structure seems to hinder progress." Yet, in the era of the Federal-city partnership and the War on Poverty, more and more programs were cutting across departmental lines. Urban renewal involved the City Planning and Housing Commissions, and the Departments of Health, Buildings and Safety Engineering, Parks and Recreation, Streets and Traffic, and Public Works. Coordination was badly needed.

To provide this coordination, the CRP report recommended the creation of a community development coordinator in the mayor's office—the role filled by

---

* Romanoff, the son of a Greek immigrant, had shared a suite of law offices with Cavanagh. Cavanagh had appointed him executive secretary at the end of 1963 when he had named Ray Girardin police commissioner to replace George Edwards. Edwards had accepted an appointment to the United States Circuit Court, the second highest judicial body in the nation.

Strichartz in practice would be written into law. CRP would take on permanent status as the research and program development arm of the mayor.

The recommendations were, of course, those desired by Cavanagh. Two months after receiving the report, the mayor chose Black as the community development coordinator. Almost simultaneously he filled the post of administrative assistant —another position created since he had taken office. Conrad Mallett moved into the executive suite.

After leaving the police department in 1957, Mallett had become social studies teacher at Cleveland Junior High School in the Sojourner Truth area of north-central Detroit. Drawing its pupils from Negro and blue-collar Polish families, the school was one of the most troubled in the city. Teacher turnover was high—among a staff of sixty-five, Mallett was one of thirty first-year teachers. The children fought, urinated behind radiators, and threw excrement into the swimming pool. The teachers were given to understand that one of the principal criteria on which they would be judged was whether they maintained order. Children were not encouraged to take books home with them—to do so they had to obtain a special pass.

The situation was even worse at Eastern High School, to which Mallett was promoted in 1962 after he obtained his master's degree. The only white children in the school were those who had been transferred from other schools because of misbehavior. The transfers were the school district's way of expelling them in fact without expelling them de jure, since whites were not going to stay in a 99 percent black school. There were children in the high schoool who were reading at third- and fourth-grade levels. Even though Eastern was one of the Great Cities schools, there were no programs to deal with that kind of educational gap. The teachers could deplore the situation, but there was nothing they could do about it.

When Mallett was teaching family structure in sociology, he invited the Planned Parenthood League to send a representative to talk to the class. There were already three girls in his class who had children, and the school was full of pregnant girls. The League sent a registered nurse, who spent six hours in the school, part of the time teaching birth control techniques to a girls' gym class. When a Catholic teacher discovered what was going on, she was furious. In the uproar that followed, Mallett was called into the principal's office and reprimanded—Michigan forbids the dissemination of birth control information in schools. The students, however, hailed him as a hero.

In April, 1964, Mallett heard that the Mayor's Youth Employment Project, started under the Area Redevelopment Administration, needed .teachers. He joined the program and, as the only staff member with a master's degree, was made supervisor of training.

The purpose of the Youth Employment Project was to train sixteen- to twenty-one-year-old high school graduates who had been unable to find work. After thorough screening and testing and a two-week program of induction into "the world of work," applicants were placed with city departments and paid twenty dollars a week for on-the-job training. Upon "graduation," they were sent on to regular employment in business and industry. The fact that nearly 80 percent of the trainees were subsequently able to obtain jobs resulted in high staff morale and a sense of accomplishment. Not until later did Mallett realize that the Youth Employment Project—like the first public housing projects in the 1930's—was skimming the cream off the top. The program was not dealing with the dropouts or the semiliterate high school graduates, but with youths who would have found jobs anyway in a resurgent economy.

With the start-up of the antipoverty program at the beginning of 1965, Mallett became executive director of staff training at the Total Action Against Poverty agency. Then, obtaining a fellowship from the Mott Foundation,* he decided to return to school to obtain his doctorate. When Cavanagh entered the Senate race, Mallett, who had never met the mayor, was attracted to his candidacy by his Vietnam stand and worked for him in Flint and Saginaw.

During the shuffle of staff positions in the mayor's office, Cavanagh indicated that he was considering adding a Negro to his personal staff. Phil Rutledge, the director of TAAP, recommended Mallett.

Black and Mallett entered the mayor's office at a time when the momentum of the Cavanagh Administration had been lost, and the War on Poverty was being crowded out by the war in Vietnam. Until well into 1965 President Johnson had proceeded on the assumption that the war would not affect his domestic programs. By 1966, however, the Vietnam War was costing between $25 and $30 billion annually, and creating snarls in the American economy.

As a consequence, the paths of the President and the proponents of domestic action were diverging. On August 23, 1966, a Midwest regional conference of directors of antipoverty Community Action Programs issued a statement calling the "War on Poverty more important than the Viet Nam War. The promised Great Society appears to border on a state of bankruptcy." [1] On the same day Mayor Cavanagh was telling a U. S. Senate subcommittee that Detroit would need $15 billion in Federal money over the next ten years, and New York City's Mayor John Lindsay requested $50 billion. But in the fall the President, plagued by inflation, skyrocketing interest rates, and a mushrooming Federal budget deficit, called the mayors of the nation's major cities to Washington and told them that they must cut back on projects funded by the Federal government. At the National League of Cities meeting in December, Cavanagh referred to programs passed but not funded by Congress and said, "The rhetoric and the money are still miles apart."

Nowhere were they further apart than in the Model Cities Program—the new designation for the Demonstration City concept.† Congressional reaction to the President's proposal for the program had at first been negative. So by the time the act was passed and signed by President Johnson on November 3, 1966, "Model Cities" had been distributed to every congressional supporter of importance. The original concept had been to concentrate large sums of money in a few cities. Instead, $400 million a year was now to be spread over seventy-five cities in the *first round*—with others to follow later. Included were such "metropolises" as Butte (population 27,000) and Helena (22,000), Montana, for Senate Majority Leader Mike Mansfield; Texarkana, Texas (32,000), for Chairman Wright Patman of the House of Representatives Banking and Currency Committee, which had been responsible for holding the hearings on the

---

* The Mott Foundation was established with one of the General Motors fortunes. It has directed its money primarily toward the Flint, Michigan, school system, and enabled it to become one of the most progressive in the United States.
† The name was changed after congressmen questioned whether it would be necessary for a city to have a "demonstration" or a riot in order to become eligible.

bill; McAlester, Oklahoma (17,000), for House Democratic Majority Leader Carl Albert; and Pikeville, Kentucky (5,000), for Chairman Carl Perkins of the House Committee on Education and Labor.

Detroit's Model City was reduced from an area encompassing the entire city to a nine-square-mile section of the inner city superimposed upon Target Area I of the antipoverty program's four target areas. The area and the population (134,000) were approximately one fifteenth of the entire city. It was the part of the city that had the greatest concentration of physical blight. It contained all of the urban renewal projects—an important consideration since, by their inclusion in the Model City, supplemental Federal funds would become available. But Twelfth Street, which had the worst social problems, and many other blighted areas had to be left out.

In effect, three classifications of financial assistance were being established. To the Model City area would go the greatest concentration of Federal aid. To the remaining three TAAP target areas and their combined population of approximately 200,000 the normal antipoverty funds were being directed. But the other poor—a significant number of Negroes and a large number of whites —who lived in low-income enclaves scattered throughout the city remained as separated and alienated from the social programs as they had been before the War on Poverty got under way.

The Model City proposal had been envisioned as a means to provide city-wide coordination of programs. Instead, it had been turned into a Frankenstein that even before being injected with life gave every indication of merely aggravating the governmental fragmentation.

Nevertheless, at the initial meeting of the Model City area residents on December 20, 1966, Mayor Cavanagh told the seventy community representatives who were gathered that he expected the program "will be the biggest rehabilitation effort in this country."

The immediate reaction from the residents was overwhelmingly negative. Their instinct was to regard Model Cities as another Establishment project that, like urban renewal, would play hob with their lives. The people who were on TAAP's Area I advisory board looked upon Model Cities as a rival that would take away their programs and their power. Whereas citizens' participation in TAAP was limited to the poor, in Model Cities all residents of the area would be given a voice. Middle- and upper-income whites and Negroes of the Lafayette Park Redevelopment Area and Wayne State University would participate, and were likely to become a dominant elite. Community Development Coordinator Harold Black had the task of organizing Model Cities. He was confronted by twenty-five organizations, some denouncing Model Cities and demanding to be left out, others denouncing Model Cities and demanding to be let in.

The West Central Organization, a church-funded Alinsky * group already locked in dispute with the city over the demolition of houses for the Wayne State University redevelopment project, suspected that Model Cities was a device for the municipal government to achieve urban renewal by another name. A delegation from the West Central Organization traveled to Lansing to meet with Governor Romney, who had expressed antipathy for the Model Cities

---

* Saul Alinsky was a Chicago social worker and rebel against the welfare matriarchy. He was one of the first to argue that the poor must organize themselves in order to obtain power.

Program. A bill was drafted for the establishment of "urban renewal councils" composed of the residents of each urban renewal area. The bill in effect applied the concept of citizens' participation to urban renewal.

Militant black organizations feared Model Cities as an infringement, and stridently opposed it. Neighborhood organizations were infuriated when they discovered their areas were being left out of Model Cities. Walter Reuther and Walker Cisler, chairman of the board of the Detroit Edison Company, spearheaded the organization of the Metropolitan Detroit Citizens Development Authority (MDCDA). It was intended as a nonprofit private corporation to channel funds into the area, much as the Citizens Redevelopment Corporation had helped get the Gratiot renewal project off the ground. The MDCDA organizers also expected to participate in the planning. Their participation was opposed by Black and many of the residents, who viewed Reuther and MDCDA as part of the Establishment.*

Night after night Black met with various groups. He attempted to explain the program to them, allay their fears, and temper their criticism (which he feared would reach the ears of the Department of Housing and Urban Development in Washington, and damage the city's application). Night after night he was criticized, shouted down, and accused of wanting to make Model Cities another TAAP, in which the citizens would have pro forma but no actual decision making power. The citizens' resentment against all government—city, state, or national—came as a shock to him. It was a resentment harbored not only by the poor, but by the middle class.

The citizens divided into two antagonistic factions—the Negro poor who exercised power in TAAP on the one side (in essence, east of Woodward Avenue) and the *integrated* militants who organized themselves into the Congress of Grass Roots Organizations on the other (the west side of Woodward). It was a division of the inner city population that had existed ever since World War I. Now it was being structuralized.

Meanwhile, another conflict was occurring in the government. Agencies that Model Cities was supposed to coordinate did not want to participate and be coordinated. Many were already involved in the War on Poverty and had no interest in yet another program.

The staff of TAAP, like the citizens, suspected that Model Cities would become a competitor to the antipoverty program. It was a suspicion that filtered down from the Office of Economic Opportunity headquarters in Washington, which feared that through Model Cities the new Department of Housing and Urban Development would try to preempt the programs. In Detroit, TAAP Director Rutledge and Housing Director Knox were old associates from Democratic party activities, and there was little friction between them. Rutledge, nevertheless, was maneuvering to give TAAP equal status with the Housing Commission not only in the Model City area but throughout the city—it was his contention that if the Housing Commission had citywide responsibility for physical (urban) renewal, then TAAP should have citywide responsibility for social renewal. With that end in mind he convinced Cavanagh to change the antipoverty agency's name from Total Action Against Poverty to the Mayor's Committee for Human Resources Development (MCHRD).

---

* It was ironic that Reuther and Cisler, representing the arch foes of labor and business a quarter century before, could now work in harmony with one another but be opposed by the underclass of the inner city.

Faced with the necessity of submitting a proposal for a planning grant to HUD in Washington, Black went ahead without consulting the fractious citizens who were demanding that they be given control of the planning process (even though they had no experience in planning). To placate them he told them that the document being submitted, despite its detailed, 275 pages, was meaningless and designed only to obtain the Federal money needed to get the project under way. As soon as Federal approval was obtained, discussion could resume on the role that the citizens would play. On April 11, 1967, the city council was pressured by the deadline into approving the "Proposal for Progress," and it was sent on to Washington.

Black had been terrified by the thought of moving into the mayor's office, but the job was not one easily refused. He did not instinctively take to power the way Strichartz did. He was a fine researcher and writer, but he did not have Strichartz's commanding personality. Strichartz had been able to come into the government and raise hell because he had had no personal relationship with the people in it. When the time came to move on he could return to Wayne State University. Black had spent twenty-four years in the Detroit government. He felt uncomfortable in dealing with men who for years had been his superiors. He could not give "orders" to Planning Director Blessing or Housing Director Knox. When Cavanagh left office, Black might be returning to his run-of-the-mill, Civil Service-protected job in the city government.

Strichartz had been Cavanagh's neighbor, and in private there was no formality between them. Whenever he had a problem, Strichartz—or Romanoff —would simply walk into Cavanagh's office. Quickly recognizing that Cavanagh would just as soon have him settle a problem or make a decision, Strichartz would say: "Jerry, what we've decided to do is . . ." Usually, Cavanagh would indicate agreement. Occasionally, he would respond: "Like hell it is!" Then there might be a hot dispute between Strichartz, Romanoff, and Cavanagh. Cavanagh enjoyed such give-and-take battles, and expected his aides to force them upon him. He lacked the patience for administration and was content to leave as much of that as possible to Romanoff and Strichartz.

When Strichartz left, the Cavanagh Administration suffered the loss of the same kind of drive, abrasiveness, and administrative talent as the Ford Motor Company when James Couzens had departed. Cavanagh was on the opposite side of the human spectrum from Henry Ford. Nevertheless, as the men who had climbed the pedestal with him fell away, he suddenly stood alone, an aura of greatness misting about him. Unlike Ford, Cavanagh remained an earthy, convivial, gregarious being who did not want to suffer the isolation of fame and be surrounded by yes-men. But the condition was such a natural concomitant of reputation and power that it was difficult to escape.

Cavanagh was a man with a national reputation, he was president of the United States Conference of Mayors, he was in demand as a speaker, and he spent a good deal of time away from the city.* Cavanagh wanted Black to make decisions. But Black was reluctant to do so. He was in no position to call the mayor "Jerry"; he never barged into his office; and he really did not know Cavanagh's mind. If Black could not make decisions, then Cavanagh

---

* Jokingly, Cavanagh's staff would greet him with such salutations as: "Mr. Mayor, we have great pleasure in welcoming you to our city."

would have to. But Cavanagh, whose record of coming to correct decisions—mostly by instinct—had been unparalleled, had been burned in the Senate race. He too was vacillating. On some days he would appear in his office with the old fire, and then things would begin to move. On others, if he had happened to have a long night's session of gin rummy with some of his premayoralty cronies, he might not show up until after lunch. In any case, he tended to give priority to whatever person or event forced itself upon him with the greatest insistence. Black and Mallett, neither of them "pushers," had difficulty cornering him. During his first seven months as Community Development Coordinator, Black saw the mayor for a total of about four hours.

By the time in mid-April, 1967, that the proposal for a Model Cities planning grant was on its way to Washington, Black was exhausted. For nearly a year he had been making arrangements for a vacation trip of several weeks to Europe and Israel. When Cavanagh heard about it, he did not want Black to go. None of the controversies in the Model City Program had been resolved. Furthermore, in the mayor's office a state of flux existed because Romanoff was leaving as executive secretary and being replaced by Bob Roselle.

Nevertheless, Black decided to go ahead with his trip. During his absence, the burden of resolving the conflicts was shifted to Mallett.

Mallett had the advantage of being a Negro, and the residents did not regard him so much as part of the municipal government's "establishment." Cavanagh had conceived of the Model City Program as a coordinating mechanism for the mayor's office, and citizen demands for control of the program had therefore been unacceptable to him. But he was losing faith that the program would be implemented in the form he had envisioned. So he allowed Mallett to negotiate an agreement with the Congress of Grass Roots Organizations. The citizens were granted "full and equal participation" in the planning and execution of programs.

When Black returned, he was out of favor with Cavanagh. He had hoped to escape from the position of community development coordinator by becoming director of the Model City Program. But the mayor now wanted a Negro for director of the program, and Mallett had already sounded out David Cason, a Wayne State University sociologist who was a friend of Housing Director Knox and an opponent of MCHRD Director Rutledge. Rutledge was proposing that MCHRD's citizens advisory council for Area 1 should become the governing board for the Model City also, a development that would give MCHRD control of the Model City Program. Rutledge had the apparent backing of the mayor. Cavanagh was trying to give something to everyone—citizens participation to the Congress of Grass Roots Organizations, the director's post to a friend of Knox, and power to Rutledge.

The intricate political maneuvering, however, further perplexed and frustrated Black, who had to deal with the disputants on a daily basis. He was now determined to resign as community development coordinator. On July 19, 1967, he announced the entire program was being turned over to the Mayor's Committee for Human Resources Development.

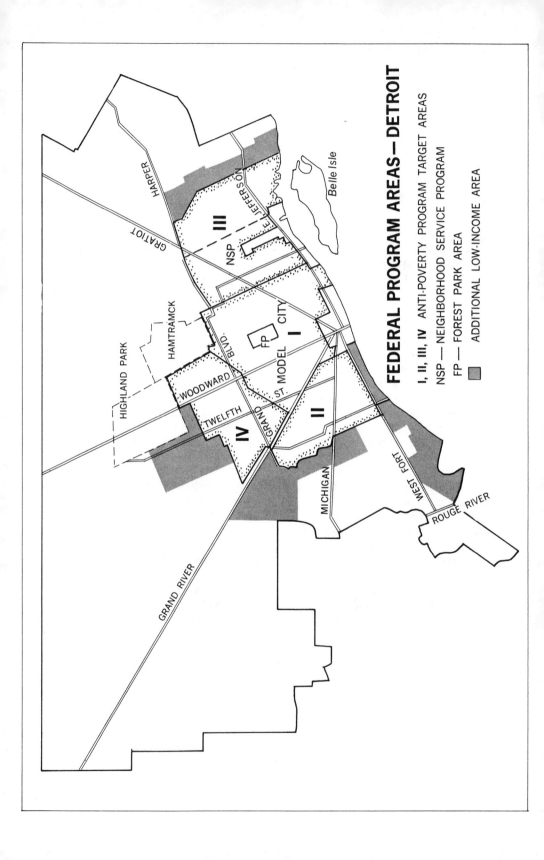

FEDERAL PROGRAM AREAS—DETROIT

I, II, III, IV ANTI-POVERTY PROGRAM TARGET AREAS

NSP —NEIGHBORHOOD SERVICE PROGRAM

FP —FOREST PARK AREA

⬛ ADDITIONAL LOW-INCOME AREA

Belle Isle

HARPER

GRATIOT

JEFFERSON

NSP

III

HAMTRAMCK

HIGHLAND PARK

WOODWARD

TWELFTH

GRAND RIVER

BLVD.

FP

CITY

MODEL

GRAND ST.

I

IV

II

MICHIGAN

WEST FORT

ROUGE RIVER

105

MCHRD

IN OPERATION FOR TWO AND A HALF YEARS, THE MAYOR'S COMMITTEE FOR Human Resources Development, or MCHRD (pronounced "Mac Heard"), had carved out a powerful constituency in the city. MCHRD had two delegate agencies: the Board of Education, and the (Catholic) Archdiocese Opportunity Program, both of which furnished classroom facilities and instruction. To MCHRD's forty-one member Policy Advisory Committee, citizens elected only sixteen members—four from each target area—and the mayor had no difficulty exercising control. But the four area advisory committees of twenty-five to thirty members each were elected strictly by residents, and it was in these that the antipoverty program had its principal effect as a catalyst of grass-roots politics.

Since the citizens participation election had been greeted by general apathy,* membership on the advisory committees had gone primarily to people who had already been politically and civically active. They represented block clubs, welfare rights groups, unionists, and civil rights organizations. Approximately half were unemployed, and many others had "undesirable," low-paying jobs. Representative of a generation with severely limited education, they had little sophistication. Meetings frequently turned into acrimonious shouting matches during which fratricidal neighborhood feuds were continued. They were dominated by the one or two most articulate and best educated persons, who tended to ride roughshod over the opposition and take on the nature of "bosses."

The area advisory committees had little power over program operations, but they did have powerful voices. Residents exercised those voices to demand what they had expected most out of the antipoverty program: jobs.

The professional positions were beyond their reach, and most of these were going to school personnel or people who in one manner or another had been

---

* Almost nowhere in the United States did even 5 percent of the eligible turn out in antipoverty program elections. The small turnouts were representative of the confusion surrounding the elections and the fact that people of limited education are less likely to participate in politics.

involved in the creation of the antipoverty program: members of civil rights organizations and unions. At first it appeared as if the residents would not obtain many of the subprofessional and semiskilled positions, either, since the Civil Service Commission demanded, in accordance with municipal regulations, that everyone must pass a test. The result of such tests would inevitably be that all but a handful of the ghetto jobs would go to whites and middle-class Negroes. Cavanagh, however, pressured Civil Service into eliminating written examinations for some of the positions.

Secretary of Labor Wirtz had been concerned that the antipoverty program would not create jobs; but it was creating jobs. Six hundred to seven hundred area residents became employed by MCHRD (or TAAP, its predecessor). Some of them were members of advisory committees. Others obtained their jobs through committee members. A half century after the WASPish Good Citizens League had succeeded in eliminating the ward system, the War on Poverty recreated it in a new form.

There was a running conflict between the committees and the professionals on the MCHRD staff as to whether money should be spent on employing residents or on programs *for* residents. The originators of the concept of "maximum feasible participation" of citizens had not envisaged that they would be creating a surrogate employment agency. There was as great a communications gap between the residents and the staff as between the middle class and ghetto dwellers everywhere. The residents could not understand why things they wanted done could not be done, and the professionals resented having to take time to explain to them over and over that there were *guidelines* that had to be followed. The explanations were especially difficult when the Office of Economic Opportunity, the Department of Housing and Urban Development, the Office of Education, the Children's Bureau, the Public Health Service, the Bureau of Apprenticeship Training, the Bureau of Work-Training Programs, the Small Business Administration, and other Federal agencies involved in the antipoverty program all issued their own individualistic guidelines. Some of them affected the same programs and conflicted, and some were repeatedly changed. Some "guidelines" were booklets of up to two hundred fifty and three hundred pages. Strichartz complained that it would take the entire year in which programs were supposed to be completed just to digest and understand the guidelines. "You people are out of your minds," he told his friends in Washington. "No city has the capability of delivering if you're going to indulge in those kinds of intellectual planning exercises." [1]

The Office of Economic Opportunity needed success models, and Detroit was one of its principal hopes. During the first year of operations, the Cavanagh Administration had no difficulty in coming to agreement with the people in Washington. But in 1966 OEO adopted the practice of other Federal agencies and divided the country into regions. A Midwest office was established in Chicago. Although officials in the regional office were supposed to make decisions, they were often afraid to exercise their power. Functioning as little more than a post office for forwarding applications, the Chicago office became a bottleneck.

Funding was a never-ending problem. Authorization for the 1965 summer program did not reach Detroit from the OEO office in Washington until June, the 1966 authorization did not arrive until July, the 1967 authorization until

June, and so it went year after year. During the 1965 fiscal year, Detroit's Community Action Program received $5.5 million in Federal funds (2.4 percent of the national allocation); in 1966, $10.8 million (1.7 percent); and in 1967, $15.7 million (1.9 percent). (Detroit contained approximately .8 percent of the American population.) The Community Action Programs were intended to give localities flexibility in programming and experimenting with new approaches. But after the initial year all the funds were absorbed by the expansion of ongoing programs like Head Start. In the OEO offices in Washington reports were piling up from "demonstration programs" carried on by communities throughout the nation but discontinued for lack of funds. (The Federal government paid 90 percent of the cost of demonstration programs. Since the local share could be "in kind," communities had to put up no cash. Following the demonstration year, however, the local share usually increased to 50 percent, and revenue-short communities almost invariably dropped the programs.)

At the start of each fiscal year in July, OEO and other Federal agencies divided appropriations among communities and programs across the nation. By May or early June, however, some of the funds were still unspent, because some localities either had not submitted applications or had failed to have their applications approved. These funds were routed into a "grab-bag" and became available to any community that submitted a program and had it approved before July 1.

As a "favored" city, Detroit could expect to be called when the grab-bagging began. One Friday afternoon in late June of 1967, four or five persons were sitting around the MCHRD office when the director of the Neighborhood Youth Corps came in.

"Who's going to Chicago on Monday to write the program?" he asked.

"What program?"

"I don't know. One for three hundred thousand dollars. I just got a call from the region. They're expecting someone."

No one had any idea what he was talking about. But on Saturday Myron Liner, MCHRD's director for Program Planning, Research, and Development, began sifting through all the programs submitted but never funded. He finally came across one for "urban beautification" that had been sent to OEO. Since the call had come not from OEO but from the regional Labor Department office, he was puzzled. He concluded, however, that the Labor Department must have unspent funds, and because the program had a component for putting people to work in parks it had been redesignated a "manpower" program. On Monday he went to Chicago and spent two days writing a program according to the specifications of the regional office. The city received $335,000.

Several months earlier Liner had submitted an application for a grant of $237,000 for an emergency family-loan program. He heard nothing more until the second week in June, when he received a new set of guidelines with a submission deadline of June 30.

His initial reaction was "to hell with it." The staff was inadequate, and the annual problems of the summer programs were coming to a head. But the next week he received a telephone call from Washington.

"Didn't you people submit a program for emergency family loans?"

"Yes."

"Fine. Could you drop it in the mail and send it to us?"

Liner mailed a copy of the program that had been subitted six months before. After it arrived in Washington, another call came.

"We can't fund this. It's far too much money!"

"How much isn't?"

"One hundred thousand dollars."

"Okay. Make it a hundred thousand."

It was difficult to explain to the Policy Advisory Committee and to the area committees why some programs were being funded while others, to which the committees had given greater priority, were not. The residents' assumption that they were being double-crossed by the MCHRD professionals and the city was not unreasonable. Yet the city, too, was suffering from a distortion of its priorities. Getting "free" money for anything was too great a temptation to resist, yet often the matching funds required from the city could have been put to better use elsewhere.

When Mayor Cavanagh, as president of the United States Conference of Mayors, testified before the Senate Subcommittee on Employment, Manpower, and Poverty in March, 1967, he felt compelled to respond to criticism of the antipoverty program. Since both the proponents and the critics of the War on Poverty were wrestling about in computer printouts and cost-benefit analyses, he came prepared with imposing sets of statistics. Four hundred thousand Detroiters (or one out of every four persons in the city) had been assisted. "Detroit's On-The-Job Training Program . . . costs approximately $378 per trainee . . . to train a person to earn $4,500 to $5,000 a year"; 635 previously unemployed or underemployed had gone through the program. The Neighborhood Youth Corps program had received $5,459,237 in grants, but "it is estimated that NYC alumni earn $10,500,000 annually and return $1,750,000 to society in the form of taxes." The Specialized Training and Employment Placement Services (STEPS) program which "utilizes an intensive follow-up technique to keep in contact with an individual while trying to find him employment and to maintain contact with him during the first sixty days on the job" had cost $175,000, but had "placed 461 persons in jobs. These jobs have a projected yearly income of $1,917,760." [2]

The roll of figures went on and on. The senators were impressed.

Those closer to the scene, such as auditors of the General Accounting Office,* and consultants employed by the Senate subcommittee were less impressed.

While in some areas residents were not being served by the programs, in others there was duplication and overlapping—the Archdiocese Opportunity Program was addressing itself to many of the same people as MCHRD and the Detroit schools. MCHRD had all but severed relations with the city's Parks and Recreation Department, whose staff, protected by Civil Service, "doesn't talk to anyone, and no one will talk to them."

Johnny Smith, living in a housing project, was being pulled six different ways. MCHRD's Youth Opportunity Program had a day camp on Belle Isle. The Parks and Recreation Department ran a basketball league. The Board of Education had recreation programs that the principal of each school operated semiautonomously. The United Community Services had its "drop-in

* The General Accounting Office is the congressional watchdog agency.

center," plus two or three other overlapping programs. Theoretically, every-one agreed that coordination was desirable. But each agency had its own staff, and no one was interested in "economy" that would result in an elimination of jobs. All the agencies were secretive, jealous of their own functions, and unwilling to take directions from anyone else, including the mayor's office.

"So while Smith is being kept out of trouble by being given a brush with which to paint penises in a Youth Opportunity art class under the label of 'black expressionism,' " said one of the mayor's aides, "Jones in the next block is being ignored and left to his own devices to steal hub caps, which may be what he'd rather do anyway." [3]

The General Accounting Office professed itself unable to comprehend the justification for the designation of the archdiocese as a delegate agency. (But then the accountants were not politicians in a city with a large number of Catholics.) The archdiocese had no previous experience running such a program, and its accounting practices and management of the program were in disarray. Ineligible people were being enrolled because the archdiocese not surprisingly failed to understand the guidelines. The Board of Education was in violation of the law by using money from one set of Federal grants to provide the matching requirements for another. The mayor's presentation had given the impression of coordination and control through a Manpower Council, a Departmental Poverty Council, and an Administrative Council; but after the summer of 1966 these were largely paper organizations.

The General Accounting Office found MCHRD's management of the programs less than satisfactory. But given the conditions of congressional funding and the bureaucratic operations of the Washington and regional offices, good management was all but impossible.

The least reliable part of Mayor Cavanagh's presentation to the senators was the cost-benefit analysis. The fighters of the War on Poverty were as statistics-happy and as loose with their figures as the fighters of the war in Vietnam.

According to MCHRD, former Neighborhood Youth Corps (NYC) members were earning $10.5 million a year. But the NYC lacked the resources to significantly improve the skills or education of enrollees, 90 percent of whom were operating intellectually at a grammar school level. (It was difficult to find NYC members who had a reading level high enough so they could be used as pages in the library; then it was discovered they could not be employed because at $1.25 per hour their pay would be higher than that of regular pages.) The Neighborhood Youth Corps' primary function was that of a "holding operation," designed to keep its participants out of trouble while employment or training could be found for them. Six months after successfully completing the program, only one fifth of the former enrollees were employed.

The Specialized Training and Employment Placement Services (STEPS) program, MCHRD said, had produced "benefits" of more than $1.9 million at a cost of $175,000. But STEPS was actually not a training program but an effort to overcome the shortcomings of the state employment service, which previously had made no effort to find jobs for the unskilled and semiskilled in the poverty area. MCHRD itself was employing some of the people being processed through the STEPS program—part of the "benefits" came from the same Federal funds as the "costs!" Even so, STEPS was able to find employment or training slots for only 10 percent of the people who registered. A congressional consultant wondered "why a new administrative structure had to be established . . . for doing things MESC [the employment service] and MCHRD were supposed to be doing all along." [4]

The Adult and Youth Employment Project, MCHRD asserted, would return $4 million in wages on an investment of $788,000. But the employment service was making little effort to place AYEP graduates, who had, on the average, a sixth-grade reading level.

(One trainee achieved a typing speed of ninety words per minute, and staffers were congratulating themselves until they discovered she could not read a word she was typing—she was merely a human copying machine.)

The use of "cost-benefit" as a criterion tended to pressure administrators of the antipoverty program into enrolling the more trainable and employable people—whereas on-the-job training for a person with reasonable reading skill cost from $200 to $400, training costs for the functionally illiterate were $1,200 to $1,700. Each year there were more than eight thousand dropouts in the Detroit school system. And with most of these disillusioned, bitter, semiliterate young men the War on Poverty had not yet begun to skirmish.

The greatest and most immediate impact of the antipoverty program was on the area residents that it itself hired. "One might suppose," wrote a congressional consultant, "that the Community Action Program is helping the [community] aides far more than it is helping anyone else." [5]

106

The Hard Corps

ONE OF THE COMMUNITY AIDES WAS NATALIE STALLINGS, THE DAUGHTER OF Donald Stallings and Irma Mirow. Of the six Stallings children, Natalie and her older brother Windsor were the only ones to graduate from high school.

In September, 1965, Natalie married Nick Palmerill. Palmerill, thin and taut, was in his early twenties. His father had disappeared, and his mother had supported five children by supplementing the welfare payments by working as a charwoman. She did not report her earnings—a failure that was, of course, illegal. But the combined incomes were just enough to bring up her children decently. Upon Nick's television image of a white world in which people remained forever young and luxuriated in material things was superimposed the vision of his mother scrubbing the floors of the office building night after night. In the mornings her fingers were so stiff that she could not bend them and her back was so sore that she could not straighten up. Nick hated the white world. Because he hated and wanted to kill, he joined the marine corps.

He was just about to be shipped overseas when he received word that his mother was critically ill. Granted an emergency leave, he found her suffering from peritonitis in Detroit General Hospital. He could not understand why the doctors, the *white* doctors, were not doing more for her.

On the eighteenth day she died. With her death, he no longer could control his hatred. When he returned to the base, a white sergeant gave him an order, and he attacked him with a bayonet. In the wild melee that followed, he cut a half dozen soldiers. Three months later he was given a psychological discharge.

Returning to Detroit, he went to work in the Dodge plant in Hamtramck. Natalie begged him not to try to buck the system. But in 1966, when she was six months pregnant, he attacked a foreman with a jagged piece of metal. The man nearly bled to death. Palmerill was sentenced to Ionia Penitentiary.

Natalie's grandfather, Wallace Mirow, helped her until after she gave birth. If the year had been 1956 instead of 1966, Natalie would have had little

choice but to go on welfare. In 1966 she was hired by the antipoverty program. Since she was unable to pass the Civil Service examination for counselor
aide, she was taken on as a community aide. Community aides were supposed
to restrict themselves to going out into the neighborhoods, finding people who
needed help, and informing them of the programs that were available. It was
the counselor aides who were to "counsel" the people and direct them to the
program or assistance suited to their needs. But, in actuality, there was no
sharp division between the jobs.

Natalie worked in Target Area IV, which encompassed the southern portion
of the Twelfth Street area. The area center was located in one wing of what
once had been Providence Hospital. Located at Fourteenth Street and Grand
Boulevard, the Catholic hospital had been abandoned in the early 1960's. The
new Providence Hospital had been erected near the intersection of two freeways in the suburban community of Southfield.

The old Providence Hospital was a huge, fortresslike brick structure. Covering an entire square block of the city, it could have barracked an army. Seven
of Jerry and Mary Cavanagh's eight children had been born in the hospital.
But now it stood forlorn and empty, a dead weight on the tax rolls, a symbol
of the decline of the city. When the hospital had been operating, the area had
been one of constant activity. The hospital pulled out; the activity ceased. The
area, with its heart removed, rapidly mortified. Through the long corridors
and myriad rooms crept the winter dampness, peeling away the layers of paint.
From somewhere deep in the bowels of the building rose a ghostly stench that
traveled first here, then there, as if in restless exploration. Occasionally, derelicts and juveniles braved the ghosts to force a window and leave bottles and
other mementos of their presence. In the once-magnificent high-vaulted chapel
in which Marie Jansen had cried because she did not want to have another
baby, the stained-glass windows were shattered. Debris littered the altar. Nearby
a large statue of Christ had been abandoned. Another statue of several hundred pounds lay cracked on the floor, its guillotined head by its side. The antipoverty center's staff, occupying the first three floors along the front of the
building, were frightened of its depths. If a fuse went out at night, no one
would venture to the back of the building to replace it until the next day.

The building created a morale problem. The uncertainty of funding and the
possible elimination of jobs created anxiety. And the people who day after
day came in to unfold their tattered lives created depression.

To Natalie came P.D., a thirty-three-year-old sign painter. An epileptic with
a drinking problem, he had had a seizure while working at a second-story
height, fallen to the ground, and badly injured himself. He had no income, no
job, no trade other than painting. What should he do?

To Natalie came Mrs. B.F., a woman on welfare who wanted a job. She
was referred to the Skills Center for training as a power sewing machine operator.
After a few weeks it became apparent that she had deep-seated psychological
problems and that nothing could be accomplished until these were dealt with.
Her training was terminated. Her welfare worker was fearful that she would
harm her children. After the initial interview, however, she refused to return
to the psychologist or to accept therapy. The antipoverty people wanted nothing
more to do with her, but she would call five or six times a day to complain
about one difficulty or another.

To Natalie came B.W. Twenty-three years old, he had been born with club-
feet. He had had two years of college in South Carolina, but he was unable

to find a job. He had gone into Goodwill's managerial program, but then had been told that there were no managerial openings, and that Goodwill had discontinued its placement program.

To Natalie came Mrs. B.D. She was in her middle fifties and terribly fat. At the age of sixteen she had been seduced by two uncles. She had contracted syphilis, but the disease had not manifested itself until she was forty-seven. Her husband had died four years before of cancer of the tongue. She had a fourteen-year-old son and an eighteen-year-old daughter who were also obese —in the neighborhood the family was mocked as "the fat ones." Her son was retarded, and she was concerned over what would happen when he reached eighteen and her welfare payments were cut off. Her daughter had cerebral palsy and was deaf, but nevertheless had been married at the age of sixteen. She had had two children, both of whom had died. Her daughter's husband was in and out of jail, and getting other girls in the neighborhood pregnant. For the staff of the antipoverty agency it was difficult to know where to start. But Mrs. B.D. did not return for her second appointment. A visit was made to her home, but no one was there. A phone call was placed. No one answered. The case was terminated.

During its first two months of operation in 1965, the center had had twenty-six thousand such appeals for help. On each one a card or folder was dutifully made out and filed. In ninety-nine out of one hundred cases there were one or two contacts, perhaps a referral, and then the person, like a moth briefly attracted to the light and then fluttering off again into the darkness, disappeared without anyone's knowing what had happened to him. That was how the statistic of four hundred thousand persons "reached" had been accumulated; a statistic that the mayor had presented to the Senate subcommittee.

Natalie had little sympathy for the people with whom she came into contact. Since they mirrored her own problems and her own life, she could not feel sympathy without becoming depressed. Reacting to older people, she sometimes had difficulty controlling her antagonism. It was *they* who had messed up the lives of their children, it was *they* who had generated the misery in which she and her friends lived. About the only excuse they had was that white society was the real culprit—and in a way Natalie hated whites as much as her husband hated them.

It was this antagonism that had driven the whites—who, in fact, made up 60 percent of the poverty area—out of the program. Appalachians and Latin Americans had participated at the beginning, but then drifted away. Blacks had established their control over the program. Blacks had been hired to staff the centers. Blacks viewed whites as having every advantage and could not understand why whites should be coming to seek help—unless they were no good and looking for handouts.

There was, in any case, too little help available. Natalie's younger brother Brett had an extensive record as a juvenile delinquent and was failing in school. But despite the plethora of government programs, he was not "reached" by any of them. He was big and strong—by the age of thirteen he was over six feet tall—but slow in maturing. On the surface he spoke and acted like a man, but the moment his bravado was pierced he bawled like a five-year-old. At the age of thirteen he propositioned girls with remarks like "Come on, old woman, let's fuck tonight!" He was antagonistic toward any man, and doubly so toward anyone who personified authority.

The school system was in a quandary how to handle an obscene, tough-acting six-footer who one moment behaved as if he were ready to wreck the building and the next had tears pouring down his face. Tested in the psychological clinic, he was bounced from school to school, assigned to "health conservation" classes, tried in a home room with a female teacher whom he propositioned, and in a home room with a male teacher whom he cursed.

"I don't like robbing and stealing," he said. "But what can you do? Around the neighborhood even the girls'd just as soon bust you on the side of the head and peck your pockets clean!"

He rationalized that "everybody does it," and concluded that "they don't do nothing to you noways." Saturdays he was on the lookout for newsboys making their collections—strong-arm robberies of newsboys are among the most frequent crimes of the inner city. He was convinced that "you take ten dollars from the [white] man, it don't mean nothing to him." His view of the American system was that "the getting" was all-important. "Man, once you got it, nobody gives a shit. . . . You kill somebody, it don't mean nothing . . . you know, you just peels off them bills, and the judge says, you know, he says 'thank you, we have just fined you two thousand dollars!'" He was critical of the schools because "They don't teach you nothing! See, they tells you all this stuff, and you asks 'em what it means, and they tells you like it means this and that, and you say what's this and that? And they don't got no answer." Since he knew he was not learning, he reasoned that the fault lay with the teachers. "See, they got all this itty-bitty shit, like rules you know, and they makes you learn them. Now what's that got to do with education? I want to take a crap, I got to go up to this woman teacher, and I got to give her my card, and I got to say, 'Lady, please let me take a crap.' Now that is *not* education."

He thought that the rules were made deliberately numerous and diverse so that they would be broken. "They got this quota system. See, they start out, and they put too many in the class, and they say that ain't gonna do. We got to get rid of some. So they put in the rules, and they know that they're gonna be broke. So they say, man, you broke the rules, we can't have that. So they put you someplace else."

He hated the tests. "Look," he said, "they ask about this stuff, but nobody never tell about it, so how can they ask it? I say, why you do this? You tell about one stuff, and ask another? And they say, well, you got to dig it yourself."

Since he hated the tests, it was before a test that he usually—subconsciously —provoked an incident. At the age of fifteen he was three years behind in school. In the fall of 1965 he slipped on a flight of stairs and landed on his back. It "messed up the tissue," and he went to a doctor and complained about pains in his neck and back. He said it was especially difficult for him to sit behind a desk, because "they don't make 'em my size." The doctor, whose marginal inner city practice had as the result of Medicaid and Medicare more than doubled,* agreed with Brett that the injury made it difficult for him to attend school. Charging him eight dollars a visit, paid by Medicaid, he told him to come to see him twice a week.

It was a solution that satisfied everyone—Brett, who no longer had to deal

---

* By 1969 some Michigan doctors were collecting as much as $4,000 in Medicaid payments weekly, and one received $169,000 during the year. On a single day in June, 1968, one Detroit doctor gave physicals and immunization shots to 47 children at $25 per child—a total of $1,175.[1]

with the frustrations of going to school and not being able to learn; the schools, which had a legal copout for no longer enrolling him; the doctor, who was paid sixteen dollars a week. But it scarcely benefited Brett. Able now to sleep in the morning, he drifted around the streets all night. In November, 1965, when a friend of Brett was arrested for burglary, Brett went down to the police station to see him at eleven o'clock at night. The police, suspecting that he had been involved, held him and placed him in the juvenile home. He claimed, however, that he had spent the evening listening to the Clay-Patterson heavyweight championship fight, and was released for lack of evidence. At three o'clock in the morning on the night after Christmas he was discovered with two other youths in a grocery store whose door had been broken open. When the three of them ran, the police opened fire. One of the boys received a superficial scalp wound, and all three were caught. The other two backed Brett's story that he had not been with them when they had broken in, but had only agreed to help carry away the goods.

"This boy lives with his grandmother, who has no control whatsoever over him," reported the two patrolmen from the police youth bureau who investigated the case. "The grandmother can no longer cope with him and wants help from the court. He will continue to repeat if he is allowed to roam the streets."

Nevertheless, Brett was returned to Freda's supervision. In the afternoons he walked the few blocks to Northern High School. There, together with other youths who were not in school, he smoked pot and waited for the girls to come out. The dropouts attracted the police, and there were clashes between them. Within the school, whose student body was 98 percent black, the situation was volatile. The administration was so fearful that it obtained continuous police protection during school hours. To the students it was but one more indication that the school was a custodial rather than a teaching institution. One of them wrote an article for the school newspaper attacking the administration for failing to provide the kind of education that the students would need to "make it" in contemporary American society and for being reactionary and unresponsive to student demands for improvement.

The principal refused to allow the article to be published. It was almost a reflex action—few bureaucracies willingly open themselves to criticism. But what happened next would have been unheard of in a white school. On April 7, 1966, the entire student body of two thousand walked out and went on strike. Supported by the black community, they set up "freedom schools."

The action was representative of the growing and organized militancy of students, and demonstrated the division between the white-dominated bureaucracy interested in the maintenance of *order,* and the black youths who were demanding that even at the risk of upheaval order must give way to *progress.* The principal, who was caught unprepared, was removed by the school administration—which was scarcely any more prepared.

Brett identified with the walkout. But, in a way, it was only one more frustration—he was not able to walk out because he was not in school. He developed the common teen-age passion for cars, and throughout the summer he was in one scrape after another. He was discovered tampering with cars. He was one of the passengers in a car stolen by a friend of his. He "returned" to its owner a car that he said had been stolen by one of his friends, and the owner rewarded him by smashing his jaw with a hammer.

In the fall of 1966 Brett was six feet three inches tall and weighed two hundred pounds. Lying about his age, he obtained a job as a laborer in a steel mill. Working the afternoon shift from 4 P.M. to midnight, he hung around the high school during the day, and the money in his pocket made him a big man with the girls. But he worked only to get money to spend—when he had money he was more interested in making it with the girls than in working. After six weeks he was laid off. In October he was once again picked up in a stolen car—and this time he was driving, and not "returning" it.

The police youth bureau recommendations and warnings kept piling up: "It appears that if this boy is not put away, he is capable of hurting someone." "The youth is well on the way down the wrong road. Court action is essential before he gets in too deep." But the Juvenile Court had no intermediate facility to which he could be sent—it either had to commit him to the reformatory and expect that he would be released fully prepared for the penitentiary, or else continue him on probation and hope for the best. (Since he was of average intelligence, Wayne County Training School was out of the question.) In any case, in another seven months he would be seventeen and out of the jurisdiction of the Juvenile Court.

In desperation, Freda "enlisted" him in the Job Corps, which was recruiting heavily in the inner city. Recruiters tended to make exaggerated promises and paint idealized pictures of the life in the Corps. Brett looked forward to playing basketball, learning to drive a truck and a tractor, and "getting to know stuff like hari kari" (karate).

The Job Corps, which Sargent Shriver had hoped would be the most visibly successful of the antipoverty programs, was turning out to be the most distressed program. It was costing between seven thousand and ten thousand dollars a year to support an enrollee—about as much as the cost of a four-year education in an American college. Since the program did not attract youths, a "hard sell" was necessary. It was difficult to fill the camps to more than half their capacity; for a time in some camps the staff members outnumbered the enrollees. The Job Corps tended to draw from the bottom of the barrel, and the Office of Economic Opportunity was shocked at just how low the level of performance at the bottom was. (One third of enrollees were illiterate, and many did not even know the letters of the alphabet. In one center, only 18 of 670 youths were functioning at the tenth-grade level.) Most enrollees suffered from a constellation of problems—nearly two thirds came from broken homes in which the head of the household had no job; the same proportion had been suspended from school; and two fifths were mentally retarded or emotionally disturbed.

For the staff of the antipoverty agency it was difficult to know where to start. The expectation that the Job Corps could be patterned on the Civilian Conservation Corps, which during the Depression had drawn tens of thousands of youths from the middle class, was unrealistic. Courses were set up on "The Principles and Theories of Atomic Energy—the Processes of Fission and Fusion," "Newton's Law of Motion," and "The Dynamic Molecular Structure of All States of Matter." Tens of thousands of textbooks were ordered: *Thevenin's Theorem; Delta and Y Transformation; Squares, Square Root, and Logarithm; Superposition Theorem; Kirchoff's Laws;* and *Theories of Relativity.* Technical-book publishers reaped a bonanza.

As inappropriate as this material was on the one hand, the basic readers were on the other. Hard-shelled ghetto youth were asked to read *Miss Ant Has on a Hat* and *This Is Ann's Pink Dress*. Despairing, the staff at the Job Corps Centers provided youths with whatever they would read or at least look at the pictures in—mostly comic books and pornography.

Brett was shipped to Fort Custer, near Battle Creek, Michigan—like most of the other centers a converted army camp. What would have benefited him most would have been a well-ordered, highly structured setting in which he received intensive counseling. What he came to instead was a permissive, confused environment in which the enrollees were given a plethora of tests but little direction. The camp's approach was to "let them do their thing" and "don't push them." Many of the youth simply took up where they left off at home. Absenteeism in the classes was 20 percent, higher than in the Detroit inner city schools.

Brett was incapable of going to sleep before two o'clock in the morning, so he stayed up and watched television, played cards, or simply roamed around. He discovered he could spend all morning in his bunk without anyone bothering him. Sometimes when he did get to class he would go to sleep there— and that, because he attended, was considered an improvement. He was as antagonistic as ever to male authority—even more so when that authority attempted to operate in an undisciplined setting. He got into one fight, then another. He went AWOL because "I'll go stir crazy if I don't get me some cock!" Week by week he became more restless. At the end of three months it was evident that he was one of the two thirds majority who would gain little benefit from the Job Corps.* His enrollment was terminated. With $150 in "readjustment pay" (accumulated at the rate of $50 per month), he was sent back to Detroit in March of 1967.

Two months later, in May, the Juvenile Court probation officer noted: "Brett Stallings has made a satisfactory adjustment at home, in school, and the community. This boy has passed his seventeenth birthday, and he has no known police contacts in over six months. It is therefore recommended that this case be dismissed and probation terminated."

---

* OEO showed a higher success rate for the Job Corps, but independent analyses by the United States Labor Department and Comptroller-General indicate significant gains made by fewer than one in three enrollees. (Christopher Weeks, a former Job Corps administrator, says that during the first twenty months of the program six enrollees failed to finish the course for every one who "graduated"—a term that the Corps applied loosely.) That, considering the backgrounds of the youths, was not a bad showing, and there were notable successes—George Foreman, who was to become world heavyweight champion, had his life redirected in the Corps. But OEO had puffed up the Job Corps beyond realistic expectations, and Congress was disappointed.

107

The Pilot Light

IN ACTUALITY, BRETT WAS ONE OF THOUSANDS OF BLACK YOUTH ROAMING THE streets. There were few jobs in which they could be usefully employed—the gap between the level of their education and the demands of a technological age continued to widen. Many of them held low-paying jobs for a few months, then lost them and were unemployed for an equal number of months. They were bounced in and out of government programs. One month they would have money and become accustomed to spending it. The next month they would be broke. By "hustling" and peddling drugs they often could obtain a larger and steadier income than by working. They were under continual pressure to get money. As they idled about, they discerned chances for an easy "hit." Sometimes they would commit a robbery or burglary on the spur of the moment. "Crimes of opportunity" occurred frequently in the inner city. Inevitably, when the number of unemployed and idle youth increased, more crimes were committed.

Throughout the nation, citizens were being made aware of a vast increase in crime, a "crime wave" the likes of which had not been seen since the 1930's. In the 1930's the awareness had come through gangsters and spectacular shoot-outs. In the 1960's it was through the steady drumming of statistics.

In 1958 the FBI had initiated a uniform method of keeping and reporting crime statistics. Until then each jurisdiction had kept statistics in its own fashion, some in detail, others carelessly. Many jurisdictions attached little significance to their statistical operations. In an era when newspapers periodically attacked police departments for failing to put down "crime waves," police deemphasized statistics. Until 1949, New York, with two and a half times the population of Chicago, was reporting about one fourth the robberies and one half the burglaries annually. The FBI declared that it did not believe the statistics. In 1950 New York switched to a central reporting system, and in one year the robbery statistics jumped 400 percent and the burglary statistics 1,300 percent.

Had every city changed simultaneously to the FBI's Uniform Crime Reports, there would have been an immediate and startling increase in the national statistics. But each city changed according to its own schedule. Some cities changed one year, others the next, and only a portion of the nation's jurisdictions were melded into the Uniform Crime Reports each year. Consequently, instead of a fantastic one-time jump in reported crimes, there was a steady upward trend. (At the end of the 1960's, by which time most cities had been included in UCR, the yearly increases leveled off.)

It was May, 1966, before Detroit, installing a computer operation, switched to the Uniform Crime Reporting method, and it was the end of the year before the changeover was completed. At the time of World War I when Couzens was police commissioner, he had spoken out against encouraging "officers to make large numbers of arrests [so as] to make crime-increasing agencies out of the police departments." He had instituted a "merit system" for precinct commanders "who maintain order and reduce the number of crimes." [1] In the half century since, there had been little change in the departmental philosophy on statistics. There was no standard procedure for precincts to report crimes, and if those precincts that had the fewest crimes were to be judged the best, then the fewer that could be reported the better. Some commanders were reporting less than 50 percent of the crimes actually occurring in their precincts.

With the introduction of Uniform Crime Reports (UCR), discretionary power of reporting or not reporting was taken away from precinct commanders. Domestic "assault" cases in which the aggrieved party refused to file a complaint usually had not been reported. In UCR they became a statistic under "aggravated assault," considered one of the seven "major" crimes. (The others are homicide, rape, robbery, burglary, grand larceny, and auto theft.) Between 1965 and 1967, assault reports from the four middle-class white precincts * doubled, accounting for one third of the citywide increase. A casual reading, therefore, might lead one to believe that the white population had suddenly turned to mayhem.

Since ninety-nine out of a hundred routine burglaries never get investigated, the tendency in the precincts had been not to report burglaries. If a window had been broken or there had been an attempt to jimmy a door, but nothing had been taken, no report was filed. If something had been taken but entry had been gained through an open door or window—the case in one third of all burglaries—the loss might have been classified as a "mysterious disappearance." If it involved an item worth less than fifty dollars, it might have been reported as "petty larceny," not a major offense. Under UCR every breaking and entering or attempt at entry was reported. The number of burglary reports from several precincts rose two and a half times, and citywide they more than doubled.

Grand larceny is the theft of an article valued at more than fifty dollars. The criterion has been held constant as the dollar declined in value and the cost of articles rose. In 1940 the value of the average theft had been twenty-six dollars; in 1965 it was eighty-four. In the same period, as the average larceny changed from "petty" to "grand" and became a "major" crime through no other factor than inflation, the number of grand larcenies in Detroit rose from 1,100 to 7,400 a year. Since, like burglary, grand larceny was a nonviolent and unobtrusive crime, it had been greatly underreported. With the introduction of UCR, it statistically doubled, to 14,800, in 1967.

---

* The Twelfth, Fourteenth, Fifteenth, and Sixteenth Precincts.

The advent of Uniform Crime Reports, therefore, brought about an "increase" in crime of 55 percent in the city between 1965 and 1967. (Other cities experienced similar "increase" as they joined UCR. Baltimore's "increase" was 41 percent; Buffalo's 95 percent; Chicago's 72 percent; Cleveland's 63 percent; and Kansas City's 202 percent.) By underreporting offenses, precinct commanders had been able to report an impressive 33 percent of crimes "cleared." With UCR, police efficiency appeared to plunge as dramatically as mayhem increased—after 1967 "clearances" were less than 20 percent.

In the past such an increase in crime might have made the police the target of a newspaper crusade. But the national focus had changed from blaming crime on the police to blaming it on Negroes, "permissiveness," and the relaxation of moral standards. Throughout its existence the police department, like other tax-funded agencies, had struggled for public funds. But in the "crime wave" of the 1960's and the anxiety it generated in Americans, the police discovered the key to the municipal treasury. The grandsons of immigrants who had hurled rocks at officers and the sons of blue-collar whites who had engaged them in hand-to-hand combat around the factories hailed the police as defenders of law and order and backed their demands for more money.

Councilwoman Mary Beck exploited the crime statistics to attack Mayor Cavanagh. A friend of the mayor's wife, Miss Beck charged Cavanagh was leading an immoral life,* and launched a recall campaign against him. She demanded that the mayor initiate a "war on crime." In the third week in April, 1967, a series of crimes exploded at Cobo Hall. They were climaxed by a robbery-murder—a fifteen-year-old white boy who had come to play in a band concert was stabbed by a fifteen-year-old Negro. The crime was one that adequate social institutions could have prevented far more easily than the police.† Nevertheless, it seemed to prove Miss Beck's assertion, "No man, woman, or child in Detroit appears to be safe."

Since 1946 the budget of the police department had nearly quadrupled, from $11 million a year to $40 million, and Cavanagh had expanded the budget more than any other mayor. Patrolmen's salaries, which had been a maximum of $3,000 a year in 1943 and $5,600 in 1957, had risen to $8,300 (in Police Commissioner Girardin's opinion equal with fringe benefits to $12,000), 80 percent more than the increase in the cost of living. The Detroit Police Officers Association, the patrolmen's union,‡ nevertheless demanded that in the forthcoming budget the pay be raised to $10,000 a year. When Cavanagh said that was impossible, there was no money available for such a raise, they went on a ticket-writing strike. When Cavanagh ordered Police Commissioner Girardin to crack down and transfer men from patrol cars to foot duty, the Police Officers Association responded, "If the mayor wants war, he will get it." In June a

---

* He wasn't. The mayor was adept at flirtation and at Irish blarney, but he was all eyes and no hands.
† The murderer was a mental defective with an IQ of 61 and a record of robbery and outbursts of violence dating back to the age of twelve. Two years before, the Juvenile Court "had made arrangements for the boy to enter Wayne County Training School . . . but at the last minute the boy's father decided against sending him. This was a voluntary petition and the Court had no control over the father's decision." The court report continued: "The boy is dangerous and the Juvenile Court simply does not have any facilities to meet his needs. The proper place for him would be a controlled setting for an indefinite period for delinquent retarded juveniles. There is no such place at the Juvenile level in Michigan." [2]
‡ There were four separate unions active in the department: one each for patrolmen, sergeants, detectives, and lieutenants.

large number of men, stricken with "blue flu," staged a sickout, the first American police strike since 1919.

Police Commissioner Ray Girardin had spent thirty years on the police beat for the Detroit *Times.* He had had a working and drinking relationship with the officers and knew many of them personally. He was generally accepted by the men, and not disliked as George Edwards had been. Still, he was not a member of the hierarchy. He had to govern through men to whom he was an "outsider." The large, drab, dusky commissioner's office tended to swallow him. A small, wizened man with such deeply etched lines that he was nicknamed "Old Prune Face," he sat behind his desk like the lonely figure in an Edward Hopper painting waiting for the next train out.

"The guys you're dependent on," said Girardin, "have been there twenty-five years. On top of that, they're bound up in a hundred years of tradition. To attempt to get the department to examine its own problems—how God-awful it was!"

Girardin knew from his association with officers how much they drank, and he himself had joined Alcoholics Anonymous. He believed "too damn much drinking" was the cause for a great deal of bad judgment and use of excessive force by officers. They would "drink while on duty, go to the back door, and hit people up for bottles." One of his first acts as commissioner was to establish a branch of Alcoholics Anonymous in the department. "We sobered up an awful lot of policemen. You can cut it down. But you can't eliminate it."

In the clannish atmosphere of the department the fact that an officer was having problems seldom came to light until he committed some act that was impossible to ignore. In the Thirteenth Precinct one sergeant acted peculiarly for months. But not until he belted a lieutenant in front of a thousand people on a picket line did twenty officers acknowledge that they had known that something was wrong with him. "No matter how awful the behavior," Girardin said, "no one will rat on anyone else. I could stop people from getting shot or beat up, but I soon realized I wasn't going to change anyone's thinking. When you talk to them about civil rights and community relations, they think you're *touched.* 'What else can you do with niggers besides hit them on the side of the head?' " [3]

To try to lessen racial tensions the Cavanagh Administration had initiated a police community relations course. Although 1,800 officers attended the twenty-hour course, they tended to look upon it as attempted brainwashing. A professor from Wayne State University was introduced to a class as "the man who's here to teach you to say 'incredible' instead of 'shit!' " [4]

Cavanagh responded to Councilwoman Beck's emphasizing of Negro crime by accusing her of trying "to fan the flames of panic." During the summer of 1966 a disturbance had been set off when police ordered a group of Negro youths to disperse from a street corner on Kercheval Avenue on the far East Side. Instead of dispersing, the youths had started to stone cars. The entire police department had been placed on alert. Cavanagh and Girardin adopted a policy of *showing* force, but avoiding mass arrests and the use of force. Antipoverty and community relations activities were intensified in the area. Trouble continued for three nights, and there were a good many broken windows and a few attempted fire bombings. But the area did not have numerous high-density apartment buildings nor a concentrated commercial district. Damped by rain, the disturbance had fizzled out largely of its own accord.

Since Detroit's reaction to the "Kercheval incident" was successful, the mayor's staff considered it the model for handling future disturbances. The United States

Conference of Mayors even issued a pamphlet, *Community Planning and Civil Disturbances,* detailing the Detroit experience for the benefit of other cities.

But as the summer of 1967 approached, Cavanagh declared he was "more fearful than at anytime in the past five years of possible civil unrest." His words were prophetic. After a spring during which disorders occurred at several Negro universities, a riot erupted in Tampa, Florida, on June 11. Other disturbances quickly followed. News media and government officials, conditioned by the riots of the three preceding summers, began keeping score. All clashes involving Negroes on the one hand and police on the other, no matter how trivial, were tallied. Incidents that previously had been reported on the inside page of a local newspaper were magnified to front-page coverage all across the nation. A fight at a dance, a dispute over a traffic accident, the breaking up of a dice game—all were metamorphosized into "riots."

By the third week of July, 1967, the "score" stood at twenty-nine, ahead of any previous year.* On July 12 the arrest of a Negro cab driver precipitated a week of violence in Newark, New Jersey, that brought death to twenty-three persons, twenty-one of them black. Television was beaming into every American home pictures of red lights and sirens, of shattered glass and billowing flames, of crackling guns and sprawling figures, of red-tipped bayonets pressed to black skins, of wide-eyed men and boys soaking in rivulets of blood. They were pictures steaming on the hot TV tubes in cramped ghetto rooms, pictures macabre and confused that like the pungent smell of frying "soul food" flowed through open windows and filled ghetto streets.

In mid-July a multiple-car accident on Detroit's Twelfth Street led to the gathering of an angry crowd of Negroes. Although no violence resulted, Conrad Mallett was concerned enough to call a meeting in the mayor's conference room. On Thursday, July 20, he met with fifteen representatives of the police and fire departments and community agencies. He presented to them a scenario in which he picked, with remarkable prescience, the corner of Twelfth Street and Clairmount Avenue as the site of an accident. When the first ambulance took a pregnant white woman instead of a profusely bleeding Negro to the hospital, onlookers started a disturbance that developed into a riot.

Mallett asked the participants in the exercise how they would react. The police and fire department officials responded confidently. They knew precisely what they would do and how they would counter the actions of the rioters.

Since June, Mallett had been supervising a "neighborhood reporting service" that was part of the Mayor's Summer Task Force. Every day from 8 A.M. to 12:30 A.M. the next morning a "hot line" was open to the executive suite. Any dangerous situation that developed would be reported within minutes.

No city had done more to ward off a riot, and none was as well prepared for the eventuality of an outbreak. Yet at a time when sparks of every kind were setting conflagrations all over the nation, no one in Detroit had examined the routine police functions to determine how they could be curtailed or altered to reduce the possibilities of an incident. Such functions were in the province of the bureaucracy, a province that policy makers invaded at their peril. The Cavanagh Administration was like a householder who is aware of a potentially explosive gas leak and lays in fire extinguishers and alerts the fire department—but then leaves the pilot light burning.

* The reader who is interested in a more detailed account of what was happening on the national scene during this period is referred to Chapter 1, "Profiles of Disorder," of the *Report of the National Advisory Commission on Civil Disorders.*

108

The Day of the Blind Pig

ON THE NIGHT OF SATURDAY, JULY 22, 1967, THE TENTH PRECINCT "CLEANUP squad" consisting of Sergeant Arthur Howison and three patrolmen was cruising along Twelfth Street. The cleanup squad was the precinct equivalent of the headquarters "vice squad"—throughout the police department there tends to be an overlapping and duplication of functions between the precinct and the more prestigious "downtown." * The vice and cleanup squads were supposed to control gambling, prostitution, illegal liquor operations, and after-hours, unlicensed "blind pigs." † Officers on the vice detail were expected to close down a reasonable number of blind pigs every month. They knew that if they didn't, they would be returned to a regular beat. Violators who were arrested were fined one hundred dollars, and the next week would be back in business. Some had been arrested as many as thirty or forty times in the revolving-door process.

The day had been warm, humid, and smoggy, and Twelfth Street—"The Strip"—was teeming with people. Miniskirted prostitutes, dope pushers, the syndicate man who provided *juice* (a loan for criminal activity), the armed robber who had just knocked off a cab driver—all blended into the swirl. At the corner of Twelfth Street and Clairmount was a nondescript building that housed the Economy Printing Company on the first floor, and above it the United Civic League for Community Action. The police had known the United Civic League for Community Action to be the front for a blind pig ever since it had been chartered a year and a half before. Sergeant Howison had raided it the first time in February, 1966. Repeatedly, thereafter, various members of the Tenth Precinct cleanup squad had attempted to gain entrance. The rival vice

* For example, if an armed robbery is committed, the scout car will take the initial report. Then the precinct cruiser—a kind of roving supervisory operation—might drop by. Then will come the precinct detectives followed, finally, by the holdup detail from downtown.
† It is impossible to estimate how much home brewing continues to take place within the limits of Detroit. One day a woman came into the mayor's office and complained to Tony Ripley, the mayor's aide, that her house was being stormed by legions of rats and roaches, which she was fighting off with a blowtorch. Investigating, Ripley discovered that in the house next door a still had burst, flooding the basement with water and mash. The mixture had fermented, and provided an ideal medium for the multiplication of insects and rodents, which overran the neighborhood.

squad, however, had staged the next successful raid, on June 3, 1967, less than two months previously.

At 10:30 P.M. on July 22, a half hour after the squad left the precinct station to begin its night's work, Patrolman Charles Henry knocked on the door of the blind pig, but was refused admittance as "unknown" and suspect—he didn't have a woman with him, he was fairly young, well dressed, and in good physical condition; all of which meant that he might be a cop. For the next five hours the four plainclothes officers busied themselves checking other tips. Usually officers on vice details knocked off about 3 A.M. to return to the station and write their reports. That was the procedure followed by several other officers who had successfully busted four *blind pigs* during the night. But before going back to the station, Patrolman Henry told Sergeant Howison he thought he might be able to gain entry now.

At 3:34 A.M. vigilance at the blind pig had wilted, and Henry was able to walk in behind three women. Ten minutes after Henry had gone inside—time enough for him to have bought a drink—Sergeant Howison radioed for the Tenth Precinct cruiser. (Another squad car also responded.) He then ordered the door of the blind pig smashed with a sledgehammer.

Once inside, the police discovered the place was being used to hold a party for servicemen, two of whom had recently returned from Vietnam. Sergeant Howison had expected to find a score of people at most, but instead he discovered eighty-two! Sergeant Howison called for a paddy wagon to take them to the station.

Over an hour and four paddy wagon trips were required to remove everyone. Police Commissioner Ray Girardin was well aware that on The Strip "you can blow a whistle at three o'clock in the morning and get two thousand people on the street." On a balmy Saturday night there was still a good deal of vehicular traffic. Cars stopped. People drifted out of all-night eating places. They looked out of their windows and came down from their apartments. About two hundred spectators gathered. Many of their comments were jocular and the mood was not "ugly." But, inevitably, as people were herded into the paddy wagon, some were jostled by the police. A college student kept shouting: "Motherfuckers! Leave my people alone!" The rumor spread that the police had manhandled a woman. There was a general air of resentment against police vice activity—an activity that was looked upon by the black community as being directed discriminatorily against Negroes.* As the last police car left the scene at five o'clock, an empty bottle smashed against its rear window. A litter basket was heaved through the window of a store. Rocks were thrown. In a few minutes the police returned to the area. A lieutenant was struck by a brick.

Within fifteen minutes all of the officials in the department were notified. At twenty minutes past five the telephone rang at Girardin's home, and he was told. By six thirty burglar alarms set off by broken windows were awakening residents of a half dozen blocks on Twelfth Street, and police officials were gathering at the musty police headquarters on Beaubien Street. Ten minutes later the Tactical Mobile Unit, the first formed in the country for just such an emergency, mobilized

---

* For all practical purposes, the police leave "private" gambling alone, and so do not intrude upon it in the "private" white clubs in which it takes place. The author one night watched a police captain and several municipal officials engage in a poker game in the civic center's Veterans Memorial Building. Later he accompanied the vice squad to try to sniff out gambling games and rent parties in Negro homes.

some of its eighty men. The night shift was held over, and the day shift for all West Side precincts was called to duty an hour and a half early. (They were due at 8 A.M.) It was the two hundred sixty-sixth anniversary of the day on which Cadillac had first stepped ashore on *de trois;* but by nightfall, July 23 would be better established as The Day of the Blind Pig.

109

"Motown, If You Don't Come Around, We Are Going To Burn You Down."

AT DAWN GIRARDIN CALLED THE MAYOR'S MANSION. CAVANAGH WAS NOT IN-clined to take chances. At seven o'clock he ordered that the state police, the Michigan National Guard, the Wayne County sheriff's office, and the FBI be notified that a possibly inflammatory situation existed in Detroit.

At eight o'clock the mayor arrived in his office. Fifteen minutes earlier Mallett had called the mayor's executive secretary, Robert Roselle, who arrived at 8:30 A.M. Already a steady stream of reports was coming in from members of the Mayor's Summer Task Force. Soon more than two hundred community leaders were circulating through the crowds on Twelfth Street. Many of them lived in the well-preserved residential districts on both sides of Twelfth Street. Among the community leaders (all Negro) were the Reverend Robert Potts, one of the organizers of the summer program; Hubert Locke, a Wayne State University professor who was serving as assistant to the police commissioner; Arthur Johnson, a civil rights leader who was deputy superintendent for school-community relations; and Representative John Conyers, Jr., a "militant" who now occupied the congressional seat held in the 1940's by Negro-baiting Representative Rudolph G. Tenerowicz. They were collecting information, trying to stifle rumors, telling the people that "nothing is going to happen," and urging them to go home.

The early reports coming into the mayor's office were not particularly discouraging. Some looting of stores whose windows had been broken earlier had occurred, but it was not widespread. At 8:25 A.M. fire broke out in a shoe store, but firemen were not interfered with as they extinguished the blaze. The question for the men in the mayor's office was what to do—and they agreed unanimously that the police should refrain from taking precipitate or provocative action.

When the cleanup squad had splintered the door of the United Civic League for Community Action, departmental strength was at its low point of the week. The twelve-hour period after 3 A.M. Sunday, when the drinking and revelry of Saturday night have ceased, is traditionally the least troublesome for police in cities everywhere, and departments have adjusted their duty hours accordingly.

When the last people were being taken from the blind pig, the department had but 272 of its 4,356 men and women on duty, and only 193 of these were on street patrol. A show of force such as that immediately staged on Kercheval Avenue the year before was impossible.

By midmorning the department had mobilized 1,122 of its men—an impressive accomplishment on a sunny eighty-six-degree day when many officers had gone on excursions out of the city. Five hundred and forty of these were at the staging area that had been established at Hermann Kiefer Hospital near Twelfth Street, or in the vicinity of the six-block area south of Clairmount in which the disturbance continued to be contained.

Several thousand persons were on Twelfth Street, but most of them were not violating any laws. A great many were women and children. They came, they went back to their apartments to eat breakfast, they returned; throughout the morning they wandered back and forth. Since it was the order to disperse that had started the trouble on Kercheval, there was no order to disperse. Girardin had made up his mind that he was not going to arrest people by the busloads for minor infractions. Three fourths of the officers were not injected into the disturbance area, but were being held in reserve.

To prevent the stoning of motorists that had been so much a part of other riots, the area was sealed off—the tactic was largely successful. To forestall a black-white confrontation like that of 1943, the bridge to Belle Isle was closed—an action that may have been a blunder, for it barred thousands from their normal place of recreation. To keep the curious and the restless from being drawn to the scene, radio and television stations were asked not to make any mention of the disturbance, and largely they complied. (No one thought to notify the police of Highland Park, whose boundaries were less than a mile from the area, and they did not find out that there was trouble until the middle of the afternoon.)

Chafing, the police stood hour after hour at sawhorses set up on the periphery. Residents, some still in their pajamas, bantered with them. Along the six blocks of shattered store windows a few people were going "shopping." At 10:30 A.M. police picked up six looters. But there was no frenzied mass looting. From 5 A.M. to noon police made only forty-four arrests, scarcely more than on any other Sunday morning.

In the nerve-racking isolation of the eleventh floor of the City-County Building, Cavanagh kept receiving reports and waiting; waiting and hoping that people would heed the community leaders who were urging them to go home.

But these community leaders were part of the "establishment," and there were other voices on Twelfth Street; voices that were telling blacks to separate themselves from the white Establishment. "The Negro is involved in a struggle for survival—a struggle to determine whether we can live in these United States," the Reverend Albert Cleage, Jr., of the Twelfth Street area's Central United Church of Christ had said three years before. Blue-eyed and light-skinned, Dr. Cleage was the son of an Indianapolis surgeon. He held a divinity degree from Oberlin, and had presided over one of the more integrated churches in the city until the white flight of the latter 1950's left him with a black congregation. Disillusioned with integration, he had turned to emphasizing his *black*ness.

In March of 1963, Dr. Cleage had identified himself with a small group of students at Wayne State University who were fed up with the snail's pace of the civil rights movement and formed a Swahilian-titled organization, UHURU. The UHURU, "Freedom Now" movement rejected black-white organizations like the NAACP and the Urban League because they were white-dominated, and urged Negroes to seize control of their own destinies. It identified with the black African nations that had just burst to life out of the shell of colonialism, and it revitalized the black consciousness of Garvey's Back to Africa crusade. (It did not propose, however, that the future of American blacks was anywhere but in the United States.) To a large degree it was the intellectual counterpart of the "Black Muslim" movement; a movement that, after having been quiescent for twenty years, had begun an extraordinary resurgence in the 1950's, when it started recruiting Negro youths in prison and acquired a talented writer, Malcolm X, as a spokesman.

The events in Birmingham, and the failure of the Detroit and Washington Freedom Marches to produce immediate benefits strengthened UHURU's arguments. (In the summer of 1963 UHURU found a cause célèbre in the shooting of an Amazonian black prostitute by a Detroit police officer. Repeatedly the organization picketed police headquarters, and once it staged a sit-in in front of the mayor's office.) The Negro had been told to make himself socially acceptable, Dr. Cleage said, and discrimination against him would cease. He learned that the bathtub was not to put coal in; he learned to take a shower and put on a clean shirt, to say "please" and "thank you"—and discrimination did not cease. The Negro had been told to obtain education, and discrimination would cease. He sent his children to school and to college—and discrimination did not cease. He had been told to take legal action, and discrimination would cease. He had won decision after decision before the Supreme Court—but the decisions had not been enforced, and discrimination did not cease. He had been told that Americans were a moral people, and if he resorted to moral persuasion, discrimination would cease. He had tried nonviolent, moral persuasion—and he had had his head cracked open and his children attacked by dogs.

"So," Dr. Cleage had said in early 1964, "we have got to do something else. . . . We have got to take independent black political action. We have got to mobilize the masses of Negro people into an independent black political movement. The masses of Negro people have got to understand that this is a power struggle, and we have got to bring to bear in this power struggle our mass political strength." [1]

It was the enunciation of "black power." Dr. Cleage became chairman of the Freedom Now party, and in 1964 he ran as its candidate for governor of Michigan.

The doctrine of black power found ready acceptance among more militant Negro college students, who had grown to manhood in a nation whose laws now decreed equality, but whose practices were still discriminatory. The doctrine lodged in the Student Nonviolent Coordinating Committee, which Dr. King had founded in 1960 as a means of mobilizing the idealism and activism of students.

Since the early 1960's, SNCC had been engaged in voter registration drives, many of them frustrated by the South's white power structure. By 1964 the SNCC-led Mississippi Freedom party was well enough organized to challenge the segregationist regulars at the Democratic party convention—a challenge that set off a chain of events that by 1972 brought the greatest internal party reform in American history. In the spring of 1966 the black-power faction, headed by West Indian-born Howard University graduate Stokely Carmichael, captured control of SNCC. In Lowndes County, Alabama, where Negroes were numerous enough to make "black power" a reality, a chapter of the Freedom party adopted a black panther as the party's symbol.

In the Negro college community even more than in the white, there was widespread opposition to the Vietnam War. Negro students not only opposed American involvement, they identified with the "Third World" of Africans and Asians. Black power and antiwar became interwoven. Members of SNCC and RAM (Revolutionary Action Movement) traveled to and were feted in Cuba, Algeria, and eastern European Communist nations. When disturbances broke out in city after American city, the black power advocates, notably Carmichael and his associate Hubert "Rap" Brown (a former student at Southern University), hailed them as the long-awaited black uprising. Rejecting the Ghandian concept of nonviolence on which Dr. King had based the civil rights movement, they preached revolution.

"This nonviolence bit is just a philanthropic hangup," Carmichael said. "I don't see why people keep thinking about that. The violence is inevitable.

"When you talk of Black Power, you talk of bringing this country to its knees. When you talk of Black Power, you talk of building a movement that will smash everything Western civilization has created. When you talk of Black Power, you talk of the black man doing whatever is necessary to get what he needs. We are fighting for our lives."

Throughout the second half of 1966 and the beginning of 1967, Carmichael and Brown traveled around the country and repeated the message. On April 18, 1967, Carmichael told a crowd in St. Petersburg:

"When they talk about law and order they not talking about justice. . . . Wherever the hunkies got injustice we gonna tear their cities up. Period."

On April 29 he spoke in a Cincinnati church:

"So that when they say . . . 'Black Power means violence.' They want us to say, 'Uh-uh, bossman, that's not what it means.' Later for you, hunky. We know what it means! . . . Black Power is the coming together of black people to fight for their liberation by any means necessary. Period. Period. Period."

On May 17 he was in Grand Rapids, Michigan.

"That's why they can't even begin to understand SNCC. 'Cause they cannot any longer decide for us the arena in which we fight. . . . Blacks in South Africa should pick up guns and shoot the hell out of every hunky in there. Shoot them, that's how you do it. But if you say that, you're violent!"

On June 29 the four-day, second annual "Black Arts Convention" opened at Dr. Cleage's church in Detroit. In the three years since he had spoken of the blacks accepting their separateness and turning it to their advantage through the development of political and financial power, the young militants had redefined black power as a revolutionary movement for the overthrow of the white power structure. In the spectrum of militants who attended the convention, Dr. Cleage found himself almost a conservative. A member of the Cincinnati chapter of SNCC declared: "We already had our riot and we're here to show you how it's done."

Shaking his fist, Rap Brown orated:

"Let white America know that the name of the game is tit-for-tat, an eye for an eye, a tooth for a tooth, and a life for a life. . . . Motown, if you don't come around, we are going to burn you down!" [2]

SNCC was a small organization, which, as soon as Carmichael and Brown started chanting, "Black power," was torn by internal dissension. It soon was in serious financial straits. The hard core of Carmichael's and Brown's followers in the organization never numbered more than about thirty. But the black-power oratory was so startling that the American media, notably television, jumped upon it and made Carmichael and Brown national figures, purportedly representing a new phenomenon: the revolutionary Negro. By the summer of 1967 the theme of violence and riot repeated and magnified by the press was creating the same kind of fear and frenzy that had swept France after the overthrow of Louis XVI, and the American South following John Brown's raid on Harpers Ferry. Like the Southerners who had not been able to keep John Brown and his small band of fanatics in perspective, millions of Americans were looking at their television screens and seeing armies of guerrillas sweeping across the land behind Carmichael and Brown. Whites raced for gun stores.* Young blacks looked about and wondered what was wrong with themselves if their city had not yet had an *uprising,* if they had not yet vented their lifetime of frustrations in an orgasm of smashing, looting, and burning.

"I saw the brothers bleeding in Newark, and I wanted to get me a gun," said seventeen-year-old Brett Stallings. With his sixteen-year-old stepcousin, Garry Gatling, he went to Twelfth Street. They saw Congressman Conyers standing on a car and telling people to "cool it." But Congressman Conyers was making little impression. His reputation as a "militant" carried no weight—the youths had never heard of him.

In Detroit unemployment reaches a peak in the summer when the automobile industry lays off men during the model changeover. In July it was 6.1 percent—and between 15 and 20 percent in the inner city.† In the very center of that inner city, a mile and a half from Twelfth Street and Clairmount, was the Kahn-designed General Motors Building, the headquarters of the world's richest and most powerful corporation. To the G.M. Building some of the world's most affluent executives drove via "Cobo's Canyons." But to the General Motors executives Twelfth Street and the people on it were as remote as if they had existed in another universe.

In the immediate vicinity of Twelfth Street and Clairmount lived approximately one thousand young men between the ages of fourteen and twenty-four. At least one in three was not in school and not employed, and most of them had not been *reached* by the antipoverty program. None of them could have said where the headquarters of General Motors was, and some of them did not know there *was* a General Motors; but all of them had been conditioned by television and the standards of American society to yearn for a Chevrolet or a Buick.

The total population of this stretch along Twelfth Street was nearly sixteen thousand, and the surrounding area had the greatest housing density and social disorganization in the city. During the preceding three years an increasing number of people had been pushed into the area as a consequence of the Wayne State University urban renewal project. Urban renewal, whose original

* Gun registrations in Detroit were up by 66 percent over 1966, and by 1968 they would be triple what they had been. In California, gun sales had more than quintupled after the Los Angeles riot.
† Inner city unemployment runs roughly triple that of the metropolitan area, and youth unemployment is about twice that of the general population.

purpose had been to provide better housing for the poor, was now razing more low-income housing units than it was creating. The proportion of households headed by women (32.5 percent) and the illegitimacy rate were the second highest in the city, and the crime rate was the highest. The Tenth Precinct had the greatest number of murders, robberies, burglaries, and auto thefts (twice the number of any other precinct), and was second in rapes and assaults.

In an alley Brett and Garry joined a gathering of youths. The youths attended either Central or Northern High Schools. Recreation facilities for them were virtually nonexistent. The Central High School area is the only one in the city that has neither a park nor a playing field. It has less than five acres of open space, one third as much as the next lowest high school area: Northern. (The average for high school areas in the newer, "outer ring" is 333 acres.) Central was the most overcrowded high school in the system. Academic achievement of students in Central and Northern was among the lowest in the city, and continuing to decline.*

Yet despite Central's poor academic standing, 46 percent of the students indicated they were planning to go on to college—the sixth highest proportion for any school in the system! It was indicative of the socioeconomic mix of the Twelfth Street area. The high school drew its students from both the top and the bottom—the crowded apartments along The Strip and the demimansions of LaSalle Boulevard two blocks to the west. The median income of students' families was $5,525, sixth lowest in the district. But while 40 percent earned less than $3,000 a year, 16 percent earned more than $10,000. The middle-class Negroes who had replaced the Jews were following in the footsteps of their academic tradition,† and the lower-class blacks who followed the middle-class were absorbing some of their ambitions. Whose fault was it that their ambitions exceeded their grasp?

To the youths with whom Brett and Garry were gathering, it was the fault of the "system," and they looked upon it as the consequence of "white oppression." Their most intimate personal experience with the "system" was in the schools, and the lower their achievement and the greater their frustration the more they felt alienated. To them integration was not only a theoretical failure; integration had brought the personal experience of white rejection. Ten years before, when they had been starting school, the Twelfth Street area had been amidst the ferment of purported integration. Many of them had experienced the bussing from school to school that the system had undertaken to keep some of its schools 95 percent white; yet even so they had attended grammar school with more whites than they had found in junior high school, and there had been more whites in junior high school than in high school. In 1967, there were but 6 whites left in a student body of 2,446 at Central High.

The white residents were gone, but the white economic structure remained. Property and businesses continued to be owned largely by whites and, notably, by Jews. It was Hastings Street twenty-four years later, Hastings Street a generation advanced in sophistication, education, and economic standing.

* Of twenty-two high schools in Detroit, Central and Northern ranked fifteenth and seventeenth according to English-test results of twelfth-grade students, but fell to eighteenth and twentieth on the basis of test results of younger, tenth-grade students.
† When Central had been the "Jewish" high school, it had been the leader in the proportion of graduates who went on to college. The new "Jewish" high school was Mumford, and it led the city in median income, value of homes, and children going on to college.

The youths had heard Carmichael and Brown proclaim the black revolution, and they had seen what they presumed to be its manifestation on television. After two years of such exposure they had no doubts about how to initiate an uprising. Hour after hour Twelfth Street resembled a town forum in which the residents debated among themselves if the time had come to stage *their* rebellion.

In an alley a youth appeared with two one-gallon jugs filled with gasoline. "The man ask me what I want the stuff for," he related, "and I tell him, shit, what you think I want it for? I run out of gas. So he says, you run out of gas, you don't need *two* gallons. And I says, shit, don't be stupid! I run out of gas in *two* cars!"

110

The Inferno of Poverty

By NOON IT WAS EVIDENT THAT THE CROWD ON TWELFTH STREET WAS NOT going to be talked into dispersing. In his office, Mayor Cavanagh's only contact with Girardin and the police was via telephone. The police commissioner was receiving information from his men in the field, and Cavanagh was getting his intelligence from the Mayor's Summer Task Force, but there was no co-ordination between them. The reports the mayor obtained from newspaper and TV reporters convinced him that the mood of the people on Twelfth Street was turning darker, and that it was doubtful passive reaction was going to succeed.

He left his office for police headquarters a half dozen blocks away. There, Girardin, too, was coming to a conclusion. He now had nearly fourteen hundred men on duty, one third of the force. On Twelfth Street the intermittent rock throwing was intensifying. But, after seven hours of confrontation, nothing had yet really *happened!* What could be the explanation?

The repetition of the revolutionary theme had made an impact upon the police fully as great as on black youth. In July, 1964, the Twelfth Street militants had organized the Medgar Evers Rifle Club for the purpose of training an "army" to invade Mississippi.* The following year the club had joined with the Revolutionary Action Movement (RAM) to form a new organization, euphemistically named the Fox and Wolf Hunt Club. RAM subtitled itself "the Black Liberation Front of the U.S.A.," and had close connections with Robert Williams, a Negro who had fled to Cuba and from there was urging revolution. Williams was writing and RAM was distributing primers on guer-rilla warfare: "The weapons of defense employed by Afro-American Freedom Fighters must consist of a poor man's arsenal. Gasoline fire bombs (Molotov cocktails), lye or acid bombs . . . can be used extensively. During the night hours such weapons thrown from roof tops will make the streets impossible for racist cops to patrol. . . . High-powered sniper rifles are readily available. Armor-piercing bullets will penetrate oil storage tanks from a distance. . . . The electrical plant should be the first target." [1]

* Medgar Evers, field secretary of the NAACP in Mississippi, was murdered in 1963 by a segregationist.

Could it be, Girardin asked himself, that this was indeed the start of revolution? That nothing was happening because the action on Twelfth Street was
"a diversionary tactic to get all our people on the west side when the main
attack would be perhaps in auto plants on the east side or something on the
east side of the city?" [2] It was along the riverfront (both east and west) that
the electric plants, pharmaceutical works, and heavy industry were located. At
12:15 P.M. Girardin ordered a large number of police officers moved from the
Twelfth Street staging area at Hermann Kiefer Hospital to strategic installations
throughout the city.

During the same hour, however, the volatile mixture on Twelfth Street south
of Clairmount exploded. Shortly before 1 P.M. flames burst from four stores.

When fire had broken out four hours earlier in the shoe store, Detroit Fire
Chief Charles J. Quinlan had promoted a Negro fire captain to acting battalion
chief and sent him in with as many of the department's Negro firemen (6
percent of the total) as he had been able to round up. Now, however, white
firemen had to be rushed into the area.

They were greeted with rocks and bottles. Several firemen and police officers
reported injuries from thrown objects.

At 1:30 P.M. the police launched a sweep to disperse the crowd. By then
it was too late. As they advanced with fixed bayonets, a rumor swept through
the throng that a man had been bayoneted. (The rumor was false.) Hostility
intensified. The police attempted to protect the firemen as they moved from
fire to fire. Twelve-man squads of officers were stationed at two-block intervals,
but they continued to make no effort to interfere with looters who were smashing store windows. The inactivity of the police emboldened the crowd. There
had been a breakdown in communications—the officers were reacting to a full-
scale riot with the same tactics they had been instructed to employ in order to
prevent a riot.

Since 9 A.M. both the Michigan State Police and the National Guard had had
liaison men at the Tenth Precinct police station. Three hundred and fifty men
assembled for their regular drill at the Detroit Artillery Armory on the city's
outskirts were ordered by Governor Romney to be held on standby alert, and
the State Police issued a similar alert order. The National Guard and State Police
made repeated inquiries whether assistance was needed. As late as 1:55 P.M.
Girardin responded no, the situation appeared to be under control.

But at two o'clock Mayor Cavanagh decided that no one any longer knew
what the situation was or could predict what turns it would take. Five minutes
later he placed a call requesting the assistance of the State Police officers.

At 3 P.M., 360 state officers were assembling at the Artillery Armory, bringing the total force there to 700 men. But by then the riot was spilling outward
from Twelfth Street like a flaming tide of oil. Westward it raced to Grand River
Boulevard and southward to Grand Boulevard, licking at the edges of the General Motors Building.

At ten minutes past four, the mayor called Governor Romney at his suburban
Bloomfield Hills home, and requested that the National Guard be brought into
the city. By 5 P.M. two hundred guardsmen were on their way to a staging area
at Central High School, and two hundred State Police officers had arrived at
the police command post at Kiefer Hospital.

Simultaneously, Mayor Cavanagh and Conrad Mallett were meeting with
approximately seventy-five members of the Mayor's Summer Task Force, and

other community leaders, representing every Negro opinion except that of the revolutionaries. Included were Detroit's two black congressmen, Charles Diggs and John Conyers Jr., the Trade Union Leadership Council's Horace Sheffield, and the youth who had led the 1966 boycott at Northern High School. Cavanagh advised them that he had asked for the National Guard and that he planned to impose a curfew. He received complete and unanimous backing, and there were calls of "do everything you have to do, just bring peace and order to our city." Several of the participants, however, remembering the 1943 riot, urged that citizens be assigned as community liaison officers to National Guard and police units. Their suggestion was ignored.

Only now were most Detroiters becoming aware that something was awry in their city. Fifty thousand had attended the Detroit Tigers-New York Yankees baseball game and a large number of them, making their way home in late afternoon via the John Lodge Freeway, could see fire after fire as they paralleled Twelfth Street.

On Twelfth Street, people were running around looting and shouting, drinking and laughing. All were swept along in the frenzy. One man stood in front of a smashed store window and yelled, "Stop it! Stop it!" to the people who were rushing past him to get in. Finally he gave up—and followed them in.

In many locations, where people were looting, the firemen were paid no heed. Elsewhere, youths hurled rocks and bottles at the men. The youths did not want the fires put out. Firemen had met similar resistance in riots as far back as the Civil War. Rig after rig radioed: "There is no police protection here at all; there isn't a policeman in the area," or, "We are getting stoned and bombed on Linwood and Clydesdale," or, "We are getting it bad. We'll try to go in and make another pass at it again."

At 4:30 P.M. Chief Quinlan ordered:

"All those companies without police protection, tell them to withdraw. Do not try to get in and extinguish the fires." [3]

The firemen pulled back from a one-hundred-square-block area to await police protection. Throughout the afternoon and evening the wind was blowing at a steady ten miles per hour with gusts up to twenty-two miles per hour. The effect was much the same as it had been in 1805. The flames spread from building to building. Two thirds of the buildings were destroyed by fires ignited someplace else.

At 7:30 P.M. Governor Romney was driven to police headquarters. At nine o'clock he went aloft in a National Guard helicopter to survey the city. By then looting had spread as far north as Seven-Mile Road and as far west as Livernois. Within another two hours it progressed to the location of the previous year's "Kercheval incident" on the East Side. From aloft, the glittering lights on the East Side presented the normal appearance of ordered patterns of streets and intersections, broad boulevards and neon concentrations of shopping districts. But as the helicopter passed west of Woodward Avenue tongues of flame swathed in smoke leaped up from the electric pattern, as if scores of short circuits had taken place. The governor was not aware that often a single arson had touched off rivers of fire. He saw "entire blocks in flames" and had the impression that "the city had been bombed." [4]

The fires were everywhere, up and down Twelfth Street, radiating out to Grand River Avenue on the west, Hamtramck on the east, and Vernor Avenue on the south. Never before in an American riot had fires wreaked such havoc on residential structures, structures almost entirely occupied by Negroes. One fire set on Twelfth Street swept down a cross street and wiped out an entire block of houses and apartment buildings. In the city, 606 dwelling units were destroyed. People saved what possessions they could and piled them in the streets. Going off to look for a place to sleep, they became violators of the 9 P.M. curfew imposed by the mayor and were arrested.

It was past 10:30 P.M. when Governor Romney, shaken, returned to police headquarters. Looting was spreading, and reports of small-arms firing were being received. The police had been placed on twelve-hour shifts, and over 1,600 men were on duty. But many were guarding installations, taking care of prisoners, and performing routine functions. Fewer than 700 were on patrol. They were augmented by a force of 750 National Guardsmen and 800 State Police officers, between half and two thirds of whom were in the streets. But 4,000 men, nearly half the state's National Guard, was still at its summer encampment at Camp Grayling, two hundred miles north of Detroit. At ten minutes before 11 P.M. Governor Romney ordered these units trucked to Detroit.

In the aging police building, desks and cabinets formed cramped mazes everywhere, and there was no empty office for the governor. So Girardin had a desk set up for Governor Romney in a corner of the commissioner's office. The corridors and offices with their faded walls, the scuffed floors, the two creeping elevators, and the lingering staleness of tens of thousands of cigars created an atmosphere straight out of the 1930's. The computer room with its blue machines, blinking lights and revolving disks, and the gleaming communications center were like transplants in an aging body.

It was in the communications center that the course of the riot was most evident. As incoming messages were received they were transmitted electronically, and written out by an automatic hand in the adjacent radio room. Above the two-man crews, each handling two precincts, hovered a huge, green-lit map of the city divided into scout-car areas. On it the location of every car was plotted. As midnight came and went, reports of riot activity continued to accelerate. Between 1 and 2 A.M. a climax was reached. During that one hour there were 238 riot-related messages sent over the radio, 96 known offenses committed, and 213 arrests.

Observing the increase of riot activity even as the number of State Police and National Guardsmen on the streets increased, Girardin, Cavanagh, and Romney were alarmed. Up-to-the-hour intelligence is difficult to obtain in any riot. All the men could go by were the reports from the communications center. They had no way of knowing that the riot was now at its crest. If there were organization to the rioting, if the riot were still gathering momentum, then the city would need more help quickly. The National Guard was already being employed in four different precincts, and the guardsmen from Camp Grayling could not be expected until midday. Who knew if there would be enough of them then?

At 2 A.M. the governor, the mayor, the police commissioner, and their staffs conferred and agreed to ask for the assistance of Federal troops. Fifteen minutes later Mayor Cavanagh telephoned Vice-President Humphrey, who was in Minneapolis. The Vice-President told Cavanagh he should contact U.S. Attorney-General Ramsey Clark through the White House switchboard. At twenty minutes before 3 A.M. Governor Romney awakened Attorney-General Clark and requested that 5,000 Federal troops be dispatched.

Clark asked the governor if he were certain he needed the troops. If they were sent, Detroit would become the only American city outside of Washington, D.C., in which Federal troops had been employed twice to quell a domestic disorder. (Actually, three times: the first occasion was in 1863.) Romney responded that he *was* certain.

But while the governor was talking to the Attorney-General, the commander of the Michigan National Guard, who had established his headquarters at the Detroit Armory more than eight miles from the police building, was telling the commanding general of the U.S. Fifth Army in Chicago that he believed his men would be able to handle the situation. When Clark received this conflicting report, he called Romney back at 3:30 A.M. and asked him to reconcile the conflict. The governor's request for troops would have to be in writing. Romney and Cavanagh, who were in the midst of a press conference they had called to announce they were asking for Federal assistance, had to backtrack and say that they were reevaluating the situation. Major General Cecil Simmons, the National Guard commander, was called to police headquarters. It was after 5 A.M. before he had been briefed, and agreed with the assessment that Federal troops would be needed.

At 5:15 A.M. the governor once more called Clark. Clark advised him to address a telegram to the President stating that he was faced with a situation of domestic violence that state and local forces could not control. Romney, rumpled and red-eyed, had been up for nearly twenty-four hours. He thought Clark was asking him to certify that a situation of domestic *insurrection* existed. (Clark may, in fact, have alluded to *insurrection,* since this is the term employed in the Constitution.) The governor was unwilling to make such a statement, and he could not say that the remainder of the National Guard, once it arrived in the city, would not be able to control the riot.

As dawn broke over the city, and the sun rose filtered through the smoke, the governor and the mayor climbed into a car for another tour and assessment. People do not riot around the clock any more than they commit crimes with equal frequency around the clock, and at 6 A.M. Monday the streets were fairly quiet. Nevertheless, fires were still burning. Looting had occurred in areas spread over half the city. Romney and Cavanagh agreed that it was impossible to predict developments.

Two telegrams were composed: one to the Attorney-General and the other to the President. There was further confusion and discussion about the language, and Romney was on the telephone twice more to Clark. (Romney "recommended" the dispatch of Federal troops. Clark advised him that he had to "request" them.) There was, Romney complained, only "a single stenographer in the office—she is not a very fast typist—and she took an inordinately long time typing that first telegram, and we couldn't get the second one out until we got the first one out." [5] Not until ten o'clock was the request dispatched to Washington. By then, looting was on the increase again.

At 3 P.M. Cyrus Vance, President Johnson's special representative, and Lieutenant General J. L. Throckmorton, commander of a five-thousand-man airborne task force, met at Selfridge Air Force Base twenty-five miles north of Detroit. The President was reluctant to involve Federal troops in quelling a riot, and he did not want to commit them unless there was an absolute need. Vance put off Romney and Cavanagh, both of whom urged that the troops be brought in immediately. At 5 P.M. Vance and General Throckmorton embarked on a two-hour tour of the city with the governor and the mayor. Nearly thirty fires were burning, but most of them were being brought under control. In most of the areas through which the party passed there was only an occasional window broken or store looted. At least half the National Guardsmen had not yet been committed. Neither Vance nor General Throckmorton believed Federal troops should be ordered into action.

Since the previous evening, guardsmen had been assigned hither and yon, twenty here and fifty there, wherever the police requested. They were ordered to follow the directions of the police, use only minimum force, and conduct themselves like soldiers. Most of them were in their middle twenties and came from lower-middle class backgrounds.* There were few Negroes among them (127 out of 9,760 men were black). For months they had heard talk of "revolution" and "guerrilla warfare." Everyone was conscious of the danger from "snipers."

Their commanding officer, General Simmons, insisted that they were "well trained." But they had had no training for the situation into which they were thrust, and between two thirds and three fourths of them felt *untrained*. None of them knew what to expect. As units were divided and dispersed, the command chain broke down. Men were posted on street corners and left there for days. Sometimes orders did not reach the men; at other times the orders seemed confused and contradictory. One officer said he was well informed so long as he still had dimes for the pay phone.

Many of the men believed themselves to be in "hostile territory," engaged in a domestic guerrilla war. They were tense and apprehensive. They were carying rifles with rounds loaded into the chambers. Repeatedly weapons were discharged accidentally. Except for a vague directive that automatic weapons were not to be fired except on an officer's orders—a directive not always obeyed—no warnings were issued on the danger of firing high-velocity weapons in a crowded city.

Men were not instructed what to do about cars that did not respond quickly enough at roadblocks. They fired shots "across the bows" of automobiles or at the tires—and the bullets headed in the direction of other guardsmen and law enforcement personnel a few blocks away. The explosions of cans and bottles in burning stores, the collapse of timbers in skeleton buildings, the knocking over of a trash barrel in an alley—any strange noise in the surrealistic configurations of darkness carried a message of danger. The men reacted as if they were on a picket line and an enemy sniper might be lurking unseen in the jungle night. They fired on "suspicion," and when one man pulled the trigger, others fired in the same direction. Hundreds of rounds were dispatched at street lights which, the men felt, exposed them to sniper fire. But once the lights had been shot out, the darkness only heightened the anxiety.

Bullets shattered windows, ricocheted from walls and streets, and seemingly —after having been shot up at street lights—rained down from rooftops. Even experienced combat veterans could not determine the origins of such fire. On

---

* Four out of five were working in skilled blue-collar or entry-level white-collar jobs. Seven of eight had joined the National Guard so as not to be drafted.

Sunday night police had continued to practice the restraints normally imposed on the use of weapons. The number of guardsmen on duty had been limited and they had been under police supervision. Firing had not been widespread. On Monday, however, all available guardsmen, many of whom had had little or no sleep during the previous night, were placed in the streets. Darkness brought an exponential increase in the amount of firing. Amidst the splat-splat sound of weapons and the whine of ricochets, guardsmen and law enforcement personnel took cover and reported that they were being pinned down by "sniper fire."

Riot activity—as measured by the number of offenses and arrests—was down to approximately half what it had been on the previous night. But because of the reports of "sniper fire," messages coming into the communications center between 9 and 11 P.M. nearly doubled over the same period twenty-four hours earlier. Occasionally, Governor Romney himself went to the radio room to pick up the action reports and take them to Vance and General Throckmorton. As the figures kept increasing, he declared:

"We've got to have those troops."

By 11 P.M. all state and city forces were committed. Vance telephoned the White House. At 11:20 P.M. President Johnson issued an executive order authorizing the use of Federal troops.

General Throckmorton, upon whom overall command now devolved, divided the city along Woodward Avenue. The army took responsibility for the eastern section. The western section—including Twelfth Street—remained under the control of the National Guard.

At 4 A.M., Tuesday, the transfer was completed. The disciplined army forces were permitted to fire only if they could see the person at whom they were firing, and reports of "sniper fire" in the city's eastern half all but ceased.

West of Woodward Avenue, however, the situation continued much as it had been. General Throckmorton ordered all rifles unloaded, but the order did not reach National Guard troops, or was ignored by them. Repeatedly the police command post at Hermann Kiefer Hospital was "besieged by sniper fire" that came from the direction of Twelfth Street. A tough, potbellied captain—a teamster in civilian life—told his men: "We've got the area from Woodward to Twelfth, and from Grand Boulevard to Clairmount. Snipers all over the place." On the police radio, a desperate voice sounded the alarm: "Snipers are all over! Snipers are all over!" [6]

The ironic tragedies of the riot went on. A private Negro guard requested assistance against rioters at a store. When a police officer and three National Guardsmen responded, he was shot dead. A four-year-old girl was machine-gunned to death when the flash of a cigarette lighter was mistaken for the firing of a weapon. A white businesswomen opened the drapes on the window of her hotel room, said, "Look at the tanks!" and toppled dead, with a bullet in her. Police killed an arson suspect, who allegedly attempted to escape while being interrogated, but attributed his death to "sniper fire." The heavy "sniper fire" reported in the vicinity of the Algiers Motel was the prologue to a tragedy in which three Negro youths consorting with two white prostitutes were killed. (Two Detroit vice squad officers were accused of murder, but acquitted.) A National Guard column led by a tank failed to verify a "sniper" report, and laid down withering machine-gun and rifle fire against one of the mansions on quiet LaSalle Boulevard. (The owners had been having difficulty with the tenants, whom they had just evicted, and who allegedly had threatened to obtain the help of the National Guard.) Amid the hail of wild firing that swept the city, a guardsman and a fireman fell fatally wounded. To a young, nervous, and excited guardsman, who was "hoping for some action," it seemed "like in the movies." *

If the initial confusion of the riot had liberated the rioters from normal restraints, the "sniper" chaos that followed dissolved some of the regulatory inhibitions of the police. Tired and exasperated, working amidst terrible tensions, some of the officers reverted to the police tactics of prior generations and scrapped "civil liberties." Prisoners were handled roughly. "Alley courts" were revived. "Sniper" suspects—who were numerous—were butted around. Verbal abuse was widespread. In one incident a National Guard unit was escorting a nurse to work when the group was halted by a police car. A police officer referred to the nurse as a "nigger bitch." A Negro guardsman told him to shut up. The officer's hand went to his gun. The guardsman swiveled his machine gun toward the police. He warned that if the officer pulled his gun, he and his fellow officers were "going to die." The officers climbed back into their car and drove off.

By 6 A.M. Tuesday the police had arrested two thirds of the total of 7,200 persons that were to be picked up during the riot. Girardin had wanted to avoid mass arrests, but a dragnet-type operation was now being conducted. Everyone was swept up regardless of identification and reason—a probation officer here, a newspaper reporter there. The jails were filled within a few hours. Prisoners were herded into the garages at precinct stations and the basement of police headquarters. As in other disturbances, the rioters were characterized by their youth. Seven hundred were sixteen years and under, and 3,100 were between the ages of seventeen and twenty-four.

Early Thursday morning, General Throckmorton succeeded in establishing control over the National Guard troops. "Sniper fire" quickly subsided. Governor Romney, Mayor Cavanagh, and Police Commissioner Girardin returned to their homes for their first substantial sleep in four days. Thousands of persons—all those except the small minority charged with serious offenses—were released from the jails.

Scores had been arrested as "snipers," and newspaper headlines had heralded their capture. But, in the light of day, they turned out to have been snipers without weapons. (There was one major shoot-out between rioters and police, but none of the rioters was captured. In another incident a man with a pistol went berserk, but his actions were only marginally connected with the riot.) One of the youths in jail, anxious for attention, told NBC News a tale about well-organized guerrillas and snipers. But the Detroit press and the FBI disproved the story.

No "snipers" were brought to trial. Charges against people arrested were dropped and cases evaporated. More than 500 of the 7,200 confined had been picked up on violations not connected with the riot. Nearly 1,800 persons were released after it was discovered they had been arrested erroneously, or had unintentionally or unavoidably violated the curfew. Another 1,800 pleaded guilty to misdemeanor charges—most of them to "entering without owner's permission." They were placed on probation, received suspended sentences, or were sentenced to the time they already had spent in jail. Only 3 percent of

* Pages 84–108 of the *Report of the National Advisory Commission on Civil Disorders* are devoted to the events in Detroit.

the cases came to trial. (Half resulted in convictions.) In hundreds of cases store owners refused to prosecute after they discovered how much time they would have to spend in court, and charges were dismissed. Fewer than 50 persons were sentenced to jail, most of them for less than three months. The longest sentence was one to fifteen years for armed robbery.

Like almost every other disorder of the 1960's, the Detroit riot had been blown out of proportion—all the more because the fire department, inadequate in size for such a conflagration, had been ineffective during the riot's early hours. Original damage estimates of $500 million were reduced by four fifths and more—opinion differed on how much a store in a declining inner city neighborhood was worth, or how much stock it might have contained.

Nearly all of the property destroyed had been built in the early part of the century and ranged from substandard to dilapidated.

"The tragedy," said one of the mayor's aides only half in jest, "was not that so much of the city was burned, but so little." He suggested that if there were another riot, the administration should consider organizing "a selective burning squad."

On Thursday afternoon (July 27), the mayor and the governor invited five hundred Detroiters, a cross-section of the community including block club leaders, militant blacks, and the heads of the major auto companies, to meet in the auditorium of the City-County Building. The riot was causing people who for years had been looking outward from the city to turn their gazes back upon it. Momentarily the riot shocked them into a determination to do something about the deterioration.

Never before had the city seen such a gathering. The leaders of the automobile industry were there: Henry Ford II; James M. Roche, president of General Motors; Lynn Townsend, president of Chrysler; Roy Chapin, Jr., president of American Motors and son of the principal founder of the erstwhile Hudson Motor Car Company. Roche pledged the "facilities, skills, resources, and people" of General Motors to "insure the prompt and effective rebuilding of Detroit." Walter Reuther, in keeping with his character, made the most expansive speech. Declaring that he had been shocked by the lack of clean-up and repair of the damage he had seen in Watts following the Los Angeles riot, he volunteered six hundred thousand labor union members for the task of "cleaning up the scars." The union members, he said, would go to work after hours and on weekends to remove the wreckage. With Public Works Commissioner Bob Toohey he worked out a plan to have union members assist in transforming the sites of eighty burned-out buildings into mini-parks. But Reuther's gung-ho projects expired in the unenthusiastic and apathetic response from union members. The mini-parks were never put in, and the clean-up in Detroit turned out to be far slower than the one in Los Angeles.

Out of the meeting came the decision to establish a "New Detroit Committee" to channel private resources into the city, and to chart its future. The committee was to be composed of all elements of the community. Its staff would come largely from manpower loaned by various corporations. Joseph L. Hudson, Jr., the thirty-six-year-old president of what had grown into the world's largest privately owned department store, was chosen chairman. William Patrick, who had been the city's first Negro councilman under the new charter, was named executive director. Detroit became the first city to organize. an "urban coalition."

In Washington, the Detroit riot stimulated the formation of a National Urban

Coalition. The concept of uniting business and government to solve the problems of the cities had been talked about since the summer of 1966, when the pressures resulting from the Vietnam War and the onset of the "white backlash" made it appear that Federal funds would be directed away from antipoverty and urban programs. Little, however, had been done to realize the concept until John Feild, a former Detroiter who was executive director of the President's Committee on Equal Employment Opportunity, was spurred to action by the riot and contacted Mayors John Lindsay of New York and Joe Barr of Pittsburgh. On July 31 an ad hoc steering committee called for a national convocation of municipal officials, urban experts, and businessmen. On August 24 more than one thousand persons met in Washington. Early in 1968 Secretary of Health, Education, and Welfare John Gardner agreed to accept the presidency of the National Urban Coalition, and in March he obtained a grant of one million dollars from the Ford Foundation to finance it.

For President Johnson it had been "a week such as no nation should live through; a time of violence and tragedy." In addition to the Detroit riot, there had been disturbances in East Harlem and Rochester, New York; Cambridge, Maryland; Toledo and Youngstown, Ohio; Phoenix, Arizona; Chicago, Illinois; and Pontiac, Flint, and Grand Rapids, Michigan. The President had done more for social programs, minorities, and the cities than any of his predecessors in the White House. He had been beguiled by a plethora of statistics like those about the four hundred thousand persons "reached" by the antipoverty program in Detroit. He was perplexed. It seemed the more he had done, the more violent and extensive the rioting had become. In five years Detroit had received more than $230 million in Federal grants, and it had produced the most explosive riot of all. The nation, said the President, was "disturbed, baffled, and dismayed." Subjected to the same influences as Ray Girardin and other Americans, he was all but convinced that the riots were being organized. To determine "What happened? Why did it happen? What can be done to prevent it from happening again and again?" he announced the appointment of a National Advisory Commission on Civil Disorders.[7]

To Cavanagh, the events of the week proved almost a relief. The pedestal on which he had been placed had disintegrated.* But he had survived. And now there was no more need of pretending. Even some of the old verve was returning, as if there had been a purification by fire. On the "Meet the Press" program he declared, "If what happened in Detroit this week happened in Washington, D.C., this might lift the veil off the eyes of the members of the Congress." (Eight months later the first part of his wish was to be granted.)

Tieless, the mayor walked up Twelfth Street and talked to its habitués. No longer was he the bright and eager Frank Merriwell who had taken office nearly six years before. His eyes were puffed, his hairline was receding (a nagging worry), his face looked coarser, and sometimes he was referred to as "Detroit Fats." (Having stopped smoking two years before, he had gained twenty pounds.) But, weathered and aged like the city itself, he was more mature and, somehow, more appealing.

"Hey, J.P. Come back here. You're all right, man!" A young black called out. Cavanagh nodded his appreciation. Already The Strip was recovering some

---

* On July 18, five days before the start of the riot, his wife, Mary, had filed for separate maintenance.

of its joie de vivre—like a sybarite two days after a particularly excessive dissipation. In the back alleys looters were peddling liquor, clothing, appliances, television sets—a peripatetic flea market was in progress. In the evening dampness an acid smell rippled out from the charcoal debris, and a sometime brewmaster murmured, "Man, I bet this stuff would make fine sour mash." There was an aura not so much of revolution, not so much of violence and law breaking, but of illicit consummation.

111

Catalogs of Failure

ON TWELFTH STREET MAYOR CAVANAGH COULD SEE SOME OF THE SOCIOLOGICAL effects of urban renewal. Much of the black vice driven from Hastings Street and Paradise Valley had lodged on The Strip. The white alcoholics forced from Michigan Avenue had scattered in several directions. Since Harold Black's suggestion that another skid row would have to be created for them had been laughed off, they had dispersed into a number of new skid rows. Some of the men had merely moved a few blocks farther out on Michigan Avenue. There they huddled in the bleak dawn on a street corner that functioned as a "slave market," where contractors could hire casual laborers at twelve dollars a day.* Other skid rows formed along once-elegant Jefferson Avenue and on Cass Avenue south of Wayne State University; one new skid row was clustered in the bars around the City-County Building and the Greyhound Bus Station. At the bus station the Negro guard swung his billy club at the derelicts, called them "goddam white bums," and chased them away.

Mayor Albert Cobo had decided to clear the drunkards from the "gateway to the city," and they had lodged almost beneath the windows of the mayor's office. On some days when Mayor Cavanagh was driven out of the parking lot in his limousine he might have seen Peter Jansen reeling down the street.

Jansen was one of the one hundred thousand identified alcoholics in Detroit and nine million in the nation. (Since many alcoholics continue to function in one fashion or another, statistics on alcoholism are not overly reliable.) The habitués of skid row were mostly middle-aged and elderly—some of them had been "social drinkers" until their forties and then tumbled over the brink. Among them were professional men—one man asking for handouts insisted he was a design engineer at Ford, and said: "I came down to the Brass Rail to get a drink. I am getting drunk, and going home in the morning." Many were pensioners. Nearly all had physical ailments. They were among the world's loneliest men—according to custom, no one paid attention to anyone else, nor

---

* Some of the contractors gave vouchers that could only be cashed in certain bars, thus encouraging the men to drink the money away.

to what was happening around him. They were easy prey for strong-arm robbers and petty thieves. If one drunk were being rolled in a doorway, a dozen others would walk by and pretend not to see.

Jansen was seventy-one years old, and most alcoholics did not live past sixty. He had been in superb physical condition in his youth, but his skin had turned parchmentlike and his face cadaverous. In the fall of 1967 he was coughing against the wind and shaking with cold. He was too sick to do even the lightest work. Sometimes he went to "Sally" (the Salvation Army); and if he had $1.15 he might bed down in the Mariner's Inn. During the day he could keep warm by climbing the stairs to the second floor of an old, rundown building two blocks from the bus station, and there amid the barren surroundings doze on a scuffed chair. It was the walk-in center maintained by the Mayor's Rehabilitation Committee on Skid Row Problems. Purportedly, the center existed to encourage alcoholics to change their ways, and it provided counseling for those who wanted it. But its very appearance mirrored the futility of the lives of those who came there. In its files were thousands of names, just as there were thousands and tens of thousands of names in the files of MCHRD, of the school system, of the Bureau of Social Services, of the Juvenile Court, and of a myriad social agencies. Yet what, in the end, they amounted to were catalogs of failure.

In the late afternoon Jansen staggered out into the street again. A dying man, he traveled in great loping strides from a lamp post to a doorway, from a doorway to a lamp post, propping himself up and gasping for air. In the setting darkness a mixture of derelicts and government workers passed him by. A half block down the street was the lighted doorway of a bar—if he could reach it, he might live another day.

Peter Jansen's daughter Rita and her husband, George Devers, had moved out of the Twelfth Street area in 1960. As a result of economic depression and the movement of people from the city, public housing projects were searching for tenants for the first time in Detroit's history. Both the Brewster and Jeffries projects were convenient to George's place of work, the Dodge plant in Hamtramck. But Brewster had always been a "Negro" project, and Jeffries had turned entirely black within five years of the attempt to convert it from "white" to "integrated." So George, Rita, and their six children moved into Herman Gardens, a "white" project in the western section of the city. That meant a daily drive of eight miles each way across the center of the city for George. The saving in rent payments was eaten up by the increased transportation costs.

The birth of three physically and mentally defective children within a period of four years—Hilda in 1955, Norman in 1957, and Laura in 1959—had shattered whatever stability the family had had. Hilda and Norman were blind and of borderline mentality (Hilda's IQ was 75 and Norman's 69), and Laura had cerebral palsy and a septal defect. Since Georgia had been born with club feet, only Trilby and Ryan were without congenital defects. With each new catastrophic arrival, George's resentment toward Rita grew. He drank more, stayed away more, and left her to cope with the children as best she could. She, groping around half blind, was incapable of coping with them. Mixing codeine, tranquilizers, and wine she was often suspended midway between the worlds of reality and dreams.

During the 1961 recession, George was laid off at Dodge. Once more a layoff and the financial problems it brought tumbled the family into a crisis. They defaulted on their rent payments. The children roamed the grounds unsupervised. Together with children of other families who had too little money, too many offspring, and not enough compatibility they formed gangs of vandals. After a screaming, knockdown fight between Rita and George, the Devers family was evicted from Herman Gardens.

They moved to the Brightmoor area of northwest Detroit. The district had been a slum ever since the tacky, foundationless frame houses had been built during the auto industry boom of the 1920's. Then George took a job as a mechanic in a small town in southeastern Michigan and moved away from his family. He sent money erratically and in small amounts. Rita's difficulties mounted. When an attendance officer visited the home in September of 1962 to determine why the children were not in school, he found Rita in bed. Physically and mentally worn out and ill, she was befuddled from pills and drugs. There was neither food nor clothing for the children.

Momentarily conscience-stricken, George returned. Since he was without a job, he applied to the welfare department. He was advised that, as was normal, the case would take two weeks to reactivate.

Desperate, he called caseworkers at the various social agencies with which the family had had contact. After assessing the situation, the Juvenile Court worker agreed that the need was immediate. He reported:

"I spoke with three individuals at the Department of Public Welfare, none of whom was able to be of any assistance except to reaffirm that the case will have to go through the proper channels, and that the Deverses could not be seen till Sept. 29. I tried to contact Miss G., case worker at Catholic Social Services, and was told that the case was closed and Miss G. no longer was on the staff. I spoke to another case worker and she said the family had been given help from time to time and termed them 'professional beggars.' I said I felt the need was dire, because of health problems of the parent, as well as of the children. She suggested I get in touch with the Society of St. Vincent de Paul."

Throughout the fall of 1962, a visitor to the Devers home might have thought himself back in the Jansen home a quarter century before. The children slept in blankets rolled up on the floor. While George sought work, the two older girls, Trilby and Georgia, stayed out of school to baby-sit. Every other week the supply of food ran out, and they went begging from door to door. Since there was inadequate fuel with which to heat the house, the pipes froze, and the family was without water. Then the pipes burst, and they were inundated.

Rita was exhausted by her ailments, exhausted from drugs, and exhausted from fighting. When a quarrel erupted, she would take Laura in her arms to shield herself so that George would not hit her. When Laura fell ill with measles and pneumonia and was taken to the hospital, neither Rita nor George made any effort to pick her up after they were notified she was ready to go home. "Home," in fact, was still without water, icy and mildewing.

The children were hardly in school at all. Hilda was supposed to be picked up daily by a taxi to be taken to special classes for the blind, but because of administrative snarls the taxi did not show up until the fall term was well under way, and then it was a day-to-day affair whether it would appear. In December, 1962, George went back to work at the Dodge plant. Rita, recovering some of her strength, assumed a measure of control of the household. The children began to attend school every day. But then, on a New Year's binge, George battered Rita so badly that she took the children and left him.

The half dozen social agencies involved with the Deverses were angry at each other, disgusted with the family, and prepared to place the blame for the chaos on everyone but themselves. The Aid-to-the-Blind worker called the case "troublesome." The worker at Catholic Social Services said the family was always "trying to pick off other agencies that do not know them." The parish priest refused to extend further assistance.

The caseworker at the Juvenile Court attempted to set up a conference of a'l the agencies involved, but—as was typical—he failed. Everyone agreed that such a conference would be desirable in order to end the duplication and confusion and to look at the family as a unit. But when it came to setting a time and place, no one had the time; no one had a room in which the half dozen or more workers could meet; everyone thought that one of the others should make the arrangements; and when the arrangements were made, two thirds of those involved protested that they would not be able to attend because the arrangements were inconvenient.

Laura had to be waited on hand and foot and watched constantly. At the age of four she could not walk, talk, control her bowel or bladder, or feed herself. The caseworker at the welfare department suggested that since she took so much of Rita's time, "she should be put away for her own good." A psychological test seemed to indicate that she had more potential than she was showing, and that her lack of ability might be due not so much to brain damage as to a "psychotic autism," stemming from her environment. A psychiatrist recommended immediate placement in Plymouth State Hospital in order to develop her potential.

But Rita was unable to discuss rationally Laura's removal from the home. She cried that she would not allow her family to be broken up and her children to be treated the way she and her brothers and sisters had been treated. Seeking solace and reassurance, she reverted to her premarital behavior and accepted comfort from any man who offered it. George drank and strayed after other women. He tried to keep the family together, but he could not work and simultaneously look after the children. The landlord claimed that the family was responsible for the damage to the house, and evicted them. Rita disappeared. For the next ten days George and the five children—Laura, fortunately, was again in the hospital—made their home in the car. He would get someone to put them up for one night. Then the next night, when there would be no one who would take them, he would park the car in front of a bar. Leaving the children cramped and huddled to sleep as best as they could, he would drink the hours away.

Shortly thereafter, Rita was discovered by the police slumped half naked in a doorway. Admitted to the drug addiction clinic at Hermann Kiefer Hospital for what was to be only the first of several stays, she spent the next few weeks being washed out and dried out.

Since that was a crisis that could not be ignored, various agencies responded with services for which George had been "begging." Just as a confluence of factors produced the sporadic catastrophes, now a combination of favorable events resulted in the fortunes of the family improving. Returning from the hospital, Rita was determined to be a good mother. During the economic boom of 1964 George worked steadily, and earned more than ever before. A year after he and the children had roamed about the city in the car, the family was buying, on a land contract, a frame house in Redford Township. In the kitchen was a new stove; in the garage a drier and washer; in the living room a large-screen television set. George was making house and car payments and paying off the $2,000 debt on the household furnishings and appliances at a rate of $100 a month for thirty-six months. As long as there was no economic downturn, as long as there were no personal mishaps, as long as the family remained on an even keel, they were payments he could just barely make. He drove thirteen miles each way to and from work, and spent nearly two hours a day on the road. But, he said, he was glad to do it so the children could have a decent place to live and a yard full of old apple trees in which to play.

A visiting nurse was assigned to the family to help care for Laura. Responding to the increased attention, Laura at the age of six began to walk. She was extraordinarily affectionate and had an instinct for endearing herself to people. Her speech was a babble of unintelligible sounds through which, with startling clarity, a "damn" or "shit" would suddenly burst.

Psychiatric counseling for the family was provided by the Kiefer Drug Addiction Clinic and by Catholic Social Services. The psychiatric caseworker from Catholic Social Services came to the house every other week to conduct sessions in group therapy. He had difficulty persuading Rita, who disliked psychological probing, to join the group. If George were home, he only inhibited the discussion. So the caseworker, a young man, did not object when he withdrew to the kitchen to drink beer. The children, sitting in a circle on the living room floor, thought the discussions great fun. Sometimes they told the truth, and sometimes they lied—the worker had difficulty knowing when it was harder to believe them. Georgia, fourteen, kept asking to talk to him alone upstairs. She pouted when he responded he would talk to her alone anyplace else.

At the end of each session, George would meet the psychiatric worker at the door, and, barring his way, ask: "And now what are you going to do about it?"

Whenever Rita saw the caseworker she would tell him that George was barhopping with girls; that George was embracing Trilby and Georgia and only waiting for the opportunity to have incestuous relations with them. By 1966 Rita was again addicted. Her eyesight had deteriorated. She could no longer read even the largest print, and had to be helped across the street. Sporadically, she continued to leave George. Since she did not trust him with the girls, she would take them with her. The task of caring for the three younger children fell to twelve-year-old Ryan. Although he was a bright youngster, he too fell behind in school.

The caseworker was more and more frustrated. The group therapy sessions were futile. George called Catholic Social Services to complain that the caseworker was storming out of the house and swearing at the children.

In the winter of 1966–1967 the transmission of George's car failed and required a major overhaul. The family was again in disarray. George was two to three months behind in payments. Medical expenses were increasing. The repair bill for the car collapsed the family's financial structure. A court judgment of $938.66 was entered against him for delinquent payments on the home. The mortgage was foreclosed. The family was evicted. When the regular summer layoff came in the automobile industry, George did not even have enough money to pay for food.

Welfare was reinstated. When George returned to work, creditors obtained so many garnishments against him that he received only thirty dollars in his weekly pay check.

During the first two months of the 1967 spring semester Georgia attended school only six days. From the age of thirteen she had "acted out" her resentment at her mother and father. She was classified as a "troublemaker." In the fall of 1967, fifteen years old, she was still in the seventh grade. She was far bigger than any of her classmates, yet unable to keep up with them in the work. To achieve status, she terrorized her classmates and established herself as the "boss." One girl became so frightened that she screamed and threw up if Georgia came near her.

Most of Georgia's teachers at Murphy Junior High School were convinced she did not lack intelligence. The principal promised to double-promote her if she would cooperate and make an effort to keep up. A request was made to have her tested by the school psychological clinic. But the clinic's backlog was so great that Georgia could not be seen before March, 1968.

She stole and extorted money from younger children. She had respect neither for adults, nor the regulations they established. "They just mess up," she said. Whenever a teacher said something with which she disagreed, she exclaimed: "Oh, shit!" She made advances to male teachers and repeatedly asked them if she could come to their homes to be tutored. She competed with the teachers for the attention of the class. She had one conference after another: with the teachers, with the counselor, with the attendance officer, with the assistant principal, with the principal. She enjoyed the conferences. But they produced no results.

Although she was but one of a handful of children with behavior problems in the school—compared to hundreds in each school in the inner city—teachers complained that she demanded too much of their time, and that the disruptions she caused made teaching impossible. By Thanksgiving she was excluded from four of her six classes. At Christmas she was suspended.

In the spring semester of 1968 she was transferred to Harding Junior High School. Whereas Murphy was considered an "elite" school, Harding, a mile and a half away in the adjacent school "constellation," drew a substantial number of Negroes from the J. W. Smith Homes, a public housing project. Any pretense that Georgia could benefit from further education along traditional lines was hypocritical. In order to satisfy the compulsory attendance law, a place had to be found for her until she reached sixteen. So she was shunted, along with other disruptive pupils, into what essentially were custodial classes.

Georgia said she would go to another school like Murphy. But she refused to go to Harding. "I'm sick of the schools!" she sobbed. "If a nigger was suspended, the Board of Education would knock itself out to assign her to the school she wanted. Everybody thinks I'm a boob. So what? I'm not!"

Georgia's father was no virulent "nigger hater." For more than twenty years George Devers had worked side by side with Negroes. Nevertheless, he would not drink with them. He had brought with him from Alabama a definite sense of whiteness, blackness, and their separateness. Georgia was more prejudiced than he. Struggling to maintain her *place* on a level above the Negroes, she felt degraded by any association, physical or categorical, with them. She resented all the talk about "doing things" for Negroes. She heard they were getting special treatment in the schools and special help in finding jobs. There was a lot of money being handed to them by the government.

George felt much the same way. All his life he had been struggling. He was grossing $175 a week, but the medical and drug bills for Rita and the three younger children came to $125 a month. His pay was being garnished for the back payments on the house in which they were no longer living. He was unable to keep up the payments on the appliances, the furniture, and the car. All went to the repossessor. He was unable to find a job in one of the newer suburban plants but continued to work at the Dodge Main Plant in Hamtramck. The plant was old and outmoded. It was a "Negro" plant, in which blacks outnumbered whites. Since he had no car, George spent almost four hours a day traveling to and from work on buses. His work and travel hours combined were greater than a workman's hours at the turn of the century. He resented young Negroes for the fancy cars they drove. He believed that the unity and militancy of Negroes were enabling them to make gains to which they weren't entitled, gains that they were making at his expense.

"Now Reuther," he said, "all he keeps talking about is the colored. They shoot and burn down half the town, and he wants us to go help clean it up. They say if they don't get jobs they're gonna riot some more, so what do the government do? It gives 'em jobs out at the Rouge and places like that, and then it gives 'em buses to ride out there. They can take those express buses and it takes 'em a half hour to get to work. And I got to ride a bus for two. And who's paying for it all? Me. I got to pay more taxes all the time so that they can chofa the colored around in style!"

(George was making no distinction between income and Social Security taxes. While the Johnson Administration was making heralded cuts in the progressive income tax, of which George paid little, the regressive Social Security tax, of which he paid as much as a single man without dependents and without problems, kept going up.)

"They got the poverty program," he declared, "and they can go and screw to their heart's content, and the government'll take care of the bastards, and all I get is shit!"

Rita had returned home at the beginning of 1968, but there were periods when she would spend days, nonfunctioning, on a codeine jag. George was trying to obtain help from the psychologist who had been counseling Rita at the drug addiction clinic. But the psychologist had taken a new job with the Board of Education, and the drug addiction clinic said they could do nothing unless Rita came in to be interviewed by his replacement. Catholic Social Services had given up and requested they be relieved of supervision of the case by the Juvenile Court. The social worker at the court was of the opinion that "they botched the job." But neither the court, nor the Detroit Department of Public Welfare, nor the Wayne County Department of Social Services, nor the Recorders Court, nor the women's division of the police department, nor the Detroit Public Schools Psychological Clinic, nor the Visiting Teachers Association, nor the Northville State Hospital had done any better.

George thought "the system" was expending all its resources to help the Negro. He had always voted Democratic. But now the Democrats seemed to be out chasing after the Negroes. "Wallace," he said, "is the only one that makes any sense." In the fall of 1968 Alabama Governor George Wallace was becoming a major force to be reckoned with in the auto plants.

He was the only candidate to be "talked up" in the bars of the lower income white areas on the edge of the city. A Wallace worker came through the neighborhood and passed out literature. She urged the people to show their independence of the CIO and UAW by rallying to Wallace when he came to Detroit.

On the night of October 29, when Wallace made his campaign appearance in the city, George and Georgia drove with a friend to Cobo Hall.

Thousands of people were milling about in the vicinity of the convention center. Although the Wallace headquarters in Detroit was nothing more than a small, ramshackle store front in Melvindale, adjacent to the Ford plant at River Rouge, there was a massive turnout of Wallace supporters. Posters proclaimed: IT TAKES COURAGE TO STAND UP FOR AMERICA—GEORGE WALLACE HAS IT. DO YOU?

Opposing Wallace, hundreds of picketers composed primarily of Wayne State University students, Negroes, and hippies, waved Nazi flags and homemade signs stating "Wallace for Halloween," and "Wallace for Fuehrer." Although there was a determined effort to bar them from the auditorium, about a thousand of them were able to infiltrate the throng of more than ten thousand that filled nearly every seat. It was the largest crowd drawn in the city by any candidate during the campaign—and Wallace had been pulling crowds like it all over the state and the "native American" belt of the Midwest.

The right-wing, segregationist American Independent party, under whose banner Wallace was running, had had its genesis in the South in the early 1960's.* But Wallace was drawing his support not only from the right-wingers, but the "left-outs." Many were blue-collar workers who rubbed shoulders with Negroes and felt threatened by them. They had few resources they could fall back on. The deterioration of the city and their neighborhoods had more serious consequences for them than for any other group—and since the spread of blight and the spread of Negroes appeared interlocked, they blamed the deterioration on the blacks. They kept hearing about tax cuts and new government programs; but the programs seemed not to reach them, and their own taxes kept going up. About half of them were union members, but they did not identify with the bureaucratic "pork choppers" who ran the unions. While the Negroes' alienation stemmed from ostracization by the majority society, the blue-collar whites felt they were the stepchildren of the system. Their gathering in Cobo Hall gave them an uncommon sense of unity, of purpose, and of belonging—it generated an electric current that hummed around the hall.

The music was country and Western. Campaign contributions were solicited in Kentucky Fried Chicken baskets. Wallace stepped onto the platform. Hundreds of balloons floated from the ceiling. Georgia screamed, and George joined in the minutes-long roar of approval. From the balcony in the rear came the rhythmic, persistent chant: "Go home, Wallace! Go home, Wallace! Go home, Wallace!"

"You anarchists better have your day now because after November fifth you're through in this country!" Wallace shouted at the hecklers.

The crowd roared.

"Sieg Heil! Sieg Heil! Sieg Heil!" the hecklers chanted.

"You're the kind of folks the people in this country are sick and tired of putting up with!"

Cheers and clapping.

"You've made it unsafe for the workingman to go to work or his wife to ride the transit system or go to the neighborhood grocer, and I can assure you

* During the 1964 campaign, the American Independent party was the only party to question the validity of the Gulf of Tonkin Incident, which led to full-scale American commitment in Vietnam.

when I become the President we're gonna restore law and order in this country!"

Roars of approval.

"Both national parties have kowtowed to every group of anarchists that have roamed the streets of Michigan. . . . That day is over in our country! . . . Not one dime of Federal tax money is going to be used to bus anybody. . . . A man's home is his castle. . . . Folks are sick and tired of the breakdown of law and order. . . . We need to let the police enforce the laws. That's all we need!"

"Fuck Wallace! Fuck Wallace! Fuck Wallace!"

Wallace was the bullfighter, taking on a thousand bulls and meeting the charges head-on. With every chant, with every visceral exchange, the emotion and the tension grew. The roar of the crowd became deeper and angrier.

"Sieg Heil! Sieg Heil! Sieg Heil!"

A fight flared up on the floor of the convention. The legions of private police patrolling the hall sprayed mace. Chairs sailed through the air. "Let the police handle it! Let the police handle it!" Wallace scurried along the stage like a harried director. "Now, you fellows, let the police handle it. . . . You came for trouble and you got it!"

"We want Wallace! We want Wallace! We want Wallace!"

As the rally ended, the police formed a solid line to keep the pro- and anti-Wallace factions apart in front of the auditorium. There was, of course, a great deal of pro-Wallace sentiment among the police. (Some police cars were being driven around with Wallace stickers). As the two sides taunted each other, a police sergeant suddenly said, "Let's go!" The line of officers charged the hecklers. Driving the hecklers across broad Jefferson Avenue, the police chased them this way and that. In the confusion and darkness hecklers and spectators became intermingled—some officers swung and punched their batons at both.

George and Georgia Devers thought the evening one of the most satisfying they had ever had. Losers all of their lives, they had for once had the exhilaration of being on the winning side.

112

The Assertion of Forest Park

WALLACE WAS ATTRACTING ONE OUT OF EVERY FIVE AMERICANS TO HIS candidacy. In Michigan, half his support came from union members, who had voted Democratic since 1932. To draw union voters back into the fold, the CIO Political Action Committee conducted a massive campaign. It warned that a vote for Wallace would be "wasted" and allow Richard Nixon, who throughout his career had been antilabor, to attain the presidency.*

When Democrat Hubert Humphrey, whose prolabor record was unquestioned, appeared in Detroit two days after Wallace, he was received with indifference. Humphrey's image had been damaged by his inability to slip away from Johnson's dominating figure and his association with the President's Vietnam policies. Michigan's Democrats were divided between the liberal hawks of the CIO, and the Cavanagh-led middle-of-the-road doves.†

While Humphrey went about attempting to patch up the party, his wife, Muriel, was scheduled to visit the juvenile home. But the Director of Intake Services did not want her subjected to the "extremely crowded conditions" under which the home was operating. On October 15 he issued a memorandum that there were to be "no more admissions to the Youth Home, the population must be reduced."

Three days later he came out with a second memorandum: "So there is no misunderstanding . . . I want you to make it extremely difficult for anyone to be admitted to the Youth Home except for an offense such as murder, rape, or felonious assault."

* One of the front runners for the Republican nomination had been Governor George Romney. Romney, making a tour of the nation's cities, had asserted he was the man best qualified to deal with urban ills. But after going to Vietnam, he tacked first this way, then that, in his position on the war. Finally he blurted that he had allowed himself to be "brainwashed" by the military. That declaration ended his chance of successfully challenging Nixon.
† Cavanagh, after hesitating, had endorsed Robert Kennedy. A few days later Kennedy was assassinated in Los Angeles. At the convention, Cavanagh gave his backing to the lost cause of Senator George McGovern.

In one week the population of the Youth Home was reduced from 250 to 180. (It had been as high as 325.) Mrs. Humphrey and her entourage of reporters did not have to see children sleeping on the floors and jammed on top of each other. They could be lectured on the theoretically efficient operations— how the home actually operated did not have to be revealed to them.

Across from the youth home was the old Polish section where Wallace Mirow years before had bought his home. Although the Polish Catholic Church still stood majestic and a few old residents remained, the area was now 92 percent Negro. Some of the frame housing was one hundred years old. Much of it had been blighted during the Depression. The foundationless one-, two-, and three-story structures had settled at various angles, like old men leaning on their canes. Here and there were huge mounds of the dead—the material carcasses of an industrial society. Automobiles, refrigerators, washing machines, television sets —all had come to spend their last, feeble days in the area before expiring. (Some homes had as many as six television sets—none of them working.) Trundled to empty lots, they were never removed, but year after year grew like surrealistic sculptures. The few that were salvageable wound up in a ramshackle second-hand store, some of whose unrestored treasures would have sold for fancy prices in a middle-class antique store. A junkman made his rounds with a horse and wagon, and on Illinois Avenue there was a stable. Since one fourth of the land stood vacant, people were able to tend "potato patches" as they had in Pingree's day.

Although the area was physically deteriorated and had a far lower per capita income than Twelfth Street, it possessed a considerable degree of stability. In its population of 6,000 were 1,100 children on welfare, but many of the residents owned their homes. Like a small town decaying in the shade of its old trees, it had little attraction for the young, who tended to move out as they grew up.

In 1965 the city designated the area as an urban renewal project and named it Forest Park. It was part of the Model City and of Target Area I of MCHRD. In the spring of 1968, after the Michigan Legislature authorized district councils for urban renewal areas, the Forest Park Citizens Planning Group was established. The state legislation was intended to give citizens a voice in the planning. But what kind of voice were they to have when the Detroit Housing Commission had responsibility for physical renewal and MCHRD for social renewal; when these agencies already were locked in a battle for control with the Model Cities Governing Board; and the Model Cities Governing Board was embroiled in conflict with MCHRD's Policy Advisory Committee? To establish ground rules as to who was to have a say on what, the Forest Park Group signed a "treaty" with the Model Cities Governing Board giving them semiautonomy to deal with their neighborhood, so long as their decisions did not go counter to the overall planning for the Model City.

In any case, it seemed an academic exercise. Had work commenced on the $11 million urban renewal propect in 1965, it could not have been completed until 1972 or 1973. But in the fall of 1968, the project was scarcely more advanced than it had been three and a half years earlier. The Detroit Housing Commission had applied for a "survey and planning" grant, and the Department of Housing and Urban Development had "reserved" $8 million to cover the Federal share of the project. But an urban renewal project has to go through eleven stages encompassing seventy-four different steps, many of them requiring the close cooperation of various city agencies: the Housing Commission, the

Planning Commission, the Controller's Office, the Public Works Department, the Water Department, the Streets and Traffic Department, the Health Department, the Corporation Counsel, the Department of Buildings and Safety Engineering, and so on.

These agencies, however, are not used to working together. They are vertically oriented, so that it is difficult to get a health inspector to talk to a housing inspector, even though both of them might be working in the same block.

Furthermore, there were feuds. The antagonism between Housing Director Knox and Planning Director Blessing continued unabated.

In 1965 Mayor Cavanagh had taken a group of planners and placed them in the Housing Commission as an "applied design" team. He hoped that they would be able to serve as a bridge between the "ideal designs" of Blessing and the practical necessity that was Knox's first consideration. But when the applied design team was implanted in the Housing Commission it began espousing the housing director's viewpoint.

To the conflict between the planning and the housing directors were now added battles between two competing design groups.

Every department tended to place priority on its own, routine functions, and to regard the "extra" work required by an extra-ordinary project like urban renewal as an imposition. Since, for some of the steps, there was no clear-cut division of responsibility between departments, there tended to be duplication on the one hand and procrastination on the other.

For an urban renewal project to progress at a steady pace, someone in the mayor's office had to supervise and coordinate it. This meant it must be regarded as a priority project. Forest Park had no priority. (For months the city's application had been "lost" in HUD's regional office in Chicago. Since no one from Detroit inquired about it, the application sat under a pile of other papers.) The city had not yet even gotten under way on Elmwood 3, a residential project of many years' standing. The Central Business District, Medical Center, and Wayne State University projects were all encountering difficulties and taking up the attention and time of the staff. The Forest Park project had been initiated in 1965 primarily to get it "on the books" so that the Federal government would "reserve" $8 million for it. Where the city would obtain the $3 million for its own share was a problem that would have to be met when the time came.

But while the project was stalled, the Forest Park area was undergoing the typical "blight by announcement." Property owners stopped making improvements. City departments exhibited lack of interest—the area had been written off, so why bother making inspections, cleaning the streets, or picking up the garbage more than absolutely necessary. Time and resources could be better spent in other neighborhoods.

The members of the Forest Park Planning Group did not know why the project was stalled. But they did not want to go on living year after year under the doom of demolition. In contrast to the residents of other urban renewal areas, many of them were planning to return to the neighborhood after it had been redeveloped, and they wanted to see that redevelopment occur in their lifetimes. The chairman of the group was fifty-six-year-old Chris Alston. (When he and his family had moved into the neighborhood in 1918, they had been greeted by two hundred curious Poles, who wanted to see what a Negro looked like.) Alston was a member of the UAW, a worker in the antipoverty program, and a Democratic party activist. He and the Group's secretary, Roy J. Robinson, decided to try to make a direct appeal to Vice-President Humphrey when he made his campaign appearance in Detroit.

On the morning of November 1, 1968, Alston and Robinson drove to the union hall where the Vice-President was to have pancakes with a delegation of steelworkers. Hundreds of people, standing behind police lines, were waiting to see Humphrey. Robinson made his way forward and told a police officer, "I've been in communication with the Vice-President, I want to see him." *

The officer thought he was a nut. But Robinson insisted that the officer call one of Humphrey's aides. A woman came over.

"I'm from Forest Park Planning, and I want to see the Vice-President," Robinson told her.

"You can't see him. He's going to make a speech."

Robinson was now in the cordoned-off area, and spotted an old schoolmate who was an official in the state party. Robinson explained the situation to him. He agreed to put Robinson into the VIP line to shake hands with the Vice-President.

Clasping hands and making "nice to see you" remarks, Humphrey came down the line. He reached Robinson.

"Mr. Vice-President, I'd like to talk to you. I'm from the Forest Park Planning Group," Robinson blurted out, and thrust a package containing Forest Park's presentation into the hands of the startled Humphrey. Humphrey agreed to read the material on the plane.

The next day HUD Secretary Robert Weaver, who was in Detroit and suddenly very much aware of Forest Park, toured the area.

Through a fluke, Forest Park had short-circuited the elaborate bureaucratic machinery. The Planning Group had bypassed the guards, the secretaries, the anterooms, and the aides that would have prevented them from reaching the Vice-President in his Executive Office Building suite in the capital. In the first week of January, 1969, the outgoing administration allocated a survey and planning grant of $400,000 to Forest Park.

The grant tangled the priorities of the city. The administration would have to find $3 to $4 million in its small capital improvements budget. Housing Director Knox was upset.

Because of the bottlenecks in urban renewal projects all across the nation, Congress a few months earlier had enacted an alternate approach to urban renewal: the Neighorhood Development Program. (At the end of 1967, although HUD had $6.25 billion "on reserve" for urban renewal projects, it had dispersed only $2.13 billion. Detroit had $133 million "reserved," but had spent only $45 million. Renewal projects in cities like Elizabeth, New Jersey, had been scheduled for as long as twelve years, but no construction had started. In 1966 HUD suspended the Cleveland program entirely because the city had cleared six thousand acres but had not rebuilt any of them.) Under the Neighborhood Development Program (NDP), a city could act to stem an area's deterioration while redevelopment was in progress. Instead of being a long-term, five- to ten-year program, it was an annual program. In urban renewal, a city had to formulate all the plans and complete the steps form A to Z before the project could commence. Under the NDP, a city could undertake clearance, renovation, and the construction of public facilities immediately on a spot basis. The NDP

* The Planning Group had addressed a telegram to Humphrey in Washington.

could cover a wide area and would not be restricted, like urban renewal, to relatively small sites. It would enable a city to draw on the funds the Federal government had "on reserve" and would require smaller capital outlays by local government.

In Detroit, the Neighborhood Development Program would have an additional advantage. Since schools were built with local funds, they could be included as part of a city's contribution of its one-third share of project costs. (A school had to be within a project area and could not have been built more than three years prior to the start of a project.) Some cities, like Chicago and New Haven, had coordinated their urban renewal projects with school construction. In Detroit, however, where the school system and the municipal government were separate, school construction had taken place in areas almost entirely without relation to urban renewal projects. The city had lost tens of millions of dollars in "school credits," which could have been applied as the local share of projects.

There were no "school credits" to be had within the Forest Park urban renewal area. But if Forest Park were included in the thirty-two-square-mile Neighborhood Development Program, whose boundaries were identical with those of the Model City, then school credits were available for a portion of the local share. Furthermore, since the three-year limitation was about to expire, these school credits had to be put to use immediately.

All through November and December of 1968, Housing Director Knox worked to transform Forest Park into a Neighborhood Development project. He did not inform the Forest Park Planning Group, but he had the support of HUD's regional office in Chicago. The HUD staff, disillusioned with urban renewal, wanted to convert as many projects as possible to NDP. As part of the Model City area, Detroit's Neighborhood Development Program would receive additional "add-on" funds from the Federal government. But without the inclusion of Forest Park, HUD's regional officials declared, the NDP project would not be funded.

To Knox and the regional officials, Robinson's cornering of the Vice-President, and Washington's decision to fund Forest Park as an urban renewal project came as a shock. Knox lamely attempted to explain why he had not told anyone in Forest Park of the change in directions. Depreciating urban renewal, Knox tried to coerce Forest Park into agreeing to the change. "The community should be well aware of HUD's lack of interest in speed and Forest Park in particular," a letter from the Housing Commission to the Forest Park Planning Group declared. Six to seven years would probably pass before site acquisition could begin, and ten years or more before the project would be completed. Furthermore, "present monies available . . . are insufficient. Under Urban Renewal, to get additional funds, it is necessary to file an amendatory application.* If these funds are not available immediately, another two-year delay would not be unusual. Also in this case the city would be obliged to provide one third of

---

* Because of the great time lag between the announcement and consummation of urban renewal projects, inflation invariably pushes costs over the original projection, and supplemental funds have to be requested from the Federal government. Since these funds are invariably granted, it has become common practice for local governments to underestimate the original costs, on the basis that the lower the cost, the greater the chance of a project's approval. This practice of underestimating and underbidding has become almost routine in dealing with the Federal government, and is employed by "grantsmen" and defense contractors alike.

this difference, and since it is already pressed to its limits in the Model Cities program, there are grave doubts that the additional one or two million dollars could be found. In this case, no additional federal money would come and the project could stop until the city's funds were then available." * [1]

Chris Alston and the Forest Park Group were infuriated. They had overcome seemingly impossible odds to get the project under way. The survey and planning funds had been approved, the $8 million grant reservation was there, but now Housing Director Knox wanted to give up all of that and accept instead a year-by-year plan of redevelopment and funding that might be aborted anywhere along the line. (If Forest Park were not continued as an urban renewal project, the grant reservation would be automatically terminated.) Knox said that the question would seem to be one "of trust between the citizens, city officers, and federal officials." But trust in Knox and the city and Federal bureaucracy was precisely what the people of Forest Park did not have. They were not going to let go of their urban renewal project, and they shouted their refusal to the city.

Knox, threatening to resign, demanded the backing of the mayor. In the past when the housing director had mentioned resigning, Cavanagh had responded soothingly. But that was when there had been a Democratic administration in Washington and Knox's political contacts had been useful. The new Secretary of Housing and Urban Development was George Romney, and Romney and Knox were long-time antagonists on the Michigan political scene. Knox's dealings with the people in the Model City area had become a liability, and Cavanagh was embarrassed by what he considered the botch Knox had made of Forest Park.

"We'll miss you, Bob," he said.

In his place, as the first Negro director of the Detroit Housing Commission, Cavanagh appointed Conrad Mallett.

---

* The communication closed with not just a mixed, but a befuddling hashed metaphor. "It would seem that this is not the case where a dog has to drop one bone in hope of getting a bigger bone, but a case where a community can either reach for an egg which with care, feeding, and luck (hope that the fox doesn't come) can possibly grow into a chicken which can be stewed; or the community can grab a hen now and plop it quickly into the pan before anything can happen to her. NDP is that hen, it's here, it's not perfect, but it's nutritious and the farmer cannot stall her preparation until she is too tough for anything but stewing."

113

The Orchestration of Housing

THE FUNCTIONS OF THE AGENCY THAT MALLET TOOK OVER HAD EXPANDED enormously in recent years. Under the jurisdiction of the Housing Commission were public housing, urban renewal, the Neighborhood Development Program, the Neighborhood Service Program, the Neighborhood Conservation Program, Model Cities, and a multitude of rent-supplement and low-income housing programs.

The pace of the city's deterioration nevertheless continued to outstrip the resources of all the programs combined. The condition of 30 percent of the city's industrial and 21 percent of its residential structures was such that they were ready or would be ready for demolition during the next ten years. (By 1987 more than half the buildings in the city should, theoretically, be torn down.) Sixty-eight thousand housing units were unfit for habitation. Although there were 381,000 households with incomes that qualified them for public housing, there were only 12,000 public housing units in the metropolitan area.

The public housing program had been created by the Federal government to enable cities to provide decent housing for the lower middle class. The program was based on the premise it would pay its own way and be self-liquidating. That premise went by the board when the occupants of the units became welfare families and people living on Social Security and small pensions. The support payments they received from the government always lagged far behind the increases in the cost of living. In 1968 Michigan was still making welfare payments on the minimum subsistence calculations based on 1960 prices—even though the cost of living had risen 15 percent since then.

The rents the tenants could afford to pay were, therefore, not keeping step with the costs the housing authorities were incurring. Every time a union won an increase in pay, or the price of a bucket of paint went up, the gap widened. In Detroit's public housing projects, an elevator maintenance man could make $20,000 a year with overtime. Between 1952 and 1969 the cost of maintenance per unit increased from $28 to $71 a year (154 percent), while the average annual income of tenant families increased only from $2,500 to $4,267 (71 percent). Detroit was faced with a $600,000 deficit in its public housing projects in 1970; and 82 of the largest 100 public housing projects in the United States were in danger of going broke.* Public housing operations might have to be suspended.

In one of his final acts of office, Knox raised rents by as much as $19 to cover rising costs. When Mallet became housing director, the tenants confronted him with a rent strike. The city council grudgingly agreed to provide a $200,000, one-time subsidy that would carry the most needy tenants through June. That, however, was but a temporary solution. If the public housing projects were to remain operable and not go the way of Pruitt-Igoe, the tenants with the lowest incomes—principally the elderly and those on welfare—might have to be evicted and replaced with people of higher income able to pay higher rents. The strike continued. Mallet considered suggesting to Cavanagh and the council that the city abandon the public housing projects to the Federal government and let the Department of Housing and Urban Development deal with the mess that was the consequence of national and state economic policies.†

While the tenants were unable to pay rents in the older projects built at a cost of ten dollars per square foot and less, construction costs of new housing intended for low- and moderate-income families was skyrocketing to fifteen and twenty dollars per square foot. Ever since Thomas Edison had asserted that he could mass produce low-cost concrete housing, scheme after scheme had been advanced to reduce housing costs by factory production, and in scheme after scheme projected savings over on-site construction had turned out to be illusory.

The Department of Housing and Urban Development nevertheless believed that a new method of lightweight construction developed by a Harvard architect, Neal Mitchell, provided the long-awaited breakthrough. HUD signed a contract with the archdiocese of Detroit and a neighborhood group for a demonstration project of seventeen houses. Costing $7.50 per square foot, they were to be the forerunner of a five-hundred-home development.

Detroit's Building and Safety Commissioner, Robert Kearns, however, refused to grant a permit to the "Phoenix" project. The construction would not conform with the city's building code, he said, and he doubted that the houses would be safe. He asked that one house be built first for testing.

Officials at HUD did not want to expend $30,000 on a test they considered redundant. For nearly a year, as the two sides battled verbally, nothing was done. Finally, HUD and Kearns agreed to have the National Bureau of Standards run a test on a mockup. The test proved Kearns essentially correct. HUD agreed to nearly double the strength of the concrete used in the construction.

---

* One project that went under was high-rise Pruitt-Igoe in St. Louis. When it opened in the early 1950's, the project had won prizes for design and was pointed to with pride. Within a few years, however, more than half the twelve thousand occupants were Negro welfare mothers. Missouri welfare payments were $75 a month for a mother with four children. The housing authority's per unit obligation was $45 a month. What happened was typical of a poor neighborhood. Unsupervised children ran wild. Vandals broke windows and ripped out fixtures. Lacking money for maintenance, the housing authority let the buildings deteriorate. As people moved out, squatters took over the empty apartments. Muggings, robberies, and murders multiplied until the high-rise buildings had one of St. Louis's highest crime rates. Within a decade of its construction, Pruitt-Igoe was one of the world's most notorious slums. In the early 1970's the project was abandoned and scheduled for demolition.
† Reacting to the nationwide problem, Senator Edward Brooke of Massachusetts introduced a measure for subsidizing tenants in public housing. Passed by Congress, the measure cost the Federal government three quarters of a billion dollars annually by 1972.

With HUD contributing $203,000, and the archdiocese $138,000, the project was now ready to proceed. A HUD official flew to Detroit to turn the first spade of earth in the groundbreaking ceremony.

Not till then was it discovered that there was no factory in Michigan or the Midwest capable of manufacturing the components for the project. If the components were to be shipped from the East, the houses might cost as much as $40 per square foot.

So Phoenix returned to the ashes. If construction costs could not be dramatically reduced, how could low-income families pay for the supposedly "low-cost" housing in the urban renewal areas?

Edward J. Robinson, executive director of the Metropolitan Detroit Citizens Development Authority,* applied himself to the problem in the Elmwood urban renewal project. The six thousand persons in Elmwood 3 (the area was being redeveloped in three phases) were mostly elderly. Fifty-five percent were more than sixty-two years old; only a few were under forty. Ninety percent were long-time residents who were not particularly unhappy with their accommodations, even though those accommodations were not up to modern standards. Their rent was low, about $35 per month—a critical consideration, since the median income was under $3,000, and a third of the families had less than $1,800 a year to live on. Given their preference, the people would have chosen to be left alone.

To the city, of course, the area was a liability. The average homeowner paid only $159 in property taxes yearly. Redevelopment would quadruple the value of the property and the revenues to be derived.

But since the people would have to go elsewhere, would not whatever area they moved to become another Elmwood? If the housing they moved into were better, would it not be housing which they would have difficulty affording? (That has been the history of people relocated as the result of urban renewal —they have had to pay more for their new accommodations, even though they could seldom afford to pay more.) Would they not then be a contributing factor to the deterioration of the area in which they relocated? Was urban renewal serving only to shuffle the poor around, and spread blight from one part of the city to another?

Obviously, these were questions the planners were not anxious to ask themselves. Since the practice of scattering residents from a renewal area all over the city had fallen into disrepute, Robinson planned to move the people from Elmwood 3 into Elmwood 2 housing as it was completed. But fewer than 20 percent of the residents in Elmwood 3 had incomes high enough to afford the new housing in Elmwood 2—even though the housing was being built under Federal subsidy programs. (The incomes of more than one in ten were so low as to make them ineligible even for public housing.)

What, then, was to be done? Robinson proposed the initiation of a two-year "income upgrading" program for more than half of the heads of household. People from forty to sixty years old with fourth- to seventh-grade educations and incomes of sixty to seventy dollars a week were to be reoriented, re-educated, and retrained. To accomplish this transformation, Robinson wanted to employ a host of agencies: MCHRD, the Housing Commission, the Health

---

* MDCDA, it may be recalled, was Walter Reuther's idea for funneling private development funds into the Model City area.

Department, the Department of Social Services, the Board of Education, the Employment Security Commission, the National Alliance of Businessmen, the New Detroit Committee, and whoever else might be roped in. "We are using housing," he said, "as the focal point for dealing with the complex problems of poverty and deprivation. In short, the people with our assistance are attempting to orchestrate the institutions, agencies and environment that serve them in a way that will produce a happy society."[1]

That was the old song of the 1930 environmentalists, embroidered with new social science flimflam. The consensus of Mallett and the mayor's staff was that—the uneconomic aspects of the proposal aside—Robinson was not versed with the realities of the institutions that he wanted to "orchestrate."

114

The Irresistible President

IN AUGUST, 1965, MAYOR CAVANAGH HAD SUBMITTED A MEMORANDUM TO President Johnson's Task Force on Housing and Urban Development. Prepared by Harold Black and the Community Renewal Program, it pointed out that there was a great need to have every person dealt with as an entity, instead of as an individual with an employment problem, a health problem, a housing problem, an education problem, a recreation problem, and so on. To implement this "wholistic" approach, the memorandum requested the Federal government to fund three "Family Service Centers." * Each center would be staffed with representatives from all the agencies.

The belief that something must be done about the proliferation of programs and "centers" was gaining strength in the President's Bureau of the Budget. The Bureau's Dr. Michael March enumerated manpower centers, human resources development centers, comprehensive health centers, parent and child centers, maternal and child health centers, youth opportunity centers, rehabilitation centers, employment subcenters, comprehensive mental health centers, supplementary education centers, and so on ad infinitum. When the Department of Health, Education, and Welfare (HEW) packed fifteen separate health programs into comprehensive health centers, the Office of Economic Opportunity (OEO) promptly funded other comprehensive health centers to fill the gaps it perceived in the HEW centers. OEO alone had eight hundred Community Action Centers in two hundred cities across the nation, but most were store front operations with little impact on the neighborhoods.

By the summer of 1966 the fragmentation of services and the lack of "one-stop" centers had been brought to the attention of President Johnson. On August 19 he spoke on "the center of our society, the American city." He declared, "I have asked the Secretary of Housing and Urban Development to set as his goal the establishment—in every ghetto of America—of a neighborhood center to service the people who live there." [1]

* The more expansive Cavanagh plans called for a network of sixteen such centers to cover the entire city.

On August 30 Executive Order 11,297 established HUD as the "convening agency" to supervise a pilot program of neighborhood service centers in fourteen cities, including Detroit. HUD was to take its own programs and those of OEO, HEW, and the Labor Department and put them all together under one roof.

For the next several months the matter languished. No agency wanted to combine its programs with somebody else's programs. The Chicago regional director of HEW jibed at the concept, writing in a memorandum:

"The Center of the Center of the Center. Someday, somewhere in one of our 100 or so large cities, someone is going to cry 'Eureka—I have found the center!' . . . a pentagon-shaped, neon-lighted sign will revolve on its rooftop, carrying the names of the participating agencies—and a giant computer with long arms, but tender hands and a soft voice, will 'reach out' to the disadvantaged, the advice-needers, and the poor who pass by."

On January 31, 1967, HUD Undersecretary Robert Wood (second in command of the agency) complained that he was receiving no cooperation, that none of the other departments were allocating any money, and that there was not a single full-time man working on the program anywhere. HUD itself was dragging its feet, and no one knew where the program was heading or whether the President really cared.

Wood, who had headed the presidential task force on urban development and was "the White House man" at HUD, was assured that the President not only cared, but that "the President's prestige is on the line in these 14 cities, and we'd better be able to show results soon." On March 22 Wood held an *emergency* "undersecretaries' meeting" with Wilbur Cohen of HEW, Jim Reynolds of Labor, and Bertram Harding of OEO; and this was followed by a *desperation* meeting. But he was unable to pry firm commitments or money out of anybody. Everyone agreed that he would do all that was possible; but what was possible was, apparently, nothing.

It was the first time the departments had been asked to work closely together on a program; and the deficiencies and distortions in the Federal structure were manifested as never before. Not only was it impossible for one department (HUD) to get other departments to commit themselves to a cooperative program, even though the President had explicitly directed them to. But the departmental structures reaching down to the local level were such as to make chaos out of attempts at coordination in the cities involved.

Each Federal department had evolved at a different time and in a different manner. The Department of Labor was formed out of four separate bureaus in 1913. The Department of Health, Education, and Welfare was a "conglomerate" woven together out of a multitude of different agencies in 1953. The Office of Economic Opportunity was created in 1964 to deal with the problems of poverty; the Department of Housing and Urban Development in 1965 to deal with the problems of the cities. (The other nine executive departments and forty-seven independent agencies had similar individual origins.) Each established its own regional substructure to suit its own needs and peculiarities. There was no attempt at uniformity. Some departments divide the United States into seven regions; others into nine. A state can be in the Central region of one department, in the Midatlantic of a second, in the Great Lakes of a third, and in the Southeastern of a fourth. Even within a department, bureaus have different regional organizations. (There are nine disparate regional organizations in the Department of Labor.) Regional offices were located in cities as much by caprice as by design—often the location was the result of an attempt to please one congressman or another. States have to deal with regional offices in as many as ten different cities.

At the same time, Federal departments—even more than municipal departments—are structured vertically. Horizontal coordination is almost impossible. Departments like Labor and HEW have never integrated themselves on the regional level. The regional administrator of the Office of Education reports to the Commissioner of Education in Washington, the regional administrator of the Children's Bureau to the chief of the Children's Bureau. The regional director of the HEW office in which they are located has little authority and virtually no control over them.

Yet, while the departmental bureaucrats in Washington procrastinated, the heads of the regional offices, scattered in cities hither and yon, were asked to pull together the seventy-six different Federal grant-in-aid programs that the Bureau of the Budget projected as likely components of the Neighborhood Service Centers. Some of these programs went through the states to the people; some through the states to the cities; some through the cities to the people; and some directly to the community action agencies and the people. Since the regional head of the Bureau of Work-Training Programs might never have met his counterpart in the Bureau of Employment Security—even though both were in the Department of Labor—the Bureau of the Budget fostered the development of Federal Regional Teams.* These "teams" were composed of the regional directors. But it was difficult for regional directors to attempt coordination of programs when there was little coordination within departments, no cooperation between departments, and chaos in regional organizations.

The Bureau of the Budget proposed that the Neighborhood Service Centers "should be made a no-nonsense test case [of] Federal interagency leadership and cooperation. . . . If this enterprise can't be made to work on a small scale, it raises bleak questions concerning the much tougher Model Cities effort." But HEW was still offering only lip service, no money; the Department of Labor suggested it might contribute $500,000, a pittance that was an insult; and OEO was sulking and refusing even to comment on the guidelines that HUD was sending out to the cities.

By the first week of April, matters had come to such a pass that Joseph A. Califano, Jr., President Johnson's special assistant in charge of domestic affairs, felt compelled to take a personal hand. He called in the Secretaries of the four departments and told them that the program was a "presidential must." They were to stop procrastinating. They were to allocate the funds—an estimated $49 million—to finance the neighborhood centers. Jay Janis, Califano's college roommate, was executive assistant to HUD Secretary Weaver, and was now assigned "leadership responsibility." The program was linked to the Office of the President as closely as it could possibly be.

On May 13, 1967, representatives of the fourteen cities were brought to Washington for a weekend meeting. Harold Black came from Detroit. Detroit's

* In an earlier attempt to establish some kind of liaison between Federal departments at the regional level, President Kennedy in 1962 had created "Federal Executive Boards," but these had been virtually stillborn.

proposal was thought to have the best concept of program coordination—not surprising since the city had originated the neighborhood center concept. But the prevailing atmosphere was one of confusion. In Detroit, the Butzel Family Service Center area was to be adjacent to the Model City area. But nine cities were planning to place the Neighborhood Service Centers within their Model Cities boundaries. The city representatives wanted to know whether the centers were to be part of the Model Cities Program, whether the Model Cities Program was to supplant them, or whether Model Cities was being abandoned. Boston could not understand why it was being asked to establish a new neighborhood center in Roxbury, when the existing OEO center there was failing for lack of funds.

HUD tried to inspire a "sense of urgency" in the cities, because Califano wanted the "core services"—the administration and staffing of the centers— to be operative by the end of August, the first anniversary of the President's announcement of the program. The cities' applications, however, had to go through forty-eight steps. The normal processing time for programs funded through the various agencies was five to twelve months. HUD promised to introduce a "simplified request procedure" for the neighborhood centers. But the Department of Labor balked, and refused to adopt the procedure.

On June 23, President Johnson announced that "proposals by 14 cities for the establishment of multi-purpose neighborhood centers in poverty neighborhoods have been approved. The four Federal agencies participating in the Pilot Program will give priority to supporting the projects from available resources and already have reserved certain funds for them. . . . [They] have worked closely together, and with city and state agencies, over the past several months to develop the program."

At the same time, the Bureau of the Budget was circulating a "confidential" memorandum:

"You should know that they did not put in the bulk of the HEW, Labor and OEO service components, for which no grants are being made."

Despite the White House pressure, the three agencies still professed themselves unable to find money in their budgets to support the neighborhood centers. Earlier in the year the Department of Labor, discovering that inner city unemployment was three times that in the nation at large, had launched a "crash urban slums employment program." To implement the program, the department was expending million of dollars to set up Concentrated Employment Program (CEP) centers. Stanley Ruttenberg, the Assistant Secretary for Manpower, did not hear about the Neighborhood Service Center Program until mid-July. The Concentrated Employment Program centers would provide one half to two thirds of the services provided under the Neighborhood Service Program. In a half dozen cities the two centers would be in conflict with each other, and in Washington, D.C., the Labor Department was building a $5.4 million Concentrated Employment Program center within two blocks of where a $5 million Neighborhood Service Center was planned. The Labor Department proposed that it be allowed simply to take over the Neighborhood Service Center program.

OEO, which in theory was part of the Office of the President, complained that its funding had not been increased as rapidly as it had projected and that all its money ($2.06 billion for the fiscal year) was committed to ongoing programs. On July 7 Califano addressed a letter to OEO Director Sargent Shriver.

Dear Sarge:

We have carefully considered your letter of June 30, 1967, protesting the funding consequences of the President's decision with respect to the 14 pilot neighborhood center programs. Demands for new and increased programs do, of course, strain the availability of funds. . . . Every budget, however, has some flexibility for changes. The OEO budget has more room for maneuver than most budgets. When the President himself identifies high priority items, we believe every effort should be made to carry out his instructions.

Califano thought OEO could afford a $5 million contribution, since it was increasing the funding for its own community action centers from $85 million to $120 for the fiscal year. But what was worrying OEO more than the money was the possibility that the Neighborhood Service Program would establish another competitive political structure in the inner city. (The Model Cities Program already challenged OEO.) Like the community action agencies and Model Cities, the Neighborhood Service Centers were to be governed with the "maximum feasible participation" of citizens. OEO was now as zealous about guarding its political power against potential usurpers as the traditional political structure had been in fighting off OEO. In Detroit the city proposed that the Butzel Family Service Center be run by MCHRD.* But the citizens—who were located in Target Area III of the antipoverty program—were so disillusioned with MCHRD and so anxious to get a piece of the political action for themselves that they vociferously opposed control by MCHRD and the Target Area III advisory committee.

On the surface, HEW was the department most amenable toward providing funds for the HUD-sponsored project. In actuality, HEW was doing a great deal of maneuvering that made it seem compliant but cost it nothing. The Detroit school system had made application for a Title III-Elementary and Secondary Education Act grant (innovative programming and supplementary educational facilities) but had been turned down at the state level. After the riot, Assistant Superintendent Louis D. Monacel went to Washington to appeal the city's case to Nolan Estes, Associate U.S. Commissioner for Elementary and Secondary Education.

"We can't fund it," Estes said. "But if you were to put the program into the contemplated Neighborhood Service Program area, that would be a different thing."

The school system had better uses for the money and did not want to tie it down in the Butzel area. "What the hell good is the money," asked Monacel, "if the program doesn't meet the needs of the school system? We're having to live with a lot of money and programs that won't do any good."

Nevertheless, since it was a question of getting money or not getting money, Monacel rewrote the proposal to fit into the Neighborhood Service Program. He went back to Estes. Estes suggested some changes. "Okay," said Monacel, "but I'll have to check it with the Federal regional team in Chicago."

"What?" asked Estes, who had never heard of the regional teams that sup-

* The Butzel Center was to be the first of the three Neighborhood Service Centers in the city.

posedly were to coordinate all the programs going into the neighborhood centers.[2]

So the Detroit school system received a three-year grant totaling six million dollars—the largest of its kind in the nation—for innovative and supplementary education programs in the Butzel Junior High School area. But by then it was the fall of 1967, and Congress, upset over the Vietnam War and inflation, was constricting funds for domestic programs. Less willing than ever to direct money toward a program not their own, OEO, HEW, and the Department of Labor continued to evade the presidential directives. In the spring of 1968 President Johnson announced he was not running for reelection. In August, Jay Janis, the presidential expediter, left the government, and with him went the last possibility of the program's success.

Lyndon B. Johnson had thought of himself as the irresistible President. But he had met an immovable bureaucracy. And inertia had triumphed.

115

The Muddled City

IN DETROIT AND SOME OF THE OTHER CITIES, BITS AND PIECES OF THE Neighborhood Service Program lingered, an arm here and a leg there, like the remnants of an infant born dismembered and without a head. HUD had no immediate intent of funding the Butzel Family Service Center. But the school system, with its six-million-dollar HEW grant, placed a Neighborhood Education Center in operation at Butzel Junior High School. At another location, MCHRD was providing "core services"—administration and intake—in a dingy store front that was simply another of the fourteen OEO neighborhood centers scattered about the city. At four additional locations there was a Nutrition and Senior Citizens Center, a Parent-Child Center, a Family Planning Center, and a Neighborhood Services Program Training Center. The people at "core services" knew nothing about the Neighborhood Education Center, and some of the staff at the Neighborhood Education Center had never heard about the Neighborhood Service Program (of which they were supposedly a part). In the final irony, the Neighborhood Service Program survived as its own worst example of the fragmentation it had been intended to correct.

With it survived the "Interagency Policy Board," the citizens participation structure that was supposed to be the governing agency for the Neighborhood Service Program. In an effort to give something to everyone, and ensure the maximum feasible chaos, the structure provided independence for the Interagency Policy Board (made up half of citizens and half of representatives from agencies with programs in the area), control for MCHRD's Target Area IV Advisory Committee, supervision for MCHRD's Policy Advisory Committee, and liaison with the Model Cities Governing Board. Not surprisingly, in December, 1968, the NSP director declared, "Our most notable achievement during the last quarter was gathering statistics showing what services were delivered." [1]

The Neighborhood Service Program was supposed to be a pilot program for the Model Cities Program.* What then of the Model Cities Program, which

---

* The intent of Model Cities was to provide additional funds for the most poverty-stricken areas and to provide coordination among all programs and agencies, Federal and local, in these areas.

required far wider and more complex coordination, and which involved not 14 cities, but 142 (following a second round of selection)?

Model Cities had one thing going for it that the Neighborhood Service Program did not—a congressional authorization of two billion dollars, spread over five years. But the multiplication of cities was making a travesty of the original concept of concentrating funds in a few critical urban areas. The program was so overcommitted and overextended that it had been diluted to the point of meaninglessness. HEW, OEO, and the Department of Labor were no more enthusiastic about channeling funds into the HUD-directed Model Cities than they were about contributing them to the HUD-coordinated Neighborhood Service Program.

At the Bureau of the Budget, William Carey, the director of the Human Resources Division, called in officials from HEW bureau by bureau and told them that the program has "presidential priority, and you must fund it."

They replied, "It can't be done." Approximately 95 percent of HEW funds were channeled through state agencies. "We can't go to the states," they contended, "and say break off the chocolates and concentrate them in two cities in the state, taking them away from existing communities. It's politically impossible unless we get add-ons [new, uncommitted funds]." [2]

Carey and H. Ralph Taylor, the assistant secretary at HUD who was in charge of the Model Cities effort, attempted to get HEW to commit $173 million of "new" money to Model Cities, but had to settle for a pledge of $65 million. The contribution promised by OEO was minuscule—$9 or $10 million, of which two thirds represented funds for programs already operating in Model City neighborhoods.

Taylor complained that the structure over which he was supposed to preside was "one of the goddam craziest things" he had ever seen. The prevailing sentiment at OEO was that Model Cities was not only a rival but an insult to the OEO operation and that it was "like inventing the wheel all over again." In order to keep the Community Action Agencies of OEO and the City Demonstration Agencies of Model Cities from cutting each other's throats, the White House conceived of having them sign *treaties*. But such high-level attempts at diplomacy had little impact on the behavior of the citizens governing agencies.

In Detroit, Harold Black had resigned as Community Development Coordinator following the riot,* and Knox's friend David Cason had been appointed director of the Model City Program. Knox advised Cason to employ his time "to make speeches. I'll handle the work." Another one of Cason's friends, State Representative David Holmes, whose district encompassed the Model City area, told him: "You let us run this program for the black folks of the inner city." The residents of the area presumed that it would be another job-generating program like MCHRD. Lena Bivens, the fierce, strident, and turretlike leader of a welfare mothers organization, demanded that the residents, despite their lack of education, be hired for the top planning positions at pay of $6,500 to $14,000 a year because they "have natural skills." [3]

The Negro political-matriarchal alliance captured control of the Election Planning Committee, which was established to prepare the election for the 108-member Citizens Governing Board. They were opposed by the west-of-Woodward Congress of Grass Roots Organizations (composed of blacks and

* Black became Model City director of Highland Park, and then established himself as a consultant in urban affairs.

Appalachian whites), by the middle-class whites of the Lafayette Park redevelopment area, by the Poles, by the Cavanagh Administration, and by Cason himself.

In the first week of December, 1967, the city received its one-year planning grant from HUD. Since it appeared that with the formation of the Citizens Governing Board the Negro matriarchy would lose control of the program, the Election Planning Committee steadfastly refused to schedule the election. When their hand was finally called and the election was scheduled for May 30, 1968, they filed suit to delay it. After the election was held, Lena Bivens went to court to protest it, because members of the Planning Committee had been barred from running for office. (She won her case.) Not until June did the Citizens Governing Board become operative, and not until September 12 did each member receive a copy of the city's application, "Proposal for Progress."

By then they had less than three months to prepare the application for the first year's action grant. Cason viewed his role as an advisor rather than a leader, and failed to control the meetings. Lena Bivens, unable to dominate the Citizens Governing Board as she dominated her MCHRD Area Advisory Committee, was a continually disruptive force. She protested, demanded votes, shouted, and talked on and on—until it seemed she might by herself sink the program. HUD's regional office in Chicago considered Detroit the showcase city, and was increasingly concerned. If the program could not be made to work in Detroit, where the idea had been conceived, where would it work? Finally there was tacit agreement that the Citizens Governing Board would stop meeting, and let eleven committees—nine of whose chairmen were white—prepare the proposals.

HUD insisted that its format be followed, but Cason's staff was unable to make heads or tails of the complex and convoluted guidelines that HUD kept sending out. "They don't know how to apply the planning process and can't explain it to the citizens," Cason lamented. "Even those citizens on the board with professional backgrounds cannot follow the technical language." [4] In desperation, HUD agreed not only to hold a training session on October 28, but to have the man who wrote the guidelines explain them. But when he appeared, the people still could comprehend little of what he was talking about; and what he was talking about seemed to have even less relation to the everyday problems in the neighborhood.

So HUD all but took over the preparation of the Detroit application. A HUD regional representative from Chicago was in the city continually to supervise, correct, and redirect the writing of the application. On a November day in a cold, bare room of the ancient office building in which the Model City staff was quartered, the HUD representative worked with Cason and his staff on the conceptualization of a "pyramid." Its foundation rested on EMPLOYMENT, HOUSING, HEALTH, and EDUCATION; from there it built up layer by layer to the IMPROVED QUALITY OF URBAN LIFE. It was the kind of intellectualizing taught by social planners, and it would go over big in Washington.

On the evening of November 17 the Model City executive board met to vote on "priorities." A huge packet of material had not been delivered to them until the night before. Few people had read much of the material and some could not understand the statements on the "priorities" on which they were to vote. One member complained, "We spent a whole year in planning—and now we have five to ten minutes to make decisions of great importance."

Cason, however, warned that because of the "change in administrations in Washington, what the new administration will do with the program is doubtful. All the time we have is now. We have to work with what we've got." Though hardly anyone understood clearly what he was voting on, priorities were allocated.

Four days later there was a meeting of the full Citizens Governing Board. By then, some of what had happened was sinking in, and one member complained, "They castrated the whole program, the way they wrote it up." Another discovered the inclusion of projects he had never heard of.

The unfortunate truth was, Mayor Cavanagh told them, that "citizens participation can be an effective barrier to action." [5] To expect more than one hundred people with widely differing social and economic backgrounds, with no experience in planning, and with a distinct lack of direction, to plan as intricate and complex a program as Model Cities had been ludicrous from the beginning.

The Citizens Governing Board ranked employment, education, and health as their number two, three, and four priorities (housing was first). But by April, 1969, HUD's regional director in Chicago still had been unable "to come up with a dime" from the Departments of Labor or HEW. The regional directors of the various HEW bureaus reiterated that all their funds were channeled through the states and that they could only "request" state agencies to make some of them available to the Model Cities Program. The state agencies said all the money was already committed. The Labor Department's regional office was dealing with five hundred sponsors of Work-Training Programs— aside from sponsors for a host of specialized programs like the Concentrated Employment Program. The staff had been complaining about the lack of funds. Yet now they were supposed to influence the states to shunt money away from the existing programs and into Model Cities. Not surprisingly, they lacked enthusiasm for such an effort.

(In Detroit, the Skills Center had facilities and equipment for 1,200 to 1,600 trainees a day, but cutbacks in funding had reduced the number to 700.)

Officials in the regional offices were apprehensive and resentful. They felt that they were caught in the middle. They did not know what was going on in Washington, and they were convinced the Washington offices did not know what was going on in the cities. They were being assigned tasks that, with the money and resources available, were impossible. They knew that there were great expectations; but that it would be difficult to meet even modest requests. "If you're really honest with the cities, what do you tell them?" asked one of the men who was supposed to coordinate the program in Detroit and twenty-three other Midwestern cities. [6]

Thus the Model Cities Program got under way. From Washington to Mayor Cavanagh's office there was a resigned expectation of its failure. Only the people in the Model City area retained a measure of belief in the pyramid topped by the "improved quality of urban life."

But, with their jealousies of each other and distrust of the city government, the Model City residents created an operating structure that seemed destined for self-destruction. To permit each of the various factions to have a measure of autonomy, the Model City was subdivided into four areas. Each of these subareas had its own staff. To oversee the entire area, the Citizens Governing

Board had a staff of forty-five. This staff was matched by a staff from the city agencies. Nobody knew who was working for whom, or who was supposed to do what.

This, then, was the program that Cavanagh and Strichartz four years earlier had conceived as a means to bring about coordination in the city.

116

Confrontation in the Schools

OF ALL THE AGENCIES OUTSIDE THE CITY GOVERNMENT, THE ONLY ONE THAT showed interest in participating in the Detroit Model City Program was the school system. Since 1964 the system had gone a long way toward ending its insular aloofness; an aloofness it had practiced since World War I, when the new city charter had separated it from municipal politics.

Much of the transformation was due to the system's new superintendent. At the close of the 1965–1966 school year—a few months after the Northern High School boycott—Dr. Brownell had resigned. Chosen to replace him was Dr. Norman Drachler, who in 1957–1958 had been director of research for the Citizens Advisory Committee on School Needs headed by George Romney.

Born in 1912 in the Ukraine, Dr. Drachler was the grandson of a mill owner, and the son of Israel Drachler, the head of education of the Jewish ministry in the Ukrainian government. Israel Drachler had learned during the Russian Revolution that he was to be purged. He had fled with his family to Poland. From there, via one of the roundabout routes made necesssary by the new American immigration laws, he had come to New York. Unable to support his family by his writings, he had moved in 1929 to Detroit to teach in the Hebrew School.

Norman Drachler had graduated from Central High School the next year. In 1936 he had graduated from Wayne State University. Like other offspring of eastern European Jewish immigrants whose educational tradition led them into the free United States public university system, he found that jobs in industry were hard to come by. Anti-Semitism was reinforced by the Depression. So like many of the others he became a teacher. His first assignment was at Poe Elementary School in the poor-white district west of Woodward Avenue. (There he was the only male teacher.) In 1951 he obtained his doctorate from the University of Michigan. Two years later he was named an elementary school principal. (Although approximately six hundred of Detroit's eleven thousand teachers were Jewish, there was no Jewish high school principal in the city until the mid-1950's.) Following his role with the Citizens Advisory

Committee, Dr. Drachler was appointed assistant superintendent in charge of school-community relations.

Dr. Drachler took over as superintendent at a time when more and more of yesterday's solutions were turning into today's failures. Ten years earlier it had been thought that if the schools could provide a middle-class environment for the children of the inner city, the environment would somehow transform them into middle-class students with middle-class habits and middle-class values. Only toward the end of the 1960's were educators beginning to realize that so long as the culture of poverty remains the same, those growing up within it will remain the same.

Both the Great Cities Program and the Federal aid programs under the Elementary and Secondary Education Act that followed were directed toward the ambiance in which the child operated and toward his "cultural enrichment"; they hoped to bridge the gap between school and community; they tried to solve special problems such as continuing education for pregnant girls—but they made minimal contributions toward basic education. To make such contributions, it was feared, would weaken local effort. There was no realization of the depth and extent of the problems. Dr. Drachler believed Federal aid to be like Mark Twain's description of the Missouri River, "a mile wide and an inch deep." [1]

The $16 to $19 million of Federal money that was coming into the school district each year in the latter 1960's represented 8 to 9 percent of the total budget, but was spread over 35 to 40 programs. In 1967, $1.5 million was going to "cultural enrichment." But the children who were being taken to concerts at a cost of $5 to $6 per head were bewildered. Half of them did not know how to read. Every year reading ability and achievement in the schools declined. It was becoming manifest not only in Detroit but throughout the nation that compensatory education did little good unless it was administered in massive doses. Dr. Marburger estimated the cost of that dose at $3,000 per child per year—a huge amount considering that the Detroit schools spent about an average of $600 per pupil annually and that the Federal contribution was only about $100 for each disadvantaged child. Three thousand dollars, however, was no more than the cost of supporting a person in most of the manpower training programs, which were remedial and limited in effect.

The Head Start Program for preschool children was an intensive approach, and many of the children made dramatic gains. But as soon as the children graduated from the program and were left with nothing but the largely negative environments of the communities in which they lived and the schools they attended, they retrogressed. By the second grade the gains were washed out.

Dr. Drachler decided something had to be done to try to preserve the gains. The ability to read was the sine qua non for success in school. Yet it was not unusual for children to reach the eighth grade without being able to write the alphabet, and by the time they were pushed on to high school the textbooks they were supposed to study might as well have been written in Sanskrit. In one school (Martin Luther King) only one of seven hundred tenth-graders was reading at grade level. Kids were being graduated from high school unable to read the words on their diplomas.

Dr. Drachler, therefore, redirected the money from "cultural enrichment" toward a reading program. To reduce the dilution of funds, he reclassified the 249 schools receiving compensatory education funds into Class A, B, and C, according to the degree of deprivation of the areas they served. Most of the funds were allocated to some seventy Class A schools, and within the schools they were concentrated in the first two grades.

The majority of teachers, however, did not know how to teach reading. If a child were not *ready* to read—that is, if he did not have the middle-class background in which he had been read to and exposed to reading material— they did not know what to do with him. (The school system experimented with five different methods of teaching reading and found that none had an advantage over another: the only variable was the teacher.) In order to initiate an intensive reading program, therefore, the first necessity was to retrain the staff.

Results were according to expectations. Between 1965 and 1969, while the average reading level of children in the city was dropping 2 months (measured in terms of grade level) as a consequence of the continuing outward movement of the middle-class population, in the hard-core Class A schools it was rising 2 months, and in Class B schools it was up 1.4 months.

In Class C schools, however—which had been deleted from the program following cutbacks in Federal funding in 1968—the reading level continued to go down. It was in these peripheral schools, mostly in areas into which the population from the inner city was pushing, that the system had the best chance of preserving the quality of education. Yet it was these schools that the system lacked funds to save.

In these schools there was confrontation not only between the white administration and the black community, but between white students and black students, and between black militants and the white community. Located in a six- to seven-mile arc from the center of the city, the schools were experiencing the transient "integration" and the accompanying overcrowding that had occurred in the Central High School area a decade earlier. Parents, teachers, and students resented what they considered the preferential treatment accorded inner city schools. Whites and middle-class Negroes both believed the schools were failing to function as well as they should. Teachers forced to operate amid inadequate facilities looked upon themselves as a persecuted minority. (In some schools the teachers' "lounge" consisted of a small, dark area in the basement amid pipes, washbasins, and jumbles of furniture and fixtures stacked to the ceiling.) Whenever a new grant went to the inner city there were "hate" calls to the administration and complaints that other schools were being relegated to second-class status.

The transformation of the peripheral schools from white to black was rapid. Cooley High School was 7 to 10 percent Negro in 1965, 30 percent in 1967, and more than 50 percent in the fall of 1969. Neither the faculty nor the students viewed the school as "integrated." The teachers thought of themselves as in the trenches of the urban battlefront. "Everyone knew that hell was coming!" one of them said. The students segregated themselves as completely as if signs had been posted. In the lunchrooms, not a black student sat at a "white" table; not a white student at a "black" table.

The principal looked upon his position as one that had changed from that of an educator to that of a politician and a policeman. The quality of education was secondary to "the keeping of the peace." Anything not nailed down was liable to be stolen, youths took out their frustrations in random vandalism, and assaults occurred in the restrooms. Dropouts returned to roam the corridors. They banged on classroom doors, invaded classes, extorted money, and sold pot. In the overcrowded hallways there was shoving and jostling, and blacks often were quick to conclude that it was not accidental.

Teachers, steeped in the culture of the middle class, were exposed to the four-letter language of the inner city and shocked to hear the opposing student body (Central High) at a football game chant: "Cooley is shit! Cooley is shit!" They felt they were being looked upon as "big old witches," and that the "youngsters are turned off and it is increasingly difficult to get through to them. You can't have to explain three thousand times and not be frustrated." They resented being called "racist pigs." They hesitated to call upon Negroes, because the black youths overreacted to being corrected or criticized. They knew some of their students were smoking marijuana, but they were just as happy to have them sitting in the class glassy-eyed and passive. A white youth noted that "some teachers have just quit teaching." Two years before, one had been "real interesting, but now she just gets out." [2]

It was an atmosphere in which militant groups could make headway organizing the students: the Malcolm X Society the blacks; the Students for a Democratic Society the left-leaning of both races; and Breakthrough the right-wing whites.

(Breakthrough had a small but active membership in the city. Its founder was Don Lobsinger, a white-collar employee of the city's Parks and Recreation Department. He had a startling resemblance to Fearless Fosdick, the jutjawed detective of the "Li'l Abner" comic strip. Following in the footsteps of Father Coughlin, Lobsinger had the same blue-collar white constituency, preached essentially the same gospel, and urged his adherents to prepare for and arm against the Negro "revolution.")

Even though each of the groups had only minor followings, they were able to precipitate major confrontations. On Malcolm X Day, February 21, 1969, black high school students from all over the city walked out to stage black-power demonstrations. At Cooley, thirty-five white kids from Breakthrough decided to hold a counterdemonstration. In the process they beat up a Negro. The blacks plotted revenge. Fights broke out. White girls, their hair sheared, ran screaming from the toilets.

Ninety percent of both black and white youths wanted nothing to do with that kind of polarization, and many would have tried to bridge the gap had they been offered any kind of support. But the principal had too few resources and was too wrapped up in the growing troubles of the school to provide it. There was little dialogue between black and white students, between students and the administration, and between the administration and the parents. Any incident in the school was likely to be exaggerated by the time it reached the community. A fight between two boys became the basis for a rumor that twelve children had been stabbed. White parents were suggesting to their sons that they should form "vigilante groups."

The turmoil in the school system led to the white population's abandonment of it. By 1970, more than 60 percent of the children in the Detroit public schools were nonwhite. The black community's dissatisfaction with the system brought demands for more black teachers and administrators, for citizens' control of the schools, and for the breaking up of the entire system.

No superintendent of the Detroit schools—and few anywhere in the United States—had ever been confronted with the difficulties that faced the short, slow-speaking, pipe-smoking Dr. Drachler. Student walkouts and demonstrations at the Public Schools Center (the administration building) were common. In the state legislature, black legislators were pushing a bill to divide the city's schools into sixteen separate districts. Voters in white sections of the city defeated one attempt after another to raise the school tax rate. The American Federation of Teachers had one of the strongest chapters in the nation. After a strike in the fall of 1967, the union had negotiated a contract raising the average teacher's salary from $8,580 to $9,505 a year, the second best in the nation among major cities.* The schools' personnel were affiliated with no fewer than thirty-four professional and labor organizations ready to defend the special interests of their members.

Thus beleaguered, Dr. Drachler proceeded on an uncharted course between change and revolution. Increasing the number of black teachers was the least problem. As more and more Negroes attended college and white female graduates refused assignments to inner city schools, the percentage of blacks on the instructional staff increased from 5 percent in 1950 to 40 percent in 1970. (In 1967, out of 1,300 new teachers hired, more than 300 were released because they would not teach at inner city schools.)

Enlarging the number of black administrators was a different matter. When Dr. Drachler took over, there were 192 Negro administrators out of a total of 1,600. Seniority rules virtually assured that the top bureaucracy would be composed of whites for another twenty years. (Until the early 1960's an educator had to have fourteen years of experience to become principal of an elementary school, and twenty years to become principal of a secondary school.) To prevent calcification, Dr. Drachler engaged in "administration packing." He created the new position of assistant regional superintendent—requiring only seven years of experience and a master's degree—and filled six of the fourteen openings with Negroes. He added thirty-five new high school administrators, most of them Negro. He elevated Negroes to two of the seven deputy superintendent positions.

In so doing he exhausted the list of Negroes who had passed the examination for administrative positions. There were, however, twenty-four whites on the list who had not yet been placed. By all precedent, they would have to be assigned before new examinations were held. Dr. Drachler disposed of precedent and scheduled further examinations to add more Negroes to the list. The white-dominated, old-line Detroit Education Association protested that this was reverse discrimination. It was. But the city, said Dr. Drachler, "no longer has time to wait."

The Detroit Federation of Teachers was troubled. But in the Federation Negroes were an ever more potent force. Dr. Drachler pointed out that the contract the Federation had signed contained a clause specifying that an integrated staff was to be achieved as quickly as possible; and that he was merely pursuing the implementation of that clause.

In this fashion he doubled the number of Negro administrators to 384 by the 1968–1969 school year. Black militants gave him grudging credit. The Reverend Dr. Cleage invited him to speak to a Black Community Educators Conference from which other whites were barred.

* Taking into account both salaries and differences in the cost of living. The San Francisco Bay area ranks first.

(A month later Dr. Drachler had to explain his appearance to the school system's principals, who were "afraid he had given away the mortgage.") [3]

By his willingness to move rapidly toward equality for blacks, Dr. Drachler gained support for a compromise plan of decentralization. To fragment the system into numerous districts with widely varying tax bases would be uneconomic and self-defeating. (Some districts would have had twice the assessed valuation per pupil as others.) But to continue in the aloof mold in which the Good Citizens League had cast the school system in order to remove it from the spoils system was equally impractical. It was a mold that had concentrated power in the hands of the educational bureaucracy and made it unresponsive to citizens' desires; and Dr. Drachler firmly believed that "historically major changes in education have come from outside of the system." [4]

Dr. Drachler supported a reorganization that would provide neighborhood control of the schools within an "umbrella" administrative structure. In the summer of 1969 the state legislature passed a bill decentralizing the Detroit school system. The central Board of Education was expanded to sixteen members—seven elected at large as before, and one member elected from each of the nine regions into which the district was subdivided. The central board continued to have responsibility for financing, labor negotiations, purchasing, and special education programs. The regions, each governed by a board of its own, were granted power to control the educational staff, determine the curriculum, choose textbooks, and determine the allocation of funds received from the district. Opponents warned that the decentralization was likely to bring back the spoils system and make the schools political footballs. And of course they were right. (Already there were bitter battles between the "ins" and the "outs" at many inner city schools. The "ins" were those who held the eight hundred teacher and community aide jobs created by Federal funds.) But blacks wanted to see for themselves if a spoils system in which they got some of the spoils would be so bad.

More and more principals and teachers were succumbing to the constant tension, taking leaves of absence, retiring, or changing jobs. (One of them was the principal at Cooley, who decided to go where the area's white student population was going—to a high school in the suburbs.) This attrition from stress was becoming a problem among both the pupils and the staff. Yet teachers disliked to refer children to the psychological clinic for fear that the referral was a reflection on themselves; principals were even more reluctant to refer teachers; and there was no one to refer principals. For years the problem had been ignored, and the education bureaucracy, like the police bureaucracy, practiced self-protection. If a teacher lay down in the aisles and refused to get up, it was because he was "tired." If a principal had a paranoid personality, the fact that he was "good old Joe" took precedence over his negative impact on the school.

In 1968, however, Dr. Drachler authorized a psychoeducational project to observe classroom behavior, identify children with psychological and learning problems, and determine what was happening in the interaction between teacher and child.

What was happening was that children from deprived homes, rejected all of their lives, were entering school expecting nothing but further rejection. They had even less frustration tolerance than their middle-class counterparts. If they "acted out" their frustrations, they were behavior problems. If, instead, they had had their natural aggressiveness beaten out of them at home, they came to school afraid to move. Unused to participating in anything, they forced the teacher to lead them step by step. In either case, the teacher was frustrated and reacted negatively. The negative reaction was what the child expected, he tuned out more, and the communications gap between child and teacher became more pronounced. The teacher thus contributed to the destruction of the child's self-concept. Even if the child entered school ready to learn, by the time he reached the second grade he was likely to have lost interest.

Conversely, a teacher in a class in which the children were failing tended to lose his sense of purpose and self-esteem. One teacher, who had been in the same school for fifteen years, had conceived of herself as a good teacher when the community was middle class. But when the neighborhood deteriorated and children from problem homes came into the class, she began to say to herself: "I was a good teacher. But these people are preventing me from fulfilling my role." Finding no reward in teaching, she and other teachers merely "put in time," and moved out at the first opportunity. A teacher's race made little difference—black teachers tended to react the same as white.

The longer a teacher remained in a deprived neighborhood, and the greater the number of "nonachievers" in the class, the lower her expectations dropped. The lower her expectations, the lower the performance of the class.

Teachers knew standard methods were not working and that there had been no major change in the educational program in twenty-five years. But they were trapped by the curriculum. "You can talk all you want about creative teaching —but in the end you'd better get through the program or else!" one said. Teachers felt abandoned and unimportant. Nobody ever asked their opinions. Discussions were always related to why children were failing, never to whether it might be the program that was not meeting the needs.

Not infrequently it was the stress of the school situation added to the stress of the home situation that brought a child to the point where he broke down and ceased to function. (But teachers seldom could understand how they themselves were a contributing factor.) A child might come into the system with an IQ of 85 and 90 and be assigned to a special class. He would "progress" from there to a class for the socially maladjusted, and finally end up in a class for the mentally handicapped.

Other children reached school age unable to communicate at all. Between 1963 and 1965 the Detroit Public Schools Speech and Hearing Clinic examined 4,300 preschool children with language problems, and of these 880 were verbally nonfunctional.

Such children usually could not be taught, and would have to be institutionalized for the remainder of their lives at a cost of $250,000 each. Yet most did not appear to have organic brain damage. Although more often than not the parents were poor, the children came from a variety of socioeconomic backgrounds. There did not seem to be a specific, identifiable constellation of causes—except that in many cases the child's withdrawal had been triggered by a traumatic illness or experience. Some had never spoken; others had been learning to speak but had suddenly stopped. What was clear was that all had blocked out their environments and retreated to worlds of their own.

In 1966, the school system received a Federal grant to try to break through to twenty of these children.

For two and a half hours a day, teachers and therapists worked with groups of two to five children. The children's behavior was bizarre. All of them were hyperactive and ignored their environment. Fearful, they slunk around like beaten animals and made animal sounds. Some of them whirled like dervishes until they fell in semitrances of exhaustion. They screamed, they jumped, they banged their heads without feeling pain. One spoke occasionally, but withdrew from reality if he were spanked. Another after being spanked demanded that his butt be kissed.

The motor functions of one child were so severely retarded that he was unable to use his tongue and did not know how to swallow—he ate like a baby bird by tilting his head back and allowing the food to trickle down his throat. Another child, even though he refused to speak and would not hear, could read with comprehension. A third occasionally uttered one word in a piercing scream: "Bullshit!"

Gradually, contact was made with some of the children. Three years after the inception of the program, three of the original twenty children were communicating and attending regular classes. Yet for every child that was being treated, 43 were not.

The number of problem children in the city increased every year. The school system's psychological staff, however, had not been augmented in thirty years, and its strength was one sixth that required by state law. The psychological clinic could handle about forty cases a week; and the case load was now backed up a full year. Children in special education classes at one time had been tested every year. Now they were tested at most every four years. There was a great need for more intensive studies of children with learning problems; but there was time for only routine testing. Even when an intensive study was made, the system lacked the ability to follow up. As in other organizations, there was a fragmentation of services—a counselor, an attendance officer, and a psychologist might all be working with the same child, but one professional would not know the other and what work he was doing with the child.

In the files were records on 180,000 children. Some of the records spanned as many as four generations of the same families. Prominent among the multi-generation failures were the children of the Jansen and Stallings families.

117

The Reunion

SINCE 1956, WHEN SHE HAD GIVEN BIRTH TO ELIZA, JOELLA JANSEN HAD produced nine of those children. After Packard had shut down, Joella and Black Bear had left Eliza with Joella's mother, Marie, and started hitchhiking around the country "seeking work." Black Bear found a job as an itinerant truck driver. Joella, once more pregnant, returned to Detroit.

What Joella needed was a stable setting with plenty of reassurance and a routine varying little from day to day. Instead, she led a totally unsettled life. Black Bear appeared and disappeared. He gave her money at varying intervals and in varying amounts. Joella was always suspended in uncertainty. She sought relief from her anxiety in companionship and sex.

At the time she had been committed to Wayne County Training School, Joella had been adjudged feeble-minded. She had never had her legal rights restored to her. Although Black Bear divorced his wife and agreed to marry her, she could not get married until those rights were restored. It was not until April, 1959, that a court hearing was held, and she was able to get married. She was then four months pregnant with her fourth child.

Number five arrived in the spring of 1961. By then, the household was a shambles. The children were dirty, neglected, and undernourished. They romped in an apartment soggy with urine and infested with flies, roaches, and rodents. With each additional child, conditions deteriorated further, and with each deterioration Joella and Black Bear blamed each other more, fought more, and took out their anger and frustrations on the children. One night Black Bear brought home a buddy, a truck driver by the name of Sumpler. Sumpler had a regular run from Houston to Detroit. Joella was pretty and only twenty-three years old. Sumpler began stopping by whenever he was in the city. A few weeks after Joella was delivered of her fifth child, he suggested to her that she needed a "vacation."

Leaving a note for Black Bear that she was going on "a trip," Joella took off with Sumpler for Houston. Black Bear was left with five children, ranging in age from five years to a few weeks.

Black Bear did the best he could. He placed the children with anyone who would take them—neighbors, Joella's sisters, her mother, Marie. The Juvenile Court returned to the case in May of 1962 when a neighbor called the police to say the baby had been boarded with her eight months previously, but Black Bear had not made any payments in four months, and she wanted someone to come and take the child.

Not until July, 1962, did Joella return to Detroit—just in time to give birth to Sumpler's child. (It was placed for adoption.) Charged with neglect and abandonment, she was sentenced to a year's probation. She went back to live with Black Bear, but stayed with him only fifteen months—time enough to bear another child. In November, 1963, Joella deserted Black Bear and the children again.

A neighbor called the police. The children were taken to the juvenile home, and then placed in various boarding homes under the supervision of the court. Black Bear was upset when he discovered what had happened to the children, and even more upset when he learned that the court intended to dun him for their care. He said he wanted Joella and the children back.

The Juvenile Court referee decided to release the two older children to Black Bear and Joella. The others were placed in white foster homes in the suburbs, where Black Bear and Joella visited them once or twice a year.

The referee suggested that two children were all the couple was capable of caring for and urged Joella not to have any more children. But pregnancy for Joella had become a natural physical condition. In ten months she gave birth to a boy.

All the children were attractive physically; and all presented behavior problems. They were immature for their ages; they were supersensitive and refused to obey; they were hostile, and hyperactive. At least one of the children needed the service of a visiting teacher. But the suburban school district refused to bear the expense of providing a visiting teacher if the child were only in the home "temporarily" and was ultimately to be returned to Detroit. The Juvenile Court probation officer professed to see "no need for a Visiting Teacher at all, since *all* children are hyperactive!"

The younger children soon forgot their parents. In October, 1965, Joella went to visit her four-year-old daughter for the first time in a year. When she reached the foster home, she saw a redheaded, blue-eyed girl playing on the lawn. "What a lovely child!" she said to the foster mother. "Whose is it?"

"Why, it's yours!" said the woman.

Black Bear was grossing $110 a week. After deductions for Social Security and union dues, the net came to about $90. He was supposed to contribute $10 a week to the cost of boarding the children. But he broke his collar bone and for several weeks he could not work. He continued to drink and to receive traffic tickets, and so periodically he was laid off. The new baby arrived. His payments became erratic, and finally ceased altogether. When the probation officer warned him that he was violating the conditions of his probation, he replied, "If the children can't be at home, I'm not going to make it easy on anyone."

During the middle 1960's the pickup in the economy enabled Black Bear to obtain a second, moonlighting job. The increased income and the fact that he was at home less reduced the friction between him and Joella. They moved from their dingy quarters near the Ambassador Bridge (where the Norveths had once lived) to a large, sparsely furnished four-bedroom house on West Grand Boulevard. Rather than pay "strangers to take care of my kids," Black Bear said he wanted the children returned to him and Joella. A new probation officer at the Juvenile Court, who had but recently taken over the case, visited the home and decided the family had stabilized. She took little consideration of the history of the family, she discounted the economics of the situation, and she failed to project what effect the addition of four more children would have upon Joella's limited capacity to function. She recommended that the children be released to their parents.

In the summer of 1966 four children who had forgotten their parents were reunited with Joella and Black Bear, who did not know their children. Just to make certain that the children returned home under auspicious circumstances, the court worker had a statutory wage assignment of $20 a week entered against Black Bear for the $514.67 (including interest) that he owed for the board of the children.

By the time school started Joella was into the fourth month of another pregnancy. When Black Bear discovered her condition, he was furious. Joella told the probation officer that "ever since the children come home he hasn't been acting normal." In fact, with seven children in the house, he was acting predictably. Although he worked at two jobs, the financial squeeze was excruciating. While the court deducted for the back board, household bills piled up. The children lacked clothing, they were malnourished, they missed school nearly half the time, they were dirty and unkempt. They were trapped in the same environment in which their mother had grown up. Their performance deteriorated. Black Bear drank more than ever, he grew angrier with each further bulge of Joella's abdomen, and he slapped her around. In February, when Joella went to the hospital to have the baby, he "celebrated" by getting drunk. He ran his truck into the rear of another vehicle. He had received four citations in the previous fifteen months, and was suspended from work. Joella refused to return to him, but instead took the baby and went to live with Rita. Black Bear applied for welfare assistance, and turned for help to the one person in the Jansen family who had a degree of stability: Katherine.

Five months after being turned down for nurse's training in June of 1960 and becoming a salesgirl at Kresge's, Katherine had met Larry Higgins. Twenty-five years old, Higgins was from a West Virginia town of twenty-five hundred population near the Kentucky border. His father and uncles were coal miners. But following the replacement of steam locomotives with G.M.'s Diesels, and the great conversion from coal to oil after World War II, one after another of the small, marginal mines had shut down. The coal mining towns of West Virginia slowly rotted and floated away in the wind like the silver towns of Nevada and the copper towns of the Upper Michigan Peninsula. Higgins and thousands of other young men began to commute to Detroit—he came when the auto industry was on the upswing and there were jobs; he went back home when there were layoffs.

Three months after they met, Katherine and Larry were married. Larry worked on the assembly line. While they were dating, he had drunk nothing more than an occasional beer. Katherine had the terrible fear that like an arm reaching up out of the swamp something would drag her back to the morass of the life from which she had been rescued only a short time before. She needed an anchor against the suction of the Jansens. She thought Larry could provide that anchor.

They had their first child in early 1963 and their second a year later. Katherine received her initial shock when she discovered that Larry drank not only beer but "boilermakers"—an explosive combination of whiskey washed down with beer. Another shock came when he revealed he intended to continue to go home every summer for six weeks during the model changeover in order to "save money," and that he expected her and the children to accompany him.

She went once. But she could not get along with his family. In many ways they reminded her of her own. The house in which the Higgins family lived was as mean and overcrowded as the house in which she had grown up. It depressed her terribly, and she went into crying spells that lasted for hours.

Every summer after 1963 they separated. She stayed in Detroit and he went back to West Virginia. She really would have liked to divorce him, but since they were Catholic—although only she went to church—she could not face the thought of divorce. For two and a half years there were no more children, but then in the fall of 1966 another arrived.

They were buying a house on a land contract in the West Grand Boulevard area, not far from where Black Bear and Joella lived. It was a typical inner city frame house, large, but deteriorating. It had no insulation, and in midwinter it cost a hundred dollars a month to heat.

Black Bear thought Katherine was wonderful. He came to her with all his and Joella's troubles, and expected her, somehow, to resolve them. Katherine would have liked nothing better than to have moved far away from her family and never again be reminded of their tribulations. But since she was the only one who had had the benefit of an "education," and was only too well aware of the inability of the members of her family to handle their lives, she felt a keen sense of responsibility. She did what she could. Yet it was an unfair burden.

When Joella learned that Black Bear was dropping by Katherine's house two or three nights a week, she suffered pangs of jealousy. She accused him of "running around with Katherine." In May, 1967, she returned to him and her children.

After a month's layoff, Black Bear had been reinstated by the trucking company. He continued to work on two jobs. On weekends Joella worked at a bar. They saw each other little, and the less they saw each other the better they got along. Gradually, their financial situation improved. Black Bear gave Joella his old 1953 Chevrolet, and began buying through the employees' credit union a 1961 Plymouth—they had joined America's two-car families! By November, 1968, Black Bear had $1,200 saved in the credit union. Making a down payment of $1,100, he bought for $10,500 the house in which he and Joella were living.

At the same time, however, he had fallen $350 in arrears on the gas and electric bills. His take-home pay from both jobs was only $7,000 a year. The little that Joella earned she spent on herself. Black Bear's and Joella's earnings put them among the "upper income" families in the inner city, but the money was far from adequate for raising eight children. The children still did not have enough to eat, they still did not have warm winter clothing, and with both parents out of the house most of the time they were as neglected as ever. Often Black Bear and Joella took out their irritation with each other on them, and "spanked" them with a paddle or a belt until they were black and blue. The children were frequently absent from school. When they did go they arrived in torn and sometimes grotesque clothing. They were bruised and they were dirty. They were failing.

In the fall of 1967 the automobile workers went on strike. In the past, when the time had come for rehiring, the automobile plants had recruited most of their unskilled and semiskilled labor from the Appalachian whites. But the Detroit riot brought the plight of the inner city Negroes to the industry's attention. Ford, Chrysler, and other plants hired thousands of unemployed blacks, and even arranged for buses to carry them to and from the plants. (It was this special hiring of Negroes that George Devers complained about.) When Larry Higgins returned to Detroit, he was unable to find work. For three months Katherine worked at the Scott Paper Company to keep the family going, and Larry took care of the children. When she returned home one evening a few days before Christmas, she found a note from her husband. He said he was going back to West Virginia, and had taken the children. She could follow him or not, as she pleased.

She went and "stole the children back," and returned to Detroit. In January of 1968 she applied for welfare.

Katherine's father, Peter Jansen, died during the winter. Her mother, Marie, lived alone in a small, cluttered room on Cass Avenue, a narrow, "white" enclave paralleling Woodward Avenue. In her midfifties, Marie worked as a waitress in a café. She seldom saw Rita, Joella, Katherine, or her son Jim, who worked as a window washer, painter, and handyman when he was not in jail. Her other children had been placed in boarding homes, and she could not even remember what they had looked like.

Several nights a week she went to the movies. After she returned home, she switched on the television set and watched movies until the early morning hours. For the first time in her life nothing interfered with her passion.

One day in the spring of 1969 she was walking the two darkened blocks from Woodward Avenue to her room. Two Negro youths followed her. Pushing her into a doorway, they grabbed at her purse. She screamed, and they panicked. One of the youths drove a knife into her chest.

She was seriously injured. When she recovered, she suffered spells of disorientation, and clearly was not able to care for herself. The hospital undertook the task of contacting her relatives. A conference was arranged.

Rita, Katherine, and Joella came. So did Elmira Lentick, Marie's younger sister, who had married Harold Lentick. Harold was a skilled worker at River Rouge. Harold and Elmira had two boys and a girl. One of the boys had graduated from college, and the other was doing well as a salesman. Harold had almost paid off the mortgage on the house in Dearborn, and he bought a new car every three or four years. He had been a member of the United Auto Workers for more than thirty years. He could recall his father's anger at "the bosses" and the stories of the labor turmoil at the Calumet and Hecla mine, and he himself had participated in the struggle to organize the UAW. Yet the union was now as much an institution as the Ford Motor Company. One seemed as firmly established as the other, and Lentick could no longer think of them as adversaries. If he had a vague sense of dissatisfaction, it was a feeling that "America's not what it used to be when I was growing up."

Another of Peter and Marie Jansen's children, Alice, came too. Alice had lived with her parents only as an infant. The Juvenile Court had placed her in a foster home, and she had rarely seen Peter and Marie. In her early thirties, she was a blonde and beautiful woman. She had graduated from a suburban high school, and married an engineer at Ford. She and her husband lived with their three children in a forty-thousand-dollar home in Southfield. Her husband did not even know her mother was still alive. When Alice saw Rita, her older sister, she thought at first that Rita must be Marie's sister. Rita's face was lined; the skin hung from her arms like flabby dough; her legs were inked with varicose veins. She wore a faded dress, whose wide skirt flapped around her calves. Since she was unable to travel by herself, Georgia had brought her. Georgia was pregnant and supposed to get married shortly.

Katherine thought she might be able to care for Marie at some time in the future, but she did not have room for her mother at the present. Alice agreed she would pay a considerable portion of the bill if Marie were placed in a nursing home. After an hour together, the women went their own ways again—Alice to Southfield, Elmira to Dearborn, Rita to western Detroit, and Joella and Katherine to Grand Boulevard.

Katherine had seldom been so depressed. In Elmira and Alice she saw the middle-class world of which she might have become a part. For a brief time, when she had been in the girls' academy, that world had seemed to be attainable. Then she had lost it; and now her worst fears were coming to pass.

One afternoon the worker from the Department of Social Services came to talk to her about her plans and about her children. The social worker asked her if the children had had their immunizations, and suddenly, to the worker's bewilderment and consternation, Katherine was crying, not for two-minutes or three, but for twenty minutes, thirty minutes, an hour. Finally she calmed down, but clung verbally to her visitor.

"Mrs. Higgins, for some reason," the social worker wrote, "started to talk about how she grew up in foster homes, and how difficult a time she had had there.

"She said that one time her mother said she wished she could go on ADC so as not to have a boyfriend hanging around. And the next thing she knew she and the other kids were being removed from the home and placed.

"She always thought that the social agencies were against her mother, and one day her mother would come back and rescue her from all of these people. She remembers the homes she lived in vividly; and it is not a good memory.

"She said she would do anything rather than have this happen to her children. And when the worker asked her what she meant by anything—she said *anything*."

118

The Welfare Murder

DURING THE TIME THAT MARIE JANSEN WAS IN DETROIT GENERAL HOSPITAL recovering from the stab wound, Irma Mirow was admitted in critical condition. Since November, 1967, she had been in and out of the hospital. She drank herself into chronic nosebleeds and bloody diarrhea. She had terrible cramps and dry heaves, and saw strange people and things. For five or six days at a time, she would be in screaming agony. After each stay in the hospital, she would remain off alcohol for two or three months. Then there would be "just one drink," followed by a two-month slide into the abyss. In the spring of 1969, a few months after her husband Donald had died suddenly, she was once more admitted to the hospital. She vomited bloody coffee grounds. Blood surged from first one orifice and then another. Clawing at the green-eyed snakes that were attacking her, she died.

Irma's daughter, Mirabel, had learned to drink while lying in bed with her mother. As a child she had hated what liquor was doing to her mother, but as she grew older she cared less. A Juvenile Court probation officer admonished her: "Don't let your children repeat your mistakes." But Mirabel was trapped in a world of mistakes. She wanted to believe the social worker who encouraged her to be a nurse's aide. But her lack of education created a chasm between even that modest ambition and its attainment. She wanted to raise her children decently; but nobody had ever taught her how to raise children. She wanted to feed and clothe and house the children adequately. But while the cost of living kept going up, she was receiving $180 a month for four persons.

Mirabel returned to prostitution to supplement her income. She hated herself, and to blot out the hate and the contradictions she drank. The more she drank, the more money she had to earn by prostitution to pay for the liquor. Although she was only in her twenties, her teeth were in an advanced state of decay and her gums were filled with abscesses. Often she drank to kill the pain. Already the teeth of her children were deteriorating too. There had never been a toothbrush in the house. Dental hygiene was as foreign to the poverty population as to the immigrants before Ford had introduced them to "sociology." Wayne

County contained 325,000 children in families with incomes under $4,000 a year, and 80 to 90 percent of these children above the age of ten were having difficulties with their teeth. In the summer of 1966 the PRESCAD (Preschool, school, and adolescent children) program was launched with a Federal grant of $4.5 million, the largest of its kind in the country. PRESCAD was supposed to be a "comprehensive health" program taking care of all the children's medical needs. But the need for dental care was so acute the directors of the program decided to concentrate the money on dental work.

Not until June, 1967, did Mirabel hear anything about the program. Then she was urged to register her children. Of course, she didn't. By the time the matter was brought up again, the program had been "closed"—there were too many children and not enough money. Then it was *open* again; then it was *closed* again; then it was only for children under nine years of age. On-again and off-again, the program provided treatment for only about eight thousand children a year.

PRESCAD's snarl resulted largely from a lack of planning. There were an inadequate number of dental personnel to care for a previously unmet need, and the Michigan Dental Association was determined to direct a considerable portion of the funds to private dentists. The original intent of the PRESCAD proposal, written by a University of Detroit Dental School professor, had been to establish public clinics throughout the county. The Dental Association managed to kill that proposal, and substitute one of its own. Patients were to be channeled to private dentists through a referral organization, the Michigan Dental Service Corporation. This corporation had never before grossed more than $35,000 a year, but was now given a $350,000 annual contract by PRESCAD. (Public clinics were set up simultaneously in six community action centers.) In May, 1967, however, PRESCAD discovered that despite the tremendous unmet dental needs of children, it had spent or allocated only about one third of its funds—the "unencumbered" sum would have to be returned to the Federal government at the end of the fiscal year on June 30. (A large part of the money that *had* been spent was not doing the children any good. Some $190,000 was used to purchase equipment for public clinics, but much of the equipment remained in crates because there were no facilities in which to set it up or dentists to make use of it. In the "out-county" areas beyond the city limits, more than $230,000 was expended without the treatment of a single child.) A frantic effort was initiated in June to have children examined· by dentists so that corrective work could be scheduled for the future, but contracted for under the current fiscal year. When the results of this pell-mell effort were tabulated in August, it was discovered that not $350,000 had been contracted for, but $896,000—the program had been filled for a year and a half ahead! In the meantime, since PRESCAD had had difficulty employing its first-year funds, the Federal government cut second-year funding to $3.95 million. As frantically as it had sought children, therefore, PRESCAD turned them away. (PRESCAD was also suffering because it paid $12 a visit, compared to the $8 paid by Medicaid. Naturally, when given a choice, practitioners and hospitals were billing PRESCAD.) Since *remedial* dental care for children would cost more than $15 million a year, the PRESCAD directors decided "to write off the population with holes in its teeth," and concentrate on preventive dental care. (The expenditure of the same amount of money would bring greater results in preventive than remedial care.) "It's an incredibly unpopular decision," said

Dr. George Pickett, Detroit Health Commissioner. "Kids will suffer unnecessarily, and end up in the acute emergency room to get their teeth yanked. But bad teeth rarely kill or disable. So they're expendable." [1]

So Mirabel's four children continued to suffer with their expendable teeth. (Mirabel had a new baby fathered by a "john" whose name she did not know.) The oldest child, Dinah, born in 1955, was quite pretty. Mirabel's brother, Brett, only five years older than Dinah, visited occasionally and brought his stepcousin, Garry Gatling, along. Garry was working as a stock boy. He liked Dinah and felt sorry for her. He bought her candy and took her to the movies. The relationship seemed innocent and platonic.

But one day in the spring of 1969 when he was out with Brett, Garry suddenly said: "I got to get some bread."

Brett asked him why.

"I messed up. Dinah's gonna drop a baby. I got to help her."

In an effort to expand his pay, Garry had gotten into a crap game and lost it all. Brett, who was once more working at a steel plant, had bought a 1961 Chevrolet for two hundred dollars. Like tens of thousands of other cars in the city, it was on its last wheels.* Brett was having a hard time making his pay last from one week to the next; and he had just found out that the car would need a new differential.

They were driving around and talking about how they might get some money. Garry suggested that they snatch some purses. Brett thought of Pepper. Pepper was so small nobody paid attention to him. He was quick, and he could run fast. They decided to pick up Pepper.

Pepper Culleran, thirteen years old, was the fifth of eleven children of Fanny Culleran and Zeb Rockhill. Rockhill had come to Detroit from the South in 1942. Three years later Fanny had followed her husband, Dick Culleran, who was in the army, to Michigan. But he deserted her, and she began living with Rockhill. Since she never divorced Culleran, all of her and Rockhill's children bore the Culleran name.

For fifteen years Rockhill had worked at the same foundry that employed Tom Winesberry, Mirabel's husband. The Culleran and Stallings children had become acquainted. When the foundry shut down in 1961, the fifty-year-old Rockhill was thrown out of work. He was an "older" worker, and he was never again able to obtain a job that lasted more than a few months. He made little more than half of the one hundred dollars a week he had been earning at the foundry.

The family had never been on welfare. Until 1962 the children had not gotten into trouble. The school system classified them in the "dull normal" range. But as the family's economic situation deteriorated, so did the performance and behavior of the children. Rockhill's lungs had been damaged by the smoke, dust, and heat of the foundry, and he had incipient bronchiectasis and emphysema. He was laid up for weeks at a time. During the winter of 1964, the family had no gas, no heat, no electricity. Fanny cooked on a tiny iron coal stove set on top of the gas range in the kitchen. The old frame house

---

* America's dilapidated cars, like dilapidated appliances and dilapidated housing, were a natural concomitant of the lower economic areas of the city. Dozens of used car lots sold vehicles from twenty-five to a few hundred dollars—and many of them scarcely lasted long enough to get the buyer home. The city annually collected twenty-five thousand abandoned cars, yet was unable to keep up. Automobiles sometimes sat for days in the middle of the streets in which they died.

projected over the counter. Throwing the overcoat open, he pulled out the .45. Holding it with both hands, he had to raise it to eye level in order to bring it above the edge of the counter.

"This is a stickup!" he shouted, his voice sounding as if it were coming out of a character in "Donald Duck."

"Like hell it is!" Rosenweiss ejaculated, and threw a seltzer bottle at him.

The gun went off. The shot reverberated in the confines of the store. The slug entered just above the druggist's right eye. As the two women ran screaming toward a rear door, Rosenweiss toppled backward and disappeared behind the counter.

Pepper ran out of the store and jumped into the car. Brett screeched out of the alley.

"I sure lit that dude up!" Pepper said. "I really lit him up!"

"You killed him?" Brett yelled.

"I sure lit him up!" Pepper kept repeating.

Garry wanted to know how much money he had gotten. But Pepper had forgotten all about the money.

The next day, when Brett found out that the druggist had been killed, he took the gun and threw it into a dump.

The three of them had spent so much time in the vicinity of the drugstore that the police had plenty of witnesses. Both Garry and Pepper had been seen by customers in the store. The police showed the witnesses mug books of youthful holdup men. But, of course, the pictures of Garry, Brett, and Pepper were not included.

The police might never have caught them, if Pepper had not gone around telling all his acquaintances that "I sure can shoot," and "I lit him up like a jukebox." Nobody was going to ignore him, abuse him, or take him lightly anymore. After a few days, the neighborhood rumors filtered down to Homicide detectives via a Juvenile Court probation officer. The detectives picked up Pepper and another boy who had been heard talking about the shooting.

Pepper's distinctive skin mottling made it easy for the two women to identify him. At first he was sullen and defiant. But as he became frightened, he admitted that he had been at the scene. He denied, however, that he had killed anybody. He said it hadn't been his idea. A detective asked him if it hadn't been he who had fired the gun. He replied no. The detective pointed out that two witnesses had seen him. "It just went off!" said Pepper. How could it have just gone off? the detective asked. "It was magical interference," said Pepper.

The two detectives treated him sympathetically. They did not laugh at him. They did not make light of him. They treated him like an adult, but at the same time did not seem to place the blame on him. Pepper regained his confidence. He felt important. From Baby-Face Nelson, he switched his identification to the detectives. He was going to help them solve the crime. Bit by bit, detail by detail he told the story.

Brett and Garry were picked up. They denied everything. Then they tried to place the blame on Pepper. Garry swore that he was innocent, that Brett had had the gun and that Pepper had done the shooting, and that he had been along only for the ride.

The room in the Juvenile Court in which Judge James Lincoln presided over hearings was small and elongated, not more than a third or a fourth the size of most regular courtrooms. At the head of the room was a table for the judge.

Placed against it in T-fashion was a long table at which the defendant, the prosecuting and defense attorneys, and other participants in the case sat. In back of the room were benches and chairs for witnesses and members of the families. In the overheated room the semiformal procedure tied judge, perpetrator, attorneys, witnesses, and members of the defendant's and the victim's families together. There was an intimacy and tension lacking in adult proceedings.

Pepper had admitted the shooting. But the defense attorney contended that he had acted without premeditation or intent; that he had been under the influence of Brett and Garry, and was being made the scapegoat.

"Didn't you tell the police officer the three of you were driving around looking for someplace to rob?" the prosecutor asked Pepper.

There was a long silence. Pepper looked down and did not answer.

Judge Lincoln interjected himself. "What did the detective ask you?"

"He ask me where was we going?" Pepper replied in a barely audible voice.

"At what point did you think there would be a holdup?"

"I had a funny feeling. But I didn't know."

"Which is the truth?" the prosecutor shot at him. "The statement you made to the detective about [Brett] Stallings having a gun and driving around looking for a place to stage a holdup, or what you're saying here?"

"Both of them."

"You were looking for someone to rob," insisted the prosecutor.

"We all was looking. But not me," said Pepper.

"Let's get it together now," Brett, who with Garry was seated in the back of the room, called out in a threatening voice.

"You *will* be quiet," said Judge Lincoln. "To intimidate a person is contempt of court."

"I have a right to talk," Brett retorted.

"I think the boy is trying to tell the truth," Judge Lincoln addressed himself to the prosecutor. "Sometimes neither the full truth nor a lie is told. What occurred may be different than what any of us suspect."

Finally, all the witnesses had been heard.

"The fact that a heinous crime was committed is not enough," said Judge Lincoln. "I have to consider the prior record of the child, the pattern of living, the maturity of the child, the best interests of public welfare and safety."

"This is a one-time offense," said the defense attorney.

"The police have connected him to numerous other offenses—purse snatchings, B and E's," asserted the prosecutor.

Judge Lincoln did not reply; but he was skeptical that juveniles were responsible for as many crimes as police claimed they admitted to—it seemed a convenient way to clear the blotter.

"I really don't want to send him to training school [the Michigan State Boys Vocational School in Lansing]," Judge Lincoln said, "because he'd learn how to jump a switch and steal a car. If he were given twenty lashes—this may sound barbaric—but most kids would rather take twenty lashes, and it would probably rehabilitate just as many of them. I have on my desk a list of seventy-nine boys whom I sent to the training school, and sixty to sixty-five of them later were picked up on major felonies."

Nevertheless, Judge Lincoln said, he had no choice. The school was the only facility available.

Pepper burst out crying. He started to run toward his father, a thin, stooped, ill-looking man at the back of the room. A bailiff grabbed Pepper. He struggled.

"Leggo!" he cried. "I want to see my old man. I want to see him—just for a minute!"

"We'd like to see our father, too," Rosenweiss's twenty-year-old daughter echoed bitterly.

Several months later, in Detroit Recorders Court (the adult court), Pepper testified against Brett and Garry. Convicted of first-degree murder, Brett and Garry were sentenced to life imprisonment.

In the routinized atmosphere of the training school in Lansing, Pepper did well. He tried to please any adult who paid attention to him and treated him with kindness. His behavior was good. His schoolwork picked up. He did not manifest any serious psychological disturbances. He acted quite differently—and was, in truth, a different person—than on the streets of Detroit. Judge Lincoln had recommended that he be held until he was nineteen (the maximum age). But in less than two years the psychologist and counselor considered him rehabilitated. They could see no further benefit to him from a continued stay at the school—and the school desperately needed every bed for new boys it was being asked to admit.

Pepper was returned to the atmosphere of his home and Detroit. The police, frustrated, cursed, tried to watch him and were convinced that within several weeks of his return he was again getting into trouble.

It was not the first case that had had such a denouement. Judge Lincoln was irate: "If a boy commits murder the week before his seventeenth birthday, he gets a few months. If he does it the week after, he gets mandatory life."

There was, however, nothing Judge Lincoln could do about it. As the only judge on the court, he headed the largest juvenile jurisdiction in the nation. (He had seven attorneys working under him as referees.) Crusty, salty, drawling his words with a country twang, he was incisive and meticulously fair.* From year to year he saw the problems of the city come before him, and year after year they went on by with little that he could do. "This court," said Lincoln, "is so inadequate that it's irrelevant."

Ten thousand youngsters yearly were processed through the juvenile home which, both legally and physically, was attached to the court. Nearly nine thousand complaints were filed annually against juveniles in the county; and 62 percent of the youths were repeaters. "The nation," said Lincoln, "is focusing on what juveniles are doing. It should look at what's being done *to* juveniles.

"There are millions of children being born who aren't wanted. They get battered and neglected. They become emotionally disturbed. They can't function in school. If they get into trouble in school, they'll wind up in court.

"The common denominator of crime is failure. Eighty-six out of every one hundred boys in the Youth Home don't graduate from high school. The most important thing is to give a boy some sense of achievement. Most of them can't

---

* Judge Lincoln had been born in 1916 on an 80-acre farm in Huron County. His mother, a school teacher, had taught Frank Murphy. When Murphy had been appointed U.S. Attorney-General, he had taken Jim Lincoln to Washington with him, and Lincoln had become the "doorman" for Murphy's senior aide, G. Mennen Williams. After World War II, Lincoln became Williams's law partner in Detroit, and in 1953 he had run for mayor against Cobo. He was a city councilman when Governor Williams appointed him judge of the Juvenile Court in 1960.

get it in school. If he were a problem child, he used to be thrown out. Now we're saying to the system that no matter what, whether he's not motivated, has got the heebie-jeebies, or is a sex maniac, you've got to hold on to him; you've got to teach him. But school is just not the bag for a lot of kids. Buffalo Bill could pull a knife in school and wind up delivering the mail. A hundred years ago the delinquent was sent out West to shoot Indians and dig potatoes. Fifty years ago he could go to a factory gate, tell them he was a farmboy, and they'd put him on. Now if he's a dropout they won't even look at him. What the hell do I do with a sixteen-year-old ninth-grader functioning at the fourth-grade level?"

If the sixteen-year-old ninth-grader functioning at the fourth-grade level were a girl, she almost inevitably became pregnant. "Thirty-five to forty years ago they used to dress virgins in the juvenile home in white, and the others in blue. Pretty soon you never saw a white dress, and even they wanted to know how you could get a blue. Now we get fourteen- and fifteen-year-old girls, and they've got more mileage on them than the C and O Railroad."

Judge Lincoln performed marriage ceremonies for three thousand pregnant teen-agers a year—and that figure represented only a portion of the total in the county. In one case, a thirteen-year-old girl and a fourteen-year-old boy of French-Canadian parentage "wanted a full-blown wedding—flowers, relatives, organ music and church bells if we'd had them. I asked them if that wasn't putting it on thick. But the mother said, 'If they're physically able to have the child, then God must have meant for them to have it. I was married at her age and we have a fine family. That's the way we do it up there.'

"So who the hell am I to interfere with local custom? People have a sense of injustice if you interfere with their lives. We're never going to solve the problem until we develop a good contraceptive gin. If I remove the children from the home, what am I going to do with them? I can't find foster homes for the Negroes, and the real hard cases nobody wants. We don't even know what constitutes *neglect*. I gave a law class at Wayne State University a case without names and dates, and in two hours they had removed the child from the home. He was Abraham Lincoln.

"I had all the propensities of a delinquent. I once nailed a neighbor's dog at two hundred yards, and I wouldn't want to get sent up for that. But the nearest neighbor was two miles away, and usually I got tired before I got there. I grew up with a kerosene lantern, an outhouse, and patches on the pants, but I never realized I was a deprived child until I became a judge. Everybody was poor. You could be proud of being 'poor but honest.' Today, television pictures a superaffluent America. It puts tremendous pressure on kids to get material things. We've made it dishonest to be poor. So people are poor and angry. If you have a society that puts a premium on material things, then you've got to give it to them, or you're going to have crime and delinquency."

One third of the space in the juvenile home was taken up by long-termers, who were supposed to be in state institutions, but whom state institutions would not accept because of overcrowding or lack of suitable programs. The Wayne County "quota" at the Boys Vocational School in Lansing (capacity four hundred) was two boys per month. In 1958, Judge Lincoln's predecessor, Judge Nathan Kaufman, had taken a busload of hard-core delinquents to the school and dumped them inside its gate. The school had sent twenty-two of them back to Detroit on a Greyhound bus—within a year, all twenty-two had been in further trouble. The state constructed a new unit for eighty-five boys at Whitmore Lake. In 1963 Judge Lincoln shipped twenty boys there with commitment papers. Sixteen of them were returned.

Judge Lincoln had no choice but to take the less violent, the lesser malefactors, the neglected and abused children, and return them under court supervision to the community. He estimated that fifty thousand children in Wayne County needed psychological treatment. But there were too few probation officers, there were no programs for the juveniles, and the after-care section was, in Lincoln's words, "paper thin and no good at all." Conditions of probation often evaporated in the lack of enforcement. Sometimes they had ironic twists. A youth reported to his probation officer for fourteen weeks in a row and became the pride of the office—and every week he was stealing a car to make the trip.

"All we're doing," said Judge Lincoln, "is shuffling juveniles around."

Brett Stallings and Garry Gatling were serving life terms in prison. Fourteen-year-old Dinah gave birth to Garry's child. Mirabel, thirty years old, had a baby only a year older than Dinah's. Dinah's child was added to the ADC welfare payments Mirabel was receiving.

Shortly before Christmas, Dinah took two dollars and went to Hudson's department store to buy presents for her mother and the baby. The vastness, the well-dressed shoppers, the multicolored piles of goods on the tables and counters frightened and bewildered her. A fantastic array of candies, nuts, and chocolates attracted her—she had never imagined that so many different kinds existed.

She had never before gone shopping in a store downtown, and she was overwhelmed. She watched the cash registers ringing up the sales, the ten- and twenty-dollar bills changing hands, and she knew she could not buy anything. She wandered from area to area, she took the elevator and went from one floor to the next. She saw perfumes and dresses, cameras and colored television sets, blouses and lingeries, dolls and teddy bears, purses and belts, maternity wear and fur-trimmed overcoats, ski pants and shoes, toys and infant wear. She took a sweater from a counter and stuffed it inside her frayed overcoat.

She no longer was going to school. Like other children in the poverty area, she had an awareness of money, an awareness that the birth of the baby had sharpened. A few weeks after Christmas, she told a sixteen-year-old girlfriend how depressed she was. "Come on," said the friend, "I'll show you how to make out. It's fun!"

So Dinah, a pretty child in a dark-blue, faded dress hung out in bars with her friend and let herself be picked up. One night in March, she was suggestively sliding her dress up to her thighs, but she was too inexperienced to know that she was picking up a member of the vice squad.

She solicited a fee of ten dollars, and found herself being hustled into a car by two Negro detectives and a sergeant. The car was parked on a side street by the rear of the bar, where a garbage bin carried the message: "Do Not Eat Food out of Garbage—25 Percent Poison." Down the block another girl was waving a flashlight at the cars that passed by. A half dozen black youths were watching, and making threatening remarks. The operation seemed more like a kidnaping than an arrest.

The tension inside the car was high. After a few months on the vice squad

the men looked upon every girl as a whore, and they made no distinction between a teen-ager of fifteen and an experienced hooker of twenty-five or thirty.

"For ten bucks you ought to sixty-nine a john," said one of the officers.

"Fuck you!" Dinah replied, frightened but trying to put up a good front.
"That's what you were going to do!"

"I'd rather go down on a whitey for four bits than on you for fifty dollars!"

"You nigger bitch!"

At police headquarters on Beaubien Street they took her to the seventh floor.
She was led to the vice bureau and placed in an inner room with a barred
window. The brown-yellow walls sucked in the fluorescent lighting. There was
a pervasive atmosphere of cheapness and age. An officer told her to empty her
purse onto the table, and out came a comb, a piece of Kleenex, two dimes and
a nickle, a good-luck charm, a key, one Tampax, and a stick of gum.

It was nearly midnight before she arrived at the intake section of the juvenile home. She was locked in the girls holding room to await an interview by
a social worker. There was only a barren bench, and the walls were scarred
with the graffiti of those who had preceded her. She did not know what would
happen to her. She wanted to see her baby. And she cried.

119

The Haves and Haves-Not

BRETT STALLINGS HAD BEEN REMOVED FROM URBAN SOCIETY. MIRABEL WAS a prostitute on Twelfth Street, and her daughter was already following in her steps. Natalie Stallings, however, was slowly separating herself from the deprivation in which she had grown up.

In the spring of 1967 her husband, Nick Palmerill, had been released from prison. He had had psychological counseling and had done a good deal of reading. If he were still angry, he had more insight and no longer blamed everything on whites. In order to be hired, he lied about his prison record. He thought that though management might find out about his record later, he would be kept on if he did a good job. He started working in a metal shop; but when his prison record was discovered, he was fired. He went to work in an auto repair shop; and he was fired.

The future looked bleak. In the meantime, the Detroit riot occurred. On October 30, 1967, following the end of the UAW strike against Ford, the company had sixty-five hundred vacancies for unskilled and low-skilled workers. Henry Ford II announced that the company would recruit five thousand workers from the inner city. Employment offices were set up at two community action centers. Written tests, previously required of all applicants, were eliminated for inner city recruits. Special bus service was initiated to River Rouge. In a miniature recreation of the scene at Highland Park in 1914, fifteen hundred persons, some of them husbands and wives, began lining up in front of the community action centers in the middle of the night.

For years Lewis F. Nicolini, Midwest regional director of the manpower program, had been unsuccessfully trying to convince industry to hire prison parolees. Now Ford reinstituted on a small scale the employment of ex-convicts, a practice that had fallen into disrepute during the tenure of Harry Bennett. The firm discovered that the parolees were generally in better physical condition than the persons hired off the street because they had received medical attention in prison. They had developed discipline that was transferable to private employment. Many of the inner city employees had difficulties similar to those of the immigrant workers two generations earlier, so there was a low-key revival of Henry Ford's "sociology." The workers were taken through an orientation program, told they must report to work *every day,* advised to buy alarm clocks (which are rarities in poverty households), and warned against spending every penny they earned and contracting debts. They were encouraged to form "buddy" systems, so that if one started slipping another would push him back onto the track. Simultaneously, foremen had to have their thinking and behavior redirected. All too often they looked upon the unskilled workers (and especially blacks) as chronic screwups. The foremen yelled at and castigated the workers, and could not care less whether they returned the next day. The company had to impress upon the foremen that it did care.

Palmerill was one of the first ex-convicts to be hired. He worked as a sweeper and was paid the entry-level wage of $3.25 an hour. His temper still flared on occasion, but he tried to direct his anger toward constructive action. Natalie had found her niche as a community aide in MCHRD. Her job was not intended to be permanent, but to train her for private employment. But like most of the other MCHRD employees she never considered that she might someday move to another job. She went to the birth control clinic established at Hermann Kiefer Hospital—she did not want to have another child and to have to quit working.

Between them, Palmerill and Natalie were earning approximately ten thousand dollars a year. They made a down payment on a modest but well-kept house in the Twelfth Street area. They bought new furniture and heavy carpets. They were proud of the house and kept it spotless. The neighborhood was divided between the "haves" and the "haves-not." The "haves" had a block club, and the "haves-not" had numerous kids. There was no communication between them, and the kids were running around uncontrolled, committing vandalism and tearing up the street.

Palmerill, who could talk the kids' language, started meeting with them and trying to restructure their activities. "If I can make it, so can you," he told them. On those who could see a possibility of graduating from high school, he made some impression. There was a dropoff in the aimless vandalism. But those who had been mired in poverty all their lives and were failing in school had difficulty believing in anything, especially themselves. When Palmerill told them they could make it, they asked:

"How?"

120

The International Fords

FORD'S PROGRAM TO EMPLOY INNER CITY RESIDENTS WAS SOON BROUGHT TO the attention of President Johnson. In the fall of 1967 Senators Clark of Pennsylvania and Javits of New York had introduced a Public Service Employment Act to initiate a massive public service employment program for the hard-core unemployed. Embroiled in the Vietnam War, the President was trying to cut back on domestic programs. He wanted nothing to do with a program that would make the Federal government the employer of last resort and cost one billion dollars a year. When Ford called the White House to suggest that the motor company's program could be expanded throughout American industry in a business-government partnership, the President seized the concept as a reasonable alternative to public service employment. On March 1, 1968, President Johnson announced the formation of the National Alliance of Businessmen to operate the JOBS (Job Opportunities in the Business Sector) program. The immediate goal was the hiring of one hundred thousand hard-core unemployed. Ford was appointed chairman of the National Alliance of Businessmen (NAB), and Leo Beebe, Ford's vice-president, became executive director.

Within two years the NAB met the goal of one hundred thousand jobs. But the Federal government was subsidizing employers $2,700 for the orientation and training of each worker—a sum equal to two thirds of the projected cost of the public service employment program. While public service employment had been intended to *create* jobs, JOBS proved to be essentially a job-redistribution program. When the economic expansion of 1968–1969 ended in the slump of 1970, JOBS had no effect on unemployment. In many cases it did, however, provide a bonanza in subsidies for employers.

(In Detroit the meat packing industry had been having difficulty hiring people—even though the pay scale was $2.80 to $4.40 per hour for unskilled jobs—because of the undesirability of the work. They had been taking everybody they could get from the inner city. Yet they now received a JOBS grant of $240,000 to train ninety people.)

601

Much of the impetus for Ford's inner city employment project and JOBS came from the New Detroit Committee. The New Detroit Committee was the organization formed by Governor Romney and Mayor Cavanagh during the week of the riot, and Henry Ford II was one of thirty-nine members. It was at a meeting of the committee that Levi Jackson, a former black football star at Yale and a Ford employee, had cornered Ford and handed him a typed proposal that the company go into the inner city to hire people.

The New Detroit Committee brought together for the first time in the history of any city diverse elements of the community. On the committee were some of the world's most powerful men of industry: James M. Roche, chairman of the board of General Motors, the world's largest corporation; Ford, chairman of the board of the Ford Motor Company, the world's third largest corporation; Lynn A. Townsend, chairman of the board of Chrysler; Walker Cisler, chairman of the board of the Detroit Edison Company; William Day, president of the Michigan Bell Telephone Company; Max M. Fisher, leading investor in the Marathon Oil Company and one of Richard Nixon's chief fund raisers and his "expert on Jewish affairs"; Joseph L. Hudson, Jr., president of the J. L. Hudson Company; Ralph T. McElvenny, chairman of the board of the Michigan Consolidated Gas Company; Stanley Winkelman, president of Winkelman Stores.

They came once a month to ultramodern McGregor Memorial Auditorium on the Wayne State University campus and crossed the catwalk to the second-floor meeting room. There, around the horseshoe arrangement of tables, they were joined by Dr. Drachler from the school district, Dr. William R. Keast, president of the university, Walter Reuther and Jack Wood from the labor movement, Edward Carey and Mel Ravitz from the city council, and the blacks from the inner city. They listened patiently to the long-winded expostulations of Lena Bivens, representing the welfare mothers and Target Area I of the antipoverty program. They tolerated with forebearance the appearance of an "honor guard" of four bereted youths brought along by the director of an inner city organization and stationed on either side of the door as if to announce the dissolution of the Kerenskyist New Detroit Committee by a black Detroit soviet.

During the first two years of its existence, the committee spent ten million dollars on projects relating to the inner city. Its principal concern was with the black population, and it supported everything from black arts and black theater to black business. It financed studies that were rehashes of studies done before, and so gave employment to social scientists. It provided money to the Detroit school system for a summer reading program, and to the health department for expanded family-planning clinics. It agreed with *Fortune* Magazine (July, 1968), that "seldom has a nation governed by rational men created an institution so erratic in its operations, and so perverse in some of its social effects, as the U.S. Welfare System," a system that "does not provide a decent standard of living on which a mother can decently house, feed, and clothe her children." It petitioned the governor "to set up a study commission to develop alternative means of delivering public assistance."

It voiced concern about the police department. William Patrick, the committee's president and a former city councilman, asserted in November, 1968, that "citizens' grievances against police practices are held more deeply today than in 1967." Winkelman said, "We're talking about the fundamental failure of the police to discipline officers. . . . The department needs to be taken apart and put together again." The committee appropriated $300,000 for a management study of the police department. Mayor Cavanagh supported the study. But the departmental bureaucracy was resolutely opposed. With the well-tested tactics of inertia, delay, and circumlocutious memoranda, they managed to frustrate the proposal until it finally faded away.

When the New Detroit Committee had been founded, there had been an assumption that its purpose was to revitalize and rebuild the city. During the second year of its existence, however, it was still wrestling with its direction and its goals. Fisher, who took over as chairman in 1969 and was a close friend of Ford, believed strongly that "we need better objectives and goals for the New Detroit Committee. We need a far larger degree of involvement with the community, and methods of communicating with all segments of the community." Certainly the committee's business members were no longer oblivious of the people on Twelfth Street. In a memorandum Fisher suggested that "the primary focus . . . will be to assist the community in the solution of the problems relating to the black minority in the metropolitan area." Since "recent events have shown that evolutionary change now seems unlikely to narrow the widening gulf of disadvantage dividing our society . . . is New Detroit committed to the principle of self-determination by the disadvantaged even if such expression of need runs counter to the traditional views of our membership? . . . How far ahead of public opinion are we prepared to stand to support this fundamental need?"

"We're here because the white community has failed," Winkelman said. "We have a tremendous job to change attitudes and institutions. We must mobilize the resources of people, not only of finances."

"We must recognize there are other disadvantaged people than black," Reuther declared. "What we're talking about is facilitating peaceful social change. Only this way can we prevent violent social change."

"The urban problem is the most complex and difficult society has ever faced," said Arjay Miller, Ford's vice-chairman of the board.

Putting the ends of his Ben Franklin half glasses in his mouth, chewing on them, twirling them around, Henry Ford II listened to the debate. His long hair slightly graying at the temples, he had the dour, contemplative, well-fed appearance of an English bulldog. (Physically, he resembled his mother and was the antithesis of his grandfather.) Ford was impatient with the workings of the committee. (He had told one of its employees: "I wouldn't take this crap if you were working for me.") He interjected: "We have to get down to programs. We have to get out and do things. I'd rather get something done than sit around and talk about it."

The need, Fisher kept emphasizing, was "to come to grips with the problems." But the business members of the committee were unable to resolve the conflict between their personal civic consciences and their corporate interests. With $1.5 million the committee established an Economic Development Corporation for the city. The fifty-one members of the board of directors included not only the business members of the committee but the chairmen of the board or presidents of Great Lakes Steel, American Motors, the Bendix Corporation, Parke-Davis, S. S. Kresge Company, the Burroughs Corporation, Kelsey-Hayes, Rockwell-Standard, the Budd Company, Wyandotte Chemical, and most of the leading banks in the city.

Yet even while they joined the Economic Development Corporation for the city, the same men continued to move their companies out of the city and expand their properties in the suburbs. The Budd Company shifted its automotive division headquarters from the city to the suburb of Troy. The Kresge Company, which had originated with a single five-and-ten-cent store on Woodward Avenue in 1899, let it be known that they were going to build a new headquarters—in the city or out. Both Mayor Cavanagh and Planning Director Blessing were ready to make every concession to keep the company in the city and proposed that the company erect its new general offices on a site to be cleared adjacent to the civic center. But the two-billion-dollar company, which had progressed from urban dime stores to suburban K-Mart discount stores, picked a thirty-acre site amid the open spaces of Troy. To build in downtown Detroit would have cost the company between one third and one half more immediately, and a far greater amount over the years in higher taxes.

The Chrysler Corporation announced plans to build an entirely new town on 1,700 acres near Troy. Included were the 774 acres of Wabeek Farm, the property purchased by James Couzens with some of the first of the fortune he had earned with the Ford Motor Company.

Ford, too, participated in facilitating the outmigration. On the remaining 2,300 unused acres of the vast property his grandfather had accumulated in Dearborn, he commenced construction in 1970 on a complex of office, commercial, and residential buildings. (One of the businesses that announced it would be making the journey to Dearborn was the Michigan Automobile Club, which had its headquarters at 139 Bagley Avenue, just a block from where Ford had constructed his first automobile. It employed eight hundred persons.)

Every day Henry II was chauffeured across the breadth of the city at seventy miles per hour from Grosse Pointe Farms to his twelfth-floor office in Dearborn. Still in his early fifties, he had been president of the company since 1945 and probably would rule over it longer than his grandfather. Under his stewardship the company had pulled even with General Motors in engineering, styling, and innovation—Ford's research department employed two hundred Ph.D.'s—if not in sales. Beginning in the mid-1950's the company introduced a remarkable number of successful new cars—the Thunderbird, the Lincoln Continental (a revival), the Falcon, the Mustang, and the Maverick. Its one great failure was the Edsel—and there Henry II had let his heart get the better of his head.

The success of the company pumped hundreds of millions of dollars into the Ford Foundation. The foundation's assets of $3 billion were four times as large as those of the Rockefeller Foundation, the next in size, and by 1970 it had made grants of $3.3 billion. Henry II had studied sociology at Yale—due to a misunderstanding over a ghostwritten thesis he never received his degree, a fact that does not seem to have had an adverse effect on his career—and through the foundation he was able to put sociology into practice as no private person had before.

The foundation's grants for higher education, elementary education (Great Cities), hospitals, and juvenile delinquency had focused attention on areas of neglect, and become a catalyst for Federal involvement. Within the walls of the foundation the thesis had been cultivated that welfare maternalism was failing and that the poor must be given a role in their own destinies; and this had become a cornerstone of the War on Poverty. The interaction between the foundation and the Federal government made the five years of the Johnson Administration a watershed in national involvement in urban affairs. It brought the nation a new awareness of the plight of the Negro—but not enough awareness of the nature of poverty in general—and it gave Henry II an influence in national politics far beyond any exercised by his grandfather. He became a "Kennedy liberal," he headed Businessmen for Johnson in 1964, and he supported Hubert Humphrey (of whom he was personally fond) in 1968. From the Kennedy Administration came McGeorge Bundy, the Ford Foundation's new president. Bundy (who had been President Kennedy's national security advisor) pushed the foundation toward more innovative and radical funding. He regarded it as an instrument for social change and as an agent for the resolution of civil conflict. He indicated that it would concentrate on the problems of poverty and the cities, and that "full equality for all American Negroes is now the most urgent domestic concern." * [1]

Henry II's rule of the Ford empire was less obtrusive and more sophisticated than that of his grandfather—but when necessary he could rule just as forcefully as the autocrat of Dearborn. River Rouge, which as a three-year-old he had helped dedicate, was still the world's most massive industrial complex. Nineteen locomotives operated on its eighty-five miles of railroad tracks. It had smoked itself gray and it had the dirt-caked look of age, but it was America's twelfth largest steel producer, third largest glass producer, and largest computer center. (It continued, also, to be one of America's worst polluters; under Michigan's Environmental Protection Act of 1970, the Wayne County Air Pollution Control Division charged Ford with 143 violations of air pollution control regulations.)

Yet River Rouge was but one part of what had become a worldwide industrial empire. Only 35,000 of Ford's 433,000 employees worked at River Rouge. More than half (208,000) of the rest were employed in Ford plants in twenty foreign countries.

Both the outmigration from the American city that had begun in the 1920's and the expansion of American industry from the United States to foreign shores reached maturity in the 1960's. The Americanization of Europe and the growth of the middle class offered enticing opportunities for investment. The number of automobiles in Europe multiplied from twenty million in 1960 to sixty million in 1970. Next to Fiat, Ford was Europe's largest producer of cars, and by 1971 one fourth of its revenues came from foreign sales. The company was spending approximately one third of its budget for capital improvement and expansion abroad, and the proportion was continuing to increase.† Its export of vehicles, 180,000 in 1929, was down to 30,000 a year, and it was importing and marketing more than double that number of European-made cars in the United States.

Between 1960 and 1965 the introduction of compact cars by American manufacturers had temporarily slowed the rise in imports. But then, inevitably,

---

* In 1967 Bundy was the chairman of the panel appointed by New York Mayor John Lindsay to draw up a decentralization plan for the city's schools; the Ford Foundation funded the Ocean Hill-Brownsville experiment that led to the conflict between Negroes seeking to establish local control of the schools and the largely Jewish United Federation of Teachers, intent on retaining the power and bureaucratic security it had achieved for itself.
† In 1972 Ford claimed to have received 4.4 billion dollars more from its foreign investments than it had spent since 1950. But what it has been exporting is jobs, and what it has been importing is profits and dividends.

the compact cars had grown bigger, more gimmicky, and more expensive—
it was the General Motors way of planned obsolescence; and as General Motors
went the other manufacturers followed. The upshot was that between 1965
and 1970 imports more than tripled—from 600,000 in 1965 to over 2 million
in 1970. By 1972 foreign manufacturers held more than 15 percent of the
American market, and the Volkswagen supplanted the Model T as the largest-
selling car in history.

Once more Ford and General Motors assembled their respective committees
for soul searching, and went back to the drawing boards. The result was the
introduction of the "subcompact" car—G.M.'s Vega and Ford's Pinto, designed
to compete directly with the imports. For General Motors the Vega presented
a dilemma—if a small, basic car with constant styling was desirable, what about
the remainder of G.M.'s line, large-sized and cosmetic? Ford had an easier
task—the company advertised the Pinto as a reincarnation of the Model T.

But whereas the Model T had set off Detroit's greatest boom, the guts of
the Pinto—its engine and transmission—were being manufactured abroad and
shipped to the United States for assembly with the rest of the car. In the five
years after 1966 Ford overseas employment climbed by 50,000, but its domestic
work force shrank by 8,000. The 10,000 to 12,000 blacks Ford hired from the
inner city were going not into new jobs but into jobs previously occupied by
someone else. The New Detroit Committee was functioning in the manner of
a small and localized foundation, but it was a poor substitute for the great
economic revitalization the city needed.

Along with the internationalization of the motor company came an internationalization of the Ford family. At a 1960 Paris party hosted by his uncle
Ernest Kanzler, Ford met vivacious Cristina Vettore Austin, an Italian divorcee.
Then in his forties, Henry II was becoming more and more of a swinger, and
less and less like his grandfather. He could put away vast quantities of Scotch,
and he drank champagne over ice. When he went out to have a good time it
was with abandon—he liked "decadent jazz" and rock, and legend has it that
he once led a Dixieland band fully clothed into a swimming pool. His wife,
Anne, was a devout Catholic, a fashion leader with seldom a hair out of place,
and a patron of the Detroit Institute of Arts and the opera. Four years after
the Paris party Ford divorced Anne, and in February, 1965, he married
Cristina. (Both were promptly excommunicated by the Catholic Church.)

In mid-December, 1965, Ford's twenty-four-year-old daughter Charlotte
married Stavros Spyros Niarchos, a fifty-six-year-old Greek who claimed to
be the world's largest shipowner. (The marriage was dissolved in less than
a year, following the birth of a child.)

A few days later, Ford's second daughter, twenty-two-year-old Anne, married Giancarlo Uzielli. Born in Italy, Uzielli had come to the United States as
a boy. A member of the New York Stock Exchange, he worked in the field
of international investments. Although he was Catholic, on his mother's side
he was a Rothschild. Henry Ford's great-granddaughter had come perilously
close to marrying an "international Jew."

121

The Twilight of the City

FOR FORD, THE FINANCIAL ASPECTS OF HIS DIVORCE PRESENTED NO PROBLEM. He made a settlement on his former wife of $16 million, which hardly made a dent in his fortune. For Jerome P. Cavanagh the matter was not so simple. After taxes, deductions, alimony, and payments for his older sons' schooling at a fashionable prep school, Cavanagh had $6,363 left for living expenses out of his $35,000-a-year salary. (The blow was cushioned by the fact that he had no housing or transportation expenses.) If Sylvester and Rose Cavanagh had come to such a parting of the ways, the consequences for Jerry and his brothers and sisters would probably have been disastrous. But upper- and middle-income people can afford mistakes that poorer people cannot.

The income from honorariums for speeches was as important as ever to the mayor, and he continued to spend a good deal of time away from the city. Bob Roselle, whom he had appointed executive secretary in June, 1967, knew the city intimately and was a good administrator. But like Harold Black he was a civil servant, and he expected to be returning to a position within the municipal bureaucracy. He acted cautiously, and strictly within regulations. He lacked the whipcracking ability of Strichartz and the political flair that Cavanagh needed and had come to expect of his executive secretary. After a year, Cavanagh eased him out and made him Commissioner of Public Works.

For eighteen months beginning during the summer of 1968, the all-important post of executive secretary remained unoccupied. Since this was the nerve center through which Cavanagh had run the city and directed the Federal-urban partnership, his control over programs and departments was reduced.

During his first four years in office the mayor had gained the reputation of an urban alchemist, who could take the dross of the city and transmute it into gold. But then the sheen began to fade, and the gold reverted to dross.

The basic problems were economic, and there was just no way to overcome them. Cavanagh continued to work hard to keep industry from moving out of the city. He succeeded in the cases of the Burroughs Corporation, and the Peerless Cement Company. But for every company that stayed, two were leaving.

(Seventy percent of industrial construction was outside Detroit.) Throughout the city there were blocks of abandoned factory buildings and warehouses, many of them standing tomblike amid residential districts. From the mayor's office Cavanagh could see on the riverfront a multistory industrial building topped by a rusting water tank, the huge PACKARD lettering slowly fading. (On East Grand Boulevard the Kahn-built Packard plant had been chopped into storage and office space for a dozen unrelated concerns.) Skirting the river were scores of acres that had passed from the Michigan Central to the New York Central, and from the New York Central to the Pennsylvania Central Railroad in two mergers over three quarters of a century. They included some of the most valuable waterfront property in the nation. Yet while the city was going broke and the Pennsylvania Central Transportation Company was slipping into bankruptcy (where it arrived in June of 1970), the land with its crisscrossing tracks was being used for switching trains.

Scores of other acres that once had made up the Potomac and Black Bottom had been cleared for urban renewal before Cavanagh had entered office, but were still being used for parking cars. The Michigan Avenue skid row district that had been bulldozed in the late 1950's was overgrown with weeds—on one block a battered sign erected over a decade before announced that this was the site of the new Federal Building.

It seemed a symbol of the Federal-urban partnership that Cavanagh had looked forward to with such anticipation in 1962. The Federal programs had come in a torrent, but they created almost as many problems as they solved. Even the progenitors of the Model Cities Program could not regard it without a kind of horror. MCHRD and the antipoverty program were ossifying into a permanent WPA, already infused with bureaucratic arteriosclerosis.

Most of the jobs in MCHRD were not supposed to be permanent. But because people lacked basic education, even after they had been *trained* they were unable to move up, and they certainly did not want to move out. A community aide worked for two years in a "temporary" position of telephone operator, and earned $5,400 a year. The permanent position paid $5,800 a year (under the city's salary schedule), and MCHRD wanted to place her in it. Civil Service, however, said it would have to hold competitive examinations—there were many persons more qualified than she, and for lower-classification jobs like clerks and secretaries there were eight applicants for each position open. Civil Service insisted that it was unethical for someone coming in through the back door of the antipoverty program—a back door that sometimes was opened by ghetto politics —to be able to obtain a permanent lease on a job. Why, they asked, didn't the girl become a telephone operator in some small establishment paying perhaps five thousand dollars a year. But that was the last thing she wanted to do. Not only would she have to take a cut in salary, but she would not feel as secure as she did in MCHRD.

MCHRD's director was inundated with paper work—in his office he virtually disappeared behind the head-high stacks of paper. To evaluate the effectiveness of its programs, MCHRD installed a computerized Management Information System (MIS). But obtaining valid and reliable data with which to program the computer was nearly impossible. So a GIGO (garbage-in, garbage-out) operation resulted. After a year, Congress's General Accounting Office concluded that MIS was a *mis*information system.

With the passage of the years, employees were more and more concerned with Civil Service examinations, job security, and status, and less and less with the program's intended purpose of assisting the population of the inner city. It was clear that the most effective way to help people out of poverty was to employ them. MCHRD did that, but there were enough low-income people in Detroit to support a score of MCHRD's.

The members of the mayor's staff had difficulty accepting that the crusading spirit of the War on Poverty was gone.* Old-line agencies tended to look down on MCHRD, and handicap its work. The Department of Social Services would not respond to calls from workers in the antipoverty program. (At the end of 1966, the city and county welfare offices finally had been merged, ending the hydra-headed structure.) But they would respond to one of the mayor's aides.

Cavanagh's addition of seven positions to the mayor's staff made possible for the first time since the days of the ward system more than cursory responses to people's complaints. Some of the callers were mentally disturbed—one woman was talked out of committing suicide—but most had legitimate complaints, and had been unable to obtain satisfaction from the municipal bureaucracy until they reached the mayor's office. The mayor's staff worked to make the bureaucracy more responsive. Sometimes the staff, too, was stymied.† Occasionally their operations produced unexpected dividends.‡

In many ways the mayor's "third team" was fully as capable and talented as his "first team" had been. But the personal gap between Cavanagh and the "third team" was even greater than between him and the "second team" —they looked upon him as the leader, not as the first among equals. They were incapable of pressuring him to make decisions—and so decisions were not made. Without an executive secretary, the staff lacked a general. As each person went about performing his own function, there was little coordination. On a day-by-day basis the mayor's office ran well enough, but it tended to be ensnared by minutiae. While skirmishes were won, the battle was being lost.

Statistics indicated that crime was continuing to increase. The city was in the grip of a siege mentality. The Detroit *News,* whose circulation was increasingly suburban, ran a daily log of crimes and listed the race of the perpetrators (mostly Negro). The feature stirred such animosity that the newspaper hired guards and initiated security procedures that would have done justice to the Pentagon. Banks, Western Union offices, lending institutions—all the places that had significant sums of cash on hand—installed bulletproof partitions and erected walls to separate themselves from the public. Insurance for plate-glass

* When one of the mayor's aides, David Nelson, went to the Bagley Recreation Center, the place looked like a pigsty. The counselor aides had nothing to do, but were sitting around complaining about the failure of the Parks and Recreation Department (which claimed it lacked the manpower) to clean up the center. Nelson did not have the courage to ask the counselors why they didn't clean up the mess themselves—he knew they would be insulted. After all, *they* were on Civil Service.

† Tenants, claiming the landlord was failing to provide upkeep and necessary repairs, went on a rent strike in a thirty-four-unit apartment building. The case went into lengthy litigation. It was the middle of winter; the landlord, saying he had no money with which to buy fuel, shut off the heat. One of the mayor's assistants called the health department to see what could be done about getting the heat restored. The only thing we can do, the health department responded, is go out with a thermometer and take the temperature of the building.

‡ In another instance when there was a complaint of no heat, an inspector was dispatched to the building. He noticed a lot of people going upstairs. The police staked out the building, and discovered the landlord was running a "shooting gallery"—a dispensary for narcotics.

windows rose astronomically, so the windows were bricked up. The multiplication of solid walls was referred to as Riot Renaissance.

In the schools, the teachers locked the doors of the classrooms to protect themselves from youths roaming the corridors. Paul Conlan, the director of the Department of Social Services, was unable to gain admittance to his own office after hours.* At MCHRD, the office of the director was locked and could be opened from the outside only with a buzzer located beneath the desk of the secretary.

There was continuing pressure to expand the police department, and to add black officers. But adding black officers was difficult while the mystery of why Negroes failed to gain acceptance remained unsolved. The mayor, therefore, appointed a Task Force on Police Recruiting and Hiring.

In 1967, 2,186 whites and 1,936 Negroes had made application for the police department. Of these, 252 whites and 71 Negroes had finally been hired. More whites than Negroes were rejected because of criminal records, and educational and physical deficiencies. Many blacks, however, were unable to cope with the written examination (483 Negroes compared to 301 whites), and at every stage of the procedure there was a gradual but distinct erosion of Negro applicants. The erosion was most noticeable during the personal investigation and oral board phases. Background investigations eliminated 29 percent of Negroes but only 11 percent of whites, and the oral board turned down 25 percent of Negroes compared to 9 percent of whites.

Since a background investigator had considerable influence in determining who would serve on the force, his was a critical position. Seventeen of the twenty investigators were white. One officer previously had slugged a black, city-employed photographer who had gone to the scene of a crime to take pictures. The department had suspended the officer. After his reinstatement he had ben placed in the "nonsensitive" investigatory position.

Most of the members of the task force—composed of whites and blacks from all walks of life—became convinced that through a variety of subtle ways Negro applicants were being discouraged. While white officers frequently were placed on the departmental payroll even before they were admitted to the police academy, the background investigations for Negroes were dragged out; blacks were not notified until the last minute that the classes were about to start. The criteria for their acceptance were stringent. (The assistant manager of a loan company was eliminated because he would purportedly be a credit risk.)

Seven members of the task force demanded that fifteen hundred Negro officers be added to the force immediately; when they were told that was a budgetary impossibility, they resigned. Moderate members of the task force and Mayor Cavanagh came to an agreement with Inspector Robert S. Quaid, personnel director of the department, that future police academy classes would have a fifty-fifty division between blacks and whites. A few weeks later it was apparent that the composition continued to favor whites by a sixty-forty ratio. Under pressure from the task force, Cavanagh sent a memo to Police Commissioner

---

* Conlan had given orders that no one was to be admitted to the building. When he tried to enter, the guard told him that the building was closed to everyone. "By whose order?" Conlan asked. "By the order of the director," the guard replied. Conlan showed him his identification. "Who am I?" he asked. "You are the director," the guard replied. "Can I get in?" "No."

Johannes Spreen * on August 9, 1968, declaring that there had been "an apparent flagrant disregard for the policy" and "a return to 'business as usual.'" He ordered that until the remaining two hundred authorized positions on the department were filled, classes were to be made up of four black officers for each white officer.

Inspector Quaid complained to Commissioner Spreen that the mayor was violating the city charter. By late October, Cavanagh's memorandum and other correspondence had been smuggled to Councilman Philip Van Antwerp, a former police officer. Van Antwerp accused the mayor of reducing the standards and destroying the morale of the department. He thought the fact that Negroes accepted by the department had increased from six in all of 1964 to ninety-one in the first eight months of 1968 showed progress was being made. The mayor, who did not want to have a public confrontation with the department, hemmed and hawed, juggled the issue, and finally dropped it like a cracked egg.

The police department had grown to the largest and most powerful agency in the city government. While, overall, municipal employment was on the decline, departmental strength grew from 3,500 in 1940 to 5,500 in 1970. The police budget multiplied from $11 million to $60.5 million (exclusive of pensions and contributions to the retirement fund.) Of this, more than $58 million was going for salaries and wages. The average police officer, who had made $6,000 in 1960, was earning more than $10,000 a decade later.

Part of the salary increase was justified by inflation and part as a means of attracting better men to the force. But much of it was due to the focus that had been placed on the police, and the astute and militant manner in which that focus was exploited by the Detroit Police Officers Association.

In a city that was the most labor-conscious in the nation, that fact was not lost on other municipal employees. For decades the government had placated employees with the argument that, although their wages might be lower than those of industrial workers, they had year-round work, job security, and fringe benefits like pensions. But industrial workers had now achieved most of these benefits. (In their latest contract, the United Auto Workers obtained a clause guaranteeing workers with seniority 95 percent of their regular pay during layoffs.) Municipal employees were impressed by the evidence that the people who were making the greatest gains were those who were the best organized and could exert the greatest muscle. During the 1950's and, especially, the 1960's, unionization spread rapidly through government. In 1965 Michigan passed a public service employment bargaining law, requiring government bodies to negotiate with unions. By the latter 1960's the Detroit government had to contend with 120 separate bargaining units.

The city had been paying 40 cents an hour less than industry to building-trades workers, but after 1968 municipal wages were pegged to industrial. Carpenters earned $6.50 an hour. The starting salary of janitors was more than $5,800 a year. Nurses at General Hospital went on strike and obtained pay increases of $1,200 to $1,900 a year. Professionals, especially in the upper grades, were unhappy as their pay increases failed to keep pace with those achieved by the unions, and began talking of forming organizations of their own.

Unlike industry, the city had no customers, only citizens to whom it could

---

* Ray Girardin's health was failing, and he had left office early in 1968.

pass on the pay hikes. In an organization in which the bureaucracy, Civil Service, and unions were now competing for status and power, productivity gains were so marginal as to be meaningless. (The city was purchasing more advanced computers, but continuing to use the same programming; so what had taken eight hours in 1952 was taking seven hours four or five models later in 1969.) Robert Banyai of the operations analysis division estimated that five million dollars a year was being lost through inefficiency in the sanitation division—but that was less than one year's increase in the payroll of the police department. City employees worked, at best, a seven-hour day (8 A.M. to 4 P.M. with lunch and coffee breaks). One minute after what has come to be celebrated as the "four o'clock stampede," the City-County Building is deserted—in some offices the lights go off automatically. (A few professionals, however, such as those in the mayor's office and in the planning department, frequently work until late at night.)

The payroll accounted for approximately half the cost of running the city, and salary increases were the major force driving up the municipal budget. But the inflation gripping the American economy also had a serious effect.When the cost of money rose, the municipal bonds that the city had been able to market for less than 2 percent in 1950 went for 6 percent in 1970. The city purchased $25 million annually in goods—from trucks and computers to typewriter ribbons, salt (for de-icing roads) and Band-Aids—and the prices kept rising. The capital improvements budget was squeezed to $21 million, the lowest since 1949.

Because the city lacked the money to buy new equipment and smog control devices, it was in the embarrassing position of being responsible for the control of air pollution while continuing to be one of the area's biggest polluters. When Morton Sterling, head of the Air Pollution Control Division, pointed his finger at a plant, the plant's executives would point their fingers back, and claim that they didn't have any money either.*

Cavanagh had taken office at a time when the city's post-World War II financial crisis was in its first stages, and had been hailed as a "wizard" for resolving it. But the resolution was temporary. By unburdening the city of its welfare department Cavanagh was able to save $15 million a year. The Detroit Street Railways, which the city had acquired in a "thirty years' war," had become uneconomic to operate as the city's population thinned out. Routes had been dropped and service curtailed, but the department still accounted for the second largest annual appropriation ($41 million) and was losing up to $5 million a year. People continued to complain about the lack of service, but the number of complainants fell—the issue of public transportation was kept alive more by city planners and urban sociologists than by the populace. (Even residents of the Model City area rated public transportation last among their priorities.) Members of the mayor's staff were urging Cavanagh to try to unload the Detroit Street Railways (whose last streetcar had been retired in 1955) upon a Metropolitan Transit Authority.

But eliminating unloved departments did nothing to solve the basic problem. "Detroit is attempting to operate in a period of inflation within relatively fixed

---

* The Chrysler foundry was one of the worst polluters. New control equipment would cost one million dollars, and take eight to nine months to install. So Sterling asked the shutdown of only one furnace. Chrysler executives replied that that furnace turned out the cam shafts for 100 percent of its automobiles, and closing it down would halt all production. The matter was dropped.

revenues," the Mayor's Task Force on City Finances reported in January, 1968. "Continued reliance on the property tax as a major revenue can only lead to fiscal disaster." In 1968 revenues from property taxes were $115 million, compared to $125 million in 1958.* A $40-million-a-year budgetary deficit was in the offing, a deficit dwarfing that incurred by the Miriani Administration.

The task force urged the mayor to ask the state legislature to double the income tax. The legislature agreed to raise the tax for residents from 1 to 2 percent, but it balked at increasing the ½ percent tax for the more than 300,000 suburbanites who worked in the city.

The increase brought income tax revenues to 73 percent of revenues derived from the property tax ($93 million versus $122 million, in 1970), and reduced the proportion of the taxes collected from property to one fourth of the total budget.† (In comparison, property taxes had accounted for 60 percent of revenues in 1933, and 37 percent in 1960.) Clearly, property taxes were playing a declining role in the financial operation of the city. Yet the widening of the differential from ½ to 1½ percent between the residential and nonresidential income tax was a further inducement for people and industry to move out of the city. "No one knows," said Bernard Klein, who had replaced Strichartz as controller, "where a diminishing return on taxation sets in." [1]

When Cavanagh had taken office in January, 1962, the Bagley Elementary School area in the Mumford High School constellation, where he and Strichartz lived, still had had less than a one-to-one-hundred ratio of Negro to white residents. It was a mixed middle-income Jewish-Catholic neighborhood (but since many of the Catholic parents preferred to send their children to parochial schools, the children tended to be segregated). It had been a low crime area of well-kept $16,000 to $30,000 homes, where people did not hesitate to go out in the evening or leave their children's toys and tricycles on the lawn. By the winter of 1963–1964, however, the number of Negro families was rapidly increasing, and a sense of unease pervaded the neighborhood. It was prevalent not only among whites but also among middle-class Negroes who, in general, were of higher socioeconomic standing than the whites. They had moved out of their old neighborhoods because they believed the schools were deteriorating, because they did not want their children associating with the lower-class children and being exposed to the raw language, violence, and drugs, and because they feared for the safety of their families. They had the same attitudes as the whites toward the lower-income blacks.

By 1965 Negroes made up about one third of the population, and both Bagley Elementary School and Mumford High School were more than half black. Teachers became discouraged, and white parents transferred their children out of the schools. (White Christian parents in the Ford High School area were upset by the influx of Jewish children from Mumford, and so transferred their children to Redford.) The Mumford area was the Twelfth Street of the 1960's. By 1969 Mumford had turned as black as Central High School had during the 1950's, and there were blocks and blocks without a white family remaining. (Nearly all who did stay had no school-age children, or were sending their

---

* Adjusting for inflation, the sum was approximately the same as the $62 million collected in 1945. The assessed valuation of property then had been $2.9 billion, compared to $4.8 billion in 1969.
† The Detroit budget is divided into the tax-supported General Fund, which accounts for about four fifths of the total, and revenue-supported departments: water, sewage disposal, the Detroit Street Railways, housing, aviation, and parking.

children to parochial school.) In a half century the black population had followed the Jewish in a wedge up Woodward Avenue all the way from Hastings Street to Mumford. The Jews had reached the city limits, and as the decade of the 1970's approached, the last two Jewish Reform congregations in the city made plans to move out and build new temples at Fourteen-Mile Road, six miles beyond the city.* Even Strichartz lost faith in the ability of the Detroit school system to educate his children, and moved to the suburbs.†

Cavanagh had accomplished the Herculean feat of expanding the municipal budget from $324 million in 1962 to $456 million in 1969 and developing the revenues to pay for the expansion. Yet the budget was still $20 million in the red, and Bernard Klein estimated an increase of 10 percent a year in revenues would be required merely to offset inflation and pay the scheduled salary increases. Every projection indicated that it would be almost impossible to obtain such increases from taxation within the city.

As the summer of 1969 approached, Cavanagh was expected to announce for reelection. But a kind of gallows' humor pervaded the executive offices. Klein suggested issuing a statement that "The New Detroit Committee is not moving to Troy." Cavanagh, addressing himself to no one in particular, asked, "Christ, can't we get Shamie (whom he had whipped in 1965) to run again?" "I've got some of my best people on his committee," Joe B. Sullivan replied.

If Cavanagh ran, the campaign would be difficult for the mayor. The exodus of whites had left the population of the city nearly 44 percent black (compared to 29 percent ten years earlier). A Negro would certainly run and draw off much of Cavanagh's support from blacks and liberals. Many whites would vote for a conservative white candidate in the primary. Cavanagh could probably win reelection as the "middle-of-the-road" candidate in a runoff, but he might not win enough votes in the primary to qualify for one of the two top spots. In contrast to the few thousand dollars his campaign had cost in 1961, the estimate for 1969 was $200,000. He had had difficulty paying off the $300,000 debt that had been left from his Senate race. He was tired. He had failed to exploit his political peak in 1965. The city's course for the 1970's seemed beset with storms.

On June 24, 1969, Cavanagh announced he would not seek reelection.

He had made many mistakes. His second term in office was affected by the disintegration of his marriage and his disjointed Senate campaign. Yet he had made his imprint on the city and its government as no other of its mayors save Pingree and Couzens. Through his articulateness and the force of his personality, he had done much to focus the nation's attention on its cities. In the end, as he sat surrounded by books like *Twenty-four Families who Inhabited the White House,* Rexford Tugwell's *How They Became President,* John F. Kennedy's *Words To Live By,* and Lyndon B. Johnson's *No Retreat from Tomorrow*—all personally inscribed—he was left with a feeling of what might have been.

In November, Wayne County Sheriff Roman Gribbs, a white who had established a reputation for upgrading blacks in his department, and Wayne County

---

* The Reform congregations are generally wealthier, more liberal, and more socially integrated than the Conservative and Orthodox congregations.
† Another outmigrant because of the schools was Berl Falbaum, the reporter who covered the mayor's office for the Detroit *News.* When Falbaum lived in northern Detroit, it had taken him one hour and fifteen minutes to reach downtown via bus. After he moved outside the city limits to Oak Park, an express bus using the freeway carried him downtown in thirty-five minutes.

Auditor Richard Austin, the first Negro certified public accountant in the state, met in the runoff for the mayor's office. Both were moderately liberal Democrats, and except for the color of their skins there was little difference between them. Gribbs defeated Austin by 6,194 votes out of the 511,766 cast, the smallest percentage in a mayoralty election in the city's modern history.*

In January, 1970, Cavanagh left the mayor's office and the mayor's mansion, and moved into a townhouse in Lafayette Park. In the urban renewal area where Donald and Irma Stallings had dwelled before they were expelled into the vortex of Twelfth Street, lived Cavanagh and Girardin, Josephine Gomon and Harold Black—the white liberals and some of the Negroes who had made it to the middle class.

Their presence made the Chrysler Elementary School a middle-class island in the inner city. But they refused to send their children on to "integrated" Miller Junior High School.

Fewer and fewer people continued to believed in school integration as a means of increasing the quality of education and providing greater equality for Negroes. When the Detroit School Board changed the feeder pattern to shift three thousand white students so as to prevent rigid segregation under the new decentralization plan, most of the remaining whites in the city rebelled. In July, 1970, the state legislature passed a law permitting students to transfer without regard to the racial composition of the schools. The coalition that passed the bill included white liberals disenchanted with integration, and Negroes more interested in black power and community control of the schools than in the racial composition of the student bodies.† In November, the citizens elected the most conservative school board in fifteen years.

Dr. Drachler had taken office in 1966 with the goal of increasing the quality of education for blacks, reducing segregation, and preventing the further flight of whites. But, by and large, the time for effective action had already passed. In 1960, 57 percent of the pupils in the public school system had been white. In 1970, 63 percent were black.‡

In the quarter century between 1945 and 1970 the school budget had risen from $39.5 million a year to $226 million, a rate of increase considerably greater than that of the municipal budget. (The municipal budget multiplied from $152 million to $485 million.) While the city had developed alternate

---

* Austin was elected secretary of state of Michigan in 1970, the first black ever to hold such a high post in the state government. In the 1973 Detroit municipal election, State Senator Coleman Young narrowly defeated Police Commissioner John Nichols to become the first black mayor in the city's history. (Young had been one of the officers placed in the stockade when blacks had tried to integrate a white officers club in Indiana during World War II.) City Council President Mel Ravitz, a white liberal, finished third in the primary, indicating that Cavanagh's assessment of his chances in the 1969 election may well have been correct.

† A new furor was generated in 1972 by a court order to integrate, through bussing, Detroit's black schools with suburban white schools.

‡   Public School Enrollment

| | 1960 | | | | 1970 | | | |
	Black	White	Total	Percent Black	Black	White	Total	Percent Black
Elementary School	87,000	103,000	190,000	46	115,000	64,000	179,000	64
High School	24,000	46,000	70,000	34	52,000	35,000	87,000	60
Total	111,000	149,000	260,000	43	167,000	99,000	266,000	63

revenues, the schools had no local source of revenue other than the property tax, which provided nearly half the district's income. (Property taxes contributed $108 million to the 1970–1971 budget, the state $90 million, the Federal government $24 million, and the county $.7 million.) While the municipal property tax rate had remained relatively stable—it rose from $21.33 per $1,000 of assessed valuation in 1945 to $24.15 in 1970—the school tax had nearly tripled, from $8.09 to $22.86, and accounted for the major portion in the rate increase (including county) from $34.14 to $54.11.

The citizens of Detroit clearly were unwilling to raise their property tax rate much above $50 to $55 *—after that level was reached in 1960, one after another proposed increase was defeated. The teachers' strike in 1967 had been settled by a contract calling for a two-step, $16 million pay increase; but in November, 1968, the voters once again turned down a rate increase, the revenues from part of which would have gone to pay the teachers. The district was left with a contract which it lacked the revenues to fulfill. So probationary personnel were dismissed and programs were cut back in order to scrape money together, and the administration began running a deficit of $4 million a year.

Dr. Drachler estimated that the school district would need at least $30 to $35 million a year just to offset inflation and meet new contract obligations. He had campaigned for the tax increases, and he had failed. He had upgraded Negro personnel. He had been hounded by the militants, and he had done everything within reason to meet their demands. He had backed decentralization of the district, but decentralization was now threatening to be merely the first step in disintegration. He was tired and discouraged. At the end of the 1970–1971 school year, he announced his retirement, and took a post with the Institute of Educational Leadership, funded by the Ford Foundation.

Both Cavanagh and Dr. Drachler had taken office with the determination to chart new courses and build a new future for the city and its institutions. Both found themselves overwhelmed and swept aside by forces over which they had no control. Twilight was settling upon the city; the twilight of an eclipse. Eventually the city may reemerge from the shadow, but it will be a different city when it does.

---

* Property was assessed at 60 percent of full value, so the actual tax was slightly over 3 percent. (A $20,000 house would be assessed at $12,000, so the tax would be approximately $650.)

VI

EPILOGUE AND PROLOGUE

I. CAPITALISM AND THE AMERICAN GENESIS

Detroit had been founded in 1701, at the beginning of a century that was to produce the most profound changes in society since the end of the Roman Empire. Throughout Europe the growth of population was generating economic problems. France, with approximately twenty-five million people, was by far the most populous country. The nation had run out of developable land. Primogeniture prevented the breakup of estates. The younger sons of noblemen had a choice between careers in the clergy or the army. The band of gentlemen "adventurers" that Antoine de la Mothe Cadillac led to *de trois* sought to establish a New France of large estates based on the feudal pattern.

In England the population had doubled, from 2.5 million to 5 million, during the sixteenth century. The economy was unable to keep pace. Prices rose astronomically. By the 1630's they were three and a half times what they had been between 1500 and 1510. The cost of some foodstuffs multiplied even more rapidly.* The value of land quadrupled.

Englishmen looked with avaricious eyes upon the vast tracts of land owned by the Catholic Church. The drain of specie to Rome contributed to the shortage of money and the rise in prices. The rituals and structure of the Church, developed for an illiterate, rural society were out of place in the growing towns. Literacy flourished among the bourgeoisie—after Gutenberg perfected the mass production of type during the middle years of the fifteenth century, the number of books printed annually rose from a few thousand to approximately one million. The break of Henry VIII with Rome and the expropriation of Church lands had the approbation of the majority of his countrymen.

The division and distribution of the Church lands earned the king the support of the new squires. The educated, fraternal bourgeoisie, however, continued to be "nonconformist." They "dissented" as much from the rule of an autocratic king as they had from the rule of an autocratic pope. During the 1630's, 8,000 middle-class Puritans emigrated to Massachusetts at a time when English settlers in North America still numbered fewer than 30,000. Whitney, Joy, Chandler,

---

* By the end of the sixteenth century eggs cost six times as much and wheat eight times as much as one hundred years earlier.

Leland—an astonishing number of prominent Americans were descended from these educated, Protestant town dwellers whose heritage was to shape the essential character of the new nation.

Spanish, Portuguese, and French colonization was financed largely by the royal treasuries. In the Lowlands and England, however, where the bourgeoisie was challenging the royal power, merchants banded together to exploit the riches of the new discoveries. Between 1600 and 1602 the British and Dutch East India Companies were founded—the dawn of capitalism was at hand. Joint stock companies were formed to colonize the North American seacoast.

North America supplied the natural resources England lacked. England had been stripped of its forests, so shipbuilding became a colonial enterprise. During the early years of the eighteenth century serious consideration was given to transferring the English iron industry to the colonies also.

Beneath the peat moss that the English population was tearing up for fuel, however, were huge beds of coal. In the 1730's Dud Dudley unearthed a century-old process for making iron with coal. Dudley's discovery transformed England from an agricultural to an industrial nation, and saved the population from the misery and starvation of the Irish. (Ireland's lack of commercial-grade coal precluded industrialization of the country.)

Between 1698 and 1769 Thomas Savery, Thomas Newcomen, and James Watt developed the steam engines that enabled the Cornish to dig their mines ever deeper, and thus support their expanding families. Capital was needed to purchase the machinery, and was supplied by the bourgeoisie who previously had invested their money in commerce. Capital provided the ties that bound formerly independent occupations and enterprises together. The capitalist bought coal to fuel the steam engine whose construction he had financed so that he could obtain tin and copper to sell to the smiths. The capitalist bought wool to farm out to spinners, transferred the yarn to the weaver for the production of cloth, and sold the cloth to the merchant and the tailor. As the "putting out" system developed, a single entrepreneur for the first time controlled manufacture from raw material to finished product.

In Europe the new economics came into conflict with the existing mercantile society. Merchant guilds (comparable in some ways to chambers of commerce) frequently controlled the politics of towns. Craft guilds established prices, regulated the number of tradesmen, and dominated the trades. Monarchs granted monopolies.

In English North America, however, the new forces were allowed free reign. Anxious to develop the colonies quickly, the British government practiced a policy of "salutary neglect." The policy was successful beyond expectation. The French colonies, hindered by royal restrictions, were swallowed by the British. By 1770 the North American population was gaining on England's—the colonies contained 2.5 million people, England 8 million. The colonies were England's principal shipbuilder and supplier of naval stores. They furnished a major portion of Europe's tobacco, rice, indigo, furs, dried fish, rum, flax, silk, and iron. They contained more blast furnaces (82) and iron forges (175) than England.

The expansion of the English colonies had precipitated the Seven Years' War (1756–1763) between England and France. It was but the latest in a series of wars in which the principal European powers engaged during much of the eighteenth century. At the conclusion of the war the British government had an unprecedented national debt of one hundred million pounds. Every new tax proposed to pay off that debt brought rioters into the streets of the English cities, and every time Parliament backtracked. Parliament's endeavors turned toward taxing the new wealth of the colonies. The bourgeois Americans, however, resisted as fiercely as the English citizens. Once more a confrontation was precipitated between royal authority and the fraternal, educated middle class who refused to accept the validity of law by fiat.

Simultaneously, conflict increased between the colonial free enterprisers and the government-regulated and guild-dominated artisans and shopkeepers of the British Isles. London artisans tried to maintain their monopolies by promoting laws prohibiting the manufacture of articles in the colonies. While the money-short colonists attempted to inflate the monetary supply, British bankers and merchants strove to prevent money from being depreciated.* A virtual state of war existed between the British East India Company, which demanded that its royal monopoly be enforced, and the Boston tea merchants, who were prospering by smuggling and by underselling the company. In retaliation for the Boston Tea Party of 1773, the British government closed the port of Boston.

The Revolution that followed signaled the advent of a new economic order and the rise to power of the middle class. England's men of industry and commerce, engaged in intercourse with the colonies and disliking government regulation of economic activities as much as the Americans, joined the Revolution in spirit. On March 9, 1776, four months before the American Declaration of Independence, Adam Smith's *An Inquiry into the Nature and Causes of the Wealth of Nations* was published in England. It was the world's first comprehensive political economy, and asserted that the government which is best regulates least. Smith postulated a natural law of economics that would go into operation as soon as "unnatural" restraints were removed. He advocated the abolition of economic controls by the central government and the end of the policy of mercantilism. This was laissez-faire.

The victory of the American Revolutionists brought into being the world's first nation based on that principle. The American Constitution established a democracy of the middle class. The American genesis coincided with the development of capitalism and industrialization. Unlike the European nations, the United States was not fettered by outmoded institutions. It did not have to contend with overpopulation—quite the opposite, it had a shortage of labor, and this shortage provided incentive to exploit the new means of production to the fullest. America rode the crest of the new economic wave, and within one hundred years the nation was the most powerful on earth.

II. THE FACTORY AND URBAN DEVELOPMENT

When production depended principally upon the workman's skills, a man's place of work was his home. The spinner, weaver, blacksmith, carpenter, or coal miner was often also a farmer. To which pursuit he devoted his time depended upon the seasons, the availability of raw materials, and the demand for his product. Essentially he was self-sufficient. Even if he were an artisan whose goods were in great demand, he was likely to retain a small plot of land—a "Pingree potato patch" he could always fall back on.

---

* Since the colonies had an unfavorable balance of trade with England, the flow of money was from America to England. The colonies had a favorable balance of trade with the Spanish West Indies, from which there was an influx of money. Since this money consisted of the Austrian silver *Thaler* (Spain and Austria were linked through the Hapsburgs), the *Thaler*, or dollar, became the American medium of exchange.

The need to provide the growing population with more and cheaper goods brought an end to the era of the home workshop and cottage industries. While the demand for cloth multiplied, weavers were stymied by the lack of yarn— one weaver kept three spinners occupied. In the early 1760's weaver James Hargreaves developed the spinning jenny, which mounted as many as eighteen spindles in place of one. As other inventions followed during the next two decades, spinning and weaving were mechanized. Water power, then steam power were harnessed to drive the heavy new machinery. Capital was required to purchase the machines, and the machines were concentrated in a single building, or "factory," * located at an advantageous site—a site on a waterway or near deposits of coal.

In the cottages the family had been a working unit. A man's wife worked by his side, and often complemented his skills. (While men wove, women spun.) The workshop was the school for his children, and they grew up learning the trade.

The factory made the spinner and the weaver noncompetitive. It forced them to abandon the spinning wheels and hand looms, and transfer their skills to the power machinery of the factory.

Since a man could not support his family on factory wages, women and children followed men into the factories. More than four out of five workers in English textile factories were women and children. (The composition of the labor force in New England was much the same.) Working twelve to fourteen hours a day, women all but abandoned their younger children to the streets. They returned to their family's one-room habitats exhausted, and saw little of either husbands or children. The hot meal became a Sunday treat.

The factory broke up the family. It destroyed the age-old structure that had enabled parents to supervise and teach their children as they worked. Family ties became tenuous. When the husband or wife was felled by sickness, or when men were laid off from work, the ties frequently dissolved.

The population's rapid growth overwhelmed the nascent industrial society. "The country has been wholly unable to find adequate employment for the numerous laborers and artificers who were able as well as willing to work," the Reverend Thomas Robert Malthus wrote in the early ninteenth century. "It is scarcely possible for [the laboring man] to marry without becoming the father of paupers." Desertions became so common that the Reverend Dr. Malthus "once heard a hard-working good, sort of man propose to do this as the best mode of providing for a wife and six children," and came to the conclusion that "if the simple fact of these frequent desertions were related in some countries, a strange inference would be drawn against the English character." [1]

To the twentieth-century reader who believes the welfare family is a recent American phenomenon, the Reverend Dr. Malthus's observations may be startling. But beggary had become widespread in England after the Catholic Church had been disestablished and the lands were no longer used to support tens of thousands of poor for whom there was no place on estates run for profit. The expropriation of Church property expelled an estimated 150,000 monks and nuns into secular society. By the second half of the sixteenth century countless men, women, and children were wandering across the country-

---

* The factory derives its name from the "factor," or agent, who provided the raw materials and machinery necessary for production.

side and along the horse trails. Since little work was available, there were at least twenty-four different kinds of beggars.* When the government of Elizabeth I discovered that even in booming London at least 10 percent of the families were in dire need, the Poor Laws were enacted. Each parish was enjoined to place a tax on land for support of the poor. The Poor Laws became the direct antecedent of the American welfare system.

In practice, the laws did little to alleviate the plight of the poor. By the end of the seventeenth century the estimated number of poor, working and nonworking, constituted more than half the population, and the cost of supporting them had increased twenty times since midcentury. The extended family group which had provided women and children with support if the husband died disappeared in impersonal urban society. Whenever a town acquired a population of a few thousand, it was forced to institute Poor Relief. Poor Relief was an apt double entendre. To reduce the burden of taxation, towns established workhouses and poorhouses, and attempted to make them self-supporting by hiring out the women, children, sick, and aged who constituted most of the poorhouse population. In the cold, dank, and sometimes nearly windowless buildings the inmates were worked fourteen hours a day. Lice, fleas, and vermin proliferated. In the putrid beds the well slept with the sick. Epidemics carried off large numbers. For an infant to survive its first year was almost unheard of. Girls as young as twelve were pressed into "forced marriages" to get them off the poor rolls. They naturally produced new swarms of children, children who soon swelled the poor rolls further.

Among the rural population sexual practices were more natural than regulated, and "Scotch marriages" without benefit of clergy were common. In both Europe and America illegitimacy was widespread. In Sweden recorded illegitimacy quadrupled between the mideighteenth and nineteenth centuries. In America, when Father Gabriel Richard arrived at the frontier post of Mackinac, he "found there a large number of children, for more than thirty of whom I supplied the ceremonies of baptism. They were over seven years of age, and most of them illegitimate. . . . I was informed that there are many others in the same condition at different places." [2]

As long as children had been absorbed into the working family unit, their increasing numbers had not drawn attention. But as soon as people were put off the land and began concentrating in towns, the multiplication of children became cause for concern. During the reign of James I in the first quarter of the seventeenth century a statute was enacted that any female vagrant giving birth to a child was to be whipped, and imprisoned for six months. Vagrants' children could be enslaved until they reached maturity.

The statute, of course, was unenforceable. In the towns the Puritans attempted to establish a sexual morality tailored to urban conditions. It was a morality difficult enough for the middle class to honor, and the poor found it largely irrelevant. Whether in seventeenth-century England or twentieth-century Detroit, rural migrants regarded pregnancy as "God's will."

III. CRIME

So the working population that factories concentrated as never before reproduced itself in unprecedented numbers. Cities whose population heretofore

---

* Among them were the Abraham Men, who pretended to be mad; the Hookers, who used hooked sticks to steal clothes out of windows; the Pryggers, who were horse thieves; and the Rufflers, who begged from the strong and stole from the weak.

AMERICAN ODYSSEY

had been measured in the tens of thousands grew to hundreds of thousands.

The productivity of machines was so much greater than the productivity of human labor that machines chronically produced more goods than the masses of people could absorb. Repetitive cycles of boom and bust resulted. Every boom drew more people into the cities; and every bust left them stranded. They had no reserves to fall back on, and no lord of the manor to tide them through. Almost any alternative seemed preferable to being committed to the workhouse. Amid social and economic turmoil, vice and prostitution were so prevalent that not more than one virgin could be found among every three or four working-class girls.

There was little separation between the working-class districts and the mansions of the nouveau riche industrialists and merchants. Even when there were no jobs for the poor, there was never a lack of opportunity for despoliation of the wealthy. So crime burst like a star shell upon the consciousness of the middle class.

Crime was directly related to industrialization. In England and Wales, 4,506 persons were committed for trial in 1805, 18,107 in 1830, and 31,309 in 1842. In Scotland, 89 persons were charged in 1819, and 4,189 in 1842. In Lancashire, crime increased six times more rapidly than the population.

The problem was equally severe in the United States. On November 23, 1854, the *Detroit Advertizer* editorialized: "Will there ever be any safety to property or life in Detroit? Probably not!" Throughout America during the last decades of the nineteenth century there were repeated expressions of alarm at the great increase in crimes and declarations of indignation at the "laxity of courts." The number of murders multiplied from 1,266 in 1880 to 7,840 in 1898.

Three factors stand out in the incidence of crime: the economy—in Detroit, every panic and depression from the 1830's on generated a "crime wave"; the social and economic divisions in the population—the greater they are, the more intense is the conflict, conflict generally expressed in the form of crime; the age of the population—the younger the population, the more crimes it commits.

With every recession, the number of major economic crimes (robbery, burglary, grand larceny) increased. The crime peaks of 1933, 1938, 1949, 1954, 1958, 1960, and 1970 all mark recessions or depressions.*

Economic recovery brought a temporary decline in crime. Because of growing productivity, however, industry failed to rehire all the men who had been laid off. Therefore, as new workers were attracted to the city during the economic resurgence, the number of crimes also began to climb again.†

Lack of employment and the propensity to commit crime are both char-

---

* The 1941 crime peak seems the exception to the rule, but can be explained by the large number of young men drawn to the city by war production. In 1945–1946, the termination of war production and the breakout of strikes created much unemployment.
† The switch to Uniform Crime Reports makes difficult any comparison between pre-1966 and post-1967 figures. A further complicating factor is inflation. During the deflationary period of the 1920's and 1930's, the number of grand larcenies (representing theft of an article of more than $50) declined from 2,812 in 1924 to 899 in 1933. The total number of larcenies, however, jumped from 11,000 in 1929 to 25,000 in 1933. Conversely, during the inflation of the 1960's, grand larceny soared from 4,800 in 1960 to 26,665 in 1970.

The author estimates that if pre-1966 reporting practices had continued to prevail and prices had not rocketed upward, the total number of major economic crimes in Detroit in 1970 would have been between 40,000 and 45,000 (instead of 100,000), an increase of 30 to 40 percent.

DETROIT—NUMBER OF MAJOR ECONOMIC CRIMES ANNUALLY

'29 '30 '32 '34 '36 '38 '40 '42 '44 '46 '48 '50 '52 '54 '56 '58 '60 '62 '64 '66 '68 '70 '72

100,000
90,000
80,000
70,000
60,000
50,000
40,000
30,000
20,000
10,000

SOURCE: DETROIT POLICE DEPARTMENT ANNUAL REPORTS

acteristic of youth. Unemployment is especially high among minority youth, who now make up the majority of juveniles in many large cities. Between 1950 and 1970, while the population of Detroit fell from 1,850,000 to 1,511,-000, the number of black males under twenty-one tripled from 49,000 to 149,000. Of the 10,258 male suspects arrested for major crimes in Detroit in 1967, more than half were between the ages of seventeen and twenty-four, and three fourths were under thirty-four. Six thousand male juveniles were picked up. Eighty percent of the men arrested for major crimes were black.

At the same time that the proportion of youth in the population increased, the alienation of black youth from white society was exacerbated. The youth were quick to flash into violence. In the climate of fear that came to grip the city, people of all kinds acquired weapons—there are now an estimated half million handguns in Detroit. A similar situation had existed during the 1920's, when the offspring of immigrants had been caught up in the gangsterism of Prohibition. In 1926, 225 murders were committed in Detroit, compared to an annual average of 87 between 1930 and 1964. Not until 1968, the year after the riot, was the 1926 record broken. By 1971, however, there were 508 murders in the city, and in 1972 there were 601—a two-year total of 1,109, compared to 988 for the entire decade of the 1950's.*

While youth commit more crimes, the victims are often older citizens, less capable of defending themselves. Between 1950 and 1970 the number of people over sixty in Detroit rose from 181,000 to 245,000. In 1950, 41 percent of the population (759,000 of 1.85 million) was under twenty-one or over sixty. By 1970 the proportion had risen to 54 percent (815,000 of 1.51 million).

Crime is a product of the sociological conflict in the cities—of inadequate education in a demanding technological society; of poverty juxtaposed to wealth; of youth divided sharply from older citizens, with many of the generation between gone to the suburbs.† One cannot treat crime as a "problem," because crime is not a cause but an effect. It is the conflict that will have to be resolved, because the incidence of crime is a manifestation of the intensity of that conflict.

IV. RIOT

As the commission of crimes multiplied in the English cities during the early nineteenth century, propertied citizens sought to protect their interests. Banding together, they hired watchmen and constables. Living in the largest city of the world's most advanced industrial nation, Londoners in 1829 organized the first metropolitan police force. The police were intended to act as the bulwark against crime; to keep crime from flooding into and disturbing the peace of the middle-class residential districts. (For decades, therefore, the police tended to leave the denizens of the slums to their own activities, so long as these did not impinge upon the tranquility of the middle class.) But under

---

* Another parallel is provided by auto theft, a crime committed primarily by youth. There were 10,840 cars stolen in 1925, a number not surpassed until 1965, when 12,661 were taken.
† There are, of course, various crosscurrents within that conflict. Older white voters turn down proposed increases in school taxes for the benefit of the large number of black youth. The more youths emerge with an inferior education from the schools, the more crimes are committed.

the best of conditions, the restraints worked only marginally. The economic disparities always generated more crime than the police were capable of restraining.

What, then, when the restraints break down?

The consequence is a volcanic eruption of crime—the riot. It is most likely to occur when war, or some other upheaval, puts additional stresses on the socioeconomic structure. War speeds up industry, and creates an economic updraft. More people flock to the cities. Inflation, however, deteriorates conditions for the poor and the unskilled even further. The ideological conflict that accompanies war also sometimes paves the way for a riot.

Thus, the anti-Negro campaign with which Northern Democrats mobilized the unskilled Irish laborers against the Civil War provided an antiwar, anti-Negro rationale for outbursts around the country. When a mob attacked and set fire to the draft office in Manhattan on July 11, 1863, the actions of the largely Irish and sympathetic police were hesitant and confused. The restraints were broken. Within hours, the heart of the city—whose two hundred thousand Irish made its East Side the most densely packed piece of land in the Western world—was in control of the mob. Smashing store windows, invading the homes of the well-to-do, setting fire to public buildings and Republican newspaper offices, lynching Negroes, the mob looted at will.

Afterward, the secretary of the New York Prison Association told an investigating committee:

"Every hiding place and nursery of crime discovered itself by immediate and active participation in the operations of the mob. Those very places and domiciles, and all that are like them, are today nurseries of crime, and of the vices and disorderly courses which lead to crime. . . ." [3]

The riots that swept America in 1919 came during boom times in the aftermath of a war that had drawn an unprecedented number of Negroes to the cities. The Harlem riot of 1935 occurred as hundreds of thousands of blacks were driven off the land and into the cities, where they were unable to find jobs.

The Detroit riot of 1943 was the culmination of the jostling for position between blacks and blue-collar whites after more than a decade of economic drought. It quickly divided into two simultaneous riots. On Hastings Street, Negroes plundered the representatives of the middle class: the Jews. On Woodward Avenue, whites attacked Negroes. On both sides, the principal participants were the young and the alienated. An arson squad officer commented that he was familiar with the white youths, who belonged to "gangs of Italians, Syrians, and others who hang around bars and poolrooms, and in 'peacetime' pull false alarms and that sort of thing." [4]

In the mid-1960's, war, economic recovery, and inflation once more precipitated turmoil in the cities. The failure of the police to react forcefully to the incident at the blind pig resulted in the breakdown of the normal restraints. In the city's most volatile and crime-prone area, the gradual increase in criminal activity between 5 A.M. and midday eventually burst into riot.

The accompanying map shows the close correlation between areas of high crime activity during normal summer months, and the areas of greatest activity during the riot (twenty or more incidents reported). There was little activity in the homogeneously poor areas of the inner city, for there was little to be looted. The rioters struck along the principal commercial streets, where the

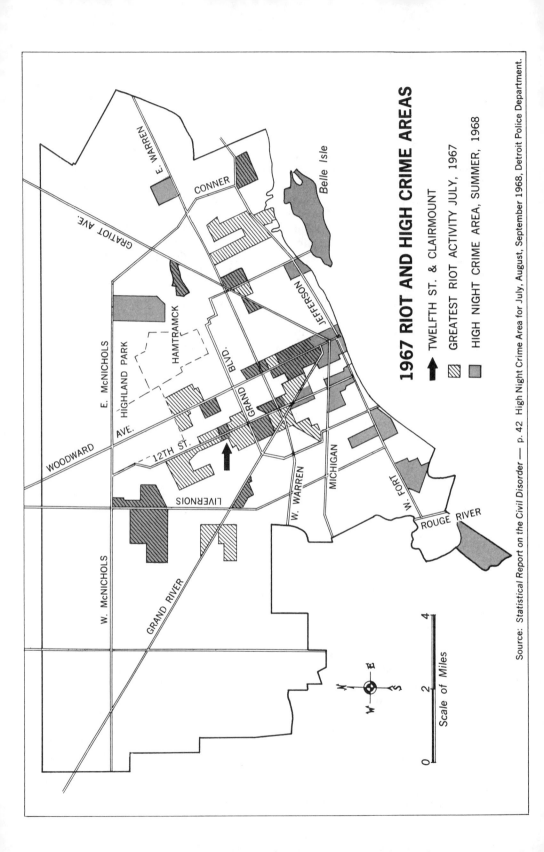

1967 RIOT AND HIGH CRIME AREAS

↑ TWELFTH ST. & CLAIRMOUNT

▨ GREATEST RIOT ACTIVITY JULY, 1967

■ HIGH NIGHT CRIME AREA, SUMMER, 1968

E. WARREN

CONNER

Belle Isle

GRATIOT AVE.

JEFFERSON

E. McNICHOLS

HIGHLAND PARK

HAMTRAMCK

GRAND BLVD.

WOODWARD AVE.

12TH ST.

W. WARREN

MICHIGAN

W. FORT

LIVERNOIS

W. McNICHOLS

GRAND RIVER

ROUGE RIVER

N E S W

Scale of Miles

0 2 4

Source: *Statistical Report on the Civil Disorder* — p. 42 High Night Crime Area for July, August, September 1968, Detroit Police Department.

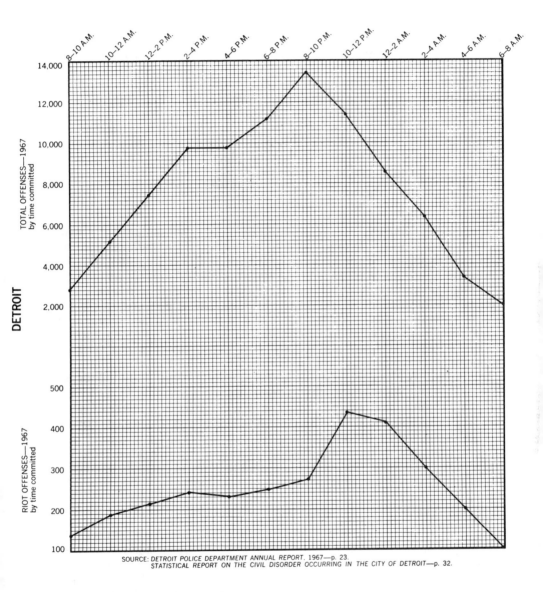

DETROIT

TOTAL OFFENSES—1967
by time committed

RIOT OFFENSES—1967
by time committed

SOURCE: DETROIT POLICE DEPARTMENT ANNUAL REPORT, 1967—p. 23.
STATISTICAL REPORT ON THE CIVIL DISORDER OCCURRING IN THE CITY OF DETROIT—p. 32.

economic establishments of the middle class remain like trading posts on black reservations. These establishments are subject to attack by burglars and robbers every day. With the riot the attacks came en masse. (In keeping with the nature of crime in the city, the first person to be killed was a sixty-eight-year-old shopkeeper, George Messerlian, beaten to death by a Negro youth.)

The only deviation from the normal geographic crime pattern by the riot was its encompassing of a much greater area. The riot did not penetrate into the high crime areas in the core of the central business district, nor into those of the low-income white population in southwest Detroit. It did not affect Belle Isle, which was closed.*

In addition to the close geographic correlation between the riot and normal crime activity, there was an almost perfect horological correlation (see graph). The top graph shows the total number of offenses during 1967 in Detroit, according to the time committed. Criminal activity picks up sharply beginning at 8 A.M., increases until midafternoon, levels off, then rises to a peak between 8 and 10 P.M. After midnight criminal activity declines, and reaches a low point between 6 and 8 A.M.

Riot activity followed the same pattern. The reason that the peak of activity was not attained until approximately two hours later is that darkness does not settle in summer until 9 P.M.†

Clearly, if law enforcement and government officials had understood that the riots were an extension of daily criminal activity, their responses should have been substantially different. In city after city the sharp tailing off in riot activity during the early morning hours has been regarded as an indication that the riot was coming under control. But in city after city, rioting resumed later in the day. The lull was merely a manifestation of normal physical exhaustion.

Had riot dynamics been understood in Detroit in 1967, state aid should have been summoned sooner. Law enforcement personnel should have been concentrated along the commercial strips bisecting low-income areas rather than scattered about the city. When Cyrus Vance and Lieutenant General J. L. Throckmorton made their assessment tour at 5 P.M., they should have taken into account that they were seeing the city at a period when there was a momentary plateau in riot activity, and that this was no measure of whether or not troops should be committed.

V. EDUCATION

A reservoir of latent criminal activity that erupts into riots all over the nation is an indication of a major breakdown in the social order. Controlling a riot is like performing an excision because an infection has been neglected.

"Indigence in the present state of society may be considered as a principal cause of the increase of crimes," London magistrate Patrick Colquoun had said during the first years of the nineteenth century.‡ [5] Malthus observed that "education appears to have a considerable effect in the prevention of crimes."

* The high crime area directly east of Hamtramck abuts the Plymouth plant.
† Also, many arrests were made for curfew violations.
‡ Colquoun was one of the first men to concern himself with the problems stemming from the rapid growth of the cities. In addition to his *Treatise on Indigence,* he wrote *A New and Appropriate System of Education for the Labouring People,* and a *Treatise on the Police of the Metropolis.*

American nineteenth-century historian Martha Lamb reported that between 1835 and 1845 "juvenile crime increased fearfully year by year." [6] The urban professional leadership of Massachusetts and Michigan warned that if children were not educated universally at public expense, they would attend "the school of vice." On the basis of that argument and the need of industry for workers who could read and add, the public school system was established.

During the nineteenth century, the schools had to struggle continually to pry funds out of begrudging taxpayers. In 1870 the average annual teacher's salary was $189, and the annual expenditure per pupil was $15.55. By 1900 salaries had risen to $325 and per-pupil expenditure to $20.21. Not until the pace of industrialization and urbanization quickened did expenditures increase rapidly. Schools were supported not only by industry, which looked toward them to provide an upgraded work force, but by the expanding middle class of homeowners, who recognized that education was essential to the future of their children. By 1930, expenditures were more than five times what they had been three decades earlier.

Industrialization and mechanization demanded a higher and higher level of education. In 1870, only one out of every fifty youths graduated from high school. By 1910, one out of every eleven was graduating. During the next thirty years, the number of high school graduates mushroomed from 156,000 to nearly 1.25 million annually. By 1940 more than half of seventeen-year-olds were receiving their diplomas, and by the 1960's the proportion climbed to better than three out of four.

Until the 1880's a high school education had been intended primarily as preparation for college. The children who entered high school came mostly from the well-to-do and had had the advantage of better teaching than was available in the public elementary schools. But as high school education came to be looked upon as an end in itself, more and more children from middle-income families were continuing their schooling. And eighteen- and nineteen-year-old girls with eighth- and ninth-grade educations were not capable of preparing children for entry into high school.

By World War I, a high school diploma was becoming a requirement for public school teachers. The Depression and World War II raised standards to a bachelor's degree (and, in some states, beyond). Persistent demands for increases both in the quantity and quality of education caused costs to rise steeply. Expenditures for public elementary and secondary education multiplied from $1 billion in 1920 to $26 billion in the mid-1960's. (Detroit's budget increased from $1 million in 1900 to $226 million in 1970.) Expenditures for higher education rose from $500 million in 1930 to approximately $10 billion in the mid-1960's.

In general property owners taxed themselves willingly to pay for the outlays. Detroit's school tax advanced from less than $7 per $1,000 of assessed valuation in 1940 to nearly $23 in 1970. Nevertheless, revenues have never kept up with the schools' needs.

To deal with the new educational realities, John Dewey at the turn of the century urged schools to stop thinking of themselves as separate, compartmentalized institutions, and integrate themselves into the children's learning experience. Dewey believed children would learn more through exposure and absorption than through being force-fed information that had little meaning for them. His philosophy presumed that when children arrived in school they would already have had positive learning experiences and that those experiences could be transferred to the school situation. It presumed that the children would have been exposed to discipline, that they would daily come to school physically and mentally prepared, that they would have constructive attitudes toward learning, and that the parents would help reinforce the work of the school.

The twentieth-century American school system that developed was geared to deal with middle-class children from stable families. It was intended to decrease the stress of the school situation for children; but it has failed, simultaneously, to teach children how to cope with stress. It avoids subjecting children to failure in small doses; but it makes it easy for teachers to allow underachievers to slide. So that failure when it comes—in the form of the realization of how far a child has fallen behind—is overwhelming for all involved.

The system is ill suited to deal with the lower economic, rural migrants to the cities. For the children of the urbanized Jewish immigrants, it provided a magic door to upward mobility.* But during the first part of the twentieth century it made dropouts of millions of French-Canadian, Hungarian, Polish, Italian, Slavic, and American-Indian children—by the eighth grade only one in five was still in school and keeping up.

A half century later, the system has similar difficulties with the children of Negro migrants. Even so, Negro youth are progressing faster than immigrant youth had progressed—by the end of the 1960's six out of ten blacks were graduating from high school.†

The American educational system thus continues to be the key to the difference between the relatively static societies of Europe and the mobile society of the United States. (Only one out of four of the fathers of graduate students in American universities in 1965 had completed college, and four out of ten had not finished high school.) In 1967 the United States had nearly 20 million of the total world high school enrollment of 111 million, and 7.9 million (twice the number of all European nations combined) of the world college enrollment of 24.3 million.‡ The famed "Yankee ingenuity" has stemmed from universal education—education that enabled people to perceive and grasp opportunities.

The successes of the educational system have also spotlighted the failures. It is not that failures have been increasing; but that the economic system, demanding continuously higher levels of performance, has been less and less tolerant of those failures. Even before Ford introduced the assembly line in 1914, the economy was having difficulty absorbing lower-grade workers. Every decade since has seen a rise in the level at which underproducers are precipitated out. As the struggle for men to keep pace with machines continues, Negroes and other contemporary migrants are faced with a greater challenge than people whose urbanization took place at an earlier age.

* According to a survey by the American Council on Education, one out of ten freshmen entering universities is Jewish, nearly four times the proportion of Jews in the general population.
† Some of these are "social promotions." Nevertheless, Negroes are doing as well as white youth did twenty-five years ago, and the gap between white and black is diminishing.
‡ Nevertheless, the Soviet Union, with 8.8 million enrolled in high school and 4.6 million in higher education, has made rapid advances. The United States and the U.S.S.R. combined account for more than half of world university enrollment.

VI. THE DUAL ECONOMY

Since the Luddites rioted in England during the Napoleonic Wars and attempted to halt industrialization by smashing machines and burning factories, the disparity in efficiency between man and machine has led to one crisis after another.

Adam Smith envisioned laissez-faire as a model of perfect and free competition. With the restrictive practices of guilds and the monopolistic grants of governments done away with, talent and enterprise would rise to the top, and the best man, the best method, the best product would emerge triumphant. But Smith failed to take human nature into account, and he preceded the age of the machine and the factory, which was to concentrate enormous power in a few hands.

The United States emerged as the world's first incarnation of Smith's free enterprise theories. The nation's genesis was a direct reaction to monopolism and governmental regulation of the economy. By the second half of the nineteenth century, however, competition in the railroad industry was leading to rate-cutting wars that frequently ended in bankruptcies. The railroad magnates concluded that they did not really like free enterprise; so they formed pools to control competition.

Other industrialists were quick to recognize the benefits that could be derived by putting an end to "ruinous competition." Industry after industry organized along monopolistic lines. Following the depression of the 1890's, the practice took on a new dimension through the formation of international cartels, designed to control marketing worldwide.

"Taylorization" and the assembly line, breeding greater and greater efficiency, widened further the gap between production and wages. All through the 1920's, the industrial elite kept the economy going by lending wage earners the money that was not being paid them. The credit economy seemed an ingenious instrument to overcome the distortions of the economic system. In reality, it only postponed the day of accounting. When the day came, the bill was so huge that it collapsed the system.

With the Great Depression, the free enterprise system split asunder. Industry rushed toward the shelter of a system of benevolent mercantilism under government protection (the NRA and the Blue Eagle), and when that system crumbled, industries continued through one device and another to administer the economy themselves. Trade associations and fair-trade laws serve the purpose admirably. The most effective means, however, is the "shared monopoly," in which a half dozen or fewer enterprises divide the market between them. It works especially well when one firm, like General Motors, dominates an industry. In the American automobile market today truly free competition is all but impossible. If Chrysler decided to challenge General Motors, G.M. could within a short time bankrupt its challenger. G.M.'s problem, in fact, is how to guide the industry so that Chrysler and American Motors can continue to function—for if Chrysler and American Motors were to fail, the government would certainly initiate antitrust action against General Motors.

So General Motors, operating on the basis of "standard volume," establishes prices and policies, and the others—with an exception now and then—follow. Since one assembly line is more or less like another and there are no engineering secrets, the final product is much the same. "Competition" is primarily a matter of styling, advertising, and *image*.

If the Depression had the effect of reducing industrial competition, it also pointed up the necessity of giving the workingman the right to organize in order to meet the power of industry with power of his own. The restrictions on immigration and the "Americanization" of the working force facilitated the organization of labor and undercut management's tactics of strikebreaking. Since the Civil War, labor and industry had been locked in mortal conflict, but the UAW victory over Ford marked the last great battle over unionization. After that, it became a question of the manner in which unions and industry would interact. Walter Reuther took the position that workers' gains would be eroded if wage increases were passed on to consumers in increased prices. But Reuther was pressured to stop bargaining on national economic terms. Thus, the repeating cycle of wage and price hikes was established. In an economy of administered prices, the cycle was one that industry had little difficulty in sustaining.

Members of the crafts and professions could not organize along the lines of industry or industrial unions. So they combated the vicissitudes of free enterprise through a variety of devices to reduce competition and stretch the available work. Craft unions reverted to the old guild practice of limiting entry to the sons of relatives and special friends, and requiring exorbitantly long apprenticeships. Frequently, they refused to adopt labor-saving devices. Painters would not use rollers or spray guns. Plumbers would not work with plastic pipe, or electricians with plastic-sheathed wire. Printers refused to accept matted type until they were able to obtain contracts requiring the setting of "bogus type" (resetting in each establishment the type for the copy in the mats), which was thrown away as soon as it had been set. Trainmen fought the undermining of their jobs by G.M.'s Diesels by demanding that each engine continue to have a fireman (even though his position was now superfluous). The union insisted that runs continue to be measured according to steam-engine schedules—so that it is common for a crew to work no more than two or three hours a day.

The professions—teachers, doctors, dentists, lawyers—used their organizations to establish standards and, in effect, set themselves up as licensing bodies for aspiring members. Although initially the establishment of standards was necessary and commendable, it gradually became a means to protect the incumbents, squelch new and "radical" concepts and ideas, and make training and entry more difficult and costly.

An industry like the automobile, highly productive, mechanized and automated, can easily grant higher wages, whether the productivity of the worker is a factor or not. Workers in less productive industries, however, then tend to demand comparable wages. Wage increases are granted regardless of productivity—otherwise the purchasing power of workers in less productive industries declines, and unemployment rises.

Other people in organized fields assure "parity" for themselves by increasing fees. They are able to make these increases stick because, in most cases, restrictive entry has created situations in which the demand exceeds the supply.

Since in the service and professional fields there have been few gains in productivity, price increases initiated by pace-setting industries in the administered economy set off even greater cost spirals elsewhere. The automobile mechanic in a service shop who achieves wage parity with the skilled worker on the assembly line does not have productive parity. Paid at an hourly rate, he takes longer and longer to deal with the more and more complex machines whose production costs are held in line by automation, but whose repair costs rise astronomically.

If the laissez-faire conditions of the pre-World War I era had continued to exist, the high American wages would be drawing workers from labor-surplus, low-wage countries to the United States. Willing to accept a lower standard of living, these workers would be employed in the less productive, labor-intensive industries, whose goods could thus be kept competitive with those turned out by high-productive industries. (These workers would also, of course, keep regenerating slums.)

Since, however, the free interplay of economic forces was restricted by immigration laws, tariffs, semimonopolies, and governmental subsidies and controls, the labor-intensive industries which could no longer import manpower commenced to export themselves. They first moved from highly organized, high-wage Northern industrial areas to the nonunion, low-wage, low-tax South. But for many that was only a temporary stopping-off place, and they continued on to Japan, Mexico, Italy, and other labor-surplus, low-wage countries. Consequently, the United States has been losing large chunks of some of its oldest industries (leather working and textiles), new industries which otherwise might have established themselves here (the transistor is an American invention, but a considerable segment of the industry has emigrated to Japan), and even portions of high-productive industries like the automobile. (The average Ford worker earns more than $40 a day in the United States, but only $8.80 a day in Mexico.)

The goods produced by these industries return to the United States as low-priced imports, and enable the high-wage American worker to further improve his standard of living. The imports provide the free-enterprise competition abandoned by administered industries. But they aggravate the plight of American labor-intensive industries and threaten to precipitate the less productive portion of the population out of the work force altogether.

In fields in which low-productive service workers are pitted against imports and high-efficiency machines, employment has steadily declined. The difference between the price of a new pair of Brazilian shoes, a Japanese radio, or a pair of pants from Hong Kong and the cost of having a used article repaired in an American service shop has narrowed to the point that it often makes more sense to discard the old and buy a new. For considerably less than a year's cost of employing a maid at the lowest acceptable salary, housewives have replaced maids with mechanical devices—vacuum cleaners, clothes washers and driers, freezers, self-cleaning and electronic ovens, dishwashers, garbage disposals, electric mixers and beaters, electric percolators, electric shoe polishers, and so on, ad infinitum. Since an electric saw or drill costs less than a single visit from a carpenter or plumber, many American homes today are better equipped than a small carpenter's or mechanic's shop a generation ago, and the do-it-yourself phenomenon blossomed.

The human problems arising out of the dual economic structure have increasingly drawn the Federal government into the social welfare field, and led to Federal attempts at managing the economy. Such governmental intervention in the economy had been a major contributing factor to the middle-class

colonists' rebellion against the British government. It was the kind of intervention that the framers of the American Constitution had thought they were
safeguarding the new nation against.

VII. THE POLITICAL SYSTEM

The intent of the Federal system was to provide a mechanism for coordination between the states, and to present a unified posture to the transoceanic
world. The Federal government was not to interject itself into the everyday
lives of the people—the Bill of Rights made that clear.

The cession of the Western lands by the original states, however, and the
establishment of a public domain controlled by the Federal government produced unexpected results. Special interests pressured the Federal government
to dispose of the lands, and the Federal government began to develop domestic
policies that no longer were necessarily channeled through state governments.
Out of the Western expansion the Jacksonian Democratic party emerged, followed by the broad Republican fusion.

That the South regarded the Civil War as the War Between the States was
not merely a matter of semantics—in the agricultural South parochialism
prevailed, and men thought of themselves as Virginians and Georgians first and
Americans second. The Republicans, to the contrary, were the political manifestation of the development of canals, railroads, telegraph lines, and industry
—the new technology that was tying the nation together. The Republican outlook was nationalistic, and they regarded the Federal government as a means
to implement nationalism.

The Republicans used the Federal control of land to provide the backing
for canal and railroad construction, and directed the Federal conduct of the
war toward the benefit of their industrial enterprises. The Railroad-industrial
Republicans manipulated the government until the Crédit Mobilier scandal
and the crash of 1873 put a temporary halt to their activities.

By then, the reaction to the Big Business-banker domination of the party
had given birth to the Liberal Republicans. The Liberals represented the intellectuals, common people, and idealists in the coalition. To compensate for
the defection of the Liberals and retain power, the regular Republicans sought
to organize the Southern Negroes.

Since the Republican party, however, embraced not only the most productive
portion of the population, but that part favoring a monopolistic and administered economy, and the Negro field hands were among the least productive
and the most unorganized, the Republican-Negro alliance was the most anom-
alous of coalitions.

The old North-South Democratic party split apart under the stresses produced by industrialization. In the South the party remained (or became, with
the addition of former Whigs) a Bourbon-controlled oligarchy. In the North
it came to represent the less productive, the unskilled and the semiskilled, the
masses operating in the free economy. In the latter 1880's, the Western miners
and farmers, fighting against a tidal wave of mechanization and economic
control, coalesced into a cousin of the Democratic party—the Populists. Gathering in the small farmers and the *menu peuple* of the South as well, the Populists
captured control of the Democratic party and threatened to put an end to the
Bourbon dominance.

While the Populists were attacking the Republican oligarchy from the outside, the Progressives were working to undermine it from the inside. The Progressives were even more fully committed to the reality of Federal power than the Railroad-industrial Republicans, but they were firm believers that that power must be applied for the public good, and not for private greed. They adhered to Henry George's philosophy that land and natural resources should be a public trust employed for the benefit of all the people.

In their time of distress during the 1890's, the Republican and Bourbon oligarchs drew together. To the Republicans, the Southern Negroes became sacrificial goats. The Bourbons, faced by the threat of a white-black Populist revolution, threw the goats to the white Populists. The Populists, climbing upward over the bodies of the Negroes, scrambled after the crumbs of political and economic power that the Bourbons judiciously scattered about. The Bourbons recognized that if they had to tax themselves for schools and a measure of social programs, the tax would be far less onerous if the benefits were restricted to one segment of the population, the white, rather than applied to all the people—white and black.

Through the first three decades of the twentieth century, both the Democrats and Republicans remained divided. The oligarchs, better financed and better organized, dominated both parties.*

Then came the Depression, and the emergence of a charismatic Progressive, Franklin D. Roosevelt. Amid a graphic demonstration that the supposedly "free enterprise" system had broken down, the Progressives, represented by Roosevelt, fused with the Populists, represented by John Nance Garner. Although the Democrats and the Republicans retained their old designations, the realignment was as epochal as if Chevrolet had chosen to merge with the Model T and been continued in production under the Ford name.

VIII. AGRICULTURE

President Hoover had clung to the concept that the Federal government was separated from the people by the states. When he protested that the American system would never be the same again if that separation were violated, he was right. The choice, however, was between bending the system to fit a modern nation in which distances no longer separated and states' boundaries were little more than conveniences, or having it drained of vitality and break. Ironically, through the Populist-Progressive fusion it was the Democrats, who had viewed the Federal government as an overbearing coupling between centralized power and big industry, who brought about concentration and dimension of that power never before envisioned.

The infusion of humanism into the Federal government (largely through Harry Hopkins) directed the government's attention not only to management of the economy but to measures of relief for the population in the subeconomy. Relief and subsidies (such as public housing) were regarded, however, as only temporary balm for casualties of the economic battles. There was little recognition that long-term economic trends were such that the subeconomic were becoming cripples for life, and no realization that Federal policies themselves might be exacerbating those trends. There was no comprehension that the

---

* Populist William Jennings Bryan captured control of the Democratic party and Progressive Theodore Roosevelt became President on the Republican ticket, but they were notable exceptions.

small farmer and the blue-collar worker were in dire straits for essentially the same reason—because machines with the capability of producing huge volumes of goods were replacing both. The agrarian population had been fighting an unequal battle against industrial productivity for a century and a half. During the 1920's the assembly line aggravated that inequality. The ability of many industries to administer prices, while farmers continued to operate in a free economy, increased it further. Unlike the factories, which shut down when consumers were no longer able to absorb the masses of goods they were turning out, farmers kept churning out record crops that sold for less and less as fewer and fewer people had money to buy them. The farmers who thereupon had no money to pay their mortgages swelled the sea of poverty-stricken in the cities.

The Federal government's solution was to convert agriculture—or at least major portions of it—into an administered industry. Parts of the agricultural "factories" were to be shut down, and their owners compensated. "Parity" was established between agricultural and industrial prices. The flow of agricultural produce was to be regulated by the government according to supply and demand in much the same fashion as industries regulated their output.

Of course, the most marginal and inefficient agricultural "factories," the ones employing the most labor, would be shut down first. Since it was the size of the "factory" and not the output that was regulated, the incentive was to utilize the land more intensively—by the late 1960's, productivity per acre was nearly twice what it had been a half century earlier. For the smaller farmers the subsidy payments were not large enough to provide anything but balm, but for the larger farmers they acted as a source of capital for investment. The farmers who had the least need for subsidies were the ones who reaped the most benefits.

Consequently, hundreds of thousands of small farmers gave up and sold out.* From Virginia to California, abandoned farmhouses bleached and rotted, while the land on which they stood continued to be farmed by larger and larger enterprises, some of them corporations. Since every decade saw a near doubling of the productivity of farm labor—in 1970, two men were able to perform the work of eleven in 1940, and one farm worker supplied thirty-nine urban dwellers (compared to a ratio of one to fourteen in France and one to seven in Russia)—the farm population fell even faster than the number of farms. In 1930, 30.5 million people, one out of every four Americans, was living on a farm. By 1970, the total was down to 9.7 million, fewer than one in twenty.

Between 1933 and the early 1970's, the Federal government spent nearly $70 billion on farm subsidies, and was continuing to spend close to $4 billion a year—providing approximately one fifth of net farm income. But the government programs only accelerated the trend toward an industrial-type structure of agriculture and set off a migration which exceeded that from Europe to America. (Between 1820 and 1960, 47 million immigrants arrived in America, of which an estimated 22 million returned to Europe, leaving a net of 25 million. Between 1920 and 1970, as the rural birth rate continued

---

* Between 1930 and 1970, while the size of the average farm grew from 151 to 383 acres, the number of farms plummeted from 6.55 million to 2.92 million. In 1949, 77 percent of farms had annual sales of less than $10,000. By 1970, only 13 percent of these remained. Between 1960 and 1970, farms grossing more than $40,000 increased from 30 to 50 percent of the total.

significantly higher than the urban, an estimated 40 million persons left American farms for the cities.)

Since Negroes generally had the smallest farms, worked the most marginal lands, and were heavily dependent on farm work for employment, the mechanization of agriculture had an especially harsh impact upon them.

When a minimum wage of $1.25 an hour for farm labor was established in 1967, plantations in the Mississippi Delta intensified their use of machinery. Approximately 8,000 families, with 54,000 members, were left jobless and homeless. The use of hand labor was all but eliminated. On one plantation, between the mid-1950's and 1960's machines replaced 446 out of the 450 cotton choppers. In Florida, orchards switched to mechanical pickers for citrus fruit. In California (where Mexican-Americans were primarily affected) the harvesting of tomatoes was mechanized. Every increase in the cost of human labor brought more use of machinery. Federal intervention and the trend toward unionization had the same effect upon agricultural labor as upon industrial—the phasing out of the unskilled. The few who were left would be better off, but the many would join the "redundant population," whose existence Malthus had recognized more than one hundred fifty years ago.

In the South, the uneasy Bourbon-Populist alliance dominated the administration of Federal programs. Disbursement of Federal funds was controlled by locally elected committees from which Negroes were excluded, and Negroes were regularly discriminated against in grants. Despite civil rights activities, Federal laws, and equal employment opportunity directives, the Agricultural Extension Service and the Employment Security Service remained almost as segregated in the 1960's as they had been in the 1930's, and provided inferior service to Negroes.

In some rural areas conditions remained similar to those from which Odie Stallings had emerged fifty years before. People lived in shacks, some of which had not even a well or a privy. Their light came from a kerosene lantern—whenever there was money enough to buy kerosene. In one Alabama county four fifths of the children were suffering from malnutrition and anemia. Some of them had a hemoglobin count only one third that of the average white child, and indicated symptoms of oxygen starvation—physical lassitude and brain damage. Negro schools continued to have as little as one third or one fourth as much money per capita spent on them as white schools. Graduates of rural and small-town Negro high schools actually were functioning at sixth- to eighth-grade levels.

In the towns, the factory owners placated the Populist whites by giving them first opportunity at jobs. Negroes were hired in fewer numbers, and usually only for lower classification jobs. (In Black Belt areas where the Negro population constituted 60 to 80 percent of the total, only slightly more than one out of every five factory workers was a Negro.) Factory managers explained that they were not discriminating, but that Negroes lacked the education and the physical and mental abilities to pass employment tests.

While hundreds of thousands of men were forced off the land and unable to obtain jobs in factories, so that their families had to go on welfare, the states resisted increasing their welfare budgets. Alabama granted a family of four $85 a month. Mississippi calculated the minimum need per person—and then made payments on the basis of 31 percent of that need! The average allotment per child was $9 a month. A family, no matter how large, could not receive more than $90.

If Negroes wanted to obtain a full measure of the Progressives' social-welfare legislation, they had to migrate to the North and the West. In the North and the West the influence of the formerly Republican Liberals and Progressives opened job opportunities to them both in government and in private industry —Negroes were still discriminated against, but the extent of discrimination was less.

So they streamed from the South into the urban areas of the North. In 1920, 6.7 million out of the nation's 10.5 million Negroes had lived in the rural South, and fewer than 1 million had lived in the central cities of the North and the West. Between 1920 and 1970, while Southern in- and outmigration of whites nearly balanced, there was a net outmigration of 5½ million blacks. Half the Negroes left the rural South as they reached the age of adulthood— a large part of an entire generation was gone. Between 1960 and 1970 nearly two thirds of the black population moved off the land. By 1970 only 940,000 Negroes were left on farms. More than 13 million of the nation's 22.6 million blacks were now living in central cities.

IX. STAGES OF THE CITY

Cities always have had difficulty handling the inmigration. The new arrivals always congregated in the oldest and most ramshackle districts. But while the middle and upper classes continued to reside in the city and there was a gradual, osmotic upward movement of the migrants, the city presented an illusion of heterogeneity.

Before 1800 most population centers were market towns whose size was limited by the extent of the areas they served. Towns that grew into cities were few—they were either seats of government like Paris and London, or crossroads of commerce like Venice and Marseilles. Since the only efficient medium of transportation was the ocean, and the growth of every community was limited by the availability of food, the commercial centers were nearly all ports. Before the sixteenth century, European trade and ports were oriented on the Mediterranean. As trade shifted to the Atlantic, the ports that grew most rapidly were those in the north and west—Lisbon, Amsterdam, Liverpool. In America, towns developed along the Atlantic coast from Boston to Charleston.

The first stage of the modern city came to an end during the latter part of the eighteenth century with the advent of the factory and steam power. To provide transportation to and from the industrial sites, artificial waterways—canals—were constructed. Steam power was applied to inland transportation —first to ships, then to railroads. The steamship and the railroad joined the factory as forces that concentrated people in great blobs of humanity, until the city was nearly unlivable. Pressure to make more intensive use of land in the urban centers led America to develop the skyscraper—and high-rise construction increased density still further. Horse-drawn vehicles congested the hearts of the cities.

By the end of the nineteenth century, urban reformers recognized that high density was a significant factor in the development of slums. Many reformers looked upon the improvement of public transportation as a panacea that would relieve congestion and put an end not only to slums, but to the problems associated with slums. To relieve street traffic, the elevated railroad and then the subway were developed. But rapid transit concentrated population along its lines in a similar fashion to the railroad. Rapid transit failed to bring about more than a limited measure of dispersal. High population density was, in fact, necessary for the economic operation of public transportation, for public transportation tended to be by nature inefficient.* Its labor force and equipment had to be sufficient to operate the system during two or three peak periods a day. Inevitably, public transportation was jam-packed and uncomfortable at peak hours, and uneconomic to operate at off-peak periods when the massive equipment often traveled three fourths empty.

The automobile, however, succeeded where rapid transit failed, and initiated the third stage of the modern city. Between 1910 and 1920 technology ceased acting as a concentrator of population. The well-to-do moved their year-round residences from the central city to their summer estates in Grosse Pointe and similar suburbs. Henry Ford's mass production of the automobile freed the middle class from the rigidities of public transportation and enabled them to acquire miniature "country places" of their own. The city accommodated the dispersal by pushing its boundaries outward.

The automobile was an excellent device to spread out the population, but it created nightmares in the high-rise urban hubs. Designed to furnish family transportation, it was inefficient for commuter and shopping trips. It took up inordinate amounts of space on streets and in parking lots. To provide rapid transportation to outlying districts, it needed a through road without cross traffic—and so the freeway was devised.

Freeways ushered in the fourth stage of the city. One of the governmental priorities after World War II was to provide the American people with better housing, and Federal policies encouraged the building of single-family homes. Building materials were relatively inexpensive. The United States had a surfeit of money, so interest rates were low. The cost of land, however, played an increasing factor in the price of housing. The farther from the city center land was located, the cheaper its price. The spread of electrification initiated by the Federal government in the 1930's radiated the conveniences of modern life to the urban borderland. With gasoline plentiful and cheap, and freeways increasing average speeds to three and four times what they were on surface streets, residential districts pushed beyond urban boundaries. The age of suburbia arrived.

The suburbs, of course, were copies of the more amenable districts within the cities, and sometimes improvements on them. They reflected the revolution brought about by the automobile, electric power, and communications. The automobile and the telephone linked former rural areas to the city. The radio, television, and high fidelity equipment transformed much of entertainment from an exercise in mass participation to a matter of private enjoyment. Gregariousness and anonymity characterized the city. Privacy and individual identity marked the suburbs.

Electricity and highways freed factories, like people, from urban confinement. Like heavenly bodies cracking under centrifugal forces, the urban mammoths threw out masses of population. New cities more manageable than the mammoths of the era between 1800 and 1950 formed. They were satellite bodies on which the great metropolitan centers maintained a gravitational pull. The

---

* Use of public transportation is directly related to population density. Fifty-five percent of workers travel on public transportation in New York City, which has a density of 4,977 persons per square mile; 32 percent in Chicago, which has a density of 1,657; 18 percent in the San Francisco Bay area, which has a density of 840; 10 percent in Denver, which has a density of 254.

central city remained a regional state of mind and a regional institution—people moved to Grosse Pointe and Warren, Southfield and Dearborn Heights, but they supported the Detroit Tigers and Lions, attended events at Cobo Hall, read the Detroit newspapers, and thought of themselves as *Detroiters.*

X. TAXATION AND MIGRATION

While one set of Federal programs was encouraging the subproductive population of the rural areas to move into the cities, another was facilitating the outflow of the middle class. The consequence has been a cross-migration: as the middle class moved out, the undereducated and underskilled moved in.

The outflow of wealth, and the contraction of the economic base as businesses and factories departed, generated difficulties for cities attempting not only to maintain the level of services, but to raise them to meet rising expectations. The greater a city's efforts, the more it exacerbated its troubles. By increasing taxation in order to provide better services for the poor—better schools, better police protection, better recreation, better health—the city only accelerated the exodus.

In Detroit—and cities like Cleveland and Newark—the movement verges, economically, on the catastrophic. Since 1950 Detroit has lost two out of every three whites between the ages of twenty-five and forty-four. Of the 834,000 whites between the ages of twenty and fifty-four, only 345,000 remain.

On the other hand, the number of the aged has continued to increase, and nearly every one of the 212,000 white children that left for the suburbs has been replaced by a black. A plurality of 484,000 that the *working* population (ages twenty-one to sixty-four) had over the *dependent* (under twenty, and over sixty-five) has turned into a virtual standoff. (If sixty-two is used as the cutoff for the working age, the *dependent* population actually outnumbers the working by 57,000.) Between 1960 and 1970, as housing discrimination in the suburbs was alleviated, even a portion of the most productive Negro population began to move out. There were 71,000 blacks between the ages of thirty and thirty-nine in Detroit in 1970 compared to 79,000 a decade earlier.

DETROIT POPULATION
(in thousands)

	1950	1970	Gain or Loss
Total	1,850	1,511	−339
White	1,447	839	−608
Black	303	660	+357
Working Pop.			
(21-64)	1,167	768	−399
Dependent Pop.			
(0-20 & 65+)	683	743	+ 60
White			
25-44	499	164	−335
20-54	834	345	−489
Under 21			
White	477	265	−212
Black	100	301	+201

Since Federal policies were a major contributing factor to the migrations, the Federal government should have assumed a major share of the burdens created by the migrations. But many of the constraints—structural, legal, psychological—to Federal involvement in domestic affairs remained. Even when the mid-1960's brought an historic shift in the Federal role in urban affairs, Federal tax and fiscal policies continued to aggravate the difficulties of the cities.

Since states and localities had already staked out the property tax (the historic tax) for their own use, the Federal government during the Civil War had imposed an income tax. The income tax was recognition that in an industrial society wealth was no longer measured solely by the ownership of property. During peacetime, however, the limited activities of the Federal government could be supported without the income tax. It was not until the massive spending during World War I that the income tax began to play a major role in the lives of Americans.

During the semihibernation of the Federal government in the 1920's, the wealth-favoring policy of Treasury Secretary Mellon once more reduced the importance of the income tax. The Depression, and the initiation of Federal programs of social welfare, necessitated a sharp increase in revenues and taxes. The top rate rose from 25 to 79 percent. The progressive tax rate in some measure reversed the financial flow from the general population to the coffers of corporations and the wealthy, and redistributed money to the sub-economy. The tax thus meliorated the fiscal distortions created by the administered economy.

The enormous expenditures for World War II (enormous, at least, at the time) brought the income tax to full flower. As the cutoff level was lowered and the labor force burgeoned, the number of returns filed more than tripled —from 15 million to 47 million. The income tax—both corporate and individual—established itself as the most productive tax ever enacted.

The end of the war, therefore, left the Federal government in excellent financial condition. Even with the advent of the Korean War, the Federal government had a surplus in five of the six years between 1946 and 1951— a total of $38 billion.

Since state and local governments had a combined revenue of but $21 billion in 1950, that $38 billion would have gone far toward easing the burden of local taxation and improving the quality of services—schools, health care, and pollution abatement. But the Federal government continued to be essentially outer-directed: it would spend billions for defense and foreign aid, but scarcely one cent to save the teeth of the nation's children. Since it was deluged by surpluses, there was no pressure for economy. There was, in fact, stimulation to find new ways of spending. During the Kennedy Administration, several leading economists propounded the theory that Federal taxes were responsible for a "fiscal drag" that was slowing economic expansion. So the rates on income and corporate taxes were cut.

But if *progressive* taxes created a "fiscal drag," how much more drag was generated by *regressive* taxes? (A tax is *regressive* when it falls comparatively more heavily on lower than higher income groups.) Traditionally, state and local governments had depended on the property tax, the most regressive of all. (It is regressive because it originated when property and landholding were a measure of wealth. The practice of heavily taxing home ownership is an essentially American development. There is little logic but much reason to it: since home ownership spread as the middle class expanded, the tax is highly remunerative, easy to administer, and almost impossible to escape.) During the Depression, when homeowners could no longer pay their property taxes, and revolted, state and local governments commenced to enact sales taxes as an alternative. The sales tax was regressive, but less so than the property tax (especially in states in which food and drugs are exempted).

Not only was the property tax regressive, but it was quite *inelastic* (it responded relatively little to up and down movements in the economy), and in the older cities its efficiency was negatively affected by inflation.

Attempting to cope with inflation, state and local governments ran in the red in nine of the years between 1950 and 1965. Property taxes were repeatedly raised, and because of the tax's regressive nature each hike discriminated more against lower income groups than the one before. (In 1964, according to calculations by the Advisory Commission on Intergovernmental Relations, typical property and sales taxes took 11.7 percent of an income from $2,000 to $3,000 a year—which was below the poverty line!—6.2 percent from $5,000 to $6,000, 5.5 percent from $9,000 to $10,000, and 4.3 percent from $15,000 to $20,000.)

Thus, while Federal revenues, derived primarily from progressive taxes, rose from $232 to $719 per capita between 1950 and 1970, an increase of 210 percent, state and local taxes, four fifths of which were regressive, burgeoned from $105 to $427 per capita, an increase of 307 percent—nearly 50 percent faster than Federal taxes! The hardest hit was that portion of the population earning $10,000 and less.

Since this low-income population composed an ever greater percentage of the central cities, the cities were, economically, the most affected. In 1959 suburban family income was 19 percent higher than central city income. As the disparity continued to increase, ten years later the figure was nearly 30 percent.*

In the Detroit area, family income in the suburbs was a fourth higher than in the central city. Yet in trying to cope with inflation and the increased services required by the growth of the "dependent" and the low-income populations, Detroit raised school and general city taxes (excluding state and county taxes) from $71 to $225 per capita between 1950 and 1970.

Since assessed valuation in the city increased only from $4 billion to $5 billion, the rise represented a near tripling of the tax burden on the individual. The urban population was paying 7 percent of its income in taxes; the suburban 5.3 percent.†

But, as the cost of general government in the city continued to grow at a faster pace than in the suburbs, the residents of the city were reaping fewer benefits. The schools were in competition for the tax dollar with the police department, and the citizens were more willing to increase revenues for the police than for the schools. Police costs in the city were more than twice per capita

---

* In the Cleveland area, where the disparity was the greatest, suburban family income was roughly double family income in the city.
† In two urban areas, the city populations paid more than twice the percentage in taxes as the suburban. In Newark, New Jersey, the figures were 13.3 and 6.5 percent, and in Washington, D.C., they were 9.7 and 4.2 percent. (Not surprisingly, these are the two cities which have the largest black majorities.) New York City dwellers had the second heaviest tax burden in the nation, paying 10.2 percent of their incomes in taxes compared to 6.7 percent for residents of the suburbs.

those in the suburbs—a burden placed on central city residents because other social problems were not being solved. In 1965 Detroit spent 38 percent more per capita than the suburbs for general government, but the suburbs spent 47 percent more than Detroit for education.

So the people streamed out of the city because they were paying more but receiving less. Businesses went after them because they were losing their more affluent customers, because they were themselves paying higher taxes, and because the purchasing power of those left behind was being taxed away. (In 1958 Detroit led the suburbs slightly in retail sales, but by 1963 the suburbs were outgrossing the central city by nearly $700 million a year.)

That was the climate in which Mayor Cavanagh had proclaimed the arrival of a new Federal-urban "partnership." The attention of the Federal government was turned toward urban problems; problems that were in fact national, and "urban" only in the sense that the economic disease afflicting the nation was most evident in the cities.

XI. THE FEDERAL SYSTEM

But the Federal government had not been structured for domestic administration. A system had to be invented. The first monetary grant to the states was made in 1879 to provide teaching materials for the blind, and another half dozen small-scale programs were initiated during the next four decades. The first major program, however, was the highway act of 1916, pushed through by Henry Joy, Chapin, and the other promoters of the Lincoln Highway. A year later the Vocational Education Act provided training for labor—both acts signified the inability of state and local bodies to deal with the national problems of an industrial age.

Not a single new aid program was established during the three business-oriented Republican administrations of the 1920's. It was the Roosevelt Administration which, for the first time, committed the Federal government to a major role in domestic affairs. During the post-World War II years that role expanded gradually. The perception of each new need generated a drive for a new grant-in-aid program. With the advent of the Johnson Administration and the Great Society, the programs more than doubled, until by 1967–1968 there were 379 with a total of 1,674 different components. There was overlapping, duplication, and confusion. There were four different programs for sewer and water systems administered by four different Federal departments (Housing and Urban Development, Agriculture, Interior, and Commerce). There were nine programs for the mentally retarded, twelve for vocational rehabilitation, and one for diseases in evergreen trees. There were one hundred thirty different manpower programs. There were programs like the Special Impact Program, designed by Senator Jacob Javits and the late Senator Robert Kennedy to help the Bedford-Stuyvesant area of New York City; but since the program could not pass Congress in such form, it was transmuted into a *national* program. (Bedford-Stuyvesant, nevertheless, received half of the first year's $25 million appropriation.) Every program had its own matching formula, uncoordinated with other programs, with the Federal contribution ranging from 30 to 100 percent. It was impossible for anyone to keep up with all the programs. It was not unusual for the staffs of congressional committees to be approached by supposedly knowledgeable people on the passage of legislation for programs that had already been enacted. In 1966 Congress passed duplicate programs for the preservation of historic sites, assigning one to the Department of the Interior and the other to HUD.

Every new program spawned a new bureaucracy. Often a lobby was the main force behind the creation of a program, and it was from the lobby that the nucleus of bureaucrats to run the program came. (If no lobby existed, the program was sure to generate one.) A close relationship—and frequently an interchangeability—developed between the Federal bureaucrats, the state bureaucrats, and the professionals in the fields for which the bureaus were established.

Little wonder that there was compartmentalization, and that for decades there was no attempt at horizontal organization. Each department and bureau laid its own pipeline to the states, and established its own regional structure and regional offices wherever and however it willed. By the mid-1960's more than half the states and cities had to deal with regional offices in six or more different locations. (For five states there were regional offices in six different cities; for seven in seven; for twelve in eight; for four in nine; and for one—Kentucky— in ten. Officials in Washington, D.C., have to deal with regional offices in eight different cities!)

The first major effort at coordination tied several agencies into the Department of Health, Education, and Welfare in 1952, but failed to bring about cooperation or unification. The bureaus functioned as independently within HEW as they had as separate agencies. The effort in 1964 to create the Office of Economic Opportunity as a coordinating and controlling mechanism foundered in the rapids of political expediency.

The bureaucracy has, in fact, become an extraconstitutional fourth arm of the Federal government.* Remote from the public, semi-insulated against the executive department whose servant it theoretically is, the bureaucracy often seems responsive and accountable only to its professional compeers and the congressional committees upon which it depends for funds.

The system concentrates enormous power in the hands of the chairmen of congressional committees. The chairman of the House Committee on Education and Labor was Carl Perkins of eastern Kentucky. Eastern Kentucky received one third of the entire national allocation of the Work Experience Program and one fifth of the Mainstream Program. When Representative Perkins complained to the Department of Labor that his district still was not getting enough money, it was explained to him that the department had already exceeded the statutory limit. "Is that so?" he said, and in the next committee hearing the section restricting allocations was amended.[7]

Participants were supposed to be limited by law to three years in the manpower training programs. Three years, presumably, was long enough for them to garner the skills necessary to obtain jobs in the labor market. But after three years no jobs were available, and seventy thousand men in eastern Kentucky were still unemployed. The men in the Mainstream Program had come to con-

---

* The bureaucrat's most prominent characteristic is his "functionalism"—he looks upon his own particular programs and functions as ends in themselves, without regard to their effectiveness or place in the larger scheme of things. According to Frank Fisher, when he took over as director of the regional HUD office in Chicago, "There were five hundred fifty people, and not one of them had ever asked himself whether what he was doing was rational or what he was accomplishing. The only criteria used was whether it fit the guidelines and the statutes."

sider the program as their job. To expel them would be to return them, with their new "skills," to welfare. So the Department of Labor made an end run around the law, and shifted the men into the Concentrated Employment Program, JOBS, and other training programs. Few of the remainder of the 1.3 million men in manpower training programs could expect such favored treatment, yet in other permanently depressed areas, such as northern Michigan, they were just as badly off. Many were being "trained" for nothing but unemployment.

When Richard Nixon took office in 1969 he was faced with an enormously expanded Federal establishment over which the President had only marginal control. The bureaucracy was overwhelmingly Democratic, and a Republican administration only cemented the bureaucrats' ties to the Democrat-controlled Congress. Theoretically within the Executive Office itself was the Office of Economic Opportunity, whose staff was the most liberal in Washington.

In an attempt to strengthen presidential control, Nixon enlarged the executive staff and expanded the role of the Bureau of the Budget (whose name was changed to the Office of Management and Budget). But the President's efforts in the domestic area were largely frustrated. The White House staff was divided between progressives like Daniel Moynihan and Robert Finch, and conservatives like John Ehrlichman and H. R. Haldeman. The division was reflected in confusing policies and directives, and contributed to the administration's inept handling of relations with Congress.

Throughout its first term the Nixon Administration was saddled with programs failing to meet the needs for which they had been created. Yet the constituencies generated by the programs made termination of them difficult, if not impossible. By 1972 the hard-liners in the White House were convinced that little could be achieved by trying to work with Congress and the bureaucracy.

A new "game plan" was devised for the second term. A large number of Nixon men would be infused into the bureaucracy. Programs would be decentralized and the flow of power toward Washington would be reversed—Nixon became the first President since Hoover to deemphasize the Federal establishment. Presidential power and executive orders would be used to present Congress with faits accompli. The President would let programs atrophy by refusing to spend funds appropriated by Congress. The Office of Economic Opportunity would be abolished and its remaining functions delegated to other agencies—there would be, in effect, a return to the status quo before 1964.

Such actions presented a direct challenge to the existing system and involved constitutional questions—even though the system and practices themselves have little constitutional base. Moreover, the actions ignored the fact that though the War on Poverty had largely not succeeded, the program had been conceived because the American economy failed to provide adequate employment and income for everyone. The failure was as evident in the 1970's as it had been in the 1960's. The Federal government itself was a major contributor to the economic distortions; distortions generating critical problems for America.

XII. THE ECONOMICS OF INFLATION

The Depression had established among economists a keen awareness of the danger of deflation. The problem seemed to be how to pour enough money into the economy to satisfy the enormous demands of American industrial production. After the economy advanced only in fits and starts during the 1950's, one school of economists convinced President Kennedy that the Federal government could "prime the pump" by reducing taxes, running a temporary deficit, and permitting mild inflation. Such a policy, it was thought, would reduce the tendency of Federal taxes to remove money from the economy and put a premature brake on expansion.

So many other inflationary pressures were at work, however, that a policy intended to allow mild inflation produced runaway inflation.

Inflationary pressures began in the administered economy in the late 1930's and matured after World War II. Once the Federal government acquiesced to labor-management negotiated wage-price increases, it had to expand the monetary supply to cover those increases—a fixed money supply concurrent with rising prices would result in recession.

Members of the organized economy reacted to higher prices by raising their fees although they did not render greater services or increase their productivity— since there was no price competition among lawyers, doctors, or dentists, they operated in effect in a fee monopoly.

The Federal government became a major contributor to fee inflation through programs like Medicare and Medicaid. Commendable and necessary as these programs are, they were enacted willy-nilly without simultaneous expansion of the inadequate number of medical practitioners.

Conversely, the programs encouraged overexpansion and overequipment of hospitals, and hospital room charges were raised again and again to pay off capital investment. Between 1965 and 1971 physicians' fees increased 46 percent and daily hospital charges 110 percent—and many people in the free enterprise economy who had to pay their own medical bills saw doctor and hospital costs pass beyond reach.*

The interjection of an administering agency into the client-professional relationship—whether that agency was the government or an insurance company —produced a huge volume of paper work that pushed costs up further. Paperwork inflation exists throughout the economy as America changes from a cash to a credit-card society—administrative costs are tacked onto the charges for goods and services.

Some inflation is the result of the growth of the nonproductive population— retirees, unemployed, and welfare recipients.† Since these are people who consume but do not produce, they generate a classic demand-type inflation on goods in short supply.

Until 1968 the impact of this inflation had been neutralized by payments into the Social Security fund. Federal revenues and expenditures were calculated according to an "administrative budget," which excluded Social Security and other trust funds. Since the trust funds normally showed a surplus, they tended to retard the inflationary effect of the deficits accumulated under the administrative budget. For example, in 1967 when the administrative budget had a deficit of $15 billion, trust funds showed a surplus of more than $6 billion.

Trying to reduce the sting of repeated Federal deficits, the Johnson Admin-

* Median earnings for physicians were $22,100 in 1959, $28,960 in 1965 when Medicare went into effect, and $41,500 in 1970.
† Between 1950 and 1970 the number of persons over sixty-five increased from twelve million to twenty million.

istration in 1968 switched to a "national income accounts" method of calculation. The new method included trust fund revenues and expenditures in reporting the Federal budget. In 1969, when the administrative budget would have shown a deficit of $5.5 billion, the national income accounts budget showed a *surplus* of $3.3 billion. In 1971, a $7 billion trust fund surplus reduced a whopping administrative budget deficit from $30 billion to $23 billion. The 1968 revision of accounting methods eliminated what had been a "hidden" brake on the inflationary effect of Federal deficits.

Primarily, inflation is the consequence of the expansion of the money supply without commensurate production of useful goods and services.* For every additional dollar placed in the economy, something must be produced on which it can be spent, else the money will drive up the prices of existing goods. (The alternative is to remove the excess money from the economy through taxation or savings.) By far the most serious inflationary pressure has been that produced by the Vietnam War and by the expansion of the defense establishment.

The American arms industry pioneered the techniques of mass production. From the midnineteenth century until World War II, American manufacturers were world suppliers of arms. They contributed to the favorable American balance of trade, and the United States profited hugely from other nations' wars. By the end of World War II, however, the American defense establishment had grown to far the largest in world history. In a world divided among defeated enemies, bankrupt allies, and Communist foes, the remaining major purchaser of weapons was the United States Government. For the first time, expenditures for armaments dominated American peacetime budgets.

Until the 1960's, American affluence and industrial dominance were so great that defense expenditures appeared to have little economic impact. In reality, revitalized German and Japanese industries were gaining rapidly. The huge American expenditures for the Vietnam War and space exploration increased the outflow of dollars to the crisis point.

Under classic wartime circumstances, the diversion of industry to arms production should have created inflationary shortages. Taxes should have been raised to sop up purchasing power and pay for the war.

Since the United States already had a large military establishment, however, much of the materiel for Vietnam could be obtained by switching from one type of arms production to another. Many of the dollars spent in Vietnam were not immediately returned to the United States, but were absorbed into the international money market, where the dollar had the same exalted status as gold. Other excess dollars that the Federal government poured into the American economy were used to purchase imported consumer goods, and these dollars also found their way overseas.

Momentarily it seemed that the Federal money managers were wizards—America was fighting a large-scale war, yet there was no shortage of consumer goods, taxes were increased only minimally and briefly, and inflation remained at an acceptable level.

Actually, the United States was able to conduct its economy as usual because of its vast reserves. But these were being depleted. The true state of affairs

---

* One factor—though not a major one—in the expansion of the money supply comes from the transformation from a cash to a credit card economy. The money that remains on deposit instead of circulating as cash can be used by banks as the base for expanding credit.

manifested itself initially in the cost of money. From World War I until after the Korean War gold had flowed into the United States, the United States had had a surfeit of money, and interest rates had generally been low. In the latter 1950's however, the American balance of payments became unfavorable, and the flow of gold was reversed. As the supply of money decreased, interest rates rose. Higher interest rates were one of the principal reasons for inflation. (A twenty-five-year, $25,000 housing loan that could have been obtained for 4.5 percent interest with monthly payments of $139 in 1950 cost $193 per month at 8 percent interest in 1969.)

Money flowed into foreign hands through war and foreign aid expenditures, through overseas investments by American firms, and through purchases of foreign goods and oil by American consumers. Since the dollar was regarded as good as gold, a reaction was delayed. But as America continued to fail to produce enough goods it could sell competitively in foreign markets and the horde of dollars kept growing, foreign bankers became restive. Inevitably, the value of the dollar in relation to the currencies of more productive countries— notably Germany and Japan—declined. The prices of imported goods shot up in America.

The mass of dollars, however, remained in foreign hands. To redress the economic balance, they had to be spent on American goods. During the early 1970's the excess dollars that had been produced by the deficit spending of the Vietnam War years and exported overseas began to return to the United States.* Since American production did not expand sufficiently to absorb the money, prices skyrocketed—there was a unique manifestation of delayed inflation. As the Japanese competed for timber, Americans paid the price for the colossal mistreatment of their natural resources—with reasonable management America could have had an ample supply of lumber. Instead, soaring costs forced even middle-class Americans to cut back their housing standards. As the waste of oil and power encouraged by American industry took its toll on domestic reserves, America was transformed from an oil-exporting to an oil-importing nation, and the price of fuel rose. As foreign nations stepped up their agricultural purchases, the culmination of decades of production cutbacks was the greatest inflation of food prices in American history. In a land of chronic agricultural surpluses and immense unused agricultural capacity, there was talk of possible food rationing. President Nixon embargoed the export of some products—a futile gesture since the inflationary pressures were simply being shifted elsewhere as long as the balance-of-trade deficit remained.

Inflation is the means the Federal government has chosen to combat the economic distortions and the tendency of money to be siphoned off from the lower half of the population to the upper 10 percent. Federal payments to the lower-income population are transfusions into the consumer economy, and act to forestall unemployment and depression. Since tax revenues, however, do not cover the cost of all the Federal programs, the government creates "new" money not warranted by industrial production, and prices rise.

Inflation is a means of taxation, one from which the Federal government reaps dividends. The family buying a house for $30,000 and selling it five years later for $40,000 pays a capital gains tax even though the increased

* Germans, Japanese, and Arabs have begun investing extensively in the United States. The first major German acquisition was the purchase of the Wyandotte Chemicals Corporation by Badische Anilin and Soda Fabrik AG for $100 million in 1969.

price is due to inflation and they make no profit. (The tax *is* forgiven if the family buys another residence for itself within one year.) The government taxes interest on savings even though the interest may be less than inflation during the year—in effect, Americans pay to keep money in the bank. The married man with two children who made $5,000 in 1950 would have to be earning $8,000 in 1970 to have the same purchasing power. In 1950 he would have paid $270 income tax. If his tax had increased on the same curve as inflation, he would have paid $464 in 1970. But because the income tax is *progressive,* and inflation advanced him from a 23 percent to a 26 percent bracket, in 1970 he was actually paying $772. Thus he was confused and angry as he kept hearing that his taxes were supposedly being *cut!* *

XIII. THE UNEQUAL BURDEN

While the Federal government pursued taxation through inflation with the progressive income tax, it promoted one increase after another in the regressive Social Security tax.

The initial tax of 1 percent—paid half by the worker and half by the employer—had been insignificant. But as inflation pushed the cost of living up, the benefit payments, never adequate, became more inadequate. When payments were increased, the trust fund faced the danger of depletion. More money had to be raised. Since 1950, taxes for Social Security have been the fastest rising in the nation.

Because the Social Security tax is calculated by applying a flat rate to a base part of a person's income, it is highly regressive. In 1950 the tax was 3 percent on the first $3,000 of income: a maximum of $90, of which the worker paid $45. By 1972 it had risen to 10.40 percent on the first $9,000 of income: a maximum of $936, of which the worker paid $468.

The Social Security increases have severely affected the progressive nature of the Federal tax system, and its ability to act as a correcting agent in economic cycles. Although in theory the Federal income tax rates rise quite steeply, in actual practice, with deductions, the curve is gradual. Combining income and Social Security taxes, the average taxpayer earning $4,000 a year pays more than 13 percent of his income in taxes; the taxpayer earning over $30,000 pays less than 21 percent.† A study by Herman P. Miller, chief of the U.S. Census Bureau's population section, and Roger Herriot indicates that, when all taxes are added together, they account for between 30 and 33 percent of income whether a person is earning $5,000 or $50,000 a year.

The Social Security increases, therefore, are reinforcing the negative economic impact of local property and sales taxes. Since Social Security has been collecting more than it pays out in benefits—in 1970 collections on all levels of government exceeded disbursements by more than $10.7 billion—it has an even greater deflationary effect on the lower income population, and the economies of the cities in which they reside, than property and sales taxes.

---

* Federal personal income tax revenues increased more than twice as fast as per capita income. Between 1950 and 1970, annual per capita income rose from $1,501 to $3,929, an increase of 161 percent. Per capita income tax revenues rose from $104 to $445, an increase of 328 percent!

† In 1970, the average taxpayer earning from $3,000 to $5,000 paid 13.2 percent of his income in Social Security and income taxes; from $5,000 to $10,000, he paid 15 percent; from $10,000 to $15,000, he paid 15.1 percent; from $15,000 to $25,000 he paid 16.6 percent; from $25,000 to $50,000, he paid 20.8 percent.[8]

Furthermore, the Social Security tax has a regressive effect not only on the working population but on business. Since employers pay 5.20 of the 10.40 percent, the tax acts, in effect, as a tax on labor. It discriminates against the employment of low-productive labor, since the employer pays the same tax on a $9,000-a-year worker as on a $15,000-a-year worker. It discriminates against less efficient, labor-intensive enterprises. (The effect is aggravated by the depreciation allowances for machinery.) Since it is a tax on production, not on profits, its costs are passed on to the consumer, thus adding to inflation.

It is an example of the manner in which the Federal government has been pursuing programs divided against themselves. At the very moment that the government directed itself to the problems in the cities, its tax and fiscal policies intensified those problems. While, through the JOBS program, it subsidizes industry to employ low-productive labor, it places an increasingly heavier tax on that labor. The consequence, by making labor more costly, can only be to bring about accelerated substitution of machinery for men, and to make American labor-intensive industries less competitive with those in foreign countries.

While the high-productive, organized and administered industries and populations swim in prosperity, unemployment continues at a high level, and the public assistance rolls burgeon. From $2.5 billion in 1950, welfare costs rose to $14.5 billion in 1970. The number of persons in the Aid for Dependent Children program multiplied from 2,233,000 to 9,657,000.

The welfare population consists largely of the people displaced by the ever greater efficiency achieved by Big Industry and Big Agriculture. Welfare is an indirect subsidy to industry and agriculture. Yet between 1960 and 1970 corporate income taxes fell from 20 to 15.7 percent of taxes collected by the Federal government. The burden of paying for welfare has fallen increasingly on the middle-income and low-income populations.

Not only the welfare population, but also a disproportionate number of the working lower income population is concentrated in the major cities. The result is an urban economy of poverty not fully integrated into the American economy. Income is lower, but taxes and costs are comparatively higher. A significant proportion of those costs provide no current benefit, but were contracted for when the cities were more affluent.

Often, during the 1940's and 1950's, fringe benefits were used to grant more without immediately having to pay more. Detroit could be generous with retirement benefits for its employees, but did not immediately have to tax the voters to pay for that generosity. In some departments, like the police and fire, early retirement (after twenty-five years' service) was used as a recruiting device.

By the latter 1960's, however, a huge bill, aggravated by inflation, was coming due. In 1969 there were 4,127 retired police and firemen, compared to 6,567 active, and the number of the retired was increasing rapidly. In the Detroit Street Railway System, the numbers were almost equal—2,322 retired, and 2,601 active. For every ten workers in the city government, there were more than four retired.

The total accrued pension liability came to $711.5 million. During year after year of tight budgets, funds set aside to meet future liabilities were insufficient. The city charter mandated that the Detroit Street Railway System operate out of its own revenues. Since there was no hope of accruing the pension liabilities from fare-box collections without an impossible increase in fares, the Cavanagh

Administration entered into a "conspiracy" with the union not to set aside the funds. Of the total liability of $79 million, $59.5 million was unfunded.

The situation in the remainder of the retirement system was only slightly better. Of the total of $711.5 million, $477.3 million was unfunded. The unfunded portion was roughly equal to the entire city budget for a year. The city's contributions to the police and fire retirement system already exceeded its capital improvements budget by nearly 50 percent! The total 1969–1970 pension appropriation of $59.4 million was more than the city's entire tax budget in 1938!

The unfunded liability represents a huge mortgage against the future. It is a mortgage being inherited by the blacks and the poor. Detroit's low-income area now encompasses a population of 350,000. In it, the median family income is $6,977 a year, less than the retirement pay of a police sergeant after thirty years' service. The unorganized, subeconomic latecomers will be required to make good on the commitments that members of the organized economy were able to exact at a more affluent time. If the overtaxed lower income population of the city continues to grow, and the economic base is not expanded, Detroit is on a collision course with fiscal disaster.*

XIV. THE CYCLE OF POVERTY

Because it is in the cities that the economic problems are being concentrated, the cities are serving to expose the rotten parts in the system. All over America the older cities are laying off workers and curtailing services. School systems are on the edge of bankruptcy. Yet the poverty of Appalachia, the Mississippi Delta, Upper Michigan, Puerto Rico, and Detroit are interrelated. Blight and decay are the manifestations not only of Hough in Cleveland, Central Avenue in Los Angeles, Harlem in New York, and the Inner Boulevard area in Detroit, but of the cores of Hamtramck and Highland Park, and towns large and small across the nation. The existence of some communities hangs on a thread. Hamtramck's problems are worse than Detroit's. The Dodge Main Plant is obsolescent, and when it shuts down, Hamtramck might as well shut down with it. Someday someone in Washington who has never heard of the Dodge Main Plant or Hamtramck will make a decision that will result in another 1.99 percent rise in the cost of operating the plant; and that will be the end.†

The cities continue to be the depots for people whose means of livelihood is destroyed by wasteful exploitation of natural resources, mechanization, pollution, and governmental policies—just as they have been for centuries.‡ The exhaustion of the Cornish mines and fisheries drove the Lenticks to Michigan's northern Peninsula, and when the mines there began to give out they migrated to Detroit. The Cavanaghs were forced to flee Ireland, and two generations

---

* The practice of being generous with retirement pay, until it comes time to pay off, is widespread. The state of Michigan is more than one billion dollars in arrears on its contributions to the teacher retirement system. The railroad retirement fund has money enough to operate only until the early 1980's. Private firms sometimes fire workers a short time before they would become eligible for retirement benefits. Some companies simply close their doors, and the employees' retirement benefits disappear like a mirage.

† The population of Hamtramck, which was once 56,000, has shrunk to 27,000, and has an excess of older people—the median age is nearly forty. The financial state of the municipality is desperate. Highland Park has shrunk from 53,000 to 35,000.

‡ In 1972 the company that previously had been California's third largest lumber producer shut down and ended the existence of another small town. "Sooner or later," a youth said without understanding the implications of his words, "everybody has to go to the city." [9]

later Sylvester Cavanagh correctly perceived that prospects were brighter in industrial Detroit than on his family's farm. William Norveth, who was made redundant by the overpopulation of Hungary and the American mechanization of agriculture, was sucked into the maws of the industrial machine. Black Bear's ancestors were deprived of their lands by the white men's guns. Odie Stallings would have starved in a Virginia economy in which he had no means of support. Wallace Mirow was expelled by a land that revolted at its rape. The Jansens became immigrants when the herring was fished out of the Baltic and the trees of Sweden's more accessible forests were felled. But in America the fisheries of the Great Lakes for which they had been recruited were murdered by pollution, and the forests were extirpated.

Over the decades, despite the multitude of tribulations, the newcomers have adapted remarkably well to industrial society. Many of the second generation have moved up to white-collar status. Urban poverty is a rung above rural poverty. There is more hope for the child of a Negro welfare mother in Detroit than there ever was for the child of a field hand in the Mississippi Delta. The Dillingham Commission would be perplexed to discover that it is the Russian Jews, transferring from the towns of Europe to the cities of America, who have demonstrated more upward mobility than any other ethnic group; that the "inferior" Poles and Italians who became concentrated in the cities have done better than the earlier-arriving, "sturdy Nordics," who settled more in rural areas; and that the Irish have had the greatest difficulty of any European immigrants in moving out of poverty.*

Harold Black and Richard Strichartz are representative of the Jewish immigrants and their children in the United States. Jerome P. Cavanagh and Conrad Mallett are outstanding examples of the upward mobility that can be achieved in an urban society by the children of rural migrants.† But for each Black and Strichartz, Cavanagh and Mallett, there is a Jansen or a Devers, a Lentick or a Stallings struggling to pull himself out of the morass. For each generation urban society has grown more complex, the skills that must be mastered more difficult, the goals to be attained more demanding, the hopes brighter but more unreachable.

Every few months President Johnson had announced the further success of the War on Poverty, and an additional percentage of people no longer living "in poverty." But, even with inflated participation figures, no more than one in ten of the poor was being "reached" by the War on Poverty.‡ Hundreds of thousands of those climbing above the official "poverty line" were doing so by no more than $200 or $300 a year. Relative to median income, the position of the poor was not improving at all. The upper third of the American population received a greater share of national income in 1969 than in 1910, and

---

* In 1970, the following percentage of each ethnic group remained below the poverty line: Russian (mostly Jewish), 4.5 percent; Polish, 5.3; Italian, 6.1; German, English, and Scottish, 8.6; French, 9.3; Irish, 10.5.

† Cavanagh has remarried and is running for governor of Michigan in 1974. Mallett is now a member of the Wayne County Board of Commissioners (formerly the Board of Supervisors).

‡ According to an internal Office of Economic Opportunity document, in 1969, 9 percent of the total need for work and training was being met; 14 percent of the need for basic employment; 7 percent of the need for vocational training; 15 percent of the need for legal services; 5 percent of the need for comprehensive health; 10 percent of the need for family planning; 1 percent of the need for adult and school-age education; and .27 percent of the need for parent-child centers.

the lower half was getting considerably less. The actual dollar gap, representing purchasing power, steadily widened.

SHARE OF TOTAL INCOME
RECEIVED BY AMERICAN POPULATION

Population	Income	
	1910	*1969*
Upper 30 percent	56 p.c.	57 p.c.
Lower 50 percent	27 p.c.	23 p.c.

The tendency has been to talk about the "welfare population" and the "poverty population" as if they were fixed bodies in the firmament of the nation. They are, in reality, composed of agitated particles moving up and down, forward and sideways, responding to conditions over which they have no control, but on which governmental policies have a great effect. An aerospace engineer can find himself a member of the long-term unemployed; his family becomes a "poverty family." A woman whose husband is felled by a catastrophic illness may be a middle-class suburban housewife one day and a "welfare mother" a few months later.

When the small foundry in which Zeb Rockhill was employed closed as the result of higher labor and production costs, the Rockhill-Culleran family was plunged through the poverty floor. The effect upon the children was predictable. Yet the family was not able to obtain even the inadequate support of the Aid for Dependent Children program—a support below the poverty line and far beneath the income considered necessary by the Department of Labor for a "minimum but adequate" standard of living. The perversities of the system are such that time and again the maximum stress is placed on marginal families—until, inevitably, they crumble.

Every family has its "stress level." If the totality of circumstances in which the family lives are above that level, the family will remain viable. If they fall below the stress level, the family is in danger of disintegrating. The birth of each child beyond the two or three that lower- and middle-income families can manage increases the stress. If the children are unwanted, the stress is intensified. If they are physically or mentally handicapped, such as the children of George and Rita Devers, the stress is made almost unbearable.

The unrealistic demands of social agencies increase the stress. Rising expectations increase the stress by elevating the level against which a family measures its own living standards. (Thus, the widening dollar gap between top and bottom is a significant factor.) Untreated illnesses and aching teeth that are "expendable" increase the stress. A family with declining or static income amid inflation increases the stress. The commitment of future income to credit payments increases the stress.

The variable with the most critical impact on the progress of lower-income families is the economy. George Devers could not afford to be laid off even for two weeks. Every time he was out of work all the gains the family made were wiped out. The effect on Georgia and the other children was to make them less and less capable of coping with school, and condemn them to repeating the lives of their parents. When Packard shut down in 1956 and Black Bear lost his job, he and Joella Jansen started on their roller-coaster ride.

When a regressive tax takes another fifty dollars a year out of the income of a marginal family, it may not seem much to a legislator. But Marie Jansen will not cut out smoking or going to the movies, and Irma Stallings will not stop drinking cheap booze. That fifty dollars is going to come out of the food the children eat and the clothes they wear. The additional deprivation increases the stress upon them, and makes it even more difficult for them to succeed in school.

In a society that emphasizes material progress and makes acquisition the goal of life, what reason for existence is there for people who have no hope of acquisition? Many attempt fulfillment through acquisition by illegal means: crime.

Inevitably, they fail there, too. The only anodyne for the failures and the hopelessness is escape: escape into alcohol, escape into movies, escape into gambling, escape into drugs. If some means of escape are addictions, and others merely obsessions or compulsions, there is not that much difference between them.

In today's educational system the children of the poor have little chance of succeeding. During the 1967–1968 school year 85 percent of the grammar school pupils in the lower income areas of Detroit were retarded in reading—by the time they reached the eighth grade they were more than two and a half years behind. Of the youths who entered high school, only 39 percent were graduating, compared to 67 percent in the city's medium-income schools, and 81 percent in the state as a whole.

Only 7 percent of dropouts were employed in white-collar jobs, where employment was expanding. Working in marginal and blue-collar jobs, often in fields in which employment was being exported, they had an unemployment rate more than 50 percent higher than high school graduates. While college graduates of minority races were rapidly achieving equality, the semieducated population of the inner city was falling further behind.*

Poverty, inferior education, and a high birth rate continuously reinforced each other. The birth rate for women who were dropouts was 68 percent higher than for college graduates. Subjected to the multiplying stresses of too little income and too many children, the families were more likely to break up. Their children then repeated the educational failure—between two thirds and four fifths of dropouts had parents who had been dropouts, and up to three fourths came from families of five or more children.

More than four fifths of Negro children and over one third of white children in families with five or more children are being reared in poverty.† "Probably no other facts link high fertility and poverty so dramatically and point up so vividly the plight of the poor," demographer Philip M. Hauser advised the U.S. Senate Committee on Government Operations.[10]

So the cycle of poverty repeated itself. The human misery, the crime, and the social turmoil expanded. The expansion was not only a product of the

---

* In 1970, the median family income of Negro college graduates was $14,470 compared to $15,841 for white graduates. The median family income of Negro high school dropouts was $6,563 compared to $9,509 for white dropouts. Median income of Detroit Negroes ranges from $22,589 in one exclusive golf course area (Palmer Park) to $1,896 in part of Forest Park.

† In Detroit, less than 10 percent of families with two children or fewer are below the poverty line, but 28 percent of families with five children, and 22 percent of those with six or more children are below.

normal growth of the population and its concentration in the urban areas, but of the interaction between the two.

It was like epidemic. The plague had always been with the people of medieval Europe, but as long as the population density was low, distance acted like a quarantine. But when the population multiplied and crowded into the cities, the black plague raced like fire through the streets. In some places it carried off half the inhabitants. The plague of social ills will not kill (except in relatively rare instances); but it will spread and multiply.

It is a multiplication that the nation cannot afford. To halt it, we are going to have to cut through the myths, and shed our illusions.

XV. MYTHS AND INSTITUTIONS

Every nation has its mythology, and the United States is no exception. Myths serve to rationalize history, to embellish it with heroic figures, and to provide explanations for events not fully understood.

To justify the separation of the Indians from their lands, the conquering white man portrayed the native American as a cruel savage and himself as the civilizer. The whites' superiority in numbers and weapons * was mythologized into the legend of cowboys and Indians. The Westerner was the "rugged individualist," and if he were worth his salt he would like Herbert Hoover or Horatio Alger succeed in becoming a millionaire.

In fact, one of the most common ways of becoming a millionaire was through the acquisition of land and exploitation of its natural resources. The origin of the wealth of Robert R. Livingston, who financed Fulton's construction of the *Clermont,* was the New York land which his ancestors acquired from the Indians. The Joys, the Wards, and the Algers, the railroad, lumber, and copper barons all derived their fortunes from the land. Had the Indians retained a significant portion of the lands or been compensated equitably for them, Indians would today compose a large percentage of America's wealthy. Instead, the Federal government acted as a redistributor of wealth—taking from the Indians and giving to the "rugged individualists" adept at extracting favors from Washington.

From the time that the Federal government financed Whitney's mass production of muskets and backed French émigré Du Pont's building of a powder works, the government has played a major role in the making of American millionaires, and in determining who was to prosper at whose expense.† For a quarter century the builders of the railroads obtained their capital through Federal land grants. Civil War expenditures for railroads led to numerous success stories like those of John S. Newberry and James McMillan. Federal expenditures in every war since have created new industrial giants. Although Henry Ford abhorred war, he accepted the Federal aid that was largely responsible for bringing the River Rouge complex into existence. The Lincoln plant was financed by the Federal government. Government contracts brought the aircraft manufacturing industry into existence during World War I, and the American aerospace industry has been heavily dependent on Washington

---

* In one California battle the arrows shot by Indians bounced off the whites whom they struck. Spanish soldiers used leather headgear and vests for protection.
† There was not a single millionaire in America at the time of the Revolutionary War. By the 1960's there were seventy-one thousand millionaires.

ever since.* The Willow Run factory that Ford built for the government during World War II is today an automatic transmission plant for General Motors. Several wars transformed the small Electric Boat Company, founded to build submarines, into the giant General Dynamics. By 1961 the mutuality of interest between a large segment of industry and the professional military had grown so extensive that President Eisenhower in his farewell address warned against the "conjunction of an immense military establishment and a large arms industry [leading to] the acquisition of unwarranted influence . . . by the military-industrial complex." [11]

The American arms industry had mass produced the guns to subdue the Indians, and after the Indians were vanquished arms manufacturers kept right on churning out tens of millions of small arms. America was saturated with guns. Out of the deadly power of guns grew the myth that Americans were an especially violent people. This myth is exposed by the record of the Spanish in their civil war, the Germans, Japanese, and Russians before and during World War II, and the participants in the Nigerian and Congon civil wars. On the other hand, all attempts to place some control over guns in America have failed in Congress because tens of thousands of people make their living through the manufacture and sale of guns, and millions of others are adherents of the "gun culture."

The man with the gun and the "rugged individualist" were elements of the same mythology—the heroic figure relying on no one but himself to make his fortune. In reality, the rugged individualist was likely to eke out a miserable existence in the mountains or the Western plains. Horatio Alger was an Eli Whitney, James F. Joy, Henry Ford, or Herbert Hoover—a man whose family had belonged to the middle class for generations, who received a good education, and was in a position to exploit opportunity when it presented itself.

During the nineteenth century, America was unquestionably the land of opportunity—its riches were vast and its population small compared to Europe's. Economics set off a great migration that Emma Lazarus † and other romantics viewed from the perspective of the small minority fleeing religious or political persecution.‡ Many immigrants who had received idealized versions of conditions in America were shocked on their arrival. One woman wrote: "I had imagined America to be a beautiful country where aesthetic qualities are on a par with money. At once on my arrival I was bitterly disappointed when I reached this mining town. . . . As I contrasted conditions here with those in my native country I began to cry." [12] She related she would have returned to Scandinavia, but had no money. Nearly half the immigrants did, in fact, go back to their native lands.

To the educated middle class who were accultured to the city, the unschooled and poverty-shackled migrants from rural areas were barbarians. "These folk have grown up in a virtually uncivilized condition. They are uncouth, improvident, and addicted to drink. . . . Everything combines to drive the _____ to drink—his lighthearted temperament, akin to that of the Mediter-

* The most recent example was the $250 million loan to save Lockheed from bankruptcy.
† The composer of the verse on the Statue of Liberty.
‡ Sometimes, as with Polish Jews, more than one factor was involved. Even in the Polish migration, however, the overriding motive was economic—many of the immigrants went not to the United States but to the two other principal industrial nations, Germany and England. Hundreds of thousands of Irish emigrants settled in England—the land of their oppressors!

ranean people, his coarseness, which drags him down virtually to the level of a savage, his contempt for all normal human pleasures . . . combined with his dirty habits and abject poverty." Insert *Negro* into the blank space, and the writer would be an American segregationist. Insert *Slovak,* and the writer would be a Viennese at the time of World War I. Insert *Irishman,* and you would have the actual writer, Friedrich Engels, expressing the almost universal nineteenth-century English opinion.[13]

In Northern Ireland, with its limited resources, the enmity between the Protestant Scotch-Irish and the Catholic Irish continues to erupt in warfare. In an America of economic opportunities, the children of the migrants were educated in the schools and attained political power, and the grandchildren sometimes grew wealthy. By the third and fourth generations the Catholics were intermarrying with the Protestants. The Lowells were speaking not only to the Cabots, but to the Kennedys.

By the third generation the newcomers were becoming urbanized in their sexual habits and acquiring the inhibitions of the middle class. Since the beginning of time, copulation had been accepted as a natural function concomitant with puberty—girls were married at the age of twelve or thirteen and boys at fifteen or sixteen. But marriage and children were at odds with the need for continuing education. Middle-class parents conditioned their children to sexual abstinence under the guise of morality. As the years of schooling were extended, so was the period of continence.

Sexual abstinence generated tremendous stresses. The Chinese men who were trapped in America without Chinese women suppressed their sexual drive in opium dens. The Occidentals relaxed with alcohol and nicotine. The middle class developed neuroses and began to frequent psychiatrists to rediscover their suppressed sexuality. Pharmaceutical firms contrived generation after generation of tranquilizers. Alcohol, tobacco, and the overuse of drugs did incalculable harm. During the 1960's the young turned to something probably less dangerous: marijuana.

But pot was prohibited. The alcohol, tobacco, and pharmaceutical lobbies were among the most powerful in the country, but there was no giant marijuana lobby. The attempted prohibition of marijuana was as futile in the 1970's as the attempted prohibition of alcohol had been in the 1920's. It had the same effect of breeding an illegal industry, increasing crime, and stigmatizing pot-smoking citizens who were otherwise law-abiding.

In the central cities, the more recent arrivals have the same difficulty as their predecessors in reducing their procreation of children. The sexual freedom of the ghetto is more natural than the sophisticated suppression endured by the middle class before the widespread distribution of contraceptives, but in a modern economy the children who are the product of those sexual practices are handicapped from the moment they are conceived. In a typical year (1967) 3,577 girls below the age of eighteen gave birth in Detroit. Of the 1,644 births by black girls, 1,457 were illegitimate; of the 1,933 births by white girls, 972 were illegitimate. (One may presume that many of the white girls contracted postpregnancy marriages.) Half the girls received no prenatal care. Coming primarily from low-income families, only one third of whom have adequate diets, they do not eat enough protein or vitamins for the optimum development of the fetus and, especially, its brain. When the child is born, it is often subjected to neglect, further malnourishment, and an inferior environment. Remedial measures taken later probably cannot undo the damage inflicted during the first two or three years of a child's life. By providing just enough support for a child to survive, but not enough for him to develop to his full potential, we are creating a monstrous world of handicapped children.

For a girl, early pregnancy almost invariably means not only a suspension of education, but further pregnancies, and damnation to poverty. In Detroit, the most pronounced difference between the white (primarily middle-income) and the black (essentially low-income) birth rate is among girls fifteen to twenty-four. In this age group the blacks have 50 percent more babies than the whites. (Judge Lincoln has suggested the development of a contraceptive gin, but contraceptive lollypops may be more effective.) Ninety-two thousand children are growing up under conditions of abysmal poverty in Detroit. That their future is clouded is an ill omen for the nation. It is a continuing tragedy, in which the epilogue of one generation is but the prologue of the next.

XVI. THE SHAPE OF THE FUTURE

Because history has been neglected, each generation tends to perceive its experiences as unique manifestations. Since the eighteenth century each generation has believed itself faced with *unprecedented* "crime waves." Each generation finds education inadequate and assumes that in the past it must have been better. Popular history has been written largely by and about the upper and middle classes—the struggles of the majority of the population have been plowed under and forgotten. The "good old times" never existed—they were times of hunger and disease, of water pollution and street pollution, of ignorance and poverty, of isolated farms and overcrowded cities, of dying children and prematurely aged women and men.

An objective examination of history provides us with experience and precedent. History is a tool, and like all tools its effectiveness depends upon the skill of the craftsman using it. Too often the logic of history has been obscured because events have been regarded as unrelated incidents. The links have been overlooked, and the connections have not been examined. Because of a lack of appreciation and understanding, history has been approached as a dead record of the past, not a vital, continuing experience that acts as a guidepost to the future.

I have tried to demonstrate the continuity, unity, and logic of history. How and why has the American system succeeded, and where has it failed? The question remains: can the failures be rectified and a course charted for the future?

The framers of the Declaration of Independence postulated a society in which "all men are created equal," and declared that government is instituted to secure for men the "unalienable rights [of] life, liberty, and the pursuit of happiness." Obviously, they were referring to *free* men in a middle-class society—a society that did not then exist but was a goal to be achieved in the future.

America has come a long way toward that achievement. For those who are in some measure created "equal," America offers more opportunity than any previous society. The standard of living of all people has continuously improved—the life of a welfare family today would seem like an unrealizable dream to the immigrants of 1900. The American system brought into existence the world's first mass middle-class society.

But a system established on the presumption that everyone has the opportunity to compete on an equal basis fails if the conditions of that competition are not equalized. America has never come close to achieving the "self-evident truth" that all men are created equal.

We can no longer ignore the inequality with which the child of a poor family is shackled at birth. We should establish as a national priority a program to improve the environment for children of low-income families. This program must aggressively encourage teen-aged girls and young women to practice birth control. It must offer to a poor woman the same medical attention a rich woman can afford. It must conduct classes in child rearing and aim to limit family size. It must provide every child with an adequate diet. It must establish centers where a child can receive the attention and stimulation he often does not in a low-income home.

We need to reinforce and upgrade the educational system not only in the ghettos but the suburbs. In the ghetto the system is inadequate because educators have had neither the wisdom nor the resources to deal with children who lack entry-level requirements—the system is like a conveyor belt that fails to pick up those who do not measure up to predetermined qualifications. In the suburbs the system has similar difficulty coping with the laggards, and also fails to challenge children more sophisticated and advanced than the youth of former generations. Since it is a mass education system, it bases its operations on a great common denominator, and is troubled by children who fall outside either the upper or lower limits. (Thomas Edison would probably be considered as much a problem child today as he was in the 1850's.) Undoubtedly the system could be improved with more financial support. But much of the money will be wasted if the educational bureaucracy is not more receptive, more flexible, and more willing to consider children as individuals.

The establishment of a system of universal education was a concomitant of the transformation of America from a rural to an urban society. The shortcomings of urban living have brought about a transition during the last half century to a mixed urban-suburban society.* The formation of suburbia marked the implementation of population dispersion that urban reformers had sought since the nineteenth century.

From most standpoints, the moderate-sized suburban community of 25,000 to 100,000 people is to be preferred over the megalopolis. Government is less impersonal and more responsive, children have more freedom, shopping is easier, air and noise pollution are less.

Because of the inefficiency of the automobile as a commuting device, however, the suburbs have spotlighted the inadequacies of public transportation—inadequacies that have always existed. The automobile did not bring on the abandonment of public transportation; public transportation brought that on itself. The automobile substituted a convenient means of transportation for an inconvenient. Yet planners of public transportation have shown little imagination. Their proposals generally encompass new versions of old failures.

---

* As previously pointed out, *urban* and *suburban* are relative terms. Many newer areas within cities are suburban in character.

Public transportation will continue to be inefficient and unsatisfactory until we apply to it the insight Edison exercised one hundred years ago in the development of the electric light. Edison recognized that the key to the widespread application of electricity was the subdivision of light, or power. Similarly, we must recognize that the widespread acceptance of public transportation depends upon its subdivision and personalization. The automobile substituted a family-sized unit for the large, inflexible, and rigidly routed conveyances of public transportation. The problem to which we should apply ourselves is reducing the automobile to an individual-sized unit that can be integrated into a transportation system.

The criticism of suburbia has stimulated a trend toward reconcentration of population in the cities. In place of high-rise, high-density and low-income developments, high-rise, high-density and high-income projects are being erected. (In Detroit, Henry Ford recently proposed the construction of a half-billion-dollar Renaissance Center in the redevelopment area once known as The Potomac.) Renaissance projects, however, have the same effect as urban renewal in pushing the low-income population from the center of the city and creating new slums farther out. Whether in Detroit, Chicago, or New York, they are but one more example of problem-shuffling instead of problem-solving. The crisis in the nation's central cities has occurred because it is in the cities that the nation's problems have become concentrated. Since the problems, however, are *national,* we must solve them on a national basis and give them national priority and national financing. As long as we try to cope with myriad symptoms instead of attacking underlying causes we shall continue to have a high percentage of failures.

Whether in business, justice, or government we operate within adversary systems that are the natural outgrowth of laissez-faire. Theoretically, all parties are given an equal opportunity in the arena, and a determination on merit follows. In actuality, the party able to spend more is often able to present its case with greater force. Money is translated into "merit," and becomes the measure of value.

Judgment dependent on such measure is inimical to the effective operation of an adversary system and will eventually destroy it. If a firm can sell an inferior product to the public because it has the financial capability to outadvertise its competitor, or one candidate has twice the money to spend on a campaign as another, merit will not prevail.

Corporations and labor unions operating in an administered economy, and organizations like the American Medical Association can marshal immense resources to lobby for favorable legislation and prevent the passage of unfavorable. The power of industry and labor tend to cancel each other out. Industry and labor come to an accommodation, but often at the expense of the third, unorganized and unrepresented party, the public. When the UAW is able to obtain comprehensive health and dental coverage for its workers, the cost of that coverage is passed on by the manufacturers to the public. The public pays not only in the increased prices of the products, but in the higher fees charged by doctors and dentists. Individuals operating in the free economy cannot contend equally. The need to redress the balance and to equalize the resources available to the adversaries is critical.

In no field has the public welfare been more subordinated to private interests than in medicine. Until the late nineteenth century the rich and the poor had a certain equality—if the poor remained untreated, the treatment received by the rich was commonly so bad as to be worse than none. Then, as rapid advances were made, medicine divided into two main branches: public health and private practice.

In public health, where the criterion was the prevention of disease and not the attainment of profit, the achievements have been tremendous. In private medicine, patients have more and more been accepted or rejected on the basis of their ability to pay. The principle was developed that the workingman should be able to pay and that the poor should be treated as charity patients. It is a principle that ignores the increasing cost of medical treatment, and the occurrence of chronic and catastrophic illnesses. In many cases a man must bankrupt and degrade himself before he can obtain public treatment for himself or his family. The consequence may be the destruction of a family, and the creation of more social problems for the nation.

A healthy population clearly is a national asset. Yet in a nation whose standards of medicine are the highest in the world, we have not established adequate treatment for all as a national goal. In trying to meet some of the needs we have instead set up a hodgepodge of categorical programs. A sixty-five-year-old sick person is eligible for treatment, but a sixty-four-year-old is not.

We should scrap most of the existing programs and substitute one comprehensive national health plan that takes into account the ability to pay but does not penalize anyone for suffering serious illness. The Federal government should reimburse an individual for all medical expenses above a fixed percentage of his income. The program can be administered through the apparatus of the Internal Revenue Service. An individual would file for reimbursement with his income tax return.* Physicians would be relieved of administration, and much of the paper work that has contributed to increased costs could be eliminated.

If we dedicate ourselves to providing people with basic services and a more balanced distribution of income we shall need fewer corrective programs—programs that have contributed to the rapid expansion of governmental bureaucracies, increased administrative snarls, and the growing complexity of Federal-state-local relations. We would consider illogical the establishment of a separate program to combat each water-borne disease rather than the assuring of a safe water supply. Yet in large areas of human and economic welfare we are pursuing the irrational course of trying to correct damage rather than preventing it.

We have much to do to restructure taxes that burden some localities and many individuals more heavily than others, and have recently become more regressive. Regressive taxation has serious economic effects. It reduces the buying power of the lower income population and so cuts consumption. It diminishes the ability of this population to accumulate savings for down payments on major purchases. It reinforces recessions. If President Herbert Hoover could suggest that earned income be taxed at a lower rate than returns from investment, the idea cannot be too radical. Yet we have been moving in the opposite direction, taxing the wage earner ever harder while providing an intricate pattern of exemptions for the recipient of unearned income.

Perhaps the most important factor in economic inequality is the imposition

---

* When necessary, filing and reimbursement can take place on a quarterly basis.

of prices and policies by forces operating in the administered and organized economies. The record of large corporations, unions, and professional organizations reveals frequent shortsightedness and occasional sacrifice of national interests for private gain. Size can be beneficial—the public is better served by four American auto manufacturers today than by dozens a half century ago. General Motors and Du Pont have conducted research and marketed new products that several smaller firms operating individually might not have been able to. A firm that dominates an industry, however, takes on the nature of a utility. The decisions of its officers affect everyone in the nation, yet usually are directed toward the best interests of the firm. Increasingly, those interests are global, not national. The decisions and practices of these corporations should, therefore, be subjected to public influence and restrictions.*

As a consequence of the growth of the administered and organized economies we have been moving steadily into an era of neo-mercantilism. In place of the urban guild structure that controlled wages and prices, we have national unions exercising great power in the setting of wages. Instead of companies with monopolistic patents from kings, we have corporations whose immense power in the market place enables them to operate as semi-monopolies. Succeeding the royal government that attempted to maintain autocratic control over trade and commerce, we have a government that tries to manage the economy through the control of money and credit; a government that because of repeated breakdowns in this economic management is being pushed toward more direct controls—which have been employed by governments for hundreds of years and have seldom worked.

The unfortunate truth is that mankind has yet to produce an economic system that has operated satisfactorily for a protracted period in the modern world. Mercantilism failed. Laissez faire did not work. Socialism is no panacea. A dual economic system is inequitable. If we are to avoid being a nation in which the individual is ground between the giant wheels of industry, labor, and bureaucracy, we must therefore preserve and strengthen free and open competition.

But we must do so within a framework of national interests and national goals. At present our mechanism to define and set those goals is inadequate. Both the executive and the legislative branches are oriented toward operations, not long-range planning. Presidents serve a maximum of eight years, and there is seldom a smooth transition from one administration to the next. (Often, of course, a President has views and aims diametrically opposed to those of his predecessor.) A good deal of the first term is occupied with preparing a record for reelection. Programs become distorted because of the lack of research, uncertainty of direction, political influences, and pressures for quick implementation—the most graphic example is the antipoverty program and its offshoots. President Nixon follows President Johnson and is appalled by the chaos and waste of money. He decides to terminate, reshape, and rechannel many of the programs. But his solutions seem little better than the problems he is trying to cope with, and he runs afoul of Congress. Congress lacks research capacity of its own,

---

* The present operation of public regulatory bodies is unsatisfactory. They are sometimes dominated by industry members, and have inadequate staffs to probe thoroughly into accounting practices. The public itself lacks the resources to counter the impressive cases for rate increases usually prepared by industry.

and its members are even more embroiled in day-to-day activities than the President.

We need a quasi-official, nonpolitical national planning body.* This institution would study problems, make long-range projections, define national goals, and recommend solutions. It would have absolute independence, but its facilities and resources would be available to Congress and the President. Its power would rest on its prestige.

We cannot afford to continue dissipating American wealth—dissipation in terms of wasteful use of resources, of idle manpower, and of artificial restriction of useful production. If nine pairs of shoes are manufactured for every ten people, one person will have to go without. If one person out of ten is too sick to work because he cannot afford medical treatment, the other nine will have to support him. No more pernicious an economic scheme could be devised than to have one third of the population support the remaining two thirds. Yet that would be the ultimate effect of the widespread implementation of retirement after twenty-five years' service—the inflationary result would be against the interest of the pensioners themselves. In the organized and administered pursuit of self-interest, fundamental economics seem to have been forgotten. So long as the whole is not expanded, whatever gains one segment of the population makes will be at the expense of another. The surest way to increase the standard of living for everyone is to check inflation and increase production. The fruits of that production should be directed toward the people most in need and toward providing essential services for everybody.

The quality of the population, the efficiency of industry, and the extent of natural resources are a far better measure of national power than the size of the military establishment. One after another the world's major commercial and industrial nations have wasted their wealth in arms production and war. When Detroit was founded in 1701, France was the Western world's leading power. The royal government used that power to engage in war after war.† The privileged classes received tax exemptions, and money was extracted from the common people through regressive taxation. The economic base failed to expand, so trades were increasingly regulated; one job was sometimes shared by two persons. Crime and vice spread over the country, and became "organized." When additional stress was generated by the new English industrial efficiency, the French economy collapsed. Revolution followed.

The nineteenth century was the century of British power. Britain built the world's largest navy and remained unchallenged until the rapid industrialization of Germany after the Franco-Prussian War. As Germany's industrial establishment overtook Britain's, Germany built a navy to challenge England's and an army to challenge France's. Two internecine world wars, from which Britain never recovered, followed.

America has been engaged in major warfare for sixteen of the thirty-two years since 1941. The defense budget has risen from $46 billion in 1960 to $80 billion annually, and former Secretary of Defense Melvin Laird asserted that progress in disarmament talks with Russia reinforces the need to expand the arms budget—reasoning that carried to its ultimate conclusion would indi-

* Possible nuclei for such a body exist in the Brookings Institution and the National Planning Association.
† France was at war for thirty-seven of the eighty-eight years between 1701 and 1789.

cate that absolute peace requires total preparation for war. While the United States has been fighting, the next three largest industrial nations—Russia, Germany, and Japan—have been at peace.

National security is a necessity. But redundant and wasteful spending for defense drains the economic lifeblood of a country. America is no longer the world's lone economic superpower. A leavening process is at work among the industrial nations. Much of the future depends on whether we regard the upsurge of other nations as a threat or a challenge. If we react to it as a threat and try to isolate ourselves, the consequences may be disastrous. If we accept it as a challenge and redirect our energies toward strengthening our population, safeguarding and restoring our natural resources, and expanding agricultural and industrial production, only good can result.

We have come to the end of an era. The need to restructure American policies to fit the new realities is critical. The American future will be shaped by our willingness to correct the errors of the past, to draw upon the experience of history, and to revive the Revolutionary conviction that this should be a land that offers not privileges to some, but equal opportunity and hope to all.

Appendix

Crime in Detroit

YEAR	MAJOR ECONOMIC CRIMES	MURDERS
1929	5,024	158
1930	5,625	114
1931	5,279	107
1932	6,746	96
1933	6,827	78
1934	5,672	60
1935	4,827	60
1936	5,152	66
1937	6,309	74
1938	7,275	55
1939	7,044	60
1940	9,004	66
1941	10,168	57
1942	8,925	48
1943	10,294	79
1944	10,617	73
1945	12,534	71
1946	13,893	85
1947	13,844	86
1948	13,969	89
1949	15,361	91
1950	14,815	97
1951	15,337	105
1952	14,068	86
1953	15,387	103
1954	17,937	95
1955	15,393	121
1956	16,955	89
1957	17,997	103
1958	21,157	91
1959	21,286	98
1960	25,288	119
1961	23,061	108
1962	26,417	112
1963	27,295	103
1964	26,747	104
1965	31,374	148
1966	50,676	175
1967	65,081	220
1968	69,366	303
1969	80,914	354
1970	100,571	412
1971	97,620	508

(Source: *Detroit Police Department Annual Reports.*)

Bibliography

CITIES—GENERAL

Advisory Commission on Intergovernmental Relations. *Urban and Rural America: Policies for Future Growth.* Washington, D.C., 1968.

AFL-CIO. *The Urban Crisis: an analysis, an answer.* Washington, D.C., 1967.

Break, George F. *Intergovernmental Fiscal Relations in the United States.* Washington, D.C., 1965.

Census Bureau: Commerce Department. *Census of Governments: Local Governments in Metropolitan Areas.* Washington, D.C., 1967.

———. *Characteristics of the Population,* Vol. 1. Washington, D.C., 1971.

———. *Governmental Finances in 1963–64.* Washington, D.C., 1965.

———. *U. S. Census of Business.* Washington, D.C., 1967.

Cleveland *Plain Dealer. Eleven Urban Mayors and Their Problems* (reprint). January 26, 29; February 2, 5, 9, 12, 16, 20, 23, 26; March 2, 1969.

Government Operations Committee, Subcommittee on Government Research, U. S. Senate. *The Rural to Urban Population Shift.* Washington, D.C., 1968.

Maxwell, James A. *Financing State and Local Governments.* Washington, D.C., 1965.

Mumford, Lewis. *The City in History.* New York, 1961.

Musgrave, Richard A. (ed.). *Essays in Fiscal Federalism.* Washington, D.C., 1965.

National Commission on Urban Problems. *Impact of the Property Tax.* Washington, D.C., 1968.

———. *Report of.* Washington, D.C., 1968.

National League of Cities and U. S. Conference of Mayors. *America's Urban Challenge: A Required National Response.* Washington, D.C., 1968.

Netzer, Dick. *Economics of the Property Tax.* Washington, D.C., 1965.

President's Committee on Urban Housing, *Report of.* Washington, D.C., 1968.

Riis, Jacob A. *The Battle with the Slum.* New York, 1902.

———. *How the Other Half Lives.* New York, 1890.

Schlesinger, Arthur M. *The Rise of the City.* New York, 1933.
Starrett, W. A. *Skyscrapers.* New York, 1928.
Sternlieb, George. *The Tenement Landlord.* New Brunswick, N. J., 1966.
Thompson, Wilbur R. *A Preface to Urban Economics.* Baltimore, 1965.
U. S. Conference of Mayors. *City Problems, the Annual Proceedings of the U. S. Conference of Mayors.* Washington, D.C., 1952–1970.

CIVIL DISORDERS

Anonymous. *A Thrilling Narrative of the Late Detroit Riot.* Detroit, 1863, and Hattiesburg, Miss., 1945.
Congressional Quarterly Service. *Urban Problems and Civil Disorders.* Washington, D. C., 1967.
Government Operations Committee, Subcommittee on Investigations, U. S. Senate. *Riots, Civil and Criminal Disorders* (Parts 5, 6 and 7). Washington, D.C., 1968.
Grimshaw, Allen. "Actions of Police and the Military in American Race Riots." *Phylon.* Fall, 1963.
———. "Changing Patterns of Racial Violence in the United States. *Notre Dame Lawyer.* Vol. XV, No. 5, 1965.
———. "Lawlessness and Violence in America." *The Journal of Negro History,* Vol. XLIV, No. 1, 1959.
Judiciary Committee, U. S. Senate. *Hearings, Anti-Riot Bill.* Washington, D.C., 1967.
Katz, William L. (ed.) *Anti-Negro Riots in the North, 1863.* New York, 1969.
Lee, Alfred M. and Humphrey, Norman D. *Race Riot Detroit, 1943.* New York, 1968.
Library of Congress Legislative Reference Service. *Civil Disorder.* Washington, D.C., 1967.
Lincoln, James H. *The Anatomy of a Riot.* New York, 1968.
Lowinger, Paul and Huige, Frida. *The National Guard in the 1967 Detroit Uprising* (Mimeographed). Detroit, 1968.
National Advisory Commission on Civil Disorders, *Report of.* Washington, D.C., 1968.
Shogan, Robert and Craig, Tom. *The Detroit Race Riot.* Philadelphia and New York, 1964.
U. S. Conference of Mayors, Community Relations Service. *Community Planning and Civil Disturbances.* Washington, D.C., 1967.

ECONOMICS AND INDUSTRY

AFL-CIO Department of Research. *Labor Looks at Automation.* Washington, D.C., 1966.
Bober, M. M. *Karl Marx's Interpretation of History.* Cambridge, Mass., 1950.
Bogart, Ernest L. *Economic History of Europe.* London, Toronto, New York, 1942.
Burlingame, Roger. *Backgrounds of Power.* New York and London, 1949.
Cabinet Committee on Price Stability. *Studies by the Staff.* Washington, D.C., 1969.
Clough, Shepard B. and Cole, Charles W. *Economic History of Europe.* Boston, 1952.

Colm, Gerhard and Gulick, Luther. *Program Planning and National Goals.* Washington, D.C., 1968.

Commerce Department. *The National Income and Product Accounts of the United States, 1929–1965.* Washington, D.C., 1966.

Evans, Trevor and Stewart, Margaret. *Pathway to Tomorrow, the Impact of Automation on People.* Oxford, 1967.

Friedman, Milton and Schwartz, Anna J. *A Monetary History of the United States, 1867–1960.* Princeton, N. J., 1963.

George, Henry Jr. *Progress and Poverty.* New York, undated.

Giedion, Siegfried. *Mechanization Takes Command.* New York, 1948.

Joint Economic Committee, Congress of the United States. *Inflation and the Price Indexes.* Washington, D.C., 1966.

Keynes, John Maynard. *General Theory of Employment, Interest, and Money.* New York, 1936.

Labor Department, Bureau of Labor Statistics. *Handbook of Labor Statistics.* Washington, D.C., 1968.

―――. Manpower Administration. *Area Trends in Employment and Unemployment.* Washington, D.C., 1967–1970.

Lecht, Leonard A. *The Dollar Cost of Our National Goals.* Washington, D.C., 1965.

―――. *Goals, Priorities, and Dollars.* New York, 1966.

Leven, Maurice; Moulton, Harold G.; and Warburton, Clark. *America's Capacity to Consume.* Washington, D.C., 1934.

Lynch, David. *The Concentration of Economic Power.* New York, 1946.

Moulton, Harold G. *Income and Economic Progress.* Washington, D.C., 1935.

National Commission on Technology, Automation, and Economic Progress. *Technology and the American Economy.* Washington, D.C., 1966.

National Planning Association, Center for Economic Projections. *Critical Geographic Dimensions of Employment and Economic Development.* Washington, D.C., 1968.

Peach, W. Nelson and Krause, Walter. *Basic Data of the American Economy.* Chicago, 1950.

Rayback, Joseph G. *A History of American Labor.* New York, 1959.

Smith, Adam. *The Wealth of Nations.* New York, 1937.

Taylor, Frederick W. *The Principles of Scientific Management.* New York and London, 1942.

Wright, Chester W. *Economic History of the United States.* New York, 1949.

EDUCATION

Dewey, John. *The School and Society.* Chicago, 1900.

Dworkin, Martin S. *Dewey on Education.* New York, 1959.

Education and Labor Committee, U. S. House of Representatives. *Compendium of Federal Education Laws.* Washington, D.C., 1967.

―――. *Federal Educational Policies, Programs, and Proposals* (3 parts). Washington, D.C., 1968.

―――. *Hearings, Elementary and Secondary Education Amendments of 1967.* Washington, D.C., 1967.

―――. *Hearings, Preschool Centers Supplementary Education Act.* Washington, D.C., 1968.

————. *Study of the United States Office of Education.* Washington, D.C., 1967.

Health, Education, and Welfare Department. *Equality of Educational Opportunity.* Washington, D.C., 1966.

Health, Education, and Welfare Department: Office of Education. *Digest of Educational Statistics.* Washington, D.C., 1968.

Keyserling, Leon H. "Achieving Nationwide Educational Excellence, a Ten-Year Plan to Save the Schools." *Changing Education,* Summer–Fall, 1968.

Mosbaek, E. J., *et al. Analyses of Compensatory Education in Five School Districts.* Office of Education, Washington, D.C., 1968.

National Education Association. *School Dropouts.* Washington, D.C., 1967.

Quattlebaum, Charles A. *Federal Educational Policies, Programs, and Proposals.* The Legislative Reference Service of the Library of Congress, Washington, D.C., 1968.

U. S. Commission on Civil Rights. *Racial Isolation in the Public Schools.* Washington, D.C., 1967.

GENERAL

Aaron, Daniel (ed.). *America in Crisis.* New York, 1952.

Bemis, Samuel F. *A Diplomatic History of the United States.* New York, 1950.

Brown, Sterling. *The Negro in Washington.* New York, 1969.

Carmichael, Stokely and Hamilton, Charles V. *Black Power.* New York, 1967.

Census Bureau: Commerce Department. *Current Population Reports: 24 Million Americans, Poverty in the United States, 1969.* Washington, D.C., 1970.

————. *Historical Statistics of the United States, Colonial Times to 1957.* Washington, D.C., 1960.

————. *Income Growth Rates in 1939 to 1968 for Persons by Occupation and Industry Groups.* Washington, D.C., 1970.

————. *Negroes in the United States, 1920–1932.* Washington, D.C., 1935.

————. *Social and Economic Conditions of Negroes in the United States.* Washington, D.C., 1968.

————. *Statistical Abstract of the United States.* Washington, D.C., 1962, 1967, 1972.

De Tocqueville, Alexis. *Democracy in America.* New York, 1966.

Dickinson, H. W. *Robert Fulton.* New York and London, 1913.

Haas, Ben. *KKK.* Evanston, Ill., 1963.

Handlin, Oscar. *Race and Nationality in American Life.* Garden City, N. Y., 1957.

Hughes, Langston. *Fight for Freedom, the Story of the NAACP.* New York, 1962.

Hulbert, Archer B. *Great American Canals.* Cleveland, 1904.

Josephson, Matthew. *Edison.* New York, 1959.

Key, V. O. Jr., *Southern Politics.* New York, 1949.

Moos, Malcolm. *The Republicans.* New York, 1956.

Munitions Industry Special Investigation Committee, U. S. Senate, *Report of.* Washington, D.C., 1936.

Myers, William Starr. *The Republican Party.* New York, 1928.

Myrdal, Gunnar; with Richard Sterner and Arnold Rose. *An American Dilemma.* New York and Evanston, 1962.

National Commission on Law Observance and Enforcement. *Official Records* (5 volumes). Washington, D.C., 1931.

Schlesinger, Arthur M. Jr. *The Coming of the New Deal.* Boston, 1958.

——. *The Crisis of the Old Order.* Boston, 1957.

——. *The Politics of Upheaval.* Boston, 1960.

Sherwood, Robert E. *Roosevelt and Hopkins.* New York, 1948.

Smith, Gene. *The Shattered Dream.* New York, 1970.

Sorensen, Theodore C. *Kennedy.* New York, 1966.

Un-American Activities Committee, U.S. House of Representatives. *Investigation of Un-American Propaganda Activities in the United States,* Vol. 6. Washington, D.C., 1939.

——. *The Present-Day Ku Klux Klan Movement.* Washington, D.C., 1967.

Westcott, Thompson. *The Life of John Fitch.* Philadelphia, 1857.

Wood, Forrest G. *Black Scare.* Berkeley and Los Angeles, 1968.

IMMIGRANTS AND THE BACKGROUND OF IMMIGRATION

Barker, T. C. and Harris, J. R. *A Merseyside Town in the Industrial Revolution, St. Helens 1750–1900.* London, 1959.

Bennett, George. *The History of Bandon.* Cork, 1869.

Benson, Adolph and Hedin, Naboth. *Americans from Sweden.* Philadelphia and New York, 1950.

Cassell's *History of England,* Vols. II, III, IV. London and New York, undated.

Cusack, M. F. *History of the City and County of Cork.* Cork, 1875.

Eden, Sir Frederick Morton. *The State of the Poor.* London, 1928.

Engels, Friedrich. *The Condition of the Working Class in England, 1844.* Oxford, 1958.

Goldenweiser, E. A. "Immigrants in Cities." *The Survey,* Vol. XXV, p. 598, October, 1910–March, 1911.

Gwynn, Stephen. *The History of Ireland.* New York, 1923.

Immigration Commission, *Reports of* (42 volumes). Washington, D.C., 1911.

——. *Conclusions and Recommendations,* Vols. 1 and 2.

——. *Emigration Conditions in Europe,* Vol. 4.

——. *Immigrants in Industries (Mining),* Vol. 16.

——. *Immigrants in Industries,* Vol. 18, Part 22.

——. *Immigrants in Cities,* Vol. 26.

——. *The Children of Immigrants in Schools,* Vol. 31.

——. *Immigration and Crime,* Vol. 36.

——. *Steerage Conditions, Importation and Harboring of Women for Immoral Purposes, Immigrant Home and Aid Societies, Immigrant Banks,* Vol. 37.

Janson, Florence B. *The Background of Swedish Immigration.* Chicago, 1931.

Lauck, W. Jett. "Industrial Communities." *The Survey,* Vol. XXV, October, 1910–March, 1911.

Leifchild, J. R. *Cornwall: Its Mines and Miners.* New York, 1968.

Lloyd, L. *Peasant Life in Sweden.* London, 1870.

Malthus, T. R. *An Essay on Population.* London and New York, 1914.

Nelson, Helge. *The Swedes and the Swedish Settlements in North America.* New York, 1943.

Roth, Cecil. *A Short History of the Jewish People.* London, 1953.

Rowe, John. *Cornwall in the Age of the Industrial Revolution.* Liverpool, 1953.

Sachar, Abram Leon. *A History of the Jews.* New York, 1967.

Stephenson, George M. *A History of American Immigration.* Boston and New York, 1926.

Willis, H. Parker. "The Findings of the Immigration Commission." *The Survey,* Vol. XXV, p. 571, October, 1910–March, 1911.

MICHIGAN HISTORY

Beck, William. "Law and Order During the 1913 Copper Strike." *Michigan History Magazine,* Vol. 54, pp. 275–292, 1970.

Brunson, Catherine C. "Sketch of Pioneer Life Among the Indians." *Michigan Pioneer and Historical Collections,* Vol. 28, pp. 161–163, 1897.

Caldwell, Helen Nichols. "Indian Reminiscences." *Michigan Pioneer and Historical Collections,* Vol. 21, pp. 297–316, 1892.

Christian, E. P. "Historical Associations Connected with Wyandotte and Vicinity." *Michigan Pioneer and Historical Collections,* Vol. 13, pp. 308–324, 1888.

Dunbar, William F. *Michigan: A History of the Wolverine State.* Grand Rapids, Mich., 1965.

Felch, Alpheus. "The Indians of Michigan and the Cession of Their Lands to the United States by Treaty." *Michigan Pioneer and Historical Collections,* Vol. 26, p. 274–297, 1894.

Forster, John H. "Life in the Copper Mines of Lake Superior." *Michigan Pioneer and Historical Collections,* Vol. 11, pp. 175–186, 1887.

Gates, William B. Jr. *Michigan Copper and Boston Dollars.* Cambridge, Mass., 1951.

Gordon, John M. with an Introduction by Douglas H. Gordon and George S. May. "The Michigan Land Rush in 1836." *Michigan History Magazine,* Vol. 43, pp. 1–42, 129–149, 257–293, 433–478, 1959.

Hyma, Dr. Albert. *Albertus C. Van Raalte.* Grand Rapids, Mich., 1947.

Leach, Carl A. "Deward, A Lumberman's Ghost Town." *Michigan History Magazine,* Vol. 28, pp. 5–19, 1944.

Lewis, Ferris E. "Frederic, A Logging Village in the Twilight of the Lumbering Era." *Michigan History Magazine,* Vol. 34, pp. 35–49, 1950.

Martin, John B. *Call It North Country.* New York, 1944.

Maybee, Rolland H. "Michigan's White Pine Era." *Michigan History Magaizne,* Vol. 43, pp. 385–432, 1959.

Niemi, Clemens. *Americanization of the Finnish People in Houghton County, Michigan.* Duluth, Minn., 1921.

Osband, Melvin D. "The Pioneer and His Work." *Michigan Pioneer and Historical Collections,* Vol. 29, pp. 709–717, 1900.

Pieters, Aleida J. *A Dutch Settlement in Michigan.* Grand Rapids, Mich. 1923.

Rowse, A. L. *The Cousin Jacks: The Cornish in America.* New York, 1969.

Sarasohn, Stephen B. and Vera H. *Political Party Patterns in Michigan.* Detroit, 1957.

Smith, Samuel L. "Pre-Historic and Modern Copper Mines of Lake Superior." *Michigan Pioneer and History Collections,* Vol. 39, pp. 137–151, 1915.

Sullivan, William A. "Copper Miners' Revolt." *Michigan History Magazine,* Vol. 43, pp. 294–319, 1959.

Todd, Arthur Cecil. *The Cornish Miner in America.* Truro, Cornwall; and Glendale, Calif., 1967.

Van Buren, A. D. P. " 'Raisings' and 'Bees' Among the Early Settlers." *Michigan Pioneer and Historical Collections,* Vol. 5, pp. 296–300, 1882.

————. "What the Pioneers Ate and How They Fared: Michigan and Cookery in the Early Days." *Michigan Pioneer and Historical Collections,* Vol. 5, pp. 293–296, 1882.

Waite, Minnie B. "Indian and Pioneer Life." *Michigan Pioneer and Historical Collections,* Vol. 38, pp. 318–321. 1912.

Webber, William. "Discovery and Development of the Salt Interest in the Saginaw Valley." *Michigan Pioneer and Historical Collections,* Vol. 4, p. 13, 1881.

Woodford, Frank B. *Alex J. Groesbeck.* Detroit, 1962.

DETROIT: AUTOMOBILE INDUSTRY

Automobile Manufacturers Association. *Automobile Facts and Figures.* Detroit, 1940 through 1972.

Beasley, Norman. *Knudsen.* New York, 1947.

Beasley, Norman and Stark, George W. *Made in Detroit.* New York, 1957.

Borth, Christy. *Masters of Mass Production.* Indianapolis and New York, 1945.

Chrysler, Walter P. with Boyden Sparks. *Life of an American Workman.* New York, 1937.

Cook, Fred J. *Walter Reuther.* Chicago, New York, London, 1963.

Drucker, Peter F. *The Concept of the Corporation.* Boston, 1960.

Federal Trade Commission. *Report on the Motor Vehicle Industry.* Washington, D.C., 1939.

Holliday, Barbara. "Harley J. Earl, the Original Car Stylist." *Detroit Magazine,* May 25, 1969.

Howe, Irving and Widick, B. J. *The UAW and Walter Reuther.* New York, 1949.

Judiciary Committee, Subcommittee on Antitrust and Monopoly, U. S. Senate. *Administered Prices: Automobiles.* Washington, D. C., 1958.

Karman, Thomas F. "The Flint Sit-Down Strike." *Michigan History Magazine,* Vol. 46, pp. 97–125 and 223–250, 1962.

King, Charles B. *Psychic Reminiscences* (privately published). Larchmont, N. Y., 1935.

Labatut, Jean and Lane, Wheaton J. (eds.). *Highways in Our National Life.* Princeton, N. J., 1950.

Leland, Mrs. Wilfred C. with Minnie D. Millbrook. *Master of Precision: Henry M. Leland.* Detroit, 1966.

Parker, John. *A History of the Packard Motor Car Company from 1899 to 1929* (Wayne State University's master's thesis). Detroit, 1949.

Pound, Arthur. *The Turning Wheel.* Garden City, N. Y., 1934.

Rae, John B. *The American Automobile.* Chicago, 1965.

————. *American Automobile Manufacturers.* Philadelphia and New York, 1959.

Reuther, Walter P. *Price Policy and Public Responsibility.* Detroit, 1958.

Rolt, L. T. C. *A Picture History of Motoring.* New York, 1956.

Sheppard, Harold L.; Louis A. Ferman and Seymour Faber. *Too Old to Work, Too Young to Retire.* Washington, D. C., 1959.

Sloan, Alfred P. Jr. with John McDonald. *My Years with General Motors.* Garden City, N. Y., 1964.

Walker, Charles R. and Guest, Robert H. *The Man on the Assembly Line.* Cambridge, Mass., 1952.

DETROIT: CAVANAGH ADMINISTRATION

Citizens Research Council of Michigan. *Urban Renewal in the City of Detroit— A Study of Administrative Organization.* Detroit, 1965.

Community Renewal Program. *Detroit: the New City.* Detroit, 1966.

———. *Detroit Study Design.* 1968.

———. *Economic Projections* (Mimeo). 1964.

———. *Population Estimates* (Mimeo). 1966.

———. *Population and Housing Study* (Mimeo). 1965.

———. *Proposal for Progress: Detroit's Application for a City Demonstration Planning Grant* (Mimeo). 1967.

———. *School Credits for Urban Renewal* (Mimeo). 1965.

———. *Second Memorandum to the Task Force: the Housing and Urban Development Act of 1965* (Mimeo). 1965.

———. *Social Renewal Progress Report* (Mimeo). 1966.

Detroit, City of. *Active Community Team* (CADY). 1962.

———. *Appearance Before the National Advisory Commission on Civil Disorders.* 1967.

Greenleigh Associates. *Home Interview Study of Low-Income Households in Detroit, Michigan.* New York and Chicago, 1965.

———. *Study of Services to Deal with Poverty in Detroit, Michigan.* New York and Chicago, 1968.

———. *A Study of United Community Services of Metropolitan Detroit.* New York and Chicago, 1968.

Llewelyn-Davies Weeks Forestier-Walker and Bor. *Elmwood's People Rebuild.* London, 1968.

Mayor's Committee for Human Resources Development. *Management Information System Narrative Report* (Mimeo). Detroit, July–September, 1968.

———. *Medical Aspects of Unemployment in Detroit* (Mimeo). 1968.

———. *Neighborhood Service Program Organizational Chart* (Mimeo). 1968.

———. *Neighborhood Service Program's Core Services Monthly Report* (Mimeo). 1968–1970.

———. *Response to the Interim Documentation Report of the Committee* [of the Michigan Legislature] *on Total Action Against Poverty* (Mimeo). 1968.

———. *Target Area 1 Monthly Report* (Mimeo). 1968–1969.

Mayor's Development Team. *Report to Mayor Jerome P. Cavanagh* (Mimeo). Detroit. 1967.

Mayor's Task Force Committee. *Detroit: the Demonstration City* (Mimeo). 1965.

Metropolitan Detroit Citizens Development Authority. *Outline of the Proposal for Upgrading Incomes of Elmwood 2 and Belle Isle Residents* (Mimeo). Detroit, 1968.

———. *Summary of OSTI Report on Social Planning and Programming for Elmwood 2* (Mimeo). Detroit, 1968.

————. *Text of Presentation by Edward J. Robinson, Executive Director, Before the New Detroit Committee* (Mimeo). August 8, 1968.

Model City Program. *Committee Report—Model Neighborhood Conference* (Mimeo). Detroit, September 18–20, 1968.

Special Committee to Investigate Irregularities in the Total Action Against Poverty Program in the City of Detroit, Michigan Legislature. *Examination of the War on Poverty*. Lansing, 1968.

Total Attack Against Poverty. *Memorandum on Poverty Program in Detroit* (Mimeo). Detroit, May 6, 1964.

Willcox, David and Jacobson, Sol. *Model Cities Program in Detroit*. Ann Arbor, 1970.

DETROIT: FORD

Anonymous. *Notes on Henry Ford and Thomas Maybury* (typewritten manuscript). Burton Historical Collection, Detroit Public Library.

Bennett, Harry with Paul Marcus. *We Never Called Him Henry*. New York, 1951.

Clancy, Louise and Davis, Florence. *The Believer, the Life Story of Mrs. Henry Ford*. New York, 1960.

Ford Foundation. *Annual Report*. New York, 1969.

————. *Ford Foundation in the 1960's: Statement of the Board of Trustees on Policies, Programs, and Operations*. New York, 1962.

————. *Report of the Study for the Ford Foundation on Policy and Program*. Detroit, Mich., 1949.

————. *The Society of the Streets*. New York, 1962.

Ford, Henry with Samuel Crowther. *My Life and Work*. Garden City, N. Y., 1922.

Ford Motor Company. *Helpful Hints and Advice to Employees*. Detroit, 1915.

Greenleaf, William. *From These Beginnings*. Detroit, 1964.

Herndon, Booton. *Ford*. New York, 1969.

Hershey, Burnet. *The Odyssey of Henry Ford and the Great Peace Ship*. New York, 1967.

Liebold, E. G. *Reminiscences* (typewritten manuscript). Ford Archives, Dearborn, Mich.

Lochner, Louis P. *Henry Ford, America's Don Quixote*. New York, 1925.

Macdonald, Dwight, *The Ford Foundation*. New York, 1956.

Marquis, Samuel S. *Henry Ford*. Boston, 1923.

Nevins, Alan and Hill, Frank E. *Ford: Decline and Rebirth*. New York, 1957.

————. *Ford: Expansion and Challenge*. New York, 1963.

————. *Ford: the Times, the Man, the Company*. New York, 1954.

Pipp, Edwin. "The Real Henry Ford." *Pipp's Weekly*. Detroit, 1932.

Quaife, M. M. *The Henry Ford Family* (typewritten manuscript). Burton Historical Collection, Detroit Public Library.

Raushenbush, Carl. *Fordism*. New York, 1937.

Ruddiman, Margaret Ford. "Memories of My Brother Henry Ford." *Michigan History Magazine*, Vol. 37, pp. 225–275, September, 1958.

Sorensen, Charles E. *My Forty Years with Ford*. New York, 1956.

Sward, Keith. *The Legend of Henry Ford*. New York and Toronto, 1948.

DETROIT: GENERAL

Census Bureau, Commerce Department. *Detailed Housing Characteristics, Michigan.* 1960 and 1970.
―――. *Detroit, Michigan Census Tracts.* 1972.
―――. *Employment Profiles of Selected Low-Income Areas, Detroit, Michigan.* 1970.
―――. *General Population Characteristics, Michigan.* 1960 and 1970.
―――. *General Social and Economic Characteristics, Michigan.* 1960 and 1970.
Detroit City Plan Commission. *Economic Base of Detroit.* 1944.
Detroit Metropolitan Area Regional Planning Commission. *Center of Population, Detroit Metropolitan Area and City of Detroit, 1930–1960* (Mimeo). 1961.
Detroit Regional Transportation and Land Use Study. *Living Patterns and Attitudes in the Detroit Region.* Detroit, 1967.
―――. *Profile of Southeastern Michigan.* Detroit, 1968.
―――. *Talus and Tomorrow.* Detroit, 1968.
Gregory, Karl D. *Detroit: Crisis in the Central City.* Fiscal Issues in the Future of Federalism. New York, 1968.
Labor Department, Manpower Administration. *Area Trends in Employment and Unemployment, Detroit.* Washington, D.C., August, 1972.
Lafayette Clinic. *12-Year Report.* Detroit, 1968.
Leggett, John C. *Class, Race, and Labor.* New York, 1968.
Michigan Department of Social Services. *Fourteenth Biennial Report.* Lansing, 1966.
Michigan Emergency Welfare Relief Commission. *Emergency Relief in Michigan, 1933–39.* Lansing, 1939.
Mowitz, Robert J. and Wright, Deil S. *Profile of a Metropolis.* Detroit, 1962.
PRESCAD Citizens Committee, *Minority Report of* (Mimeo). Detroit, 1968.
―――. *Report of* (Mimeo). Detroit, 1968.
Rankin, Louis. "Detroit Nationality Groups." *Michigan History Magazine,* Vol. 23, June, 1939.
Wayne County Board of Auditors. *Audit Report of Project PRESCAD.* Detroit, 1968.
―――. *Views in Regard to the Wayne County Child Development Center.* Detroit, 1968.
Wayne County Child Development Center. *Study of Objectives and Programs, 1926–1968* (Mimeo). Detroit, 1968.
Wayne County Child Development Center Citizens Review Committee, *Report and Recommendations of.* Detroit, 1968.
Wayne County Professional Committee. *In Behalf of the Children at the Wayne County Training School* (Mimeo). Detroit, 1967.

DETROIT: GOVERNMENT

Detroit, City of. *Annual Financial Report for 1970.* Detroit, 1971.
―――. *Budget, 1968–1969.*
―――. Budget History, 1929–1969 (prepared by the Director of the Budget for the author).

Detroit City Plan Commission. *Citizen Participation in the Planning Process* (Mimeo).

————. *Commercial Renewal*. Detroit, 1958.

————. *Long and Short Range Goals* (Mimeo). Detroit, 1967.

————. *Official Master Plan*. Detroit, 1951.

————. *Population Capacity*. Detroit, 1954.

————. *Population Change by Census Tracts, City of Detroit, 1930–1960* (Mimeo). Detroit, 1963.

————. *Renewal and Revenue*. Detroit, 1962.

————. *Residential Densities Table by 1960 Census Tracts, City of Detroit* (Mimeo). 1966.

————. *Summary of Major Comments and Recommendations, Analysis of Mayor's Development Team Report* (Mimeo). Detroit, 1967.

Detroit Civil Service Commission. *Organization Charts of the City of Detroit*. 1968.

Detroit Department of Health. *Air Pollution Control Division Progress Report*. 1967.

————. *Annual Report, Public Health and Hospitals*. 1965.

————. *Data Book*. 1967.

————. *Status of Detroit General Hospital* (Mimeo). 1967.

Detroit Housing Commission. *Forest Park Rehabilitation Project Number 2, Survey and Planning Application*. 1965.

————. *Gratiot Redevelopment Project: Final Project Report*. 1964.

————. *The History, Organization, and Function of the Detroit Housing Commission* (Mimeo).

————. *Letter, Re: the Possible Inclusion of Forest Park II in the 1969 Neighborhood Development Program*. February 19, 1969.

————. *Memorandum of Understanding, Forest Park Number 2 Citizens Planning Group*. August 14, 1968.

————. *Summary of Detroit's Urban Renewal Program* (Mimeo).

————. *Tour of Detroit's Urban Renewal Projects*.

————. *Urban Renewal and Tax Revenue*.

Eyre, Virginia L. *Tax Delinquency in the Second Ward of Detroit*. Detroit Bureau of Government Research Report Number 139. 1935.

Jenkins, Bette Smith. *The Racial Policies of the Detroit Housing Commission and Their Administration* (Wayne State University master's thesis). Detroit, 1950.

Ketcham, Dorothy. *A Manual of the Government of Detroit*. Detroit Bureau of Government Research Report Number 163. 1943.

Leonard, J. M. and Mohaupt, Rosina. *Cost of Living Salary Plans for Municipal Employees*. Detroit Bureau of Government Research Report Number 162. 1942.

————. *Exemption of Homesteads for Taxation*. Detroit Bureau of Government Research Report Number 144. 1937.

————. *Redistricting Detroit for Representation in the State Legislature*. Detroit Bureau of Government Research Report Number 156. 1941.

Upson, Lent D. *Growth of a City Government*. Detroit Bureau of Government Research Report Number 164. 1942.

Wengert, Egbert S. *Financial Problems of the City of Detroit in the Depression*. Detroit Bureau of Government Research Report Number 151. 1939.

DETROIT: HISTORY

Bald, F. Clever. *The Great Fire of 1805.* Detroit, 1951.

Bancroft, William. "Memoir of Captain Samuel Ward." *Michigan Pioneer and Historical Collections,* Vol. 21, pp. 336–351, 1892.

Banking and Currency Committee, U. S. Senate. *Hearings, Practices of Stock Exchanges: Banking Operations and Practices.* Washington, D.C., 1934.

Barnard, Harry. *Independent Man, the Life of Senator James Couzens.* New York, 1958.

Bingay, Malcolm W. *Detroit Is My Own Home Town.* Indianapolis and New York, 1940.

Burton, Clarence. *The City of Detroit, Michigan 1701–1922.* Detroit, 1922.

Burton, C. M. "Detroit in the Year 1832." *Michigan Pioneer and Historical Collections,* Vol. 28, pp. 163–171, 1897.

Catlin, George B. *The Story of Detroit.* Detroit, 1926.

Dain, Floyd R. *Detroit and the Westward Movement.* Detroit, 1951.

Detroit *Post and Tribune. Life of Zachariah Chandler.* Detroit, 1880.

Farmer, Silas. *The History of Detroit and Michigan* (2 volumes). Detroit, 1889.

Ferman, Louis A. *Death of a Newspaper: the Story of the Detroit Times.* Kalamazoo, 1963.

Ford, Henry A. "Detroit in 1838." *Michigan Pioneer and Historical Collections,* Vol. 10, pp. 97–104, 1886.

Franks, Carl D. "Marker to First Mile of Concrete Road." *Michigan History Magazine,* Vol. 43, p. 109, 1959.

Garrity, Leona. *The Story of the Poor Commission of Detroit, 1880–1918* (Wayne State University master's thesis). Detroit, 1940.

Girardin, J. A. "Life and Times of Father Gabriel Richard." *Michigan Pioneer and Historical Collections,* Vol. 1, pp. 481–495, 1874–1876.

————. "Slavery in Detroit." *Michigan Pioneer and Historical Collections,* Vol. 1, pp. 415–417, 1874–1876.

Glazer, Sidney. *Detroit: a Study in Urban Development.* New York, 1965.

Haigh, Henry A. "The Michigan Club." *Michigan History Magazine,* Vol. 6, pp. 540–557, 1922.

Hamer, Alvin C. (ed.). *Detroit Murders.* New York, 1948.

Harris, T. George. *Romney's Way.* Englewood Cliffs, N. J., 1967.

Hecock, Donald S. *Review of the 1939 Mayoralty Election.* Detroit Bureau of Government Research Report Number 174. 1940.

Heineman, David E. "Jewish Beginnings in Michigan Before 1850." *American Jewish Historical Society,* No. 13, 1905.

Heyda, Marie. "Senator McMillan and the Flowering of the Spoils System." *Michigan History Magazine,* Vol. 54, pp. 183–200, 1970.

Holli, Melvin G. *Reform in Detroit.* New York, 1969.

Katz, Irving I. *The Beth El Story.* Detroit, 1955.

Lane, William H. "A History of the Electric Service of Detroit." Detroit Bureau of Government Research, Number 142, 1937.

Lodge, John C. *I Remember Detroit.* Detroit, 1949.

Lovett, William P. *Detroit Rules Itself.* Boston, 1930.

Lunt, Richard D. *The High Ministry of Government: the Political Career of Frank Murphy.* Detroit, 1965.

McNaughton, Frank. *Mennen Williams of Michigan.* New York, 1960.

Miller, Raymond C. *Kilowatts at Work, a History of the Detroit Edison Company.* Detroit, 1957.

Moore, Charles. "James M'Millan, United States Senator from Michigan." *Michigan Pioneer and Historical Collections,* Vol. 39, pp. 173–187, 1915.

Moran, J. Bell. *The Moran Family.* Detroit, 1949.

Mugglebee, Ruth. *Father Coughlin.* Garden City, N. Y., 1933.

Neville, Howard R. *The Detroit Banking Collapse of 1933.* East Lansing, Mich., 1960.

O'Geran, Graeme. *History of the Detroit Street Railways.* Detroit, 1931.

Pargellis, Stanley. *Father Gabriel Richard.* Detroit, 1950.

Pound, Arthur. *Detroit, Dynamic City.* New York and London, 1940.

Quaife, M. M. *This Is Detroit.* Detroit, 1951.

Rockaway, Robert A. "The Detroit Jewish Ghetto Before World War I." *Michigan History Magazine,* Vol. 52, pp. 28–36, 1968.

Smith, Carl. O. and Sarasohn, Stephen B. "Hate Propaganda in Detroit." *Public Opinion Quarterly,* Spring, 1946, pp. 24–52.

Spivak, John L. *Shrine of the Silver Dollar.* New York, 1940.

Stark, George W. *Detroit at the Century's Turn.* Detroit, 1951.

Trevelyan, Harry A. *Detroit Voters and Recent Elections.* Detroit Bureau of Government Research, Report Number 150. 1938.

Tull, Charles J. *Father Coughlin and the New Deal.* Syracuse, N. Y., 1965.

Wilson, Edmund. *American Earthquake.* Garden City, N. Y., 1958.

Wood, Arthur E. *Hamtramck, Then and Now.* New York, 1955.

Young, Cynthia B. "WWJ, Pioneer in Broadcasting." *Michigan History Magazine,* Vol. 44, pp. 411–433, 1960.

DETROIT: NEGROES

Dancy, John C. *Sand Against the Wind.* Detroit, 1966.

Darrow, Clarence. *The Story of My Life.* New York, 1932.

Detroit Regional Transportation and Land Use Study. *Comparison, Analysis, and Discussion of the Characteristics of the White and the Negro Population in the Detroit Metropolitan Area* (Mimeo.). Detroit, 1967.

Detroit Urban League. *The Detroit Low-Income Negro Family.* Detroit, 1966.

——. *A Profile of the Detroit Negro, 1959–1967.* Detroit, 1967.

Haynes, George E. *Negro Newcomers in Detroit.* New York, 1969.

Henderson, George. *12th Street, an Analysis of a Changing Neighborhood.* Detroit, 1961.

Hoult, Thomas F. and Mayer, Albert J. *The Population Revolution in Detroit.* Detroit, 1963.

——. *Race and Residence in Detroit.* Detroit, 1962.

Lincoln, Eric C. *The Black Muslims in America.* Boston, 1963.

Louis, Joe. *My Life Story.* New York, 1947.

Mallas, Aris A. Jr.; Rea McCain and Margaret K. Hedden. *Forty Years in Politics.* Detroit, 1957.

Michigan State Advisory Committee to the U. S. Commission on Civil Rights. *Employment Problems of Nonwhite Youth.* Washington, D.C., 1969.

Northrup, Herbert R. *The Negro in the Automobile Industry.* Philadelphia, 1968.

United Community Services. *Social Characteristics of Communities in the Detroit Area* (Mimeo.).

U. S. Commission on Civil Rights. *Hearings, Detroit, Michigan, 1960.* Washington, D.C., 1961.

Wolf, Eleanor and Lebeaux, Charles. *Change and Renewal in an Urban Society.* New York, 1969.

DETROIT: POLICE DEPARTMENT

Branton, Robert C. *The Development of the Detroit Police Department in the Nineteenth Century* (Wayne State University master's thesis). 1937.

Citizens Committee for Equal Opportunity. *The Police, Law Enforcement, and the Detroit Community.* Detroit, 1965.

Detroit Police Department. *Annual Report.* 1929 through 1972.

———. *Report on Civil Emergency, April 5–11, 1968.*

———. *Statistical Report on the Civil Disorder Occurring in the City of Detroit, July, 1967.*

———. *Story of the Detroit Police Department, 1916–1917.*

Edwards, George. "Order and Civil Liberties: A Complex Role for the Police." *Michigan Law Review,* Vol. 64, No. 1, November, 1965.

Searles, John R. and Leonard, J. M. *Experiments in the Mental Testing of Detroit Policemen.* Detroit Bureau of Government Research, No. 141, 1936.

Special Task Force on Police Recruiting and Hiring, *Report of.* Detroit, August 14, 1968.

DETROIT: RAILROAD HISTORY

Anonymous. "James F. Joy Tells how He Went into the Railroad Business." *Michigan Pioneer and Historical Collections,* Vol. 22, pp. 297–304, 1894.

Harlow, Alvin F. *The Road of the Century.* New York, 1947.

Hirshfeld, Charles. *The Great Railroad Conspiracy.* East Lansing, Michigan, 1953.

Lee, Helen Bourne Joy. *The Joy Genealogy.* Essex, Conn., 1968.

Overton, Richard. *Burlington Route.* New York, 1965.

Pearson, Henry G. *An American Railroad Builder: John Murray Forbes.* Boston and New York, 1911.

Stevens, Frank W. *The Beginnings of the New York Central Railroad.* New York, 1926.

Thompson, Slason. *A Short History of American Railways.* Chicago, 1925.

DETROIT: SCHOOLS

Brownell, Dr. Samuel M. *Pursuing Excellence in Education: the Superintendent's Ten-Year Report, 1956–66.* Detroit, 1966.

Dain, Floyd R. *Education in the Wilderness.* Lansing, 1968.

Detroit Board of Education. *Budgets,* 1895–1970.

———. *The Constant Search, the Story of Federal Aid to Detroit Schools.* 1968.

———. *One Hundred Years, the Story of the Detroit Public Schools, 1842–1942.* Detroit, 1942.

———. *Report of the High School Study Commission.* 1968.

Detroit Public Schools. *Achievements and Aptitudes of Detroit Public School Pupils* (Mimeo.). 1966.

————. *Evaluation of the Language Retardation Unit of the Communication Skills Center Project* (Mimeo.). 1968.

————. *Fact Pack* (Mimeo.). 1968.

————. *Great Cities School Improvement Project.* 1966–1967.

————. *Neighborhood Educational Center.* 1967.

————. *Programs Operated by the Detroit Public Schools* (Mimeo.). 1969.

————. *Projects and Studies Completed or Underway in the Detroit Public Schools in 1967–68* (Mimeo.).

————. *Racial Distribution of Students and Personnel in the Detroit Public School* (Mimeo.). 1967.

————. *Relationship Between Family Incomes of School Neighborhoods and Reading Achievement.* 1968.

————. *Relationship Between Family Incomes of School Neighborhoods and School Achievement Means* (Mimeo.). 1968.

————. *Relationship of Income to Some Indices of High School Success* (Mimeo.). 1968.

————. *Summary of Project Evaluation, ESEA, Title I* (Mimeo.). 1967, 1968.

————. *Testing in Detroit Schools* (Mimeo.). 1968.

Disbrow, Donald. *Schools for an Urban Society.* Lansing, 1968.

Lee, Ralph. "Stirrings in the Big Cities: Detroit." *National Education Association Journal,* Vol. 51, March, 1962.

Moehlman, Arthur B. *Public Education in Detroit.* Bloomington, Ill., 1925.

Pierce, John D. "Origin and Progress of the Michigan School System." *Michigan Pioneer and Historical Collections,* Vol. 1, p. 37, 1874–1876.

Starring, Charles and Knauss, James O. *Michigan's Search for Educational Standards.* Lansing, 1969.

Wilkins, William D. "Traditions and Reminiscences of the Public Schools of Detroit." *Michigan Pioneer and Historical Collections,* Vol. 1, pp. 448–466, 1874–1876.

FEDERAL GOVERNMENT: ANTIPOVERTY PROGRAM

Advisory Commission on Intergovernmental Relations. *Intergovernmental Relations in the Poverty Program.* Washington, D.C., 1966.

Campbell, Arthur A. "The Role of Family Planning in the Reduction of Poverty." *Journal of Marriage and the Family.* May, 1968.

Comptroller-General of the United States. *Need for Improvements in Certain Neighborhood Youth Corps Operations in Detroit, Michigan.* Washington, D.C., 1968.

————. *Review of Community Action Program in Detroit, Michigan.* Washington, D.C., 1968.

————. *Review of Economic Opportunity Programs.* Washington, D.C., 1969.

Education and Labor Committee, Subcommittee on the War on Poverty Program, U. S. House of Representatives. *Hearing, Economic Opportunity Act of 1964.* Washington, D.C., 1964.

Labor and Public Welfare Committee, Subcommittee on Employment, Manpower, and Poverty, U. S. Senate. *Examination of the War on Poverty* (15 parts). Washington, D.C., 1967.

————. *Hearings on Hunger and Malnutrition in the United States.* Washington, D.C., 1968.

————. *Toward Economic Security for the Poor*. Washington, D.C., 1968.

Levine, Robert A. *Evaluating the War on Poverty* (OEO internal document). Washington, D.C., 1967.

Moynihan, Daniel P. *Maximum Feasible Misunderstanding, Community Action in the War on Poverty*. New York, 1969.

Office of Economic Opportunity. *Monitoring Branch Abstracts* (Mimeo.). Washington, D.C., 1967, 1968, 1969.

————. *Organizing Communities for Action*. Washington, D.C., 1968.

Weeks, Christopher. *Job Corps*. Boston, 1967.

FEDERAL GOVERNMENT: PROGRAMS AND POLICY

Agriculture Committee, U. S. Senate. *Hearings, General Farm Legislation*. Washington, D.C., 1937.

Agriculture Committee, Subcommittee on Rural Development, U. S. House of Representatives. *Hearings on Effect of Federal Programs on Rural America*. Washington, D.C., 1967.

Congressional Quarterly Service. *Federal Economic Policy*. Washington, D.C., 1967.

Dorfman, Robert (ed.). *Measuring Benefits of Government Investments*. Washington, D.C., 1963.

Education and Labor Committee, U. S. House of Representatives. *Federal Labor Laws*. Washington, D.C., 1967.

Interdepartmental Committee on Children and Youth: Health, Education, and Welfare Department. *Federal Programs Assisting Children and Youth*. Washington, D.C., 1967.

Labor Department. *The Anvil and the Plow*. Washington, D.C., 1963.

Labor Department, Manpower Administration. *Manpower Report of the President*. Washington, D.C., 1968.

Levitan, Sar A. and Mangum, Garth L. *Making Sense of Federal Manpower Policy*. Ann Arbor and Detroit, Mich., 1967.

Office of the Federal Register, General Services Administration. *U. S. Government Organization Manual*. Washington, D.C., 1969.

Office of the President. *Economic Report of the President together with the Annual Report of the Council of Economic Advisers*. Washington, D.C., 1964 through 1971.

President's Commission on Income Maintenance Programs. *Poverty Amid Plenty*. Washington, D.C., 1969.

Sundquist, James L. *Politics and Policy*. Washington, D.C., 1968.

FEDERAL GOVERNMENT: URBAN AFFAIRS

Advisory Commission on Intergovernmental Relations. *Apportionment of State Legislatures*. Washington, D.C., 1962.

————. *Fiscal Balance in the American Federal System* (2 volumes). Washington, D.C., 1967.

————. *Governmental Structure, Organization, and Planning in Metropolitan Areas*. Washington, D.C., 1961.

————. *Metropolitan America: Challenge to Federalism*. Washington, D.C., 1966.

————. *Economic Disparities: Implications for Intergovernmental Relations in Central Cities and Suburbs.* Washington, D.C., 1965.

Banking and Currency Committee, U. S. House of Representatives. *Basic Laws and Authorities on Housing and Urban Development.* Washington, D.C., 1968.

————. *Demonstration Cities and Metropolitan Development Act of 1966.* Washington, D.C., 1966.

————. *Hearings, Demonstration Cities, Housing and Urban Development, and Urban Mass Transit.* Washington, D.C., 1966.

————. *Hearings, Housing Act of 1954.* Washington, D.C., 1954.

————. *Hearings, to Create a U. S. Housing Authority.* Washington, D.C., 1937.

Banking and Currency Committee, Subcommittee on Housing, U. S. House of Representatives. *Hearings on the Housing and Urban Development Act of 1965.* Washington, D.C., 1965.

Banking and Currency Committee, U. S. Senate. *Progress Report on Federal Housing Programs.* Washington, D.C., 1967.

Banking and Currency Committee, Subcommittee on Housing and Urban Affairs, U. S. Senate. *Congress and American Housing, 1892–1967.* Washington, D.C., 1967.

Education and Labor Committee, U. S. Senate. *Hearings, to Create a U. S. Housing Authority.* Washington, D.C., 1936.

Government Operations Committee, U. S. Senate. *Unshackling Local Government.* Washington, D.C.,1968.

Government Operations Committee, Subcommittee on Executive Reorganization, U. S. Senate. *Federal Role in Urban Affairs* (21 parts). Washington, D.C., 1967.

Government Operations Committee, Subcommittee on Intergovernmental Relations. *The Federal System as Seen by Federal Aid Officials.* Washington, D.C., 1965.

————. *Hearings, Creative Federalism.* Washington, D.C., 1967.

————. *Impact of Federal Urban Development Programs on Local Government Organization and Planning.* Washington, D.C., 1964.

Housing and Urban Development Department. *Improving the Quality of Urban Life—a Program Guide to Model Neighborhoods in Demonstration Cities.* Washington, D.C., 1967.

————. *Model Cities Planning Requirements, CDA Letter #1.* Washington, D.C., 1967.

————. *Plant Relocation and the Core City Worker.* Washington, D.C., 1967.

————. *Report of Task Force on Departmental Field Structure* (internal document). 1966.

————. *Report of Task Force on Metropolitan Development* (internal document). 1966.

————. *Report of Task Force on Renewal and Housing Assistance* (internal document). 1966.

————. *Science and the City.* Washington, D.C., 1967.

————. *Urban Renewal Directory.* Washington, D.C., 1967.

Joint Economic Committee, U. S. Congress. *Federal Programs for the Development of Human Resources* (3 volumes). Washington, D.C., 1966.

March, Dr. Michael S. "The Neighborhood Center Concept." *Public Welfare,* January, 1968.

President's Commission on Law Enforcement and Administration of Justice. *The Challenge of Crime in a Free Society.* Washington, D.C., 1967.

———. *Task Force Report: The Courts.* Washington, D.C., 1967.

———. *Task Force Report: Juvenile Delinquency and Youth Crime.* Washington, D.C., 1967.

———. *Task Force Report: the Police.* Washington, D.C., 1967.

Rothenberg, Jerome. *Economic Evaluation of Urban Renewal.* Washington, D.C., 1967.

Task Force on Metropolitan Development, *Report of.* Washington, D.C., 1966.

Tax Foundation, Inc. *Medicaid: State Programs After Two Years.* New York, 1968.

Wright, Deil S. *Federal Grants-in-Aid: Perspectives and Alternatives.* Washington, D.C., 1968.

Source Notes

A NUMBER OF CONSIDERATIONS DICTATED THE STYLE OF THE SOURCE NOTES. RAISED NUMBERS have been kept to a minimum within the text so as not to disturb the reader. They are used to identify the sources of quotes, plus a limited amount of other material. Most identification is made in the Source Notes by referring to the text by page and paragraph. Since limitations of space played a major factor throughout the book, references are grouped together at the end of each paragraph or section dealing with a unified subject. References are generally given in the order they occur, and not according to the regular order of page numbers in a book. (For example: DF: Nevins, *Ford Expansion* 315-16, 262, 605.)

Because of the large number of sources, references are identified according to the section of the bibliography where the work appears. Thus, "DH" refers to "DETROIT: HISTORY." When necessary, more than the initial letters may be used. To distinguish "DETROIT: GENERAL" from "DETROIT: GOVERNMENT," the designations "D GEN" and "D GOV" are employed.

Usually the name of the author or the publishing agency serves to identify a work. When, however, there is more than one work by an author, as much of the title as necessary for identification is given.

Material obtained by the author through an interview or discussion is identified by the full name of the person making the statement. Thus, "Jerome P. Cavanagh" indicates that Mayor Jerome P. Cavanagh supplied the information.

The designation "Author's Research" identifies material obtained from the files of the Juvenile Court, Wayne County Department of Social Services, the Detroit Public Schools, the Detroit Police Department, and interviews used to compile the histories of families whose real names cannot be disclosed.

In affixing paragraph numbers, a paragraph carried over from a previous page is considered as the first paragraph on a new page.

EXAMPLES:

P. 238. ¶ 7. DF: Nevins, *Ford Expansion* 410-11, 415; Sward 196. DA: Sloan 162.

¶ References are to DETROIT: FORD (DF), books by Alan Nevins, *Ford: Expansion and Challenge* (pages 410-411, and 415), and by Keith Sward (page 196); and to DETROIT: AUTOMOBILE INDUSTRY (DA), the book by Alfred P. Sloan, Jr. (page 162).

P. 476. ¶ 1. Kermit Gordon. FG PP: Labor, *Manpower Report* 308.

¶ References are to material obtained by the author from an interview with Kermit Gordon; and to the FEDERAL GOVERNMENT: PROGRAMS AND POLICY section (FG PP), the Labor Department Manpower Administration's *Manpower Report of the President* (page 308).

SOURCE NOTES: ABBREVIATIONS OF BIBLIOGRAPHICAL SECTIONS

CIT	CITIES—GENERAL
CD	CIVIL DISORDERS
EC	ECONOMICS AND INDUSTRY
ED	EDUCATION
GEN	GENERAL
IM	IMMIGRANTS AND THE BACKGROUND OF IMMIGRATION
MH	MICHIGAN HISTORY
DA	DETROIT: AUTOMOBILE INDUSTRY
D CAV	DETROIT: CAVANAGH ADMINISTRATION
DF	DETROIT: FORD
D GEN	DETROIT: GENERAL
D GOV	DETROIT: GOVERNMENT
DH	DETROIT: HISTORY
DN	DETROIT: NEGROES
DP	DETROIT: POLICE DEPARTMENT
DR	DETROIT: RAILROAD HISTORY
DS	DETROIT: SCHOOLS
FG AP	FEDERAL GOVERNMENT: ANTIPOVERTY PROGRAM
FG PP	FEDERAL GOVERNMENT: PROGRAMS AND POLICY
FG UA	FEDERAL GOVERNMENT: URBAN AFFAIRS

Introduction

1.* DH: Wilson 232.

1. The Shantyman

1. *Michigan History Magazine,* Vol. 28: 101.
2. MH: Leach 14.

P. 6. ¶ 1. MH: Dunbar 481, 504, 469-70, 476; Leach 5-19. D GEN: Michigan Emergency 96-97. Author's Research.
P. 7. ¶ 2. DH: Garrity 27. DF: Nevins, *Ford Times* 523. DA: Beasley, *Made* 212, 218. MH: Dunbar, 569-70; Author's Research.

2. The Paris of the West

1. DH: Farmer, Vol. 1: 26.
2. DH: Farmer, Vol. 1: 287.
3. DH: Farmer, Vol. 1: 345.

P. 9. ¶ 4. DH: Farmer, Vol. 1: 489-90, 25-26, 30, 333-34; Quaife 28.
P. 10. ¶ 2. DH: Farmer, Vol. 1: 15-16, 333, 527, 12, 321-22, 331.
P. 10. ¶ 3. DH: Farmer, Vol. 1: 338, 706, 767-68.
P. 11. ¶ 1. DS: Dain 23. EC: Wright 67. MH: Osband 709-17. DH: Catlin 69-72; Farmer, Vol. 1: 243-49, 261, 280; Girardin, *Slavery* 415.
P. 11. ¶ 3. GEN: Westcott. EC: Burlingame 106; Wright 277.
P. 11. ¶ 6. EC: Wright 207. DH: Farmer, Vol. 1: 879. DS: Dain 58 ff. DH: Catlin 129-30.
P. 12. ¶ 4. Johnson, Allen (ed.), *Dictionary of American Biography* (New York: 1964), Vol. 10: 157-60; Vol. 8: 526-28. EC: Burlingame 79-81, 85.
P. 13. ¶ 3. DH: Catlin 131. DS: Dain 58 ff. DH: Farmer, Vol. 1: 284, 281, 287; Glazer 24; Dain 5. GEN: Hulbert 56.
P. 14. ¶ 3. DH: Farmer, Vol. 1: 181-83, 201, 340, 62, 556. DS: Moehlman 32-34, 40-41; Dain 41, 88; Detroit Board of Education, *One Hundred Years* 4-5.
P. 14. ¶ 4. DS: Moehlman 33, 40; Dain 79. DH: Farmer, Vol. 1: 182.
P. 15. ¶ 2. DH: Farmer, Vol. 1: 201, 838, 769-70; Quaife 35; Catlin 238.

---

* Numbers without page reference (i.e., 1., 2., etc.) refer to the raised numbers in the text.

P. 15. ❝ 3. DH: Catlin 231; Farmer, Vol. 1: 847.

P. 16. ❝ 3. DH: Farmer, Vol. 1: 345; Catlin 250-55. Johnson, *op. cit.*, Vol. 2: 563.

P. 16. ❝ 8. DH: Pargellis. MH: Dunbar 277, 247-48, 278. GEN: Hulbert 135. DS: Dain 124; Moehlman 36. DH: Dain 15-16; Catlin 263, 126, 281.

P. 17. ¶ 2. MH: Dunbar 328. DH: Farmer, Vol. 1: 889, 15-16.

3. The Irish Aphrodisiac

1. IM: Bennett 96, 344.
2. Kaplow, Jeffry, *New Perspectives on the French Revolution* (New York: 1965), p. 260.

P. 19. ¶ 7. EC: Wright 46. IM: Gwynn 234, 235, 257, 354-57, 270-71, 370-71, 422; Cassell's, Vol. 4: 139-40.

P. 19. ❝ 8. IM: Gwynn 323. EC: George 126.

P. 20. ¶ 4. IM: Gwynn 331, 428, 281, 395, 459. EC: Burlingame 45; Giedion 36-38; Bogart 51-52.

P. 20. ¶ 6. Johnson, *op. cit.*, Vol. 10: 157-60. EC: Wright, 220-21; Burlingame 71-73; Bogart 53.

P. 21. ¶ 6. IM: Gwynn 458, 462, 436; Cusack 481; Immigration Commission, Vol. 1: 66-96. EC: Wright 69, 223, 248, 214, 215; Bogart 103. DF: Ruddiman 271. Connolly, John, "William C. Maybury," *Michigan Pioneer and Historical Collections*, Vol. 38: 714-16.

4. The Warm Wave of the White Man

1. MH: Hyma 119.
2. *Ibid.*, 118.
3. MH: Dunbar 322-23.
4. MH: Gordon 6-12.
5. DH: Catlin 255, 257.
6. MH: Dunbar 330. EC: Wright 398.

P. 22. ¶ 3. DR: Harlow 78. MH: Dunbar 249-50. DH: Farmer, Vol. 1: 335-36, 770.

P. 23. ¶ 5. DH: Farmer, Vol. 1: 11. GEN: De Tocqueville 745, 741. MH: Dunbar 258; Van Buren, *What the Pioneers Ate* 296.

P. 24. ¶ 3. GEN: De Tocqueville 741. MH: Hyma III, 162, 118; Van Buren, *What the Pioneers Ate* 296; Caldwell 297-316; Brunson 161-63. DH: Dain 18; Farmer, Vol. 1: 324.

P. 24. ¶ 5. MH: Dunbar 249-50. DH: Burton, C. M. 171; Farmer, Vol. 1: 848-49.

P. 26. ¶ 2. EC: Wright 253. Johnson, *op. cit.*, Vol. 2: 563. DH: Catlin 250-58. MH: Gates 2; Felch 274-97; Caldwell 297-316.

P. 26. ¶ 5. DR: Pearson 19-20. DH: Ford 97-104. EC: Wright 217; Rayback 75, 76; Bogart 147. GEN: De Tocqueville 744. DH: Farmer, Vol. 1: 893, 15; Ford 97-104; Catlin 364-65, 354. MH: Dunbar 333-35. DA: Rolt 12.

P. 27. ¶7. MH: Dunbar 335-36, 324-26. EC: Wright 385, 386; Rayback 77. DH: Catlin 358, 361; Farmer, Vol. 1: 154, 850-52; Pound 166-68.

P. 28. ¶ 2. MH: Dunbar 330-33; Farmer, Vol. 1: 896; Catlin 369-70.

P. 28. ¶ 3. EC: Wright 279.

5. The Epidemic Tax

1. DA: Labatut 80.

P. 29. ¶ 1. MH: Pieters 39.

P. 30. ¶ 6. DH: Catlin 298-301, 284-85, 315-19; Farmer, Vol. 1: 48-49; Burton, C. M. 163-71. DS: Dain 199.

P. 31. ¶ 1. IM: Engels 104; Barker 282. Russell, John, *The Early Irish of Detroit*, manuscript, Burton Historical Collection, Detroit Public Library.

P. 32. ¶ 3. DH: Pargellis; Catlin 319-20, 317, 318; Farmer, Vol. 1: 644, 648, 151-53, 155, 203. MH: Dunbar 285. DP: Branton 12.

P. 32. ¶ 5. Johnson, *op. cit.*, Vol. 7: 248. IM: Stephenson 104; Immigration Comm., Vol. 2: 561. EC: Rayback 93-94.

6. Liberty and Learning

1. GEN: Katz 103-04. DS: Moehlman 82.
2. GEN: Katz 100.
3. DS: Dain 281.

P. 33. ¶ 2. GEN: Census, *Historical Statistics,* Chapter Z. IM: Cassell's, Vol. 2: 325, 548-49. DS: Moehlman 48.

P. 34. ¶ 2. MH: Dunbar 317-18. DS: Dain 140; DS: Moehlman 52, 55, 67, 36; Pierce 37-45; Det. Bd. of Ed., *One Hundred Years* 5; Starring 34. DH: Catlin 380.

P. 35. ¶ 1. DS: Det. Bd. of Ed., *One Hundred Years* 6-11; Dain 250, 280-81; Moehlman 72-78; Starring 5. Johnson, *op. cit.,* Vol. 5: 254.

P. 36. ¶ 1. IM: Barker 282-83; Gwynn 425, 453, 451, 461, 463; Engels 307. EC: Wright 236-37. DH: Catlin 464.

P. 36 ¶ 3. IM: Barker 280, 279; Immigration Comm. Vol. 1: 65-96; Gwynn 453, 461; Stephenson 20.

P. 37. ¶ 3. IM: Stephenson 249; Immigration Comm. Vol. 2: 589-92; Todd 47. DF: Nevins, *Ford Times* 33. GEN: De Tocqueville 737-39. EC: Wright 278. MH: Dunbar 359-63. DH: Catlin 393.

7. The Heathen Altar of the Michigan Central

1. DR: Hirshfeld 5.
2. DR: Hirshfeld 76.

P. 38. ¶ 2. DR: Harlow 228. EC: Wright 276.

P. 38. ¶ 4. DH: Catlin 403. MH: Dunbar 363, 498-99. Johnson, *op. cit.,* Vol. 2: 339-40.

P. 40. ¶ 2. Johnson, *op. cit.,* Vol. 3: 193-94, Vol. 6: 607-09. EC: Burlingame 167-68.

P. 41. ¶ 2. DH: Catlin 415-16; Farmer, Vol. 1: 154, Vol. 2: 1059-62. DS: Dain 250.

P. 41. ¶ 5. DR: Anonymous 297-304; Overton 28; Pearson 24, 2-9, 67, 40; Harlow 75; Stevens 401. DH: Catlin 414.

P. 42. ¶ 6. DH: Catlin 416-17; Farmer, Vol. 1: 898-99. DR: Harlow 215, 225, 73, 78, 270-71; Pearson 42.

P. 43. ¶ 2. DR: Anonymous 297-304; Thompson 120, 124; Pearson 71-73; Overton 19, 12; Harlow 222. DH: Farmer, Vol. 1: 898. Joy, J. R., *Thomas Joy and His Descendants* (privately published).

P. 44. ¶ 10. MH: Dunbar 381. DR: Hirshfeld 4-6, 9-12, 13, 15, 17, 20, 24-26, 41-44, 49, 52, 55-56, 75-76, 82, 101. DH: Catlin 466-68; Detroit Post 47; Farmer, Vol. 1: 900.

8. The Republican Genesis

1. MH: Pieters 31.
2. GEN: Brown 69.
3. EC: Wright 304.
4. DH: Catlin 510.
5. GEN: Myers 48-51; Moos 11. DH: Det. Post 109-13. DR: Hirshfeld 114, 116.

P. 45. ¶ 2. EC: Bogart 215-16. GEN: Census, *Statistical Abstract,* 1967, p. 95.

P. 46. ¶ 5. IM: Stephenson 106-07. DH: Det. Post 80-82.

P. 47. ¶ 6. DH: Farmer, Vol. 1: 49-50; Catlin 431, 427.

P. 48. ¶ 1. IM: Stephenson 100-03, 111; Immigration Comm., Vol. 2: 562-63.

P. 48. ¶ 5. DS: Moehlman 90-92, 68; Wilkins 459-60. IM: Stephenson 101. DH: Catlin 438.

P. 49. ¶ 3. DR: Pearson 40, 44, 67, 70, 75, 84; Overton 30, 32, 45; Harlow 228, 258. DH: Farmer, Vol. 1: 903, 1059-62. Joy, *op. cit.*

P. 50. ¶ 1. DR: Overton 18, 54, 10; Pearson 28 ff.; Harlow 228. IM: Stephenson 47-48, 116-17. EC: Wright 67, 431.

P. 51. ¶ 3. EC: Wright 304. CIT: Schlesinger 9. DN: Dancy 43. GEN: Moos 8-9.

P. 52. ¶ 1. GEN: Myers 38, 36; Moos 13. DH: Det. Post 99, 101-03; Catlin 468-70; Farmer, Vol. 1: 826.

P. 53. ¶ 2. DH: Det. Post 91. EC: Rayback 98-99. GEN: Moos 31-33. IM: Stephenson 110. MH: Dunbar 429-30.

P. 53. ¶ 5. EC: Wright 304. DH: Pound 187-88; Farmer, Vol. 1: 346; Catlin 321-22; Det. Post 75-76. MH: Dunbar 428.

9. The Predictable War

1. GEN: Myers 55.
2. IM: Stephenson 112, 113; Immigration Comm., Vol. 2: 564. GEN: Moos 29, 36-37.
3. DR: Pearson 109.
4. GEN: Katz 120.
5. Congressional *Globe,* 35th Congress, 1st Session, March 4, 1858.
6. EC: Wright 358.
7. DH: Det. Post 186.
8. MH: Dunbar 455. DH: Catlin 526.

P. 55. ¶ 3. DH: Det. Post 115-16; Farmer, Vol. 1: 841. GEN: Moos 10, 13. DR: Hirshfeld 106-08, 117.
P. 56. ¶ 4. GEN: Myers 39. IM: Immigration Comm., Vol. 2: 363; Stephenson 114-15.
P. 56. ¶ 5. MH: Dunbar 428. DH: Farmer, Vol. 1: 347; Det. Post 120-22.
P. 57. ¶ 1. GEN: Katz 112. DR: Pearson 145, 113.
P. 57. ¶ 2. DR: Overton 54. DH: Det. Post 143.
P. 57. ¶ 6. DN: Dancy 45. DH: Farmer, Vol. 1: 347-48.
P. 58. ¶ 4. EC: Wright 306. GEN: Myrdal 444; Katz 125-29, 123.
P. 58. ¶ 6. GEN: Moos 81, 55, 74-75.
P. 59. ¶ 4. EC: Wright 431-32, 317-18. DH: Catlin 514. DR: Overton 63, 76.
P. 60. ¶ 2. MH: Dunbar 448. DH: Catlin 515-16. IM: Stephenson 47-48, 129.
P. 60. ¶ 8. DH: Farmer, Vol. 2: 1059. DR: Overton 83. GEN: Katz 93. IM: Stephenson 135-37. EC: Rayback 109.
P. 61. ¶ 1. EC: Burlingame 159, 162-65, 173.
P. 61. ¶ 4. DH: Catlin 524; Pound 191. DF: Nevins, *Ford Times* 22. DR: Pearson 119.
P. 61. ¶ 7. DH: Burton 791. DF: Anonymous; Nevins, *Ford Times* 39-42, 22; Ruddiman 234 ff. EC: Giedion 131, 145.

10. The Education of Thomas Edison

P. 62. ¶ 5. Johnson, *op. cit.,* Vol. 7: 249. DH: Farmer, Vol. 1: 883. DR: Harlow 228, 258.
P. 63. ¶ 1. EC: Wright 331; Burlingame 174. IM: Benson 165.
P. 64. ¶ 5. GEN: Josephson 1-22, 26-27, 33, 39-41. D GOV: Ketcham 48. DH: Pound 181; Catlin 503, 400-01; Farmer, Vol. 1: 507-08. EC: Burlingame 171. DR: Harlow 228, 232. MN: Dunbar 435.

11. The Great Boom

P. 65. ¶ 2. DH: Det. Post 157. MH: Gates 15.
P. 66. ¶ 2. IM: Todd 119. MH: Gates 3, 19; Leach 5-19. DR: Pearson 99. DH: Bancroft 336-51; Catlin 497-98; Glazer 123. DF: Nevins, *Ford Expansion* 289.
P. 66. ¶ 7. DH: Catlin 651-52; Det. *Post and Tribune* 85; Farmer, Vol. 2: 1063-67; Moore 173-87; Heyda 183-200.
P. 67. ¶ 1. DH: Farmer, Vol. 1: 807, 806, 813.

12. The Coming of the "Cousin Jacks"

1. Journal of Henri A. Hobart, Burton Historical Collection, Det. Public Library.

P. 68. ¶ 1. IM: Rowe 152, 312, 211. MH: Todd 19. Author's Research.
P. 69. ¶ 3. IM: Rowe 71-78, 68, 153, 155; Leifchild 45-51, 143-46, 156-57, 285-86. MH: Rowse 161.
P. 70. ¶ 2. IM: Rowe 231, 149, 156-58; Leifchild 270, 182-83, 215-16, 226-27.
P. 70. ¶ 6. MH: Gates 7, 100; Rowse 166, 17; Todd 47, 120, 127, 20, 19. IM: Rowe 308, 316, 317, 311, 321.
P. 71. ¶ 3. MH: Todd 122, 120; Rowse 170, 342; Martin 87-88; Gates 98-99, 67.

13. The Irish Riots

1. GEN: Myers 89.
2. CD: Anonymous.
3. GEN: Myrdal 292.

P. 73. ¶ 1. EC: Wright 314; Burlingame 177-79; Friedman 75; Labor *Handbook* 236. Johnson, *op. cit.,* Vol. 5: 284-85. DH: Glazer 70. DS: Moehlman 101, 104; Starring 13.
P. 73. ¶ 6. GEN: Myers 136; Wood 22-24, 54. IM: Stephenson 138.
P. 75. ¶ 1. DH: Farmer, Vol. 1: 181, 348, 307-08; Catlin 527-29; Pound 192. CD: Anonymous; Katz 5-13. DN: Mallas 2-8.
P. 75. ¶ 2. IM: Engels 146. CD: Grimshaw *Lawlessness.* National Advisory Commission on Civil Disorders, *Miscellaneous Papers.* DH: Farmer, Vol. 1: 204.

14. Republican: Spelled "R A I L R O A D"

1. DS: Moehlman 113; Starring 101.
2. DH: Lodge 183; Catlin 580.
3. IM: Stephenson 258-59.
4. DS: Moehlman 101.

P. 77. ¶ 1. DR: Pearson 125; Overton 78, 110, 68-69, 85-91, 106. DH: Farmer, Vol. 2: 1059-62; Vol. 1: 806.
P. 77. ¶ 2. CIT: Schlesinger 28. DR: Overton 102. IM: Immigration Comm., Vol. 2: 385; Stephenson 71-72.
P. 77. ¶ 6. EC: Clough 565. IM: Janson 274-76; Immigration Comm., Vol. 2: 594-95; Barker 370.
P. 78. ¶ 2. EC: Giedion 145, 214-16. DH: Catlin 545. IM: Barker 281.
P. 78. ¶ 6. GEN: Moos 144. EC: Wright 507-08; Burlingame 267. DR: Overton 113-14.
P. 79. ¶ 1. GEN: Moos 137.
P. 79. ¶ 5. DH: Det. Post 180, 290; Farmer, Vol. 2: 1059. CIT: Schlesinger 164-65. GEN: Myrdal 228.
P. 80. ¶ 1. GEN: Haas 11-12.
P. 80. ¶ 2. GEN: Moos 129; Wood 82-90. DS: Moehlman 111. DN: Mallas 12 ff.
P. 81. ¶ 1. DR: Harlow 234, 238; Overton 125-38. EC: Burlingame 200. GEN: Myers 210-11; Moos 140-43.
P. 81. ¶ 3. DH: Det. Post 337-38. GEN: Moos 148-52.

15. A Ford Comes to the City

1. DS: Starring 16-17.
2. DS: Det. Bd. of Ed., *One Hundred Years* 19.
3. GEN: Myers 222.

P. 82. ¶ 2. MH: Van Buren, *What the Pioneers Ate* 293-96; Webber 13.
P. 83. ¶ 2. DF: Nevins, *Ford Times* 44-45. DS: Starring 25, 16-18, 20; Moehlman 100, 101, 113; Det. Bd. of Ed., *One Hundred Years* 18.
P. 84. ¶ 1. CIT: Schlesinger 41-42. EC: George 323.
P. 84. ¶ 7. DF: Nevins, *Ford Times* 54, 73-74, 79-81. IM: Rowe 102-10, 124. DA: Rolt 12-13. DH: Catlin 657. DR: Overton 114. EC: Wright 480-81.

16. The Subdivision of Light

1. Josephson 212.

P. 86. ¶ 3. DH: Lane 3-5. Johnson, *op. cit.,* Vol. 10: 168-69. GEN: Josephson 177.
P. 87. ¶ 5. GEN: Josephson 74-84, 178-80, 183, 176, 161-74, 187-89.
P. 88. ¶ 3. GEN: Josephson 208-09, 199, 212, 218-31.

17. The View from the Tower

1. DF: Nevins, *Ford Times* 107.

P. 90. ¶ 1. DH: Lane 9, 2; Moran 90-91; Lodge 73-74; Catlin 573-75; O'Geran 21-25.
P. 90. ¶ 4. DF: Nevins, *Ford Times* 83-84, 62-69. DH: Pound 228-29, 270; Catlin 499.
D GEN: Detroit City Plan 3-5.
P. 90. ¶ 6. DH: Pound 270. DF: Nevins 87-90. DA: Federal Trade Commission 622.
P. 91. ¶ 4. DF: Nevins, *Ford Times* 109. DH: Lodge 114.
P. 91. ¶ 8. DH: Quaife 61; Catlin 563-64, 553. D GOV: Upson. DS: Moehlman 22.
MH: Dunbar 492.
P. 92. ¶ 4. DH: Lodge 61; Miller 4-5; Lane 26; Moran 102. DF: Nevins, *Ford Times*
122, 108-10.

18. The Industrial Aristocrats

P. 93. ¶ 3. DH: Farmer, Vol. 1: 804, 806, 807-24, Vol. 2: 1204.
P. 94. ¶ 4. DH: Farmer, Vol. 1: 773-76, 831, Vol. 2: 1153-54; Catlin 653-55, 664-65;
Lodge 121-22. MH: Dunbar 593.
P. 94. ¶ 7. DH: Farmer, Vol. 2: 1153-54, Vol. 1: 813; Catlin 476-77.
P. 95. ¶ 1. DF: Nevins, *Ford Times* 123. DH: Glazer 50; Catlin 657.
P. 95. ¶ 3. EC: Wright 490, 879. GEN: National Commission, Vol. 4: 574; De Tocque-
ville 737-39.
P. 95. ¶ 8. DH: Quaife 83; Lane 17, Miller 5, 8, 12-14. Stonehouse, Merlin, "Michigan
Excursion to Riverside, California," *Michigan History Magazine,* Vol. 45: 193-94 (1961).
GEN: Josephson 248. Joy, *op. cit.*

19. The Reformation of the City

1. GEN: Myers 288.
2. CIT: Schlesinger 115-16, 361-63.
3. DH: Bingay 240.

P. 96. ¶ 2. EC: Wright 480-81, 453. CIT: Schlesinger 28. IM: Benson 159.
P. 97. ¶ 2. IM: Janson 222, 229, 280, 315, 283; Lloyd 365, 87, 94-95, 147, 151, 368, 346,
370.
P. 97. ¶ 5. IM: Janson 265, 274, 279-80, 321-26, 336; Benson 159, 165; Nelson 123.
P. 98. ¶ 6. EC: Rayback 111, 118-19, 129, 132, 134-36, 143-44, 162, 167-68.
P. 99. ¶ 2. CIT: Schlesinger 65-66, 73. EC: Rayback 168-69.
P. 99. ¶ 6. DH: Haigh 540-57; Farmer, Vol. 1: 117.
P. 99. ¶ 7. CIT: Schlesinger 126. DH: Pound 254.
P. 100. ¶ 4. DH: Lovett 63-65, 21; Bingay 328-29. CIT: Schlesinger 390.
P. 100. ¶ 8. MH: Sarasohn 9-10. DH: O'Geran 61-63; Catlin 591-92.

20. The Strong Mayor

1. EC: George 541-42.

P. 101. ¶ 1. DH: Holli 129-30; Lovett 23.
P. 101. ¶ 3. DA: Beasley, *Made* 16-17. DH: Lodge 122; Bingay 301.
P. 102. ¶ 1. DH: Bingay 235. MH: Dunbar 585. CIT: Schlesinger 282, 140; Starrett 24,
27, 29.
P. 102. ¶ 2. DH: Catlin 487. CIT: Schlesinger 103.
P. 102. ¶ 3. CIT: Schlesinger 216. DH: Catlin 394, 395. Hurd, Dr. Henry M., "A History
of the Asylums for the Insane in Michigan," *Michigan Pioneer and Historical Collec-
tions,* Vol. 13: 292 ff. (1888).
P. 102. ¶ 4. DH: Lodge 189; Quaife 147.
P. 103. ¶ 2. DH: Farmer, Vol. 1: 927-30; Moran 90-91; Catlin 593-96; Lodge 189;
Bingay 232. DA: Beasley, *Made* 22; Labatut 85, 218. CIT: Schlesinger 313. IM: Barker
462. DF: Nevins, *Ford Times* 122-24.
P. 104. ¶ 1. DH: Bingay 232; Lodge 116-17; Catlin 610-11; O'Geran 64-65.
P. 104. ¶ 4. MH: Dunbar 530. DH: Holli 128-29, 76, 78-79; Miller 29-33; Catlin 601-03.
P. 104. ¶ 5. CIT: Schlesinger 91. DH: Holli 37; Catlin 598. EC: Clough 332. Johnson,
op. cit., Vol. 10: 168-69.

P. 105. ¶ 3. MH: Dunbar 604. DH: Catlin 617-18; O'Geran 78-87; Bingay 236. EC: Rayback 155, 177.

21. A School of Philosophy

1. DN: Mallas 12, 21.

P. 106. ¶ 2. GEN: Myers 314; Moos 196. MH: Sarasohn 1, 70.
P. 106. ¶ 5. EC: Wright 487, 492; Clough 564. IM: Barker 440, 448.
P. 107. ¶ 1. EC: Clough 767, 538-39; Bogart 6, 314, 330, 530, 549, 559.
P. 107. ¶ 3. EC: Bogart 237; Wright 601; Labor *Handbook* 236; Rayback 179-80; Friedman 116.
P. 107. ¶ 4. EC: Wright 544, 483. DH: Moore 180.
P. 108. ¶ 1. CIT: Schlesinger 13-15.
P. 108. ¶ 8. CIT: Schlesinger 19-20. GEN: Myrdal 452-53; Myers 313-14; Moos 195-96; Key 540-41, 553. DH: Moore 180. EC: Friedman 106.
P. 109. ¶ 2. CIT: Schlesinger 384. DN: Dancy 86-87. GEN: Myrdal 452. DH: Holli 72-76.
P. 109. ¶ 5. DN: Mallas 12, 21, 27-29, 84-87, 35, 43.

22. An Electric Beginning

P. 110. ¶ 4. DF: Ruddiman 264; Nevins, *Ford Times* 110, 118, 144-46. DH: Miller 16-17. DA: King.
P. 111. ¶ 4. DF: Nevins, *Ford Times* 144, 97, 126. DA: Rae, *The American Automobile* 7-8; Rae, *American Automobile Manufacturers* 8, 24-25, 29-30; Fed. Trade Comm. 907-09.
P. 111. ¶ 7. DH: Miller 43. DF: Nevins, *Ford Times* 145-46, 142; Clancy 38-39. DH: Pound 273-74.

23. Pingree's Progress

1. CIT: Schlesinger 104.
2. DP: Detroit Police Department, *Story* 299-300.
3. DH: Holli 67.
4. CIT: Schlesinger 21-22. IM: Stephenson 270.
5. DH: Bingay 237-39.

P. 112. ¶ 2. EC: Friedman 108; Wright 706. GEN: Moos 201.
P. 112. ¶ 3. DH: Catlin 631; Holli 63-64; Garrity 20.
P. 113. ¶ 6. DH: Holli 57-58, 62-64, 69, 72; Garrity 16; Catlin 616. IM: Stephenson 148. DA: Beasley, *Made* 20.
P. 114. ¶ 1. DH: Holli 64-66.
P. 114. ¶ 3. DH: Holli 67, 65; Bingay 245. IM: Stephenson 145-46. CIT: Schlesinger 346-47. GEN: Moos 205.
P. 114. ¶ 5. DS: Moehlman 144. DH: Holli 186-88, 112-14; Catlin 612. CIT: Schlesinger 390.
P. 115. ¶ 5. DH: Bingay 236; Lovett 19-20. DS: Moehlman 141-52. IM: Immigration Comm., Vol. 31: 5-7.
P. 115. ¶ 9. DH: Bingay 237; Miller 36, 38, 55-56; Catlin 604-05; Burton, Clarence 783. DF: Nevins, *Ford Times* 135. Connolly, John, "William C. Maybury," *Michigan Pioneer and Historical Collections,* Vol. 38: 714-16 (1912).

24. The Olds-Powered Ford Cadillac

1. DA: King 19.
2. GEN: Josephson 406.
3. GEN: Moos 218.
4. DH: Bingay 239-40.
5. CIT: Schlesinger 71.

P. 116. ¶ 1. DH: Miller 161-62, 15.
P. 117. ¶ 1. DA: Rae, *Amer. Auto. Mfrs.* 28-30, 10. DF: Nevins, *Ford Times* 146, 150-51. DH: Pound 271.

P. 117. ¶ 6. DA: King 15-20. DF: Nevins, *Ford Times* 154-56, 160, 166; Ruddiman 268-69.

P. 117. ¶ 10. DH: Miller 43, 44, 46.

P. 118. ¶ 1. GEN: Josephson 386-93, 351-53, 358-61. DH: Miller 25. DF: Nevins, *Ford Times* 166.

P. 118. ¶ 7. EC: Wright 468; Burlingame 262. GEN: Moos 181. CIT: Schlesinger 24, 47-49, 370-73, 3-4.

P. 119. ¶ 1. EC: Rayback 195-96, 201-04. DH: Catlin 611-12; Bingay 234.

P. 119. ¶ 3. DH: Holli 138-40, 194-95. MH: Dunbar 531-33.

P. 119. ¶ 8. GEN: Myers 341; Moos 213, 215-17, 218-19. CIT: Schlesinger 405, 185, 252-53, 189. DH: Catlin 628. Johnson, *op. cit.,* Vol. 8: 519-20.

P. 120. ¶ 3. DF: Sward 12; Nevins, *Ford Times* 170-72, 174. DA: Rae, *Amer. Auto. Mfrs.* 29; King. MH: Dunbar 535. DH: Moran 79, 126.

P. 120. ¶ 5. DH: Miller 47-48, 96-98, 161-62. DF: Nevins, *Ford Times* 175, 144. MH: Gates 119, 225. DA: Rae, *Amer. Auto. Mfrs.* 30-31.

P. 120. ¶ 6. DA: Beasley, *Made* 89-90; Rae, *Amer. Auto. Mfrs.* 12-13.

P. 121. ¶ 2. DA: Beasley, *Made* 52. DF: Nevins, *Ford Times* 204, 206; Sward 15.

P. 122. ¶ 6. DF: Nevins, *Ford Times* 210-11, 190-91, 277. CIT: Schlesinger 71. DA: Leland 21-40, 44-45, 52-53, 62-63; Beasley, *Made* 48; Rae, *Amer. Auto. Mfrs.* 31-32. DH: Pound 277-78.

P. 122. ¶ 8. DF: Nevins, *Ford Times* 213. DA: Leland 67, 69; Fed. Trade Comm. 910; Beasley, *Made* 89.

25. The Mile-A-Minute Company

1. Simonds, William A., *Henry Ford, His Life, His Work, His Genius* (Indianapolis and New York: 1943), p. 75.

P. 123. ¶ 4. DF: Nevins, *Ford Times* 205, 213-14, 225, 229, 233; Sward 15-16. DA: Beasley, *Made* 26.

P. 124. ¶ 6. DF: Nevins, *Ford Times* 229, 243-44. DH: Bingay 116-18; Barnard 18-22, 26-28.

P. 125. ¶ 5. DF: Nevins, *Ford Times* 230-32, 235-40. DH: Barnard 38, 45, 39; Farmer, Vol. 1: 173, 324; Vol. 2: 1190; Quaife 113. MH: Felch 289. DA: Beasley, *Made* 85.

P. 126. ¶ 2. DF: Nevins, *Ford Times* 246. DH: Barnard 47-48.

26. The Joy of Packard

P. 127. ¶ 5. DA: Rae, *Amer. Auto. Mfrs.* 29-30, 12-13, 22-23; Parker 30-34; Fed. Trade Comm. 733-34. Johnson, *op. cit.,* Vol. 7: 128-29. EC: Borth 105.

P. 128. ¶ 1. DH: Catlin 550-51.

P. 128. ¶ 8. DH: Farmer, Vol. 1: 477. EC: Borth 98-103, 107. DA: Parker 17; Beasley, *Made* 74-78, 104-05.

27. The Making of Detroit

P. 129. ¶ 2. DA: Beasley, *Made* 56, 83, 49. DF: Nevins, *Ford Times* 234. Johnson, *op. cit.,* Vol. 6: 436-37.

P. 130. ¶ 2. Johnson, *op. cit.,* Vol. 8: 74-75. DA: Rae, *The Amer. Auto.* 11; Rae, *Amer. Auto. Mfrs.* 10-28. DF: Nevins, *Ford Times* 194.

P. 130. ¶ 3. DA: Rae, *Amer. Auto. Mfrs.* 68-70.

P. 130. ¶ 5. DA: Labatut 79, 86; Rae, *Amer. Auto. Mfrs.* 11.

P. 130. ¶ 7. DF: Nevins, *Ford Times* 515.

P. 131. ¶ 2. DA: Rae, *Amer. Auto. Mfrs.* 62-65, 32; Beasley, *Made* 106; Leland 99.

P. 131. ¶ 5. DA: Sloan 5-6.

P. 131. ¶ 6. DF: Nevins, *Ford Times* 270. DH: Pound 281.

28. The Wretched Refuse

1. IM: Immigration Comm., Vol. 37: 338.

2. IM: Janson 234.

3. IM: Immigration Comm., Vol. 4: 150.

P. 132. ¶ 2. IM: Immigration Comm., Vol. 4: 361-65.
P. 133. ¶ 8. IM: Immigration Comm., Vol. 4: 79, 97-102. Author's Research.
P. 134. ¶ 2. IM: Immigration Comm., Vol. 4: 164, 169-70, 55, 158-60.
P. 134. ¶ 7. IM: Immigration Comm., Vol. 37: 6-22, 67-74.
P. 135. ¶ 9. CIT: Schlesinger 16. IM: Janson 253-54; Immigration Comm., Vol. 2: 443-49.
P. 136. ¶ 4. IM: Immigration Comm., Vol. 37: 209-34, 305-06.
P. 137. ¶ 1. CIT: Riis, *How* 136-45, 120-33.
P. 137. ¶ 3. Author's Research.

29. The Posthumous Revolution

1. *The Survey,* Oct. 1, 1910, p. 70. IM: Lauck 585.
2. IM: Immigration Comm., Vol. 2: 497-98.
3. *The Survey,* Oct. 1, 1910, p. 4.
4. DS: Moehlman 166.
5. DF: Nevins, *Ford Times* 519.
6. CIT: Riis, *How* 180, 43; Riis, *Battle* 185-86.
7. IM: Immigration Comm., Vol. 31: 5-9, 12-14.
8. IM: Immigration Comm., Vol. 31: 8-9.

P. 138. ¶ 1. D GOV: Upson. CIT: Riis, *Battle* 54; Riis, *How* 275; Schlesinger 93. DH: O'Geran 201.
P. 139. ¶6. CIT: Riis, *Battle* 69-74; Riis, *How* 87. DH: Farmer, Vol. 1: 662. Author's Research.
P. 140. ¶ 3. EC: Wright 591. CIT: Schlesinger 161-62; Riis, *Battle* 344. IM: Immigration Comm., Vol. 1: 214.
P. 141. ¶ 2. CIT: Riis, *How* 113. DS: Moehlman 141; Det. Bd. of Ed., *One Hundred Years* 32. IM: Immigration Comm., Vol. 31: 11-12.
P. 141. ¶ 6. DS: Det. Bd. of Ed., *One Hundred Years* 46. IM: Immigration Comm., Vol. 31: 8-12.
P. 142. ¶ 4. DS: Moehlman 161-62. DH: Holli 198, 204, 197, 212; Catlin 636-37. MH: Sarasohn 11-13.
P. 142. ¶ 6. DH: Catlin 638-39; Holli 213. MH: Dunbar 632, 707-08. DS: Disbrow 136.
P. 142. ¶ 7. DS: Starring 42; Disbrow 12, 23-26. MH: Dunbar 702.
P. 143. ¶ 1. ED: HEW, *Digest* 52.

30. A Car for All People

P. 144. ¶ 1. DH: Lodge 116-17. DF: Nevins, *Ford Times* 340.
P. 144. ¶ 4. DF: Nevins, *Ford Times* 269; Marquis 122-23.
P. 145. ¶ 1. DF: Nevins, *Ford Times* 274. DH: Barnard 60.
P. 145. ¶ 3. DF: Nevins, *Ford Times* 275-76, 323-24.
P. 290. ¶ 9. DH: Barnard 61-62, 64. DF: Nevins, *Ford Times* 278-79, 329-31.
P. 146. ¶ 3. DF: Nevins, *Ford Times* 281, 334-35, 331, 644-50; Sward 32-33. DA: Beasley, *Made* 141.
P. 146. ¶ 5. DA: Beasley, *Made* 139-40.
P. 146. ¶ 7. DF: Nevins, *Ford Times* 644-50, 354-55.
P. 147. ¶ 6. DF: Nevins, *Ford Times* 387-405; Sward 27. EC: Wright 544.
P. 148. ¶ 3. DF: Nevins, *Ford Times* 447, 484, 644-50. DA: Beasley, *Made* 165, Labatut 102. DH: Lodge 116-17; Franks 109.
P. 148. ¶ 6. GEN: Josephson 423-24. DF: Bennett 111.

31. The Birth of Empire

P. 149. ¶ 2. EC: Wright 554, 557; Lynch 167, 127; Clough 645. DA: Rae, *Amer. Auto. Mfrs.* 11. GEN: Katz 133-34; Munitions 21, 222. Johnson, *op. cit.,* Vol. 3: 177-78.
P. 150. ¶ 6. DA: Beasley, *Made* 178; Leland 100, 95, 15; Fed. Trade Comm. 450-51. DH: Barnard 73-75; Pound 293-96. DF: Nevins, *Ford Times* 150, 385.
P. 151. ¶ 2. DA: Sloan 5-8.

P. 151. ¶7. DA: Chrysler 18-31, 83-84, 138, 99-100, 106-08, 127, 132-37, 145. DH: Bingay 67.

32. The Union Wreckers Association

1. EC: Labor, *Handbook* 301. GEN: Census Bureau, *Historical Statistics,* D 735-40, p. 97.
2. EC: Wright 716.

P. 152. ¶3. DA: Rae, *Amer. Auto. Mfrs.* 11, 68-69, 72-79, 29, 92-96; Rae, *The Amer. Auto.* 27-28, 45.
P. 153. ¶1. MH: Dunbar 563-64. DA: Beasley, *Made* 236.
P. 153. ¶3. DA: Fed. Trade Comm. 628. DF: Nevins, *Ford Times* 345-46, 644-50.
P. 154. ¶1. DF: Nevins, *Ford Times* 407-09, 494, 458-60. DA: Beasley, *Knudsen* 5, 17-28, 53-56. GEN: Josephson 340-41.
P. 154. ¶4. EC: Rayback 208.
P. 155. ¶3. DH: Moran 134. DF: Nevins 377-78, 514-15. EC: Wright 716. Detroit *News,* May 3, 1909.

33. The Strike Against the "Widow Maker"

1. MH: Sullivan 298.
2. MH: Sullivan 296.

P. 156. ¶1. EC: Rayback 237-38, 243.
P. 157. ¶3. MH: Gates 110, 45, 56-60, 67, 111-12; Forster 175-86. IM: Immigration Comm., Vol. 16: 83.
P. 157. ¶6. MH: Todd 128-29; Gates 111. IM: Immigration Comm., Vol. 16: 84.
P. 158. ¶3. MH: Sullivan 294-95; Gates 218, 121, 126, 129.
P. 158. ¶9. MH: Gates 131-33; Beck 279, 284-85; Sullivan 298-300.
P. 159. ¶2. MH: Sullivan 296; Gates 133; Beck 286-89.
P. 160. ¶4. *The New York Times,* Dec. 25, 1913. MH: Beck 291; Gates 134. Author's Research.

34. The Dawn of the Assembly Line

1. DF: Nevins, *Ford Times* 644-50.
2. EC: Taylor 46.

P. 161. ¶1. DA: Fed. Trade Comm. 629-30. DF: Nevins, *Ford Times* 452-57.
P. 162. ¶2. EC: Taylor 39 ff. DF: Nevins, *Ford Times* 468-69; Sward 34.
P. 162. ¶6. EC: Clough 541; Taylor 70-72; Giedion 97, 92. DF: Nevins, *Ford Times* 456; Sward 39, 35-36.
P. 163. ¶3. DH: Miller 64-65, 159-60, 163, 149.
P. 163. ¶5. DH: Miller 149. DF: Sward 36-37.
P. 164. ¶1. DF: Nevins, *Ford Times* 644-50, 529; Sward 39, 45. DH: Glazer 69; Barnard 88.
P. 164. ¶7. DF: Nevins, *Ford Times* 532-33, 529. DH: Barnard 89-92. DA: Beasley, *Made* 216. *The New York Times,* Jan. 6, 1914. Det. *News,* Jan. 6, 1914.

35. The $5 Day

1. DF: Marquis 152.
2. DF: Marquis 151.

P. 169. ¶3. DH: Garrity 109; Pound 317. DF: Nevins, *Ford Times* 527, 522; Sward 50-51.
P. 170. ¶7. DA: Beasley, *Made* 212, 218. DF: Sward 53-55; Nevins, *Ford Times* 543-44. *The New York Times,* Jan. 12, 13, 1914. Det. *News,* Jan. 12, 13, 1914. Author's Research.
P. 173. ¶4. DA: Beasley, *Made* 217-18. DF: Nevins, *Ford Times* 473; Sward 37. Author's Research.
P. 174. ¶2. Author's Research.

P. 175. ¶ 2. DF: Ford Motor Company 11-20, 25-30; Nevins, *Ford Times* 558, 534-36.
P. 175. ¶ 3. *The New York Times,* Jan. 9, 10, 1914.
P. 176. ¶ 3. DF: Nevins, *Ford Times* 534, 554-56; Ford Motor Co. 1-9, 11; Sward 57-60.
DH: Barnard 93-94.
P. 176. ¶ 7. Author's Research.

36. The Americanization of Detroit

1. DF: Ford 129.
2. IM: Immigration Comm., Vol. 4: 307, 332.
3. IM: Sachar 310.

P. 177. ¶ 4. DF: Nevins 550; Sward 56; Ford 129. DH: Barnard 88. D GEN: Rankin.
IM: Immigration Comm., Vol. 4: 290-93, 332; Stephenson 74-75; Sachar 224; Roth
289-90.
P. 178. ¶3. IM: Immigration Comm., Vol. 4: 266, 286, 314-16, 309-10, 330, 307, 343,
272-76, 279; Sachar 321-22, 314; Stephenson 77-78.
P. 178. ¶ 8. Harold Black. DF: Ford Motor Co. 11, 25-30, 9; Nevins, *Ford Times* 557-58.
D GEN: Rankin. DS: Disbrow 48.

37. The American War

1. Detroit *Free Press,* Aug. 22, Sept. 1, 5, 1915. DF: Sward 84; Liebold 280. DA: Parker
93.
2. DF: Liebold 258.
3. DF: Lochner 42.
4. DF: Lochner 87.

P. 180. ¶ 1. DH: Garrity 27, 31, 87-89, 93. DS: Disbrow 48.
P. 180. ¶ 6. DA: Labatut 223. GEN: Munitions 33, 235.
P. 180. ¶ 7. EC: Bogart 530; Clough 538-39, 767; Friedman 199.
P. 180. ¶ 8. GEN: Munitions 39-40, 237.
P. 181. ¶ 2. DF: Nevins, *Ford Times* 568-69, 644-50; Sward 55, 462.
P. 182. ¶ 2. DF: Lochner 6, 10-27; Hershey 61-62; Liebold 250-56.
P. 182. ¶ 6. DF: Lochner 43; Hershey 75, 92.
P. 182. ¶ 7. DF: Liebold 258 ff.; Herndon 164-65.
P. 183. ¶ 2. DH: Barnard 80. DF: Nevins, *Ford Expansion* 609; Sward 91, 88.
P. 183. ¶ 7. DF: Lochner 67, 8; Hershey 132, 97, 203; Liebold 279.

38. "No Stockholders . . . No Parasites"

1. DH: Barnard 99.

P. 184. ¶ 4. DH: Barnard 76-81, 67-68; Sward 43-44, 65.
P. 184. ¶ 6. DF: Nevins, *Ford Times* 581. DH: Barnard 85-86.
P. 185. ¶ 6. DF: Nevins, *Ford Times* 568; Sward 66-69. DA: Beasley, *Made* 256-57; Rae,
Amer. Auto. Mfrs. 56-57. DH: Lodge 124-25.

39. The Three T's

1. MH: Dunbar 683-84.
2. IM: Immigration Comm., Vol. 37: 82-83, 67, 123.
3. IM: Immigration Comm., Vol. 37: 142, 83, 77. CIT: Schlesinger 116.
4. DP: Searles 3.

P. 186. ¶ 2. DH: O'Geran 263, 279-80; Barnard 84-85, 104-05.
P. 186. ¶ 4. DA: Beasley, *Made* 225; Leland 156-60. DH: Bingay 205-06; Lodge 84-87;
Lovett 86-87.
P. 187. ¶ 2. MH: Dunbar 612. DH: Holli 96-98.
P. 187. ¶ 3. ED: HEW, *Digest* 28. DS: Disbrow 25.
P. 187. ¶ 4. DS: Det. Bd. of Ed., *One Hundred Years* 15; Disbrow 226.
P. 187. ¶ 6. DH: Lovett 71-83.

P. 188. ¶ 2. GEN: Census, *Statistical Abstract* 1967, pp. 24, 33. IM: *Immigration Comm.,* Vol. 1: 97. DH: Lovett 27.

P. 188. ¶ 2. CIT: Schlesinger 157; Riis, *How* 217 ff. DH: Lovett 216; Lodge 191. DA: Beasley, *Made* 178.

P. 189. ¶ 3. DP: Det. Police Dept., *Story* 263, 265.

P. 190. ¶ 1. DF: Det. Police Dept., *Story* 92; Searles 42. DH: Catlin 671-73; Lodge 80; Barnard 106. DA: Beasley, *Made* 231-32.

P. 190. ¶ 2. DH: Barnard 108-10.

40. The City at War

1. DP: Det. Police Dept., *Story* 17, 104.
2. DP: Det. Police Dept., *Story* 10, 13, 21.
3. IM: Stephenson 212.

P. 191. ¶ 2. EC: Friedman 199, 221.

P. 182. ¶ 2. DA: Rae, *The Amer. Auto.* 72-73; Leland 175-81, 189-91. DF: Sward 96; Nevins, *Ford Expansion* 63-64, 72.

P. 192. ¶ 5. DA: Automobile Manufacturers Association 3; Labatut 223-24; Rae, *The Amer. Auto.* 71.

P. 192. ¶ 9. DF: Nevins, *Ford Times* 258, 485-87. DA: Rae, *The Amer. Auto.* 51-52; Auto. Mfrs. Assoc. 19; Labatut 91.

P. 193. ¶ 2. MH: Dunbar 566.

P. 193. ¶ 4. DH: O'Geran 381-82.

P. 193. ¶ 7. DH: Moran 84.

P. 194. ¶ 1. DH: Quaife 80; Moran 79. DP: Det. Police Dept., *Story* 98, 108.

P. 194. ¶ 2. DH: Barnard 110; Quaife 151. DP: Det. Police Dept., *Story* 17, 99.

P. 194. ¶ 4. DA: Leland 175-81. DF: Nevins, *Ford Expansion* 687. EC: Wright 754. DS: Disbrow 79. DN: Dancy 51-54. GEN: Myrdal 1115-18.

P. 195. ¶ 1. EC: Friedman 221; Labor, *Handbook* 236. DH: Garrity 33.

P. 195. ¶ 2. DS: Moehlman 193, 206; Disbrow 138.

P. 195. ¶ 4. DP: Det. Police Dept., *Story* 7, 14, 17, 290.

P. 196. ¶ 6. DH: Glazer 108. IM: Stephenson 202-10, 222-23. DS: Disbrow 92, 48. MH: Dunbar 689.

41. The Progressive Tide

1. DH: Barnard 96-97.
2. *The New York Times,* Jan. 6, 1914.

P. 197. ¶ 3. MH: Dunbar 541. GEN: Moos 275; Schlesinger, *Crisis* 37-41. FG PP: Labor, *Anvil* 3-4; Education and Labor Committee 88-90. DF: Nevins, *Ford Times* 519-20.

P. 198. ¶ 4. DS: Disbrow 228. DH: Barnard 115-16; Bingay 120; O'Geran 201, 271-72.

P. 198. ¶ 6. DN: Mallas 36-43; Dancy 103-04, 61-63. Det. *Free Press,* Alfred Pelham file.

P. 199. ¶ 6. DN: Dancy 88, 51; Haynes 13, 14, 16. GEN: Myrdal 819-22, 837. DF: Nevins, *Ford Expansion* 539.

42. "A Great Business Is Really Too Big To Be Human"

1. DF: Lochner 119.
2. MH: Sarasohn 20.
3. DF: Nevins, *Ford Expansion* 525.

P. 201. ¶ 3. MH: Sarasohn 19-20; Dunbar 544. DA: Rae, *The Amer. Auto.* 71. DF: Nevins, *Ford Times* 510, 644-50; Sward 116-21. DH: Barnard 136-37.

P. 201. ¶ 6. DH: Beasley, *Made* 257; Barnard 130. DF: Sward 71-74.

P. 202. ¶ 1. DF: Nevins, *Ford Expansion* 217-26, 231, 204-16, 282-87, 253-54; Sward 132-35. DA: Beasley, *Knudsen* 70.

P. 202. ¶ 2. EC: Friedman 229-30; Peach 145.

P. 202. ¶ 7. DA: Judiciary 52-53; Fed. Trade Comm. 641. EC: Friedman 232. DF: Sward 75-76.

P. 203. ¶ 7. DF: Marquis 143, 174-76; Nevins, *Ford Expansion* 349-50, 326, 333; Bennett 24; Sward 75-80; Ford 263.

43. The "American Plan"

P. 204. ¶ 3. DF: Bennett 108-09. EC: Rayback 279, 283-90; Labor, *Handbook* 301.
P. 205. ¶ 2. IM: Sachar 308, 297; Immigration Comm., Vol. 4: 309-10, 321-25. EC: Bogart 226; Rayback 283, 290-91. GEN: Myrdal 1118, 1123.
P. 205. ¶ 5. GEN: Schlesinger, *Crisis* 42-43, 49, 51. EC: Rayback 290.
P. 205. ¶ 7. DS: Disbrow 49, 138-39. DH: Barnard 124. GEN: Schlesinger, *Crisis* 41. EC: Labor, *Handbook* 166.

44. The "International Jewish Conspiracy"

1. DF: Lochner 212.
2. DA: Beasley, *Knudsen* 109.
3. DF: Nevins, *Ford Expansion* 124.
4. DF: Sward 101.
5. DF: Sward 104.
6. DF: Sward 144.
7. DF: Nevins, *Ford Expansion* 168, 222; Liebold 257, 399; Sward 118, 119; Bennett 58.
8. DF: Ford 250-52.
9. DF: Liebold 442.
10. Ford, Henry. *The International Jew.* Chs. 11, 16, 19, 20, 21, 23.*
11. *Ibid.,* Ch. 16.
12. DH: Katz 54-56; Farmer, Vol. 1: 868-69; Heineman 59-63.
13. DF: Bennett 47.
14. Hitler, Adolf, *Mein Kampf* (Boston: 1962), p. 639.
15. Shirer, William L., *The Rise and Fall of the Third Reich* (Greenwich, Conn.: 1960), p. 209. DF: Sward 159-60, 451.
16. DF: Liebold 472-73.

P. 207. ¶ 2. DH: Moran 80. DA: Leland 198-205, 227-34, 129-33; Fed. Trade Comm. 643-45. DF: Sward 163-70.
P. 207. ¶ 6. Det. *Free Press,* Liebold file. DF: Liebold 1-21, 511 ff.; Bennett 48.
P. 207. ¶ 8. DA: Beasley, *Knudsen* 68, 93; Rae, *Amer. Auto. Mfrs.* 132.
P. 208. ¶ 5. DF: Nevins, *Ford Expansion* 124-27; Sward 140-45.
P. 209. ¶ 2. DF: Sward 100-04; Nevins, *Ford Expansion* 117, 132.
P. 210. ¶ 2. DF: Sward 149; Liebold 481; Bennett 47-48.
P. 210. ¶ 5. DF: Nevins, *Ford Expansion* 311-15, 210; Sward 146.
P. 211. ¶ 3. DF: Liebold 452-55.
P. 211. ¶ 7. DH: Katz 44-46. Det. *News,* March 23, 1902.
P. 212. ¶ 3. DF: Liebold 452-55, 471, 1534; DF: Nevins, *Ford Expansion* 315-16, 262, 605; Sward 147, 149, 157; Bennett 48-54; Ford 250-52.

45. The Scab Millionaire

1. GEN: Josephson 312.

P. 214. ¶ 1. DH: Barnard 120-22. D GOV: Upson.
P. 214. ¶ 3. D GOV: Ketcham 51.
P. 214. ¶ 5. DH: Lane 69; Miller 210-11.
P. 214. ¶ 7. DA: Labatut 224. DH: Quaife 153.
P. 215. ¶ 5. GEN: National Comm., Vol. 4: 575. MH: Dunbar 685, 650-51. DA: Beasley, *Made* 252-53.
P. 215. ¶ 6. DH: Barnard 130 ff.: O'Geran XIII, 363, 367, 377. D GOV: Ketcham 52 ff.
P. 216. ¶ 4. DH: Barnard 118-20, 136-38; Bingay 123. DF: Sward 121-22.

* Copies of *The International Jew* are difficult to obtain, and the author worked with a serialized version without page numbers. Only chapter references can, therefore, be given.

46. The Government of Business

1. GEN: Schlesinger, *Crisis* 51.
2. GEN: Moos 323.
3. DF: Sward 131
4. DF: Liebold 511.
5. GEN: Schlesinger, *Crisis* 58.
6. GEN: Munitions 272.
7. DH: Barnard 154.

P. 217. ¶ 4. DH: Barnard 157. DF: Sward 126, 125, 123.
P. 218. ¶ 9. DF: Nevins, *Ford Expansion* 303-05; Sward 127-31. GEN: Schlesinger, *Coming* 319-22. DH: Barnard 145-46.
P. 219. ¶ 2. GEN: Schlesinger, *Crisis* 57. EC: Wright 658-61; Bogart 489; Clough 767.
P. 220. ¶ 1. GEN: Munitions 264-66. EC: Wright 577. GEN: Moos 357.

47. The Source of All Evils

1. IM: Goldenweiser 598.
2. IM: Lauck 584-85.
3. IM: Lauck 584.
4. IM: Lauck 584, 586.
5. IM: Willis 574-75.
6. IM: Immigration Comm., Vol. 2: 243, 251.
7. IM: Immigration Comm., Vol. 36: 8, 265.
8. IM: Immigration Comm., Vol. 1: 13-14.
9. IM: Immigration Comm., Vol. 1: 242.
10. IM: Immigration Comm., Vol. 4: 21.
11. IM: Immigration Comm., Vol. 4: 186, 378.
12. IM: Willis 573.
13. IM: Nelson 48.
14. Hitler, *op. cit.*, 440.

P. 222. ¶ 2. IM: Stephenson 162; Immigration Comm., Vol. 26: 141-50; Vol. 36: 2, 233, 251.
P. 222. ¶ 5. IM: Immigration Comm., Vol. 36: 2, 25, 19-20, 17, 1, 8, 254-57.
P. 223. ¶ 4. IM: Stephenson 202-10; Immigration Comm.: Vol. 4: 33-34, 28; Vol. 1: 23; Vol. 26: 4.
P. 223. ¶ 8. IM: Nelson 45, 49, 50, 57.
P. 224. ¶ 4. IM: Stephenson 185-89. GEN: Census, *Statistical Abstract,* 1967, pp. 91-94.

48. The Age of Intolerance

1. GEN: Census, *Negroes* 7, 48.
2. GEN: Schlesinger, *Crisis* 99.

P. 225. ¶ 1. DS: Moehlman 188.
P. 226. ¶ 3. DH: Miller 148-49; Young 415-16. EC: Giedion 590-93.
P. 228. ¶ 1. GEN: Myrdal 231, 235, 1112-18. DN: Northrup 8-9. Author's Research.
P. 229. ¶ 3. Davis, Forrest, "Labor Spies and the Black Legion," *New Republic,* June 17, 1936. GEN: Haas 59-63, 69-73; Schlesinger, *Crisis* 99-100; Moos 354.

49. Sweet Justice

1. GEN: Census, *Negroes* 78-86.
2. GEN: Census, *Negroes* 213, 239.
3. DN: Dancy 30.
4. DN: Dancy 218.

P. 231. ¶ 5. Author's Research.

P. 231. ¶ 6. DN: Dancy 155, 152, 135, 58-59; Haynes 21-25; U.S. Commission 114. D GEN: Census, *Census Tracts, Detroit SMSA* 25-26.
P. 232. ¶ 5. DN: Dancy 27, 56.
P. 233. ¶ 2. DN: Dancy 21-24, 28.
P. 234. ¶ 4. Josephine Gomon. DN: Darrow 22-30, 301-11. DH: Lunt 25.

50. One Family—Like Cain and Abel

1. DF: Marquis 77-78; Nevins, *Ford Times* 575; Nevins, *Ford Expansion* 490-91. DA: Howe 90.
2. DF: Nevins, *Ford Expansion* 408.
3. DF: Nevins, *Ford Expansion* 321; Liebold 487. DA: Beasley, *Made* 302-03.
4. DF: Liebold 492.

P. 235. Footnote. DH: Woodford 119; Lodge 109-11.
P. 236. ¶ 4. DF: Bennett 22; Nevins, *Ford Expansion* 482, 410, 500; Nevins, *Ford Decline* 57-59.
P. 236. ¶ 7. DF: Nevins, *Ford Expansion* 238-46.
P. 236. ¶ 8. DA: Sloan 153. DF: Nevins, *Ford Expansion* 264.
P. 236. ¶ 9. DA: Auto. Mfrs. Assoc. 59.
P. 237. ¶ 2. DA: Sloan 158-62.
P. 237. ¶ 5. DA: Auto. Mfrs. Assoc. 19. DH: O'Geran 381-82. DR: Overton 374. MH: Dunbar 569-70.
P. 238. ¶ 1. DF: Nevins, *Ford Expansion* 386, 416-17; Sward 196-98. GEN: Census, *Statistical Abstract,* 1967, p. 24.
P. 238. ¶ 7. DF: Nevins, *Ford Expansion* 410-11, 415; Sward 196. DA: Sloan 162.
P. 238. ¶ 9. DF: Nevins, *Ford Expansion* 317.
P. 239. ¶ 2. DF: Bennett 1-17, 173, 24, 93; Nevins, *Ford Expansion* 270-74.
P. 239. ¶ 4. DF: Liebold 495; Sward 152-57; Bennett 58.
P. 239. ¶ 11. DF: Bennett 55, 48-54, 101; Liebold 487.
P. 240. ¶ 2. DA: Sloan 69; Rae, *The Amer. Auto.* 99. DF: Bennett 96; Nevins, *Ford Expansion* 430-32.

51. The Model of the Modern Corporation

1. GEN: Munitions 171.

P. 241. ¶ 5. DA: Beasley, *Made* 218, 233-34; Fed. Trade Comm. 419-25; Sloan 9-11. DH: Pound 300; Bingay 59.
P. 242. ¶ 1. DA: Sloan 15, 17-18, 20-24.
P. 242. ¶ 4. DA: Sloan 25-31, 171, 62, 69.
P. 242. ¶ 8. DA: Sloan 33, 41, 35, 14; Fed. Trade Comm. 427, 426; Judiciary 7-8. GEN: Munitions 20, 22-23.
P. 243. ¶ 2. DA: Beasley, *Knudsen* 115; Sloan 45, 67, 83. DF: Nevins, *Ford Expansion* 404.
P. 243. ¶ 4. DA: Drucker 1-20; Sloan 99-130.
P. 243. ¶ 5. DA: Sloan 143; Judiciary 74-76.
P. 243. ¶ 6. DF: Nevins, *Ford Expansion* 403.
P. 244. ¶ 1. DA: Sloan 38; Rae, *Amer. Auto. Mfrs.* 166-68, 171-72, 181-85; Beasley, *Made* 297. DF: Nevins, *Ford Expansion* 392.
P. 244. ¶ 4. DA: Chrysler 161, 164, 175, 181-89, 191-96; Sloan 27, 162; Rae, *Amer. Auto. Mfrs.* 143-48, 181-82, 132; Beasley, *Made* 298-301; Fed. Trade Comm. 549-621, 428-29. DH: Pound 300-01.

52. An Aristocracy of Wealth

1. EC: Peach 149. D GOV: Upson.
2. DH: Barnard 161, 163, 166-67, 188; Bingay 126-27. GEN: Schlesinger, *Crisis* 65.
3. GEN: Schlesinger, *Crisis* 113.

P. 245. ¶ 1. DA: Judiciary 152; Sloan 302-03, 150-51.

P. 246. ¶ 1. GEN: Moos 357; Schlesinger, *Crisis* 63, 253-54; Census, *Historical Statistics,* Y 254-57, p. 711. DH: Barnard 266. Johnson, *op. cit.,* Vol. 11: 449.
P. 246. ¶ 6. EC: Wright 584; Moulton 65; Peach 59, 65. DA: Cook 73.
P. 246. ¶ 7. EC: Lynch 89; Labor, *Handbook* 67, 166; Moulton 65; Peach 217.
P. 247. ¶ 3. EC: Peach 37; Leven 123, 56. DF: Sward 69, 345.

53. The Curse of Progress

P. 248. ¶ 2. DA: Auto. Mfrs. Assoc. 3. DF: Nevins, *Ford Expansion* 453; Sward 200-01, 205. EC: Peach 59, 191, 193, 217.
P. 248. ¶ 3. DF: Sward 175-76, 312; Raushenbush 9; Nevins, *Ford Expansion* 527, 514. Author's Research.
P. 249. ¶ 2. Author's Research.
P. 249. Footnote. DS: Disbrow 181.
P. 249. ¶ 3. DH: O'Geran 377-78.
P. 250. ¶ 1. EC: Peach 233, 225, 239; Leven 173, 176. Author's Research.
P. 250. ¶ 3. EC: Peach 235, 237.
P. 252. ¶ 5. Author's Research.

54. American Roulette

P. 253. ¶ 3. DF: Nevins, *Ford Expansion* 438; Sward 199. DA: Cook 21, 35-38.
P. 253. ¶ 4. DF: Nevins, *Ford Expansion* 294, 593.
P. 254. ¶ 1. DF: Sward 204; Nevins, *Ford Expansion* 453, 461, 463.
P. 254. ¶ 4. EC: Peach 99, 121; Leven 87, 93. DA: Rae, *The Amer. Auto.* 109.
P. 254. ¶ 6. EC: Peach 179; Friedman 288. GEN: Census, *Historical Statistics* N 1-28, p. 379. D GOV: Leonard, *Exemption;* Det. City Plan, *Renewal and Revenue* 119.
P. 254. ¶ 8. DA: Sloan 323-27. DF: Nevins, *Ford Expansion* 559. EC: Clough 734-35; Friedman 273, 290.
P. 255. ¶ 2. EC. Peach 123, 229, 115; Leven 58-61; Wright 685. DF: Sward 245. DH: Banking, Pt. 9, p. 4543.
P. 255. ¶ 5. DF: Nevins, *Ford Expansion* 465.
P. 255. ¶ 6. DF: Nevins, *Ford Expansion* 467; Raushenbush 10-11; Sward 216-17. DA: Auto. Mfrs. Assoc. 3.
P. 255. ¶ 10. DA: Sloan 162; Fed. Trade Comm. 54, 285-90, 1022-57. DF: Nevins, *Ford Expansion* 469-75, 266; Sward 206, 215, 216. EC: Peach 193.
P. 256. ¶ 1. D GEN: Det. City Plan 8. DA: Parker 84-86.
P. 256. ¶ 2. DA: Federal Trade Comm. 36, 507, 649; Judiciary 108-10; Pound 355-56. EC: Moulton 146. *The New York Times,* Feb. 13, 1927.
P. 256. ¶ 3. EC: Peach 99. GEN: Census, *Historical Statistics* X 343-347, p. 657.
P. 256. ¶ 4. GEN: Schlesinger, *Coming* 436-37. DH: Barnard 265.
P. 257. ¶ 2. EC: Friedman 260, 290, 254-66. DA: Sloan 170-72.
P. 257. ¶ 4. GEN: Josephson 479; Census, *Historical Statistics* S 81-93, p. 511; R 90-98, p. 491. DF: Nevins, *Ford Expansion* 503.
P. 257. ¶ 5. GEN: Josephson 480.

55. The Lowering of the Boom

1. *Literary Digest,* Nov. 9, 1929. GEN: Schlesinger, *Crisis* 164; Smith 58.
2. GEN: Schlesinger, *Crisis* 165.

P. 258. ¶ 3. EC: Friedman 305, 335; Peach 95. GEN: Schlesinger, *Crisis* 158-59. *Variety,* Oct. 30, 1929.
P. 259. ¶ 1. DA: Judiciary 204; Fed. Trade Comm. 419. D GOV: Wengert 1. DH: Glazer 104. EC: Burlingame 287. GEN: Census, *Historical Statistics* M 133-137, p. 361. DF: Nevins, *Ford Decline* 3.
P. 259. ¶ 2. DA: Auto. Mfrs. Assoc. 3. D GEN: Mich. Emergency 85.
P. 259. ¶ 5. DF: Nevins, *Ford Expansion* 529; Sward 218.
P. 259. ¶ 6. EC: Peach 59.
P. 260. ¶ 4. DF: Nevins, *Ford Expansion* 571. DA: Fed. Trade Comm. 189-91. GEN: Census, *Historical Statistics* P 250-306, p. 422. EC: Commerce 94, 114.

P. 260. ¶ 8. D GEN: Mich. Emergency 85.
P. 260. ¶ 11. DA: Sloan 172-77. EC: Peach 191.

56. The $150 Marriage

P. 263. ¶ 4. Author's Research.

57. Blood and Gin

1. GEN: National Comm., Vol. 4: 340, 582; Vol. 1: 323.
2. GEN: National Comm., Vol. 1: 324.

P. 264. ¶ 3. GEN: National Comm., Vol. 4: 294. DH: Lovett 29.
P. 265. ¶ 2. GEN: National Comm., Vol. 1: 322-26; Vol. 4: 228-41, 303, 311, 331-33.
P. 265. ¶ 4. GEN: National Comm., Vol. 1: 25-27, 268. DP: Det. Police Dept. *Annual Report,* 1929. *The New York Times,* May 3, 1928.
P. 266. ¶ 1. DH: Wood 49. GEN: National Comm., Vol. 4: 260. DP: Searles 3, 8, 24, 32.
P. 266. ¶ 3. GEN: National Comm., Vol. 4: 581.
P. 266. ¶ 5. DH: Lovett 220-22.
P. 267. ¶ 1. Josephine Gomon. DH: Glazer 98; Lovett 213; Lodge 94. DP: Det. Police Dept., *Annual Reports.* GEN: National Comm., Vol. 5: 111-20.
P. 267. ¶ 6. Josephine Gomon. DF: Bennett 57. DH: Hamer 121-25; Lovett 235; Lunt 28.

58. The Flapping of the Hoover Flags

P. 268. ¶ 2. EC: Labor, *Handbook* 67; Commerce 90-91, 94.
P. 269. ¶ 1. D GOV: Wengert 2, 3, 9, 48, 55.
P. 269. ¶ 6. Josephine Gomon. DH: Lunt 30, 34-36; Glazer 97-100.
P. 271. ¶ 3. D GOV: Upson; Wengert 36. DH: Lunt 32.
P. 271. ¶ 5. Josephine Gomon. DH: Lunt 34. DF: Sward 223. GEN: Schlesinger, *Crisis* 177.
P. 272. ¶ 6. Author's Research.

59. The Ford Circus

P. 273. ¶ 1. DH: Lunt 79. GEN: Schlesinger, *Crisis* 278.
P. 273. ¶ 3. DH: Lunt 32, 35. DF: Raushenbush 51; Sward 226-27.
P. 274. ¶ 7. Josephine Gomon. D GOV: Wengert 45. DF: Bennett 18. DH: Lunt 32.
P. 274. ¶ 8. DF: Raushenbush 16; Sward 227-28; Bennett 68.
P. 275. ¶ 3. DF: Bennett 82, 83, 93, 42, 97, 84, 18, 110-11; Nevins, *Ford Expansion* 591; *Ford Decline* 233-38; Herndon 161; Liebold 1055-58.
P. 275. ¶ 5. DA: Fed. Trade Comm. 189-91. DF: Nevins, *Ford Expansion* 571, 573, 578.
P. 275. ¶ 6. DF: Sward 225, 232. D GEN: Mich. Emergency 1, 87.
P. 275. ¶ 8. DH: Lunt 32, 37, 42-43, 39.
P. 276. ¶ 1. DH: Barnard 203; Lunt 37.
P. 276. ¶ 2. D GOV: Wengert 45, 15-16; Eyre 1. DH: Lunt 50-51, 54-55.

60. The Patriarch of Inkster

1. DF: Liebold 1432.

P. 278. ¶ 3. DF: Nevins, *Ford Expansion* 594; Liebold 1410-32; Sward 228-30. Author's Research.
P. 278. ¶ 8. DF: Nevins, *Ford Expansion* 490. DN: Lincoln 10-11, 81, 91.
P. 279. ¶ 1. DN: Lincoln 57-65. GEN: Myrdal 746-49.
P. 279. ¶ 7. DN: Lincoln 12, 14-16.

61. A First-Class Promoter

P. 281. ¶ 1. Jerome P. Cavanagh; Rose Cavanagh.
P. 281. ¶ 4. DH: Mugglebee 147, 154, 158, 161-62.

P. 281. ¶ 8. DH: Mugglebee 164, 166, 167, 143-46, 231-34, 265, 192-95; Tull 4, 45. GEN: Schlesinger, *Politics* 17-18.

P. 282. ¶ 1. DH: Mugglebee 202, 172-79; Tull 20.

P. 282. ¶ 2. DH: Tull 6-7, 14; Mugglebee 262. GEN: Schlesinger, *Politics* 17-18.

P. 282. ¶ 4. DH: Tull 15.

62. The Hunger March

1. GEN: Schlesinger, *Crisis* 185.
2. GEN: Schlesinger, *Crisis* 179.

P. 283. ¶ 3. DH: Lunt 33, 53. DS: Disbrow 236. DF: Sward 223.

P. 284. ¶ 1. D GOV: Eyre; Wengert 36. DH: Lunt 51, 79.

P. 284. ¶ 2. DH: Lunt 53.

P. 285. ¶ 7. DF: Nevins, *Ford Decline* 32-33; Sward 231-32, 228-29, 241, 316, 232-36; Bennett 93. DH: Lunt 43. DA: Fed. Trade Comm. 664, 668. Det. *News,* Det. *Free Press,* March 8-9, 1932.

P. 285. ¶ 9. DH: Lunt 66-67. DF: Sward 240.

P. 286. ¶ 1. DH: Lunt 65. DF: Sward 238-39.

P. 286. ¶ 2. DF: Raushenbush 26, 49; Sward 230, 295, 319.

63. The Verge of Destruction

1. DH: Lunt, 59-60. Det. *News,* June 2, 1932.
2. GEN: Schlesinger, *Crisis* 242.

P. 287. ¶ 1. DH: Lunt 29. EC: Commerce 78, 40, 44. DA: Judiciary 141.

P. 287. ¶ 3. D GOV: Wengert 24-27, 55. DH: Lunt 54-57, 70.

P. 288. ¶ 2. DH: Barnard 204; Lunt 58-60. GEN: Schlesinger, *Crisis* 229 ff. Josephine Gomon.

P. 289. ¶ 1. GEN: Moos 385; Schlesinger, *Crisis* 164. DA: Fed. Trade Comm. 35; Judiciary 168-69. EC: Peach 121.

P. 289. ¶ 3. EC: Bogart 658; Clough 815; Commerce 52; Friedman 317; Peach 95. GEN: Moos 380.

P. 290. ¶ 4. GEN: Schlesinger, *Crisis* 182, 417. DH: Lunt 73. FG PP: Ed. & Labor Com. 103-04.

64. "In No Year Did the Corporation Fail To Earn a Profit"

1. DA: Sloan 199.

P. 291. ¶ 1. D GOV: Wengert 5.

P. 291. ¶ 2. DF: Nevins, *Ford Expansion* 586. DA: Fed. Trade Comm. 546, 507; Judiciary 108-10. EC: Commerce 126.

P. 291. ¶ 4. EC: Commerce 94, 102. DA: Auto Mfrs. Assoc. 3.

P. 292. ¶ 1. DA: Rae, *Amer. Auto. Mfrs.* 193; Judiciary 9; Fed. Trade Comm: 742. DF: Nevins, *Ford Expansion* 572.

P. 292. ¶ 3. DA: Rae, *Amer. Auto. Mfrs.* 194, 198-99; Judiciary 4, 8-10. Johnson, *op. cit.,* Vol. 10: 417-18.

P. 292. ¶ 6. DR: Overton 380, 402, 393, 396-97.

P. 293. ¶ 2. DA: Sloan 362-65, 341-53; Judiciary 26-28, 172-73. GEN: Munitions 23; Schlesinger, *Coming* 448-55.

P. 293. ¶ 4. DA: Sloan 354-60.

P. 294. ¶ 1. DA: Sloan 221-24; Fed. Trade Comm. 428, 478; Rae, *Amer. Auto. Mfrs.* 255.

65. The Coming of Christ's Deal

1. GEN: Schlesinger, *Crisis* 264.
2. GEN: Schlesinger, *Crisis* 259.
3. GEN: Schlesinger, *Crisis* 204, 268.
4. GEN: Smith 90.

5. GEN: Schlesinger, *Crisis* 314; *Politics* 23.

P. 295. ¶ 1. EC: Lynch 209. DA: Judiciary 203. GEN: Schlesinger, *Crisis* 266-68.
P. 296. ¶ 1. GEN: Smith 135.
P. 296. ¶ 7. GEN: Schlesinger, *Crisis* 273-76.
P. 297. ¶ 2. GEN: Schlesinger, *Crisis* 304-12.

66. The End of Illusion

1. GEN: Schlesinger, *Crisis* 209, 210, 213.

P. 298. ¶ 2. DH: Lunt 61, 73. D GOV: Wengert 9, 36.
P. 298. ¶ 3. DH: Lunt 62. D GOV: Leonard, *Exemption* 1. MH: Dunbar 636.
P. 298. ¶ 4. D GEN: Mich. Emergency 85. DH: Barnard 204. EC: Rayback 314.
P. 299. ¶ 2. GEN: Schlesinger, *Crisis* 432.
P. 299. ¶ 7. DA: Cook 18, 48-50.
P. 300. ¶ 2. GEN: Schlesinger, *Crisis* 434; Moos 388.
P. 300. ¶ 4. DA: Cook 50.

67. The Collapse of the Pyramids

1. DH: Neville 35.
2. DH: Banking, Pt. 10, p. 4702.
3. DH: Banking, Pt. 9, pp. 4545, 4551, 4573.
4. GEN: Schlesinger, *Crisis* 476; Smith 225.

P. 301. ¶ 3. DH: Neville 48; Lunt 78; Howe 94. DF: Sward 220-21; Nevins, *Ford Decline* 36-37. Author's Research.
P. 301. ¶ 4. D GOV: Wengert 41, 13.
P. 302. ¶ 1. DH: Neville 45. EC: Friedman 325.
P. 302. ¶ 2. DH: Neville 3.
P. 302. ¶ 4. DF: Sward 245, 250. DH: Neville 5, 11-19.
P. 303. ¶ 1. DF: Sward 247. DH: Banking, Pt. 10, pp. 4600, 4612; Neville 36-37.
P. 303. ¶ 4. DF: Sward 245-46. DH: Neville 40, 25-31, 37-38; Banking, Pt. 9, p. 4560.
P. 303. ¶ 6. DH: Neville 34-35.
P. 304. ¶ 1. GEN: Schlesinger, *Crisis* 237-38. DH: Barnard 204; Banking, Pt. 9, p. 4555. DA: Rae, *Amer. Auto. Mfrs.* 193-94.
P. 304. ¶ 2. GEN: Schlesinger, *Coming* 438. DF: Sward 256. DH: Banking, Pt. 10, p. 4712.
P. 304. ¶ 5. DH: Banking, Pt. 9, pp. 4561-63.
P. 304. ¶ 7. DH: Neville 52; Barnard 216, 225; Banking, Pt. 9, p. 4569.
P. 305. ¶ 2. DH: Barnard 223, 226-27; Banking, Pt. 10, pp. 4663-66, 4685-86, Pt. 9, pp. 4563, 4572; Neville 53; Bingay 129. DF: Sward 249. EC: Friedman 320.
P. 306. ¶ 1. DF: Liebold, Ch. 21; Sward 251-52; Nevins, *Ford Decline* 12-14. DH: Neville 54; Barnard 229; Bingay 129; Banking, Pt. 10, pp. 4692-96.
P. 306. ¶ 4. DH: Banking, Pt. 10, pp. 4700-01; Barnard 243; Neville 55.
P. 306. ¶ 6. DH: Neville 56, 57; Bingay 49-50. MH: Dunbar 675.

68. The Faded Mask

1. GEN: Schlesinger, *Coming* 13.
2. Josephine Gomon.
3. *Ibid.*

P. 309. ¶ 2. DH: Lunt 75, 79. D GOV: Wengert 5, 18, 27. EC: Friedman 325.
P. 309. ¶ 4. *The New York Times,* March 13, 1933.
P. 310. ¶ 1. DF: Nevins, *Ford Decline* 15; Liebold, Ch. 21; Bennett 99-101. Det. *Free Press,* Liebold file. DH: Barnard 252.
P. 310. ¶ 6. GEN: Schlesinger, *Coming* 337-40.
P. 311. ¶ 1. D GOV: Wengert 36. Det. *Free Press,* Cobo file. GEN: Schlesinger, *Coming* 297-98.

P. 311. ¶ 6. D GOV: Wengert 24-27; Detroit Housing Commission, *History*. Banking & Currency Committee, Subcommittee on Housing, *Congress and American Housing* 5. DH: Glazer 104. Josephine Gomon.
P. 312. ¶ 4. D GOV: Det. Housing Comm., *History*.

69. The Bubbling Earth, the Drifting Land

1. FG PP: Agriculture Committee, *Hearings, General Farm Legislation* 172.
2. FG PP: Agric. Com., *op. cit.*, 214.

P. 313. ¶ 1. GEN: Schlesinger, *Coming* 42-45, 65-66; *Crisis* 459-60.
P. 313. ¶ 5. GEN: Schlesinger, *Coming* 59-64.
P. 314. ¶ 5. EC: Peach 181, 227, 229, 237; Labor, *Handbook* 79.
P. 315. ¶ 2. GEN: Schlesinger, *Coming* 50-59; *Politics* 433; Myrdal, 370, 372. EC: Peach 225, 227, 229, 233.
P. 316. ¶ 7. Author's Research.

70. The Destroyer of the Spirit

1. GEN: Schlesinger, *Politics* 268.

P. 317. ¶ 1. D GOV: Upson; Wengert 34; Leonard, *Exemption* 11. DS: Disbrow 121; Det. Bd. of Ed., *Budgets*.
P. 317. ¶ 4. GEN: Schlesinger, *Coming* 264-67. DS: Disbrow 109. EC: Rayback 322.
P. 318. ¶ 3. GEN: Schlesinger, *Coming* 270-71. D GEN: Mich. Emergency 30-32, 85. DP: Det. Police Dept., *Annual Reports*.
P. 318. ¶ 4. D GEN: Mich. Emergency 4-5.
P. 319. ¶ 1. GEN: Schlesinger, *Politics* 264; *Coming* 287-88. DF: Raushenbush 44. D GOV: Ketcham 51.
P. 319. ¶ 6. GEN: Schlesinger, *Politics* 266, 272. EC: Commerce 52.

71. The National Runaround

1. GEN: Schlesinger, *Coming* 102.
2. DF: Nevins, *Ford Decline* 44.

P. 321. ¶ 3. GEN: Schlesinger, *Coming* 115-16, 125-35. EC: Lynch 86. DF: Nevins, *Ford Decline* 38-41.
P. 321. ¶ 8. DA: Howe 48. GEN: Schlesinger, *Coming* 117. DF: Nevins, *Ford Expansion* 535; *Ford Decline* 18-21, 42, 48-49; Raushenbush 18.
P. 322. ¶ 1. EC: Rayback 330. DF: Nevins, *Ford Decline* 43-47; Raushenbush 21.
P. 322. ¶ 4. D GOV: Wengert 42. GEN: Census, *Historical Statistics* H 199-206, p. 200. EC: Peach 175; Commerce 40. DA: Auto. Mfrs. Assoc. 3.
P. 322. ¶ 5. DA: Sloan 200-01.
P. 322. ¶ 6. GEN: Myrdal 398.
P. 323. ¶ 2. EC: Peach 191, 59; Commerce 94, 118; Labor, *Handbook* 67. D GEN: Det. City Plan 22.

72. "Roosevelt or Ruin"

1. *The New York Times*, Nov. 28, 1933. DH: Mugglebee 325. GEN: Schlesinger, *Politics* 23.
2. GEN: Schlesinger, *Coming* 201.
3. GEN: Schlesinger, *Politics* 608.
4. GEN: Schlesinger, *Politics* 66.
5. Det. *News*, Sept. 1, 1936.
6. DF: Greenleaf 181-82.
7. DF: Greenleaf 188.

P. 324. ¶ 3. EC: Friedman 465, 470.
P. 325. ¶ 1. DH: Spivak 23. GEN: Schlesinger, *Politics* 27.
P. 325. ¶ 3. DH: Tull 56, 91; Lunt 124; Mugglebee 345. GEN: Schlesinger, *Politics* 250.

P. 325. ¶ 5. DH: Tull 61, 69, 93, 96. GEN: Schlesinger, *Politics* 24-26, 112-14, 117-19.
P. 326. ¶ 1. GEN: Schlesinger, *Politics* 30-37. EC: Commerce 2, 52, 54.
P. 326. ¶ 4. GEN: Schlesinger, *Politics* 47, 63; Aaron 313.
P. 326. ¶ 6. Burton Historical Collection, Det. Public Library, *Black Legion* file.
P. 327. ¶ 1. GEN: Schlesinger, *Coming* 386-94. DA: Howe 49.
P. 327. ¶ 5. Burton Historical Collection, *op. cit.* GEN: Aaron 305-07. DA: Howe 8.
DH: Hamer 159-78.
P. 327. ¶ 6. GEN: Schlesinger, *Politics* 80-81; Un-American, *Investigation* 3708 ff., 3786,
3824. DF: Bennett 118, 131; Sward 373-74.
P. 328. ¶ 1. DF: Liebold 1406.
P. 328. ¶ 5. DF: Nevins, *Ford Decline* 411, 413; *Ford Expansion* 493; Greenleaf 181-87,
177; Macdonald 130. Det. *Free Press,* Cameron file.

73. The Middle of the Road

1. GEN: Schlesinger, *Politics* 519.
2. GEN: Schlesinger, *Politics* 620, 625, 629, 630.
3. GEN: Schlesinger, *Politics* 638-39.

P. 329. ¶ 2. GEN: Schlesinger, *Politics* 341, 555.
P. 330. ¶ 3. GEN: Myrdal 503.
P. 330. ¶ 4. GEN: Hughes 76; Myrdal 307.
P. 330. ¶ 5. GEN: Schlesinger, *Politics* 433, 435-36; Myrdal 365.
P. 331. ¶ 1. GEN: Schlesinger, *Politics* 433-34, 436-38; Hughes 35; Census, *Historical
Statistics* H 452-54.
P. 331. ¶ 2. DN: Mallas 52-68.
P. 331. ¶ 5. IM: Stephenson 83-84; Sachar 363-64.
P. 332. ¶ 7. Harold Black.
P. 333. ¶ 3. Author's Research.
P. 333. ¶ 5. DH: Lunt 126, 132-33, 136; Barnard 307, 321. GEN: Moos 400-01.
P. 333. ¶ 6. EC: Commerce 126. DA: Sloan 200.
P. 334. ¶ 1. DH: Parker 91-93. Johnson, *op. cit.,* Vol. 11: 354-55.
P. 334. ¶ 2. GEN: Schlesinger, *Politics* 518-23.
P. 335. ¶ 1. DH: Lunt 135. EC: Commerce 106; Peach 37, 59; Labor, *Handbook* 67.
P. 335. ¶ 2. DF: Sward 347. Rose Cavanagh. Jerome P. Cavanagh.
P. 335. ¶ 3. DH: Lunt 137. GEN: Moos 388.

74. The Labor of Union

1. DN: Darrow 29.
2. GEN: Schlesinger, *Coming* 412.
3. DA: Cook 81.

P. 336. ¶ 2. DH: Barnard 323. Det. *Free Press,* Oct. 23-26, 1936.
P. 337. ¶ 1. GEN: Myrdal 495.
P. 337. ¶ 3. ED: HEW, *Digest* 52. DS: Disbrow 115. GEN: Census, *Statistical Abstract*
1967, p. 365.
P. 338. ¶ 1. DS: Disbrow 20. EC: Friedman 444.
P. 339. ¶ 1. FG PP: Ed. & Labor Com. 106-11; Labor, *Anvil* 73-86. GEN: Schlesinger,
Politics 260, 290-92.
P. 339. ¶ 3. DA: Cook 74; Howe 49-50.
P. 339. ¶ 6. DA: Howe 49. DH: Pound 319. IM: Sachar 634-35. EC: Rayback 328-29.
P. 340. ¶ 1. DA: Cook 74-76. EC: Peach 187; Commerce 90. FG UA: Ed. & Labor Com.,
Hearings, testimony of Harry C. Bates, April 20, 1936.
P. 340. ¶ 4. GEN: Schlesinger, *Coming* 411-15. DA: Howe 51-52.
P. 340. ¶ 7. DA: Howe 51-53; Cook 74-76. DF: Sward 381.
P. 341. ¶ 3. DH: Pound 330-31. DA: Howe 53; Cook 78-80.
P. 342. ¶ 1. George Edwards, Jr.
P. 342. ¶ 5. Walter Reuther. DA: Cook 82; Howe 54-55.

75. The Sparks of Flint

1. GEN: Schlesinger, *Coming* 405-06.
2. DA: Fed. Trade Comm. 34.
3. EC: Lynch 254.
4. DA: Cook 74.
5. DH: Lunt 171.
6. DA: Cook 97; Howe 60.
7. DA: Cook 99.
8. DA: Cook 98; Howe 61.

P. 343. ¶ 2. DA: Cook 87, 84; Howe 55; Rae, *Amer. Auto. Mfrs.* 168. DH: Lunt 163. MH: Dunbar 552.
P. 344. ¶ 1. DA: Drucker, 154 ff.; Cook 85-86. DH: Pound 322.
P. 344. ¶ 5. DA: Drucker 123.
P. 344. ¶ 6. EC: Lynch 86, 145-50.
P. 344. ¶ 8. EC: Lynch 160-61, 165-66, 222-23.
P. 345. ¶ 3. DH: Pound 321, 324; Lunt 163. DA: Cook 86.
P. 346. ¶ 2. DA: Howe 56-67; Cook 74, 87-88. DA: Karman 109-10, 104. DH: Lunt 166-67. DF: Raushenbush 38.
P. 346. ¶ 7. DH: Lunt 168. DA: Karman 111-12. DA: Cook 88-90. GEN: Schlesinger, *Coming* 416.
P. 347. ¶ 1. DH: Lunt 169. DA: Cook 93.
P. 347. ¶ 3. DH: Lunt 169. DA: Karman 123; Howe 56-57.
P. 347. ¶ 9. DH: Lunt 172. DA: Howe 58; Cook 95; Karman 231-32.
P. 348. ¶ 5. DA: Cook 96. Walter Reuther. Det. *Free Press,* Feb. 2-5, 1937.
P. 348. ¶ 10. DF: Nevins, *Ford Decline* 134. DA: Howe 59-60.
P. 349. ¶ 6. DH: Lunt 173-74; Pound 325-26. DA: Cook 98-99; Howe 61.
P. 350. ¶ 2. DA: Howe 61; Cook 98. DH: Lunt 174-75.
P. 350. ¶ 6. DH: Lunt 175-79. DA: Cook 99; Sloan 200.

76. The Battle of the Overpass

1. DF: Nevins, *Ford Decline* 141, 239; Sward 396.

P. 351. ¶ 3. DA: Howe 62. DH: Lunt 181-82.
P. 352. ¶ 1. DF: Bennett 34; Sward 319, 373. MH: Sarasohn 27-28.
P. 352. ¶ 2. DF: Sward 295-98; Raushenbush 16-17, 24-28, 34. DA: Howe 92.
P. 353. ¶ 3. DF: Raushenbush 24-28, 4; Nevins, *Ford Decline* 28-29, 139-44; Sward 389-95, 398-99. DA: Cook 101-06. DH: Quaife 127.

77. The Permanent Depression

1. D GEN: Mich. Emergency 44, 106.
2. D GEN: Mich. Emergency 84.

P. 358. ¶ 2. Author's Research. D GEN: Mich. Emergency 96, 100, 42-43.
P. 358. ¶ 3. EC: Commerce 52, 130.
P. 359. ¶ 3. EC: Peach 37; Commerce 52; Friedman 493. D GEN: Det. City Plan 22. FG UA: Ed. & Labor Com., *Hearings,* April 20, 1936. GEN: Census, *Historical Statistics,* H 199-206, p. 200. DA: Auto. Mfrs. Assoc. 3.
P. 359. ¶ 4. D GEN: Mich. Emergency 107-09. Det. *Free Press,* March 11, 1938. EC: Friedman 493.
P. 361. ¶ 2. Author's Research.

78. Monuments to Genius

1. FG UA: Ed. & Labor Com., *Hearings;* testimony of Jacob O. Pedersen, April 29, 1936.
2. *The New York Times,* June 29, 1936.
3. FG UA: Bkg. & Cur. Com., *Hearings, To Create a U.S. Housing Authority.* Aug. 5, 1937.

4. *Ibid.*
5. FG UA: Bkg. & Cur. Com., *Hearings, To Create a U.S. Housing Authority.* Aug. 3, 1937.

P. 362. ¶ 2. D GOV: Det. Housing Com., *History.* FG UA: Bkg. & Cur. Com., *Hearings, To Create a U.S. Housing Authority;* testimony of John L. Lewis, Samuel F. Clabaugh, A. R. Clas, Josephine Gomon, Aug. 3-6, 1937.
P. 363. ¶ 4. FG UA: Bkg. & Cur. Com., *op. cit.,* testimony of Miles Frisbie, Aug. 4, 1937. Josephine Gomon.
P. 363. ¶ 6. FG UA: Ed. & Labor Com., *Hearings;* remarks of Sen. Robert F. Wagner, testimony of Miles Frisbie, Helen Alfred, Josephine Gomon, A. R. Clas, April 20-21, 1936.
P. 363. ¶ 7. FG UA: Bkg. & Cur. Com., *op. cit.,* testimony of Harold Ickes and Dr. Julius Fleischmann, Aug. 5, 1937. Ed. & Labor Com., *Hearings;* testimony of New York Conference of Mayors, April 21, 1936.
P. 364. ¶ 6. FG UA: Ed. & Labor Com., *Hearings;* testimony of Walter White, Ernest J. Bohn, Rabbi Edward L. Israel, April 21, 1936. Bkg. & Cur. Com., *op. cit.,* testimony of J. C. de Holl, Aug. 6, 1937; Dr. Julius Fleischmann, Aug. 5, 1937.
P. 364. ¶ 8. Josephine Gomon. Bkg. & Cur. Com., *op cit.,* testimony of William Green, Aug. 3, 1937; Frank W. Hancock, Jr., Aug. 5, 1937.

79. "The End of the Ford Motor Company"

1. DH: Tull 196.
2. DF: Liebold 461.
3. DH: Tull 197-98, 212.
4. DH: Spivak 111.

P. 366. ¶ 1. DH: Trevelyan 13-14; Hecock 1. DF: Raushenbush 60.
P. 367. ¶ 1. DA: Cook 115. DH: Bingay 345. Det. *Free Press,* Reading file. Ray Girardin.
P. 367. ¶ 2. DA: Cook 107-09.
P. 367. ¶ 3. DF: Sward 398-99; Bennett 114-15.
P. 367. ¶ 5. DF: Sward 398-99, 382-84; Bennett 110-11. DA: Howe 68-78.
P. 368. ¶ 3. DF: Raushenbush 32-33. DH: Spivak 108, 115, 135, 145, 127; Tull 177, 180, 189, 193.
P. 368. ¶ 4. DF: Bennett 128, 141-42, 130; Nevins, *Ford Decline* 181; Liebold 1408. DH: Spivak 130. Carlson, John R., *Under Cover* (New York: 1943), p. 322.
P. 368. ¶ 7. DF: Nevins, *Ford Decline* 168; Sward 452-53. Det. *Free Press,* Liebold file.
P. 369. ¶ 5. DA: Howe 75-77; Beasley, *Knudsen* 194; Cook 121. DH: Spivak 108-11, 117. DF: Nevins, *Ford Expansion* 562.
P. 369. ¶ 6. DA: Howe 77-78. DH: Spivak 122-23. DF: Bennett 114-16; Sward 382-84; Liebold 1066.
P. 369. ¶ 8. DF: Nevins, *Ford Decline* 160; Sward 402; Bennett 117.
P. 370. ¶ 2. DF: Sward 404; Nevins, *Ford Decline* 161. DA: Howe 101-04. Det. *Free Press,* April 2, 1941.
P. 370. ¶ 5. DF: Sward 408-09, 412-14; Nevins, *Ford Decline* 161; Liebold 1066 ff.
P. 370. ¶ 9. DF: Sward 410, 307; Nevins, *Ford Decline* 151-55. DA: Howe 207-10, 219. DN: Northrup 32.
P. 371. ¶ 2. DA: Howe 104, 216-17. DF: Sward 326, 411, 414; Nevins, *Ford Decline* 163.
P. 371. ¶ 8. DS: Det. Bd. of Ed., *One Hundred Years* 54. Harold Black. Rose Cavanagh. Jerome P. Cavanagh.
P. 372. ¶ 2. Det. *Free Press,* April 12-14, 1941. DF: Liebold 1065; Nevins, *Ford Decline* 164; Sward 417.
P. 372. ¶ 3. DF: Bennett 120, 125; Nevins, *Ford Decline* 183-84, 165.
P. 372. ¶ 5. DF: Bennett 136, 118; Nevins, *Ford Decline* 166-67; Sward 419-21.

80. Sojourner Truth

1. Det. *Free Press,* Jan. 31, 1942.
2. CD: Shogan 1.

P. 374. ¶ 2. George Edwards, Jr. Det. *Free Press,* Edwards file.

P. 374. ¶ 3. D GOV: Det. Housing Com., *History; Urban Renewal* 119-20; Ketcham 40-41.
P. 374. ¶ 4. DH: Wood 104-05, 49, 60, 65, 84, 86. DA: Howe 33-34, 12-13. D GOV: Jenkins 81.
P. 375. ¶ 1. EC: Myrdal 851-52, 300. DA: Howe 219.
P. 375. ¶ 3. D GOV: Jenkins 83-85. DA: Howe 34.
P. 375. ¶ 4. DA: Howe 8. D GOV: Jenkins 107, 94.
P. 375. ¶ 7. D GOV: Jenkins 86, 88. CD: Lee 74; Shogan 30. DA: Howe 34.

81. "Detroit is Dynamite"

1. CD: Shogan 6-7.
2. CD: Shogan 32. GEN: Hughes 96.
3. *PM,* June 27, 1943. *Life,* Aug. 18, 1942. Det. *Free Press,* June 4, 1943.
4. CD: Lee 81.
5. CD: Shogan 101, 87. Det. *Free Press,* July 1, 1943.
6. CD: Lee 56.
7. Det. *Free Press,* July 27-28, 1943. CD: Lee 65, 69.
8. *American Labor News,* Aug. 10, 1943.

P. 376. ¶ 1. CD: Shogan 26.
P. 377. ¶ 2. DF: Sward 430-32; Nevins, *Ford Decline* 215-18. DH: Bingay 303-09. DN: Dancy 91-92.
P. 377. ¶ 3. CD: Shogan 26. DN: Detroit Urban League, *Profile* 21.
P. 378. ¶ 2. Author's Research. CD: Lee 93. DN: Dancy 202.
P. 378. ¶ 4. CD: Lee 8. DN: Dancy 201; Northrup 18-19. Det. *Free Press,* May 2, 1942. DA: Howe 220-21.
P. 378. ¶ 5. DH: Tull 235. CD: Lee 63. Det. *Free Press,* Gerald L. K. Smith file.
P. 379. ¶ 2. GEN: Hughes 95. DA: Howe 221.
P. 379. ¶ 4. DA: Howe 221.
P. 379. ¶ 5. Det. *Free Press,* June 14, 16, 1943.
P. 380. ¶ 4. DH: Quaife 101. CD: Lee 26-28; Shogan 35-42. Det. *Free Press,* June 21, 1943. Det. *News,* June 21, 22, 1943.
P. 381. ¶ 1. Author's Research. D GEN: Hughes 93-94. CD: Lee 90-91.
P. 381. ¶ 2. Det. *Free Press,* Oct. 19, 1943.
P. 381. ¶ 6. DH: Quaife 157. CD: Lee 28; Shogan 46. Harold Black. Det. *Free Press,* June 21-22, 1943. Det. *News,* June 22, 1943.
P. 383. ¶ 4. Author's Research. CD: Shogan 54-55.
P. 383. ¶ 5. CD: Shogan 69-70; Lee 29.
P. 383. ¶ 8. CD: Shogan 51-53, 62.
P. 384. ¶ 3. Author's Research. CD: Shogan 56-63. Det. *Free Press,* June 22-23, 1943.
P. 384. ¶ 5. CD: Lee 30; Shogan 70. George Edwards, Jr.
P. 385. ¶ 1. CD: Lee 58, 39; Shogan 74-77, 79.
P. 385. ¶ 4. CD: Lee 33, 36; Shogan 78-79. Det. *News,* June 22, 1943.
P. 385. ¶ 5. CD: Lee 42-43, 84.
P. 385. ¶ 6. CD: Lee 82.
P. 386. ¶ 5. George Edwards, Jr. CD: Lee 54.

82. The Chameleons

P. 391. ¶ 2. DN: Dancy 222, 225. Conrad Mallett. Mrs. Mary Lonnie Mallett.

83. A Master Plan

1. DA: Cook 140
2. DH: Smith 43-44.

P. 392. ¶ 3. Harold Black.
P. 392. ¶ 4. D GOV: Ketcham. D CAV: Citizens Research 51-53.
P. 393. ¶ 1. D GOV: Upson; Detroit Budget History. Det. *Free Press,* Jeffries file.
P. 393. ¶ 3. EC: Labor, *Handbook* 236. DA: Cook 146-47.

P. 393. ¶ 4. DH: Smith 24 ff.
P. 394. ¶ 1. D GOV: Jenkins 107. Michigan *Chronicle,* Sept. 29, 1945. CD: Shogan 125.
P. 394. ¶ 2. DH: Smith 47-50. Det. *Free Press,* Frankensteen file.
P. 394. ¶ 4. DH: Smith 35-37, 40-42.
P. 394. ¶ 6. Det. *Free Press,* Frankensteen file; Edwards file. DH: Smith 47-50.

84. Metamorphosis and Death

1. DA: Howe 142; Sloan 406.
2. DA: Sloan 398.
3. DA: Cook 149; Howe 134.
4. DF: Liebold 1434.

P. 395. ¶ 1. EC: Labor, *Handbook* 301. DA: Cook 146-47; Howe 127-30.
P. 396. ¶ 4. DA: Cook 153, 150, 160; Howe 142, 137, 177-78; Sloan 395-97.
P. 397. ¶ 1. DA: Auto. Mfrs. Assoc. 3; Judiciary 108-10. EC: Commerce 127-28, 107-08.
P. 397. ¶ 4. DF: Nevins, *Ford Decline* 307, 224.
P. 397. ¶ 6. DF: Nevins, *Ford Decline* 242-46, 265-66, 111-16, 248-52; Bennett 164.
P. 398. ¶ 1. DF: Bennett 173-75, 154; Nevins, *Ford Decline* 258-65.
P. 398. ¶ 3. DF: Herndon 27, 185; Nevins, *Ford Decline* 266-69, 328, 308-15.
P. 398. ¶ 4. DF: Nevins, *Ford Decline* 344-45.

85. The "Detroit Plan"

1. D GOV: Det. City Plan, *Official Master Plan* 85.

P. 400. ¶ 1. DF: Nevins, *Ford Times* 644-50; *Decline* 287-90. GEN: Bemis 718. EC: Commerce 32-33; Wright 839; Peach 121, 227. DA: Auto. Mfrs. Assoc. 3.
P. 400. ¶ 2. Charles Blessing.
P. 401. ¶ 5. DH: Glazer 115. D CAV: Community Renewal, *Detroit: the New City* 75. D GOV: Det. City Plan, *Renewal* 15.
P. 402. ¶ 2. D GEN: Mowitz 14. D GOV: Det. City Plan, *Renewal* 105. D CAV: Community Renewal, *op. cit.,* 13, 19.
P. 402. ¶ 3. D GEN: Mowitz 20-24.
P. 402. ¶ 4. DA: Howe 19. D GOV: Det. City Plan, *Renewal* 119. DN: Det. Urban League, *Profile* 21. CD: Shogan 127.
P. 403. Footnote†. MH: Dunbar 650; Sarasohn 30-32. Ray Girardin.
P. 403. ¶ 2. DA: Howe 25. D GEN: Mowitz 650. MH: Sarasohn 55. DH: McNaughton 102-05, 93, 26-31, 74-75.
P. 404. ¶ 1. DA: Howe 247-54, 258, 230, 228-30.
P. 404. ¶ 5. George Edwards, Jr. Det. *Free Press,* Edwards file; Cobo file. D GEN: Mowitz 144, 149.
P. 405. ¶ 2. D GEN: Mowitz 646.
P. 405. ¶ 3. DH: McNaughton 129-32; 220-21.

86. The Jurisdiction of the Juvenile Court

P. 407. Footnote. William H. Bannon.
P. 408. ¶ 4. Author's Research.
P. 409. ¶ 3. D GEN: Mowitz 17, 30, 45.
P. 412. ¶ 3. Author's Research.

87. A Black Man on a White Force

P. 413. ¶ 5. Conrad Mallett. DP: Det. Police Dept., *Annual Reports.*
P. 414. ¶ 3. DN: U.S. Comm. 335, 361-62, 413-14, 417-18, 366, 384, 408.
P. 415. ¶ 1. Conrad Mallett.
P. 415. ¶ 2. DN: U.S. Comm. 381, 324-26.
P. 415. ¶ 7. Conrad Mallett.

88. The Master Mistake

1. D GEN: Mowitz 121.
2. D GEN: Mowitz 123.

P. 416. ¶ 2. D GEN: Mowitz 101, 103, 110-11, 107. D CAV: Community Renewal, *Detroit: the New City* 19.
P. 417. ¶ 3. D GEN: Mowitz 111-13, 125. Harold Black. Robert G. Hoffman.
P. 417. ¶ 8. D GEN: Mowitz 127, 124, 138.
P. 418. ¶ 1. D GEN: Mowitz 129-32.

89. The Inner City Syndrome

1. D GEN: Wayne County Child Development Center Citizens Review Committee 18.

P. 422. ¶ 5. Author's Research.
P. 423. ¶ 1. DS: Disbrow 178, 181. D GEN: Wayne County Child Development Center 1-2.
P. 423. ¶ 3. D GEN: Wayne County Child Development Center 2-3, 8. Wayne County Child Development Center Citizens Review Com. 50-51. *Characteristics of the Wayne County Child Development Center Resident Population* (Mimeo), Aug. 30, 1968, pp. 2, 8-9.
P. 423. ¶ 4. *Characteristics, op. cit.,* 7, 11-14.
P. 423. ¶ 5. D GEN: Wayne County Child Development Center Citizens Review Com. 21, 25-26, 50.
P. 424. ¶ 2. *Report on Wayne County Child Development Center* by William L. Cahalan, Prosecuting Attorney, Feb. 16, 1967. D GEN: Wayne County Professional Committee 5-6, 8-9; Wayne County Child Development Center 16-19, 34, 37.
P. 424. ¶ 5. D GEN: Wayne County Child Development Center Citizens Review Com. 50.
P. 426. ¶ 4. DR: Harlow 222. DA: Sheppard 10-12, 14-16. Author's Research.

90. "What's Good for General Motors . . ."

1. DA: Holliday 16.
2. DA: Sheppard 3.
3. DA: Rae, *The Amer. Auto.* 204; Pound 332.

P. 427. ¶ 5. DA: Holliday 8-16; Sloan 268-69.
P. 428. ¶ 2. DA: Judiciary 95-96, 121-22, 147, 129, 26-28, 111-12.
P. 428. ¶ 3. DA: Judiciary 8-10, 175; Sheppard 3.
P. 429. ¶ 3. DA: Auto. Mfrs. Assoc. 3.
P. 429. Footnote. DA: Auto. Mfrs. Assoc. 3. EC: Commerce 108-09; Labor, *Handbook* 236.
P. 430. ¶ 3. DA: Auto. Mfrs. Assoc. 3, 5; Rae, *The Amer. Auto.* 168-70. DN: Northrup 22-23. Cavanagh Administration, miscellaneous papers.

91. The Bad Seed

P. 434. ¶ 7. Author's Research.

92. The Crossroads of the City

P. 435. ¶ 4. Det. *Free Press,* Cobo file. Harold Black. Frank Beckman.
P. 436. ¶ 4. Charles Blessing.
P. 436. ¶ 6. Harold Black.
P. 437. ¶ 4. DN: U.S. Comm. 180, 184, 135, 147, 144-45.
P. 438. ¶ 2. DS: Det. Bd. of Ed., *Budgets;* Disbrow 240. DN: U.S. Comm. 187. MH: Harris 89-152, 212.
P. 439. ¶ 1. DN: U.S. Comm. 152, 170-78. DS: Disbrow 240; Lee 18. DF: Ford Foundation, *Society* 22.

P. 439. ¶ 2. DS: Det. Bd. of Ed., *Budgets;* Brownell 138-39. DN: U.S. Comm. 149-61.
P. 439. ¶ 5. Dr. Norman Drachler. DN: U.S. Comm. 140-46, 148, 156, 188, 191.
P. 439. Footnote. D GEN: Myrdal v, vi.
P. 440. ¶ 4. DS: Det. Bd. of Ed., *Constant Search* 4. DN: U.S. Comm. 171-77. Dr. Carl Marburger.

93. The Ford Foundation

1. DF: Ford Foundation, *Report of the Study* 17, 38-39.
2. DF: Ford Foundation, *op. cit.,* 44, 91.

P. 441. ¶ 2. DF: Macdonald 130-33, 10-11.
P. 442. ¶ 2. DF: Macdonald 141, 112.
P. 442. ¶ 3. DF: Macdonald 4, 29-35, 73; Ford Foundation, *Report of the Study* 66.
P. 442. ¶ 5. DF: Macdonald 3-4; Nevins, *Ford Decline* 417.
P. 442. ¶ 6. DF: Macdonald 161.
P. 443. ¶ 3. Paul Ylvisaker. James Sundquist.

94. The Big Builder

P. 444. ¶ 1. D GOV: Det. City Plan, *Renewal* 38. D GEN: Mowitz 59, 66, 64.
P. 444. ¶ 3. D GEN: Mowitz 65-66, 71. Det. *Free Press,* Cobo file.
P. 445. ¶ 1. D GEN: Mowitz 73-74.
P. 445. ¶ 5. Det. *Free Press,* Cobo file. D GEN: Mowitz 171 ff., 223-28.

95. Jerry the Giant Killer

1. DN: U.S. Comm. 399, 401.
2. FG UA: Government Operations Committee, *Federal Role,* Pt. 7, p. 1554.

P. 446. ¶ 1. D GOV: Detroit, *Budgets;* Det. City Plan, *Renewal* 10, 19, 102.
P. 446. Footnote‡. DS: Disbrow 14. DH: McNaughton 20, 16, 10, 15, 1-2.
P. 447. ¶ 1. Det. *Free Press,* Miriani file. Cavanagh file.
P. 447. ¶ 2. Det. *Free Press,* Miriani file.
P. 448. ¶ 4. Jerome P. Cavanagh. Mrs. Rose Cavanagh. Joe B. Sullivan.
P. 448. ¶ 7. Det. *Free Press,* Cavanagh file.
P. 448. ¶ 9. DN: Detroit Urban League, Profile 34; *Detroit Low-Income* 21.
P. 448. ¶ 10. DP: Det. Police Dept., *Annual Reports.*
P. 449. ¶ 1. DN: U.S. Comm. 312.
P. 449. ¶ 4. DN: Det. Urban League, *Profile* 21.
P. 449. ¶ 6. Richard Strichartz. Joe B. Sullivan. Frank Beckman. Det. *Free Press,* Cavanagh file.
P. 450. ¶ 1. Det. *Free Press,* Alfred Pelham file.
P. 451. ¶ 1. Jerome P. Cavanagh. Richard Strichartz. George Edwards, Jr. Joe B. Sullivan. Det. *Free Press,* Edwards file.
P. 451. ¶ 3. Cavanagh Administration, miscellaneous papers.
P. 452. ¶ 4. Jerome P. Cavanagh. Richard Strichartz. Joe B. Sullivan. MH: Dunbar 653-56. Det. *Free Press,* Cavanagh file.
P. 452. ¶ 5. Mel Ravitz. Jerome P. Cavanagh. Joe B. Sullivan.

96. The Embattled City

1. DH: Ferman 47.
2. Richard Strichartz.

P. 453. ¶ 3. EC: Peach 99, 121. GEN: Census, *Statistical Abstract,* 1967, p. 814.
P. 454. Footnotes * and †. EC: Labor, *Handbook* 94, 338.
P. 454. ¶ 4. GEN: Census, *Statistical Abstract,* 1967, pp. 829-32.
P. 454. ¶ 6. EC: Commerce 103-05. DA: Auto. Mfrs. Assoc. 3. D CAV: Community Renewal, *Population and Housing,* Table V. Cavanagh Administration, miscellaneous papers.

P. 455. ¶ 2. DH: Ferman 9-10. Ray Girardin.
P. 455. ¶ 3. DH: Ferman 60.
P. 455. ¶ 5. DH: Ferman 12-29, 47.
P. 456. ¶ 1. James T. Trainor. Ray Girardin. DH: Farmer, Vol. 1: 205, 644.
P. 456. ¶ 5. Jerome P. Cavanagh. Richard Strichartz. *Look,* Sept. 11, 1962.

97. "What About the Poverty Problem?"

1. Walter Heller, address at Indiana State College, March 25, 1965.

P. 459. ¶ 3. FG PP: Congressional Quarterly 51; Sundquist 63-73. EC: Commerce 103-05.
P. 460. ¶ 1. EC: Commerce 20-21, 112-13; Labor, *Handbook* 22.
P. 460. ¶ 3. FG PP: Sundquist 85-97, 44-46; Congressional Quarterly 56-58.
P. 460. ¶ 4. GEN: Census, *Statistical Abstract,* 1967, pp. 814-815.
P. 460. ¶ 6. James L. Sundquist. Kermit Gordon. Cavanagh Administration, miscellaneous papers.

98. "Twelfth Street Is Not the Milky Way"

P. 461. Footnote. EC: Labor, *Handbook* 255, 295.
P. 465. ¶ 4. Author's Research.

99. The River of Hate

1. DN: U.S. Comm. 243.
2. Judge James Lincoln.
3. Det. *News,* June 8, 1963.
4. Det. *News,* June 24, 1963.

P. 466. ¶ 2. DP: Det. Police Dept., *Annual Reports;* Edwards 53.
P. 467. Footnote. Joe B. Sullivan.
P. 467. ¶ 9. George Edwards, Jr.
P. 468. ¶ 1. ED: U.S. Comm. 7.
P. 468. ¶ 3. DN: Hoult 7; U.S. Comm. 246, 254-59, 476-80, 490-97.
P. 469. ¶ 2. DN: Northrup 45, 58-59; U.S. Comm. 63-66.
P. 469. ¶ 3. DN: U.S. Comm. 114-18.
P. 469. ¶ 4. DN: U.S. Comm. 64; Northrup 12, 31.
P. 469. ¶ 5. DS: Lee 18. DN: Northrup 54; Det. Urban League, *Profile* 37, 36; U.S. Comm. 87, 63-65, 71.
P. 470. ¶ 2. DN: Det. Urban League, *Profile* 28; Northrup 38; U.S. Comm. 92. D CAV: Detroit, *Active Community Team,* Appendix "C." Detroit Public Schools, *Cumulative End of Grade Survival for the Class of 1966* (Mimeo). Judge James Lincoln.
P. 470. ¶ 4. DN: Det. Urban League, *Detroit Low-Income Negro* 19; *Profile* 49; U.S. Comm. 122. FG UA: Government Operations, *Federal Role,* Pt. 3, pp. 674-90.
P. 470. ¶ 5. DN: Wolf 381. GEN: Census, *Statistical Abstract,* 1967, p. 333.

100. An Unconditional War on Poverty

1. D CAV: Detroit, *Active Community Team* 8.
2. William Capron.
3. FG PP: Sundquist 137.
4. James L. Sundquist.
5. Kermit Gordon.
6. Richard Boone.

P. 472. ¶ 3. James L. Sundquist. William Capron. CIT: Government Operations 22. FG UA: Sundquist 135-36. GEN: Census, *Statistical Abstract,* 1967, pp. 332-34.
P. 473. ¶ 4. Richard Strichartz. Robert Roselle. D CAV: Detroit, *Active Community Team.*
P. 474. ¶ 3. William Capron. James L. Sundquist. FG PP: Sundquist 137.
P. 474. ¶ 5. Dr. Michael S. March.
P. 474. ¶ 7. William B. Cannon. David Hackett.

P. 475. ¶ 1. Paul Ylvisaker. Kermit Gordon. FG PP: Sundquist 111.
P. 475. ¶ 2. William Capron.
P. 475. ¶ 4. David Hackett. Richard Boone. James L. Sundquist.
P. 476. ¶ 1. Kermit Gordon. FG PP: Labor, *Manpower Report* 308.
P. 476. ¶ 4. Paul Ylvisaker. Richard Boone.
P. 477. ¶ 3. William Capron. James L. Sundquist.
P. 477. ¶ 5. William Capron. Richard Boone. James L. Sundquist. FG PP: Sundquist 74-75.

101. A Social Portrait

1. Jerome P. Cavanagh testimony, National Advisory Commission on Civil Disorders.
2. FG PP: Congressional Quarterly 60.
3. Harold Black.
4. Robert Roselle.

P. 479. ¶ 3. Richard Strichartz.
P. 480. ¶ 1. Charles Blessing.
P. 480. ¶ 3. Charles Blessing. Harold Black. James Wiley. Richard Strichartz. Robert Roselle.
P. 481. ¶ 1. Jerome P. Cavanagh. Robert Roselle. Richard Strichartz. Charles Blessing. Harold Black.
P. 481. ¶ 4. Robert Roselle.
P. 481. ¶ 5. Harold Black.
P. 482. ¶ 1. EC: Commerce 102-05; Labor, *Handbook* 286, 291, 296. FG PP: Labor, *Manpower* 288. D CAV: Greenleigh, *Home Interview* 28, 20, 31, 22.
P. 482. ¶ 2. D CAV: Greenleigh, *op. cit.*, 83, 86, 17-18.
P. 482. ¶ 3. D CAV: Greenleigh, *op. cit.*, 40.
P. 483. ¶ 2. DS: Disbrow 243. D CAV: Greenleigh, *op. cit.*, 55, 57.
P. 483. ¶ 3. D CAV: Greenleigh, *op. cit.*, 63.
P. 483. ¶ 5. D CAV: Greenleigh, *op. cit.*, 83, 73, 91, 60-61. Cavanagh Administration, miscellaneous papers.
P. 484. ¶ 1. D CAV: Greenleigh, *op. cit.*, 63, 74, 90-91, 101.
P. 484. ¶ 3. DN: Det. Urban League, *Profile* 31.

102. The Bridging of the Moat

1. DS: Det. Bd. of Ed., *Constant Search* 5.
2. Stewart McClure.
3. ED: Ed. & Labor Com., *Federal Educational Policies*, Pt. 1, p. 42.

P. 485. ¶ 2. Dr. Carl Marburger. DS: Det. Bd. of Ed., *Constant Search* 14.
P. 486. ¶ 1. Dr. Carl Marburger.
P. 486. ¶ 2. ED: Ed. & Labor Com., *op. cit.*, Pt. 1, pp. 14, 20-22.
P. 486. ¶ 8. ED: Ed. & Labor Com., *op. cit.*, Pt. 1, p. 25.
P. 487. ¶ 2. Dr. Carl Marburger. Jack Conway. FG PP: Sundquist 211.
P. 487. ¶ 5. William Bozman. Richard Strichartz. Robert Roselle. Jerome P. Cavanagh. FG AP: Labor and Public Welfare, *Examination*, Pt. 6, pp. 1713-20.
P. 488. ¶ 2. ED: Ed. & Labor Com., *op. cit.*, 70-71; *Study of the U.S. Office of Education* 4, 23. FG PP: Sundquist 214, 217. John Gardner. Harold Howe. Samuel Halperin. Stewart McClure. Dr. Carl Marburger.

103. The City of Promise

1. Robert Wood. Jack Conway.
2. Jerome P. Cavanagh.
3. Richard Strichartz. Anthony Ripley.

P. 489. ¶ 2. Jerome P. Cavanagh. Robert Wood. Dwight Ink. FG UA: Advisory Commission, *Metropolitan America* 2.
P. 490. ¶ 1. Cavanagh Administration, miscellaneous papers. EC: Commerce 102-05. DA: Auto Mfrs. Assoc. 3. FG UA: Labor, *Manpower* 288. DN: Hoult, *Population* 1.
P. 490. ¶ 2. Cavanagh Administration, miscellaneous papers. Det. *Free Press*, May 5, 1965.

P. 490. ¶ 4. Det. *Free Press*, July 24-Aug. 2, 1965.

P. 491. ¶ 2. *Look*, Sept. 21, 1965. *Time*, Sept. 24, 1965. Det. *Free Press*, Cavanagh file.

P. 491. ¶ 4. Det. *Free Press*, Cavanagh file.

P. 491. ¶ 6. Jerome P. Cavanagh. Robert Wood. Jack Conway. Richard Strichartz.

P. 492. ¶ 1. Cavanagh Administration, miscellaneous papers.

P. 492. ¶ 4. Robert Wood. Kermit Gordon. Frank Beckman. FG AP: Labor and Public Welfare, *Examination*, Pt. 1, p. 123. D CAV: Mayor's Task Force.

P. 493. ¶ 1. FG UA: Government Operations, *Federal Role*, Pt. 19, p. 4135.

P. 493. ¶ 2. Detroit Regional Planning Commission, *Annual Survey of Building Permits*. FG UA: Advisory Comm., *Fiscal Balance*, Vol. 2: 53; Government Operations, *Federal Role*, Pt. 19, p. 4135. D CAV: Community Renewal, *Detroit: the New City* 62. Charles Blessing. Jerome P. Cavanagh.

P. 493. Footnote. Jerome P. Cavanagh.

P. 493. ¶ 5. Richard Strichartz. Conrad Mallett.

P. 494. ¶ 7. Det. *Free Press*, Jan. 28, 1966. Jerome P. Cavanagh.

P. 494. ¶ 8. Jack Casey.

P. 495. ¶ 6. Josephine Gomon. Jerome P. Cavanagh.

P. 495. ¶ 8. Jerome P. Cavanagh.

P. 496. Footnote. Philip Rutledge.

P. 496. ¶ 3. Det. *Free Press*, July 5, 1966.

P. 496. ¶ 4. Det. *Free Press*, Aug. 5, 1966.

104. The Changing of the Guard

1. Det. *Free Press*, Aug. 24, 1966.

P. 497. ¶ 2. Richard Strichartz.

P. 497. ¶ 3. D CAV: Community Renewal, *Detroit: the New City* 124.

P. 498. ¶ 6. Conrad Mallett.

P. 499. ¶ 2. D CAV: Greenleigh, *Study of Services* 68. Conrad Mallett. DS: Disbrow 218.

P. 499. ¶ 5. Cavanagh Administration, miscellaneous papers. Jerome P. Cavanagh. FG UA: Government Operations, *Federal Role*, Pt. 3, pp. 632-33.

P. 500. ¶ 2. Robert Wood. H. Ralph Taylor. Harold Black.

P. 501. ¶ 5. Cavanagh Administration, miscellaneous papers. Harold Black. Richard Strichartz.

P. 501. ¶ 6. Philip Rutledge. Richard Simmons. Harold Black. Carl Westman. Robert Knox.

P. 502. ¶ 3. Harold Black. Mel Ravitz. Richard Strichartz.

P. 503. ¶ 1. Conrad Mallett. David Nelson. James T. Trainor. Harold Black.

P. 503. ¶ 3. Harold Black.

P. 503. ¶ 4. Conrad Mallett. Jerome P. Cavanagh. D CAV: Willcox 116-19.

P. 503. ¶ 6. Philip Rutledge. Harold Black. Conrad Mallett. David Cason.

105. MCHRD

1. Richard Strichartz.
2. FG AP: Labor and Public Welfare, *Examination*, Pt. 1, pp. 87-97.
3. David Nelson.
4. FG AP: Labor and Public Welfare, *Examination*, Pt. 6, p. 1812.
5. FG AP: Labor and Public Welfare, *Examination*, Pt. 6, p. 1841.

P. 506. ¶ 2. FG AP: Labor and Public Welfare, *Examination*, Pt. 6, pp. 1713-20, 1751, 1746-47, 1725-26, 1815. Robert A. Levine. William Bozman. Charles A. Mayer.

P. 506. ¶ 4. FG AP: Labor and Public Welfare, *Examination*, Pt. 1, pp. 249, 263. Robert A. Levine. Robert Perrin. Richard Strichartz. Robert Roselle.

P. 507. ¶ 1. FG AP: Comptroller General, *Review of Community Action* 3. Robert A. Levine.

P. 508. ¶ 7. Myron Liner. Leon Shearer. Ralph Rosenfeld.

P. 509. ¶ 4. David Nelson. FG AP: Comptroller General, *Review of Community Action* 17, 34-38; Labor and Public Welfare, *Examination*, Pt. 1, p. 96; Pt. 6, p. 1797.

P. 510. ¶ 2. FG AP: Labor and Public Welfare, *Examination*, Pt. 1, pp. 95-97; Pt. 6, pp. 1805-06, 1808-12.

P. 510. ¶ 4. FG UA: Government Operations, *Federal Role*, Pt. 19, p. 4183. FG AP: Comptroller General, *Need* 25. Det. Public Schools, *Annual School Holding Power Report*, 1965-1966.

106. The Hard Corps

1. D GEN: PRESCAD, *Report*, statement of Wayne County Supervisor Thomas Turner. Statement of Sen. Charles Zollar, chairman, Michigan Senate Appropriations Committee, November, 1969.

P. 513. ¶ 2. Author's Research.
P. 513. ¶ 3. Richard Simmons, Jr.
P. 515. ¶ 2. Author's Research.
P. 515. ¶ 5. DS: Det. Bd. of Ed., *Report* 3-4. Stan Webb.
P. 516. ¶ 3. Author's Research.
P. 517. ¶ 1. FG AP: Labor and Public Welfare, *Examination*, Pt. 9, pp. 3024-25, 3000-01, 3011. Comptroller-General of the United States, *Review of the Activities of the Job Corps Men's Center, Tongue Point, Oregon* (Washington, D.C.: 1968), p. 7; *Review of Selected Activities at the Parks Job Corps Center* (Washington, D.C.: 1967), pp. 39, 74-76.
P. 517. Footnote. FG UA: Government Operations, *Federal Role*, Pt. 19, p. 3008. FG AP: Weeks 239.
P. 517. ¶ 4. Author's Research.

107. The Pilot Light

1. DP: Det. Police Dept., *Story* 10, 13, 21.
2. Probate Court, Juvenile Division, memorandum of Aug. 29, 1967.
3. Ray Girardin.
4. Hubert Locke.

P. 518. ¶ 3. FG UA: President's Commission, *Challenge of Crime* 26-27.
P. 519. ¶ 3. DP: Det. Police Dept., *Annual Report*, 1967.
P. 519. ¶ 5. DP: Det. Police Dept. *Annual Reports*. Lt. Fred Schieman, Det. Police Dept. FG UA: President's Comm., *op. cit.*, 19.
P. 520. ¶ 1. FG UA: President's Comm., *op. cit.*, 25. DP: Det. Police Dept., *Annual Reports*.
P. 520. ¶ 3. Det. *Free Press*, April 16, 23, 1967.
P. 521. ¶ 1. D GOV: Detroit City Budget History. DP: Det. Police Dept., *Annual Report*, 1967, p. 3. Ray Girardin. Jerome P. Cavanagh. Det. *Free Press*, May 26, 1967.
P. 521. ¶ 4. Ray Girardin.
P. 521. ¶ 5. Judge Henry Heading.
P. 521. ¶ 6. FG AP: Labor and Public Welfare, *Examination*, Pt. 1, pp. 109-10.
P. 521. ¶ 7. Det. *Free Press*, April 16, 1967. FG UA: Government Operations, *Federal Role*, Pt. 3, pp. 637-41.
P. 522. ¶ 3. Det. *Free Press*, May 3, 1967. CD: Congressional Quarterly 3-6.
P. 522. ¶ 6. Conrad Mallett.

108. The Day of the Blind Pig

P. 525. ¶ 1. CD: Government Operations, Pt. 6, pp. 1347-58, 1453-59. D CAV: Detroit, *Appearance*. Ray Girardin. DP: Det. Police Dept., *Statistical Report*, pp. ii-iv.

109. "Motown, If You Don't Come Around, We Are Going To Burn You Down."

1. *Liberator*, April, 1964.
2. CD: Government Operations, Pt. 6, pp. 1415-16; Library of Congress, testimony of J. Edgar Hoover before House of Representatives Subcommittee on Appropriations, Feb. 16, 1967. National Advisory Comm. on Civil Disorders, miscellaneous material.

P. 526. ¶ 2. Conrad Mallett. Robert Roselle. Jerome P. Cavanagh. Ray Girardin. Hubert Locke. Rep. John Conyers, Jr.

P. 527. ¶ 2. DP: Det. Police Dept., *Statistical Report*—"Chronology and Manpower Report"; and p. iii.

P. 527. ¶ 3. Ray Girardin.

P. 527. ¶ 5. CD: National Advisory Comm. 88-89. DP: Det. Police Dept., *Statistical Report*—"Time. Analysis of Arrests."

P. 528. ¶ 2. CD: Government Operations, Pt. 6, pp. 1398-1402.

P. 530. Footnote*. Det. Police Dept., *Firearms Survey. U.S. News and World Report*, Sept. 6, 1965.

P. 531. ¶ 1. Author's Research. CD: Government Operations, Pt. 5, pp. 1327, 1226. FG UA: Government Operations, *Federal Role*, Pt. 19, p. 3929. D CAV: Detroit, *Appearance*—"Statistical Profile"; Community Renewal, *Population Estimates.* United Community Services of Detroit, *Social Characteristics of Communities in the Detroit Area* (Mimeo). Detroit Health Department, *Illegitimate Live Births* (Mimeo). DP: Det. Police Dept., *Annual Report*, 1967, pp. 25-26.

P. 531. ¶ 3. DS: Det. Bd. of Ed., *Report* 17, 19, 75, 107, 163, 166, 194, 201, 218.

P. 531. ¶ 4. DS: Det. Bd. of Ed., *Report* 293.

P. 532. ¶ 2. Author's interview of Twelfth St. youths, July 28, 1967.

110. The Inferno of Poverty

1. CD: Government Operations, Pt. 6, pp. 1407-08.
2. Ray Girardin.
3. Detroit Fire Department, tape recording of radio messages.
4. CD: National Advisory Comm. 92.
5. CD: Government Operations, Pt. 5, p. 1254.
6. Det. *Free Press*, articles by Saul Friedman, July 27-28, 1967. CD: National Advisory Comm. 536, 538. Los Angeles *Times*, July 30, 1967. Jerome P. Cavanagh. David Ginsburg, executive director, National Advisory Comm. on Civil Disorders.

P. 534. ¶ 1. Ray Girardin. Jerome P. Cavanagh. Robert Roselle. Conrad Mallett. CD: Government Operations, Pt. 6, pp. 1404-08, 1414-15.

P. 534. ¶ 3. D CAV: Detroit, *Appearance.*

P. 534. ¶ 5. Stan Webb.

P. 534. ¶ 9. D CAV: Detroit, *Appearance.* CD: Government Operations, Pt. 5, pp. 1216-18, 1230-32, Pt. 6, pp. 1453-59.

P. 535. ¶ 1. Conrad Mallett. Stan Webb.

P. 535. ¶ 7. DP: Det. Police Dept., *Statistical Report* pp. 51-52.

P. 536. ¶ 1. D CAV: Detroit, *Appearance*—"Damage Assessment."

P. 536. ¶ 2. CD: Government Operations, Pt. 5, 1252. Testimony of Gov. George Romney, National Advisory Comm. on Civil Disorders.

P. 536. ¶ 4. Ray Girardin. DP: Det. Police Dept., *Statistical Report* pp. 53, 32, 11.

P. 537. ¶ 6. CD: Government Operations, Pt. 5, pp. 1252-54. Testimony of Gov. George Romney, National Advisory Comm. on Civil Disorders.

P. 538. ¶ 2. CD: Government Operations, Pt. 5, pp. 1254-55, 1269; Pt. 7, pp. 1508-09.

P. 539. ¶ 1. CD: Government Operations, Pt. 7, pp. 1503-06; Lowinger. D CAV: Detroit, *Appearance.*

P. 539. ¶ 3. CD: Government Operations, Pt. 5, p. 1255. DP: Det. Police Dept., *Statistical Report* p. 53.

P. 539. ¶ 6. CD: Government Operations, Pt. 7, pp. 1509-12.

P. 540. ¶ 1. D CAV: Detroit, *Appearance.* Det. *Free Press*, article by Saul Friedman, July 28, 1967.

P. 540. ¶ 2. CD: Lowinger 13.

P. 540. ¶ 3. DP: Det. Police Dept., *Statistical Report* pp. 1, 11.

P. 541. ¶ 1. CD: Government Operations, Pt. 5, pp. 1312-25, 1345-46; Pt. 7, pp. 1585-87. William Cahalan. Judge Henry L. Heading.

P. 541. ¶ 6. Det. *Free Press*, July 29, 1967.

P. 542. ¶ 1. John Gardner. John Gunther. John Feild. Ron Linton.

P. 542. ¶ 3. "Meet the Press," July 30, 1967.

P. 543. ¶ 1. Jerome P. Cavanagh. Conrad Mallett. Author's Observations.

111. Catalogs of Failure

P. 544. ¶ 1. Delbert R. Jay.
P. 552. ¶ 10. Author's Research. The description of the Wallace rally is from the author's notes and tape recording.

112. The Assertion of Forest Park

1. D GOV: Det. Housing Comm., *Letter.*

P. 553. ¶ 1. Det. *News,* Oct. 27, 1968.
P. 553. ¶ 4. Memorandums of Oct. 15 and 18, 1968.
P. 554. ¶ 4. D GOV: Det. Housing Comm., *Forest Park.*
P. 555. ¶ 1. D CAV: Citizens Research 21-24.
P. 555. ¶ 7. Conrad Mallett. Robert Knox.
P. 556. ¶ 10. Chris Alston. Roy J. Robinson. Det. *News,* Nov. 2, 9, 1968, Jan. 8, 1969. D GOV: Det. Housing Comm., *Memorandum.* Letter to Christopher Alson from Robert McCabe, Deputy Assistant Secretary for Urban Renewal, Nov. 14, 1968. Telegram to Robert Knox from Sen. Philip A. Hart and Rep. Charles Diggs, Jr.
P. 557. ¶ 1. Robert Wood. FG UA: Bkg. & Cur. Com., *Hearings on the Housing and Urban Development Act of 1965,* pp. 752-60; Housing and Urban Development, *Urban Renewal Directory* 1, 81.
P. 557. ¶ 2. D CAV: Community Renewal, *School Credits.*
P. 557. ¶ 4. Ed Levin.
P. 557. Footnote. Robert E. McCabe. Philip N. Brownstein.
P. 558. ¶ 5. Jerome P. Cavanagh. Conrad Mallett. Robert Knox. Richard Strichartz.

113. The Orchestration of Housing

1. D CAV: Metropolitan Detroit, *Text of Presentation.*

P. 559. ¶ 2. D GOV: Det. City Plan, *Renewal* 116. D CAV: Metropolitan Det., *Text of Presentation.*
P. 560. ¶ 2. Conrad Mallett. Robert Knox.
P. 560. Footnote*. Robert Wood. FG UA: Government Operations, *Federal Role,* Pt. 9, pp. 2013-48.
P. 561. ¶ 3. Dr. Robert Kearns. Robert Wood. H. Ralph Taylor. Thomas Rogers. Robert Knox. Robert G. Hoffman. "Phoenix: Legend of Low Cost Housing Delays," *Engineering News Record,* Aug. 29, 1968.
P. 562. ¶ 2. D GOV: Det. Housing Comm., *Urban Renewal and Tax Revenue; Tour of Detroit's Urban Renewal Projects.* Conrad Mallett. Robert Knox. Edward J. Robinson. James L. Trainor. D CAV: Llewelyn-Davies.

114. The Irresistible President

1. FG UA: Government Operations, *Federal Role,* Pt. 18, p. 3651.
2. Dr. Louis D. Monacel.

P. 563. ¶ 1. D CAV: Community Renewal, *Second Memorandum.*
Author's note: Many persons in the federal government contributed their knowledge, as well as various documents, to the writing of this chapter. Considerations of confidentiality preclude their identification.

115. The Muddled City

1. D CAV: Mayor's Committee, *Neighborhood Service Program's Core Services Monthly Report,* Dec. 1968.
2. William D. Carey.
3. D CAV: Willcox 129, 130, 147.
4. D CAV: Willcox 341.
5. Author's notes of meeting.

6. Bob Ford.

P. 569. ¶ 1. DS: Det. Bd. of Ed., *Constant Search* 95-96. D CAV: Mayor's Committee, *op. cit.,* Feb. 1969.

P. 569. ¶ 2. D CAV: Mayor's Committee, *Neighborhood Service Program Organizational Chart.*

P. 570. ¶ 6. William D. Casey. H. Ralph Taylor. Natalie Spingarn. Philip Rutledge. William Bozman. Alexander J. Green.

P. 571. ¶ 2. D CAV: Willcox 151 ff., 189-90.

P. 572. ¶ 3. Author's notes on meetings.

P. 572. ¶ 4. Lewis F. Nicolini. Alan Goldfarb.

P. 572. ¶ 5. Dr. Norman Drachler.

116. Confrontation in the Schools

1. Dr. Norman Drachler.
2. Author's discussions with faculty and students.
3. Dr. Norman Drachler.
4. Dr. Norman Drachler.

P. 575. ¶ 1. Dr. Norman Drachler.

P. 575. ¶ 4. Dr. Norman Drachler. Dr. Carl Marburger. Dr. William Wattenberg. DS: Detroit Public Schools, *Achievements and Aptitudes; Programs Operated.*

P. 576. ¶ 4. Dr. Norman Drachler. Dr. Robert S. Lankton. DS: Det. Bd. of Ed., *Constant Search* 32.

P. 578. ¶ 1. Dr. Norman Drachler. DS: Det. Public Schools, *Fact Pack* 15. ED: National Education Association, *Economic Status* 56.

P. 579. ¶ 3. Dr. Norman Drachler. Mrs. Dorothy Ware. Dr. James Neubacher. Mrs. Mary Ellen Riordan.

P. 579. ¶ 4. Mrs. Dorothy Ware. Conrad Mallett.

P. 580. ¶ 4. Mrs. Elsie M. Jinks. Mrs. Dorothy Ware. Miss Ann McCarthy. Maurice Silver. Louis Starks. Joseph McGlynn. Charles Reich. Nettye Buchalter.

P. 581. ¶ 3. Dr. Theodore Mandell. DS: Det. Public Schools, *Evaluation.* Miscellaneous documents, Language Retardation Unit.

P. 581. ¶ 5. Mrs. Elsie Jinks. Mrs. Dorothy Ware. Miss Ann McCarthy.

117. The Reunion

P. 587. ¶ 8. Author's Research.

118. The Welfare Murder

1. Dr. George Pickett.

P. 588. ¶ 2. Author's Research.

P. 589. ¶ 1. D GEN: PRESCAD, *Report* 13-14, 1, 27.

P. 590. ¶ 1. Supervisor Paul Silver. Dr. George Pickett. D GEN: PRESCAD, *Report* 8, 17; Wayne County Board, *Audit Report* 2. Statements of Supervisors Paul Silver and Thomas Turner.

P. 590. Footnote. James L. Trainor.

P. 597. ¶ 3. Judge James Lincoln. Author's Research and Observations.

P. 598. ¶ 8. Author's Research and Observations.

119. The Haves and Haves-not

P. 600. ¶ 4. Author's Research.

120. The International Fords

1. *The New York Times* Magazine, April 20, 1969.

P. 601. ¶ 2. Jack Howard. Stanley Ruttenberg. Philip Rutledge. John Feild. DF: Herndon 25, 337-38.

P. 601. ¶ 3. Chris Alston.

P. 602. ¶ 1. DF: Herndon 39-40, 102-03.

P. 602. ¶ 3. Author's Observations.

P. 602. ¶ 4. New Detroit Committee Agenda, Oct. 3, 1968, pp. 1-8.

P. 603. ¶ 1. New Detroit Committee meeting, Nov. 8, 1968.

P. 603. ¶ 2. Max M. Fisher, Memorandum to Board of Trustees, Nov. 1, 1968.

P. 603. ¶ 6. New Detroit Committee meeting, Nov. 8, 1968; Agenda "D," Nov. 8, 1968. DF: Herndon 334.

P. 604. ¶ 5. DF: Herndon 12, 354.

P. 605. ¶ 1. DF: Herndon 326. *The New York Times,* Dec. 23, 1968.

P. 605. Footnote*. DF: Herndon 359.

P. 605. ¶ 2. DN: Northrup 14. DF: Herndon 12. *The New York Times,* July 16, 1970.

P. 605. ¶ 3. Los Angeles *Times,* July 2, 1972.

P. 605. ¶ 4. *The New York Times,* Dec. 12, 1968.

P. 606. ¶ 1. DA: Auto. Mfrs. Assoc.

P. 606. ¶ 3. Los Angeles *Times,* July 2, 1972.

P. 606. ¶ 4. DF: Herndon 27. *The New York Times* Magazine, Oct. 19, 1969.

P. 606. ¶ 6. *The New York Times,* Feb. 21, Oct. 27, Dec. 17, 1965. DF: Herndon 393.

121. The Twilight of the City

1. Bernard Klein.

P. 608. ¶ 4. James D. Wiley. Civil Service Commission Examiner Joseph Nowakowski.

P. 608. ¶ 5. Chuck Allegrino.

P. 609. ¶ 3. Sandy McClure. David Nelson.

P. 610. ¶ 6. Ernest C. Browne. Robert Banyai. DP: Special Task Force.

P. 610. Footnote. Paul Conlan.

P. 611. ¶ 1. Jerome P. Cavanagh.

P. 611. ¶ 2. Philip Van Antwerp, "Report to the Common Council on the Lowering of Recruiting Standards and Morale of the Detroit Police Department," Oct. 24, 1968.

P. 611. ¶ 3. D GOV: Detroit, *Annual Financial Report* 40. DP: Det. Police Dept., *Annual Reports.*

P. 611. ¶ 6. Al Legatt. Edward P. Henry.

P. 612. ¶ 2. D GOV: Detroit, *Annual Financial Report* 96-101. Detroit, Budget History. Bernard Klein. Joe B. Sullivan. Walter I. Stecher.

P. 612. ¶ 3. Morton Sterling.

P. 612. ¶ 4. D GOV: Detroit, *Annual Financial Report* 19-20; Detroit, *Budget* ii-iv. Bernard Klein. Walter I. Stecher. Robert Toohey.

P. 613. ¶ 2. Mayor's Task Force on City Finances, *Interim Report,* Jan. 9, 1968. D GOV: Detroit, *Budget* vi-vii.

P. 613. ¶ 3. D GOV: Detroit, Budget History.

P. 613. ¶ 4. DN: Wolf 2-3, 21-24, 37, 56-57.

P. 614. ¶ 1. DN: Wolf 28-29, 32. *The New York Times,* April 15, 1968. D GEN: *Census Tracts, Detroit, Michigan.* Richard Strichartz.

P. 614. ¶ 2. Bernard Klein.

P. 614. ¶ 3. Jerome P. Cavanagh. Bernard Klein. Joe B. Sullivan.

P. 615. ¶ 1. *The New York Times,* Nov. 5, 6, 1969.

P. 615. ¶ 4. Dr. Norman Drachler.

P. 615. ¶ 5. D GEN: *General Social and Economic Characteristics,* 1960, pp. 389-90; 1970, p. 307.

P. 616. ¶ 1. DS: Det. Bd. of Ed., *Budgets.* DG: Detroit, *Budget* vi-viii.

P. 616. ¶ 3. Dr. Norman Drachler.

VI. EPILOGUE AND PROLOGUE

1. IM: Malthus 57, 65, 203.

2. DH: Girardin, "Life and Times" 484.

3. CIT: Riis, *How* 2.

4. CD: Lee 81.
5. IM: Malthus 176.
6. IM: Malthus 259. CIT: Riis, *How* 14.
7. Philip Rutledge.
8. Author's calculations from 1972 *Statistical Abstract,* pp. 283, and 392-94.
9. Los Angeles *Times,* Dec. 1, 1972.
10. FG UA: Government Operations, *Federal Role,* Pt. 14, p. 3015.
11. *The New York Times,* Jan. 18, 1961.
12. MH: Niemi 12.
13. IM: Engels 104, 106.

P. 619. ¶ 3. IM: Cassell's, Vol. II: 343-44, 400, 402.
P. 620. ¶ 1. GEN: Census, *Historical Statistics,* Ch. "Z."
P. 620. ¶ 2. IM: Cassell's, Vol. II: 398.
P. 620. ¶ 4. IM: Cassell's, Vol. IV: 167.
P. 621. ¶ 1. IM: Cassell's, Vol. IV: 164-65, 178 ff. EC: Wright 96.
P. 621. ¶ 5. IM: Barker 3-4.
P. 622. ¶ 4. IM: Engels 12, 159-60.
P. 623. ¶ 1. IM: Cassell's, Vol. II: 343; Eden 26-27, 21.
P. 623. ¶ 2. IM: Eden 39-40; Malthus 203; Barker 141.
P. 623. ¶ 3. IM: Lloyd 346-47.
P. 623. ¶ 4. IM: Eden 24, 10-11; Cassell's, Vol. II: 402-03.
P. 624. ¶ 2. IM: Malthus 177; Engels 167.
P. 624. ¶ 4. IM: Engels 146-47.
P. 624. ¶ 5. DP: Branton 281. CIT: Schlesinger 114, 115.
P. 624. ¶ 8. DP: Det. Police Dept., *Annual Reports.*
P. 626. ¶ 1. DP: Det. Police Dept., *Annual Report,* 1967, pp. 31-33, 43.
P. 626. ¶ 2. DP: Det. Police Dept., *Annual Reports.*
P. 626. ¶ 3. D GEN: Census, *General Population Characteristics,* 1950, p. 68; 1960, p. 60; 1970, p. 83.
P. 631. ¶ 2. ED: HEW, *Digest* 28-29.
P. 630. Footnote‡. Stephens, Sir Leslie, and Lee, Sir Sidney (eds.), *Dictionary of National Biography* (Oxford, England: 1917), Vol. IV.
P. 631. ¶ 6. ED: HEW, Digest, 52, 59, 69. DS: Det. Bd. of Ed., *Budgets.*
P. 632. ¶ 4. GEN: Census, *Social and Economic Conditions of Negroes* 18.
P. 632. ¶ 5. ED: HEW, *Digest* 75. *United Nations Statistical Yearbook,* 1971, pp. 752-53.
P. 635. ¶ 3. Los Angeles *Times,* July 2, 1972.
P. 638. ¶ 3. FG UA: Government Operations, *Federal Role,* Pt. 18, p. 3750.
P. 638. ¶ 4. GEN: Census, *Statistical Abstract,* 1967, pp. 607, 605; 1972, pp. 572, 590, 598, xxii. FG UA: Government Operations, *Federal Role,* Pt. 18, p. 3750.
P. 639. ¶1. GEN: Census, *Statistical Abstract,* 1972, pp. 596, 53. CIT: Government Operations 7, 77-79, 112.
P. 639. ¶ 3. FG AP: Labor and Public Welfare, *Examination,* Pt. 1, pp. 158, 248; Pt. 9, pp. 2983-84.
P. 639. ¶ 7. CIT: Government Operations 55-60. FG AP: Labor and Public Welfare, *Examination,* Pt. 1, p. 159.
P. 640. ¶ 2. CIT: Government Operations 19-22. GEN: Census, *Statistical Abstract* pp. 584-85, 16, 26; General Population Characteristics, U.S. Summary, 1960, Table 44; 1970, Table 48.
P. 641. Footnote. CIT: Break 194.
P. 642. Table. D GEN: Census, General Population Characteristics, 1950, p. 68; 1960, p. 60; 1970, p. 83.
P. 643. ¶ 4. FG UA: Advisory Comm., *Fiscal Balance,* Vol. 1: 105-06.
P. 643. ¶ 6. EC: Commerce 52-55.
P. 644. ¶ 3. EC: Commerce 54-55. FG UA: Advisory Comm., *Fiscal Balance,* Vol. 1: 122-23.
P. 644. ¶ 4. GEN: Census, *Statistical Abstract,* 1967, p. 418; 1972, p. 409.
P. 644. ¶ 5. FG UA: Advisory Comm., *Fiscal Balance,* Vol. 2, 43-45.
P. 644. ¶ 6. FG UA: Advisory Comm., *Fiscal Balance,* Vol. 2: 197-98.
P. 644. ¶ 7. FG UA: Advisory Comm., *Fiscal Balance,* Vol. 2: 80.
P. 645. ¶ 2. FG UA: Advisory Comm., *Fiscal Balance,* Vol. 2: 51, 87, 104-05, 108.

D GOV: Detroit, *Budget* vii; *Annual Financial Report* 4. DS: Det. Bd. of Ed., *Budget*, 1971.

P. 646. ¶ 1. FG UA: Advisory Comm., *Fiscal Balance*, Vol. 1: 151, 153, 337-44. James D. Wiley. Philip Rutledge.

P. 646. ¶ 3. FG UA: Advisory Comm., *Fiscal Balance*, Vol. 1: 182.

P. 646. ¶ 5. FG UA: Advisory Comm., *Fiscal Balance*, Vol. 1: 190.

P. 647. ¶ 1. Philip Rutledge. Lewis Nicolini.

P. 648. ¶ 6. GEN: Census, *Statistical Abstract*, 1972, pp. 32, 65, 68.

P. 649. ¶ 1. FG PP: Congressional Quarterly 9, 85. GEN: Census, *Statistical Abstract*, 1972, p. 386.

P. 650. Footnote. Los Angeles *Times*, July 25, 1973.

P. 651. ¶ 1. GEN: Census, *Statistical Abstract*, 1967, pp. 397, 321; 1972, pp. 349, 391, 409, 418.

P. 651. ¶ 4. GEN: Census, *Statistical Abstract*, 1972, p. 283.

P. 651. ¶ 5. Herman P. Miller. David Broder in Los Angeles *Times*, June 7, 1971.

P. 651. ¶ 6. Commerce Department, Office of Business Economics, *Survey of Current Business*, July, 1971, p. 28.

P. 652. ¶ 3. GEN: Census, *Statistical Abstract*, 1972, pp. 291-95.

P. 652. ¶ 4. GEN: Census, *Statistical Abstract*, 1967, p. 418; 1972, p. 409.

P. 653. ¶ 2. D GOV: Detroit, *Annual Financial Report* 15.

P. 653. ¶ 3. D GEN: Census, *Employment Profiles* 106.

P. 654. Footnote*. GEN: Census, *Statistical Abstract*, 1972, p. 333.

P. 655. ¶ 1. FG PP: President's Comm. 32, 37, 39. EC: Peach 37. GEN: Census, *Statistical Abstract*, 1972, p. 324.

P. 656. Footnote*. GEN: Census, *Statistical Abstract*, 1972, p. 325. D GEN: Census Tracts, 1972, pp. P 335, 337.

P. 656. ¶ 6. ED: National Education Assoc. 8, 23, 27, 38, 52; HEW, *Digest* 14. DS: Det. Public Schools, *Relationship of Income to Some Indices; Relationship Between Family Incomes of School Neighborhoods and Reading Achievements.*

P. 656. Footnote†. D GEN: Census, *Employment Profiles* 172.

P. 657. Footnote†. GEN: Census, *Statistical Abstract*, 1972, p. 336. EC: Wright 851.

P. 660. ¶ 1. FG PP: President's Comm. 15-17. Dr. Margaret Zolliker.

P. 660. ¶ 2. D GEN: Census, *General Social and Economic Characteristics*, 1970, pp. 24/255, 24/369.

P. 663. ¶ 6. GEN: Moos 380-81.

Index